an Encyclopaedia of

THE WINES
AND
DOMAINES
OF FRANCE

an Encyclopaedia of

THE WINES AND DOMAINES OF FRANCE

CLIVE COATES MW

CASSELL&CO

First published in the United Kingdom in 2000 by Cassell & Co

A CIP catalogue record for this book is available from the British Library

ISBN 0 304 35441 4

Design director David Rowley
Editorial director Susan Haynes
Editor Fiona Holman
Typeset and designed by Nigel Soper
Art editor Briony Chappell
Maps by Eugene Fleury and M L Design
Indexer Dawn Butcher
Typeset in SpectrumMT
Printed in France

Cassell & Co
Wellington House
125 Strand
London
WC2R 0BB

PREFACE

In 1991 I published *The Wines of France*. In a sense this is a second edition. But while much of the preamble – the history and general description of each *appellation* – only needed to be gently brought up to date, the commentary on the leading estates, as well as the general presentation has been completely rewritten and repackaged. And with certain chapters, notably those on the South of France from Biarritz to Nice, so much has changed in just a decade that whole sections have had to be totally rewritten. Thus the change of title as this is an entirely new book.

OTHER BOOKS BY CLIVE COATES
Grands Vins, The Finest Châteaux of Bordeaux and Their Wines
Côte d'Or, A Celebration of the Great Wines of Burgundy
Both published by Weidenfeld & Nicolson and the University of California Press.

AUTHOR'S ACKNOWLEDGEMENTS

This book is dedicated to the *vignerons* of France, without whose generosity, hospitality, encouragement and general enthusiasm for their wines and the wines of their peers, this book could never have been written.

I would also like to thank Catherine Manac'h of Food and Wines of France (UK) and the various *comités* of all the *appellations* and regions in France. Tom Stevenson's encyclopaedic knowledge of Champagne is much appreciated. Charles Sydney, broker of the wines of the Loire, made no end of useful suggestions. Liz Morcom MW and Paul and Jeanne Strang pointed me in the right direction in the Languedoc/Roussillon and the South-West respectively. Becky Wasserman and Russell Hone are my best friends, as well as my keenest spies in Burgundy, and Liz Berry MW has been a font of knowledge both about Alsace and the Midi, as well as a generous host whenever I have been in Saint-Martin-de-Crau.

I would also acknowledge my professional friends, the buyers and directors of the serious wine businesses in Great Britain. I have pillaged their lists to see who they are buying from, as I have also heeded the recommendations in other journals and books, notably the *Revue du Vin de France*, the *Guide Hachette* and *Le Classement* of Michel Bettane and Thierry Dessauve, plus Jacqueline Friedrich on the Loire and Robert Parker on the Rhône (about the only books on French wines which are reasonably up to date).

Finally my secretary Sonia Portalès. This is the third book we have produced together. Without her I would be lost. Merci!

But, and this is a big but, these are my own notes, assessments and ratings and not anyone else's. I have been there and found out for myself. I have tasted. What follows on the subsequent pages is my own opinion.

CONTENTS

READERS' NOTES

STAR RATINGS

I have considered a number of ways of assessing and noting the domaines and merchants singled out in this book.

A precise mark, whether out of 20 or 100, seemed to me to be too exact. We are, after all, talking generalities here. You can give precise marks to wines, but not to the overall performance of an estate or a merchant as a whole. Stars out of five, as in, for instance, books as diverse as Michael Broadbent's *Great Wine Book* or Robert Parker's *Wines of the Rhône Valley*, I also found wanting. One star was equivalent to 'average'. I wanted to single out the above-average! So I have adopted what I might call the Michelin Three Star System, familiar to all readers who have bought their red guides, and to readers of French wine journals and annuals such as the *Revue du Vin de France*, the *Guide Hachette* and *Le Classement*, the yearly guide by Michel Bettane and Thierry Dessauve.

PRODUCER RATINGS

★★★	The very best: excellent by any standards.
★★	Very good: can be thoroughly relied on.
★	Good: one of the top producers in the area.
No star but mentioned	A producer worthy of consideration.

SPELLING IDIOSYNCRASIES

France is notoriously haphazard over spelling. Vineyard or domaine names can be either singular or plural – Griotte or Griottes; hyphenated or not – Cheval Blanc or Cheval-Blanc, Beaux-Monts or Beaumonts; they can incorporate the definite article or not, and can even use prepositions such as *Aux* or *En* rather than *Le* or *Les*.

By and large I have tried to follow what the growers themselves put on their labels, except where I know them to be in error, e.g. Clos Vougeot instead of the more correct Clos de Vougeot. But sometimes I have never seen, or have forgotten, what was on the label.

You will notice therefore a number of alternating spellings in the pages that follow. But this is one of the charms of France.

LIST OF MAPS

INTRODUCTION

France produces the finest wines in the world. That is my thesis. Moreover it does it in a volume and in a variety that no other country can even think of rivalling. There are just under 900,000 hectares of vineyard in France, creating an annual volume of some 60 million hectolitres of wine. Fifty-two per cent of this surface area is authorised for wine of *appellation contrôlée* or VDQS standard. Forty-six per cent of the total volume produced is of this quality. This is the equivalent of some 276 million cases of quality wine. No other country can claim this amount of top standard wine.

There are said to be as many as a thousand different varieties of vine planted in Italy. France has fewer, but it has many more that produce wine of yardstick quality; many more that winemakers in the 'New World' – the United States, Australasia and South America – want to import and try out for themselves. What other country can rival the glorious variegation of Cabernet Sauvignon, Pinot Noir, Syrah, Merlot, Cabernet Franc, Tannat, Gamay, Malbec (Auxerrois), Mourvèdre and Grenache for red wines; of Chardonnay, Sauvignon Blanc, Sémillon, Chenin, Roussanne, Viognier, Gros and Petit Manseng, Gewurztraminer, Pinot Gris and Riesling for whites? Only Germany, with its own version of Riesling, and Italy with its Sangiovese Grosso and Nebbiolo, and California with its Zinfandel can offer serious additions to this list of first-division grape varieties.

And there is more. At the everyday, affordable level, despite savage competition from places as far apart as Bulgaria and Chile, France can more than hold its own. Certainly the wine flavours are more natural, less 'manufactured' in the bottles I buy from the South of France.

The first country to implement legislation codifying viticultural and vinification practices and protecting geographical names of origin, France today has some 450 different *appellations d'origine*. In many regions there is an additional hierarchical system, singling out the best land, the finest vineyards and domaines from the rest. The fact that a wine comes from a *premier* or *grand cru* vineyard or a classed growth estate does not in itself ensure that it is of top quality, but it must be of considerable help to the consumer in choosing what to buy and what to avoid. The diversity of different *appellations* is complex, but the range of styles and tastes is unrivalled.

Finally and this may indeed be the explanation for France's preeminence – the country has been growing vines and exporting fine wine far longer than most. Once again only the Rhineland, one or two isolated pockets in Italy, and the fortified wine centres of Jerez, Oporto and Madeira have as long a history of quality wine production as Bordeaux, Burgundy, the Rhône and Champagne.

Vinous France can be separated as Caesar divided Gaul: into three parts. There is the north, the *départements* which front the English Channel – which the French, with an atypical lack of chauvinism, call La Manche. Here there are no vines. Next there is the bulk of France – from the point of view of area – where the vine is occasionally the supreme crop, but where in the main the vineyards are interspersed with woodland and meadow, fruit trees, cereal crops and market gardens. And finally there is the South, paradoxically called the Midi, the land of the olive as well as the vine. Here, between the seaside resorts and the rocky *garrigues* in the foothills of the Alps, the Cévennes and the Pyrenees the vine is supreme, the land monocultural, producing millions and millions of hectolitres of largely indifferent, insipid, barely legitimate wine. Yet here can also be found some of the most exciting, value-for-money wines in the whole of France.

FRANCE

N

Seine
AISNE
Aisne
Reims
Épernay
MARNE
Paris
SEINE-
ET-
MARNE
CHAMPAGNE
AUBE
Troyes
MEUSE
MOSELLE
LORRAINE
BAS-RHIN
Toul
Strasbourg
MEURTHE-
ET-MOSELLE
ALSACE
HAUTE-
MARNE
Seine
Colmar
HAUT-
RHIN
SARTHE
Sarthe
Orléans
LOIRET
YONNE
Auxerre
Chablis
BURGUNDY
HAUTE-SAÔNE
LOIRE VALLEY
LOIR-
ET-CHER
LOIRE-
ATLANTIQUE
Angers
Loire
CÔTE-D'OR
Saône
Besançon
DOUBS
Ancenis
Nantes
MAINE-
ET-LOIRE
Tours
INDRE-
ET-LOIRE
Cher
Sancerre
NIÈVRE
Dijon
Beaune
VENDÉE
DEUX-
SÈVRES
VIENNE
Poitiers
INDRE
Creuse
Vienne
LOIRE VALLEY
CHER
Loire
ALLIER
St-Pourçain-
sur-Sioule
BURGUNDY
SAÔNE-ET-LOIRE
Mâcon
AIN
Arbois
JURA
JURA
HAUTE-
SAVOIE
Annecy
ATLANTIC
OCEAN
CHARENTE-
MARITIME
CHARENTE
Cognac
HAUTE-
VIENNE
CORRÈZE
Villefranche-
sur-Saône
Roanne
BEAUJOLAIS
RHÔNE
Lyon
Clermont-
Ferrand
AUVERGNE
PUY-DE-DÔME
LOIRE
Vienne
SAVOIE
Chambéry
SAVOIE
ISÈRE
BORDEAUX
Isle
GIRONDE
Libourne
Bordeaux
Langon
Garonne
Bergerac
DORDOGNE
Dordogne
LOT
SOUTH-WEST
Lot
Allier
Loire
RHÔNE
Valence
Die
DRÔME
Montélimar
RHÔNE
VALLEY
HAUTES-
ALPES
Durance
LOT-ET-
GARONNE
TARN-ET-
GARONNE
Cahors
AVEYRON
Tarn
Orange
VAUCLUSE
Avignon
ALPES-
DE-HAUTE-
PROVENCE
ALPES-
MARITIMES
LANDES
SOUTH-WEST
Baïse
Gaillac
TARN
GARD
Nîmes
BOUCHES-
DU-RHÔNE
PROVENCE
Nice
GERS
Toulouse
HAUTE-
GARONNE
LANGUEDOC
HÉRAULT
Montpellier
Aix-en-
Provence
Draguignan
VAR
Pau
PYRÉNÉES-
ATLANTIQUES
Garonne
HAUTES-
PYRÉNÉES
AUDE
Limoux
Marseille
Toulon
ARIÈGE
MEDITERRANEAN
SEA
ROUSSILLON
Perpignan
PYRÉNÉES-
ORIENTALES
Banyuls

0   120km
0   80miles

CORSICA
Patrimonio
HAUTE
CORSE
Ajaccio
CORSE
DU-SUD

Fine wine, good wine, wine that is worth drinking – call it what you will – comes from all over France, from the Minervois as well as the Médoc, from Bandol as well as Beaune, from Cahors as well as Champagne. The country is prolific; prolific in its number of different soils, grape varieties and methods of making wine. There is a wealth – perhaps unrivalled throughout the world – of good wine; some, obviously, is classic, rare, expensive; more, perhaps more than some people realise, is remarkable value, within the means of anyone who cares to drink wine regularly. I have attempted to note all the best growers in every single *appellation*.

It is the variety of French wine which fascinates me. For most of the twenty years that I spent as a wine merchant before 'retiring' to become a full-time wine writer at the end of 1984 I specialised in the wines of France. Every year I would spend weeks if not months touring round the highways and byways of France sniffing out good growers in unexpected areas, importing their wines and – with a reasonable degree of success – introducing them into the English market. It would be rash to be too positive, but I think that I may have been the first to ship the wines of Fronton and the Côtes Roannaises, Bellet, Bugey and Vins de L'Orléanais to Britain. I hope I also did something to give the wines of Bandol the full recognition that they deserve.

Unearthing the best sources was sometimes difficult, often frustrating and inevitably tiring; but always – and there is no other word for it – fun. I remember the first time I seriously investigated the wines of Cahors in south-west France. Armed with a list from the local *Syndicat d'Initiative* or tourist office, I arrived in the town on a bleak and crisp February afternoon, and, as was my custom, descended to the local one-star restaurant for a meal in the evening. I had discovered that you could rely on the indigenous gastronomic centres to list at least most of the good local growers in their wine lists. A little preliminary tasting would prepare me – by setting a few yardsticks – for what I would uncover during the next couple of days.

The restaurant (it has since disappeared from the guides) was a long, thin, dark cavern in the old town of Cahors. Business was quiet in February, and apart from a quartet of local businessmen I was the sole client. On the wine list was a choice of nine Cahors wines, but at a combined price of a bottle of decent Meursault (which they didn't have) or a *flacon* of Champagne. I ordered all nine wines. '*Grandes bouteilles?*' asked the incredulous Madame (there were no halves). '*Oui*', I nodded.

Madame stopped occasionally to check that I was not drinking myself insensible and eventually her husband, the chef, ambled by. I had already explained my purpose was degustatory rather than inebriation and I didn't have to push him too hard before he began telling me who was who in the Cahors *vignoble*. The local quartet soon joined us, finished up my nine bottles, and before too long my list of sixty-odd growers to visit had been whittled down to a nucleus of eight.

In return I was fed countless different twenty-year-old vintage Armagnacs – down the side of the dining-room was a low shelf ranked with large bottles the size of *impériales* in which it is customary to imprison this nectar – and given the run-down on the local political situation, the world and the universe as it appeared to the inhabitants of south-west France. The next day I swiftly snapped up the best available grower in the area, and, having saved a day on my schedule, celebrated by touring the magnificent Gorges du Tarn and some of its extraordinary grottoes. It had certainly been an evening well spent.

While it never occurred to me in those far-off days that one day I would attempt to write a book on the whole of France's wines, it was nevertheless a private ambition to visit and taste extensively in every single *appellation contrôlée* and VDQS (Vins Délimités de Qualité Supérieure). Finally in the autumn of 1982 I arrived at Irouléguy at the Basque end of the Pyrenees. I had made it! (Not that the journey was worth it, as it happens.)

I have made many other wine excursions: to the vineyard on top of the battlements of the Château at Angers, to that in Montmartre in Paris (on the Rue Gordon Bennett, would you believe), to several vineyards in the Savoie which proclaim themselves as the highest vineyard in the country and to another near Collioure which lies both in France and in Spain. This pilgrimage has been the result of a love of France, its people, its food, its wines, its countryside and its climate. Long may this love affair continue!

The French vineyard scene and the standard and styles of its wines develop and change at a relentless pace with which no one individual can keep up. Though I have spent a great deal of time in the wine regions of France in the last three and a half decades no single person can cover every producer, every region even, every year; every rising star, every change of management, every declining reputation. It would be like attempting a one-man Michelin Guide.

I have followed up the suggestions of my friends, consulted the wine lists of merchants I trust and restaurants I approve and attempted to examine each wine regon in as much depth as possible. Every producer discussed or recommended in the following pages is personally known to me as are the wines they have produced in the last decade. But there is bound to be the odd important producer who has been unwittingly excluded. My apologies to them in advance. The mistakes will, I trust, be rectified in a subsequent edition of this book.

History

The history of wine in France is inextricably bound up with the political and socio-economic evolution of the country. It is estimated that one in twelve of the adult population is involved directly or indirectly in the wine business. The vine was introduced by Phoenician and Greek traders. From about 600 BC onwards they formed settlements along the Mediterranean coast. Wine was certainly imported. Whether and indeed when the vine was introduced is less certain, but amphorae, coins and other artefacts dating from the pre-Roman period have been found as far north as Burgundy.

The subjugation of the northern part of the country by Julius Caesar in the middle of the first century BC — Roman power had already been long established in the Midi — followed by the colonisation of the whole of Gaul in the time of Augustus and his great general, Agrippa, brought the techniques of vine cultivation and wine production to France; and the impetus was swift.

At the time of the birth of Christ there is no clear evidence of vines in France outside the Midi; beyond Vienne to the north, or Gaillac to the west. But by AD 71 Pliny records that there were vines in Bordeaux and in the vineyards in the vicinity of Augustodunum (present-day Autun in Burgundy), capital of the Aedui, the Romans' first allies in Gaul; and the vine had reached Paris (Lutetia) and Trier (Augusta Treverorum) by the turn of the century.

It is customary to consider the decline and fall of the Roman Empire and the replacement of its civilisation in France by the ravaging incursions of barbarian tribes such as the Alamans, the Goths, the Visigoths and the Franks as one of the world's all time great disasters. This is not wholly true. These tribes were not just old enemies, waiting impatiently on the Empire's borders for authority to crumble, but customers as well. When the Roman legions departed the vineyards were not completely destroyed, nor were all their magnificent constructions put to the torch. The barbarians, for the most part, simply moved in to fill the vacuum. Moreover, one great Roman institution remained in Gaul, the established Christian church. With typical efficiency the Romans had created a system of dioceses throughout the country, a hierarchical system of bishops and priests. One of the greatest achievements of the early Christian church was the maintenance of organized agriculture, of which the traditions of viticulture and viniculture were a vital part, throughout the Dark Ages.

By the time of the re-emergence of 'civilisation' around the time of Charles Martel and his grandson Charlemagne and the establishment of the Holy Roman (and Christian) Empire in AD 800, the focus of Western Europe had moved to Aachen, and it was the Rhineland that experienced the first expansion of viticulture since Roman times. That in France followed somewhat later. In northern and eastern France the driving force was the church. The great abbey at Cluny in the Mâconnais was founded in AD 910 and its tentacles rapidly spread as it spawned a multitude of sister, subsidiary establishments through Europe. Two centuries later the rival Cistercian order was formed at Cîteaux near Dijon. The church was financed by a system of tithes. In theory the laity had to pay a tenth of their agricultural income, in cash or in goods, to the ecclesiastical authorities. In practice the percentage was less, and there were other ways of meeting one's obligations or of avoiding them.

The church soon grew fat. As their economic influence grew, so did their political clout. And their landholdings increased likewise, swelled by donations from the aristocracy, anxious to ensure their favourable reception in the life to come. Wine was a valuable commodity and the church gave every encouragement to the establishment of vineyards. Its influence, particularly in Burgundy, was paramount.

Meanwhile Bordeaux, in the South-West, slumbered in the backwaters. The region had begun as an *emporium*, a depot through which the wines of the Haut Pays further inland (Cahors, Gaillac and the Dordogne) were exported. The vines of the Gironde region around the city itself were few. Even by the time of the famous union between Henry Plantagenet and Eleanor of Aquitaine in 1152 the situation had little changed. There were vineyards in the Saint-Emilion area and in the Entre-Deux-Mers, but few in the Graves, except to the south near Langon, and none in the marshy Médoc.

It was the arrival of the English which produced the decisive change. Exports expanded, not just to the British Isles but to the Netherlands and the Hanseatic ports, and the vineyard area soon increased to meet the demand for wine. Twice a year a vast fleet – 900 ships in AD 1300 – sailed from Bordeaux with the latest vintage. By the middle of the fourteenth century, as much land was under vine in the Gironde as exists today. The Bordelais were soon imposing taxes and other restrictions on the wines from the inland regions in order to maintain premier position for their own local produce. The position did not radically change even when the English lost the South-West at the end of the Hundred Years War in 1453.

For the next two hundred years, despite the decline in the influence of the church, changing fashions on the export market – most of England and northern Europe turned to the richer but not yet fortified wines of Iberia – and the arrival of distilled wines, Cognac and other brandies, the pattern of life of the French *vigneron* and his patron and the way he made his wine hardly changed. Wine was made in a fairly artisanal way, shipped or otherwise transported in wooden casks and consumed as early as possible, before it went off. The wine was anonymous, identified only by the area of origin. The rise of individual estates, the emergence of a hierarchy separating the best from the mundane, and the concept of wine as a product of quality which could last, indeed could improve with keeping, had to wait until the reinvention of the glass bottle and the rediscovery of the sealing properties of cork around 1650. From this period on, in the economic glory of the Sun King and his successors, the concept of fine wine grew apace. In the more leisured pursuits of the aristocracy the appreciation of wine and food – gastronomy – began to take its place in the art of good living. The rising merchant classes were not slow to join in. The eighteenth century saw an enormous expansion of monocultural vineyard estates in the newly drained Médoc, the emergence of named domaines in the Rhône, the development of Champagne as the drink we know today and the creation of a number of aristocratic, as opposed to ecclesiastical, domaines in Burgundy.

Then came Revolution. The old order crumbled. Church land, and that of the old aristocracy who had emigrated, was sequestered and sold as *biens nationaux*. A new moneyed class, soon ennobled, swiftly moved in to take the place of the old. Little changed: much less than we are given to believe. In Bordeaux the effects were barely noticeable. A few proprietors went to the guillotine, but rather more properties changed hands in the economic depression of the 1830s than during Napoleonic times. In Burgundy where the ecclesiastical landholding was a small proportion of what it had been at its zenith, but nevertheless the equivalent of some 10,000 hectares, perhaps a third of the vineyard changed hands. Most was sold in significant pieces to the *nouveaux* riches, the *haute bourgeoisie*. The socializing, the democratisation of land, if that had been an object of the Revolution, did not immediately come about. What the new order did introduce, its effect to be insidious, a canker which was ultimately to disrupt almost the whole of the French *vignoble*, was the Code Napoléon, a change in the laws of inheritance. Primogeniture was abolished. Henceforth estates would have to be equally divided among the heirs. The consequences were to be far-reaching. They still are today.

The nineteenth century saw a rise in the power of the wine merchant and his increasing involvement as vineyard proprietor, the gradual implementation of more scientific and mechanised techniques of viticulture and vinification, the elimination of lesser strains and the concentration on particular noble grape varieties in each major *vignoble*, and a vast expansion of communication, particularly with the arrival of the railway. The first half of the century saw not so much an expansion of the area of vineyard under cultivation but of consolidation, vineyards being rationalised and set apart from other crops in a more efficient manner. Population and prosperity grew, and with it the demand for wine. Each vineyard area, finally, began to produce wines with their own individual characters.

Nemesis was to follow. Three great scourges, the cryptogamic diseases of oidium and mildew bracketing the more catastrophic phylloxera epidemic, followed by the Franco-Prussian war of 1870-1871 and the economic depression which it left in its wake, changed the face, the prosperity and the socio-economic parameters of French viticulture. The last thirty years of the century reduced the French vineyard to a state of abject crisis from which it was not fully to recover until the 1960s.

The convulsions caused by phylloxera were the most far-reaching. Phylloxera is an aphid, an insect with a very complicated life cycle. In both the nymph and the adult states the insect sucks the sap out of the roots of the vine, forming galls on these roots which eventually kill the plant. Once it has arrived in the vineyard it is ineradicable. The only solution, it was eventually found, was to graft the noble *Vitis vinifera* cutting into a more resistant non-*vinifera* (American) rootstock.

The effect of this climactic event, the sheer cost of reconstructing vineyards which had ceased to produce, especially in the unfortunate economic situation which prevailed, was to produce a major contraction of the French *vignoble*. Many of the lesser, more northerly French vineyards had found life tough going since the time the wines of the Midi could be rapidly brought up to Paris and the other major conurbations of the north by the railway. They were never reconstituted. In the 1840s vineyards extended uninterruptedly from Sens to Dijon. Today only Chablis and a few neighbouring hectares are left. Even Chablis almost ceased to exist. The same can be said of Cahors, Madiran and other important, but only latterly fashionable, vineyard areas.

Elsewhere the consequences were equally monumental. While in Bordeaux the large estates, owned by the new aristocracy or the wealthy merchant classes, managed to survive more or less unscathed, the large estates in Burgundy were sold up. This began a process of fragmentation which has resulted in, to take a single example, the fact that the 50-odd hectares of Clos Vougeot have no less than eighty owners today.

For seventy years, until the late 1950s, the life of the French vineyard proprietor and merchant was an unhappy one. Making and selling wine was barely profitable. More and more vineyards fell into disuse, particularly those which were impossible to work mechanically such as the steep slopes of Côte-Rôtie in the northern Rhône, as the younger generation emigrated into the factories of the nearby cities. There was a mass evacuation of the countryside in favour of the town throughout France. With the flower of French manhood slaughtered on the Western Front between 1914 and 1918 economic privation became yet more acute. Even in Bordeaux, hitherto largely immune and protected by the importance of its export market, the wolf was at the gate. By 1945 a quarter of the sixty classed growths listed in the 1855 Classification existed in name only. The vineyards and *chais* suffered from a lack of investment, the quality of the wine being further diminished by a run of unsuccessful vintages in the 1930s.

Meanwhile, beginning in Champagne before the First World War, altruistically encouraged by the Baron le Roy de Boiseaumarie in Châteauneuf-du-Pape in the 1920s, and finally promulgated in the mid-1930s, the French had codified their viticultural and vinicultural practices, established the right to legally protected regional and communal wine names, and introduced the *Comité National des Appellations d'Origine*. The Loi Capus, named after its godfather Joseph Capus, was passed in 1935. After the Second World War the *Comité* became an *Institut* (often abbreviated to INAO), and it continues today as the governing body of French wine and the model for similar developments in wine-producing countries throughout the world.

The last forty years have seen changes as far-reaching as any of the previous two hundred and fifty. Most fundamental of all has been in the understanding of what precisely happens when the juice of the grape is fermented into wine, the increasing control over the processes of nature, the implementation of new technology and the realisation that *élevage* – which one can roughly translate as what goes on during the period between winemaking and wine-bottling – is as important as vinification itself. Financed by increasing prosperity and profitability, the result has been an enormous increase in the consistency of wine quality, whether at the level of the basic wines produced by the co-operatives or at classed growth or *premier cru* level. In 1959 it was hard to find drinkable French wine outside the better wines of the mainstream areas, and many of them were rustic and sulphury. Today, from Muscadet to Bellet, from Irouléguy to Alsace, and especially in the lesser areas in between, there is a wealth of good, honest, carefully made wine. The change has been dramatic.

Fashions have changed. Beaujolais and Muscadet, to take two examples, were rarely seen outside their areas of origin in the 1940s. These wines were sold by the glass, direct from the cask, in the bistros of Lyon and Nantes. They were rarely exported. Today 55 per cent of Beaujolais is sold abroad, most of it as Nouveau. The central Loire wines of Sancerre and Pouilly-Fumé, unheard of forty years ago, are today widely distributed, both within and without metropolitan France. There is increasing interest in the wines of the Midi, the South-West and other hitherto 'lesser' areas.

The pattern of drinking has changed both in France and elsewhere. The French man (and woman) drinks less than he used to – but still rather more than everybody except his counterpart in Italy – but he drinks better. Consumption of *vin ordinaire* is on the decline: of *appellation* wines on the increase. In the non-wine-making countries of northern Europe, in the Americas, in Australasia and the Far East, the market base has expanded. In Britain – and we lag behind the Netherlands and other countries with a less puritanical attitude to wine taxation – the consumption of table wine is today 16 litres a year, and 10 million people drink wine on a regular basis. This is an increase in sales of nearly 500 per cent since 1970. Once again the selection has evolved: less *vin ordinaire*, more *vins d'appellation*. And despite the increasing competition of better and better wines from other countries France continues to hold its own. Thirty-two per cent of British wine consumption is of French wine.

The way French wines are marketed by those who make them has also changed, and radically too. Domaine bottling is on the increase and merchant bottling on the decline. More and more wines are marketed direct by the producer. The opportunity provided by the Internet is only just beginning to be appreciated. More and more estates in more and more areas now have their own personality and individuality unsubmerged with the wine of their neighbours. The pride that comes with domaine bottling has encouraged perfectionism. It has widened the diversity and also increased the quality of wines available. And prices have risen too.

This is a prosperous time for the French *vigneron*. The pace of these developments is both exhilarating and breathtaking. What is encouraging is that the profits have been ploughed back into a continuing search after higher standards and the implementation of all the resources of modern science and technology, both in the vineyard and the *chais*, to achieve them.

Today the French winemaker is expertly trained, insatiably curious and often surprisingly knowledgeable about wines made elsewhere. He is increasingly dedicated, and rightly confident in his ability to compete in the world markets. The future looks rosy.

A YEAR IN THE VINEYARD

Good wine is produced from ripe, healthy, concentrated grapes. The aim of viticulture is to produce fruit in as optimum a condition as possible at harvest time, to produce as much as is compatible with the highest quality – but not too much, for quality is inversely proportional to quantity – and to mitigate the vagaries of the climate and the depredations of pests and diseases.

The first element to consider is the soil. The vine will thrive on a wide range of geological structures and compositions, but some varieties do better on some soils than on others. Cabernet Sauvignon, for instance, while it has a tolerance for limestone and marl (limestone-clay mixtures) and even for loam (sand-clay mixtures), provided the soils are not too cool, performs to its most elegant capacity on well-drained gravel. Hence its preponderance in the Médoc and the Graves areas of Bordeaux. Gamay is found in the marly soils of the Loire and Ardèche and in the undulating limestone hills of the Mâconnais and the lower Beaujolais; but it produces its greatest definition on the granite slopes of the Beaujolais-Villages area. Syrah thrives on the granite debris of the northern Rhône Valley, Pinot Noir on a subtle mixture of limestone scree, marl and older alluvial deposits which you can only find in Burgundy. Where the soil is purer limestone Chardonnay will perform better, as it will in the chalk of Champagne or the marly Kimmeridge clay of Chablis.

In general the soil needs to be poor in nitrogenous matter. Above all it must be well-drained, particularly in the north of the country and in other pockets where the rainfall is higher. Aspect is important. An orientation towards the east or south-east is ideal. The first rays of the morning will warm up the ground, drive away the mist and ensure that maximum use is made of the heat of the sun. Moreover the vineyard must be protected from wind, and the prevailing wind, in general in France, approaches from the west. It is therefore no coincidence that many of the greatest vineyards lie halfway down the south-eastern-facing slopes of river valleys. The slope aids drainage, trees at the top of the slope protect against the prevailing wind, and the nearby water protects equally against frost in winter and spring and drought in the later part of the summer.

Having chosen his site, installed a draining system and prepared his land, if necessary by manuring and adjusting the chemical composition and certainly by ensuring that it is free of disease, the grower's next task is the choice of grape variety and clone or strain of that particular variety, and the selection of a rootstock to go with it. The former choice will, of course, be determined by the local *appellation contrôlée* laws. A permanent result of the phylloxera epidemic is that all vine varieties in France (except in one or two isolated pockets, particularly where the soil is predominantly sandy, for the aphid cannot thrive here) are today grafted on to American, phylloxera-resistant rootstocks.

While it is fair to say that over the last thirty years the developments in viniculture have outstripped the evolution of viticulture, there has nevertheless been considerable research into the production of disease-resistant clones which can produce quantity without sacrificing quality, and the propagation of suitable rootstocks which are compatible, both with the clone and with the chemical and physical composition of the soil. Grafting normally takes place at the horticulturalist's greenhouse, not in the vineyard.

With considerations of mechanical tending of the vineyard, and, indeed, increasingly today, mechanical harvesting of the vintage, determining the space between the vines and the space between the rows, the vineyard is then planted. The amount of vines per given area varies greatly. Half as many vines can exploit the same amount of soil and produce as much wine as double the quantity. But in the better areas the density tends to be greater. The closer together, the more the vine is encouraged to develop a deeply penetrating root system. It will then extract the maximum complexity from soil and subsoil and be more resistant to temporary drought and floods.

Over the next few years, as the vine slowly develops into a mature plant, it is carefully pruned and trained into a particular shape. There are, in essence, two basic pruning methods: long- or cane-pruning, and short- or spur-pruning; and two basic shapes. Cane-pruning lends itself to the ultimate formation of a hedge shape, the canes – one or two with about six buds on each – being tied to a series of horizontal wires stretched along the row of the vines. This is known as the Guyot system. Spur-pruning or the Gobelet method produces a free-standing bush shape. There are six or so short spurs, each with two or so buds. A compromise between the two, giving short spurs on horizontal branches which can be trained on wires, is the Cordon de Royat system.

The vine flowers, and therefore will ultimately fruit, on the previous year's wood. The object of pruning is to select the best of this wood, to cut it back, eliminating all the rest, and to reduce the eventual crop to a potential of six to a dozen bunches of grapes per vine.

The yearly cycle of the vine begins after the harvest. With the onset of the cold weather of winter the vine has become dormant, the sap has descended into the roots of the vine and the process of tidying up, cutting away the dead wood and preparing the vineyard for next year's harvest can begin. The roots will be earthed up to protect them against frost, manure and other fertilisers can be ploughed in, and stakes and wires can be renewed if necessary. This is the time to rip up old vines which are dead or beyond their useful life and to begin to prepare sections of the vineyard for replanting in the spring after a year or two's rest. It is also the time to replace soil which may have been washed down the slopes by the rain of the previous season. Throughout the winter pruning takes place. It must be finished before the warmer weather returns again in the spring and the sap of the vine begins to rise anew.

In March the vine begins to wake up from its winter dormancy. A further ploughing is undertaken, this time to weed and aerate the soil and to uncover the base of the vine. The buds begin to swell, and will eventually burst in mid-April to reveal a small cluster of tiny leaves. This is when the danger of frost is at its greatest. The vine itself can withstand winter temperatures as low as minus 20°C but the embryonic leaf-cluster is susceptible to just the slightest descent below zero.

From the emergence of the leaves the vineyard is regularly sprayed: with sulphur against oidium, with copper sulphate (Bordeaux mixture) against mildew, and with other chemicals against red spider, moths and other insects. Alternatively pest damage can be reduced by the introduction of predators or by the use of pheremones to create sexual confusion in the insects and therefore a failure to propagate. Later on the fruit may be sprayed to harden its skin and prevent the emergence of rot. Increasingly, particularly in the South of France where the risk of insect depredation is less and the climate drier, vineyards – and indeed the winemaking that follows – are run on organic and ecological principles and chemical treatments are kept to a minimum.

In June the vine flowers, and this is one of the most critical times in the yearly cycle. Warm, dry weather is required to ensure that the fruit setting, which follows the flowering, takes place swiftly and successfully. If the weather is cold and humid the flowers may not set into fruit (*coulure*) or the fruit may remain as small, green, bullet-hard berries and not develop (*millerandage*). Moreover, should the flowering be prolonged the result will be bunches of uneven ripeness at the time of the harvest, compromising the decision of when to pick.

Throughout the summer spraying continues, particularly if the weather is inclement; the vineyard is ploughed to aerate the soil and eliminate weeds; the shoots are trained on to the wires, so that they do not break off in the wind, and the vegetation is trimmed back so that the vine can concentrate its resources into producing fruit. Increasingly in the best vineyards today there is a 'green harvest', an elimination of excess bunches before they develop and change colour, in order to reduce the final crop and so concentrate the eventual wine.

This colour change (*véraison*) takes place in August. Grapes as green as Granny Smith apples turn red and eventually black, or else soften into a greeny gold. From then it is seven weeks or so to the harvest (100 to 110 days after the flowering). Spraying must soon cease. The work in the vineyard is now over. All one can do is to pray for fine weather. Whatever might have happened earlier in the season the result will only have affected the quantity to be harvested. The weather from the *véraison* onwards is critical for the quality. What is required during these weeks is an abundance of sunshine, to ripen the fruit, an absence of excessive rain, which would only expand the grapes and dilute the wine, and an absence of humidity, which would encourage rot.

In about the third week of September the harvest starts. Preliminary tests to establish the sugar and acidity contents of the grapes will have taken place to ensure that ripeness and concentration are at their optimum at the time of collection. The weather forecast is anxiously studied. A preliminary passage through the vineyard to eliminate the diseased or otherwise inadequate bunches or part of bunches, and therefore make the life of the picker easier, is often undertaken. And when the time is ripe the vintage begins. The result of a year's hard labour is soon evident.

Today the majority of French vineyards, like the majority outside the country, is harvested by machine. Only in the top estates of Bordeaux and Burgundy and elsewhere, or where the land is inappropriate – and of course in places which produce individual bunch-selected sweet wines such as Sauternes – does harvesting continue by hand. And even here, for instance among the classed growths of the Haut-Médoc, mechanical harvesters are increasingly seen.

The advantage of mechanical harvesting is its convenience and its speed. One machine can do the work of twenty-five manual pickers and removes the stems from the bunches of grapes too. It can work twenty-four hours a day, if desired; and the new, second generation of machines, if correctly driven, does little harm to the vines. Mechanical harvesting can mean a later start to the harvest and a quicker conclusion, concentrating collection at the optimum state of the fruit's ripeness. This is the future.

HOW WINE IS MADE

Wine is produced by fermenting the juice of freshly gathered grapes. It sounds simple. But in fact it is extremely complicated. Though fine wine has been produced for centuries, it is only in the last forty years that we have come fully to understand both the alcoholic fermentation and that of malic acid to lactic acid which normally follows. Yeasts excrete enzymes which cause the sugar in the grape juice (or must) to turn into alcohol. The chemical process is very complicated. The reaction is exothermic, producing heat, so needs to be controlled. Carbon dioxide is also produced and there is an additional 3 per cent of other chemical by-products.

It is this 3 per cent of 'other' which is crucial. Alcohol has no flavour, nor does water, and the grape juice and therefore the wine is 85 per cent or so water. It is in the 3 per cent of other that you will find the colour and the flavour. The reason the fermentation process needs to be controlled is not only that at too high temperatures the process will 'stick' and the danger of

acetifaction (the production of vinegar) will arise, but that the flavour elements are very volatile. They need to be prevented from evaporating into the air. They need to be preserved in the wine. Moreover, the extraction of colour, tannins and flavour from the skins of the grape varies with both the temperature, pressure and availability of oxygen and with the length of maceration of these skins with the fermenting must.

There is a further problem. The effect of oxygen on wine will cause further chemical reactions to take place. Wine (alcohol) is only a halfway house between sugar and vinegar. While a little oxygenation is necessary for maturation, at all times during vinification and when the wine is retained in bulk thereafter, evolving and undergoing the various treatments which take place before it is bottled, the winemaker must ensure that the wine is uncontaminated by too much oxygen. He or she must not unduly expose the wine to air. Control, and the equipment with which to do this, as well as a thorough understanding of the process, is crucial.

Making Red Wine

Vinification

On arrival at the *cuverie* or vinification centre, the grape bunches are dumped into a V-shaped trough and churned by means of a revolving vice through a *fouloir-égrappoir*. This pulls off the stalks and gently breaks the skin of the grape berry. Only rarely outside Burgundy — and today it is rare *inside* Burgundy as well — is the must (or grape juice) vinified with the stalks. There is enough tannin in the skins already.

The produce of different grapes, different sections of the vineyard, and, particularly, vines of different age, will be vinified separately. For red wines, there are two concurrent aspects to vinification: the fermentation itself — the grape sugar being converted to alcohol — and maceration, the length of time the must is in contact with the skins, yielding tannin, colour and extract from the pulp. The temperature is important, for the reasons outlined above.

Today the finer red wines are usually vinified at about 30°C, allowing the temperature to rise no higher than 33°C before cooling. Some estates prefer to ferment between 26°C and 28°C. The lighter red wines, where excessive tannin is to be avoided, are vinified at a lower temperature of 25°C or less. The need for control of temperature, as well as the ability to fully clean and sterilise the fermenting receptacle, has led to a movement away from the more traditional oak to the adoption of stainless-steel or enamel-lined metal fermentation vats, which are easily cooled by running cold water down the outside, or by means of an enveloping, thermostatically controlled 'cummerbund'.

Periodically during fermentation the juice is pumped over the floating mass of skins, pips and stalks, if any, or this cap or *chapeau* is pushed down into the must and broken up, a process called *pigeage*. This is to combine the colour-retaining components with the must, equalise the temperature and assist the release of colour, tannin and extract from the skins. The current trend is to 'pump over' more frequently, but to macerate in total for a shorter time before running the liquid off the skins. The length of maceration (or *cuvaison*) will vary from three or four days for a light red wine such as Beaujolais or *vins de pays* from the South of France to as much as four weeks in the case of a top red Bordeaux.

When the fermentation is over, the juice is then run off into a clean, empty vat or barrel. This juice is the *vin de goutte*. The residue of skins is then pressed. The *vin de presse* that results is important. It will be firmer, more tannic and more acidic than the free-run juice, and a proportion will normally be blended back in varying quantities, or added periodically when the wine is later racked. The failure to add *vin de presse* may result in a rather weak, ephemeral wine, however enjoyable and supple it may be in its youth.

Carbonic Maceration

Carbonic maceration or *macération carbonique*, though a technique which is hardly used for the finest wines, particularly those intended to be wines for ageing, is now increasingly employed where the object is to produce fruity, soft, red wines for early drinking. This technique is discussed in more detail in the chapter on Beaujolais (see page 239).

In brief, on arrival at the *cuverie* the bunches of grapes are not crushed, but poured into the vats whole. These vats are normally closed to the air, allowing the carbon dioxide produced by the fermentation process to escape, but not the oxygen in the air to come into contact with the fruit.

The first part of the fermentation takes place within the skins of the grapes, in an atmosphere of carbon dioxide. This produces colour and extract but not much tannin. After a few days the free-flow juice is decanted off, the residue is pressed, and the fermentation process proceeds as normal. Often wine fermented by carbonic maceration is later blended with wine vinified in the natural way at the time of the *égalisage* or blending.

Cold Maceration

A further technique, employed particularly in Burgundy, is cold maceration or *macération à froid*. The principle is to maximise extraction of colour and aroma before the fermentation process takes place and without producing an excess of tannin at the same time. It is normally cool in Burgundy at the time of the harvest, and the lightly crushed grapes or whole bunches, or a proportion of the two, are left for a few days to macerate with the free-run juice, no deliberate steps being taken to start the fermentation process early. Some Burgundian growers, following the counsels of a local *oenologue* Guy Accad, deliberately prolong this maceration, and ensure that it takes place at an even colder temperature.

Chaptalisation

Chaptalisation is the addition of sugar to a fermenting must and is a practice permitted for white and rosé wines as well as for red. The process is not intended to make sweet wine but to make one with a higher level of alcohol. In vintages unblessed by a sunny autumn there is not enough natural sugar in the fruit to produce a wine with a sufficiently stable level of alcohol, say 12° or so. It is now customary everywhere in France except in parts of the Midi where it is forbidden to add sugar to the must, to the equivalent of a degree of alcohol or so or more, even in years when the grapes are fully ripe. It is said to knit the wine together. Moreover, if the sugar is added, not at the beginning of the fermentation but towards the end, it will extend the process, thus helping to extract more tannin (because the temperature will increase) and give both added density and added richness (eventually) to the wine.

Micro-Oxygenation and Délestage

These are two new-ish techniques, particularly popular in the South-West. Grapes such as the Tannat are quite the opposite of the Pinot Noir. While the Pinot needs to be vinified and reared in the absence of oxygen, once the fermentation gets under way, the Tannat, and to some extent the Syrah and both Cabernet varieties, need more aeration. The normal process would be to rack more frequently, but to carry this to excess, with all the pumping and general disturbance that would be involved, would tire the wine out.

So we have *délestage*, which I would describe as a wholesale pumping-over process. The entire vat of wine is run off, the cap falls to the bottom, where it is broken up, and the wine then poured back on top of it, all this hardly taking a minute or two. This produces better results than a more gentle pumping over, and can be employed where the vat is closed at the top, and *pigeage* (treading down of the cap) cannot be employed.

Micro-oxygenation consists of introducing a small cylinder into the middle of the tank of wine (both during and after fermentation and maceration). Oxygen is leaked in and gently bubbles up through the wine. Patrick Ducourneau in Madiran is one of the pioneers of this technique. It has certainly led to a considerable improvement in the local wines.

Elevage

Once the fermentation process is complete the must is now wine and it must be looked after with meticulous care until it is ready for bottling, a process that must be done at the right time and with correct attention to detail. I am convinced that as much potentially good wine is ruined by incorrect or simply sloppy cellarwork during the *élevage* as by poor vinification before or inferior storage afterwards.

After fermentation the first thing is to ensure that the wine is clean, in the sense of free of potential chemical or bacteriological contamination, and that it has completed its malolactic fermentation. This 'second' or malolactic fermentation, which also gives off carbon dioxide, often takes place immediately following the sugar-to-alcohol fermentation, and can be encouraged by warming the must or the surrounding environment to between 18° and 20°C, and the addition of an artificial malolactic bacterium to get the fermentation going. The result is to lower the apparent acidity by a degree or two; so rounding off the wine and softening it up. In many white wines, particularly those of the South with an already low acidity level, this would be a mistake, but with reds the malolactic fermentation is generally encouraged.

The next step is the *égalisage* or blending. This takes place normally during the winter a few months after the harvest, though in some regions it takes place just before bottling. This is the moment of truth – the creation of the château or domaine wine, the blending together of the constituent parts from different grape varieties (if there are more than one), vine ages and sections of the vineyard. A large property might have as many as thirty vats-worth of wine to choose from, and not all of these may be suitable. If the weather has not been perfect, or if much of the vineyard consists of immature vines – less than ten or even fifteen years old in a top growth – many will not be of the required standard for the *grand vin* or top wine.

Having made the blend (and we are assuming wine of some pretension here: lesser wines are stored in bulk), the wine is transferred to oak barrels in which it may well have been lying before the *égalisage* – and allowed to mature and settle out its sediment, or lees. The barrels will need constant topping up, to make up for evaporation, particularly in the first few months, and for this reason they are first stored with the bung-hole upright, loosely covered by a glass stopper or rubber bung. Later, a wooden, more permanent bung will be driven into this hole, and the casks moved over so the bung is on the side or, having taken up enough wood, the wine will be transferred back to tank.

One of the questions consistently asked of a proprietor or his cellar manager is the proportion of new oak hogsheads he uses each year. As a new cask now costs upwards of 3500 francs, the provision of a large proportion of new oak is a major financial undertaking. Nevertheless, the extra muscle and tannin, coupled with the flavour the oak gives to a wine, is an essential ingredient in the taste of a fine red wine. A few of the very top estates invariably put their top wine entirely into new oak. For most producers, a proportion of between a quarter and a half, depending on the quality and style of the vintage, is normal. More would impart too much of a *boisé* (woody) smell to the wine. This view would be echoed by many in Burgundy and elsewhere. Nevertheless, there has been a trend toward the use of more new wood. On the other hand, together with more new wood has come a reduction in the time the wine spends there. Ageing used to be for a minimum of two years. Today it is frequently as much as six months less before bottling, and the wine may well have been run off into older casks or into vat after only a year to avoid taking up too much taste of the oak.

The major French oak forests lie in the centre of the country. Limousin imparts a very marked oak flavour and is not used for fine wine. Tronçais, Nevers and Allier are widely found, the latter being the most delicate and is largely used for white wines. Elsewhere in France Burgundian oak and oak from the Vosges are used.

During the first year of a wine's life, it will be racked to separate the wine from its lees, and also to transfer it from new to old oak and vice versa, so that all the wine spends an equal amount of time in wood of different ages. Big full wines such as Bordeaux throw more sediment than lighter wines such as Burgundy. In Bordeaux the wine will be racked every three months in the first year, in Burgundy every six months or less. In principle the less you move or manipulate the wine the better. During the second year, the racking is less frequent, but additionally the wine is 'fined', traditionally with beaten white of egg for fine wines, to coagulate and deposit further unstable elements. Lesser wines are fined with isinglass, casein (milk powder), bentonite and other natural or proprietary substances.

Bottling

The date of bottling is an important matter which has only received sufficient attention relatively recently. I still do not consider that it is flexible enough to allow for variations between one vintage and the next. A wine matures much quicker in cask than in bottle, and a variation of six or even three months in the date of bottling can hence have a decisive effect on the eventual date of maturity and on the balance of the wine.

A concentrated, tannic wine from a Bordeaux vintage such as 1990 may need a full two years or even more in cask before it is ready for bottling, but equally a light vintage, particularly one that is feeble in acidity, a 1997 Côte Chalonnaise, for example, needs early bottling; and Beaujolais is bottled almost as soon as it is stable. Most top Bordeaux châteaux and their Côte d'Or equivalents in Burgundy bottle during the spring or early summer of the second year, when the wine is between fifteen and twenty-one months old. If you wait any longer the wine may dry out and become astringent, having lost some of its fruit before it is ready to drink.

When to Drink the Wine

Once a wine has been bottled, when will it be ready for drinking? And perhaps more important, how long will it be at peak after that? It has for long been the general rule that a wine such as a good Second or Third Growth Médoc from a good vintage like 1995 or 1996 requires ten years from the date of harvest to mature; a First Growth fifteen or more; and lesser Médocs, Saint-Emilions and Pomerols from five to ten years. *Petits châteaux* are at their best between three and six years after the harvest. These figures would be less in a softer, less tannic vintage such as 1993, and proportionately more in a big, firm vintage such as 1990. These figures would similarly apply to wine from the northern Rhône. For Burgundy they should be reduced by a third. Thereafter, a well-made, well-stored wine will last for at least as long as it has taken to mature. The proportion between the time a wine will live once mature and the time it has taken to reach maturity increases with the quality of the wine and the vintage, so that a top wine from an excellent red Bordeaux vintage, 1990, ready in 2010, instead of having thereafter a twenty-year life at peak, may have as much as forty, or twice the length of time it took to mature, before beginning to decline. Provided the storage is correct most well-balanced wines will last much longer than most people expect. It is harmony, which means a good acidity level, not size, which enables a wine to last.

When you prefer to drink your wine is a matter of personal taste. While I incline more to the French taste – which to some in England and elsewhere seems a predilection for infanticide – I normally stick to the Bordeaux ten-year rule, and its equivalent elsewhere. I prefer to drink a wine at the beginning of its 'at peak' plateau, rather than at the very end.

MAKING ROSÉ WINE

The normal process for making rosé begins as for red wine: but the must is racked off the skins after only a matter of hours (somewhere between six and twenty-four hours). Thereafter the juice is run off and the vinification proceeds as for a dry white wine. Most rosé is made for early drinking and few age with any dignity.

MAKING DRY WHITE WINE

Vinification

The grapes which will produce dry white wine normally reach maturity a few days before the red varieties, and the precise date for top quality is even more crucial in order that the exact balance between sugar and acidity can be obtained.

With the trend in the 1960s towards drier, crisper wines came an unfortunate move in the Loire, Bordeaux and elsewhere towards picking a few days in advance of the optimum moment in order to make wines with a good refreshing acidity. This was sadly carried a bit too far and the results, too often, were wines with a rasping, malic acidity and a consequent lack of ripe fruit. The wines were too green. As the grape ripens the malic acidity changes into tartaric acidity. Now, with the help of mechanical harvesting, the grower can wait longer without the risk of prolonging the collection of the crop beyond the desired period. It is now appreciated that once the correct maturity has been reached, provided the climatic conditions are favourable, the acidity, now essentially tartaric rather than malic, will not continue to diminish and may even concentrate further to give a wine with both ripeness and balance. Growers now concentrate on the flavour optimum.

White wines are vinified without their skins, and the first procedure is to press them as soon as possible after arrival from the vineyard, normally in some form of horizontal cylindrical apparatus. The juice is then run off and allowed to settle (a process called *débourbage*) for twenty-four hours so that the solid matter falls to the bottom before the rest is vinified. Except in the top estates where fermentation takes place in oak barrels, vinification takes place in vat or tank, often in anaerobic conditions, and for white wines must proceed at a reduced temperature in order to prolong the process as long as possible, thus preventing loss of the volatile elements which impart flavour and aroma, and maximising the intensity of the fruit.

The common temperature for the controlled fermentation of most white wines is between 18° and 20°C. For a long time it has been accepted that the lower the temperature of fermentation the more the volatile, flavour-enhancing chemicals in the fruit are preserved in the resulting wine. It is not the lower temperature *per se*, however, but the prolongation of the fermentation which is important. The longer the fermentation, the more complex the flavour. 'Artificial' yeasts are now widely employed, for they make the fermentation easier to control and produce wines of greater fruit definition and finesse, at the expense, perhaps, of individuality.

Today in order to maintain a crisper acidity in the finished wine the second, malolactic fermentation is discouraged for many fine white wines in Bordeaux, Jurançon, Alsace, the Rhône and the Midi, even in the Mâconnais and the Côte d'Or in some vintages, though it is necessary for more northern wines such as Sancerre and Chablis. Whether the wine is matured in cask or in tank, bottling takes place much earlier than for reds, often as early as the following spring. The aim is to preserve freshness and fruit and to minimise oxidation. Only the best, oak-vinified and oak-aged wines will develop in bottle.

Macération préfermentaire or skin contact before fermentation is a white wine technique that has become increasingly popular. It is now recognised that most of the flavour-producing elements in the pulp of the grape lie near or within the skin and this technique allows white grape juice to remain in contact with the grape skins for a few hours before pressing. It is a process which needs to be handled with great care, for bruised or rotten berries will taint the whole wine. The results though are most rewarding: wines of greater complexity and depth of flavour. Increased character can also be produced by leaving the new white wine on its fine lees (*sur lie*) for as long as possible before the first racking. The wine feeds off this sediment, mainly dead yeast cells, and becomes richer and fuller in flavour. In Bordeaux, Burgundy and elsewhere the wine might be kept on its lees until midsummer before the first racking.

Another development after leaving the wine for several months on its fine lees is to bottle without racking first. The result, once again, is an enhancement of the complexity. Muscadet has long been bottled *sur lie* in March or so six months after the vintage.

The bane of white wine has been the over-use of sulphur. Sulphur is a necessary ingredient in the preservation of wine. It protects it against oxidation and bacterial infection, but too heavy a hand with it will kill the wine. The sulphur will bind in with the wine, destroying the freshness, the nuances of the fruit, and producing a sickly, heavy 'wet-wool' flavour. This used to be particularly prevalent in Bordeaux. Thankfully, after years of maltreating their white wines, the Bordeaux winemakers are beginning to realise – as their counterparts in the Loire and southern Burgundy did years ago – that, well-handled, dry and sweet white wine does not require as much sulphur to protect it as they thought. More careful winemaking, in anaerobic conditions and with a cleaner must, enables the winemaker to reduce his recourse to sulphur dioxide during the *élevage*. Healthy wine, correctly balanced, requires less sulphur. If the Loire and Burgundian winemakers can do it, why can't the Bordelais? The penny is beginning to drop. Fewer and fewer dry white Graves – though there are still far too many depressing examples – taste of nothing but sulphur dioxide.

Elevage

The use of oak, new or newish, is another relatively recent development for white wine. Prior to the 1960s, wood – old barrels for the most part – was the most common receptacle for *élevage* and transporting wine. The fashion then swung to the tank, whether enamelled or stainless steel, and the concrete vat. All the old, diseased, bug-infected barrels were burned, and probably a good thing too. Only the very top wine estates persisted with using oak for their dry white wines.

But oak, new oak, adds weight, complexity of flavour, depth and class. More and more wines, even in less usual places like Sancerre and Alsace, are using wood. And, of course, the wine should be fermented as well as matured in cask. The wood flavours derived thereby are more delicate and complex and exist in greater harmony with the rest of the flavour ingredients of the wine. Oak should be *de rigueur* for any white wine aspiring to quality status, as it is in the *appellation* of Limoux in the Languedoc.

Bottling

White wines are generally bottled much earlier than reds: the vast majority, those not matured in oak, within six months of vinification. Most of the rest of the fine dry wines are bottled the following autumn or in the spring thereafter. Only the richest sweet wines such as those of Sauternes are given more than eighteen months in cask.

When to Drink the Wine

When should you drink white wine? The lesser wines, like 'small' white wines all over the world, are essentially made one year for drinking the next. Within twelve months after bottling, i.e. eighteen months after the harvest, they will begin to lose their youthful fruity freshness. This applies to most Sauvignon wines, to Muscadet and Mâcon, to the whites of Bergerac, Gaillac and the Midi, and to the standard Alsace *cuvées*.

Grander white wines, those that have been fermented and matured in oak, can, and must, be kept for a period. Often they enter a rather dumb phase after bottling, and for two or three years they will appear rather clumsy, particularly if they have been bottled with a little too much sulphur, as is still, sadly, often the case. Lesser vintages will be at their best between three and eight years after the harvest. The best white wines need longer before they are fully ready, and will keep for a decade or more after that.

MAKING SWEET WINE

The world's greatest sweet white wines are rare, highly prized, expensive to produce and infrequent in occurrence. That they appear at all is a tribute to the dedication and patience of the few growers who specialise in them, and is a consequence of a particular mesoclimate acting on a small number of specific grape varieties, the result of an Indian summer of misty mornings and warm balmy afternoons continuing long after the rest of the *vignerons* have cleared their vines and are busy in the cellars nurturing the birth of their new vintage. The French examples come mainly from the Loire and Sauternes.

The great sweet wines are not merely sweet. If this were all, the addition of sugar syrup to a finished dry wine would be all that was necessary. Indeed, this is how cheap sweet wines are made. But these the consumer will soon find bland and cloying.

Noble Rot

The finest dessert wines are the result of a particular phenomenon, the attack on the ripe, late-harvested fruit by a fungus known as *Botrytis cinerea*. It produces what is known in France as *pourriture noble* and in Germany as *Edelfäule*, both of which can be translated as 'noble rot'. Leave any fruit on the tree after it has ripened and eventually it will rot. This rot (*pourriture grise*), however, will not be 'noble'; the fruit will be ruined and the taste disgusting. In certain parts of the vineyard areas of the world though, in the right climatic conditions, the noble rot will occur and this in Bordeaux will produce the great Sauternes, in the Loire Valley will produce the sweet wines of the Layon and Vouvray and in Alsace will produce Sélections de Grains Nobles.

What is required is a particular mesoclimate. The grapes are left on the vine after the normal harvesting time for the production of dry white wine. The conditions thereafter need to combine both warmth and humidity. It must continue fine and sunny long into the autumn but not be too dry. Most high-quality vineyard areas, however, are near the extremes of viable grape production; in poor years the fruit does not ripen sufficiently and the later the harvest the greater the risk that summer will have finished and autumn rains and chilly winter weather will have set in. This further complicates matters for the quality sweet wine producer. He needs not just a fine late summer but a prolonged and clement autumn. These occur rarely. Two years out of three, or even three out of four, are good years for red and dry white wines. For great sweet wines, the regularity is hardly one in three or even one in four.

When the noble rot fungus attacks the ripe grapes, they first darken in colour. From golden, they turn a burnished, almost purple brown. Then the surface appears to get cloudy, the skin begins to wither and get mouldy as the spores of the fungus multiply, feeding on the sugar in the berry. Finally, the grape becomes shrivelled like a raisin and completely decomposed. The noble rot does not have a very prepossessing appearance!

Unfortunately, it does not strike with equal regularity and precision over the whole vineyard or even over the whole of a single bunch of grapes. This necessitates picking over the vineyard a number of times in order to select each bunch, part bunch or even, at Château d'Yquem, each individual berry, separately. A prolonged harvest is therefore implicit in the production of noble rot wines. In some cases it will continue not just into November but even into December.

The effect of this noble rot attack is to alter the chemical and physical composition of the grape and therefore, obviously, the taste of the wine. First, the water content of the berries is considerably reduced. Second, the acidities are changed and, third, the quantity of higher sugars such as glycerine is increased. The net effect is to create a very small quantity of juice with a sugar content equivalent to an alcohol level which in a top Sauternes will be well above 20°. This produces a wine with an actual alcohol level of 14 or 15° or so and 4 or 5° (higher in the most successful vintages) of unfermented sugar. This is the sweetness. The other effect of the noble rot is to combine this sweetness with a luscious, spicy, complex, individual flavour and a high, naturally ripe acidity level.

There is much talk in Sauternes today of a new technique called cryoextraction. Briefly the principle is that juice heavy in sugars and glycerine freezes at a lower temperature than water. Thus, should you have a situation where it rains during the harvest, if you are able to freeze the grapes to a certain temperature and then press them carefully you should be able to capture the concentrated, Sauternes-producing juice without it being diluted by the rain, for this rain will be frozen into ice-crystals and will not flow off during the pressing: a sort of artificial Eiswein, in fact.

Sweet wines by their very nature are an aberration. Contrary to all normal agricultural principles and practices the grower deliberately allows his harvest to rot. He has to wait until he is at the mercy of the elements as autumn evolves into winter: 'We are all playing poker with God', as one grower once told me. All too often a state of rot which was incipiently noble can be turned by bad weather into ignoble. This is where cryoextraction comes in. It is not intended to replace normal harvesting and pressing in fine weather, but it will enable a grower to rescue his harvest if the climatic conditions turn against him. Of course, the majority of sweet and semi-sweet wines are made from grapes which, while ripe, are not affected by noble rot. They are sweet because the fermentation process is arrested before all the sugar is converted into alcohol. This can be done by increasing the sulphur content and/or filtering out the active yeasts.

The fermentation of sweet white wine proceeds in general along the same lines as that for dry white wines. Crushing has to be slow, repeated and gentle – often, paradoxically, the best juice does not come from the first pressing – and the wine is often chilled or centrifuged to eliminate the gross lees rather than being allowed to settle of its own accord. This is in order to prevent oxidation. The fermentation is slow, often difficult. It is important to preserve the correct balance between alcohol and sugar. A Coteaux du Layon with, say, 12.5° of alcohol can support only a maximum 35 grams of sugar per litre. This wine would be called *moelleux* (medium sweet) but not *doux* (very sweet).

A *doux* Vouvray, such as those of 1989 and 1990, with say 50 grams of sugar per litre, will need to be more alcoholic. A Sauternes with 14 to 15° of alcohol needs to be really luscious or it will appear oily and heavy.

Once the wine has been made it takes longer than a dry one to settle down and stabilise. Moreover it is susceptible to further fermentation as, by its very nature, it will contain a large amount of unfermented sugar. It needs therefore to be carefully nurtured, its sulphur level maintained at a relatively high level to preserve it. Exposure to the air must be avoided at all costs.

Nevertheless maturation in (at least partially) new oak, and often for a year and a half or more, does wonders for the richest and most concentrated of these sweet wines. No classy Sauternes should be matured without oak. The lighter sweet wines of the Loire see less oak, if any, and are bottled sooner.

Passerillage

In some parts of France, in the Jurançon and elsewhere in the South-West, for instance, sweet wines are produced without being attacked by *pourriture noble*. The grapes merely dry out and concentrate on the vine without rotting. This method is called *passerillage*. The effect, however – a higher level of sugar and acidity in the reduced volume of juice, and hence a sweet wine – is the same, though the wines will not be as complex as those originating from nobly-rotten grapes.

Ageing of Sweet Wines

Sweet white wines need maturing. Though often delicious young they mature so well and can reach such levels of complexity that it is a tragedy to pull the cork too soon. A medium-sweet Loire wine may be mature at five years. Ten is the minimum for a *doux*, for a good Sauternes and for a top Alsace selected late-harvest wine. And they will last. A twenty-year-old Sauternes of a top vintage like 1990, 1989 or 1988 will still be a virile teenager. These wines will keep for fifty years.

MAKING SPARKLING WINE

A sparkling wine is produced by adding further yeasts and sugar to a young finished still wine, thus causing a second fermentation. The carbon dioxide so produced is not allowed to escape until the final bottle is opened by the consumer. The gas then rises up in the form of a *mousse* of tiny bubbles.

There are essentially two ways of making sparkling wine. In the first, the Champagne or Traditional method, the second fermentation takes place in individual bottles (see page 546). In the second, the second fermentation takes place in bulk, in a sealed tank, and the wine is eventually transferred in to bottle under pressure. This cheaper method is known as the *cuve close* or Charmat method. Most *appellation contrôlée* sparkling wines, including the Crémants of the Loire, Burgundy and Alsace, Blanquette de Limoux and, of course, Champagne, must be made by the first method. For some curious reason, and it cannot just be the quality of the fruit in the first place, non-Traditional method sparkling wines are usually of very inferior quality.

GRAPE VARIETIES

The grape variety – or mix of grape varieties (called *encépagement* in French) – is the single most important contributor to both the flavour and the character of a wine. The soil is important, as is the expertise and techniques of vine-growing (*la viticulture* in French) and winemaking (*la vinification* in French). In France the weather is paramount in determining the quality of the vintage. But the grape variety contributes most to the style of the wine. The following pages cover the main quality grape varieties planted in France.

RED VARIETIES

CABERNET FRANC

Location: Bordeaux; Bordeaux satellites; Madiran; Touraine (Chinon and Bourgueil); Anjou (Saumur-Champigny, Anjou-Villages and also for Cabernet Rosé d'Anjou).

This vine is the 'poor country cousin' of Cabernet Sauvignon, and shares many of its characteristics, though wine from it is less positive and less distinctive. In Bordeaux, though losing ground on the left bank in the Médoc, on the right bank in Saint-Emilion and Pomerol it is widely preferred to Cabernet Sauvignon. Here it is called Bouchet and thrives better than Cabernet Sauvignon on the more limestone and clay-based soils. Wine made from it is softer, more subtle and more aromatic. It is for this reason, as well as for its shorter growing cycle, that, much further north in the Loire Valley, Cabernet Franc is the grape used for the wines of Chinon and Bourgueil in the Touraine.

The bunch is looser, the grapes still small, but larger than those of Cabernet Sauvignon, and the resulting wine is more fragrant but less coloured, less full and less tannic. It develops faster than Cabernet Sauvignon. The vine is cane-pruned.

CABERNET SAUVIGNON

Location: Bordeaux, particularly in the Médoc and Graves areas; Bordeaux satellites such as Bergerac and Buzet; widely used in Provence and the Languedoc-Roussillon as a *cépage améliorateur* or on its own for *vin de pays* wines.

Though not the most widely planted grape in the Gironde (Merlot is the most popular Bordeaux grape variety), Cabernet Sauvignon is accepted as the classic red Bordeaux grape. It is a vigorous but small producer, which develops late in the season – thus an advantage against spring frosts – and ripens late. It flourishes on most types of soil, consistently showing its style and quality, as evidenced by the wide adoption of this grape outside the Bordeaux area, as a *cépage améliorateur* in the Midi, and in Australia and California. It is less susceptible to *coulure* (failure of the flower to set into fruit) or to *pourriture grise* (grey rot) than Merlot, but more so to powdery mildew. The grape cluster is cylindrical-conical, made up of small round berries, very black in colour. The vine is cane-pruned.

This is the grape which gives red Bordeaux its particular blackcurrant taste. It provides the firmness, the tannin and the backbone. It gives the colour and the acidity, from whence comes the longevity, the depth, the finesse and the complexity of top Bordeaux wine.

CARIGNAN

Location: throughout the South of France.

Like the Grenache, Carignan is of Spanish origin (its Spanish name is Cariñena). But today it is probably the most widely planted red wine variety in France. It buds late, thus being protected against spring frosts, but is susceptible to both mildew and oidium. *Coulure* is not a problem, however, and as a result it tends to over-produce. Restrained harvests will give a wine of good colour (the skins are thick), extract, alcohol and tannin.

Though frowned on in some parts of the South of France, Carignan is an essential ingredient in the vineyards of the Languedoc and the Roussillon, both for *vins ordinaires* and *vins d'appellation*. and is often produced by carbonic maceration methods. Here it is cane- or Cordon du Royat-pruned, facilitating machine-harvesting.

CINSAULT

Location: Southern Rhône; Provence; Languedoc-Roussillon.

Cinsault – some authorities prefer to spell it Cinsaut without the 'l' – is, with the superior Syrah and Mourvèdre, the variety most widely recommended in the southern Rhône as an accessory to the Grenache. Like the Grenache but unlike the other two, the wine it produces is low in tannin, but it is less affected by *coulure* and rot. It produces a wine with a better acidity and colour and rather more stylish fruit. The wine has rather an innocuous character and does not age well, particularly if cropped to the limit. It is often exiled from the red *cuvée* into the rosé. The vine is spur-pruned.

DURAS

Location: Gaillac; other South-West vineyards.

Together with the Braucol (see Fer Servadou) the Duras is one of the mainstays of red Gaillac wine. Wine made from Duras (not to be confused with the AC Côtes de Duras) is medium-bodied and fruity, and ages fast as the acidity level is low. It is cane-pruned.

FER SERVADOU

Location: western Languedoc; South-West.

Known as the Pinenc in Madiran and the Braucol in Gaillac and Marcillac, the Fer Servadou produces sturdy, somewhat rustic wine of size rather than nuance, and is now declining in importance. This is an accessory variety in Madiran, the Béarn, Gaillac and the vineyards of the Aveyron. It is also authorised in the Côtes du Cabardès. It is cane-pruned.

GAMAY

Location: Beaujolais; Mâconnais; Lyonnais; Savoie; Ardèche (*vin de pays*); Languedoc-Roussillon (*vin de pays*); Gaillac; Loire, particularly the Côte Roannaise, Forez and Haut-Poitou.

If the Pinot Noir is aristocratic, however much it may hint at having been born as the result of a dalliance with a member of a visiting circus, the Gamay is a solid, expansive and reliable member of the *bourgeoisie*. There are a number of Gamay varieties. The best and the one grown in Beaujolais is the Gamay Noir à Jus Blanc.

It is a vigorous, productive variety which ripens early. It is susceptible to spring frost, but is able to produce a second generation of buds to replace those which have been lost, so a serious deterioration in yield after poor weather is hardly ever a problem. It produces a medium-sized, compact cluster of berries, somewhat cylindrical, which makes a lightish wine of highish acidity, an abundant, crisp, cherry-like fruit, and very low tannin, which is at its best very young, often as soon as it has settled down after bottling. Gamay should be ripe but never sweet.

The Gamay is grown throughout France except in Alsace, Provence and Bordeaux, but comes into its own on the granitic soils of the northern Beaujolais and when vinified by carbonic maceration methods. It is also grown widely in the Mâconnais and to an extent on the lesser soils further north in Burgundy. In the Côte d'Or and the Côte Chalonnaise wines from Gamay are often blended with Pinot Noir (two-thirds of Gamay to one-third Pinot Noir) to make Bourgogne Passetoutgrains. This is one of the mismatches of the wine world, in my view, producing something both acid and rustic but it may be that the constituent parts – the grapes for the wines by implication of its name coming from the worst sited vineyards – were just as poor. Unlike the other Burgundian varieties the Gamay is spur-pruned.

GRENACHE

Location: Southern Rhône; Provence; Languedoc-Roussillon.

Though the Grenache originated in Spain, where under the name Garnacha it is one of that country's most popular red wine varieties, it has conquered southern France. This is the staple quality grape not only of Châteauneuf-du-Pape and Côtes du Rhône but of Côtes de Provence and the entire Languedoc-Roussillon.

Spur-pruned and trained to the Gobelet (bush) shape, Grenache is a fairly early developer though a late ripener. It is hardy, vigorous and adaptable, its major disadvantage being its lack of resistance to *coulure* and a tendency to rot if the weather changes to wet and

humid in the run-up to the harvest. A Grenache wine – and this is the reason why it is invariably blended with other varieties – has a wild, spicy, almost burned, slightly sweet character; very alcoholic on the one hand but blowsy because of a lack of acidity on the other and not particularly tannic.

The Lladoner-Pelut is, if not the same variety, at least a very close cousin.

MALBEC

Location: Cahors; Loire; Bordeaux; Bordeaux satellites.

This is the principal grape of Cahors, where it is called the Auxerrois or the Cot, and is grown in the Loire, where it is known as the Cot. In Bordeaux it is also authorised but it is little grown in the top properties, particularly in the Médoc, though it can be found in small proportions in the top estates of Saint-Emilion and Pomerol, where it is known as the Pressac. The berries are large and the cluster loose. Merlot is prone to *coulure*, downy mildew and rot. The quantity of wine which results is large, compared to other Bordeaux varieties. Malbec is quite rich in tannin and colour, but with less intensity of aroma and with much less finesse. In the Loire and Bordeaux the wine is only medium in body. In the best part of Cahors, on the baked limestone flanks or *causses* the grape makes wine that is rather more beefy. The vine is cane-pruned.

MERLOT

Location: Bordeaux, particularly in Saint-Emilion, Pomerol and the rest of the Libournais; Bordeaux satellites; Cahors; Languedoc-Roussillon (as a *cépage améliorateur* or on its own for *vin de pays* wines).

The Merlot is the leading grape of the Dordogne side of the Bordeaux region and the most widely planted across the area as a whole. It is a vigorous, productive vine, which buds early – thus rendering it liable to spring frost damage – and ripens earlier than both the Cabernets. It is susceptible to *coulure*, downy mildew and botrytis (rot) which can cause considerable damage if there is rain at the time of harvest. It is less adaptable to different soils.

The grape cluster is cylindrical, but looser than Cabernet Sauvignon and Franc, the other main red Bordeaux grapes, and the berries are round, but larger, and less intensely coloured. A Merlot wine is generally a degree or two higher in alcohol than wine from either Cabernet variety, less acidic, less tannic and less muscular. It is softer, fatter and more aromatic in character, and it matures faster. The vine is cane-pruned.

MOURVÈDRE

Location: Southern Rhône; Provence, especially in Bandol; Languedoc-Roussillon.

Mourvèdre is a variety of Spanish origin and is a difficult plant to rear. Trained by either Gobelet or Cordon du Royat, it buds late but also ripens late. Even in the magnificent Bandol sun it does not often reach full maturity before the last week of September. It is a fussy plant, susceptible to mildew and oidium, though less to *coulure*, preferring a sheltered spot and a deep, well-drained stony soil, and is sensitive to prolonged summer drought. The wine is full, quite alcoholic and rather bitter and dense at first. Underneath it is rich and classy, but patience is needed before the full glories are evident.

NÉGRETTE

Location: Fronton; also found in Cahors, Gaillac and elsewhere in the South-West.

The Négrette produces an easily quaffable wine that is soft and fruity, without tannin but also without a very pronounced acidity and so is incapable of ageing well. When young, crisp and intelligently made, the wine can be a delicious *petit vin*. The Négrette is cane- (single-Guyot) pruned.

PETIT VERDOT

Location: Bordeaux (Médoc only).

This variety is of minor importance, but is included here so that all the five Bordeaux red varieties are listed. Petit Verdot is a sort of super-concentrated Cabernet Sauvignon, which has all but disappeared in the Bordeaux vineyards except in some of the top Médoc estates. It is difficult to grow, prone to disease, and ripens last of all, often not completely successfully.

Some growers swear by it, saying it brings finesse, acidity, alcoholic concentration and backbone. Others, like Jean-Louis Charmolüé at Château Montrose or Robert Dousson, the former owner of Château de Pez, who have each carried out tests to discern the development of blends with or without wine from this grape, have decided it is not for them. As the late Peter Sichel of Château Palmer ruefully pointed out, in the good vintages when everything ripens successfully, Petit Verdot is superfluous; in the poor years, when you need it, it does not ripen at all. Nevertheless, he added, a mixture of grape varieties, each budding, flowering and ripening at a different time, acts as a kind of insurance against sudden attacks of frost, hail and other climate hazards. The vine is cane-pruned.

PINOT MEUNIER

Location: Champagne.

Readers may be surprised to read (I certainly was when I was first told) that it is the Meunier or hairy Pinot and not the Pinot Noir or the Chardonnay which is the most widely planted grape variety in Champagne. It buds later, so suiting sites vulnerable to frost and thriving in years when *coulure* has been a problem, and ensuring a larger and more consistent crop than the Pinot Noir. The variety shares many of the characteristics of its noble cousin but matures slower in the vineyard, so producing a wine of lower alcohol and higher acidity. This makes it rather more aromatic, though less long lasting. Fine for a non-vintage blend, but its comparative lack of finesse as well as staying power render it unsuitable for fine vintage wines. It is cane-pruned.

PINOT NOIR

Location: Burgundy; Champagne; Sancerre and other *appellations* of the Central Loire; Alsace; Jura; South of France, particularly Limoux.

Pinot Noir is said to be an old variety, close to the types the Romans brought with them when Burgundy was first planted with vines. It can be traced back in records to the early Middle Ages when there were a number of ducal edicts promoting the Pinot and outlawing the ignoble Gamay in the Côte d'Or. The variety is sensitive to cold, both during the winter and during the flowering. It buds early, making spring frost a potential hazard, and ripens early. Pinot Noir produces a small, cylindrical cluster of densely packed, slightly oval berries. As a result of the berries being close together, and particularly as many of the newer strains of Pinot Noir have thinner skins than hitherto, grey rot can be a serious problem if the weather turns humid towards harvest time.

As important are two other traits. Wine made from Pinot Noir is much more susceptible than most other varieties to over-production. The concentration and character dissolve rapidly if the yield is excessive. The introduction of high-yielding clones, particularly the infamous Pinot Droit, has been one of the banes of post-war Burgundy. Moreover, Pinot Noir is very susceptible to the temperature as it nears the end of its ripening cycle. As with other varieties the wine can be mean and unripe if the sun fails to shine, but if the weather is too hot and roasted a Pinot Noir wine is prone to becoming coarse and leaden-footed. For this reason it is rarely successful outside the Burgundy region.

A Pinot Noir wine is rarely a blockbuster. Finesse rather than muscle is the keynote. The flavour of young Pinot Noir wine is of slightly sweet, freshly crushed, soft summer fruits; a fragrant, silky, multi-faceted and delicately elegant combination of raspberries, strawberries, mulberries and plums. Burgundy is feminine while red Bordeaux and Hermitage are masculine. Concentrated young Burgundy often offers up a hint of coffee. The elusive character can often, though, be swamped by excessive maceration or by too much new oak.

As a Pinot Noir wine matures, an animal, gamey, almost vegetal aspect evolves. The fruit flavours deepen, incorporating hints of damson and blackberry, and the whole thing becomes much more sensuous. Pinot Noir also makes an attractive *rosé* wine. The vine is cane-pruned, or trained to a Cordon du Royat, in order to space the fruit out more evenly.

POULSARD, TROUSSEAU AND MONDEUSE
Location: Jura; Savoie.
These three grapes are the indigenous varieties of the

red wines of the Jura and the Savoie. None is particularly distinguished. The first two are found in the Jura and the Mondeuse in Savoie. The Poulsard is prone to frost because it buds early, to *coulure* and to rot, because the skin is thin. The wine is reasonably perfumed, light in body but oxidises quickly. It makes a pretty but essentially uninspiring red which is more akin to a *rosé*.

Trousseau is a moderately producing variety with a thicker skin, producing fullish, well-coloured wine which needs time to soften. The wine is rustic though, and it does not age well, losing colour and also oxidising fast. In the Jura both these varieties are losing out to the Pinot Noir; and a good thing too. Both are cane-pruned.

The Mondeuse is confined to the Savoie, though it appears under the name of Refosco in northern Italy. It is a vigorous variety, and can produce wine with good body, colour and fruit, though rarely in the cool alpine climates of the Savoie. Here the wine is all too often weak, tart and attenuated, and without any potential for ageing. The vine is spur-pruned.

SYRAH
Location: Rhône Valley, particularly in the northern section; Provence and the Languedoc-Roussillon; Gaillac.
The Syrah is one of the three great black grapes of France, similar in quality and depth of character to the Pinot Noir and Cabernet Sauvignon. It is the classic variety of all the *appellations* of the northern Rhône and is now increasingly used as a *cépage améliorateur* in the southern Rhône, Languedoc-Roussillon and Provence. It is said to have originated in either Syracuse in Sicily or Shiraz in Persia (hence the grape's famous Australian name of Shiraz), or even both, but has certainly been established in the Rhône Valley for many centuries, if not since Roman times. Prior to the phylloxera epidemic it was distributed even more widely in France.

The Syrah is not a productive variety and, indeed, loses much of its character when grown on more fertile, alluvial or gravel soils rather than on the essentially granite-based rock of the northern Rhône. It is susceptible to *coulure* but resistant to mildew and oidium. The berries are small and densely purple in colour and give a wine which is solid, tannic, full-bodied and long-tasting. When young, the wines have a youthful, even raw, slightly 'green' damson or blackcurrant leaf aroma. On ageing the flavour mellows, softens and becomes more obviously rich as the wine takes on the extra complexity of age. Syrah wines need a long time to mature but their character is noble and aristocratic and worth the patience. The Syrah is both spur- (Gobelet) and cane-pruned, or trained to the Cordon du Royat.

TANNAT

Location: Madiran, Irouléguy, Béarn; elsewhere in the South-West.

The Tannat is the classic red wine variety of the extreme South-West of France. It buds and ripens late, in cool vintages not entirely successfully, but when it does the leaves turn completely red, a fiery russet, and seem to shimmer in the late afternoon sun of a glorious autumn day. Tannat produces a deeply coloured, full-bodied, tannic wine, with high acidity and alcohol. Modern methods have tamed what used to be rather a brutal wine and shown that Tannat is a grape variety of high quality, producing richly fruity, long-lasting wine. The Tannat is cane-pruned.

WHITE VARIETIES

ALIGOTÉ

Location: Burgundy.

Aligoté is an old Burgundian variety of very secondary importance, producing only generic wine. It has diminished in favour in recent years. Aligoté is a resistant grape which crops well, ripening early to produce a light, *primeur*-style wine with a slightly herbal flavour and rather higher levels of acidity than the Chardonnay. The variety needs good weather in the run-up to the harvst otherwise the wine can be somewhat tart.

There is a certain amount of Aligoté in odd parcels throughout the region. Only in the Auxerrois and in Bouzeron in the northern Côte Chalonnaise is it a speciality; Pernand-Vergelesses in the Côte de Beaune used to be another commune boasting fine Aligoté, but in recent years, as elsewhere, the variety has tended to be

replaced with Chardonnay. Aligoté is the traditional wine for mixing with a little Crème de Cassis to make Kir. The vine is spur-pruned.

BOURBOULENC

Location: Southern Rhône; Languedoc; Cassis.

Bourboulenc is losing favour. The wine tends to be a little oily and alcoholic, hard and somewhat fruitless. In a blend it can add body, but rather at the expense of elegance. It is known as the Doucillon in Cassis. It is spur-pruned.

CHARDONNAY

Location: Burgundy; Champagne; Jura; Savoie; Ardèche (*vin de pays*); Loire (*vin de pays*); Limoux; South of France (*vin de pays*); increasingly elsewhere.

The first thing to get straight about Chardonnay is that it has nothing to do with the Pinot family. The phrase Pinot-Chardonnay is a misnomer. Chardonnay is currently the most fashionable white wine variety in the world. It is probably now grown in every single wine-making region in France save for Bordeaux, the northern Rhône and parts of the South-West (it is now even allowed in Bergerac for *vin de pays*) as well as almost everywhere else.

Chardonnay is a fairly vigorous variety. It starts and finishes its growing season just a little after the Pinot Noir but is nevertheless also susceptible to spring frost, particularly in the cooler climate of Chablis, but is more hardy to extreme winter temperatures. *Coulure* is also a problem. It forms a small, relatively compact, winged-cylindrical cluster of small berries, not as densely closed as that of the Pinot Noir, and so is less susceptible to grey rot, though in the Mâconnais heat in the run-up to the vintage has occasionally produced *pourriture noble*.

Chardonnay grows well on all calcareous-chalky soils and is in general a much more adaptable variety than Pinot Noir, performing equally well in California as in Champagne and Chablis, though there is a danger of excessively high degrees of alcohol in hotter conditions, as much in Pouilly-Fuissé as in the Napa Valley. The best Chardonnay wines are both fermented and matured in wood, a percentage of which is new. It is the blend of subtle, ripe, opulent, nutty-buttery fruit gently supported by oak which is the true taste of fine Chardonnay and one of the great white wine flavours of the world. It ages very well in bottle. Chardonnay is cane-pruned.

CHENIN BLANC

Location: Loire, particularly Touraine and Anjou.
Though there is a great deal more Sauvignon and Muscadet under cultivation than Chenin Blanc, it is Chenin which immediately springs to mind when one thinks of the Loire. It is the top white wine grape of Anjou and Touraine, exclusively producing the wines of Vouvray and Montlouis, Coteaux du Layon and Savennières, as well as the other quality white wines of the area. It is a vigorous, reasonably high-yielding variety that buds early, rendering it susceptible to spring frost. It is sensitive to both mildews though resistant to *coulure* and, most importantly, prone to rot. This is both its greatest advantage and its chief drawback. If the autumn weather is benign the grower can wait for an attack of *pourriture noble*. If not, and in the Loire we are almost at the northernmost limit of viable viticulture – so the risk is even higher than in Bordeaux – the rot will be grey, ignoble, and the Vouvray or Coteaux du Layon producer is wisest to avoid the risk and make a wine which is *sec-tendre* (dry but soft) or *demi-sec*.

Chenin wines have another failing. For some reason the flavour absorbs sulphur, becoming hard, neutral and somewhat sickly if the winemaker has over-protected his wine. The flavour is essentially fuller, richer and sweeter-smelling than Sauvignon, even if the wine is dry. It reminds me of a mixture of Victoria plums, greengages and something herbal and flowery such as camomile. There is a tart acidity in Chenin wines which admirably balances the more peachy, nectarine fruit of the sweeter versions, but the drier wines can be somewhat lean if the autumn weather has not provided enough sun. While some growers make an off-dry wine for everyday drinking, the best dry Chenins in Vouvray and Savennières may need five years to mature properly, longer even than most Chardonnays. It is spur-pruned.

CLAIRETTE

Location: Languedoc; Roussillon; Southern Rhône; Provence; Cassis; Palette.
Clairette was once the most widely-planted quality white grape variety throughout the South of France. Correctly vinified it can produce a pleasant, slightly appley wine, but the acidity is low and the wine a little light and characterless. It can still be found: indeed there continue to be two separate Clairette *appellations* (Clairette de Die and du Languedoc) but winemakers are now more interested in other varieties. It is cane-pruned.

COLOMBARD

Location: South-West; Bordeaux.
A healthy, vigorous, high-yielding variety: permitted in Bordeaux but useful in the South-West (though not used in Armagnac). It produces simple but fruity wines with reasonable acidity. It is cane- pruned.

GEWURZTRAMINER

Location: Alsace.
Nowhere else in the world does the Gewurztraminer reach such an apogee of quality than in Alsace. With its easily enjoyed, memorable, spicy flavour, Gewurztraminer is the ambassador of Alsace; as the late Jean Hugel, head of Hugel, the long-established Alsace merchants, wrote, 'every man's Grand Vin'.

The flavour is attractive and the wine, when well made, a delight. The Gewurztraminer is said to be a form – a sort of particularly spicy cousin – of the Traminer grape, a variety which has been indigenous to Alsace since the Middle Ages. The Traminer may possibly originally have come from the village of Tramin or Termano in the Italian Alto-Adige – it is certainly still widely planted there – or this may be pure coincidence. As Gewurztraminer, the grape has had its own individuality for at least a century or more, when it first appeared on wine lists as a superior and more expensive alternative to Traminer. For years the names Traminer and Gewurztraminer were interchangeable in Alsace, the latter name – for *Gewurz* is German for 'spice' – being the spicier example. Since 1973 all wine has been labelled as Gewurztraminer.

It is not an easy variety to cultivate. Though vigorous and thriving on most soils, particularly those heavy with clay, it is prone to frost in the spring because the buds break early, and also to powdery mildew. More importantly it is also more susceptible than most to *coulure*. In 1990, and again in 1994 and 1995, there was a tiny Gewurztraminer crop in Alsace as a result of poor weather in June.

Gewurztraminer requires a particularly good autumn in order fully to ripen. When this happens, the small, rather loose bunch of small, thick-skinned grapes will turn salmon pink in colour, leading some to mistake them for unripe red grapes. Because of this late ripening, I often find merchants' basic Gewurztraminer to be a little insufficient in fruit, thus sometimes a little bitter. The Reserve wines are invariably better value for money and will keep. The better examples still will develop for five years or more, and last for twenty.

Gewurztraminer varies widely in style, largely because of the soil on which it is grown. Some *négociants*, having allowed a malolactic fermentation to occur, produce a soft, scented wine. Others make a more masculine example, firmer and with higher acidity, longer-tasting. Others still produce a very aromatic Gewurztraminer; some, even the rather over-perfumed wine the locals call *pommadé*. Above all Gewurztraminer is unmistakable. It is fat, scented, aromatic and spicy. It is mouth-filling, strong and flamboyant. There is nothing particularly subtle or elegant about a Gewurztraminer wine but there is much which is irresistible, even seductive. The variety is cane-pruned.

GROS PLANT

Location: Muscadet; Cognac.

A variety of high acidity, low alcohol and not much interest, also known as the Folle Blanche in the Charente. It is cane-pruned.

MACCABÉO

Location: Roussillon; Languedoc.

Known in Catalonian Spain as the Viura, the Maccabéo or Maccabeu is particularly found in the Roussillon as one of the base varieties for the *appellation contrôlée* white. It

is light, *primeur* and fruity, with good acidity and more interest than most of the local white varieties. The Maccabéo is cane-pruned.

GROS MANSENG AND PETIT MANSENG

Location: Jurançon; elsewhere in the South-West.

The Petit Manseng is the one with the smaller berries, as you might expect, and it is also the superior variety. Unfortunately it is the more difficult of the two to grow and much the lower yielder. The skins of both, but particularly of Petit Manseng, are thick, so the berries dry up rather than produce *pourriture noble* in the best vintages. Both varieties produce wines with plenty of interest, flavour and quality. The character is herbal and gently spicy, with good levels of both alcohol and acidity. There is a tendency today to use a majority of Gros Manseng in the blend for a dry wine and Petit Manseng if the aim is a sweet wine. Both Mansengs are cane-pruned.

MAUZAC

Location: Limoux; Gaillac; elsewhere in the South-West.

Mauzac is a vigorous variety which ripens late and produces a crisp, somewhat neutral, lightish wine with quite a high acidity. The flavour is herbal and appley; and the wines are best drunk young while they are fresh. As a wine with high acidity Mauzac is the traditional base for the sparkling wines of Limoux. In Gaillac the wine is often slightly *pétillant* or *perlé*. The variety is spur-pruned.

MUSCADET

Location: Muscadet.

Muscadet is the name of a wine and a vineyard area as well as a grape. It is an interloper in the Pays Nantais at the western end of the Loire Valley, having arrived from Burgundy in the early eighteenth century. The variety is, in fact, the white Gamay or Melon de Bourgogne.

Muscadet is resistant to frost, moderately vigorous and buds and ripens early. It is susceptible to both mildews and to rot, but does not suffer unduly from *coulure*. Muscadet wine has a flavour which is somewhat neutral, but fresh and soft, not overly acidic. It needs drinking early. The vine is spur-pruned.

MUSCADELLE

Location: Bordeaux; Monbazillac and other Bordeaux satellites.

The Muscadelle has nothing in common, despite the similarity of spelling, with either the Muscadet of the Pays Nantais or the various varieties of Muscat. It is moderately vigorous but very productive, develops late, and produces a large, loose, conical cluster of sizeable round berries. It is susceptible to *coulure*, powdery mildew, *pourriture grise* and botrytis (*pourriture noble*) while being less prone to downy mildew. You will rarely come across the Muscadelle in Bordeaux except in small proportions in the sweet white wine areas of Bordeaux. Even here it is frowned upon at the highest level, for it is considered to produce coarse wine; very perfumed, but lacking finesse. In Monbazillac and Saussignac in the Bergerac region it is more highly regarded. It is cane-pruned.

MUSCAT

Location : Alsace; southern Rhône and Languedoc-Roussillon for *vins doux naturels* and *vins de pays*.

There is a phrase in the Song of Solomon, 'a fountain of gardens', which to me admirably summarizes the flavour of dry Muscat wines. Muscat makes the most grapey of all wines, for wines do not normally taste of grapes. Normally, in the Midi and elsewhere around the Mediterranean, it is found as a sweet wine. In these regions – Beaumes-de-Venise, Rivesaltes, Frontignan and Lunel – the fermentation of the must is arrested by fortification with brandy, producing a naturally sweet wine with an alcohol level of just over 15°. These are called *vins doux naturels*.

There are many, many different varieties of Muscat grape. In Alsace there are two, the Muscat à Petits Grains, which is also grown in Beaumes-de-Venise and Frontignan, and the Muscat Ottonel. The resulting wine is always dry. Neither variety is easy to grow in the Alsace climate. Both are rather particular about the soil they prefer and are very prone to *coulure*, mildew and rot, sometimes failing to produce at all. The Muscat à Petits Grains, perhaps the older variety of the two in the region, ripens late, a further disadvantage, and so has

been largely replaced since the late nineteenth century by the Ottonel, a variety developed from the Chasselas, which develops earlier and produces more regularly. I find the Ottonel wine less fine, less distinctive, coarser, and it is sad that more hardy strains of the true Muscat d'Alsace have not so far been developed. A good Muscat from Alsace will have a wonderfully fresh, flowery, sweet grapey nose – there are elements of honeysuckle – and yet be dry on the palate. It makes a perfect aperitif, and is best drunk young.

In Roussillon both *vins doux naturels* and dry *vins de pays* are produced from Muscat à Petits Grains and the less subtle but hardier Muscat d'Alexandrie. All these three Muscat varieties are spur-pruned.

PICPOUL

Location: Languedoc; Southern Rhône; Charente; Pays Nantais.

Picpoul produces a fresh wine, good in acidity if deficient in most other interesting parts such as fruit. It is authorised in Châteauneuf-du-Pape and is found in the Languedoc where there is a separate white sub-*appellation* called Picpoul de Pinet. In the Charente (Cognac area) it is known as the Folle Blanche. and in the Pays Nantais – the Muscadet region – it is called the Gros Plant. It is cane-pruned.

PINOT BLANC AND PINOT AUXERROIS

Location: Alsace; Burgundy.

Clevner, or Klevner, is the Alsace name for wine which can come from a number of members of the Pinot family. Normally it is made from the Pinot Blanc which originated in Burgundy or from its slightly spicier cousin, the Pinot Auxerrois. Clevner can also be made from the Pinot Noir vinified as a white wine, or from the Pinot Gris.

Whatever the blend, the wine can be called either Clevner or Pinot Blanc, and normally the latter for the export markets. Pinot Blanc is more productive than Pinot Auxerrois but Auxerrois gives a slightly higher alcohol degree and marginally lower acidity, though in neither variety is the wine's acidity level very high. Clevner wine has the typical, rather foursquare Alsace character, fuller and more interesting than Sylvaner, and also used for carafe wine. It is soft, fruity, supple and fairly low in acidity. It is best drunk young while it still preserves its youthful freshness. Today it is the basis for most 'house' Alsace blends.

Production of Pinot Blanc has increased considerably in Alsace in the last twenty years as it can be planted on soils generally unfavourable to other varieties and it has a good resistance to frost, though it is susceptible to a number of fungoid diseases. Pinot Blanc forms the base for most Crémant d'Alsace, the local sparkling wine. Both varieties are cane-pruned.

PINOT GRIS

Location: Alsace; Burgundy.

That the wine from the Pinot Gris came to be called Tokay d'Alsace in Alsace is explained by local tradition that the variety was brought back by Baron Lazari de Schwendi who led an expedition of French mercenaries which captured the town of Tokay from the Turkish invaders in 1565. Sadly for the story, Pinot Gris has no connection at all with the Furmint, the real Tokay grape, it being the same as the Szukebarat of Hungary's Lake Balaton region, the Ruländer of Germany and the Malvoisie of the Loire Valley. Despite recent EU directives, endeavouring to prohibit the use of the title Tokay d'Alsace, the locals still persist with using the name.

Pinot Gris ripens early but produces feebly and is prone to disease. The wine is full, fat, rich and spicy with a sort of barley sugar after-taste, and a fairly high level of alcohol. Its lack of acidity prevents Tokay d'Alsace from being as interesting and as satisfying as the wines made from Riesling and Gewurztraminer. Nevertheless, it is a 'first division' Alsace variety, with a lot more character than either the Pinot Blanc or the Pinot Auxerrois.

Though not widely planted, Pinot Gris is one of three varieties in Alsace which are regularly made into Vendange Tardive and Sélection de Grains Nobles wines (the other two are Riesling and Gewurztraminer) and will develop in bottle.

In Burgundy it is known as Pinot Beurot, but is not very widely planted and is now discouraged. It is cane-pruned.

RIESLING

Location: Alsace.

The noble Riesling, producer of nearly all Germany's finest wines, is equally at home in Alsace. While, to the outsider, Gewurztraminer may be the most 'typical' Alsace grape, the locals are normally proudest of their Riesling wines. Though it has been grown there since 1477, and widely since the mid-eighteenth century, Riesling has only been a major force in Alsace since the 1920s. The Riesling prefers a well-drained slope, generally of a limestone nature. Yet it will thrive on the volcanic soil of the famous Rangen vineyard at Thann, on the granitic soil of the Brand vineyard at Turckheim, on the gravelly alluvial soil of the Herrenweg in Turckheim, on the chalky clay of the Clos Hauserer, as well as the limestone of the Hengst vineyard, both in Wintzenheim. The Turkheim producer Zind-Humbrecht has vineyards planted with Riesling on all these sites. A comparative tasting of all their different Rieslings, each made in the same way, but each with its own particular characteristics and nuances, is a fascinating experience.

The Riesling vine is hardy and resistant to disease, and though a relatively shy cropper compared with the Sylvaner or Pinot Gris, it is regular. It ripens late, but — a great advantage in a northern climate — it continues to develop even in fairly cool autumns. When allowed to come to full maturity it will give a wine of extraordinary finesse and complexity of fruit, with a complex nose, and a rich, full flavour balanced with a high level of acidity, giving an excellent length on the palate. In Alsace, unlike on the Rhine and the Mosel, the must is allowed to ferment completely, any residual sugar, in the case of Vendange Tardive or Sélection de Grains Nobles wines, being natural, the sugar of perfect ripeness.

An Alsace Riesling can be anything from a classy but essentially rather four-square wine, albeit with the characteristic clean, slightly austere fruit of the Riesling grape, to a wine of superlative quality, one of the really great wines of the world. Even in poor years like 1991, a Riesling from a good site such as Trimbach's Clos Sainte Hune can be remarkably fine, while the wines of the other Alsace grapes remain no better than undistinguished. The Riesling is cane-pruned.

ROLLE

Location: Languedoc; Provence; Bellet; Corsica.

Also known as the Vermentino and supposed to be the same as Malvasia, Rolle is authorised for Bellet, and now increasingly found elsewhere in the Midi. The Rolle is a more-than-useful variety, producing an aromatic wine of generous body (and no lack of acidity if not over-produced) which takes wood fermentation and ageing well. It is cane-pruned.

ROUSSANNE AND MARSANNE

Location: Rhône; Savoie; Languedoc-Roussillon.

It is convenient to treat these two varieties together for, outside Condrieu and Château Grillet where the Viognier is grown, they produce all the white wine *appellations* of the northern Rhône. Roussanne is the classy variety but very susceptible to oidium, and even now that more resistant clones have been developed, a poor cropper. Its wine is delicate and fragrant, with a crisp mountain herbs flavour, a refreshing acidity and a depth of character which means that not only can it be delicious young, but it will age; though it seems to go through a curious adolescent phase in the middle. In the Rhône it is almost entirely confined to the Hermitage hill, but it is becoming increasingly common in the Languedoc-Roussillon for *vins de pays*.

Elsewhere in the northern Rhône the Marsanne has taken over. More vigorous and more productive than the Roussanne, the Marsanne ripens almost too easily. There is a tendency to produce wines with a little too much alcohol and not enough acidity. Blended half with Roussanne and correctly vinified as in the top wines like Jaboulet's Hermitage, Le Chevalier de Sterimberg, its threatening coarseness can be contained. Elsewhere the wine needs to be bottled and consumed early before it maderizes.

In the Savoie, where the Roussanne is known as the Roussette, the wines, of whichever origin, are lighter, more ephemeral, and have a mountain herbs flavour. Like the Roussanne the Marsanne is found in the Languedoc-Roussillon, and some enterprising producers of *vins de pays* make some interesting examples. Both Roussanne and Marsanne are cane-pruned.

SACY

Location: Saint-Pourçain-sur-Sioule; Auxerrois.

Though not allowed in the Auxerrois for *appellation contrôlée* Bourgogne Blanc Sacy is permitted for the Crémant. In Saint-Pourçain-sur-Sioule it is known as the Trésallier. It has a tart acidity and a slightly off crab-apple-quince flavour. It is cane-pruned.

SAUVIGNON BLANC

Location: Bordeaux, Bergerac, Duras and other Bordeaux satellites; Gaillac; Touraine; Central Loire; Auxerre (Sauvignon de Saint-Bris); Provence and Languedoc-Roussillon as a *cépage améliorateur* or as *vin de pays*.

The Sauvignon Blanc, to differentiate it from other Sauvignons (Sauvignon Gris is a spicier, more aromatic cousin found in Bordeaux), is a vigorous variety which matures early, forming a compact, conical cluster of small round berries. According to leading ampelographers it is subject to *coulure*, but in my experience the size of the crop in Bordeaux does not seem to vary nearly as much as a result of poor flowering as does the Merlot, for example, and in the Loire crops suffer more as a result of frost, so no doubt more *coulure*-resistant strains have been developed. Oidium is more of a problem. It is also prone to botrytis, though not so much as Sémillon.

The Sauvignon grape produces a wine with a very individual flavour: steely, grassy, high in acidity, very flinty and aromatic. Words like gooseberry, blackcurrant leaf, even cat's pee are employed. As such the dry, stainless-steel-aged, youthfully bottled Sauvignon is a wine now widely seen, though the Bordeaux version is somewhat fuller and less racy than that of the Touraine and Central Loire, and in Bordeaux many seemingly pure Sauvignons have a little Sémillon in the blend to round the wine off. Strange as it may seem for a white wine, this variety produces a wine with a certain amount of tannin, and as a result of this, vinification and *élevage* (initial maturing) of pure Sauvignon in new oak is a procedure which needs to be handled with care. Combined with Sémillon in various proportions and fermented and aged in wood, Sauvignon produces the great white Graves. Sauvignon is cane-pruned.

SAVAGNIN

Location: Jura.

The Savagnin Blanc is said by ampelographical experts to be the same as the Traminer of Alsace. (Do not confuse it with the Savagnin Rosé or the Klevner of Heiligenstein which makes a particular, rather uncommon wine in Alsace. This is said not to be a true relation.) Legend has it that Savagnin was brought from Hungary to France by Benedictine monks in the tenth century. It is a late developer and a poor cropper but produces a wine powerful in both alcohol and flavour. I find it has little in common with the Traminer, but that is not to say that it does not have either quality or individuality. The wine is full and has a peculiar spicy nuttiness that reminds me of green walnuts. You will rarely see it on its own as a table wine for it is normally the minor partner in a Chardonnay/Savagnin blend. As the 'onlie begetter' of the Jura *vins jaunes* it is incomparable. The Savagnin is cane-pruned.

SÉMILLON

Location: Bordeaux; Bergerac and other Bordeaux satellites.

Sémillon is the base for all Bordeaux's great sweet wines, though its value for dry wine production is only just beginning to be appreciated once again. This is the most widely planted white grape in the Bordeaux area. Sémillon is a vigorous, productive variety. It is spur-pruned; and pruned very hard in Sauternes to reduce the crop to a minimum. It produces a cylindrical bunch of round berries, noticeably larger than the Sauvignon Blanc. These tend to develop a pinkish shade at full maturity, turning to browny-purple with over-ripeness. It is a hardy variety but susceptible to rot, both *pourriture grise* and *pourriture noble*, as it has a thin skin.

Poorly vinified, dry Sémillon wines can lack freshness and bouquet, character, breed and acidity. The result is heavy, neutral and dull. Correctly vinified, as increasingly this variety is in the Graves and the Entre-Deux-Mers, the results are totally different. The wines, though dry, are rich, fat and aromatic, with almost tropical, nutty fruit flavours and quite sufficient acidity. Good dry Sémillon is very classy, a far more interesting wine in my view than dry Sauvignon, and it has been under-rated in Bordeaux. It has taken the Australians, where for many years the variety has been grown in the Hunter Valley, to show the Bordeaux wine producers the potential for this grape.

SYLVANER

Location: Alsace.

Sylvaner is a variety which is less popular than it was a couple of decades or so ago. Having been No 1 in Alsace it is now No 4, after Riesling, Pinot Blanc and Gewurztraminer. Its origin is said to be Austria or Transylvania, and it only arrived in Alsace in force after the Franco-Prussian war (1870-1871) when the region was under German rule. Without being a hardy plant, it is a grape which gives a high yield, even in cool conditions, and it is also resistant to rot. It ripens later than most of the rest of the Alsace grapes. It is usually cane-pruned.

Sylvaner wine has a low alcohol but a refreshing acidity, making it an excellent *carafe* wine. Some really fine Sylvaners are suitable for maturing in bottle, but these are rare. Most Sylvaner, soft, fruity and easy to drink, is best consumed young.

UGNI BLANC

Location: Charente; Bordeaux; South-West; Languedoc; Roussillon; Provence; Cognac.

Known as the Trebbiano in Italy, Ugni is the most widely planted white grape variety in France, responsible for almost all Cognac and much of Armagnac. Made into a dry white wine it can be pleasantly fruity in a high acid, *primeur* way. It makes a good foil to the Colombard grape in Vin de Pays des Côtes de Gascogne. In the Midi its main usefulness is this high acidity, a factor many of the other varieties lack. In Cognac it is known as the Saint-Emilion. It is cane-pruned.

VIOGNIER

Location: Condrieu and Château-Grillet; southern Rhône; Provence; Languedoc-Roussillon.

This is an intriguing variety. The Viognier produces one of the most deliciously fragrant and complex wines in the whole world (in Condrieu and Château Grillet), but with such a grudging attitude towards quantity that even the most altruistic millionaire must view it with suspicion. Viognier is difficult to establish, though once it has settled in it is capable of living to a grand old age. It is susceptible to both *coulure* and *millerandage*, and even when the flowering takes place successfully the variety only ripens with difficulty, and the yield is consequently very low. The wine, though, is of the highest quality, full-bodied, quite alcoholic and rich, yet at the same time delicate, flowery and with a touch of citrus. It has a flavour of great individuality and elegance. The drawback is low acidity. So most examples do not keep. Today, happily, more productive, less susceptible strains of Viognier have been developed and planting Viognier is now a commerical propostion. I am pleased to see that estates in the southern Rhône and in the Midi such as Mas de Daumas Gassac at Aniane, Château Sainte-Anne at Saint-Gervais and the Perrin family in their Coudoulet vineyard are encouraging this variety. It is widely grown in the Ardèche and increasingly fashionable in the Languedoc. It is cane-pruned.

THE FRENCH LAWS OF WINE

Progressively since the beginning of the twentieth century – gathering momentum in the early 1930s and finally being enacted in its present form in 1936 – the government of France, in the form of the *Institut National des Appellations d'Origine* (INAO) together with local representatives, developed a system of wine laws. While these regulations do affect the standard of the wines, their concept was not to offer a guarantee of quality. The purpose was to endeavour to protect the geographical origin of the wines against fraud and to determine the often time-honoured ways in which the wines were made and the grape varieties used. There are four standards of wine.

1. APPELLATION CONTRÔLÉE

The best are those with the designation *Appellation d'Origine Contrôlée* or AOC, often shortened simply to *Appellation Contrôlée* or AC. This has covered all the mainstream areas of France since 1935 and is slowly but surely being extended to the lesser regions. Over 40 per cent of the total wine production of France is now AC. The total area delimited is some 472,000 hectares (335 separate *appellations*) and the total production is some 54.3 million hectolitres per annum.

2. VINS DÉLIMITÉS DE QUALITÉ SUPÉRIEURE

The second category after AC wines, dating from 1949, is that of the *Vins Délimités de Qualité Supérieure* or VDQS. These are the wines of the lesser areas of France. As standards rise more and more VDQS are being promoted to AC. Only 0.9 per cent of France's production is now VDQS: half a million hectolitres and 9000 hectares.

3. VINS DE PAYS

Vins de pays, the third category, are a superior form of *vins ordinaires*. Higher yields and a more liberal choice of grape varieties are allowed than for VDQS and AC wines but each wine must pass a tasting test. Enterprising growers in the South and South-West, where most of these wines are found, often produce some very interesting *vins de pays*, largely because they can be made with a higher percentage of non-indigenous quality grapes than the local AC and VDQS regulations allow. Twenty-seven per cent of all French wine produced (nearly 14 million hectolitres) falls into this category.

The concept of *vins de pays* was devised in 1973. There are now over 140, which I feel is so large a number as to be almost self-defeating, particularly as it is hard to differentiate between the styles of a great number of them. They fall into three categories: regional (from a large wine area, covering more than one *département*); departmental (covering the wines of a whole *département*), and zonal (limited to a small district, perhaps even just one commune). (See page 584 for a full list.)

Vins de pays vary in style, quality, pretension and price. Most of the examples from the South of France are red wines intended for early drinking; those from the Loire are similar white wines; good quaffing bottles with nothing more to say for themselves. Here and there you will find better examples, especially varietal wines from Cabernet Sauvignon, Chardonnay and Viognier. In the Midi there are an increasing number of quality wines which sell for consequently higher prices.

4. VINS DE TABLE, VIN ORDINAIRES AND VINS DE CONSOMMATION COURANTE

This category covers the remainder and includes wine for distilling into brandy – Cognac from the Charentes, Armagnac from Gascony and a little Fine elsewhere. Five million hectolitres are produced (plus 9 million of wine destined to be fortified). Most is produced in the Midi and consumed within France. The domestic market for this wine has declined. The French now drink less in total, but more wines of better quality, as in other wine-producing countries.

AC and VDQS Specifications

The specifications cover the following categories:

Area of production This defines the area entitled to a particular *appellation*, in principle restricting the land only to suitable vineyard sites.

Grape varieties This lists which grape varieties may be planted in order to qualify for the *appellation*. In practice this means a list of 'recommended' varieties together with, in some cases, an additional list of varieties 'permitted' in small proportions. Often these 'permitted' varieties are to be slowly phased out by a given date.

Viticultural regulations This lays down the density of the vines per given area and determines how they should be planted, pruned and treated.

Ripeness of the fruit This determines the minimum alcohol level of the wine before chaptalisation. The grape juice must have enough natural sugar to produce a wine which will reach the minimum alcohol level before chaptalisation. In some areas in the South of France chaptalisation is not permitted. The amount by which a wine can be chaptalized is also regulated.

Quantity This sets maximum yields per given area. It is expressed in hectolitres of juice per hectare. This is explained more fully below.

Winemaking This determines what is and is not allowed during the vinification and maturation process for each *appellation*.

Age of commercialisation This regulates the minimum age at which a wine can be put on the market.

Tasting and chemical analysis All wines must pass both a tasting test – in practice this seems more to be directed towards typicity, i.e. that it demonstrates the style of the grape or grapes from which it originates, than (high) quality – and satisfy the authorities by its chemical analysis. This was introduced in 1974.

Declaration of stocks and yields Growers need to make a declaration of their production each vintage and of their unsold stocks at 31 August each year.

The Appellation System Today

The authorised maximum yield per given area has always been the most thorny of the legislative problems and the one most open to abuse. Prior to 1974 the 'Cascade' system was in operation. A grower producing more than the permitted quantity of a top *appellation* could declare the maximum for that *appellation* and the remainder under a lower category where the restrictions on the yield were not quite so strict – and if there was still some wine over, that would be declared as a generic wine. Thus, to take a Burgundian example, let us suppose a grower in Chambertin-Clos de Bèze, a *grand cru* in Gevrey-Chambertin, produced 50 hectolitres from his one hectare of vines. A maximum of 30 hectolitres would be declared as Clos de Bèze, a further 5 (because the legislation allowed 35 hectolitres per hectare) as village Gevrey, and 15 as Bourgogne Rouge, for the allowable limit for the generic wine was 50 hectolitres per hectare. In theory it was, or could have been, all the same wine. In practice the Cascade system was rampant with fraud, thousands of casks or cases being exported as 'Bourgogne No 9', with a nod and a wink that it was 'surplus production'. This was labelled and eventually sold as Nuits-Saint-Georges or some other name. Today an alternative, marginally more satisfactory system is in practice. (What prevents it from being more satisfactory still is that the yields are too lenient.) In essence there is more flexibility. The basic permitted yield (*rendement de base*) remains. Each year the local growers' syndicate will propose an annual yield (*rendement annuel*) to the INAO (*Institut National des Appellations d'Origine*). This figure will take into account the actual climatic conditions of the year. The figure can indeed in theory be less than the basic yield. But in practice it is invariably higher – or the same. On top of this a grower is permitted to produce a fixed percentage more, usually 20 per cent. If the grower decides to apply for this *plafond limite de classement* (PLC), all his wine must pass a tasting test. If it is rejected it must be distilled. In the statistics used in this book the 'Maximum Yield' is the *rendement de base*.

The main criticism of the AC laws is that they protect the grower rather than the consumer. There are a number of improvements that would help to redress the balance. The first and most important one would be to include on the various legislative bodies, controlling syndicates and tasting committees qualified representatives who can speak and argue from the point of view of the consumer and who have no commercial axes to grind. Tasting certificates of approval should be based on quality as well as on typicity rather than on an absence of obvious flaws. Wines should also be sampled after bottling. The authorities should have the power to demote a wine, though its origins and style may be totally authentic, solely on the basis of quality.

We live in a time when, with the help of modern science, yields are plentiful; but often they are excessive. Whatever the growers and their oenologists may argue, there is a point where quantity becomes inversely proportional to quality – when the heavily laden vines have to struggle to achieve a reasonable level of alcohol and are then chaptalized up to the limit to reach the point where the wine is stable. When additionally they do not have a natural balancing level of acidity, no wine of real quality and concentration can result. Maximum allowable yields need to be reduced, the 20 per cent PLC should be abolished for 'quality' wine, and more rigorous pruning and obligatory crop-thinning after a successful flowering must be introduced. Anyone who produces over the allowable limit should be threatened with automatic rejection of the entire crop.

A further improvement would be the introduction of compulsory estate bottling of all classified, *premier cru* (in Burgundian terms) or other wines which are to be dignified with a single domaine or site-name label. All other wines of *appellation* or VDQS quality should be bottled in the area of their origin (as already is decreed for Alsace). This should help to guarantee origin and authenticity. It will also concentrate the mind of both grower and *négociant*, and that might not be a bad thing. The designations 'domaine' (which can mean almost anything and is therefore valueless and meaningless) and *mise en bouteille à la propriété* need to be tightened up. The use of *sous marques* (second labels) needs to be examined, and the practice of some organizations and co-operatives using other 'invented' names, which might make the consumer think that it is an individual grower's wine, must be prohibited. The information on the wine label could also be improved to the benefit of the consumer. We already have informative back labels on many wines from California and Australia which the French could do well to copy.

All this might sound as if I consider that the intention of those in the wine business is to mislead the consumer and foist him or herself off with inferior or fraudulent wine. And that the consumers are themselves being fooled. This is in no way so. The wine trade in my experience is a very honourable one.

The vast majority of the producers are doing their very best to make as good a wine as they possibly can. The buyers select with care and their marketeers – for we live in a competitive world – must make sure they can sell it at a reasonable price or they will go out of business. Nor are the consumers such fools. Most of them can tell good from bad and will recognize quality and reject the inferior.

As a result of modern methods, a widening of the market and increasing knowledge on both sides the standard of wine has increased out of all proportion in the four decades since I started regularly drinking wine. But it could improve even further. And today as we are being asked to pay very high prices for the best, we are surely entitled to demand that we do get commensurate quality in the bottle.

BORDEAUX

ORDEAUX IS BY FAR THE LARGEST FINE WINE REGION IN FRANCE. It is also, arguably, the greatest, and as such, again a matter for dispute, the finest in the world. Bordeaux produces all the three main types of wine, red, dry white and luscious sweet white wine. At the top levels these are the most aristocratic, the most profound and the most sumptuous of all wines.

It is the number and variety of its finest wines that, for me, makes Bordeaux the most impressive wine area of all. Burgundy has as many quality wine growers and top domaines, but production is on a very much smaller scale: a few casks rather than several dozen *tonneaux*. One single vineyard, itself much less extensive than a Bordeaux estate, may in Burgundy be divided among a couple of dozen owners. In Bordeaux vineyards belong to one owner and the economies of scale make it much easier for the top growers to be as rigorous as possible in their selection of which *cuvées* will go into the *grand vin* and which will be rejected.

There are some 154 classed growth estates in Bordeaux; 61 Médocs, 28 Sauternes, 53 Saint-Emilions and a dozen Graves. Add to this the top wines of Pomerol – which has never been classified – and the best of the *bourgeois* estates, many of whom produce wine of similar quality, and you have perhaps 250 single wine names producing at the highest level. Multiply that figure by the number of vintages drinkable or not yet mature that may be on the market, and you will have upwards of 5000 different wines. Each will be constantly changing as it gradually ages; and of all wines Bordeaux, whether red or sweet white – and indeed the top dry whites as well – has the greatest capacity to age, acquiring further depth, complexity and uniqueness of character as it does so. Every year a new crop will unleash another substantial batch of wines to be appreciated.

But this is only the tip of the iceberg. This cream will represent perhaps 5 per cent – but as much as 26 million bottles in total – of the annual harvest. Underneath that lies the unsung Bordeaux – good, if not fine, but still worthy of recognition. Not perhaps the sort of wines to which wine writers will

devote pages of purple prose, nor drinkers any abject ceremony, but bottle after bottle of the most part solidly dependable wine at prices we can all afford to dispense regularly.

Bordeaux is both a city and the name of wine. The city, eighth largest in France, and until recently one of its major ports, lies on a bend of the river Garonne in south-west France. The Garonne flows north-westwards from the middle of the Pyrenees into the Atlantic Ocean. Some 10 kilometres north of Bordeaux it is joined by the last of its great tributaries, the river Dordogne. Together these form the estuary of the Gironde, from which comes the name of the *département* of which Bordeaux is the capital.

The Gironde *département* (with the exception of the coastal area) corresponds with the wine-growing region of Bordeaux. Roughly 110,000 hectares of land are planted with vines, producing, during the 1990s, an average of over 6 million hectolitres of AC wine per annum, about 22 per cent of the total AC production of France. This is approximately twice as much as that of Burgundy (including Beaujolais) and half as much again as the Rhône Valley. For example, Château Brane-Cantenac, one of the largest of the Bordeaux classed growths, produces over 40,000 cases of wine a year, as much as the total production of the Hermitage *appellation* in the Rhône Valley.

About 85 per cent of the region's AC harvest is red wine. This makes it by far the largest quality red wine area of France. The Gironde's production of over 5 million hectolitres of *appellation contrôlée* red wine dwarfs that of Burgundy's mere half a million hectolitres of Pinot Noir. Unlike Burgundy – indeed unlike much of the rest of France – Bordeaux is an area of largely proprietorial rather than peasant ownership and hence is one of relatively large estates, often long-established, self-sufficient in wine terms and which sell their wines under their own 'château' names. Cocks and Féret, the 'bible of Bordeaux', lists some 4200 single vineyards and the proprietors thereof, and this itself is only the cream of around 12,500 growers who officially declare a crop each vintage.

History

In books devoted solely to the wines of Bordeaux, the history of the region and its produce has been covered with great depth and authority. I shall not attempt to emulate them. I refer readers to both these lucid accounts and acknowledge my debt to them in preparing the resume which follows.

It seems likely that Bordeaux was a wine-trading centre before it was a vine-growing region. The western side of the region is very flat, and in early Roman times it would have been marshy, covered in forest and infested with mosquitoes. The soil was poor and the climate less propitious for the cultivation of the vine than the higher ground, the Haut Pays further to the south and west. At the start Bordeaux was an *emporium*, important primarily as a port. It is therefore probable that it was not until the third century AD that the vine began to be widely planted in the locality. Ausonius, poet, consul and tutor to Roman emperors, owned vineyards in the area in the fourth century, though whether this was at Château Ausone is a matter for dispute. In one of his poems he refers not to the Dordogne but to the Garonne flowing gently at the bottom of his garden. Yet the most impressive Roman ruins outside Bordeaux are to be found in the grounds of Château La Gaffelière, at the foot of the Château Ausone escarpment.

Historical details during the next several hundred years, as elsewhere in the Europe of the Dark Ages, are sparse. There was an expansion of the vineyard in the eleventh century, but it was the arrival of the English after the marriage of the redoubtable Eleanor of Aquitaine to Henry Plantagenet in 1152 that had the profoundest effect. For three centuries the Bordeaux vineyards came under the jurisdiction of the English crown. England became the Gironde's most important export market, and each year, shortly after the harvest, before the winter had set in, a vast fleet would transport the cream of the crop, first chiefly to Bristol and Southampton, later to London. During the thirteenth, fourteenth and fifteenth centuries the vine gradually replaced all other forms of agriculture in the area, and

though at first most of the wine shipped to England seems to have come from further north, from the Poitou and the Charente, Bordeaux soon became the major point of departure. For many hundreds of years, long after the departure of the English in 1453, wine was France's leading export, Britain its most important customer and Bordeaux the chief exporter.

Not all the wine exported was strictly 'Bordeaux', however; much was the produce of the Haut Pays wine of the Dordogne, the Lot, the Tarn and the upper Garonne. These had to pay a tax, higher if from the French side of whatever was the border between the French and the English at the time, and faced other restrictions, such as being embargoed from shipment until after the Gironde harvest had left. Nevertheless, the whole of the South-West of France looked to England, and later to the Low Countries, Hamburg and the Baltic ports, for its market. Communications overland were cumbersome, hazardous and prolonged, and the French crown bought its wine from nearer at hand, from the upper Loire, Champagne and Burgundy.

Sensibly, even after the expulsion of the English after the battle of Castillon in 1453, the French kings took care not to disrupt the Bordeaux trade. The local inhabitants had never considered themselves anything other than Gascon, neither English nor French. The privileges the Bordeaux merchants had enjoyed under the English were confirmed, and after an initial bout of petty commercial warfare the French realised that they were now competing on their most important export market with wines from the Iberian peninsula and elsewhere.

The English remained customers for the finest Bordeaux wines even after the rise of the Dutch as an economic power in the seventeenth century and the various economic treaties discriminating against the French and in favour of Portugal which culminated in the Methuen Treaty in 1703. The Dutch became Bordeaux's major customer, but their requirements were for cheap wines, largely white, much of which was re-exported to Scandinavia and the Hanseatic ports.

The last quarter of the seventeenth and the first half of the eighteenth centuries was the period of the establishment of most of the great estates, that were to become the *crus classés* in 1855. Prior to this period the quality red wines had come from the upper Graves, surrounding the town of Bordeaux. Dutch engineers, with their experience in the Low Countries, drained the Médoc, formerly a land of marshes liable to widespread flooding at the time of spring tides, thus exposing the mounds of almost pure gravel, excellent for the vine, on which the great properties are centred to this day.

Château Haut-Brion in the Graves and then owned by the influential Pontac family, was the first of the Bordeaux estates to achieve renown and the first in English literature to be specifically named, the diarist Samuel Pepys enjoying the wine at the Royal Oak Tavern in 1663. Forty years later the London Gazette advertised the sale of Lafite, Margaux and Latour wines, as well as 'Pontac', looted from ships captured in the War of Spanish Succession. These estates were all owned by a new aristocracy, the *noblesse de la robe*. As the seventeenth century had progressed, a new breed of moneyed class had replaced the old *noblesse d'épée*. These families, of largely merchant origin, owed their power to their place in the Bordeaux *parlement*, their wealth to their land. Increasingly during the eighteenth century, suitable terrain in the Médoc was converted into monocultural vineyards, and after the French Revolution this expansion continued, but gradually, in Saint-Emilion, Pomerol and the Léognan part of the Graves.

The Revolution and the Napoleonic wars, though serious for the wine trade, left the top growths relatively unscathed. A few proprietors were guillotined, others emigrated and had their estates sequestered, as were those vineyards in ecclesiastical ownership. Though business suffered, there was little social upheaval. The great estates preserved their unity and remained the property of the moneyed classes. Bordeaux is a region of large domaines, *bourgeois* in ownership and vinously self-sufficient; Burgundy is a region of much fragmented vineyards in largely peasant possession.

The nineteenth century saw three major scourges in the vineyards, the arrival of a new generation of proprietors, industrialists or those who had made their money out of the wine trade itself, and the beginning of the adoption of modern mechanical and scientific methods of tilling the land and making the wine.

The first of the great natural disasters was the arrival of oidium in the early 1850s. Oidium, or powdery mildew, is a cryptogamic disease which affects both leaves and grapes. The leaves shrivel and drop off; the fruit is split and dries up. Though the solution, the application of sulphur, was soon discovered, production was decimated and prices rose steeply, never to return to their previous levels.

Though phylloxera, a member of the aphid family, was first discovered in France in 1863, it did not make its appearance in the Gironde until 1869, and did not really begin to cause serious damage in the Médoc until a decade later. Phylloxera is the greatest pest of them all, for, unlike oidium and mildew, which, like a spring frost attack, bad weather during the flowering or hail in late summer, only affect a single year's harvest, the phylloxera kills the plant itself. Potentially its ravages are catastrophic. It is not for nothing that its cognomen is *Vastastrix*. Phylloxera arrived in Europe from America, and it was in America that the imagination of the Bordeaux viticulturalist Leo Laliman found the solution to the problem, astonishingly as early as 1871. This was to graft the noble European varieties of the *vinifera* vine on to American non-*vinifera* rootstocks. Opposition to this radical proposal seemed solid until, despairing of finding an alternative solution, the growers had to face the inevitable. By 1882 97.5 per cent of the Gironde had been over-run by the louse, but it was only gradually, far more gradually in the top estates than most people realise, that grafted vines began to be introduced. As late as the 1890s *vignes françaises* were still being planted. Château Latour did not begin to plant grafted vines seriously until 1901 and it took several decades completely to replace the non-grafted old French vines.

Meanwhile Bordeaux had been hit by the third of its plagues. Downy mildew or peronospera arrived in the South of France in 1882, and seems to have spread rapidly west to the Gironde. Like oidium it is a cryptogamic disease, but affecting mainly the leaves. An antidote, copper sulphate solution, was soon discovered, and by 1888 the outbreak was under control.

As important as this succession of natural disasters were the economic consequences. Bordeaux, indeed the whole of France south of Paris, had many more hectares of land under vine in the 1850s than in 1900 or even today. In hard-nosed financial terms the arrival of phylloxera could be termed salutary. Uneconomic vineyards were allowed to decay; their owners and their workers forced to seek alternative employment. The human corollary compounded by the Franco-Prussian War and by a recession in wine prices which remained until the mid-1950s, is incalculable. This cloud of misery which hung over the peasant *vigneron* for three successive generations still continues as a folk memory.

It was not just the smallholder who was affected by this lack of prosperity. Though Bordeaux was not in general as badly off as elsewhere in France, owing to the reputation of its wines and the fact that the majority of its reds could mature in bottle, it was more dependent on its export markets. Demand from Germany, a major Bordeaux customer, collapsed after the First World War, the British market was moribund before the war and declined afterwards, and sales to pre- Prohibition America were negligible. The 1930s world recession, followed by the Second World War, forced even well-known classed growths almost out of business.

All this seems hardly credible today. Rising standards of living, appreciation of wine as part of the art of good living, a widening of the consumer base and the emergence of the Far East as well as the United States as customers for the top growths have transformed the scene. At the bottom of the pyramid a minor change in the ratio of the price of Bordeaux Rouge to Côtes du Rhône or Beaujolais, coupled with a plentiful harvest, can still cause problems. At the top end, a handful of proprietors seem to think they can get away with anything. Prices of First Growths and the best of the rest have been rising at an alarming rate alongside a succession of good but also highly plentiful vintages. It is now apparent that even the 'second best' Bordeaux are wines which most of us can only afford to drink rarely. And with prices of new wines almost as expensive as those now reaching maturity it hardly seems worthwhile to bother to buy them *en primeur*.

Coupled with this there is a sad trend. With death duties being what they are more and more estates are now owned by insurance companies and multinationals rather than by their original families.

One benefit, though, has been that the whole of Bordeaux, from First Growth to the regional co-operative, is making better wine. Scientific progress in vineyard and *chai*, the arrival of the trained *oenologue* (wine chemist), the financial means and the moral duty to make a rigorous selection of the *grand vin* have led to fewer poor vintages, more wine and a higher quality product. Some of the proprietors of the most sought-after wines may believe they can get away with murder. At least those who sell them are fully aware of the competition from elsewhere in the world.

THE WINES

Red Wines

There are two quite separate winemaking districts in Bordeaux as far as the top red wines are concerned. West of the Garonne and Gironde, on a low-lying, gravel-covered peninsula, stretch the vineyards of the Graves and the Médoc, on either side of the city of Bordeaux. The best wines of the Médoc come from six communes, each of which has its own particular character, described in detail on page 68 onwards. The estuarial parishes of Margaux, Saint-Julien, Pauillac and Saint-Estèphe contain the majority of the most respected estates. In the Graves, the best wines are found in Léognan, and closer to Bordeaux in Pessac and Talence in the conglomerate *appellation* of Pessac-Léognan.

Fifty kilometres away, north of the Dordogne river, lies a quite separate region covering the wines of Saint-Emilion and Pomerol which, in their own but different ways, are the equal of the Médoc and the Graves. Saint-

BORDEAUX

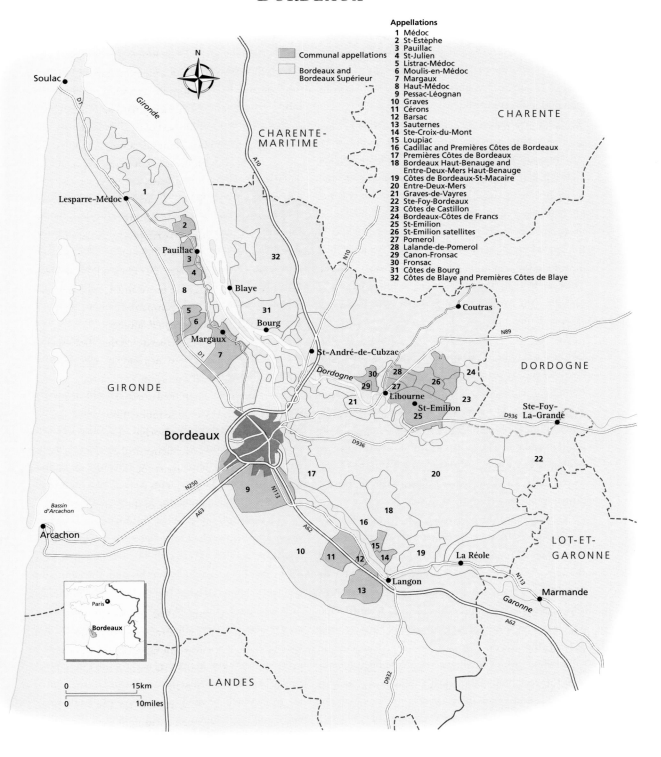

Appellations

1 Médoc
2 St-Estèphe
3 Pauillac
4 St-Julien
5 Listrac-Médoc
6 Moulis-en-Médoc
7 Margaux
8 Haut-Médoc
9 Pessac-Léognan
10 Graves
11 Cérons
12 Barsac
13 Sauternes
14 Ste-Croix-du-Mont
15 Loupiac
16 Cadillac and Premières Côtes de Bordeaux
17 Premières Côtes de Bordeaux
18 Bordeaux Haut-Benauge and
   Entre-Deux-Mers Haut-Benauge
19 Côtes de Bordeaux-St-Macaire
20 Entre-Deux-Mers
21 Graves-de-Vayres
22 Ste-Foy-Bordeaux
23 Côtes de Castillon
24 Bordeaux-Côtes de Francs
25 St-Emilion
26 St-Emilion satellites
27 Pomerol
28 Lalande-de-Pomerol
29 Canon-Fronsac
30 Fronsac
31 Côtes de Bourg
32 Côtes de Blaye and Premières Côtes de Blaye

Communal appellations

Bordeaux and
Bordeaux Supérieur

Emilion itself is divided into an easterly section, known as the Côtes Saint-Emilion, on the slopes around the town of Saint-Emilion itself, the Sables Anciennes to the north and the Graves Saint-Emilion, 4 kilometres to the west on the border of Pomerol. Pomerol, north of the port of Libourne, has only recently received its due recognition for the quality of its wines.

Médoc and Graves wines, based on Cabernet Sauvignon, are full, firm and tannic when young, even austere. Saint-Emilion wines may be equally abundant and rich, but lack the muscle and backbone of their westerly neighbours. Based on the Merlot, their wines are fruitcakey rather than blackcurrant in flavour, more aromatic in character. Most mature faster and do not last as long. Pomerol wines, from a clay rather than limestone soil, are fuller than those of Saint-Emilion. They can be rich, fat and succulent, as full as Graves or Margaux (the two lightest wines of the west bank) and as long-lasting.

Adjacent to Saint-Emilion and Pomerol are the Libournais satellites. Lalande-de Pomerol, Fronsac and Canon-Fronsac produce lesser wines in the style of Pomerol. Surrounding Saint-Emilion are Montagne-Saint-Emilion, which absorbed Saint-Georges-Saint-Emilion and Parsac-Saint-Emilion in 1972, Lussac-Saint-Emilion and Puisseguin-Saint-Emilion. Some of these wines are as good as ordinary Saint-Emilions themselves, but in the main those with a simple Saint-Emilion AC are more consistently reliable.

North-west of the Libournais, on the right bank of the Gironde estuary, lie the districts of Bourg and Blaye. East of Saint-Emilion in the direction of Bergerac and the department of the Dordogne are the Côtes de Castillon and the Côtes de Francs. A further useful red wine *appellation* is the Premières Côtes de Bordeaux, which lies on the right or east bank of the Garonne opposite the Graves.

All these are now thriving areas, providing *petit château* wines of great interest at prices hardly far removed from that of Bordeaux Supérieur. These are wines which can be bought and drunk regularly, rather than being preserved for special occasions. Land in these areas is cheap compared with the astronomical prices now being paid for classed growths in the Médoc. Able young men and women, suitably trained, have moved in, or taken over from their less expert parents.

The remainder of the Gironde region, with the exception of the coastal area, is authorised for the production of Bordeaux and Bordeaux Supérieur. Entre-Deux-Mers is a white wine *appellation* only and any red wines produced there will be simply Bordeaux or Bordeaux Supérieur.

White Wines

The Graves, stretching south from the suburbs of Bordeaux down the west side of the Garonne as far as Langon, produces the best dry white wines of Bordeaux as well as red wines; though to many people's surprise more red wine is made than white. Its northern half, from the city itself down to La Brède, is called Pessac-Léognan. For many years the dry white wines continued to be made by rustic, old-fashioned methods. Quite deservedly, they fell out of fashion. Recently there has been a dramatic improvement in the wine, and a revival of the region's fortunes.

Within the Graves, towards the southern end, is the enclave of Sauternes and Barsac, origin of the world's richest and most sumptuous sweet white wines. Lesser, medium sweet white wines are made nearby at Cérons, and on the opposite bank of the Garonne at Sainte-Croix-du-Mont, Loupiac and part of the Premières Côtes de Bordeaux, under the Cadillac *appellation*.

The peninsula between the Dordogne and Garonne rivers is known as the Entre-Deux-Mers. This generic *appellation*, like that of Graves and Graves Supérieures, is used solely for white wines. Yet this is another source of good *petit château* red wine, labelled simply as Bordeaux or Bordeaux Supérieur. Within the Entre-Deux-Mers are four districts: Graves de Vayres, opposite Fronsac and the town of Libourne; Sainte-Foy-Bordeaux, at the extreme east below Montravel in the Dordogne *département*; Côtes de Bordeaux-Saint-Macaire in the south, taking over where the Premières Côtes de Bordeaux ends; and Haut-Benauge, a sub-region of the Entre-Deux-Mers. In total, in 1998 there were 43 *appellations* within the Gironde.

Surface Area and Production

The largest Bordeaux harvest of *appellation contrôlée* wine in modern times took place in 1997. Of a total of 6.68 million hectolitres just over 86 per cent was red wine (including a little rosé), the highest proportion ever – during the 1980s about 20 per cent of the Gironde crop was white, but as recently as the late 1960s more white wine than red wine was produced in the area. Most of this wine is sold as Bordeaux or Bordeaux Supérieur. The combined production of the 'quality' areas (the Médoc, Graves, Saint-Emilion, Pomerol, Sauternes and Barsac) was only some 1.42 million hectolitres, 21 per cent of the grand total – and it is arguable how much of the generic wines from Graves, Saint-Emilion and Médoc can be described as 'quality' wine.

The decades since the Second World War have seen a number of parallel trends in the Bordeaux region. The total surface area under vine decreased from nearly 140,000 hectares – the peak was in 1950 – to under 100,000 in the late 1970s and early 1980s. It has since risen again to around 115,000 hectares. But the surface area producing AC wine has steadily increased and now stands at 98 per cent of this total.

As well as increased surface area clonal selection and better vineyard husbandry have meant that the production of AC wine has more than tripled – the average yearly yield in the five years from 1945 to 1949 was just over 2 million hectolitres. In the five years between 1994 and 1998 it was almost 6.4 million hectolitres. At the same time there has been a dramatic shift away from white to red wine – from one-third of the harvest being red Bordeaux to about 85 per cent. In the five years from 1994 to 1998 more *appellation contrôlée* red wine was produced in the Bordeaux area than in the twenty vintages from 1945 to 1964.

It is the change from white to red, despite the increased fashion for white wine drinking in the 1980s, which is the most curious and significant of these trends. Prior to the Second World War, oceans of generic Graves, Entre-Deux-Mers and Bordeaux Blanc, produced with various levels of sweetness from dry to almost luscious, provided France and its export markets with most of its staple white wine-drinking at a level of quality that was just above *ordinaire*.

The fashion then changed to something a bit lighter and cleaner. While the French domestic preference moved away from Bordeaux white to other whites such as Muscadet and Mâcon Blanc, other countries turned to the wines of Germany and Yugoslavia. White Bordeaux became almost unsaleable, fetching, at its cheapest level, no more than *vin ordinaire*. The growers began to switch to making red wines, and 1962 remains the only vintage of white Bordeaux totalling over 2 million hectolitres.

SURFACE AREA AND PRODUCTION (1998 HARVEST)

APPELLATIONS	SURFACE AREA (HA)		PRODUCTION (HL)	
	RED & ROSÉ	WHITE	RED & ROSÉ	WHITE
REGIONAL WINES				
BORDEAUX	39,023	9045	2,421,912	539,377
BORDEAUX CLAIRET	1611		102,686	
CRÉMANT DE BORDEAUX	6	92	–	5752
BORDEAUX SUPÉRIEUR	9215	43	544,796	1695
CÔTES DE BORDEAUX-SAINT-MACAIRE	–	60	–	2354
ENTRE-DEUX-MERS, HAUT-BENAUGE	–	1819	–	110,407
SAINTE-FOY-BORDEAUX	168	41	10,261	2032

→

APPELLATIONS	SURFACE AREA (HA)		PRODUCTION (HL)	
	RED & ROSÉ	WHITE	RED & ROSÉ	WHITE
CÔTES				
Blaye/Côtes de Blaye }			11,839	
Premières Côtes de Blaye	4912	438	299,810	12,053
Côtes de Castillon	2925	–	172,324	–
Bordeaux-Côtes de Francs	471	14	27,667	–
Bourg, Côtes de Bourg	3765	32	226,648	1615
Graves de Vayres	446	147	25,323	8550
Premières Côtes de Bordeaux	3034	387	171,594	
MÉDOC/GRAVES				
Graves	2197	939	124,692	50,590
Graves Supérieures	–	465	–	19,356
Pessac-Léognan	1040	280	51,170	14,192
Médoc	4822	–	290,598	–
Margaux	1355	–	68,231	–
Saint-Julien	906	–	48,216	–
Pauillac	1170	–	65,417	–
Saint-Estèphe	1229	–	68,946	–
Listrac	644	–	37,997	–
Moulis	557	–	32,129	–
LIBOURNAIS				
Canon-Fronsac	302	–	16,881	–
Fronsac	824	–	46,566	–
Pomerol	784	–	36,066	–
Lalande-de-Pomerol	1111	–	56,152	–
Saint-Emilion	2048	–		–
Saint-Emilion Grand Cru }	3421	–	273,611	–
Lussac-Saint-Emilion	1428	–	84,837	–
Montagne-Saint-Emilion	1565	–	91,346	–
Puisseguin-Saint-Emilion	736	–	42,524	–
Saint-Georges-Saint-Emilion	172	–	10,118	–
SWEET WHITE WINES				
Sauternes	–	1639	–	36,214
Barsac	–	601	–	14,268
Cérons	–	73	–	2421
Sainte-Croix-du-Mont	–	465	–	16,436
Loupiac	–	419	–	14,214
Cadillac	–	221	–	6885
TOTAL	96,165	17,219	5,698,480	870,250
TOTAL RED AND WHITE WINES	113,384		6,568,730	

The Style of the Wine

The word 'claret' means any red Bordeaux wine. The word is derived from the French *clairet*, indicating a lightish red wine as opposed to the fuller, more robust wines formerly produced in the hinterland beyond the Bordeaux area, but shipped through the same port.

Bordeaux, unlike many other top red French wines – Burgundy and Hermitage, for example – is made from a mixture of grapes. The red wines are produced from Cabernet Sauvignon, Cabernet Franc and Merlot, with Petit Verdot used in small proportions in many of the top Médoc estates, and Malbec found in some of the lesser properties of the Saint-Emilion and Pomerol *appellations* and the Libournais. Some years, such as 1998, favour the Merlot; others, such as 1996, the Cabernet. In general, the wines of the Médoc are largely produced from Cabernet Sauvignon with some Cabernet Franc and Merlot. The Libournais wines are mainly made from the Merlot, with Cabernet Franc as the additional variety, but little Cabernet Sauvignon except in rare cases.

The quality of the final wine depends on the quality of these grapes at harvest time. The purpose of all viticultural procedures is to produce as much fruit as is consistent with quality – for, to a very large extent, quality is inversely proportional to quantity – in as perfect a condition as possible on the date that they are picked.

The character of a wine depends on a number of other things, most importantly the soil and, as vital in viticulture, the subsoil. Soils in the Bordeaux region combine, in one form and proportion or another, the following ingredients: gravel (of various types), sand, clay and limestone.

The Médoc and the Graves are based on the first two, on a subsoil of gravel, alios (a hard, iron-rich sandstone), marl, clay or sand; Saint-Emilion and Pomerol soils contain more limestone, especially round the town of Saint-Emilion itself, and there is also more clay. Gravel and sand are present to a lesser extent. The subsoil consists of limestone, though in the Graves area of Saint-Emilion and in Pomerol there is gravel and clay.

Of equal importance to the chemical constituents of the soil is its aspect: the relation of the vineyard to the rays of the sun, and its protection from wind, hail and particularly frost; and the efficiency of its drainage. Unlike many other vineyards in France and Germany, most of the top Bordeaux vineyards lie on flat ground, not on a slope so much as a small mound, rarely more than a few metres above the surrounding countryside. Thus there is no natural protection from the prevailing weather, and severe frost can damage large tracts of vineyard, as it did spectacularly in Saint-Emilion and Pomerol in 1956 and throughout the region in 1977 and 1991. The Médoc is well drained and can withstand heavy rain better in wet years such as 1991, 1992 and 1993 than can the heavier clay or limestone soil of Pomerol and Saint-Emilion. On the contrary, these latter areas can cope with severe drought, as in 1989 and in 1985, better than the Médoc.

The climate in Bordeaux is conditioned by the nearby Atlantic Ocean, and is, in general, less extreme than in Burgundy, and better both in terms of a higher average temperature and less severe bouts of rainfall. Unlike in Burgundy, where the red and white wine harvests often run concurrently, the harvest in Bordeaux always begins with the dry white wines, usually between 10 and 20 September. When the red wine vintage begins a week or so later, the Merlot grapes are picked before Cabernet, the Libournais area usually beginning a few days before the Médoc and the Graves. The sweet wine harvest commences last of all and can last throughout October even into November.

Compared with Burgundy, winemaking in Bordeaux is on a much larger scale: a domaine of 20 (or greatly more) hectares may make only two wines, the *grand vin* and a second wine; while in Burgundy an estate half the size or even smaller may have as many as ten different wines to offer. In general in Bordeaux the vats are closed rather than open during fermentation, as is often the case in Burgundy, the fruit for red wines is almost invariably entirely destalked and vinification temperatures are high (30°C or so) for the top red wines. The malolactic fermentation seems to follow more easily, permitting an early *égalisage*, or blending of the vats of different grape varieties.

A relatively recent development in the leading estates has been the concept of a second wine. With increased prosperity and perfectionism only the very best vats are today assembled into the *grand vin*. The rejected wine, from younger vines or less successful parts of the vineyard, is bottled under another name. Today just about every top estates produces a second wine. In good vintages and from the top estates these can be worth buying. Even if they do not show the depth of the *grand vin* they will normally share its elegance. The second wines are listed in the château descriptions within each *appellation*.

When to Drink the Wines

Fine red Bordeaux is a much fuller, more tannic wine than red Burgundy. It has a deeper colour, the best wines remaining purple-hued for many years. It needs time to mature. Lesser red Bordeaux, the generic wines and the lightest *petits châteaux*, will be ready for drinking a couple of years or so after the harvest. The *bourgeois* wines will be mature at three to six years, the classed growths after five to ten years. The wines of lighter vintages, of course, will mature sooner than those of fuller years.

While there is a much smaller proportion of top dry whites than there is in Burgundy these too need time (a minimum of five years), though most of Bordeaux's dry white wine harvest is bottled early, having not been vinified or matured in oak, and is intended for early drinking. A good Sauternes has the capacity for long ageing. The best, like the best red wines, need to be kept for a minimum of a decade.

Bordeaux Vintages for Red and Dry White Wines

In recent vintages the dry white wine harvest can be divided between those châteaux that picked very early – even in August and were not caught by rain in the 1991-1996 period (these are fine and will keep), and the rest that did not. Wines from the former group are scarce, fine and expensive. The other wines have been disappointing. 1986 and 1990 are the best vintages. Apart from the 1996 and 1997, other years will probably be already getting tired.

1998 A very large crop, and an uneven one. After torrid weather in August the first two weeks of September were unsettled. There was then a ten-day period of fine weather during which most of the Saint-Emilion and Pomerol part of the Bordeaux region, as well as the dry white wines, enjoyed an easy harvest. Rain then set in again just as the Médoc-Graves harvest was getting into its stride. The result is the best Libournais vintage since 1990, very good dry white wines but only intermittently very good red wines in the Médoc and Graves. The wines are expensive.

1997 A record crop: the largest vintage ever, with nearly 6.7 million hectolitres of wine produced. It was a very early harvest, but the most extended one in recent memory. After a very early bud-break the flowering commenced in mid-May, but the fruit-setting was prolonged by adverse weather, and this was reflected in state of ripeness at vintage time. A variable result therefore for both red and dry whites, with the top properties proportionately more successful than the lesser estates. Some very good wines. Continuing high prices made this a vintage of very questionable value.

1996 A large harvest which was only just below the record one of 1995. After fine weather during the flowering the summer was cool and wet, and the harvest was saved by a largely dry, sunny but cool September. Rain at the end of the month affected the Libournais vineyards. A fine October enabled the later-developing Cabernets in the Médoc to mature to an excellent ripe and healthy condition. The results therefore are variable: largely disappointing in Pomerol and Saint-Emilion, average in the Graves and southern Médoc, but very fine – up to 1990 levels – in Pauillac, Saint-Estèphe and Saint-Julien where the wines will keep well. An average vintage for dry white wines. Prices were unprecedentedly high.

1995 A record vintage: for the first time the total crop exceeded 6.5 million hectolitres. The summer was largely dry, but, for the fifth year in succession, rain in September dashed hopes of a really spectacular quality harvest. Overall the results are more even than in 1996: good to very good in the Libournais, especially in Pomerol, good in the Graves for both red and dry white, good to very good in the Médoc, particularly in Saint-Julien, Pauillac and Saint-Estèphe. The red wines will evolve in the medium to long term, well in advance of the best 1996s. Prices were high.

1994 A splendid, hot, dry summer led everyone to hope for a high quality vintage. Sadly it was not to be. It began raining on 9 September and hardly ceased until the end of the month. Modern methods, however, can ensure at least acceptable wine, provided, as in 1994, there is no rot. The results are heterogeneous. Acidity levels are low; some of the tannins are not really properly ripe. But the wines, if lacking real character, are at least clean. They will evolve in the medium term. The dry whites are adequate. The yield was large.

1993 Another large vintage, and another where summer expectations were dashed by a rainy September. Indeed there was even more rain than in 1994, though less than in 1992. At first the wines were lean and skinny. A year on they had taken up a bit more new oak from the cask than young Bordeaux usually does, and were pleasantly juicy if one-dimensional. By 1997, though, a lot of the fruit had dried out. An unexciting vintage, though with a little more substance than the 1992s. Again the dry whites were adequate. The wines are as good as ever they will be and should be drunk soon.

1992 This year saw the rainiest September of the 1991-1996 period: indeed, a record 279mm. The result is a poor vintage of hollow, watery wines which are already showing age. So are the dry white wines, which were better.

1991 Following April frosts, a small vintage. After this disaster the summer was fine, raising hopes of a small-but-beautiful vintage like 1961. But there was rain in the second half of September right through the harvest, which was late. Many Saint-Emilion and Pomerol estates did not produce a *grand vin*. The best wines – more interesting than those produced in 1992 and 1993 – come from those estates in the Médoc nearest to the Gironde estuary and least affected by the frost. These are now ready, and worth investigating. The remainder are dull and now old. There were some reasonable dry whites but these are now showing age.

1990 A harvest which was very large, early and of consistently very fine quality – for dry white wines as well as for red wines. It was a hot summer, but the wines were not as stressed as in 1989, and the more mature tannins

as a result are one of the reasons this vintage generally has the edge on 1989. The reds are big, rich and classy, and will slow to mature, but will last well. Though not as expensive as the 1989s at the outset, prices are now rather higher, indeed the highest of recent years apart from the 1982s.

1989 A very large vintage again, and early one, and a successful one, though a little uneven, and for the most part eclipsed by 1990. A hot dry summer produced fruit at the time of the vintage which was physiologically ripe (the sugar/acidity ratio) but was not completely phenolically ripe (i.e. the quality of the tannins). As a result, though the Saint-Emilions and Pomerols are fine, as are most Graves, some Médoc wines exhibit rather hard dry tannins. Acidity levels are marginally lower than in the 1990 vintage too. A fine red wine vintage nevertheless, which is only now beginning to mature. The dry whites, though rich, lacked a bit of zip and have aged fast. Prices at the outset were high.

1988 A large harvest. After a very rainy first half of the year the Cabernets struggled to achieve full maturity, and there was some rain at the end of September and again in October. Medium to medium-full red wines which were rather austere at the outset. This higher than normal acidity has preserved the fruit and finesse, and at ten years old the best wines now show a lot of interest, though the lesser wines are proportionately more boring. These best wines are only just ready and will keep well. Very good dry white wines. Unjustly ignored at present, the best wines are excellent value.

1987 A medium-sized vintage, spoiled by rain. In their prime the reds provided light, pleasant wines. Most are now too old. Not of note in dry whites either.

1986 A huge crop: in terms of yield per hectare the largest ever. There was a thunderstorm towards the end of September, just as the red wine harvest was due to start. This posed problems in the Graves and in the Libournais where the rain was at its heaviest. The northern Médoc escaped unscathed. Excellently concentrated, long-lasting wines in Saint-Julien and Pauillac, as good, if different from, 1982. This is where the 1986 harvest is at its best. Good but inconsistent quality elsewhere in the Médoc. In general, the Graves and the Libournais wines are somewhat diluted and not as good as those of 1985. Fine, elegant quality, too, in the dry white wines. **1985** In general the wines evolved in the medium term and are now in their prime. A very big crop, and an exceptionally dry end to the ripening season. In contrast to 1986, the Merlots were more successful than the Cabernets. Very good quality in Saint-Emilion and Pomerol. Also very good in the Graves and Margaux, though in Saint-Julien and Pauillac the 1996 vintage is very much better. This is not a heavyweight year but the wines have balance and elegance. Very good dry white wines, fuller and richer than those of 1986.

GOOD, EARLIER RED WINE VINTAGES

1983 is very good in the southern Médoc and the Graves, but disappointing elsewhere in Bordeaux. 1982 is superb, but many of the Saint-Emilion and Pomerol wines lack grip. 1981 has held up surprisingly well. The best years prior to 1981 are 1978, 1975, 1970, 1966, 1964 (Libournais only), 1961 and 1959.

CLASSIFICATIONS

Since the creation of primarily monocultural, winemaking estates in the last years of the seventeenth and the first half of the eighteenth centuries, the wines of these properties have been categorised and classified by the Bordeaux brokers and *négociants*. These lists were based on the prices the wines would fetch and were no doubt of use in the continual battle between the proprietor or his bailiff and the *négoce* in Bordeaux. Once the price had been fixed for one wine, prices for the rest would fall into place according to the unofficial lists circulating at the time. This was the price at which the haggling would commence. These lists were fluid and they altered with the times. The names of properties come and go, reputations are made and lost, and the effects of neglect and dedication can be clearly seen.

The first 'official' classification is that of 1855. In this year, the new French Second Empire sent to Bordeaux for a 'representative selection of the wines of the *département* of the Gironde' for display at the Paris Exhibition, the Exposition Universelle. The selection was to include not only examples of the commune wines, but also a list of the *crus classés*. At the behest of the Chamber of Commerce, the Bordeaux brokers produced a list of the top red and top sweet white wines, the dry wines not being considered of *cru classé* standard. In the red wine list, reproduced in an updated form right, there are five categories, and, counting the divided Rauzan and Léoville vineyards as single estates, there are sixty-one proper-

ties. It is by accident — and the prices the wines fetched — that all but one of the wines come from the Médoc. It was never intended to be a classification of Médoc wines only, as many people now believe.

At the same time the top sweet white wines were classified. These were all wines of Sauternes and Barsac. Château d'Yquem was put into a class of its own: *grand premier cru*. Then followed what are today, allowing for changes, twenty-four more properties, eleven *premiers crus* and thirteen *deuxièmes crus*.

For some reason, the 1855 Classification has assumed permanent status. Some châteaux mention their position on their label, and all wine books and wine lists refer to it. The reputation of some wines is unduly enhanced by having been chosen as a Second or Fifth Growth in 1855, while others now producing better wine were excluded. Various authorities have long called for a reclassification, but with the sole exception of Mouton-Rothschild's elevation to First Growth status in 1973, and despite various abortive attempts in the 1960s and 1970s initiated by the INAO (Institut National des Apellations d'Origine) nothing has yet resulted.

Meanwhile, in 1959 (revised in 1969, 1985 and 1996) the INAO classified the wines of Saint-Emilion; the Graves region was classified in 1953 and 1959 and is now well overdue for reclassification; and in 1932, 1966, 1978, 1984 and again as this book goes to press, attempts were made to classify the lesser growths of the Médoc. Pomerol has never had an official classification.

THE 1855 CLASSIFICATION OF
THE RED WINES OF BORDEAUX

This is the original list of 1855, along with the 1973 incorporation of Château Mouton-Rothschild. It takes into account divisions and other changes since 1855.

CHÂTEAU	COMMUNE	HECTARES	CASES
PREMIERS CRUS (FIRST GROWTHS)			
CHÂTEAU LAFITE-ROTHSCHILD	PAUILLAC	70	36,000
CHÂTEAU LATOUR	PAUILLAC	65	36,700
CHÂTEAU MOUTON-ROTHSCHILD (1973)	PAUILLAC	75	27,500
CHÂTEAU MARGAUX	MARGAUX	78	33,300
CHÂTEAU HAUT-BRION	PESSAC-LÉOGNAN	43	16,000
DEUXIÈMES CRUS (SECOND GROWTHS)			
CHÂTEAU RAUZAN-SÉGLA	MARGAUX	49	22,200
CHÂTEAU RAUZAN-GASSIES	MARGAUX	28	13,300
CHÂTEAU LÉOVILLE-LAS-CASES	SAINT-JULIEN	95	44,800
CHÂTEAU LÉOVILLE-POYFERRÉ	SAINT-JULIEN	80	44,400
CHÂTEAU LÉOVILLE-BARTON	SAINT-JULIEN	47	20,800
CHÂTEAU DURFORT-VIVENS	MARGAUX	30	16,500
CHÂTEAU LASCOMBES	MARGAUX	83	49,100
CHÂTEAU GRUAUD-LAROSE	SAINT-JULIEN	82	51,000
CHÂTEAU BRANE-CANTENAC	CANTENAC-MARGAUX	85	50,000
CHÂTEAU PICHON-LONGUEVILLE (BARON)	PAUILLAC	50	20,000
CHÂTEAU PICHON-LONGUEVILLE, COMTESSE DE LALANDE	PAUILLAC	83	50,000
CHÂTEAU DUCRU-BEAUCAILLOU	SAINT-JULIEN	50	19,000
CHÂTEAU COS D'ESTOURNEL	SAINT-ESTÈPHE	64	25,000
CHÂTEAU MONTROSE	SAINT-ESTÈPHE	68	37,100
TROISIÈMES CRUS (THIRD GROWTHS)			
CHÂTEAU KIRWAN	CANTENAC-MARGAUX	35	18,900
CHÂTEAU D'ISSAN	CANTENAC-MARGAUX	30	12,500
CHÂTEAU LAGRANGE	SAINT-JULIEN	109	66,700
CHÂTEAU LANGOA-BARTON	SAINT-JULIEN	17	7100
CHÂTEAU GISCOURS	LABARDE-MARGAUX	82	44,400
CHÂTEAU MALESCOT-SAINT-EXUPÉRY	MARGAUX	24	14,000
CHÂTEAU BOYD-CANTENAC	CANTENAC	18	8000
CHÂTEAU CANTENAC-BROWN	CANTENAC-MARGAUX	32	12,000

→

CHÂTEAU PALMER	CANTENAC-MARGAUX	43	18,000
CHÂTEAU LA LAGUNE	LUDON	70	38,900
CHÂTEAU DESMIRAIL	MARGAUX	28	15,400
CHÂTEAU CALON-SÉGUR	SAINT-ESTÈPHE	58	25,000
CHÂTEAU FERRIÈRE	MARGAUX	8	4000
CHÂTEAU MARQUIS D'ALESME-BECKER	MARGAUX	17	96,000

QUATRIÈMES CRUS (FOURTH GROWTHS)

CHÂTEAU TALBOT	SAINT-JULIEN	102	54,200
CHÂTEAU SAINT-PIERRE	SAINT-JULIEN	17	8000
CHÂTEAU BRANAIRE (DUCRU)	SAINT-JULIEN	50	25,000
CHÂTEAU DUHART-MILON-ROTHSCHILD	PAUILLAC	64	17,000
CHÂTEAU POUGET	CANTENAC	11	4900
CHÂTEAU LA TOUR-CARNET	SAINT-LAURENT	40	20,000
CHÂTEAU LAFON-ROCHET	SAINT-ESTÈPHE	30	22,200
CHÂTEAU BEYCHEVELLE	SAINT-JULIEN	90	55,600
CHÂTEAU PRIEURÉ-LICHINE	CANTENAC-MARGAUX	67	38,300
CHÂTEAU MARQUIS-DE-TERME	MARGAUX	35	14,400

CINQUIÈMES CRUS (FIFTH GROWTHS)

CHÂTEAU PONTET-CANET	PAUILLAC	77	38,900
CHÂTEAU BATAILLEY	PAUILLAC	60	20,000
CHÂTEAU HAUT-BATAILLEY	PAUILLAC	22	10,000
CHÂTEAU GRAND-PUY-LACOSTE	PAUILLAC	50	16,700
CHÂTEAU GRAND-PUY-DUCASSE	PAUILLAC	40	14,200
CHÂTEAU LYNCH-BAGES	PAUILLAC	90	35,000
CHÂTEAU LYNCH-MOUSSAS	PAUILLAC	30	17,800
CHÂTEAU DAUZAC	LABARDE	40	20,000
CHÂTEAU D'ARMAILHAC	PAUILLAC	50	19,200
CHÂTEAU DU TERTRE	ARSAC	50	20,600
CHÂTEAU HAUT-BAGES-LIBÉRAL	PAUILLAC	27	13,300
CHÂTEAU PÉDESCLAUX	PAUILLAC	9	5800
CHÂTEAU BELGRAVE	SAINT-LAURENT (HAUT-MÉDOC)	54	20,000
CHÂTEAU DE CAMENSAC	SAINT-LAURENT (HAUT-MÉDOC)	75	29,200
CHÂTEAU COS LABORY	SAINT-ESTÈPHE	18	10,000
CHÂTEAU CLERC-MILON	PAUILLAC	30	13,300
CHÂTEAU CROIZET-BAGES	PAUILLAC	26	15,600
CHÂTEAU CANTEMERLE	MACAU (HAUT-MÉDOC)	69	44,400

THE 1855 CLASSIFICATION OF THE SAUTERNES

This is the original list, but brought up to date to take account of divisions and other changes.

CHÂTEAU	COMMUNE	HECTARES	CASES
PREMIER GRAND CRU (FIRST GREAT GROWTH)			
CHÂTEAU D'YQUEM	SAUTERNES	113	8200
PREMIERS CRUS (FIRST GROWTHS)			
CHÂTEAU LA TOUR-BLANCHE	BOMMES	34	6700
CHÂTEAU LAFAURIE-PEYRAGUEY	BOMMES	40	7900
CHÂTEAU CLOS HAUT-PEYRAGUEY	BOMMES	23	2800
CHÂTEAU DE RAYNE-VIGNEAU	BOMMES	79	6700
CHÂTEAU SUDUIRAUT	PREIGNAC	87	10,000
CHÂTEAU COUTET	BARSAC	39	7000
CHÂTEAU CLIMENS	BARSAC	29	5600
CHÂTEAU GUIRAUD	SAUTERNES	100	16,100
CHÂTEAU RIEUSSEC	FARGUES	75	14,000
CHÂTEAU SIGALAS-RABAUD	BOMMES	14	2900
CHÂTEAU RABAUD-PROMIS	BOMMES	33	500
DEUXIÈMES CRUS (SECOND GROWTHS)			
CHÂTEAU MYRAT	BARSAC	22	3200
CHÂTEAU DOISY-VÉDRINES	BARSAC	27	1500
CHÂTEAU DOISY-DAËNE	BARSAC	15	2400
CHÂTEAU DOISY-DUBROCA	BARSAC	3	500
CHÂTEAU D'ARCHE	SAUTERNES	29	2200
CHÂTEAU FILHOT	SAUTERNES	60	10,000
CHÂTEAU BROUSTET	BARSAC	16	3000
CHÂTEAU NAIRAC	BARSAC	17	1800
CHÂTEAU CAILLOU	BARSAC	13	3600
CHÂTEAU SUAU	BARSAC	8	2200
CHÂTEAU DE MALLE	PREIGNAC	50	5000
CHÂTEAU ROMER-DU-HAYOT	FARGUES	16	4200
CHÂTEAU LAMOTHE-DESPUJOLS	SAUTERNES	8	1700
CHÂTEAU LAMOTHE-GUIGNARD	SAUTERNES	17	4000

THE 1959 CLASSIFICATION OF THE GRAVES

Château Haut-Brion did not wish to be included in the classification for white wine as production at the château was too tiny (800 cases a year today).

CLASSIFIED RED WINES	COMMUNE	HECTARES	CASES
		(RED & WHITE VARIETIES COMBINED)	
Château Bouscaut	Cadaujac	45	22,200
Château Carbonnieux	Léognan	90	22,000
Domaine de Chevalier	Léognan	35	10,000
Château de Fieuzal	Léognan	45	12,200
Château Haut-Bailly	Léognan	28	15,000
Château Haut-Brion	Pessac	46	16,000
Château Malartic-Lagravière	Léognan	19	6000
Château La Mission-Haut-Brion	Pessac	21	7500
Château Olivier	Léognan	45	13,000
Château Pape-Clément	Pessac	33	13,500
Château Smith-Haut-Lafitte	Martillac	55	23,000
Château La Tour-Haut-Brion	Talence	5	2500
Château La Tour-Martillac	Martillac	36	15,000

CLASSIFIED WHITE WINES	COMMUNE	HECTARES	CASES
Château Bouscaut	Cadaujac	–	4400
Château Carbonnieux	Léognan	–	22,000
Domaine de Chevalier	Léognan	–	1500
Château Couhins	Villenave-d'Ornon	8.5 (WHITE ONLY)	1000
Château Couhins-Lurton	Villenave-d'Ornon	5.5 (WHITE ONLY)	2100
Château Laville-Haut-Brion	Talence	3.7 (WHITE ONLY)	1100
Château Malartic-Lagravière	Léognan	–	1500
Château Olivier	Léognan	–	10,000
Château La Tour-Martillac	Martillac	–	5000

THE 1996 CLASSIFICATON OF SAINT-EMILION

The wines of Saint-Emilion were first classified in 1959, and this classification was revised in 1969, 1985 and 1996. The *Premiers grands crus classés* are divided into two sections, A and B.

PREMIERS GRANDS CRUS CLASSÉS
(FIRST GREAT GROWTHS)

A

Château Ausone
Château Cheval-Blanc

B

Château Angélus
Château Beau-Séjour-Bécot
Château Beauséjour-Duffau-Lagarrosse
Château Belair
Château Canon
Clos Fourtet
Château Figeac
Château La Gaffelière
Château Magdelaine
Château Pavie
Château Trottevieille

GRANDS CRUS CLASSÉS
(GREAT GROWTHS)

Château L'Arrosée
Château Balestard-La-Tonnelle
Château Bellevue
Château Bergat
Château Berliquet
Château Cadet Bon
Château Cadet-Piola
Château Canon-La-Gaffelière
Château Cap de Mourlin
Château Chauvin
Château La Clotte
Château La Clusière
Château Corbin
Château Corbin-Michotte
Château La Couspaude
Château Curé Bon
Couvent des Jacobins
Château Dassault
Château La Dominique
Château Faurie de Souchard
Château Fonplégade
Château Fonroque
Château Franc-Mayne
Château Grand-Mayne
Château Grand-Pontet
Château Les Grandes Murailles
Château Guadet-Saint-Julien
Château Haut-Corbin
Château Haut-Sarpe
Clos des Jacobins
Château Lamarzelle
Château Laniote

Château Larcis-Ducasse
Château Larmande
Château Laroque
Château Laroze
Château Matras
Château Moulin-du-Cadet
Clos de L'Oratoire
Château Pavie-Decesse
Château Pavie-Macquin
Château Petit-Faurie-de-Soutard
Château Le Prieuré
Château Ripeau
Château Saint-Georges-Côte-Pavie
Clos Saint-Martin
Château La Serre
Château Soutard
Château Tertre-Daugay
Château La Tour-du-Pin-Figeac (Giraud-Belivier)
Château La Tour-du-Pin-Figeac (J M Moueix)
Château La Tour-Figeac
Château Troplong-Mondot
Château Villemaurine
Château Yon-Figeac

THE CRUS BOURGEOIS OF THE MÉDOC AND HAUT-MÉDOC

In 1932 six properties in the Haut-Médoc were classified as *crus bourgeois exceptionnels*, and others in both the Haut-Médoc and the Bas-Médoc into *crus bourgeois* and *crus bourgeois supérieurs*. In the 1960s this list was expanded, and in 1978 was replaced by a division into the categories of *cru bourgeois*, *cru grand bourgeois* and *cru grand bourgeois exceptionnel*. Only properties in the Haut-Médoc could be considered for the latter category, and these wines had to be château-bottled. A number of the better growths (e.g. Château Gloria) declined to be considered for the 1978 classification, fearing that inclusion on this list would preclude consideration in a revision of the *crus classés*. All this then changed in 1984. European law decreed that there should be one category only: that of *cru bourgeois*. Since then there has been an internal list of members of the Syndicat of Cru Bourgeois. As this book goes to press moves are afoot for this list to be officially revised. Here is a list of current members (listed by commune):

AC MÉDOC

BÉGADAN: Châteaux Le Barrail, des Bertins, de By, des Cabans, Cailloux de By, La Clare, La Gorre, Greysac, Haut-Peyrillat, Laffitte-Laujac, Lalande-Robin, Laujac, du Monthil, Moulin de La Roque, Patache d'Aux, Le Pey, Plagnac, Rollan de By, La Roque-de-By, La Tour-de-By, Vieux-Robin and Vieux-Château-Landon.

BLAIGNAN: Châteaux Blaignan, Canteloup, La Cardonne, La Gorce, Grivière, Haut-Myles, Lalande d'Auvion, Normandin, Pontet, Prieuré, Ramafort, Rose de France, Tour Haut-Caussan and des Tourelles.

CIVRAC-EN-MÉDOC: Châteaux Bornac, La Chandellière, d'Escurac and de Panigon.

COUQUÈQUES: Châteaux de Conques, Les Moines and Les Ormes-Sorbet.

JAU-DIGNAC-ET-LOIRAC: Châteaux Fergraves, Gravelongue, Haut-Brisey, Lacombe-Noaillac, Listran, Moulin de Noaillac, Nausicaa, Noaillac, La Pirouette, Saint Aubin, Segue-Longue, Sestignan and Les Traverses.

LESPARRE-MÉDOC: Châteaux Preuillac and Vernous.

ORDONNAC: Châteaux de La Croix, Fontis, Gallais Bellevue, Goudy La Cardonne, Lassalle, Pey-Martin, Potensac, Taffard de Blaignan and Terre Rouge.

PRIGNAC-EN-MÉDOC: Châteaux Chantelys, La Fontaine de L'Aubier, Haut-Garin, Hourbanon, Lafon and Tour Prignac.

QUEYRAC: Château Carcanieux.

SAINT-CHRISTOLY-MÉDOC: Châteaux Le Boscq, Les Grands-Chênes, Guiraud-Peyrebrune, Haut-Canteloup, du Moulin, Moulin de Castillon, Les Mourlanes, du Perier, Saint-Bonnet, Tour-Blanche and La Valière.

SAINT-GERMAIN D'ESTEUIL: Châteaux Brie-Caillou, Castéra and Hauterive.

SAINT-YZANS-DE-MÉDOC: Châteaux des Brousteras, La Croix du Chevalier, Haut-Maurac, Lestruelle, Loudenne, Mazails, La Mothe, Moulin de Bel Air, Le Plantey, Quintaine-Mazails, La Ribaud, Sigognac and Les Tuileries.

VALEYRAC: Châteaux Bellegrave, Bellerive, Bellevue, Le Bourdieu, Lousteauneuf, Sipian, Le Temple and Valeyrac.

VENSAC: Châteaux Comtesse de Gombaud, David and de Taste.

AC HAUT-MÉDOC

ARCINS: Châteaux d'Arcins, Arnauld, Barreyres, Tour Bellevue, Tour du Mayne and Tour du Roc.

ARSAC: Château Le Monteil d'Arsac.

AVENSAN: Châteaux Citran, Meyre, Moulins de Citran and Villegeorge.

BLANQUEFORT: Châteaux Breillan, Dillon, Magnol and Saint-Ahon.

CISSAC-MÉDOC: Châteaux Abiet, du Breuil, Le Chêne, Cissac, Hanteillan, Haut-Logat, Laborde, Lamothe-Cissac, Landat, de Martiny, Moulin du Breuil, Puy Castéra, La Tonnelle, Tour du Mirail, Tour Saint-Joseph and de Villambis.

CUSSAC-FORT-MÉDOC: Châteaux Aney, d'Arvigny, Beaumont, Bel-Air, Fort de Vauban, Julien, Lamothe-Bergeron, du Moulin Rouge, du Raux, Romefort and Tour du Haut-Moulin.

LAMARQUE: Châteaux du Cartillon, de Lamarque and Malescasse.

LISTRAC-MÉDOC: Château Peyre-Labade.

LUDON-MÉDOC: Châteaux d'Agassac, d'Arche and Paloumey.

MACAU: Châteaux Cambon La Pelouse, Dasvin Bel Air and Maucamps.

PAREMPUYRE: Château Clément-Pichon.

LE PIAN-MÉDOC: Châteaux Barthez, Laffitte-Canteloup, Lemoine-Nexon, de Malleret and Sénéjac.

SAINT-LAURENT-MÉDOC: Châteaux Balac, Barateau, Caronne-Sainte-Gemme, Labat, Lagrave-Genestra, Larose-Mascard, Larose-Perganson, Larose-Sieujan and Larose-Trintaudon.

SAINT-SAUVEUR: Châteaux Fonpiqueyre, Fontesteau, Fournas-Bernadotte, La Grave, Haut-Laborde, Haut-Madrac, Hourtin-Ducasse, Lieujean, Liversan, Peyrabon, Peyrahaut, Ramage-La-Batisse and Tourteran.

SAINT-SEURIN-DE-CADOURNE: Châteaux d'Aurilhac, Bel-Orme-Tronquoy-Lalande, Bonneau-Livran, Charmail, Coufran, Dilhac, La Fagotte, Grand-Moulin, Grandis, Lestage-Simon, Marquis de Cadourne, Muret, Perselan, Plantey de La Croix, Pontoise-Cabarrus, Puy-Medulli, La Rose-Maréchale, Saint-Paul, Senilhac, Soudars, Troupian and Verdignan.

LE TAILLAN-MÉDOC: Châteaux La Dame Blanche and du Taillan.

VERTHEUIL: Châteaux de L'Abbaye, Le Bourdieu-Vertheuil, La Gravière, Haut-Vignoble du Parc, Le Meynieu, Reysson and Le Souley-Sainte-Croix.

AC MOULIS-EN-MÉDOC

Châteaux Anthonic, Biston-Brillette, Brillette, Caroline, Chasse-Spleen, Chemin-Royal, Duplessis, Dutruch Grand-Poujeaux, Franquet Grand-Poujeaux, Malmaison, Maucaillou, Moulin-à-Vent, Moulin de Saint-Vincent, Moulis, Poujeaux and La Salle de Poujeaux.

AC LISTRAC-MÉDOC

Châteaux La Bécade, Bellevue-Lafont, Cantegric, Cap-Léon-Veyrin, Clarke, de Corde, L'Ermitage, Fonréaud, Fourcas-Dupré, Fourcas-Hosten, Fourcas-Loubaney, Les Hauts Marcieux, Lafon, Lalande, La Lauzette, Lestage, Liouner, Mayne-Lalande, Moulin-de-Laborde, Peyredon-Lagravette, Reverdi, Saronsot-Dupré and Semeillan-Mazeau.

AC SAINT-ESTÈPHE

Châteaux Andron-Blanquet, Beau-Site-Haut-Vignoble, Beausite, Le Boscq, Canteloup, Capbern-Gasqueton, Chambert-Marbuzet, La Commanderie, Coutelin-Merville, Le Crock, Domeyne, Haut-Baradieu, Haut-Beauséjour, Haut-Coteau, Haut-Marbuzet, Les Hauts de Pez, La Haye, Lilian Ladouys, Mac-Carthy, de Marbuzet, Meyney, Morin, Les Ormes-de-Pez, de Pez, Phelan-Ségur, Picard, Pomys, La Rousselière, Saint-Estèphe, Saint-Roch, Ségur de Cabanac, Tour de Marbuzet, Tour de Pez, Tour des Termes, Tour du Haut-Vignoble, Tronquoy-Lalande and La Villotte.

AC PAUILLAC

Châteaux Artigues, Belle-Rose, Bernadotte, Chanteclerc-Milon, Colombier-Monpelou, La Fleur-Milon, Fonbadet, Haut-Bages-Monpelou, Pibran and du Plantey.

AC SAINT-JULIEN

Châteaux La Bridane, du Glana, Moulin de La Rose, Moulin-Riche, Sirène and Terrey-Gros-Cailloux.

AC MARGAUX

Châteaux d'Arsac, Deyrem-Valentin, Haut-Breton Larigaudière, La Gurgue, Labégorce, Labégorce-Zédé, Larruau, Marsac-Seguineau, Martinens, Monbrison, Paveil-de-Luze, Pontet-Chappaz, Tayac and La Tour de-Mons,.

AUTHOR'S CLASSIFICATION

I first produced a comprehensive personal list of the top red wines of the whole Bordeaux area in my book *Claret* published in 1982. I confined myself to the top sixty or so wines, the same number as the brokers in 1855, and I divided them into four categories: First Growths, Outstanding Growths, Exceptional Growths and Very Fine Growths. The list was based on the performance and prices of the properties concerned during the 1960s and 1970s and allowed for their particular standing in 1982. Since then, seventeen more vintages have arrived and we can now evaluate the mature wines of the 1980s as well as those made earlier. We have also had a chance to see vintages such as 1995 and 1996 in bottle. Here is this revision based on the quality, reputation and prices of the properties concerned over the last decade or so and with particular reference to the château's standing in 1999. The wines are listed in alphabetical order within each category.

First Growths (the Undisputed Top Red Wines of Bordeaux)

Médoc
Château Lafite-Rothschild
Château Latour
Château Léoville-Las-Cases
Château Margaux

Graves
Château Haut-Brion

Saint-Emilion
Château Cheval-Blanc

Pomerol
Château Petrus

Outstanding Growths

These are the super-seconds, wines which, more than occasionally, produce wine of First Growth quality. One could argue very forcibly that in terms of absolute quality (if there is such a thing), some at least should be included in the category above. Prices, however, push the First Growths into a category apart.

Médoc
Château Cos d'Estournel
Château Ducru-Beaucaillou
Château Grand-Puy-Lacoste
Château Léoville-Barton
Château Léoville-Poyferré
Château Mouton-Rothschild
Château Palmer
Château Pichon-Longueville,
   Comtesse de Lalande
Château Rauzan-Ségla

Graves
Domaine de Chevalier
Château La Mission-Haut-Brion

Saint-Emilion
Château Magdelaine

Pomerol
Château L'Evangile
Château La Fleur-Pétrus
Château Lafleur
Château Latour-à-Pomerol
Château Trotanoy
Vieux-Château-Certan

Exceptional Growths

These wines are often as fine as those above if not as prestigious nor as expensive.

Médoc
Château Clerc-Milon
Château Gruaud-Larose
Château Haut-Batailley

Château Haut-Marbuzet
Château Lagrange
Château La Lagune
Château Langoa-Barton

Chateau Lynch-Bages
Château Malescot-
   Saint-Exupéry
Château Montrose

CHÂTEAU PICHON-LONGUEVILLE
   (BARON)
CHÂTEAU PONTET-CANET
CHÂTEAU SOCIANDO-MALLET
CHÂTEAU TALBOT

GRAVES
CHÂTEAU DE FIEUZAL
CHÂTEAU HAUT-BAILLY
CHÂTEAU PAPE-CLÉMENT
CHÂTEAU LA TOUR-HAUT-BRION

SAINT-EMILION
CHÂTEAU ANGÉLUS
CHÂTEAU L'ARROSÉE
CHÂTEAU AUSONE
CHÂTEAU BEAUSÉJOUR-DUFFAU-
   LAGARROSSE
CHÂTEAU CANON
CHÂTEAU FIGEAC
LA MONDOTTE
CHÂTEAU PAVIE
CHÂTEAU LE TERTRE-ROTEBOEUF
CHÂTEAU TROPLONG-MONDOT

POMEROL
CHÂTEAU CERTAN-DE-MAY
CHÂTEAU CLINET
CHÂTEAU LA CONSEILLANTE
CLOS L'EGLISE
CHÂTEAU LA FLEUR-DE-GAY
CHÂTEAU GAZIN
LE PIN

VERY FINE GROWTHS

Many of these châteaux regularly produce wine in the higher 'Exceptional' category.

MÉDOC
CHÂTEAU D'ANGLUDET
CHÂTEAU D'ARMAILHAC
CHÂTEAU BATAILLEY
CHÂTEAU BEYCHEVELLE
CHÂTEAU BOYD-CANTENAC
CHÂTEAU BRANAIRE
CHÂTEAU BRANE-CANTENAC
CHÂTEAU CALON-SÉGUR
CHÂTEAU CANTEMERLE
CHÂTEAU CHASSE-SPLEEN
CHÂTEAU COS-LABORY
CHÂTEAU DAUZAC
CHÂTEAU DESMIRAIL
CHÂTEAU DUHART-MILON
CHÂTEAU DURFORT-VIVENS
CHÂTEAU FONBADET
CHÂTEAU GISCOURS
CHÂTEAU GLORIA
CHÂTEAU D'ISSAN
CHÂTEAU LABÉGORCE-ZÉDÉ
CHÂTEAU MONBRISON
CHÂTEAU DE PEZ
CHÂTEAU POTENSAC
CHÂTEAU POUGET
CHÂTEAU POUJEAUX
CHÂTEAU PRIEURÉ-LICHINE
CHÂTEAU SAINT-PIERRE
CHÂTEAU DU TERTRE
CHÂTEAU LA TOUR-DE-MONS

GRAVES
CHÂTEAU BOUSCAUT
CHÂTEAU CARBONNIEUX
CHÂTEAU LARRIVET-HAUT-BRION
CHÂTEAU LA LOUVIÈRE
CHÂTEAU MALARTIC-LAGRAVIÈRE
CHÂTEAU OLIVIER
CHATEAU SMITH-HAUT-LAFITTE
CHÂTEAU LA TOUR-MARTILLAC

SAINT-EMILION
CHÂTEAU BEAU-SÉJOUR-BÉCOT
CHÂTEAU BELAIR
CHATEAU BERLIQUET
CHÂTEAU CADET-BON
CHÂTEAU CADET-PIOLA
CHÂTEAU CANON-LA-GAFFELIÈRE
CHÂTEAU CURÉ-BON
CHÂTEAU DASSAULT
CHÂTEAU LA DOMINIQUE
CHÂTEAU FONROQUE
CLOS FOURTET
CHÂTEAU LA GAFFELIÈRE
LA GOMERIE
CHÂTEAU GRAND-MAYNE
CHÂTEAU LARCIS-DUCASSE
CHÂTEAU LARMANDE
CLOS DE L'ORATOIRE
CHÂTEAU PAVIE-DECESSE
CHÂTEAU PAVIE-MACQUIN
CLOS SAINT-MARTIN

CHÂTEAU LA SERRE
CHÂTEAU SOUTARD
CHÂTEAU TERTRE-DAUGAY
CHÂTEAU LA TOUR-FIGEAC
CHÂTEAU TROTTEVIEILLE
CHÂTEAU DE VALANDRAUD

POMEROL
CHÂTEAU BEAUREGARD
CHÂTEAU LE BON-PASTEUR
CHÂTEAU CERTAN-GIRAUD (NOW
   CHATEAU HOSANNA)
CLOS DU CLOCHER
CHÂTEAU LA CROIX-DE-GAY
CHÂTEAU L'ENCLOS
CHÂTEAU LE GAY
CHÂTEAU LA GRAVE-à-POMEROL
CHÂTEAU LAGRANGE
CHÂTEAU NENIN
CHÂTEAU LA POINTE
CLOS RENÉ

FRONSAC
CHÂTEAU CANON (MOUEIX)
CHÂTEAU CANON-DE-BREM
CHÂTEAU DALEM
CHÂTEAU FONTENIL
CHÂTEAU LA RIVIÈRE
CHÂTEAU VILLARS

The Wine Regions

MÉDOC

Surface Area (1998): 4822 ha.
Production (1998): 290,598 hl.
Colour: Red (the white wines are AC Bordeaux or Bordeaux Supérieur).
Grape Varieties: Cabernet Sauvignon, Cabernet Franc, Merlot, Malbec and Petit Verdot.
Maximum Yield: 50 hl/ha.
Minimum Alcohol Level: 10°.

The Médoc (also called Médoc Maritime or Bas-Médoc to differentiate it from the Haut-Médoc) begins where the Haut-Médoc leaves off, north of Saint-Estèphe, and runs from Saint-Yzans and Saint-Germain d'Esteins all the way up to Soulac at the tip of the peninsula.

Viticulturally, as well as in terms of prestige, it is a minor area compared with its more famous neighbour to the south. There are fourteen wine-producing communes, with a total area under vine of some 4800 hectares, producing some 300,000 hectolitres a year. The *appellation* covers red wines only. It is a part of the world which few outsiders ever visit. The countryside is low-lying, flat and open to the skies. Even more than the Haut-Médoc, the atmosphere often resembles that of Holland. Fields of pasture cover the land more than vines, interspersed with copses, hamlets and the occasional wine-producing farmhouse. It is peaceful but bleak and remote.

Nevertheless, the wines are well worth investigating, for they are inexpensive, and no serious list of Bordeaux *petits châteaux* will be without one or two of the better examples. Like the more famous estates to the south Cabernet Sauvignon and Cabernet Franc form the bulk of the plantings, together with Merlot and a little Malbec, and this mixture of varieties gives the wine body and backbone, albeit at a lower level of breed and concentration than in Pauillac or Margaux. The wines will have a similar blackcurranty taste, but usually without the oak element found in the better wines from further south. Most are at their best after five years.

Leading Médoc Producers

CHÂTEAU POTENSAC

Commune: Ordonnac.
Owners: Delon family.
Surface Area under Vine: 52 ha – 60% Cabernet Sauvignon, 15% Cabernet Franc and 25% Merlot.
Second Wines: Château Lasalle and Château Gaillas-Bellevue.
Classification: Cru Bourgeois.

Owned by the Delons of Château Léoville-Las-Cases and managed with the same dedication it is not surprising that Château Potensac is the leading estate in the Médoc. Twenty per cent of the barrels are new each year. The wine is very classy, and needs six to seven years to mature.

Other wines CHÂTEAU LÉOVILLE-LAS-CASES (SAINT-JULIEN) AND CHÂTEAU NENIN (POMEROL).

CHÂTEAU TOUR-HAUT-CAUSSAN

Commune: Blaignan.
Owner: Philippe Courrian.
Surface Area under Vine: 17 ha – 50% Cabernet Sauvignon and 50% Merlot.
Second Wine: Château La Landotte.
Classification: Cru Bourgeois.

Lying on a splendid plateau dominated by a working windmill this vineyard is under the inspired management of Philippe Courrian. Since the mid-1980s Tour-Haut-Caussan has established itself as the closest rival in the Médoc to Château Potensac (see above). The wine is lush, concentrated and oaky (one-third of the casks are new).

Other wine CHÂTEAU CASCARDAIS (CORBIÈRES).

Other Producers of note

CHÂTEAU LA CARDONNE (BLAIGNAN), CHÂTEAU CASTÉRA (SAINT-GERMAIN-D'ESTEUIL), CHÂTEAU LA CLARE (BÉGADAN), CHÂTEAU FONTIS (ORDONNAC), CHÂTEAU LES GRANDS-CHÊNES (SAINT-CHRISTOLY-MÉDOC), CHÂTEAU

GREYSAC (BÉGADAN), CHÂTEAU LAUJAC (BÉGADAN), CHÂTEAU LOUDENNE (SAINT-YZANS-DE-MÉDOC), CHÂTEAU DU MONTHIL (BÉGADAN), CHÂTEAU NOAILLAC (JAU-DIGNAC-ET-LOIRAC), CHÂTEAU LES ORMES-SORBET (COUQUÈQUES), CHÂTEAU PATACHE D'AUX (BÉGADAN), CHÂTEAU PONTET (BLAIGNAN), CHÂTEAU RAMAFORT (BLAIGNAN), CHÂTEAU ROLLAN DE BY (BÉGADAN), CHÂTEAU SIGOGNAC (SAINT-YZANS-DE-MÉDOC), CHÂTEAU LA TOUR-DE-BY (BÉGADAN), CHÂTEAU LA TOUR-SAINT-BONNET (SAINT-CHRISTOLY-MÉDOC), VIEUX CHÂTEAU LANDON (BÉGADAN) AND CHÂTEAU VIEUX-ROBIN (BÉGADAN); PLUS IMPORTANT CO-OPERATIVES AT BÉGADAN, ORDONNAC, SAINT-YZANS, QUEYRAC, DRIGNAC AND GAILLAN.

HAUT-MÉDOC

Surface Area (1998): 4277 ha.
Production (1998): 249,962 hl.
Colour: Red (the white wines are AC Bordeaux or Bordeaux Supérieur).
Grape Varieties: Cabernet Sauvignon, Cabernet Franc, Merlot, Malbec and Petit Verdot.
Maximum Yield: 48 hl/ha.
Minimum Alcohol Level: 10°.

The Haut-Médoc begins at the Jalle de Blanquefort, north of Bordeaux, and continues to Saint-Seurin-de-Cadourne, a distance of some 50 kilometres as the crow flies. The vineyards stretch back from the Gironde estuary on a series of rippling mounds or *croupes* of gravel banks as far as the D1/N215, the main road from Bordeaux to Le Verdon and the ferry across the mouth of the estuary over into the Charente country.

This is the largest, greatest and most concentrated red wine area on earth. Once the traveller from Bordeaux reaches the first of the classed growths, Château La Lagune in the commune of Ludon some half an hour's drive away from the city centre, the vines and the great names continue almost uninterruptedly until you pass Châteaux Coufran and Soudars in the hamlet of Cadourne and cross into the Bas-Médoc. To the right, particularly from Saint-Julien onwards, the great

vineyards lie close to the water. The brown, sluggish, shallow estuary, within which lie long sandbanks or marshy islands, covered with tangled undergrowth, can clearly be seen. Behind, to the left, the vineyards continue until the gravel gives way to sand and pines. 'The best vines are those which can view the water' is a much repeated quotation and in general this is so. Those properties whose land lies on the first *croupe* facing the Gironde, produce the wines with the greatest complexity of character and depth of flavour. Those from the plateau behind often have more body, but have less finesse. In principle those from the five parishes which make up the *appellation* Margaux and those from Macau and Ludon in the south of the Haut Médoc are more delicate than those further north.

This is a countryside dominated by fine wine. The estates are large, and can boast long histories. There are many fine parks and elegant buildings. It was in the Médoc that the *noblesse de la robe*, the wealthy Bordelais in the eighteenth century, established their country estates. During the nineteenth century a new breed of the moneyed classes, whose wealth was based in finance and industry or in wine, replaced those who had died out or disappeared. These in their turn have been superseded by multinationals, insurance companies and other conglomerates in the post-Second World War era. The Haut-Médoc is not only more homogenous but more alive, more vigorous than the sleepy, more desolate countryside of the Médoc further north. The villages are larger and those who do not work in the *chais* and vineyards of the great estates commute to Bordeaux. There is an element of creeping suburbia, particularly close to the great city and the industrial developments that lie on its outskirts.

The Haut-Médoc consists of twenty-nine communes; some 10,100 hectares of vineyard produce an annual total of about 500,000 hectolitres of wine. Some 2800 hectares, a third of the land under vine, is classed growth. The majority of these estates lie in the four great communes of Margaux, Saint-Julien, Pauillac and Saint-Estèphe. Each of these has a separate superior *appellation* to that of Haut-Médoc, as additionally do the communes of Moulis and Listrac. Outside these six communes which are entitled to their own individual *appellation*, there are a further twenty-three communes whose *appellation* is simply Haut-Médoc. Most of these form a line behind the more famous parishes, lying on what one might term the third and fourth ridge of gravel mounds as they ripple away from the Gironde estuary. Two lie south of Margaux (Macau and Ludon); others (Cussac, Lamarque, Arcins) lie between Margaux and Saint-Julien. Saint-Seurin-La-Cadourne is north of Saint-Estèphe.

The Haut-Médoc is the Bordeaux heartland of Cabernet Sauvignon. Together with Cabernet Franc, balanced with a proportion of Merlot, and, in the best properties, combined with the flavour of new oak, this produces the blackcurrant-blackberry fruit, and the austere, firm, tannic, full-bodied character which is associated with the words 'claret' or 'Red Bordeaux' the world over.

Leading Haut-Médoc Producers

CHÂTEAU BELGRAVE
Commune: Saint-Laurent.
Owners: Groupe CVBG.
Surface Area under Vine: 3 ha – 40% Cabernet Sauvignon, 20% Cabernet Franc, 35% Merlot and 5% Petit Verdot.
Second Wine: Diane de Belgrave.
Classification: Cinquième Cru (1855).
Château Belgrave lies in Saint-Laurent, just west of the Saint-Julien boundary and has been the subject of a major investment since changing ownership in 1979. This is now being reflected in the quality of the wine, which has improved considerably in the 1990s.
Other wines CHÂTEAU LE BOSQ (SAINT-ESTÈPHE); CHÂTEAU LA GARDE (PESSAC-LÉOGNAN) AND OTHERS.

CHÂTEAU CAMENSAC
Commune: Saint-Laurent.
Owners: Forner family.
Surface Area under Vine: 65 ha – 60% Cabernet Sauvignon, 15% Cabernet Franc and 25% Merlot.
Second Wine: La Closerie de Camensac.
Classification: Cinquième Cru (1885).

Château Camensac was acquired by the Forner family in 1964. It was in a somewhat dilapidated condition at the time, necessitating an almost complete replanting of the vineyard, as well as a new *cuverie* and cellars. Not surprisingly, quality has improved, but Château Camensac is still a long way from being a super-star.

CHÂTEAU CANTEMERLE
Commune: Macau.
Owners: SMABTP.
Surface Area under Vine: 67 ha – 35% Cabernet Sauvignon, 23% Cabernet Franc, 40% Merlot and 2% Petit Verdot.
Second Wine: Baron Villeneuve de Cantemerle.
Classification: Cinquième Cru (1855).
Under the Dubos/Binaud ownership, which lasted until 1982, Château Cantemerle was undercapitalised (by the end the vineyard had contracted to 23 ha) but still made very elegant, soft, fragrant wine. Money is now no longer a problem and investment has been made. But in the process they have lost the soul of the wine. It is good, but no more. I wait in hope.
Other wines CHÂTEAU HAUT-CORBIN AND CHÂTEAU LE JURAT (BOTH SAINT-EMILION).

★ CHÂTEAU LA LAGUNE
Commune: Ludon.
Owners: Ducellier family.
Surface Area under Vine: 72 ha – 60% Cabernet Sauvignon, 10% Cabernet Franc, 20% Merlot and 10% Petit Verdot.
Second Wine: Château Ludon Pomiès Agassac.
Classification: Troisième Cru (1855).
Château La Lagune is yet another property which has been rescued from dereliction – this time by Georges Brunet in 1954. Hardly had he done so than he sold up to the Ducellier family of Champagne Ayala. Since then, apart from a blip in the mid-1990s – a result of a sudden drop in the average age of the vines – Château La Lagune has consistently produced very good if never quite super-second quality. The wine is medium bodied, juicy, oaky, fresh and full of charm. It lasts well and is deservedly popular.

THE MÉDOC AND NORTHERN MÉDOC

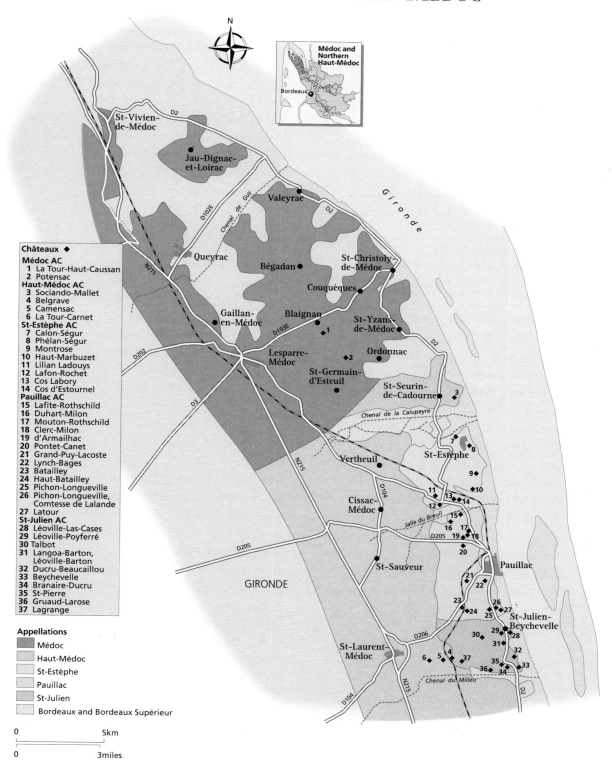

N

Médoc and
Northern
Haut-Médoc

Bordeaux

St-Vivien-
de-Médoc

Jau-Dignac-
et-Loirac

Valeyrac

Gironde

Queyrac

Bégadan

St-Christoly-
de-Médoc

Couquèques

Châteaux ◆

Médoc AC
1 La Tour-Haut-Caussan
2 Potensac
Haut-Médoc AC
3 Sociando-Mallet
4 Belgrave
5 Camensac
6 La Tour-Carnet
St-Estèphe AC
7 Calon-Ségur
8 Phélan-Ségur
9 Montrose
10 Haut-Marbuzet
11 Lilian Ladouys
12 Lafon-Rochet
13 Cos Labory
14 Cos d'Estournel
Pauillac AC
15 Lafite-Rothschild
16 Duhart-Milon
17 Mouton-Rothschild
18 Clerc-Milon
19 d'Armailhac
20 Pontet-Canet
21 Grand-Puy-Lacoste
22 Lynch-Bages
23 Batailley
24 Haut-Batailley
25 Pichon-Longueville
26 Pichon-Longueville,
   Comtesse de Lalande
27 Latour
St-Julien AC
28 Léoville-Las-Cases
29 Léoville-Poyferré
30 Talbot
31 Langoa-Barton,
   Léoville-Barton
32 Ducru-Beaucaillou
33 Beychevelle
34 Branaire-Ducru
35 St-Pierre
36 Gruaud-Larose
37 Lagrange

Gaillan-
en-Médoc

Blaignan

St-Yzans-
de-Médoc

1

Lesparre-
Médoc

2

Ordonnac

St-Germain-
d'Esteuil

St-Seurin-
de-Cadourne

3

Chenal de la Calupeyre

Vertheuil

7

St-Estèphe

8

9

10

Cissac-
Médoc

11

13

12

14

Jalle du Breuil

15

16 17

19 18

20

St-Sauveur

21

22

Pauillac

23

24

25

26

27

St-Julien-
Beychevelle

29 28

30

31

32

33

34

35

36

37

4

5

6

St-Laurent-
Médoc

GIRONDE

Chenal du Milieu

Appellations

- Médoc
- Haut-Médoc
- St-Estèphe
- Pauillac
- St-Julien
- Bordeaux and Bordeaux Supérieur

0 ————— 5km

0 ————— 3miles

★ CHÂTEAU SOCIANDO-MALLET

Commune: Saint-Seurin-de-Cadourne.
Owner: Jean Gautreau.
Surface Area under Vine: 45 ha – 60% Cabernet Sauvignon, 8% Cabernet Franc, 30% Merlot and 2% Petit Verdot.
Second Wine: La Demoiselle de Sociando-Mallet.

Jean Gautreau acquired the almost derelict Château Sociando-Mallet in 1969 and has since developed it into this leading Haut-Médoc estate. The wine is full, oaky, Cabernet-flavoured and has surprising depth and elegance. The site, a gravel *croupe* directly overlooking the Gironde estuary in Saint-Seurin-de-Cadourne, north of Saint-Estèphe, contains less clay in the soil than in neighbouring estates and perhaps this explains why the wine is superior. Or do the other estates just not try hard enough?

CHÂTEAU LA TOUR-CARNET

Commune: Saint-Laurent.
Owner: Marie-Claire Pellegrin.
Surface Area under Vine: 42 ha – 53% Cabernet Sauvignon, 10% Cabernet Franc, 33% Merlot and 4% Petit Verdot.
Second Wine: Les Douves de Carnet.
Classification: Quatrième Cru (1855).

Château La Tour-Carnet is a proper castle, with a moat, and lies next to Château Camensac in Saint-Laurent, west of Saint-Julien. For a long time quality here was in the doldrums. Occasionally there was a glimmer suggesting that things had turned the corner. The wine is better than it used to be but there is still a long way to go before it justifies its classed growth status. The vineyard is in a frost pocket, which does not help.

Other Producers of note

CHÂTEAU ARNAULD (ARCINS), CHÂTEAU BEAUMONT (CUSSAC-FORT-MÉDOC), CHÂTEAU BERNADOTTE (SAINT-SAVEUR), CHÂTEAU CARONNE-SAINTE-GEMME (SAINT-LAURENT), CHÂTEAU CHARMAIL (SAINT-SEURIN), CHÂTEAU CISSAC (CISSAC), CHÂTEAU CITRAN (AVENSAN), CHÂTEAU COUFRAN (SAINT-SEURIN), CHÂTEAU HANTEILLAN (VERTHEUIL), CHÂTEAU DE LAMARQUE (LAMARQUE), CHÂTEAU CLÉMONT-PICHON (PAREMPUYRE), CHÂTEAU LAMOTHE-BERGERON (CUSSAC-FORT-MÉDOC), CHÂTEAU LANESSAN (CUSSAC-FORT-MÉDOC), CHÂTEAU LAROSE-TRINTAUDON (SAINT-LAURENT), CHÂTEAU LESTAGE-SIMON (SAINT-SEURIN), CHÂTEAU MALESCASSE (LAMARQUE), CHÂTEAU MAUCAMPS (MACAU), CHÂTEAU DU MOULIN ROUGE (CISSAC-FORT-MÉDOC), CHÂTEAU RAMAGE-LA-BATISSE (SAINT-SAVEUR), CHÂTEAU SÉNÉJAC (LE PIAN), CHÂTEAU SOUDARS (SAINT-SEURIN), CHÂTEAU TOUR DU HAUT-MOULIN (CUSSAC-FORT-MÉDOC), CHÂTEAU VERDIGNAN (SAINT-SEURIN) AND CHÂTEAU VILLEGEORGE (AVENSAN).

SAINT-ESTÈPHE

Surface Area (1998): 1229 ha.
Production (1998): 68,946 hl.
Colour: Red (The white wines are AC Bordeaux or Bordeaux Supérieur).
Grape Varieties: Cabernet Sauvignon, Cabernet Franc, Merlot, Malbec and Petit Verdot.
Maximum Yield: 45 hl/ha.
Minimum Alcohol Level: 10.5°.

Saint-Estèphe is the largest and most northerly of the four great Haut-Médoc communes. It has long suffered by comparison with the others. Writers extol the magnificence of Pauillac, the breed of Saint-Julien, the subtlety and fragrance of Margaux. Yet they do not warm to Saint-Estèphe. Saint-Estèphe can only boast five classed growths (two Seconds, a Third, a Fourth and Fifth) and would not manage to scrape many more if there were to be a reclassification. The commune is dominated by a large cluster of good-but-never great *bourgeois* growths, many extensive in area, regularly exported and deservedly popular. But these are middle-class wines rather than aristocrats.

The soil in Saint-Estèphe is varied. In the south-east corner of the *appellation* it is heavy gravel on the hard sandstone base rich in iron known as *alios*, similar to that in Pauillac. Progressively west and north it contains more clay, less gravel, becomes heavier and more fertile. In parts there is limestone. Naturally the style of the wines varies too. Although in general there is more Merlot here than elsewhere in the Haut-Médoc, there are nevertheless many properties with 70 per cent or more Cabernet Sauvignon and Cabernet Franc.

Compared with Pauillacs the wines are in general tougher and denser, though not necessarily fuller. They are more aromatic and less elegant. They are firm, full and tannic but in a less distinguished way; less obviously richly blackcurrant in flavour, and more robust and spicy – even sweeter – in character. Some Saint-Estèphes do not age too gracefully. That said, the best wines – Cos d'Estoumel clearly, and Montrose also – both from the south-eastern end of the parish, are as good, and can last as well, as the very greatest of their peers elsewhere. Overall in the commune there has been an encouraging change for the better in recent years.

Leading Saint-Estèphe Producers

CHÂTEAU CALON-SÉGUR
Owners: Gasqueton family.
Surface Area under Vine: 74 ha – 65% Cabernet Sauvignon, 15% Cabernet Franc and 20% Merlot.
Second Wines: Mademoiselle de Calon, Marquis de Calon and Saint-Estèphe de Calon La Chapelle.
Classification: Troisième Cru (1855).
The oldest property in the commune is Calon-Ségur, whose vineyards, surrounding an elegant château, lie north of the village, making it the last of the classed growths as one journeys from the Haut-Médoc into the Bas-Médoc. Quality was fine here in the years after the Second World War. Then too much Merlot was planted, a bias which has since been corrected, and standards slipped. They have since improved, but only a little.and there is still some way to go to realise its full potential. The wine is full, spicy and gamey but lacks real finesse.

★★ CHÂTEAU COS D'ESTOURNEL
Owners: Groupe Taillan.
Surface Area under Vine: 65 ha – 60% Cabernet Sauvignon, 2% Cabernet Franc and 38% Merlot.
Second Wine: Les Pagodes de Cos.
Classification: Deuxième Cru (1855).

The oriental-style temple which is the Cos d'Estournel *chai* stands out as one arrives in Saint-Estèphe from the south. This is the home of what is clearly the commune's best wine, and has been consistently so since Bruno Prats took over in 1971. The family sold out in 1998 but his son Jean-Guillaume continues as manager. Other Saint-Estèphes may be burly, muscular and coarse, but Cos is a wine of ripe tannins, elegant, sophisticated fruit with a spice which distinguishes itself from the Pauillacs and Saint-Juliens further south.

CHÂTEAU COS LABORY
Owners: Audoy family.
Surface Area under Vine: 18 ha – 50% Cabernet Sauvignon, 15% Cabernet Franc, 30% Merlot and 5% Petit Verdot.
Second Wine: Le Charme Labory.
Classification: Cinquième Cru (1855).
Cos Labory can be a charming, elegant wine and very good value, but it is never a blockbuster. The vineyard stretches behind the château, sandwiched between vines belonging to the other Cos towards the Audoys' sister property, Andron-Blanquet.
Other wine CHÂTEAU ANDRON-BLANQUET (SAINT-ESTÈPHE).

★ CHÂTEAU HAUT-MARBUZET
Owner: Henri Dubosq.
Surface Area under Vine: 50 ha – 50% Cabernet Sauvignon, 10% Cabernet Franc and 40% Merlot.
Second Wine: La Rose MacCarthy.
Classification: Cru Bourgeois.
Passionate, perfectionistic winemaking and lots of new oak have brought Haut-Marbuzet to the forefront since the 1980s. But in fact it has been making very good wine since it was acquired by Hervé Dubosq, father of Henri, in 1952. Today it is consistently among the top three in the commune. It is a very individual wine however: disarmingly seductive. Happily in this case the new oaky lushness is more than just make-up.
Other wines CHÂTEAU CHAMBERT-MARBUZET, CHÂTEAU MACCARTHY AND CHÂTEAU TOUR DE MARBUZET (ALL SAINT-ESTÈPHE).

CHÂTEAU LAFON-ROCHET

Owners: Tesseron family.
Surface Area under Vine: 40 ha – 56% Cabernet Sauvignon, 4% Cabernet Franc and 40% Merlot.
Second Wine: No 2 du Château Lafon-Rochet.
Classification: Quatrième Cru (1855).

Château Lafon-Rochet has been almost completely resurrected since Guy Tesseron bought it in 1959. At first he planted too much Cabernet Sauvignon, but this has now been rectified, and the wine is no longer as hard as it used to be. It still has a way to go before it shows the finesse of its stablemate, Château Pontet-Canet.
Other wine CHÂTEAU PONTET-CANET (PAUILLAC).

CHÂTEAU LILIAN-LADOUYS

Owner: Banque Populaire, Paris.
Surface Area under Vine: 48 ha – 58% Cabernet Sauvignon, 5% Cabernet Franc and 37% Merlot.
Second Wine: La Devise de Lilian.
Classification: Cru Bourgeois.

Château Ladouys was acquired by Christian Thiéblot in 1989, and enlarged, renovated, up-dated and christened in the years to follow. From the very first vintage under the Thiéblot regime it established itself in the top rank of Saint-Estèphes and this quality has been continued under the new owners who took over in 1996.

★ CHÂTEAU MONTROSE

Owners: Charmolüe family.
Surface Area under Vine: 68 ha – 65% Cabernet Sauvignon, 10% Cabernet Franc and 25% Merlot.
Second Wine: La Dame de Montrose.
Classification: Deuxième Cru (1855).

The vineyard of Château Montrose lies very close to the estuary and as a consequence enjoys a benign mesoclimate, not, for instance, being frosted nearly as severely as its neighbours in 1991 or 1956. The wine has had a tendency to be very big and tannic, these tannins obscuring the richness of the fruit and never seeming to mellow. Since 1982 there has been a movement to subdue this tendency. They got it spot on in 1990 and have usually been fairly nearly there, as in the 1986 and 1996. Avoid the 1983 and 1985 though. Here the wine was too weak.

CHÂTEAU PHÉLAN-SÉGUR

Owner: Xavier Gardinier.
Surface Area under Vine: 66 ha – 60% Cabernet Sauvignon, 10% Cabernet Franc and 30% Merlot.
Second Wine: Frank Phélan.
Classification: Cru Bourgeois.

Château Phélan-Ségur has proven in the past that it can make wine of good classed growth standard (1959, 1961). After years of neglect it was acquired by the Gardinier family in 1985. Since then there has been a major investment in château and *chais*. The wines are now beginning to realise their potential.

Other Producers of note

CHÂTEAU LE BOSCQ, CHÂTEAU COUTELIN-MERVILLE, CHÂTEAU LE CROCK, CHÂTEAU LA HAYE, CHÂTEAU MARBUZET, CHÂTEAU MEYNEY, CHÂTEAU LES ORMES-DE-PEZ, CHÂTEAU DE PEZ, CHÂTEAU SÉGUR-DE-CABANAC AND CHÂTEAU TOUR-DES-TERMES.

PAUILLAC

Surface Area (1998): 1170 ha.
Production (1998): 65,417 hl.
Colour: Red (The white wines are AC Bordeaux or Bordeaux Supérieur).
Grape Varieties: Cabernet Sauvignon, Cabernet Franc, Merlot, Malbec and Petit Verdot.
Maximum Yield: 45 hl/ha.
Minimum Alcoholic Level: 10.5°.

The commune of Pauillac lies between Saint-Julien and Saint-Estèphe some 45 kilometres north of Bordeaux. The vineyards of the three parishes are in fact contiguous, the vines of Léoville-Las-Cases in Saint-Julien marching with those of Latour, separated only by a narrow gully; those of Lafite facing those of Cos d' Estournel in Saint-Estèphe across a stream, the Jalle de Breuil. Pauillac is not the largest of the main communes – that honour falls to Margaux in size but Saint-Estèphe in volume of production; but it is the most important. Pauillac contains three of the four First Growths and no fewer than fifteen other classified châteaux, almost a third of the 1855 Classification. It also boasts a number of good *bourgeois* properties.

The commune is split in two by a stream, the Pibran, which flows diagonally across the parish in a north-easterly direction, debouching into the Gironde at the northern end of the town of Pauillac itself. North and west of this stream the land rises steeply (in Médocain terms) to some 27 metres above sea level, and includes the vineyards of both the Rothschilds and Pontet-Canet. South and east lie the Bages and Grand-Puy-Lacoste plateau, the Batailleys, the Pichons and Château Latour. The Pauillac soil is heavy gravel, thicker to the north than to the south, based on a subsoil of larger stones, and iron-based sand. The wines of Pauillac are archetype Bordeaux and the taste of Cabernet Sauvignon, which in some cases – as at Châteaux Mouton-Rothschild and Latour – form the vast part of the *encépagement*. The wines are full-bodied, dense and tannic; austere when young, rich and distinguished when mature; and the longest-lived of all Bordeaux wines. At their best they are the fullest and most concentrated of all red wines.

Leading Pauillac Producers

CHÂTEAU D'ARMAILHAC

Owner: Baronne Philippine de Rothschild.
Surface Area under Vine: 49 ha – 49% Cabernet Sauvignon, 23% Cabernet Franc, 26% Merlot and 2% Petit Verdot.
Classification: Cinquième Cru (1855).
Baron Philippe de Rothschild bought this property, then called Mouton d'Armailhacq, in 1934. The land lies between Châteaux Mouton-Rothschild and Pontet-Canet. It has since had three changes of name: to Mouton Baron Philippe in 1956 and then Baronne Philippe, in honour of his late wife in 1975. It reverted to simple Armailhac, without the final Q, in 1989. Made by the Mouton team, the wine is of medium weight, usually one of the better, more elegant Fifths Growths. Currently its other stablemate, Château Clerc-Milon, makes better, more concentrated wine.
Other wines CHÂTEAU CLERC-MILON AND CHÂTEAU MOUTON-ROTHSCHILD (BOTH PAUILLAC).

CHÂTEAU BATAILLEY

Owner: Émile Castéja.
Surface Area under Vine: 55 ha – 70% Cabernet Sauvignon, 3% Cabernet Franc, 25% Merlot and 2% Petit Verdot.
Second Wine: Plaisance Saint-Lambert.
Classification: Cinquième Cru (1855).
This is the largest part of the divided Batailley domaine, the separation having occurred in 1942, and the wine is sold, not on the open market, but through *négociants* Borie-Manoux, the family wine business. Château Batailley's quality does not aspire to super-second status, but neither does its price. It is a medium bodied, mellow, fruity wine which is generally very good value.
Other wines CHÂTEAU DU DOMAINE DE L'EGLISE (POMEROL), CHÂTEAU HAUT-BAGES-MONPELOU, CHÂTEAU LYNCH-MOUSSAS (BOTH PAUILLAC), CHÂTEAU TROTTEVIEILLE (SAINT-EMILION) AND OTHERS.

★ CHÂTEAU CLERC-MILON

Owner: Baronne Philippine de Rothschild.
Surface Area under Vine: 32 ha – 50% Cabernet Sauvignon, 13% Cabernet Franc, 34% Merlot and 3% Petit Verdot.
Classification: Cinquième Cru (1855).
A modest château, but with an up-to-date *cuvier*, owned by the Rothschilds of Mouton since 1970. This is one of the best value châteaux in Bordeaux, regularly making full, rich, concentrated wine, almost of super-second quality, but at a much more reasonable price.
Other wines: CHÂTEAU D'ARMAILHAC AND CHÂTEAU MOUTON-ROTHSCHILD (BOTH PAUILLAC).

★ CHÂTEAU DUHART-MILON

Owners: Domaines Barons de Rothschild.
Surface Area under Vine: 65 ha – 65% Cabernet Sauvignon, 5% Cabernet Franc and 30% Merlot.
Second Wine: Moulin de Duhart.
Classification: Quatrième Cru (1855).
Château Duhart-Milon, which was bought by the Rothschilds of Lafite in 1962, occupies land between Châteaux Lafite and Mouton-Rothschild and the eastern boundary of Pauillac. For many years the wine was rather hard

and green, the vintages of the late 1980s and 1990s have seen this character moderated, allowing finesse to come forward. It is nevertheless, as a result of the location of the vineyard, a firmer, more masculine wine than Lafite. Recent vintages have been of a high standard.

Other wines CHÂTEAU L'EVANGILE (POMEROL) AND CHÂTEAU LAFITE-ROTHSCHILD (PAUILLAC).

★★ CHÂTEAU GRAND-PUY-LACOSTE

Owners: Borie family.
Surface Area under Vine: 50 ha – 75% Cabernet Sauvignon and 25% Merlot.
Second Wine: Lacoste-Borie.
Classification: Cinquième Cru (1855).

This estate was acquired by the late Jean-Eugène Borie of Château Ducru-Beaucaillou in 1978. It had a fine reputation then – with Lynch-Bages the best of the Fifth Growths – and an even better one now. Xavier Borie is in charge, as he is at Ducru-Beaucaillou, and he produces a wine of real Pauillac size and great Cabernet breeding, splendidly elegant and concentrated, and very consistent. There seems to have been no trouble with chlorine taints recently, unlike at Ducru-Beaucaillou.

Other wines CHÂTEAU DUCLUZEAU (LISTRAC), CHÂTEAU DUCRU-BEAUCAILLOU (SAINT-JULIEN) AND CHÂTEAU HAUT-BATAILLEY (PAUILLAC).

★ CHÂTEAU HAUT-BATAILLEY

Owners: Borie family.
Surface Area under Vine: 22 ha – 65% Cabernet Sauvignon, 10% Cabernet Franc and 25% Merlot.
Second Wine: Château La Tour d'Aspic.
Classification: Cinquième Cru (1855).

This estate was separated from Château Batailley in 1942, when the Borie brothers split their assets. It has always produced a fuller, rather austere wine, which has needed time to mature and which was never as classy or as concentrated as Château Grand-Puy-Lacoste. The 1996 and 1997 suddenly showed a change: more charm and succulence without any dilution of structure.

Other wines CHÂTEAU DUCLUZEAU (LISTRAC), CHÂTEAU DUCRU-BEAUCAILLOU (SAINT-JULIEN) AND CHÂTEAU GRAND-PUY-LACOSTE (PAUILLAC).

★★★ CHÂTEAU LAFITE-ROTHSCHILD

Owners: Domaines Barons de Rothschild.
Surface Area under Vine: 94 ha – 70% Cabernet Sauvignon, 10% Cabernet Franc and 20% Merlot.
Second Wine: Carruades de Lafite.
Classification: Premier Cru (1855).

Château Lafite can be as great as Château Latour, but great in a completely different way. Where Latour is firm, aloof and austere, Lafite is more approachable and supremely elegant. Vintages from 1963 to 1977 are not up to par, but prior to this, exceptionally in 1953, 1959 and 1961, and subsequently, almost without exception since 1978, Lafite is as great as its reputation: the first of the firsts in the 1855 Classification.

Other wines CHÂTEAU DUHART-MILON (PAUILLAC), CHÂTEAU L'EVANGILE (POMEROL) AND CHÂTEAU RIEUSSEC (SAUTERNES).

★★★ CHÂTEAU LATOUR

Owner: François Pinault.
Surface Area under Vine: 65 ha – 80% Cabernet Sauvignon, 4% Cabernet Franc, 15% Merlot and 1% Petit Verdot.
Second Wine: Les Forts de Latour.
Classification: Premier Cru (1855).

This is the greatest Bordeaux of them all, with not only a reputation for the longest-lived, most austere at first, most dignified and aristocratic of all Gironde wines, but also an uncanny ability to produce surprisingly splendid wines even in the most mediocre of vintages. Quality during the 1980s was not as it should be (that is, it was one of the top three if not *the* top of the entire region) but the 1990 reaffirmed pole position with a bang and vintages since then have been true to real form.

Savage selection – the property is healthily open in its statement of overall *rendement* and percentage used in the *grand vin* – and a perfectionistic and motivated team led by Frédéric Engerer ensure that Latour today will never produce anything less than great wine. But it needs time before it is ready. There has been evidence of chlorine contamination in some recent vintages (e.g. 1994) of the second wine: Les Forts de Latour.

Other wine A PAUILLAC DE LATOUR IS OFTEN PRODUCED.

★ Château Lynch-Bages

Owners: Jean-Michel Cazes and family.
Surface Area under Vine: 90 ha – 75% Cabernet
Sauvignon, 10% Cabernet Franc and 15% Merlot.
Second Wine: Château Haut-Bages-Averous.
Classification: Cinquième Cru (1855).

The Cazes family arrived at Lynch-Bages in 1934, first renting it and in 1939 buying it outright. Since then they have taken the reputation of Lynch-Bages up from Fifth Growth to super-second. The wine is lusher and spicier than Grand-Puy-Lacoste, but perhaps not quite so elegant. But at its best it can be splendidly seductive. Recent vintages, though, have lacked a bit of character.

Other wines BLANC DE LYNCH-BAGES (BORDEAUX), CHÂTEAU CORDEILLAN-BAGES (PAUILLAC) AND CHÂTEAU LES ORMES-DE-PEZ (SAINT-ESTÈPHE).

★★ Château Mouton-Rothschild

Owner: Baroness Philippine de Rothschild.
Surface Area under Vine: 79 ha – 76% Cabernet
Sauvignon, 9% Cabernet Franc, 13% Merlot and
2% Petit Verdot.
Second Wine: Le Petit Mouton.
Classification: Premier Cru (1855, amended in 1973).

Apart from the Barton châteaux, this is the only Bordeaux estate to be in the same hands as it was at the time of the 1855 Classification. Then it was placed at the top of the Second Growths.

After fifty years of lobbying the late Baron Philippe de Rothschild succeeded in having the 1855 Classification amended in 1973. Château Mouton-Rothschild had been unofficially accepted as a First Growth for a century or more. Quality can be breathtakingly brilliant here as in 1982 and 1986. But then again mystifyingly humdrum as in 1983, 1985 and 1989. I cannot explain the inconsistency. Currently the last really exciting vintage from Mouton-Rothschild was the 1990.

The museum at Mouton-Rothschild is an eclectic collection of objects, all with a wine connection and is a must for every tourist in the region.

Other wines AILE D'ARGENT (A WHITE WINE MADE ON THE PROPERTY), CHÂTEAU D'ARMAILHAC AND CHÂTEAU CLERC-MILON (BOTH PAUILLAC).

★ Château Pichon-Longueville (Baron)

Owners: AXA Millésimes.
Surface Area under Vine: 60 ha – 75% Cabernet
Franc and 25% Merlot.
Second Wine: Les Tourelles de Longueville.
Classification: Deuxième Cru (1855).

Château Pichon-Longueville (the 'Baron' has now been suppressed) was the first venture by the insurance company AXA into the world of wine in 1987. Since then day-to-day management has been in the hands of the team of Château Lynch-Bages and a brand new and very elegant winery complex was built in time for the 1992 vintage. This is the senior and more masculine of the two Pichons, with land immediately adjacent to that of Château Latour. An excellent 1990 – a true Pauillac – showed the potential, but vintages since then have not been proportionately of such quality.

Other wines CHÂTEAU CANTENAC-BROWN (MARGAUX), CHÂTEAU PETIT-VILLAGE (POMEROL), CHÂTEAU SUDUIRAUT (SAUTERNES) AND OTHERS.

★★ Château Pichon-Longueville, Comtesse de Lalande

Owners: Lencquesaing family.
Surface Area under Vine: 75 ha – 45% Cabernet
Sauvignon, 12% Cabernet Franc, 35% Merlot and
8% Petit Verdot.
Second Wine: Réserve de La Comtesse.
Classification: Deuxième Cru (1855).

Since May-Éliane de Lencquesaing took over the family property in 1978 hardly a foot has been put wrong. Right from this first vintage the wine achieved super-second status, and only in 1990 and 1989 (both just a little lightweight) and in 1998 has this not been repeated. The Merlot is to the fore, producing a ripe and succulent wine, marvellously elegant and complex in its fruit. It is not a blockbuster nor is it austere. But it is very fine.

Other wine CHÂTEAU BERNADOTTE (HAUT-MÉDOC).

★ Château Pontet-Canet

Owners: Tesseron family.
Surface Area under Vine: 78 ha – 63% Cabernet

Sauvignon, 5% Cabernet Franc and 32% Merlot.
Second Wine: Les Hauts de Pontet.
Classification: Cinquième Cru (1855).
Over the last fifteen years the quality has been steadily improving here (the Cabernet percentage has also been reduced in favour of Merlot) and Château Pontet-Canet, always a good dependable wine, can now be justly regarded as producing wine well above its Fifth Growth status. This extra sophistication deserves more recognition. Prices are still reasonable.
Other wines Château Lafon-Rochet (Saint-Estèphe).

Other Producers of note
Château La Bécasse, Château Cordeillan-Bages, Château La Couronne, Château La Fleur-Milon, Château Fonbadet, Château Grand-Puy-Ducasse, Château Haut-Bages-Libéral and Château Pibran.

Under-Achieving Classed Growths
Château Croizet-Bages, Château Lynch-Moussas and Château Pédesclaux (all Fifth Growths).

Saint-Julien

Surface Area (1998): 906 ha.
Production (1998): 48,216 hl.
Colour: Red (the white wines are AC Bordeaux or Bordeaux Supérieur).
Grape Varieties: Cabernet Sauvignon, Cabernet Franc, Merlot, Malbec and Petit Verdot.
Maximum Yield: 45 hl/ha.
Minimum Alcohol Level: 10.5°.

Saint-Julien lies immediately to the south of Pauillac and is the smallest of the four main Haut-Médoc communes in terms of its production. The commune is compact and dominated by its eleven classed growths, all of which produce excellent wine and many of which produce wine above their 1855 Classification level. There are five Second Growths, two Thirds and four Fourths.

At the northern end lie the three Léoville estates, at the southern end Beychevelle, Ducru-Beaucaillou and Gruaud-Larose. Langoa is in the middle, between the villages of Saint-Julien and Beychevelle; set back from the river are Talbot and Lagrange. The soil is predominantly gravel, particularly nearer to the Gironde, where it is based on a subsoil of the iron-based sandstone known as *alios* and clay. Further inland the soil has less gravel and more sand, and beneath this is a richer subsoil containing clay, *alios*, and occasionally marl.

Saint-Julien wines are the closest to those of Pauillac in character, and like Pauillac they contain high proportions of Cabernet Sauvignon. Indeed, with the exception of such First Growths as Mouton-Rothschild, Latour and Lafite, there is not a great deal of difference in weight or style between the wines of the two communes. Properties such as Léoville-Las-Cases and Léoville-Barton can produce wine every bit as full-bodied and slow maturing as Lynch-Bages and Grand-Puy-Lacoste in Pauillac.

The quintessence of a wine from Saint-Julien is its balance and its finesse. The wines are well-coloured, have plenty of body, are full of fruit, rich and elegant. It is harmony rather than power which gives longevity; so Saint-Juliens, if without the firmness and reserve of a great Pauillac, nevertheless keep exceptionally well.

Leading Saint-Julien Producers

Château Beychevelle
Owners: Grands Millésimes de France.
Surface Area under Vine: 85 ha – 60% Cabernet Sauvignon, 8% Cabernet Franc, 28% Merlot and 4% Petit Verdot.
Second Wine: Amiral de Beychevelle.
Classification: Quatrième Cru (1855).
Château Beychevelle is frustrating. It is usually – but not always – of very good quality. But both its situation and the reputation of old bottles of the 1940s and 1950s indicate that it could be even better: though only a Fourth Growth in 1855, a super-second today. Long run at second hand, and today the property of an insurance company, one longs for the personal commitment and perfectionism of a proprietor on the spot as at neighbouring Château Ducru-Beaucaillou.

Other wines BRULIÈRES DE BEYCHEVELLE AND CHÂTEAU BEAUMONT (BOTH HAUT-MÉDOC).

CHÂTEAU BRANAIRE
Owner: Patrick Maroteaux.
Surface Area under Vine: 52 ha – 70% Cabernet Sauvignon, 5% Cabernet Franc, 22% Merlot and 3% Petit Verdot.
Second Wine: Château Duluc.
Classification: Quatrième Cru (1855).
This somewhat parcellated estate has been owned by its present proprietors since 1988. A splendid new winery has been constructed behind the elegant early nineteenth-century façade of the château itself. Resident manager Philippe Dhalluin and his team now produce a consistently reliable wine, worthy of its 1855 Third Growth status. The wine can be a little dense in its youth but all it needs is time.
Other wine CHÂTEAU LA ROSE DE FRANCE (HAUT-MÉDOC).

★★ CHÂTEAU DUCRU-BEAUCAILLOU
Owners: The family of the late Jean-Eugène Borie.
Surface Area under Vine: 50 ha – 65% Cabernet Sauvignon, 5% Cabernet Franc, 25% Merlot and 5% Petit Verdot.
Second Wine: Château La Croix.
Classification: Deuxième Cru (1855).
That Château Ducru-Beaucaillou is no longer the top wine in Saint-Julien is not through any falling off in its excellence, but due to the ascendance of Léoville-Las-Cases since 1975. This meticulously crafted, splendidly elegant wine has been consistently of super second quality since the late 1940s – for instance, there was a perfectly sumptuous 1961 and a truly deliciously harmonious 1970 – with the exception of the 1988, 1989 and 1990, affected by the chlorine taint; this sadly only publicly accepted by the Borie family a number of years subsequently. Vintages since then – 1995, 1996 and 1998 in particular – have been very fine. This is the quintessential Saint-Julien: yardstick Bordeaux.
Other wines CHÂTEAU LA COURONNE (PAUILLAC), CHÂTEAU DUCLUZEAU (LISTRAC), CHÂTEAU GRAND-PUY-

LACOSTE (PAUILLAC), CHÂTEAU HAUT-BATAILLEY (PAUILLAC) AND CHÂTEAU LALANDE-BORIE (SAINT-JULIEN).

★ CHÂTEAU GRUAUD-LAROSE
Owners: Groupe Taillan.
Surface Area under Vine: 82 ha – 60% Cabernet Sauvignon, 7% Cabernet Franc, 30% Merlot and 3% Petit Verdot.
Second Wine: Sarget de Gruaud-Larose.
Classification: Deuxième Cru (1855).
Hitherto owned by the Cordier family, and still marketed by Domaines Cordier, this is a large estate with a long and honourable tradition of making good wine. The wine is always full and tannic: in some vintages it can be somewhat sturdy, solid and over-extracted – at the expense of its finesse – and it always needs time to mature. Given this time it can be glorious, but often it can taste more 'Cordier' than Saint-Julien.
Other wine CHÂTEAU MALESCASSE (HAUT-MÉDOC).

★ CHÂTEAU LAGRANGE
Owners: Suntory.
Surface Area under Vine: 113 ha – 66% Cabernet Sauvignon, 27% Merlot and 7% Petit Verdot.
Second Wine: Les Fiefs de Lagrange.
Classification: Troisième Cru (1855).
This is a sadly dilapidated estate with a splendidly eccentric label, Château Lagrange was taken in hand, many millions being spent, by Suntory, the giant Japanese whisky company, in 1984. The property had an excellent reputation in the mists of history, and has now proved that this is no mere myth. Resident manager Marcel Ducasse makes a prudent selection – much of this vineyard being young vines – and the wines are elegant, rich and repay storage. They are also good value.

★ CHÂTEAU LANGOA-BARTON
Owner: Anthony Barton.
Surface Area under Vine: 20 ha – 71% Cabernet Sauvignon, 8% Cabernet Franc and 21% Merlot.
Second Wine: Lady Langoa.
Classification: Troisième Cru (1855).

Though taking second place to Léoville-Barton – a Third Growth rather than a Second, and proof that the 1855 Classification can still have validity – Langoa-Barton is nevertheless a thoroughly delicious Saint-Julien: a little softer, a little more feminine, a little earlier to develop. The 1979, for various internal logistical reasons is actually better than the Léoville. Since Anthony Barton took over in 1983, this has been consistently reliable and splendid value.

Other wine CHÂTEAU LÉOVILLE-BARTON (SAINT-JULIEN).

★★ CHÂTEAU LÉOVILLE-BARTON
Owner: Anthony Barton.
Surface Area under Vine: 48 ha – 72% Cabernet Sauvignon, 8% Cabernet Franc and 20% Merlot.
Second Wine: La Réserve de Léoville-Barton.
Classification: Deuxième Cru (1855).
Magnificent – and splendid value – during the 1940s and 1950s, Léoville-Barton's quality dipped somewhat through a lack of investment and selection until Anthony Barton took over from his uncle Ronald in 1983. Since then it has been very firmly back at the top of the super-seconds, and still sells for prices which are remarkably reasonable, both at the outset and subsequently at auction, compared with Ducru-Beaucaillou and Léoville-Las-Cases. Based at Château Langoa-Barton, and run in tandem, this Léoville is a full, rich, aristocratic wine which needs a good dozen years in a good vintage before it is ready. All vintages since 1985 can be enthusiastically recommended.

Other wine CHÂTEAU LANGOA-BARTON (SAINT-JULIEN).

★★★ CHÂTEAU LÉOVILLE-LAS-CASES
Owners: Michel Delon and family.
Surface Area under Vine: 97 ha – 65% Cabernet Sauvignon, 13% Cabernet Franc, 19% Merlot and 3% Petit Verdot.
Second Wines: Clos du Marquis.
Classification: Deuxième Cru (1855).
Since Michel Delon took over from his father in 1975, Léoville-Las-Cases has not put a foot wrong, and today it is the one wine in Bordeaux which deserves to be

promoted to the First Growth category. The nucleus of the estate is the Le Grand Clos de Léoville vineyard, which lies immediately to the south of Château Latour. Time and time again, especially since 1978, blind tastings have placed the wine into the top three or four reds from the whole of the Médoc and Graves regions and this is due, in no small part, to the rigour of selection. Often hardly 40 per cent of the total crop is deemed worthy to go into the *grand vin*. Léoville-Las-Cases is a Saint-Julien of Pauillac depth and substance, with a breed only equalled today by Château Latour.

Other wines CHÂTEAU POTENSAC (MÉDOC), CHÂTEAU DU GRAND PARC AND DOMAINE DE BIGARNON FOR WINE OF LÉOVILLE-LAS-CASES NOT INCLUDED IN THE *grand vin*.

★★ CHÂTEAU LÉOVILLE-POYFERRÉ
Owners: Cuvelier family.
Surface Area under Vine: 80 ha – 65% Cabernet Sauvignon, 2% Cabernet Franc, 25% Merlot and 8% Petit Verdot.
Second Wine: Château Moulin-Riche.
Classification: Deuxième Cru (1855).
From phylloxera times until the Second World War this estate was regarded as the best of the Léovilles, and it continued to provide noteworthy wines until the early 1960s. It then seemed to go off the boil until the arrival of Didier Cuvelier in the early 1980s. It has since retained its super-second status, though now as the third Léoville in the hierarchy. The wines are softer, more succulent and less Cabernet and tannic than the other two, but aromatic and complex, with no lack of finesse.

Other wine CHÂTEAU LE CROCK (SAINT-ESTÈPHE).

CHÂTEAU SAINT-PIERRE
Owners: Héritiers Martin-Triaud family.
Surface Area under Vine: 17 ha – 70% Cabernet Sauvignon, 10% Cabernet Franc and 20% Merlot.
Classification: Troisième Cru (1855).
Henri Martin, who had built up Château Gloria from scratch in the 1940s and 1950s, finally realised his ambition to be a proprietor of a classed growth in 1983, when he bought Saint-Pierre. It is now run by his son-in-law. I have very fond memories of the Saint-Pierres of the

1960s and 1970s, which I regularly bought. Since then I have much admired some vintages but have found others less exciting. The 1994 vintage had a chlorine taint, as did the wine from the sister Château Gloria.

Other wine CHÂTEAU GLORIA (SAINT-JULIEN).

★ CHÂTEAU TALBOT

Owners: Lorraine Rustmann-Cordier and Nancy Bignon-Cordier.
Surface Area under Vine: 107 ha – 66% Cabernet Sauvignon, 3% Cabernet Franc, 24% Merlot and 5% Petit Verdot and 2% Malbec.
Second Wine: Le Connétable de Talbot.
Classification: Quatrième Cru (1855).

When the Cordiers relinquished control of Château Gruaud-Larose and their other Bordeaux estates in the 1993 they retained Talbot which had been in their possession since 1918. Somehow this independence has added a lustre to this always reliable wine which hitherto was missing. I have much admired the wines of the late 1990s, though I would not put the quality on a super-second pedestal. Caillou Blanc is a rare Médoc white, and well-made, too. From Sauvignon Blanc, it is vinified in oak and matured on its lees until bottling.

Other wines CHÂTEAU TALBOT CAILLOU BLANC (BORDEAUX) AND CHÂTEAU SÉNÉJAC (HAUT-MÉDOC).

Other Producers of note

CHÂTEAU DU GLANA, CHÂTEAU GLORIA, CHÂTEAU LALANDE-BORIE, CHÂTEAU MOULIN DE LA ROSE AND CHÂTEAU TERREY-GROS-CAILLOUX (ALSO SOLD AS CHÂTEAU HORTEVIE).

MARGAUX

Surface Area (1998): 1355 ha.
Production (1998): 68,231 hl.
Colour: Red (The white wines are AC Bordeaux or Bordeaux Supérieur).
Grape Varieties: Cabernet Sauvignon, Cabernet Franc, Merlot, Malbec and Petit Verdot.
Maximum Yield: 45 hl/ha.
Minimum Alcohol Level: 10.5°.

While the other three great communes of the Haut-Médoc form a continuous chain of vineyard – from Beychevelle in Saint-Julien north to Calon-Ségur in Saint-Estèphe – Margaux lies separately to the south. In between, close to the estuary, much of the land is too marshy for vines, the gravel *croupes* less well defined, and no great properties are to be found. The *appellation* covers five communes – as well as Margaux itself, Labarde, Arsac and Cantenac, the communes to the south, and Soussans, Margaux's neighbour to the north. This conglomeration of parishes boasts no fewer than twenty classed growths: one First (Château Margaux), five Seconds, no fewer than nine Thirds, three Fourths and two Fifths. Some of these, like some of Pauillac's Fifth Growths, are relatively obscure, small in production terms, and little seen on the market or at auction. Others are very large, like Château Brane-Cantenac, or, like Château Palmer, deservedly extremely fashionable.

The soil varies within Margaux but is generally a sandy gravel, thinner than in Saint Julien and Pauillac, and lighter in colour. This lies on a base which in Margaux itself is partly marl, partly clay. Elsewhere the subsoil is sometimes gravel, sometimes iron-rich sandstone *alios*, and in Labarde is sand and *graviers* (grit).

I find it difficult to generalise about the style of Margaux wines, for they vary greatly. While on the whole they are softer, have less backbone, and develop sooner than Saint Juliens, and also have less of the pronounced Cabernet Sauvignon-oak flavour (one is supposed to find a scent of violets in a Margaux), there are some Margaux wines – Lascombes for example – which are every bit as 'big' as wines from further north in the Haut-Médoc. The classic character of the commune, however, which many call feminine, can be found at Château Margaux itself, Château Palmer, and in wines like Issan. These have an inherent delicacy and elegance right from the start, which is not to say they do not have plenty of body and potential for ageing well.

On the whole the Margaux vineyards are planted with more Merlot and less Cabernet than further north, and this gives a 'soft fruits' flavour, also found in wines of the Graves. In general, Margaux is less successful than Pauillac and Saint-Julien in lighter, poorer years.

Leading Margaux Producers

★ Château d'Angludet

Commune: Cantenac.
Owners: Sichel family.
Surface Area under Vine: 32 ha – 58% Cabernet Sauvignon, 5% Cabernet Franc, 35% Merlot and 2% Petit Verdot.
Second Wine: La Ferme d'Angludet.
Classification: Cru Bourgeois.

Almost derelict in 1961 when bought by the late Peter Sichel, the vineyard of Château d'Angludet lies on a gravel plateau where the communal boundaries of Labarde, Cantenac and Arsac meet. The wine is fullish, rich and robust, in all the best senses of this term, needs time to mature, and has for long been a major contender for upgrading to *cru classé*. It is also both consistent and well priced.

Other wine Château Palmer (Margaux).

★ Château Brane-Cantenac

Commune: Cantenac.
Owner: Henri Lurton.
Surface Area under Vine: 85 ha – 70% Cabernet Sauvignon, 10% Cabernet Franc and 20% Merlot.
Second Wines: Le Baron de Brane and Château Notton.
Classification: Deuxième Cru (1855).

A Second Growth but one whose quality was for some time a long way from being 'super', Brane-Cantenac has shown in the past that it can produce elegant wine, on the delicate and fragrant side as befits Cantenac. Sadly it is variable, all too often being rather lean and thin, without either depth or finesse. In the late 1990s, however, things were beginning to look up.

Château Cantenac-Brown

Commune: Cantenac.
Owner: AXA Millésimes.
Surface Area under Vine: 52 ha – 65% Cabernet Sauvignon, 10% Cabernet Franc and 25% Merlot.
Second Wine: Château Canuet.
Classification: Troisième Cru (1855).

Since changing ownership in 1987 Château Cantenac-Brown has been the subject of major investment, without, sadly, producing much of an improvement in the character and quality of the wine.

Other wines Château Petit-Village (Pomerol), Château Pichon-Longueville (Pauillac), Château Suduiraut (Sauternes) and others.

★ Château Dauzac

Commune: Labarde.
Owners: MAIF.
Surface Area under Vine: 45 ha – 58% Cabernet Sauvignon, 5% Cabernet Franc and 37% Merlot.
Second Wine: Labastide-Dauzac.
Classification: Cinquième Cru (1855).

This château was an under-performer until it was acquired by an insurance company in 1989, followed in 1992 by the appointment of André Lurton, of Châteaux Bonnet, La Louvière and others, to supervise. Château Dauzac is now producing very stylish wines. These are in true Margaux style, of medium weight but with expressive, balanced fruit. Prices are still reasonable.

Other wine Château Labarde (Margaux).

★ Château Durfort-Vivens

Commune: Margaux.
Owner: Gonzague Lurton.
Surface Area under Vine: 30 ha – 65% Cabernet Sauvignon, 15% Cabernet Franc and 20% Merlot.
Second Wines: Second de Durfort and Domaine de Cure Bourse.
Classification: Deuxième Cru (1855).

This is one of several properties owned by the children of Lucien Lurton, brother of André above. Lurton inherited Château Brane-Cantenac and proceeded to build up an empire so each of his ten children could inherit a château. Like many of these châteaux, Durfort-Vivens has been far from super-second quality, though standards have much improved in the late 1990s since Gonzague Lurton took over. The wine is fuller than Château Brane-Cantenac, despite the fact that their vineyards very largely march side by side, but the tannins can – or used to – lack sophistication.

SOUTHERN HAUT-MÉDOC

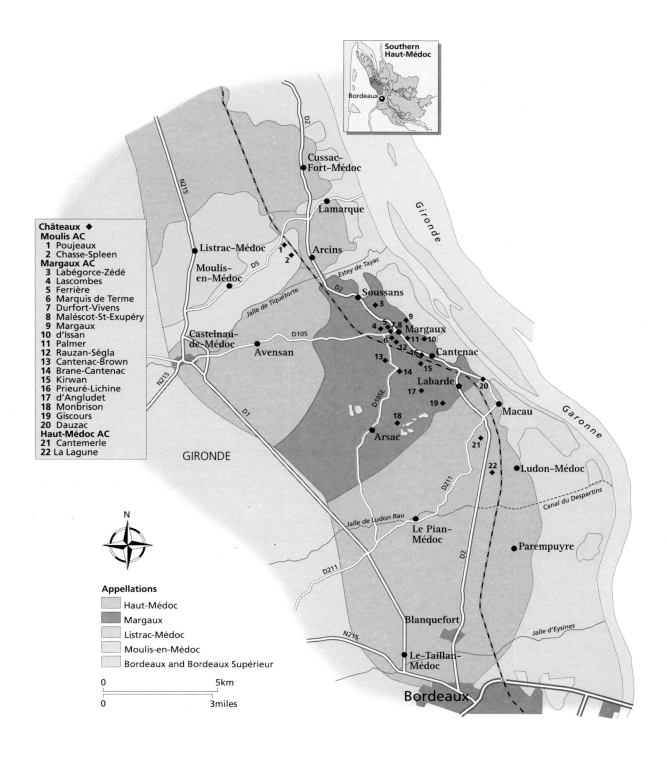

Southern Haut-Médoc

Bordeaux

Cussac-Fort-Médoc

Lamarque

Châteaux ◆
Moulis AC
 1 Poujeaux
 2 Chasse-Spleen
Margaux AC
 3 Labégorce-Zédé
 4 Lascombes
 5 Ferrière
 6 Marquis de Terme
 7 Durfort-Vivens
 8 Maléscot-St-Exupéry
 9 Margaux
 10 d'Issan
 11 Palmer
 12 Rauzan-Ségla
 13 Cantenac-Brown
 14 Brane-Cantenac
 15 Kirwan
 16 Prieuré-Lichine
 17 d'Angludet
 18 Monbrison
 19 Giscours
 20 Dauzac
Haut-Médoc AC
 21 Cantemerle
 22 La Lagune

Listrac-Médoc

Arcins

Moulis-en-Médoc

Estey de Tayac

Soussans

Jalle de Tiquetorte

Castelnau-de-Médoc

Avensan

Margaux

Cantenac

Labarde

Macau

Arsac

Gironde

Garonne

Ludon-Médoc

Canal du Despartins

Le Pian-Médoc

Parempuyre

Jalle de Ludon Rau

GIRONDE

N

Appellations
 Haut-Médoc
 Margaux
 Listrac-Médoc
 Moulis-en-Médoc
 Bordeaux and Bordeaux Supérieur

Blanquefort

Jalle d'Eysines

Le-Taillan-Médoc

0   5km
0   3miles

Bordeaux

★ CHÂTEAU FERRIÈRE

Commune: Margaux.

Owners: Merlaut/Villars family.

Surface Area under Vine: 10 ha – 75% Cabernet Sauvignon, 20% Merlot and 5% Petit Verdot.

Second Wine: Les Remparts de Ferrières.

Classification: Troisième Cru (1855).

This property was leased to Château Lascombes and rarely seen until 1992, when it changed hands and administration was entrusted to Claire Villars. Since then there have been some delightful wines, full of creamy, concentrated old-vine fruit, which are well worth seeking out.

Other wines CHÂTEAU CHASSE-SPLEEN (MOULIS), CHÂTEAU CITRAN (AVENSAN), CHÂTEAU LA GURGUE (MARGAUX) AND CHÂTEAU HAUT-BAGES-LIBÉRAL (PAUILLAC).

CHÂTEAU GISCOURS

Commune: Labarde.

Owner: Eric Albade Jelgersma.

Surface Area under Vine: 80.5 ha – 55% Cabernet Sauvignon, 5% Cabernet Franc, 35% Merlot and 5% Petit Verdot.

Second Wine: La Sirène de Giscours.

Classification: Troisième Cru (1855).

Having been resurrected by Nicolas Tari in the 1950s, Château Giscours produced very ordinary wine in the 1970s and 1980s under his son Pierre. The Tari family then ran into financial difficulties, and in 1995 a Dutchman Eric Albada Jelgerma took over. Things have now begun to improve.

Other wine CHÂTEAU DU TERTRE (MARGAUX).

CHÂTEAU D'ISSAN

Commune: Cantenac.

Owners: Cruse family.

Surface Area under Vine: 52 ha –75% Cabernet Sauvignon and 25% Merlot.

Second Wine: Château La Candale.

Classification: Troisième Cru (1855).

The château is a fine building, surrounded by a moat. Unusually for Margaux, the vineyard is in one block, and is encircled by a stone wall. The wine can be elegant and fragrant, if of medium rather than full body. But it often fails to live up to its early promise.

CHÂTEAU KIRWAN

Commune: Cantenac.

Owner: Jean-Henri Schÿler.

Surface Area under Vine: 35 ha – 40% Cabernet Sauvignon, 20% Cabernet Franc, 30% Merlot and 10% Petit Verdot.

Second Wines: Les Charmes de Kirwan.

Classification: Troisième Cru (1855).

In 1994 the insurance group GAN became involved here, only for the Schÿler family to buy back their share a couple of years later. This proved to be the shot in the arm needed by the estate. Having been one of the *appellation*'s many under-achievers things are now looking up: the tannins are riper and the fruit more clearly defined.

★ CHÂTEAU LABÉGORCE-ZÉDÉ

Commune: Soussans.

Owners: Thienpont family.

Surface Area under Vine: 27.5 ha – 50% Cabernet Sauvignon, 10% Cabernet Franc, 35% Merlot and 5% Petit Verdot.

Second Wine: Domaine Zédé.

Classification: Cru Bourgeois.

Luc Thienpont arrived here in 1979 and ever since the wine has been worth looking out for. It is a consistent, medium-bodied wine of ample fruit and style which is now better than many of Margaux's classed growths.

Other wines CHÂTEAU LE PIN, VIEUX-CHÂTEAU-CERTAN (BOTH POMEROL), CHÂTEAU LES CHARMES GODARD, CHÂTEAU LA CLAVERIE AND CHÂTEAU PUYGUÉRAUD (ALL BORDEAUX-CÔTES DE FRANCS).

CHÂTEAU LASCOMBES

Commune: Margaux.

Owner: Bass.

Surface Area under Vine: 83 ha – 55% Cabernet Sauvignon, 40% Merlot and 5% Petit Verdot.

Second Wine: Château Segonnes.

Classification: Deuxième Cru (1855).

Much of the increase in the vineyard since the purchase by a consortium lead by Alexis Lichine in 1952 had been into areas incapable of making great wine. However, during the time of René Vanetelle as manager (1985-1997) it was decided to restrict the area producing the *grand vin* just to the plateau immediately in front of the château, this being obviously *cru classé*-potential *terroir*. As a result of this and other improvements – a new *cuvier* in 1987, air conditioning in the *chai* in 1997 – Château Lascombes has improved. It is a fairly sizeable wine for Margaux and can still sometimes lack delicacy.

★ CHÂTEAU MALESCOT-SAINT-EXUPÉRY
Commune: Margaux.

Owner: Roger Zuger and family.

Surface Area under Vine: 31 ha – 50% Cabernet Sauvignon, 10% Cabernet Franc, 35% Merlot and 5% Petit Verdot.

Second Wines: Dame de Malescota and Château Loyac.

Classification: Troisième Cru (1855).

Château Malescot-Saint-Exupéry's fine reputation began to sink in the 1970s and 1980s. Since Roger Zuger's son Jean-Luc took over from his father in 1991, there has been a more severe selection and a general greater attention to detail. Recent vintages have been very good. This is a fullish wine, rich, succulent and multi-dimensional, today one of the top half-a-dozen in the *appellation*.

Other wine DOMAINE DU BALARDIN (BORDEAUX SUPÉRIEUR).

★★★ CHÂTEAU MARGAUX
Commune: Margaux.

Owners: Angelli and Mentzelopoulos families.

Surface Area under Vine: 90 ha – 75% Cabernet Sauvignon, 20% Merlot and 5% Petit Verdot.

Second Wine: Pavillon Rouge du Château Margaux.

Classification: Premier Cru (1855).

This famous property, like Château Lafite, suffered a dip in quality between 1963 and 1978, when it was bought from the Ginestet family by André Mentzelopoulos. The new regime (Mentzelopoulos sadly died in 1980, but

his energy and perfectionism continued with his wife Laura and daughter Corinne) built a new underground second year cellar, renewed the wooden fermentation vats and shrewdly appointed the greatly talented Paul Pontallier as director of operations. Since 1978 quality has consistently been at a very high level indeed. It is now apparent that Château Margaux is not the delicate wine we all thought it was but one of quite full body and strength, as much as Château Lafite, for instance. But the elegance and the very pure fruit typical of the commune is nevertheless unmistakably there.

Other wine PAVILLON BLANC DU CHÂTEAU MARGAUX.

CHÂTEAU MARQUIS DE TERME
Commune: Margaux.

Owners: Seneclauze family.

Surface Area under Vine: 35 ha – 55% Cabernet Sauvignon, 3% Cabernet Franc, 35% Merlot and 7% Petit Verdot.

Second Wine: Château des Gondats.

Classification: Quatrième Cru (1855).

The vines of Château Marquis de Terme are well placed, and there is no reason why in more sensitive hands the wine should not be as good as that of Château Malescot, or at least Lascombes (there is a large plot next to the latter château). As it is we have a wine of size and robustness, not lacking in rich fruit, but without much finesse.

★ CHÂTEAU MONBRISON
Commune: Arsac.

Owners: Mrs Elizabeth Davis and Sons.

Surface Area under Vine: 3.2 ha – 50% Cabernet Sauvignon, 15% Cabernet Franc, 30% Merlot and 5% Petit Verdot.

Second Wine: Bouquet de Monbrison.

Classification: Cru Bourgeois.

Jean-Luc Vonderheyden, son of Elizabeth Davis, died tragically young in 1992. Since then his brother Laurent has been the winemaker. It took him a few years to recapture the flair which had been so apparent in the Monbrisons of the later 1980s but this is now back in the wines. Coming from Arsac the wine is big and plentiful, but also rich and elegant.

★★ Château Palmer

Commune: Cantenac.

Owners: Mahler-Besse and Sichel families.

Surface Area under Vine: 45 ha – 55% Cabernet Sauvignon, 5% Cabernet Franc and 40% Merlot.

Second Wine: La Réserve du Général.

Classification: Troisième Cru (1855).

Château Palmer was perhaps the first property to attract the phrase 'super-second', with the excellence of its wines of the 1960s, particularly the 1961 and the 1966. It has continued to produce distinguished wine ever since. The style is lighter than that of Château Margaux, the vines being mainly in Cantenac and not in Margaux itself, but with great intensity, breeding and intensity of fruit. This is one of the purest, most elegant wines in the whole Bordeaux region.

Other wine Château d'Angludet.

Château Prieuré-Lichine

Commune: Cantenac.

Owner: Ballande group.

Surface Area under Vine: 68 ha – 52% Cabernet Sauvignon, 4% Cabernet Franc, 39% Merlot and 5% Petit Verdot.

Second Wine: Château de Clairefond.

Classification: Quatrième Cru (1855).

The property has been considerably enlarged since it was acquired by Alexis Lichine in 1951 – it was sold by his son, Sacha, in 1999 – and is now one of the most scattered estates in the *appellation*. Much of this land is incapable of producing great wine, and this is the château's undoing. The wine is competently made, but lacks real class. Prices, however, are not excessive, and this is one of the more welcoming estates, open to visitors with or without appointment all the year round.

★★ Château Rauzan-Ségla

Commune: Margaux.

Owners: Wertheimer family.

Surface Area under Vine: 45 ha – 63% Cabernet Sauvignon, 2% Cabernet Franc and 35% Merlot.

Second Wine: Ségla.

Classification: Deuxième Cru (1855).

Much had been done by the former proprietors – a new cellar and *cuvier* in 1983 and drainage in the vineyards – and quality had risen considerably as a result. Then the château was sold to the Wertheimer brothers, owners of Chanel, in 1994, who entrusted David Orr and John Kolasa, ex-Château Latour, with the job of running it. Matters have further improved and Rauzan-Ségla is now a rival to Château Palmer for the number two position in Margaux. The wine is fullish, rich and sophisticated, intense and long on the palate.

Other wine Château Canon (Saint-Emilion).

Other Producers of note

Château Bel Air Marquis d'Aligre (Soussans), Château Boyd-Cantenac (Cantenac), Château Desmirail (Cantenac), Château Deyrem-Valentin (Soussans), Château La Gurgue (Margaux), Château Haut-Breton-Larigaudière (Soussans), Château Labégorce (Margaux), Château Marsac-Seguineau (Soussans), Château Martinens (Cantenac), Château Paveil-de-Luze (Soussans), Château Pouget (Cantenac), Château du Tertre (Arsac) and Château La Tour-de-Mons (Soussans).

Underachieving Classed Growths

Château Marquis d'Alesme-Becker (Margaux) and Château Rauzan-Gassies (Margaux).

Moulis and Listrac

Surface Area (1998): (Moulis) 557 ha; (Listrac) 644 ha.

Production (1998): (Moulis) 32,129 hl; (Listrac) 37,997 hl.

Colour: Red (the white wines are AC Bordeaux or Bordeaux Supérieur).

Grape Varieties: Cabernet Sauvignon, Cabernet Franc, Merlot, Malbec and Petit Verdot.

Maximum Yield: 45 hl/ha.

Minimum Alcohol Level: 10.5°.

Moulis and Listrac lie inland adjacent to one another in the Haut-Médoc between Margaux and Saint-Julien.

Both *appellations* produce fairly full, sturdy wines though those of Moulis are finer – the explanation being that this commune's soil is a purer gravel from being closer to the estuary – and it possesses at least two good estates, both *crus bourgeois*.

Leading Moulis Producers

★ CHÂTEAU CHASSE-SPLEEN

Owners: Villars/Merlaut families.
Surface Area under Vine: 75 ha– 65% Cabernet Sauvignon, 30% Merlot and 5% Petit Verdot.
Second Wine: L'Ermitage de Chasse-Spleen.
Classification: Cru Bourgeois.

Claire Villars has proved a worthy successor to her mother Bernadette, who did so much to put Château Chasse-Spleen on the map. She is now in charge of a large stable of properties, all of them over-achievers. There is ample, rich fruit here, plus a sophistication of tannins rare in Moulis. It is this which distinguishes Château Chasse-Spleen from most of its peers.

Other wines CHÂTEAU CITRAN (HAUT-MÉDOC), CHÂTEAU FERRIÈRE, CHÂTEAU LA GURGUE (BOTH MARGAUX) AND CHÂTEAU HAUT-BAGES-LIBÉRAL (PAUILLAC).

★ CHÂTEAU POUJEAUX

Owners: Thiel family.
Surface Area under Vine: 52 ha – 50% Cabernet Sauvignon, 5% Cabernet Franc, 40% Merlot and 5% Petit Verdot.
Second Wine: La Salle de Poujeaux.
Classification: Cru Bourgeois.

Today's generation of Thiels have achieved at Château Poujeaux what the late Bernadette Villars and her daughter Claire have done at neighbouring Château Chasse-Spleen: raised the quality from being that of a rustic country wine to one of classed growth. There is a healthy rivalry between the properties which is all to the wine-lover's advantage. Poujeaux is a rounder, lusher, oakier wine; Chasse-Spleen is more austere, but perhaps with more depth.

Other wine CHÂTEAU ARNAULD (HAUT-MÉDOC).

Other Producers of note

CHÂTEAU ANTHONIC, CHÂTEAU BISTON-BRILLETTE, CHÂTEAU DUPLESSIS, CHÂTEAU DUTRUCH-GRAND-POUJEAUX, CHÂTEAU GRESSIER-GRAND-POUJEAUX, CHÂTEAU MAUCAILLOU AND CHÂTEAU MOULIN-à-VENT.

Listrac Producers of note

CHÂTEAU CLARKE, CHÂTEAU DUCLUZEAU, CHÂTEAU FONRÉAUD, CHÂTEAU FOURCAS-DUPRÉ, CHÂTEAU FOURCAS-HOSTEN, CHÂTEAU LESTAGE, CHÂTEAU SARANSOT-DUPRÉ AND CHÂTEAU SÉMEILLAN-MAZEAU.

GRAVES

RED

Surface Area (1998): 2197 ha.
Production (1998): 12,492 hl.
Colour: Red.
Grape Varieties: Cabernet Sauvignon, Cabernet Franc, Merlot, Malbec and Petit Verdot.
Maximum Yield: 50 hl/ha.
Minimum Alcohol Level: 10°.

WHITE

Surface Area (1998): 939 ha.
Production (1998): 50,590 hl.
Colour: White (dry).
Grape Varieties: Sauvignon Blanc, Sauvignon Gris, Sémillon and Muscadelle.
Maximum Yield: 50 hl/ha.
Minimum Alcohol Level: 11°.

GRAVES SUPÉRIEURES

Surface Area (1998): 465 ha.
Production (1998): 19,356 hl.
Colour: White (semi-sweet).
Grape Varieties: Sauvignon Blanc, Sauvignon Gris, Sémillon and Muscadelle.
Maximum Yield: 50 hl/ha.
Minimum Alcohol Level: 12°.

The Graves region commences a few kilometres north of the city of Bordeaux – although nowadays few vineyards so close to the city have survived the increasing sprawl of suburbs, industrial estates and shopping precincts – and continues south, round the back of the sweet white wine *appellations* of Cérons, Barsac and Sauternes as far south as Langon.

This is a much more interesting landscape than the Médoc, and far richer in history. There is more for the tourist to see – the ancient fortress at Roquetaillade, castles at Villandraut and Budos, the cathedral at Bazas and the early Gothic church at Uzeste, where Clément V, the Gascon Pope, lies buried. And of course there is the lovely moated Château de La Brède, home of the seventeenth-century French statesman and philosopher, Montesquieu, and perhaps the greatest tourist attraction in the entire Gironde.

The Graves is both hillier and more wooded than the Médoc. The countryside becomes gradually more undulating as you travel south, oak and silver birch progressively giving way to pine as you approach the forests of the Landes, whose sandy soils form a natural limit to the vineyard area. The soil within Graves is similar to that of the Médoc. As might be expected from its name, the area is composed of ridges of gravel rippling away from the river Garonne. This is mainly combined with and based on sand or sandstone although there is also clay. The soil to the south nearer Langon contains more limestone and is perhaps more suitable for white wines than red, though both are made in the area.

The vineyards share the land with pasture and arable crops. There are fields of maize and market gardens. In the northern part of the Graves, immediately outside the motorway which encircles Bordeaux and extending down to Léognan and Cadaujac the region is heavily populated. In the south away from the city the atmosphere is more pastoral. This is a larger area than the Haut-Médoc – 55 kilometres from north to south and 20 kilometres at its widest east-west point. But there are fewer vines. Much of the best vineyard area close to Bordeaux has disappeared in the expansion of the city and the creation of the airport at Mérignac. At the beginning of the twentieth century there were 168 properties or individual growers recorded in the Mérignac-Pessac-Talence-Gradignan sector in what are now the suburbs.

Today there are only nine. Production in the Graves is less than half that of the Haut-Médoc.

The Graves is commonly thought to be a white wine region even though more red wine is actually produced. Certainly the generic wine, hugely popular a generation or two ago before the rise of Liebfraumilch and the vogue for Muscadet and Mâcon, was, and still is, a white wine – though there is nothing to stop red wines being labelled simply as Graves. Today if a white wine is labelled 'Graves', the wine will be dry, and probably in a dark green glass bottle. If labelled 'Graves Supérieures' it can only be a medium, almost medium-sweet wine, and will be in a clear bottle.

Château Haut-Brion was included in the Bordeaux red wine Classification of 1855, at a time when the rest of what are now the leading estates further south, with the exception of Château Carbonnieux, had only recently been formed. After the Second World War, like those of Saint-Emilion the Graves proprietors lobbied for a separate classification. This was granted in 1953 and revised in 1959, adding a white wine section. There is one category only, that of *cru classé*. Sadly, unlike the classification of Saint-Emilion, no clause was included ensuring a periodic revision. This is now long overdue. There are not only one or two red wine *bourgeois* Graves estates such as Château La Louvière which deserve promotion to *cru classé* status, but, more importantly, many white wines which deserve recognition.

In the Graves, as opposed to Pessac-Léognan, the most successful wines are the whites and this is where the potential for improvement is the greatest. The reds are worthy but lack real definition.

Graves Producers of note (mainly for white wines)
Château d'Archambeau (Illats), Château Le Bonnat (Saint-Selve), Château Cabannieux (Portets), Château de Chantegrive (Podensac), Château Ferrande (Castres), Clos Floridène (Poujols-sur-Ciron), Château de Landiras (Landiras), Château Magneau/ Cuvée Julien (La Brède), Château Montalivet (Poujols-sur-Ciron), Château Rahoul (Portets), Château Respide-Médeville (Roaillan) and Château Roquetaillade-La-Grange (Mazères).

PESSAC-LÉOGNAN

RED

Surface Area (1998): 1040 ha.
Production (1998): 51,170 hl.
Colour: Red.
Grape Varieties: Cabernet Sauvignon, Cabernet Franc, Merlot, Malbec and Petit Verdot.
Maximum Yield: 45 hl/ha.
Minimum Alcohol Level: 10°.

WHITE

Surface Area (1998): 280 ha.
Production (1998): 14,192 hl.
Colour: White.
Grape Varieties: Sauvignon Blanc, Sauvignon Gris, Sémillon and Muscadelle.
Maximum Yield: 48 hl/ha.
Minimum Alcohol Level: 11°.

In 1984 the INAO issued a decree permitting the Graves estates in the communes of Pessac and Léognan to add the name of their commune to that of Graves on the labels of their wines. (For some time there had been an insistence by the growers in the 'Graves du Nord' that their wine was superior to that of their neighbours to the south, and they lobbied for an official distinction between the two parts of the region, similar to that between the Haut and Bas-Médoc.). Three years later the separate Pessac-Léognan *appellation* was created to cover ten communes – Pessac and Léognan, plus Talence, Gradignan, Villenave d'Ornon, Cadaujac, Martillac, Mérignac, Canéjan and Saint-Médard d'Eyrans. The Graves has been cut in two, and all the Graves classed growths are found in Pessac-Léognan.

Leading Pessac-Léognan Producers

CHÂTEAU CARBONNIEUX

Commune: Léognan.
Owners: S.C. des Grandes Graves/Perrin family.
Surface Area under Vine: 90 ha – (red)
60% Cabernet Sauvignon, 7% Cabernet Franc,
30% Merlot, 2% Malbec and 1% Petit Verdot;
(white) 60% Sauvignon Blanc, 38% Sémillon and
2% Muscadelle.
Second Wine: La Tour Léognan.
Classification: Cru Classé (red and white).

This is not only the largest property in Pessac-Léognan, it is also the only classed growth to offer a serious amount of white wine (22,000 cases a year) rather than a token few hundred cases. The red wine is a typical Graves: medium-bodied, accessible and fruity, with a slightly earthy flavour. The white wine has vastly improved since 1988 and is gently oaky, ripe and minerally. Both are made for drinking in the medium term.
Other wines CHÂTEAU HAUT-VIGNEAU, CHÂTEAU LE PAPE AND CHÂTEAU LE SARTRE (ALL PESSAC-LÉOGNAN).

CHÂTEAU LES CARMES HAUT-BRION

Commune: Pessac.
Owners: Chantecaille family.
Surface Area under Vine: 4.5 ha – 40% Cabernet Sauvignon, 10% Cabernet Franc and 50% Merlot.
Second Wine: Le Clos des Carmes.

This tiny estate lies next to Haut-Brion itself in the Bordeaux suburbs, with the small winery on the opposite side of the park to the nineteenth-century château. The wine is a contender for elevation to *cru classé*: quite firm with good tannins and refinement. It keeps well and can be enjoyed well beyond its tenth birthday.

★★ DOMAINE DE CHEVALIER

Commune: Léognan.
Owners: Bernard family.
Surface Area under Vine: 35 ha – (red)
65% Cabernet Sauvignon, 5% Cabernet Franc and 30% Merlot; (white) 70% Sauvignon Blanc and 30% Sémillon.
Second Wine: L'Esprit de Chevalier.
Classification: Cru Classé (red and white).

South and west of the town of Léognan surrounded by pine forest – and often affected by frost – stands Chevalier, for some reason a domaine rather than a château. The wine has real elegance, with a silky-smooth texture, refined fruit and lots of dimension. All this is within a

Graves and Pessac-Léognan

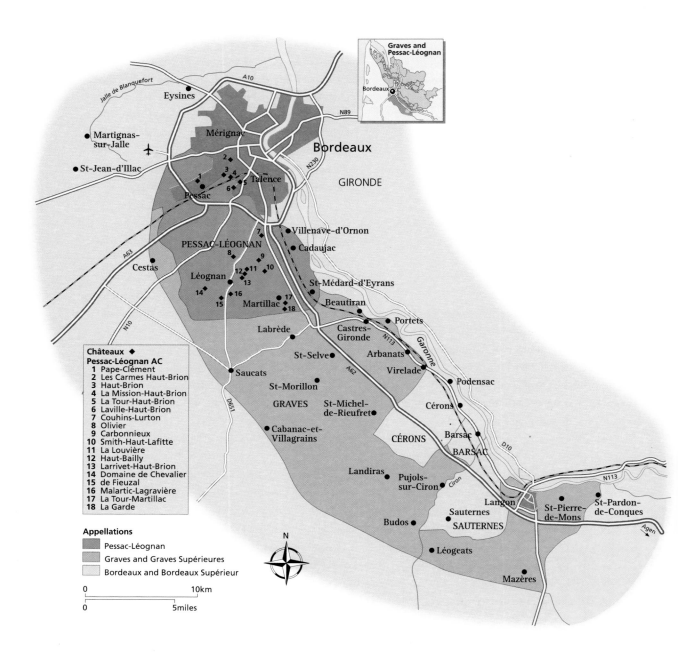

Châteaux ◆
Pessac-Léognan AC
1 Pape-Clément
2 Les Carmes Haut-Brion
3 Haut-Brion
4 La Mission-Haut-Brion
5 La Tour-Haut-Brion
6 Laville-Haut-Brion
7 Couhins-Lurton
8 Olivier
9 Carbonnieux
10 Smith-Haut-Lafitte
11 La Louvière
12 Haut-Bailly
13 Larrivet-Haut-Brion
14 Domaine de Chevalier
15 de Fieuzal
16 Malartic-Lagravière
17 La Tour-Martillac
18 La Garde

Appellations
　Pessac-Léognan
　Graves and Graves Supérieures
　Bordeaux and Bordeaux Supérieur

0　　　　　　　10km
0　　　　　5miles

structure which is not a blockbuster, but is by no means lacking intensity. The white wine, too, is fine and one of the few in Bordeaux made for the long term. The white wine is justifiably expensive, but the red is remarkably cheap by modern standards for such finesse.

Other wine DOMAINE DE LA SOLITUDE (PESSAC-LÉOGNAN).

★ CHÂTEAU COUHINS-LURTON
Commune: Villenave d'Ornon.
Owner: André Lurton.
Surface Area under Vine: 0.5 ha – 100% Sauvignon Blanc.
Second Wine: Château Cantebau.
Classification: Cru Classé (white).

The Château Couhins estate is split between the Institut National de La Recherche Agronomique (INRA), whose wine (and it is unexciting) is sold to the staff there, and André Lurton's parcel. This Couhins is a fine example of white Graves. The soil is gravel and the grapes are collected by successive *passages* through the vines and then vinified in wood, half of which is new. As with all top white Bordeaux, there is no malolactic fermentation. The result is a firm, individual wine of great character, which can keep for up to ten years or more.

Other wines CHÂTEAU DE CRUZEAU, CHÂTEAU LA LOUVIÈRE and CHÂTEAU ROCHEMORIN (all PESSAC-LÉOGNAN) AND CHÂTEAU BONNET (ENTRE-DEUX-MERS).

★ CHÂTEAU DE FIEUZAL
Commune: Léognan.
Owner: SA Château de Fieuzal (Fructivie).
Surface Area under Vine: 45 ha – (red)
60% Cabernet Sauvignon, 5% Cabernet Franc, 30% Merlot and 5% Petit Verdot ; (white)
50% Sauvignon Blanc and 50% Sémillon.
Second Wine: L'Abeille de Fieuzal.
Classification: Cru Classé (red).

Gérard Gribelin has run this château since 1974, and owned it until it was sold to a French insurance company in 1994. The red wine is full and rich, with a tendency to robustness, but nevertheless it is still a thoroughly satisfactory wine. The white, which is not *cru classé*, and of which only 3000 cases are made a year, is yet more impressive, typically fruity, full, lush and oaky. It keeps better than most *cru classé* Graves.

Other wines CHÂTEAU LE BONNAT (GRAVES) AND CHÂTEAU HAUT-GARDÈRE (PESSAC-LÉOGNAN).

CHÂTEAU LA GARDE
Commune: Martillac.
Owners: Dourthe Frères/CVBG.
Surface Area under Vine: 45 ha – (red)
65% Cabernet Sauvignon and 35% Merlot;
(white) 100% Sauvignon Blanc.
Second Wine: Château Naudin Larchey.

Dourthe Frères bought the Château La Garde from the *négociants* Eschenhauer in 1990, since when there has been a considerable increase in quality. The best *cuvées* of the red wine are bottled as Réserve du Château. This is rich, plump and quite oaky. The white (all bottled as Réserve du Château) is gently oaky and very stylish: for drinking within three or four years of the vintage.

Other wines CHÂTEAU BELGRAVE (HAUT-MÉDOC) AND OTHERS.

★ CHÂTEAU HAUT-BAILLY
Commune: Léognan.
Owner: Robert J. Wilmers.
Surface Area under Vine: 28 ha – 65% Cabernet Sauvignon, 10% Cabernet Franc and 25% Merlot.
Second Wine: La Parde de Haut-Bailly.
Classification: Cru Classé (red).

Château Haut-Bailly is the only *cru classé* Graves not to make a white wine. It lies between Châteaux La Louvière and Larrivet-Haut-Brion on the road between Léognan and Château Carbonnieux at the highest point of a gentle gravel rise. Some 15 per cent of the vines are over a century old. Having been owned for nearly fifty years by Jean Sanders and his family, it was acquired by an American banker in 1997, but Sanders continues on a consultancy basis for the time being. This is one of the Graves' best red wines: velvety rich, ample, gently oaky and of great elegance and intensity.

Other wines CHÂTEAU DE COURBON (GRAVES) AND CHÂTEAU DU MAYNE (SAUTERNES).

★★★ CHÂTEAU HAUT-BRION

Commune: Pessac.

Owner: Domaine Clarence Dillon.

Surface Area under Vine: 46 ha – (red)
45% Cabernet Sauvignon, 18% Cabernet Franc
and 37% Merlot; (white) 37% Sauvignon Blanc and
63% Sémillon.

Second Wine: Le Bahans de Château Haut-Brion.

**Classification: Premier Cru (1855); Cru Classé
(red).**

Château Haut-Brion is the *fons et origo* of quality Bordeaux. The estate was vinously monocultural long before the rest, as early as the 1650s, and was the first to sell its wine under a specific property name. Now in the suburbs of Bordeaux, and superbly managed by successive generations of the Delmas family, it has succeeded in keeping itself up to date in cellar and vineyard while maintaining a consistency of quality at a very high level. Haut-Brion *rouge* is a wine of medium-full body, great concentration and elegance and enormous subtlety. The white is not *cru classé* and at most there are 800 cases produced a year. Currently much of the vineyard is young vines. It is a wine to put alongside a top Burgundy *grand cru* and needs ten years to develop.

Other wines CHÂTEAU LAVILLE-HAUT-BRION, CHÂTEAU LA MISSION-HAUT-BRION AND CHÂTEAU LA TOUR-HAUT-BRION (ALL PESSAC-LÉOGNAN).

CHÂTEAU LARRIVET-HAUT-BRION

Commune: Léognan.

Owners: Andros.

Surface Area under Vine: 5.3 ha – (red)
55% Cabernet Sauvignon and 45% Merlot;
(white) 60% Sauvignon Blanc, 35% Sémillon
and 5% Muscadelle.

Second Wine: Domaine de Larrivet.

Together with its neighbour Château La Louvière and Les Carmes-Haut-Brion, Château Larrivet is a contender for upgrading to *cru classé* status, should this ever occur. Today's fine quality was established by François Boutemy who managed the estate until he left to set up Château Haut-Lagrange close by in 1989. The red is of medium body, plump and stylish; the white is a good

'modern' style of Graves: clean, oaky, elegant and slightly tropical in its fruit.

CHÂTEAU LAVILLE-HAUT-BRION — *See* CHÂTEAU LA MISSION-HAUT-BRION

CHÂTEAU LA LOUVIÈRE

Commune: Léognan.

Owner: André Lurton.

Surface Area under Vine: 50 ha – (red)
64% Cabernet Sauvignon, 3% Cabernet Franc,
30% Merlot and 3% Petit Verdot; (white)
85% Sauvignon Blanc and 15% Sémillon.

Second Wine: L de Louvière.

André Lurton bought this derelict estate adjacent to Haut-Bailly in 1965 and has since restored the elegant château, replanted the vineyard, and installed a modern winery. Quality is now equal to the general run of Graves *crus classés*. The red is fresh, fruity and of medium body; the white stylish, balanced, crisp and gently oaky. Both will develop in the medium term, two years for the white wines and five for the reds.

Other wines CHÂTEAU BONNET (ENTRE-DEUX-MERS), CHÂTEAU COUHINS-LURTON, CHÂTEAU DE CRUZEAU AND CHÂTEAU DE ROCHEMORIN (ALL PESSAC-LÉOGNAN).

CHÂTEAU MALARTIC-LAGRAVIÈRE

Commune: Léognan.

Owner: Alfred Alexandre Bonnie.

Surface Area under Vine: 19 ha – (red)
50% Cabernet Sauvignon, 25% Cabernet Franc and
25% Merlot; (white) 85% Sauvignon Blanc and
15% Sémillon.

Second Wine: Le Sillage de Malartic.

Classification: Cru Classé (red and white).

Château Malartic-Lagravière has been through difficult times in recent years, but under its new owners, who arrived in 1997 and now with a new winery, is undergoing a happy renaissance. The red wine here has had a tendency to sturdiness and inelegant tannins; the white used to be 100 per cent Sauvignon Blanc, not integrated with its oak, and sulphury to boot. Recent vintages suggest that there is a new elegance in both wines.

★★ CHÂTEAU LAVILLE-HAUT-BRION

Commune: Talence.

Owners: Domaine Clarence Dillon.

Surface Area under Vine: 3.7 ha – 30% Sauvignon
Blanc and 70% Sémillon.

Classification: Cru Classé (white).

★★ CHÂTEAU LA MISSION-HAUT-BRION

Commune: Talence.

Owners: Domaine Clarence Dillon.

Surface Area under Vine: 20.9 ha – 48% Cabernet
Sauvignon, 7% Cabernet Franc and 45% Merlot.

Second Wine: La Chapelle de La Mission-Haut-
Brion.

Classification: Cru Classé (red).

★ CHÂTEAU LA TOUR-HAUT-BRION

Commune: Talence.

Owners: Domaine Clarence Dillon.

Surface Area under Vine: 4.9 ha – 42% Cabernet
Sauvignon, 35% Cabernet Franc and 23% Merlot.

Classification: Cru Classé (red).

One estate: three wines. For many years the property of
the Woltner family, during which time the name La
Tour-Haut-Brion was used for the second wine of La
Mission-Haut-Brion (it now comes from a separate
plot), the domaine was sold to the owners of neighbouring Château Haut-Brion in 1983.

Despite the same management, and the fact that the
plots of vines dovetail into one another, the wines
remain quite distinct, La Mission-Haut-Brion being
firmer, more high-toned, more *nerveux*, Haut-Brion
being more composed, more classy. Laville-Haut-Brion
is one of the great white wines of the world, a rare Bordeaux needing a decade to mature. Château La Tour-
Haut-Brion has a true Graves earthiness and is now
quite distinct from La Mission-Haut-Brion.

Other wine CHÂTEAU HAUT-BRION (PESSAC-LÉOGNAN).

CHÂTEAU OLIVIER

Commune: Léognan.

Owner: Jean-Jacques de Bethmann.

Surface Area under Vine: 45 ha – (red)

65% Cabernet Sauvignon, 35% Merlot; (white)
30% Sauvignon Blanc, 65% Sémillon and
5% Muscadelle.

Second Wine: Réserve d'O du Château Olivier.

Classification: Cru Classé (red and white).

This is a proper château, part medieval, part Renaissance
and surrounded by a moat. The Bethmann family used
to rent it to the *négociants* Eschenhauer, and have only
been been in charge on their own since 1982. There is a
magic *terroir* here, and slowly but surely de Bethmann is
realising its full potential. The wines of the 1990s, both
red and white, are very promising.

★ CHÂTEAU PAPE-CLÉMENT

Commune: Pessac.

Owners: Léo Montagne and Bernard Magrez.

Surface Area under Vine: 32.5 ha – (red)
60% Cabernet Sauvignon and 40% Merlot; (white)
45% Sauvignon Blanc, 45% Sémillon and
10% Muscadelle.

Second Wine: Le Clémentin du Pape-Clément.

Classification: Cru Classé (red).

After a decade in the doldrums Château Pape-Clément
was revived under the management of Bernard Pujols,
who arrived in 1984 and who now makes one of the best
wines in the *appellation*. The wine is full, firm and rich,
concentrated and assertive. There is an increasing
amount of white wine made but the blend varies alarmingly (67 per cent Sémillon in 1997 and 62 per cent
Sauvignon in 1996), making it impossible to define its
general character.

Other wine CHÂTEAU POUMEY (PESSAC-LÉOGNAN).

CHÂTEAU SMITH-HAUT-LAFITTE

Commune: Martillac.

Owners: Daniel and Florence Cathiard.

Surface Area under Vine: 55 ha – (red)
55% Cabernet Sauvignon, 10% Cabernet Franc and
35% Merlot; (white) 100% Sauvignon Blanc.

Second Wine: Les Hauts de Smith.

Classification: Cru Classé (red).

Daniel and Florence Cathiard bought the Martillac
estate of Smith from the *négociants* Eschenhauer in 1990

and have continued the programme of investment which had been introduced by the previous owners. Château Smith-Haut-Lafitte red is never a very full wine. Under the new owners it has, however, become more refined. Similarly the white (2200 cases a year) is made for early drinking. It is fragrant and gently oaky.

In 1990 the Cathiards and their partners opened a new five-star hotel and spa, Les Sources de Caudalie, on the estate.

Other wine CHÂTEAU CANTELYS (PESSAC-LÉOGNAN).

CHÂTEAU LA TOUR-MARTILLAC
Commune: Martillac.
Owners: Kressmann family.
Surface Area under Vine: 36 ha – (red)
59% Cabernet Sauvignon, 35% Merlot and
6% Malbec; (white) 35% Sauvignon Blanc,
60% Sémillon and 5% Muscadelle .
Second Wine: Château La Grave-Martillac.
Classification: Cru Classé (red and white).

This is another property where quality has improved during the 1990s, the red wine becoming more sophisticated and the white cleaner. The red wine is now plump, generous and medium-bodied. The white has at least the potential to age well. Currently it is made to be at its best after three or four years.

Other wine CHÂTEAU LESPAULT (PESSAC-LÉOGNAN).

Other Producers of note
CHÂTEAU BROWN (LÉOGNAN), CHÂTEAU CANTELYS (MARTILLAC), CHÂTEAU DE CRUZEAU (SAINT-MÉDARD-DE-EYRANS), CHÂTEAU DE FRANCE (LÉOGNAN), CHÂTEAU HAUT-BERGEY (LÉOGNAN), CHÂTEAU HAUT-GARDÈRE (LÉOGNAN), CHÂTEAU HAUT-LAGRANGE (LÉOGNAN), CHÂTEAU LESPAULT (MARTILLAC), CLOS MARSALETTE (LÉOGNAN), CHÂTEAU LE PAPE (LÉOGNAN), CHÂTEAU PIQUE-CAILLOU (MÉRIGNAC), CHÂTEAU PONTAC MONPLAISIR (VILLENAVE D'ORNON), CHÂTEAU DE ROCHEMORIN (MARTILLAC), CHÂTEAU LE SARTRE (LÉOGNAN) AND DOMAINE DE LA SOLITUDE (MARTILLAC).

Underachieving Classed Growth
CHÂTEAU BOUSCAUT (CADAUJAC).

SAUTERNES AND BARSAC

Surface Area (1998): 1639 ha plus 601 ha (Barsac).
Production (1998): 36,214 hl plus 14,268 ha (Barsac).
Colour and Style: Sweet white.
Grape Varieties: Sémillon, Sauvignon Blanc and Muscadelle.
Maximum Yield: 25 hl/ha.
Minimum Alcoholic Level: 13°.

In the south of the Graves, on the left bank of the river Garonne just above the town of Langon, lies the Sauternes district, home of the greatest, richest and most luscious sweet wines of the world. Surrounding Sauternes on either side of the river are the other, but lesser sweet wine areas of Bordeaux: Cérons, Loupiac and Sainte-Croix-du-Mont. Here the wines are less intensely sweet, less concentrated, less honeyed, but they can nevertheless be fine wines in their own right.

Sauternes and the other sweet wines of the region are the result of botrytis-affected grapes. The harvest is deliberately put off until late in the season, allowing the grapes to become affected by noble rot. What produces the mesoclimate necessary for its production is a little river, hardly more than a stream, called the Ciron. The Ciron arises out of a spring deep in the Landes and flows into the Garonne between the villages of Barsac and Preignac. The waters are cold; when they meet the warmer Garonne the atmosphere becomes suffused in mist, particularly in the early morning. This creates the humidity necessary for the production of the *Botrytis cinerea* fungus and noble rot.

Sauternes can be made from three grape varieties: Sémillon, Sauvignon Blanc and Muscadelle, but Sémillon is the main variety as it is the most susceptible to rot. It is very rigorously pruned to reduce the yield, more so than Sauvignon (Muscadelle is present only in small amounts and disapproved of by the leading châteaux), and so while the average *encépagement* in the vineyard might be 85 per cent Sémillon to 15 per cent Sauvignon the blend in the wine might be 75 to 25 per cent.

The *appellation* of Sauternes consists of five communes. Of these the largest, and an *appellation* in its own right, is Barsac. Barsac lies to the north of Sauternes, on the bank of the Garonne, its vineyards stretching back to the motorway. To the south is Preignac, also on the river bank, but with its best vineyards inland from the *autoroute* where it marches with the commune of Sauternes. On the other sides of Sauternes are the communes of Fargues and Bommes.

The Sauternes is a laid-back, idle, bucolic region, seemingly one of the backwaters of Bordeaux, despite the world-wide fame of its wines. The region is attractive, undulating and well-wooded. Each of the important classed growths occupies its own little hillock, the less well-exposed valleys being left to pasture or planted with maize and wheat rather than with vines. The roads in between the fields and vineyards are narrow and winding and it is easy to lose one's way.

Until recently the fortunes of the Sauternes region were in the doldrums. After a fine run of vintages between the end of the Second World War and the early 1960s, successful years became sparse. The market for sweet wines evaporated. Life became increasingly uneconomic. One Second Growth, Château de Myrat, grubbed up its vines and gave up entirely (though it has been recently resurrected). Others gave up even the pretence of producing serious wine. Many changed hands – four classed growths in 1971 alone. Not only was production unprofitable, but the owners seemed to have lost faith in their product. There was no combined marketing effort, indeed little communication between one owner and another. I remember as late as 1982 introducing one château proprietor to his neighbour. In the ten years one had lived in the region (he was one of the 1971 arrivals: the other had been resident far longer) they had never actually met!

Today the position is different. There is a new mood of buoyancy, profitability and confidence in the air. In part this is a question of new blood and new brooms, the arrival of a new generation and outsiders such as the Rothschilds at Rieussec and AXA at Suduiraut. They were helped by one good (1985) and five excellent (1983, 1986, 1988, 1989, 1990) vintages in eight years for which they asked and readily obtained economically realistic prices (sadly, there has only been one excellent

vintage – 1997 – since). These prices enabled investment in new oak and refrigerated stabilisation equipment, made it a commercial possibility to wait for the arrival of an abundance of *pourriture noble* and to pick over each row of vines a number of times, and allowed for a severe selection of only the best *cuvées* for the *grand vin*. There has been a revolution in Sauternes since the mid-1980s, equivalent to that which has taken place in the Graves with the dry white wines. For the first time for a generation most of the classed growths – indeed nearly every single one of them – are making fine wine. The future looks exciting.

Sauternes will always be expensive. If in the Médoc and the Graves a yield of one bottle of wine per vine is the norm in the top properties, in the Sauternes the yield will be only a third or less. One glass of wine per vine, they will tell you at Château d'Yquem. In Sauternes the harvesting costs are higher and successful vintages rarer. For these reasons we must be prepared to pay high prices for good Sauternes or the wine will cease to exist.

There are significant differences between the style of wines produced in the five Sauternes communes. Sauternes itself is the fullest, the richest, the most concentrated, especially at Château d'Yquem, but potentially, at least, also in the other top estates. Fargues, nearby, as characterised by Château Rieussec, Yquem's immediate neighbour, produces wines the closest in character. Those of Bommes (Lafaurie-Peyraguey, Rayne-Vigneau, Sigalas-Rabaud and Rabaud-Promis) and Preignac (Suduiraut) are ample and plump, marginally less honeyed, a little more flowery. Barsac is an *appellation* in its own right. The properties here have a choice whether to label their wines Sauternes or Barsac. Its wines (Climens, Coutet, Doisy-Daëne and Nairac) are the most racy of them all, the least luscious. But it is in fact difficult, as well as dangerous, to generalise. Because of the prolonged harvest, where one grower may wait and have his patience rewarded, or his neighbour pick early and avoid the terrible consequences of a change in climate, Sauternes is not only much less consistent from vintage to vintage but also between one château and its neighbour.

When to Drink the Wines

When should you drink your fine Sauternes? The wines are full-bodied, alcoholic, high in sugar and high in balancing acidity. They are big wines, in short. It is infanticide to drink the richest, best-balanced vintages too early; before ten years old in fact. Château d'Yquem, however, is an exception. The wines are twice as concentrated as the rest of Sauternes and so the timescales need to be doubled.

On the other hand, I consider the lesser Sauternes vintages are at their best young. The wines may be sweet but they will not be as honeyed and luscious nor as harmonious. Wines from these years may coarsen as they age. Drink them young, at the age of five years or so, and you will enjoy their youthful freshness and fragrance.

Sauternes Vintages

1998 Certainly potentially a very good vintage. The wines showed well in April 1999, with no lack of either noble rot nor balancing acidity.

1997 The first really fine vintage since 1990. At its very best inland in the communes of Sauternes, Fargues and Bommes rather than nearer the river Garonne in Barsac. Needs a decade to mature.

1996 The wines showed well in April 1997, indicating a lighter vintage but one with style and at least some botrytis. A year on many seemed a bit coarse and clumsy. Time will tell when the wines have settled down after bottling.

1995 A vintage of medium-sweet wines with only a little botrytis. Some interesting wines at the best levels but not really a serious sweet wine year. For drinking soon.

1994 to 1991 Rainy weather at vintage time induced the wrong sort of rot. One or two properties such as Climens produced the odd pleasant sweetish wines, but none with any real Sauternes character.

1990 The last and perhaps greatest of a magnificent trio: 1988, 1989 and 1990. Never before have we had three top vintages in a row. Full, rich, very concentrated wines with excellent supporting acidity and real finesse. Will last fifty years or more. Start drinking the lesser wines now. Leave the best until 2005 or later.

1989 Splendidly ripe, rich wines, luscious and honeyed.

Perhaps the 1990 have a little more elegance, but it is a close run thing. The wines are similar in size and should be consumed over the same timescale.

1988 A slightly lighter vintage with very good noble rot and an excellent supporting acidity. The wines have a delightful flowery fragrance and real breed and length. All but the very biggest wines are now just beginning to mature. Drink over the next thirty to forty years.

1987 Not a Sauternes vintage.

1986 A vintage much in the mould of 1988 but not quite as fine. There are, nevertheless, some very lovely wines which are now just about ready. Drink over the next twenty years.

1985 A vintage of full, sweet wines but without much noble rot flavour. Now ready. Drink until 2010.

1984 Not a Sauternes vintage.

1983 A potentially great vintage, but not all the top properties were performing as well as they do today, so the results are patchy. The best are rich and full with plenty of botrytis. They are ready now and will last another twenty years.

GOOD, EARLIER VINTAGES
1976, 1975, 1971, 1967, 1962 and 1959.

Leading Sauternes and Barsac Producers

CHÂTEAU D'ARCHE
Commune: Sauternes.
Owners: Bastit-St-Martin family/Pierre Perromat.
Surface Area under Vine: 29 ha – 70% Semillon, 29% Sauvignon Blanc and 1% Muscadelle.
Second wine: Cru de Braneyre.
Classification: Deuxième Cru (1855).

Château d'Arche produces a round, ripe, honeyed, gently oaky wine of medium weight and intensity, and like many in the region has much improved in quality over the last twenty years.

CHÂTEAU BASTOR-LAMONTAGNE
Commune: Preignac.
Owners: Crédit Foncier de France.

Surface Area under Vine: 50 ha – 78% Sémillon, 17% Sauvignon Blanc and 5% Muscadelle.
Second wine: Les Remparts de Bastor.

Bastor-Lamontagne, located near Suduiraut in Preignac, is one of the best and most reliable of the non-classed growths. The wine shows good noble rot here, medium weight and honeyed, peachy fruit.
Other wines CHÂTEAU BEAUREGARD (POMEROL) AND CHÂTEAU SAINT-ROBERT (GRAVES).

CHÂTEAU CAILLOU
Commune: Barsac.
Owners: Bravo family.
Surface Area under Vine: 13 ha – 90% Sémillon and 10% Sauvignon Blanc.
Second wine: Château Haut-Mayne.
Classification: Deuxième Cru (1855).

Caillou can produce very good fullish, concentrated wine, akin to Climens, whose vineyards are close by. In most successful vintages, however, the best barrels are creamed off into a *tête de cuvée* (formerly called Crème de Tête, now Private Cuvée) leaving a coarser, harder wine for bottling as plain Château Caillou.

CHÂTEAU CLOS HAUT-PEYRAGUEY
Commune: Bommes.
Owners: Pauly family.
Surface Area under Vine: 23 ha – 83% Sémillon, 15% Sauvignon Blanc and 2% Muscadelle.
Second wine: Château Haut-Bommes.
Classification: Premier Cru (1855).

While not always in the very top flight of the First Growths Clos Haut-Peyraguey can occasionally surprise you, as it did when I sampled the 1997s for the first time blind. It is neither as luscious or as oaky as Lafaurie-Peyraguey from which the estate was split in 1878, but the wine is normally plump, sweet, elegant and fruity.

★★ CHÂTEAU CLIMENS
Commune: Barsac.
Owners: Brigitte and Bérénice Lurton.
Surface Area under Vine: 29 ha – 100% Sémillon.
Second wine: Les Cyprès de Climens.

Classification: Premier Cru (1855).

Climens is not merely the best wine in Barsac but probably, after Château d'Yquem, the best of the whole Sauternes area. No *grand vin* was declared in mediocre vintages such as 1993, 1992, 1987 and 1984 and even in other years, the selection is rigorous. The wine combines the lusciousness of Sauternes with the raciness of Barsac and is rich, honeyed and peachy. The great trio of vintages 1990, 1989 and 1988 are simply splendid – 1997 is fine too. Though sometimes adolescently awkward in its youth Climens will last for decades. Of all Sauternes it is one of the most consistent.
Other wine CHÂTEAU DOISY-DUBROCA (BARSAC).

★ CHÂTEAU COUTET
Commune: Barsac.
Owners: Baly family.
Surface Area under Vine: 38.5 ha – 75% Sémillon, 23% Sauvignon Blanc and 2% Muscadelle.
Second wine: La Chartreuse de Château Coutet.
Classification: Premier Cru (1855).

Château Coutet stands a few hundred metres nearer to the river Garonne from Climens and is the only other First Growth Barsac. The wine is just a little lighter, but very elegant. In exceptional vintages a small amount of Cuvée Madame, the result of a single vineyard visit, is produced. This is a wine which, at its best, has monumental intensity and concentration.

★ CHÂTEAU DOISY-DAËNE
Commune: Barsac.
Owners: Dubourdieu family.
Surface Area under Vine: 15 ha – 100% Sémillon.
Classification: Deuxième Cru (1855).

Doisy-Daëne is a wine of medium lusciousness and concentration but marvellously elegant, flowery fruit and good intensity: a wine which is really peachy. In great years a super cuvée called L'Extravagance is produced. There is also a Sauvignon-based wine called Doisy-Daëne Sec and intermittently a Cuvée Saint-Martin from late-picked, non-botrytis-affected grapes which is also made into a dry wine.
Other wine CHÂTEAU CANTEGRIL (SAUTERNES).

★ CHÂTEAU DOISY-DUBROCA

Commune: Barsac.

Owners: Brigitte and Bérénice Lurton.

Surface Area under Vine: 3.3 ha – 100% Sémillon.

Classification: Deuxième Cru (1855).

Doisy-Dubroca is made at Château Climens and though rarely seen, as hardly 600 cases a year are made, the two wines have much in common, though there is less new oak used for the Doisy-Dubroca.

Other wine CHÂTEAU CLIMENS (BARSAC).

★ CHÂTEAU DOISY-VÉDRINES

Commune: Barsac.

Owners: Pierre Castéja.

Surface Area under Vine: 27 ha – 80% Sémillon, 15% Sauvignon Blanc and 5% Muscadelle .

Classification: Deuxième Cru (1855).

This wine is fuller and lusher than Doisy-Daëne, despite the presence of Sauvignon in the blend, and in the best vintages is a splendidly rich, honeyed wine, yet with all the Barsac elegance. It is consistent too.

★ CHÂTEAU DE FARGUES

Commune: Fargues.

Owners: Lur-Saluces family.

Surface Area under Vine: 15 ha – 80% Sémillon and 20% Sauvignon Blanc.

Second wine: Guilhem de Fargues.

Not classed in 1855 because Sauternes was not made here then (this is a post-1942 development) Fargues uses secondhand barrels from Yquem (the two châteaux were under the same ownership until 1999) but is otherwise made with the same attention to detail. Tasted separately the wines seem very alike. Alongside each other the extra intensity, but most of all the extra elegance of Yquem becomes apparent. But this is still a wine of top *premier cru* quality: rich, oaky and opulent.

CHÂTEAU GILETTE

Commune: Preignac.

Owner: Christian Médeville.

Surface Area under Vine: 4.5 ha – 90% Sémillon, 8% Sauvignon Blanc and 2% Muscadelle .

Production is idiosyncratic here, the wine being aged in glass-lined concrete vats, often for at least fifteen years before bottling. The top vintages bear the designation Crème de Tête. The colour is golden amber and the wines are sweet and tangy, though not necessarily with much of a taste of noble rot. I find they lack elegance.

Other wines CHÂTEAU LES JUSTICES (SAUTERNES) AND CHÂTEAU RESPIDE-MÉDEVILLE (GRAVES).

CHÂTEAU GUIRAUD

Commune: Sauternes.

Owners: Narby family.

Surface Area under Vine: 100 ha – 65% Sémillon and 35% Sauvignon Blanc.

Second wine: Le Dauphin du Château Guiraud.

Classification: Premier Cru (1855).

The Narby family acquired this run-down estate down the road from Yquem in July 1981. At the time there was far too much Sauvignon in the vineyard and so a dry white Bordeaux, G de Château Guiraud, was created, and is still made. Guiraud is a rich, full wine, with a tendency to a rather heavy colour, quite early on, as at Rieussec. It is reliable, but lacks a little refinement.

★★ CHÂTEAU LAFAURIE-PEYRAGUEY

Commune: Bommes.

Owners: Domaines Cordier.

Surface Area under Vine: 40 ha – 90% Sémillon, 5% Sauvignon Blanc and 5% Muscadelle .

Second wine: La Chapelle de Lafaurie.

Classification: Premier Cru (1855).

Lafaurie-Peyraguey is one of the best and most reliable of the First Growth Sauternes: rich, intense, classy, honeyed and concentrated. The crenellated battlements look too good to be true, but they are genuine in parts.

Other wine CLOS DES JACOBINS (SAINT-EMILION).

★ CHÂTEAU LAMOTHE-GUIGNARD

Commune: Sauternes.

Owners: Philippe and Jacques Guignard.

Surface Area under Vine: 17 ha – 90% Sémillon, 5% Sauvignon Blanc and 5% Muscadelle .

Classification: Deuxième Cru (1855).

SAUTERNES AND OTHER SWEET WHITE WINE AREAS

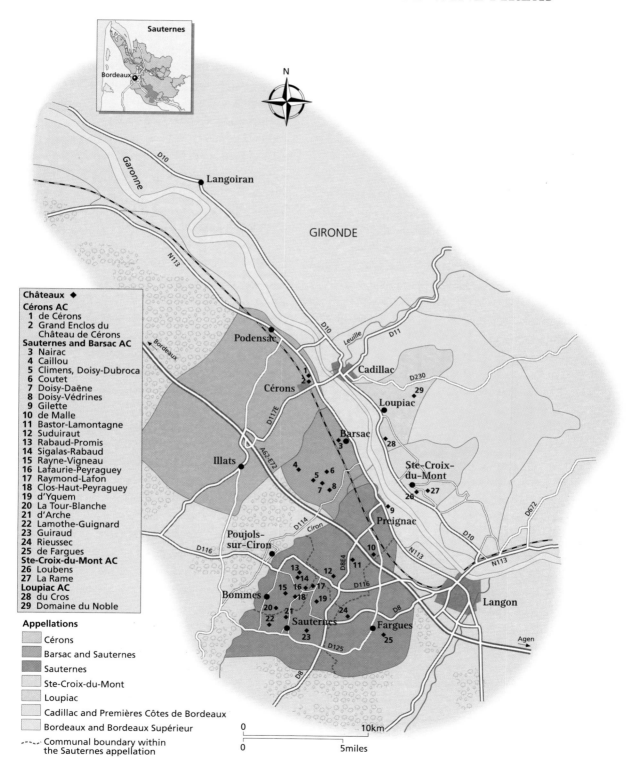

Sauternes

Bordeaux

N

Garonne

D10

Langoiran

GIRONDE

Châteaux ◆

Cérons AC
1 de Cérons
2 Grand Enclos du
  Château de Cérons

Sauternes and Barsac AC
3 Nairac
4 Caillou
5 Climens, Doisy-Dubroca
6 Coutet
7 Doisy-Daëne
8 Doisy-Védrines
9 Gilette
10 de Malle
11 Bastor-Lamontagne
12 Suduiraut
13 Rabaud-Promis
14 Sigalas-Rabaud
15 Rayne-Vigneau
16 Lafaurie-Peyraguey
17 Raymond-Lafon
18 Clos-Haut-Peyraguey
19 d'Yquem
20 La Tour-Blanche
21 d'Arche
22 Lamothe-Guignard
23 Guiraud
24 Rieussec
25 de Fargues

Ste-Croix-du-Mont AC
26 Loubens
27 La Rame

Loupiac AC
28 du Cros
29 Domaine du Noble

Podensac

Cadillac

D230

29

Loupiac

Cérons

D117E

Barsac

28

Ste-Croix-
du-Mont

Illats

4

5   6

7   8

26   27

9

Preignac

Poujols-
sur-Ciron

D114

Ciron

10

D8E4

11

D116

13

14

12

15   16   17

18   19

20   21

22

24

Sauternes

Fargues

25

Bommes

23

D125

Langon

N113

Agen

Appellations

Cérons

Barsac and Sauternes

Sauternes

Ste-Croix-du-Mont

Loupiac

Cadillac and Premières Côtes de Bordeaux

Bordeaux and Bordeaux Supérieur

- - - - - Communal boundary within
         the Sauternes appellation

0   10km

0   5miles

95

The Guignard brothers bought this half of the divided Lamothe estate in 1981, and have produced very good wine in all the suitable vintages since, and at generous prices. The style is on the light side for a true Sauternes, but balanced, stylish and fruity.

Other wines CHÂTEAU DE ROLLAND (BARSAC) AND CHÂTEAU DE ROQUETAILLADE LA GRANGE (GRAVES).

★ CHÂTEAU DE MALLE

Commune: Preignac.
Owner: Comtesse de Bournazel.
Surface Area under Vine: 50 ha — 75% Sémillon and 25% Sauvignon Blanc.
Second wine: Château de Sainte-Hélène.
Classification: Deuxième Cru (1855).

The château is a very fine building dating from the early seventeenth century, and is a national monument, open to the public in the summer. The wine is racy and Barsac-like (although the vineyard straddles the communes of Preignac, Fargues and Toulenne) and can have great elegance and intensity. Real progress has been made here in the last fifteen years. Sauternes is now profitable, and the proceeds have been invested in the vineyard and *chais*.

Other wines CHÂTEAU DE CARDAILLAN (RED GRAVES) AND M DE MALLE (WHITE GRAVES).

★ CHÂTEAU NAIRAC

Commune: Barsac.
Owners: Nicole Tari.
Surface Area under Vine: 17 ha — 88% Sémillon, 9% Sauvignon Blanc and 3% Muscadelle.
Classification: Deuxième Cru (1855).

This is the nearest classed growth to the river Garonne, and the only property directly on the N113, the main Bordeaux-Langon road. The elegant mansion in the classical style dates from 1776. Tom Heeter and his wife Nicole bought the run-down estate in 1971 and it was Tom's dedication in the 1970s which put Nairac on the map. Since their divorce Nicole has managed it on her own, now helped by their son, Nicolas. Nairac is a firm wine, sometimes very oaky in its youth, with good botrytis-affected fruit, body and extract.

★ CHÂTEAU RABAUD-PROMIS

Commune: Bommes.
Owners: Philippe Dejean.
Surface Area under Vine: 33 ha — 80% Sémillon, 18% Sauvignon Blanc and 2% Muscadelle .
Second wines: Domaine de L'Estremade and Château Bequet.
Classification: Premier Cru (1855).

Château Rabaud-Promis is another of the wines which has improved out of all proportion since the Sauternes renaissance began in 1982. Under Philippe Dejean's able direction we now have a very typical Bommes-style wine: plump, medium-bodied, ample, honeyed and rich. There is plenty of depth and elegance as well.

CHÂTEAU RAYMOND-LAFON

Commune: Sauternes.
Owners: Meslier family.
Surface Area under Vine: 18 ha — 80% Sémillon and 20% Sauvignon Blanc.
Second wine: Château Lafon-Laroze.

Here is a proof of the crucial importance of *terroir*. The property and its vineyards lie at the bottom of the Yquem hill. The wine is made with the same dedication. Pierre Meslier, who bought the estate in 1972, was for many years the *régisseur* or bailiff at Yquem and so knows exactly what needs to be done. And yet the wine, rich and sweet as it is, lacks real class. It is good — even very good — but it will never be great.

★ CHÂTEAU RAYNE-VIGNEAU

Commune: Bommes.
Owners: Mestrezat.
Surface Area under Vine: 79 ha — 75% Sémillon, 23% Sauvignon Blanc and 2% Muscadelle.
Second wine: Clos L'Abeilley.
Classification: Premier Cru (1855).

Rayne-Vigneau produces a lightish, elegant, very floral style of Sauternes. This is not to say that there is a lack of depth or intensity: far from it, as the 1997 shows. This is yet another property whose reputation was zero in the early 1980s but which has made great strides since.

Other wines CHÂTEAU GRAND-PUY-DUCASSE

(PAUILLAC), CHÂTEAU LAMOTHE-BERGERON (HAUT-MÉDOC) AND CHÂTEAU MARSAC-SEGUINEAU (MARGAUX).

★★ CHÂTEAU RIEUSSEC

Commune: Fargues.
Owners: Domaines Barons de Rothschild.
Surface Area under Vine: 75 ha – 90% Sémillon, 7% Sauvignon Blanc and 3% Muscadelle.
Second wine: Clos Labère.
Classification: Premier Cru (1855).

The only classed growth in the commune of Fargues, Rieussec occupies the *croupe* immediately south of Château d'Yquem, and comes the closest in style to that miraculous creation. Resurrected by Albert Vuillier in the 1970s, acquired by the Domaines Rothschild in 1984, Rieussec is full, rich and firm, very concentrated, very honeyed and with very good noble rot flavours. This is one of the slowest Sauternes to mature.

★ CHÂTEAU SIGALAS-RABAUD

Commune: Bommes.
Owners: Marquis Lambert des Granges family.
Surface Area under Vine: 14 ha – 98% Sémillon and 2% Sauvignon Blanc.
Classification: Premier Cru (1855).

Since 1994 the wine has been made for the Lambert des Granges family by Domaines Cordier, who are next door at Lafaurie-Peyraguey. This was one of the few Sauternes which did not go downhill in quality in the 1960s and 1970s, and this good track record has been continued since. It is full and rich, more like Lafaurie than Rayne-Vigneau, another neighbour, and often of splendid depth and concentration.

★ CHÂTEAU SUDUIRAUT

Commune: Preignac.
Owners: AXA Millésimes.
Surface Area under Vine: 87 ha – 80% Sémillon and 20% Sauvignon Blanc.
Second wine: Castelnau de Suduiraut.
Classification: Premier Cru (1855).

The chateau is a fine building, with even finer gardens laid out by Le Nôtre, and the estate, bordering on

Yquem, is the largest in Preignac. It was bought by AXA from the Fonquernie family in 1992. Somewhat uneven before, and notorious for picking early (so the wine had little noble rot), the new regime has improved things. The wine is sweet, plump and peachy and now has greater concentration. Sometimes a special wine (Crème de Tête) is produced.

Other wines: CHÂTEAU CANTENAC-BROWN (MARGAUX), CHÂTEAU PETIT-VILLAGE (POMEROL) AND CHÂTEAU PICHON-LONGUEVILLE (PAUILLAC).

★ CHÂTEAU LA TOUR-BLANCHE

Commune: Bommes.
Owners: Ministry of Agriculture.
Surface Area under Vine: 34 ha – 77% Sémillon, 20% Sauvignon Blanc and 3% Muscadelle.
Second wine: Mademoiselle de St Marc.
Classification: Premier Cru (1855).

La Tour-Blanche is home to a school of viticulture and oenology having been donated to the government for this purpose in 1909. Great strides have been made since 1983 and the wines are now rich, fullish and quite oaky (often with a hint of mint) with good noble rot flavours.

★★★ CHÂTEAU D'YQUEM

Commune: Sauternes.
Owners: L V M H group.
Surface Area under Vine: 113 ha – 80% Sémillon and 20% Sauvignon Blanc.
Classification: Premier Cru Supérieur (1855).

Yquem is sweet wine at its greatest, the product of ultra-perfectionism, an attention to detail which even at Yquem's prices must be hardly economic. Picking here is berry by berry of only botrytis-affected fruit, and yields amount to one glass of wine per vine (and a small glass at that!) as opposed to three-quarters to one bottle if the property had been producing red or white Graves. The wine is kept in new oak casks for three years or more, and no one is allowed to sample it until it has been released. It will last for fifty years or more. Despite a change of ownership in 1999, Comte Alexandre de Lur-Saluces continues to manage his former estate.

Other wine Y (YGREC), A DRY WHITE WINE.

Other Producers of note

CRU BARRÉJATS (POUJOLS-SUR-CIRON), CHÂTEAU
CANTEGRIL (POUJOLS-SUR-CIRON), CHÂTEAU GRAVAS
(BARSAC), CHÂTEAU HAUT-BERGERON (PREIGNAC),
CHÂTEAU LIOT (BARSAC), CHÂTEAU DE MAYNE (BARSAC),
CHÂTEAU MENOTA (BARSAC), CHÂTEAU MYRAT (BARSAC),
CHÂTEAU PIADA (BARSAC), CHÂTEAU ROUMIEU-LACOSTE
(BARSAC) AND CHÂTEAU SAINT-AMAND (PREIGNAC).

Underachieving Classed Growths

CHÂTEAU BROUSTET (BARSAC), CHÂTEAU FILHOT
(SAUTERNES), CHÂTEAU LAMOTHE (SAUTERNES),
CHÂTEAU ROMER DU HAYOT (FARGUES) AND CHÂTEAU
SUAU (BARSAC).

CÉRONS

Surface Area (1998): 73 ha.
Production (1997): 2421 hl.
Colour and Style: Sweet white.
**Grape Varieties: Sémillon, Sauvignon Blanc and
Muscadelle.**
Maximum Yield: 40 hl/ha.
Minimum Alcohol Level: 12.5°.

North of Barsac is Cérons, both a village and a sweet
wine *appellation*. The wine can be also be made in Illats
and Podensac and all three villages can also produce dry
white and red Graves and Graves Supérieures. Little
Cérons is produced, barely one-twentieth that of
Sauternes and most leading estates choose to make dry
Graves instead. Demand and prices being low, the proprietors cannot afford several visits to the vineyard nor
new oak. Cérons wine is therefore sweet but lacks a
noticeable flavour of botrytis. It is best drunk young,
chilled, as an aperitif.

Leading Cérons Producers

CHÂTEAU DE CÉRONS
Owner: Jean Perromat.
**Surface Area under Vine: 10 ha – 70% Sémillon and
30% Sauvignon Blanc.**

Château de Cérons was originally part of the same property as the estate below, but was divided when the main
road was built through the village in the mid-nineteenth century. Quality has improved in recent years,
especially since reverting to fermentation in wood in
1990 (this time in new or newish oak). This has been the
best vintage so far. A white Graves, called Château de
Calvimont, is produced in the less good vintages.

GRAND ENCLOS DU CHÂTEAU DE CÉRONS
Owner: Olivier Lataste.
**Surface Area under Vine: 1.5 ha – 80% Sémillon
and 20% Sauvignon Blanc.**

Most of the vineyard produces a white Graves called
Château Lamouroux but a very small amount of sweet
wine is made from vines planted in 1921. The 1990 Grand
Enclos du Château Cérons is delicious.

SAINTE-CROIX-DU-MONT AND LOUPIAC

**Surface Area (1998): (Sainte-Croix-du-Mont)
465 ha; (Loupiac): 419 ha.**
**Production (1998): (Sainte-Croix-du-Mont) 16,436
hl; (Loupiac): 14,214 hl.**
Colour and Style: Sweet white.
**Grape Varieties: Sémillon, Sauvignon Blanc and
Muscadelle.**
Maximum Yield: 40 hl/ha.
Minimum Alcohol Level: 13°.

Rather larger, rather better and altogether more vigorous than Cérons are the neighbouring *appellations* of
Sainte-Croix-du-Mont and Loupiac on the other side of
the river Garonne. The communes lie adjacent to one
another on the top of a steep bank above a bend in the
river opposite Barsac and Preignac. From the top of the
hill there is a superb view over the Sauternes area and
out towards the pine forests of the Landes.

There is little to distinguish between the wines of one
commune and the other, and in style, quality and
lusciousness they come between the sweet wines of

Cérons and Sauternes. Indeed, many of the best properties produce wine of equal quality to the *bourgeois* Sauternes châteaux. These sweet wines should be drunk young and chilled as an aperitif, like those of Cérons.

Leading Sainte-Croix-du-Mont Producers

CHÂTEAU LOUBENS
Owner: Arnaud de Sèze.
Surface Area under Vine: 21 ha – 97% Sémillon and 3% Sauvignon Blanc.
Second Wine: Château des Tours.
You get a splendid view over the river Garonne and the Sauternes district from the terrace in front of Château Loubens. Tunnelled into the cliffs behind are several galleries which would make a splendid barrel cellar. The shame is that the wine is produced in tank rather than oak. It is a very good sweet wine – *élevé en fûts de chêne*, or aged in oak, and it would be even better.

CHÂTEAU LA RAME
Owner: Yves Armand.
Surface Area under Vine: 20 ha – 75% Sémillon and 25% Sauvignon Blanc.
Château La Rame is aged, as it should be, in barrel, a third of which is new each year, and the wine is stylish and floral. In good years a 'Réserve' bottling is made.

Other Producers of note
CHÂTEAU CRABITAN-BELLEVUE – CUVÉE SPÉCIALE, CHÂTEAU GRAND-PEYROT AND CHÂTEAU LA GRAVE.

Leading Loupiac Producers

CHÂTEAU DU CROS
Owner: Boyer family.
Surface Area under Vine: 43 ha – 70% Sémillon, 20% Sauvignon Blanc and 10% Muscadelle.
Second Wine: Château Ségur du Cros.
This is one of the most reliable estates in the commune, producing a wine with a depth to withstand quite a lot of new oak (50 per cent upwards) which is what it is

given in the best vintages. The property also produces very good dry wines.

DOMAINE DU NOBLE
Owner: Patrick Dejean.
Surface Area under Vine: 14 ha – 85% Sémillon and 15% Sauvignon Blanc.
Second Wine: Château du Gascon.
This is the brother of Philippe Dejean of Château Rabaud-Promis, and the ancestral home of the Dejeans, if this doesn't sound too grand. Patrick Dejean makes one of the best Loupiacs, a wine that will keep for ten years in good vintages. There are sometimes both oaked and unoaked *cuvées*.

Other Producers of note
CHÂTEAU GRAND-PEYRUCHET – CUVÉE MARIE-CHARLOTTE, CLOS JEAN, CHÂTEAU MÉMOIRES – SÉLECTION DES GRAINS NOBLES – AND CHÂTEAU DE RICAUD.

CADILLAC

Surface Area (1998): 221 ha.
Production (1997): 6885 hl.
Colour and Style: Sweet white.
Grape Varieties: Sémillon, Sauvignon Blanc and Muscadelle.
Maximum Yield: 40 hl/ha.
Minimum Alcohol Level: 12°.

North of Loupiac lies the village of Cadillac. This is a curious, and recent (1973) *appellation*. Cadillac, like most of the right bank of the Garonne between Bordeaux and Langon (with the exception of Loupiac and Sainte-Croix-du-Mont) was, and continues to be, part of the Premières Côtes de Bordeaux AC. Effectively, since 1973, the southern half of this area, comprising some twenty-one communes, is now allowed to produce a Cérons-type sweet wine under the *appellation* of Cadillac. Few growers seem to be interested. Chateau Carsin at Rions, under its Australian winemaker, Mandy Jones, is one of the few. Her wine has the weight and concentration of a Loupiac.

ENTRE-DEUX-MERS

Surface Area (1998): 1819 ha.
Production (1997): 110,241 hl.
Colour: White.
Grape Varieties: Sémillon, Sauvignon Blanc, Muscadelle, Merlot Blanc, Colombard, Ugni Blanc and Mauzac.
Maximum Yield: 60 hl/ha.
Minimum Alcohol Level: 10°.

Between the seas, or more correctly, between the rivers, Garonne and Dordogne, lies the Entre-Deux-Mers. This is a prosperous landscape of farms and orchards and vineyards, of spinneys, copses and large forests, of running rivers and sudden hidden valleys. It is undulating, even hilly in parts. There are pleasant country farmsteads, elegant manors, imposing ruins and medieval churches. It is a rich land of mixed agriculture and it is where I would like to live if I were to settle in Bordeaux.

Yet it was not always as benign and prosperous an area as it seems today. The area, and the *appellation*, is a white wine region but the demand for white Bordeaux wines has contracted. Much of the Bordeaux change-over in the vineyards from white vines to red in the last generation or so has occurred in the Entre-Deux-Mers. For some time it has been more profitable to produce either red wine, simply labelled as Bordeaux or Bordeaux Supérieur, or even larger quantities of non-*appellation* white wine, than Entre-Deux-Mers AC, which must be a dry white wine. The co-operative at Rauzan in the middle of the area and one of the largest and most up to date in the Gironde, produces over 80,000 hectolitres of Bordeaux Rouge but only hardly 10,000 of Entre-Deux-Mers.

Happily in recent years, with the arrival of the trained oenologist, increasing use of the mechanical harvester and controlled vinification methods in modern equipment (paid for by subsidies from the EU), both yields and quality have been increased while unit costs have been reduced. Moreover, albeit slowly, Entre-Deux-Mers is now beginning to recapture a wider market – though many proprietors prefer to label their white wines as Bordeaux. It seems to sell better. It is once again an economic proposition for the *vigneron* to concentrate on quality rather than quantity. The region is beginning to thrive.

The Entre-Deux-Mers is triangular in shape, occupying most of the land between the two rivers with the departmental border with the Lot-et-Garonne as its base in the south-east corner. There are various sub-regions such as the Haut-Benauge, Saint-Macaire, Sainte-Foy-Bordeaux and the Graves de Vayres, as well as the sweet wine areas of Sainte Croix-du-Mont, Loupiac and Cadillac. On the right bank of the Garonne, opposite the Graves, lies the *appellation* of the Premières Côtes de Bordeaux. Sainte-Foy-Bordeaux, at the extreme east of the region, and the Graves de Vayres opposite Libourne, are *appellations* for both red and white wines, though rarely seen. Haut-Benauge lies behind the Premières Côtes at its southern end and continues into Saint-Macaire. These *appellations* are for white wines only. Production of Saint-Macaire and Sainte-Foy is minuscule.

The Entre-Deux-Mers is the largest region in the Gironde. The soil structure is complex, essentially loam or marl with patches of gravel; occasionally *boulbènes*, a sort of sand-clay mixture which can compact almost to a concrete-like substance and is hence very difficult to work. The vines are trained high, spaced far apart to assist mechanical cultivation, and grass is allowed to grow in between the rows of vines. It makes quite a different picture from the immaculate, flat, intensively cultivated but essentially arid-looking Médoc .

Entre-Deux Mers Producers for Good, Modern, Dry, White Bordeaux

CHÂTEAU BAUDUC – CUVÉE LES TROIS HECTARES (CRÉON), CHÂTEAU BONNET/ANDRÉ LURTON – RÉSERVE (GRÉZILLAC), CHÂTEAU DU CARPIA (CASTILLON-DE-CASTETS), CHÂTEAU MOULIN DE LAUNAY (SOUSSAC), CHÂTEAU RAUZAN-DESPAGNE (NAUJAN-ET-POSTILLAC), CHÂTEAU ROQUEFORT – CUVÉE SPÉCIALE (LUGASSON), CHÂTEAU THIEULEY – CUVÉE FRANCIS COURSELLE (LA SAUVE-MAJEURE), CHÂTEAU TOUR-DE-MIRAMBEAU – CUVÉE PASSION (NAUJAN-ET-POSTILLAC) AND CHÂTEAU TURCAUD – CUVÉE BOIS (LA SAUVE-MAJEURE).

PREMIÈRES CÔTES DE BORDEAUX

RED

Surface Area (1998): 3034 ha.
Production (1998): 171,594 hl.
Colour: Red.
Grape Varieties: Cabernet Sauvignon, Cabernet Franc, Merlot, Malbec and Petit Verdot.
Maximum Yield: 50 hl/ha.
Minimum Alcohol Level: 10.5°.

WHITE

Surface Area (1998): 387 ha.
Production (1998): 13,777 hl.
Colour: White.
Grape Varieties: Sauvignon Blanc, Sauvignon Gris, Sémillon and Muscadelle.
Maximum Yield: 55 hl/ha.
Minimum Alcohol Level: 12°.

Along the right bank of the Garonne, all the way from Saint-Maixant opposite the town of Langon to Bassens north of Bordeaux, a distance of some 60 kilometres, the land rises steeply away from the river and, at the top of the slope, stretches inland for a few kilometres. This narrow strip is the region of the Premières Côtes de Bordeaux, interrupted only by the indentations of Sainte-Croix-du-Mont and Loupiac. Twenty-one communes in the southern half of the region can use the Cadillac *appellation* for their sweet white wines.

This is an interesting region, not only because of the attractive scenery, similar to that of the Entre-Deux-Mers, but also because of the wines. A significant proportion of gravel in the soil gives the reds more definition and character than most of the *petits châteaux* of Bordeaux. There are white wines too, but these must be off-dry, if not medium-sweet, and can often be quite sweet, a style which finds little demand these days.

Those producers in the Premières Côtes de Bordeaux who do produce a dry white wine, such as Denis Dubourdieu at the excellent Château Reynon at Béguey, can only call it Bordeaux Blanc.

Premieres Côtes de Bordeaux producers of note for Good, Modern, Dry, White Bordeaux
CHÂTEAU DE BIROT (BÉGUEY), CHÂTEAU CARSIN (RIONS), CHÂTEAU CAYLA (RIONS), CHÂTEAU DU JUGE (CADILLAC) AND CHÂTEAU REYNON (BÉGUEY).

SAINT-EMILION

SAINT-EMILION

Surface Area (1998): 2048 ha.
Production (1998): 115,764 hl.
Colour: Red.
Grape Varieties: Merlot, Cabernet Franc (Bouchet), Cabernet Sauvignon and Malbec (Pressac).
Maximum Yield: 45 hl/ha.
Minimum Alcohol Level: 11°.

SAINT-EMILION GRAND CRU

Surface Area (1998): 3421 ha.
Production (1998): 157,847 hl.
Colour: Red.
Grape Varieties: Merlot, Cabernet Franc (Bouchet), Cabernet Sauvignon and Malbec (Pressac).
Maximum Yield: 40 hl/ha.
Minimum Alcohol Level: 11.5°.

Some 40 kilometres east of Bordeaux, across the peninsula of the Entre-Deux-Mers, can be found the sizeable, bustling but architecturally nondescript town of Libourne, centre both geographically and commercially of the Right Bank. The portmanteau phrase Dordogne or Libournais wines means those of Saint-Emilion, Pomerol, Fronsac and their satellites.

For centuries this region was, literally, a backwater. The wines were the poor country cousins of those of the Graves and the Médoc. Holdings were small and ownership in the hands of the peasants or local *petite bourgeoisie*. Communications with Bordeaux were tedious – there was neither a bridge across the Dordogne at Libourne nor one across the Garonne at Bordeaux until 1820 or so. And the wines had little impact on the

Bordeaux marketplace as a result. While the extensive, aristocrat-owned, monocultural estates of the Médoc found equally well to-do customers in Britain and Ireland, the artisanal produce of the Libournais was shipped as generic wine to the burghers of Holland, Bremen and the Hanseatic ports. The area remained one of mixed farming until much later than the Médoc and the Graves, few domaines having any individual reputation until the 1830s or 1840s.

Not surprisingly, when the Bordeaux brokers drew up the 1855 Classification, the wines of the Libournais were ignored. It was not until post-phylloxera times towards the end of the nineteenth century that prices began to match those of even the lesser Médoc Classed Growths, and only since the Second World War that there has been parity. The Libournais remains a wine region of small estates, of charming but largely unsophisticated and architecturally undistinguished dwellings, but one with often surprisingly lengthy family histories of ownership.

Some 6 kilometres north-east of Libourne lies the ancient walled town of Saint-Emilion. In contrast with Libourne Saint-Emilion is almost too self-consciously picturesque. Wine has been made here since Gallo-Roman times. Whether the poet and statesman Ausonius, after whom one of the area's most prestigious estates is named, ever had a vineyard in Saint-Emilion is a matter for dispute, but there is plenty of archaeological evidence to support a history of almost two millennia of continuous vine cultivation.

Above Château Ausone on the plateau you can see ancient trenches excavated out of the limestone bedrock. These were filled with earth and planted with fruit trees such as apples, pears, cherries and peaches. Vines were then trained up the trees and on to overhanging trellises in a sort of pergola system. Not long ago, not at Château Ausone but in the vineyard of Château La Gaffelière, another Saint-Emilion First Growth, an impressive mosaic showing a vineyard scene, was partially uncovered. This is no longer on view to the tourist, sadly, having been earthed up to await a more comprehensive dig in the future when techniques are yet more advanced.

The town itself is named after the hermit, Aemilianus, who lived in the eighth century. Deciding to retire from life completely he sought a quiet spot where he could calmly meditate on the cares of the world. He found his site, a grotto in a limestone bluff above the valley of the Dordogne. Today this is the town of Saint-Emilion. Above the hermit's cell, excavated deep into the rock, is a vast, underground monolithic church, the largest in Europe. Surrounding this the steep, cobbled streets and houses cling to the sides of a defile in the slope. The narrow alleys are filled with shops selling the celebrated local macaroons as well as wine and cans of *confit d'oie*, *cèpes* and *pâté de foie gras*.

From the Eglise Collégiale and Place Pioceau at the top of the town the view south is spectacular: the celebrated classed growths on the plateau and the slopes, lesser vineyards on the valley floor and finally the Dordogne, glinting away in the distance. You can also look directly down to the Place du Marché. Here, outside the Eglise Monolithique, the Jurade of Saint-Emilion congregate four times a year in their red ceremonial robes to proclaim the commencement of the harvest in September and command the ritual burning of an old wooden barrel, commemorating the old days when the Jurade (and not some bureaucrat in Paris or Brussels) held power over the legislation of the local wines.

Saint-Emilion, though by no means the largest in overall surface area, is the most compact and the most intensely cultivated *appellation* in Bordeaux. There is hardly a spare field which is not covered in neat rows of vines. The area forms a rough rectangle only 10 kilometres by 5, yet there are more than 5400 hectares of vines. By comparison, the entire Haut-Médoc (measuring 50 kilometres from Blanquefort to Saint-Estèphe) has not even double the amount under cultivation, about 10,200 hectares of vines.

Moreover, in contrast to the rolling gravel plateaux of the Médoc, where the châteaux holdings are large and the atmosphere is aristocratic, Saint-Emilion is a region of the small peasant proprietor. The 5400 hectares are divided among a thousand or more different owners, some 25 per cent of whom are members of the thriving local co-operative.

Geographically and also in terms of the style of its wines, Saint-Emilion can be divided into three main areas. South of the town itself, the land falls away abruptly towards the river Dordogne. The best vineyards lie either on these slopes or occupy the plateau on the other three sides of the town. This is the area known as the Côtes-Saint-Emilion. Here the soil consists of a thin layer of limestone debris on a solid limestone rock base, into which many a quarry has been hewn and is now used for cellaring the wine. Mixed with the limestone is a certain amount of clay. There is more sand as you descend down the slope into the valley. All but two of Saint-Emilion's First Growths lie in the Côtes. To the west of the Côtes, adjacent to Pomerol, is the smaller area of Graves-Saint-Emilion. As the name suggests, there is gravel in the soil. There is less limestone and clay than in the best sites of the Côtes but more sand. The subsoil is of the same composition. This area is almost entirely occupied by two First Growths, Châteaux Cheval-Blanc and Figeac.

Between these two areas, but largely north and west of the town itself, lies an area of old weathered sand known as the *sables anciens*, similar to that found in the Graves-Saint-Emilion, but without the gravel and on a base of limestone. The sand here is distinct from the more alluvial soil to the south of Saint-Emilion. Wines from here are good, if not of the very highest quality. There are no First Growths.

The wines of Saint-Emilion – and indeed the whole of the Libournais – are made from the three great red varieties of the Bordeaux area, but in a different proportion to that used in the Médoc. In the Médoc the Cabernet Sauvignon is king, occupying between 60 and 80 per cent of the vineyards; Merlot is an important subsidiary; Cabernet Franc is out of favour. In Saint-Emilion the Merlot is the most widely planted variety, with Cabernet Franc the main additional grape, while Cabernet Sauvignon is hardly used at all. The reason for the choice of Cabernet Franc rather than Sauvignon is the difference in soil structure. Cabernet Sauvignon thrives in the gravelly soils of the Médoc but Cabernet Franc performs far better in the predominantly limestone but colder soils of the Saint-Emilion area, where it is known

locally as the Bouchet. It also matures sooner than the Cabernet Sauvignon. The two main areas of Saint-Emilion, the Côtes and the Graves, produce quite different wines; though with the exception of Châteaux Cheval-Blanc and Figeac the top growths have similar *encépagements*, of roughly 50 to 70 per cent Merlot and 30 to 50 per cent Cabernet Franc or Bouchet.

The Côtes wines can vary depending whether the vineyard is largely or indeed entirely on the plateau or mostly on the slope. Some of the plateau wines can be very full and sturdy like Château Canon and Clos Fourtet. Mostly, though, all these Côtes wines start off well-coloured, quite full, without being particularly densely structured, and develop quickly, being ready for drinking a few years earlier than a Médoc or Graves of similar standing. In character they are loose-knit, somewhat warmer and sweeter than in the Médoc, with a spicy, fruit-caky flavour which derives from the predominant Merlot grape. A good First Growth from a successful vintage needs to be kept eight years or so before it is ready for drinking. It will keep well for at least a decade after that if properly stored. The wines from châteaux located on the *sables anciens* are similar but both less intense and less stylish.

The much smaller area of Graves-Saint-Emilion really needs to be considered as a quite separate sector. The wines have more power and are fuller and more concentrated, richer and firmer than those of the Côtes. These Saint-Emilions are more similar to Pomerols, their nearest neighbours. They tend to require a couple of years longer to mature and last better.

The lesser wines of the Saint-Emilion area, and this applies to the satellites as well as to Saint-Emilion itself, are predominantly Merlot-based, loose-knit, gentle wines without a great deal of grip. In weaker years they can rapidly become attenuated – but, at least, unlike a lesser Médoc in a poor year, they do not have unpleasant unripe tannins. Personally I find Fronsacs and lesser Pomerols have more interest than these wines.

It is commonly but erroneously believed that the famous 1855 Classification of Bordeaux was of the Médoc only, with Château Haut-Brion being smuggled in on the old-boy network because it was too important to be left out. In fact, the Classification was of all the red wines of Bordeaux. It was simply that the Libournais wines were not then considered fashionable and fetched low prices at that time. Indeed, at the time it was the wines of Fronsac which fared better.

Anxious not to be left out for ever, the local growers lobbied for their own separate classification in the 1950s. This is under the ultimate control of the INAO and is supposed to be revised every ten years. In fact the original classification of 1954 (promulgated in 1959) was revised in 1969, again in 1985, and again in 1996. The wines and growths of Saint-Emilion are divided into four categories: *premiers grands crus classés* (itself subdivided into categories A and B), *grands crus classés*, *grands crus* and plain or generic Saint-Emilion. (See page 59.)

The two Category 'A' are Château Ausone in the Côtes and Château Cheval-Blanc in the Graves-Saint-Emilion. These wines sell for almost double the price of the others. Prices are equivalent to those of Château Haut-Brion and the First Growths in the Médoc.

Of the *premiers grands crus classés* I would class Canon, Figeac and Magdelaine in a class above the rest and equivalent to the 'super-seconds' of the Médoc, wines such as Châteaux Ducru-Beaucaillou, Léoville-Las-Cases, Palmer and Pichon-Longueville, Comtesse de Lalande. Châteaux Angélus, Beauséjour-Duffau-Lagarrosse and Pavie are very good, Belair is elegant if somewhat unconcentrated and Clos Fourtet is fuller and improving. In my view the remaining properties should be demoted into a lower division with the best châteaux from the next category.

This list of *grands crus classés* is far too cumbersome, not least because many of the properties are very small and their wines rarely encountered. The best ought to be separated out into a superior classification (and into which châteaux Trottevieille and others should be demoted from *premiers grands crus classés*). These highfliers are, in alphabetical order: L'Arrosée, Berliquet, Cadet-Piola, Canon-La-Gaffelière, Clos de L'Oratoire, Dassault, La Dominique, Fonplégade, Fonroque, Larcis-Ducasse, Larmande, Laroze, La Mondotte, Pavie-Decesse, Pavie-Macquin, La Serre, Soutard, Tertre-Daugay, Le Tertre-Roteboeuf and Troplong-Mondot.

The next category below *grands crus classés* is *grands crus*. This is a misleading title, for there is little *grand* about these wines. The wines are ordinary, equivalent to the *petits châteaux* found in the northern part of the Médoc, in Bourg and Blaye and the other lesser areas of the Gironde. To be classified as *grand cru* the wines have to attain a requisite level of alcohol, pass a chemical analysis and be approved by a tasting panel. There are some 200 châteaux in this category.

Finally, there is the simple Saint-Emilion classification. This is simple generic wine, without a property name, and normally appears under the label of a local merchant or co operative. These wines are good daily drinking, but nothing more pretentious than that.

Leading Saint-Emilion Producers

★ CHÂTEAU ANGÉLUS

Owners: Boüard de Laforest family.
Surface Area under Vine: 26 ha – 50% Merlot, 45% Cabernet Franc and 5% Cabernet Sauvignon.
Second Wine: Le Carillon de L'Angélus.
Classification: Premier Grand Cru Classé B.
This estate has only come to the fore since the early 1980s, but has come so far forward that it was rewarded with promotion to the ranks of *premier grand cru* in 1996. The vineyard lies below Château Beauséjour-Duffau-Lagarrosse, half on the slope, half at its foot. The wine is rich, oaky, generous and opulent and its current status is certainly deserved.
Other wines CHÂTEAU LA FLEUR DE BOUARD (LALANDE-DE-POMEROL) AND CHÂTEAU DE FRANC (BORDEAUX-CÔTES DE FRANCS).

★ CHÂTEAU L'ARROSÉE

Owner: François Rodhain.
Surface Area under Vine: 10 ha – 55% Merlot, 15% Cabernet Franc and 30% Cabernet Sauvignon.
Classification: Grand Cru Classé.
There is no château as such at L'Arrosée, merely the winery which adjoins a cottage for one of the vineyard workers. Lying on the slope south of the town of Saint-Emilion, carefully made – you need patience to wait for

the Cabernet Sauvignon to be fully ripe, says Monsieur Rodhain – L'Arrosée is rich and oaky, with good acidity. It is frequently of *premier cru* quality.

★ CHÂTEAU AUSONE

Owner: Alain Vauthier.
Surface Area under Vine: 7.3 ha – 60% Merlot and 40% Cabernet Franc.
Classification: Premier Grand Cru Classé A.

There is a mystery about Château Ausone. The site is magnificent, the vineyard is old, the wine frequently spectacular at the outset. But then it fails to live up to it early promise. Is the cellar too damp, too mouldy? In 1997 Alain Vauthier took complete control, sacked the winemaker Pascal Delbeck and installed Michel Rolland as consultant. He also decided to keep the wine in a drier cellar during the winter. The result of these changes was a different style of Ausone: bigger, but perhaps less refined. We wait to see how these vintages will show with five years in bottle.

★ CHÂTEAU BEAU-SÉJOUR-BÉCOT
★ LA GOMERIE

Owners: Gérard and Dominique Bécot.
Surface Area under Vine: 16.5 ha – 70% Merlot, 24% Cabernet Franc and 6% Cabernet Sauvignon.
Second Wine: Tournelles des Moines.
Classification: Premier Grand Cru Classé B.

Demoted in 1985, because the vineyards were extended (this was not allowed in the *appellation* rules of the time but these have since been altered) and promoted again in 1996, this Beau-Séjour produces a lighter, lusher, oakier but perhaps simpler wine than Beauséjour-Duffau-Lagarrosse. It is for drinking in the medium term, from six years on rather than ten. La Gomerie is a special selection from a particular vineyard. It is rich and very concentrated, in the modern lush and glossy style.
Other wine CHÂTEAU GRAND-PONTET (SAINT-EMILION).

★ CHÂTEAU BEAUSÉJOUR-DUFFAU-LAGARROSSE

Owner: Jean-Michel Dubos.

Surface Area under Vine: 7 ha – 55% Merlot, 30% Cabernet Franc and 15% Cabernet Sauvignon.
Second Wine: La Croix de Mazerat.
Classification: Premier Grand Cru Classé B.

This Beauséjour has always been an intensely coloured, firm, tannic wine. It used to be too hard, I suspect because the Cabernet Sauvignon was not sufficiently ripe when picked, but has become more refined in the last fifteen years. The tannins are riper, the wine richer. This wine lasts longer than most Saint-Emilions. It fully deserves its current classification.

CHÂTEAU BELAIR

Owner: Mme Dubois-Challon.
Surface Area under Vine: 12.6 ha – 70% Merlot and 30% Cabernet Sauvignon.
Classification: Premier Grand Cru Classé B.

Until 1997 this was the sister château of Ausone, both wines being made by the winemaker, Pascal Delbeck. He continues here and, indeed, lives in the château itself. Despite the vineyard being as much on the plateau (alongside Château Canon and other sturdy Saint-Émilions) as on the slope, Château Belair is a wine of medium body only. It can be elegant and fragrant, but sometimes it is a little weak.
Other wine CHÂTEAU TOUR DU PAS SAINT-GEORGES (MONTAGNE SAINT-EMILION).

★ CHÂTEAU BERLIQUET

Owner: Patrick de Lesquen.
Surface Area under Vine: 9 ha – 70% Merlot, 23% Cabernet Franc and 7% Cabernet Sauvignon.
Second Wine: Les Ailes de Berliquet.
Classification: Grand Cru Classé.

Until September 1996 Château Berliquet was made by the local co-operative. The winemaking was then entrusted to Patrick Valette (he had just done the *élevage* of the 1996) and with his very first vintage, the 1997, he put Berliquet on the map. The vineyard lies on the slope next to Château Magdelaine, and the wine enjoyed a high reputation a century ago. This is certainly a candidate for promotion to *premier grand cru classé*, next time around, perhaps.

★ CHÂTEAU CANON

Owners: Wertheimer family.
Surface Area under Vine: 18 ha – 55% Merlot and
45% Cabernet Franc.
Second Wine: Château J. Kanon.
Classification: Premier Grand Cru Classé B.

This fine property with a fine reputation was sold by the Fournier family to the Wertheimers, owners of Chanel, in 1996, only for them to find one or two vintages, notably the 1994, had suffered a chlorine taint. The first few vintages under the new regime were disappointing, but at its best, as it proved in the 1980s, Château Canon is one of the few Saint-Emilions which can combine fullness and concentration with depth and refinement.
Other wine CHÂTEAU RAUZAN-SÉGLA (MARGAUX).

CHÂTEAU CANON-LA-GAFFELIÈRE
★ LA MONDOTTE

Owners: Comte Von Neipperg family.
Surface Area under Vine: 19.5 ha – 55% Merlot,
40% Cabernet Franc and 5% Cabernet Sauvignon.
Second Wine: Côte Migon La Gaffelière.
Classification: Grand Cru Classé.

Stephan Von Neipperg produces very good wine from this estate on the flatter land below Château La Gaffelière. It is lush and oaky and ranks high up at the top with the other *grands crus classés*, though his other, newer, estate, Clos de L'Oratoire is even better.

Since the 1996 vintage he has produced an even superior wine, called La Mondotte, from a 4.5 hectare parcel of vines on the top of the plateau between Châteaux Troplong-Mondot and Pavie-Decesse and planted in the ratio of 75 per cent Merlot and 25 per cent Cabernet Franc. The wine, lush, concentrated and oaky, in the modern style, is certainly a contender for *premier grand cru classé* in due course.
Other wine CLOS DE L'ORATOIRE (SAINT-EMILION).

★★★ CHÂTEAU CHEVAL-BLANC

Owners: MM. Bernard Arnault & Albert Frère.
Surface Area under Vine: 36 ha – 39% Merlot,
57% Cabernet Franc, 1% Cabernet Sauvignon and
3% Malbec.

Second Wine: Petit-Cheval.
Classification: Premier Grand Cru Classé A.

Château Cheval-Blanc is perhaps the only truly great wine made from a base of Cabernet Franc. The wine has been made since the early 1990s by the youthful and talented Pierre Lurton, a member of a many-tentacled Bordeaux wine family, and he has carried on the good work of Jacques Hébrard. In all these years there has hardly been a failure, and wines like the 1947 are legendary. The vineyard lies on the westerly borders of Saint-Emilion, on gravelly soil between Châteaux Figeac and L'Evangile, and produces a wine of size and generosity but with great depth and class. This is the longest-lasting of all the Libournais wines but while pre-Second World War, indeed 1920s bottles of Château Latour and the other Médoc/Graves First Growths are still splendid, the limit for Cheval-Blanc is fifty years.

★ CHÂTEAU FIGEAC

Owners: Manoncourt family.
Surface Area under Vine: 40 ha – 30% Merlot,
35% Cabernet Franc and 35% Cabernet Sauvignon.
Second Wine: La Grange Neuve de Figeac.
Classification: Premier Grand Cru Classé B.

Adjacent to Château Cheval-Blanc, and sharing its gravelly soil, Château Figeac has occasionally produced wine as grand as its illustrious neighbour, but suffers in some vintages from its high (by Libournais standards) percentage of Cabernet Sauvignon. This gives a firm, blackcurranty, good acidity element, but can sometimes also add a hard herbaceousness to the character of the wine. Quality is variable, therefore, but the 1990 and the 1982 are very good indeed.

CLOS FOURTET

Owners: Lurton family.
Surface Area under Vine: 19 ha – 72% Merlot,
22% Cabernet Franc and 6% Cabernet Sauvignon.
Second Wine: Domaine de Martialis.
Classification: Premier Grand Cru Classé B.

Clos Fourtet lies on the plateau next to the church of Saint-Emilion, with an impressive cellar quarried out of the rock underneath its vines. For a long time the wine

SAINT-EMILION AND SATELLITE AREAS

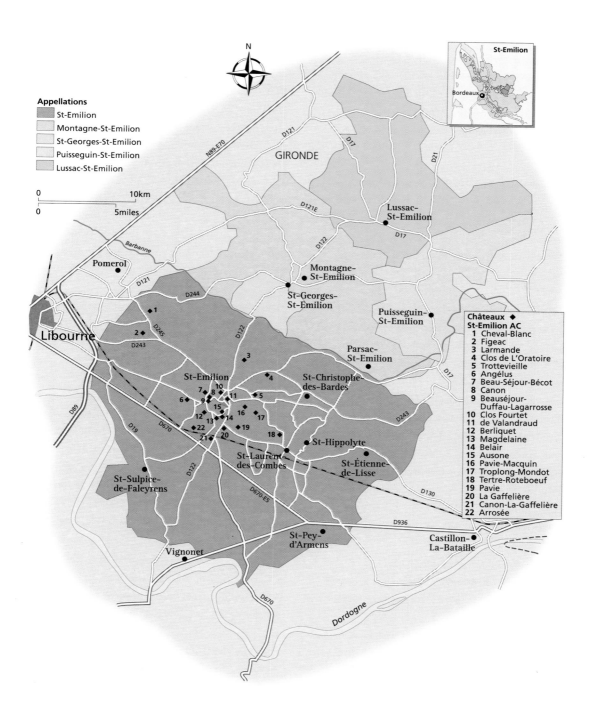

N

St-Emilion

Bordeaux

Appellations

St-Emilion

Montagne-St-Emilion

St-Georges-St-Emilion

Puisseguin-St-Emilion

Lussac-St-Emilion

0   10km

0   5miles

GIRONDE

Lussac-
St-Emilion

Pomerol

Barbanne

Montagne-
St-Emilion

St-Georges-
St-Emilion

Puisseguin-
St-Emilion

Libourne

Parsac-
St-Emilion

St-Emilion

St-Christophe-
des-Bardes

St-Hippolyte

St-Laurent-
des-Combes

St-Étienne-
de-Lisse

St-Sulpice-
de-Faleyrens

St-Pey-
d'Armens

Castillon-
La-Bataille

Vignonet

Dordogne

Châteaux ◆
St-Emilion AC
1 Cheval-Blanc
2 Figeac
3 Larmande
4 Clos de L'Oratoire
5 Trottevieille
6 Angélus
7 Beau-Séjour-Bécot
8 Canon
9 Beauséjour-
   Duffau-Lagarrosse
10 Clos Fourtet
11 de Valandraud
12 Berliquet
13 Magdelaine
14 Belair
15 Ausone
16 Pavie-Macquin
17 Troplong-Mondot
18 Tertre-Roteboeuf
19 Pavie
20 La Gaffelière
21 Canon-La-Gaffelière
22 Arrosée

was full but burly and rustic. In the 1990s standards improved, the fruit became lusher and more refined and the tannins more sophisticated.

CHÂTEAU LA GAFFELIÈRE

Owner: Léo de Malet Roquefort.
Surface Area under Vine: 22.1 ha – 65% Merlot,
30% Cabernet Franc and 5% Cabernet Sauvignon.
Second Wine: Clos La Gaffelière.
Classification: Premier Grand Cru Classé B.

The vineyards of La Gaffelière lie partly on the slope below Château Belair, partly on flatter, more sandy soil further down the slope from Château Pavie and produce a fruity wine of medium weight. More often than not, however, the wine lacks both intensity and real First Growth class.

Other wines CHÂTEAU TERTRE-DAUGAY (SAINT-EMILION).

CHÂTEAU LARMANDE

Owner: Groupe d'Assurance La Mondiale.
Surface Area under Vine: 25 ha – 65% Merlot,
30% Cabernet Franc and 5% Cabernet Sauvignon.
Second Wine: Le Cadet de Larmande.
Classification: Grand Cru Classé.

Situated north of the town on old, weathered sand mixed with clay, hemmed in by the vineyards of other *grands crus classés*, Larmande has a long history of making one of the best of the non-*premier cru* wines. Sixty per cent of the *grand vin*, after the second wine has been excluded, is aged in new wood. The wine is rich, full and succulent. It keeps better than most of its peers.

★★ CHÂTEAU MAGDELAINE

Owners: Ets. J P Moueix.
Surface Area under Vine: 10.4 ha – 90% Merlot and 10% Cabernet Franc.
Classification: Premier Grand Cru Classé B.

In the hands of the excellent Moueix team Château Magdelaine is regularly one of the very best Saint-Emilions. The vineyard, largely Merlot, lies half on the plateau, half on the slope directly south of Château Canon. The wine has considerable class, intensity and concentration, while remaining essentially velvety and soft-centred. It keeps well.

Other wines CHÂTEAU FONROQUE (SAINT-EMILION), CHÂTEAU LA FLEUR-PÉTRUS, CHÂTEAU LA GRAVE-À-POMEROL, CHÂTEAU LA TOUR-À-POMEROL, CHÂTEAU TROTANOY (ALL POMEROL) AND OTHERS.

★ CLOS DE L'ORATOIRE

Owners: Comte Von Neipperg family.
Surface Area under Vine: 10.3 ha – 75% Merlot and 25% Cabernet Franc.
Classification: Grand Cru Classé.

Since its acquisition by Stephan Von Neipperg of Château Canon-La-Gaffelière in 1991 this property, which lies between Châteaux Soutard and Dassault, has been given a new lease of life. Ironically it now produces better wine, because the land is superior to Château Canon-La-Gaffelière. This is one of the *appellation*'s new stars.

Other wines CHÂTEAU CANON-LA-GAFFELIÈRE AND LA MONDOTTE (SAINT-EMILION).

★ CHÂTEAU PAVIE

Owner: Gérard Perse.
Surface Area under Vine: 35 ha – 55% Merlot, 25% Cabernet Franc and 20% Cabernet Sauvignon.
Classification: Premier Grand Cru Classé B.

Gérard Perse of Château Monbousquet acquired Pavie-Decesse in 1997 and Pavie itself in 1998. Prior to this, run by Jean-Paul Valette, Château Pavie had shown itself to be one of the best of the First Growths B châteaux: never a blockbuster, but regularly balanced and refined, with very good concentrated fresh fruit. I look forward with great interest to tasting the wines of the new regime with three or four years' bottle age.

Other wines CHÂTEAUX LA CLUSERIE, MONBOUSQUET AND PAVIE-DECESSE (ALL SAINT-EMILION).

★ CHÂTEAU PAVIE-MACQUIN

Owners: Corre-Macquin family.
Surface Area under Vine: 15 ha – 70% Merlot, 25% Cabernet Franc and 5% Cabernet Sauvignon.
Second Wine: Les Chênes de Macquin.

Classification: Grand Cru Classé.

Nicolas Thienpont, cousin of Alexandre and co-owner with him of Vieux-Château-Certan, is in charge here, and since 1990 the quality has dramatically improved. The vineyard is well situated up on the plateau east of the town of Saint-Emilion, next to Troplong-Mondot. This is a firm wine, with depth and finesse, and it is now a contender for elevation to *premier cru*.

★ CHÂTEAU LE TERTRE-ROTEBOEUF
Commune: Saint-Laurent-des-Combes.
Owner: François Mitjaville.
Surface Area under Vine: 0.7 ha – 80% Merlot and 20% Cabernet Franc.
Classification: Grand Cru.

A marvellous south-facing, sloping site, old vines, low yields, organic viticulture and, above all, a passionate perfectionism have brought this estate to *premier cru* quality since 1985. François Mitjaville is not interested in getting his property upgraded however and he already has no difficulty selling his wine at a high *premier cru* price. The wine is full, tannic, rich and long-lasting.
Other wine CHÂTEAU ROC DE CAMBES (CÔTES DE BOURG).

★ CHÂTEAU TROPLONG-MONDOT
Owner: Christine Valette.
Surface Area under Vine: 30 ha – 80% Merlot, 10% Cabernet Franc and 10% Cabernet Sauvignon.
Second Wine: Château Mondot.
Classification: Grand Cru Classé.

Here is one of the main contenders for promotion to *premier grand cru classé*. For the last fifteen years no effort has been spared here and the quality has been very high. The vineyard lies around an ugly water-tower on a high plateau to the east of the town of Saint-Emilion, and the wine is full, rich, gently oaky, concentrated and very stylish. It needs seven to eight years to mature.

CHÂTEAU TROTTEVIEILLE
Owners: Castéja family.
Surface Area under Vine: 10 ha – 50% Merlot, 45% Cabernet Franc and 5% Cabernet Sauvignon.

Classification: Premier Cru Classé B.

The small vineyard lies away from the other *premiers crus* (though surrounded by *grands crus*) north-east of the town. The wine is of medium body, sound and fruity, but rarely offers great intensity or excitement.
Other wines CHÂTEAU BATAILLEY (PAUILLAC), DOMAINE DE L'EGLISE (POMEROL) AND OTHERS.

★ CHÂTEAU DE VALANDRAUD
Owners: Jean-Luc and Murielle Thunevin.
Surface Area under Vine: 2.6 ha – 75% Merlot, 20% Cabernet Franc and 5% Cabernet Sauvignon.
Second Wine: Virginie de Valandraud.
Classification: Grand Cru.

De Valandraud is the first and most notorious of a new breed of Bordeaux wines, known as *vins garagistes*. These are produced in minuscule quantities, are fat, concentrated, lush and highly extracted, and matured in entirely new oak. They sell to the gullible at ridiculous prices, higher even than Château Cheval-Blanc.

The minuscule vineyard covers no fewer than ten plots, some in inferior sandy soils well south of the town towards the river Dordogne. The techniques include high extract and lots of new oak – 'I admit it is no more than a *vin de technique*, not a *vin de terroir*,' says Thunevin. But he is not complaining about the prices he can demand for his wine!

Other Producers of note
CHÂTEAU BALESTARD-LA-TONNELLE*, CHÂTEAU CADET-BON*, CHÂTEAU CADET-PIOLA*, CHÂTEAU CAP-DE-MOURLIN*, CHÂTEAU CHAUVIN*, CHÂTEAU DE LA COUSPAUDE*, CHÂTEAU CURÉ-BON*, CHÂTEAU DASSAULT*, CHÂTEAU LA DOMINIQUE*, CHÂTEAU FERRAN-LARTIGUE (VIGNONNET), CHÂTEAU FONROQUE*, CHÂTEAU FRANC-MAYNE*, CHÂTEAU GRAND-MAYNE*, CHÂTEAU LARCIS-DUCASSE*, CHÂTEAU MONBOUSQUET (SAINT-SULPICE-DE-FALEYRENS), CHÂTEAU MOULIN-DU-CADET*, CHÂTEAU PAVIE-DECESSE*, CHÂTEAU ROLLAND-MAILLET (POMEROL), CLOS SAINT-MARTIN*, CHÂTEAU LA SERRE*, CHÂTEAU SOUTARD*, CHÂTEAU TERTRE-DAUGAY*, CHÂTEAU TEYSSIER (VIGNONNET) AND CHÂTEAU LA TOUR-FIGEAC*.
* in the commune of Saint-Emilion.

The Saint-Emilion Satellites

Lussac-Saint-Emilion
Surface Area (1998): 1428 ha.
Production (1998): 84,837 hl.

Montagne-Saint-Emilion
Surface Area (1998): 1565 ha.
Production (1998): 91,346 hl.

Puisseguin-Saint-Emilion
Surface Area (1998): 736 ha.
Production (1998): 42,524 hl.

Saint-Georges-Saint-Emilion
Surface Area (1998): 172 ha.
Production (1998): 10,118 hl.
For all the above:
Colour: Red.
Grape Varieties: Merlot, Cabernet Franc (Bouchet), Cabernet Sauvignon and Malbec (Pressac).
Maximum Yield: 45 hl/ha.
Minimum Alcohol Level: 11°.

Above and behind Saint-Emilion are the Saint-Emilion satellites: Montagne (Montagne-Saint-Emilion having absorbed the smaller neighbouring commune of Parsac in 1972), Lussac, Puisseguin and Saint-Georges (producers in Saint-Georges can also use the Montagne *appellation*). All these communes can add the name Saint-Emilion to their own. Here there are some large estates, for this area was only developed more recently, and by the moneyed classes of the late nineteenth century. There are some fine buildings and some good wine, often better than that from the more alluvial, soils between Saint-Emilion itself and the river Dordogne.

In general the *encépagement* contains more Merlot and less Cabernet than in the heart of Saint-Emilion. The wines are round and generous, though sometimes both rather diffuse and lacking finesse. They are best drunk young, within three to six years after the vintage.

Saint-Emilion Satellite Producers of note
Lussac-Saint-Emilion Château Lionnat.
Montagne-Saint-Emilion Château Faizeau, Château de Maison Neuve, Château de Musset (Parsac) and Château du Roudier.
Saint-Georges-Saint-Emilion Château Saint-Georges and Château Tour du Pas Saint-Georges.

Pomerol

Surface Area (1998): 784 ha.
Production (1998): 36,066 hl.
Colour: Red.
Grape Varieties: Merlot, Cabernet Franc (Bouchet), Cabernet Sauvignon and Malbec (Pressac).
Maximum Yield: 42 hl/ha.
Minimum Alcohol Degree: 10.5°.

Pomerol is a strange area. If one excludes the vineyard of its greatest domaine, Château Petrus, it has no focus. Travelling north out of Libourne along the D244 towards Montagne-Saint-Emilion you pass a few vineyards and then come to the village of Catusseau. At this point the road forks. Between these two roads, about half a kilometre away on the highest ground of the area, lies Château Petrus surrounded by most of the rest of the top Pomerol domaines. This is the nucleus of the area. A little further on, to the left, there is a church and a few houses. This is all there is of Pomerol as a village.

Pomerol is by far the smallest of Bordeaux's top wine regions. It is a compact commune of relatively small estates, many of which are now owned, managed or marketed by the excellent firm of Jean-Pierre Moueix in Libourne. The heart of the area is a gravel and clay plateau which lies on a hard, iron-rich base known as *crasse de fer* or *machefer* and which slopes down to the more alluvial sandy soils of the Dordogne, Isle and Barbanne rivers on three sides, and adjoins the Graves-Saint-Emilion vineyards on the east. The area measures barely three kilometres by four and consists of some 800 hectares of vines. This is hardly one-seventh of the whole of Saint-Emilion, and roughly comparable with the smallest Médoc commune, Saint-Julien.

Pomerol's worldwide fame is recent. While a number of the leading growths can trace their history to before the French Revolution, the vineyards were neglected until very recently. Pomerol was only recognised as an area in its own right in 1923 and as late as 1943 when a list of comparative prices was produced for the Vichy Government, Petrus could only command the price of a Second Growth Médoc and the next category of top Pomerols below Petrus, Vieux-Château-Certan and La Conseillante, for example, were rated the equivalent of Giscours and La Lagune. It took two people – Madame Loubat, owner of Château Petrus, and her ally Jean-Pierre Moueix – plus two enthusiasts, Ronald Avery and Harry Waugh, to transform the situation. Yet Pomerol is still a sleepy backwater, with few imposing estates.

If forty years ago the wines were barely recognised as being part of the Bordeaux pantheon, today they are much in demand. The prodigious price of Petrus at auction and the quality of the other top Pomerols hardly need pointing out any longer. On the other hand, as the vast majority of the properties are so tiny, barely a dozen hectares in surface at their largest, some wines are rarely encountered. Look at any list of old wines: plenty of Médocs, few Pomerols. The main grape is the Merlot, the principal subsidiary variety the Cabernet Franc (here as in Saint-Emilion called the Bouchet). You may also find a few rows of Malbec (here known as the Pressac). One or two estates such as Vieux-Château-Certan have Cabernet Sauvignon, but in general this does not do as well on this side of the Gironde as the Cabernet Franc.

Pomerol wines are subtly different from those across the border in Saint-Emilion, particularly those from the limestone rock and *sables anciens* (weathered sandstone) around the town of Saint-Emilion itself. Saint-Emilions are in general soft, aromatic, plump, fleshy and slightly spicy. Compared with the deeper-coloured, intense, firm, blackcurranty Médocs they are looser-knit, quicker to mature and do not last as long. Pomerols in many respects are a sort of halfway house. They are fresher and more solid than Saint-Emilions, richer, more plummy and less fruitcakey in flavour. Compared with the Médocs on the other hand, they are more obviously velvety but have less austerity and backbone. The concentration of fruit is more apparent, particularly when the wines are young, because it is less hidden by the tannin. I find the style delicious and the wines of increasingly high quality.

There has never been a Pomerol classification.

Leading Pomerol Producers

CHÂTEAU BEAUREGARD
Owner: Crédit Foncier de France.
Surface Area under Vine: 17 ha – 60% Merlot, 30% Cabernet Franc and 10% Cabernet Sauvignon.
Second Wine: Le Benjamin de Beauregard.
Château Beauregard lies just off the main plateau behind Château Petit-Village and produces a reliable, fullish, fruity wine which is usually just off the first division. There has been a distinct improvement since 1985.
Other wine CHÂTEAU BASTOR-LAMONTAGNE (SAUTERNES).

CHÂTEAU LE BON-PASTEUR
Owner: Rolland family.
Surface Area under Vine: 6.7 ha – 80% Merlot and 20% Cabernet Franc.
This is the leading estate of local but world-renowned oenologists Michel and Dany Rolland. It lies on clay-gravel soil at the extreme north-east of the *appellation*, near where Pomerol meets Lalande-de-Pomerol, Saint-Emilion and Montagne-Saint-Emilion. Rolland believes in picking late, so there is an element of over-ripeness in the fruit, and extended macerations. This is in total contrast to the philosophy of the Moueix team at Petrus, Trotanoy and other chateaux. The result here is a wine of fine colour and impressive intensity of fruit. Half the wine each year is aged in new oak.
Other wines CHÂTEAU BERTINAU-SAINT-VINCENT (LALANDE-DE-POMEROL), CHÂTEAU FONTENIL (FRONSAC) AND CHÂTEAU ROLLAND-MAILLET (SAINT-EMILION).

★ CHÂTEAU CERTAN-DE-MAY
Owner: Mme Odette Barreau-Badar.
Surface Area under Vine: 5 ha – 70% Merlot, 25% Cabernet Franc and 5% Cabernet Sauvignon.

This small estate has now been run by Jean-Luc Barreau-Badar for over twenty years, and in this time he has hardly failed to make a wine in the top rank. The wine is richer and more opulent than its neighbour, Vieux-Château-Certan, and is ready sooner. It is nevertheless full, concentrated, very distinguished and lasts well.

★ CHÂTEAU CLINET

Owner: GAN.
Surface Area under Vine: 9 ha – 75% Merlot, 10% Cabernet Franc and 15% Cabernet Sauvignon.
Second Wine: Fleur de Clinet.

Though owned by an insurance company since 1991, the wine continues to be made by Jean-Michel Arcaute, the son-in-law of the previous owner, together with his friend, the wine consultant Michel Rolland. The result is a deeply coloured, quite extracted, plump, oaky wine. There is plenty of concentrated fruit here but sometimes one wishes for a little more elegance.

Other wine CHÂTEAU LA CROIX-DE-CASSE (POMEROL).

★ CHÂTEAU LA CONSEILLANTE

Owners: Nicolas family.
Surface Area under Vine: 12 ha – 65% Merlot, 30% Cabernet Franc and 5% Malbec.

Adjoining Petrus, L'Evangile and Vieux-Château-Certan it is not surprising that this is one of the top Pomerols. The wine is lighter than its neighbours, but usually one with intensity, elegance and velvety-textured fruit. Subtlety, not muscle, is the keynote.

CHÂTEAU LA CROIX-DE-GAY
★ CHÂTEAU LA FLEUR-DE-GAY

Owner: Noël Reynaud.
Surface Area under Vine: 12 ha – 80% Merlot, 10% Cabernet Franc and 10% Cabernet Sauvignon.

Château La Croix-de-Gay is a good 'second division' Pomerol, quite full, sometimes lacking real elegance. A distinctly superior super-*cuvée*, La Fleur-de-Gay, is produced from the best part of the vineyard, from 100 per cent Merlot, aged entirely in new wood.

Other wine CHÂTEAU FAIZEAU (MONTAGNE-SAINT-EMILION).

★ CLOS L'EGLISE

Owner: Sylvain Garcin-Cathiard.
Surface Area under Vine: 6 ha – 57% Merlot, 36% Cabernet Franc and 7% Cabernet Sauvignon.

Clos L'Eglise was acquired by Madame Garcin-Cathiard in January 1997, since when an entirely new winery has been constructed. Always a good wine, if never quite in the top rank, recent vintages have shown its true potential: full, concentrated and lush, with no lack of class.

Other wine CHÂTEAU HAUT-BERGEY (PESSAC-LÉOGNAN).

★★ CHÂTEAU L'EGLISE-CLINET

Owner: Denis Durantou.
Surface Area under Vine: 6 ha – 80% Merlot and 20% Cabernet Franc.

Denis Durantou took over this reliable if rarely very exciting second-division Pomerol in 1983. He has slowly but surely refined the style and the wine has been in the top rank since 1989 or so, and now fetches prices to match. The wine is medium-full, with very lovely intense fruit and a lot of depth and class. La Petite Eglise is a separate property.

Other wine LA CHÉNADE MADE FROM BOUGHT-IN WINE (LALANDE-DE-POMEROL).

CHÂTEAU L'ENCLOS

Owner: Weydert family.
Surface Area under Vine: 9.5 ha – 82% Merlot, 17% Cabernet Franc and 1% Malbec.

While much of the Enclos vineyard lies west of the N98 Libourne to Périgueux main road, on soil which is quite sandy, there is an important parcel which lies near the Pomerol church, and it this which gives the wine from L'Enclos its class. It is carefully made (particularly as far as the yield is concerned), matured in one-third new oak, and the result is a wine of medium weight, elegance and harmony.

★★ CHÂTEAU L'EVANGILE

Owners: Domaines Barons de Rothschild.
Surface Area under Vine: 14.1 ha – 78% Merlot and 22% Cabernet Franc.
Second Wine: Blazon de L'Evangile.

Lying as it does between Châteaux Cheval-Blanc and Petrus, you would expect the vineyard of L'Evangile to produce great wine, and so it does, but it has taken some time to do so. It used to have a rather dense herbaceous character in the old days, when there was rather more Cabernet, including Cabernet Sauvignon in the *encépagement*. Since the Rothschilds of Château Lafite acquired a majority shareholding in 1990 the style has been refined, and the wine is richer. But it is only since the mid-1990s that the potential has been fully realised.

Other wines CHÂTEAU DUHART-MILON, CHÂTEAU LAFITE-ROTHSCHILD (BOTH PAUILLAC) AND CHÂTEAU RIEUSSEC (SAUTERNES).

★★ CHÂTEAU LA FLEUR-PETRUS

Owners: Ets. J P Moueix.

Surface Area under Vine: 13.6 ha – 90% Merlot and 10% Cabernet Franc.

Château La Fleur-Petrus acquired 4.4 hectares from Château Le Gay in 1994 bringing it up to its present size. This is one of the best wines in the vast and distinguished Moueix stable. Quality dipped a little in the mid-to-end 1980s – perhaps the average age of the vines was not as old as it should be – but is now back at the top level. The wine is never a blockbuster, but always one of silky intensity, and ripe, rich, classy Merlot fruit.

Other wines CHÂTEAU MAGDELAINE (SAINT-EMILION), CHÂTEAU PETRUS, CHÂTEAU TROTANOY (BOTH POMEROL) AND OTHERS.

★ CHÂTEAU GAZIN

Owners: De Bailliencourt family.

Surface Area under Vine: 26 ha – 80% Merlot, 15% Cabernet Franc and 5% Cabernet Sauvignon.

Second Wine: L'Hospitalet de Gazin.

Nothing exciting was made here until they asked the Moueix team (Ets. J P Moueix sells much of the wine) to help advise in the mid-1980s. Together with the establishment of a second wine the standard has much improved. Medium weight with generous ripe fruit is the style today. The vineyard marches with that of Châteaux Petrus and L'Evangile on the north-eastern side of the commune.

★ CHÂTEAU LA GRAVE-À-POMEROL

Owner: Christian Moueix.

Surface Area under Vine: 8.4 ha – 85% Merlot and 15% Cabernet Franc.

Christian Moueix has been the owner of this attractive property situated in one block near the N98 main road since 1971. During the 1990s the stylishly fruity and medium-bodied wine has progressed in quality from the second division to the first during the 1990s.

Other wines CHÂTEAU LA FLEUR-PETRUS, CHÂTEAU PETRUS, CHÂTEAU TROTANOY (ALL POMEROL), CHÂTEAU MAGDELAINE (SAINT-EMILION) AND OTHERS.

★★ CHÂTEAU LAFLEUR

Owners: Marie Robin/Jacques Guinaudeau.

Surface Area under Vine: 4.5 ha – 50% Merlot and 50% Cabernet Franc.

Second Wine: Pensées de Lafleur.

Though of a completely different character, owing as much as anything to the quite different *encépagement*, Château Lafleur is perhaps the only wine to rival Petrus today, certainly in terms of its weight, intensity, concentration and long adolescence. The wine is made by a nephew of the long-time owner, together with advice from the Moueix team, who market the wine.

Other wine CHÂTEAU LE GAY (POMEROL).

CHÂTEAU LAGRANGE

Owner: Ets. J P Moueix.

Surface Area under Vine: 8.2 ha – 95% Merlot and 5% Cabernet Franc.

Château Lagrange in Pomerol, not to be confused with Château Lagrange in Saint-Julien, is a worthy member of the 'second' division of Pomerol estates. Despite the high Merlot content it possesses a backbone, a richness and capacity to age well which some of its peers do not. One-third new oak is used every year.

★★ CHÂTEAU LATOUR-À-POMEROL

Owners: Mme Lily Lacoste-Loubat/Ets. J P Moueix.

Surface Area under Vine: 7.9 ha – 90% Merlot and 10% Cabernet Franc.

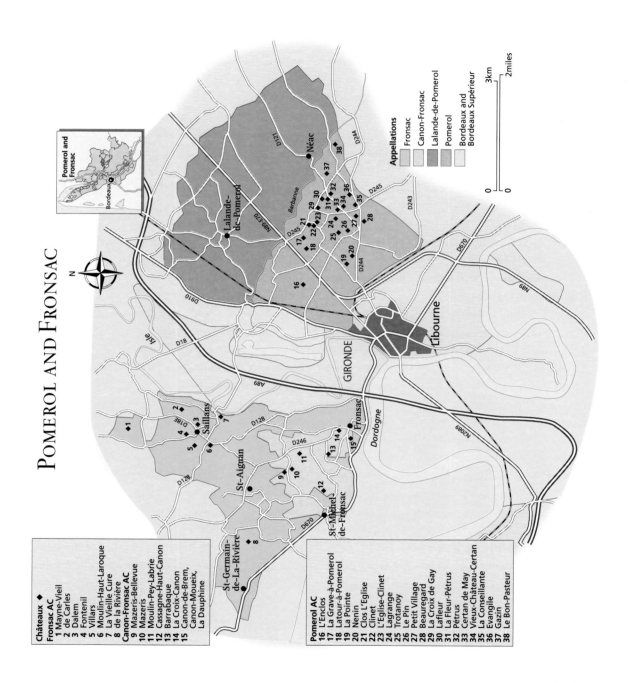

Pomerol and Fronsac

Appellations

Fronsac
Canon-Fronsac
Lalande-de-Pomerol
Pomerol
Bordeaux and
Bordeaux Supérieur

Pomerol and Fronsac

Bordeaux

Lalande-
de-Pomerol

Néac

Libourne

GIRONDE

Fronsac

St-Michel
de-Fronsac

St-Aignan

Saillans

St-Germain-
de-La-Rivière

Isle

Dordogne

Châteaux ◆

Fronsac AC
1 Mayne-Vieil
2 de Carles
3 Dalem
4 Fontenil
5 Villars
6 Moulin-Haut-Laroque
7 La Vieille Cure
8 de la Rivière

Canon-Fronsac AC
9 Mazeris-Bellevue
10 Mazeris
11 Moulin-Pey-Labrie
12 Cassagne-Haut-Canon
13 Barrabaque
14 La Croix-Canon
15 Canon-de-Brem,
    Canon-Moueix,
    La Dauphine

Pomerol AC
16 L'Enclos
17 La Grave-à-Pomerol
18 Latour-à-Pomerol
19 La Pointe
20 Nenin
21 Clos L'Eglise
22 Clinet
23 L'Eglise-Clinet
24 Lagrange
25 Trotanoy
26 Le Pin
27 Petit Village
28 Beauregard
29 La Croix de Gay
30 Lafleur
31 La Fleur-Pétrus
32 Pétrus
33 Certan de May
34 Vieux-Château-Certan
35 La Conseillante
36 Evangile
37 Gazin
38 Le Bon-Pasteur

This is another of the top Pomerol estates in the Moueix portfolio. Some of the vines lie down by the N89, next to Château La Grave, but the main segment is alongside the church near the various Clinet and L'Eglise châteaux. I frequently taste this wine alongside La Fleur-Petrus. Sometimes one is superior, sometimes the other. Latour is a little fuller; La Fleur-Petrus more refined.

Other wines CHÂTEAU LA FLEUR-PETRUS, CHÂTEAU PETRUS, CHÂTEAU TROTANOY (ALL POMEROL), CHÂTEAU MAGDELAINE (SAINT-EMILION) AND OTHERS.

★ CHÂTEAU NENIN
Owner: Michel Delon.
Surface Area under Vine: 25 ha — 70% Merlot, 20% Cabernet Franc and 10% Cabernet Sauvignon.
Second Wine: Les Fugues de Nenin.
Until 1997 this property, large for a Pomerol estate, and lying next to Château La Pointe between the Libourne suburbs and Catusseau, was an underachiever. Michel Delon of Château Léoville-Las-Cases has rapidly put things right. This is a fullish wine, rich and concentrated.
Other wines CHÂTEAU LÉOVILLE-LAS-CASES (SAINT-JULIEN) AND CHÂTEAU POTENSAC (MÉDOC).

CHÂTEAU PETIT-VILLAGE
Owners: AXA Millésimes.
Surface Area under Vine: 11 ha — 80% Merlot, 10% Cabernet Franc and 10% Cabernet Sauvignon.
Located in its own triangle bordered by Vieux-Château-Certan, Certan-de-May, Le Pin and Beauregard, this property should produce fine wine, and it did in the 1950s and 1960s when owned by the Prats family of Château Cos d'Estournel. Under the AXA umbrella it has lost its soul.
Other wines CHÂTEAU CANTENAC-BROWN (MARGAUX), CHÂTEAU PICHON-LONGUEVILLE (PAUILLAC), CHÂTEAU SUDUIRAUT (SAUTERNES) AND OTHERS.

★★★ CHÂTEAU PETRUS
Owners: Mme Lily Lacoste-Loubat family and Ets. J P Moueix.
Surface Area under Vine: 11.4 ha — 95% Merlot and 5% Cabernet Franc.

This unassuming, uninhabited château marks the focal point of Pomerol. Here the soil is clay. The surrounding vineyards contain some gravel, and then there is more and more sand (and less exciting wine) as one falls off the plateau to the north, south and west (east lies Château Cheval-Blanc).

For long the senior estate in Pomerol, Petrus is today the most expensive and the most soughtafter Bordeaux in the world. Since 1964 the majority of the shares have been owned by the Moueix family and the Moueix team has made the wine. The attention to detail here is almost excessive. One reads of helicopters generating wind to dry the grapes after rain, plastic sheeting on the ground to stop this rain reaching down as far as the roots, and sees pictures showing draconian green pruning. The wine is magnificent, as good as pure Merlot (which is what it usually is) can be: extremely concentrated and rich, needing fifteen years to mature.

Other wines CHÂTEAU LA FLEUR-PETRUS, CHÂTEAU LATOUR-à-POMEROL, CHÂTEAU TROTANOY (ALL POMEROL), CHÂTEAU MAGDELAINE (SAINT-EMILION) AND OTHERS.

★ CHÂTEAU LE PIN
Owner: Jacques Thienpont.
Surface Area under Vine: 2 ha — 92% Merlot and 8% Cabernet Franc.
Château Le Pin is very good: rich, oaky and opulent. But, in my view, it is not as good as the high price it commands suggests it is. The property was acquired in 1979 before which the wine had been sold off in bulk. The first widely distributed vintage was the 1981 and very soon the world was clamouring for the wine. With only some 30 barrels per annum demand soon forced the prices into the stratosphere.

CHÂTEAU LA POINTE
Owner: d'Arfeuille family.
Surface Area under Vine: 23 ha — 75% Merlot and 25% Cabernet Franc.
Second Wine: La Pointe Riffat.
La Pointe lies near Chateau Nenin on the Libournais side of the hamlet of Catusseau, and is likewise a large estate for the area. The d'Arfeuilles are also *négociants* in

Libourne. The wine is medium weight, lush, elegant and fruity, one of the best of the 'second division' Pomerols.
Other wines CHÂTEAU LA SERRE (SAINT-EMILION) AND CHÂTEAU TOUMALIN (FRONSAC).

★★ CHÂTEAU TROTANOY
Owners: Ets. J P Moueix.
Surface Area under Vine: 8 ha – 90% Merlot and 10% Cabernet Franc.

Though Trotanoy's vineyard is not quite on the central Pomerol plateau the wine is better, and sells for a higher price than La Fleur-Petrus, also in the Moueix stable. This is a splendid, opulent, rich Pomerol: medium-full and with a great deal of class. Some vintages, such as the 1982, developed surprisingly early. This was already delicious in 1990. Trotanoy, nevertheless, keeps very well.
Other wines CHÂTEAU LA FLEUR-PETRUS, CHÂTEAU PETRUS (BOTH POMEROL), CHÂTEAU MAGDELAINE (SAINT-EMILION) AND OTHERS.

★★ VIEUX-CHÂTEAU-CERTAN
Owners: Thienpont family.
Surface Area under Vine: 13.5 ha – 60% Merlot, 30% Cabernet Franc and 10% Cabernet Sauvignon.
Second Wine: La Gravette de Certan.

This is one of my personal favourites among the stellar Pomerols. I always seem to mark it very highly in blind tastings. It made a very fine 1982 (and some splendid earlier vintages) and has not put a foot wrong since Alexandre Thienpont took over from his father in 1985. Alexandre is a perfectionist. The wine is classic, with very classy fruit, and a backbone and acidity due to the high proportion of Cabernet. It keeps extremely well.

Other Producers of note
CHÂTEAU BOURGNEUF-VAYRON*, CHÂTEAU LA CABANNE*, CHÂTEAU CERTAN-GIRAUD*, CLOS DU CLOCHER*, CHÂTEAU FEYTIT-CLINET*, CHÂTEAU LE GAY*, CHÂTEAU GUILLOT-CLAUZEL*, CHÂTEAU HAUT-TROPCHAUD*, CHÂTEAU LAFLEUR-GAZIN*, CHÂTEAU PLINCE (LIBOURNE), CLOS RENÉ*, CHÂTEAU ROUGET*, CHÂTEAU LA VIOLETTE* AND CHÂTEAU VRAI-CROIX-DE-GAY*.
* in the commune of Pomerol.

LALANDE-DE-POMEROL

Surface Area (1998): 1111 ha.
Production (1998): 56,152 hl.
Colour: Red.
Grape Varieties: Merlot, Cabernet Franc (Bouchet), Cabernet Sauvignon and Malbec (Pressac).
Maximum Yield: 42 hl/ha.
Minimum Alcohol Level: 10.5°.

Across the river Barbanne to the north of Pomerol are two areas which are now incorporated into one, Néac having been absorbed into Lalande-de-Pomerol (an easier name to sell, no doubt) in the 1980s. The wines, naturally, are like lesser Pomerols, plump and fruity, without seeming to be too Merlot-based and loose-knit in character. They are attractive and stylish, at their best between three and eight years old, and we shall see a lot more of them in the years to come.

Lalande-de-Pomerol Producers of note
CHÂTEAU L'ANCIEN*, CHÂTEAU BERTINEAU-SAINT-VINCENT*, CHÂTEAU CANON-CHAIGNEAU (NÉAC), CHÂTEAU DE CHAMBRUN (NÉAC), LA CHÉNADE* (NÉGOCIANT WINE FROM DENIS DURANTOU OF CHÂTEAU L'EGLISE-CLINET), CHÂTEAU LA FLEUR DE BOUARD*, CHÂTEAU LA FLEUR-SAINT-GEORGES (NÉAC), CHÂTEAU GARRAUD (NÉAC), CHÂTEAU GRAND-ORMEAU*, CHÂTEAU HAUT-CHAIGNEAU (NÉAC), CHÂTEAU PERRON*, CHÂTEAU PERRON-LA-FLEUR*, CHÂTEAU LA SERGUE* AND CHÂTEAU SIAURAC (NÉAC).
* in the commune of Lalande-de-Pomerol.

FRONSAC AND CANON-FRONSAC

Surface Area (1998): (Canon-Fronsac) 302 ha; (Fronsac) 824 ha.
Production (1998): (Canon-Fronsac) 16,881 hl; (Fronsac) 46,566 hl.
Colour: Red.

Grape Varieties: Merlot, Cabernet Franc (Bouchet), Cabernet Sauvignon and Malbec (Pressac).
Maximum Yield: 42 hl/ha.
Minimum Alcohol Level: 11°.

Of all the non-classic areas of Bordeaux – outside the areas of Haut-Médoc, Pessac-Léognan, Saint-Emilion and Pomerol – Fronsac wines have the most definition, the most personality. The wines have fruit, character and charm and are increasingly well made. A good Fronsac wine will usually cost less than a Médoc *cru bourgeois* or a minor Saint-Emilion *grand cru classé* and is normally a better wine. So the area has value for money, too, on its side. There has been considerable investment in the area and the wines deserve to be better known.

Fronsac lies west of Pomerol, across the river Isle, a tributary of the Dordogne which it joins at Libourne. Viewed from the river or from the opposite bank in the Entre-Deux-Mers, you can see the land rising sharply. On this limestone bluff, the Tertre de Fronsac, and on the land behind it descending gradually towards the village of Galgon, are the Fronsac vineyards. The Fronsac plateau dominates a bend in the Dordogne and the surrounding countryside. Over twelve centuries ago, the Emperor Charlemagne commanded a fortress to be built to control the neighbouring area and to defend the Libournais against marauding pirates. The site was known as Fransiacus.

In 1623 the fortified castle which had evolved from Charlemagne's stockade was razed to the ground. Ten years later the great Cardinal de Richelieu bought the land – and the title of Duke of Fronsac – for the children of his younger sister. In the Fronsac area there are many elegant eighteenth and early nineteenth-century buildings. The countryside is also attractive, with carefully tended vineyards interspersed with woodland and smaller, more formal parks surrounding the larger mansions. The views from the higher ground across to the Entre-Deux-Mers and along the Dordogne in both directions are well worth a detour.

Two centuries ago Fronsac's leading wines were the stars of the Libournais. References to Canon meant

Fronsac's most famous wine owned by the Fontemoing family and not the Saint-Emilion *premier cru*. Indeed, the very first Bordeaux wine to appear in a Christie's catalogue refers to 'a hogshead of Canon Claret'. This can only be the Fronsac wine, for what is now the estate in Saint-Emilion was known as the Domaine de Saint-Martin until 1857.

The rise in fame of Saint-Emilion wines in the mid-nineteenth century and those of Pomerol somewhat later was paralleled by a decline in the prestige of Fronsac. By the end of the century, a good Fronsac wine could fetch between 500 and 1000 francs a *tonneau*, roughly equivalent to a Pomerol satellite or Saint-Emilion *grand cru*, but by the 1950s the price was little more than that of Bordeaux Supérieur. Most wines were sold in bulk to the *négociants*, standards were poor and the wine rustic. It was not until after the frost disaster of 1956 when Fronsac, because of its elevated position, was affected least of all the Libournais wine areas – but still severely enough – that an organised effort to improve standards and promote the wines was made.

The real progress has begun more recently and is still accelerating. Comparisons of comprehensive tastings I have made over the years since the mid-1970s show more and more establishments vinifying under controlled conditions, investing in new oak casks and producing wine to be reckoned with. Fronsac has also begun to attract the investor in real estate. The excellent company of Jean-Pierre Moueix, established in Libourne, has long been a source of good Fronsac wines. They are now the owners of several estates, as are the d'Arfeuilles, *négociants* and owners of Château La Pointe in Pomerol. As well as Moueix other Libournais merchants such as Horeau-Beylot, Janoueix, Armand Moueix and René Germain are also owners or farmers of wine estates in the Fronsac area.

Fronsac is about the same size as Pomerol and consists of two *appellations* spread over six communes. The better of the two *appellations*, in theory if not necessarily in practice, is Canon-Fronsac, formerly known as Côtes Canon-Fronsac, and comes from the two communes of Saint-Michel-de-Fronsac and Fronsac itself. Surrounding Canon-Fronsac and producing about two-and-a-half times as much wine is plain Fronsac *appellation contrôlée* which, until 1976, was known as Côtes de Fronsac. This *appellation* covers part of the commune of Fronsac plus La Rivière, Saint-Germain-La-Rivière, Saint-Aignan, Saillans and part of Galgon. The soil is clayey-limestone, with some sand on the lower-lying land nearest to the Dordogne, on a limestone base, the Molasses de Frondasais. Like Saint-Emilion, the area is honeycombed with quarries and man-made caves, many of which are now used for the cultivation of mushrooms, as well as for storing wine.

Where Fronsac differs from the rest of the lesser Libournais wines is in its *encépagement*. While the remainder of the region concentrates on the Merlot, with the Cabernet Franc (or Bouchet) as an important subsidiary grape and Malbec (or Pressac) as a minor partner, Fronsac wines have somewhat less Merlot and many have Cabernet Sauvignon as well as Cabernet Franc, though growers, as in Saint-Emilion, consider the latter superior for their terrain. This blend of grapes gives the wine more backbone and a better acidity than the wines from the satellite Saint-Emilion *appellations*, a more masculine richness and longer life.

Leading Fronsac and Canon-Fronsac Producers

Château Barrabaque
Appellation: Canon-Fronsac; commune: Fronsac.
Owner: Bernard Noël.
Surface Area under Vine: 9 ha – 70% Merlot,
20% Cabernet Franc and 10% Cabernet Sauvignon.
Second Wine: B de Barrabaque.
Barrabaque is a substantial château up on the hill above Fronsac, overlooking the river Dordogne. Bernard Joël and his team produce a nicely substantial, sometimes slightly four-square wine under the basic Barrabaque name. Rather better is the new oaky Cuvée Prestige.

Château Canon-de-Brem
Château de La Dauphine
Appellation: Canon-Fronsac; commune: Fronsac.
Owner: Ets. J P Moueix.

Surface Area under Vine: 4.7 ha – 65% Merlot and
35% Cabernet Franc.
Château Canon-de-Brem lies on the main road between Fronsac and Saint-Michel with its vineyard on the slopes in front of it. What lies on the flat land running down to the river is the vineyard of Château de La Dauphine (AC Fronsac). In old editions of *Cocks and Féret*, the Bordeaux bible, the frontage of the elegant, Empire-style château illustrated Canon-de-Brem, the rear façade La Dauphine. The property makes a rich, generous wine, consistently one of the *appellation*'s best and most attractive examples.
Other wines Château Canon-Moueix, Château La Croix-Canon (both Canon-Fronsac), Château Trotanoy (Pomerol) and others.

Château Canon-Moueix
Appellation: Canon-Fronsac; commune: Fronsac.
Owner: Ets. J P Moueix.
Surface Area under Vine: 4 ha – 90% Merlot and
10% Cabernet Franc.
Owned by the same Ets. J P Moueix of Châteaux Canon-de-Brem and La Croix-Canon, and with vineyards very near to the former this is always one of the most refined and profound wines of the *appellation*, and it is usually priced accordingly. Confusingly Christian Moueix personally owns the separate and minuscule (1.2 ha) Château Canon. This is even better.
Other wines Château Canon-de-Brem, Château de La Dauphine and Château La Croix-Canon (all Canon-Fronsac), Château Trotanoy (Pomerol) and others.

Château de Carles
Appellation: Fronsac; commune: Saillans.
Owners: Antoine Chastenet de Castaing &
Stéphane Droulers.
Surface Area under Vine: 20 ha – 65% Merlot,
30% Cabernet Franc and 5% Malbec.
The château is medieval in origin with round towers at either end. The wine is plump and attractive. The Chastenet de Castaing and Droulers families also produce an oaky *tête de cuvée* called Château Haut de Carles.

Château Cassagne-Haut-Canon

Appellation: Canon-Fronsac; commune: Saint-Michel-de-Fronsac.

Owner: Jean-Jacques Duplessis.

Surface Area under Vine: 13 ha – 70% Merlot, 25% Cabernet Franc and 5% Cabernet Sauvignon.

Cassagne is old French for oak, and there are some venerable examples in the park of this attractive mid-nineteenth-century château. My experience of Jean-Jacques Dubois' wines rests entirely on the Cuvée La Truffière, in which there is 20 per cent of Cabernet Sauvignon and quite a bit more new wood. This is a sturdy wine with plenty of depth.

Château La Croix-Canon

Appellation: Canon-Fronsac; commune: Fronsac.
Owner: Ets. J P Moueix.

Surface Area under Vine: 14 ha – 70% Merlot, 25% Cabernet Franc and 5% Cabernet Sauvignon.

Second Wine: Château Bodet.

The latest (1995) Fronsac acquisition by Ets. J P Moueix, Château La Croix-Canon (formerly called Château Charlemagne) is potentially the best of all the Moueix Fronsac estates, the vineyard being splendidly situated in a little amphitheatre above the river Dordogne and most of the vines being of considerable age. This is a rich, generous, fruity and very classy wine.

Other wines Château Canon-de-Brem, Château de La Dauphine and Château Canon-Moueix (all Canon-Fronsac), Château Trotanoy (Pomerol) and others.

Château Dalem

Appellation: Fronsac; commune: Saillans.
Owner: Michel Rullier.

Surface Area under Vine: 14.5 ha – 85% Merlot, 10% Cabernet Franc and 5% Cabernet Sauvignon.

Second Wine: Château La Longua.

Michel Rullier's property is situated near Châteaux Villars and La Vieille Cure, equally consistent properties. The wine has for a long time been one of the most reliable Fronsacs. I have notes going back to 1971 when I first sampled (and bought) the 1970. It is round and full of fruit. One-quarter of the casks are new each year.

Other wine Château de La Huste (Fronsac).

Château Fontenil

Appellation: Fronsac; commune: Saillans.
Owners: Michel and Dany Rolland.

Surface Area under Vine: 8.5 ha – 85% Merlot and 15% Cabernet Franc.

Michel Rolland is one of Bordeaux's best-known oenologists and he now consults for wineries all around the world. His wife Dany is a wine chemist, too. Fontenil was acquired by the Rollands in 1986, since when they have enlarged the vineyard by a third. The wine is reliable. Never a blockbuster, it is always balanced and succulent, with a good base of oak.

Other wines Château Bertineau-Saint-Vincent (Lalande-de-Pomerol), Château Le Bon-Pasteur (Pomerol) and Chateau Rolland-Maillet (Saint-Emilion).

Château Mayne-Vieil

Appellation: Fronsac; commune: Galgon.
Owners: Sèze family.

Surface Area under Vine: 41 ha – 90% Merlot and 10% Cabernet Franc.

Second Wine: Château Moire-Martin.

This was one of the 1970 Fronsacs I bought, a purchase which turned out highly satisfactorily. Only later did I visit the Sèze family in their elegant 1860 *chartreuse* in Galgon, right at the northern limits of the *appellation*. Today there is a delicious, *super-cuvée* called Cuvée Aliénor.

Château Mazeris

Appellation: Canon-Fronsac; commune: Saint-Michel-de-Fronsac.

Owner: Christian de Cournuaud.

Surface Area under Vine: 15 ha – 85% Merlot and 15% Cabernet Franc.

Both Mazeris châteaux (see below) lie up on the slopes above Saint-Michel-de-Fronsac, the vineyards facing west over the river Dordogne. Christian de Cournuaud's wine, like Château de Carles, is sold through merchants Ets. J P Moueix and the château can call on the Moueix team for advice. The wine, refined and supple, is all the better as a result. La Part des Anges (the angels' share) is a *cuvée* from forty- to eighty-year-old vines. The family have owned the property since 1800.

CHÂTEAU MAZERIS-BELLEVUE

Appellation: Canon-Fronsac; commune: Saint-Michel-de-Fronsac.
Owner: Jacques Bussier.
Surface Area under Vine: 11 ha – 45% Merlot, 15% Cabernet Franc, 35% Cabernet Sauvignon and 5% Malbec.

Jacques Bussier, whose family have been here since 1848, makes quite a different wine from Christian de Cournuaud at Château Mazeris. The blend contains far more Cabernet, and Sauvignon at that, and far more new wood. This Fronsac wine needs time to mature and is proportionally better in the better vintages.

CHÂTEAU MOULIN-HAUT-LAROQUE

Appellation: Fronsac; commune: Saillans.
Owner: Jean-Noël Hervé.
Surface Area under Vine: 15 ha – 65% Merlot, 20% Cabernet Franc, 10% Cabernet Sauvignon and 5% Malbec.
Second Wine: Château Hervé-Laroque.

Jean-Noël Hervé's wine is another example of the strength in depth of wines from Saillans: once again these are wines of plump fruit, gently oaky (one-third new oak barrels each year) and medium to medium-full body. These are stylish examples for the medium term.

CHÂTEAU MOULIN-PEY-LABRIE

Appellation: Canon-Fronsac; commune: Fronsac.
Owners: B. & G. Hubau.
Surface Area under Vine: 6.7 ha – 70% Merlot, 10% Cabernet Franc and 20% Cabernet Sauvignon.
Second Wine: Château Moulin.

The Hubau family make their best wine, indeed one of the *appellation*'s top examples, here. A severe selection and one-third new oak each year produces a wine with more depth and concentration than most. It should not be confused with its neighbour, Château Pey-Labrie.

Other wines CHÂTEAU HAUT-LARIVEAU AND CHÂTEAU COMBES-CANON (BOTH FRONSAC).

CHÂTEAU DE LA RIVIÈRE

Appellation: Fronsac; commune: La Rivière.
Owner: Jean Leprince.
Surface Area under Vine: 53 ha – 65% Merlot, 12% Cabernet Franc, 15% Cabernet Sauvignon and 8% Malbec.
Second Wine: Château Prince de La Rivière.

The much-turreted Château de La Rivière dates from 1560 and dominates the parishes of La Rivière and Saint-Germain. For a long time it was run by the mercurial, fiercely proud Jacques Borie who used to embarrass his guests by serving his wine blind alongside First Growth Médocs. Borie sold out to Jean Leprince at the end of 1994. This is a big wine which keeps well. The grapes are machine-harvested, which is a pity as a severe sorting of the best grapes from the rest is then almost impossible.

CHÂTEAU LA VIEILLE CURE

Appellation: Fronsac; commune: Saillans.
Owners: Colin Ferenbach and associates.
Surface Area under Vine: 19 ha – 80% Merlot, 15% Cabernet Franc and 5% Cabernet Sauvignon.
Second Wine: Château Coutreau.

Much money has been invested in Château La Vieille Cure since it was taken over by a consortium of Americans in 1986. The improvement in quality is now clear to anyone who tries this charming, medium-bodied, fruity wine. Prices are not unreasonable either.

CHÂTEAU VILLARS

Appellation: Fronsac; commune: Saillans.
Owner: Jean-Claude Gaudrie.
Surface Area under Vine: 29.5 ha – 70% Merlot, 20% Cabernet Franc and 10% Cabernet Sauvignon.
Second Wine: Château Moulin-Haut-Villars.

Château Villars has been established longer than most in Saillans. The vines are old, the wine is given one-third new oak and the results are rich and substantial. The wine keeps better than most Fronsacs, up to fifteen years in the best vintages.

Other Producers of note

Fronsac CHÂTEAU CARDENEAU (SAILLANS), CHÂTEAU JEANDEMAN (FRONSAC), CHÂTEAU RICHOTEY — CUVÉE PRESTIGE (SAINT-MICHEL-DE-FRONSAC), CLOS DU ROY (SAILLANS) AND CHÂTEAU LES TROIX-CROIX (FRONSAC).

Canon-Fronsac CHÂTEAU LA FLEUR-CAILLEAU (FRONSAC), CHÂTEAU PAVILLON (FRONSAC), CHÂTEAU TOUMALIN (FRONSAC), CHÂTEAU VRAI-CANON-BOUCHÉ (FRONSAC) AND CHÂTEAU VRAI-CANON-BOYER (SAINT-MICHEL-DE-FRONSAC).

CÔTES DE CASTILLON

Surface Area (1998): 2925 ha.
Production (1998): 172,324 hl.
Colour: Red.
Grape Varieties: Merlot, Cabernet Franc (Bouchet), Cabernet Sauvignon and Malbec (Pressac).
Maximum Yield: 50 hl/ha.
Minimum Alcohol Level: 11.5°.

East of Saint-Emilion, further upstream towards the boundary with the *département* of Dordogne and the Bergerac region, is the Côtes de Castillon, an up-and-coming *appellation*. Castillon itself, an attractive outpost at the eastern extremity of the Bordeaux vineyards, is the site of the famous battle of 1453, commemorated in Shakespeare's play, *Henry VI Part One*, when after three centuries of hegemony the English were finally driven out of Bordeaux. The date, 17 July 1453, should be commemorated by claret lovers every year! The French can celebrate, English-speaking people can hold a wake.

The Castillon wines are interesting, increasingly well made and some of the best value for money among the myriad *petits châteaux*. The soil consists of gravel, sand and marl nearer the river, and becomes progressively more calcareous as the land rises to the north. The *appellation* spreads over eight communes.

Côtes de Castillon Producers of note

CHÂTEAU D'AIGUILHE (SAINT-PHILIPPE D'AIGUILHE), CHÂTEAU DE BELCIER (LES SALLES DE CASTILLON),

CHÂTEAU LAPEYRONIE (SAINTE-COLOMBE), CHÂTEAU DE PITRAY (GARDEGAN-ET-TOURTIRAC), CHÂTEAU POUPILLE (SAINTE-COLOMBE) AND CHÂTEAU ROCHER-BELLEVUE (SAINT-MAGNE-DE-CASTILLON).

BORDEAUX-CÔTES DE FRANCS

Surface Area (1998): (Red) 471 ha; (white) 14 ha.
Production (1998): (Red) 27,667 hl; (white) 525 hl.
Colour: Red.
Grape Varieties: (Red) Merlot, Cabernet Franc (Bouchet), Cabernet Sauvignon and Malbec (Pressac); (white) Sauvignon Blanc, Sémillon, Muscadelle, Ugni Blanc and Colombard.
Maximum Yield: 50 hl/ha.
Minimum Alcohol Level: 11°.

East of the Saint-Emilion satellites of Puisseguin and Lussac, Bordeaux-Côtes de Francs was created as a separate *appellation* in 1967. There are three communes, that of Montbadon having been moved from Côtes de Francs to Côtes de Castillon in 1976. This is an expanding *appellation* which has attracted several enterprising younger Libournais winemakers. The wines are good value.

Bordeaux-Côtes de Francs Producers of note

CHÂTEAU LES CHARMES-GODARD (SAINT-CIBARD), CHÂTEAU DE FRANCS (FRANCS), CHÂTEAU LACLAVERIE (SAINT-CIBARD), CHÂTEAU LA PRADE (SAINT-CIBARD) AND CHÂTEAU PUYGUÉRAUD (SAINT-CIBARD).

BOURG AND BLAYE
BOURG

Surface Area (1998): (Red) 3765 ha; (white) 32 ha.
Production (1998): (Red) 226,648 hl; (white) 1615 hl.
Colour: Red and white.
Grape Varieties: (Red) Merlot, Cabernet Franc (Bouchet), Cabernet Sauvignon and Malbec (Pressac); (white) Sauvignon Blanc, Sémillon, Muscadelle, Ugni Blanc and Colombard.

Maximum Yield: (Red) 50 hl/ha; (white) 60 hl/ha.
Minimum Alcohol Level: (Red) 10.5°; (white) 11°.

PREMIÈRES CÔTES DE BLAYE, CÔTES DE BLAYE, BLAYE

Surface Area (1998): (Red) 4912 ha ; (white) 438 ha.
Production (1998): (Red) 299,810 hl; (white) 23,892 hl.
Colour: Red and white.
Grape Varieties: (Red) Merlot, Cabernet Franc
(Bouchet), Cabernet Sauvignon and Malbec
(Pressac); (white) Sauvignon Blanc, Sémillon,
Muscadelle, Ugni Blanc and Colombard.
Maximum Yield: (Red) 50 hl/ha; (white) 60 hl/ha .
Minimum Alcohol Level: (Red) 10°; (white) 11°.

The up-and-coming areas of Bourg and Blaye lie on the right bank of the Gironde estuary and the river Dordogne. There is only one Bourg *appellation*, Côtes de Bourg (though it can be described in three ways: Côtes de Bourg, Bourg or Bourgeais), but a number for the wines of Blaye, of which Premières Côtes de Blaye is the most important. The wines are predominantly red. This is a thriving, attractive region of small villages, gently undulating countryside and neat little wine estates. Blaye is the larger of the two geographically, five times the size of its neighbour, yet produces only a marginally greater quantity of wine.

The town itself, an active fishing port, especially for *alose* (shad) during its restricted spring season and for sturgeon from which comes the local caviar, lies alongside a vast Gallo-Roman castrum, re-fortified in the seventeenth century by Vauban, the military architect.

The wines of Blaye are said to be inferior to the best of the Côtes de Bourg, but the leading estates, most of which are in the southern part of the region — much of the north is forest — are in my view the equal of the best of the Bourg. There is little difference in character between the wines of the two *appellations*. Côtes de Bourg is a more compact area and forms a semi-circle round the town of Bourg itself. The countryside is quite hilly, and there are even one or two grottoes and prehistoric caves. It is much more extensively planted than the Blaye. There are many estates whose wines are excellent

value for money. This is an active and improving area, perhaps destined to take the place of Fronsac, when the Fronsac area is fully discovered, as the 'best value' in Bordeaux. In general, like most *petits châteaux*, the wines are at their best between three and six years of the harvest.

Leading Bourg Producer

CHÂTEAU ROC DE CAMBES
Commune: Bourg.
Owner: François Mitjaville.
Surface Area under Vine: 9.6 ha – 65% Merlot,
20% Cabernet Sauvignon, 10% Cabernet Franc and
5% Malbec.
The vineyard of Roc de Cambes lies in a couple of natural amphitheatres overlooking the Gironde estuary. Like most of its neighbours, the vineyard produced unremarkable wine until the current owner took over, in the person of Francois Mitjaville of Château Terte-Roteboeuf in 1988. He set about reducing yields in the vineyard and and delaying the harvest until the grapes were really ripe (sometimes he picks a month later than his neighbours). The results are startling. The wine is better than most Saint-Emilion *grands crus classés*.
Other wine CHÂTEAU TERTRE-ROTEBOEUF (SAINT-EMILION).

Côtes de Bourg Producers of note
CHÂTEAU BRULESECAILLE (TAURIAC), CHÂTEAU FALFAS (BAYON-SUR-GIRONDE), CHÂTEAU GRAND-LAUNAY — RÉSERVE LION NOIR (TEUILLAC), CHÂTEAU GUERRY (TAURIAC), CHÂTEAU MACAY (SAMONAC) AND CHÂTEAU ROUSSET — GRANDE RÉSERVE (SAMONAC).

Côtes de Blaye Producers of note
CHÂTEAU LES BERTRANDS (REIGNAC), CHÂTEAU CHARRON — LES GRUPPE CUVÉE (SAINT-MARTIN-LACASSUADE), CHÂTEAU HAUT-BERTINERIE (CUBZENAIS), CHÂTEAU HAUT-SOCIONDO (CARS), CHÂTEAU LES JONQUEYRES (SAINT-PAUL-DE-BLAYE), CHÂTEAU PERENNE — CUVÉE PRESTIGE (SAINT-GENÈS-DE-BLAYE), CHÂTEAU SEGONZAC (SAINT-GENÈS-DE-BLAYE) AND CHÂTEAU DES TOURTES (SAINT-CAPRAIS-DE-BLAYE).

GENERIC BORDEAUX

BORDEAUX ROUGE/BORDEAUX BLANC

Surface Area (1998): (Red) 39,023 ha; (white) 9045 ha.

Production (1998): (Red) 2,421,902 hl; (white) 539,377 hl.

Colour: Red and white.

Maximum Yield: (Red) 55 hl/ha; (white) 65 hl/ha.

Minimum Alcohol Level: (Red) 9.5°; (white) 11°.

BORDEAUX SUPÉRIEUR

Surface Area (1998): (Red and rosé) 9215 ha; (white) 545 ha.

Production (1998): (Red and rosé) 544,796 hl; (white) 1695 hl.

Colour: Red, rosé and white.

Maximum Yield: 50 hl/ha.

Minimum Alcohol Level: (Red and rosé) 10°; (white) 12°.

BORDEAUX CLAIRET OR ROSÉ

Surface Area (1998): 1611 ha.

Production (1998): 102,686 hl.

Colour: Rosé.

Maximum Yield: 55 hl/ha.

Minimum Alcohol Level: 9.5°.

CRÉMANT DE BORDEAUX

Surface Area (1998): (Rosé) 6 ha; (white) 92 ha.

Production (1998): (Rosé) 168 hl; (white) 5752 hl.

Colour: Rosé and white.

Maximum Yield: 65 hl/ha.

Minimum Alcohol Level: 9.5° as still wine.

FOR ALL THE ABOVE:

Grape Varieties: (Red and rosé) Cabernet Sauvignon, Cabernet Franc, Carmenère, Merlot, Malbec and Petit Verdot; (white) Sémillon, Sauvignon Blanc, Muscadelle plus (maximum in total of 30%) Merlot Blanc, Colombard, Mauzac Ondenc, Ugni Blanc (Saint-Emilion des Charentes). These subsidiary varieties are not permitted for Bordeaux Supérieur.

With over 48,000 hectares of vines, today producing almost 3 million hectolitres of wine in an average vintage, Bordeaux is by quite a long way the largest *appellation* in France. Côtes du Rhône is the only other *appellation contrôlée* with an annual production of over 2 million hectolitres.

This is your basic Bordeaux *rouge* (and to a lesser extent *blanc* and rosé), the standby of many a wine list. It should be at least dependable. It is, after all, what you judge a winebuyer's expertise by – for all you need to buy Château Lafite and the like is a chequebook. Sadly, the price the wine fetches does not enable the grower to be as painstaking as he or she should be and today much of the production at this basic level is substandard. The consumer can do better elsewhere.

Bordeaux Supérieur is much the same, only with half a degree extra of alcohol for the red wine. There is only a small quantity of Crémant and it is rarely seen. Although made by the Traditional or Champagne method, it is not as exciting as other Crémants from Burgundy, the Loire and Alsace.

VINS DE PAYS

Vin de Pays de La Gironde

I have never encountered this departmental *vin de pays*, and was unaware it existed until I started researching all the *vins de pays* for my *Wines of France* (1991). The wine can be red, rosé and white, from the usual Bordeaux grape varieties, and comes from vineyards in the *département* not classified for AC Bordeaux.

Vin de Pays Charentais

Another *vin de pays* is produced in the Charente (Cognac country), just to the north of the Gironde. Like its Armagnac equivalent in Gascony, this *vin de pays* is the base white wine, before distillation, and likewise the grape is the Ugni Blanc, locally called the Saint-Emilion. The local co-operatives are the chief sources of this wine. I find the Gascon wine rather more interesting and, in my experience, white Vin de Pays Charentais is shallow and acid. Red and rosé wines are also authorised. They are thin and rustic.

BURGUNDY

B URGUNDY IS IN MANY WAYS THE MOST CONFUSING, the most frustrating, the most inconsistent and the most individual of all the world's great winemaking areas. The wines can be sublime; so often they are disappointing. The best are difficult to obtain and they are certainly expensive. The region is complex, as is the structure of its wine economy. There is no easy classification of the best hundred or so wines or properties towards which to point the newcomer; indeed there is a plethora of *appellations*, villages, vineyards and producers. Yet the consumer should not allow himself to be put off. Great bottles of red Burgundy may seem far rarer than red Bordeaux, but when they come they are nectar. They are worth searching for.

The individuality and the inconsistency of red Burgundy arises from the Pinot Noir grape and the wine it produces. When the season is fine, the yield is restricted and the wine-maturing is expert, the wine can be exquisite. When the reverse is the case, to a greater extent than in Bordeaux, the result is drear. Good Pinot Noirs now hail from elsewhere in the world, from California and the Pacific North-West in the United States, from Australia and New Zealand, from Sancerre and Alsace in France, even from Eastern Europe. But they are good rather than great. So far Burgundy seems to be the only region which can produce great Pinot Noir.

The frustration and confusion of Burgundy lies in its size and diversity. It is a small area, smaller than we realise. The whole region, including Beaujolais, which should really be regarded as a separate vineyard area, produces less than half the wine of Bordeaux; excluding Beaujolais the fraction is more like one-fifth. Moreover, Burgundy is a fragmented region. In Bordeaux and elsewhere in France there is generally one *appellation* per district with a large number of sizeable estates, most of which are self-sufficient in wine terms. Each estate will produce only one or two wines and under a clearly recognisable château or domaine name. In Burgundy, each village – and indeed some of the best individual *climats* or vineyards – may have its own *appellation*. These vineyards are themselves tiny, and will be divided

among dozens of different owners. One domaine of no more than a few hectares may have its holdings spread over a number of different villages and vineyards. The result is a multitude of different wines, whose production figures are numbered in dozens rather than in thousands of cases. The consequence of this lack of economy of scale is a further reduction in the possibility of great wine. If a domaine only makes three casks of Chambertin what does it use for topping up? Can it afford to isolate the yield of the younger vines? How can it properly control the fermentation of such a small quantity of must?

Historically, the solution to this problem has lain in the hands of the local merchant or *négociant*. The merchant will buy up small parcels of wine and blend them together, or increasingly these days enter into a contract with a grower to purchase his grapes and vinify them together with others. Thus this complex fragmentation is transformed into quantities of uniform wine of a more sensible commercial size which the merchant will market under his own name. A large company such as Maison Louis Jadot may have contracts with a dozen or more growers in Meursault or Gevrey-Chambertin. They will produce just one village wine from each of these communes, but there will be enough for all their potential customers. How very sensible, you might think.

Yet there are a number of disadvantages. There are first good *négociants* and bad *négociants* just as there are good growers and bad growers. There are those who are prepared to pay up to a quality and those who insist on buying down to a price. Sadly there are some who are not above a bit of sly manipulation, promoting a village wine to a higher *premier cru*, or even blending in a bit of wine from outside the region, though this is rarer these days than it used to be. It is true to say that there is more genuine merchant Burgundy on the market than there was a generation or more ago. What is not true is that the standard of quality – the sheer palatability – of ordinary merchant Burgundy wine has improved. Regrettably most is very disappointing.

BURGUNDY

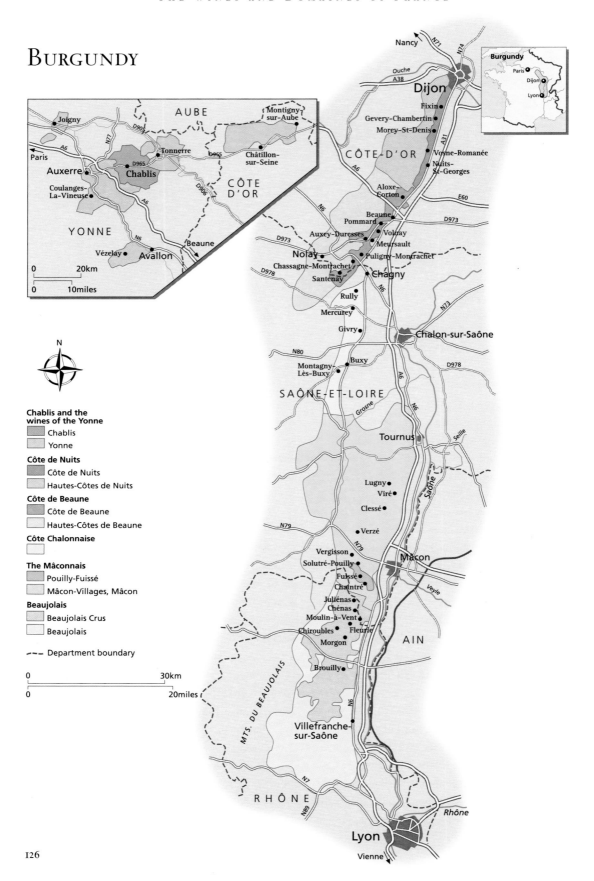

Chablis and the wines of the Yonne
- Chablis
- Yonne

Côte de Nuits
- Côte de Nuits
- Hautes-Côtes de Nuits

Côte de Beaune
- Côte de Beaune
- Hautes-Côtes de Beaune

Côte Chalonnaise

The Mâconnais
- Pouilly-Fuissé
- Mâcon-Villages, Mâcon

Beaujolais
- Beaujolais Crus
- Beaujolais

--- Department boundary

There are further drawbacks to merchant Burgundy wine. The individuality of the grower's wine is submerged into the melting-pot of the blend. It will take on the house style of that particular merchant. If I buy a wine from, say, two neighbouring châteaux in Saint-Julien, each will express its own character, influenced by its soil, the personality and skill of the winemaker (and, in this case, the *encépagement*). Each will be different. But both will be recognisably Saint-Julien. In Burgundy on the other hand, it is usually far easier to pick out the same *négociant* in a range of wines than to pick out the village from whence the wines have come. Too often the house style obliterates the communal character. Finally there is yet another important deterrent to buying merchant wine, however easier it may be so to do. The best are even more expensive than the best grower's wines — and these are expensive enough.

Yet for all its exasperation Burgundy is a delightful area, and the rewards for those who travel there and are prepared to devote a little time to uncovering its secrets and to seeking out the best growers are great. It is, for a start, a much more attractive part of the world than Bordeaux. The food is better and the region abounds in friendly little *auberges* and bistros where you can eat not only stylishly and abundantly, but inexpensively. The growers themselves, once you have broken down the traditional French suspicion of foreigners and outsiders, are genuinely welcoming. There is little of the *de haut en bas* stand-offish reception one occasionally meets in the grand châteaux of Bordeaux.

Geographically there is nothing homogenous about Burgundy. The region extends from Sens in the north to Lyon in the south; from the banks of the upper Loire to the foothills of the Jura. It includes the forests, the valleys and the escarpments of the Morvan as well as the rolling pastures of the Charollais and the marshy *étangs* of the Bresse. It is an area rich in history and in ecclesiastical architecture; of the abbey of Cluny, the basilica of Sainte-Madelaine at Vezelay, the Hôtel-Dieu in Beaune and the palace of the Dukes of Burgundy in Dijon. And of the more humble and charming but no less impressive Romanesque churches of the Brionnais and southern Mâconnais. Gastronomically Burgundy is

a plentiful and rich part of France. There are the plump, sleek, coffee-coloured Charollais cattle, the *appellation contrôlée* corn-fed chickens of the Bresse, the smoked Morvan hams, *jambons persillés* and *escargots*, and a multitude of cheeses and freshwater fish. In the north among the Auxerrois vineyards you will see cherry trees and in the south in the Beaujolais you will find walnut and almond orchards. Throughout Burgundy the locals will devote a substantial portion of their garden to the cultivation of fresh vegetables, and the most gastronomic will have their favourite place in the woods for wild mushrooms and toadstools, *chanterelles*, *morilles* and *cèpes*.

And, of course, there is the wine. There are superlative reds (Chambertin and Romanée-Conti) and incomparable whites (Le Montrachet and Corton-Charlemagne). But there are also plenty of increasingly good bottles at a more affordable price: Givry, Mercurey, and to a lesser extent, Rully in the Côte Chalonnaise produce red wine from the Pinot Noir which if not as concentrated or as full-bodied as a Gevrey-Chambertin, will nevertheless have all the delicate fruit of this fascinating variety; and have the advantage of maturing sooner. Chorey, Savigny, Santenay and Maranges offer similar bargains.

For Chardonnay lovers there are the wines of Pouilly-Fuissé, Saint-Véran, Rully and Mercurey, as well as those of Saint-Aubin, Saint-Romain, Auxey-Duresses and Pernand-Vergelesses, plus a little bit of Fixin and Marsannay at the northern end of the Côte de Nuits.

Bear in mind also that you may well get a much better wine under a simple 'Bourgogne' label from a high-class domaine than something supposedly more distinguished but at an inflated price from a less reputable source. These top domaines are meticulous about separating the not-quite-so-good from the best; but the lesser *cuvées* can nevertheless prove excellent value for money. You need to buy from a specialist, though, someone who has done his homework and has built up a personal relationship with a grower and his family over a number of years. In Burgundy, rather more than elsewhere in France, small is beautiful. Good growers' wines are often better and cheaper than the equivalent from a *négociant*. The difficulty is running them to earth.

HISTORY

The origins of Burgundian viticulture lie buried in history but there is little in the way of actual evidence. Wine enjoyment by the locals obviously preceded actual cultivation, but it is difficult to pinpoint precisely when the first vines were planted on the slopes of the Côte d'Or. It was not until after Caesar's great victory at Alesia in 52 BC and the imposition of Roman subjugation in Gaul, that conditions became ripe for such a long-term project as the cultivation of the vine. Phoenician traders from the Levant had brought wine to France some five centuries previously, setting up a trading station at Marseille from which they travelled up through France and even across the Channel in search of tin from Cornwall. It seems clear that the Phoenicians also introduced the vine and viticultural techniques to southern France.

But how long did it take for this culture to spread up the Rhône Valley and into Burgundy? It is not until the second century AD that there is firm evidence of local viticulture in Burgundy.

But there is another theory – a seductive local tradition which still continues today – that the vine was brought back from northern Italy by a returning Celtic tribe, the Aedui, in about 200 BC. The ancestors of the Aedui, seduced by the wine they had enjoyed at the hands of itinerant travellers, had invaded the rich plains of Lombardy some two hundred years previously. Forced north later by the expanding Roman Empire, some returned to their homeland. And, having abandoned their nomadic instincts in the meanwhile and learned about viticulture, it was natural that they should return bringing with them the vine.

Whatever the origins, the vine was certainly firmly established by AD150. A panegyric thanking the Emperor Constantine for reducing taxes in the locality in AD 312 gives a convincing illustration of not only long-established but well-regarded vineyards.

Burgundy seems to have survived the fall of the Roman Empire and subsequent barbarian invasion with comparative ease. Indeed it was one of these tribes, in the interregnum between the Romans and the arrival of the Frankish King Clovis in the early sixth century, which has given the area its name. The Burgondes were an obscure people who settled in the region in the second half of the fifth century. They had arrived via Germany and the Rhône Valley and remained until AD 534 when they were defeated in battle and absorbed into the Frankish kingdom. From Clovis onwards the story has two themes: the evolution of Burgundy as a political entity – first an independent kingdom until the early eighth century, and then an autonomous duchy, considerably enlarged by dynastic marriages in the later Middle Ages – and the rise of the influence of the church. In no other region of France was the church to play such an important role. Its power was immense, its viticultural holdings huge, and its hegemony, alongside the equally significant estates of the local nobility, was to continue until the French Revolution.

The first records of gifts of land including vines to a local Burgundian abbey date from AD 587, when Gontran, king of Burgundy, made a donation to the Abbey of Saint Benigne in Dijon. From then on the gifts came thick and fast. The Emperor Charlemagne donated part of the hillside between Pernand and Aloxe to the Abbey of Saulieu in AD 775, and with the rise of Cluny, founded by the Benedictines in AD 910 in the Mâconnais and the breakaway Cistercian abbey near Nuits-Saint-Georges at Cîteaux, founded in AD 1098, the development of the vineyards increased as did the fame of their wines.

Burgundy reached its apogee under the successive reigns of the four royal Valois Dukes, Philip the Bold (*Le Hardi*) (1364-1404) John the Fearless (*Sans Peur*) (1404-1419), Philip the Good (1419-1467) and Charles the Bold (*Le Téméraire*) (1467-1477). The four built up an empire which stretched from Holland to Savoy. Their power was immense, greater in influence, in land and in wealth, than their nominal liege-lords, the kings of France themselves, with whom they were normally at loggerheads, if not actually at war. It was Philip the

Good who appointed an Autun minor nobleman, Nicolas Rolin, as his chancellor, the controller of his court and its exchequer, and the most influential official post in Burgundy. In 1443 Rolin endowed a religious foundation and hospital, the Hôtel-Dieu, in Beaune. This was the origin of what is now the famous Hospices. While Rolin did not in fact donate any vineyards (though both he and his wife Guigone de Salins are commemorated in two of the wines sold by the Hospices), this charitable institution soon began to receive gifts of land and now possesses 62 hectares, all except three in the Côte de Beaune. The auction of the wines made from the Hospices' vineyard holdings is traditionally held during the weekend of the Trois Glorieuses in November and is normally regarded as setting the trend for the price of the Burgundian vintage as a whole.

Valois Burgundy collapsed with the death of Charles the Bold before the walls of Nancy in 1477. His infant daughter was already betrothed to the Hapsburg Emperor Maximilian of Austria. The duke had no other heirs, and in the vacuum Burgundy was rapidly annexed into the kingdom of France. Nevertheless it was some time before the wines of Burgundy were more appreciated in Paris than in their traditional export markets of the Low Countries and Flanders – markets which are still vigorous today. There had been a significant Protestant population in Burgundy, and the expulsion of the Huguenots from France after the Revocation of the Edict of Nantes in 1685 only served to increase the opportunity of sales abroad. It was not until the eighteenth century, following the success of the surgeon Fagon in curing Louis XIV of a fistula by dosing him with Romanée-Saint-Vivant, coupled with the improvement in communications between Burgundy and the capital, that the wines began to be preferred in Paris to those of the Loire.

The consequences of the French Revolution were decisive and far-reaching, not only in the ownership and structure of the Burgundian vineyards but on the market for its wines. Both the church and the aristocracy were dispossessed of their land. The great estates were broken up and sold off, though at first the best individual vineyards were not fragmented. This happened later as a result of the Code Napoléon, the change in the French laws of inheritance promulgated in 1790. Primogeniture was abolished. Henceforth a man's estate must be divided equally among his children.

The result, two centuries on, is that the Burgundian vineyard is the biggest and most complicated jigsaw in the world. Vineyards, parts of vineyards, even individual rows of vines have been divided and sub-divided over the generations as the effect of the Code Napoléon has remorselessly surged on. Today some of the holdings are so small that it is inevitable that fraud must occur and that the yield of one *climat* (vineyard) must be vinified with the crop of another. The most notorious example of the Code Napoléon is Clos Vougeot. This vineyard, the largest of the Côte de Nuits' *grands crus*, was not broken up until 1889, when it was sold off to six different owners. The 50 or so hectares are now divided into over a hundred different plots, shared between some eighty different owners.

Having lost one market, the church and nobility, Burgundy was soon to gain another. Napoleon was said to drink only Chambertin, and this helped to promote the wines of this commune. With the rise in population and the arrival of nineteenth-century *bourgeois* prosperity the demand for Burgundy grew: so much so that abuse became rife. Blending with inferior wine became widespread. With the fragmentation of the vineyards came the rise of the *négociant*, the activities of the most nefarious of which, in the days before the *appellation contrôlée* laws, could not be controlled.

As elsewhere in France, the triple scourges of oidium, phylloxera and mildew dealt a devastating blow to Burgundy. In Burgundy the effect was yet more severe as a result of the opening up of the Paris-Lyon-Marseille railway line in 1856, bringing cheap Midi wines within easy reach of the capital. The result was a contraction of the Burgundian vineyard. Hitherto vines had continued uninterruptedly from Sens, north of Chablis, as far south as Dijon. Before phylloxera there had been 31,000 hectares of vineyards in the Côte d'Or and 40,000 in the Yonne, most of them, it is fair to say, planted with inferior varieties producing *vin ordinaire*, not with Pinot Noir or Chardonnay. In the harsh economic conditions which were to follow and continue until the 1950s even the vineyards in Chablis itself almost disappeared. Even today in the Côte d'Or there are only some 8500 hectares of *appellation contrôlée* vineyards. Phylloxera, however, had one positive consequence. It reduced the area under vine to only the most suitable sites.

The 1980s have seen some dramatic changes in Burgundy. Led by growers such as Henri Gouges and the Marquis d'Angerville in the 1930s and encouraged by buyers such as Frank Schoonmaker and Alexis Lichine, the best estates were encouraged to forsake their traditional customer, the Beaune *négociant*, and to mature, bottle and sell their wine direct. Since 1975 this move-

ment has accelerated. It is now estimated that 40 per cent of the Côte d'Or crop is estate-bottled and the percentage of the better wines is even greater.

There has been a dramatic improvement in the quality of the winemaking and a lessening of the traditional Burgundian suspicion of outsiders and petty jealousies among neighbours. The new generation of winemakers have all been to wine school together and friendships have been made between former rival families. They have formed unofficial tasting groups, they exchange information among themselves and even travel abroad to other winemaking regions to see how the Pinot Noir is grown elsewhere.

THE WINES

Burgundy consists of five main wine regions – or four if you regard the Beaujolais as a separate area as many do. These are Chablis, the Côte d'Or, the Côte Chalonnaise, the Mâconnais and finally the Beaujolais. Chablis and its satellites, the red and white wines of the Auxerrois and Saint-Bris, lie isolated from the rest of Burgundy some 130 kilometres northwest of Dijon, almost halfway to Paris. The remaining four regions merge into one another in a north-south line between Dijon and Lyon on the western side of the valley of the river Saône.

Unlike Bordeaux and the southern Rhône Burgundy is not a very intensive vineyard area. Only 2 per cent of the *département* of the Côte d'Or is vineyard, and not much more in either the Saône-et-Loire (covering the Chalonnais and Mâconnais regions) or in the Rhône (confusingly the Beaujolais vineyards are in the Rhône *département*). Looking at a wine map, the area seems to be one continual vineyard south of Dijon but it is only in the best sites that the vine has been left to flourish. Largely these exist on the slopes where the uplands to the west fall down into the flatter plains of the east. Up in the hills it is too exposed and too cold for vines and in the lowlands it is too marshy and too alluvial.

The heart of Burgundy is the Côte d'Or, the Golden Slope. The Côte d'Or is not so much a ridge of hills as

the eastern perimeter of the hilly plateau known as the Morvan. It extends south of Dijon, through Nuits-Saint-Georges and Beaune, and finally peters out just below Santenay, west of Chagny, a distance as the crow flies of 55 kilometres. The vines lie on the eastern or south-eastern-facing slopes of this ridge, facing towards the flat lands of the Saône. At the top of the slope the soil is too barren and exposed, at the bottom it is too rich and alluvial. Only in a narrow band – hardly a kilometre or two wide – between the two extremes is the vine planted. Only in an even more confined position on mid-slope at about 275 metres above sea level do all the ingredients of soil, drainage, aspect, protection and mesoclimate unite to provide the perfect environment needed for wines of quality.

The soil structure of the Côte d'Or is limestone, but limestone of a wide number of different origins, constituencies and admixtures. It is a complex mixture of elements of different rocks which have outcropped and decomposed, been washed down the slope and been carried back up again. This scree has been mixed with marl, clay, sand and pebbles. Broadly speaking at the top of the slope is the most calcareous and the surface layer above the bedrock is at its thinnest; at the bottom there is more silt and clay and the soil is deeper. It is also more humid here. In general white wines will do best where

SURFACE AREA AND PRODUCTION (1998 HARVEST)

APPELLATIONS	SURFACE AREA (HA)		PRODUCTION (HL)	
	RED & ROSÉ	WHITE	RED & ROSÉ	WHITE
GENERIC WINES (BOURGOGNE)				
(INCLUDING HAUTES-CÔTES)				
YONNE	581	775	32,309	53,855
CÔTE D'OR	2190	1321	113,281	83,706
SAÔNE-ET-LOIRE	2292	1923	132,942	114,251
TOTAL GENERIC WINES	9082		530,344	
CHABLIS				
PETIT CHABLIS	–	506	–	29,057
CHABLIS	–	2716	–	160,972
CHABLIS PREMIER CRU	–	739	–	42,460
CHABLIS GRAND CRU	–	106	–	5080
TOTAL CHABLIS	–	4067	–	237,569
IRANCY	122		6415	
SAUVIGNON-DE-SAINT-BRIS	–	97	–	6872
CÔTE D'OR				
CÔTE DE NUITS, VILLAGE WINES	1173	38	51,546	1787
CÔTE DE NUITS, PREMIERS CRUS	388	8	15,017	315
CÔTE DE BEAUNE, VILLAGE WINES	1398	635	62,011	29,904
CÔTE DE BEAUNE, PREMIERS CRUS	969	411	39,898	18,674
GRANDS CRUS	360	84	11,907	3664
TOTAL CÔTE D'OR	4288	906	180,379	54,344
	5194		234,723	
SAÔNE-ET-LOIRE				
CÔTE CHALONNAISE	763	633	37,832	31,684
MÂCONNAIS	765	4766	45,149	277,349
REST OF CÔTE D'OR (MARANGES)	164	3	7500	128
TOTAL SAÔNE-ET-LOIRE	1692	5424	90,481	309,161
	7116		399,642	
BEAUJOLAIS				
BEAUJOLAIS, BEAUJOLAIS SUPÉRIEUR	10,182	141	662,890	9059
BEAUJOLAIS-VILLAGES	6101	46	361,389	2983
BEAUJOLAIS CRUS	6394	–	366,974	–
TOTAL BEAUJOLAIS	22,683	187	1,391,253	12,042
	22,830		1,403,295	
COTEAUX DU LYONNAIS	304	25	19,363	1587
TOTAL RED AND WHITE WINES	34,152	14,964	1,966,423	873,387
TOTAL BURGUNDY	49,116		2,839,810	

the limestone is dominant or even chalky; red wines are more suitable where there is more clay or marl.

The Côte d'Or is divided in two by marble quarries at Corgoloin and Comblanchien to form the Côte de Nuits in the north and the Côte de Beaune in the south. The Côte de Nuits is narrower and steeper and faces predominantly east, the Côte de Beaune is wider, more gently sloping and faces more to the south. This is predominantly a red wine region. Excluding generic wine, 75 per cent of the production is red. Almost all the white wine comes from the four Côte de Beaune communes of Meursault, Puligny-Montrachet, Chassagne-Montrachet and Pernand-Vergelesses. But only Meursault and Puligny-Montrachet are predominantly white wine communes.

Up in the hills behind the towns of Nuits-Saint-Georges and Beaune are the Hautes-Côtes, logically divided into the Hautes-Côtes de Nuits and the Hautes-Côtes de Beaune. This is a relatively new winemaking area, the *appellations* dating only from 1961. Modern techniques, particularly those of using clones more resistant to the cooler mesoclimates in these uplands and mechanical harvesting, have made wine production in the Hautes-Côtes more viable. The wine made here is almost entirely red.

Across the river Dheune and the Canal du Centre from Santenay at the southern end of the Côte de Beaune lies the commune of Bouzeron, the northernmost wine commune in the Côte Chalonnaise. The soil structure is similar but this is a much smaller vineyard area. There are only another four Chalonnais communes which produce wine, yet the distance from Bouzeron in the north to Montagny in the south is as much as from Santenay to Beaune. The vineyards are restricted to the best sites which lie mainly on the west side of the road which runs down from Chagny towards Cluny, the D981. Paradoxically it is marginally colder in the Côte Chalonnaise than further north, so the harvest begins a week or so later than in the Côte de Nuits, itself a week after the Côte de Beaune. The wines have less definition, less body and less concentration. They are predominantly red, even though this has traditionally been the centre for the sparkling wines of Burgundy.

As the Chalonnais hills lie separate from the Côte d'Or, so the Mâconnais hills are themselves distinct from those of the Chalonnais, across the valley of the river Grosne. The Mâconnais soil is limestone again but the wines are largely white, particularly in the south around the Pouilly-Fuissé *appellation*. The area begins to the west of Tournus and effectively ends when the limestone gives way to the granite of the Beaujolais just below Mâcon and Pouilly-Fuissé on the borders of the Saône-et-Loire et Rhône *départements*.

Finally we come to the Beaujolais. On a map the area seems to be no larger than the Mâconnais, yet this is a much more intensively cultivated vineyard area. The region can be divided into two: the northern, superior half, based on granite soil, and the southern section which is once again limestone. Beaujolais is one of the world's most successful and popular wines.

Surface Area and Production

Slowly but surely since the end of the Second World War, and particularly since 1970, the whole Burgundian vineyard area has expanded, to a point where it has now reach saturation point, at least as far as non-generic wines are concerned. Chablis, in particular, has increased in size almost beyond recognition.

Inevitably, this increase in surface area has led to an increase in production. The first generation of disease-resistant clones has produced yields that are too high and quality has been compromised. Growers have learned that the Pinot Noir cannot be pushed too far, and the most dedicated are increasingly conscientious about keeping yields in check. The average yield in a top red wine *grand cru* is perhaps 30 hl/ha, 60 per cent of that in a top Bordeaux estate. Today's top growers will prune and then de-bud (leaving it to a 'green harvest' in July is a waste of time,) to six bunches for Pinot Noir and eight for Chardonnay. This will give roughly 35hl/ha of red wine and 42hl/ha for white: the *rendement de base*.

The harvest of 1982, when over 3 million hectolitres of wine were produced in Burgundy and 309,000 hectolitres in the Côte d'Or (not including generic wine), looks like remaining Burgundy's largest crop for some time to come.

WINEMAKING

The general principles for the vinification and maturation of red and white wines are covered on pages 19-25 but throughout Burgundy you will find much less conformity between one cellar and the next. It is a region of passionate individualists, each with his own views on how the wine should be made. This is one of its fascinations. The structure of the Burgundian vineyard does not lend itself to anything on a large scale. Thus not only are there few harvesting machines, except in Chablis and the Mâconnais, but neither are there batteries of large stainless-steel fermentation vats except in those establishments belonging to either major *négociants* who buy in grapes or to the larger co-operatives. Winemaking is much more artisanal, more modest than in Bordeaux.

Both hail and the incidence of rot are more prevalent in Burgundy than in Bordeaux, and the necessity of picking through the fruit, either in the vineyard or on arrival at the winery, is therefore of crucial importance. This process is known as *triage*. In some years as much as a third of the crop might be rejected. Red wines are normally vinified in small wooden *foudres* with removable tops, metal vats or large casks. Leaving a proportion of the stalks in the macerating wine, in order to extract more body and tannin, is also a more usual occurrence in Burgundy than in Bordeaux, though declining. The breaking-up of the *chapeau* or cap of grape skins which floats up to the top of the vat during fermentation (called *pigeage*) is achieved by the use of poles or even by feet, the men balancing themselves on the top of the fermenting must and treading down the *chapeau* for half an hour to an hour two or three times a day.

In order to increase the ratio of pulp to juice and to concentrate the eventual wine in abundant vintages, a process called *saigner* (to bleed) is also performed. Before fermentation a certain proportion, between 5 and 15 per cent of the free-run juice, is tapped off. This is separately fermented and will result in a rather weak rosé wine, but it means that the remainder of the wine will be more concentrated. A new and better technique but more expensive than *saigner*, is to invest in a concentrating machine. This eliminates excess water but without having to warm up the wine. While these are useful, indeed admirable techniques, the processes are criticised in some quarters for being no substitute for severe pruning, followed by crop-thinning when necessary during the summer before the harvest.

The use of 100 per cent new oak is less prevalent in Burgundy than in Bordeaux. While some estates such as the Domaine de La Romanée-Conti, swear by it, others will cite the delicacy of the Pinot Noir and the care required not to dominate its flavour with the taste of new wood as a reason for not using so much wood. In most estates only the *grands crus* are totally matured in new wood. There are some winemakers who abjure it entirely. For the same reason, that the Pinot Noir is a less tannic, less substantial wine, bottling takes place a few months earlier, twelve to eighteen months after the vintage being the norm rather than eighteen to twenty-four months as in Bordeaux.

White wines are vinified very much in a conventional way: pressing, *débourbage* (settling of the lees), fermentation in wood for the top wines, in tank for the lesser wines, and earlier bottling than for the reds. Nearly all the top, even village, white wines of the Côte de Beaune are fermented and matured in wood, and the practice is spreading south to the Côte Chalonnaise and to Pouilly-Fuissé. Unlike in Bordeaux, where the malolactic fermentation of the top white wines is often avoided this often takes place in Burgundy in order to ensure the correct acidity level. There are some growers who make the error of excessively warming the cellar in order to induce this to occur soon after the first fermentation. This often produces a rather cooked, oaky flavour and results in a wine which is a bit flabby.

Négociant means merchant in French and, traditionally in Burgundy, the merchant not only deals in the wine, he is responsible for its maturation (*élevage*) and eventual bottling, so you may see the words *négociant-éleveur* on the label. Today many merchants are also important vineyard owners as well and also vinify the grapes of those suppliers contracted to them. As the fragmentation of the Burgundian vineyards increased and the size of the domaines declined, the importance of the merchant rose. He would buy the wines from a large range of small domaines, and blend them into *cuvées* of economic size for the mass market. The role of the *négociant* here, in fine wines as well as in basic Burgundy, is of far greater importance than anywhere else in France outside Champagne and Alsace.

Most of the major Burgundian merchants have their headquarters in the centre of the Côte d'Or in the towns of Beaune or Nuits-Saint-Georges.

The Style of the Wine

Red Burgundy is made exclusively from the Pinot Noir grape. There are one or two minor exceptions – in the Yonne some rare local grapes can be incorporated into the blend; in the Beaujolais for some obscure reason the wines of the *cru* villages (made from the Gamay) can be declassified to Bourgogne Rouge; elsewhere the Pinot Liebault and Pinot Beurot (the Pinot Gris or Tokay d' Alsace) are allowed – but essentially the Pinot Noir makes red Burgundy and red Burgundy tastes of the Pinot Noir. Red Burgundy is a wine of finesse, subtlety, delicacy, fragrance and complexity: not, essentially, a wine of power and substance. Yes, it is a wine of concentration and intensity of flavour, but this comes in terms of a precious stone rather than a lump of granite.

Despite the difficulties of production and the susceptibilities of the Pinot Noir to overproduction, vagaries of climate and poor vinification, there is one important feature that saves the day: the fact that mature, low-yielding vines in the best *climats* in Burgundy will always produce wine of subtlety and depth, even if the climatic conditions are inauspicious – provided of course the fruit does not rot. In this respect red Burgundy is helped by the fact that it is not as tannic a wine as Bordeaux. It is essentially a wine of elegance, and this elegance is not swamped by unripe tannins in unripe vintages. In contrast with Bordeaux I would rather drink a wine of a top *climat* in a poor vintage than a village or communal wine of a great

vintage. Even in the worst years good winemaking, old vines and prestigious land will produce wine of individuality and finesse. And even if the wine is a bit lean at the outset, a few years in bottle will round it off. Moreover, the competence of the grower is all-important and the name of the producer is the most vital piece of information on the label. For this reason vintage charts in Burgundy are even more misleading than they are in other wine regions.

While the lesser white wines of Burgundy are vinified in stainless steel or concrete vats and bottled early without ever coming into contact with oak, the best wines are both fermented and matured in wood, a percentage of which is new. It is the blend of subtle, ripe, opulent, nutty, buttery fruit and oak which is the true taste of fine white Burgundy, one of the great wines of the world. It ages very well in bottle.

The flavours of different white Burgundies obviously vary according to where the grapes are grown as well as to how the wine is made. Chablis will be crisper and more racy; the acidity level will be higher – though the Chardonnay does not produce excessively acidic-tasting wine – and the wine will be less fat. Classic Côte de Beaune will be the most complex and perfectly balanced of all white Burgundy, and the wines of the Côte Chalonnaise and Mâconnais will have less depth and mature faster. Côte Chalonnaise is leaner and less easy to drink than the riper wines of the Mâconnais.

There is also a little Burgundy rosé made mainly from Pinot Noir. Most of it comes from Marsannay at the northern end of the Côte de Nuits and the wine is raspberry/strawberry-flavoured, racy and elegant. I find it delicious. It is for early drinking.

Crémant de Bourgogne is the regional sparkling wine (there are lesser, branded sparkling wines made in the region but not with wine from the region). Crémant de Bourgogne is made by the Traditional or Champagne method, as are Crémant de La Loire and Crémant d' Alsace, and like Champagne, the second fermentation takes place in the bottle. All the Burgundian white grape varieties can be employed, but often a mixture is used, the higher acidity of the Aligoté and other grapes blending with the fatness of the Chardonnay.

When to Drink the Wines

Red Burgundy matures faster than red Bordeaux but this is not to say that it does not last as long. Moreover, though it never has the intensity of colour of a red Bordeaux, the colour seems to be more stable and, indeed, even to deepen, at least initially, as the wine ages. Côte de Beaunes are less full than Côte de Nuits, and mature faster. *Premier cru* wines are normally more advanced than *grand cru*, and village wines are ready for drinking earlier still, as you would expect.

Burgundy is such a complex area, with so many different styles of wine, that it is almost impossible to generalise about how long to suggest a wine should be kept. I would start drinking a red village wine from a lighter Côte de Beaune commune such as Volnay but from a good vintage five years after the harvest. The fullest *grands crus* of the Côte de Nuits — say Chambertin — would need twelve years. In lesser vintages the wines will mature more quickly. The top white wines will also develop in bottle: a *premier cru* Chablis for four years, a *grand cru* for seven or eight before fully mature. White wines from the Côte de Beaune should be kept for six years for a *premier cru* and ten years for a *grand cru*.

Beaujolais and Mâconnais (both red and white) are made for drinking early, as early as a month after the harvest in the case of Beaujolais Nouveau. Exceptionally, the weightier Beaujolais *crus* such as Moulin-à-Vent will keep for several years. But it is best to consume them, and most of the white wines except the very finest Pouilly-Fuissés, within eighteen months or two years of the harvest. Crémant de Bourgogne is normally produced as a non-vintage wine and is intended to be drunk within a year or two of bottling.

Burgundy Vintages

1998 The weather posed problems throughout the growing season. There was frost at Easter, which halved the crop in some *climats* on the slope, the *premiers crus* being more advanced than the vines on the flat land below. The damage affected the Pinot Noir wines in the Côte de Nuits and Pommard and Volnay in the Côte de Beaune, but mostly Chardonnays in Meursault and Puligny-Montrachet. Chardonnays in the Côte

Chalonnaise and the Mâconnais were also affected. This was followed by hail in Chablis in May, by serious outbreaks of oidium and excessively hot weather in August. The first half of September was rainy, but the skies cleared just in time for the Côte d'Or harvest. Here we have very good, rich reds and clean, fruity whites, both somewhat like the 1997s but with more to them. The Côte Chalonnaise wines are good, but no better than the 1997s. The Chablis, largely picked when the rain returned at the end of September, are of average quality, for early drinking.

1997 An early harvest, and not an excessive one. The spring was fine, but the weather was poor during the flowering of the Pinot Noir, though better later for Chardonnay. The harvest weather was excellent, offering the prospect of the third fine vintage in a row. The red wines started out with low acidities — and a more uneven state of ripeness — and are more variable than the whites. Both will evolve in the medium term.

A fine vintage in Chablis, smaller in volume than 1966. A good vintage in the Côte Chalonnaise and in the Mâconnais. A very good vintage in the Beaujolais.

1996 A large vintage, and a highly successful one. The run-up to the harvest was characterised by very sunny days and cool nights. This produced very healthy fruit, concentrated in both sugar and acidity. Fine red wines of medium weight, very pure fruit and the capacity to age well. Very good fresh, peachy-appley white wines, though some show the size of the harvest and lack backbone. A very good year indeed for generic wines and the Côte Chalonnaise, especially in red.

An excellent, though large vintage in Chablis. A very good Beaujolais vintage.

1995 A small crop as a result of poor weather during the flowering. The white wines are excellent, the best since 1985; firm and concentrated, with the ability to age. The reds are of medium-full weight with good tannins and abundant plump fruit: generous and seductive. They will need time. Rain at the end of the picking diluted some of the last-to-be-cleared plots in the Côte de Nuits: the village wines from Vosne-Romanée northwards.

A very good vintage in Chablis and the Beaujolais.
1994 An average-sized crop and of average quality, rain

interfering with the harvest and causing premature botrytis. The white wines are ripe but lack depth and definition. Most are now ready for drinking. The reds are variable, but better in the Côte de Nuits than the Côte de Beaune where in many cases they are to be preferred to those of 1992. These are soft, plump, medium-bodied wines which will be at their best between now and 2005.

Similar average quality in the Beaujolais and Chablis.

1993 A crop of normal size, but of exciting quality in Pinot Noir. The white wine harvest, except for those *climats* on the Meursault-Puligny border, which suffered hail damage, was rather more abundant, and the wines proportionately more dilute.

The red wines are structured, have good tannins, abundant ripe fruit and firm acidity. This is a consistently fine vintage in the Côte d'Or which still needs keeping and will last very well. Start drinking the village wines from 2000, the better wines from 2002. There are some unexpectedly good white wines, with concentration as well as grip, from Meursault-Perrières and neighbouring *climats*. Though lean at first, they have put on weight in bottle. These will keep well. The remainder are ready now and should be drunk soon. A good year in Beaujolais. An average vintage in Chablis.

1992 A large crop of red wine, but not quite so prolific in white. Ten days of great heat before an early harvest benefited the Chardonnays, which are rich and ample, even concentrated, though without quite the acidity level of a great vintage. There was then rain, and this affected the Pinot Noirs. These are of medium weight, round and plump, pleasant but with less *terroir* definition than usual. They are now for the most part fully ready. The very best wines can still be held.

An above-average vintage in Beaujolais, average in Chablis. Both are now showing their age.

1991 Born under the shadow of the great 1990 harvest. it was perhaps inevitable that the 1991s would be unjustly scorned. It was a small vintage, and the climatic conditions were not perfect, with hail in Chambolle in midsummer and rain at the beginning and at the end of the harvest. The red wines have good colour and structure, some of the tannins are little hard, but there is

good fruit and grip to give underlying support. They are just beginning to come round. They should last well. Certainly a very good vintage.

The white wines are less interesting: they lack ripeness and real concentration. Drink them soon.

An average vintage in Chablis. A very good vintage in the Beaujolais.

1990 A large vintage. Magnificent in red; fine in white. Though the flowering weather was mixed, the rest of the summer was dry and hot and the berries were small and concentrated, giving a low juice to solid ratio in the fermenting must. As a result the wines were densely coloured, full-bodied, rich and concentrated, with, because of the heat, an almost cooked-fruit flavour. Highly successful both hierarchically and geographically. 1990 is better than any of the rest of the red Burgundian vintages produced in the previous thirty years, and it has not been surpassed since.

The white wines also are fine, though most growers now marginally prefer their 1989s; full, balanced, rich and classy. Both red and white wines are wines for the long term. Even in 1998, only a few village wines are yet at their peak. A fine vintage in Chablis. A very good vintage in Beaujolais, but now getting old.

1989 A large vintage, though not as abundant as 1990. Very good indeed in red, even better in white (the best between 1985 and 1995) where, at least in Meursault and Chassagne, the quantity produced was less excessive than in the Pinot Noirs. It was a largely dry and hot summer, and it was very warm at harvest. The Pinot Noir skins were thin, and the acidities on the low side. Nevertheless the best growers made wines with no lack of colour or staying power, and, after eleven years these are only just beginning to come into their own. The whites have grip and concentration and are real keepers: more so than 1990 and 1992. In both colours quality increases more than proportionately as one climbs up the hierarchy. Good Chablis. Beaujolais now old.

1988 An average sized red wine crop but a large white wine crop. After a successful flowering the summer was mixed, but the vintage weather was largely clement. The red wines have high acidities, seemed a bit austere to begin with, and have taken their time to come round.

They are only just ready, twelve years on. But now one can see the balance and finesse one always suspected. These red wines are better than 1989 and 1985, as good as 1993, so only just below the 1990, the best in recent memory. The character however is more classic.

There are some fine white wines, but generally one can see the size of the crop. Most are correct, but dull, and will not improve. A very good vintage in Chablis. Beaujolais now old.

Earlier Vintages
Both the 1987 and 1986 vintages were affected by indifferent weather in September and are now old in both colours. Initially the white 1986s promised much, but they have not aged gracefully.

The 1985 whites are fine and still vigorous. The best reds are very good, but only the finest promise much life beyond 2003. These are ample, fruity wines, but in many cases lack vigour as they were low in acidity. 1984 was the last really poor Burgundian vintage. The 1983 reds are tannic and muscular, in some cases with a hint of undergrowth or mould or even hail. The whites were alcoholic and overblown and are now past their best. 1982 was abundant. Only a few reds still hold up, but there are some good white wines. 1981 was short in quantity and weak in quality.

Earlier Vintages of Note for Red Wines
1978, 1976 (tannins a bit hard), 1971 (uneven and now weakening), 1969, 1966, 1964, 1962, 1961, 1959, 1952, 1949.

CLASSIFICATIONS

The layman, recently introduced to the intricacies of Burgundy, may find the *appellations* of the region rather daunting. Many more seasoned wine lovers still do. There are two main reasons for this. Most of the villages have adopted the name of their most celebrated vineyard as a suffix (for example Aloxe-Corton) and in Burgundy vineyards rather than individual estates are classified as *grand* and *premier cru*. An additional but less important complication is that there is frequently a choice of alternative spellings for names of individual vineyards.

It was a wily Burgundian mayor who first decided to aggrandise the reputation of the wines of his village by tagging on the name of its most famous growth to that of the commune. Gevrey was the first and it was re-christened Gevrey-Chambertin in 1847. Soon nearly all the others were following suit. Vosne became Vosne-Romanée; Aloxe, Aloxe-Corton, and both Puligny and Chassagne claimed Montrachet. The last was the village of Morey which acquired Saint-Denis in 1926. This may be smart marketing, but is confusing for the consumer, doubly so when there are hyphenated *grand cru* names as in the commune of Gevrey. Thus Gevrey-Chambertin is a village wine, Charmes-Chambertin a *grand cru*.

General Regional Appellations
At the bottom of the Burgundian AC hierarchy lie the generic wines. First comes Bourgogne Grand Ordinaire or Bourgogne Ordinaire. These names are synonymous. There is little grand about the wine and it is little seen. It can come in red, white and rosé, the red and rosé made largely from Gamay, the white from a mixture of varieties, mainly Aligoté. Production is declining as the more noble Pinot Noir and Chardonnay replace the minor grape varieties in the region. This is the cheapest wine in Burgundy and my advice is to pay a little more for the next category, AC Bourgogne, which is distinctly superior. The majority of Burgundy's generic wines fall into this category. With minor variations, Bourgogne Rouge comes from Pinot Noir and Bourgogne Blanc has to come from Chardonnay and/or, occasionally, Pinot Blanc. Bourgogne Aligoté comes from Aligoté. Roughly 47 per cent of Bourgogne comes from the Saône-et-Loire *département*, 37 per cent from the Côte d'Or and 16 per cent from the Yonne.

Simple Bourgogne Rouge or Blanc can be an extremely good wine. All the top domaines produce a little generic wine, from their younger vines or less good vats as well as from their lesser vineyards, but it is vinified and matured with the same care as that bestowed on their grander *cuvées*. These wines can seem expensive but often offer a much better glass of wine than a more pretentious label from a lesser grower or less reputable merchant. They should be regarded in the same light as the second wines produced by the top Bordeaux châteaux.

Less expensive, but equally commendable can be the top of the range generic wines of the better merchants and those of co-operatives such as that of Buxy in the Côte Chalonnaise. Like the top generic wines of the leading domaines these wines can also be aged in oak to give them a sheen of extra class. Bourgogne Passetoutgrains is a mixture of Gamay and Pinot Noir, normally in the ratio of two-thirds Gamay to one-third Pinot Noir. Whether because the vines are located in less favourable sites or because they are young, I have always found the wines disappointing.

Specific Regional Appellations

Superior generic wines can come with a specific note of their origin. Bourgogne-Hautes Côtes de Nuits and Bourgogne-Hautes Côtes de Beaune come from the hills behind the main Côte d'Or vineyards and are for both red and white wines. Bourgogne-Côte Chalonnaise covers red or white wines from the whole Chalonnaise region. From the Yonne *département* comes Bourgogne-Côtes d'Auxerre which can be both red or white.

Until Marsannay, at the north of the Côte de Nuits, was promoted to a full village *appellation* in 1986, there was additionally the *appellation* of Bourgogne Rosé de Marsannay. These wines using the name of Bourgogne with a region of origin are roughly analogous to the regional wines of Chablis, Mâcon and Beaujolais.

There is no regional *appellation* covering the whole of the Côte d'Or, though there is the tiny *appellation* of Côte de Beaune for wine coming from a small parcel of vines on the east side of the town of Beaune itself.

Instead, for the wines of the lesser villages of the Côte d'Or, there are the two *appellations* of Côte de Beaune-Villages and Côte de Nuits-Villages. These cover wines coming either from a single specified village or from a blend of several villages.

Village Appellations

The hierarchy then ascends to the wines made from the grapes of a single village: for example, Vosne-Romanée, Gevrey-Chambertin, Nuits-Saint-Georges in the Côte de Nuits and Volnay and Meursault in the Côte de Beaune.

Premiers Crus

Within these villages or communes, certain vineyards or *climats*, to use the Burgundian expression, are classified as *premiers crus*. The name of a specific *premier cru* will appear on the label after the village name. If the wine is a blend of several *premier cru* vineyards, the label will state simply *premier cru* after the village name.

Many villages have a large number of these vineyards. There are more than 450 in the Côte d'Or (including nearly 330 in the Côte de Beaune). Gevrey Chambertin has 26, Nuits-Saint-Georges 37 and Beaune 44. However, to confuse matters, some of the vineyards are classified as partly *premier cru* and partly AC village wine. There are also *premier cru* vineyards in Chablis.

The classification of both *premier cru* and *grand cru* forms part of the *appellation contrôlée* regulations. This means that, for example, a wine labelled Beaune Grèves will be, in fact, 'appellation Beaune Premier Cru Grèves contrôlée', and will state this somewhere on the label, even if in smaller print.

Grands Crus

At the top of the classification are the *grands crus*, found only in Chablis and the Côte d'Or. Unlike the *premiers crus*, the Côte d'Or *grands crus* do not need to be qualified with the name of the village on the label – the vineyard name is sufficient. There are now thirty *grands crus* in the Côte d'Or, of which two (Le Musigny and Corton) produce both red and white wine. The rest are for either red or white wine only. Most *grands crus* are in the Côte de Nuits and their total surface area is about 450 hectares. Each is entitled to its own separate *appellation contrôlée* (one of them, La Romanée, at 0.8 hectare, is the smallest *appellation contrôlée* in France). In Chablis there are seven *grands crus*, totalling just over 100 hectares, producing white only.

CÔTE D'OR GRANDS CRUS (1998 HARVEST)

APPELLATIONS	RED OR WHITE	COMMUNE	SURFACE AREA (HA)	PRODUCTION (HL)
CÔTE DE NUITS				
BONNES-MARES	RED	CHAMBOLLE-MUSIGNY & MOREY-SAINT-DENIS	15.0	407
CHAMBERTIN	RED	GEVREY-CHAMBERTIN	13.0	364
CHAMBERTIN, CLOS DE BÈZE	RED	GEVREY-CHAMBERTIN	14.2	390
CHAPELLE-CHAMBERTIN	RED	GEVREY-CHAMBERTIN	5.5	150
CHARMES-CHAMBERTIN & MAZOYÈRES-CHAMBERTIN	RED	GEVREY-CHAMBERTIN	28.6	1016
CLOS DE LA ROCHE	RED	MOREY-SAINT-DENIS	16.0	458
CLOS DU TART	RED	MOREY-SAINT-DENIS	7.1	198
CLOS DES LAMBRAYS	RED	MOREY-SAINT-DENIS	8.2	235
CLOS SAINT-DENIS	RED	MOREY-SAINT-DENIS	6.1	183
CLOS DE VOUGEOT	RED	VOUGEOT	49.9	1618
ECHEZEAUX	RED	FLAGEY-ECHEZEAUX	34.3	1102
LA GRANDE RUE	RED	VOSNE-ROMANÉE	1.7	53
GRANDS-ECHEZEAUX	RED	FLAGEY-ECHEZEAUX	7.6	225
GRIOTTES-CHAMBERTIN	RED	GEVREY-CHAMBERTIN	2.7	96
LATRICIÈRES-CHAMBERTIN	RED	GEVREY-CHAMBERTIN	6.7	235
MAZIS-CHAMBERTIN	RED	GEVREY-CHAMBERTIN	8.7	283
LE MUSIGNY	RED	CHAMBOLLE-MUSIGNY	9.8	212
	WHITE	CHAMBOLLE-MUSIGNY	0.4	7
RICHEBOURG	RED	VOSNE-ROMANÉE	7.7	249
LA ROMANÉE	RED	VOSNE-ROMANÉE	0.8	31
LA ROMANÉE-CONTI	RED	VOSNE-ROMANÉE	1.6	40
ROMANÉE-SAINT-VIVANT	RED	VOSNE-ROMANÉE	9.0	250
RUCHOTTES-CHAMBERTIN	RED	GEVREY-CHAMBERTIN	3.3	89
LA TÂCHE	RED	VOSNE-ROMANÉE	5.9	138
CÔTE DE BEAUNE				
BÂTARD-MONTRACHET	WHITE	PULIGNY-MONTRACHET & CHASSAGNE-MONTRACHET	11.9	504
BIENVENUES-BÂTARD-MONTRACHET	WHITE	PULIGNY-MONTRACHET	3.7	174
CHEVALIER-MONTRACHET	WHITE	PULIGNY-MONTRACHET	7.3	245
CORTON	RED	ALOXE-CORTON, LADOIX & PERNAND-VERGELESSES	94.8	3539
	WHITE	ALOXE-CORTON, LADOIX & PERNAND-VERGELESSES	2.0	88
CORTON-CHARLEMAGNE (OR CHARLEMAGNE)	WHITE	ALOXE-CORTON & PERNAND-VERGELESSES	51.0	2325
CRIOTS-BÂTARD-MONTRACHET	WHITE	CHASSAGNE-MONTRACHET	1.6	75
LE MONTRACHET	WHITE	PULIGNY-MONTRACHET & CHASSAGNE-MONTRACHET	6.2	245

The Wine Regions

Generic Bourgogne

Bourgogne Rouge
Surface Area (1998): (Côte d'Or) 822 ha; (Saône-et-Loire) 924 ha; (Yonne) 349 ha; total of 2095 ha.
Production (1998): (Côte d'Or) 45,657 hl; (Saône-et-Loire) 54,562 hl; (Yonne) 22,845 hl; total of 123,064 hl.
Colour: Red.
Grape Varieties: Pinot Noir, plus César and Tressot in the Yonne.
Maximum Yield: 50 hl/ha.
Minimum Alcohol Level: 10°.

Quality within this catch-all *appellation* can vary from the delicious (from vines located just a metre outside the Volnay *appellation* and made by a master winemaker such as Michel Lafarge) to the very ordinary. Most Bourgogne Rouge comes from inferior, often humid, land on the wrong side of the tracks. Taste before you buy and be prepared to pay more for the examples from better growers. (Officially, Beaujolais *cru* from Gamay can be downgraded to Bourgogne Rouge but none has been so declared for at least five years.)

Bourgogne Grand Ordinaire
Surface Area (1998): 184 ha.
Production (1998): (Red and rosé) 9258 hl; (white) 2460 hl.
Colour: Red, rosé and white.
Grape Varieties: (Red and rosé) Gamay, Pinot Noir, plus César and Tressot in the Yonne; (white) Chardonnay and Pinot Blanc.
Maximum Yield: (Red and rosé) 55 hl/ha; (white) 60 hl/ha.
Minimum Alcohol Level: (Red and rosé) 9°; (white) 9.5°.

This is the bottom rung of the Burgundian wine hierarchy. You will rarely encounter it, except in bulk from a co-operative. Resist the temptation at all costs.

Bourgogne Passetoutgrain
Surface Area (1998): 1242 ha.
Production (1998): (Côte d'Or) 20,606 hl; (Saône-et-Loire) 43,764; (Yonne) 2293 hl; total of 66,663 hl.
Colour: Red.
Grape Varieties: Gamay and Pinot Noir (minimum of one-third).
Maximum Yield: 55 hl/ha.
Minimum Alcohol Level: 9.5°.

A blend of Gamay and Pinot Noir might promise to be barely drinkable. In practise as this wine is largely from grapes which barely ripen in the coolest parts of the Burgundy vineyards the results are usually worse. Someone must like it, for the amount produced each year is not negligible.

Bourgogne Blanc
Surface Area (1998): (Côte d'Or) 290 ha; (Saône-et-Loire) 236 ha; (Yonne) 346 ha; total of 872 ha.
Production (1998): (Côte d'Or) 17,551 hl; (Saône-et-Loire) 14,940 hl; (Yonne) 24,719 hl; total of 57,210 hl.
Colour: White.
Grape Variety: Chardonnay.
Maximum Yield: 55 hl/ha.
Minimum Alcohol Level: 10.5°.

There is a world of difference between the wines of ace Côte de Beaune producers such as Patrick Javillier and Domaine Leflaive and those of third-rate merchants or a not-so-good Mâconnais co-operative.

Bourgogne Aligoté
Surface Area (1998): 1556 ha.
Production (1998): (Côte d'Or) 40,465 hl; (Saône-et-Loire) 36,763 hl; (Yonne) 18,188 hl; total of 95,416 hl.
Colour: White.
Grape Variety: Aligoté.
Maximum Yield: 60 hl/ha.
Minimum Alcohol Level: 9.5°.

More Aligote is produced than Bourgogne Blanc and most is consumed locally for the wine is rarely seen abroad, Its tart, appley flavour suits the warm summers of southern Burgundy but has no appeal in cooler, more northern climes. A local drink, named after a priest and famous Resistance hero, is kir, Aligoté laced with half a teaspoonful per glass of crème de cassis, the local blackcurrant liqueur.

CRÉMANT DE BOURGOGNE

Surface Area (1998): 454 ha.
Production (1998): (Côte d'Or) 13,178 hl; (Saône-et-Loire) 28,985 hl; (Yonne) 9913 hl; total of 52,076 hl.
Colour: Rosé and white.
Grape Varieties: (White) Pinot Noir, Pinot Blanc and Chardonnay plus Melon and Sacy in the Yonne; (rosé) all these varieties plus Gamay.
Maximum Yield: 55 hl/ha.
Minimum Alcohol Level: 10°.

Sparkling wines have been made in Burgundy since the 1820s, the best ones by the Traditional or Champagne method when the second fermentation takes place in bottle. In 1975 the superior *appellation* of Crémant de Bourgogne was created to improve on what had been called Bourgogne Mousseux. Only the juice from the first pressing is used. The wine must pass a tasting inspection and be aged for nine months before release.

Crémant de Bourgogne Producers of note
THE CAVE DE BAILLY IS A MAJOR SOURCE, AS ARE THE FIRMS OF MONGEOIN IN NUITS-SAINT-GEORGES AND DELORME AND VEUVE AMBAL, BOTH IN RULLY. THERE IS A SURPRISINGLY GOOD CO-OPERATIVE AT PRUSLY NEAR CHATILLON (NOT A PART OF BURGUNDY MUCH KNOWN FOR ITS WINE) AND OTHERS IN THE MÂCONNAIS. GOOD INDIVIDUAL PRODUCERS INCLUDE PAUL CHOLLET (SAVIGNY-LÈS-BEAUNE), CHRISTIAN AND BRUNO DENIZOT (BISSEY-SOUS-CRUCHAUD), BERNARD DURY (MERCEUIL) AND FRÉDÉRIC TROUILLET (POUILLY).

CHABLIS AND THE YONNE

Equidistant between Champagne, Sancerre at the eastern end of the Loire Valley and the Côte d'Or, the isolated region of Chablis lies on the banks of the small river Serein in the Yonne *département*. A dozen kilometres away, the Paris-Lyon *autoroute* cuts a great concrete swathe across the fields of wheat, maize and pasture. Across the *autoroute* you come to the busy city of Auxerre, dominated by its cathedral of Saint-Etienne.

But Chablis lies in a backwater. The town is sleepy and rural – there is nothing really to distinguish it from a hundred other small towns in arable France, except that the wine produced here from a single noble grape variety, Chardonnay, has become one of the world's best-known dry white wines. Chardonnay thrives in the Chablis soil which is a highly individual mixture of chalky limestone and clay.

A century or more ago, before the arrival of phylloxera, the Burgundian vineyard began at Sens and continued, uninterrupted, through the Auxerrois and down to Montbard and Dijon. There were then in the Yonne as many as 40,000 hectares under vine. Much of the resulting wine, no doubt, was thin and very ordinary, destined to be consumed direct from the cask in the *comptoirs* of Paris and the other towns of northern France. Chablis and the other local vineyards benefited greatly from this close proximity to the capital, but, with the arrival of the phylloxera louse – rather later than in the Côte d'Or, for it did not seriously begin to affect the Chablis vines until 1893 – coupled with increasing competition from the Midi once the railway system connecting Paris with the Midi had been completed, most of the Yonne vineyards disappeared. This decline was further accentuated by the First World War and the resulting economic stagnation and rural depopulation. By 1945, when a particularly savage frost totally destroyed the potential harvest – not a single bottle of Chablis was produced in this vintage – the total area under vine was down to less than 500 hectares. As late as the severe winter of 1956 the locals were skiing down what is now the *grand cru* of Les Clos in February.

Since then, however, there has been a gradual but accelerating increase in the total area of vineyards to 4067 hectares in 1998. As more efficient methods of combating the ever present threat of frost damage have been devised, as greater control of other potential depredations of the yield has been introduced and as more prolific strains of Chardonnay have been planted, production has risen disproportionately from an average of around 24,000 hectolitres per annum in the 1960s to almost ten times as much in the late 1990s.

A Question of Soil

The heartland of the Chablis region is the south-west-facing slope north of the town. Here all the *grands crus* are situated in a continuous line, adjacent to some of the best of the *premier cru* vineyards. These famous vineyards lie on a soil of crumbly limestone, grey or even white in colour, which is named after a small village in Dorset, Kimmeridge. Elsewhere, particularly at Beines to the east and the communes of Maligny, Villy and Lignorettes to the north, the soil has a different appearance, being more sandy in colour and is marginally different – Portlandian limestone as opposed to Kimmeridgian.

There has been much argument over whether the wines from Portlandian soils are as good as those from Kimmeridgian. At times there has been heated opposition, even lawsuits, between those who favour a strict delimitation of Chablis and those who favour expanding the vineyards. The first camp stresses the overriding importance of Kimmeridgian soil, the second believes that an extension of the Chablis vineyards over further suitable slopes of Portlandian soil will relieve pressure on the existing vineyard and better enable the whole community to exploit and benefit from the worldwide renown of its wine. Each grower will probably be a member of one of the two rival *syndicats* or producer groups. Le Syndicat de Défense de L'Appellation Chablis, as its name implies, is in favour of the strict delimitation of Chablis and is now led by Jean-Bernard Marchive of

Domaine des Malandes. The second group, La Fédération des Viticulteurs Chablisiens, is led by Jean Durup of Domaine de L'Eglantière in Maligny.

Following a decision by the INAO in 1978 which effectively diminished the importance of the soil in favour of mesoclimate and aspect when considering a further revision of the area, the expansionists are in the ascendant. Since then the total vineyard area has tripled. New *premiers crus* have appeared on the scene. No-one who has tasted the new *premier cru* Vau de Vey alongside other *premiers crus* such as Vaillons or Montmains from the same grower, can be in any doubt that it is at least as good. Whether this extension of vineyard area will help to avoid some of the extreme fluctuations in the price of Chablis we have seen in the past remains to be seen. Greater stability, in my view, is crucial to the continuing commercial success of the wine.

So too is a higher and more consistent level of quality. The run of recent vintages has been kind, but half the vines, especially the ones for ordinary Chablis, are young, and production figures tend to be much higher than in the Côte de Beaune (58 hl/ha in 1998), inevitably necessitating chaptalisation up to the limit, even in the very best vintages.

The Danger of Frost

The Chablis vineyards lie very close to the northernmost limit for cultivating the vine successfully. The vine will not start to develop in the early spring until the average temperature reaches 10°C and the fruit must ripen before the leaves begin to fall in the autumn. The incidence of frost, therefore, is an important concern. Chablis, particularly the lower slopes adjacent to the river Serein, lies in a frost pocket. The *grand cru* vineyards are the most susceptible but even on the higher plateaux used for the generic wine or plain Chablis, the young shoots are vulnerable from the time they break out of the buds in late March through until the middle of May. The exposure and angle of the slope is critical and there are a number of techniques the grower can use in order to protect his vines from being harmed.

The most primitive method is simply to install a little fuel burner or a paraffin *chaufferette* in the vineyard.

CHABLIS GRANDS CRUS

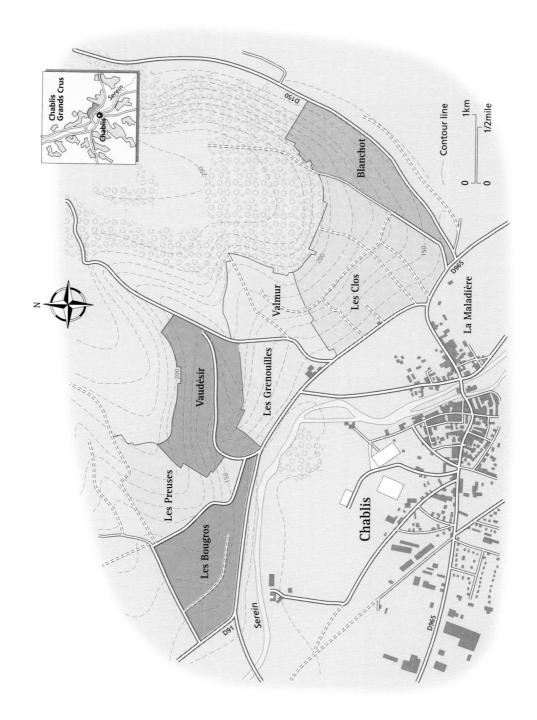

Chablis
Grands Crus

Serein

Chablis

Blanchot

D150

Valmur

Les Clos

La Maladière

D965

Vaudésir

Les Grenouilles

Les Preuses

Les Bougros

Chablis

Serein

D91

D965

N

Contour line

1km

1/2mile

0

0

150

200

250

More recently automatic fuel-heating systems connected to a nearby tank, and infrared devices have been installed in some vineyards. These are expensive both in fuel and in labour but are effective.

Another technique is the aspersion method. A system of water sprinklers is set up in the vineyard and connected to a supply of water. (There is a large reservoir outside Beines which serves over 80 hectares of vines, chiefly in the *premier cru* Fourchaume.) When the temperature descends to zero, the system sprays the vines with a continual fine stream of water. Water freezes at zero but the vine buds will not suffer until the temperature sinks below minus 5°C by which time the bud is protected by a snug coating of ice.

There are some Chablis producers who argue that regularly imprisoning the embryonic leaf cluster in ice for five or six hours a day, perhaps for a month or more, will do it no good. Despite the difficulties of keeping the nozzles unblocked, this is a technique which has spread rapidly since its introduction in the late 1970s. Installation costs are high and maintenance is crucial but operating expenses are minimal.

CHABLIS GRAND CRU

Surface Area (1998): 106 ha – Blanchot 14 ha, Les Bougros 14 ha, Les Clos 27 ha, Les Grenouilles 10 ha, Les Preuses 12 ha, Vaudésir 15 ha and Valmur 14 ha.
Production (1998): 5080 hl.
Colour: White.
Grape Variety: Chardonnay.
Maximum Yield: 45 hl/ha.
Minimum Alcohol Level: 11°.

There are currently over 4000 hectares of vineyard in production in the Chablis area. Just over a hundred of these are the *grand cru* vineyards, a continuous slope of undulating vines facing south-west, north of and directly overlooking the town itself.

Looking up at the slope from the town these *grands crus* are, from left to right: Les Bougros, Les Preuses incorporating La Moutonne of Domaine Long-Depaquit, Vaudésir, Les Grenouilles, Valmur, Les Clos and Blan-chot. It is generally agreed that Les Clos is the best, producing the most powerful and long-lasting wines and with the most intensity and richest flavour. Valmur and Vaudésir are also highly regarded (Valmur, in particular, also needs time to age). Les Preuses and Les Grenouilles produce more floral and delicate wines. Les Bougros and Blanchots are the least fine.

Opinions and, quite naturally, it is difficult to find a grower who is totally objective. Michel Remon of the *négociant* Albert Pic, who can afford to be more dispassionate than most as this firm does not own any vineyards at all, describes wine from Blanchots as the most rustic and he condemns Les Grenouilles for its lack of class; in his opinion, it is only a *grand cru* because it lies alongside the rest. He says that Les Clos is racy and the most *nerveux*; Vaudésir is the roundest and richest but occasionally is a bit heavy; Les Preuses is similar but with less style; Les Bougros produces wine somewhat like it on its upper slopes but is more like Les Grenouilles on the lower land. Monsieur Remon gives first prize to Valmur – the most elegant wine and full of depth.

The important grower William Fèvre sees three different categories. He puts Les Clos at the top of the list, describing it as intense and long on the palate, with a toasted, gamey flavour. Bougros is *tendre* and *douceâtre* (soft and sweetish) with elements of chocolate. The wine is less steely and more obviously fruity than Preuses. Grenouilles and Vaudésir come somewhere between the two in style – less powerful than Les Clos, with more delicate and floral perfumes and a touch of violets. Christian Moreau of the *négociant* J Moreau simply says that Les Clos, Valmur and Vaudésir are the three finest *climats* and the remainder do not merit *grand cru* prices. Jean-Pierre Simonnet, an important *négociant-éleveur*, finds the quality-price ratio for all the *grands crus* to have ceased to be useful. These wines are difficult to buy, finance or sell, he will tell you. He concentrates now on *premiers crus*.

CHABLIS PREMIER CRU

Surface Area (1998): 739 ha.
Production (1998): 42,460 hl.
Colour: White.

Grape Variety: Chardonnay.
Maximum Yield: 50 hl/ha.
Minimum Alcohol Level: 10.5°.

In 1998 there were 739 hectares of *premier cru* vineyards, 70 per cent more than in 1978. In 1967, to facilitate their commercialisation, what was then a total of twenty-six original *lieux-dits* (site names) was reduced to eleven *premiers crus*. The grower now had a choice before him. He could either use the main *premier cru* name on the label – which would additionally allow him to blend the wine from several subsidiary vineyards under this title – or he could continue to use the old *lieu-dit*. In 1986 this list was extended to include seven other sites, some of which incorporated several *lieux-dits*. Today there are 40 *lieux-dits* but generally only 17 names in common usage.

Of these, the longest established – and still considered the best today – are Fourchaume, Montée de Tonnerre and Mont de Milieu. It is no coincidence that these three *premiers crus* all lie on the right bank of the Serein above and below the *grands crus*, facing south-west like the *grands crus*. The largest and most important of the rest, Beauroy, Vau de Vey, Côte de Léchet, Vaillons and Montmains, are all in side valleys on the left bank and face south-east. The wines from Vaillons and Montmains are better than the rest though the first results from Vau de Vey are promising. These wines are shorter in flavour, less powerful, more floral than those on the right bank of the Serein. When made from ripe grapes, they have a peachy, Granny Smith appley flavour while a Fourchaume wine is rich and plump and Montée de Tonnerre and Mont de Milieu are firm, nutty and steely, and are the closest in style to Les Clos, the best *grand cru*.

CHABLIS AND PETIT CHABLIS

Surface Area (1998): (Chablis) 2716 ha; (Petit Chablis) 506 ha.
Production (1998): (Chablis) 160,972 hl; (Petit Chablis) 29,057 hl.
Colour: White.

Grape Variety: Chardonnay.
Maximum Yield: 50 hl/ha.
Minimum Alcohol Level: (Chablis) 10°; (Petit Chablis) 9.5°.

Not surprisingly, the largest increase in Chablis' surface area in recent years has been in those vineyards which produce generic Chablis. Since 1978 there has been more than a 300 per cent increase to 2716 hectares.

The area delimited as Petit Chablis, the lowest ranking Chablis *appellation*, has tended to fluctuate greatly. New vineyards have come into production while others have been upgraded to Chablis or declassified entirely. There were 184 hectares in 1976, decreasing to only 113 in 1981 and we were lead to believe that the authorities were going to eliminate this *appellation* entirely. However, as the result of new vineyards being authorised the figure has risen to 506 hectares today. Good intentions have found it hard to compete with local politics. Petit Chablis wine is dry and crisp, but not as intensely flavoured as Chablis and should be drunk young.

To Oak the Wines or Not

As well as the feud between the restrictionists and the expansionists there has been vehement debate about whether Chablis should or should not be vinified and matured in whole or in part in new or newish wood. William Fèvre used to lead the oak faction as he did the restrictionists. As the largest owner of *grand cru* vineyards, he was able to control the vinification of his wine from the start as well as the *élevage* (most of the *négociants* buy must, not grapes) and he fermented all his own *grands crus* in wood. All his wines were partly matured in oak as well. This approach is being continued, but with a lighter hand, by the new management (see page 150).

The non-oak faction has many supporters, including large landholders such as Jean Durup, the top grower Louis Michel and *négociants* such as J Moreau, Michel Laroche and Michel Remon of Albert Pic who also trade as A Regnard et Fils. All these producers do not use any new oak at all. Their wine spends all its life in *cuve*, stainless steel or glass and tile-lined concrete vat. Others, such as the much-respected growers François Raveneau

CHABLIS PREMIERS CRUS

LIEU-DIT/	COMMUNE	OPTIONAL PREMIER CRU NAME
RIGHT BANK OF SEREIN		
BERDIOT	FYÉ	
CHAPELOT	FYÉ	MONTÉE DE TONNERRE
CÔTE DE BRÉCHAIN	FYÉ	MONTÉE DE TONNERRE
CÔTE DE FONTENAY	FONTENAY	FOURCHAUME
CÔTE DE PRÉS GIROTS	FLEYS	LES FOURNEAUX
CÔTE DE VAUBAROUSSE	FYÉ	
FOURCHAUME	LA CHAPELLE VAUPELTEIGNE	
LES FOURNEAUX	FLEYS	
L'HOMME MORT	MALIGNY	FOURCHAUME
MONT DE MILIEU	FLEYS	
MONTÉE DE TONNERRE	FYÉ	
MOREIN	FLEYS	LES FOURNEAUX
PIED D'ALOUE	FYÉ	MONTÉE DE TONNERRE
VAUCOUPIN	CHICHÉE	
VAULORENT	POINCHY	FOURCHAUME
VAUPOULENT	LA CHAPELLE VAUPELTEIGNE	FOURCHAUME
LEFT BANK OF SEREIN		
LES BEAUREGARDS	COURGIS	
BEAUROY	POINCHY	
BEUGNONS	CHABLIS	VAILLONS
BUTTEAUX	CHABLIS	MONTMAINS
CHÂTAINS	CHABLIS	VAILLONS
CHAUME DE TALVAT	COURGIS	
CÔTE DE CUISSY	COURGIS	LES BEAUREGARDS
CÔTE DE JOUAN	COURGIS	
CÔTE DE LÉCHET	MILLY	
CÔTE DE SAVANT	BEINE	BEAUROY
LES EPINOTTES	CHABLIS	LES BEAUREGARDS
FORÊT	CHABLIS	MONTMAINS
LES LYS	CHABLIS	VAILLONS
MÉLINOTS	CHABLIS	VAILLONS
MONTMAINS	CHABLIS	
RONCIÈRES	CHABLIS	VAILLONS
SÉCHET	CHABLIS	VAILLONS
TROESME	BEINE	BEAUROY
VAILLONS	CHABLIS	
VAU DE VEY	BEINE	
VAU LIGNEAU	BEINE	
VAUGIRAUT	CHICHÉE	VOSGROS
VAUX RAGONS	BEINE	VAU DE VEY
VOSGROS	CHICHÉE	

CHABLIS PREMIERS CRUS

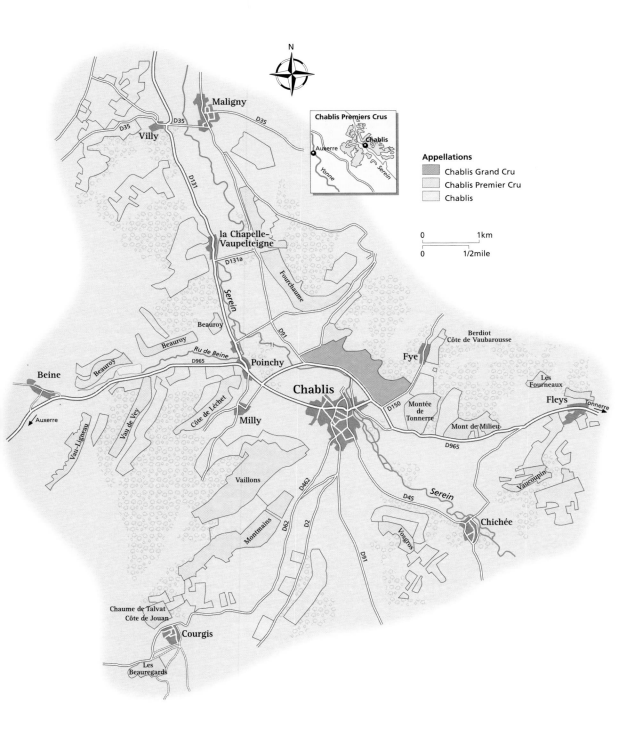

Chablis Premiers Crus

Chablis

Auxerre · Chablis

Yonne · Serein

Appellations

- Chablis Grand Cru
- Chablis Premier Cru
- Chablis

0 — 1km
0 — 1/2mile

Maligny

Villy

D35 · D35 · D35

D131

la Chapelle-
Vaupelteigne

D131a

Fourchaume

Serein

Beauroy

Beauroy

Ru de Beine

D91

Beauroy

D965

Poinchy

Beine

Vau-Ligneau

Vau de Vey

Côte de Léchet

Milly

Auxerre

Chablis

Vaillons

Montmains

D62

D2

D462

Chaume de Talvat
Côte de Jouan

Courgis

Les
Beauregards

Vosgros

D91

D45

Serein

Chichée

Berdiot
Côte de Vaubarousse

Fye

Les
Fourneaux

Montée
de
Tonnerre

Mont de Milieu

D150

D965

Fleys

Tonnerre

Vaucoupin

and René et Vincent Dauvissat use oak, but it is old not new, and it imparts no oaky taste to the wine.

The general belief of the non-oak faction is that Chablis should not try to ape the whites from the Côte de Beaune. Chablis should be as natural a wine as possible; its flavours are subtle and delicate and its essential gun-flinty, steely character should not be swamped by the supplementary aromas which result from vinifying or maturing the wine in oak.

There are arguments in favour of both sides. I have had many a well matured, non oak-aged Chablis which have proved that tank-matured wine need not be ephemeral. Ageing potential is as much a result of the correct balance between fruit and acidity (plenty of each and plenty of concentration) as of maturation and fermentation in wood *per se*. On the other hand, the extra weight and tannins added by the wood do help, especially in the weaker vintages. Fèvre's wines and those of Joseph Drouhin in Beaune, an important Chablis proprietor and also a believer in new wood, do keep extremely well. Moreover, their capacity for ageing is not so dependent on the vagaries of the vintage.

New oak is not used for the lesser wines but today more and more growers – and also the important co-operative, La Chablisienne – produce at least one special *cuvée* which has been *élevé en fût de chêne*.

The Style of the Wine

Chablis, at its best, is a magnificent wine and is quite unique. The colour should be a full, in the sense of quite viscous, greeny-gold. The aromas should combine steeliness and richness, gun-flint, grilled nuts and crisp toast. The flavour should be long, individual and complex. Above all, the wine should be totally dry but without greenness. The after-taste must be rich rather than mean, ample rather than hard, generous rather than soulless. Chablis should be subtle rather than obvious, reserved rather than too obviously charming.

When to Drink Chablis

Top quality Chablis – the *grands crus*, the best *premiers crus*, from a fine vintage and a star-rated grower or merchant – will last a long time, rather longer than one would

expect. A *cuvée* of Fourchaume 1978 I chose at La Chablisienne was still alive and delicious in 1990. Sadly, these wines are the tip of the iceberg. There is much rather thin and weedy wine being bottled as *appellation contrôlée* Chablis.

The general rule is (after the vintage)

Petit Chablis	Six months to two and half years
Chablis	One to four years
Chablis premier cru	Three to eight years
Chablis grand cru	Five to twelve years

Leading Chablis Producers

Many wine writers have been too diffident or too polite to come out into the open with a hierarchy of the top Chablis growers and *négociants*. The position is complicated for various reasons; first, the controversy over whether the wine should be matured in wood or not; second, the arm's-length presence of the *négociants* in Beaune and Nuits-Saint-Georges, all of whom sell Chablis but few of whom, except Drouhin, own any Chablis vineyards; and third, the presence of a very powerful local co-operative, La Chablisienne, which accounts for one-third of the Chablis crop and, not unnaturally, has a major influence on the annual price of the wine.

La Chablisienne was my major Chablis supplier throughout most of my professional life and I never found anything in the quality of its best wines – obviously with such a large business you have to pick and choose – which was not of the very highest standard. You may criticise the co-operative for its policy of allowing commercial buyers to choose the name of one of the co-operative's members to put on its label: for example Fèvre Frères for Fourchaume which, together with *mise en bouteille à la propriété* and no note of La Chablisienne, is certainly misleading, but you cannot deny that the wine can be as good as anything the *appellation* can produce.

★ DOMAINE J BILLAUD-SIMON
Owner: Billaud-Simon family.
Surface Area under Vine: 20 ha – Chablis,
Blanchots (20 a), Chablis, Les Clos (50 a), Chablis,
Les Preuses (50 a), Chablis, Vaudésir (80 a), Chablis

premiers crus Fourchaume, Montée de Tonnerre, Mont de Milieu and Vaillons, Chablis, including Cuvée Spéciale Jules Simon, and Petit Chablis. Alongside the gently flowing river Serein is the modern Billaud-Simon winery, now run by Samuel Billaud, grandson of Jules, and his uncle Bernard. The wines, from prized old vines, are fermented in thermo-regulated stainless steel vats, following a serious débourbage (several days at 1°C), with some of the special cuvées such as the Blanchots being vinified and raised in oak. These are very pure, mineral, elegant wines. They last well.

★ LA CHABLISIENNE

Members: 300.

Surface Area under Vine: 1200 ha – Chablis, Blanchots (1 ha), Chablis, Bougros (25 a), Chablis, Les Clos (50 a), Chablis, Château de Grenouilles (7.50 ha), Chablis, Les Preuses (4 ha), Chablis, Valmur (25 a), Chablis, Vaudésir (50 a), Chablis premiers crus Fourchaume, Les Lys, Mont de Milieu, Montée de Tonnerre, Vaillons, Vaulovent and others, Chablis including Vieilles Vignes, and Petit Chablis.

Founded in 1923 and responsible for one-third of the total Chablis production, La Chablisienne is both well-established and very powerful. Once you have joined the co-operative it is both difficult and expensive to withdraw and set up independently. Thankfully this is a modern and high quality establishment, sensitively run by Hervé Tucki – who took over from his father, Michel in 1989 – and his team. Wines are vinified both in tank and in new oak. One of the top cuvées is Château de Grenouilles. La Chablisienne is a prime source of Chablis, much used by Burgundy merchants, but also selling a large part of its production as bottled wine.

★★ DOMAINE RENÉ & VINCENT DAUVISSAT

Owners: René & Vincent Dauvissat.

Surface Area under Vine: 11 ha – Chablis, Les Clos (1.7 ha), Chablis, Les Preuses (96 a), Chablis premiers crus La Forêt, Séchet and Vaillons, Chablis and Petit Chablis.

This famous domaine has been estate-bottling longer than most, since the time of grandfather Robert Dauvissat in 1931. It is now run by René and his son Vincent. The wines are all vinified in wood, but it is old wood, so there is no obvious oaky taste, and bottled after twelve to fifteen months. The vines have an average age of forty years, and are some of the few in Chablis still entirely hand-picked. The Dauvissat style is for long-lasting, complex, minerally wines, of very high quality.

★ DOMAINE DANIEL-ETIENNE DEFAIX

Commune: Milly.

Owner: Daniel Defaix.

Surface Area under Vine: 25 ha – Chablis, Blanchots (25 a), Chablis premiers crus Côte de Léchet, Les Lys and Vaillons, Chablis, including Vieilles Vignes, and Petit Chablis.

This is an individual domaine, run by a man with individual ideas. 'If a vigneron works his premiers and grands crus in exactly the same way, it would be very hard to tell which is the better. The reason why the grands crus produce better wine is not so much the site as the greater care – lower rendement and so forth – with which they are treated'. So says Daniel Defaix, a staunch believer in old vines, natural yeasts, working by gravity, no use of oak, and keeping the wine in tank two years before bottling in order to make something which will last. Some of them do keep surprisingly well.

DOMAINE JEAN-PAUL DROIN

Owner: Jean-Paul Droin.

Surface Area under Vine: 20 ha – Chablis, Blanchots (17 a), Chablis, Les Clos (99 a), Chablis, Grenouille (48 a), Chablis, Valmur (1.03 ha), Chablis, Vaudésir (1.04 ha), Chablis premiers crus Côte de Léchet, Fourchaume, Montée de Tonnerre, Montmains, Vaillons and Vosgros, Chablis and Petit Chablis.

De père en fils depuis 1697 (from father to son since 1697) is grandly announced on the brochure: twelve generations (the thirteenth, son Benoît, will soon join his father) in 300 years. Droin harvests his grands crus by hand, the rest of his vines by machine. The better wines are vinified in wood, wholly or partly, but very few wines show much evidence of this. These full, elegant and steely wines last well. The *grands crus* will keep ten years.

★ DOMAINE/MAISON JOSEPH DROUHIN DOMAINE DE VAUDON

Communes: Chablis and Beaune.
Surface Area under Vine: 45 ha – Chablis, Bougros (30 a), Chablis, Les Clos (1.30 ha), Chablis, Les Preuses (30 a), Chablis, Vaudésir (1.40 ha), Chablis *premiers crus* Mont de Milieu, Montée de Tonnerre, Montmains, Monein, Séchet and Vaillons, and Chablis, including Domaine de Vaudon.

Drouhin are one of the few Beaune *négociants* who have their own domaine and a press-house in the Chablis area, the must being transported to Beaune the next day after *débourbage* for fermentation in their cellars there. The top wines have a gentle period of ageing in one- or two-year-old wood, to leave a hardly perceptible flavour of new oak, and are bottled after eight to nine months. The Domaine de Vaudon is a special *cuvée* originally from vines below Mont de Milieu and Montée de Tonnerre. The wines are on the delicate side but with all the intensity and elegance that we have come to associate with this excellent establishment.

★ DOMAINE GÉRARD DUPLESSIS

Owner: Gérard Duplessis.
Surface Area under Vine: 7 ha – Chablis, Les Clos (33 a), Chablis *premiers crus* Fourchaume, Montée de Tonnerre and Montmains, and Chablis.

Gérard Duplessis presides over the family domaine whose premises lie next to those of Billaud-Simon on the Quai de Reugny in Chablis. The wines are vinified in tank and matured in old wood. These are firm, long-lasting wines. This is a very good source of Chablis.

★ DOMAINE WILLIAM FÈVRE

Owner: Henriot family.
Surface Area under Vine: 60 ha – Chablis, Bougros (6.10 ha), Chablis, Les Clos (4 ha), Chablis, Grenouilles (57 a), Chablis, Les Preuses (2.40 ha),

Chablis, Valmur (1.66 ha), Chablis, Vaudésir (1.20 ha), Chablis *premiers crus* Beauroy, Fourchaume, Côte de Léchet, Les Lys, Mont de Milieu, Montée de Tonnerre, Montmains, Vaillons and Vaucoupin, Chablis and Petit Chablis.

This important domaine, the largest *grand cru* owner outside the Chablisienne co-operative, was sold to the Henriot family, owners of Henriot Champagne and also of the Beaune *négociant*, Bouchard Père et Fils, in 1998. Prior to this it belonged to William Fèvre, patron of both the oaky faction and the anti-expansionists in Chablis. I find the wines less oaky – for the better – than they used to be. They are now also bottled later, the *grands crus* up to fifteen months after the vintage, and this has given an extra polish to their style. Now they are definitely Chablis wines instead of some mongrel crossbreed. Some of the wines are sold under the Domaine de La Maladière label, as well as subsidiary labels Ancien Domaine Auffrey and Jeanne-Paule Filipi.

★ DOMAINE JEAN-PIERRE GROSSOT

Commune: Fleys.
Owner: Jean-Pierre Grossot.
Surface Area under Vine: 18 ha – Chablis *premiers crus* Fourchaume, Fourneau, Mont de Milieu, Côte de Troesmes and Vaucoupin, Chablis, including La Part des Anges and Grossot, and Petit Chablis.

The Grossot domaine lies at the extreme western end of Fleys, under the *climat* of Fourneaux. Vinification is partly in tank, partly in oak, the Grossot *cuvée* being particularly oaky, but the rest of the range much less so. Bottling takes place in December, fifteen months after the harvest, and the wines are then held back a further year before release. I like the style here, the wines are appropriately steely, even in a *tendre* vintage like 1997.

★ DOMAINE DES MALANDES

Owner: Lyne & Jean-Bernard Marchive.
Surface Area under Vine: 25 ha – Chablis, Les Clos (53 a), Chablis, Vaudésir (90 a), Chablis *premiers crus* Fourchaume, Côte de Léchet, Montmains and Vau-de-Vey, Chablis and Petit Chablis.

This highly regarded domaine was inherited by Lyne Marchive from her family, the Tremblays of La Chapelle-Vaupelteigne, and re-named, so as not to be in competition, in 1986. There is no wood used, vinification being in stainless-steel or enamel-lined metal tanks. Bottling takes place from June onwards after the harvest. 'You should harvest Fourchaume early, because it is a warm area, and the risk of over-ripeness is high,' says Jean-Bernard Marchive, a thoughtful man, who as an outsider is able to take a detached view.

★ DOMAINE DES MARRONNIERS

Commune: Préhy.
Owner: Bernard Légland.
Surface Area under Vine: 18 ha – Chablis *premiers crus* Côte de Jouan and Montmains, Chablis and Petit Chablis.

Bernard Légland's parents were polyculturalists: Préhy lies beyond the other end of the Montmains slope from Chablis, and there were few vines planted here at the time. He decided to become a *vigneron* and planted his first vines in 1976. No oak is used at all. The wines are finely poised, elegant and thoughtfully made by an intelligent man. The domaine deserves to be better known.

★★ DOMAINE LOUIS MICHEL & FILS

Owner: Jean-Loup Michel.
Surface Area under Vine: 23 ha – Chablis, Les Clos (50 a), Chablis, Grenouilles (55 a), Chablis, Vaudésir (1.20 ha), Chablis *premiers crus* Fourchaume, Forêts, Montée de Tonnerre, Montmains and Vaillons, Chablis and Petit Chablis.

This is a brilliant consistent estate, where there is no use of wood (the barrels in the cellar are only for show). The wines are vinified in a temperature-controlled room full of stainless steel vats of different sizes and not bottled until a year to eighteen months afterwards – or even later. The magnificently austere and steely wines keep much longer than most Chablis.

★ DOMAINE LOUIS MOREAU

Commune: Beines.
Owners: Louis & Anne Moreau.

Surface Area under Vine: 120 ha – Chablis, Les Blanchots (50 a), Clos des Hospices *monopole* (1 ha), Chablis, Les Clos (2.50 ha), Chablis, Valmur (1 ha), Chablis *premiers crus* Les Fourneaux, Vaillons and Vaulignot, Chablis and Petit Chablis.

It is important to draw the distinction between the merchant firm of J Moreau & Fils, which today belongs to Jean-Claude Boisset of Nuits-Saint-Georges, and the vineyard of the Moreau family, currently owned by Jean-Jacques Moreau and his brother Christian. Currently the plum sites – all the *grands crus* and the Vaillons – are on lease to J Moreau & Fils until 2004.

Meanwhile, in Beines, Louis Moreau (son of Jean-Jacques) and his wife Anne set up on their own in 1994. They took over the Domaine de Biéville and the Domaine du Cèdre Doré and produce very stylish, unoaked wines for drinking early.

★ DOMAINE PINSON

Owner: Christophe & Laurent Pinson.
Surface Area under Vine: 11 ha – Chablis, Les Clos (2.50 ha), Chablis *premiers crus* Forêt, Mont de Milieu, Montmains and Vaillons (young vines at present), and Chablis.

This long-established domaine is now run by the young and energetic brothers Christophe and Laurent Pinson. Vinification is in enamelled steel *cuves*, but all the wines, except for the straight Chablis, then spend some time in *barrique*. The result is wines of immediate attraction, but nonetheless serious and profound. They keep longer than most – Les Clos for up to ten years.

★★ DOMAINE FRANÇOIS RAVENEAU

Owner: François Raveneau.
Surface Area under Vine: 7 ha – Chablis, Blanchot (75 a), Chablis, Les Clos (50 a), Chablis, Valmur (75 a), and Chablis *premiers crus* Butteaux, Chapelot, La Forêt, Montée de Tonnerre, Montmains and Vaillons.

After a period when the wines were sold either under the name of François Raveneau or that of Jean-Marie, father and son, things have been resolved: Domaine François Raveneau is now the registered name.

This estate enjoys the reputation of being the best within the town of Chablis. This is one of the few Chablis domaines to pick the grapes entirely by hand, not that Jean-Marie has anything against machines (it is just that his vineyards are rather steep). He prefers to pick early and chaptalise than pick over-ripe fruit with low acidity. The wine is vinified in tank but reared in old wood, and then bottled after eighteen months. One of the keys is a low yield. You don't make fine bottles out of dilute wine. These are splendidly backward, concentrated, steely wines. Don't pull the cork too soon. There is often a protracted period of adolescence when the wines taste too sulphury.

★ DOMAINE SERVIN

Owner: François Servin.
Surface Area under Vine: 32 ha – Chablis, Blanchot (90 a), Chablis, Bougros (65 a), Chablis, Les Clos (88 a), Chablis, Les Preuses (86 a), Chablis *premiers crus* **Forêts, Montée de Tonnerre and Vaillons, and Chablis.**

Depending on the vintage, most of the better wines are vinified using a varying proportion of *barrique*: the *grands crus* usually 100 per cent, the *premiers crus* less. The wines are bottled between July and September following the harvest. These are neat, clean, stylish, fruity wines, evolving in the medium rather than the very long term.

Other Producers of note

DOMAINE BARAT/ MICHEL BARAT (MILLY), DOMAINE PASCAL BOUCHARD (CHABLIS), DOMAINE DE CHANTEMERLE/ ADHÉMAR BOUDIN (LA CHAPELLE-VAUPELTEIGNE), DOMAINE JEAN COLLET (CHABLIS), DOMAINE DE LA CONCIÈRGERIE/CHRISTIAN ADINE (CHABLIS), DOMAINE DANIEL DAMPT (MILLY), DOMAINE JEAN & SÉBASTIEN DAUVISSAT (CHABLIS), DOMAINE BERNARD DEFAIX ET FILS (MILLY), DOMAINE JEAN DURUP & FILS (MALIGNY), DOMAINE RAOUL GAUTHERIN (CHABLIS), DOMAINE ALAIN GEOFFROY (BEINES), DOMAINE LAROCHE (CHABLIS), DOMAINE LONG-DEPAQUIT (CHABLIS), DOMAINE SYLVAIN MOSNIER (BEINES), DOMAINE GILBERT PICQ & SES FILS (CHICHÉE), DOMAINE DENIS POMMIER (POINCHY), DOMAINE FRANCINE & OLIVIER SAVARY (MALIGNY), DOMAINE PHILIPPE TESTUT (CHABLIS), DOMAINE GÉRARD TREMBLAY (POINCHY), DOMAINE LAURENT TRIBUT (POINCHY), DOMAINE VOCORET (CHABLIS) AND DOMAINE YVON VOCORET (MALIGNY).

OTHER YONNE WINES

After Chablis the other wines of the Yonne can be divided into two groups: the village *appellations* (Irancy and Saint-Bris) and the generic Bourgogne wines – some of the Bourgogne wines can also be labelled with the name of the village, e.g. Bourgogne-Coulanges-La-Vineuse and others with the phrase Côtes d'Auxerre. Most Côtes d'Auxerre wine does indeed come from the land south of Auxerre, but there are isolated pockets at Vézelay, Joigny, Epineuil near Tonnerre, and even Chatillon-sur-Seine. None of these areas is very large, the grand total of all these vineyards comprising some 870 hectares producing 50,000 hectolitres of wine, half of it red and rosé, half of it white.

These figures, however, do not include sparkling wine. The Auxerrois, the western side of the region, is a centre for excellent Crémant de Bourgogne, produced by the Cave de Bailly, near Saint-Bris-Le-Vineux. Much of Burgundy's 600 hectares and 32,000 hectolitres given over to sparkling wine must originate from this establishment. Official figures, however, do not give us the exact details. The combination of a calcareous rich, marly soil and the cool climate produces grapes with the high acidity, which though a disadvantage for still wine, is essential for sparkling wine.

Outside Chablis, then, vines are scarce. In the Yonne we are rapidly approaching the northernmost point at which the vine will ripen sufficiently to produce palatable wine. There is competition from cereals and pasture, and the vine can thrive only in the most favourable sheltered, south-facing pockets.

As well as the Pinot Noir, the Chardonnay and the Aligoté, a number of rustic grape varieties, long since dispensed with elsewhere, continue to survive here. The César is used to beef up the colour and the alcohol level of red wine. Officially there is also Tressot, though this is hardly seen today. Two white grape varieties, the Sacy (called Tresallier in Saint-Pourçain in the Upper Loire) and the Melon (better known as Muscadet) are permitted for Crémant, as is the Gamay for the rosé. And then there is Sauvignon Blanc (see Saint-Bris, below).

IRANCY

Surface Area (1998): 122 ha.
Production (1998): 6415 hl.
Colour: Red.
Grape Varieties: Pinot Noir and César.
Maximum Yield: 55 hl/ha.
Minimum Alcohol Level: 10°.

Irancy lies 10 kilometres south-east of Auxerre and is visually one of France's vineyard gems. Above the village a natural amphitheatre faces due south and captures all the available sun. The slopes are full of vines and cherry trees with a little road winding down from the forest above. In the spring, when the wildflowers are out, the place is enchanting. You can also eat very well at the Auberge des Tilleuils beside the river Yonne in the village of Vincelottes below Irancy. The wine, which is more than a sort of half rosé. is clearly the best Auxerrois red. Drink it at between two and five years old.

SAUVIGNON DE SAINT-BRIS

Surface Area (1998): 97 ha.
Production (1998): 6872 hl.
Colour: White.
Grape Variety: Sauvignon Blanc.
Maximum Yield: 60 hl/ha.
Minimum Alcohol Level: 9.5°.

This is a curious *appellation*. Until 1995 it was Burgundy's sole VDQS, relegated to the second rank because Sauvignon Blanc is not considered properly Burgundian — except that we are only 130 kilometres west of Pouilly-sur-Loire, home to some of France's best Sauvignon Blanc wine, and the Nièvre *département* has always historically been part of greater Burgundy. Nevertheless, here we have a wine from a variety not permitted elsewhere

in Burgundy. In the past it has had some difficulty competing with the improved quality of the local Chardonnay wines, and the fact that Sauvignon is not allowed in the local Crémant has tended to discourage growers from planting it. Promotion to *appellation contrôlée* has given Sauvignon de Saint-Bris a shot in the arm, though, and the surface area of vines is increasing.

Saint-Bris-Le-Vineux lies on the road from Auxerre to Irancy and is both a substantial and a pretty town. We are in the centre of the Côtes d'Auxerre here and most of the local growers produce Bourgogne wine as well as the local Sauvignon. It can be an attractive wine, but it has more in common with a generic Sauvignon de Touraine than with a higher quality Sancerre.

REGIONAL BOURGOGNE

BOURGOGNE CÔTES D'AUXERRE, BOURGOGNE CHITRY, BOURGOGNE COULANGES-LA-VINEUSE, BOURGOGNE SAINT-BRIS, BOURGOGNE EPINEUIL, BOURGOGNE CÔTE SAINT-JACQUES AND BOURGOGNE VÉZELAY

(For production figures see page 131.)

Chitry lies on the Chablis side of Saint-Bris and Irancy, Coulanges-La-Vineuse on the other, some 8 kilometres due south of Auxerre. Together with Saint-Bris-Le-Vineux and eight other communes not grand enough to be allowed to use their name on the label they comprise the Côtes d'Auxerre region. This is the home of increasing stylish light Chardonnays and almost *vin de l'année* Pinots, best drunk cool in the summer following the vintage.

Coulanges-La-Vineuse has made a speciality of its reds, and obviously has ambitions to join Irancy as an *appellation* in its own right. At Chitry we are on the borders of the Chablis *appellation*, and, not surprisingly, the bias is towards Chardonnay. Epineuil and Tonnerre, the former virtually a suburb of the latter, produce a small amount of Pinot Noir from the south-facing slopes above the river Armançon. This, too, is a light wine for early drinking and can also have elegance.

The vineyards at Côte Saint-Jacques, above Joigny to the north, and Vézelay to the south, are recently planted and minuscule, the effort of a few brave pioneering spirits who would have us remember what an important *vignoble* the Yonne was in pre-phylloxera days. Not surprisingly the two local Michelin chefs, Marc Meneau of L'Espérance at Saint-Père near Vézelay and Michel Lorain of, appropriately, La Côte Saint-Jacques at Joigny, are in the forefront of this revival.

Leading Yonne Producers

SICA du Vignoble Auxerrois Cave de Bailly

Commune: Bailly.
Members: 80.
Surface Area under Vine: 350 ha – Crémant de Bourgogne, Bourgogne Aligoté and Sauvignon de Saint-Bris.

Founded in 1971, this co-operative produces the best Crémant de Bourgogne. The up-to-date premises, with cellars cut out of an old limestone quarry into which, at least partly, you can drive your car, are worth a visit.

Domaine Anita & Jean-Pierre Colinot

Commune: Irancy.
Owner: Anita & Jean-Pierre Colinot.
Surface Area under Vine: 8 ha – Irancy, including Côte du Moutier, Les Mazelots and Palotte.

This is the source of the best Irancy wine, produced from 95 per cent Pinot Noir and 5 per cent César, with the *cuvée* from the best parcels being vinified and bottled separately. The Colinots are charming, irrepressible and passionate about their wine, which is made without using any wood.

Domaine Ghislaine & Jean-Hugues Goisot

Commune: Saint-Bris-Le-Vineux.
Owners: Ghislaine & Jean-Hugues Goisot.
Surface Area under Vine: 24 ha – Bourgogne Côte d'Auxerre, Bourgogne Aligoté and Sauvignon de Saint-Bris.

This is a splendid source of neatly made, elegant Bourgogne wine. The Goisots live in Saint-Bris, but wine sold under this label only represents a third of their production. The best Côte d'Auxerre are sold under the name Corps de Garde and with a few years in bottle these are admirable wines.

Other Yonne Producers of note

DOMAINE DE L'ABBAYE DU PETIT QUINCY/DOMINIQUE GRUHIER (EPINEUIL), DOMAINE RENÉ BON – FOR COULANGES-LA-VINEUSE (MIGÉ), DOMAINE FRANCK CHALMEAU (CHITRY), DOMAINE DU CLOS DU ROI/MICHEL BERNARD (COULANGES-LA-VINEUSE), DOMAINE ANNE & ARNAUD GOISOT (SAINT-BRIS-LE-VINEUX), DOMAINE JOËL & DAVID GRIFFE (CHITRY), DOMAINE ALAIN MATHIAS (EPINEUIL), DOMAINE MARC MENEAU (VÉZELAY), DOMAINE JACKY RENARD (SAINT-BRIS-LE-VINEUX) AND DOMAINE JEAN-PIERRE SORIN (SAINT-BRIS-LE-VINEUX).

CÔTE DE NUITS

The Côte de Nuits begins at Marsannay, just south of Dijon, and continues for some 22 kilometres to Corgoloin, about half-way between Nuits-Saint-Georges and Beaune. The heart of the Côte de Nuits is one of the greatest red wine areas in the world. From the village of Gevrey-Chambertin southwards, the famous names ring out: Morey-Saint-Denis, Chambolle-Musigny, Vosne-Romanée and Vougeot.

Above and behind these villages, neatly parcelled behind crumbling dry-stone walls, every available scrap of land is planted with vines. In winter, the land is bare and bleak, the fields broken up by little bonfires of prunings as the plants are ruthlessly close-cropped to stunted stumps. In high summer, the green vines, a hedge of opportunity, rustle gently in the breeze. In late autumn, the wine now actually bubbling away in the growers'

CÔTE D'OR YIELDS AND ALCOHOL LEVELS

APPELLATIONS	MAXIMUM YIELD	MINIMUM ALCOHOL LEVEL
RED WINES		
BOURGOGNE	55 HL/HA	RED & ROSÉ 10°
BOURGOGNE HAUTES-CÔTES	50 HL/HA	10°
BOURGOGNE PASSETOUTGRAINS	55 HL/HA	9.5°
BOURGOGNE ORDINAIRE	55 HL/HA	9°
VILLAGE WINES	42 HL/HA	10.5°
PREMIERS CRUS	42 HL/HA	11°
GRANDS CRUS	35 HL/HA	11.5°
WHITE WINES		
BOURGOGNE BLANC	60 HL/HA	CHARDONNAY 10.5°, ALIGOTÉ 9.5°
BOURGOGNE HAUTES-CÔTES	55 HL/HA	10.5°
BOURGOGNE ORDINAIRE	60 HL/HA	9.5°
VILLAGE WINES	45 HL/HA	11°
PREMIERS CRUS	45 HL/HA	11.5°
GRANDS CRUS	42 HL/HA	11.5°
		LE MONTRACHET & 12°
		CHEVALIER-MONTRACHET

cellars, the vineyards are stripped and savaged but the colours are flame and russet in the low cool sun.

The *climats* which give the best wines lie on mid-slope, sheltered from the prevailing winds from the west by the forest which crowns the topmost ridges. From La Tâche at the southern end of Vosne-Romanée northwards to Mazis on the edge of the village of Gevrey-Chambertin is an almost unbroken line of red *grands crus*. Only in Corton, further south in the Côte de Beaune, is there another *grand cru* for red wine.

The Côte de Nuits is half the size of the Côte de Beaune, with some 1815 hectares of vines (excluding the vines producing straight Bourgogne). The vineyards are not only narrower, from east to west, but also steeper, and sloping more to the east rather than to the south-east. Production is almost entirely of red wine. There is some rosé in Marsannay, and the odd few hundred cases of white, but this latter is more of a curiosity than a commercial proposition. In general the Côte de Nuits reds are fuller, firmer, richer and more concentrated than those of the Côte de Beaune. They need longer before they are ready but consequently last better.

CÔTE DE NUITS-VILLAGES

Surface Area (1998): 160 ha.

Production (1998): (Red) 6845 hl; (white) 198 hl.

Colour: Red and white.

Grape Varieties: (Red) Pinot Noir; (white) Chardonnay.

This useful local *appellation* is used for the minor villages. Though not as well known as the Côte de Beaune-Villages, Côte de Nuits-Villages provides an inexpensive introduction to the greater wines of the Côte, and is often as good as a village wine from a more important commune at half the price. The wines can come from Fixin and Brochon in the north and from Prissey, Comblanchien and Corgoloin in the south. Fixin wines can also be sold under their own name. The wine can be somewhat four-square, even a bit rustic, but is fuller than wine from the Hautes-Côtes. In theory there is a tiny amount of white wine as well as the red.

Côte de Nuits-Villages Producers of note

DENIS BACHELET, MICHEL ESMONIN ET FILLE, PHILIPPE

ROSSIGNOL (ALL GEVREY-CHAMBERTIN), CHOPIN ET FILS, DANIEL CHOPIN-GROFFIER (BOTH COMBLANCHIEN), DOMAINE DE L'ARLOT, JEAN-JACQUES CONFURON, PHILIPPE GAVIGNET, DANIEL RION (ALL NUITS-SAINT-GEORGES), AND ROBERT JAYER-GILLES (MAGNY-LÈS-VILLERS).

MARSANNAY

Surface Area (1998): 225 ha.
Production (1998): (Red) 6085 hl; (rosé) 3231 hl; (white) 1308 hl.
Colour: Red, rosé and white.
Grape Varieties: (Red and rosé) Pinot Noir; (white) Chardonnay.

The Côte d'Or officially begins in the suburbs of Dijon, but the first commune of importance is Marsannay. Until 1986 Marsannay could only use the simple Bourgogne *appellation* for its wines. In that year, as a result of some successful lobbying by the local growers, it was decided not to promote the village wines to Côte de Nuits-Villages which might have been logical, but to award them an *appellation* in their own right. The wines are much lighter than the wines of Côte de Nuits-Villages, and all the better for not being too fleshy.

The village has long been renowned for its rosé, one of the most delicious in France. The Pinot Noir produces a delightful rosé, dry but full of fruit and fragrance and for drinking within a couple of years of the vintage, like all rosés. Marsannay had made a speciality of this wine, for which it had had a separate *appellation*, Bourgogne, Marsannay Rosé. Production had been in decline for some years, and before the promotion of the village to its own *appellation contrôlée* in 1987 only some 15 per cent of the harvest was made into pink wine. Since then its fortunes seem to have revived. Many of the vines in the next-door village of Couchey are *appellation* Marsannay.

Leading Marsannay Producers

★ DOMAINE BRUNO CLAIR
Owner: Bruno Clair.
Surface Area under Vine: 20 ha, owned and *en*

fermage – Chambertin, Clos-de-Bèze (1 ha), Corton-Charlemagne (34 a), Gevrey-Chambertin *premier cru* Clos-Saint-Jacques, Les Cazetiers and Clos-du-Fonteny *monopole*, Savigny-Lès-Beaune *premier cru* La Dominode, village Morey-Saint-Denis in the *lieu-dit* En La Route de Vergy (red), village Morey-Saint-Denis (white), village Chambolle-Musigny in the *lieu-dit* Les Veroilles, village Vosne-Romanée in the *lieu-dit* Les Champs-Perdrix, village Aloxe-Corton, Marsannay, including the *lieux-dits* Les Grasses-Têtes, Les Longeroies and Les Vaudenelles (all red) and Marsannay (white and rosé).

In the early 1980s the well-known Domaine Clair-Daü was split up, the result of family difficulties. Some was sold to Maison Louis Jadot, who also leases another part. Bernard Clair took the important holding in Bonnes-Mares and leases this to the Domaine Fougeray de Beauclair. Bruno, his son, has inherited the rest of the domaine, and has since expanded. The wines are pure, elegant, if sometimes a little austere when young and last well. They have rapidly improved since Bruno has been on his own, and were a triumphant success in 1996, and again in 1998.

★ DOMAINE PHILIPPE NADDEF
Commune: Couchey.
Owner: Philippe Naddef.
Surface Area under Vine: 5 ha, owned and *en fermage/métayage* – Mazis-Chambertin (40 a), Gevrey-Chambertin *premier cru* Les Cazetiers and Les Champeaux, village Gevrey-Chambertin, including Vieilles Vignes, village Fixin and Marsannay (red).

Philippe Naddef is lean, dark, intense and perfectionistic. He took over his patrimony – it mainly comes from his maternal grandfather – in 1983. The wines are well-coloured, full and concentrated and markedly oaky.

Other Producers of note
DOMAINE BART, RÉGIS BOUVIER, DOMAINE FOUGERAY-DE-BEAUCLAIR, ANDRÉ GEOFFROY, ALAIN GUYARD AND DOMAINE HUGUENOT (ALL MARSANNAY).

FIXIN

Surface Area (1998): *Premiers crus* 19 ha; village wine 80 ha.

Production (1998): *Premiers crus* (red) 676 hl, (white) 27 hl; village wine (red) 3414 hl, (white) 71 hl.

Colour: Red and white.

Grape Varieties: (Red) Pinot Noir; (white) Chardonnay.

Premiers Crus There are eight, in whole or part – Les Arvelets, Clos du Chapitre (*monopole*), Les Hervelets, Les Meix-Bas, Clos Napoléon (*monopole*), Clos de La Perrière (*monopole*), Queue de Hareng (in the commune of Brochon) and En Suchot. Les Meix-Bas, Queue de Hareng and En Suchot are very tiny – wine from Les Meix-Bas is always sold as Les Hervelets and Queue de Hareng and En Suchot lie within the Clos de La Perrière.

Fixin – pronounced 'Fissin' – is the next commune south on the Côte after Marsannay. Its wines can claim either the village *appellation* or that of Côte de Nuits-Villages. The village has Napoleonic connections. Some 150 years ago Claude Noisot, a local aristocrat who fought alongside Napoleon in many battles and even accompanied him in exile to Elba, arrived back in the village. He proceeded to rechristen the name of one of his vineyards Clos Napoléon, install a small museum of memorabilia and commission a statue for the local village square. All this did much to help the esteem of the local wine. Clos du Chapitre, not Clos Napoléon, is probably Fixin's best *premier cru*.

The locals refer to the style of Fixin as *sauvage*: robust, full, gamey, somewhat four-square, and the *premier crus*, lying above the village on a fairly steep slope, all produce wine that is very strong. The village wines come from vineyards which are lower down, on more clayey soil and are meaty in texture; similar to those of Gevrey-Chambertin, but with less concentration and finesse.

Fixin Producers of note
VINCENT ET DENIS BERTHAUT, PIERRE GELIN AND ANDRÉ MOLIN.

GEVREY-CHAMBERTIN

Surface Area (1998): *Grands crus* 82 ha; *premiers crus* 78 ha; village wine 329 ha.

Production (1998): *Grands crus* 2842 hl; *premiers crus* 3055 hl; village wine 14,779 hl.

Colour: Red.

Grape Variety: Pinot Noir.

Premiers Crus There are twenty-six *premiers crus*. in whole or in part. In alphabetical order they are: Bel-Air (part), La Bossière (part), Les Cazetiers, Les Champeaux, Les Champitenois (more commonly known as La Petite-Chapelle), Les Champonnets, Chapître, Les Cherbaudes, Au Cloiseau, La Combe-aux-Moines, Aux Combottes, Les Corbeaux (part), Le Craipillot, Les Ergot, Les Estournelles (-Saint-Jacques), Le Fonteny, Les Goulots, Lavaux-Saint-Jacques, La Perrière, Les Petits-Cazetiers, La Plantigone (also known as Les Issarts), Le Poissenot, Clos Prieur (part), La Romanée (part), Clos Saint-Jacques and Clos des Varoilles.

Grands Crus There are eight or nine *grands crus*: Chambertin, Chambertin Clos de Bèze, Chapelle-Chambertin, Charmes-Chambertin (incorporating Mazoyères-Chambertin), Griottes-Chambertin, Latricières-Chambertin, Mazis-Chambertin and Ruchottes-Chambertin.

Travelling south from Fixin to Gevrey we come to the beginning of the finest sector of Burgundy vineyards. Gevrey is the largest of the great communes of the Côte de Nuits (possessing eight out of the twenty-three Côte de Nuits *grands crus*) and vies with Vosne-Romanée as being the most important one of all – the pinnacle of Pinot Noir.

The name Gevrey comes from Gabriacus, a name dating from Gallo-Roman times and which was first recorded in AD 640. About this time, the Abbey of Bèze was given land by Duke Amalgaire of Burgundy which the monks then planted with vines. Shortly after, so the tale runs, a peasant named Bertin decided that he, too, would plant vines on his neighbouring plot of land. From the Campus or Champ Bertin comes the name of Chambertin, Gevrey's greatest vineyard.

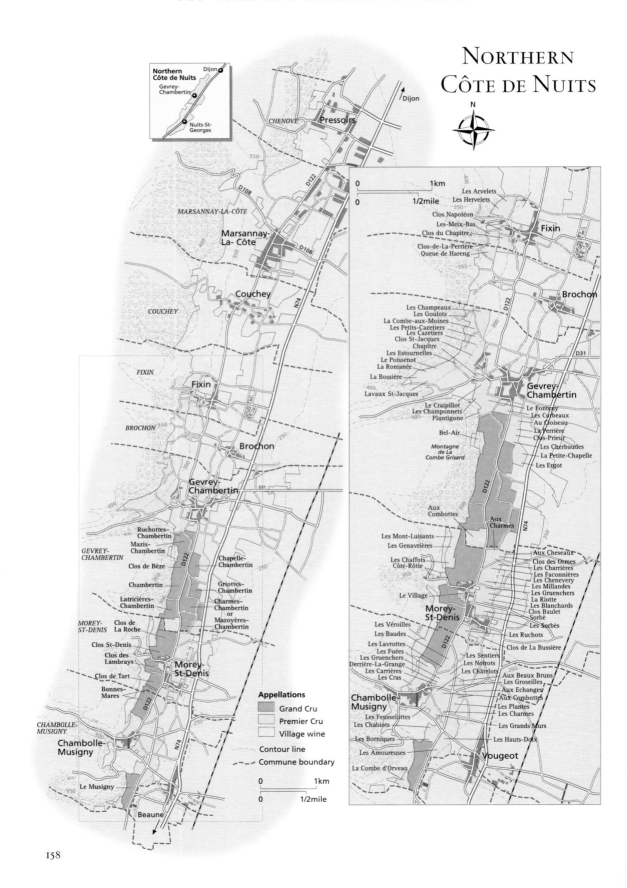

NORTHERN CÔTE DE NUITS

N

In 894, the Abbey of Sainte-Bénigne was donated land by another Burgundian duke, Richard le Justicier. This abbey soon came under the jurisdiction of the great ecclesiastical establishment at Cluny. In the Middle Ages the Abbey of Bèze sold their vineyards to the cathedral chapter of Saint Mammés at Langres, who remained the nominal proprietors until the French Revolution. During the seventeenth century, the chapter leased out these and other vineyards in their possession and, in 1731 the bulk of the Clos de Bèze passed to Claude Jobert. Jobert was an important official in the royal court at Versailles and soon became its Burgundian supplier. Under his forceful promotion, the reputation of the local wines increased by leaps and bounds. Exceptionally, the Jobert domaine survived the French Revolution intact while most of the remaining estates, more directly in ecclesiastical hands prior to the Terror in 1793, were sequestered and broken up. Napoleon's predilection for Chambertin is well known. He is reputed to have drunk little else. It would seem that the Emperor drank his Chambertin – five or six years old and bottled with an embossed 'N' – much diluted with water.

During the nineteenth century, as a result of the Code Napoléon and the laws of inheritance, the vineyards of Gevrey were divided and sub-divided among more and more owners. By 1850, there were nine owners in the 28 hectares of Le Chambertin and Clos-de-Bèze. By 1900 the number had grown to nineteen and today, the figure is twenty-five.

The wine of Chambertin and Clos-de-Bèze, not least as a result of its Napoleonic patronage, has a great reputation. Understandably, the neighbouring wines have sought to share its glory. In 1847 the village of Gevrey was allowed to add Chambertin to its name. Subsequently, a number of neighbouring grands crus were, similarly, allowed to add the magic name of the top vineyard onto their own. Only Clos de Bèze, equal to Le Chambertin in prestige, is allowed to place the name of Chambertin before its own and, indeed, its wines can be sold as Chambertin without the Clos de Bèze. The other grands crus may only add Chambertin after their own.

Together, the grand cru vineyards produce about 25 per cent of the total yield of red grand cru Burgundy.

Compared with Bordeaux it is a drop in the ocean. Château Lafite on its own can produce as much. These eight vineyards stretch in a line south of the village along the little road which connects Gevrey with Morey. Ruchottes, Mazis, Clos de Bèze, Chambertin itself and Latricières lie upward of this road. La Chapelle, Griottes, Charmes and Mazoyères are on the downward side.

What is the difference between the various grands crus? While the answer is made more complex by the myriad different owners, ages of vineyard and vinification methods, any explanation is essentially due to variations in exposure and altitude of the vineyards and subtle alterations in soil structure. The soil is a Bajocian limestone covered by a thin layer of earth comprised of a mixture of pebbles, flint, chalk, clay and limestone debris; the higher up the slope the lower the clay content. Few would deny that Chambertin and Clos de Bèze are the best grands crus. I rate Mazis and Ruchottes next. Charmes and Griottes (most of Mazoyères is sold as Charmes), if not Chapelle, produce a more feminine wine, less powerful, less intensely flavoured and, in my experience, less full-bodied. Latricières has an almost robust touch.

Much of the village wine, in contrast to the rest of the Côte de Nuits, comes from the east of the main Dijon to Nuits-Saint-Georges road. Gevrey's vineyards also extend north into the commune of Brochon.

The best section of the premiers crus lies above the village up in the valley of the Combe aux Moines. The slope here is steep but sheltered, and many of these vineyards (Clos Saint-Jacques, Lavaux-Saint-Jacques, Estournelles and Cazetiers) produce wine every bit as good as the lesser grands crus. Most of those who own vines in Clos Saint-Jacques as well as in Charmes or Chapelle consider the Clos Saint-Jacques to be superior, will give its wine the benefit of 100 per cent new oak and consider it an error that it was not given grand cru status when the legislation was drawn up in the 1930s.

Leading Gevrey-Chambertin Producers

★ DOMAINE DENIS BACHELET
Owner: Denis Bachelet.
Surface Area under Vine: 3 ha, owned – Charmes-

Chambertin (43 a), Gevrey-Chambertin *premier cru* Les Corbeaux, village Gevrey-Chambertin and Côte de Nuits-Villages.

Denis Bachelet took over his small family domaine – it largely came from his grandparents – in 1983, when he was in his twenties. It has been enlarged a little since, but the operation remains essentially that of a one-man band. Bachelet is a perfectionist. His wines are never blockbusters but intense, subtle, harmonious and of great elegance. The Charmes is a real gem: a ravishing wine which really sings – sensuous in the best sense.

★ DOMAINE ALAIN BURGUET

Owner: Alain Burguet.

Surface Area inder Vine: 5.35 ha, owned and *en fermage* – Gevrey-Chambertin *premier cru* Les Champeaux, and village Gevrey-Chambertin, including Vieilles Vignes and the *lieux-dits* Les Billards and Les Regnards.

After quarrelling with his father, Alain Burguet went off on his own, tending the vines for a neighbour, Gabriel Tortochot while he built up his own domaine. Alain is in his late forties, short, solid, quietly determined, even grim. So is the wine: full, muscular, uncompromising, sturdy, concentrated and long-lasting.

★ DOMAINE CLAUDE DUGAT

Owner: Claude Dugat.

Surface Area inder Vine: 4 ha, owned – Charmes-Chambertin (42 a), Griottes-Chambertin (16 a), Gevrey-Chambertin *premier cru* Lavaux-Saint-Jacques, and village Gevrey-Chambertin.

Cousin of Bernard (see below), Claude Dugat cellars his wine in the beautifully restored Cellier de Dîmes, up by the church. The Griottes is bottled under the name of Françoise, his sister. These are very rich, concentrated wines; they have marvellously classy fruit and good grip.

★ DOMAINE BERNARD DUGAT-PY

Owner: Bernard Dugat.

Surface Area inder Vine: 6 ha, owned and *en fermage* – Chambertin (5 a), Charmes-Chambertin (49 a), Mazis-Chambertin (18 a),

Gevrey-Chambertin *premiers crus* Lavaux-Saint-Jacques and Petite-Chapelle, and village Gevrey-Chambertin, including Vieilles Vignes.

The wine here is stocked in cask in the magnificent cellars of the crypt of the church of an erstwhile *leprosarium*. The wines have the concentration typical of old vines and minimum yields. They are abundantly fruity, very stylish and well balanced. This is a classy establishment presided over by a charming couple.

DOMAINE MICHEL ESMONIN ET FILLE

Owner: Michel and Sylvie Esmonin.

Surface Area under Vine: 6.63 ha: owned and *en fermage/métayage* – Gevrey-Chambertin *premier cru* Clos-Saint-Jacques, village Gevrey-Chambertin and Côte de Nuits-Villages.

Fille is the attractive Sylvie, daughter of Michel, qualified both as an *ingénieur agronome* and an oenologist. She took charge in 1989, since when the domaine has increasingly bottled more and more of its own wine (and now 100 per cent) and made serious wine. The atmosphere is tidy, competent and quietly confident; the wines suitably more feminine and elegant when they are young than *chez* the cousins below.

★ DOMAINE DES ESTOURNELLES, FRÉDÉRIC ESMONIN

Owner: André and Frédéric Esmonin.

Surface Area under Vine: 7 ha, owned and *en métayage* – Griottes-Chambertin (59 a), Mazis-Chambertin (42 a), Ruchottes-Chambertin (42 a), Gevrey-Chambertin *premier cru* Les Champonnets, Les Estournelles-Saint-Jacques and Lavaux-Saint-Jacques, and village Gevrey-Chambertin.

There are at least three noteworthy aspects to this fine domaine. First it farms for the Hospices de Beaune, and also for the Thomas family, donors of the Hospices' Mazis. Second it owns the lion's share of the *premier cru* Estournelles, and probably makes the best wine from it. Last it is the only domaine where you can sample Griottes, Mazis and Ruchottes, the best three *grands crus* outside the big two in my view, alongside each other. I see from my notes that each year I seem to prefer a different one. The home team prefers the Ruchottes, which are the oldest vines.

★ DOMAINE JEAN-CLAUDE FOURRIER
Owner: Jean-Claude Fourrier.
Surface Area under Vine: 9 ha, owned – Griottes-Chambertin (26 a), Gevrey-Chambertin *premier cru* Clos Saint-Jacques, La Combe-aux-Moines, Les Cherbaudes and Les Champeaux (the last two currently blended together as *premier cru*), village Gevrey-Chambertin, including the *lieu-dit* Aux Echezeaux, village Morey-Saint-Denis, village Chambolle-Musigny and Vougeot *premier cru* Les Petits Vougeots.

Here is another once-fine domaine which declined in the 1980s and now, with a change of generation, is back on the map. Jean-Claude's son, Jean-Marie, is now in charge. A few handfuls of unstemmed bunches are left in the vats, the rest destalked and after three to five days' cold maceration the fermentation is allowed to rise to 34°C and the *cuvaison* prolonged to extract the *matière*. This domaine dislikes using new oak, and believes in bottling after twenty months in cask.

★ DOMAINE VINCENT GÉANTET-PANSIOT
Owner: Vincent Géantet-Pansiot.
Surface Area under Vine: 13 ha, owned and *en fermage* – Charmes-Chambertin (50 a), Gevrey-Chambertin *premier cru* Le Poissonot, village Gevrey-Chambertin, including the *lieu-dit* Les Jeunes-Rois and Vieilles Vignes, Chambolle-Musigny *premier cru* village Chambolle-Musigny and Marsannay.

Vincent Géantet took over the domaine in 1982 from his father Edmond and things have gently been improving ever since, especially since 1990. The wines are intensely flavoured but not blockbusters. There is succulent perfumed fruit and good balance. A very good domaine.

★★ DOMAINE DENIS MORTET
Owner: Denis Mortet.
Surface Area under Vine: 10 ha, owned and *en*

fermage – Chambertin (15 a), Clos de Vougeot (31 a), Gevrey-Chambertin *premier cru* Lavaux-Saint-Jacques and Les Champeaux, village Gevrey-Chambertin, including the *lieux-dits* En Champs Vieilles Vignes, Au Velle and En Motrot *monopole*, Chambolle-Musigny *premier cru* Aux Beaux-Bruns, and Marsannay.

What was formerly the Domaine Charles Mortet et Fils was divided after the 1991 harvest, Denis Mortet (born in 1956) and his younger brother Thierry having decided to go their separate ways. Denis was then lucky enough to be approached by a neighbour about to retire, and has since taken this 4.5-hectare domaine *en fermage*.

The results here have been fine for some time and now they are brilliant. Total destemming, four to six days of pre-fermentation maceration, a thirteen- to fifteen-day *cuvaison*, at a maximum temperature of 32°C, and a percentage of new oak which varies from 25-80 per cent, depending on the *cuvée*. There has been a change in the origin of the wood used as well as a mixture for the lesser wines – Vosges wood is used for the best wines. There is no filtration and sometimes no fining.

But of course great winemaking cannot be encapsulated in a single paragraph. It is about a meticulous attention to detail from the vineyard onward, a very low yield, a very severe selection of fruit, and, above all, flair and imagination. Our man has got this in spades. The wines are full-bodied, concentrated, harmonious, intensely flavoured and splendidly elegant. The 1993s, the first vintage with the additional parcels of land, were particularly exciting.

★ DOMAINE JOSEPH ROTY
Owner: Joseph Roty.
Surface Area under Vine: 7.80 ha, owned and *en fermage* – Charmes-Chambertin (16 a), Griottes-Chambertin (8 a), Mazis-Chambertin (12 a), Gevrey Chambertin *premier cru* Le Fonteny, village Gevrey-Chambertin, including the *lieux-dits* Les Champs-Chenys, Clos-Prieur and Brunelle, and Marsannay.

Joseph Roty is one of Burgundy's *enfants terribles* – arrogant, voluble, excitable, quick to take offence (even when none was intended), impossible to pin down, infuriating but at the same time lovable. It is difficult to get into his cellar, but once in it is almost impossible to get out. I think I hold the world record for the shortest visit: one and a half hours. I should long ago have given up on this difficult, touchy and exasperating man. But he does make very good wine.

Roty's wines are very distinctive. They are full, very intense, very perfumed and very harmonious. They are certainly immensely seductive. Sometimes, though, I find them just a touch sweet, just a shade over-oaky. Roty only started in 1968, his father having died when he was a child, and my experience of old, mature Rotys is scant. I look forward to seeing the vintages of the late 1980s when they are fully mature. Perhaps then I'll award him two stars.

★★★ DOMAINE ARMAND ROUSSEAU
Owner: Charles Rousseau.

Surface Area under Vine: 14 ha, owned – Chambertin (2.20 ha), Chambertin Clos-de-Bèze (1.50 ha), Charmes-Chambertin (1.36 ha), Mazis-Chambertin (53 a), Ruchottes-Chambertin, Clos-des-Ruchottes (1.06 ha), Clos-de-La-Roche (1.48 ha), Gevrey-Chambertin *premier cru* Clos-Saint-Jacques, Les Cazetiers and Lavaux-Saint-Jacques, and village Gevrey-Chambertin.

A visit to taste in Charles Rousseau's cellar is one of the delights of every Burgundy visit. This is a domaine with a track record of producing fine wine which dates back to the 1930s, when Charles' father Armand was one of the very first in the region to start bottling his own wine. Armand died in 1959 at the age of seventy-five, and the mantle passed to Charles, born in 1922, a short man with a large head, a voluble expansive presence and a lush squeaky laugh. Waiting in the wings, so to speak, for Charles is still firmly in charge, is his son Eric.

Some 15 per cent of the stems are retained, to aid fermentation as much as anything else. The *cuvaison* lasts fifteen days, at a maximum temperature of 31°C, and the top three wines. the third being the Clos-Saint-Jacques (not the Mazis or the Ruchottes) get 100 per cent new wood. But it all starts in the vineyard, says

Charles, with a low yield which is established early in the season, by hard pruning and debudding. He does not like the current fashion for green harvesting.

Rousseau's wines are rich in colour, pure in texture, never over-oaked, always concentrated, balanced, vigorous and very classy. The wines are distinctive, each expressing their individual *terroirs*. This is superb wine-making, from one of the gentlemen of Burgundy.

★ DOMAINE CHRISTIAN SÉRAFIN
Owner: Christian Sérafin.

Surface Area under Vine: 4.70 ha, owned and *en fermage* – Charmes-Chambertin (31 a), Gevrey-Chambertin *premier cru* Les Cazetiers and Le Fonteny, village Gevrey-Chambertin including the *lieu-dit* Les Corbeaux and Vieilles Vignes.

Stanislaus Sérafin arrived from Poland before the Second World War (the family are cousins of the Heresztyns who have a domaine in the village), worked first as a mason but in 1947 bought a piece of land and set himself up as a *vigneron*. He gradually built up an estate which his son Christian inherited in 1988 (he had already been responsible for the wine for a decade or more). It was then generally considered to be a good rather than an exciting domaine. The 1990s have seen a distinct improvement, as if Christian had been somewhat constrained in the past. The wines are full-bodied, oaky, meaty and abundantly rich, with a good touch of spice. The village Gevrey-Chambertin from old vines is usually better than the Fonteny.

★ DOMAINE JEAN & JEAN-LOUIS TRAPET
Owner: Jean and Jean-Louis Trapet.

Surface Area under Vine: 12 ha, owned – Chambertin (1.9 ha), Chapelle-Chambertin (60 a), Latricières-Chambertin (75 a), Gevrey-Chambertin *premier cru* La Petite Chapelle and Clos Prieur, village Gevrey-Chambertin and Marsannay.

This is much the better half of the old Trapet domaine (the other half is Rossignol-Trapet), divided in 1990. Standards are now back to where they used to be in the 1950s. Since 1990, when Jean-Louis took over, yields have been cut and the viticultural approach has been more and more biodynamic.

Other Producers of note

Lucien Boillot et Fils, Philippe Charlopin-Parizot, Pierre Damoy, Dominique Gallois, Gérard Harmand-Geoffroy, Bernard Maume and Thierry Mortet.

MOREY-SAINT-DENIS

Surface Area (1998): *Grands crus* 37 ha; *premiers crus* 40 ha; village wine 54 ha.

Production (1998): *Grands crus* 1121 hl (excluding Bonnes-Mares); *premiers crus* (red) 1471 hl and (white) 34 hl; village wine (red) 2078 hl and (white) 123 hl.

Colour: Red and white.

Grape Varieties: (red) Pinot Noir; (white) Chardonnay.

Premiers Crus There are twenty *premiers crus* today, a number having been absorbed into Clos Saint-Denis and Clos de La Roche over the years. In alphabetical order they are: Clos Baulet, Les Blanchards, Clos de La Bussière, Les Chaffots, Aux Charmes, Les Charrières, Les Chenevery, Aux Cheseaux, Côte-Rôtie, Les Faconnières, Les Genavrières, Les Gruenchers, Les Millandes, Les Mont-Luisants, Clos des Ormes, La Riotte, Les Ruchots, Sorbè, Les Sorbès and Le Village. In 1995 the local growers' syndicate lodged an application for the reclassification as *premier cru* of part (2.5 ha) of the *climat* of En la Rue de Vergy, above the *grand cru* of Clos de Tart.

Grands Crus Morey has four *grands crus*, plus a small part of Bonnes-Mares (the rest lies in Chambolle-Musigny). From the north they are: Clos de La Roche, Clos Saint-Denis, Clos des Lambrays and Clos de Tart.

Sandwiched between Gevrey and Chambolle, Morey has never received the recognition it deserves. This is curious, as there are four *grands crus* plus a small section of the Bonnes-Mares *grand cru*, most of which lies in Chambolle, and it produces very good red wine which, at best, can combine the concentration and the delicacy of both of its neighbours. There is a tiny amount of white wine.

The origins of Morey are closely connected with the Cistercian abbey of Cîteaux and with their benefactors, the Seigneurs of Vergy. Between the two of them they held authority over the village and its land until the French Revolution. This ecclesiastical heritage is echoed in the many Clos or walled vineyards with their attendant buildings, which still exist today.

Only the excellent Gevrey-Chambertin *premier cru* Aux Combottes separates the Latricières-Chambertin *grand cru* from Clos de La Roche, after which the *grands crus* follow in a line above the Route des Vins or D122 which runs through the village, until the *climat* of Bonnes-Mares spreads over into Chambolle-Musigny. In general Clos de La Roche, not Clos Saint-Denis from which the village has prized its suffix, is considered the best wine. Both these *grands crus* are in the hands of a number of proprietors, while Clos des Lambrays and Clos du Tart are, rarely for Burgundy, both *monopoles*.

In the main the *premiers crus* lie further down the slope from the *grands crus* and the wines display the same characteristics of their neighbours – firmer to the north and more fragrant to the south.

Leading Morey-Saint-Denis Producers

★★ DOMAINE DUJAC

Owner: Jacques Seysses.

Surface Area under Vine: 11.50 ha, owned and (Vosne-Romanée only) *en fermage* – Clos de La Roche (1.95 ha), Clos-Saint-Denis (1.47 ha), Charmes-Chambertin (70 a), Bonnes-Mares (43 a), Echezeaux (69 a), Gevrey-Chambertin *premier cru* Les Combottes, Morey-Saint-Denis *premier cru*, Chambolle-Musigny *premier cru* Les Gruenchers, Vosne-Romanée *premier cru* Les Beaumonts, village Morey-Saint-Denis, including white, and Chambolle-Musigny.

This perfectionist domaine has only been in existence for little over twenty-five years, when Jacques Seysses' father bought the Domaine Marcel Graillet for his son. Traditional in some ways (100 per cent of stems retained), ultra modern in others (clonal selection, cultured yeasts, low-temperature fermentation, enzymes to clarify the wine) and with a healthily biological approach to viticulture under the vineyard manager Christophe Morin, the Dujac wines, almost entirely matured in new oak, are strikingly individual. Never very deep in colour – because of the retained stems – they are nevertheless intense, perfumed, silky-smooth and impeccably balanced.

There is a small associate *négociant* company, Druid Wine, which specialises in wines from Meursault.

★ DOMAINE ROBERT GROFFIER PÈRE ET FILS

Owner: Robert Groffier.
Surface Area under Vine: 8 ha, owned –
Chambertin Clos-de-Bèze (41 a), Bonnes-Mares
(98 a), Chambolle-Musigny *premier cru* in Les
Amoureuses, Les Hauts-Doix and Les Sentiers,
and village Gevrey-Chambertin.

This Morey-based domaine is singular in that it owns not one vine in the commune. What it does possess is good-sized plots in all the *climats* it is present in, including the largest single slice of Chambolle-Musigny, Les Amoureuses (1.09 ha). As you drive up the hill from Vougeot to Chambolle you will see Robert Groffier's large hoarding advertising this wine. In all other ways Robert, who works alongside his forty-year-old son Serge, is self-effacing, somewhat shy and gentle, and the wines are like the man himself: not rugged blockbusters, but pure, intense, understated and elegant.

DOMAINE DES LAMBRAYS

Owner: Günter Freund.
Surface Area under Vine: 10.7 ha, owned – Clos
des Lambrays (8.70 ha), Morey-Saint-Denis
premier cru*, Puligny-Montrachet *premier cru
Les Caillerets and Les Folatières, and village
Morey-Saint-Denis.

Owners of virtually the monopoly of the Clos des Lambrays, this domaine was acquired by the German Günter Freund from the Saier family in 1997. Left derelict after the Second World War the majority of the Clos was replanted in the early 1980s and only now are the vines reaching a respectable average age. Today we can see that the wine is fragrant and supple: a true Morey-Saint-Denis; it is more akin to Clos Saint-Denis than to Clos de Tart and Bonnes-Mares.

★ DOMAINE HUBERT LIGNIER

Owner: Hubert Lignier.
Surface Area under Vine: 7.70 ha, owned and *en*
***métayage* – Clos de La Roche (80 a), Charmes-**
Chambertin (10 a), Morey-Saint-Denis *premier*
***cru* Les Chaffots, Les Façonnières and**
Les Chenevery, Gevrey-Chambertin *premier cru*
Les Combottes, Chambolle-Musigny *premier cru*
Les Baudes, and village Morey-Saint-Denis,
Gevrey-Chambertin and Chambolle-Musigny.

Although always reliable, quality at this estate has shown a distinct improvement since Hubert's son Romain took over winemaking responsibility in 1991. Rich, generous, quite oaky wines are the style here.

★ DOMAINE HENRI PERROT-MINOT

Owner: Henri Perrot-Minot.
Surface Area under Vine: 5 ha, owned – Charmes-
Chambertin (1.56 ha), Morey-Saint-Denis *premier*
cru* La Riotte, Chambolle-Musigny *premier cru
La Combe-d'Orveau and Les Fuées, village Morey-
Saint-Denis in the *lieu-dit* En La Rue de Vergy,
and village Gevrey-Chambertin and Chambolle-
Musigny.

Henri Perrot-Minot has now been joined by his son Christophe. This change has brought a distinct improvement in the wines, and the domaine has stopped selling in bulk. Some 20-30 per cent of the stems are retained, the fermentation temperature is allowed to rise to 32°C, after four to five days' cold maceration, and 30-40 per cent new wood is utilised. The wines are nicely rich, individual and stylish. This is the best source for that elusive Chambolle *premier cru* La Combe d'Orveau: the vines lie above and adjacent to Le Musigny itself.

★ DOMAINE PONSOT

Owner: Jean-Marie Ponsot.
Surface Area under Vine: 8.73 ha, owned and *en*
***métayage* – (owned) Clos de La Roche (3.31 ha),**

Chapelle-Chambertin (47 a), Morey-Saint-Denis *premier cru* Les Mont-Luisants (red and white), village Gevrey-Chambertin and Morey-Saint-Denis. *En métayage* from the Mercier family (sold as Domaine Chézeaux) – Griottes-Chambertin (89 a), Clos-Saint-Denis (32 a) and Chambolle-Musigny *premier cru* Les Charmes (58 a); formerly *en métayage* elsewhere, but no longer exploited – Latricières-Chambertin (32 a) and Chambolle-Musigny *premier cru* Les Charmes.

Quality has blown hot and cold here in the 1990s, but at its best it can be glorious, and now that Laurent Ponsot, son of Jean-Marie (mayor of Morey) is more able to take decisions, I hope for less disappointment in the future.

The domaine has pioneered clonal selection, the mother plants being its own finest old vines. There are, you will be firmly told, 'no rules' in the winemaking here. De-stemming is optional, there is a maximum temperature of 30°C during the *cuvaison*, very little new oak, and neither fining nor filtration. The wines are very individual: rich, exotic and spicy. Sometimes they work, sometimes they don't. Beware also of other wines under the Chézeaux label. Not all are the Ponsots' creation.

DOMAINE DU CLOS DE TART

Owner: Mommessin S A.
Surface Area under Vine: 7.5 ha – monopoly of Mommessin S A.

The Clos de Tart *grand cru* lies directly above the village. Curiously, the vines are planted north-south rather than the more usual direction of up and down the slope. The large, impressive, two-level cellar is nineteenth century, but the buildings opposite, comprising the offices and lodging for some of the vineyard workers, are medieval, once a monastic *dortoir*. This is a full wine, sturdier than the neighbouring Clos des Lambrays. It has had a tendency to be a little robust, but a new manager, Sylvain Pithiot, who arrived in 1995, has refined matters.

Other Producers of note

PIERRE AMIOT & FILS, GEORGES LIGNIER, DOMAINE LIGNIER-MICHELOT, MICHEL MAGNIEN, JEAN RAPHET AND BERNARD SERVEAU.

CHAMBOLLE-MUSIGNY

Surface Area (1998): *Grands crus* 25.2 ha; *premiers crus* 51 ha; village wine 96 ha.
Production (1998): *Grands crus* (red) 625 hl and (white) 7 hl; *premiers crus* 1811 hl; village wine 3778 hl.
Colour: Red. White wine (from Chardonnay) can be produced only in Le Musigny *grand cru*.
Grape Variety: (Red) Pinot Noir.
Premiers Crus There are twenty-three *premiers crus*, in whole or in part. In alphabetical order they are: Les Amoureuses, Les Baudes, Aux Beaux Bruns (part), Les Borniques, Les Carrières, Les Chabiots, Les Charmes, Les Châtelots, La Combe d'Orveau (part), Aux (or Les) Combottes (part), Les Cras (part), Aux Echanges, Les Feusselottes, Les Fuées, Les Grands Murs, Derrière-La-Grange, Les Groseilles, Les Gruenchers, Les Hauts-Doix, Les Lavrottes, Les Noirots, Les Plantes, Les Sentiers and Les Véroilles (part).
Grands crus Chambolle-Musigny possesses two grands crus: Bonnes-Mares of which 1.6 out of 15 ha lies in the neighbouring commune of Morey-Saint-Denis, and Le Musigny, most of which is owned by de Vogüé.

Geographically Chambolle is a large commune, but is split in two by a narrow valley which seeps out of the upland plateau, thus turning a substantial part of the hillside round to face north, making it unsuitable for the production of high quality wine. The village name comes from Campus Ebulliens or Champ Bouillant: not so much boiling as bubbling, indicating that after a violent storm the little river Grosne would burst its banks and flood the surrounding fields. Like Morey much of the land was under the control of the monks of Cîteaux until sequestered at the time of the French Revolution.

Bonnes-Mares is the fuller of the two *grands crus*, and the more reserved when young, though it is less substantial than Clos de La Roche or the Gevrey *grands crus*. At its best Le Musigny is one of the most ravishing wines of Burgundy: delicate, feminine and fragrant, all silk and lace, the epitome of finesse. The soil in Chambolle contains more limestone, less clay than most of the other

Côte de Nuits communes, and as a result all Chambolle should be exemplified by subtlety rather than power – the Côte de Nuits' equivalent to Volnay in the Côte de Beaune. There is a little white Musigny made from Chardonnay. It is extremely expensive and overpriced.

The best of the *premiers crus* are Les Amoureuses, which lies just below the northern end of Le Musigny, and Les Charmes, which is across the little road leading up from Vougeot. As the names suggest, wines from these two *climats* are similarly soft and feminine, though less intensely flavoured than Le Musigny. The important *premiers crus* on the Bonnes-Mares side are Cras, Fuées, Baudes and Sentiers.

Leading Chambolle-Musigny Producers

★ DOMAINE GHISLAINE BARTHOD

Owner: Ghislaine Barthod.
Surface Area under Vine: 6.6ha, owned and *en fermage* – Chambolle-Musigny *premiers crus* Les Charmes, Les Cras, Les Fuées, Les Véroilles, Aux Beaux-Bruns, Les Baudes and Les Châtelots, and village Chambolle-Musigny.

Ghislaine Barthod took over the winemaking here from her late father Gaston in 1987, and from the 1992 vintage onwards the labels bear her name and not her father's. What has happened at this domaine since 1987 is exemplary of modern-day Burgundy. Ghislaine went to wine school – Gaston, though, once a soldier, had no theoretical qualifications. The vineyard yields are now much lower than they used to be. Other changes include a *table de tri*, more control over vinification temperatures, more *pigeage* and less *remontage*; estate-bottling rather than contract-bottling and fining and filtering only when absolutely necessary.

The result has been a leap in quality from the merely good to the definitely fine, making this cellar a splendid place to compare the nuances between different Chambolle *premiers crus*. In addition to the wines listed above there is some young vine Combottes and a splendid Bourgogne Rouge from a *lieu-dit* called Les Bons-Bâtons located on the other side of the N74 main road.

★★ DOMAINE JACQUES-FRÉDÉRIC MUGNIER

Owner: Jacques-Frédéric Mugnier.
Surface Area under Vine: 4 ha, owned – Le Musigny (1.15 ha), Bonnes-Mares (1.35 ha), Chambolle-Musigny *premiers crus* Les Amoureuses, Les Fuées and Les Plantes, and village Chambolle-Musigny.

The Mugnier domaine occupies the Château de Chambolle-Musigny, a rather gaunt pile built in 1709 with a splendid, if rather sparsely filled, cellar in the basement. The vines used to be farmed by others, but in 1984 Freddy Mugnier returned to take over. He supplements his living by working as an airline pilot three days a week. Quality has improved dramatically, and now more than matches the impressive landholdings. The wines are very pure and have excellent finesse.

★★ DOMAINE GEORGES ROUMIER ET FILS

Owner: Jean-Marie and Christophe Roumier.
Surface Area under Vine: 14.2 ha, owned and *en fermage* (and *en métayage* under the label of Christophe Roumier: see wines*) – Le Musigny (10 a), Bonnes-Mares (1.5 a), Clos de Vougeot (32 a), Corton-Charlemagne (20 a), Chambolle-Musigny *premiers crus* Les Amoureuses and Les Cras, Morey-Saint-Denis *premier cru monopole* Clos-de-La-Bussière, village Chambolle-Musigny, Ruchottes-Chambertin* (two-thirds of 1.54 ha), and Charmes-Chambertin* (half of 0.27 ha).

This is one of Burgundy's most important domaines, run by Jean-Marie Roumier and his son Christophe, who has been making the wine since 1982. The wine is atypical Chambolle: substantial and quite sturdy. Catch them in their adolescence and they can be a bit heavy, a bit four-square. Let them mature properly for ten years or so and you are in for a treat.

★★★ DOMAINE COMTE GEORGES DE VOGÜÉ

Owner: Ladoucette family.
Surface Area under Vine: 12 ha, owned –

Le Musigny (7.14 ha), Bonnes-Mares (2.67 ha), Chambolle-Musigny *premier cru* Les Amoureuses (and also Les Baudes and Les Fuées, but this goes into the village wine), and village Chambolle-Musigny.

This famous domaine can trace its ancestry back to the Middle Ages, and occupies a Renaissance courtyard – the château is no longer inhabited – in the middle of the village. The cellars are substantial and impressive.

The domaine went through a long period when the wine was not up to standard but things were taken in hand in the late 1980s, and from 1989 the team of François Millet in the cellar, Jean-Luc Pépin in the office and Elizabeth de Ladoucette, daughter of the late Comte, have not put a foot wrong. The 1990 Musigny is one of the truly great Burgundies it has been my privilege to drink young.

Other Producers of note

DOMAINE AMIOT-SERVELLE, PIERRE BERTHEAU ET FILS AND DANIEL MOINE-HUDELOT.

VOUGEOT

Surface Area (1998): *Grand cru* 50 ha; *premiers crus* 12 ha; village wine 3 ha.
Production (1998): *Grand cru* 1691 hl; *premiers crus* (red) 363 hl and (white) 130 hl; village wine (red) 91 hl and (white) 45 hl.
Colour: Clos de Vougeot is red only. Vougeot and Vougeot *premiers crus* can be red or white.
Grape Varieties: (Red) Pinot Noir; (white) Chardonnay.
Premiers crus There are four *premiers crus:* Les Cras, Clos de La Perrière, Les Petits Vougeots (in part) and Les Vignes Blanches (Le Clos Blanc),
Grand cru Clos de Vougeot.

While Chambolle is at the top of the slope, the hamlet of Vougeot, hardly more than a main street off which there are a couple of alleyways, lies down on the N74 main road, though thankfully for its few dozen inhabitants, the through traffic now by-passes the village.

Vougeot is dominated by its *grand cru*, Clos de Vougeot, which accounts for four-fifths of the commune's production of red wine. *Premiers crus* account for most of the rest and there is little if any village wine.

By the beginning of the twelfth century, the centre of the western world was the Abbey of Cluny in the southern Mâconnais. Founded by the followers of Saint Benedict in AD 910, Cluny was the wealthiest and most powerful religious settlement in Christendom.

Elsewhere in France, however, there were Benedictines who felt that with such power had come a relaxation in the strict monastic virtues laid down by their founder Saint. Humility, obedience, silence, even chastity, had been forgotten, replaced by rich living, sumptuous eating and drinking and a worldliness far removed from the original objective. One such was Robert, Abbot of Molesmes, a monastery north of Dijon between Langres and Les Riceys. Robert had attempted unsuccessfully to reform the way of life at Molesmes but he found that only a few of his fellow monks wished to return to the simple life. In 1098, with some twenty companions, he left Molesmes and established a reformed commune on the flat plains of eastern Burgundy, in a clearing within forests of oaks and marshy reedlands. From the ancient French word for reed, *cistel*, the name evolved to the Latin *Cistercus*. The new order became known as the Cistercians and the new abbey renamed Cîteaux.

But at Cîteaux the land was unsuitable for the vine. Following the Vouge river upstream, the monks explored the higher ground to the west. Eventually they settled on some uncultivated slopes, bartered with four Burgundian landowners and acquired a few hectares of land. This was the nucleus of Clos de Vougeot.

The monastery soon started receiving gifts of adjoining land suitable for the vine. The poverty, industry, austerity and saintliness of the Cistercians contrasted well with the opulent high life of the other religious orders. Donors shrewdly decided that the appropriate gesture in this world would be recompensed when it might be needed later and the vineyard grew. Around 1160, a press house was constructed but it was not until 1336 that the vineyard took the form we know today and, later still, that the famous wall, forming the Clos, was eventually completed. Finally, in Renaissance times, the château was constructed, affording guest rooms for the abbot and distinguished visitors. The château is now the headquarters of the Chevaliers de Tastevin, Burgundy's leading wine promotion fraternity.

Clos de Vougeot, by now a vineyard of some 50 hectares, remained in the ownership of the Cistercians until the Revolution in 1789 when it was sequestered and put up for sale as a *bien national*. In 1791 it was bought by a Parisian banker, one Jean Foquard, for the huge sum of 1,140,600 livres, payable in *assignats* (paper money). Foquard, it appears, never settled his debt and the authorities turned to Lambert Goblet, the monk cellarist or Magister Celarii, to continue to administer the estate. A year later the vineyard passed to the brothers Ravel but after the Restoration in 1815, Clos de Vougeot changed hands yet again, the Ravels and their associates having been continually in dispute over money and responsibilities over a period of twenty-five years.

This time Clos de Vougeot's proprietor was a man of financial substance. Jules Ouvrard was the local *député* (Member of Parliament) for much of his career. He took the ownership of his important vineyard with the seriousness that it deserved and he also owned land in Corton, Chambertin and Volnay as well as being the owner of the Romanée-Conti *grand cru* which he vinified at Clos de Vougeot. After Ouvrard's death in 1860, there was the usual difficulty about inheritance and this was not finally resolved until 1889. For the first time the land was divided. Originally there were six purchasers, five Burgundian wine merchants and one other; but these six soon became fifteen and now there are eighty: an average of 0.6 hectares or 200 cases per proprietor.

Clos de Vougeot is the largest *grand cru* in the Côte de Nuits and the only one whose land runs from the slope right down to the main road running between Nuits-Saint-Georges and Dijon. Not surprisingly over such a large area, the soil structure is complex and there are differences in aspect and drainage. Add to these the many different owners, each making an individual wine, and you can see why there are variations from one grower's Clos de Vougeot to another's.

At the top and best part of the Clos, where the vineyard borders the *grands crus* of Grands-Echezeaux to the south and Le Musigny to the north, the soil is a pebbly, oolitic limestone of Bathonian origin. There is little clay. Halfway down the slope, the soil becomes marl, that is a mixture of limestone and clay but of a different origin – Bajocian; however, there are still pebbles here so the land drains well. Further down the slope still the soil is less good; it becomes more alluvial and drains less well. Understandably, Clos de Vougeot wines from this lower part of the vineyard are criticised. The critics argue that this land is not worthy of its *grand cru* status, pointing out that over the wall to the south the vineyards are only entitled to the plain village Vosne-Romanée *appellation*. If the Clos had not been one large vineyard, contained within its retaining walls, it would never have been decreed *grand cru* in its entirety.

Tradition has it that the original ecclesiastical proprietors produced three wines: Cuvée des Papes from the top or best land, Cuvée des Rois from the middle and Cuvée des Moines, the only one sold commercially, from the lower slopes. Some people suggest the division was, in fact, vertical, as you face up the slope, not horizontal. Is the wine from the lower, flatter slope, inferior? In practice as well as in principle, yes; but it nevertheless remains more important to choose your grower rather than the location within the vineyard.

Currently, no fewer than twenty-three of the Clos owners possess holdings which are smaller than a quarter of a hectare. One-third of a hectare will produce, before evaporation, racking and other losses, five or six small barrels or *pièces* of wine. What do you do if you are one of these owners and some of your land is under young vines? Do you sacrifice a third of your crop? Is it too cynical to suggest that only a few Burgundians are saintly enough to be as perfectionist as this?

At its best, Clos de Vougeot can rank among the greatest red Burgundies, alongside Chambertin and the best Vosne-Romanée. But it rarely does so. Normally though, I would put it in the second division of *grands crus*, comparable with those of Morey and Corton, or indeed its neighbours Echezeaux and Grands-Echezeaux. In style, the wine is plumper and lusher than

Chambertin or La Tâche, less firm, less intensely flavoured and with less definition. It also does not possess the cumulative complexity and fragrance of Musigny. Yet when rich, fullish and generous, with a fruit which is half redolent of soft, red, summer berries and half that of blackberries and chocolate, plus undertones of toffee, liquorice, burnt nuts and even coffee (a promising sign in a young Burgundy), the wine can be immensely enjoyable. Sadly, because of the vineyard's size and renown and the multiplicity of owners, it is one of the most abused names in the area.

Clos de Vougeot Producers of note

DOMAINE AMIOT-SERVELLE, ROBERT ARNOUX, MAISON BOUCHARD PÈRE ET FILS, DANIEL CHOPIN, JACKY CONFURON-COTÉTIDOT, JEAN-JACQUES CONFURON, MAISON JOSEPH DROUHIN, RENÉ ENGEL, MAISON FAIVELEY, JEAN GRIVOT, ANNE GROS, DOMAINE GROS FRÈRE ET SOEUR, MICHEL GROS, ALFRED HAEGELYN-JAYER, ALAIN HUDELOT-NOËLLAT, MAISON LOUIS JADOT, DOMAINE LEROY, DOMAINE MÉO-CAMUZET, DENIS MORTET, DR GEORGES MUGNERET, DOMAINE MONGEARD-MUGNERET, GEORGES ROUMIER, DOMAINE THOMAS-MOILLARD AND CHÂTEAU DE LA TOUR.

The village and *premier cru* wines of Vougeot are of less interest than Clos de Vougeot. Even when tasting in the cellars of the best growers Vougeot wines seem to lack depth, vigour and intensity and you return with relief to the wines of Chambolle and Vosne, the adjacent communes.

Leading Vougeot Producer

★ DOMAINE ALAIN HUDELOT-NOËLLAT

Owner: Alain Hudelot-Noëllat.
Surface Area under Vine: 10 ha, owned and *en fermage* – Richebourg (28 a), Romanée-Saint-Vivant (48 a), Clos de Vougeot (1.05 ha), Vosne-Romanée *premier cru* Les Suchots,
Les Beaumonts and Les Malconsorts, Nuits-Saints-Georges *premier cru* Les Murgers,
Chambolle-Musigny *premier cru* Les Charmes,

and village Vosne-Romanée, Chambolle-Musigny and Vougeot (Les Petits-Vougeots).

Despite occasional inconsistency in the past – but since 1989 things have been more regular here – this is definitely one of the top domaines in Burgundy, for when Alain Hudelot's top wines are singing they are truly magnificent. Hudelot retains about 10 per cent of the stems, believes in a long maceration at up to 32°C, and gives his *grands crus* 100 per cent new oak. He neither fines not filters. These are wines of great flair and concentration: full, opulent and multi-dimensional. the only weak point is the Vougeot. But that is the fault of the soil, not the winemaking of Alain Hudelot.

FLAGEY-ECHEZEAUX

Surface Area (1998): *Grands crus* 41 ha.
Production (1998): *Grands crus* 1327 hl.
Colour: *Grands crus* Echezeaux and Grands-Echezeaux for red wines only.
Grape Variety: Pinot Noir.

If Vougeot is governed by its Clos, the commune of Flagey is even more curiously laid out. The village lies in flatlands on the wrong side (east side) of the railway and is surrounded by maize fields and orchards, not vineyards. Flagey's vineyards lie back on the west side of the railway, the right side, and consist solely of two *grands crus* which lie south-west of Clos de Vougeot, completely isolated from the village. All the other Flagey wine is sold as Vosne-Romanée, the next village to the south.

Grands-Echezeaux lies halfway up the slope, immediately above Clos de Vougeot and Echezeaux is even higher up. Wine from Grands-Echezeaux is considered to be the better of the two and fetches higher prices. It could well be argued that many an Echezeaux wine is as good as a Grands-Echezeaux, that the best sections of its vineyard are as capable of producing wines as fine as those from Grands-Echezeaux, but in general, Grands-Echezeaux is worth the extra money.

I find both wines sturdier and more robust – even sauvage – than their immediate neighbours; there is more clay in the stony soil. And the result – in

Southern
Côte de Nuits

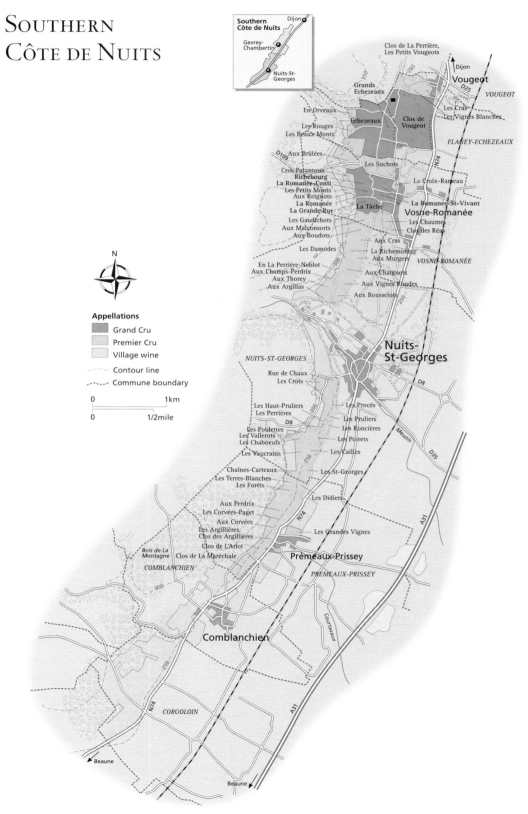

Southern
Côte de Nuits

Dijon

Gevrey-
Chambertin

Nuits-St-
Georges

Clos de La Perrière,
Les Petits Vougeots

Dijon

Vougeot

VOUGEOT

Grands
Echezeaux

Les Cras
Les Vignes Blanches

En Orveaux

Echezeaux

Clos de
Vougeot

FLAGEY-ECHEZEAUX

Les Rouges
Les Beaux Monts

Aux Brûlées

Les Suchots

La Croix-Rameau

Cros Parantoux
Richebourg
La Romanée-Conti
Les Petits Monts
Aux Reignots
La Romanée
La Grande Rue

La Tâche

La Romanée-St-Vivant

Vosne-Romanée

Les Chaumes
Clos des Réas

Les Gaudichots
Aux Malconsorts
Aux Boudots

Aux Cras

Les Damodes

La Richemone
Aux Murgers

VOSNE-ROMANÉE

En La Perrière-Noblot
Aux Champs-Perdrix
Aux Thorey
Aux Argillas

Aux Chaignots

Aux Vignes Rondes

Aux Bousselots

Appellations

- Grand Cru
- Premier Cru
- Village wine
- Contour line
- Commune boundary

0   1km
0   1/2mile

NUITS-ST-GEORGES

Nuits-
St-Georges

Rue de Chaux
Les Crots

D8

Les Procès

Les Haut-Pruliers
Les Perrières

Les Pruliers

Les Poulettes
Les Vallerots
Les Chaboeufs

Les Roncières

Les Poirets

Les Vaucrains

Les Cailles

Chaînes-Carteaux
Les Terres-Blanches
Les Forêts

Les St-Georges

Les Didiers

Aux Perdrix
Les Corvées-Paget
Aux Corvées
Les Argillières,
Clos des Argillières
Clos de L'Arlot

Les Grandes Vignes

Bois de La
Montagne   Clos de La Maréchale

Prémeaux-Prissey

COMBLANCHIEN

PRÉMEAUX-PRISSEY

Comblanchien

Courtavaux

CORGOLOIN

Beaune

Beaune

Echezeaux certainly – is a wine of less finesse, sometimes hardly worth the *grand cru* designation. In fairness, this is the least expensive of all Côte de Nuits *grand cru* wines and often no more expensive than a good Vosne-Romanée *premier cru*. In good hands, though, both these wines can represent excellent value. Most Vosne-Romanée growers own land in one or other of the Echezeaux vineyards.

Leading Flagey-Echezeaux Producer

★★ DOMAINE EMMANUEL ROUGET

Owner: Emmanuel Rouget.

Surface Area under Vine: 7 ha, owned and *en fermage/métayage* – Echezeaux (1.43 ha), Vosne-Romanée *premier cru* Les Beaumonts and Cros Parentoux, village Vosne-Romanée, Nuits-Saint-Georges and Savigny-Lès-Beaune.

It was only by accident that the genial, bullet-headed Henri Jayer (born 1922) became a winemaker and hence a guru. Youngest of three, he was approached during the war by Monsieur Camuzet, mayor of Vosne: 'Would you like to look after my vines for me?' So a share-cropping lease was drawn up which was to last until the late 1980s. In the meantime he made the wines of his elder brothers: Georges and Lucien.

Henri has now retired, and family vines are tended by his nephew Emmanuel Rouget, who lives in the old Gouroux premises in Flagey. A little Echezeaux is still bottled under the Henri Jayer name and this is a separate *cuvée*. But the names of Georges and Lucien Jayer are no more. The rest is bottled as Rouget.

Jayer's reputation, so high today, dates from the time he altered his vinification methods towards the end of the 1970s to include total destemming, a week long cold maceration before fermentation, lots of new oak, no filtration and hand-bottling. And in addition, he paid meticulous attention to cleanliness, such as keeping the wine topped up regularly in cask. Emmanuel Rouget continues to make the wine in the same way.

The resulting wines are rich in colour and aroma, opulently oaky, full but not aggressively tannic and vibrantly intense in flavour. The Cros Parentoux is the real star, even better than the Echezeaux. I have found no diminution of quality since Rouget has been in charge. If anything, the use of new oak is more sensitive. Some of Jayer's wines, the 1985s, for instance, were over-oaked and did not age gracefully.

VOSNE-ROMANÉE

Surface Area (1998): *Grands crus* 27 ha; *premiers crus* 54 ha; village wine 99 ha.

Production (1998): *Grands crus* 761 hl; *premiers crus* 2026 hl; village wine 4215 hl.

Colour: Red.

Grape Variety: Pinot Noir.

Premiers crus There are eleven *premiers crus* in Vosne-Romanée. In alphabetical order they are: Les Beaux-Monts, Aux Brulées, Les Chaumes, La Croix-Rameau, Cros Parantoux, Les Gaudichots, Aux Malconsorts, Les Petits Monts, Clos des Réas, Aux Reignots and Les Suchots. There are a further two in Flagey-Echezeaux, sold as Vosne-Romanée: Les Rouges and En Orveaux.

Grands crus There are six *grands crus*: La Grande-Rue, La Romanée-Saint-Vivant, Richebourg, La Tâche, La Romanée and La Romanée-Conti.

Vosne-Romanée is the southernmost of the six great communes of the Côte de Nuits and perhaps the greatest of them all. The village itself is small and tranquil, set back a few hundred metres from the main road. On either side of the village lie the *premiers crus*; above and behind the houses are the celebrated *grands crus*, which produce some of the finest wines of the Côte de Nuits.

Vosne is mentioned in documents as early as the seventh century, and, like much of the surrounding area, came under the control of the Abbey of Cîteaux during the Cistercian heyday. Later on it suffered badly at the hands of both Austrian troops in Napoleonic times and German troops in 1870. Little remains of the original medieval village. Chambolle, with its steep streets and narrow cul de sacs, has more charm. Morey, with its wide main street and many substantial medieval and Renaissance courtyards, is more imposing.

The Abbé Courtépée, in the late eighteenth century, said of Vosne-Romanée *'Il n'y a pas de vin commun'* (there are no common wines in the village). The wines were famous then – Louis XV's cousin, the Prince de Conti, owned a large area of La Romanée – and they are highly regarded now. The village possesses a large number of excellent growers. Growers, however, cannot produce fine wine without having prime land. The Vosne mixture is as good as you can get: a well-drained slope with the right exposure, facing east or south-east, and lying approximately 250 to 300 metres above sea level, and soil which essentially an oolitic, iron-rich limestone on a base of marl, rock and pebbles. The vineyards are sheltered from the west and north by the trees on the top of the slope and the *grand cru* vineyards, plumb in the middle of the slope, are in the best position of all.

Nearest to the village is Romanée-Saint-Vivant, the largest *grand cru*. Further up the slope is the tiny, gently sloping La Romanée-Conti and the even smaller La Romanée, at less than one hectare the smallest individual *appellation* in France. As the hill curves round to the right to face more north-east than south-east lies the steeper Richebourg. To the left, across the narrow row of vines which make up the newest *grand cru* vineyard, La Grande-Rue, runs the slope of La Tâche, which is again steep at the top. On either side of this memorable roll-call of names are two of Vosne's top *premiers crus*: Les Malconsorts, which borders one of Nuits-Saint-Georges' best *premiers crus*, Les Boudots, and to the north Les Suchots, which borders the *grand cru* Echezeaux. Four of the *grands crus* are under single ownership. La Romanée-Conti and La Tâche are owned by the Domaine de La Romanée-Conti. La Romanée belongs to the Comte Liger-Belair's Domaine de Vosne-Romanée whose wine is sold by the *négociant*, Bouchard Père et Fils. La Grande-Rue is owned by the Lamarche family.

Romanée-Conti is the best and most expensive *grand cru*, selling for more than twice that of La Tâche and three times that of the Domaine de La Romanée-Conti's Richebourg or Romanée-Saint-Vivant wines. At a price which is four times that of Château Lafite it is probably the most expensive wine on earth, and therefore should be sublime. It often is: the most intensely and subtly perfumed, the richest and most concentrated, the most explosively flavoured and the most persistently long on the palate of all Burgundy. The very best vintages take fifteen years to mature.

La Tâche runs at a very close second, and is significantly superior to the other Domaine de La Romanée-Conti wines, good as they are: Richebourg, whether from the hands of the Domaine de La Romanée-Conti or others, is opulent and velvety; Romanée-Saint-Vivant is lighter and more feminine, akin to Le Musigny. All have a finesse missing in either the Domaine's or other growers' two Echezeaux *grands crus* and a definition lacking in all but the very best Clos de Vougeots.

Among the thirteen *premiers crus*, Les Malconsorts, already mentioned as being one of the Vosne's best, has as its neighbours the *premiers crus* of Chaumes and Clos des Réas, the latter solely owned by the excellent Domaine Gros. Above Les Suchots, the other top *premier cru*, are the *premiers crus* of Les Beaumonts – technically partly in the commune of Flagey but selling its wine as Vosne – and Les Brûlées.

Leading Vosne-Romanée Producers

★ DOMAINE ROBERT ARNOUX

Owner: Arnoux family.

Surface Area under Vine: 12 ha, owned and *en fermage*/*métayage* – Romanée-Saint-Vivant (35 a), Echezeaux (79 a), Clos de Vougeot (43 a) (top), Vosne-Romanée *premiers crus* Les Suchots and Les Chaumes, Nuits-Saint-Georges *premiers crus* Les Corvées-Pagets and Les Procès, village Vosne-Romanée, including the *lieu-dit* Les Maizières, and village Nuits-Saint-Georges, including the *lieu-dit* Les Poisets.

Robert Arnoux, who died in 1995 aged sixty-four, was a large and somewhat intimidating man on first acquaintance. He had doubled the land he farmed since taking over from his father in the 1950s, and this has necessitated frequent extensions to the cellar underneath his house, set back from the Nuits-Dijon main road. He has been succeeded by his son-in-law, Pascal Lachaux.

I have had fine quality here in the past, particularly from its Romanée-Saint-Vivant and its Suchots, from old vines at the top of the vineyard. The wines are rich, sturdy and tannic, mixed with a good dollop of new oak (50 per cent for the *grands crus*), perhaps a little on the robust side, and need time to mature. Good but not great would be an apt summary of the wines of the 1980s, but since then there has been a distinct improvement, especially since 1993: Lachaux does a fine job.

★ DOMAINE SYLVAIN CATHIARD
Owner: Cathiard family.
Surface Area under Vine: 5.5 ha, owned and *en fermage/métayage* – Romanée-Saint-Vivant (17 a), Vosne-Romanée *premiers crus* Les Suchots, Les Reignots, Les Malconsorts and En Orveaux, Nuits-Saint-Georges *premier cru* Les Murgers, and village Vosne-Romanée, Chambolle-Musigny and Nuits-Saint-Georges.

Sylvain Cathiard, a quiet serious man with an unfortunate stutter, in his mid-forties, now farms almost all the land formerly controlled by his father André. He is also a *métayer* for the Moillard holdings in Les Malconsorts, Nuits-Saint-Georges Clos-de-Thorey and in Romanée-Saint-Vivant, But all these grapes go to Moillard for vinification. These are wines of concentration and elegance which will keep well. This good domaine is also a source of that *rara avis*, the En Orveaux *premier cru*.

★ DOMAINE BRUNO CLAVELIER
Owner: Bruno Clavelier.
Surface Area under Vine: 6.5 ha, owned and *en fermage/métayage* – Corton, Rognets (33 a), Vosne-Romanée *premiers crus* Les Beaux-Monts and Les Brûlées, Nuits-Saint-Georges *premier cru* Aux Cras, Chambolle-Musigny *premier cru* La Combe-d'Orveau, Gevrey-Chambertin *premier cru* Les Corbeaux, and village Vosne-Romanée, including the *lieux-dits* La Montagne *monopole* and Les Hautes-Maizières.

Bruno Clavelier (born in 1964), a qualified oenologist, took over the vines belonging to his parents and maternal grandparents (Brosson) in 1987 and has since enlarged this domaine by extending it into Nuits-Saint-Georges and Gevrey-Chambertin. He has also increased the percentage of the wine sold in bottle.

The average age of the vines is old. Ninety per cent of the grapes are destemmed and the wine is vinified traditionally at 28-30°C and matured using a maximum of 30 per cent new oak. The wines are unfiltered and are full, rich and perfumed, This is quality from a rising star.

★ DOMAINE JACKY CONFURON-COTÉTIDOT
Owner: Jacky Confuron-Cotétidot.
Surface Area under Vine: 11 ha, owned and *en fermage/métayage* – Charmes-Chambertin (39.30 a), Mazis-Chambertin (9.50 a), Clos de Vougeot (25.39 a), Echezeaux (47.52 a), Gevrey-Chambertin *premiers crus* Craipillot and Lavaux-Saint-Jacques, Vosne-Romanée *premier cru* Les Suchots, Nuits-Saint-Georges *premiers crus* Les Murgers and Vignes-Rondes, and village Vosne-Romanée, Chambolle-Musigny, Nuits-Saint-Georges and Gevrey-Chambertin.

The irrepressible and engaging Jacky Confuron, born in 1936, is married to Bernadette and although she didn't bring any vines with her as a dowry, he has added her maiden name to the domaine name in order to avoid confusion with other Confurons.

Accad is an oenologist whose theories of bringing life back to the soil, and fixing colouring and flavouring by a prolonged pre-fermentation cold-soaking were much in vogue in Burgundy in the 1980s. Jacky Confuron claims that he is not so much a disciple of the so-called Accad method of cold pre-fermentation maceration as Accad's mentor. He was cold macerating long before Accad came on the scene!

Confuron thrives on eccentricity. Underneath there is a slight chip on his shoulder, but also a serious passion for old vines, low grape yields, long *cuvaisons* and no filtration. There is minimal use of new oak and the wines are bottled later than most. In 1994 this Confuron family took over some land in Gevrey-Chambertin and at the same time his son Yves began to take over running the domaine.

★★ DOMAINE RENÉ ENGEL

Owner: Engel family.

Surface Area under Vine: 7 ha, owned – Clos de
Vougeot (1.37 ha), Grands-Echezeaux (50 a),
Echezeaux (55 a), Vosne-Romanée *premier cru*
Les Brûlées, and village Vosne-Romanée.

In the two decades since he has been in charge, Philippe
Engel (born in 1955) has transformed this domaine,
which then sold much of its wine in bulk, from the very
good, to the very serious indeed. All the wine is now bottled at the domaine. The grapes are destemmed and
given a couple of days to macerate before fermentation
starts. Maceration then lasts up to three weeks and 30-50
per cent new oak is used for maturing the wine. The
wines have great intensity, splendid style and individuality, and real power to last. In a visit to Burgundy in
November 1993 his 1992s, harvested at 32 hl/ha in an
otherwise abundant vintage, were the best range of
wines I sampled, along with those of Leroy.

★ DOMAINE FOREY PÈRE ET FILS

Owner: Forey family.

Surface Area under Vine: 9.35 ha, owned and *en
métayage* – Clos de Vougeot (32 a), Echezeaux
(38 a), Vosne-Romanée *premier cru* Les
Gaudichots, Nuits-Saint-Georges *premiers crus*
Les Saint-Georges and Les Perrières, Morey-Saint-
Denis *premier cru*, and village Vosne-Romanée,
Nuits-Saint-Georges and Morey-Saint-Denis.

The tall dark Régis Forey (born in 1960) is married to
Chantal Jacob of the Jacob domaine in Echevronne. But
the two domaines are kept separate. Forey now has a
new cellar on the other side of the village from the
Château de Vosne-Romanée where he made his wine
until 1999. Until 1999 Forey was also responsible for the
vines and winemaking in La Romanée and Les Gaudichots for the Château de Vosne-Romanée. The *élevage*
and bottling of these wines is by Bouchard Père et Fils.

He practises partial destemming, some pre-fermentation maceration, and long *cuvaisons*, resulting in full,
rich concentrated wines which keep well. I find the Gaudichots better than the Echezeaux, as well as being more
individual. The vines adjoin those of La Tâche.

★★ DOMAINE JEAN GRIVOT

Owner: Grivot family.

Surface Area under Vine: 14 ha, owned
(the domaine is *fermier* for the Grivot family
vineyard) – Richebourg (31 a), Clos de Vougeot
(1.86 ha), Echezeaux (61 a), Vosne-Romanée
premiers crus Les Beaux-Monts, Les Brûlées,
Les Chaumes, Les Suchots and Les Rouges, Nuits-
Saint-Georges *premiers crus* Les Boudots,
Les Pruliers and Les Roncières, village Vosne-
Romanée including the *lieu-dit* Les Bossières,
village Nuits-Saint-Georges including the *lieux-
dits* Les Lavières and Les Charmois, and village
Chambolle-Musigny in the *lieu-dit* La Combe
d'Orveau.

The lean, somewhat serious Etienne Grivot and his
ascetic, bearded father Jean have been producing excellent wine at this domaine for many years. A change in
vinification methods in 1987, when Etienne adopted the
cold, pre-fermentation maceration technique, has not
affected the quality. Until 1988 some of the wines
(Echezeaux and Vosne-Romanée *premier cru* Les Rouges)
were labelled Jacqueline Jayer: Mademoiselle Jayer being
Madame Jean Grivot's aunt.

Almost entirely destemmed, the must is cold macerated for a few days, the length depending on the
vintage and vinified at between 28° and 32°C. The wine is
then kept in a maximum of one-quarter new wood (10
per cent for the lesser wines) until the first racking.
These elegant, perfumed, distinctive wines are proof, if
such were still required, of the efficacy of the so-called
Accad method. This is a fine source.

★★ DOMAINE ANNE GROS

Owner: François and Anne Gros.

Surface Area under Vine: 5 ha, owned and *en
fermage* – Richebourg (60 a), Clos de Vougeot
(93 a), and village Vosne-Romanée and
Chambolle-Musigny.

The petite, charming and attractive Anne Gros has been
in charge here since 1988, this estate having been
detached from the old Louis Gros domaine in 1963. Prior
to her arrival the domaine disposed of half of its wine in

bulk. Anne is now selling all the wine in bottle and from 1995 the labels bear her name alone.

Some 20 per cent of the stems are retained, the fermentation temperatures are allowed to climb up to 32°C, and 90 per cent new wood is used for the *grands crus*. There has been a considerable improvement in a short space of time, and we can now see a sure touch here, producing fragrant wines whose characteristic is intensity and finesse rather than power. A fine source.

★ Domaine Michel Gros
Owner: Jean Gros family.
Surface Area under Vine: 17.6 ha, owned and *en fermage* – Clos de Vougeot (21 a), Vosne-Romanée *premier cru monopole* Clos de Réas (2.12 ha), and village Vosne-Romanée, Nuits-Saint-Georges and Chambolle-Musigny; plus a substantial holding in the Hautes-Côtes de Nuits.

This splendid estate was once called after Jean Gros, Michel's father, and from the mid-1980s until recently the wines were bottled under either name. Today the name of Jean Gros is no more, and the domaine has lost its Richebourg (to Michel's sister A F Gros of Pommard) in order to preserve the monopoly of the Clos de Réas. The domaine's hallmark is very pure, very intense wines with great breed.

Domaine François Lamarche
Owner: François Lamarche family.
Surface Area under Vine: 8.2 ha, owned and *en fermage* – La Grande-Rue *monopole* (1.65 ha), Clos de Vougeot (1.36 ha), Grands-Echezeaux (30 a); Echezeaux (1.10 ha), Vosne-Romanée *premiers crus* Les Suchots, Les Chaumes and Les Malconsorts, and village Vosne-Romanée.

In 1990 François Lamarche, his sister Geneviève and his wife Marie-Blanche were finally rewarded in their efforts to persuade the authorities to elevate La Grande-Rue to *grand cru* status, a task neglected by the older generation of the family in the 1930s. François has modified the winemaking methods since he has been in charge. The fruit is now entirely destemmed, the percentage of new oak has been raised – to 40 per cent overall – and the

wine is bottled earlier, after eighteen months. All this is as it should be but quality, nevertheless, once very fine at this domaine, still leaves something to be desired. I find the wines lack breed and definition. and even in 1990 some were far too weedy. Future vintages, however, suggest this domaine may have turned the corner. But there is still a way to go. The 1993s showed better than expected in bottle.

★★★ Domaine Leroy
Owner: Leroy and Bize families.
Surface Area under Vine: 22.4 ha, owned – Chambertin (50 a), Latricières-Chambertin (57 a), Clos de La Roche (67 a), Musigny (27 a), Clos de Vougeot (1.91 ha), Richebourg (78 a), Romanée-Saint-Vivant (99 a), Corton-Renardes (50 a), Corton-Charlemagne (43 a), Gevrey-Chambertin *premier cru* Les Combottes, Chambolle-Musigny *premier cru* Les Charmes, Vosne-Romanée *premiers crus* Les Beaux-Monts and Les Brûlées, Nuits-Saints-Georges *premiers crus* Les Boudots and Les Vignerondes, Savigny-Lès-Beaune *premier cru* Les Narbantons, Volnay *premier cru* Santenots, village Gevrey-Chambertin, village Chambolle-Musigny in the *lieu-dit* Les Fremières, village Vosne-Romanée in the *lieu-dit* Les Genevrières, village Nuits-Saint-Georges in the *lieux-dits* Les Lavières, Aux Allots and Au Bas-de-Combe, village Pommard in the *lieux-dits* Les Vignots and Les Trois Follots and Auxey-Duresses (white). In addition, Madame Bize-Leroy's other estate, the Domaine d'Auvenay, has important holdings in Mazis-Chambertin, Bonnes-Mares, Chevalier-Montrachet, Criots-Bâtard-Montrachet, Puligny-Montrachet *premier cru* Les Folatières and Meursault.

This is one of the greatest estates in Burgundy. Lalou Bize, part owner, and until 1993 joint manager with Aubert de Villaine of the Domaine de La Romanée-Conti, bought the moribund 12-hectare Domaine Charles Noëllat in Vosne-Romanée for 65 million francs in 1988. Part of the finance came from the sale of one-third of Leroy SA to her Japanese agents Takashimaya.

The next year there was a further acquisition: 19 million francs for the 2.5-hectare Domaine Philippe Remy in Gevrey-Chambertin. More land in Musigny followed the year after, altogether creating one of the most impressive ranges of wine to be seen in one cellar.

The wines are magnificently impressive, too. The old vines have been jealously preserved. The yields are cut to the quick, and reduced even further by the domaine's insistence on cultivation according to biodynamic principles. There is no destemming, a long *cuvaison* and plenty of new oak. The results are breathtakingly intense, pure and concentrated, and curiously quite different in style from those at the Domaine de La Romanée-Conti, despite the approach being superficially similar.

★★ DOMAINE MÉO-CAMUZET

Owner: Méo-Camuzet family.
Surface Area under Vine: 15 ha, owned and *en fermage* – Richebourg (35 a), Clos de Vougeot (3.03 ha, 2.20 ha exploited), Corton (45 a), Vosne-Romanée *premiers crus* in Cros-Parentoux, Aux Brûlées and Les Chaumes, Nuits-Saint-Georges *premiers crus* Aux Boudots and Aux Murgers, and village Vosne-Romanée and Nuits-Saint-Georges.

This is a fine domaine, but one which has only been selling its wine in bottle for a little over a decade. The urbane, silver-haired Jean Méo, civil servant and politician, and great-nephew of Etienne Camuzet, inherited a domaine which was largely leased out *en métayage* to Henri Jayer, the Faurois family, Jean Tardy and others. Up to 1983 his own share was sold in bulk to merchants. From the 1988 vintage onward the *métayage* arrangements began to come to an end and Jean-Nicolas Méo (born in 1964) son of Jean, arrived to take charge, helped by the avuncular genius of Henri Jayer. (See Domaine Emmanuel Rouget page 171.)

The wine is made in the Jayer way: total destemming, several days' cold maceration, long *cuvaison*s and lots of new oak. And the results are exciting. It is only with the Clos de Vougeot in recent years that I have occasionally had any qualms. And this is curious, for the domaine has a huge holding here, ideally placed adjacent to the château, with all the economies of scale one could wish.

★ DOMAINE GÉRARD MUGNERET

Owner: Gérard Mugneret.
Surace Area under Vine: 8.5 ha, owned and *en fermage/métayage* – Echezeaux (65 a), Vosne-Romanée *premiers crus* Les Brûlées and Les Suchots, Nuits-Saint-Georges *premiers crus* Les Chaignots and Les Boudots, Chambolle-Musigny *premier cru* Les Charmes, Savigny-Lès-Beaune *premier cru* Les Gravins, and village Vosne-Romanée and Gevrey-Chambertin.

Gérard Mugneret, an energetic, welcoming man in his forties, is one of the *métayers* of his late uncle Dr George Mugneret's estate. The fruit is totally destemmed, given a few days' cold maceration before fermentation (up to 34°C) and a long maceration. The wine is matured in an average of one-third new oak. The results are impressive: pure, focused, rich and stylish. Sadly the wine is rarely found on the export market. Having had problems with payment Gérard Mugneret now concentrates on selling direct to his French customers and others who call at the domaine.

★★ DR GEORGES MUGNERET/ MUGNERET-GIBOURG

Owner: Madame Jacqueline Mugneret and family.
Surace Area under Vine: 8.9 ha, owned – Clos de Vougeot (34 a), Ruchottes-Chambertin (0.64 a), Echezeaux (1.25 a), Chambolle-Musigny *premier cru* Les Feusselots, Nuits-Saint-Georges *premiers crus* Les Vignes-Rondes and Les Chaignots, and village Vosne-Romanée.

The charming, hospitable and elegant Mugneret ladies, Jacqueline and her daughters Marie-Christine and Marie-Andrée, produce meticulously crafted wines from the yield of their estate, most of which is tended either *en métayage* or *à la tâche* by other *vignerons*.

The fruit is entirely destemmed, cold macerated for two or three days, and fermented using cultured yeasts at a temperature of up to 33°C. There is a healthy percentage of new oak: from 20 per cent up to 80 per cent for the top wines. The wines are fullish, concentrated, very stylish and extremely well balanced: delicious examples of pure Pinot Noir. A fine domaine.

★★★ DOMAINE DE LA ROMANÉE-CONTI

Owners: de Villaine and Leroy/Bize/Roch families.
Surface Area under Vine: 25.6 ha, owned and *en fermage* – La Romanée-Conti *monopole* (1.81 ha), La Tâche *monopole* (6.06 ha), Romanée-Saint-Vivant (5.28 ha), Grands-Echezeaux (3.53 ha), Echezeaux (4.67 ha) and Le Montrachet (68 a); plus other land in Vosne-Romanée, the produce of which is sold off in bulk/or farmed by others.

This is the most famous wine name in Burgundy, and one of its largest and longest-established domaines: probably *the* largest in terms of *grand cru* ownership. Jointly owned by the de Villaine and Leroy/Bize/Roch families and administered by the scholarly Aubert de Villaine (born in 1939) and Henri-Frédérick Roch (born in 1962), the DRC (or Domaine Romanée-Conti) produces some of the most sought-after wines in the world, albeit at an unapologetically high price,

There is never any destemming here. After a careful *triage* (sorting out of the sub-standard fruit) the must is left for five or six days at a low temperature, then fermented at up to 33°C, now with mechanical *pigeage* two or three times a day, before being matured entirely in new oak for eighteen months.

Are the wines worth these high prices? For the sublimely individual, poised and intensely flavoured Romanée-Conti itself, and the lusher but equally magical La Tâche, the answer is indisputably yes. For the other wines, where there is competition at less greedy levels, the response is moot. You can often do better elsewhere. And then there is a question of style. The 100 per cent stems sometimes leave an unmistakable taste. This is not to the taste of the more modern school of Burgundian winemakers who have adopted Henri Jayer as their guru. But the beauty of Burgundy is its diversity. There is plenty of room for both. And the DRC at its best produces prodigiously fine wine.

Other Producers of note

JEAN-YVES BIZOT, PATRICE CACHEUX-SIRUGUE, DOMAINE DU CLOS FRANTIN, FRANCOIS GERBET, DOMAINE GROS FRÈRE & SOEUR, ALFRED HAEGELEN-JAYER, DOMAINE MANIÈRE-NOIROT, DOMAINE MONGEARD-MUGNERET, DENIS & DOMINIQUE MUGNERET, PERNIN-ROSSIN, ARNELLE & BERNARD RION, JEAN TARDY, FABRICE VIGOT AND CHÂTEAU DE VOSNE-ROMANÉE.

NUITS-SAINT-GEORGES

Surface Area (1998): *Premiers crus* 142 ha, village wine 162 ha.
Production (1998): *Premiers crus* (red) 5619 hl and (white) 123 hl, village wine (red) 7029 hl and (white) 39 hl.
Colours: Red and white.
Grape Varieties: (red) Pinot Noir;
(white) Chardonnay.

Premiers crus There are thirty-eight *premiers crus*, in whole or in part. I have divided them into three areas:
Northern Nuits-Saint-Georges Aux Argillas (Les Argillas is a village Nuits), Aux Boudots, Aux Bousselots, Aux Chaignots, Aux Champs-Perdrix (part), Aux Cras, Les Damodes (part), Aux Murgers, En La Perrière-Noblot (part), La Richemone, Aux Thorey (part) and Aux Vignes Rondes.

Middle Nuits-Saint-Georges Les Cailles, Les Chaboeufs, Chaînes-Carteaux, Les Crots (part), Les Perrières, Les Poirets (or Porrets), Les Poulettes (part), Les Procés, Les Pruliers, Les Haut-Pruliers (part), Les Roncières, Rue de Chaux, Les Saint-Georges, Les Vallerots (part) and Les Vaucrains.

Prémeaux Les Argillières, Clos des Argillières, Clos de L'Arlot (*monopole*), Aux Corvées, Les Corvées-Paget, Les Didiers, Les Forêts, Les Grandes Vignes (part), Clos de La Maréchale (*monopole*), Aux Perdrix and Les Terres-Blanches (part).

A number of growers boast monopolies over a particular sub-section or *clos* within a particular *premier cru*. Others are sold under other main names. Among these latter wines can be numbered: the Château Gris of Lupe-Cholet, a 2.80 ha enclosure within Les Crots; the Clos-Saint-Marc, which lies within the Corvées and is an exclusivity of Maison Bouchard Père et Fils of Beaune; and another part of the Corvées known as the Clos-des-Corvées which is owned by the Thomas family, was hitherto a monopoly of Maison Jadot and is now operated by the Domaine Prieuré-Roch. Moreover, a couple of vineyards close to Les Saint-Georges itself have slyly, like the town of Nuits, added Saint-Georges to their title as if it were some magic road to everlasting success. Thus Le Poirets or Porrets (despite being separated from it by Les Cailles) and Les Forêts (despite being separated from it by Les Didiers) are more often than not suffixed 'Saint-Georges'. It is amazing what you get away with!

Nuits-Saint-Georges is an industrial conglomeration rather than a winemaking village and is the commercial centre of the Côte de Nuits. It is a bustling, busy, friendly town, less self-conscious than Beaune. Nuits-Saint-Georges' vineyards stretch on either side of a gap in the Côte, and on the southern side of the town continue into the commune of Prémeaux, whose wines are also entitled to the Nuits-Saint-Georges *appellation*.

The original Nuits was a Gallo-Roman villa further out in the plain. The name though has no nocturnal connections and is more likely to be either a corruption of the Celtic *un win*, a stream in a valley, or else to have something to do with nuts from the French word, *noix*. In the early Middle Ages the area was the fief of Hugues, sire of Vergy, who donated much of the land to the local monastery of Saint-Denis and the priory of Saint-Vivant, and a village slowly began to expand further up the valley of the river Meuzin in the site it occupies today. Though Nuits was originally fortified, it lost its strategic importance when the Duchy of Franche-Comté was absorbed into the kingdom of France in 1678. It was no longer a frontier outpost and the walls surrounding it were slowly dismantled. As a result, and the fact that the main road thunders right through its centre, Nuits has little of Beaune's medieval attraction.

Nuits-Saint-Georges has no *grands crus* but, instead, an impressive list of twenty-seven *premiers crus*, plus another ten in Prémeaux. On the northern side, the vineyards cover a wide area from east to west. The *premiers crus* here lie at the top of the slope. The best known include Boudots, Richemone, Murgers, Damodes and Chaignots. South of the town the vineyards begin again and the slope is narrower. Here are the *premiers crus* of Pruliers, Roncières, Poirets, Vaucrains, Cailles and Les Saint-

Georges itself, the most renowned. Across the commune boundary into Prémeaux the slope becomes steeper at first and the vineyards are more confined. Here you will find the *premiers crus* of Les Forêts, Perdrix, Corvées, Argillières and two which have single owners: Clos de L'Arlot and Clos de La Maréchale. Clos de La Maréchale faces south-east rather than east like the others, and the slope is once again quite gentle.

The soil structure of the Nuits-Saint-Georges vineyards is as complex as any in Burgundy, for the distance from Les Boudots on the boundary with Vosne in the north to Clos de La Maréchale in the south of Prémeaux is six kilometres as the crow flies. North of the town the subsoil, like that of Vosne, is essentially Bajocian in origin, covered with a mixture of pebbles, silt, limestone debris and clay. Here the wines have a lot in common with those from neighbouring vineyards across the commune boundary, but the further south you go the level of clay in the soil increases, and the soil becomes richer and heavier. As a result the wines have a tendency to be four-square. South of Nuits-Saint-Georges the limestone is either Bathonian or the harder Comblanchien type. Here and there the surface soil contains sand which moderates the effect of the clay. Across into Prémeaux the soil is thin on the higher slopes as the vineyards lie on rock. Lower down on the gentler slopes the soil has more clay and marl.

The authorities were quite correct not to make any vineyard in Nuits-Saint-Georges a *grand cru*. At their best, wines from the top *premiers crus*, from Les Saint-Georges, Vaucrains and Pruliers in the centre, for instance, or from Boudots in the north, can have concentration and finesse as well as richness and structure, but there is always a certain minerally, gamey robustness about a Nuits *premier cru*, an aspect of leaden-footedness that detracts from the class, the definition, the flair. It would be fair to point out though that as a consequence of the huge popularity of the name, there has been much abuse. More sin has been committed in the name of Nuits-Saint-Georges than in the name of all the other villages in Burgundy put together. Not everything is the fault of the genuine wines themselves, and there are an increasing number of good individual properties.

A few estates make a little white wine. Robert Chevillon, Henri Gouges and the Domaine de L'Arlot are the best-known. Gouges' wine comes from some Pinot Noir vines which mutated into producing white grapes. The Clos de L'Arlot white comes from Chardonnay and Pinot Beurot. Chevillon's is from pure Chardonnay. All are excellent but difficult to come by.

With Prémeaux we come to the end of not only the Côte de Nuits *premiers crus* but also of the villages which are entitled to their own individual *appellation*. Much of the best land of the Côte here is now given over to marble quarrying and such wines as are produced in the villages of Prissey, Comblanchien and Corgoloin are only entitled to the *appellation* of Côte de Nuits-Villages.

Leading Nuits-Saint-Georges Producers

★ DOMAINE DE L'ARLOT

Commune: Prémeaux.
Owner: AXA Millésimes.
**Surface Area under Vine: 14 ha, owned –
Romanée-Saint-Vivant (25 a), Vosne-Romanée
premier cru Les Suchots, Nuits-Saint-Georges
premiers crus Clos-des-Forêts-Saint-Georges
monopole, Clos de L'Arlot *monopole* (red and
white), Côte de Nuits-Villages in the *monopole*
Clos-du-Chapeau, and Beaune *premier cru* Les
Grèves.**
In 1987 the insurance group AXA, owners of Bordeaux's Château Pichon-Longueville (Baron) and other estates, bought the moribund Clos de L'Arlot, and installed Jean-Pierre de Smet, a disciple of Jacques Seysses of Domaine Dujac, to run it.

The cellar is splendid (so is the newly restored château) and Smet's winemaking is meticulous, closely following his master's methods. This is an address for those who wish to be seduced by a lighter style of Nuits wine (especially the Clos de L'Arlot itself), not for those who seek hand-to-hand combat. There is also – and in reasonable quantity, for a whole hectare is under vine, though some is young vines at present – a white Nuits-Saint-Georges. This is quite unlike a Meursault or Puligny – it is racy but without the fat, nutty undertones.

★ DOMAINE JEAN CHAUVENET

Owner: Chauvenet family.
**Surface Area under Vine: 9.50 ha, owned and *en
fermage/métayage* – Nuits-Saint-Georges
premiers crus Rue de Chaux, Les Damodes,
Les Bousselots, Les Perrières and Les Vaucrains,
and village Nuits-Saint-Georges and Vosne-
Romanée.**
Jean Chauvenet's wines are made by his handsome son-in-law, Christophe Drag. Since 1990 the grapes have been completely destemmed. The fermentation takes place after a few days of cold soaking and is controlled at 28°-34°C. Ageing then takes place in from 10 to 25 per cent new oak. Chauvenet continues to sell 60 per cent of his village Nuits (of which he owns 7.20 ha of vines) in bulk to local merchants.

Things have much improved here in recent years. The tannins are more sophisticated, the fruit expression richer and more classy, the flavours more complex: all because there is more attention to detail, more control and no stems. This is a very good place to study the differences between various Nuits *premiers crus*.

★ DOMAINE ROBERT CHEVILLON

Owner: Chevillon family.
**Surface Area under Vine: 13 ha, owned and *en
fermage/métayage* – Nuits-Saint-Georges
premiers crus Les Saint-Georges, Les Cailles,
Les Vaucrains, Les Roncières, Les Pruliers,
Les Perrières, Les Chaignots and Les Bousselots,
and village Nuits-Saint-Georges (red and white).**
This is a splendid domaine with very old vines (seventy-five years in the case of the first three wines above) and producing a marvellous palette of *premiers crus*. A small percentage of stems is retained, there is no cold maceration, the fermentation temperatures are held between 30° and 33°C and one-third new wood is used for ageing. There is nothing special about the recipe, but the results are rich, opulent, classy and individual wines. And there is that *rara avis*, a white Nuits-Saint-Georges.

Robert Chevillon, now approaching retirement, is beginning to take a back seat and let his sons, Bertrand and Denis, take charge.

★★ Domaine Jean-Jacques Confuron

Commune: Prémeaux.

Owner: Confuron-Meunier family.

Surface Area under Vine: 7 ha, owned – Romanée-Saint-Vivant (50 a), Clos de Vougeot (50 a), Vosne-Romanée *premier cru* Les Beaux-Monts, Chambolle-Musigny *premier cru* (from Les Châtelots and Les Feusselots), Nuits-Saint-Georges *premiers crus* Les Boudots and Les Chaboeufs, village Chambolle-Musigny, village Nuits-Saint-Georges in the *lieu-dit* Les Fleuriers, and Côte de Nuits-Villages.

The origins of this domaine lie with the Noëllat estate in Vosne-Romanée, and the vines have passed through the female line for a couple of generations since then. The owners are Alain (who took over in 1988) and Sophie Meunier, *née* Confuron. Quality has improved considerably in recent years, helped by a new *cuverie* and extended cellar, and is now of the very highest order, with low harvests and a firmly *biologique* approach to the viticulture. A small percentage of the stems is left, the wine cold macerated for five days, fermentation temperatures are maintained at 30°C and up to 100 per cent new oak is used.

In the early 1990s Meunier used to produce a special oaky *cuvée* for the American market. This has now been discontinued. The quality of the wines is classy, poised and very fine. He also has a *négociant*'s licence (under the name of Féry-Meunier) and a separate cellar at Echevronne in the Hautes-Côtes for the Côte de Beaune wine he buys in.

★★ Domaine Joseph Faiveley

Owner: Faiveley family.

Surface Area under Vine: 115 ha, owned and *en fermage* – Chambertin Clos-de-Bèze (1.29 ha), Latricières-Chambertin (1.21 ha), Mazis-Chambertin (1.20 ha), Le Musigny (3 a), Clos de Vougeot (1.28 ha), Echezeaux (87 a), Corton, Clos-des-Cortons-Faiveley *monopole* (2.97 ha), Corton-Charlemagne (53 a), Gevrey-Chambertin *premiers crus* in Les Cazetiers and La Combe-aux-Moines, Chambertin-Musigny *premiers crus* Les Fuées and La Combe-d'Orveau, Nuits-Saint-Georges *premiers crus* Les Saint-Georges, Les Porrets-Saint-Georges, Les Damodes, Clos de la Maréchale *monopole* and Aux Vignes-Rondes, village Gevrey-Chambertin including the *lieu-dit* Les Marchais, and village Nuits-Saint-Georges including the *lieux-dits* Les Argillats, Les Lavières and Les Athées; plus a large domaine based in Mercurey in the Côte Chalonnaise, some of the wine of which is sold under the name of Domaine de La Croix-Jacquelet.

While Maison Faiveley is a *négociant* François Faiveley is in the fortunate position of being able to supply most of his requirements – certainly at the top end of the scale – from his own family domaine. And he intends to keep it that way. He has no wish to expand beyond a point where he feels he cannot personally supervise and guarantee the evolution and quality of every bottle that leaves his cellar door. This is one of greatest sources of quality in the whole of Burgundy. The wines are outstandingly clean, rich, balanced and concentrated, and the best are hand-bottled without filtration.

★★ Domaine Henri Gouges

Owner: Gouges family.

Surface Area under Vine: 14.50 ha, *en fermage* (family owned) – Nuits-Saint-Georges *premiers crus* Les Saint-Georges, Les Vaucrains, Chaines-Carteaux, Clos-de-Porrets-Saint-Georges *monopole*, Les Pruliers, Les Chaignots and Les Perrières (white), and village Nuits-Saint-Georges.

If domaines could be *doyens*, this would be the *doyen* of the commune, having bottled and sold its wine direct since the 1920s. Today the two cousins – Pierre, who looks after the vines, and Christian, the wine – are in charge, grandsons of the late Henri who died in 1967. Pierre was one of the first to advocate the use of ray-grass in the vineyard to reduce the effects of erosion.

After a blip in the early 1980s quality is back on song here, and the results are magnificent, but not for those who expect plump, vibrant, oaky wines. The Gouges style is for austerity, depth, breed and a minimum of new oak. Patience is required, and expected.

HOSPICES DE NUITS-SAINT-GEORGES

Surface Area under Vine: 8.10 ha, owned – Nuits-Saint-Georges *premiers crus* Les Saint-Georges, Les Didiers *monopole*, Les Forêts, La Rue de Chaux, Les Boudots, Les Murgers, Les Corvées-Pagets and Aux Vignes-Rondes, and village Nuits-Saint-Georges.

Smaller and less well-known than the Hospices de Beaune, but with a rather better track record of quality winemaking in recent years, this is a fine estate. The *premiers crus*, under the names of their donors, are sold by auction on the Sunday prior to Palm Sunday, after a tasting at the Château de Clos de Vougeot. In the long run the quality of the wine depends, of course, on who does the subsequent *élevage*. As with its Beaune counterpart, there is a danger of over-oaking the wines.

★ MAISON DOMINIQUE LAURENT

Owner: Dominique Laurent.

Dominique Laurent – his notice board slyly says Dom. Laurent, leading the innocent to believe he is a domaine – is a new star in the Côte d'Or firmament. Formerly a pastry chef, and with the girth to prove it, he was bitten by the wine bug, moved to Nuits, and set about buying up the odd cask here and there from some of the leading growers in the Côte de Nuits. Quantities are minuscule, the approach is determinedly 'hands-off', and the wines are for those who like lots of oak (Laurent often racks from new to new, i.e. to give his wines, as he puts it, '200 per cent' new oak). It is early days, for his first vintage was in 1992 but the results are undeniably pure, concentrated and of high quality.

★ DOMAINE DANIEL RION ET FILS

Commune: Prémeaux.
Owner: Rion family.
Surface Area under Vine: 18.62 ha, owned – Clos de Vougeot (55a), Echezeaux (34a), Chambolle-Musigny *premier cru* Les Charmes, Vosne-Romanée *premiers crus* Les Chaumes and Les Beaux-Monts, Nuits-Saint-Georges *premiers crus* Clos-des-Argillières, Les Vignes-Rondes, Les Haut-Pruliers, Les Terres-Blanches (red and

white), village Chambolle-Musigny, village Vosne-Romanée, village Nuits-Saint-Georges including the *lieux-dits* Les Lavières and Les Grandes-Vignes, and Côte de Nuits-Villages.

This is an important domaine, whose public face is Patrice Rion, one of three brothers who work with their father out of a large, modern, Swiss chalet-style building up on the main road just above the Grandes-Vignes *climat*. Quality is high and dependable, and if I find a 'house style' in the wines, a family resemblance, I don't quibble too much because the wines are clean and fruity and the tannins have become increasingly sophisticated over the years. Patrice has a tiny individual domaine: Michelle et Patrice Rion.

★ DOMAINE THOMAS-MOILLARD

Owner: Thomas-Moillard family.
Surface Area under Vine: 32.74 ha, almost entirely owned (only some Hautes-Côtes is farmed) – Chambertin (5 a), Chambertin Clos-de-Bèze (24 a), Romanée-Saint-Vivant (17 a), Bonnes-Mares (15 a), Clos de Vougeot (60 a), Corton Clos-du-Roi (84 a), Corton-Charlemagne (23 a), Vosne-Romanée *premiers crus* Les Malconsorts and Les Beaux-Monts, Nuits-Saint-Georges *premiers crus* Clos-de-Thorey *monopole*, Clos-des-Grandes-Vignes *monopole*, Les Forêts and Les Richemones, Beaune *premier cru* Les Grèves, and village Nuits-Saint-Georges and Savigny-Lès-Beaune (red and white).

This is an impressive line-up of wines, and very impressive quality. The wines here are intensely coloured, pure, backward and very concentrated, with a sort of cool aloofness which comes from relatively lowish fermentation temperatures (below rather than above 30°C), no stems and long *cuvaisons*. About 30 per cent new oak is used, so this element does not get exaggerated either. The wines take a long time to come round.

Most of this domaine is cultivated by outsiders on a *métayage* basis, but Thomas-Moillard, the domaine end of *négociants* Moillard-Grivot, have arranged things so that they buy in the *métayer*'s share of the grapes and vinify it all themselves.

Other Producers of note

BERTRAND AMBOISE, HUBERT CHAUVENET-CHOPIN, MACHARD DE GRAMONT, FERNAND LECHENEAUT ET FILS, ALAIN MICHELOT, HENRI ET GILLES REMORIQUET AND MICHELLE ET PATRICE RION.

Comblanchien Producers of note

DOMAINE CHOPIN & FILS AND JEAN-MARC MILLOT.

HAUTES-CÔTES DE NUITS AND HAUTES-CÔTES DE BEAUNE

Surface Area (1998): Hautes-Côtes de Nuits 643 ha; Hautes-Côtes de Beaune 487 ha.
Production (1998): Hautes-Côtes de Nuits (red and rosé) 22,573 hl and (white) 5735 hl; Hautes-Côtes de Beaune (red and rosé) 17,932 hl and (white) 5637 hl.
Colours: Red, rosé and white.
Grape varieties: (Red) Pinot Noir; (white) Chardonnay.

Above and behind the Côte d'Or in the Hautes-Côtes the countryside is peaceful and pastoral. There are valleys and plateaux, pastures and woodlands, rocky outcrops and gently sloping fields. Up here it is cooler, often more exposed, and the soils are less fine, less complex. Only in carefully selected sites is the aspect suitable for the vine. This is the area known as Hautes-Côtes.

There have always been vines in the Hautes-Côtes. Before phylloxera there were as many as 4500 hectares, though much was planted with non 'noble' grapes. But then, as elsewhere, the vineyards declined and as recently as 1968 there were barely 500 hectares of vines.

This was the nadir, but resurrection was already at hand. *Appellation contrôlée*, with the prefix Bourgogne, had been bestowed on the Hautes-Côtes in 1961, and in 1968 a co-operative cellar called Les Caves des Hautes-Côtes – not up in the back of beyond but sensibly on the main road outside Beaune where no passerby could fail to notice it – was established. This now vinifies and sells 25 per cent of the combined *appellation*. Meanwhile, at the research station at Echevronne above Pernand-Vergelesses suitable clones of Pinot Noir were developed and trials were carried out with high-trained vines, thus avoiding the worst of the frost and, because they would be planted further apart for mechanical cultivation, thus economising on the expense of planting and maintaining new vineyards. Since then the fortunes of the Hautes-Côtes have blossomed.

From a geographical point of view the two parts of the Hautes-Côtes do not quite correspond with the division between the Côte de Nuits and the Côte de Beaune. The northern section, the Hautes-Côtes de Nuits, begins at Ruelle-Vergy above Chambolle and continues to Echevronne and Magny-Les-Villers. Echevronne is in the Hautes-Côtes de Beaune while the land at Magny is divided between the two. There is then a separate section of the Hautes-Côtes de Beaune which begins at Mavilly-Mandelot above Beaune and extends south to Sampigny-Lès-Maranges and Cheilly-Lès-Maranges near Santenay.

There is some white Hautes-Côtes wine and a smidgen of rosé, but these are less successful than the red. The red wine is the corner-stone of both *appellations* and the key to their deserved recent success, especially in a warm, ripe year like 1990 or 1996 – the wines are then delicious, and some of the best value in Burgundy. Avoid the wines of a cold, rainy vintage.

The best wines of Les Caves des Hautes-Côtes, who supply much of the *négociant* wine, can be very good value for money in these good vintages. Elsewhere in the Hautes-Côtes there are enterprising growers, some of whom sell Côte d'Or wines as well. Equally producers in the Côte d'Or offer Hautes-Côtes wines as well.

Hautes-Côtes Producers of note

DENIS CARRÉ (MAZILLY-MELOISEY), LUCIEN JACOB (ECHEVRONNE), ROBERT JAYER-GILLES & CLAUDE CORNU (MAGNY-LES-VILLERS), JEAN JOILLOT & FRANÇOIS CHARLES (NANTOUX), CLAUDE NOUVEAU (MARCHEZEUIL), MICHEL SERVEAU (LA ROCHEPOT), DOMAINE THEVENOT-LE-BRUN (MAREY-LES-FUSSY), DOMAINE DU VAL VERGY/YVES CHALEY (CURTIL-VERGY) AND THIERRY VIGOT-BATTAULT (MESSANGES).

CÔTE DE BEAUNE

The Côte de Beaune begins with a bang at Ladoix with the hill of Corton and continues down beyond Santenay until the hills peter out at Cheilly-Lès-Maranges, a distance of 26 kilometres as the crow flies. This is a region of richly fruity, elegant, but essentially soft-centred red wines, neither as concentrated nor as long-lasting as those of the Côte de Nuits.

In the northern part of the Côte de Beaune, on the hill of Corton and in the surrounding *premiers crus* in the village of Aloxe, the wines are firmer than they are further south, a transition between those of the Côte de Beaune and the Côte de Nuits. From Savigny onwards, interrupted only by the *autoroute* which surges out of the Morvan hills, the Côte continues through Beaune and Pommard to beyond Volnay, producing almost entirely red wines. We then come to the magnificent trio of Meursault, Puligny and Chassagne, source of the Chardonnay grape at its finest and the greatest dry white wines in the world. Above Meursault one section of the vineyard continues through Monthelie and Auxey-Duresses to Saint-Romain. South of Puligny Saint-Romain lies up in the valley of the N6 main road. Further south, after Chassagne, lies Santenay.

Such is the renown of the Côte de Beaune white wines – and with the exception of Corton all the *grands crus* in the Côte de Beaune are white rather than red – it is easy to forget that three-quarters of the wine produced in Côte de Beaune is red. The Côte de Beaune is still part of the Pinot Noir's noble fief, even if on this occasion it has a mighty consort.

The Côte de Beaune is twice as large as the Côte de Nuits: it is both wider and more gently sloping, and the orientation is more to the south-east than the east. In the Côte de Beaune more of the vineyards are not only on the flat land at the bottom of the slope but also up in little gorges in the Côte, and in the lesser, tucked-away communes such as Saint-Aubin and Saint-Romain, Auxey-Duresses, Monthelie and Pernand-Vergelesses, there is some splendid value wine to be found, especially in a good vintage.

CÔTE DE BEAUNE

Surface Area (1998): 14 ha.
Production (1998): 659 hl.
Colour: Red.
Grape Variety: Pinot Noir.

This is a very rare and justly obscure *appellation*. The vineyards lie up in the hills above the town of Beaune. Most of the wines I have seen are unremarkable and should really be downgraded into Hautes-Côtes.

Côte de Beaune Producer of note
MAISON JOSEPH DROUHIN.

CÔTE DE BEAUNE-VILLAGES

Surface Area (1998): 12 ha.
Production (1998): 613 hl.
Colour: Red.
Grape Variety: Pinot Noir.

Côte de Beaune-Villages is a much more important *appellation* than its counterpart in the Côte de Nuits. It covers the red wine of the following sixteen villages: Auxey-Duresses, Blagny, Chassagne-Montrachet, Cheilly-Lès-Maranges, Chorey-Lès-Beaune, Dezize-Lès-Maranges, Ladoix-Serrigny, Meursault, Monthelie, Pernand-Vergelesses, Puligny-Montrachet, Saint-Aubin, Saint-Romain, Sampigny-Lès-Maranges, Santenay and Savigny-Lès-Beaune.

As production figures cover the original village growers' declarations, it is not possible to give an accurate figure of how much wine is eventually sold under this name. It is an *appellation* which you will more likely come across under a *négociant*'s or co-operative's label than under that of a private grower, for these producers will buy lesser village wines, originally declared by the grower under those of a village name, from a number of sources to blend under the Côte de Beaune-Villages label. Chorey and Maranges are the main sources of these wines. It is generally a soft, unpretentious wine for early drinking, and fills a gap between Hautes-Côtes and the least expensive village wines.

Côte de Beaune-Villages Producers of note
MAISON BOUCHARD PÈRE ET FILS, MAISON CHAMPY PÈRE ET FILS, MAISON LOUIS JADOT AND OTHER *négociants*.

LADOIX-SERRIGNY

Surface Area (1998): *Premiers crus* 14 ha; village wine 84 ha.
Production (1998): *Premiers crus* (red) 619 hl and (white) 39 hl; village wine (red) 3190 hl and (white) 673 hl.
Colour: Red and white.
Grape Varieties: (Red) Pinot Noir; (white) Chardonnay.
Premiers crus There are seven *premiers crus*, in whole or in part. At the northern end are Le Clou d'Orge (part), La Corvée (part) and La Micaude. On the Corton side lies Les Hautes Mourottes (part) and Les Basses Mourottes (both of which are an extension of Corton), Bois-Roussot (part) and Les Joyeuses (part). Early in 2000 a further 10 hectares of *premier cru* on the Corton side was authorized by the INAO.

Unlike other villages of the Côte d'Or, Ladoix, the most northerly Côte de Beaune commune, has adopted the name of Serrigny, a neighbouring hamlet, and not that of its most important vineyard. Ladoix lies on the main road between Nuits-Saint-Georges and Beaune and Serrigny is down in the plain, surrounding an attractive, small Louis XIV château belonging to the Prince Florent de Mérôde, an important grower in Corton.

Ladoix lies immediately under the Corton hill and the Rognet, Vergennes and Maréchaudes sections of the Corton *grand cru* rise up directly behind the village. Although within the Ladoix communal boundaries the lower sections of this slope are, confusingly, *appellation*

premier cru Aloxe rather than Ladoix. Ladoix has seven *premiers crus*, to the north, on either side of the D115c road which leads up into the Hautes-Côtes. You will rarely come across them, and unless you stop to buy wine in the village you will not often find Ladoix itself – much of the village wine is sold as Côte de Beaune-Villages.

Leading Ladoix-Serrigny Producer

PRINCE FLORENT DE MÉRÔDE
Owner: Florent de Mérôde family.
Surface Area under Vine: 11.38 ha, owned and leased out en *métayage* – Corton, Clos du Roi (57 a), Corton, Les Bressandes (1.19 ha), Corton, Les Renardes (51 a), Corton, Les Maréchaudes (1.53 ha), Aloxe-Corton *premier cru*, village Pommard in the *lieu-dit* Clos de La Platière, Ladoix *premier cru* (white) Les Hautes-Mourottes, and village Ladoix (red) in the *lieu-dit* Les Chaillots.
Prince Florent de Mérôde lives in the château de Serrigny, a splendid moated castle, partly dating from the Middle Ages. His family has been here since 1700, and his wife is a member of the Lur-Saluces family which until recently owned Château d'Yquem in Sauternes.

The quality of the wine has blown hot and cold here in recent years. Today the grapes are totally destemmed, having been picked over to discard the unripe, rotten or bruised on a *table de tri*. There is a new winemaker, young Didier Burrell (it used to be Pierre Bitouzet of Savigny, into whose family hands some of the vines are leased out on a share-cropping basis), one-quarter new oak is used and the wines are unfiltered. The wines are now made in a spacious, insulated and temperature-controlled *chai* converted out of old stables and cowsheds, with an impressive cellar at the end, opposite the château. At their best the wines are well coloured, rich, concentrated, individual and stylish. This is potentially one of the best sources for a range of quality Corton.

Other Producers of note
DOMAINE CACHAT-OCQUIDANT ET FILS, DOMAINE CAPITAIN-GAGNEROT FILS, ROBERT AND RAYMOND JACOB, JEAN-PIERRE MALDANT AND ANDRÉ ET RENÉ NUDANT.

ALOXE-CORTON

Surface Area (1998): Corton *grand cru* (red)
95 ha and (white) 2 ha; Corton-Charlemagne or
Charlemagne *grand cru* (white) 51 ha; *premiers
crus* 33 ha; village wines 88 ha.

Production (1998): Corton *grand cru* (red)
3539 hl and (white) 88 hl; Corton-Charlemagne or
Charlemagne *grand cru* (white) 2325 hl; *premiers
crus* (red) 1541 hl; village wine (red) 4053 hl and
(white) 25 hl.

Colour: Red and white.

Grape Varieties: (Red) Pinot Noir and (white)
Chardonnay.

Premiers crus There are thirteen *premiers crus*, in whole
or in part, some of which are technically in the commune of Ladoix. In Aloxe-Corton there are Les Chaillots
(part), Les Fournières, Les Guérets, Les Maréchaudes,
Clos des Maréchaudes, Les Meix (Clos-du-Chapitre), Les
Paulands (part), Les Valozières and Les Vercots. In Ladoix
there is more of the Clos des Maréchaudes and Les
Maréchaudes plus La Coutière, Les Petites Lolières, Les
Moutottes and La Toppe au Vert.

Many of these *premiers crus* are the lesser, downward
slopes of areas which are *grand cru* Corton and share their
names. Confusingly, at least one – Paulands – is *grand cru*
at the top, *premier cru* in the middle but only village *appellation contrôlée* at the bottom.

Grands Crus Six kilometres to the north of Beaune,
clearly visible by anybody descending the slope on the
autoroute, the lone hill of Corton marks the north end of
the Côte de Beaune. Densely wooded at its summit, oval
in shape, with the sharp ends facing south-west and
north-east, the steeply inclined surfaces of the Corton
hill form the largest *grand cru* in the whole of Burgundy.

Corton is a confusing *appellation*. The *grand cru* is spread
over three communes, Ladoix, Aloxe and Pernand, and
covers both red and white wines. The white wine can be
occasionally found labelled simply as Corton, usually as
Corton-Charlemagne or, rarely but theoretically, as
plain Charlemagne. The red wine, though technically
appellation Corton, can also appear under a number of

names: as Le Corton, a particular *lieu-dit*, as Corton followed by the name of a *lieu-dit* such as Corton-Clos du
Roi, or as Corton without the definite article, a blend of
several *grand cru lieux-dits*. To further complicate matters,
Maison Louis Latour, an important landowner in Aloxe,
produces a wine named after their domaine headquarters, Château Corton-Grancey.

Charlemagne, Charles the First and the Great, as was
befitting for a man who was Holy Roman Emperor and
effectively the ruler of the Western civilised world, was a
giant of a man. He towered over his subjects, dominating them as much physically as by the force of his
personality. One of his many domaines and the one producing one of his favourite wines was at Corton, itself
named, one interpretation suggests, after an obscure
first century Roman emperor named Orthon: Curtis
(domaine) d'Orthon becoming contracted to Corton.

The story is related that, as with certain vineyards in
Germany, noticing the snows were always the first to
melt on this particular slope, Charlemagne ordered
vines to be planted there, and lo, these produced excellent wine. At the time the wine produced was red, but,
as Charlemagne grew older, and his beard whiter, his
wife Liutgarde, ever watchful over the dignity of her
spouse, objected to the majesty of her emperor being
degraded by red wine stains on his beard and suggested
that he switched to consuming white wine. White
grapes were then planted on a section of the hill,
Corton-Charlemagne was born, and it continues still.

In reality, white wine from the Chardonnay grape on
the hill of Corton is a recent development. Jullien, in his
Topographie de Tous les Vignobles Connus in 1816, makes no
mention of white Corton. By the mid-nineteenth century, however, Chardonnay had arrived. Dr Lavalle, in
his *Histoire et Statistique de la Vigne et des Grands Vins de la Côte
d'Or* of 1855, speaks of Pinot Noir on the mid-slope and
lower ground and what he terms Pinot Blanc on the
upper parts. In the 16-hectare section of Corton-
Charlemagne in the commune of Aloxe, Messieurs
Gouveau, de Grancey, Chantrier, Jules Pautet and the
Hospices de Beaune are listed as the main owners, while
in the 19 hectares of land across the border in Pernand
only Monsieur Bonneau-Véry (now the Bonneau du

Martray family) is worthy of note. By the end of the nineteenth century the owners included Louis Latour, with the Grancey domaine, and Jules Senard, two families who are still important proprietors in the area.

Chardonnay is planted on the upper slopes in a whitish-coloured, marly soil with a high calcareous content on a hard limestone rock base. Further down the slope there is more iron and clay in the soil, and the colour of the earth is redder. Here Pinot Noir produces better wine, particularly on the more easterly-facing slopes above Aloxe and Ladoix. Today, however, growers in Le Corton and elsewhere can get a better price for white wine than for red, and there is a gradual changeover to Chardonnay in the vineyards at the top of the slope on the Aloxe side. On the Pernand flank of the Corton hill the soil is flinty, and the wine will have more austerity and be steelier than that coming from above Aloxe. The whites from Aloxe *climats* are softer in their youth and develop faster.

Nevertheless, Corton-Charlemagne or should be, a firm, full, masculine wine, perhaps even slower to mature than Le Montrachet; more closed and less accessible, but opening out after five years or so to give a wine of marvellous richness, albeit always with a certain amount of steely reserve behind the opulence. The best wines need at least ten years to mature, and it is a shame to waste them by drinking them any sooner.

Red Corton is the biggest and firmest of all the Côte de Beaune reds. It is an austere wine, and you can taste the iron in the soil, but at the same time it is rich and will eventually become opulent. There are some twenty separate *lieux-dits*, the best being Clos du Roi, Bressandes, Renardes, Perrières and Pougets as well as Le Corton.

Corton Producers of note

MAISON BOUCHARD PÈRE ET FILS, DOMAINE CHANDON DE BRIAILLES, MAISON JOSEPH DROUHIN, PIERRE DUBREUIL-FONTAINE, JOSEPH FAIVELEY, PRINCE FLORENT DE MÉRÔDE, MAISON LOUIS JADOT, MICHEL JUILLOT, LEROY, MAILLARD PÈRE ET FILS, MÉO-CAMUZET, ROLAND RAPET, MAISON REMOISSENET PÈRE ET FILS (FROM DOMAINE BARON THÉNARD), COMTE SENARD AND DOMAINE THOMAS-MOILLARD.

Corton-Charlemagne Producers of note

ADRIAN AND JEAN-CLAUDE BELLAND, PIERRE BITOUZET, DOMAINE BONNEAU DU MARTRAY, MAISON BOUCHARD PÈRE ET FILS, BRUNO CLAIR, JEAN-FRANÇOIS COCHE-DURY, MAISON JOSEPH DROUHIN, PIERRE DUBREUIL-FONTAINE, DOMAINE JOSEPH FAIVELEY, MAISON LOUIS JADOT, PATRICK JAVILLIER, MICHEL JUILLOT, MAISON LOUIS LATOUR, DOMAINE LEROY, ROLAND RAPET, MAISON REMOISSENET PÈRE ET FILS, CHRISTOPHE ROUMIER, DOMAINE THOMAS-MOILLARD AND DOMAINE TOLLOT-BEAUT. THE HOSPICES DE BEAUNE (SEE PAGE 195) PRODUCE TWO RED CUVÉES (DR PESTE AND CHARLOTTE DUMAY) AND TWO WHITE (FRANÇOISE DE SALINS AND PAUL CHANSON). SUBJECT TO THE ÉLEVAGE THESE WINES CAN ALSO BE RECOMMENDED.

Leading Aloxe-Corton Producers

MAISON LOUIS LATOUR

Owner: Latour family.

Surface Area under Vine: 45 ha, owned and *en fermage* – Chambertin (80 a), Romanée-Saint-Vivant, Les Quatre-Journeaux (1 ha), Corton (15 ha), mainly sold as Château Corton-Grancey, Corton, Clos-de-La-Vigne-au-Saint *monopole* (2.66 ha), Corton-Charlemagne (9 ha), Chevalier-Montrachet, Les Demoiselles (50 a), Aloxe-Corton *premiers crus* Les Chaillots and Les Fournières, Pernand-Vergelesses *premier cru* Ile-des-Vergelesses, Beaune *premiers crus* Vignes-Franches, Les Perrières, Clos-du-Roi and Les Grèves, Pommard *premier cru* Les Epenots, and village Aloxe-Corton and Volnay.

Maison Louis Latour is one of Burgundy's major *négociants*. This sizeable domaine, based in Aloxe-Corton, provides about 10 per cent of the firm's turnover, perhaps a quarter of its Burgundian requirements.

Latour is notorious for its policy of pasteurising its reds (to 70°C) and these are never very highly coloured, but often a bit heavy in alcohol. Sometimes I find them somewhat confected and lacking freshness, though the top wines (the Romanée-Saint-Vivant and the Chambertin, but not the Corton-Grancey) used to be very good indeed.

NORTHERN CÔTE DE BEAUNE

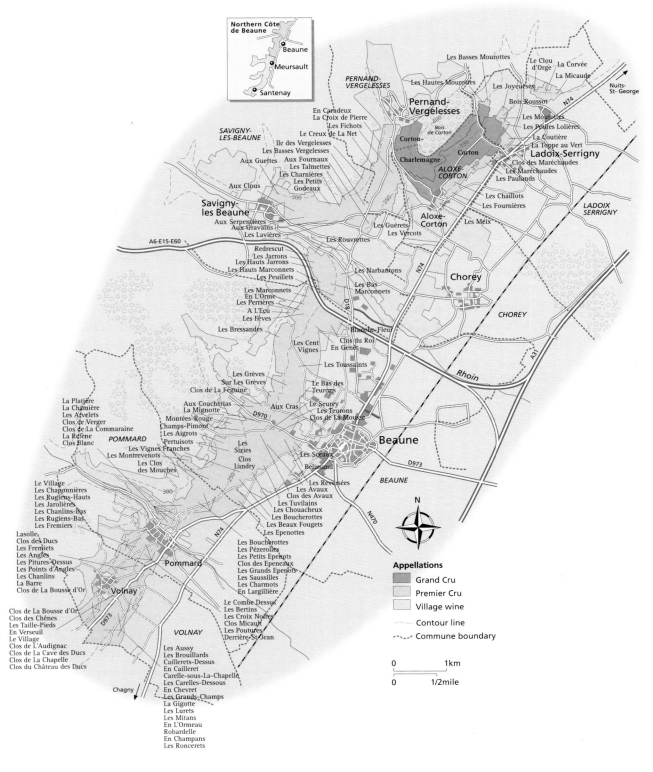

Northern Côte
de Beaune

○ Beaune

○ Meursault

○ Santenay

Les Basses Mourottes
Le Clou
d'Orge   La Corvée
La Micaude
Les Hautes Mourottes
PERNAND-
VERGELESSES
Les Joyeueses
Pernand-
Vergelesses   Bois Roussot
Les Moutottes
En Caradeux   Les Petites Lolières
La Croix de Pierre   La Coutière
SAVIGNY-   Les Fichots   La Toppe au Vert
LES-BEAUNE   Le Creux de La Net   Bois
de Corton
Ile des Vergelesses   Corton-   Ladoix-Serrigny
Les Basses Vergelesses   Charlemagne   Corton   Clos des Maréchaudes
Aux Guettes   Aux Fournaux   Les Maréchaudes
Les Talmettes   Charlemagne   ALOXE-   Les Paulands
Les Charnières   CORTON
Les Petits   Les Chaillots
Godeaux   Les Fournières   LADOIX
Aux Clous   SERRIGNY
Savigny-   Aloxe-
les Beaune   Corton   Les Meix
Aux Serpentières   Les Guérets
Aux Gravains   Les Vercots
Les Lavières
A6-E15-E60   Les Rouvrettes
Redrescut
Les Jarrons   Les Narbantons
Les Hauts Jarrons   Chorey
Les Hauts Marconnets   Les Bas
Les Peuillets   Marconnets   CHOREY
Les Marconnets
En L'Orme   Blanche-Fleur
Les Perrières   Clos du Roi   Rhoin
A L'Ecu   En Genet
Les Fèves
Les Bressandes   Les Cent   Les Toussaints
Vignes
Les Grèves   Le Bas des
Sur Les Grèves   Teurons
Clos de La Féguine
La Platière   Aux Couchérias   Le Seurey
La Chanière   La Mignotte   Aux Cras   Les Teurons
Les Arvelets   Montées-Rouge   Clos de La Mousse
Clos de Verger   Champs-Pimont
Clos de La Commaraine Les Aigrots   Beaune
La Réfène   Pertuisots   Les
Clos Blanc   POMMARD   Les Vignes Franches Sizies
Les Montrevenots   Clos   D973
Les Chanlins   Landry   Les Sceaux
Le Village   Les Clos   Bélissand
Les Chaponnières   des Mouches   BEAUNE
Les Rugiens-Hauts   Les Reversées
Les Jarolières   Les Avaux
Les Chanlins-Bas   Clos des Avaux
Les Rugiens-Bas   Les Tuvilains
Les Fremiers   Les Chouacheux
Lasolle   Les Boucherottes
Clos des Ducs   Les Beaux Fougets
Les Fremiets   Les Epenottes
Les Angles
Les Pitures-Dessus   Pommard   Les Boucherottes
Les Points d'Angles   Les Pézerolles
Les Chanlins   Les Petits Epenots
La Barre   Clos des Epeneaux
Clos de La Bousse d'Or   Les Grands Epenots
Volnay   Les Saussilles
Clos de La Bousse d'Or   Les Charmots
Clos des Chênes   En Largillière
Les Taille-Pieds
En Verseuil   Le Combe Dessus
Le Village   Les Bertins
Clos de L'Audignac   Les Croix Noires
Clos de La Cave des Ducs   Clos Micault
Clos de La Chapelle   VOLNAY   Les Poutures
Clos du Château des Ducs   Derrière-St-Jean
Chagny
Les Aussy
Les Brouillards
Caillerets-Dessus
En Cailleret
Carelle-sous-La-Chapelle
Les Carelles-Dessous
En Chevret
Les Grands-Champs
La Gigotte
Les Lurets
Les Mitans
En L'Ormeau
Robardelle
En Champans
Les Roncerets

Nuits-
St- George

N

Appellations

◼ Grand Cru

◼ Premier Cru

◻ Village wine

- - - Contour line

- - - Commune boundary

0   1km

0   1/2mile

Latour's whites have always been more reliable, though again I find them sometimes a bit over-alcoholic, occasionally a bit sulphury. Standards of both the reds and whites dipped in the mid-1980s. I regret I have not seen anything to enthuse me for some time.

DOMAINE DU COMTE SENARD

Owner: Senard family.
Surface Area under Vine: 8.70 ha, owned –
Corton, Clos-du-Roi (64 a), Corton,
Les Bressandes (63 a), Corton, En Charlemagne
(red) (40 a), Corton, Clos-de-Meix (1.65 ha),
Corton, from Les Paulands (63 a), Corton Blanc,
from the Clos-de-Meix (45 a), Aloxe-Corton
premier cru **Les Valozières, Beaune** *premier cru*
Les Coucherias, and village Aloxe-Corton (red
and white) and Chorey-Lès-Beaune.

The sympathetic Philippe Senard, today a youthful fifty-year-old, turned to the the oenologist Guy Accad for advice in 1988, and it took him a couple of years to adapt Accad's general principles to his own estate. There is no excessive new oak. The wines are bottled after a period as long as two years, without fining or filtration. The wines now taste much more 'typical' of Pinot Noir right from the start, and have colour, intensity and plenty of individuality and elegance – a good source of fine Cortons.

Other Producers of note

COLIN PÈRE ET FILS, FRANCK FOLLIN-ARVELET AND DIDIER MEUNEVEAUX.

PERNAND-VERGELESSES

Surface Area (1998): *Premiers crus* 47 ha; village
wine 74 ha.
Production (1998): *Premiers crus* (red) 1789 hl and
(white) 286 hl; village wine (red) 1956 hl and
(white) 1397 hl.
Colour: Red and white.
Grape Varieties: (Red) Pinot Noir and (white)
Chardonnay.
Premiers crus There are six *premiers crus* in whole or in
part: En Caradeux (part), Le Creux de La Net (part), La

Croix de Pierre, Les Fichots, Ile des Vergelesses and Les Vergelesses or Les Basses-Vergelesses.

Pernand is a pretty little village full of sharp corners and steep alleyways which clings to the side of a slope on the western side of the hill of Corton. The village overlooks the Charlemagne part of the Corton *grand cru*, which looms up on the other side of a little valley. Pernand also commands a fine view back over the flatter land towards Beaune. Apart from Corton and Corton-Charlemagne, most of Pernand's vineyards are on the east-facing slopes of the Bois Noël which separates the village from Savigny. Here are the six *premiers crus*, of which the best is the Ile des Vergelesses. There is rather more communal land up and behind the village than one realises, where the vines of Pernand flow imperceptibly into those of the Hautes-Côtes. Here there are also the remaining vines of Aligoté, for which Pernand used to have a fine reputation. Most of this Aligoté has now been replaced by Chardonnay, for which the growers can demand a higher price.

Village Pernand wine, whether white or red – the former represents about 40 per cent of the production – can be somewhat lean in lesser years, but is usually good value. The *premiers crus*, particularly the Ile des Vergelesses, are a different matter, and are very similar to Corton in flavour, the red with hints of damson and black cherry on the palate. These wines can be very fine, and can represent excellent value.

Leading Pernand-Vergelesses Producers

★★ DOMAINE BONNEAU DU MARTRAY

Owner: Jean-Charles Le Bault de La Morinière
and family.
Surface Area under Vine: 11 ha, owned – Corton-
Charlemagne (9.5 ha) and Corton (red) (1.5 ha).
Apart from Domaine de La Romanée-Conti, no other domaine in Burgundy sells only *grand cru* wine. The domaine's land on the Corton hill straddles the Pernand-Aloxe border and produces exemplary Corton-Charlemagne, vinified in oak, of course, of which one-third is new each year. In 1994 there was a

dual change of generation here, Jean Le Bault de La Morinière, who had inherited the domaine from his aunt, giving way to his son Jean-Charles, while Henri Brochon in the cellar ceded responsibility to his sons Bernard and Jean-Pierre. Having reduced the area planted to Pinot Noir at the bottom of the slope, retaining the oldest vines, and making other improvements, the red wine, which had tended to be a bit feeble, is getting better. But it is for its white wine that this domaine gains two stars. For a long time this has been by far and away the best Corton-Charlemagne not made in such minuscule quantities that it is impossible to find.

★ DOMAINE RAPET PÈRE ET FILS

Owner: Rapet family.

Surface Area under Vine: 19 ha, *en fermage –* Corton-Charlemagne (2.50 ha), Corton, from Les Pougets and Les Perrières (1.25 ha), Pernand-Vergelesses *premiers crus* Ile-des-Vergelesses and Les Vergelesses, Pernand-Vergelesses *premier cru* (white) Les Caradeux, Beaune *premier cru* Clos-du-Roi, and village Aloxe-Corton, Savigny-Lès-Beaune and Pernand-Vergelesses (red and white). The Rapets have been making wine at this important domaine for two centuries and for a long time were no more than competent. Vincent Rapet has now joined his father. Some 20 per cent of the stems are retained, the red wine fermented at a maximum of 33°C and about 20-30 per cent of new wood is used, depending on the *appellation*. The wines are bottled after a year or so. Since 1993 and Vincent's arrival, however, there has been a distinct improvement, both in the whites and the reds.

Other Producers of note

MARIUS DELARCHE PÈRE & FILS, DENIS PÈRE & FILS, PIERRE DUBREUIL-FONTAINE, ROGER JAFFELIN & FILS, PIERRE MAREY & FILS, RÉGIS PAVELOT & FILS AND DOMAINE ROLLIN PÈRE & FILS.

SAVIGNY-LÈS-BEAUNE

Surface Area (1998): *Premiers crus* 136 ha; village wine 208 ha.

Production (1998): *Premiers crus* (red) 5694 hl and (white) 315 hl; village wine (red) 8509 hl and (white) 1311 hl.

Colour: Red and white.

Grape Varieties: (Red) Pinot Noir and (white) Chardonnay.

Premiers crus There are twenty-two *premiers crus*, in whole or in part. On the Pernand side are La Bataillière (part of Les Vergelesses), Champ-Chevrey (part of Aux Fourneaux), Les Charnières, Aux Clous, Aux Fourneaux (part), Aux Gravains, Aux Guettes (part), Les Lavières, Les Petits Godeaux, Aux Serpentières, Les Talmettes (part of Les Vergelesses), Aux Vergelesses and Les Basses-Vergelesses. On the Mont Battois slope are La Dominode (part of Les Hauts Jarrons), Les Hauts Jarrons, Les Jarrons, Les Bas Marconnets, Les Hauts Marconnets, Les Narbantons, Les Peuillets (part), Redrescut (or Redrescul) and Les Rouvrettes (part).

Up at the beginning of the valley of the river Rhoin, 6 kilometres north-west of Beaune, lies Savigny, one of the larger of the Côte de Beaune communes. It is a modest village but flanked by a rather impressive castle dating partly from the fourteenth century. Savigny's main claim to fame is the invention of the first viticultural tractor in the mid-nineteenth century, following which vines in the surrounding vineyards were first planted in rows .

The main vineyards lie on either side of the village. To the north they continue on from the Pernand vineyards on the south-eastern or south-facing slopes of the Bois Noël. On the other side of the village the vineyards adjoin those of Beaune and face north-east. Here the soil tends to be more sandy and less pebbly. Above the vineyards, on this side, halfway up the Mont Battois, the *autoroute* thunders down from the Morvan into the plain of Beaune. There is, incidentally, a rest-site up here called the Aire de Savigny-Lès-Galloises, from which there is a splendid panorama towards the hill of Corton. If you stop here you will find yourself exactly halfway between Lille and Marseille.

There is a distinct difference in character between the wines from one side of Savigny and the other. Those vineyards lying below the Bois Noël – Vergelesses, Lavières, Serpentières and Guettes are the most important – produce lighter and more elegant wines than those under Mont Battois – Marconnets, Les Dominodes, Narbantons and Peuillets. These can be firm and hard, even a little *sauvage*, with a marked *goût de terroir*. In general Savigny's wines are not as fine as those of Beaune, Pommard and Volnay, but they are also less expensive. The best are excellent value. They mature in the medium term, similar to the wines of Beaune.

There is also a little white wine which has a slightly spicy flavour and resembles that of Beaune.

Leading Savigny-Lès-Beaune Producers

★ DOMAINE SIMON BIZE

Owner: Bize family.
Surace Area under Vine: 22 ha, owned and *en fermage/métayage* – Latricières-Chambertin (32 a), Savigny-Lès-Beaune *premiers crus* Les Vergelesses, Aux Fourneaux, Les Serpentières, Les Guettes and Les Marconnets, village Savigny-Lès-Beaune (red and white) including the *lieu-dit* Les Grands-Liards (red), and village Aloxe-Corton in the *lieu-dit* Les Suchots.

The wines were very good here twenty and thirty years ago when the late Simon Bize was in charge – I have fond memories of the 1971 Vergelesses – but are even better now. His son Patrick is one Burgundy's most sensitive and perfectionist winemakers, ever seeking to add a touch here, modify a detail there. This is clearly Savigny's best domaine.

Only the grapes from the younger vines – which for Patrick means anything under twenty years – are destemmed. There is a long *cuvaison*, controlled at 30°-33°C, and 50 per cent new wood is used each year. Bize's wines are understated, slow to evolve, a little austere at the start, but they are beautifully poised and clear-cut in their flavours, with the individual characters of the five *premiers crus* visible for all to see. The Vergelesses is usually the best. He makes excellent generic Bourgogne, including whites from both Chardonnay and Pinot Beurot. This domaine is not to be missed.

★ DOMAINE CHANDON DE BRIAILLES

Owner: de Nicolaÿ family.
Surface Area under Vine: 13 ha, owned – Corton, Clos-du-Roi (44 a), Corton, Les Bressandes (1.74 ha), Corton, Les Maréchaudes (39 a), Corton (white) (25 a), Corton-Charlemagne (11 a), Aloxe-Corton *premier cru* Les Valozières, Pernand-Vergelesses *premiers crus* Ile-des-Vergelesses and Les Basses-Vergelesses, Savigny-Lès-Beaune *premiers crus* Les Lavières and Aux Fourneaux, and village Savigny-Lès-Beaune including the *lieu-dit* Aux Fourneaux.

This important property is owned by Count Aymar-Claude and Nadine de Nicolay (pronounced Nicolaï) and their four children, and it is Nadine and her youngest daughter Claude who are in charge, together with cellarmaster Jean-Claude Bouveret, known to one and all, even himself, for obvious reasons, as Kojak. Progress has been impressive here during the 1990s and this is now a prime source for Ile-des-Vergelesses (of which they are the largest landowner) and a clutch of excellent Cortons.

★ DOMAINE JEAN-MARC PAVELOT

Owner: Pavelot family.
Surface Area under Vine: 12 ha, owned and *en fermage* – Savigny-Lès-Beaune *premiers crus* Les Dominodes, Aux Guettes, Les Narbantons, Les Peuillets and Aux Gravains, Pernand-Vergelesses *premier cru* Les Vergelesses, and village Savigny-Lès-Beaune (red and white).

This is another top Savigny domaine which produces wine without the hard *sauvage* aspect found in many young Savigny wines. Jean-Marc Pavelot's wines are elegant, plump and understated, letting all the fruit sing out, yet never simple. There is depth here and the wines last well into their second decade.

★ DOMAINE MAURICE ECARD

Owner: Ecard family.
Surface Area under Vine: 13 ha, owned and *en fermage* – Savigny-Lès-Beaune *premiers crus* Les Serpentières, Les Narbantons, Les Jarrons,

Les Hauts-Jarrons (white), Les Peuillets and Les Clous, and village Savigny-Lès-Beaune (red and white).

The rotund, bluff, genial Maurice Ecard works with his son Michel (under whose name some of the wines now appear). This is a modern, efficient set-up, and somehow you know you have stumbled on a good source of wine even before you have sampled a single cask. Some 30 per cent stalks are retained, there is a twelve-day *cuvaison* at temperatures up to 33°C and 15 per cent new oak is used each year. The results are plump, fruity wines for the medium term.

Other Producers of note
PIERRE BITOUZET, LUCIEN CAMUS-BROCHON, DOMAINE CAPRON-CHARCOUSSET, JEAN-JACQUES GIRARD AND PHILIPPE GIRARD.

CHOREY-LÈS-BEAUNE

Surface Area (1998): Village wines 133 ha.
Production (1998): (Red) 6020 hl; (white) 186 hl.
Colour: Red and white.
Grape Varieties: (Red) Pinot Noir and (white) Chardonnay.

Chorey-Lès-Beaune – the Lès denoting 'near' – is another village with most of its wine finding its way into *négociant* Côte de Beaune-Villages. The *appellation* has flat, fairly alluvial soil mainly on the 'wrong' side of the Beaune-Nuits highway. There are no *premiers crus* but there is a fine château which is the headquarters of Domaine Germain and a bed and breakfast hotel. Most of the wine is a soft, inexpensive, easy-to-drink red for drinking young and chilled, like Beaujolais.

Leading Chorey-Lès-Beaune Producers

★ CHATEAU DE CHOREY-LÈS-BEAUNE DOMAINE JACQUES GERMAIN
Owner: Germain family.
Surface Area under Vine: 7 ha, owned and *en fermage* – Beaune *premiers crus*
Les Boucherottes, Les Vignes-Franches, Les Cras,
Les Teurons, Les Cent-Vignes and Sur-Les-Grèves (white), Aloxe-Corton *premier cru* Les Valozières, and village Chorey-Lès-Beaune and Pernand-Vergelesses (white).

Not surprisingly, the Château de Chorey is the most impressive edifice in the village: a properly moated castle, medieval in origin, in a fine park. The wines of François Germain (son of Jacques) and his son Benoît, now partially stored in the fine cellars of the defunct Tollot-Voarick domaine, are finely balanced, expressive in their fruit and very elegant. This is not only a fine source for *premier cru* Beaune, but also a supplier of delicious white Pernand-Vergelesses.

DOMAINE TOLLOT-BEAUT & FILS
Owner: Tollot-Beaut family.
Surface Area under Vine: 22.28 ha, owned and *en fermage* – Corton-Charlemagne (24 a), Corton, Les Bressandes (91 a), Corton (60 a), Aloxe-Corton *premiers crus* Les Vercost and Les Fournières, Beaune *premiers crus* Les Grèves and Clos-du-Roi, Savigny-Lès-Beaune *premiers crus* Les Lavières and Champs-Chevrey *monopole*, village Aloxe-Corton, village Beaune in the *lieu-dit* Blanche-Fleur, village Savigny-Lès-Beaune and village Chorey-Lès-Beaune.

This is a well-known and very reliable estate. The large Tollot family work hard, do not spend their money on fripperies and keep an immaculate cellar. The wines – 10-20 per cent destemming, eight to twelve days' *cuvaison* at up to 32°C for the reds, and between 10 and 50 per cent new oak each year– have a particular signature: round, gently oaky, just slightly sweet in character and texture and will never disappoint. But like a Bordeaux Classed Growth – La Lagune, for example – which never quite gives you super-second excitement, so the Tollot wines never make the hair on the back of your neck tingle. Nevertheless, this is a good source and the Chorey-Lès-Beaune is a good example of basic red Burgundy.

Other Producers of note
DOMAINE ARNOUX PÈRE ET FILS, DANIEL LARGEOT, DOMAINE MAILLARD PÈRE & FILS AND RENÉ PODECHARD.

Beaune

Surface Area (1998): *Premiers crus* 307 ha; village wines 93 ha.

Production (1998): *Premiers crus* (red) 10,555 hl and (white) 1060 hl; village wines (red) 3567 hl and (white) 346 hl.

Colour: Red and white.

Grape Varieties: (Red) Pinot Noir and (white) Chardonnay.

Premiers crus There are forty-four *climats* which, in whole or in part, are entitled to the *premier cru* label. In alphabetical order these are: Les Aigrots, Les Avaux, Clos des Avaux, Les Beaux-Fougets (part), Bellisand, Blanche-Fleur (part), Les Boucherottes, Les Bressandes (part), Les Cent-Vignes, Champs-Pimont, Les Chouacheux, Aux Couchérias, Aux Cras, A l'Ecu (part), Clos de L'Ecu, Les Epenottes (part), Clos de La Féguine (Aux Couchérias), Les Fèves, En Genêt, Les Grèves, Sur Les Grèves (part), Clos Landry or Clos-Saint-Landry, Les Marconnets, La Mignotte, Montées-Rouge (part), Les Montrevenots or Montremenots, Les Clos des Mouches, Clos de La Mousse, En L'Orme, Les Perrières, Pertuisots, Les Reversées, Clos-du-Roi (part), Clos-Sainte-Anne (Sur-Les-Grèves), Les Sceaux, Le Seurey, Les Sizies, Les Teurons, Le Bas des Teurons, Les Toussaints, Les Tuvilains, Clos des Ursules (Les Vignes Franches), La Vigne-de-L'Enfant-Jésus (Grèves) and Les Vignes Franches.

Though Dijon is the departmental capital of the Côte d'Or, Beaune is the wine capital of Burgundy. Inside the old walled town the atmosphere is still largely medieval. Outside market days, and away from the Place Carnot and the few shopping streets that surround it, Beaune is a sleepy, shuttered town, full of hidden alleys, quiet Renaissance courtyards and ecclesiastical reminders of its glorious religious and aristocratic past. There is a fine church, the Collégiale Notre-Dame, dating from the twelfth century. There is a Musée du Vin, housed in a mansion formerly owned by the dukes of Burgundy in the fifteenth and sixteenth centuries. The Hôtel de Ville was once a convent and another, the Couvent des Cordeliers, houses one of Beaune's wine firms, and is a

trap for the unwary tourist. And of course there is the Hôtel-Dieu, heart of the Hospices de Beaune, one of the most magnificent wine monuments in the world.

Each year Beaune explodes into life during the weekend of the *Trois Glorieuses*, three extravagant feasts which surround the Hospices de Beaune charity auction on the third Sunday in November. The town teems with people: local growers who have come to show their wines to the massed throngs in the Hôtel de Ville or in the rather more sedate surroundings of the Salle des Jeunes Professionnels; and also tourists, agents, buyers and friends of the local *négociants*, most of whom have their headquarters in the centre of Beaune, though today their actual cellars are housed in modern warehouses on the outskirts of town. Everybody is there. For one hectic week countless gallons of wine are drunk or sampled and spat and it is impossible to find a parking space for your car, let alone a bed for the night. And then life returns to normal.

Beaune lies on a natural crossroads. It was where the old east-west road from Besançon to Autun met the north-south road from Champagne and Dijon to Lyon and Marseille; there was the added benefit of two natural springs which had their sources in the hills nearby. Colonised by the Romans as Belna or Belno Castrium in AD 40, the influence of Beaune grew as the importance of Autun, the capital of Burgundy in Gallo-Roman days, fell, particularly after Autun's destruction by the sons of Clovis in the sixth century. Even then the vine was already important in the region.

Until the Dukes of Burgundy moved to Dijon in the fourteenth century, Beaune was in all senses the capital of Burgundy. In 1395 Philippe Le Hardi published an ordinance prohibiting the plantation of the ignoble Gamay in favour of the noble Pinot, and from then on the best sites of the Côte d'Or were exclusively planted with members of the Pinot or Chardonnay family and the wines accordingly grew in fame.

Beaune is the Côte d'Or's third largest commune after Gevrey and Meursault. The slope of *premier cru* vineyards extends from the boundary with Savigny-Lès-Beaune at the northern end towards the border with Pommard at the southern end and is divided in half by the D70 which leads up to Bouze in the Hautes-Côtes and on to Bligny-sur-Ouche. The soil structure, based on limestone, is complex. In general it is thin to the north (in the Marconnets, Clos du Roi, Fèves and Bressandes *premiers crus*), especially on the steeper, upper part of the slope, and the vine roots have to search deep into the soil to find their nutrient. Wines from these slopes are full, firm, even solid at the outset, and need time to mature. In the middle section of *premiers crus* (Toussaints, Grèves, Teurons), there is some gravel (as the name Grèves indicates) and the wine is of medium weight, plump and succulent. Bouchard Père's Vigne de L'Enfant Jésus wine comes from an enclave in the Grèves vineyard. South of the D70 there is some sand in the sloping *climat* of Montée Rouge, and also in Aigrots, Pertuisots and the upper part of Vignes Franches. Mid-slope (in the *premiers crus* of Clos des Mouches, Vignes-Franches, Sizies and Avaux) the soil is very stony and hard to work; while at the southern end and lower down the slope (the *premiers crus* of Boucherottes, Epenottes and Chouacheux), there is more clay and less gravel. Here the soil is deep, and production can be excessive if not restricted. This section of the vineyards is known as Le Puit (meaning the 'well') de Beaune, and produces soft wines which mature rapidly.

Though the colour of the soil is mainly a reddish brown, there are parts where it is a whitish marl, more suitable for the Chardonnay grape than the Pinot Noir. On the upper part of the Clos des Mouches Maison Drouhin have vines which produce their celebrated white Beaune wine whose flavour is somewhat more spicy than that of a Meursault. It also tends to mature more quickly. Bouchard Père & Fils have white wine vines in the vineyards of Tulivans, Jadot in the upper part of the Grèves.

Which are the best *climats*? Dr Morelot in 1831 cited Clos de La Mousse (a small vineyard now solely owned by Bouchard Père et Fils), Teurons, Cras, Grèves, Fèves, Perrières, Cent-Vignes, Clos du Roi and Marconnets, all of which have the capacity to produce exquisite wines. Dr Lavalle in 1855 lists Fèves, Grèves, Crais (now Cras) and Champs-Pimonts as the leading wines. Camille Rodier, writing in 1920, says that the best is Fèves, with

its finesse and delicate aroma; Grèves produces a very complete wine, with more body but not without finesse and velvet (*velouté*); Marconnets, on the Savigny border, is closed and solid, full but *bouqueté*. Clos des Mouches, at the southern end adjoining Pommard, is full-bodied, fruity and very elegant. Others (Cras, Champimonts, Clos du Roi, Avaux, Aigrots) are supple and perfumed, and 'easy to drink' – a familiar phrase for damning with faint praise, I have always thought. He adds Marconnets, Bressandes and Clos des Mouches to Dr Lavalle's list of top wines. Poupon and Forgeot in their book, *The Wines of Burgundy* (1964) list Marconnets, Fèves, Bressandes, Grèves and Teurons as the best.

I would certainly agree with this final five, and would add Vignes Franches and Clos des Mouches, with the rider that, as always in Burgundy, the grower or *négociant* is of equal importance as the actual source. The *négociant* Jadot has always has a good range of Beaune *premiers crus*, as does the *négociant* Albert Morot, whose Beaune wines come from the 7-hectare family domaine and include Cent-Vignes, Grèves, Toussaints, Bressandes, Marconnets and Teurons. Bouchard Père et Fils is the largest landowner in the commune of Beaune, with 48 hectares of *premiers crus*. Chanson comes next with 26 hectares, including the majority of Fèves which they sell as Clos des Fèves. The Hospices de Beaune have eight cuvées of Beaune and possess 19 hectares of vineyards. Drouhin have 15 hectares, Patriarche 12, Jadot 9, Louis Latour just over 4 and Remoissenet a couple of hectares: most of the best land is owned by the *négociants*.

How do the wines of Beaune compare with other wines of the Côte d'Or? I find that in style they come midway between those of Pommard and those of Volnay, both communes to the south of Beaune. Pommard wines, particularly those of Rugiens, but equally from the upper part of Epenots and elsewhere, are rich and sturdy. They can be somewhat four-square, but there should always be muscle. Volnay wines, on the other hand, are elegance personified: fragrance, delicacy, subtlety and finesse are the keynotes. The wines of Beaune are varied but they lie somewhere between these two. Only rarely do they reach the quality of the best of these other two communes.

Leading Beaune Producers

★ MAISON BOUCHARD PÈRE ET FILS

Owner: Henriot family.

Surface Area under Vine: 93 ha, owned –
Chambertin (15 a), Bonnes-Mares (24 a), Clos de
Vougeot (23 a), Le Corton (3.94 ha), Corton-
Charlemagne (3.09 ha), Le Montrachet (1.10 ha),
Chevalier-Montrachet (2.02 ha), Bâtard-
Montrachet (8 a), Savigny-Lès-Beaune *premier
cru* Les Lavières, Beaune *premiers crus* Les
Teurons, Les Grèves, Les Grèves, La Vigne de
L'Enfant Jésus *monopole*, Marconnets, Clos-de-
La-Mousse *monopole* and Clos-Saint-Landry
(white) *monopole* and Beaune-du-Château,
Pommard *premiers crus* Les Rugiens and Les
Combes, Volnay *premiers crus* Les Caillerets
(Ancienne Cuvée Carnot), Enchevret, Les Tailles-
Pieds, Le Chanlin and Les Fremiets Clos-de-La-
Rougeotte *monopole*, Meursault *premier cru*
Les Genevrières, and village Chambolle-Musigny,
Aloxe-Corton in the *lieu-dit* Les Paulands,
Ladoix in the *lieu-dit* Clos-Royer and Beaune.
Beaune du Château is a blended red from either 30
hectares of *premier cru* Pinot Noir (Les Aigrots, Le Sizies,
Les Peruisots, Les Avaux, Les Seurey, Clos-du-Roi, Les
Cent-Vignes, En Genêt, Bressandes, Toussaints, Sur-Les-
Grèves, Champs-Pimont, Le Bas-des-Teurons, A L'Ecu,
Les Teurons, Les Reversées and Les Beaux-Fougets) or
white from 4 hectares of *premier cru* Chardonnay (Les
Aigrots and Les Sizies). Bouchard Père et Fils are also
éleveurs and bottlers of the wines of the Château de
Vosne-Romanée (La Romanée *monopole* and Vosne-
Romanée Aux Reignots) and the Domaine du
Clos-Saint-Marc in Nuits-Saint-Georges (Clos-Saint-
Marc *monopole* and Les Argillières). Finally they make and
distribute the wines of the 30-hectare domaine of
Ropiteau-Mignon in Meursault and the Château de
Mandelot in the Hautes-Côtes and were pioneers with
Aligoté de Bouzeron in the Côte de Chalonnaise.

I have had plenty of splendid Bouchard wines of the
1940s, 1950s and early 1960s, and would still be happy to
chance my arm today if any of these happened to come
my way. But more recently, ever since I started writing
my magazine *The Vine* in 1985, I have found the wines no
better than competent, though occasionally there have
been glimmers on the horizon. This is despite a splendid modern vinification centre and a change of policy
from buying wine to vinifying bought-in grapes or must
alongside the grapes from its own vineyards. Something
was missing.

In 1995 the firm was taken over by the Henriot family
of Champagne. Since then there has been a sea-change
in quality. This venerable company is now clearly back
where it should be.

MAISON CHAMPY PÈRE ET FILS

Owner: Meurgey family.

Champy is the oldest *négociant* in Burgundy and has
archives dating back to 1720. Somewhat moribund, it
was acquired by Jadot in the late 1980s, who were interested in their vineyards. Jadot kept these, and some
interesting reserves of old bottles dating back to the
mid-nineteenth century, but sold the remainder – both
name and cellars – in 1990 to Henri Meurgey, a well-
recognised oenologist and broker, and his son Pierre.

What Champy offers today is a wide range of well-
priced, well-chosen wines ranging from generics
upwards, but not too far upwards. The emphasis is on
affordable village wines rather than on a glitzy range of
grands crus. They buy wine rather than must or grapes,
and more than once when I have correctly guessed the
source, I have noticed that the wine in the Champy cellar showed better than it did in its original home, which
I might have visited a day or two previously.

DIVA, handling estate-bottled Burgundy, is another
Meurgey concern.

★★ MAISON JOSEPH DROUHIN

Owner: Drouhin family.

Surface Area under Vine: 63.2 ha, owned and *en
fermage* – Chambertin, Clos-de-Bèze (13 a),
Griottes-Chambertin (53 a), Bonnes-Mares (24 a),
Le Musigny (68 a), Grands-Echezeaux (48 a),
Echezeaux (46 a), Clos de Vougeot (91 a), Corton,
Bressandes (26 a), Corton-Charlemagne (34 a),

Bâtard-Montrachet (10 a), Chambolle-Musigny *premier cru* including Les Amoureuses, Vosne-Romanée *premier cru* Les Petits-Monts, Volnay *premier cru* Clos-de-Chênes, Beaune *premier cru* including Clos-des-Mouches (red and white) and Les Grèves, and village Chambolle-Musigny, Vougeot, Chorey-Lès-Beaune and Beaune; plus a domaine of 35.83 ha in Chablis.

The firm dates from 1880, when Joseph Drouhin took over an already well-established Burgundian house, and then acquired the old cellars of the dukes of Burgundy, near the Collégiale Notre-Dame. This is one of the most perfectionist and least paternalistic of the Beaune merchants, dealing in nothing but Burgundy and Beaujolais, not even generic Bourgogne.

The wines are now made in modern premises on the outskirts of Beaune, under the supervision of Robert Jousset-Drouhin, head of the firm, his son Philippe, who is responsible for the vineyards, and Laurence Jobard, chief winemaker, and are as good as any in the Côte, equally fine in both colours. Drouhin's daughter Véronique is responsible for the company's Oregon winery, Domaine Drouhin. Drouhin also distributes the wines of Domaine Marquis de Laguiche in Chassagne-Montrachet.

Maison Camille Giroud

Owner: Giroud family.

Surface Area under Vine: 32 a, owned – Beaune *premier cru* Les Cras.

Old-fashioned, in the best sense of the word, is how I would describe the wines of this merchant. Until recently Bernard and François Giroud always bought made wine for ageing. Now with a new extension to the *cuverie* completed in 1996 they buy grapes but the style of the resulting wines does not seem to have changed, however. They tend to be well-coloured, rich, full and long-lasting, sometimes a bit too robust. There is little new oak here, and the wines are bottled later than most. I have had some fine old bottles here, though others have been a bit tough.

There is now an embryonic domaine here: 32 a of Beaune *premier cru* Les Cras.

Hospices de Beaune

The Hospices de Beaune comprises two charitable institutions, the Hôtel-Dieu, founded in 1443 by Nicolas Rolin, chancellor of Philippe Le Hardi, Duke of Burgundy, and his wife Guigone de Salins, and the Hospice de la Charité, endowed by Antoine Rousseau and his wife Barbe Deslandes in the seventeenth century.

The Hôtel-Dieu is a remarkable building in the centre of Beaune and is one of the world's great wine tourist attractions. It is no longer used as a charitable institution for the sick and poor but is preserved as a museum. The central feature of the building is a huge dormitory, the Grande Salle or Chambre des Pauvres, its walls lined with curiously wide yet short beds – the inmates slept two to a bed – each with a sight of the altar in the chapel at the far end so that, though bedridden, they could participate in the services.

Over the years both these institutions were the fortunate recipients of vineyards, and the holdings now total some 62 hectares, nearly all of it *premier cru*, making the Hospices one of the largest domaines in Burgundy. The holdings are split into thirty-eight different wines, most of which are blends of a number of different vineyards within the same commune. They are sold each year under the name of major benefactors to the Hospices, by auction on the Sunday afternoon (and well into the evening: this is a lengthy, tedious *auction à la chandelle*) on the third weekend of November. In 1998 577 casks were auctioned. This is not the whole production as the wine from the younger vines is disposed of in bulk to the local *négociants*. The auction is the central event of the weekend of the Trois Glorieuses and traditionally sets the trend of prices for the vintage in Burgundy, though the actual levels paid are always grossly inflated.

The wines are sold when they are barely a month old, and as crucial as their initial quality is the competence of the firm who will then look after it. It is wise to choose a merchant you can trust. The following wines are blends from the sites listed after the *cuvée* name.

Red Wine Cuvées

Charlotte Dumay Corton Les Renardes (2 ha), Corton Les Bressandes (1 ha) and Corton Clos-du-Roi (1.4 ha).

Docteur Peste Corton Les Bressandes (1 ha), Corton Les Chaumes and Les Voirosses (1 ha), Corton Clos-du-Roi (1.5 ha), Corton La Fièvre (0.4 ha) and Corton Les Grèves (0.1 ha).

Rameau-Lamarosse Pernand-Vergelesses Les Basses-Vergelesses (0.65 ha).

Fouquerand Savigny-Lès-Beaune Les Basses-Vergelesses (1 ha), Savigny-Lès-Beaune Les Talmettes (0.65 ha), Savigny-Lès-Beaune Aux Gravains (0.33 ha) and Savigny-Lès-Beaune Aux Serpentières (0.14 ha).

Arthur Girard Savigny-Lès-Beaune Les Peuillets (1 ha) and Savigny-Lès-Beaune Les Marconnets (0.8 ha).

Nicolas Rolin Beaune Les Cent-Vignes (1.4 ha), Beaune Les Grèves (0.33 ha), Beaune En Genêt (0.2 ha), Beaune Les Teurons (0.5 ha) and Beaune Les Bressandes (0.14).

Guigone de Salins Beaune Les Bressandes (1.2 ha), Beaune Les Seurey (0.8 ha) and Beaune Les Champs-Pinots (0.6 ha).

Clos des Avaux Beaune Les Avaux (2 ha).

Brunet Beaune Les Teurons (0.5 ha), Beaune Les Bressandes (0.5 ha) and Beaune Les Cent-Vignes (0.5 ha).

Maurice Drouhin Beaune Les Avaux (1 ha), Beaune Les Boucherottes (0.65 ha), Beaunes Les Champs-Pimont (0.6 ha) and Beaune Les Grèves (0.25 ha).

Hugues et Louis Bétault Beaune Les Grèves (1.1 ha), Beaune La Mignotte (0.54 ha), Beaune Les Aigrots (0.4 ha) and Beaune Clos-des-Mouches (0.33 ha).

Rousseau-Deslandes Beaune Les Cent-Vignes (1 ha), Beaune Les Montrevenots (0.65 ha) and Beaune La Mignotte (0.4 ha).

Dames Hospitalières Beaune Les Bressandes (1 ha), Beaune La Mignotte (1.13 ha) and Beaune Les Teurons (0.5 ha).

Dames de La Charité Pommard Les Petits-Epenots (0.4 ha), Pommard Les Rugiens (0.33 ha), Pommard Les Noizons (0.25 ha), Pommard La Refène (0.35 ha) and Pommard Les Combes-Dessus (0.2 ha).

Billardet Pommard Les Petits-Epenots (0.65 ha), Pommard Les Noizons (0.5 ha), Pommard Les Arvelets (0.4 ha) and Pommard Les Rugiens (0.35 ha).

Blondeau Volnay Les Champans (0.6 ha), Volnay Les Taille-Pieds (0.6 ha), Volnay Le Ronceret (0.35 ha) and Volnay En L'Ormeau (0.25 ha).

Général Muteau Volnay Le Village (0.8 ha), Volnay Le Carelle-sous-la-Chapelle (0.35 ha), Volnay Les Caillerets-Dessus (0.2 ha), Volnay Le Fremiet (0.2 ha) and Volnay Les Taille-Pieds (0.2 ha).

Jehan de Massol Volnay Les Santenots (0.65 ha) and Les Plures (0.25 ha).

Gauvain Volnay Les Santenots (0.65 ha) and Les Plures (0.75 ha).

Lebelins Monthelie Les Duresses (0.5 ha).

Madelaine Collignon Mazis-Chambertin (1.75 ha).

Cyrot-Chaudron Beaune Les Montrevenots (1 ha).

Raymond Cyrot Pommard *premier cru* (0.65 ha) and Pommard (1.10 ha).

Suzanne Chaudron Pommard (1.37 ha).

Cyrot Chaudron et Georges Kritter Clos de La Roche (0.4 ha).

White Wine Cuvées

Françoise de Salins Corton-Charlemagne (0.4 ha).

Baudot Meursault Les Genevrières-Dessus (0.65 ha) and Meursault Les Genevrières-Dessous (0.75 ha).

Philippe le Bon Meursault Les Genevrières-Dessus (0.13 ha) and Meursault Les Genevrières-Dessous (0.4 ha).

De Balizère de Lanlay Meursault Les Charmes-Dessus (0.5 ha) and Meursault Les Charmes-Dessous (0.4 ha).

Albert Grivault Meursault Les Charmes-Dessus (0.5 ha).

Jehan Humblot Meursault Les Poruzots (0.5 ha) and Meursault Les Grands-Charrons (0.1 ha).

Loppin Meursault Les Criots (0.35 ha) and Meursault Les Peutes-Vignes (0.2 ha).

Goureau Meursault Les Poruzots (0.35 ha) and Meursault Les Grand-Charrons (0.1 ha).

Paul Chanson Corton Blanc Les Vergennes (1.35 ha).

Dames de Flandres Bâtard-Montrachet (0.35 ha).

François Poisard Pouilly-Fuissé (4 ha).

In recent years, the quality of the Hospices' wines has been much criticised, and rightly so. But in 1993 and 1994 a new winemaking centre, away from the centre of Beaune, was constructed. At the same time André Porcheret, who had been the Hospices' winemaker until seduced away by Lalou Bize to be her righthand man at

Domaine Leroy, was hired back. It became apparent that he was to be given greater control of the *vignerons* who tended the Hospices' vines (the job is leased out to locals who have neighbouring vines on an *à la tâche* basis), and that a more rigorous attitude towards yield was to be inaugurated. A *table de tri* was installed at the winery and Porcheret decided to prolong the *cuvaison* following the fermentation. It seems that a corner has been turned. Some are now beginning to suggest that the Hospices should act like a proper domaine, and look after the vines up to the time of bottling. To the Beaune *négoce*, of course, this is anathema, as it usurps their traditional role, indeed *raison d'être*. One further point of controversy is the Hospices' policy of ageing all their wine in 100 per cent new oak — this, critics argue, is fine for Mazis-Chambertin in a year like 1990, but inappropriate for an Auxey-Duresses in a much lighter year. Personally I find many of the Hospices' wines hopelessly over-oaked, even when racked into old wood immediately on receipt into the purchaser's cellar (this has to be by 15 January following the sale). Porcheret retired in 1999 and perhaps his successor, Roland Masse, who formerly worked at the Domaine Bertagna in Vougeot, will be able to change this policy.

★★ Maison Louis Jadot

Owner: Kopf family.
Surface Area under Vine: 59.44 ha, owned and *en fermage*. This land is split between five domaines.

Domaine Louis Jadot

Surface Area under Vine: 23.62 ha — Chambertin Clos-de-Bèze (42 a), Chapelle-Chambertin (39 a), Bonnes-Mares (27 a), Le Musigny (17 a), Echezeaux (35 a), Clos de Vougeot (2.15 ha), Gevrey-Chambertin *premiers crus* Clos-Saint-Jacques, Les Cazetiers, La Combe-aux-Moines, Lavaux-Saint-Jacques, Les Estournelles-Saint-Jacques and Les Poissenots, Chambolle-Musigny *premier cru* Les Amoureuses, Savigny-Lès-Beaune *premier cru* La Dominode, Beaune *premiers crus* Les Avaux and Les Teurons, Marsannay (red, white and rosé), and village Chambolle and Santenay, in the *lieu-dit* Clos-de-Malte (red and white).

Domaine des Héritiers Louis Jadot

Surface Area under Vine: 16.58 ha — Corton-Charlemagne (1.88 ha), Corton, Les Pougets (1.54 ha), Chevalier-Montrachet, Les Demoiselles (51 a), Pernand-Vergelesses *premier cru* Clos-de-La-Croix-de-Pierre (in En Caradeux), Beaune *premiers crus* Les Bressandes, Les Teurons, Clos-des-Couchéreaux (in Les Couchérias), Les Boucherottes, Le Chouacheux and Clos des Ursules (in Les Vignes-Franches), and Puligny-Montrachet *premier cru* Les Folatières.

Domaine André Gagey

Surface Area under Vine: 3.67 ha — Clos-Saint-Denis (17 a), Chambolle-Musigny *premier cru* Les Baudes, Nuits-Saint-Georges *premier cru* Les Boudots, Beaune *premiers crus* Clos de Couchereaux (in Les Couchérias), Les Cent Vignes and Les Grèves (white), Puligny-Montrachet *premier cru* Le Champs-Gain, and village Chambolle-Musigny.

Domaine Robert Tourlière

Surface Area under Vine: 2.87 ha — Clos de Vougeot (64 a), Beaune *premiers crus* Les Grèves (red and white), Les Toussaints and Les Tuvelains.

Domaine Duc de Magenta

Surface Area under Vine: 12.70 ha — Chassagne-Montrachet *premier cru* Morgeots 'Clos de La Chapelle' (red and white), Puligny-Montrachet *premier cru* Clos de La Garenne, village Puligny-Montrachet, Meursault and Auxey-Duresses.

The winemaker here is the candid and enthusiastic Jacques Lardière who is a fountain of knowledge and a man of genius. You will learn more about Burgundy in a morning tasting wine with him than in five years' trekking around the region on your own. And you will never be less than highly satisfied with his wines. This is a perfectionist.

As you sample what is an exhaustive range and make your comments, you will often be told that, yes, probably, this *premier cru* (not quite up to stuff) will probably be downgraded to the village *cuvée*; with this wine he did such-and-such, with another something quite different.

★ Domaine Albert Morot

Owner: Chopin family.

Surface Area under Vine: 7 ha, owned – Beaune *premiers cru*s Les Teurons, Les Grèves, Les Toussaints, Les Bressandes, Les Cent-Vignes and Les Marconnets, and Savigny-Lès-Beaune *premier cru* in Les Vergelesses 'La Bataillière'.

Once a *négociant*, this family firm now exists as a domaine, owning only *premier cru* vines. Operating out of the gauntly gothic Château de La Creusotte, on the road to Bouze-Lès-Beaune, it is run by Mademoiselle Françoise Choppin. Delicious wines, each one with an individuality of its own, can be found here.

★ Maison Remoissenet Père & Fils

Owner: Roland Remoissenet and family.

Surface Area under Vine: 2.50 ha, owned – Beaune *premiers crus* Les Marconnets, Les Grèves, Les Toussaints and En Genêt.

Courtier as well as *négociant* (for a long time this firm was the supplier/broker for Nicolas, the French wine firm), Remoissenet buys wine, not must or grapes. Roland Remoissenet, today in his sixties, is shrewd, a man of frequent collecting enthusiasms, and a cat who walks by himself, decidedly not part of the sometimes self-important Beaune *négociant* 'mafia'. The firms distributes the wines of the Domaine Baron Thénard and these – Le Montrachet, Corton Clos-du-Roi and Grands-Echezeaux – are often the best wines. Today the problems of supply, with all of the growers bottling all their best wines, must be becoming increasingly acute, but you can still buy some very fine wines under the Remoissenet label, particularly in white, and which keep remarkably well.

Other Producers of note

Domaine Carré-Courbin, Maison Chanson Père et Fils, La Compagnie Les Vins d'Autrefois, Domaine Michel Duchot, Maison Jaffelin and Domaine Jean-Claude Rateau.

Pommard

Surface Area (1998): *Premiers crus* 112 ha; village wines 201 ha.

Production (1998): *Premiers crus* 4401 hl; village wines 8367 hl.

Colour: Red.

Grape Variety: Pinot Noir.

Premiers crus There are twenty-eight *premiers crus*, in whole or in part. These are as follows: Les Arvelets, Les Bertins, Clos Blanc, Les Boucherottes, La Chamière (part), Les Chanlins-Bas (part), Les Chaponnières, Les Charmots, Le Combe-Dessus, Clos de La Commaraine, Les Croix Noires, Derrière-Saint-Jean, Clos des Epeneaux, Les Fremiers, Les Grands Epenots, Les Jarolières, En Largillière (Les Argillières), Clos Micot or Micault, Les Petits Epenots, Les Pézerolles, La Platière (part), Les Poutures, La Refène, Les Rugiens-Bas, Les Rugiens-Hauts (part), Les Saussilles, Clos de Verger and Le Village.

South of Beaune we come to the best red wine villages of the Côte de Beaune after the *grands crus* of Corton – Pommard and Volnay. The name Pommard is of malic origin (Pommarium, Pommone or Polmario) but there are few apple orchards today, every square metre being given over to producing one of the most popular red Burgundies.

The two best *premiers crus* (Epenots and Rugiens) are at opposite ends of the commune. At the northern Beaune end, largely behind a stone wall, lies Epenots, and above it Pezerolles; while Charmots and Arvelets, facing more to the south, are round the corner overlooking the river Dheune and the valley up to Meloissey in the Hautes-Côtes. On the southern side are Rugiens, Chanlins, Fremiers, Jarolières and Chaponnières.

Rugiens and Epenots – more particularly Les Grands Epenots and Les Rugiens Bas – produce the best Pommard wines, and would be contenders with one or two of the better Volnay *climats* for elevation to *grand cru* status. The soil structure of the Pommard *premiers crus* is complicated Burgundian limestone, stony in parts (dolomitic containing a high proportion of carbonate of magnesium), elsewhere comprising an iron-rich oolite.

To the south of the village the land rises more steeply and the vineyards face due east. The soil here is red in colour – hence the name Rugiens – because of the iron it contains. On the Beaune side the vineyards face more to the south and the slope is more gentle. In general the soil is more clayey than in Volnay or Beaune and it is this which gives Pommard wine its full, sturdy character.

Pommard wines are closed, well-coloured and long-lasting compared with those of Volnay and Beaune. They can also be a bit solid, robust and alcoholic: four-square wines which lack grace. The wines are expensive, because of the demand from the American market but when they are good they are rich, fat and succulent. Sadly the name is often abused, and you can pay a high price for an indifferent wine.

Leading Pommard Producers

★★ DOMAINE DU COMTE ARMAND DOMAINE DU CLOS DES EPENEAUX

Owner: Comte Armand.

Surface Area under Vine: 10 ha, owned – Pommard *premier cru* Clos des Epeneaux *monopole*, village Pommard, Volnay *premier cru* Les Fremiets, village Volnay, village Meursault in the *lieu-dit* Les Meix-Chavaux, Auxey-Duresses *premier cru* (red), and village Auxey-Duresses (white).

Until 1994 this was an estate which existed on its one single monopoly, the Clos des Epeneaux, but it has now begun to expand. In 1985 the Count, a Parisian lawyer in his forties, had the perspicacity, when the standards were not what they should have been, to employ the young French-Canadian Pascal Marchand as his manager and wine-maker. Since then the improvement has been exponential. The Clos is in the best bit of the Epenots *premier cru* (note the idiosyncratic spelling) and the wine is of a size and intensity that few others manage to achieve, yet retaining all the inherent finesse of the *climat*.

Pascal Marchand left to take over responsibility for the Boisset/Ponnelle domaine in Nuits-Saint-Georges in 1999. His successor is Benjamin Laroux.

★ DOMAINE JEAN-MARC BOILLOT

Owner: Jean-Marc Boillot.

Surface Area under Vine: 10.50 ha, owned and *en fermage* – Bâtard-Montrachet (18 a), Beaune *premier cru* Les Montrevenots, Pommard *premiers cru* s Les Rugiens, Les Saussilles and Les Jarolières, Volnay *premiers crus* Les Pitures, Carelle sous La Chapelle and Le Ronceret, Puligny-Montrachet *premiers cru*s La Truffière, Les Referts, Les Champs-Canet and Les Combottes, Beaune *premier cru* (white), and village Pommard, Volnay, Meursault, Puligny-Montrachet and Chassagne-Montrachet.

This is one of the very few top-quality domaines in Burgundy to make equally good red and white wines. Jean-Marc is part of the extended Boillot family, with cousins who make wine in Gevrey, a brother who makes wine in Volnay and a brother-in-law (Gérard Boudot of Domaine Etienne Sauzet) who makes wine in Puligny-Montrachet. Some of Jean-Marc's estate comes from the division of this latter domaine.

The Pinot Noirs are destemmed totally, given a week-long maceration at ambient temperatures and then vinified at 33°-35°C. There is some 20-25 per cent new wood each year for both red and white wines. Jean-Marc has not been in business on his account long (from 1984 to 1988 being winemaker for Olivier Leflaive Frères), but I have a high respect for what he does. He told me once that he considers his Pommard, Saussilles produces better wine in softer vintages, such as 1989 or 1992, than in a firmer one, which is an interesting point. Boillot also has a *négociant* licence but seems to use it mostly for white wines from the Côte Chalonnaise and also from Puligny-Montrachet.

At the time of writing the white Beaune *premier cru* is young vines.

★ DOMAINE DE COURCEL

Owner: Courcel family.

Surface Area under Vine: 6 ha, owned – Pommard *premiers crus* Les Epenots, Les Rugiens and Les Fremiers (also Les Croix-Noires but currently not bottled by the domaine), and village Pommard.

Like the Comte Armand (see page 199), the Courcels are absentee landlords. Gilles de Courcel, the member of the family who takes charge of the domaine, spends most of his life as an export manager for Calvet (a Bordeaux *négociant*). The man on the spot in Pommard is Yves Tavant who took over from his father in 1971, supervised by Yves Confuron of Vosne-Romanée.

The domaine owns a large slice of Epenots, just on the Beaune side of the Clos des Epeneaux, in what they label as the Grand-Clos-des-Epenots. But their best wine is their Rugiens, perhaps the best example of this top Pommard vineyard. The wine is proof that Rugiens would be a worthy contender for *grand cru* status.

Other Producers of note

DOMAINE BILLARD-GONNET, DOMAINE COSTE-CAUMARTIN, DOMAINE JEAN GARAUDET, DOMAINE MICHEL GAUNOUX, DOMAINE A F GROS, DOMAINE JEAN-LUC JOILLOT, DOMAINE PARENT, DOMAINE FRANÇOIS PARENT, DOMAINE DANIEL REBOURGEON-MURE and DOMAINE ALETH LE ROYER-GIRARDIN.

VOLNAY

Surface Area (1998): *Premiers crus* 126 ha; village wine 92 ha.

Production (1998): *Premiers crus* 4408 hl; village wine 4021 hl.

Colour: Red.

Grape Variety: Pinot Noir.

Premiers crus There are thirty-three *premiers crus*, in whole or in part, as follows: Les Angles, Clos de L'Audignac, Les Aussy (part), La Barre (Clos de La Barre), Clos de La Bousse d'Or, Les Brouillards (part), Caillerets-Dessus (including the Clos des Soixante Ouvrées), En Cailleret, Carelle-sous-La-Chapelle, Les Carelles-Dessous (part), Clos de La Cave des Ducs, En Champans, Les Chanlins (part), Clos de La Chapelle, Clos du Château des Ducs, En Chevret, Clos des Chênes (part), Clos des Ducs, Les Fremiets, Les Fremiets (Clos de La Rougeotte), La Gigotte (part), Les Grands Champs (part), Lasolle (part), Les Lurets (part), Les Mitans, En L'Ormeau, Les Pitures-Dessus, Les Pointes d'Angles,

Robardelle (part), Les Roncerets, Les Taille-Pieds, En Verseuil (Clos du Verseuil) and Le Village (part). In the commune of Meursault, the following *climats* when planted with Pinot Noir have the right to the *appellation* Volnay Santenots: Clos des Santenots, Les Plures or Pitures, Les Santenots-Blancs, Les Santenots Dessous, Les Santenots du Milieu and Les Vignes Blanches.

With Volnay we come to one of the most delightful wines and one of the most rewarding communes in the Côte d'Or. There are a large number of very fine and dedicated growers in the village, and the wine they produce is the epitome of elegance and delicacy, the most fragrant and seductively feminine expression of the Pinot Noir in Burgundy. Volnay is as far removed as it can possibly be from the souped up, 'old fashioned' brews which were fraudulently bottled as non-*appellation* Burgundy in our grandparents' day.

Volnay is a small village tucked into the top of its slope above the vineyards and away from the main road. The name comes from a Celtic or early Gallic water god, de Volen. The village appears in medieval times as Vollenay and was spelt Voulenay by Thomas Jefferson when he toured France just prior to the French Revolution.

Hugues IV, one of the early Burgundian dukes, built a hunting lodge up in the hills in about 1250, and it is largely from the stones of this edifice, long since demolished, that the local houses are constructed. Much of the village dates from the seventeenth and eighteenth centuries. There are some fine mansions and imposing courtyards sheltered behind tall gates and thick walls.

Domaine-bottling in Burgundy can be said to have begun in Volnay. The present Marquis d'Angerville's father was a constant critic of the cynical fraud being perpetrated by the local merchants in the 1930s. As a result they refused to accept his wine, and so he was forced to bottle it himself and to look outside the local *négoce* for his markets. He was soon joined by other growers, including his friends Henri Gouges of Nuits-Saint-Georges and Armand Rousseau of Gevrey-Chambertin who were being similarly shunned. Encouraged by Raymond Baudoin, the French wine writer and consultant to many top restaurants, by the

American wine importer Frank Schoonmaker and later by Alexis Lichine, these fine growers were eventually joined by more and more of the top estates, leading to the situation today where almost everyone who makes good wine bottles and sells at least some of it himself and one suspects that some of the Beaune *négociants* are increasingly hard-pressed to find good wine to mature and sell. The tables have well and truly been turned! D'Angerville was also a pioneer of clonal selection and has a particular low-yielding, high-quality strain, the Pinot d'Angerville, named in his honour.

At the southern end of this commune, the Volnay *premiers crus* overflow into the neighbouring commune of Meursault. The three vineyards of Santenots, Pitures and Cras can be planted with both Pinot Noir and Chardonnay. If the wine is red it is labelled as Volnay. Any white wine goes under the Meursault name. Apart from Santenots the best of the *premiers crus* are generally regarded to be the Cailleret Dessus and the Clos des Chênes, the latter lying higher up above Cailleret Dessus at the southern end of the commune. Here you will find a poor but well-exposed, very stony, reddish soil of Bathonian origin on a rocky base, on a definite south-east-facing slope. It is the lightness of the soil throughout the Volnay vineyards that largely contributes to the delicacy and finesse of the wines.

Nearer to the village are the *premiers crus* of Taillepieds and the Clos de La Bousse d'Or – a name which has nothing to do with anything golden but derives from *bousse terre* or good soil in the local patois. On the northern Pommard side are the *premiers crus* of Clos de Ducs, Pitures, Chanlins and Fremiets. Here the wines are generally just a shade sturdier than those from the southern side.

Leading Volnay Producers

★★ DOMAINE DU MARQUIS D'ANGERVILLE
Owner: Family of the Marquis d'Angerville.
Surface Area under Vine: 15 ha, owned – Volnay *premiers crus* Clos des Ducs *monopole*, Les Champans, Les Fremiets, Les Taille-Pieds,

Les Caillerets, En L'Ormeau, Les Angles and Les Pitures, Pommard *premier cru* Les Combes, and Meursault *premier cru* Les Santenots.

This estate has been in the same hands – the D'Angervilles inheriting it by marriage – since 1905, and has hardly changed throughout this time. The current Marquis, Jacques, took over on his father's death in 1952.

Pride of place in the portfolio is the Clos des Ducs, a *monopole* lying next to the Angerville château. This is a magnificent wine, with a depth and firmness perfectly in harmony with the usual pure Pinot fragrance of Volnay. The rest of the range – the lesser Volnays being combined and sold as *premier cru* – is fine too.

★★ DOMAINE MICHEL LAFARGE
Owner: Lafarge family.
Surface Area under Vine: 10 ha, owned and *en fermage* – Volnay *premiers crus* Clos des Chênes and Clos du Château des Ducs *monopole*, Volnay *premier cru* , Beaune *premier cru* Les Grèves, Pommard *premier cru* Les Pézerolles, village Volnay including Vendange Selectionnée, and village Meursault.

Year after year, Michel Lafarge and his son Frédéric produce some of the most delicious wines in the village, all the way from a splendid Bourgogne *rouge* to the yardstick Clos des Chênes. There have been Lafarges based in Volnay since before the French Revolution. Michel himself, now seventy, took over the domaine on his father's death in 1967, and has since bought his brothers out. Like his father before him, he has gently expanded the size of the domaine. Like him, he has also served as mayor of the village.

'Are there any secrets?' you ask Michel. 'Only old vines and a small crop', he answers. 'Pick early when the weather is bad. And as late as possible if it fine.'

★★ DOMAINE HUBERT DE MONTILLE
Owner: de Montille family.
Surface Area under Vine: 7.5 ha, owned – Volnay *premiers crus* Les Tailles-Pieds, Les Champans and Les Mitans, Volnay *premier cru* , Pommard *premiers crus* Les Rugiens, Les Pézerolles and

Les Grand-Epenots, and Puligny-Montrachet *premier cru* Les Caillerets.

This is another great Volnay estate, well known for its policy of minimal chaptalisation. This makes for very pure wines, perhaps a little lean and austere in their youth, but which mature magnificently. Responsibility is now shared between the Maître himself (Hubert de Montille, now retired, was a top Dijon lawyer), his son Etienne and his daughter Alix. The Puligny was acquired from the Domaine Chartron in 1993.

DOMAINE DE LA POUSSE D'OR
Owner: Patrick Landanger.
Surface Area under Vine: 13.0 ha, owned – Corton Bressandes (50 a), Corton Clos du Roi (3 ha of which 1.70 ha exploited), Volnay *premiers crus* Clos de La Bousse d'Or *monopole*, Caillerets, Clos-des-Soixante-Ouvrées *monopole*, Les Caillerets and Clos de L'Audignac *monopole*, Pommard *premier cru* Les Jarollières, and Santenay *premiers crus* Les Gravières and Clos-des-Tavannes.

Until late 1997, and the untimely death of Gérard Potel at the age of sixty-two, this property was run by Potel and his son Nicolas and was one of the most progressive of the top domaines in Burgundy. It has since been sold to Patrick Landanger. Standards, I fear, have fallen. Let us hope this descent is only temporary.

Other Producers of note
DOMAINE VINCENT BITOUZET-PRIEUR, DOMAINE JEAN BOILLOT, DOMAINE JEAN-MARC BOULEY, DOMAINE REYANNE ET PASCAL BOULEY, DOMAINE YVON CLERGET, DOMAINE ROBLET-MONNOT, DOMAINE RÉGIS ROSSIGNOL-CHANGARNIER AND DOMAINE JOSEPH VOILLOT.

MONTHELIE

Surface Area (1998): *Premiers crus* 26 ha; village wines 91 ha.
Production (1998): *Premiers crus* (red) 1099 hl and (white) 32 hl; village wines (red) 3495 hl and (white) 313 hl.

Colour: Red and white.
Grape Varieties: (Red) Pinot Noir and (white) Chardonnay.
Premiers crus There are eleven *premiers crus*, in whole or in part: Le Cas-Rougeot, Les Champs-Fuillots, Le Château Gaillard, Les Duresses (part), Le Clos Gauthey, Le Meix-Bataille, Les Riottes, La Taupine, Sur-La-Velle, Les Vignes Rondes and Le Village (part). Several are small and obscure. All except Les Duresses lie above the village on the extension of the Volnay *côte*.

Monthelie is the first commune after Volnay as the road to Autun begins to ascend into the uplands of the Hautes-Côtes. It is an attractive village set back from the main road and fits snugly in between two slopes of vineyards. Those on the northern side are a continuation of Volnay, though the slope is less steep and faces due south rather than south-east. On the other side of Monthelie the vineyards face more to the north-east and join those of Auxey-Duresses.

The best *premiers crus* are Sur La Velle and Les Champs Fuillot and are an extension of Volnay, Clos de Chênes and Cailleret. The wine from these two *climats* is really very similar to Volnay, though a little lighter and with not quite so much definition. From the rest of its vineyards the wine can occasionally suffer from a lack of real ripeness and concentration, yet in good years can be excellent value at two-thirds or less the price of its more famous neighbour.

Leading Monthelie Producer

★ DOMAINE DIDIER DARVIOT-PERRIN
Owner: Darviot-Perrin family.
Surface Area under Vine: 8 ha, owned and *en fermage* – Volnay *premiers crus* La Gigotte *monopole* and Les Santenots, Beaune *premier cru* Les Belisands, Chassagne-Montrachet *premiers crus* Les Bondues (red) and Blanchots-Dessus (white), Meursault *premier cru* Les Charmes, village Volnay, Beaune, Monthelie (red and white), Meursault and Chassagne-Montrachet (white).

Didier Darviot produces very pure, stylish wines, true to their origins from his estate, much of which is inherited through his wife's family (the Perrin-Ponsots of Meursault). Apart from the Monthelies, of which there is not much, the average age of vines is a respectable forty-five years. From this very good source the Chassagne-Montrachet Blanchots-Dessus is delicious.

Other Producers of note

DOMAINE ERIC BOIGELOT, DOMAINE MAURICE DESCHAMPS, DOMAINE PAUL GARAUDET, DOMAINE MONTHELIE-DOUHAIRET, DOMAINE J & A PARENT AND DOMAINE ERIC DE SUREMAIN AT THE CHÂTEAU DE MONTHELIE.

AUXEY-DURESSES

Surface Area (1998): *Premiers crus* 26 ha; village wines 110 ha.

Production (1998): *Premiers crus* (red) 1100 hl and (white) 41 hl; village wines (red) 3162 hl and (white) 1710 hl.

Colour: Red and white.

Grape Varieties: (Red) Pinot Noir and (white) Chardonnay.

Premiers crus There are nine *premiers crus*, in whole or in part, as follows: Les Bréterins (part), La Chapelle, Climat du Val, Les Bas des Duresses, Les Duresses (part), Les Ecusseaux (part), Les Grands-Champs, Reugne (part) and Clos du Val.

Auxey-Duresses – the first word is pronounced 'Aussey' – lies a little further along the D973 in a little valley between the Mont Melian and the Montagne du Bourdon. The latter is an extension of the Monthelie slope and faces east and then south. On it lie Auxey's nine *premiers crus* and the production is largely of red wine. Across the valley the vineyards face north, and here the Chardonnay is widely planted, as it is further round the hill above the village of Meursault.

The three best *premiers crus* are Les Duresses, La Chapelle and du Val. About two-thirds of the village wine is red, a lightish red similar to Monthelie's village

wine; a little green in the poorer years but of value and consequence when the sun shines sufficiently to ripen the grapes. Less heat is required to mature the Chardonnay, and the white wines are, consequently, more consistent. This can be a good inexpensive substitute for Meursault. Auxey is an up-and-coming *appellation*. The visitor should take note that almost everyone in the village is called Prunier!

★★★ DOMAINE D'AUVENAY
MAISON LEROY

Owners: Domaine d'Auvenay: Bize-Leroy family; Maison Leroy: Bize-Leroy and Roch families.

Surface Area under Vine: (Domaine d'Auvenay) 3.88 ha, owned – Bonnes-Mares (26 a), Mazis-Chambertin (26 a), Chevalier-Montrachet (16 a), Criots-Bâtard-Montrachet (6 a), Meursault *premier cru* Gouttes d'Or, Puligny-Montrachet *premier cru* Folatières, and village Meursault and Auxey-Duresses.

With Madame Lalou Bize-Leroy's acquisition in 1988 of the Charles Noëllat domaine in Vosne-Romanée (see Domaine Leroy page 175), one suspects that Maison Leroy, the merchant arm of the business, may not be buying much wine today but substantial stocks of high-quality old Burgundies still remain in the cellar to sell.

The Leroy style has always been for wines which last well, bought in as wine when the vintage was a good one and the quality appropriate. Here is a treasure trove, but an expensive one. While Leroy, *négociant* and domaine, is jointly owned by Madame Bize-Leroy, her sister and other shareholders, the Domaine d'Auvenay belongs to Lalou and her husband Maurice. The wines are as exceptional as they are in Vosne-Romanée, and are made in a *chai* on the family farm up above Saint-Romain.

Other Producers of note

DOMAINE ALAIN CREUSEFOND, DOMAINE JEAN-PIERRE DICONNE, DOMAINE ANDRÉ ET BERNARD LABRY, DOMAINE HENRI LATOUR, DOMAINE JEAN-PIERRE PRUNIER, DOMAINE MICHEL PRUNIER, DOMAINE PASCAL PRUNIER, DOMAINE PHILIPPE PRUNIER-DAMY, DOMAINE VINCENT PRUNIER AND DOMAINE DOMINIQUE ET VINCENT ROY.

SAINT-ROMAIN

Surface Area (1998): Village wines 86 ha.
Production (1998): (Red) 2183 hl; (white) 2129 hl.
Colour: Red and white.
Grape Varieties: (Red) Pinot Noir; (white) Chardonnay.

Saint-Romain is really part of the Hautes-Côtes, but has enjoyed full *appellation contrôlée* status in its own right since 1967. After Auxey-Duresses the road divides and the right-hand fork leads to the village of Saint-Romain, surrounded by cliffs and perched below the remains of an impressive fortified château. Below the village are the best sectors of the vineyards which are entitled to the local *appellation*. There are no *premiers crus*.

Though roughly the same amount of red and white wine is produced, the Chardonnay has the greatest reputation, and in the best vintages this can be a useful and less expensive substitute for Meursault and Puligny.

Saint-Romain Producers of note
DOMAINE GERMAIN PÈRE ET FILS, DOMAINE ALAIN GRAS AND DOMAINE GUYOT PÈRE ET FILS.

MEURSAULT

Surface Area (1998): *Premiers crus* 104 ha; village wines 269 ha.
Production (1998): *Premiers crus* (red) 88 hl and (white) 3913 hl; village wines (red) 562 hl and (white) 10,937 hl.
Colour: Red and white.
Grape Varieties: (Red) Pinot Noir and (white) Chardonnay.
Premiers crus Meursault and Blagny (for it is convenient to include Blagny here – though the terrain and wines will be discussed on page 209) possess twenty-nine *premiers crus*, including the various Santenots and Les Plures which when planted with Pinot Noir are sold as Volnay Les Santenots. These are discussed under Volnay (see page 200). In Meursault the *premiers crus* are: Les Bouchères, Les Caillerets, Les Charmes-Dessous,

Les Charmes-Dessus, Les Chaumes de Narvaux (Genevrières), Les Chaumes des Perrières, Les Cras, Les Genevrières-Dessous, Les Genevrières-Dessus, Les Gouttes-d'Or, Aux Perrières, Clos des Perrières, Les Perrières-Dessous, Les Perrières-Dessus, Les Plures, Les Poruzots, Les Poruzots-Dessous, Les Poruzots-Dessus, Clos Richemont, Les Santenots Blanc and Les Santenots du Milieu.

All the above *premiers crus* can be both red or white. In practice only the *climats* near Volnay (Santenots, Les Plures, Les Cras and Clos Richemont) are planted with Pinot Noir. However, while Meursault Les Cras, Meursault Les Caillerets and so on can be red or white, Meursault Les Santenots can only be white. If red, the wine is labelled as Volnay. In Blagny, all the *premiers crus* (Sous Blagny, Sous Le Dos de L'Ane, La Jeunelotte and La Pièce sous Le Bois) have the right to the *appellation* Meursault-Blagny *premier cru* if planted with Chardonnay. For red Blagny see page 209.

Choose selectively and you will perceive a natural progression in the Côte de Beaune. First come the sturdy reds of Pommard; then the more elegant, softer red wines of Volnay; and finally the whites of Meursault. Meursault produces almost as much white wine as all the other communes of the Côte de Beaune put together. It is a large village – only Gevrey and Beaune have more land under vines in the Côte d'Or – and with a seemingly limitless number of individual growers. Since 1983 I have visited fifteen to twenty Meursault proprietors a year, usually eliminating three or four from the previous season in order to add on new names. I have still not got to the bottom of the list.

The name Meursault – Murrisault or Murassalt in old documents – is derived according to some authorities from the Latin *muris saltus* meaning 'mouse jump'. Like the majority of the communes of the Côte d'Or, the history of Meursault is closely associated with the church. Even before there was a vine at Clos de Vougeot, the new Cistercian abbey at Cîteaux, founded by the ascetic Robert de Molesmes in 1098 as a breakaway from the more comfortable order of the Benedictines at Cluny, had received a gift of land and vineyards in

Meursault from the duke of Burgundy. This was followed by further legacies in the next few centuries with the result that after Vougeot, Meursault was Cîteaux's most important viticultural holding, a situation which continued until the French Revolution. Moreover, Meursault rather than Puligny is the heart of the Hospices de Beaune's white grape holdings. Though most of Meursault is entitled to produce red wine or white, the commune seems always to have concentrated on white wines. Thomas Jefferson was told when he visited the area in 1787 that there was 'too much stone' in the soil for red wine production. No doubt the locals would have produced red wine if they could, for the former was much the more popular then. Volnay sold for 300 francs the cask but even the best Meursault (Jefferson refers specifically to Goutte d'Or) could fetch only 150.

The commune is divided into two distinct sections by the village itself. The smaller northern part is an extension of the Volnay-Monthelie slope as it falls gently towards the south-east. The soil is a similar reddish-brown limestone containing both pebbles and clay, and is more suitable for red wines than white. Here you will find the *premiers crus* of Santenots, Pitures and Les Cras. The red wine produced here is sold as Volnay.

South of the village the soil is lighter in colour, rocky rather than pebbly, and the aspect is more east or north-east. The vines lie sheltered under the forest of the Montagne du Chatelet de Montméllian, on the one side of which is the hamlet of Blagny and on the other the village of Auxey. The best vineyards are located below Blagny where the soil is at its lightest and stoniest. Perrières lies above Charmes on the boundary with Puligny, followed, as one moves north towards the village, by Genevrières, Poruzots, Bouchères and Goutte d'Or. All these are *premiers crus* for white wine only.

The large, sprawling village of Meursault lies between the two sections of the vineyards and contains a number of fine buildings, some dating back to the fifteenth and sixteenth centuries. Chief of these is the seventeenth-century Château de Meursault, now owned by the successors to André Boisseaux of the *négociant* Patriarche Père et Fils and housing an art gallery as well as a tasting centre. Across the N74 is the village of

L'Hôpital de Meursault where you can see the ecclesiastical remains of the old leprosarium and eat at the Relais de La Diligence. In the Château de Meursault the third and least stuffy of the Trois Glorieuses banquets, the Paulée, is held at lunchtime on the Monday after the Hospices de Beaune auction. This is the party for the *vignerons*. Everyone brings his own wine and shares it with his neighbours. The last time I attended, I counted afterwards no fewer than fifty-seven tasting notes in my notebook, from Aligoté to a pre-First World War Pommard, my descriptions becoming progressively more indecipherable as the afternoon progressed!

The best *premier cru* is Perrières, normally a beautifully elegant, minerally, racy wine, followed closely by Genevrières, fatter and more sumptuous. Charmes is a large vineyard with the result that the wine can vary, for part of the vineyard, the Charmes-Dessous, is a little too far down the slope for really high-quality wine. Below it the land very soon becomes simple *appellation* Bourgogne. Poruzots and Goutte d'Or are more solid wines with less distinction and finesse but in good hands (and from the old vines and a restricted yield) can be equally fine. The best of the village *climats*, and you will often see these stated on the label – forming a sort of separate category between *premier cru* and anonymous village Meursault – are Les Chevalières, Les Tessons and Les Grands Charrons, which continue the line of the *premiers crus*. I often prefer the racier village wines from Narvaux and Tillets which come from higher up the slope.

In all, a Meursault should be an ample, round, ripe and fruity wine, with a rich, buttery flavour well supported but not overwhelmed by new oak; and with a good balancing acidity. There is a wide variation between the exciting and the bland and the wine can occasionally be a little too fat and heavy, the broadness of its style not matched with sufficient acidity. The plain village wines can be somewhat empty and anonymous.

Leading Meursault Producers

★ DOMAINE ROBERT AMPEAU ET FILS
Owner: Ampeau family.
Surface Area under Vine: 10 ha, owned – Puligny-

Southern Côte de Beaune

Southern Côte
de Beaune

Beaune
Meursault
Santenay

CÔTE D'OR

MONTHÉLIE

Les Vignes Rondes
Sur-La-Velle
Les Riottes
Le Meix-Bataille
Le Village
Le Château Gaillard
Le Clos Gauthey
Le Cas-Rougeot
La Taupine
Les Champs-Fuillots

St-Romain

Les Bas des Duresses
Les Duresses
Les Ecusseaux
Les Grands Champs
Reugne

Les Duresses

Monthélie

Les Caillerets
Clos des Santenots

Clos du Val
Climat du Val
Les Bréterins

La Chapelle

Les Santenots
Dessous
Les Santenots-Blanc
Les Santenots
du Milieu

Les Bouchères
Les Poruzots
Les Chaumes de Narvaux

Auxey-
Duresses

Les Cras

Les Plures
Clos Richemont

Sous Roche Dumay
Les Champelots
En Montceau
Sur Gamay

Les Chaumes des Perrières
Aux Perrières
Les Perrières Dessous
Les Perrières Dessus
Clos des Perrières

AUXEY-
DURESSES

Les Gouttes d'Or

MEURSAULT

Meursault

Les Chalumeaux
Hameau-de-Blagny
Sous Le Puits
La Truffière
Les Feux-Bois
En La Richarde
Sous Le Courthil

Sous Le Dos de L'Ane
La Jeunelotte
Sous Blagny
La Pièce sous Le Bois

Les Poruzots-Dessus

Derrière La Tour, En Créot, Bas de Vermarin-à-L'Est
Sur Le Sentier du Clou, Les Puits, Les Castets,
Le Village, Derrière chez Edouard, Marinot,
Les Perrières, Echaille, Les Frionnes, En La Ranché,
En Champs, Les Travers de Marinot, Vignes Moingeon

Les Poruzots Dessous
Les Genevrières-Dessus
Les Genevrières-Dessous

Le Champ Gain
Clos de Meix
Le Chavillion
La Garenne

Les Charmes-Dessus
Les Charmes-Dessous

La Chatenière
Les Cortons
En Remilly
Les Murgers des Dents de Chien
Les Combes au Sud
Le Charmois
Le Bas de Gamay à L'Est
Les Petangerets
En Vollon à L'Est

Gamay

Blagny

Les Referts
Les Champs-Canet
Les Combettes
Les Perrières
Clos de La Garenne
La Jacquelotte

Les Folatières
Au Chaniot
Les Caillerets
Chevalier-Montrachet

St-Aubin

En Remilly

Les Pucelles

Les Combards, Les Pasquelles,
Les Chaumées, Vigne-Derrière,
Clos St-Jean, Les Petangerets,
Les Reluchets, Les Murées

Puligny-Montrachet

PULIGNY-
MONTRACHET

Les Petits-Fairendes, Les Fairendes,
En Cailleret, En Virondot, Les Crets,
Le Champ-Gain, La Grande-Montagne,
Tonton Marcel, Les Places, Les Grandes Ruchottes,
La Maltroie, La Romanée, Bois de Chassagne,
Les Embazées, Les Baudines, Clos Pitois,
Francemont, Le Grand Clos, Tête du Clos,
Les Petits Clos

ST-AUBIN

Bienvenues-Bâtard-Montrachet
Montrachet
Les Demoiselles
Bâtard-Montrachet
Vide-Bourse
Criots-Bâtard-Montrachet

Blanchot-Dessus
Les Macherelles
Les Chenevottes
Les Dents-de-Chien
Les Vergers
Les Commes
Les Bondues

CÔTE D'OR

SANTENAY

Bois
de la
Comme

Chassagne-
Montrachet

CHASSAGNE-
MONTRACHET

La Boudriotte
Les Morgeots
Vigne Blanche
Les Chaumes
La Chapelle
La Guerchère
La Roquemaure
Les Criottes
Champ Jendreau

DEZIZE-LES-
MARANGES

La Comme
Comme-Dessus
Beauregard

Abbaye de
Morgeots

Les Fourneaux

La Maladière
Beaurepaire
Clos Faubard

Clos Grand
Rousseau
La Fuissière

Le Chainey

Clos Château
Les Brussonnes
Les Boirettes
La Grande-Borne
La Cardeuse

N

Le Clos de La Fuissière

Haut

Santenay

Le Clos
des Loyères

Les Gravières

Chagny

Dezize-
Lès-Maranges

Petit Clos
Rousseau

Les Clos
des Mouches

Clos des Tavannes

Sampigny

D113

Les-Passe-Temps

Dheune

Clos de
La Boutière

SAMPIGNY-
LES-
MARANGES

Les Clos
Roussots

SAÔNE-ET-LOIRE

CHEILLY-LES-
MARANGES

Cheilly

D143

Appellations

▨	Grand Cru
▨	Premier Cru
▨	Village wine
—	Contour line
– · –	Department boundary
- - -	Commune boundary

0   1km
0   1/2mile

Montrachet *premier cru* Les Combottes,
Meursault *premiers crus* Les Perrières,
Les Charmes and La Pièce-sous-Le-Bois, Volnay
premier cru Les Santenots, Beaune *premier cru*
Clos-du-Roi, Savigny-Lès-Beaune *premier cru*
Les Lavières, Auxey-Duresses *premier cru*
Les Ecusseaux, Blagny *premier cru* La Pièce-sous-
Le-Bois, and village Meursault and Pommard.

The Ampeaus, Robert and his son Michel, do not sell *en
primeur*, unlike many other growers, holding back the
vintage until they deem it ready for drinking. Moreover
as a buyer you cannot cherry-pick. you must take red as
well as white, off-vintages as well as the good years. This
is less of an imposition than it might be. Quality is high,
even in the off-vintages, and the wines are built to last. I
would much rather be offered, say, a 1994 from here
than a supposedly better 1995 from many another
Meursault establishment.

★ DOMAINE MICHEL BOUZEREAU ET FILS
Owner: Bouzereau family.
Surface Area under Vine: 11 ha, owned and *en
fermage* – Meursault *premiers crus* Les Perrières,
Les Genevrières and Les Charmes, Blagny,
Puligny-Montrachet *premiers crus* Le Champ-
Gain and Le Cailleret, Beaune *premiers crus* Les
Vignes-Franches and Les Epenottes, village
Meursault including the *lieux-dits* Le Limouzin.
Les Tessons and Les Grands-Charrons, and village
Pommard and Volnay.

This is the best of the Bouzereau cellars (there are many
others in the village). Michel and his son Jean-Baptiste
recently acquired a pneumatic press and this has further
accentuated the quality here. These are fine, racy, stylish wines which can be kept longer than most. A
domaine to watch.

★ DOMAINE YVES BOYER-MARTENOT
Owner: Boyer-Martenot family.
Surface Area under Vine: 8.5 ha, owned and *en
fermage/métayage* – Meursault *premiers crus* Les
Perrières, Les Charmes and Les Genevrières,
Puligny-Montrachet *premier cru* Le Cailleret,

Auxey-Duresses *premier cru* Les Ecusseaux,
village Meursault including the *lieux-dits* Les
Narvaux, Le Pré-de-Manche and L'Ormeau, and
village Pommard, Puligny-Montrachet and
Auxey-Duresses.

When I first started visiting Meursault regularly I found
the wines of the diminutive Yves Boyer merely average.
I called to taste the 1992s after an absence of a few years
and found exciting things, and this progress has been
confirmed by the wines since. This is now one the best
sources in the village and the wines keep well.

★★ DOMAINE JEAN-FRANÇOIS COCHE-DURY
Owner: Coche-Dury family.
Surface Area under Vine: 9 ha, owned and *en
fermage* – Corton-Charlemagne (30 a), Meursault
premier cru Les Perrières, Volnay *premier cru*
(from Clos-de-Chênes and Taille-Pieds), village
Meursault including the *lieux-dits* Les Rougeots,
Les Chevalières, Les Vireuils, Les Luchets and Les
Narvaux, and village Auxey-Duresses (red and
white) and Monthelie.

'Creamy, subtle and delicious' is how the wine writer
Anthony Hanson describes Jean-François Coche's white
wines. Here is a master winemaker, a thinker and a perfectionist. The man is shy and self-effacing. There is no
bombast, no *chi-chi* and the results are excellent. Don't
miss his red wines either.

★ DOMAINE PATRICK JAVILLIER
Owner: Patrick Javillier family.
Surface Area under Vine: 8.6 ha, owned and *en
fermage/métayage* – Corton-Charlemagne (30 a),
Meursault *premier cru* Les Charmes, village
Meursault including the *lieux-dits* Les Narvaux,
Les Casses-Têtes, Les Clous, Les Tillets, Les
Murgers and Clos-du-Cromin, village Puligny-
Montrachet, village Pommard, Savigny-Lès-
Beaune *premier cru* Les Serpentières and village
Savigny-Lès-Beaune (red and white).

The engaging and capable Patrick Javillier not only vinifies *climat* by *climat* but even cask by cask, treating each

one differently in order to build up something of even greater complexity when the final blend is settled. He makes splendid wines, and wines which last well. The Corton-Charlemagne is a recent acquisition.

★ DOMAINE CHARLES ET RÉMI JOBARD

Owner: Charles Jobard family.

Surface Area under Vine: 7 ha, owned and *en fermage* – Meursault *premiers crus* Les Charmes, Les Genevrières and Les Poruzots, and village Meursault including the *lieu-dit* Les Chevalières.

Charles Jobard is the brother of François (see below) and works his domaine with his son Rémi. Each year one-sixth new oak is used here and the wines are bottled after twelve months. A good source.

★ DOMAINE FRANÇOIS JOBARD

Owner: François Jobard family.

Surface Area under Vine: 4.71 ha, owned and *en métayage* – Meursault *premiers crus* Les Charmes, Les Genevrières, Les Poruzots and La Pièce-sous-Le-Bois (bottled as Blagny), and village Meursault.

The rather diffident, shy François Jobard makes fine and marvellously long-lasting wines, and keeps them at least eighteen months in cask before he bottles them. These wines are not for those who like fleshy, oaky Burgundy.

★★★ DOMAINE DES COMTES LAFON

Owner: Lafon family.

Surface Area under Vine: 13 ha, owned – Le Montrachet (32 a), Meursault *premiers crus* Les Perrières, Les Charmes, Les Genevrières and Les Gouttes d'Or (the latter currently young vines), Puligny-Montrachet *premier cru* Champs-Gain, village Meursault including the *lieux-dits* Clos-de-la-Barre and Désirée, Volnay *premiers crus* Santenots-du-Milieu, Les Champans and Clos-des-Chênes, and Monthelie *premier cru* Les Duresses.

This great domaine is one the very few indisputably three-star white wine estates in Burgundy. But it is of equal importance for red wine. The white wines are held

eighteen months in cask (the deep, cold cellar helps) and are minimally handled. What makes this domaine so superior to the rest? First, it is the personnel: Dominique, who has been in charge since 1982, is a man of rare flair and intelligence, as is his father. Second, the low yield is of undoubted importance, as it rarely exceeds 40 hl/ha here. But, above all, it is attention to detail – and a refusal to compromise or cut corners. In 1999 the domaine acquired a vineyard in the Mâconnais.

★ DOMAINE THIERRY MATROT

Owner: Matrot family.

Surface Area under Vine: 18.2 ha, owned – Meursault *premiers crus* Les Perrières, Les Charmes and Blagny, Puligny-Montrachet *premiers crus* Les Chalumeaux and Les Combettes, Volnay *premier cru* Les Santenots, Blagny *premier cru* La Pièce-sous-Le-Bois, and village Meursault and Auxey-Duresses.

The wine is made by Thierry; but the labels can state Joseph (grandfather), Pierre (father) or Thierry himself, depending on the importer. It is all the same wine. This is old-fashioned winemaking in the best sense of the word: wines made for the long term, with minimal use of new wood and no concessions to being *flatteur* when they are young. Both reds and whites are very good here: but they require patience. As from the 2000 vintage the estate will lose some of its vines as Thierry's aunt and sister set up together independently of the domaine.

★ DOMAINE PIERRE MOREY
MOREY-BLANC, SA

Owner: Morey family.

Surface Area under Vine: 8.24 ha, owned and *en fermage/métayage* – Bâtard-Montrachet (48 a), Meursault *premier cru* Les Perrières, village Meursault including the *lieu-dit* Les Tessons, Pommard *premier cru* Les Epenots, and village Monthelie.

The Morey family were long time *métayers* for the Domaine des Comtes Lafon. Now this arrangement has come to an end Pierre Morey has set up a small *négociant* business to compensate for what he can no longer supply. He is also *régisseur* for the Domaine Leflaive in Puligny-Montrachet. Morey combines these separate activities with great skill. He is a fine winemaker.

★ DOMAINE GUY ROULOT

Owner: Roulot family.
Surface Area under Vine: 11.4 ha, owned –
Meursault *premiers crus* Les Perrières and Les Charmes, village Meursault including the *lieux-dits* Les Tessons, Clos-de-Mont-Plaisir *monopole*, Les Luchets, Les Tillets, Les Vireuils and Les Meix-Chavaux, village Monthelie (red) and Auxey-Duresses (red).

This excellent domaine making a splendid range of Meursault wines is now run by Jean-Marc Roulot. Impeccable and conscientious winemaking produces wines that last well.

Other Producers of note

DOMAINE PHILIPPE BALLOT, DOMAINE GUY BOCARD, DOMAINE PIERRE BOILLOT, DOMAINE ROGER CAILLOT-MOREY, DOMAINE ALAIN COCHE-BIZOUARD, DOMAINE ARNAUD ENTE, DOMAINE JEAN-PHILIPPE FICHET, DOMAINE JEAN-MICHEL GAUNOUX, CHÂTEAU GÉNOT-BOULANGER, DOMAINE HENRI GERMAIN ET FILS, DOMAINE ALBERT GRIVAULT, DOMAINE LATOUR-GIRAUD, DOMAINE FRANÇOIS MIKULSKI, DOMAINE RENÉ MONNIER, DOMAINE MOREY-JOBARD AND DOMAINE ALAIN PATRIARCHE.

BLAGNY

Surface Area (1998) *Premiers crus* 6 ha; village wines 1 ha.
Production (1998): *Premiers crus* 207 hl; village wines 37 hl.
Colour: Red. If white the wine is sold as Puligny or Meursault.
Grape Variety: Pinot Noir.
Premiers crus Blagny possesses seven *premiers crus* in whole or in part. These are: La Garenne or Sous-La-Garenne, Puligny-Montrachet (9.87 ha); Hameau-de-Blagny, Puligny-Montrachet (4.27 ha); La Jeunelotte, Meursault (5.05 ha); La Pièce-sous-Le-Bois, Meursault

(11.15 ha); Sous Blagny, Meursault (2.21 ha); Sous-Le-Dos-d'Ane, Meursault (5.03 ha) and Sous-Le-Puits, Puligny-Montrachet (6.80 ha).

Up in the hills between Meursault and Puligny lies the hamlet of Blagny. Blagny is a curious *appellation*, solely for red wines. Most of the wine produced, though, is white and is sold either as Meursault-Blagny *premier cru* or as Puligny-Montrachet, the boundary between Meursault and Puligny running right through the hamlet. The red is fairly sturdy, a sort of cross between Chassagne and Pommard. It is certainly more interesting than red Meursault. One of the best-known Meursault-Blagny wines is made by Maison Louis Latour, which makes and sells the wines of the Château de Blagny estate. Good Blagny *rouge* can be found *chez* Ampeau and Matrot in Meursault and Leflaive in Puligny.

PULIGNY-MONTRACHET

Surface Area (1998): *Grands crus* 31 ha; *premiers crus* 94 ha; village wines 109 ha.
Production (1998): *Grands crus* (white, including Chassagne-Montrachet) 1243 hl; *premiers crus* (red) 8 hl and (white) 3890 hl; village wines (red) 56 hl and (white) 5611 hl.
Colour: Red and white.
Grape Varieties: (Red) Pinot Noir and (white) Chardonnay.
Premiers Crus Puligny-Montrachet possesses twenty-three *premiers crus* in whole or in part: Les Caillerets, Les Chalumeaux (part), Le Champ Gain, Les Champs-Canet, Au Chaniot (in Les Folatières), Le Chavillion, Les Combettes, Les Demoiselles (in Les Caillerets), Les Folatières (part), La Garenne, Clos de La Garenne, Hameau de Blagny, La Jaquelotte (in Les Champs-Canet), Clos de Meix (in Les Pucelles), Clos de La Mouchère (in Les Perrières), Les Perrières, Les Peux-Bois (in Les Folatières), Les Pucelles, Sous Les Puits, Les Referts, En La Richarde (part, in Les Folatières), Sous Le Courthil (in Les Chalumeaux) and La Truffière. Red wine from the *climats* of La Garenne, Hameau-de-Blagny and Sous Les Puits are sold as Blagny *premier cru*, and not

Puligny *rouge*. Apart from a little red *premier cru* from Les Caillerets, all *premier cru* Puligny-Montrachet is white.

Grands crus There are five *grands crus* on the Puligny-Chassagne border: Le Montrachet, Chevalier-Montrachet, Bâtard-Montrachet, Bienvenues-Bâtard-Montrachet and Criots-Bâtard-Montrachet. Le Montrachet and Bâtard-Montrachet straddle the commune boundary, with half their land in each commune. Chevalier and Bienvenues lie entirely in Puligny; and Criots entirely in Chassagne.

Puligny-Montrachet is the greatest white wine commune on earth. Though it is considerably smaller than either of its neighbours, Meursault and Chassagne, the village can boast two of Burgundy's six white wine *grands crus*, Chevalier-Montrachet and Bienvenues-Bâtard-Montrachet, plus roughly half, and, so the authorities would have us believe, best sections of two of the others, Bâtard-Montrachet and Le Montrachet itself. Puligny's *grands crus* lie at the southern end of the commune, overlapping into Chassagne, and this is where the Chardonnay grape realises its most regal and supreme expression: this is wine to drink on bended knees and with heartfelt and humble thanks.

The origin of the village is Gallo-Roman. In the first few centuries after the birth of Christ the vine was first commercially planted in the area and the village was known as Puliniacus. Subsequently, particularly during the Dark Ages, it was the local Cistercian monastery at the Abbey of Maizières which carried on the traditions of viticulture and viniculture. From time to time, the abbey would receive bequests of land.

At the time of the French Revolution the local seignior was the Marquis d'Agrain, who emigrated to Austria to escape from the Terror. One aristocrat who remained behind was Charles de La Guiche who had married into the Clermont-Montoison family, the largest owners of Le Montrachet itself. His luck ran out, however, and he was guillotined in 1794. But perhaps because he had remained in France and not emigrated, his land was not seized. The Laguiche family remain the principal owners of Le Montrachet, with 2 hectares, one-quarter of this remarkable vineyard. There are now sixteen other owners of Le Montrachet. How do you begin to describe something as exquisite as Le Montrachet? It is, first, a wine of great reserve and, second, one not lacking in power. It can be misleadingly dumb when immature, and only after seven or eight years does it begin to open out to reveal the depth of character and complexity of flavour within. When mature it is a wine of astonishing richness and concentration, utterly disarming in its perfection.

Above Le Montrachet lies Chevalier-Montrachet whose wine is second only in quality to Le Montrachet itself. Below is Bâtard-Montrachet, within whose boundaries is the Bienvenues *grand cru*.

The *premiers crus* extend along the road towards Meursault on the same level as the *grands crus*. Those nearest to the *grands crus*, Caillerets and Pucelles, have the highest reputation. Les Demoiselles is an enclave within the former, and is only produced by three *vignerons*, the best by the Domaine Colin-Deléger of Chassagne. Next come Clavoillon and Folatières, above which are Champ-Gain, Truffières and La Garenne. Nearer to Meursault are Perrières, Referts, Champ-Canet and Combettes. These *premiers crus* can produce very fine wine. Combettes is the softest and roundest, an ample generous hazel nutty wine which is similar to its neighbour, the Perrières vineyards in Meursault. The wines from vineyards higher up the slope such as La Garenne and Champ-Gain are lighter, more racy and mature earlier. There is something nervous, coltish, about their character. Folatières and Clavoillon are quite firm, rich and plump in character. They have plenty of finesse and keep well. Of all these, Caillerets, Pucelles and Combettes are the nearest thing to a *grand cru* at half the price. And from a master vinifier they are much, much better value. Like the *grands crus*, they, too, need keeping for at least half a dozen years. Too many of Puligny's great wines are drunk too young. It is tragic.

The village of Puligny is spread out and the houses seem less huddled together than in most other villages in Burgundy. It lies lower down the slope from the vineyards and because of a high water table the 'cellars' must be at ground level, yet still occasionally get flooded. There is a fine local restaurant, Le Montrachet.

Leading Puligny-Montrachet Producers

★ DOMAINE LOUIS CARILLON ET FILS
Owner: Carillon family.
Surface Area under Vine: 12 ha, owned –
Bienvenues-Bâtard-Montrachet (11 a), Puligny-
Montrachet *premiers crus* Les Combettes, Les
Perrières, Les Champs-Canet, Le Champ-Gain and
Les Referts, Chassagne-Montrachet *premier cru*
Les Macherelles (white), Saint-Aubin *premier cru*
Les Pitangerets (red), Mercurey *premier cru* Les
Champs-Martin, and village Puligny-Montrachet
and Chassagne-Montrachet (red and white).

The Carillon family have been resident in the village
since 1632 and Jacques, grandson of Louis, is now in
charge of the winemaking. The wines are fine but
understated. I quickly learned a lesson that it was a mistake to dismiss them for not flamboyantly displaying a
lush personality when in cask, for when I sampled them
blind in bottle later they always came out near the top.
Now I know better, and admire them from the outset.

MAISON CHARTRON ET TRÉBUCHET SA
Owners: Louis Trébuchet, René Chartron and
associates.

Louis Trébuchet, who had worked in Beaune for other
merchants, joined forces with René Chartron in 1984.
The firm has always concentrated on white wines and,
of course, the plums are those of the Chartron domaine
(Chevalier-Montrachet, Caillerets and Pucelles). The
policy is to bottle early. When I am in Burgundy in June,
wines here all the way up to the *premiers crus* are frequently already in bottle. They are clean, but something
in the winemaking has emasculated them, and they do
not last in bottle. One cannot help comparing Chartron
et Trébuchet with Olivier Leflaive Frères, set up at the
same time and also concentrating on white wines (and
about 200 metres away as the crow flies). Olivier
Leflaive's Burgundies are real wines, Chartron et
Trébuchet's are empty and soulless.

★ DOMAINE LEFLAIVE
Owner: Leflaive family.

Surface Area under Vine: 21 ha, owned – Le
Montrachet (8 a), Chevalier-Montrachet (1.91 ha),
Bâtard-Montrachet (2.00 ha), Bienvenues-Bâtard-
Montrachet (1.15 ha), Puligny-Montrachet
premiers crus Les Pucelles, Les Combettes, Les
Folatières, Le Clavoillon and Les Chalumeaux,
Blagny *premier cru*, and village Puligny-
Montrachet.

This is a famous domaine, which has seen much change
in recent years. Standards have not been what they were
in the 1960s and 1970s. Vincent Leflaive, doyen of the village and a man of great charm and wit, lost a long battle
with cancer in 1993 aged eighty-two. The mantle first
passed to his daughter Anne-Claude and nephew
Olivier, it being the custom of the domaine to have *co-
gérants*, but Olivier has now left to concentrate on his
own business (see below). There is a new *régisseur*, Pierre
Morey of Meursault and since 1990 cultivation has been
gradually converted to biodynamic lines.

There is certainly a perfectionism when it comes to
cellar practice. The *cave* is air-conditioned and scrupu-
lously tidy (no spitting on the floor but into a bucket,
no pouring back what you have not tasted into the barrel). But in the vineyards yields are definitely on the
high side, declarations from the Clavoillon *climat*, which
is 80 per cent owned by Leflaive, regularly being one of
the highest of all the Puligny-Montrachet *premiers crus*.

Leflaive wines always taste well in cask, but of late
have not aged well. The last really satisfactory vintage –
by which I mean wines with aspirations to greatness –
was 1985. But I have high hopes of the vintages since
1995, which indicate a return to greatness.

MAISON OLIVIER LEFLAIVE FRÈRES
Owner: Olivier Leflaive and associates.
Surface Area under Vine: 8.75 ha, owned and *en
fermage* – Meursault *premier cru* Les Poruzots,
Chassagne-Montrachet *premier cru* Les
Chaumées, village Puligny-Montrachet and
Chassagne-Montrachet (red and white).

Created in 1984, and with Jean-Marc Boillot of Pommard as winemaker, this merchant which has since built
up its own domaine, showed right from the start that it

could produce high quality. Franck Grux took over as winemaker in 1988, and if anything standards are even higher today. There is a wide range of wines, mainly white.

★ DOMAINE PAUL PERNOT ET FILS

Owner: Pernot family.

Surface Area under Vine: 19 ha, owned and *en fermage* – Bâtard-Montrachet (60 a), Bienvenues-Bâtard-Montrachet (38 a), Puligny-Montrachet *premiers crus* Les Pucelles, Les Folatières, Les Champs-Canet, La Garenne and Les Chalumeaux, Meursault *premier cru* Blagny, Blagny *premier cru* La Pièce-sous-Le-Bois, Volnay *premier cru* Les Carelles, Beaune *premiers crus* Les Teurons, Clos-du-Dessous-des-Marconnets and Les Reversées, and village Puligny-Montrachet, Pommard in the *lieu-dit* Les Noizons, Beaune and Santenay.

This large and expanding domaine must be a boon to the Beaune *négoce*, for quality is very high and Paul Pernot and his three sons only keep back some 20 per cent of the crop to bottle themselves. I have consistent, enthusiastic notes about the wines. The Bâtard, though the results are very good, is relatively young vines. Currently the Bienvenues is the best wine here.

★ DOMAINE ETIENNE SAUZET

Owner: Sauzet, Boillot and Boudot families.

Surface Area under Vine: 8 ha, owned – Bâtard-Montrachet (18 a), Bienvenues-Bâtard-Montrachet (15 a), Puligny-Montrachet *premiers crus* Les Combottes, Les Champs-Canet, Les Referts and Les Perrières, and village Puligny-Montrachet and Chassagne-Montrachet.

Gérard Boudot, married to a granddaughter of the late Etienne Sauzet, is one of Puligny's most gifted winemakers, and produced his twenty-fifth vintage in 1998. The estate lost a third of holdings to Jean-Marc Boillot, Boudot's brother-in-law in 1990, but Boudot has compensated by acquiring a merchant's licence, so he can buy in to fill up the gaps. These are splendid wines here. The Perrières is currently from young vines.

Other Producers of note

DOMAINE GÉRARD CHAVY ET FILS, DOMAINE PHILIPPE CHAVY, DOMAINE HENRI CLERC AND CHÂTEAU DE PULIGNY-MONTRACHET.

SAINT-AUBIN

Surface Area (1998): *Premiers crus* 105 ha; village wines 40 ha.

Production (1998): *Premiers crus* (red) 1715 hl and (white) 3438 hl; village wines (red) 1002 hl and (white) 816 hl.

Colour: Red and white.

Grape Varieties: (Red) Pinot Noir and (white) Chardonnay.

Premiers crus There are twenty-nine *premiers crus*, in whole or in part. These are: Le Bas de Gamay à L'Est, Les Castets (part), Les Champelots, En Champs, Le Charmois, La Chatenière, Les Combes au Sud, Les Cortons, En Créot, Derrière chez Edouard, Derrière La Tour, Echaille, Les Frionnes, Sur Gamay, Marinot, En Montceau, Les Murgers des Dents de Chien, Les Perrières, Les Petangerets, Les Puits (part), En La Ranché, En Remilly, Sous Roche Dumay, Sur Le Sentier du Clou, Les Travers de Marinot, Bas-de-Vermarin-à-L'Est (part), Vignes Moingeon, Le Village (part) and En-Vollon-à-L'Est.

The N6 main road from Changy to Auxerre cuts a great swathe through what is technically the commune of Chassagne – there are Chassagne vineyards on the northern side – but what feels like the border between Chassagne and Puligny. The Mont-Rachet hill curves round to face south and up a little defile lies the hamlet of Gamay. The main road continues round to the left, and we come to the village of Saint-Aubin.

Saint-Aubin is another of those neglected lesser Burgundian communes, but in my view, it is the one which merits the most serious consideration, particularly for its white wine. Both the village and the communal land are quite extensive. But, because of the sinuous layout of the hills, not all the land faces in the right direction and is suitable for the vine. Indeed, too much has been classified as *premier cru*. There are a number of separate parcels, one extending along the Chassagne slope, another on the south and west side of the Mont-Rachet while a third lies above the village of Saint-Aubin.

The red wine is light and fragrant with a certain earthy quality, a sort of cross between Chassagne and Volnay but with less definition than either. The white wine is much more interesting. The wine from the Charmois *climat*, an extension of the Chassagne slope, is much like a lesser Chassagne, as you might expect. The wines from the other well-known *premiers crus* — En Remilly, Les Murgers, Les Dents de Chien, La Chatenière — have much in common with those of Puligny. These can be excellent value and rather more interesting than those of Saint-Romain, Auxey and Monthelie, even than many a village Meursault.

Leading Saint-Aubin Producers

★ Domaine Hubert Lamy-Monnot

Owner: Lamy-Monnot family.

Surdace Area under Vine: 13 ha, owned and *en fermage* – Criots-Bâtard-Montrachet (5 a), Chassagne-Montrachet *premier cru* (white) Les Macherelles, Saint-Aubin *premiers crus* (white) Les Murgers-des-Dents-de-Chien, En Remilly, Clos-de-La-Chatenière, Les Cortons and Les Frionnes, Saint-Aubin *premier cru* (red) Les Castets, and village Puligny-Montrachet, Chassagne-Montrachet (red), Saint-Aubin (red and white) and Santenay.

Jean, the father of Hubert and René Lamy, was one the first producers in the village to start domaine-bottling his own wines. For a long time this was a reasonably dependable if rarely exciting domaine. But the recent arrival of Olivier, Hubert's son, as winemaker is edging quality forward. With a modern, custom-built cellar on three floors and plenty of space, this domaine has begun to go places.

★ Domaine Marc Colin

Owner: Colin family.

Surface Area under Vine: 16 ha, owned and *en fermage* – Le Montrachet (11 a), Bâtard-Montrachet (9 a), Chassagne-Montrachet *premiers crus* (white) Les Caillerets and Le Champ-Gain, Puligny-Montrachet *premier cru* La Garenne, Saint-Aubin *premiers crus* En Remilly, La Chatenière, Les Combes, Les Charmois, Les Cortons and En Montceau, Saint-Aubin *premier cru*, and village Puligny-Montrachet, Saint-Aubin (red) and Santenay.

Marc Colin has recently enlarged his cellar, installing a new pneumatic press, and has been joined by his sons, Pierre-Yves and Joseph. The Bâtard-Montrachet belongs to his cousin Pierre. Michel Colin of Chassagne is another cousin. Most of the vines, and certainly the more illustrious parcels, are Chardonnay. A good address. Colin also now has a merchant's licence.

Other Producers of note

Domaine Jean-Claude Bachelet, Domaine Gilles Bouton, Domaine Sylvie Langoureau and Domaine Larue.

Chassagne-Montrachet

Surface Area (1998): *Premiers crus* 141 ha and village wines 147.5 ha.

Production (1998): *Premiers crus* (red) 1806 hl and (white) 5251 hl; village wines (red) 4286 hl and (white) 2936 hl.

Colour: Red and white.

Grape Varieties: (Red) Pinot Noir and (white) Chardonnay.

Premiers crus There are a great many: indeed a record fifty-two, but you will rarely see most of them, for many have the right to be sold under a more familiar name such as Morgeots. In alphabetical order they are: Abbaye de Morgeots, Les Baudines, Blanchot-Dessus, Les Boirettes, Bois de Chassagne, Les Bondues, La Grande-Borne, La Boudriotte, Les Brussonnes, En Cailleret, La Cardeuse, Le Champ-Gain, Champ Jendreau, La Chapelle, Clos Château, Les Chaumées, Les Chaumes,

Les Chenevottes, Les Combards, Les Commes, Les Crets, Les Criottes, Les Dents-de-Chien, Les Embazées (or Embrazées), Les Fairendes, Francemont, Le Grand Clos, La Grande-Montagne, Les Grandes Ruchottes, La Guer-chère, Les Macherelles, La Maltroie, Les Morgeots, Les Murées, Les Pasquelles, Les Petangerets, Les Petits Clos, Les Petits-Fairendes, Clos Pitois, Les Places, Les Rebichets, En Remilly, La Romanée, La Roquemaure, Clos Saint-Jean, Tête du Clos, Tonton Marcel, Les Vergers, Vide-Bourse, Vigne Blanche, Vigne-Derrière and En Virondot.

Grands crus See under Puligny-Montrachet page 210. Half of Le Montrachet, half of Bâtard-Montrachet and all of Criots-Bâtard-Montrachet lie in the commune of Chassagne-Montrachet.

Chassagne-Montrachet is the last-but-one important commune of the Côte d'Or before the hills peter out at Dézize, Cheilly and Sampigny-Lès-Maranges, and it is the third of the three great neighbouring white wine villages after Meursault and Puligny.

Divided by the N6, the main road between Chagny and Chalon to the south and Autun and Auxerre to the west and north-west, now to a large extent superseded by the A6 *autoroute*, Chassagne produces both red and white wine. Historically its vineyards have always been planted with Pinot Noir but today more and more Chardonnay can be found, and it is the white wines which have the greater renown and fetch the higher prices. This is not just because of the proximity of the great white wine *grands crus* of Le Montrachet and Bâtard-Montrachet, both of which straddle the commune boundary between Puligny and Chassagne, nor solely as a result of the current demand for fine white Burgundy. The white wines, simply, are better. The reds are good, full-bodied, stalwart, workhorse examples of the Pinot Noir, occasionally rustic. They are similar in a way to those of Pommard or even the less distinctive examples of the Côte d'Or such as Fixin. The white wines, too, are full and firm; less definitive perhaps than those of Puligny, but with a better grip than many Meursaults.

Like so many places in this part of France the village has had a turbulent history. It was known as Cassaneas in AD 886. Towards the end of the fifteenth century the local *seigneur* was Jean de Chalone, Prince of Orange. His castle at the top of the hill, surrounded by what was then the village of 'Chaissaigne', was besieged by the army of Louis XI, for the Prince had sided with Louis' rival, Margaret of Burgundy. After much fighting the locals had to capitulate, and as punishment their village was razed to the ground. Eventually a new village grew up halfway down the slope. This was largely monastic in its origins. The Abbot of Maizières, recognising the value of the local terrain for vines, cleared much of the hillside, planted vines and built a local priory, the Abbaye de Morgeots, to house the brothers who worked on the vineyards. A sister establishment was established by the Abbess of Saint-Jean-Le-Grand. Morgeots and Clos Saint-Jean remain two of the largest and most important *premiers crus* in Chassagne.

Historically Chassagne was a red wine village like most in the Côte d'Or. Montrachet seems always to have been renowned for its white wines, but elsewhere, except in Meursault, the wine that was made was red.

Jullien in his *Topographie de Tous les Vignobles Connus* of 1816 makes no mention of white wines in the village apart from Le Montrachet and its satellites. This dearth of Chardonnay is confirmed by Dr Lavalle, who wrote one of the most interesting books on Burgundy in 1855: 'If one excepts the vineyards producing the white wine called Montrachet, one only finds a few *ouvrées* here and there in pinot *blanc*, as in Ruchotte, for example . . . everywhere the pinot noir is planted in the good sites and the gamay in the poorer soils.' However, he also mentions that Chassagne is the commune in Burgundy with the most Pinot Beurot or Pinot Gris (the so-called Tokay d'Alsace), also a white grape.

Old men with long memories of the village and its wines can remember when it was first decided to move from red wine to white. It was after the phylloxera epidemic when the vineyards were being replanted. Was this perhaps, I suggested, because the Chardonnay took to its graft better than the Pinot Noir? For this was one of the explanations why Sancerre, originally a red wine area, became a white wine one. No, they replied, merely a response to changing fashion. By the time the laws of *appellation contrôlée* were introduced in 1936 some 20 to 25 per cent of Chassagne's vineyards produced white wine. And, unlike most of the villages in the Côte d'Or (save Musigny and part of the *climat* of Corton and Corton-Charlemagne), the top vineyards of Chassagne are allowed to produce *premier cru* wine of either colour. Since the Second World War the move to white wine has accelerated. The grower Albert Morey, father of today's Bernard and Jean-Marc, remembers that when he bought his plot of Caillerets in 1949 the entire *climat* was planted in Pinot Noir. Today it produces one of the best Chardonnays in the commune. Fifty years ago 30 per cent of the village and *premier cru* wine was white. Today more white wine than red is produced. The reason is self-evident. A village Chassagne can today command 70 francs a bottle if it is white but only 40 francs if it is red. For a *premier cru* wine the gap is wider still: red wine from Morgeots at 68 francs and white wine from Caillerets at 120 francs – almost double the price.

Chassagne is one of the largest of the Côte de Beaune communes. The soil structure of its vineyards is complex. The rocky subsoil, like most of Burgundy, is basically an oolitic limestone. At Chassagne you can see a quarry halfway up the slope above the village, which produces polished slabs of pink, beige or grey marble-like stone used for local gravestones and fireplaces. The surface soil, essentially limestone debris, can have varying amounts of clay, chalk (the word 'criot' is a corruption of the French word *craie*, meaning chalk), as well as changing colour; the heavier *terres rouges* being found lower down the slope at Morgeots, while higher up along the line from Embrazées through Ruchottes to Caillerets you will find the lighter *terres blanches*. In general it is here in the leaner, more chalky soils of the upper slopes south of the village that the best white wines have their origins.

North of the village the slope from the top of Clos Saint-Jean down through Les Vergers and Les Chenevottes to the N6 is gentler, the soil contains both clay and gravel, and the Pinot Noir comes into its own, as it does at Morgeots, though much of this *climat* is now planted to Chardonnay. Finally, round towards the border with the commune of Saint-Aubin, across which is

this village's best *climat*, Les Charmois, the higher slopes above Les Chaumées have recently been reclaimed from the scrub. Again this cooler, north-east-facing slope has been found to produce good racy white wines.

The only *grand cru* exclusively in Chassagne is Criots-Bâtard-Montrachet. It is the smallest *grand cru* in the Côte d'Or, apart from La Romanée, and the least well known. The wine is the most delicate of the local *grands crus*, I would suggest, racier and leaner than Bâtard, as well as lighter in weight.

The best *premiers crus* for red wines are Clos Saint-Jean, Les Rebichots, Les Vergers, Les Chenevottes and Les Macherelles, plus La Maltroie, La Boudriotte and Morgeots. For white wines the best ones are Les Embrazées, La Romanée, La Grande-Montagne, Les Grandes-Ruchottes, Les Caillerets and Les Champs-Gain, plus Morgeots again.

In Chassagne the white wines are more distinctive than the reds. In general they are full and firm; more akin to Puligny than to the softer, rounder wines of Meursault. From the top of the slope on the Saint-Aubin side of the commune vineyards such as Les Chaumées produce lightish, racy wines with a touch of peach or crab apple, while from vines lower down, for example, in Chenevottes, the wine is plumper and sometimes a touch four-square. For the best of the more masculine versions of white Chassagne you need to go to Les Morgeots; Caillerets is flowery, racy and feminine; Embrazées all finesse and lighter still; while in Champs-Gain, halfway up the slope, you will get an elegant compromise: fullish, plump, succulent wines. My vote would go to the wines from Caillerets, which are offered by many producers. My specific preferences for the best individual Chassagne *premier cru* wines, however, would go to Michel Colin's En Remilly and Didier Darviot's (of Monthelie) Blanchot-Dessus.

The village of Chassagne is rich in variations on the names of Gagnard, Delagrange, Bachelet and Ramonet. Domaines are divided as one generation succeeds another or unites by marriage, the husband tagging his wife's maiden name on to his when she has brought some vineyards with her as her dowry. It can sometimes be very confusing.

Leading Chassagne-Montrachet Producers

★ DOMAINE MICHEL COLIN-DELÉGER

Owner: Colin-Deléger family.
Surface Area under Vine: 19.4 ha, owned and *en fermage* – Chevalier-Montrachet (16 a),
Chassagne-Montrachet *premiers crus* (white)
En Remilly, Les Morgeots, Les Chenevottes,
Les Vergers, La Maltroie and Les Chaumées,
Chassagne-Montrachet *premiers crus* (red)
Les Morgeots and La Maltroie, Puligny-
Montrachet *premiers crus* Les Demoiselles and
La Truffière, Saint-Aubin *premiers crus*
Les Charmois and Les Combes, Santenay *premier
cru* Les Gravières, Maranges *premier cru*,
and village Chassagne-Montrachet (red and
white) and Santenay.

Michael Colin is *fermier* for a firm called CCI Saint-
Abdon, whose owners live in the north of France. The
Demoiselles appears under his mother's name
(Françoise) and some of the Chevalier under the name
of Georges Deléger, though it all now made by Michel
Colin. This is one the best cellars in the village, with a
splendid range of (mainly white) wines on offer. Balance
and intensity of flavours are the keys here. Colin is one
of the few producers to make a white Morgeots which
is not heavy.

★ DOMAINE JEAN-NOËL GAGNARD

Owners: Jean-Noël Gagnard and family.
Surface Area under Vine: 8.5 ha, owned – Bâtard-
Montrachet (37 a), Chassagne-Montrachet
premiers crus (white) Les Caillerets,
Les Morgeots, Les Chevenottes, La Maltroie and
Le Champ-Gain, Chassagne-Montrachet *premiers
crus* (red) Clos-Saint-Jean, Les Morgeots and
La Maltroie, village Chassagne-Montrachet (red
and white), and Santenay *premier cru* Clos-des-
Tavannes.

Jean-Noël is Jacques Gagnard's brother, a little taller, a
little less solid, and a little less blunt in his disposition.
The wines are different too: somewhat fuller and richer,

less delicate, less easy to enjoy when they are young. But
this is another very good source of white Burgundy.
Recent vintages have been most impressive. The arrival
of his daughter Caroline – she has been in charge of the
winemaking since 1995 – has nudged quality up a notch
or two. Sadly, the reds are currently less impressive.

★ DOMAINE JACQUES GAGNARD-DELAGRANGE

Owner: Gagnard-Delagrange.
Surface Area under Vine: 4 ha, owned –
Le Montrachet (8 a), Bâtard-Montrachet (26 a),
Chassagne-Montrachet *premiers crus* (white)
La Boudriotte, Les Morgeots, Chassagne-
Montrachet *premier cru*, Volnay *premier cru*
Les Champans, and village Chassagne-
Montrachet (red and white).

Jacques Gagnard, brother of Jean-Noël (see below) and
father-in-law of Jean-Marc Blain and Richard Fontaine,
is a bluff, no-nonsense *vigneron*, now approaching retirement. Much of his domaine has now been passed to the
next generation. What he does still produce shows the
hand of a master.

DOMAINE DU MARQUIS DE LAGUICHE

Owner: Marquis de Laguiche family.
Surface Area under Vine: 4.75 ha, owned – Le
Montrachet (2 ha), Chassagne-Montrachet
premier cru Morgeots (red and white), and
village Chassagne-Montrachet (white).

This famous estate sells its grapes under contract to Maison Joseph Drouhin of Beaune. Is this perhaps the best
example of Montrachet? While the vines are looked after
by the domaine's own team, the vinicultural programme is a joint effort between Philippe Drouhin and
the Marquis, and it is Drouhin's team which harvests the
fruit and makes the wine in their cellars in Beaune.

★ DOMAINE MICHEL NIELLON

Owner: Niellon family.
Surface Area under Vine: 5 ha, owned –
Chevalier-Montrachet (22 a), Bâtard-Montrachet
(12 a), Chassagne-Montrachet *premiers crus*

(white) Clos-Saint-Jean, Le Champ-Gain, La Maltroie and Les Vergers, Chassagne-Montrachet *premiers crus* (red) La Maltroie and Clos-Saint-Jean, and village Chassagne-Montrachet (red and white).

Michel Niellon's cellars are almost as small as his domaine. He has two, one underneath his house, the other next to it, and both are exceedingly cramped. He believes in old vines and low yields. Small is beautiful in this case. The Champ-Gain is currently young vines.

★ DOMAINE JEAN ET JEAN-MARC PILLOT

Owner: Pillot family.

Surface Area under Vine: 10 ha, owned and *en fermage/métayage* – Chassagne-Montrachet *premiers crus* (white) Les Caillerets, Les Morgeots, Le Champ-Gain, Les Vergers, Les Chevenottes and Les Macherelles, Chassagne-Montrachet *premiers crus* (red) Les Macherelles and Les Morgeots, and village Chassagne-Montrachet (red and white), Santenay (red) and Puligny-Montrachet.

Jean-Marc Pillot, a trained oenologist, has taken over from his father Jean, and at the same time the domaine has relocated to a new, spacious cellar down on the flat land nearer to Chagny. Real progress has been made and the wines are now very good.

★★ DOMAINE RAMONET

Owner: Ramonet family.

Surface Area under Vine: 17 ha, owned – Le Montrachet (25 a), Bâtard-Montrachet (70 a), Bienvenues-Bâtard-Montrachet (33 a), Chassagne-Montrachet *premiers crus* (white) Les Grand-Ruchottes, Les Caillerets, Les Vergers, Les Chaumées, La Boudriotte, Les Morgeots, La Boudriotte and Clos Saint-Jean, Puligny-Montrachet *premier cru* Les Champs-Canet, Saint-Aubin *premier cru* (white) Les Charmois, and village Chassagne-Montrachet (red and white) and Puligny-Montrachet.

Noël and Jean-Claude Ramonet took over from their much revered grandfather, Pierre ('Père'), the creator of this marvellous estate, in 1984. Nothing much has changed since then, except that nowadays all the wines are bottled on the spot (previously some buyers employed a local contract bottler).

The beauty of the Ramonet wines is that they are totally individual: more Ramonet than Chassagne. The work is done by instinct, not by the book. And neither Ramonet has had any technical training. Risks are taken, and they do not always succeed. But when they (usually) do, they are brilliant.

Other Producers of note

DOMAINE GUY AMIOT-BONFILS, DOMAINE BACHELET-RAMONET, DOMAINE JEAN-MARC BLAIN-GAGNARD, DOMAINE VINCENT DANCER, DOMAINE RICHARD FONTAINE-GAGNARD, DOMAINE FRANÇOIS & VINCENT JOUARD, DOMAINE RENÉ LAMY-PILLOT, CHÂTEAU DE LA MALTROYE, DOMAINE BERNARD MOREY, DOMAINE MARC MOREY, DOMAINE MICHEL MOREY-COFFINET, DOMAINE FERNAND ET LAURENT PILLOT AND DOMAINE PAUL PILLOT.

SANTENAY

Surface Area (1998): *Premiers crus* 137 ha; village wines 164 ha.

Production (1998): *Premiers crus* (red) 5694 hl and (white) 315 hl; village wines (red) 6474 hl and (white) 938 hl.

Colour: Red and white.

Grape Varieties: (Red) Pinot Noir and (white) Chardonnay.

Premiers crus Santenay has fourteen *premiers crus*, in whole or in part. These are: Beauregard, Beaurepaire, Le Chainey (Clos Grand Rousseau) (part), La Comme, Comme-Dessus (part), Clos Faubard, Les Fourneaux, Clos Grand Rousseau, Les Gravières, La Maladière, Clos des Mouches, Les Passe-Temps, Petit Clos Rousseau and Clos des Tavannes.

With Santenay we come to the last of the important villages of the Côte d'Or. In fact we come to two, because there is Santenay-Le-Haut and Santenay-Le-Bas, with a kilometre of vineyard between them. The upper part is a straggly hamlet of narrow winding streets and ancient patched-up houses. Santenay-Le-Bas is rather grander. It boasts the ruins of an old castle fortified by Philippe Le Hardi in the thirteenth century and the oldest plane tree in France, said to have been planted by Henri IV in 1599. The village has been a spa since Roman times. The spring water is extremely salty but is said to relieve the symptoms of gout and rheumatism.

The vineyards of Santenay continue the Côte below Chassagne, the slope gradually shifting its orientation so that the exposure is more south than east. In the northern part of the vineyards the soil contains gravel over marly limestone – hence the name Les Gravières for one of the best-known *premiers crus*. This is the best sector. There is a local saying that the top wines of Santenay come from east of the belfry. West of the village the soil is richer and browner in colour: the wines from here have less finesse.

Most of the wine produced in Santenay is red. This can range from being rather dense and burly to something with really quite a lot of finesse, rather less sturdy and rather more stylish than the red wine found in Chassagne. Nowadays there is very good value to be found in Santenay.

Leading Santenay Producer

★ DOMAINE VINCENT GIRARDIN
Owner: Vincent Girardin and family.
Surface Area under Vine: 14 ha, owned and *en fermage* – Santenay *premiers crus* Les Gravières, La Maladière and Clos du Beauregard (white), Maranges *premiers crus* Le Clos-des-Loyères and Clos-Roussots, Pommard *premier cru* Les Chanlins, Beaune *premier cru* Clos-des-Vignes-Franches, Chassagne-Montrachet *premier cru* (red and white) Les Morgeots, and village Santenay (red and white) including the *lieu-dit* Clos-de-la-Confrérie, Pommard in the *lieu-dit* Clos-des-Lambos, Meursault in the *lieu-dit* Les Narvaux and Beaune.
Vincent Girardin is a rising star. In 1994 he acquired a new house, new winemaking premises, a very attractive

wife, Véronique, more land (the Beaunes and Pommards) and a merchant's licence. This is the best address in the village today: the wines are very well-balanced and very stylish. The merchant wines are fine too, very typical of their origins.

Other Producers of note
DOMAINE ROGER BELLAND, DOMAINE PHILIPPE BRENOT, DOMAINE RENÉ LEQUIN-COLIN AND DOMAINE LOUIS MUZARD.

MARANGES

Surface Area (1998): *Premiers crus* 53.3 ha; village wines 113.4 ha.
Production (1998): *Premiers crus* (red) 2400 hl and (white) 31 hl; village wines (red) 5100 hl and (white) 97 hl.
Colour: Red and white.
Grape Varieties: (Red) Pinot Noir and (white) Chardonnay.
Premiers crus There are six *premiers crus*: Clos de La Boutière, La Fuissière, Clos de La Fuissière, Le Clos des Loyères, Le Clos des Rois and Les Clos Roussots.

Maranges is a recent *appellation* (1989), combining the previous separate ones for the villages of Dezize-Lès-Maranges, Cheilly-Lès-Maranges and Sampigny-Lès-Maranges. These three obscure villages, whose red wine has nearly always been bottled as Côte-de-Beaune-Villages rather than under their own village names, are where the golden slope of the Côte d'Or comes to an end. Administratively these villages lie in the *département* of Saône-et-Loire rather than Côte d'Or. The wines are well-coloured and sturdy, sharing some of the earthy rustic character of the lesser Santenays from the western end of this commune.

Maranges Producers of note
DOMAINE BERNARD BACHELET ET FILS, DOMAINE MAURICE CHARLEUX, DOMAINE FERNAND CHEVROT, DOMAINE YVON ET CHANTAL CONTAT-GRANGE, DOMAINE EDMUND MONNOT AND DOMAINE CLAUDE NOUVEAU.

CÔTE CHALONNAISE

The Côte Chalonnaise, or Région de Mercurey, to give it its alternative name, has long been a well-known 'forgotten area', though this may seem paradoxical. While everyone acknowledges that it is worth investigating, few merchants seem to bother to go prospecting. There are many well-known growers whose wines are hardly ever exported.

The Côte Chalonnaise begins at the southern tip of the Côte de Beaune but on a different ridge of hills slightly to the east. The vineyards lie on the most favoured parts of a series of hummocky hills, roughly following the line of the D981 road which runs due south from Chagny down to Cluny. The main wine villages, each with their own separate *appellation contrôlée*, are Bouzeron, Rully, Mercurey, Givry and Montagny. Total production is small, less than a third of that of the Côte d'Or. Up until 1990, unlike the Mâconnais and Chablis, but like the Côte d'Or, there was no regional *appellation* for the generic wines of the Côte Chalonnaise: they were labelled anonymously as Bourgogne Rouge, Bourgogne Blanc and so on. Since then there has been a separate *appellation*, Bourgogne-Côte Chalonnaise.

In general there is little difference between the wines of the Côte Chalonnaise and the lighter wines of the Côte de Beaune. Broadly, the soils are the same, a mixture of different limestones and gravel and limestone mixed with clay. The grape varieties, Pinot Noir and Chardonnay, are used in both regions. The main difference is the mesoclimate of the vineyards. Lying at somewhere between 220 and 340 metres, their altitude is much the same as that of the Côte d'Or vineyards (though certain authorities would have you believe they are significantly higher) but they are less sheltered from the prevailing westerly wind, and, despite being further to the south, need more hours of sun to ripen fully and as a consequence are picked later.

The Côte Chalonnaise is not a monocultural vine-growing area. The surface under vine declined considerably after the phylloxera epidemic in the 1880s, and though it has increased in the last twenty years it is still but a shadow of what it was a century ago. There were 600 hectares under vine in Rully in 1860. Today there are 310. Instead, the vine occupies the particularly favoured sites — sheltered, well-exposed, gently sloping to the east or south-east, and on geologically suitable, well-drained soil. This is the theory, at any rate. In practice, if a *vigneron* has so many hectares, absolutely every square metre will be planted, whether it is suitable or

YIELDS AND ALCOHOL LEVELS (CÔTE CHALONNAISE)

	MAXIMUM YIELD	MINIMUM ALCOHOL LEVEL
RED WINES		
GENERIC WINES	55 HL/HA	10°
VILLAGE WINES	45 HL/HA	10.5°
PREMIERS CRUS	45 HL/HA	11°
WHITE WINES		
GENERIC WINES	60 HL/HA	CHARDONNAY 10.5°
		ALIGOTÉ 9.5°
VILLAGE WINES	50 HL/HA	11°
	55 HL/HA BOUZERON	11°
PREMIERS CRUS	50	11.5°

SURFACE AREA AND PRODUCTION (1998 HARVEST)

APPELLATIONS	SURFACE AREA (HA)		PRODUCTION (HL)	
	RED & ROSÉ	WHITE	RED & ROSÉ	WHITE
BOUZERON	–	56	–	3337
RULLY	108	202	4181	6880
RULLY PREMIER CRU			1038	2993
MERCUREY	468	62	17,535	2317
MERCUREY PREMIER CRU			6248	488
GIVRY	187	36	4748	1301
GIVRY PREMIER CRU			4082	352
MONTAGNY	–	277	–	3975
MONTAGNY PREMIER CRU	–		–	10,041
TOTAL	763	633	37,832	31,684
	1396		69,516	

not, provided the law allows him to. At the same time the machinations of SAFER, a French bureaucratic body which authorises transfers of land and changes in use, together with the chauvinistic attitude of the local left-wing political parties, means that it is difficult to increase the area under vine, much of which would be suitable, and hard for outsiders to come in and set themselves up as new domaines. As a result, demand for the wine always exceeds supply.

BOUZERON

Surface Area (1998): 56 ha.
Production (1998): 3337 hl.
Colour: White.
Grape Variety: Aligoté.

Travelling south the first village in the Côte Chalonnaise is Bouzeron. The vines are found on the slopes of a valley which lies parallel with and between those of Santenay and Rully. The area has long been renowned for its Aligoté wine, its reputation being acknowledged by the Abbé Courtépée in the eighteenth century; and in 1979 a special Bourgogne Aligoté de Bouzeron *appellation* was established. At the time there were less than 20 hectares of Aligoté here, but this has now grown to 56 hectares. In 1998 the *appellation* name was shortened to plain Bouzeron and it remains a decree for Aligoté only. The local Chardonnay and Pinot Noir wines are labelled Bourgogne, Côte Chalonnaise.

According to Aubert de Villaine, the doyen of the village as well as co-proprietor of the Domaine de La Romanée-Conti in Vosne-Romanée, it is important to choose the right strain of Aligoté. The Aligoté Doré is much superior to the Aligoté Vert and gives a wine of greater perfume and elegance. The soil is also important. Here at Bouzeron it is marly with a high proportion of limestone, and very little surface soil before you strike the bedrock. This helps temper the normally vigorous Aligoté grape, producing a rather more concentrated wine than elsewhere.

Leading Bouzeron Producer

★ DOMAINE A ET P DE VILLAINE
Owner: A and P de Villaine.
Surface Area under Vine: 18.5 ha – Mercurey Les Montots (red), Rully *premier cru* Clos Saint-Jacques (white), Bourgogne Rouge La Digoine, Bourgogne Blanc Les Clous and Bourgogne Aligoté.

Aubert de Villaine produces some of the best generic wines in Burgundy, and if anything were proof that there is something special in the Bouzeron soil, not just for Aligoté, but for Pinot Noir and Chardonnay, it can be found in his wines. They have all the elegance and concentration of fruit, if not, of course the volume and staying power, of much more illustrious growths.

Other producers of note

MAISON BOUCHARD PÈRE ET FILS (BEAUNE).

RULLY

Surface Area (1998): (Red) 108 ha and (white) 202 ha.
Production (1998): (Red) 5219 hl and (white) 9873 hl.
Colour: Red and white.
Grape Varieties: (Red) Pinot Noir and (white) Chardonnay.
Premiers crus There are twenty-three *premiers crus* in Rully. In alphabetical order they are: Les Agneux, La Bressande, Clos du Chaigne, Le Champ-Clou, Le Chapitre, Les Cloux, Les Ecloseaux, La Fosse, Grésigny, Margoté, Marissou, Le Meix-Caillet, Molesme, Le Mont-Palais, Les Pierres, Pillot, Préau, La Pucelle (or Les Pucelles), Rabourcé, Raclot, La Renarde, Clos Saint-Jacques and Vauvry.

The vineyards of Rully begin in the suburbs of Chagny and continue south to the boundary with Mercurey. The Montagne de La Folie divides Rully from Bouzeron, and at the north end of this ridge, underneath a large water tower which can be seen for miles around, the Noël-Bouton family produces some of Rully's best wines at the Domaine de La Folie. A few kilometres further on is the village itself, dominated by two châteaux, behind which is the slope of the *premiers crus*.

Rully produces roughly 65 per cent white wine, 35 per cent red. The reds are lighter than those of Mercurey and Givry, rather better, proportionately, in the warmer vintages. In cold years they can be a little ungenerous, though thankfully better made these days since almost every grower now destems completely. More consistently successful are the white wines. I find these more interesting than those of Montagny, their main rival in the Côte Chalonnaise. Their character is lemony-crisp and floral, ripe but lean rather than four-square. With a

judicious use of new oak this can be a major alternative to Saint-Aubin and other similar wines in the Côte de Beaune, and at a fairer price.

Rully has historically been a major source of sparkling wine for which you need not very ripe grapes and a high acidity level, which is what you get if you over-crop. It is cooler here than in the Côte de Beaune.

Leading Rully Producers

★ DOMAINE JEAN-CLAUDE BRELIÈRE

Owner: Brelière family.
Surface Area under Vine: 7.5 ha – Rully *premiers crus* Champ-Cloux (red), Margoté (white) and Préau (red), and Rully (red and white) La Barre.
Jean-Claude Brelière's first vintage was 1973. He is not too keen on new oak and keeps some of the wine in tank in order to preserve its freshness. This is one of the few domaines in Rully where the red wines are as good as the whites, one of the reasons being, I am sure, Brelière's low target of 40 hl/ha as a yield for his Pinot Noir. Currently the Champ-Cloux is young vines. The mesoclimate in this vineyard is warm, and Brelière has recently switched from Chardonnay to Pinot Noir here.

★ DOMAINE DE LA FOLIE

Owner: Noël-Bouton family.
Surface Area under Vine: 18 ha – Rully *premiers crus* Clos Saint-Jacques and Clos du Chaigne *monopole* (both white), Rully Clos de Bellecroix *monopole* (red and white), and Bourgogne Aligoté.
Jérôme Noël-Bouton, a Parisian lawyer, runs the family property, at the very north of the *appellation*, and quality is now back to the level of the 1970s. The Clos de Bellecroix red is only of medium body. It can be elegant but also be a bit too slight. This domaine earns its star for the Clos Saint-Jacques, a delicious, gently oaky, elegant, flowery white and one of the best white Rully wines.

★ DOMAINE HENRI & PAUL JACQUESSON

Owner: Jacquesson family.
Surface Area under Vine: 9.5 ha – Rully *premiers*

crus Grésigny, Les Pucelles and Cloux (all white), and Rully Les Chaponnières (red).

This is perhaps the most reliable of the Rully domaines. Now run by son Paul, though father Henri is still very active – he can't resist coming to help taste – this is an immaculately clean and precise set-up. All the grapes are hand-picked, the reds are entirely destemmed, the use of oak just right and the wines equally fine whether red or white. The red Chaponnières, though only village *appellation contrôlée,* is of top *premier cru* standard here.

Other Producers of note

Domaine Belleville, Domaine Raymond Bêtes, Domaine Michel Briday, Domaine Jean Daux, Domaine Raymond & Vincent Dureuil-Janthial, Domaine de La Renarde (André Delorme) and Château de Rully (produced by Maison Rodet in Mercurey).

Mercurey

Surface Area (1998): (Red) 468 ha; (white) 62 ha.
Production (1998): (Red) 23,783 hl; (white) 2805 hl.
Colour: Red and white.
Grape Varieties: (Red) Pinot Noir and (white) Chardonnay.
Premiers crus There are thirty *premiers crus*: Clos des Barraults, La Bondue, Les Byots, La Cailloute, Champ-Martins, La Chassière, Clos Château de Montaigu, Les Combins, Les Crêts, Les Croichots, Clos L'Evêque, Clos des Fourneaux, Grand Clos Fourtoul, Griffères, La Levrière, Clos de Marcilly, La Mission, Clos des Montaigus, Clos des Myglands, Les Naugues, Clos de Paradis, Les Puillets, Clos du Roi (or Clos du Roy), Les Ruelles, Les Saumonts, En Sazenay, Clos Tonnerre, Les Vasées, Les Velley and Clos Voyens.

The village takes its name from Mercury, the Roman god and winged messenger, who was also the god of commerce and there is supposed to have been a Gallo-Roman temple in the *climat* of Clos Voyens, on the site of today's windmill. Mercurey is a sizeable commune, larger than Gevrey-Chambertin, Meursault or Beaune, the biggest ones in the Côte d'Or. It produces twice as much wine as either Nuits-Saint-Georges or Pommard and makes almost entirely red wine. The commune straddles the D978, the main road from Chalon to Autun, and includes the villages of Bourgneuf-Val d'Or and Saint-Martin-sous-Montaigu. As there is more wine to sell, and as a number of well-known Burgundy *négociants*, particularly Faiveley, have vineyards in the commune, this is the Côte Chalonnaise's best-known red wine. It is also the most expensive. Whether the quality is worth the extra money is a moot point.

Mercurey is the most structured of the Chalonnaise red wines, and this, in leaner years, can take the form of a rather stringy and skeletal character, lacking fruit and flesh. At its best it is rich and ample, though with a certain earthiness: the best of the Côte Chalonnaise reds. The whites are similar to those of Rully, but a little fatter. Like the other Côte Chalonnaise wines, quality has much improved in the last twenty-five years or so as prices and profitability have risen.

Leading Mercurey Producers

★ Domaine de La Croix Jacquelet Maison Joseph Faiveley
Owner: Faiveley family.
Surface Area under Vine: 50 ha – Mercurey *premiers crus* Clos du Roy and Clos des Myglands *monopole* (both red), Mercurey red including La Framboisière, Clos Rond and Les Mauvarennes, all *monopole,* Mercurey white including Clos Rochette *monopole,* Rully (red and white) and Mercurey.

This is one of the best domaines in the village. The wines receive all the attention and perfectionism that Faiveley's Côte de Nuits wines enjoy (see page 180), and are impeccable examples. They will keep, too, for up to ten years for the reds in the best vintages.

★ Domaine Emile Juillot
Owner: Jean-Claude Theulot and family.
Surface Area under Vine: 11.5 ha – Mercurey *premiers crus* La Cailloute *monopole* (red and

CÔTE CHALONNAISE

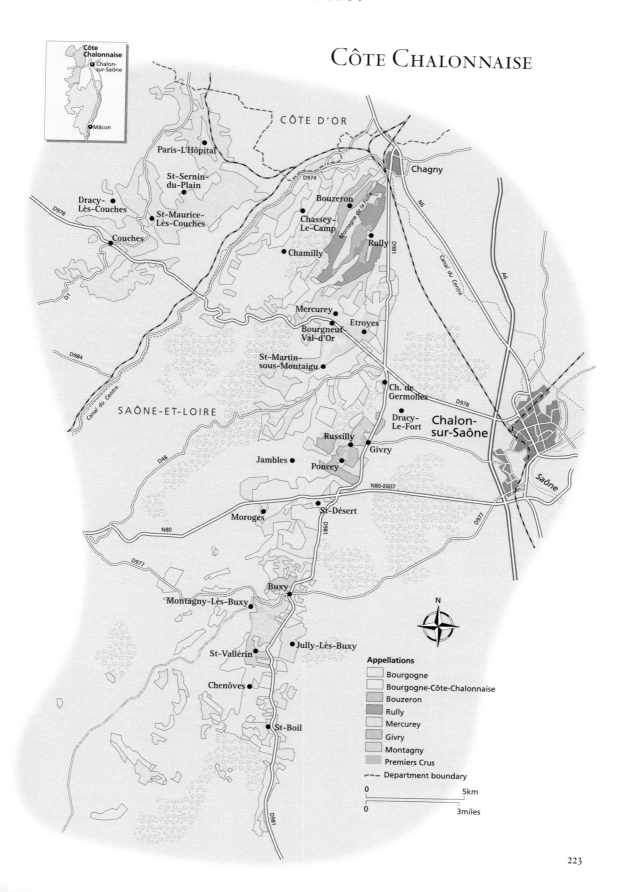

Côte
Chalonnaise

Chalon-
sur-Saône

Mâcon

CÔTE D'OR

Paris-L'Hôpital

Chagny

St-Sernin-
du-Plain

D974

Bouzeron

Dracy-
Lès-Couches

Chassey-
Le-Camp

N6

St-Maurice-
Lès-Couches

Rully

Montagne de la Folie

D981

Couches

Chamilly

Canal du Centre

A6

Mercurey

Etroyes

Bourgneuf-
Val-d'Or

D984

St-Martin-
sous-Montaigu

SAÔNE-ET-LOIRE

Ch. de
Germolles

Canal du Centre

Dracy-
Le-Fort

D978

Chalon-
sur-Saône

Russilly

Givry

Jambles

Poncey

D48

Saône

N80-E607

Moroges

St-Désert

D977

N80

D981

D977

Buxy

Montagny-Lès-Buxy

N

St-Vallérin

Jully-Lès-Buxy

Chenôves

Appellations

Bourgogne
Bourgogne-Côte-Chalonnaise
Bouzeron
Rully
Mercurey
Givry
Montagny
Premiers Crus
Department boundary

St-Boil

D981

0   5km

0   3miles

white), Champ-Martin (red), Combins (red), Les Croichots (red) and Mercurey (red and white).

Jean-Claude and Nathalie Theulot, no relation to the late Emile Juillot, run this domaine from premises just behind the local one-star hostelry the Val d'Or. In 1997 they decided to eliminate the cold-soaking followed by a shortened *cuvaison* to prevent the wines becoming too hard and tannic. But I would not accuse their 1996s of having this characteristic. The Combins is the best of the three *premier cru* reds. The Cailloute white is good too.

★ DOMAINE MICHEL JUILLOT

Owner: Juillot family.

Surface Area under Vine: 30 ha, owned – Mercurey *premiers crus* Clos des Barraults, Les Champ-Martins (both red and white), Clos du Roi (red), Clos Tonnerre (red), Mercurey (red) including Cuvée Vieilles Vignes and (white); *en fermage* in Aloxe-Corton – Corton-Perrières (1.20 ha) and Corton-Charlemagne (80 a).

There have been Juillots in the village since 1404, and this senior branch of the family has been domaine-bottling longer than most. The winemaking is now controlled by Laurent, son of Michel, and his approach is to pick early rather than too late, for a 15 day-*cuvaison* after four or five days' cold-soaking and to use natural yeasts and up to one-third new wood. Yields are low here (37 hl/ha overall in 1997, for instance). Unusually, he is not a great believer in *bâtonnage* (stirring up of the lees in the early months after the wine is made) for white wine and believes that it merely releases flavours into the 'open' at the start which he would prefer remain in the wine until it is fully mature.

I find the wines consistently some of the best in the Côte Chalonnaise with plenty of purity and elegance (the Cortons are very good, too) – the Clos des Barraults is usually just that little bit better than the Champ-Martins. Cousins run domaines in Givry (Laborde-Juillot) and Montagny (Bertrand Juillot).

★ DOMAINE JEAN & FRANÇOIS RAQUILLET

Owner: Raquillet family.

Surface Area under Vine: 10 ha – Mercurey

premiers crus Les Velley (red and white), Les Puillets, Les Vasées and Les Nauges, Mercurey (red) including a Cuvée Vieilles Vignes and white.

A new modern cellar near the church houses the Raquillet wines. François Raquillet prefers to harvest early to preserve the grapes' acidity and to prevent over-ripeness. He also curtails his yields to 40 hl/ha or so. One-fifth new wood is used each year. The Nauges may not be the fullest of the Raquillet wines, but it is the most elegant.

★ MAISON ANTONIN RODET

Maison Rodet owns, partly owns or runs the following: Château de Chamirey (Mercurey) 35 ha; Château de Rully (Rully) 45 ha; Domaine du Château de Mercey (Maranges) 44 ha; Domaine Jacques Prieur (Meursault) 14 ha; plus a small range of other Côte d'Or wines, both red and white.

Bertrand Devillard and Nadine Gublin, who is in charge of the winemaking, make a fine team at this *négociant* which is partly owned by the Champagne house of Laurent-Perrier. The standard of wine is high.

Other Producers of note

DOMAINE BERTRAND-JUILLOT, DOMAINE BRINTET, DOMAINE JEAN-PIERRE CHARTON, DOMAINE PATRICK GUILLOT, DOMAINE JEANNIN-NALTET PÈRE & FILS, DOMAINE LABORDE-JUILLOT, DOMAINE BRUNO LORENZON, DOMAINE JEAN MARÉCHAL AND DOMAINE DU MEIX-FOULOT/YVES DE LAUNAY.

GIVRY

Surface Area (1998): (Red) 187 ha; (white) 36 ha.
Production (1998): (Red) 8830 hl; (white) 1653 hl.
Colour: Red and white.
Grape Varieties: (Red) Pinot Noir and (white) Chardonnay.
Premiers crus There are twenty-two *premiers crus*: Clos de La Barraude, Les Berges, Boix Chevaux, Bois Gauthier, Clos du Cellier aux Moines, Clos Charlé, Clos du Cras Long, Les Grandes Vignes, Grands Prétants, Clos

Jus, Clos Marceaux, Marole, Petit Marole, Petits Prétants, Clos Salomon, Clos Saint-Paul, Clos Saint-Pierre, Clos Les Servoisines, Vaux, Clos du Vernoy, En Vignes Rouge and Le Vigron.

The town of Givry lies on the D981, the Chagny to Cluny road and is a bustling place. Its vineyards begin north of the town, in the commune of Dracy-Le-Fort, and continue southwards before the slopes curve round to the west in the commune of Jambles. Between Givry and Jambles lies the suburban hamlet of Poncey. Many of the *premiers crus* – Clos Salomon, for instance – are monopolies. The wines of Givry can be the most charming and the most stylish of the Côte Chalonnaise, though in structure more in the style of Rully than of Mercurey. Unlike Rully, most of the wine is red.

The soil here is just beginning to change from that of the marl and chalky limestone of northern Burgundy to the richer, more sandy limestone of the Mâconnais. As in Mercurey, however, there is a little clay, and consequently the wines are predominantly red. Contrary to elsewhere in the Côte d'Or and Côte Chalonnaise, according to the authoritative book *Terroirs et Vins de France* (Ed. Charles Pomerol, 1984), it is the land which has the least clay which produces the best reds of Givry.

Leading Givry Producers

★ Domaine du Gardin

Owner: du Gardin family.
Surface Area under Vine: 7 ha – Givry *premier cru* Clos Salomon *monopole* (red).

This domaine enjoys a splendid site on a protected, rolling slope exposed to the south-east a kilometre away from the centre of Givry, and is a very old vineyard indeed. Hughes Salomon sold some wine to the Pope in 1375. Today Madame Jacqueline du Gardin casts a watchful eye while her son Ludovic makes the wine. There is a low yield (38 hl/ha in 1997), 100 per cent destemming, natural yeasts, a few days' cold maceration, 20 to 25 per cent new wood and bottling after 18 months with no fining or filtration. The wines are very good and they keep well.

★ Domaine Jean-Marc & Vincent Joblot

Owner: Joblot family.
Surface Area under Vine: 13 ha – Givry *premiers crus* Clos Marole, Clos de Bois-Chevaux, Clos des Celliers aux Moines (all red) and Clos de La Servoisine (red and white), and Givry (red and white).

There was a time when I found the Joblots' wines far too oaky (the 1985s, for instance). Today this is no longer the case. Vineyard yields are low and the family prefer to pick early in order to keep grape acidity in check. They now only give the wines one-third new wood each year. You can definitely still taste the effect of this oakiness, but, thankfully, it is no longer exaggerated.

★ Domaine François Lumpp

Owner: François Lumpp.
Surface Area under Vine: 7 ha – Givry *premiers crus* Clos Jus, Clos du Cras Long (both red), Crausot (red and white) and Petit Marole (white), Givry (red) including Le Pied du Clou and (white).

François Lumpp and his brother Vincent divided their 1990 harvest and have operated independently since then, François being the one to move away from the family home in Poncey. He now has a new winery on the outskirts of Givry on the main road to Buxy and the south, complete with a pneumatic press.

He vinifies his white wines in wood – they are perhaps the best in the whole *appellation* – and uses one-third new wood for the reds. These, too, are pure, stylish and impressive.

Domaine Thénard

Owner: Bordeaux-Montrieux family.
Surface Area under Vine: 22 ha – Le Montrachet (1.83 ha), Grands-Echezeaux (54 a), Corton Clos du Roi (90 a), Pernand-Vergelesses *premier cru* Ile de Vergelesses (85 a), Chassagne-Montrachet *premier cru* Clos Saint-Jean, Givry *premiers crus* Clos Saint-Pierre *monopole*, Le Cellier aux Moines and Les Boix Chevaux (all red), and Givry (red and white).

Much of the wine from this domaine is sold and bottled by Roland Remoissenet & Fils of Beaune, and are some of this *négociant*'s most successful wines. Other merchants are also allowed to buy wines here, and the domaine has become a major source of Montrachet.

The cellar is impressive, the Givrys being raised *en foudre*. The quality of both the domaine wines and those sold under the Remoissenet label is dependable and good – the Remoissonet wines perhaps having the edge. The Bordeaux-Montrieux family also own a 5-hectare estate in Mercurey.

Other Producers of note

DOMAINE CHOFFLET-VALDENAIRE, DOMAINE MICHEL DERAIN (SAINT-DÉSERT), DOMAINE THIERRY LESPINASSE, DOMAINE GÉRARD & LAURENT PARIZE, DOMAINE JEAN-PAUL RAGOT AND DOMAINE MICHEL SARRAZIN & FILS.

MONTAGNY

Surface Area (1998): 277 ha.
Production (1998): 14,016 hl.
Colour: White.
Grape Variety: Chardonnay.

Beyond Givry there is a gap of half a dozen kilometres before reaching Montagny. The hillsides of Saint-Désert and Moroges are the source of some splendid generic wines. A few kilometres on is Buxy, the capital of the Montagny *appellation*.

Until 1991 almost all Montagny was sold as *premier cru*. This had nothing to do with the wine's geographical source: it merely had to come from grapes with a minimum potential alcoholic content of 11.5°. Now the land has been classified and there are 53 slopes deemed *premier cru*, far too large a number. The best known is Les Coères. These *premier cru* vineyards lie on a series of south-east-facing hills below the village of Buxy in the communes of Montagny, Bully, Jully-Lès-Buxy and Saint-Vallerin.

This is potentially the best as well as the most substantial white wine of the Côte Chalonnaise. It can be less crisp and flowery than Rully, fatter and more honeyed, sometimes nutty and sometimes broader. In the

hands of a good merchant who is prepared to age the wine in newish wood, a Montagny wine can be every bit as good as a lesser village wine from the Côte de Beaune – and excellent value, too.

★ CAVE DES VIGNERONS DE BUXY

Members: 135.
Surface Area under Vine: 860 ha – Montagny *premiers crus* **Les Coères and Les Chagnots, Montagny, Rully (red and white), Mercurey (red) and Givry (red).**

Not surprisingly, this large co-operative, dating from 1929, is the chief source of wine fromt he Montagny *appellation*. It also produces substantial quantities of generic Bourgogne. Under the management of Roger Rageot, standards are high.

The co-operative now also makes and bottles the wine for the top-quality Veuve Steinmaier domaine, at the estate.

Other Producers of note

DOMAINE MICHEL GOUBARD – BOURGOGNE CÔTE CHALONNAISE WINES ONLY (SAINT-DÉSERT) AND CHÂTEAU DE LA SAULE/ALAIN ROY.

BOURGOGNE-CÔTE CHALONNAISE

Surface Area (1998): (Red and rosé) 385 ha; (white) 128 ha.
Production (1998): (Red and rosé) 22,934 hl; (white) 7235 hl.
Colour: Red and white.
Grape Varieties: (Red) Pinot Noir and (white) Chardonnay.

In 1990 it was decided to distinguish the Côte Chalonnaise generic wines from the other Bourgogne wines. The area covers land in forty-four communes in the Saône-et-Loire *département* surrounding the land already delimited for the five Chalonnaise communal *appellations*. The *appellation* is still very small compared with those of Mâcon and Mâcon-Villages.

THE MÂCONNAIS

The lush, rolling limestone hills of the Mâconnais form a natural interlude between the Côte d'Or and its satellite, the Côte Chalonnaise, and the granite bedrock of the Beaujolais region further south. As in the Côte d'Or, the white grape is the Chardonnay; as in the Beaujolais the red wines are predominantly produced from the Gamay. Climatically as well as geographically this is an area in transition between the north and south of France. It can be unexpectedly bitter in the winter, and spring frosts are an ever-present threat, but it is warm and balmy in high summer, and autumns are normally benign. I have picnicked in the shadows of the magnificent ruins of the Abbey of Cluny in late October. But I have had to scrape early-morning ice off my car windscreen in March.

This is a rich, polycultural region, extending from Sennecy-Le-Grand north of Tournus to the boundary between the Saône-et-Loire and Rhône *départements* south of Mâcon, reaching as far as Saint-Gengoux-Le-National and Salornay-sur-Guye, north-west of Cluny and confined by the river Saône to the east. The vine shares the countryside with Charollais cattle — Charolles itself is along the road from Mâcon to Paray-Le-Monial — and pasture alternates with fields of corn and maize and orchards of nuts and fruit; there are woods and meadows, sleepy villages each with its very own Romanesque church, or so it seems, and a large native population of goats.

Vinously this is a plentiful region; by no means as abundant as Beaujolais, but at least as generous as the Côte d'Or and the Côte Chalonnaise put together, for as well as a production of more than 300,000 hectolitres under the various Mâconnais *appellations*, the bulk of the Saône-et-Loire *département*'s yield of Bourgogne in its various forms comes from here. The wines are for the most part white, and largely produced by co-operatives, and they are increasingly well made. But they are wines for daily drinking in the year after the vintage. Only in the south, in Pouilly-Fuissé and its satellite *appellations*, do the

Mâconnais wines possess serious character. Only here will you find many individual domaines with winemakers who vinify and mature their wines in new wood.

The landscape is at its most dramatic here in this southern part of the region. Aeons ago the undulating Jurassic limestone subsoil of the Mâconnais was forced up against the Hercynian granite bedrock of the Beaujolais. What is left after several millennia of erosion are two huge 500-metre cliffs looming above the villages of Vergisson and Solutré and the vineyards of Pouilly-Fuissé. On the lower slopes at the foot of these two rocks the vine is ideally exposed, bathed in sunshine from morning to night. Pouilly-Fuissé itself is rich in pre-history. Solutré has given its name to a culture of the Stone Age, a period in the Upper Paleolithic between 15,000 and 12,000 BC. Solutréan man was one of the first to use flint arrowheads, and he formed needles out of reindeer bone. Hunting to him meant rounding up the local fauna — wild horses and various species of deer — and he would then chase them to the top of the slope, create a hullabaloo by means of fire and loud noises and panic the animals into jumping over the cliff to their deaths. At the foot of Solutré there is an ossuary a metre thick and over a hectare in extent, a rather macabre memorial estimated at over 100,000 animal skeletons.

The vine arrived in Roman times but it was not until the founding of the abbey at Cluny in AD 910 that the Mâconnais became an important wine producing region. It marked the start of an enormous expansion of the Benedictine movement, which at its height, with Cluny as its capital, held jurisdiction over 20,000 monks and 2000 dependent establishments stretching from Portugal to Poland. Cluny and the other local churches — this area is a goldmine for anyone interested in Romanesque and early Gothic architecture — needed wine. The abbey itself housed 460 monks in 1155 and the abbot was said to be even more powerful than the Pope. The entertainment budget must have been colossal and surely absorbed most of what was produced locally. It was only after the decline of Cluny's importance in the fifteenth and sixteenth centuries that it became necessary for the local growers to export their wines to other parts of France and elsewhere. Deprived of access to Franche-Comté and Alsace by the restrictive customs barriers so prevalent under the Ancien Régime, and obstructed from the nearby Pays Lyonnais, which was to all intents and purposes closed to wines made outside its jurisdiction, the Mâconnais wines were sent to Paris.

Communications were almost impossible. To reach the river Loire, the gateway to the north, the casks would either have to be sent across country to Paray-Le-Monial and Digoin. Alternatively they were sent up the Saône to Chalon, thence to Dijon and over the hills to the Seine at Chatillon. The Canal du Centre which connects the Saône with the Loire was not opened until 1794. All three rivers were subject to flooding in the spring and drought in late summer. There were losses through accidents, faulty casks and robbery. Wine had to be set aside for consumption by the carriers en route, and the expense by way of local tolls and taxes or simply bribery was enormous. The journey would often take several months, by which time the wine was probably off: such that was left.

One of the local heroes was Claude Brosse. Brosse, a giant of a man, had difficulty disposing of his harvest, and in 1660 decided to take it to the Court at Versailles. He yoked up his oxen, loaded his wagon with casks of his Mâcon and set off, braving the atrocious roads and the brigands who lay in wait for the unwary traveller. The journey took him a month. Once at Versailles he met with little success, until his bulk attracted the attention of the Sun King. Louis XIV liked the wine, which he found better than those of the Loire currently fashionable, and gave him an order for more wine. His sycophantic courtiers followed suit. Brosse had ensured the commercial future of the Mâconnais wines.

The wine, though, was almost certainly red. White wines, until the time of the phylloxera epidemic, were of very secondary importance, fetching only half the price or less. Only in isolated pockets was the production of white wine a sensible proposition. André Jullien (*Topographie de Tous Les Vignobles Connus*, 1816) states that the local Mâcon wine was generally red, and only mentions Pouilly, Fuissé and some of the adjoining communes as growths for white wine. Even by the end of the nineteenth century, eighty odd years later, the position had little changed. As late as 1952 red wine made up 60 per cent of Mâconnais production.

Today the position is different. Mâcon Rouge finds few customers. If in Claude Brosse's day it might have been made from Pinot Noir it is now made from Gamay, and you only have to sneak a red Mâcon into a tasting of Beaujolais-Villages wines to see the difference. The Gamay produces a rather more interesting wine in the granite soil of Beaujolais than it does in a limestone Mâconnais vineyard. And the fashion for Chardonnay is today seemingly inexhaustible. Seventy per cent of the

SURFACE AREA AND PRODUCTION (1998 HARVEST)

	SURFACE AREA (HA)		PRODUCTION (HL)	
APPELLATIONS	RED	WHITE	RED	WHITE
POUILLY-FUISSÉ	-	776	-	43,256
POUILLY-VINZELLES	-	49	-	2455
POUILLY-LOCHÉ	-	29	-	1443
SAINT-VÉRAN	-	531	-	36,237
VIRÉ-CLESSÉ	-	540	-	7163
MÂCON-VILLAGES	-	2644	-	175,121
MÂCON/MÂCON SUPÉRIEUR	765	197	45,149	11,674
TOTAL	765	4766	45,149	277,349
	5531		322,488	

Mâconnais wine is now white and the percentage is increasing. The variety is exclusively Chardonnay for the communal *appellations*, with Pinot Blanc additionally permitted for the generic Mâcon *appellations*. Currently the Mâconnais is planted with 67 per cent Chardonnay (including a small little Pinot Blanc), half a per cent of Aligoté, 25 per cent Gamay and 7.5 per cent Pinot Noir.

There are, in addition, 4215 hectares of vineyards in the Saône-et-Loire producing Bourgogne (red, white and Aligoté), Bourgogne Passetoutgrains and Bourgogne Grand Ordinaire. Most of these vineyards are in the Mâconnais rather than the Côte Chalonnaise. The average annual production of these generic wines is 250,000 hectolitres.

MÂCONNAIS YIELDS AND ALCOHOL LEVELS

APPELLATIONS	MAXIMUM YIELD	MINIMUM ALCOHOL LEVEL
RED WINES		
MÂCON	50 HL/HA	$10°$
MÂCON SUPÉRIEUR	50 HL/HA	$10.5°$
WHITE WINES		
MÂCON	50 HL/HA	$10.5°$
MÂCON BLANC-VILLAGES	50 HL/HA	$11°$
VIRÉ-CLESSÉ	50 HL/HA	$10°$
SAINT-VÉRAN	45 HL/HA	$11°$
POUILLY-FUISSÉ	45 HL/HA	$11°$
POUILLY-VINZELLES	45 HL/HA	$11°$
POUILLY-LOCHÉ	45 HL/HA	$11°$

MÂCON AND MÂCON SUPÉRIEUR

Surface Area (1998): (Red) 765 ha; (white) 197 ha.
Production (1998): (Red) Mâcon 1146 hl; Mâcon Supérieur 28,214 hl; Mâcon with communal name 15,789 hl; (white) Mâcon 1900 hl; Mâcon Supérieur 9774 hl.
Colour: Red and white.
Grape Varieties: (Red and rosé) Gamay and Pinot Noir; (white) Chardonnay.

Red Mâcon can either be basic Mâcon Rouge or Mâcon Rouge Supérieur, the latter indicating a higher alcohol level and forming the vast majority of this joint *appellation*. While in theory the wine can come from Pinot Noir, in practice it is made from Gamay, the wine made from Pinot Noir being sold as Bourgogne Rouge and attracting a higher price. Red Mâcon is a robust, earthy sort of

wine, fuller than Beaujolais and without its class, certainly when compared with Beaujolais-Villages.

Mâcon Blanc and Mâcon Blanc Supérieur, the latter being higher in alcohol, come from that part of the region outside the delimited Mâcon Blanc-Villages area. The wines are less fine, but then they are cheaper. All these wines are for drinking early, within two years of the harvest.

MÂCON BLANC-VILLAGES

Surface Area (1998): 2644 ha.
Production (1998): 175,121 hl.
Colour: White.
Grape Variety: Chardonnay.

Well-made Mâcon Blanc-Villages is an ideal, all-purpose wine, and is consumed in great quantities at Château Coates. This is Chardonnay at its most appealing: soft

The Mâconnais

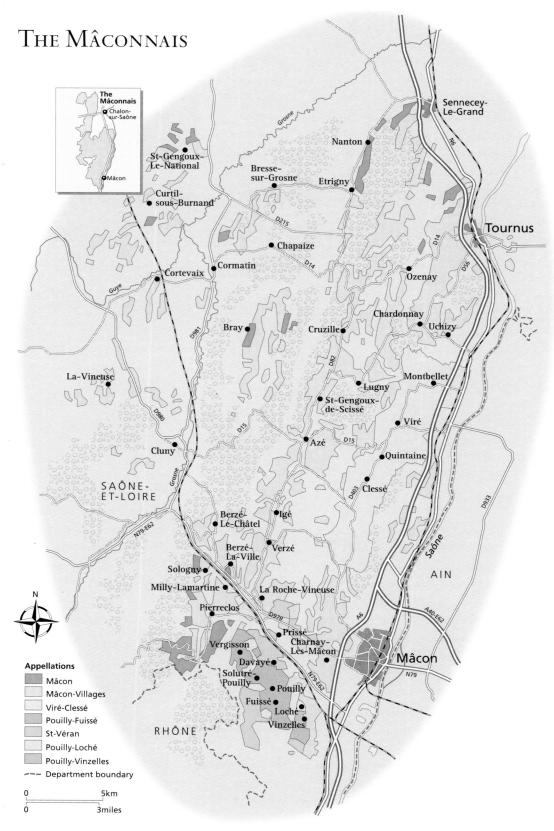

The Mâconnais
Chalon-sur-Saône
Mâcon

Sennecey-Le-Grand

Nanton

St-Gengoux-Le-National

Bresse-sur-Grosne

Etrigny

Curtil-sous-Burnand

Tournus

Chapaize

Cormatin

Ozenay

Cortevaix

Chardonnay

Uchizy

Bray

Cruzille

La-Vineuse

Montbellet

Lugny

St-Gengoux-de-Scissé

Viré

Azé

Quintaine

Cluny

SAÔNE-ET-LOIRE

Clessé

Berzé-Le-Châtel

Igé

Berzé-La-Ville

Verzé

AIN

Sologny

Milly-Lamartine

La-Roche-Vineuse

Pierreclos

Prissé

Charnay-Lès-Mâcon

Vergisson

Mâcon

Davayé

Solutré-Pouilly

Pouilly

Fuissé

Loché

Vinzelles

RHÔNE

Saône

Appellations

- Mâcon
- Mâcon-Villages
- Viré-Clessé
- Pouilly-Fuissé
- St-Véran
- Pouilly-Loché
- Pouilly-Vinzelles
- - - Department boundary

0   5km

0   3miles

and crisp, reliable year in year out, never unduly acidic, invariably plump and fruity: a wine of quality and interest but a wine without pretension.

The best Mâcon Blanc comes from a delimited region of forty villages which lie mainly in the southern section of the region, beginning at the village of Chardonnay, after which the grape variety itself might have been named, and continuing south to the boundary with Beaujolais. The wine can be labelled as Mâcon Blanc-Villages, or as Mâcon followed by the name of the village. Forty is a large number and in practice the most commonly found names are Lugny and Prissé, though I have seen both Mâcon-Fuissé and Mâcon-Vinzelles, *appellation*s easily confused with Pouilly-Fuissé and Pouilly-Vinzelles. Some villages, such as Romanèche-Thorins and Saint-Amour, are really part of the Beaujolais region and produce little white wine.

The wines vary in style from commune to commune as well as from winemaker to winemaker (though this is a region dominated by co-operatives). Those of Lugny are rich and nutty, fuller than the more fragrant delicate wines of Prissé to the south, for instance. Apart from selling wine directly under their own label, the co-operatives are the chief source of supply to the local Mâcon or Beaujolais merchants, or those based further north in Beaune or Nuits-Saint-Georges.

Maconnais Producers of note
Co-operatives AZÉ, CHAINTRÉ, CHARNY-LÈS-MÂCON, CHARDONNAY, IGÉ, LUGNY, PRISSÉ AND VINZELLES.
Merchants MAISON JOSEPH DROUHIN (BEAUNE), GEORGES DUBOEUF (ROMANÈCHE-THORINS), MAISON LOUIS JADOT (BEAUNE), MAISON LOUIS LATOUR — ESPECIALLY MÂCON-LUGNY LES GENEVRIÈRES(BEAUNE), LORON & FILS (PONTANEVAUX), MOMMESSIN (CHARNAY-LÈS-MÂCON), P SARRAU (ROMANÈCHE-THORINS), LOUIS TÊTE (SAINT-DIDIER-SUR-BEAUJEU) AND TRENEL & FILS (CHARNAY-LÈS-MÂCON).
Growers DOMAINE DE LA BRUYÈRE/PAUL-HENRI BORIE (IGÉ), DOMAINE DE DEMESSEY (CRUZILLE), DOMAINE ISABELLE & VINCENT GREAUZARD (LA ROCHE-VINEUSE), DOMAINE GILES LENOIR (PIERRECLOS), DOMAINE ROBERT MARTIN (DAVAYÉ), DOMAINE OLIVIER MERLIN (LA ROCHE-VINEUSE), DOMAINE TALMARD (UCHIZY) AND DOMAINE DU TERROIR DE JOCELYN/DAVID & ANNIE MARTINOT (BUSSIÈRES). DOMINIQUE LAFON OF MEURSAULT BOUGHT A DOMAINE IN MILLY-LAMARTINE IN 1999. SEE ALSO UN EVENTAIL (PAGE 243) AND GROWERS IN THE POUILLY-FUISSÉ AREA (PAGE 233).

VIRÉ-CLESSÉ

Surface Area (1998): 540 ha (potentially: this figure does not conform with the 1998 declaration).
Production (1998): 7163 hl.
Colour: White.
Grape Variety: Chardonnay.

This new *appellation* (1997) covers vineyards in what were hitherto two of the best Mâcon-Villages. No further tightening of the regulations is proposed beyond those of Mâcon Blanc-Villages, however, so this is just another new name to remember. One hopes it is not the start of a gaderene rush by other Mâconnais villages. Drink the wines within three years of the harvest.

Leading Viré-Clessé Producers

★ DOMAINE ANDRÉ BONHOMME
Commune: Viré.
Owner: André Bonhomme family.
Surface Area under Vine: 9 ha – Viré-Clessé including Cuvée Vieilles Vignes and Cuvée Spéciale.

André Bonhomme, having completed forty-two years at the helm, is now officially retired, and his son Pascal is in charge of the winemaking. The two superior wines are vinified partly in barrel, the Vieilles Vignes using new wood. Old vines and careful handling produce wines of exemplary style which keep well.

★ DOMAINE DE LA BON-GRAN
DOMAINE EMILIAN GILLET
JEAN THÉVENET
Commune: Quintaine.
Owner: Jean Thévenet.

Surface Area under Vine: 15 ha – Viré-Clessé and sweeter wines called Levronté and Botrytis.

Jean Thévenet is one of the anarchists of the wine world. As he produces both Mâcon-Viré and Mâcon-Clessé he will have to find new names to differentiate these two wines now that the new *appellation*, which he was against, is up and running. 'And is there any room for my sweeter wines?' he demands. I find all his wines delicious.

Other Producers of note

DOMAINE GUILLEMOT-MICHEL (CLESSÉ), DOMAINE DE ROALLY/HENRI GOYARD (VIRÉ), CAVE DE VIRÉ AND CAVE LA VIGNE-BLANCHE (CLESSÉ).

SAINT-VÉRAN

Surface Area (1998): 531 ha.
Production (1998): 36,237 hl.
Colour: White.
Grape Variety: Chardonnay.

The *appellation* of Saint-Véran, created in 1971, was one of the first in France whose wines had to be approved by a tasting panel, now compulsory everywhere else. It was carved out of various villages in the southern Mâcon-Villages area adjacent to Pouilly-Fuissé, many of which overlapped into neighbouring Beaujolais. Some of the white wines here had formerly been labelled Beaujolais Blanc, which as a consequence is much less common. The Saint-Véran villages are Chânes, Chasselas, Leynes, Saint-Amour, Saint-Vérand (with a 'd'), plus part of Solutré not entitled to produce Pouilly-Fuissé, and Davaye and Prissé north of the Pouilly-Fuissé area. Beaujolais Blanc now comes from the following four communes: Saint-Amour and Chânes (both also authorised for Saint-Véran), Crèches and Chaintré, some of whose vineyards can also make Pouilly-Fuissé.

As you might expect, the wines of Saint-Véran are a sort of halfway house between those of Mâcon-Villages and Pouilly-Fuissé though prices are nearer to the former than the latter. Saint-Véran is very good value.

Producers of note SEE POUILLY-FUISSÉ PAGE 233.

POUILLY-LOCHÉ AND POUILLY-VINZELLES

Surface Area (1998): (Loché) 29 ha; (Vinzelles) 49 ha.
Production (1998): (Loché) 1443 hl; (Vinzelles) 2455 hl.
Colour: White.
Grape Variety: Chardonnay.

The villages of Loché and Vinzelles are satellites of the four Pouilly-Fuissé communes. As they are separated from the hamlet of Pouilly itself by the commune of Fuissé one finds it hard not to accuse them of special pleading in their selection of the famous Pouilly prefix. No doubt Fuissé would not have worked quite such effective magic! The magic, though, doesn't seem to be that potent. These are two very small *appellations*, and though one does see Pouilly-Vinzelles I have rarely encountered Pouilly-Loché.

In general you will pay higher prices for these wines than for Saint-Véran, but you do not necessarily get better wine. There is a certain coarseness in both Pouilly-Loché and Pouilly-Vinzelles and a lack of zip, which I find neither in good Saint-Véran nor in the lighter styles of Pouilly-Fuissé. For some reason, the wine of Pouilly-Loché can be labelled as Pouilly-Vinzelles; but not vice versa. Drink within four years of the harvest.

Producers of note SEE POUILLY-FUISSÉ PAGE 233.

POUILLY-FUISSÉ

Surface Area (1998): 776 ha.
Production (1998): 43,256 hl.
Colour: White.
Grape Variety: Chardonnay.

Despite not being an easy name for English speakers to pronounce, Pouilly-Fuissé is a wine of enormous popularity on the export market, particularly in the United States. This is for two reasons: first it is made from the ever-popular Chardonnay, and second – normally, at any rate – it occupies the perfect psychological position on many a restaurant wine list. Pouilly-Fuissé is neither so inexpensive that it appears mean to select it, nor is it too expensive.

But it is not always so. Such is the demand, the growers have sometimes let the blood rush to their heads. Prices have regularly see-sawed between the normal and the ridiculous. The 1978s and the 1985s were only two recent examples when prices hit the roof but at least these were good vintages. The 1972s were another story. There is usually some trigger to cause this high price: a small crop or a winter frost after the vintage. Whatever the excuse the effect is an over-reaction. As a result the bottom falls out of the market, sales evaporate to a dribble and one has to wait for a couple of vintages before reason once more rears its noble head. One began to wonder whether the growers would ever learn. But since 1985 price movements have been more stable or at least along the lines of other white Burgundies.

The Pouilly-Fuissé vineyards extend over four communes. Running from north-west to south-east these are Vergisson, Solutré, Fuissé and Chaintré, the latter lying below Vinzelles. Pouilly itself is a small hamlet on the Solutré-Fuissé border.

Dominating the area are the twin cliffs of Vergisson and Solutré. On the lower slopes beneath these crags the vines are well protected and enjoy sunshine from morning to night. With the benefit of a warmer climate than in the Côte Chalonnaise or the Côte d'Or to add to this excellent exposure the Chardonnay grape often ripens to a potential 14° of alcohol. This is a dangerous drawback as Pouilly-Fuissé wines can be too heavy — carthorses rather than thoroughbreds — and a problem that has been recognised for some time. André Jullien commented in 1816 that the wines are rich, elegant, full-bodied and attractive; they have a good *bouquet*, but 'they are accused, with reason, of being too *fumeux* [alcoholic]'. There have even been vintages such as 1983 when the wines had an element of *pourriture noble* or noble rot.

There are small differences between the wines of the four communes. Fuissé has the best reputation; Chaintré the least. Solutré produces the wines with the most body, but additionally has a tendency to coarseness; those of Vergisson have the most delicacy; in Fuissé there

is some clay so the wines from here are structured; those of Pouilly are more *tendre* and have more finesse. As always, the quality of the winemaking is as important as the specific geographical origin.

There are fundamental differences in winemaking techniques. Elsewhere in the Mâconnais the wines rarely see any wood. Stainless steel or concrete is the order of the day rather than oak, and the wines are generally bottled by May following the vintage. Some Pouilly-Fuissé is made in this way and some is made as in the Côte d'Or with vinification and *élevage* in oak. Some Pouilly-Fuissé winemakers use a combination of methods — oak-fermented wine being blended later with wine which has not seen wood to produce a uniform blend, and more and more oak being used for the superior *cuvées*.

Pouilly-Fuissé is rarely a wine which you would term elegant. While there are plenty of lighter, more *primeur* Pouilly-Fuissé wines — wines similar to Saint-Véran, in fact — the more typical wine is often larger than life: full-bodied, fat, rich, exotic and often leaving the mouth with a burn of alcohol. It is an ample wine, but too often it will have a decided lack of acidity and will age badly. The happy medium, a wine that proves that it can keep, without losing elegance, freshness or fruit, is hard to find. The best are listed below.

Leading Pouilly-Fuissé Producers

★ DOMAINE ROGER CORDIER

Commune: Fuissé.

Owner: Cordier family.

Surface Area under Vine: 10.5 ha, in 45 parcels — Pouilly-Fuissé including Les Menetrières, Vigne Blanche and Cuvée Vieilles Vignes, Pouilly-Loché, Saint-Véran Clos à La Côte, Mâcon-Fuissé and Mâcon-Blanc.

Christophe Cordier has now joined his father at this impeccably run estate whose headquarters overlook the village of Fuissé on the south side. The vineyard yields are low, picking is by *tri*, crushing takes place in a pneumatic press and the wine is vinified in *foudres* or small oak barrels (the Cordiers like to use wood from the Jupille

POUILLY-FUISSÉ

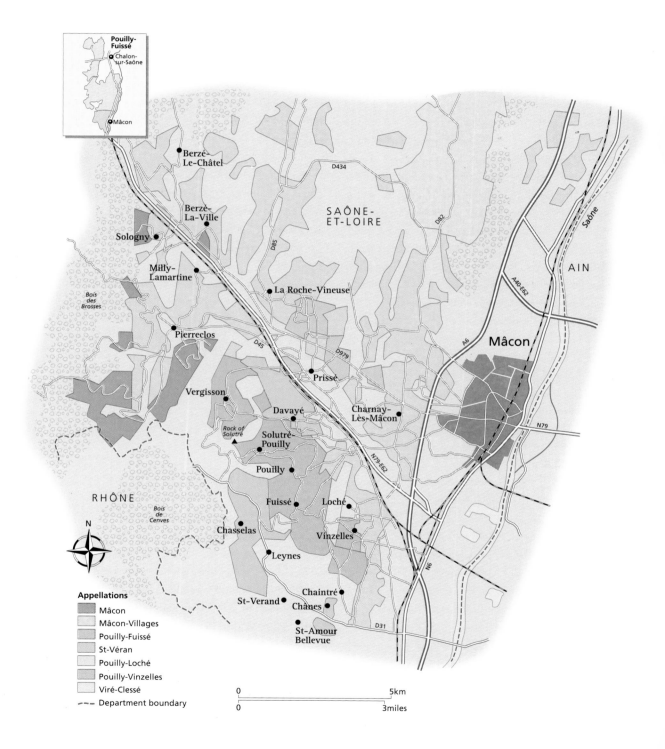

Pouilly-Fuissé

Chalon-sur-Saône

Mâcon

Berzé-Le-Châtel

D434

SAÔNE-ET-LOIRE

Berzé-La-Ville

D82

Sologny

D85

Milly-Lamartine

AIN

La Roche-Vineuse

Saône

Bois des Brosses

A40-E62

Pierreclos

D45

A6

D979

Mâcon

Prissé

Vergisson

Davayé

Charnay-Lès-Mâcon

Rock of Solutré

Solutré-Pouilly

N79

Pouilly

N79-E62

RHÔNE

Bois de Cenves

Fuissé

Loché

N

Chasselas

Vinzelles

Leynes

N6

Chaintré

St-Verand

Chânes

St-Amour Bellevue

D31

Appellations

Mâcon
Mâcon-Villages
Pouilly-Fuissé
St-Véran
Pouilly-Loché
Pouilly-Vinzelles
Viré-Clessé
- - - Department boundary

0   5km
0   3miles

forest, an unusual choice) without any exaggerated proportion of new wood. The best wines are kept for up to eighteen months before bottling. These are stylish, minerally wines of high quality.

★ DOMAINE CORSIN
Commune: Davayé.
Owner: Corsin family.
Surface Area under Vine: 12 ha – Pouilly-Fuissé, Saint-Véran (sometimes with two different *cuvées*) and Mâcon-Villages.

During the thirty years I have known the Corsin family André has succeeded Joseph and in his turn he has been succeeded by his sons Gilles and Jean-Jacques. The domaine used to be based in Pouilly but is now located in the centre of Davayé. These are beautifully clean, pure, concentrated wines, the Pouilly-Fuissé being fermented in half wood and half tank, and I have always found them irresistible.

★ DOMAINE J A FERRET
Commune: Fuissé.
Owner: Ferret family.
Surface Area under Vine: 15 ha – Pouilly-Fuissé including Les Menetrières, Tournant de Pouilly, Les Perrières and Les Clos. These *cuvées* can be further aggrandised with the words 'Hors Classe' or 'Tête de Cuvée'.

Mademoiselle Colette Ferret sold her dental practice in Mâcon to come and assist her ageing mama in 1992, and has been in charge at the domaine since her mother died the following year. Using an average of 50 per cent new wood, Mademoiselle Ferret produces wines of opulence, real depth and concentration. They are bottled after eighteen months or so and keep very well.

★★ CHÂTEAU DE FUISSÉ
Commune: Fuissé.
Owner: Vincent family.
Surface Area under Vine: 40 ha – Pouilly-Fuissé including Château de Fuissé Vieilles Vignes, Château de Fuissé Les Brûlées, Les Combettes, Les Clos and Cuvée Vieilles Vignes, Saint-Véran

Domaine de Morats, Mâcon Blanc-Villages, Morgon and Juliénas; plus a small *négociant* business.

This domaine has been in the hands of the Vincent family since 1852 and is the most important one in the Mâconnais. Estate-bottling the wines has been practised here for more than thirty years. Based on the grapes from Château de Fuissé vineyards, which have been considerably expanded in recent years, Jean-Jacques Vincent makes wines for keeping. The malolactic fermentations are blocked so that they do not take place and the use of sulphur is somewhat heavier than that of his neighbours, which can give the wines a troubled adolescence. He can now offer six different Pouilly-Fuissés from his own land. The Beaujolais are made by traditional methods too.

As well as the domaine wines, there are now merchant wines too. Some of these can be very good – the single-vineyard Saint-Véran, Domaine de Morats, for instance. But not always. Nevertheless, the wines from this domaine are proof that great Chardonnay which can last does not end at the Abbaye de Morgeots in Chassagne-Montrachet.

★ DOMAINE JEAN-MARIE GUFFENS-HEYNEN
Commune: Vergisson.
Owner: Jean-Marie Guffens-Heynen and family.
Surface Area under Vine: 3 ha – Pouilly-Fuissé including Clos des Petits Croux, La Roche and Les Crays, and Mâcon-Pierreclos including Le Chavigne.

Jean-Marie Guffens and his wife, Germaine, are both Belgian, arriving in the Mâconnais in 1976 when he was aged twenty-two. Almost immediately the name began to be talked about. I remember the wines were very expensive but they were brilliant. The man is brash, arrogant and uncouth, but he is also very lovable, and an ultra-perfectionistic winemaker.

Yields are cut to the quick. The pressing is slow and very gentle and the resulting wines can live for a decade. Small is beautiful here, very beautiful and very individual indeed. (See also Maison Verget page 236.)

★ DOMAINE PASCAL RENAUD

Commune: Pouilly.
Owner: Renaud family.
Surface Area under Vine: 13 ha — Pouilly-Fuissé including Aux Chailloux and Cuvée Vieilles Vignes, and Mâcon-Solutré.

Pascal Renaud bought this domaine in 1988 from Monsieur Balladur, where he had been a share-cropper and he had already made a reputation for himself as a careful, conscientious winemaker. Only a modicum of new wood is used and these are nicely pure, beautifully balanced wines, bottled quite early, in the summer after the vintage, for the medium rather than the long term.

★ DOMAINE THIBERT PÈRE & FILS

Commune: Fuissé.
Owner: Thibert family.
Surface Area under Vine: 13 ha — Pouilly-Fuissé including Vignes Blanches and Cuvée Vieilles Vignes, Pouilly-Vinzelles, Mâcon-Fuissé and Mâcon-Blanc.

There are two Thibert domaines in the village — this one is run by Christophe, who took over from his father René in 1990. Since then more and more of the wine has been sold in bottle. The better wines are vinified entirely in wood, but the percentage of new oak is minimal. The lesser wines are fermented in *foudre*. I like the style of these clean, pure, ample, elegant wines. The Vieilles Vignes vines really are old for once: from sixty to eighty years of age.

★ DOMAINE VALETTE

Commune: Chaintré.
Owner: Valette family.
Surface Area under Vine: 12 ha — Pouilly-Fuissé including Clos de M. Noly, Clos Reyssier and Tradition, Pouilly-Vinzelles and Mâcon-Chaintré Vieilles Vignes.

This domaine, run by Gérard Valette and his son Philippe, is relatively new, having detached itself from the local co-operative to go it alone in 1992. The Pouilly-Fuissé Clos Reyssier is fermented in wood, one-third of which is new, the Mâcon mainly in *cuve* and the other

cuvées in a mixture of the two. These are clean, balanced wines with plenty of depth: one of the 'secrets' being the low vineyard yield. Even in 1996, a prolific vintage, it was only 45 hl/ha.

★ MAISON VERGET

Commune: Sologny.
Owner: Jean-Marie Guffens-Heynen and associates.

In 1991, Jean-Marie Guffens (see page 235) started a merchant's business dealing in white wine, sourced from Mâcon to Chablis. Guffens likes to work alongside his chosen growers to ensure that the yields are kept low and the grapes picked at the optimum moment. He buys either grapes or must for fermenting at Sologny.

The results can be fine, but can also be variable, as he is the first to admit. Sometimes he has to accept fruit that is less than brilliant quality at village or *premier cru* level from his supplier growers in order to get hold of the top *appellations*.

Other Pouilly-Fuissé/Pouilly-Loché/Pouilly-Vinzelles/Saint-Véran Producers of note

MAISON AUVIGNE/BURRIER REVEL & CIE. (CHARNAY-LÈS-MÂCON), DOMAINE DANIEL BARRAUD (VERGISSON), DOMAINE ROBERT DENOGENT (FUISSÉ) DOMAINE GILLES & JOËL DENUZILLER (SOLUTRÉ), DOMAINE DES DEUX-ROCHES/ CHRISTIAN COLLOWAY & JEAN-LUC TERRIER (DAVAYÉ), DOMAINE DE FUSSIACUS/JEAN-PAUL PAQUET (FUISSÉ), DOMAINE DES GERBEAUX/JEAN-MICHEL & BÉATRICE DROUHIN (SOLUTRÉ), DOMAINE GONON (VERGISSON), DOMAINE MARC GREFFET (SOLUTRÉ), DOMAINE THIERRY GUÉRIN (VERGISSON), DOMAINE ROGER LASSARAT (VERGISSON), DOMAINE LÉGER-PLUMET (SOLUTRÉ), DOMAINE ROGER LUQUET (FUISSÉ), DOMAINE MANCIAT-PONCET (CHARNAY-LÈS-MÂCON), DOMAINE MARCEL PERRET (POUILLY), DOMAINE DE POUILLY/ ANDRÉ BESSON (POUILLY), DOMAINE JACQUES SAUMAIZE (VERGISSON), DOMAINE ROGER SAUMAIZE-MICHELIN (VERGISSON), DOMAINE JEAN-PIERRE SÈVE (FUISSÉ), DOMAINE LA SOUFRANDISE/FRANÇOIS & NICOLAS MELIN (FUISSÉ) AND DOMAINE DES VALANGES/MICHEL PAQUET (DAVAYÉ).

BEAUJOLAIS

There are two places on the long trek from Paris south to the Mediterranean coast where I always feel one moves from one climate zone to another. One is obvious, and will be recognised by anyone who has made this journey. Somewhere between Valence and Montélimar in the Rhône Valley the countryside and the weather changes: you enter Provence. Further north there is another more subtle transition – round about Mâcon the air becomes sweeter and warmer as you journey south, the countryside is lusher and riper, small vineyards alternate with tiny villages and with copses of deciduous trees and meadows occupied by a few dozen Charollais cattle.

Instead of the broad, treeless, windswept expanses of northern France, or the regimented, dry stone-wall-divided vineyards of the Côte d'Or, the whole thing is more haphazard. The elements which make up the landscape come in smaller pieces and the countryside is noticeably more undulating. Even the buildings have changed. Roofs are flatter, the brick a softer shade of pink or dull brown changing as one travels further south to a golden yellow; backdoors are open, the windows less firmly shuttered; chairs and tables under the refreshing shade of a tree indicate that more life is spent outside in the open. There is an assumption of sun. This is the hospitable and now prosperous region of Beaujolais – home to one of the world's most popular wines.

It was not always thus. It is difficult to realise that only since the Second World War has Beaujolais been widely drunk outside Lyon and the surrounding countryside. Only since then has the wine been regarded as more than just a relatively unimportant local *vin de pays*. Indeed it has been suggested that vines were first widely planted on a commercial scale only as recently as the early nineteenth century. Before the Revolution it was one of the most wretched and sparsely populated regions of France, comments Anthony Hanson in his book, *Burgundy* (1982). Two things then happened. The large aristocratic estates were divided up and sold to the local peasantry, and with the elimination of internal customs barriers and improvements to the local roads it became easier to open up markets in Paris and elsewhere, especially after the arrival of the railway.

For some reason – a combination of ignorance, convenience, inertia and habit – Beaujolais is regarded as part of Burgundy. This is a misnomer. Geographically, yes, they are adjacent, but geologically and climatically they are poles apart. More important the wine is vastly different. It is made from a different grape and it is vinified in a different way. It need hardly be said that as a consequence the flavour of a true Beaujolais is totally unlike that of a true Burgundy even if the two bottles might hail from the same merchant in Beaune. Beaujolais is a separate entity, even if the custom has decreed that somehow it must be slipped in as a sort of Burgundian lesser relation.

Beaujolais is a large and prolific region. It produces as much red wine as Burgundy proper, i.e. the Yonne, the Côte d'Or and the Saône-et-Loire *départements* put together. It is a prosperous region. Fifty per cent of the harvest is exported and about the same proportion is annually sold as Beaujolais Nouveau, shipped in mid-November and drunk by Christmas: good cashflow for one and all.

The area is bounded by the river Saône to the east (in practice the vines stop at the N6 between Mâcon and Lyon) and by the upper slopes of the Monts du Beaujolais to the west, where vines are cultivated up to an altitude of about 500 metres. To the north there is no real dividing line. At some point roughly due west of Mâcon the Chardonnay, the main Mâconnais grape, gives way to the Gamay. To the south there is a somewhat arbitrary line along the N7 which runs between Lyon and Roanne. South of this the Monts du Beaujolais become the Monts du Lyonnais, and Beaujolais becomes Coteaux du Lyonnais.

Except for a minute amount of Chardonnay-based Beaujolais Blanc on the Mâconnais border, and an equally tiny amount of rosé, all Beaujolais is red, both rosé and red made from the Gamay Noir à Jus Blanc.

NORTHERN BEAUJOLAIS

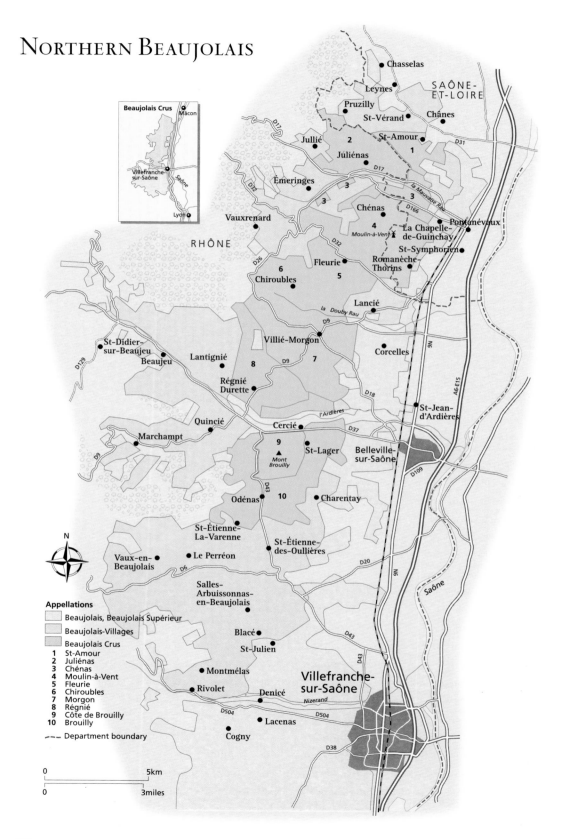

Beaujolais Crus
Mâcon
Villefranche-
sur-Saône
Saône
Lyon

Chasselas

SAÔNE-
ET-LOIRE

Leynes
Pruzilly
St-Vérand   Chânes
Jullié   2   St-Amour
          Juliénas   1
          D17   D31
Émeringes   3   la Mauvaise Rau
          3   3
          3   D166
          Chénas   Pontanévaux
Vauxrenard   4   La Chapelle-
RHÔNE   Moulin-à-Vent   de-Guinchay
          D32   St-Symphorien
          Fleurie   Romanèche-
          5   Thorins
          6
          Chiroubles
          la Douby Rau
          Lancié
          D9
          Villié-Morgon
St-Didier-   Corcelles
sur-Beaujeu
Beaujeu   Lantignié   8   7
          D9
          Régnié
          Durette   D18
          l'Ardières
Quincié
          Cercié   D37
Marchampt   St-Jean-
          9   d'Ardières
          Mont   St-Lager
          Brouilly   Belleville-
          sur-Saône
          10
Odénas   Charentay   D109
St-Étienne-
La-Varenne   St-Étienne-
Vaux-en-   Le Perréon   des-Oullières
Beaujolais   D6   D20
          Saône
Salles-
Arbuissonnas-
en-Beaujolais   N6

N

Appellations

Beaujolais, Beaujolais Supérieur   Blacé
Beaujolais-Villages   St-Julien
Beaujolais Crus
1   St-Amour   Montmélas
2   Juliénas   Denicé   Villefranche-
3   Chénas   Rivolet   sur-Saône
4   Moulin-à-Vent   Nizerand
5   Fleurie   D504
6   Chiroubles   D504
7   Morgon   Lacenas
8   Régnié   D38
9   Côte de Brouilly   Cogny
10   Brouilly

- - - Department boundary

0   5km
0   3miles

BEAUJOLAIS SURFACE AREA AND PRODUCTION (1998)

APPELLATIONS	SURFACE AREA (HA)		PRODUCTION (HL)	
	RED & ROSÉ	WHITE	RED & ROSÉ	WHITE
BEAUJOLAIS	10,076	–	656,342	–
BEAUJOLAIS SUPÉRIEUR	106	–	6548	–
BEAUJOLAIS BLANC	–	141	–	9059
BEAUJOLAIS-VILLAGES	6107	46	361,389	2983
BEAUJOLAIS CRU	6394	–	366,974	–
BROUILLY	1296	–	75,017	–
CHIROUBLES	378	–	21,696	–
CHÉNAS	281	–	16,256	–
CÔTE DE BROUILLY	312	–	18,096	–
FLEURIE	847	–	48,635	–
JULIÉNAS	602	–	34,809	–
MORGON	1119	–	63,167	–
MOULIN-à-VENT	655	–	37,400	–
RÉGNIÉ	587	–	33,807	–
SAINT-AMOUR	317	–	18,091	–
TOTAL	22,870		1,403,295	

Elsewhere in the world this Gamay produces rather a dull wine. In the Loire it is light, often with rather more pronounced acidity than ripe fruit and one dimensional – a *carafe* wine with little individuality. In the Ardèche or further south Gamay may ripen more easily, but additional sun does not bring additional character or elegance to the wine. Only in Beaujolais does the Gamay come into its own.

The reason is a particular vinification process, an adaptation of the classic system of carbonic maceration. In Beaujolais vinification takes place in a small closed vat, ideally no larger than 60 hectolitres. These are filled, but not filled to bursting, with whole, uncrushed, un-destalked bunches of grapes. The weight of the grapes releases some juice and this, warmed if necessary to get the fermentation going, is pumped over the mass of fruit. Carbon dioxide is formed by the fermentation which subsequently takes place, largely within the grapes themselves, and this blankets the top of the vats, enabling the process to take place in anaerobic conditions. The ideal temperature, controlled in the best

establishments, is between 25° and 28°C. Maceration takes place for five to six days, after which the free-run juice, now about 50 per cent of the eventual total, is racked off. The remaining pulp is pressed to extract further juice, this is added to the free-run juice and the fermentation process continues normally.

Today, practically all Beaujolais is produced by this 'semi-maceration' method, as it is known, as is also, for instance, much of the Carignan wine in the Midi. Few Beaujolais wines, except for the top domaines of the firmer *crus*, are matured in oak. One or two estates such as Jadot's Château des Jacques in Moulin-à-Vent and the Beaujolais made by Château de Fuissé in Pouilly-Fuissé remain faithful to the traditional vinification techniques for red wine as practised further north in the Côte Chalonnaise or in the Côte d'Or. These wines are quite different, having a size and, particularly, a tannin content and potential for development that 'modern' Beaujolais does not possess. I do not think, though, that they are necessarily any better for it. Good Beaujolais is a wine with a natural 11 to 11.5° of alcohol which has probably been chaptalised up by another degree. It is a light red wine, not at all tannic, purple in colour, abundantly fruity and not a bit heavy or sweet. It is bottled relatively quickly.

The bottling machines do not stand idle after the Nouveau rush in November after the harvest but move straight into bottling the generic wines for consumption immediately after Christmas. By Easter even the most solid Moulin-à-Vent is usually in bottle.

And it is a wine for drinking early. Beaujolais, whatever its designation, is a wine whose charm and character are in its youthful, perfumed, immediately appealing fruit. It is soft and should be utterly delicious and *gouleyant* (gulpable). Because Beaujolais is a wine without tannin, without structure, without real concentration and richness it will not age. It will not be transformed into something of depth and complexity by being imprisoned in bottle. It will merely get dreary. Some will tell you a fine Moulin-à-Vent will change into something resembling a Pinot Noir Burgundy if given age. It won't. This is not to say the wines won't keep; any wine of balance and fruit will last if stored correctly. But it won't improve. On the contrary it will merely become a rather strange brew of indeterminate character, of academic interest only. Most Beaujolais should be drunk within a year or at most two after the vintage.

BEAUJOLAIS AND BEAUJOLAIS-VILLAGES

BEAUJOLAIS
Surface Area (1998): (Red) 10,011 ha; (rosé) 65 ha.
Production (1998): (Red) 652,185; (rosé) 4157 hl.
Colour: Red and rosé.
Grape Variety: Gamay Noir à Jus Blanc.
Maximum Yield: 55 hl/ha.
Minimum Alcohol Level: 10°.

BEAUJOLAIS SUPÉRIEUR
Surface Area (1998): 106 ha.
Production (1998): 6548 hl.
Colour: Red.

Grape Variety: Gamay Noir à Jus Blanc.
Maximum Yield: 55 hl/ha.
Minimum Alcohol Level: 10.5°.

BEAUJOLAIS BLANC
Surface Area (1998): 141 ha.
Production (1998): 9059 hl.
Colour: White.
Grape Variety: Chardonnay.
Maximum Yield: 55 hl/ha.
Minimum Alcohol Level: 10.5°.

BEAUJOLAIS-VILLAGES
Surface Area (1998): (Red) 6096 ha; rosé 11 ha; (white) 46 ha.
Production (1998): (Red) 360,733 hl; rosé 656 hl; (white) 2983 hl.
Colour: Red.
Grape Variety: Gamay Noir à Jus Blanc.
Maximum Yield: 50 hl/ha.
Minimum Alcohol Level: 10.5°.

The most important distinction in Beaujolais is between plain Beaujolais (or Beaujolais Supérieur, an *appellation* rarely seen) and Beaujolais-Villages. This is not so much a question of alcoholic levels, though there are differences, as of location, geology and viticultural practices.

The northern part of the Beaujolais hills is formed of granite rock. The Mâconnais hills are limestone, the lower part of the Beaujolais region is sedimentary clay and more limestone. Between the two, roughly between latitudinal lines running west of Villefranche and Mâcon, lies the Beaujolais-Villages area. This is the true heartland of the Gamay.

Here the vine is pruned to the *taille gobelet*, no more than five stumps each with two fruit-bearing buds. Further south in the Bas-Beaujolais, the *taille guyot* or long cane-pruning, is permitted. The wine is lighter. Most is sold if not as Nouveau in the winter and spring following the harvest, and is tired by the summer holidays. Drink a simple Beaujolais without pomp or ceremony. Do not look for majesty or complexity. Drink it cool and drink it soon.

Beaujolais-Villages is altogether different. It is Beaujolais' greatest bargain. For hardly one franc more you will get a wine of much greater consequence. For a start the soil north of the river Nizerand, which flows out of the Beaujolais hills into the Saône at Villefranche, is granite-based. This gives the wine an added individuality, an added bite. The wines are a little bit fuller and a lot more concentrated. More importantly they have a great deal more character. I don't understand why anyone bothers with straight Beaujolais except for Nouveau. Beaujolais-Villages can come from any one of thirty-seven different communes, and you occasionally see it with the name of the commune hyphenated onto the word Beaujolais instead of 'Villages'. Those villages nearest to the Brouillys *crus* towards the south of the region seem to produce the most interesting wine. Many growers here produce both Brouilly, Côte de Brouilly and Beaujolais-Villages.

BEAUJOLAIS CRUS

Surface Area (1998): 6394 ha.
Production (1998): 366,741 hl.
Colour: Red.
Grape Variety: Gamay Noir à Jus Blanc.
Maximum Yield: 48 hl/ha.
Minimum Alcohol Level: 10.5°.

There are ten Beaujolais *crus*. The villages run in a line from Saint-Amour in the north on the Mâconnais border to Brouilly in the south, and occupy the best, north-eastern section of the Beaujolais-Villages area.

In ascending order of weight and approximate price (Fleurie is more expensive than Moulin-à-Vent) these are: Brouilly, Côte de Brouilly, Chiroubles, Régnié, Morgon, Fleurie, Juliénas, Saint-Amour, Chénas and Moulin-à-Vent.

Brouilly is the largest and southernmost *cru*, extending through a number of neighbouring communes round the conical hill of Mont Brouilly. The wine is crisp and flowery, light in style, but not without zip. I find Côte de Brouilly, the wine from the slopes of Mont Brouilly itself, normally has more definition as well as

power, and it is usually just a little more expensive. Régnié is a relatively new *appellation,* created in 1988, and lies between Brouilly and Morgon, but slightly to the west, overlapping into the commune of Durette. For some time this had been regarded as the best sector for Beaujolais-Villages and it has now become Beaujolais' tenth *cru.* The wines are similar in style to those of Brouilly.

Moving north you next come to the large and well-known *cru* of Morgon. The district is divided by the Mont du Py, south of which is the hamlet of Bas-Morgon. Here the wines tend to be lighter, more like Brouilly, than those made on the slopes of the hill or to the north round the more important village of Villié-Morgon. These denser Morgon wines can be quite hard when young and often are not at their best until the late summer or autumn after the vintage. The reason for this is said to be Morgon's own particular soil, a disintegrated schist called *rochepourrie.* Prices of Morgon today no longer command quite the premium over Côte de Brouilly that they used to but I find the wines more interesting.

Chiroubles lies up in the hills north-west of Morgon and south-west of Fleurie. Very popular in France, and consequently expensive, it never seems to have really caught on abroad. In style the wines are like a soft, even more gently fruity version of Fleurie. They develop early. At their best they are wines of real delicacy and finesse, but for early drinking.

Fleurie – ah, what a success story! The easiest *cru* to pronounce; one of the easiest to enjoy; certainly the easiest wine to sell; and now more expensive than Moulin-à-Vent, hitherto the most expensive of all Beaujolais *crus.* The name suggests the wine to be flowery. I find it the epitome of gentle, velvety fruit. A good Fleurie is a wine of medium weight which has an ample flavour absolutely crammed full with this fruit and is overwhelmingly seductive. Some Fleurie wines can be delicious as early as the spring after the vintage. Others need keeping for another six months.

Fleurie has a well-known co-operative, for many years presided over by the late Madame Marguerite Chabert, a lady of formidable force and personality. Overlooking the village is the Chapelle de La Madone perched on top of a little hill. The vineyard on the slopes of this hill is an important *lieu-dit* and source of many of Fleurie's best wines.

Moulin-à-Vent and Chénas have become almost interchangeable; Chénas, from the French word for oak (*chêne*), comes from the higher ground above the village itself and Moulin-à-Vent from the flatter land running down towards Romanèche-Thorins. The surface soil at Moulin-à-Vent is a curious pink sand, the colour coming from a high incidence of manganese in the soil. There is no village of Moulin-à-Vent, merely the famous ruined windmill.

Moulin-à-Vent is the most structured, the most powerful, and up to now the most I expensive of all the *crus*, while Chénas is a little lighter, as well as having less definition. Moulin-à-Vent has the deepest colour, the most body, the richest fruit, and normally needs a year before it shows itself at its best. Is it the best Beaujolais? For those to whom size or power in a wine is all-important, the answer is probably yes. I prefer to be caressed rather than bludgeoned and usually I'd rather cuddle up with a good Fleurie.

Juliénas is the most underrated of the Beaujolais *crus*. Currently sold for the same amount as Brouilly (indeed Brouilly, Côte de Brouilly, Morgon and Juliénas are all more or less the same price, while Chiroubles is 10 per cent more, Moulin-à-Vent 20 to 25 per cent more and Fleurie 25 to 30 per cent more) it is surely underpriced. The vineyards lie on high ground north and west of Chénas. The wines have a firm, full structure, not as rich or powerful as Moulin-à-Vent, nor as seductively fruity as Fleurie, but develop to wines of considerable depth, at their best by no means inferior to the best of these two communes. Like Chiroubles, and for the same reason — the vines being on higher ground — Juliénas often does better than its neighbours in years of great heat prior to the vintage and indeed in other years spoiled by rain. Even in well-nigh 'perfect' years, Juliénas can be the most successful *cru*.

With Saint-Amour, a small commune, we are at the northernmost limits of the granitic soil and the Beaujolais vineyards. The wines have something of the character of Mâconnais Gamay — they are fullish and more sturdy, less racy than the other Beaujolais *crus*.

Leading Beaujolais Producers

Traditionally the chief source of good Beaujolais has been the *négociant*. While the Côte d'Or-based Burgundian merchant will invariably have a range of Beaujolais on his list it is my experience that most of these wines leave something to be desired. Like the *négociants'* Burgundies there is more of a common denominator - the house style - in their wines and less of the individuality that there should be from *cru* to *cru*.

Better are the local merchants, specialists as they should be in the wines of the region, and best still those such as Duboeuf who are able to offer a range of individual growers' wines. Better still, perhaps, are the individual growers who go it alone.

Meanwhile, there are the thriving local co-operative organisations — there are eighteen co-operative cellars in Beaujolais. These are free to sell individually as well as to supply the local merchants with bulk wine. Though not as well known as their counterparts in the Mâconnais, many — such as the one at Fleurie for example — can justly be proud of what they do.

★★ ETS. GEORGES DUBOEUF

Commune: Romanèche-Thorins.
Owner: Duboeuf family.
Surface Area under Vine: 3 ha — Pouilly-Fuissé.
Georges Duboeuf matures, bottles and distributes the wines of the following domaines, almost all exclusively.
Beaujolais Cave Saint-Laurent-d'Oingt, Château de Buffavent and Château de Vernay.
Beaujolais-Villages Domaine des Sablons, Château Grande Grange, Château des Vierres, Domaine de Croix Charnay, Domaine de La Roche, Domaine des Pins and Château des Varennes.
Brouilly Domaine de Combillaty, Domaine des Nazins, Château de Nervers, Château de Pierreux, Domaine de La Roche, Château Terrière and Domaine de Voujon.
Côte de Brouilly Domaine des Berthaudières, Domaine de La Feuillée and Domaine de La Madone.
Régnié Domaine de Buyats, Domaine du Colombier and Domaine du Potet.
Chiroubles Domaine Desmures, Château de Javernand and Domaine Côtes de Tempéré.

Morgon Domaine de Bellevue, Domaine de La Chaponne, Domaine Jean Descombes, Domaine Vatoux and Domaine des Versauds.

Fleurie Château de Bachelards, Château de Deduits, Château du Grand Pré, Clos des Quatre Vents and Domaine des Quatre Vents.

Juliénas Domaine Joubert, Domaine de La Pierre, Château des Poupets and Domaine de La Seigneurie.

Chénas Domaine des Darroux, Manoir des Journets and Domaine Combe Rémont.

Moulin-à-Vent Domaine Labruyère, Domaine des Rosiers and Domaine de La Tour de Bief.

Saint-Amour Domaine de L'Ancien Relais, Domaine du Paradis, Domaine du Père Louis, Domaine des Pins, Domaine de La Pirolette and Domaine des Sablons.

Beaujolais Blanc Domaine Verchère de Savy.

Macon Villages Domaine des Chenevrières, Domaine Lenoir and Domaine Thomas.

Saint-Véran Domaine de La Batie, Domaine Saint-Martin and Domaine Val Lamartinien.

Pouilly-Fuissé Domaine Roger Duboeuf, Domaine Béranger, Domaine Bessard, Clos Reissier and Domaine de La Vieille Eglise.

The king of Beaujolais is Georges Duboeuf. The rise, expansion and success of the Duboeuf empire over the last thirty years has been remarkable and he now controls perhaps as much as 10 per cent of the entire annual Beaujolais business. His family are winemakers in Pouilly-Fuissé. Leaving his elder brother to manage the vineyard, Duboeuf set up as a broker in the 1960s. To brokering he added contract-bottling, moving round from property to property with a mobile machine in order to be able to offer his growers the marketing advantage of being able to print *Mis en Bouteille au Domaine* on their labels. From then it was a small step to marketing their wines himself.

Duboeuf's genius is his ability to judge a wine, often before the fermentation is completed, and his unerring nose for the very best. An assiduous competition participant, his wines regularly win more gold medals in one season at the various fairs in Villefranche, Mâcon and elsewhere than others in a lifetime. Invariably Duboeuf wines win the Prix Bacchus (for the best Beaujolais *cru* of the year) and the Coupe Dailly (the best Saint-Véran). Inevitably, the range of different wines Duboeuf can offer is wider than most. What is remarkable is that, despite the size of the operation today, there seems to be no deterioration in quality.

★ UN EVENTAIL DE VIGNERONS PRODUCTEURS
Commune: Corcelles.

The Eventail (the word means a 'fan' in French) is an important marketing organization for a group of independent growers in the Beaujolais and Mâconnais regions. There is a common warehouse in Corcelles where their wines are fined, bottled, stored and eventually despatched from. The standard of the Eventail's wines is generally high.

Members of the Eventail include Lionel Bertrand (Brouilly), Jean-Charles Braillon (Régnié), Jean Briday (Moulin-à-Vent), Paul Broyer (Mâcon-Solutré), Michel Brugne (Moulin-à-Vent), Bernard Castel (Saint-Véran), Château de Chénas (Chénas), André Depardon (Fleurie, La Madone, Mâcon-Solutré, Saint-Véran and Pouilly-Fuissé), Fabrice Ducroux (Brouilly), Claude Echalier (Beaujolais-Villages), François Ferrand – Beaujolais Blanc (Saint-Jean-des-Vignes), François Fichet (Mâcon-Villages), Christian Flany (Moulin-à-Vent), Henri Fontaine (Beaujolais-Villages), Claude Fortune (Beaujolais-Villages), Château Gaillard/Jacques & Pierre Montange (Beaujolais), Château Gaillard/Jean-Louis Brun (Morgon), Louis Gemillon (Beaujolais and Morgon), Philippe Gobet (Chiroubles), Domaine du Grand-Chêne/André Jaffre (Beaujolais-Villages), André Large (Brouilly and Côte de Brouilly), J F Michaud (Beaujolais), René Monnet (Juliénas), Domaine de Montgenas (Fleurie), Patissier Family (Saint-Amour, Juliénas and Beaujolais-Villages), Domaine Pelletier (Juliénas), Domaine du Petit Pressoir, Daniel Mathon (Brouilly and Côte de Brouilly), Domaine de La Roche Combe, Alain Passot (Chiroubles), Georges Ross (Chénas), René Savoye (Chiroubles), Jean-Luc Tissier (Saint-Véran), Domaine de La Tour Carré/Paul Carnin (Pouilly-Fuissé), André Vaisse (Fleurie) and Domaine du Vieux Bourg/Michel Tondu (Beaujolais).

★ CHÂTEAU DES JACQUES
Commune: Moulin-à-Vent.
Owner: Maison Louis Jadot.
Surface Area under Vine: 27 ha – Moulin-à-Vent and Beaujolais Blanc.

This important domaine in Moulin-à-Vent was acquired by the *négociant* Maison Louis Jadot of Beaune in 1996. The style of the wine is Beaujolais made by Burgundian, not by local *macération carbonique* methods and, for once, very successfully, the wines produced are splendidly rich in fruit and, unusually for Beaujolais with the structure to last for six to seven years or so.

Other Producers of note
Co-operatives FLEURIE AND CELLIER DES SAMSONS (QUINCIÉ).
Merchants LORON & FILS (PONTANEVAUX), LOUIS TÊTE (SAINT-DIDIER-SUR-BEAUJEU) AND TRENEL FILS (CHARNAY-LÈS-MÂCON).
Growers AS WELL AS THE FOLLOWING SEE ALSO DUBOEUF AND EVENTAIL ON PAGE 243.
Beaujolais-Villages
PIERRE-MARIE CHERMETTE – FLEURIE AND MOULIN-À-VENT (SAINT-VÉRAND), HENRY FESSY (SAINT-JEAN-D'ARDIÈRES) AND DOMAINE DES TERRES DORÉES/JEAN-PAUL BRUN (CHARNAY).
Brouilly
ALAIN MICHAUD AND LAURENT MARTRAY.
Côte de Brouilly
JEAN-CHARLES PIVOT – ALSO BEAUJOLAIS-VILLAGES (QUINCIÉ), OLIVIER RAVIER (CERVÉ), CHÂTEAU THIVIN/CLAUDE GEOFFRAY – ALSO BROUILLY AND BEAUJOLAIS-VILLAGES (ODENAS) AND DOMAINE DE LA VOUTE DES CROZES/NICOLE CHANNION (CERCIÉ).
Chénas
DOMAINE CHAMPAGNON – ALSO MOULIN-À-VENT, CHÂTEAU DES JEAN LORON, HUBERT LAPIERRE – ALSO MOULIN-À-VENT AND BERNARD SANTÉ – ALSO JULIÉNAS.
Chiroubles
DOMAINE DE LA COMBE AU LOUP, MÉZIAT PÈRE & FILS AND CHÂTEAU DE RAOUSSET.
Fleurie
DOMAINE BERROD – ALSO MOULIN-À-VENT AND

BEAUJOLAIS-VILLAGES, MICHEL CHIGNARD, JEAN-MARC DÉPRES, FERNAND GRAVAILLON – ALSO CHIROUBLES AND MORGON, AND DOMAINE DU POINT DU JOUR/GUY & JOCELYNE DEPARDON.
Juliénas
GÉRARD & JOELLE DESCOMBES – ALSO BEAUJOLAIS-VILLAGES, CHÂTEAU DE JULIÉNAS, JACQUES PERRACHON – ALSO MOULIN-À-VENT, AND MORGON, AND MICHEL TÊTE.
Morgon
JEAN-CLAUDE DESVIGNES, JEAN FOILLARD, MARCEL LAPIERRE, DOMAINE PIRON AND PIERRE SAVOYE.
Moulin-à-Vent
FERNAND CHARVET, DOMAINE DESPERRIER, DOMAINE LES FINES GRAVES, JACKY JANODET – ALSO CHÉNAS AND BEAUJOLAIS-VILLAGES, PAUL JANIN, CHÂTEAU DU MOULIN-À-VENT AND FLORNOY BLOUD.
Régnié
DOMAINE DES HOSPICES DE BEAUJEU AND DOMAINE PASSOT LES RAMPAUX.
Saint-Amour
DOMAINE DE LA CAVE LAMARTINE AND ANDRÉ POITEVIN.

COTEAUX DU LYONNAIS

Surface Area (1998): (Red and rosé) 304 ha; (white) 25 ha.
Production (1998): (Red and rosé) 19,363 hl; (white) 1587 hl.
Grape Varieties: (Red and rosé) Gamay Noir à Jus Blanc and (white) Chardonnay, Aligoté and Melon (Gamay Blanc).
Maximum Yield: 60 hl/ha.
Minimum Alcolhol Level: (Red and rosé) 10°; (white) 9.5°.

South of Beaujolais, stretching round the western hills and suburbs of the vast city of Lyon, is the Coteaux du Lyonnais, promoted from VDQS to full *appellation contrôlée* in 1984. The wine is largely red, made from the Gamay grape and is similar in style to an ordinary Beaujolais, though it is normally lighter and more ephemeral. Since gaining its *appellation* production has expanded and the quality of the wine has improved, though it is still rarely seen outside the region. The local co-operatives, such as the Sain-Bel, are the main source, but the wines are also sold by some Beaujolais merchants such as Georges Duboeuf. The two most important private estates are those of at the Domaine du Clos Saint-Marc at Taluyers and Etienne das Costas et Fils at Millery.

VINS DE PAYS

Vin de Pays de L'Yonne
This is a white wine – a sort of young-vine Chablis – from the Chablis-Auxerre area, and in my experience usually comes from the Chardonnay grape. I have seen some interesting wines. William Fèvre, the Chablis producer now owned by the Henriot family from Champagne, makes an oaky Vin de Pays de L'Yonne. The wine from Domaine Laroche is another good example.

Vin de Pays de La Côte d'Or
This is one of the more obscure *vins de pays* and I have rarely seen it in Burgundy, let alone elsewhere. The red wine comes from Pinot Noir and Gamay and the white from Chardonnay and Aligoté. Most of the wine comes from the co-operative at Sainte-Marie-La-Blanche in the plain east of Beaune – their Pinot Noir is a little rustic but not too bad. Thierry Vigot at Messanges in the Hautes-Côtes de Nuits makes a Chardonnay.

THE LOIRE VALLEY

THE URBAN CENTRE OF FRANCE IS, OF COURSE, PARIS; the spiritual heart is Reims where the French kings were crowned – or perhaps the Basilica of Saint-Denis outside Paris, where their mortal remains lay buried until desecrated during the Revolution. But for nine hundred years between the time when Charles Martel defeated the Moors at Poitiers in AD 732 and the ascent to the throne of the Sun King, Louis XIV in 1643 the Loire Valley was the focus, the amphitheatre on which the history of France was enacted in peace and in war, in public and in private. In the castle of Chinon, Henry Plantagenet, having imprisoned his wife, the redoubtable Eleanor of Aquitaine, in England, died a solitary death, attended only by the faithful William Marshall. In Chinon 250 years later, Joan of Arc identified her dauphin cowering among his courtiers. At Blois François I presided over a Renaissance court of quite spectacular expenditure, even attracting Leonardo da Vinci who spent the last years of his life in France and is buried at Amboise. At Nantes the famous Edict of 1598 was enacted by that cool and imaginative genius Henri IV, ensuring freedom of religious worship and expression and ensuring at least a respite in the internecine wars between Catholics and Protestants.

It was in the Loire Valley that the court collected and royalty received; where monarchs hunted, the company feasted and enemies intrigued. It was to châteaux in the Loire – thus far and no further, for it would have been uncharitable to isolate them entirely from civilisation – that royal mistresses were banished when they fell out of favour, and dowager queens were relegated when a new king took over in case they should exert too much influence over the new order. Most important for French cuisine, it was Henri II's Italian wife, Catherine de Medici, who imported Italian chefs to teach the French how to cook meals fit for royalty, and thus laid the basis for what is still today the most creative and imaginative cooking in the world.

The heyday of the Loire was the period of the later Valois kings – from the accession of Charles VIII (1483) to the murder of Henri III (1589). The sixteenth century was the period of completion of the

great Renaissance palaces of Azay-Le-Rideau, Chambord, Chenonceau, Valençay, Villandry and many others. It was not until after the accession of Henri IV in 1589 that the Loire began to decline and the sphere of influence moved to the Ile-de-France nearer Paris.

The development of Versailles under Louis XIV seventy years later was the most important factor in this decline. From then on the 'Garden of France' ceased to be the playground of its kings. The brilliant originality of the designs which flourished under François I (1515-1547) gave way to the spacious, elegant and classic, but essentially *bourgeois* architecture which marks the town planning of Saumur, Tours and Orléans: form without flair. From then on, particularly after Napoleonic times and as France became increasingly industrialised, the Loire remained a cultural backwater and its castles crumbled. The importance of its wines diminished as those of the rest of France found access to Paris easier; and as the era of great wine emerged in the pre-phylloxera years of the mid-nineteenth century, the Loire was forgotten. It was not until the 1960s that wines such as Sancerre and Savennières, even Muscadet and Vouvray, began to be widely exported outside the region. Yet the Loire Valley is a vast and rewarding area. Rich and varied in its beauty, historically fascinating in its echoes of the past, and with a vast array of wines, the Loire is indeed the 'Garden of France'.

The techniques of viticulture and vinification are said to have been first brought to the Loire by Julius Caesar (there is a Porte César in Sancerre) but it was a few hundred years later before there were any signs of intensive planting of vines in the surrounding countryside. This is credited to the Bishop, later Saint, Martin who founded an abbey in Tours in AD 372. Saint Martin is also the focus of one of wine history's most charming legends — one day he left his donkey tethered to a row of vines , on which the animal duly feasted, not having been fed that morning. In due course these truncated vines produced excellent grapes, if in small quantity. Thus did mankind discover the virtures of pruning.

THE WINES

The Loire is the longest river in France. It rises in the *département* of the Ardèche, on the slopes of the Gerbier de Jonc, a 1551-metre volcanic peak in the Massif Central a few dozen kilometres south-east of Le Puy. Here it is separated by merely a mountain ridge or two from the dusty wastes of the broad, industrialised Rhône. The Loire flows first north, then west for some 600 kilometres before it discharges into the Bay of Biscay at Saint-Nazaire. It flows north for half this distance, until just before Orléans, where it is barely an hour's drive from Paris, then west through the château country of the Touraine and the Anjou, and finally through the Muscadet vineyards of the Pays Nantais.

The tributaries of the Loire are of great importance from a wine point of view, be they little more than streams, such as the Layon, or wide imposing rivers in their own right such as the Cher. The Loire and its contributory waters drain almost a quarter of the entire land mass of France, and hence wines from Clermont-Ferrand and Poitiers have as much right to be called *vins de Loire* as those of Tours and Angers. The most important tributaries are the Allier, the Cher, the Indre, the Creuse, the Maine (itself only 10 kilometres long, but formed by the junction of the Mayenne and the Sarthe) and the Sèvre Nantaise. All, except the Maine, flow in from the south.

The Loire basin consists of all the land north of Limoges, west of Vézelay and south of Le Mans. It is a vast area, with some 300,000 growers and 180,000 hectares of vines, producing in an average year such as 1998 nearly three million hectolitres of *appellation contrôlée* wine (10 per cent of the total AC production of France) and 5000 hectolitres of VDQS wine. Additionally, the Loire Valley may produce as much as 600,000 hectolitres of *vin de pays* wine and 450,000 million hectolitres of *vin de table*.

The Loire Valley is commonly thought of as a white wine area, a sort of complement to the Rhône Valley, whose wines are almost entirely red. This is erroneous. Even allowing for the fact that French government statistics do not differentiate between red and rosé wine, and the enormous popularity of Anjou rosé, there is much red wine produced in the Loire, and only 58 per cent of the total production is white.

The wines can be divided into five main regions (though the location of some of the more outlying *appellations* within these regions is somewhat arbitrary). I have taken the logical order from the source of the Loire towards the coast.

The Upper Reaches and The Auvergne

AC Côtes Roannaises and Côtes du Forez (from 1999).

VDQS Côtes d'Auvergne, Saint-Pourçain and Châteaumeillant.

Centre Loire or Sancerrois

AC Sancerre, Pouilly-Fumé, Blanc-Fumé de Pouilly or Pouilly-Blanc-Fumé, Pouilly-sur-Loire, Menetou-Salon, Quincy and Reuilly.

VDQS Coteaux du Giennois or Côtes de Gien and Vin de L'Orléanais.

Touraine

AC Bourgueil, Saint-Nicolas-de-Bourgueil, Chinon, Montlouis, Vouvray, Touraine, Touraine-Azay-Le-Rideau, Touraine-Amboise, Touraine-Mesland, Cheverny, Cour-Cheverny, Coteaux du Loir and Jasnières. Plus *appellations* for *pétillant* and *mousseux* wines from Montlouis and Vouvray, as well as generic Touraine.

VDQS Coteaux du Vendômois and Valençay.

Anjou and Saumur

AC Coteaux du Layon, Coteaux du Layon-Villages, Bonnezeaux, Quarts de Chaume, Coteaux de L'Aubance, Saumur, Saumur-Champigny, Coteaux de Saumur, Cabernet de Saumur, Savennières, Anjou, Anjou-Villages, Anjou Coteaux de La Loire, Anjou Gamay and Cabernet d'Anjou. Plus *appellations* for *pétillant* and *mousseux* wines from Saumur and generic Anjou.

SURFACE AREA AND PRODUCTION (1998 HARVEST)

APPELLATIONS	SURFACE AREA (HA)		PRODUCTION (HL)	
	RED & ROSÉ	WHITE	RED & ROSÉ	WHITE
THE UPPER REACHES AND THE AUVERGNE				
CÔTES DU FOREZ (VDQS, AC FROM 1999)	196	–	8177	–
CÔTES ROANNAISES	166	–	8885	–
SAINT-POURÇAIN (VDQS)		530	20,565	6298
CHÂTEAUMEILLANT (VDQS)	81	–	4046	–
CÔTES D'AUVERGNE (VDQS)		395	15,938	1165
TOTAL	(443)		57,611	7463
		1368		65,074
THE CENTRE				
SANCERRE	511	1889	31,367	126,649
POUILLY-FUMÉ	–	973	–	69,364
POUILLY-SUR-LOIRE	–	49	–	15,263
MENETOU-SALON	126	221	7963	14,421
QUINCY	–	167	–	10,257
REUILLY	58	77	3330	5295
COTEAUX DU GIENNOIS (VDQS)	90	50	4799	3333
VINS DE L'ORLÉANAIS (VDQS)	119	24	4593	934
TOTAL	904	3450	52,052	245,516
		4354		297,568
TOURAINE				
VOUVRAY	–	923	–	46,913
VOUVRAY MOUSSEUX	–	1124	–	72,159
MONTLOUIS	–	189	–	7255
MONTLOUIS MOUSSEUX	–	155	–	8609
CHINON	2074	22	111,119	1083
BOURGUEIL	1292	–	71,186	–
SAINT-NICOLAS-DE-BOURGUEIL	929	–	53,572	–
TOURAINE	3083	2009	183,000	122,351
TOURAINE MOUSSEUX	68	565	3829	32,740
TOURAINE-AMBOISE	184	34	10,751	1332
TOURAINE-AZAY-LE-RIDEAU	31	24	1527	961
TOURAINE-MESLAND	105	14	5752	641
CHEVERNY	230	172	12,299	9039
COUR-CHEVERNY	–	43	–	1982
JASNIÈRES	–	50	–	2096
COTEAUX DU LOIR	38	29	1555	1012
CRÉMANT DE LOIRE (TOURAINE)	2	70	1702	35,319
ROSÉ DE LOIRE (TOURAINE)	11	–	4461	–
COTEAUX DU VENDÔMOIS (VDQS)	120	17	7515	1115
VALENÇAY (VDQS)	98	31	5711	2135
TOTAL	8255	5471	473,999	346,742
		13,726		820,741

→

Appellations	Surface Area (ha)		Production (hl)	
	Red & Rosé	White	Red & Rosé	White
Anjou				
Saumur	870	356	55,452	23,312
Saumur-Champigny	1375	–	78,715	–
Cabernet de Saumur	95	–	6294	–
Coteaux de Saumur	–	3	–	138
Saumur Mousseux	1133	3362	75,605	–
Anjou	1751	1067	99,666	58,234
Rosé d'Anjou	2069	–	129,511	–
Anjou Mousseux	66	151	3307	–
Anjou Gamay	307	–	16,784	–
Anjou-Villages	180	–	8741	–
Anjou-Villages Brissac	98	–	4771	–
Cabernet d'Anjou	2448	–	142,568	–
Anjou Coteaux de la Loire	–	40	–	1064
Coteaux du Layon and				
Coteaux du Layon-Villages	–	1853	–	52,772
Quarts de Chaume	–	40	–	693
Bonnezeaux	–	99	–	2365
Coteaux de l'Aubance	–	152	–	4660
Savennières	–	130	–	3878
Rosé de Loire (Anjou)	810	–	48,941	–
Crémant de Loire (Anjou)	–	413	–	25,716
Haut-Poitou (VDQS)	443		16,265	17,081
Coteaux d'Ancenis (VDQS)	257		15,366	226
Vins du Thoursais (VDQS)	24		569	435
Total	(10,003)	(4153)	622,395	269,486
	16,079		891,881	
Pays Nantais				
Muscadet de Sèvre-et-Maine	–	10,544	–	541,613
Muscadet des Coteaux de Loire	–	354	–	17,144
Muscadet des Côtes de Grand Lieu	–	334	–	15,263
Muscadet	–	1689	–	115,207
Gros Plant du Pays Nantais (VDQS)	–	2538	–	156,758
Fiefs Vendéens (VDQS)	415		17,692	3096
Total		(15,459)	17,692	849,081
	15,874		866,773	
	(19,605)	(31,533)	1,223,749	1,718,288
Grand Total	51,401		2,942,037	

VDQS Haut Poitou, Coteaux d'Ancenis and Vins du Thouarsais.

PAYS NANTAIS

AC Muscadet, Muscadet des Coteaux de La Loire, Muscadet de Sèvre-et-Maine and Muscadet Côtes de Grand Lieu.

VDQS Gros Plant du Pays Nantais and Fiefs Vendéens.

Wines from Anjou and Touraine can be blended to make Crémant de Loire (sparkling) and Rosé de Loire. There is no generic Loire AC for still white and red wines.

Surface Area and Production

A comparison of today's figures and those of a decade ago shows a considerable increase at the quality end and in the fashionable *appellations*. The areas under vine in Sancerre and Pouilly-Fumé have increased by 36 and 55 per cent respectively, Vouvray 15 per cent, Chinon 28 per cent, Bourgueil and Saint-Nicolas 23 per cent and Savennières an amazing 69 per cent.

When to Drink the Wines

Fifty-eight per cent of Loire wine is white and most is made for early drinking; much of the rest is rosé or a simple red, and also for early drinking. The wines made for keeping are the serious reds – Chinon, Bourgueil, Saint-Nicolas-de-Bourgueil and Saumur-Champigny, the medium-sweet or *doux* whites of Vouvray and the best parts of the Coteaux du Layon (such as Bonnezeaux and Quarts de Chaume), plus the dry white wines of Savennières and a few of the best dry Vouvrays.

With modern winemaking methods there is little fluctuation in quality between one year and the next when it comes to wine destined for quick consumption. One year's Cabernet Rosé d'Anjou or Sauvignon de Touraine will taste much like the next. Rarely will the vintage be so abysmal that Sancerre or Muscadet cannot be enjoyed. Most of these wines are made one year for drinking the next, and by the time this vintage is put on the market, six months or so after the grapes have been picked, the previous year's wine should be finished up. It will already have begun to lose its freshness. Vintage charts for these types of wine are redundant.

There are a few dry white Loire wines which repay keeping. One or two Pouilly-Fumés are now vinified and/or aged in oak: the top Ladoucette wine, Baron de L, and the Silex Cuvée of Didier Dagueneau are examples. These wines will safely last for three or four years, sometimes longer. Some dry Vouvrays, those of André Foreau for instance, will keep even longer, as much as a decade in the best vintages and so will the firmer Savennières, such as Nicolas Joly's La Roche-aux-Moines.

The sweeter wines will also keep well; the *moelleux* (medium-sweet) wines for five or perhaps ten years, and those which are truly *doux* (luscious) for decades, particularly Vouvray, which tends to be fuller than Coteaux du Layon. The great *doux* vintages of the century are 1921 and 1947. These wines are still fresh. Those of 1989 and 1990, almost as good, are still not ready.

Fine Loire vintages for the serious reds are few and far between, though thanks to modern winemaking techniques, good years are now increasingly frequent. Light reds such as Anjou Cabernet, Touraine Gamay and red Sancerre are meant for drinking, if not in the summer after the vintage, then within a couple of years. The sun does not shine sufficiently this far north to fully concentrate the grapes, and if the grower attempts to produce a lasting, tannic wine from only moderately ripened fruit he will make something overbalanced and astringent. Only rarely are we fortunate enough to get red Loire wines which can be guaranteed a lifespan longer than a Bordeaux *bourgeois* château wine, that is more than seven or eight years.

Loire Vintages

Savennières and dry Vouvray
1997, 1996, 1995, 1990, 1989, 1988, 1986, 1985, 1983, 1982, 1978 and 1976.

Coteaux du Layon and the sweet wines of Vouvray
1997, 1996, 1995, 1990, 1989, 1988, 1985, 1983, 1982, 1976, 1975, 1971, 1969, 1964, 1959, 1947 and 1921.

Chinon, Bourgueil and other top red wines
1998, 1997, 1996, 1995, 1990, 1989, 1988, 1986, 1985, 1983, 1982, 1978 and 1976. Older vintages will be showing age.

The Wine Regions
THE UPPER REACHES AND THE AUVERGNE

In contrast to the valley of the lower Rhône, only a few dozen kilometres to the east, the countryside of the source of the Loire is entirely different, a land of birch, ash and fir, rather than cypress, olive and pine: not in the least Mediterranean. Far off the beaten tourist track, this is a remote part of France. There are hills and valleys, freshly rushing streams abundant in fish and *écrevisses*, meadows and pasturelands with goats and sheep, but, as yet, no vines. It is cold and damp in winter, cool and fragrant even in the height of summer. There are few large towns and these are old, with fine Romanesque churches, touched with an element of the Byzantine brought back by returning Crusaders, and with the remains of crumbling castles, originally the fortresses of mountain brigand lords. There is little heavy industry to despoil the view or desecrate the beauty of the surroundings. It is a soft, romantic part of France, as far from the bustle of Paris as it is from the broad elegant acres of the châteaux country of the Loire.

The Côtes d'Auvergne are the first important vineyards of the Upper Loire and lie in the valley of one of the Loire's largest tributaries, the Allier, in the *département* of Puy-de-Dôme around Clermont-Ferrand. Some 50 kilometres to the east, across the Monts du Forez near the town of Boën in the *département* of Loire, is the Côtes du Forez. North of the Côtes d'Auvergne lie the vineyards of Saint-Pourçain along the banks of the river Sioule, a tributary of the Allier south of Moulins. North of the Côtes du Forez is the Côtes Roannaises, west of Roanne, home of one of France's gastronomic Meccas, the restaurant Les Frères Troisgros. A hundred kilometres west of Saint-Pourçain, almost where the four *départements* of Indre, Cher, Creuse and Allier meet, is the isolated district of Châteaumeillant. As yet, in our journey down the Loire, most of the wines are not

prestigious enough nor expensive enough, nor the areas large enough, to be anything more than VDQS. Two areas (Côtes Roannaises and Côtes du Forez) were promoted to *appellation contrôlée* in the 1990s.

CÔTES DU FOREZ

Surface Area (1998): 196 ha.
Production (1998): 8177 hl.
Colour: Red and rosé.
Grape Varieties: Gamay à Jus Blanc and other Gamays.
Maximum Yield: 55 hl/ha.
Minimum Alcohol Level: 9°.

North of Saint-Etienne the Loire Valley widens, dividing the Monts du Lyonnais on the east from the Monts du Forez on the west. On the south-eastern-facing slopes of the Monts du Forez, some 15 kilometres or so as the crow flies from the river itself and on its right bank, lie the Côtes du Forez vineyards. The holdings are scattered over twenty-one communes between Boën-sur-Lignon and Montbrison in the *département* of Loire, on soil which is clayey limestone or clayey sand on a granitic base. Forez is neither a very large nor very exciting region. Most of the wine is made by the local co-operative at Trélins, a suburb of Boën, as *vin de table* or Vin de Pays d'Urfé. Founded in 1962 the co-operative has 260 members. I find Côtes du Forez one of the least inspiring of all France's VDQS wines and its promotion to AC in 1999 unjustified. The wine from the co-operative is light, dull and an example of carbonic maceration at its worst, giving a flavour which is both rubbery and tasting of boiled sweets. The few growers' wines I have seen have been coarse and robust, inky and farmyardy. Their scruffy premises and rather cavalier attitude towards the possibility of bacterial contamination of wine do not engender much enthusiasm for the *appellation's* future.

CÔTES ROANNAISES

Surface Area (1998): 166 ha.
Production (1998): 8885 hl.
Colour: Red and rosé.
Grape Variet ies: Gamay à Jus Blanc and other Gamays.
Maximum Yield: 55 hl/ha.
Minimum Alcohol Level: 9°.

After the Côtes du Forez, continuing north for some 50 kilometres, we come to the Côtes Roannaises which is in the area of Roanne, still in the *département* of Loire. The alluvial flat land of the Loire Valley is several kilometres wide at this point, and the vineyards are planted in the granitic-based foothills of the Monts de La Madeleine some 10 kilometres to the west in twenty-five communes between La Picaudière and Bully. The chief wine centre is Renaison.

The area is small, with some hundred or so growers and 166 hectares of vineyards, planted with various forms of Gamay. The wines are red and rosé, and the best, from the Gamay Noir à Jus Blanc, the true Beaujolais grape, can be the nearest rival to the lighter Beaujolais *crus* such as Brouilly and Chiroubles. Much of the wine, however, is rustic in character, rough and farmyardy in taste, and not really worthy of its *appellation*.

Leading Côtes Roannaises Producer

DOMAINE ROBERT SÉROL & FILS
Commune: Renaison.
Owner: Robert Sérol.
Surface Area under Vine: 5 ha.
Wines: Côtes Roannaises including Cuvée Troisgros and Cuvée Vieilles Vignes.
After many years of supplying the Troisgros house wine, Robert Sérol managed to persuade the family who run this famous Michelin three-star restaurant to join him

in the development of a new vineyard. This means he now has more wine to sell to others. Vibrant with fruit, soft and elegant, the wines are yardstick examples of Côtes Roannaises.

Other Producers of note
DOMAINE ALAIN DEMON (AMBIERLE), DOMAINE DU PAVILLON/MAURICE LUTZ (AMBIERLE) AND DOMAINE DE LA PAROISSE/ROBERT CHAUCESSE (RENAISON).

CÔTES D'AUVERGNE

Surface Area (1998): 395 ha.
Production (1998): (Red and rosé) 15,938 hl; (white) 1165 hl.
Colour: Red, rosé and white.
Grape Varieties: (Red and rosé) Gamay Noir à Jus Blanc and Pinot Noir; (white) Chardonnay.
Maximum Yield: 45 hl/ha.
Minimum Alcohol Level: 9°.

Eighty kilometres to the west of the Côtes du Forez, in the shadow of the Puy-de-Dôme and overlooking the valley of the river Allier, is the noisy, unattractive, sprawling conglomeration of Clermont-Ferrand, birthplace of the seventeenth-century author Blaise Pascal and capital of the Auvergne. Now more famous as the base for the giant Michelin tyre empire, a century ago before the invasion of phylloxera, Clermont-Ferrand was the centre of a thriving wine region, the fifth largest in France.

Today, at an average of 17,000 hectolitres per annum, wine production is a vestige of what it once was, and the reputation equally diminished. Rarely, if ever, will you find Auvergne wines for sale outside the local area. This is, I regret to report, no injustice. The majority of the wine is a rather dull rosé from the Gamay grape. Coarse reds are made from Gamay and the Pinot Noir; they are either rather heavy and robust from individual growers, or lighter and somewhat better made using carbonic maceration from the two co-operatives. There is a Chardonnay-based white, but the examples I have seen do not enthuse me.

The region is a sprawling one, covering some fifty-three communes in the *département* of Puy-de-Dôme, scattered between Châtelguyon in the north and Saint-Germain-Lembron, a distance of about 60 kilometres. The soil is varied: in parts granitic sand, elsewhere limestone or marl, or even volcanic debris. The land is dry and well drained, with the vineyards exposed to the south or south-east. Vineyards, perhaps, is an exaggeration, the average plot is tiny, the farming polycultural, and such wine that is made here is mainly *ordinaire* for private consumption.

Within the broad *appellation* of Côtes d'Auvergne are five sub-areas, whose red and rosé wines must achieve an alcohol level half a degree higher to gain this superior and more precise geographical designation. From north to south these are: Côtes d'Auvergne-Madargues (communes of Saint-Hippolyte and Chatelguyon near Riom); Côtes d'Auvergne-Châteaugay (communes of Ménétrol, Châteaugay and the north part of Cébazat, north of Clermont-Ferrand); Côtes d'Auvergne-Chanturgues (the slopes of the Puy de Chanturgue immediately north of Clermont-Ferrand); Côtes d' Auvergne-Corent (communes of Corent, Les Martres-de-Veyre, La Sauvetat and Veyre-Monton, south of Clermont-Ferrand); and Côtes d'Auvergne-Boudes (communes of Boudes, Chalus and Saint-Hérent, west of Saint-Germain-Lembron). Chanturgues is said to be the best red, even being classed by the writer Jullien in the early nineteenth century alongside the third class châteaux of Bordeaux. Corent is the best-known rosé. Most of the white wine comes from Sauvagnat-Sainte-Marthe north of Issoire. In total some 2000 hectares are planted with vineyards, almost entirely with Gamay, and only one-fifth of these produce VDQS wine.

In my experience the best sources of Côtes d' Auvergne are the two co-operatives: La Clermontoise at Aubière, south of Clermont-Ferrand, founded in 1935, and the Cave Coopérative des Coteaux d'Auvergne or Cave Saint-Verny at Veyre-Monton near Corent, founded in 1951. Between them they produce about two-fifths of the area's VDQS total, and a little Vin de Pays du Puy-de-Dôme. In all, however, this is not a very exciting wine region, and I fear it will not become so until some eccentric (and rich) perfectionist arrives to take it by the scruff of its neck.

Other Producers of note

DOMAINE MICHEL BELLARD (ROMAGNAT), DOMAINE BOULIN-CONSTANT (RIOM), DOMAINE HENRI BOUCHEY (AUBIÈRE), DOMAINE ODETTE & GILLES MIOLANNE/GAEC DE LA SARDISSÈRE (NESCHERS) AND DOMAINE JEAN-PIERRE & MARC PRADIER (LES MARTRES-DE-VEYRE).

SAINT-POURÇAIN-SUR-SIOULE

Surface Area (1998): 530 ha.
Production (1998): (Red and rosé) 20,565 hl; (white) 6298 hl.
Colour: Red, rosé and white.
Grape Varieties: (Red and rosé) Pinot Noir and Gamay à Jus Blanc; (white) Tressalier, Saint-Pierre Doré, Aligoté, Chardonnay and Sauvignon Blanc.
Maximum Yield: 50 hl/ha.
Minimum Alcohol Level: 9.5°.

About 60 kilometres north of Clermont-Ferrand, along the road to Moulins in the *département* of Allier, lies Saint-Pourçain on the Sioule, a tributary of the river Allier. Here we are in the Bourbonnais, the northern foothills of the Auvergne, a gently rolling, often densely wooded land (the forest of Tronçais producing some of the best oak for wine barrels lies to the north-west) and at first sight the countryside seems to be agricultural with no sign of any vineyards. Cows graze, maize grows, other vegetables and cereals are cultivated.

The vineyards are scattered over a region some 45 kilometres long by 8 kilometres wide, on the left bank of the rivers Sioule, Bouble and Allier, either side of Saint-Pourçain between Moulins and Chantelle. There is no obvious centre to the region and many of the vineyards are little more than a few hundred square metres. Most of the vineyard owners grow other crops as well.

Saint-Pourçain, like the wines of the Auvergne, enjoyed a greater reputation in the past than it does today. The *vignoble* claims Gallo-Roman if not Phoenician origin, and the wine was for many centuries served at the table of kings of France. At the end of the eighteenth century the vines covered 8000 hectares, and could be compared, in the opinion of the writer Jullien, or so local legend would have us believe, with the best of the Mâconnais in good years. Sadly both the size of the vineyards and their fame have declined since then.

Nineteen communes are included in the Saint-Pourçain *appellation*, yet hardly 1000 hectares are planted with vines and only about half of this produces wine of VDQS standard. The co-operative (the Union des Vignerons), set up in 1952 when the area first acquired the status of VDQS, is by a long way the leading producer, but in recent years an increasing number of growers are beginning to vinify and bottle their own wine, and to sell direct.

The soil is essentially clay and limestone, forming part of the Limagne, a zone which has subsided in the crystalline shelf of the Massif Central. To the north-west this soil is poor and infertile, and the land undulating, while closer to the Sioule the vineyards are more stony and steeply sloping, giving a sunny exposure to the south and east. Nearer to Saint-Pourçain the soil is richer and more fertile. While the *appellation* produces red and rosé from Gamay and Pinot Noir, the white wine is the most interesting. Though several grapes are authorized, including Chardonnay, Aligoté and Saint-Pierre-Doré, the traditional grape for this white wine is the Tressalier (known as the Sacy in the Chablis area) which (the maximum allowed is 50 per cent) is blended with Sauvignon Blanc to give the authentic taste of Saint-Pourçain.

Saint-Pourçain white has a pronounced racy acidity, and a delicate, if not weak, structure. Yet it can be interesting and individual in a good vintage, and if from a producer with up-to-date equipment and winemaking expertise. The taste is more fragrant and herbal than a wine from Sauvignon Blanc alone, though similar, and a suggestion of some alpine flower such as gentian can be perceived by those imaginative enough to notice it. It needs to be good though, for the growers' wines are more expensive than Sauvignon from Touraine or Haut-Poitou, and much of their wine is somewhat rough and ready, and would have been better if it had been vinified and bottled by the perfectly acceptable, if not inspiring co-operative. In a region which is relatively unimportant commercially, I dealt personally with a number of growers during the time I was a wine merchant. Largely this was due to an inability to find anyone with both the size of vineyards and the quantity of wine made to give me continuity of supply and quality.

Leading Saint-Pourçain-sur-Sioule Producer

DOMAINE DE BELLEVUE
Commune: Meillard.
Owner: Jean-Louis Pétillat.
Surface Area under Vine: 17 ha.
Wines: Saint-Pourçain including Grande Réserve (white), Grande Réserve Pinot Noir (red) and Cuvée Spéciale.
This is the leading domaine in the area. In some ways it is atypical, the white being a blend of half Chardonnay and half Sauvignon Blanc, with no Tressalier, and the reds are pure Pinot Noir. But they are fine examples.

Other Producers of note
DOMAINE JOSEPH & JEAN-PIERRE LAURENT (SAULCET), DOMAINE FRANÇOIS RAY (SAULCET) AND UNION DES VIGNERONS DE SAINT-POURÇAIN-SUR-SIOULE.

CHÂTEAUMEILLANT

Surface Area (1998): 81 ha.
Production (1998): 4046 hl.
Colour: Red and rosé.
Grape Varieties: Gamay Noir à Jus Blanc, Pinot Noir and Pinot Gris.
Maximum Yield: 45 hl/ha.
Minimum Alcohol Level: 9°.

Near where the *département* of Cher meets three others (Indre, Creuse and Allier) lies the rather obscure VDQS of Châteaumeillant. Four of the eight communes entitled to the *appellation* are in the Cher, the other four across the border in the Indre, all lying on both sides of the D943 about halfway between Montluçon and Châteauroux. The wines are generally rosé, normally from the Gamay grape alone or from a Passetoutgrains mixture of two-thirds Gamay and one-third Pinot Noir.

From my experience they are light, rather dull and a little coarse, and I am not surprised their reputation is small and their consumption is but local. Once again the local co-operative, the Cave des Vins de Châteaumeillant, is the largest producer. Its Pinot Gris rosé, under the name Domaine du Parc, is not bad.

THE CENTRAL LOIRE

On the left bank of the river Loire, some 50 kilometres north of Nevers in the *département* of Cher, lie the Sancerre vineyards; on the opposite bank in the *département* of Nièvre are the vineyards of Pouilly-Fumé. These are the first great wines of the river. Further to the south-west, on the road to Bourges, is Menetou-Salon. Yet further west still, across the Bourges-Orléans *autoroute*, lies Quincy on the banks of the river Cher and Reuilly on the river Arnon.

All these *appellations* produce white wine, either wholly or predominantly, and with the exception of a small amount at Pouilly the grape used is Sauvignon Blanc, locally known as the Blanc Fumé. It is commonly believed that the name refers to something smoky in the aroma of the wine. This is not so: the *fumé* refers to the grey-green bloom on the ripening Sauvignon grape. Sauvignon Blanc, perhaps the most important quality white wine grape of western France, is in its element on the limestone soils of these central vineyards.

Away from the more alluvial, sandy, clayey soils of the Touraine, Poitou and Bordeaux, it can lose the greenness, the coarseness, the rasping acidity and the pong of cats that can frequently be encountered elsewhere. The acidity, of course, remains, but is coupled with a racy delicacy redolent of currants, gooseberries, even, say some, of rhubarb or asparagus. The wine is altogether more elegant; crisp and fresh but not mean, and light but not thin, and this comes together with the same gun-flint aroma one finds in Chablis. This last characteristic is no coincidence: the soils are very similar. Until a decade or so ago, the white wines of the area, with the exception of Ladoucette's Baron de L (see page 264), were entirely made and reared in tank; no oak was used. Led by Didier Dagueneau, the genius who showed France (not just the locals) how to achieve the difficult integration of Sauvignon Blanc and new oak (see page 263), a large number now produce oaky versions of their Pouilly-Fumés and Sancerres. Some are delicious but not all. Taste before you buy!

Of the five *appellations*, Sancerre and Pouilly-Fumé are the best known, produce the better wine, and are by far the largest. Menetou-Salon, Quincy and Reuilly, with only some few dozen growers apiece, are rarely seen outside the area, and only shipped by a few specialists. Their wines, by and large, lack the definition of their more important neighbours, and fetch prices about halfway between those of Sancerre and Pouilly-Fumé and the leading Sauvignon wines of the Touraine.

SANCERRE

Surface Area (1998): (Red and rosé) 511 ha; (white) 1889 ha.
Production (1998): (Red and rosé) 31,367; (white) 126,649 hl.
Colour: Red, rosé and white.
Grape Varieties: (Red and rosé) Pinot Noir; (white) Sauvignon Blanc.
Maximum Yield: (Red and rosé) 55 hl/ha; (white) 60 hl/ha.
Minimum Alcohol Level: (Red and rosé) 10°; (white) 10.5°.

Overlooking the Loire, at the centre of a series of undulating hills and valleys, lies the ancient town of Sancerre, strategically positioned on the highest hill of all, over

300 metres above sea level. The town is a maze of narrow streets with limestone buildings enclosing private, medieval courtyards. All the streets seem to lead to the shaded Esplanade de la Porte César and the nearby gardens of the ruined chateau of the tenth-century Count of Champagne, Thibault le Tricheur. This is a magnificent spot to gaze over the Loire Valley and to appreciate the military importance of the site. Below, the lazy river meanders between the reeds and the sandbanks, opposite lie the woods and vineyards of Tracy, the northernmost commune of Pouilly, topped by the spire of the church of Saint-Thibault.

Sancerre has had a turbulent history, particularly during the Wars of Religion in the sixteenth and seventeenth centuries, when it was a centre for the Reformed Church. In 1573, after having failed to take the town by force, the royal Catholic army under Charles IX besieged Sancerre for seven months. Starvation eventually led to capitulation, but not before half the population were dead, sick or wounded, and the survivors, having exhausted their bread and eaten all their domestic animals, had had to resort to eating rats, mice and even voles. In 1621 Sancerre was again attacked, this time by the Prince de Condé, and the castle totally destroyed, except for the twelfth-century Tour des Fiefs. Many of the Protestant families left for Switzerland and the Low Countries, despite the Edict of Nantes, and the town ceased to be a significant Protestant centre.

Though geographically part of western France, historically the region was part of the ancient Duchy of Burgundy, and in pre-phylloxera times vineyards continued intermittently across the hills of the Nièvre to Avallon and beyond. Hence, for the red wines, the Pinot Noir grape and, originally, for the whites, that dull, workhorse grape of Alsace and the Alps, the Chasselas. Historically, too, on the Sancerre side of the Loire at least, this was a red wine-producing area, but in the lean times at the beginning of the twentieth century it was found that white wine was easier to sell, and that the Sauvignon vine took to its graft onto American rootstock more successfully than either the Pinot Noir or the Chasselas. In immediate post-phylloxera times this grafting was done in the vineyard, rather than as today

in the nursery or greenhouse. From 1900 Sauvignon began to take over as the dominant variety in Sancerre. Prior to this and to the enforcement of the *appellation contrôlée* laws, much of the white wine from either Chasselas or Sauvignon had been sent to Champagne for blending.

In 1936 Sancerre achieved *appellation contrôlée* status for its white wine (exclusively from Sauvignon), but it was not until 1959 that AC for red and rosé from the Pinot Noir was granted. Such had been the swing of the pendulum, the red by then had gone almost entirely out of fashion; even when retained by a grower, the Pinot Noir was relegated to poor slopes with unsuitable soil and aspect, contrary to the normal practice which would, logically, put red grape varieties on the sunniest slopes as a red grape normally requires a higher quantity of sunshine to ripen it. The 1936 *appellation* regulations stipulated the best sites for the Sauvignon and, strangely, this law remained after 1959, and was not revoked until 1982. Now growers are free to choose which variety to plant and where to plant it.

After phylloxera, the Sancerre vineyards declined, as did many elsewhere in France. From 1700 hectares in 1893, the area under vine declined to little more than 600 hectares in 1960s, and the wine was rarely seen abroad. In the worldwide boom of the early 1960s, Sancerre and Pouilly-Fumé were in the vanguard; the wines enjoyed enormous popularity. It is hard to believe with Sancerre or Pouilly-Fumé, if not both, today *de rigueur* on every wine list, that as late as 1959 only half a dozen growers exported their wine beyond Paris. Prices of Sancerre have also risen sharply, by as much as, if not more than, fine white wines in general. Sancerre is now quite an expensive bottle of wine, more than Mâcon-Villages, sometimes even more than *premier cru* Chablis. Producers should beware of killing the goose that lays the golden eggs. The reds and rosé have made a comeback. Today around 20 per cent of Sancerre is red and rosé while a generation ago it was less than 10 per cent.

The Sancerre vineyards cover fourteen communes: Bannay, Bué, Crézancy, Menetou-Ratel, Ménétréol, Montigny, Saint-Satur, Sainte-Gemme, Sancerre, Sury-en-Vaux, Thauvenay, Veaugues, Verdigny and Vinon. Some of these villages (Montigny and Vinon, for

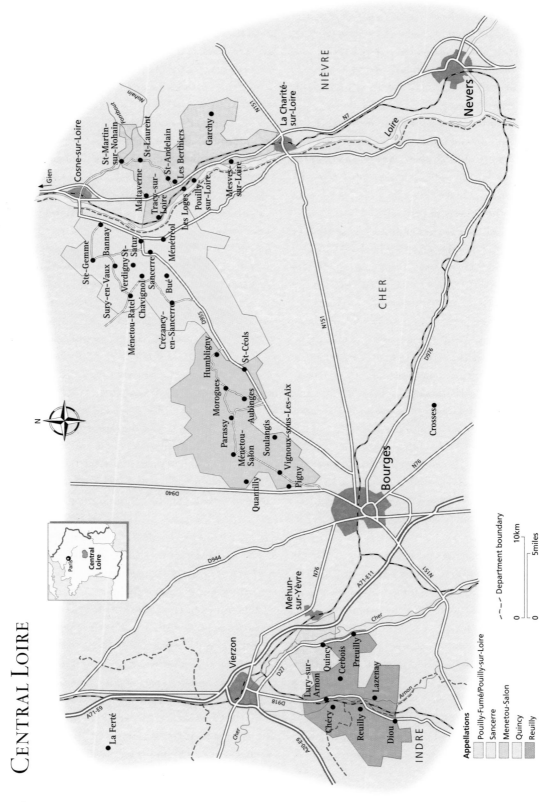

CENTRAL LOIRE

NIÈVRE

Nevers

La Charité-sur-Loire

Garchy

St-Martin-
sur-Nohain

St-Laurent

St-Andelain

Les Berthiers

Cosne-sur-Loire

Gien

Maltaverne

Tracy-sur-
Loire

Les Loges

Pouilly-
sur-Loire

Mesves-
sur-Loire

Ménétréol

Loire

Ste-Gemme

Bannay

Verdigny St-
Satur

Sancerre

Sury-en-Vaux

Ménetou-Ratel

Chavignol

Bué

Crézancy-
en-Sancerre

CHER

Humbligny

St-Céols

Parassy

Morogues

Aubinges

Soulangis

Vignoux-sous-Les-Aix

Ménetou-
Salon

Pigny

Quantilly

Crosses

Bourges

Mehun-
sur-Yèvre

Cher

Vierzon

La Ferté

Lury-sur-
Arnon

Quincy

Cerbois

Preuilly

Lazenay

Chéry

Reuilly

Diou

Arnon

INDRE

Paris

Central
Loire

Department boundary

10km

5miles

0

0

Appellations

Pouilly-Fumé/Pouilly-sur-Loire

Sancerre

Menetou-Salon

Quincy

Reuilly

example) are of minor importance, but Crézancy, Sancerre, Verdigny and Sury-en-Vaux each have over 100 hectares of vines, and Bué over 200 hectares.

The vines lie on undulating slopes, exposed to the east, south and west, and protected from the north and north-west by higher hills and trees. The soil is essentially limestone, mixed with clay; the higher up the slope the soil contains more pure limestone, the lower down the more clay. The best wine comes from the vineyards on the higher slopes and has more finesse, is more racy and more delicate.

Within this limestone generalisation, there are a number of sub-divisions. Roughly 40 per cent of the vineyards, particularly at Chavignol (a village, not a commune, and famous for its goat's cheese), Sury-en-Vaux and parts of Bué and Verdigny, is a soil called *terres blanches*, a clayey marl sometimes mixed with gravel. These are the highest slopes, and the most westerly. Centrally, particularly at Bué, and also making up another 40 per cent of the vineyards, a very stony soil predominates: these are called *caillottes*, and are often fossils. To the west, at Saint-Satur, Ménétréol, Thauveney, and part of Sancerre itself, the soil is flinty, very stony, and mixed with sand on a limestone base. Sainte-Gemme, to the north, is predominantly siliceous and, in contrast to the rest of the region, presents a red aspect, while the rest is grey. The soil here is less good quality but easier to work than the more precipitous slopes around the town of Sancerre itself.

Each of the three main soil types produces wine with a slightly different character. The *caillottes* soil gives a very perfumed wine, delicate in style, vigorously fruity and at its best young. The *terres blanches* make a firmer wine, sometimes a bit rustic, while the flinty soil gives a wine which is less perfumed but has more depth, and which keeps well. This is also the best soil for red wine.

Sancerre has many well-known *lieux-dits*, vineyard sites split up among a number of growers. The best known are Clos du Chêne Marchand and Le Grand Chemarin in Bué, Clos du Roy in Crézancy, Les Mont Damnés in Verdigny and Chavignol, Clos Beaujeu in Chavignol and Clos du Paradis in Sancerre. Most of these deserve to be singled out.

Red and Rosé Wines

Sancerre red and rosé wines are more variable in quality than the whites. Despite considerable replanting on better sites during the 1990s, this inconsistency must owe as much to poor viticultural origins as to bad winemaking, though young vines must also, if only temporarily, play their part. This is a cool climate – Sancerre, though on the same latitude as Dijon, suffers a significantly lower mean temperature during the summer months – and the wines can consequently lack 'flesh'. In poor years, in my view, rosé does better than red.

Sancerre rosé can be one of the most agreeable and elegant French rosés and a good one can certainly rival those of Marsannay in the Côte d'Or. Pinot Noir makes an attractive rosé – all flowers (violets) and summer fruits (cherry, strawberry and raspberry).

In years when there is enough sunshine and heat to ripen the grapes fully, fragrant, stylish, light red wine is made, similar in structure to a Côte Chalonnaise wine. Nowadays, with modern vinification techniques such as *chauffage de la vendange* (must-warming) which extracts more of the colour, fruit and extract, but less tannin, the reds are successful more regularly. With better handling techniques and earlier bottling, the rather rustic, attenuated Sancerre reds of yesteryear are less common, and the wines can be recommended as an alternative to a lesser Burgundy. They are ready within a couple of years or so and can last up to ten. Good recent vintages have included 1997, 1996 and 1995. Older vintages, for the most part, will be now a bit astringent.

White Wines

Sancerre is best known as a white wine region. The wine is vinified at a low temperature – between 18° and 20°C or so – to preserve as much of the volatile, aromatic compounds as possible. It is then matured in concrete vats, or, increasingly nowadays, in stainless steel, and bottled early for drinking young. In very ripe years like 1989 the malolactic fermentation is discouraged; in other years it is vital lest the wine become too lean and ungenerous. Similarly, in some years the wine is at its best in the summer after the vintage. In most years, though, a further two or three months in bottle will beneficially round off and soften the wines' dominant acidity. Few vintages should be kept more than a further year or two, not because they deteriorate, but because they lose their essential fresh, crisp, elegant, Sauvignon cut, which, to me, is the characteristic style of the wine.

Is there any material difference between the wines of Sancerre and Pouilly-Fumé, its neighbour across the river? Some authorities would have us believe that 'Sancerre normally has more body and drive (and higher acidity) than Pouilly-Fumé' (Hugh Johnson's *Wine Companion*). In general I find Sancerres marginally softer and riper; Pouilly-Fumés steelier, more racy. In vintages with a deficiency of acidity such as 1989, Pouilly-Fumé is often the better, in leaner years the opposite is sometimes true. But there is no hard and fast rule to differentiate between the two wines. Most of us, I fear, would be hard put to sort out a mixed blind tasting of samples into the two communes. Which is the better? Pouilly-Fumé is usually a franc or so cheaper, and perhaps, because it is more assertive and more angular, less easy to drink, and consequently less popular. In my view, however, there is more difference in quality between the peak wines and the run-of-the mill ones in either region than between the peaks or even the averages themselves.

The Use of Oak

Until a decade ago, Sancerre and Pouilly-Fumé, and indeed all the Sauvignons of the Loire, were fermented and aged without using oak. After a controlled vinification in stainless steel tanks the wine was allowed to settle, decanted off its gross lees into another tank from which it was bottled six months later, in most years, and among the better growers, without having undergone its malolactic fermentation.

Today in both Sancerre and Pouilly, some growers produce an oaky *cuvée*. Sometimes this works, sometimes it doesn't – as the Bordelais and the Californians have discovered, oak and Sauvignon are a difficult match. The wine has to be concentrated and substantial enough for the flavours to marry. Didier Dagueneau in Pouilly and Vincent Pinard in Sancerre produce the best oaky wines.

Leading Sancerre Producers

★ DOMAINE HENRI BOURGEOIS
Commune: Chavignol.
Owner: Jean-Marie Bourgeois.
Surface Area under Vine: 64 ha.
Wines: Sancerre including La Vigne Blanche, Grande Réserve, Les MD (Monts Damnés), La Bourgeoise, Etienne Henri and Sancerre d'Antan.
This is an ambitious and quality house, merchant as well as domaine. There is a wide range of wines, the better ones from special sites such as the MD. La Bourgeoise comes from old vines in Saint-Satur and Cuvée Etienne Henri is an oak-vinified version of the same wine. Bourgeois also sells the wines of Domaine Laporte – of these I prefer the Domaine du Rochoy and La Creste de Laporte wines to the Clos La Comtesse.

★ DOMAINE COTAT FRÈRES
Commune: Chavignol.
Owners: Francis, Paul & François Cotat.
Surface Area under Vine: 4 ha.
Wines: Sancerre including La Grande Côte, Les Monts Damnés, Le Cul de Beaujeu and Cuvée Spéciale.
These are Sancerres with originality: hand-picked, barrel-fermented, unfined, unfiltered, often not entirely dry and built to last. You will find alternative first names along with the Cotat name on different *lieu-dit* bottlings, but it is all the same domaine. These are very individual wines and are rapidly becoming a cult.

★ DOMAINE LUCIEN CROCHET
Commune: Bué.
Owners: Lucien & Gilles Crochet.
Surface Area under Vine: 33 ha.
Wines: Sancerre including La Croix du Roy and Cuvée Prestige.
The Crochet family are merchants as well as growers, but the special label wines come entirely from their own estate and are denoted by an oak tree on the label. These are elegant, minerally wines, the Cuvée Spéciale ageing very much better than most Sancerres.

DOMAINE GITTON PÈRE & FILS

Commune: Ménétréol.

Owner: Pascal Gitton.

Surface Area under Vine: 40 ha.

Wines: Sancerre including Les Belles Dames, Les Herses, La Vigne du Larrey and Galinot.

Pascal Gitton believes passionately in *terroir* and also in picking his Sauvignons at the peak of ripeness. He bottles each parcel from his extensive holding separately. Les Belles Dames is for early drinking. La Vigne du Larrey and Les Herses are for the longer term. The Galinot is *'grand cru'* in his view. There are a number of other wines as well as those listed above.

★ DOMAINE ALPHONSE MELLOT

Commune: Sancerre.

Owner: Alphonse Mellot.

Surface Area under Vine: 50 ha.

Wines: Sancerre including La Moussière and Cuvée Edmond.

Alphonse Mellot claims to be the eighteenth Alphonse Mellot in a direct line. As well as the domaine there is a *négociant* business, but the special *cuvées* are from their own vineyards. The Domaine de La Moussière is clean, pure and positive, an exemplary Sancerre. The Cuvée Edmond, from old vines, is partially fermented in wood.

DOMAINE DE MONTIGNY

Commune: Montigny.

Owner: Henri Natter.

Surface Area under Vine: 20 ha.

Wines: Sancerre including La Croix au Garde and François de la Grange.

François Natter, and his wife Cécile, are outsiders who bought land in the area in the mid-1980s and established themselves at Montigny, where Sancerre borders the Menetou-Salon *appellation*. These are rich, ample wines, yet with plenty of vigour underneath.

★ DOMAINE VINCENT PINARD

Commune: Bué.

Owner: Vincent Pinard.

Surface Area under Vine: 12 ha.

Wines: Sancerre including Cuvée Florès, Cuvée Nuance and Cuvée Harmonie.

Vincent Pinard's top vineyards are in the Clos du Chêne-Marchand *lieu-dit*, from which come the three special *cuvées*. He was one of the first Sancerre winemakers to vinify in barrel and remains one of the few to have achieved the correct oak balance. Cuvée Florès (made without oak) is concentrated, flowery and old-viney; Nuance is a mixture of one-third barrel- and two-thirds tank-fermented wine and is subtle and persistent; Harmonie is entirely vinified in wood and is an exotic, more obviously oaky wine. There is splendid finesse throughout the range and these wines are much in demand.

DOMAINE PAUL PRIEUR & FILS

Commune: Verdigny.

Owner: Paul Prieur.

Surface Area under Vine: 6.5 ha.

Wines: Sancerre.

These are good, crisp, dependable whites, even better rosés and truly exceptional reds.

DOMAINE DE SAINT-PIERRE

Commune: Verdigny.

Owners: Pierre, Didier and Philippe Prieur.

Surface Area under Vine: 6.50 ha.

Wines: Sancerre including Cuvée Maréchal-Prieur.

Father Pierre has now retired and his sons Didier and Philippe are in charge. They produce elegant, crisp, steely white wines, the Cuvée Maréchal-Prieur being oak-fermented, and good juicy reds and rosés.

★ DOMAINE VACHERON

Commune: Sancerre.

Owners: Jean-Louis & Denis Vacheron.

Surface Area under Vine: 36 ha.

Wines: Sancerre including Les Romains, Les Paradis (both white) and Belle Dame (red).

The Vacheron family produced the best wine in Sancerre when I first got to know them in the 1960s, and still do today. Few other Sancerres are as definitive, as pure, and as elegant as these wines. Occasionally you could find better whites but very rarely better reds. The vines were planted on the best sites, and are now of venerable age.

Other Producers of note

Domaine Jean-Paul Balland (Bué), Domaine Etienne Daulny (Verdigny), Les Celliers Saint-Romble/André Dezat & Fils (Verdigny), Domaine Fournier Père & Fils (Verdigny), Domaine Joseph Mellot Père & Fils (Sancerre), Domaine des Petits Perriers/André Vatan (Verdigny), Domaine du P'tit Roy and Domaine de Maimbray/Pierre & Alain Dezat (Sury-en-Vaux), Domaine Jean Reverdy (Verdigny), Domaine Pascal & Nicolas Reverdy (Sury-en-Vaux), Domaine Roger Reverdy-Cadet (Verdigny), Domaine Reverdy-Ducroux (Verdigny) and Domaine Michel Thomas & Fils (Sury-en-Vaux).

Pouilly-Fumé and Pouilly-sur-Loire

Pouilly-Fumé
Surface Area (1998): 973 ha.
Production (1998): 69,364 hl.
Colour: White.
Grape Variety: Sauvignon Blanc.
Maximum Yield: 60 hl/ha.
Minimum Alcohol Level: 10.5°.

Pouilly-sur-Loire
Surface Area (1998): 49 ha.
Production (1998): 15,263 hl.
Colour: White.
Grape Variety: Chasselas.
Maximum Yield: 60 hl/ha.
Minimum Alcohol Level: 9°.

Opposite Sancerre, on the eastern bank of the Loire, lie the communes which comprise the wine district of Pouilly-sur-Loire. Pouilly-sur-Loire – to differentiate it from countless other Pouillys, of which the best known from the wine point of view is Pouilly-Fuissé in the Mâconnais – is derived from the Latin Pauliaca Villa, but who this Roman Paul was, and whether it has any connection with Saint Paul, is not known. Nevertheless, it is highly probable that vineyards were established here in Gallo-Roman times. In the eleventh century the Pouilly area was owned by a Baron Humbault, who perished in the First Crusade. His estates then passed into the hands of the Benedictine abbey at La Charité-sur-Loire, some 30 kilometres to the south, in whose control they remained until the French Revolution. Under the monks' careful auspices, the area under vine was extended and a reputation established for the wine. Meanwhile to the north of the vineyards, at Tracy, the Estutt d'Assay family, of Scottish antecedents, established themselves in the late sixteenth century, while in 1785 the Ladoucettes, a Burgundian family, arrived at the Château de Nozet.

Despite the presence of these aristocratic landowners, Pouilly remains firmly a peasant winemaking area, and lives in friendly rivalry with its neighbour, Sancerre, across the river: 'Water divides us, wine unites us', is a local saying. Until 1973, the town was a bustling noisy place on the N7, but it now seems practically deserted, the caravans and juggernauts storming past on the bypass and leaving it in tranquillity.

Pouilly appears to have always produced only white wine. Jullien in his *Topographie de Tous les Vignobles Connus* (1816) speaks of white wines with a light gun-flint flavour, and an annual production of 40,000 hectolitres, mostly exported to Paris, a mere 200 kilometres to the north. In the mid-nineteenth century, before the phylloxera invasion, the vineyards covered over 1000 hectares, nine-tenths planted with Chasselas.

As at Sancerre, the vineyards declined during the first half of the twentieth century, and Sauvignon Blanc gradually took over as the dominant variety. Unlike Sancerre, however, Chasselas has not entirely disappeared. There are two *appellations*: Pouilly-sur-Loire, from the Chasselas grape, and Pouilly (Blanc) Fumé, or Blanc Fumé de Pouilly, from the Sauvignon. The proportions, however, are the reverse of what they were a century ago, and little, if any, Chasselas is now being planted. The area achieved *appellation contrôlée* status in 1937 for both ACs. Rather more land was authorised for potential production than is under vine today, and there is considerable scope for development.

Frost is a great danger, more so than in Sancerre because the terrain is less protected from the elements. Almost every year there is some damage. Every now and then – the last time was in 1985 – the effect is catastrophic. This has been a deterrent against expanding the vineyards, despite the wines' increasing popularity.

Pouilly-sur-Loire is made from the Chasselas grape. The wine is low in alcohol and acidity, and somewhat neutral in flavour. Nevertheless as a wine for quaffing *en primeur*, it has its place. It is certainly, currently, better vinified than many alpine Chasselas wines, and is consequently fresher and more attractive, with a similar gunflint character to the Blanc Fumé wines. If it was as cheap as generic Muscadet – which it isn't, for the prices asked are comparable to single-vineyard Muscadet *sur lie* wines – I am sure it could establish a place on the market. As it is, Pouilly-sur-Loire is rarely seen, and hardly ever exported. Growers have increasingly switched over to Sauvignon in recent years and Pouilly-sur-Loire will, I expect, soon be only a memory.

The Pouilly-sur-Loire vineyards extend over seven communes: Pouilly, including the hamlet of Les Loges, Saint-Andelain, Tracy-sur-Loire, Saint-Laurent, Saint-Martin-sur-Nohain, Garchy and Mesves-sur-Loire. The first three are the most important, with Saint-Andelain the largest; in Saint-Martin and Saint-Laurent the ground is flatter and largely falls to the north and east towards the river Nohain. The incidence of frost here is higher.

For the most part the ground is less hilly than at Sancerre, and the vineyards rise more gently. They lie less on slopes facing the river than on the plateau above. Only at Les Loges and Les Berthiers, two of the leading Pouilly sites, does one get the feeling of exposed, *côtes* vineyards that is prevalent on the other side of the river.

As at Sancerre, the soil is essentially a limestone-clay mixture, predominantly marl, *caillottes* and Kimmeridgian clay, giving way to sandy clay soil in the commune of Tracy to the north. In general, the clay content is higher, the limestone content lower than at Sancerre, and the result is a wine which is normally fuller, perhaps richer in alcohol, but less delicate.

Leading Pouilly-Fumé and Pouilly-sur-Loire Producers

★ DOMAINE ALAIN CAILBOURDIN

Commune: Maltaverne.
Owner: Alain Cailbourdin.
Surface Area under Vine: 9 ha.
Wines: Pouilly-Fumé including Cuvée de Boisfleury, Les Cris, Les Cornets and Cuvée Vieilles Vinifié en Fûts de Chêne.

The somewhat reserved Alain Cailbourdin came from Paris a decade ago, and quickly demonstrated that outsiders, perhaps because they could look at things afresh, could rival the locals. The four superior *cuvées* come from four different *lieux-dits*. I like the minerally Les Cris very much.

DOMAINE JEAN-CLAUDE CHATELAIN

Commune: Saint-Andelain.
Owner: Jean-Claude Chatelain.
Surface Area under Vine: 20 ha.
Wines: Pouilly-Fumé including Les Charmes, Cuvée Prestige and Vin de Pays des Coteaux Charitois Chardonnay and Pinot Noir.

Jean-Claude Chatelain, both merchant and grower, buys in roughly the same amount of wine that he produces himself, but his better *cuvées* come from his own vineyards. The Charmes is partly fermented in wood and the Cuvée Prestige from old vines and hand-picked grapes. The *vins de pays* are from very young vines.

★★★ DOMAINE DIDIER DAGUENEAU

Commune: Saint-Andelain.
Owner: Didier Dagueneau.
Surface Area under Vine: 13.5 ha.
Wines: Pouilly-Fumé including En Chailloux, Buisson Menard, Pur Sang and Cuvée Silex.

Didier Dagueneau is the world's greatest producer of Sauvignon Blanc wine – and by quite a long way. He is rebellious, perfectionistic, meticulous, competitive and very much given to criticising his neighbours for sloppy workmanship and over-production. With his unkempt red beard and long hair he is more than just playing the rebel. He is a Calvanistic judge and jury over all the others who produce less good wine than they could.

He has been in business since 1982. Vine density in his vineyards is up to 14,000 plants per hectare; yields are a maximum of 45 hl/ha (very low for the area) and picking is by a series of *passages* through the vineyard, when the grapes are at their aromatic perfection. Thereafter the vinification depends on the grapes themselves. There is no malolactic fermentation and the top three *cuvées* are barrel-fermented. There is a price to be paid for all this, of course, but if ever you need proof that Sauvignon can make great wine, this is the place to come.

CHÂTEAU FAVRAY
Commune: Saint-Martin-sur-Nohain.
Owner: Quentin David.
Surface Area under Vine: 12 ha.
Wines: Pouilly-Fumé.

At the northern end of the *appellation*, the vines of this domaine are secondary to a much larger planting of cereal crops. Quentin David produces a lean but racy and stylish Pouilly-Fumé, for early drinking.

SCEA FIGÉAT
Commune: Pouilly-sur-Loire.
Owners: Edmond & André Figéat.
Surface Area under Vine: 12 ha.
Wines: Pouilly-Fumé including Coques Vieilles, Champ du Roi and Vieilles Vignes and Pouilly-sur-Loire.

The Figéats produce ample, ripe wines, often of fine quality, from their vineyards in Pouilly and Les Loges.

DOMAINE DE LADOUCETTE
CHÂTEAU DU NOZET
Commune: Saint-Andelain.
Owner: Baron Patrick de Ladoucette.
Surface Area under Vine: 65 ha.
Wines: Pouilly-Fumé including Cuvée Baron de L.

Twenty five years ago the Ladoucettes at Château de Nozet were the only family in the Pouilly *appellation* to have more than 10 hectares under vine. They have now been joined by Château de Tracy, Domaine de La Moynerie, Didier Dagueneau and several others. The development of the Ladoucette family business is one of post-war France's biggest wine success stories. The current head, Baron Patrick de Ladoucette, took over control in 1972, at the age of twenty-one. At the time the estate had a fine reputation for Pouilly-Fumé, but had largely been left in the hands of a resident manager, Patrick's father having emigrated to the Argentine in 1947 where he made a fortune breeding cattle.

Patrick invested heavily in plant and machinery, installing thermostatically controlled, stainless-steel fermentation tanks, glass-lined vats for storage and an automatic bottling line. He also set about expanding his sales with remorseless energy to the extent that he now buys in as much wine (65 ha-worth), as he produces at the Château de Nozet. He has also diversified into Sancerre, under the Comte Lafond label (the name of an ancestor, once governor of the French Bank, who ordered the demolition of the old château and the construction of the present multi-turreted Château de Nozet); into the wines of the Touraine, under the Baron Briare brand name as well as the firm of Marc Brédif in Vouvray; into Chablis (Albert Pic); and into Cognac, jointly with Gonzalez Byass. The top Pouilly wine is the oak-aged 'Baron de L', sold in an old-fashioned, embossed, dumpy bottle similar in shape to that of Dom Pérignon Champagne.

DOMAINE MASSON-BLONDELET
Commune: Pouilly-sur-Loire.
Owner: Jean-Michel Masson.
Surface Area under Vine: 18.2 ha.
Wines: Pouilly-Fumé including Les Pierres Blanches, Les Angelots, Villa Paudus and Tradition Cullus, and Sancerre.

Jean-Michel Masson married Mademoiselle Blondelet and found himself in charge of a sizeable domaine. It was a challenge but one he cheerfully accepted, and this is now one of the best Pouilly domaines. There are several bottlings of separate *lieux-dits* and these are generally plump, juicy wines for drinking reasonably quickly. Tradition Cullus is partly fermented in barrel and is one of the better examples of oaky Pouilly.

CHÂTEAU DE TRACY

Commune: Tracy-sur-Loire.

Owner: Comtesse Alain d'Estuff d'Assay.

Surface Area under Vine: 33 ha.

Wines: Pouilly-Fumé.

The romantic Château de Tracy is a much finer build-ing than the Disneyesque Château de Nozet, and its roots go deep into Pouilly's history, wine having been made here since the fourteenth century. We are at the northern end of the *appellation* and from these flinty soils a racy minerally wine is what you expect and what you get. The wine could have more definition, I feel; but if the vintages of the late 1990s are anything to go by the winemaking has been refined.

Other Pouilly-Fumé Producers of note

DOMAINE DES BERTHIERS/JEAN-CLAUDE DAGUENEAU (SAINT-ANDELAIN), DOMAINE FRANÇOIS BLANCHET (POUILLY-SUR-LOIRE), DOMAINE GILLES BLANCHET (LES BERTHIERS), CAVE DE POUILLY-SUR-LOIRE – LES MOULINS-À-VENT (POUILLY-SUR-LOIRE), DOMAINE SERGE DAGUENEAU & FILLES (LES BERTHIERS), DOMAINE GÉRARD MAUROY (POUILLY-SUR-LOIRE), DOMAINE LA MOYNERIE/MICHEL REDDE (POUILLY-SUR-LOIRE), DOMAINE GUY SAGET (POUILLY-SUR-LOIRE), DOMAINE HERVÉ SEGUIN (POUILLY-SUR-LOIRE), DOMAINE ANDRÉ THÉVENEAU (LES CHAILLOUX IN SANCERRE) AND DOMAINE TINEL-BLONDELET (POUILLY-SUR-LOIRE).

MENETOU-SALON

Surface Area (1998): (Red and rosé) 126 ha; (white) 221 ha.

Production (1998): (Red & rosé) 7963 hl; (white) 14,421 hl.

Colour: Red, rosé and white.

Grape Varieties: (Red and rosé) Pinot Noir; (white) Sauvignon Blanc.

Maximum Yield: 60 hl/ha.

Minimum Alcohol Level: 10.5°.

Menetou-Salon, Quincy and Reuilly suffer from being regarded as the poor country cousins of Sancerre. The wines are made from the same grapes and in the same way, on largely the same types of soil and in more or less the same climatic conditions. By comparison with Sancerre and Pouilly-Fumé the districts are much smaller, and, probably because they were situated fur-ther from the Loire, the wines have never attained the popularity of their famous neighbours. The general view is that, pleasant as they might be, none of these wines will ever quite have the class or definition of a Sancerre. As a result, understandably, prices are cheaper.

However, is there necessarily anything wrong in being a cheap substitute? Without the fame of Sancerre, the wines of these three cousins would not be as well known as they are, or fetch the prices they now do.

Closest to Sancerre geographically, and most like its wines in style, is Menetou-Salon. The vineyards lie some 30 kilometres to the south-west on the road to the city of Bourges and cover a mere 350 hectares – one-seventh of Sancerre. At first sight, driving across the undulating hills on the D955, the vines are hard to spot. The heart of the *appellation*, in the commune of Morogues, lies off the road to the north, but even here the land is poly-cultural. The ground is flatter than at Sancerre, and the vineyards need woods to protect them from the cold winds from the north and east. The countryside feels less open, more rural. The soil, though essentially calcare-ous, is darker and richer.

Menetou-Salon itself is a comfortable, sleepy French provincial town, with little to attract the tourist except for an impressive Renaissance château.

Menetou-Salon's vines are planted in the communes of Menetou-Salon itself, Morogues (the two most important), Aubignes, Humbligny (the closest parish to Sancerre), Parassy, Pigny, Quantilly, Saint-Céols, Soulangis and Vignoux-sous-Les-Aix. *Appellation contrôlée* was granted in 1959 and production, together with the vineyard area, has been increasing rapidly since then (100 hectares in 1988 had increased to almost 250 hectares in 1998).

White Menetou-Salon is an attractive wine, sharing all the elegance and charm of Sancerre, while adding its own floral touch. I find it the most worthwhile, as well as the most consistent, of Sancerre's 'country cousins',

265

and the closest to Sancerre in character as well as quality. It has less body and flesh than its famous neighbour and the result is a wine more *primeur* in style: often, as in a year with low acidity like 1997, a wine which can be drunk as early as January, only four months after the harvest. The reds and rosés can also be delicious, and are considered by some to be superior to those of Sancerre.

Leading Menetou-Salon Producers

Domaine de Chatenoy
Owners: Bernard & Pierre Clément.
Surface Area under Vine: 10 ha.
Wines: Menetou-Salon including Cuvée Vinifié en Fûts de Chêne.
These are elegant white wines, produced partly by skin contact during pre-fermentation. There is an oaky red wine *cuvée* as well as the white wine one.

Domaine Jean-Paul Gilbert
Owner: Jean-Paul Gilbert.
Surface Area under Vine: 15 ha.
Wines: Menetou-Salon.
This is the estate which proves that Menetou-Salon reds are as good as those of Sancerre, and will improve on keeping for five years.

Domaine Henri Pellé
Commune: Morogues.
Owner: Henri Pellé.
Surface Area under Vine: 53 ha.
Wines: Menetou-Salon including Clos des Blanchais and Clos de Ratier, and Sancerre including La Croix-du-Garde.
Henri Pellé is the largest and most important grower in Menetou-Salon, responsible for about a quarter of the *appellation*'s total production. He sets a high standard for the rest of the producers, and even his basic wines are good. The Clos des Blanchais is particularly noteworthy.

Domaine La Tour Saint-Martin
Commune: Crosses.
Owners: Albane & Bertrand Minchin.

Surface Area under Vine: 6.5 ha.
Wines: Menetou-Salon.
Good reds and rosés and even better whites are produced here. I have admired the Minchins' wines ever since I once mistook their white for Vacheron's Sancerre.

Other Producers of note
GAEC des Brangers/Georges Chavet & Fils and Domaine Jean Teiller & Fils (both Menetou-Salon).

Quincy

Surface Area (1998): 167 ha.
Production (1998): 10,257 hl.
Colour: White.
Grape Variety: Sauvignon Blanc.
Maximum Yield: 60 hl/ha.
Minimum Alcohol Level: 10.5°.

Quincy lies 40 kilometres west of Menetou-Salon, south of Vierzon on the left bank of the river Cher. Quincy's chief claim to fame is that it was the second winemaking area in France (after Châteauneuf-du-Pape) to achieve *appellation contrôlée* status, in 1936. Why such an obscure *appellation* should have been so singled out is curious. The village has a long history of serious winemaking, stemming from the time it was an adjunct to the local Cistercian Abbey of Beauvoir in the Middle Ages, and the wines are said to have been exported to Paris and the royal court as early as the end of the sixteenth century. This tradition continues today, with nearly every family in the village involved in wine in one form or another.

Quincy can only be white and is made within the single commune of Quincy itself (apart from a few plots in neighbouring Brinay) on soil less calcareous and with more sand and gravel than at Reuilly or the other vineyards of the Central Loire region. Indeed much of the vineyard area lies in what was once the bed of the river Cher. Despite this I find Quincy the closest to Pouilly-Fumé of all the 'country cousins': the wine is light, racy and steely with a pronounced acidity and more than a hint of gunflint; occasionally, in poorer years (and this is a fault of Reuilly, too) there is a lack of ripeness. The vintage starts a week or so later than in Sancerre, but even this delay, in cold years, is not enough to ensure ripe grapes.

Quincy and its neighbour also suffer more from frost than do Sancerre and Pouilly, and at Quincy the danger is particularly prevalent as the vineyards are on flatter land and closer to the river. In 1977, 1984 and again in 1995 the crop was barely half its usual size.

Quincy Producers of note

DOMAINE DES BRUNIERS/JÉRÔME DE LA CHAISE, DOMAINE CLAUDE HOUSSIER, DOMAINE MARDON, DOMAINE PHILIPPE PORTIER (BRINAY) AND DOMAINE JEAN-MICHEL SORBE (REUILLY).

REUILLY

Surface Area (1998): (Red and rosé) 58 ha; (white) 221 ha.
Production (1998): (Red and rosé) 3330 hl; (white) 595 hl.
Colour: Red, rosé and white.
Grape Varieties: (Red and rosé) Pinot Noir and Pinot Gris; (white) Sauvignon Blanc.
Maximum Yield: (Red and rosé) 55 hl/ha; (white) 60 hl/ha.
Minimum Alcohol Level: (Red and rosé) 10°; (white) 10.5°.

Reuilly lies on higher ground a further 10 kilometres to the south-west of Quincy, above the river Arnon on the borders of the *départements* of Cher and Indre. It is the smallest *appellation* of Sancerre's three poor relations, despite having doubled in size in the last ten years. Further land is planted with Gamay and produces *vins de pays*. The *appellation* comprises seven communes: Reuilly and Diou in the Indre and Cerbois, Lury-sur-Arnon, Preuilly, Chery and Lazenay in the Cher.

Most of the vineyards are around the village of Reuilly itself, broken up into tiny smallholdings amid pasture and arable land, trees and orchards on the left bank of the river. This is rural France at its most typical;

self-sufficient and suspicious of change and also of any foreigners – though with a few grudging overtures to the increasing importance of the tourist, be he or she only from Paris.

Sauvignon Blanc grapes from the predominantly limestone soil of the *appellation* produces a vegetal, herby white wine which is lighter and leaner than Sancerre and Pouilly-Fumé, with its own *goût de terroir*. It is rarely more than a competent, attractive wine, lacking both the depth and length of its illustrious competitors and the charm of Menetou-Salon. The best it can aspire to is a healthy austerity, crisp and fresh in the spring and early summer following the vintage, before the earthy, rather rustic flavours begin to predominate.

I find the rosé more interesting (there is little red) which is produced, not from Pinot Noir, but from Pinot Gris. This grape, which also makes the so-called Tokay d'Alsace wine in Alsace, has an orange-brown skin when ripe, and produces a wine with a delicate salmon pink colour and a refreshing slightly spicy fruit. It is both individual and full of character – an interesting wine which is well worth seeking out.

Leading Reuilly Producer

DOMAINE CLAUDE LAFOND
Owner: Claude Lafond.
Surface Area under Vine: 25 ha.
Wines: Reuilly including La Raie, Clos des Messieurs (both white), La Grande Pièce (rosé) and Les Grandes Vignes (red).

Claude Lafond is by far the largest producer and most dynamic wine personality in the area. As well as his own expanding domaine, he is also a merchant and this side of the business is becoming more important. He is probably already responsible for a quarter of the entire Reuilly *appellation*. Happily, the wines, in all three colours, are very good.

Other Producers of note

DOMAINE GÉRARD CORDIER (LA FERTÉ), DOMAINE JACQUES RENAUDAT (DIOU) AND DOMAINE JEAN-MICHEL SORBE (PREUILLY). (SEE ALSO QUINCY.)

VIN DE L'ORLÉANAIS

Surface Area (1998): (Red and rosé) 119 ha; (white) 24 ha.

Production (1998): (Red and rosé) 4593 hl; (white) 934 hl.

Colour: Red, rosé and white.

Grape Varieties: (Red and rosé) Pinot Noir (Auvernat Rouge), Pinot Meunier (Gris Meunier) and Cabernet Franc (Noir Dur); (white) Chardonnay (Auvernat Blanc), Pinot Blanc and Pinot Gris (both called Auvernat Gris).

Maximum Yield: 45 hl/ha.

Minimum Alcohol Level: (Red) 9°; (white and rosé) 10°.

The Orléanais region, so important in the days of the Ancien Régime, has, like many French vineyards at the northern limits of cultivation, suffered from the twin blows of phylloxera and the easier access to northern France of the inevitably cheaper and more consistent wines of the Midi.

Today production is barely 1 per cent of what it was a century or more ago. The wine industry, however, is thriving, thanks to the tourists, and, no doubt, to the easily recognisable geographical name. It is a region of the *petit vigneron* who offers *dégustation libre* and *vente directe* to passersby. Reds, rosés and a small number of whites from a number of different grape varieties can be found, along with the local asparagus and other market garden produce. And the wines are by no means beneath consideration. In my experience of the Montigny wines (see below) they should be drunk early.

The region stretches, on both sides of the river Loire, from Mardie, east of Orléans, to Tavers, a kilometre or two downstream from Beaugency, and covers some twenty-five communes in the *département* of Loiret. Most of the vineyards lie on plateaux of limestone, clay, gravel or sand mixtures, a small distance away from the Loire itself, and exposed to the south and south-east. While some 400 hectares are authorized for the *appellation*, only about one-third is currently planted. Yet if the price of asparagus or *petits pois*, the main crops of the region, were to fall, I have no doubt we would see an abrupt change.

The Vin de L'Orléanais has been VDQS since 1951, and about 80 per cent of the wine comes from two co-operatives, Les Vignerons de La Grand' Maison at Mareau-aux-Prés and Covifruit at Olivet. The Montigny family at the Clos Saint-Fiacre domaine at Mareau-aux-Prés is one of the few local producers to export its wines.

COTEAUX DU GIENNOIS OR CÔTES DE GIEN

Surface Area (1998): (Red and rosé) 90 ha; (white) 50 ha.

Production (1998): (Red and rosé) 4799 hl; (white) 3333 hl.

Colour: Red, rosé and white.

Grape Varieties: (Red and rosé) Gamay Noir à Jus Blanc and Pinot Noir (the red must be a blend of the two); (white) Sauvignon Blanc and Chenin Blanc.

Maximum Yield: 45 hl/ha.

Minimum Alcohol Level: (Red) 9°; (white and rosé) 10°.

The Coteaux du Giennois or Côtes de Gien is a wine region which straddles the *départements* of Nièvre and Loiret, beginning at Cosne, where Pouilly-Fumé leaves off, and continuing north through sixteen communes until Gien. The best sector of vineyards lies east of Cosne itself, in the commune of Saint-Père, where the land contains both clay and limestone; further downstream the soil is richer and more alluvial and the banks are of sand and gravel, resulting in a wine that is thinner and less distinctive.

This is not a large *appellation*, and is a shadow of what it was in pre-phylloxera days, when, like the Vin de L' Orléanais, close proximity to Paris ensured a ready market for the wines. Most of the wines are vinified by the co-operative at Pouilly-sur-Loire.

Coteaux du Giennois Producers of note
DOMAINE ALAIN PAULAT (SAINT-PÈRE) AND DOMAINE POUPAT PÈRE & FILS (RIVOTTE).

TOURAINE

The Touraine, home of Vouvray, Montlouis and the great red Loire wines – Chinon, Bourgueil and Saint-Nicolas de-Bourgueil – broadly occupies the *départements* of Indre-et-Loire and Loir-et-Cher, with the city of Tours as its geographical focus.

This is the region of most of the grand palaces, castles and stately homes of the Loire Valley; of Chambord, a heavy, formal, Renaissance pile; Chenonceau, the intimate, unpretentious love-nest of Henry II and Diane de Poitiers; the classic symmetry of Cheverney; the mysterious, fairytale atmosphere of Ussé; the elegant charm of Azay-Le-Rideau; the doom-laden fortresses of Sully, Loches and Montreuil-Bellay; the feudal baronial keep of Chaumont; the abbey at Fontevraud, home of the tombs of the English Henry II, Eleanor of Aquitaine and Richard the Lionheart, as well as the most extraordinary Romanesque kitchen; and perhaps best of all, the castle at Chinon, now a ruin but once the largest and finest fortification in medieval France. The Touraine, or Jardin de la France, as Rabelais, the famous sixteenth-century French author, called it, is suffused with history, irradiated with flowers, particularly in the late spring, and fertile with vegetables and fruit, not only of the vine. It is a beautiful countryside of fine forests, some rather formal to English eyes and some particularly impressive gardens, such as that at Villandry.

Above all, the Touraine is a countryside of rivers, for the land is divided by the great tributaries of the Loire such as the Vienne, the Indre and the Cher. Along the banks of these fine waters lie the vineyards of the Touraine; from Candes-Saint-Martin in the west as far as Chambord in the east; from Valençay, Saint-Hippolyte and Richelieu in the south, to Neuillé-Pont-Pierre and Château-Renault in the north. Also included in the Touraine are the small *appellations* of Coteaux du Loir, Jasnières and Coteaux du Vendômois which lie further still to the north along the river Loir (le Loir), not to be confused with the Loire (la Loire) itself.

To the west, on the borders of Anjou/Saumur, are the great red wine areas, Chinon, Bourgueil and Saint-Nicolas-de-Bourgueil; in the centre the great white wine areas, Vouvray and Montlouis; to the south-east, particularly along the banks of the river Cher, are the vineyards which produce quantities of often excellent Sauvignon and Gamay de Touraine. Though the Touraine, in extent, appears larger than Anjou and Muscadet, in terms of surface area for wine production it is smaller than either. The vine has to share its place with other crops, and with grazing cattle.

VOUVRAY

Surface Area (1998): (still) 923 ha. For Vouvray *mousseux* **see page 291.**
Production (1998): (still) 46,913 hl. For Vouvray *mousseux* **see page 291.**
Colour: White.
Grape Variety: Chenin Blanc.
Maximum Yield: 52 hl/ha.
Minimum Alcohol Level: 11°.

Vouvray is the leading white wine of the Touraine and the largest of its major *appellations*. The village of Vouvray lies 10 kilometres east of the sprawling city of Tours on the north bank of the Loire. The vineyards are on a plateau above and behind the village itself, where many of its houses are wholly or partly built into the limestone rock-face. Underneath the plateau are a number of large and impressive cellars, originally hewn out to provide stone for the houses, and now providing ideal conditions for maturing wine. Vouvray has its origins in the Abbey of Saint-Martin in Tours, founded in AD 372, to whom the hamlet of Vobridius was given by Charlemagne in 887. Vines, however, were probably first planted in the region in Roman times, again by the clergy, and, as elsewhere in France, it was they who were the dominant influence in the production of wine right up until the time of the Revolution. Legend has it that it was Saint Martin himself who planted the first vines on the slopes above the village. Legend also has it that it was his donkey who, by eating many of the shoots of a particular row of vines, showed Saint Martin the benefits of pruning. Rabelais, born near Chinon and lover of all things sensual, wrote of Vouvray: 'Oh, gentle white wine. Upon my soul, this is a wine like taffeta.' Interestingly, he mentions elsewhere that the wine was made from Pineau, a local synonym for Chenin Blanc, the grape still used today.

Despite the proximity of Paris, and the presence of the aristocracy in their fine châteaux, much of the local production was exported to Holland shortly after the vintage, a state of affairs which persisted until the end of the nineteenth century. According to the writer, Jullien in 1816, most of the wine of the eastern Touraine was sold as Vouvray, whether it came from Vouvray itself or from further south along the banks of the Cher, a fraud still in practice over a hundred years later, according to Morton Shand, writing in the late 1920s.

As the Loire was a region almost entirely ignored by most of the nineteenth-century wine writers, it is difficult to decide precisely when and how the vinification of sweet wine evolved. Certainly by the end of the century the sweet wines were well known, and by this time, too, the area had already begun to make sparkling wines, a style which now makes up well over 50 per cent of the *appellation*.

Appellation contrôlée was conferred on Vouvray in 1936, and the land was restricted then to eight communes: Vouvray itself; Rochecorbon, Vernou-sur-Brenne, Sainte-Radegonde (now part of the suburbs of Tours), Chançay, Noisay, Reugny and part of Parçay-Meslay. The vineyards lie on the plateau above the N152 which runs immediately along the north bank of the river. This plateau is broken up by a number of small valleys running south into the Loire, among which are the Vallée Coquette, the valley of the river Brenne, which runs down through Vernou, the Vallée Chartier, and the smaller valleys of the Vaugondy, the Raye, the Cousse and the Vaux, small streams which themselves flow into the Brenne.

The soil is largely siliceous clay or calcareous clay. The best terrains are known as the *perruches*, and consist of large amounts of flint, particularly at the surface. The second best sites, or *aubuis*, are purer limestone. This is the *tuffe*, and it is from the subsoil under these that the marvellous cellars have been hewn. Both of these soils drain well and are excellent for producing quality Vouvray. The remaining vineyards, those with inferior aspect, or with a less-favoured soil containing more sand and gravel, are used to produce the wine destined to become *pétillant* or *mousseux*. In general, the best communes are those of Rochecorbon with a lot of *perruches* soil, Vouvray with *aubuis* and Vernou whose soil is more varied. The terrain further inland does not have the concentration of limestone sufficient to produce still wines of quality.

Vouvray is an *appellation* with many *lieux-dits*, but, unlike Sancerre, most of these are exclusive to a particular proprietor. The writer Brejoux in *Les Vins de la France* lists some forty-six, of which twenty-seven are in Vouvray and a further twelve in Rochecorbon. Those which are familiar, such as Clos Baudoin, Clos du Bourg and Clos Le Mont, I only know as wines of a single estate.

Vouvray is a versatile wine; albeit white only, it comes in a range of sweetness levels, from bone dry to *doux*, and can be still, *pétillant* (2.5 kg/cm^2 pressure) or *mousseux* (4.5 kg/cm^2). Moreover, within the still wines there are those which are ready for drinking almost as soon as they have been bottled and those more 'serious' wines which benefit from up to five or even ten years in bottle, even when made in the *sec* style.

All Vouvray is made exclusively from the Chenin Blanc or, as it is known locally, the Pineau de la Loire. This is a grape which normally produces a fairly firm, four-square wine, a bit hard in its youth and not taking kindly to the sulphuring essential in the *élevage* of a wine. Chenin appears to eat sulphur, and the taste lingers more than it does with other grapes, such as Muscadet or Chardonnay, for instance. Badly made, over-sulphured Vouvray has a smell and taste of wet wool or wet dogs. It is fortunate that a well made Vouvray ages well, for it may take years to throw off the sulphury taste. Once this has occurred, or if the wine is tasted young, in cask, the true flavour of the Chenin can be discerned – full, ripe, Victoria plummy or greengage with a hint of quince, camomile or mint (the French suggest

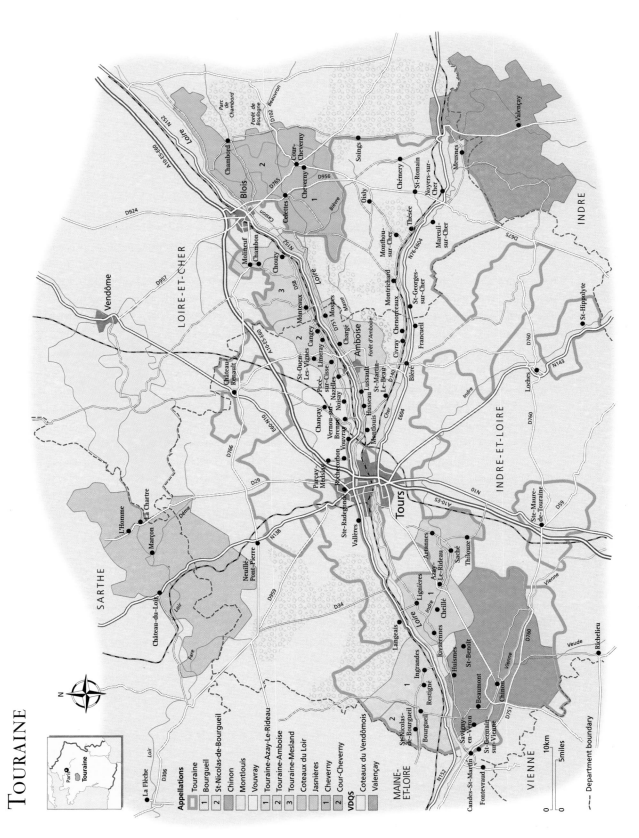

TOURAINE

Touraine

Appellations

Touraine
1 Bourgueil
2 St-Nicolas-de-Bourgueil
Chinon
Montlouis
Vouvray
1 Touraine-Azay-Le-Rideau
2 Touraine-Amboise
3 Touraine-Mesland
Jasnières
1 Coteaux du Loir
2 Cheverny
Cour-Cheverny

VDQS

Coteaux du Vendômois
Valençay

--- Department boundary

girofle or wallflower), with, if the wine be sweeter, overtones of flowers, honey, fruit salad and lanolin.

There are two styles of still Vouvray. More common, and the less expensive one, is a soft, young wine, bottled early for drinking soon, and fermented and matured entirely in tank. It is normally *demi-sec*, with about 15g to 25g of residual sugar. The wine is light in alcohol, and sweet only because the fermentation has been arrested, not because the grapes were over-ripe. This style is sold by the two local co-operatives and Loire *négociants*.

Behind this 'commercial' Vouvray lie the wines of the better growers. Here the wine is sweet or not according to the vineyard site and the weather leading up to the harvest. In less good years like 1994 most of the wine will be made *sec*; in better years more wine will be *demi-sec*. The *secs* will either be full, properly dry, and will need time to soften, or *sec-tendre*, a sort of off-dry (not as sweet as *demi-sec*) and plumper, more approachable when the wine is young. In exceptional years such as 1989 and 1990 these growers will have their patience rewarded. A proportion of the crop will be attacked by *Botrytis cinerea* or *pourriture noble* (noble rot), and some enchanting, honeyed, rich, semi-sweet wines, *moelleux* or even *doux* (luscious), will result. These Vouvrays are always big, firm wines, austere when young, masculine in character and long-lived.

Leading Vouvray Producers

DOMAINE ALLIAS PÈRE & FILS
Owners: Daniel & Dominique Allias.
Surface Area under Vine: 12 ha.
Wines: Vouvray including Clos du Petit-Mont.
Father and son, Daniel and Dominique Allias, live half way up the Vallée Coquette with vineyards on the plateau at the top of the slope. These dry wines mature quite early and have plenty of upfront fruit and a good racy finish. There is also good sparkling Vouvray. I loved their sweet wines of 1989 and 1990.

★ DOMAINE DES AUBUISIÈRES
Owner: Bernard Fouquet.
Surface Area under Vine: 20 ha.

Wines Vouvray including Le Bouchet, Le Marigny, Le Plan de Jean and Cuvée Alexandre.
Bernard and his father developed their own strain of Chenin in the 1980s and have had a singular success with it, the *sec* Le Marigny nearly always being one of the best of the vintage. The *demi-sec* Le Bouchet is regularly equally as fine in its own way. Le Plan de Jean and Cuvée Alexandre are *moelleux* wines.

CLOS BAUDOIN
Owner: Prince Philippe Poniatowski.
Surface Area under Vine: 13.5 ha.
Wines: Vouvray including Aigle d'Or (*mousseux*), Clos des Patys, Clos de L'Avenir and Clos Baudoin.
A former industrialist, Prince Poniatowski is a direct descendant of the last king of Poland. His Vouvray residence is built half inside the rock and half on top and must be damp, especially in the winter. I find his dry wines sometimes rather lean, too austere. He only makes sweeter wines in the very best years.

DOMAINE BOURILLON-DORLÉANS
Commune: Rochecorbon.
Owner: Frédéric Bourillon.
Surface Area under Vine: 18 ha.
Wines: Vouvray including La Coulée d'Or and Le Prestige Bleu (*mousseux*).
I have particularly liked the sweeter wines here in recent years (and can say a good word for the *mousseux* too). Much progress has been made here in the last decade.

DOMAINE MARC BRÉDIF
Commune: Rochecorbon.
Owner: Patrick de Ladoucette.
Surface Area under Vine: 20 ha.
Wines: Vouvray including *mousseux*.
This well-established Vouvray estate was taken over in 1980 after the retirement of Jacques Cartier, who had married a Brédif daughter, and the owner is now Patrick de Ladoucette of Pouilly-Fumé's Château de Nozet (see page 264). The firm now operates as a *négociant* as well as a domaine. It continues as a prime source of quality Vouvray, both sweet and dry.

VIGNOBLES BRISBARRE

Owner: Philippe Brisbarre.
Surface Area under Vine: 18 ha.
Wines: Vouvray including *mousseux*.

Gérard Brisbarre retired in the mid-1990s and has handed over responsibility to his son, Philippe. The dry wine is in the *sec-tendre* mode, flowery and fruity. There are good sweeter wines and sparkling examples.

DOMAINE LE CAPITAINE

Commune: Rochecorbon.
Owners: Alain & Christophe Le Capitaine.
Surface Area under Vine: 17 ha.
Wines: Vouvray.

This domaine has only been in existence since 1989, but it quickly established a reputation for quality and consistency. There are good dry wines, which keep well, and even better sweeter ones.

★ DOMAINE DIDIER CHAMPALOU

Owners: Didier & Catherine Champalou.
Surface Area under Vine: 10 ha.
Wines: Vouvray including Cuvée des Fondraux and Cuvée Cathérine Champalou.

The charming Champalous can now boast a domaine whose quality is second to none in the *appellation*, although it was only created as recently as 1984. The Cuvée des Fondraux is a *demi-sec* wine of brilliant intensity and harmony, a wine to be kept for a minimum of a decade (not that it isn't already delicious at five years!). The sweeter *cuvées*, such as Catherine Champalou, are splendidly honeyed – Didier Champalou waiting for proper botrytis to become established before picking the grapes – as well as being very elegant and well-balanced.

DOMAINE THIERRY COSME

Commune: Noisay.
Owner: Thierry Cosme.
Surface Area under Vine: 5 ha – Vouvray.

Thierry Cosme is another relatively recent arrival on the Vouvray scene, and being located at Noisay, tends to be overlooked. I admire his wines across the range and they last well. The Cabane Noire is particularly fine.

★★ CLOS NAUDIN

Owners: André & Philippe Foreau.
Surface Area under Vine: 12 ha.
Wines: Vouvray including Goutte d'Or and *mousseux*.

André Foreau's wines are the ultimate Vouvrays. The dry wines, seemingly austere in their youth, blossom out, given time, and are superbly food friendly. The *demi-secs* are also better after a decade. As for the *moelleux*! Foreau seemingly bottled cask by cask in 1989 and 1990, there were so many individual examples. The Goutte d'Or 1990 was as concentrated as a Tokaji Essenz.

CHÂTEAU GAUDRELLE

Owner: Alexandre Monmousseau.
Surface Area under Vine: 14 ha.
Wines: Vouvray including Clos le Vigneau, Réserve Passerillé and Vendange Tardive.

Alexandre's father headed the eponymous sparkling wine firm, based in Montrichard. His uncle Patrick is boss of another sparkling wine firm, Bouvet-Ladubay in Saumur. There are no really *sec* wines here – but the *demi-sec* is flowery and crisp. The nobly rotten Vendange Tardive is far more interesting than the Passerillé.

★★ DOMAINE HUET

Owner: Noël Pinguet.
Surface Area under Vine: 35 ha.
Wines: Vouvray including Le Haut-Lieu, Clos du Bourg and Le Mont.

Now in his eighties, Gaston Huet was the long-time mayor of Vouvray and the *appellation*'s representative on many a committee. He also successfully prevented the Train à Grande Vitesse railway line (TGV) from passing through the Vouvray vineyards. His son-in-law, Noël Pinguet, who took over in the early 1980s, has improved even on Huet's high standards as a winemaker, in particular by changing the culture of the vines to biodynamism. The three single vineyards, although situated close to one another, each produce quite distinct wines. To compare the steely, minerally Clos du Bourg with the intense, florally Le Haut-Lieu (both a touch more interesting than Le Mont) is a delight.

DOMAINE JARRY
Owner: Daniel Jarry.
Surface Area under Vine: 10 ha.
Wines: Vouvray including *mousseux*.

This domaine produces good dryish wine in the *sec-tendre* mode as well as very good sparkling wines.

DOMAINE FRANCIS MABILLE
Commune: Vernou-sur-Brenne.
Owner: Francis Mabille.
Surface Area under Vine: 13 ha.
Wines: Vouvray including *mousseux*.

Francis Mabille took over from his parents in 1986. I like the style of his wines. The dry examples need as much as five years to reach maturity but they have depth, and keep well.

DOMAINE PICHOT
LES LARMES DE BACCHUS
Owners: Jean-Claude & Christophe Pichot.
Surface Area under Vine: 15 ha.
Wines: Vouvray.

Father and son Pichot preside over a splendid series of cellars, one of which houses a medieval *pressoir*. These are good dry wines and even better sweet ones.

Other Producers of note
DOMAINE JEAN-CLAUDE AUBERT (VOUVRAY), DOMAINE D'ORFEUILLES/BERNARD HÉRIVAULT (REUGNY), DOMAINE FRANÇOIS PINON (VERNOU), DOMAINE DE LA ROBINIÈRE/VINCENT RAIMBAULT (CHANÇAY), DOMAINE LA SABOTERIE/CHRISTIAN CHAUSSARD (ROCHECORBON), DOMAINE DE VAUGONDY/PHILIPPE PERDRIAUX (VERNOU-SUR-BRENNE), DOMAINE VIGNEAU-CHEVREAU/ JEAN-MICHEL VIGNEAU (VERNOU) AND DOMAINE DU VIKING/LIONEL GAUTHIER (REUGNY).

MONTLOUIS

Surface Area (1998): (still) 189 ha. For Montlouis *mousseux* see page 291.
Production (1998): (still) 7255 hl. For Montlouis *mousseux* see page 291.

Colour: White.
Grape Variety: Chenin Blanc.
Maximum Yield: 52 hl/ha.
Minimum Alcohol Level: 10.5°.

Opposite Vouvray, on land bound by the Loire and Cher rivers, by the suburbs of Tours to the west and the Forêt d'Amboise to the east, is Montlouis, Vouvray's rather forgotten and smaller cousin. There is little to differentiate the wines of Montlouis from the less expensive, quicker-maturing wines of Vouvray. The soil is broadly the same, though sandier; the grape variety, the Chenin, is the same, and the mesoclimate can hardly be materially different. Indeed until *appellation contrôlée* was awarded in 1938, Montlouis wine was sold under the name of its illustrious neighbour, and fetched proportionately higher prices because of it. The imposition of AC, against the wishes of the local growers, suddenly leaving them with the problem of selling their wine under a totally unknown name, was a setback from which Montlouis has still not completely recovered. This disadvantage is compounded by the fact that the area is rather off the beaten track. If the tourist wants to visit Montlouis after Vouvray, he must go west to Tours to cross the river or continue on to Amboise and then double back. There is only a railway bridge across the Loire at Montlouis and I suspect most people leave Montlouis off their itinerary. Certainly I have found the growers rather surprised to receive a British wine buyer!

Montlouis has three communes: Montlouis itself, which lies almost directly across the Loire from Vouvray, Lussault, upstream towards Amboise, and Saint-Martin-Le-Beau, on the river Cher. These parish divisions are somewhat arbitrary. In essence, the vineyard area consists of a limestone-clay plateau which overlaps the three communes. This lies at some 60 to 50 metres in altitude and falls more sharply northwards towards the Loire, more gently towards the Cher. About half of the wine is made as *mousseux* or *pétillant* (see page 291).

Montlouis wine is some 10 per cent cheaper than Vouvray, and, as such, excellent value. Nearly all of it is dry (in a *sec-tendre* sense) or *demi-sec*. Few growers seek to risk all for the precarious and perhaps hard-to-sell possibility of making *moelleux* or *doux* wine. Many growers offer Touraine (Sauvignon, Gamay, Cabernet Franc) and/or *vin de pays* wines as well. Montlouis seems to be more prone to frost than Vouvray and both the 1991 and 1997 vintages were severely affected.

Leading Montlouis Producers

DOMAINE DE LA BIGARRIÈRE

Commune: Saint-Martin-Le-Beau.
Owner: Claude Boureau.
Surface Area under Vine: 5 ha.
Wines: Montlouis including Les Chaumodières and Les Maisonnettes, Montlouis *mousseux* and Touraine (red).

Standards can be a bit uneven here but I have had some very good wines from the 1989 and 1990 vintages, and again good 1995s, particularly the old-vine, *demi-sec* Les Chaumodières, and 1996s.

★ DOMAINE DELÉTANG

Commune: Saint-Martin-Le-Beau.
Owner: Olivier Delétang.
Surface Area under Vine: 22 ha.
Wines: Montlouis including Saint-Martin and Les Batisses, Montlouis *pétillant*, Cabernet de Touraine and Sauvignon de Touraine.

Three generations have preceded Olivier Delétang at this fine domaine. Go for the superior *cuvées* from the *lieu-dit* Les Batisses: these wines are steely in the dry version and luscious when *moelleux*. There are good generic Touraine wines too.

DOMAINE DE L'ENTRE-COEURS

Commune: Saint-Martin-Le-Beau.
Owner: Alain Lelarge.
Surface Area under Vine: 16 ha.
Wines: Montlouis including Clos de La Touche and Taille aux Loups.

Alain Lelarge, a trained oenologist, set up on his own in 1988, and has quickly established himself in the top rank of the *appellation*. These are very well-made, clean wines. He also makes good, sparkling wine.

DOMAINE CHRISTIAN GALLIOT

Commune: Saint-Martin-Le-Beau.
Owner: Christian Galliot.
Surface Area under Vine: 6 ha.
Wines: Montlouis.

Racy, fragrant, flowery wines are to be found here – the *sec* and *demi-sec* wines are nicely minerally. The *moelleux* will keep for a decade or more.

★ CLOS HABERT

Commune: Montlouis-sur-Loire.
Owner: François Chidaine.
Surface Area under Vine: 5 ha.
Wines: Montlouis including Taille du Loup, Les Choisilles and Cuvée de Lys, Montlouis *mousseux* and Gamay de Touraine.

Father and son, Yves and François Chidaine produce some of the best wines in Montlouis. They are bottled under either of their names, but essentially all the wines are from the same cellar. They keep well.

DOMAINE ALAIN JOULIN

Commune: Saint-Martin-Le-Beau.
Owner: Alain Joulin.
Surface Area under Vine: 6 ha.
Wines: Montlouis including Sélection Vieilles Vignes and Cuvée Cristal.

This good domaine makes a particularly good Vieilles Vignes wine which, in 1995, was a delicious *moelleux*. The Cuvée Cristal is a *vendange tardive* wine, picked at the end of November.

DOMAINE DES LIARDS

Commune: Saint-Martin-Le-Beau.
Owners: Berger Frères.
Surface Area under Vine: 21 ha.
Wines: Montlouis including Vieilles Vignes and Grains Nobles de Pineau and Montlouis *mousseux*.

There are two separate operations here: the wines of the family domaine which are well-made and built to last and a *négociant* business producing sparkling wine, both Montlouis and Touraine.

★ Domaine Moyer

Commune: Montlouis-sur-Loire.
Owner: Dominique Moyer.
Surface Area under Vine: 12 ha.
Wines: Montlouis including Cuvée Vieilles Vignes.

This well-established domaine is based in a very elegant Renaissance mansion built by the Duc de Choiseul in 1620. The wines are understated, very well balanced and splendidly elegant.

Domaine de La Taille aux Loups

Commune: Husseau.
Owner: Jacky Blot.
Surface Area under Vine: 7 ha.
Wines: Montlouis.

This domaine has already had an eventful history in its short life. It was created from scratch by ex-Barons de Rothschild employee Christian Prudhomme in 1988 and after he was forced to sell out in 1991 was rescued by Jacky Blot. The wines are quite markedly woody but not without quality.

Vouvray and Montlouis Vintages

1998 This is a less successful vintage for white wines, especially the sweeter versions, than for red. There was rather too much rain when the grapes for the dry wines were being collected, and the weather did not really improve sufficiently thereafter.

1997 A warm, indeed hot, end to the season, with the addition of a little rain to encourage the development of noble rot. These are soft, sweet, juicy wines for the medium term.

1996 This is a splendid vintage for sweet Vouvrays and Montlouis, the best since 1990. The wines have good backbone and acidity which well support the sweetness. They will keep very well.

1995 After a good summer September was uneven, but fine weather returned in October. A fine year for both dry and sweet wines and again they will keep well.

1994 Frost hit both Vouvray and Montlouis, the latter severely, and after a good summer the autumn was rainy. Not a successful year. Drink up.

1993 Very little really sweet wine, but there are some commendable *secs* and *demi-secs*. Drink soon.

1992 Again very few sweet wines. Some decent dry and *sec-tendre* wines were made but they tend to lack concentration. The wines are showing age now.

1991 Frost severely reduced the harvest. What was left was almost entirely dry and *demi-sec*. Drink up.

1990 A great vintage and large quantities of firm, rich, balanced *moelleux*, even *doux* wines were made. These are only just beginning to come round.

1989 Another great vintage. Some growers did not make the most of it, but learned from it and succeeded better in 1990 — which makes 1990 more satisfactory as a whole. But there are lots and lots of wines to be enjoyed here in the years to come. Like 1990, a vintage to keep.

1988 A splendid year for *sec* and *demi-sec*, and one which though delicious reasonably young, does not seem to be ageing. Many of the firmer wines can still be kept for some time.

Good, Earlier Vintages

These are the notable earlier vintages: 1985, 1982, 1976, 1975, 1971, 1969, 1964 and 1959.

Chinon and Bourgueil

While the Loire is generally thought of as predominantly a white wine region it does in fact produce almost as much red and rosé wine as white. There are good Pinot Noirs from Sancerre and some of its satellites and up-and-coming Cabernets from the Anjou and Saumur regions, but it is arguably in the Touraine that the reds are at their most interesting. A succession of fine vintages a decade ago (1988, 1989 and 1990) plus four very good recent years (1993, 1995, 1996, 1997 and, it would seem, 1998 also) and a new breed of enthusiastic young winemakers have shown the potential of Loire reds. That they are still inexpensive makes them even more worth seeking out.

The great red wines of the Touraine come from the western end near where the river Vienne flows into the Loire. The two largest and most important areas are Bourgueil, on the north bank of the Loire, along with the adjacent *appellation* of Saint-Nicolas-de-Bourgueil, and Chinon, from either bank of the Vienne. Adjacent to the west, but technically in Anjou rather than Touraine, lies Saumur and especially for good red wines Saumur-Champigny.

Grape Varieties

All these three increasingly popular and well-made red wines are made almost exclusively from the Cabernet Franc grape, locally known as the Breton. Cabernet Franc originates in Bordeaux, where in the Médoc it is a subsidiary to the Cabernet Sauvignon, and in Saint-Emilion, under the name of Bouchet, it is planted alongside the Merlot. Here in the Loire Valley, the Breton is pruned to one long cane, with seven or eight buds (the *guyot simple* method) and produces a wine which everyone from Rabelais in the sixteenth century onwards has compared to raspberries.

The Breton is a hardy but relatively late-maturing plant. This might seem a disadvantage in a northerly red wine district such as this, but the variety is resistant to rot and so can take advantage of Indian summers, giving a must of good colour, alcohol and fruit, with a tannin content which is not too hard or unyielding. The result is a wine which does not take too long to mature. Cabernet Franc can even be made into a *vin de l'année*, for drinking cool in the summer following the vintage.

There are two hypotheses for Cabernet Franc's local name of Breton. The first story relates how Cardinal Richelieu sent his *intendant*, or local administrator, to Bordeaux in 1631 to bring back a better grape variety than the then widely planted Pineau d'Aunis and Cot (otherwise the Malbec of Bordeaux and Auxerrois of Cahors). The intendant was the Abbé Breton.

This story is flatly contradicted by references in Rabelais' *Gargantua*, written a century earlier in 1534 – 'This excellent Breton wine, which doesn't come from Brittany but from this fine countryside of Véron' (the Chinon area). The late Monsieur Ory, president of the Saint-Nicolas-de-Bourgueil viticultural syndicate as well as mayor of the village, considered that the name did originate from Brittany, for the Bretons were Bourgueil's principal customers. There was also a vineyard on the Presqu'Ile de Rhuys, in the Morbihan in south Brittany, whose fruity wine was said to resemble that of the Touraine and where the local monastery was of the same order, the Benedictines, as that of Bourgueil. What is still to be established is how the vine came to be transplanted from Aquitaine, but it is said to have been first planted in the Loire Valley by the Abbot of Bourgueil, Bauly, in about 1090.

The standard of the Touraine reds has increased immeasurably in recent years. A generation ago it was only in the best of years, in 1964, for example, which is still well remembered as a classic, that good wine was made. In lesser years the wine was thin and astringent, lacking an essential element of fatness and richness, and so lacking charm. It aged badly, tending to attenuate and dry out. Vinification methods have improved. Nowadays the *cuvaison*, the time the wine macerates on its skins, is shorter, the temperature is better controlled, being warmed if necessary to extract a maximum of fruit as quickly as possible, and the wines are, as a result, more fruity, more supple, more attractive; above all, more consistent. Touraine reds can now be enjoyed in every vintage, and one can look forward to wines for keeping in most years.

CHINON

Surface Area (1998): (Red and rosé) 2074 ha; (white) 22 ha.

Production (1998): (Red and rosé) 111,119 hl; (white) 1083 hl.

Colour: Red, rosé and white.

Grape Varieties: (Red and rosé) Cabernet Franc and Cabernet Sauvignon; (white) Chenin Blanc.

Maximum Yield: 55 hl/ha.

Minimum Alcohol Level: 9.5°.

Wine has been made in the Chinon area since Gallo-Roman times, as the unearthing of a small Gallic vase in the shape of a bunch of grapes has shown. The town of Chinon has been a strategic point since at least then, the existing castle being constructed on Roman fortifications, largely during the time of the Plantagenet king of England, Henry II in the twelfth century. Henry and his turbulent family based themselves in Chinon rather than in England, and both he and his son, Richard the Lionheart, died in the castle and are buried in nearby Fontevraud. No doubt the regular presence of the English court ensured a ready market for the local wine, a taste which they took back with them to England under King John 'Lackland' when Chinon was lost, after an eight-month siege, to the French king, Philippe-Auguste in 1205.

Two centuries later, Chinon castle was again to become a focal point. At France's lowest ebb in the Hundred Years War against the English, the dauphin Charles had brought his court to Chinon and summoned the Estates General from the central and southern parts of the country still faithful to him to vote money for the relief of Orléans, besieged by the English and the Burgundians under Lord Salisbury.

With his confidence restored first by the faith and consequently by the successful exploits of Joan of Arc, Charles and his army were able to turn the course of the war, and eventually to drive the English out of most of France. The dauphin's revival began with the well-known story, set in Chinon castle, of how Joan recognised the king, though without his finery, and lurking among his courtiers. Later the castle was allowed to fall into ruins. Cardinal Richelieu had much of it demolished in order to build the town named after him 40 kilometres to the south. For nearly three centuries the castle remained in the family of his descendants who neglected it. Today the castle is owned by the state and is slowly being restored.

The wine of Chinon is inseparable from the sixteenth-century author Rabelais. He was born at La Devinière, a few kilometres to the south of the town, and spent his childhood in Chinon, interrupted only when he left to complete his studies in Angers and Montpellier. His books are liberally sprinkled with references to the wines, and by way of response the town has erected a statue of him, and the local wine promotional organisation is called Les Entonneurs Rabelaisiens de Chinon. (An *entonneur* is someone who sings the praises of someone or something.)

Chinon lies on the river Vienne, some 12 kilometres before this river reaches the Loire at Candes, and is more of a Vienne wine than a Loire wine. The vineyards cover some 2000 hectares, double the area of twenty years ago, and run from the communes of Savigny, Avoine, Beaumont, Huismes and Saint-Benoît, north of Chinon, all the way along the north bank of the Vienne, through the villages of Cravant, Panzoult, Avon-Les-Roches and Crouzilles. Crossing the river, the *appellation* returns along the south bank through Theneuil, L'Ile-Bouchard, Tavant, Sazilly, Anche, Ligré, Marçay, Rivière and La Roche-Clermault.

The Chinon vines are planted in a number of soils. Closest to the Vienne the terrain is sand mixed with gravel. From here come light wines, short lived and for early drinking. Further up the slope the soil has more clay in it, mixed with sand, gravel and limestone: medium-weight wines, with depth and finesse. From the limestone slopes come wines with the most weight and character, full-bodied wines which need five years to mature and will keep, in the best years, for twenty. These *vins de tuffe* are the great Chinons, but they are rare and expensive, and, dare I say it, only worth it in an exceptional autumn when it has been dry and sunny enough to concentrate fully the ripeness of the fruit. Happily (see page 276), there have been plenty of these recently. In most years, and with most growers, a judicious blend of the upper slopes and the plateau produces the best wine; from the lower slopes a delightful carafe wine for the local restaurants and the bistros of Paris is made, to be drunk in the year after the vintage.

Apart from Rabelais and his raspberries, what does Chinon taste like, and how does it differ from Bourgueil? Chinon for me *does* have a taste of raspberries, but this is mixed with other fruit, strawberries and mulberries, blackcurrants and plums, overlaid with a slightly spurious perfumed quality I associate with violet cachous. When you get a very dense Chinon for ageing other flavours and spices intrude, including chocolate and earth (which can be clean or rustic depending on the winemaker). Above all, Chinon is, or should be, a supple wine; essentially, however youthful and muscular, a wine with a soft centre. Bourgueil wines are more austere, more sinewy, normally fuller. I find Bourgueil wines less appealing, and also less successful in the lesser years. This might be my limited experience of growers; it might be the soil or mesoclimate; it may also be a failure of the Bourgueil growers to adapt their vinification to the production of a lighter, more supple wine when the condition of the fruit warrants it.

Unlike Bourgueil and Saint-Nicolas, Chinon can be rosé and white, as well as red. In practice there is very little of either of these colours.

Leading Chinon Producers

DOMAINE PHILIPPE ALLIET
Commune: Cravant-Les-Coteaux.
Owner: Philippe Alliet.
Surface Area under Vine: 9 ha.
Wines: Chinon including Vieilles Vignes and Coteaux de Noiré.

Philippe Alliet's wines are not for those seeking muscle and weight in their wines but for those with a taste for cedary elegance, subtlety and balance. His vines are situated on clay and gravel, even sand, not limestone. There are three *cuvées* – a fairly simple, young-vine wine; a Vieilles Vignes, aged in one-year-old wood, nicely fat and concentrated; and the Coteaux de Noire, which has had twelve months' ageing in somewhat newer oak. This is a rich, plump, oaky wine with good depth and well worth seeking out.

★ DOMAINE BERNARD BAUDRY & FILS
Commune: Cravant-Les-Coteaux.
Owners: Bernard & Mathieu Baudry.
Surface Area under Vine: 25 ha.
Wines: Chinon including Les Grézeaux and La Croix Boissée.

Matthieu, the *fils*, has recently joined his father at this well-respected domaine. The style here is for elegance and finesse, rather than muscle, and this is well expressed both in the Cuvée Les Grézeaux, from gravel soil and matured in 600-hectolitre barrels, and in the more sizeable La Croix Boissée, from the limestone slopes. A good address.

★★ DOMAINE & MAISON COULY-DUTHEIL
Owners: Pierre, Jacques & Bertrand Couly.
Surface Area under Vine: 83 ha.
Wines: Chinon including Les Gravières, Baronnie Madelaine, Domaine René Couly, Domaine de La Diligence, Clos de L'Olive and Clos de L'Echo, and Saumur-Champigny.

Couly-Dutheil is a *négociant* as well as a grower, but one of the best sources of Chinon in the area, as it has been for several generations. They buy in wine, of course, and this forms the base for the Gravières and the superior Baronnie Madelaine wines. Their vineyards are picked by hand. The wines are then matured in 50-hectolitre oak barrels and range from the Domaine René Couly through the fruity and feminine Domaine de La Diligence to the firmer, richer Clos de L'Olive, from a 3-hectare site with limestone-based soil between Chinon and Cravant-Les-Coteaux. The top wine comes from the slightly more clayey, 17-hectare Clos de L' Echo vineyard in Chinon itself: it is a powerful wine which in the best vintages needs a decade to mature.

★★ DOMAINE CHARLES JOGUET
Commune: Sazilly.
Owners: Charles Joguet & Alain Delaunay.
Surface Area under Vine: 34 ha.
Wines: Chinon including Cuvée Terroir, Clos de La Cure, Varennes du Grand Clos, Clos du Chêne Vert and Clos de La Dioterie.

Charles Joguet was one of the first growers in the area to start bottling his own wines, rather than selling in bulk to the *négociants*, and certainly the first to isolate the wines of different parcels separately. Now he is in semi-retirement and the day-to-day cellar jobs are carried out by Alain Delaunay. The wines range from non-oak-aged *primeur cuvées* from the young vines to the Clos du Chêne Vert, from a 2-hectare plot made up of a mixture of clay, chalk and silica – and the venerable 900-year-old tree, after which the vineyard is named, still exists there – and the Clos de La Dioterie, from eighty-year-old vines. These are serious wines, rich, concentrated and elegant and some of Chinon's best.

DOMAINE LE MOULIN-À-TAN

Commune: Cravant-Les-Coteaux.
Owner: Pierre Sourdais.
Surface Area under Vine: 25 ha.
Wines: Chinon including Cuvée Tradition and
Cuvée Stanislaus.

This domaine makes three *cuvées*: unoaked Les Rosiers for early drinking, from young vines located on sand and gravel; Cuvée Tradition, a blend of vines from the plain and the slopes, which is a good meaty example with plenty of depth; and finally, full, rich and classy Cuvée Stanislaus, named after a great-grandfather.

DOMAINE DE LA ROCHE HONNEUR

Commune: Savigny-en-Véron.
Owner: Stéphane Mureau.
Surface Area under Vine: 15 ha.
Wines: Chinon including Cuvée de Pacques,
Cuvée Rubis and Diamant Prestige.

There are three *cuvées* here. The Cuvée de Pacques, or 'Easter' blend, is from young vines: ripe and soft it is for early drinking like a Beaujolais (serve it cool, too); Cuvée Rubis, from older vines on a more limestone rocky soil, is plump and succulent: it is matured in wood, as is the richer and more substantial Diamant Prestige, a complex, rather fine Chinon.

DOMAINE WILFRID ROUSSE

Commune: Savigny-en-Véron.
Owner: Wilfrid Rousse.
Surface Area under Vine: 11 ha.
Wines: Chinon including Cuvée Pacques, Cuvée
Terroir and Cuvée Vieilles Vignes.

The Cuvée Pacques, or 'Easter' blend, is for drinking young. More serious is the oak-aged Cuvée Terroir. The Vieilles Vignes, which has its malolactic fermentation in barrel, as is the fashion nowadays, I find wholly admirable.

DOMAINE SERGE & BRUNO SOURDAIS

Owners: Serge & Bruno Sourdais.
Surface Area under Vine: 19 ha.
Wines: Chinon including Le Logis de La

Bouchardière, Cuvée du Chêne Vert, Cuvée
Le Clos and Cuvée Les Cornuelles Vieilles Vignes.
Father and son Serge and Bruno Sourdais produce several different *cuvées*. The Logis de La Bouchardière is a stylish basic example and the Chêne Vert is from young vines but a better *terroir*. The Clos is from further up the slope and on very flinty soil and the fine, old-vine *cuvée*, named after the flat limestone, is rich, concentrated and oaky.

Other Producers of note

DOMAINE DE LA BONNELIÈRE FROM MAISON PIERRE PLOUZEAU (LA ROCHE-CLERMAULT), DOMAINE PHILIPPE BROCOURT (RIVIÈRE), DOMAINE GUY COTON (CROUZILLES), CHÂTEAU DE LA GRILLE (CHINON), DOMAINE NICOLAS GROSBOIS (PANZOULT), DOMAINE PATRICK LAMBERT (CRAVANT-LES-COTEAUX), DOMAINE DE LA NOBLAIE/PIERRE MANZAGOL-BILLARD (LIGRÉ), DOMAINE DE LA PERRIÈRE/JEAN & CHRISTOPHE BAUDRY (CRAVANT-LES-COTEAUX), DOMAINE PIERRE PRIEUR (SAVIGNY-EN-VÉRON), DOMAINE DU RAIFAULT (SIC)/ JEAN-MAURICE RAFFAULT (SAVIGNY-EN-VÉRON), DOMAINE OLGA RAFFAULT (SAVIGNY-EN-VÉRON) AND CHÂTEAU DE VAUGAUDRY (CHINON).

BOURGUEIL AND SAINT-NICOLAS-DE-BOURGUEIL

Surface Area (1998): (Bourgueil) 1292 ha;
(Saint-Nicolas-de-Bourgueil) 929 ha.
Production (1998): (Bourgueil) 71,186 hl;
(Saint-Nicolas-de-Bourgueil) 53,572 hl.
Colour: Red.
Grape Varieties: Cabernet Franc and Cabernet
Sauvignon.
Maximum Yield: 55 hl/ha.
Minimum Alcohol Level: 9.5°.

North and west of Chinon, on the north bank of the Loire, lie the *appellations* of Bourgueil and Saint-Nicolas-de-Bourgueil. Those who make wine in Saint-Nicolas will argue that their wine is superior, more elegant and delicate to straight Bourgueil. There is, in truth, no discernible difference between the two. The soils are the same and the *encépagement* identical – Cabernet Franc almost exclusively, though Cabernet Sauvignon is also authorised. Saint-Nicolas used to have a more restricted yield and is marginally more expensive. According to the late Alexis Lichine, wine writer and merchant, the separate *appellation* for Saint-Nicolas is explained by the fact that when the INAO was codifying the Touraine region, the mayor of Saint-Nicolas-de-Bourgueil, Monsieur Ory, was the largest vineyard holder and successfully lobbied for his own communal *appellation*.

Bourgueil is spread over the communes of Saint-Nicolas-de-Bourgueil, Bourgueil, Benais, Restigné, Ingrandes and Saint-Patrice, on a straight west-east line parallel to the Loire, plus the less important communes of Chouze and La Chapelle on the edge of the river. As in Chinon the soil varies between sand (*sables limoneux*), locally known as *varennes*, nearest to the Loire, gravels of various sizes in the centre, and limestone *tuffe* over which is flinty clay on the higher slopes. Many growers have cellars underneath their vineyards in old quarries. The summit of the slope is densely covered with trees and shrub, giving the vineyards protection from the north.

If it is difficult to distinguish between Saint-Nicolas and the rest of Bourgueil, and indeed as in Chinon, it is easier to tell the difference between the wines from different soils. Again, most growers have vineyards on two or more sites, and make a blend between them, or produce a *primeur* wine from the lighter soil, and a more substantial wine from the *tuffe*.

Leading Bourgueil Producers

★ DOMAINE YANNICK AMIRAULT
Owner: Yannick Amirault.
Surface Area under Vine: 16 ha.
Wines: Bourgueil, including Les Quartiers and Le Grand Clos, and Saint-Nicolas-de-Bourgueil including Les Malgagnes.
The quiet, *sympathique* Yannick Amirault is based in Bourgueil itself, but his domaine includes a very

seductive, old-vine wine from Saint-Nicolas-de-Bourgueil called Les Malgagnes. There are several Bourgueil *cuvées*: La Source (from young vines), and then three different superior wines: Les Quartiers, from old vines on the limestone *tuffe*; Le Grand Clos, from old vines on clay-sandstone soil; and La Petite Cave, old vines on a clay-sandstone over limestone soil. Each is stylish and subtly different, bottled without filtration. In general, if one is forced to generalise, Saint-Nicolas produces a lighter, more high-toned aromatic wine than Bourgueil.

DOMAINE AUDEBERT & FILS
Owners: Jean-Claude & François Audebert.
Surface Area under Vine: 41 ha.
Wines: Saint-Nicolas-de-Bourgueil including La Conférie, Bourgueil including Domaine du Grand Clos and La Marquise, and Chinon including Les Perruches.
A merchant and this only for Touriane and Anjou wines, Audebert relies on its own domaine for the three local wines, storing them, in an old-fashioned manner, mainly in old *demi-muids* rather than new barrels. But at the top levels these are good wines.

★ DOMAINE CATHÉRINE ET PIERRE BRETON
Commune: Restigné.
Owners: Cathérine & Pierre Breton.
Surface Area under Vine: 13.5 ha.
Wines: Bourgueil including Les Galichets, Sénéchal, Nuits d'Ivresse, Grand Mont and Perrières and Chinon including Beaumont and Cuvée Picasses.
As well as their domaine at Restigné, the Bretons also look after 5 hectares of vineyards at Beaumont in the Chinon *appellation*. All the vineyards are farmed organically and the wines made in a neat modern cellar adjacent to their house, and stored in a mixture of stainless steel, *foudres* and small oak barrels, of which a percentage is new in the top *cuvées*.

There are a number of the top wines, the wines being made separately according to the different soil types and the age of the vines. The rich and plump Cuvée Les Galichets comes from old vines on gravel; the Clos Sénéchal comes from thirty-year-old vines on marl and is ripe, elegant, persistent. The curiously termed Cuvée Nuits d'Ivresse ('Drunken or passionate nights') is made without using any sulphur dioxide. It is firm and solid but not without richness. Grand Mont is perhaps the biggest of the Breton Bourgueils, but the Cuvée des Perrières (from fifty-year-old vines on clay-sandstone soil) is perhaps the lushest wine. A fine domaine.

Domaine de La Butte
Owners: Gilbert & Didier Griffon.
Surface Area under Vine: 14 ha.
Wines: Bourgueil.

The splendidly-sited Butte vineyard produces one of Bourgueil's best wines – a wine of gentle oak, powerful flavours and real elegance.

Domaine de La Chevalerie
Commune: Restigné.
Owner: Pierre Caslot.
Surface Area under Vine: 18 ha.
Wines: Bourgueil including Cuvée du Peu Muleau, Cuvée La Bretesche, Cuvée Les Galichets and Cuvée Vieilles Vignes.

There have been Caslots in Bourgueil since 1640. Pierre seems to be the best of the current generation. There are several wines corresponding to different *lieux-dits* and soils, progressively fuller and more intense as the proportion of *tuffe* increases. The old-vine *cuvée* is rich and masculine and needs a minimum of seven years' ageing.

★ Domaine Pierre-Jacques Druet
Commune: Benais.
Owner: Pierre-Jacques Druet.
Surface Area under Vine: 22 ha.
Wines: Bourgueil including Cent Boisselées, Grands Monts and Vaumoreau, and Chinon including Clos de Danzay.

Pierre-Jacques Druet is the leading grower in Benais and also produces a little Chinon (from old vines in the Clos de Danzay). Yields are very low here, the grapes

destemmed and the wine made by regular punching down (*pigeage*) during fermentation. Thereafter it can be variously stored: in stainless steel for the young-vine *cuvée* Cent Boisselées, in 700-litre barrels, some new, for the Grands Monts and in normal-sized, 300-litre barrels, again some new, for three years, for the old-vine Vaumoreau. This is a spectacular wine: rich, fat yet minerally and very individual. Given the appropriate vintage you could keep this wine for a decade or more.

★ Domaine de La Lande
Owners: Marc & François Delaunay.
Surface Area under Vine: 14 ha.
Wines: Bourgueil including Cuvée des Pins, Cuvée des Graviers and Cuvée Prestige.

The estate of Marc Delaunay and his son François includes 1 hectare of vines in Saint-Nicolas-de-Bourgueil and 1.5 hectares in Chinon, and they produce very well-mannered, silky-smooth Bourgueils which you could mistake for Chinons. The Saint-Nicolas is for early drinking, sooner than the basic Bourgueil *cuvée*, which, despite being from young vines, has structure and succulence. There are three superior wines: Cuvée des Pins, Cuvée des Graviers (not produced in 1997 because of hail problems) and the old-vine Cuvée Prestige: profound, ample and rich. A very good source.

Domaine Nau Frères
Commune: Ingrandes-de-Touraine.
Owners: Abel, Bertrand & Patrice Nau.
Surface Area under Vine: 20 ha.
Wines: Bourgueil including Les Varennes, Les Blottières and Vieilles Vignes.

'We want to bring out all the fruit', say the Nau brothers. The wines are soft and ample and stylish, but perhaps could be more concentrated.

Domaine des Raguenières
Commune: Benais.
Owners: D Maître-Gadaux & R Viemont.
Surface Area under Vine: 18 ha.
Wines: Bourgueil including Cuvée Clos de La Cure.

The *élevage* of these wines takes place in 600-litre newish barrels, double the normal size. The wines are stylish and nicely substantial.

Other Producers of note

DOMAINE CASLOT-BOURDIN (LA CHAPELLE-SUR-LOIRE), DOMAINE DE LA CHANTELEUSERIE/THIERRY BOUCARD (BENAIS), DOMAINE DU CHÊNE ARRAULT/CHRISTOPHE DESCHAMPS (BENAIS), DOMAINE DES FORGES/JEAN-YVES BILLET (RESTIGNÉ), DOMAINE DE LA GAUCHERIE/RÉGIS MUREAU (INGRANDES-DE-TOURAINE) AND DOMAINE DU ROCHOUARD/GUY DUVEAU (BOURGUEIL).

Leading Saint-Nicolas-de-Bourgueil Producers

★ DOMAINE DU BOURG

Owners: Jean-Paul & Frédéric Mabileau & Fils.
Surface Area under Vine: 15 ha.
Wines: Saint-Nicolas-de-Bourgueil including Cuvée Les Gravières, Cuvée Prestige, Cuvée Rouillères and Cuvée Eclipse.

The son Frédéric has now assumed responsibility at this domaine, and half the wines have his name on the label. Things were good in the father's days, but have reached an even higher level recently, with some new wood now used in the top *cuvées* such as the Cuvée Prestige and the Cuvée Eclipse. Some consider Saint-Nicolas wines to be lighter than Bourgueils but these ones show plenty of body as well as depth.

DOMAINE MAX COGNARD-TALUAU

Owner: Max Cognard.
Surface Area under Vine: 7 ha.
Wines: Saint-Nicolas-de-Bourgueil including Cuvée des Malgagnes and Bourgueil.

This dependable domaine produces fairly sturdy wines. The Cuvée des Malgagnes, from selected parcels of vines and older ones at that, is worth the extra cost.

★ VIGNOBLE DE LA JARNOTERIE

Owners: Jean-Claude Mabileau & Didier Rozé.
Surface Area under Vine: 22 ha.

Wines: Saint-Nicolas-de-Bourgueil including Cuvée Concerto and Cuvée de L'An 2000.

Didier Rozé, Mabileau's son-in-law, is now in charge here. The wines are aged in 450-hectolitre-old *tonneaux* (a sort of magnum-sized barrel). The superior *cuvée*, called Concerto, comes from fifty-to-eighty-year-old vines and is firm, rich yet velvety-smooth. Cuvée de L'An 2000 was produced in 1996 for the millennium. It is a delicious wine and and will be at its peak in 2000.

★ DOMAINE JOËL TALUAU

Owner: Joël Taluau & Thierry Foltzenlogel.
Surface Area under Vine: 10 ha.
Wines: Saint-Nicolas-de-Bourgueil including Cuvée Vieilles Vignes.

Joël Taluau could be termed the grandfather of Saint-Nicolas-de-Bourgueil as this estate was the first to bottle its own wine. Taluau is now helped by his son-in-law, Thierry Foltzenlogel. They eschew using oak and bottle early direct from the stainless steel vat, commenting that 'We want to bring out all the fruit.' There are three *cuvées*, of which the Vieilles Vignes, naturally, has the most depth.

Other Producers of note

DOMAINE DE LA COTELLERAIE-VALLÉE/CLAUDE VALLÉE, DOMAINE PASCAL LORIEUX AND CLOS DES QUARTERONS/ CLAUDE & THIERRY AMIRAULT. SEE ALSO BOURGUEIL PAGE 280.

Chinon, Bourgueil and Saint-Nicolas-de-Bourgueil Vintages

1998 Weather conditions during the flowering were uneven, but a fine, hot August provided the base for a successful vintage which even some rain at the end of September could not undermine. So far it is early days.

1997 Not as fine as 1996 but still a very good vintage, picked in warm conditions. The wines are round, plump and supple and will be ready in the medium term.

1996 A great vintage: the best since 1990. Warm sunny days at the end of September, interrupted by cool nights, have produced full, concentrated wine with good grip. For the long term.

1995 Another fine vintage. July and August were hot, September unsettled, but nevertheless the wines are rich and full and deeply coloured. They will last well.

1994 A short crop, badly affected by rain in September, after a very hot and dry summer. Some good wines, but the overall picture is patchy. Now ready: drink soon.

1993 A cool September, with rain at times, did not promise much. In fact the vintage has turned out very satisfactorily. Nice firm wines which are only now beginning to come round.

1992 A prolific crop, producing consequently diffuse wine. Now ready: drink up.

1991 A very small vintage as a result of frost. There was then rain at the end of the harvest. Best forgotten though there are some exceptions.

1990 and 1989 Two great vintages. Both abundant and the product of early harvests after long, hot summers: the wines full, rich and succulent. The 1989s are perhaps the more luscious, the 1990s firmer and longer-lasting. Still plenty of life left.

1988 Yet another fine year, but one in total contrast in style to the two above: leaner and more classic, less voluptuous. A smaller crop shows in the concentration of the wines. Still vigorous.

GOOD, EARLIER VINTAGES
1986, 1985, 1976, 1971, 1969, 1964 and 1959.

TOURAINE-MESLAND

Surface Area (1998): (Red and rosé) 105 ha; (white) 14 ha.

Production (1998): (Red and rosé) 5752 hl; (white) 641 hl.

Colour: Red, rosé and white.

Grape Varieties: (Red) Gamay Noir à Jus Blanc, Cabernet Franc and Cot; (rosé) Gamay Noir à Jus Blanc, Cot and Cabernet Franc; (white) Chenin Blanc, Sauvignon Blanc and Chardonnay.

Maximum Yield: (Red and rosé) 55 hl/ha; (white) 60 hl/ha.

Minimum Alcohol Level: (Red and rosé) 9.5°; (white) 10°.

Between Amboise and Blois, on the north bank of the Loire, lies Mesland, the first of three small vineyard areas (the others are Amboise and Azay-Le-Rideau) which have been singled out from generic Touraine wine. These three communes can add their name to the Touraine *appellation* provided they have an extra half a degree of alcohol. Touraine-Mesland is the largest of the three. Why these three should have been so selected seems somewhat arbitrary, for there seems neither a significant increase in quality between these and 'ordinary' Touraines – there are poor and exciting growers on both sides – nor is there a particularly special or individual style of wine. No doubt political pressure and good relations with the powers in the INAO have played their part and the reward to the growers of Mesland, Amboise and Azay is an extra *franc* or two per bottle.

The vines producing AC Touraine-Mesland lie in the communes of Mesland itself, Chambon, Chouzy, Molineuf, Monteaux and Onzain, on a soil which is predominantly clay mixed with sand or limestone.

Since 1994, while the white wines can continue to be made from just Chenin Blanc, as well as a blend of the three recommended varieties, producers have been encouraged to make the red as a blend with a minimum of 60 per cent Gamay. The red wine makes up the bulk of the production.

The Onzain co-operative produces about one-third of all Touraine-Mesland. The quality of their wine has been variable and with their resources it should be more consistently of high quality. Other Mesland producers are equally inconsistent.

Leading Touraine-Mesland Producers

CLOS DE LA BRIDERIE
Commune: Monteaux.
Owner: François Girault.
Surface Area under Vine: 12 ha.
Wines: Touraine-Mesland (red, rosé and white).
The Giraults run their estate on biodynamic lines, but with oak casks in the cellar. There is an interesting barrel-fermented white, made with the maximum 15 per cent Chardonnay allowed by the *appellation* and with

the lees roused periodically (*bâtonnage*). The red, made from one-third each Cabernet Franc, Cot and Gamay, is ample proof that this *encépagement* (a recent innovation) can work very well.

CHÂTEAU GAILLARD

Commune: Mesland.
Owner: Béatrice & Vincent Girault.
Surface Area under Vine: 40 ha.
Wines: Touraine-Mesland including Cuvée
Vieilles Vignes (red) and Crémant de La Loire.

Béatrice and Vincent Girault, the son of François Girault above, bought this estate in 1984, and have since transformed the vineyard to biodynamic methods. There is no small wood used in the cellar as the Giraults believe that it adds nothing to the wine. I think it would improve the Vieilles Vignes *cuvée* even more.

Other Producers of note

DOMAINE DE LUSQUENEAU/LATREUILLE FAMILY (MESLAND), DOMAINE DU PARADIS/PHILIPPE SOUCIOU (ONZAIN) AND DOMAINE DES TERRES NOIRES/REDIGUÈRE BROTHERS (ONZAIN).

TOURAINE-AMBOISE

Surface Area (1998): (Red and rosé) 184 ha; (white) 24 ha.
Production (1998): (Red and rosé) 10,751 hl; (white) 1332 hl.
Colour: Red, rosé and white.
Grape Varieties: (Red and rosé) Gamay Noir Jus à Blanc, Cabernet Franc, Cabernet Sauvignon and Cot; (white) Chenin Blanc.
Maximum Yield: (Red and rosé) 55 hl/ha; (white) 60 hl/ha.
Minimum Alcohol Level: (Red and rosé) 9.5°; (white) 10°.

Michel Debré, mayor in 1954, is credited with the creation of the separate *appellation* of Touraine-Amboise halfway between Tours and Blois. This is a small but expanding region on both sides of the river, centred

round the bustling town of Amboise which is dominated by its impressive castle overlooking the river.

Again, like Mesland, its neighbour slightly upstream, the region is more noticeable for other tourist attractions than its wine, for the castle at Amboise truly *vaut le voyage*, and the Leonardo da Vinci museum – the great man was invited here by François I in 1515 and died at Amboise four years later – is equally worth a visit.

The *appellation* covers eight communes (Amboise, Chargé, Cangey, Limeray, Mosnes, Nazelles, Pocé-sur-Cisse and Saint-Buen-Les-Vignes) and the same grapes, grown roughly in the same proportions and regulations, are authorized as in Mesland, except that only Chenin is allowed for the white. Interesting red wines are now made with a mixture of Gamay, Cabernet Franc and Cot. This blend is often labelled as Cuvée François 1er.

Leading Touraine-Amboise Producer

DOMAINE DUTERTRE

Commune: Limeray.
Owners: Jacques & Gilles Dutertre.
Surface Area under Vine: 32 ha.
Wines: Touraine-Amboise including Cuvée François 1er, Cuvée Prestige and Clos du Pavillon (white).

Jacques Dutertre is the leading grower in the *appellation*, and one of the originators of the blended style, Cuvée François 1er. The 1990 was delicious. I also admire his old-vine Clos du Pavillon, from 100 per cent Chenin.

Other Producers of note

DOMAINE DE LA GABILLIÈRE (AMBOISE), DOMAINE CATHERINE MOREAU (CANGEY) AND CHÂTEAU DE LA ROCHE – BELONGING TO THE NÉGOCIANT CHAINIER (AMBOISE).

TOURAINE-AZAY-LE-RIDEAU

Surface Area (1998): (Rosé) 31 ha; (white) 24 ha.
Production (1998): (Rosé) 1527 hl; (white) 961 hl.

Colour: Rosé and white.

Grape Varieties: (Rosé) Groslot (or Grolleau), Cot, Gamay and Cabernet Franc; (white) Chenin Blanc.

Maximum Yield: 55 hl/ha.

Minimum Alcohol Level: (Rosé) 9°; (white) 10°.

Azay-Le-Rideau's superb Renaissance chateau, built on the banks of the river Indre south-west of Tours, is justly one of the most popular in the Loire. Tourists flock by the coachload to be conducted in the rather grudging French manner round its beautiful rooms, now somewhat denuded of furniture but still containing a few enviable examples as well as some fine tapestries and chimneypieces.

The wine, however, is less well known. The area is smaller even than Amboise, though spread over eight communes (Azay-Le-Rideau, Artannes, Cheillé, Lignières, Ravarennes, Saché, Thilouze and Vallères). The *appellation* excludes red wine and white wine was authorised in 1953 before the rosé in 1977. The white can vary in style from bone dry to appreciably sweet, depending on the weather and the inclination of the growers. The rosé received its *appellation* in 1976 and must be made primarily from the Groslot, not the classiest of varieties, together with Gamay, Cot and Cabernet Franc.

Producers of note

Château de L'Aulée/Mme Lallier-Deutz (Azay-Le-Rideau), Domaine Marc Badiller/La Cave des Vallées (Cheillé), Domaine Robert Denis (Cheillé) and Domaine Pascal Pibaleau (Azay-Le-Rideau).

Touraine

Surface Area (1998): (Red and rosé) 3083 ha; (white) 2009 ha. See also Touraine *mousseux* page 291.

Production (1998): (Red and rosé) 183,000 hl; (white) 122,351 hl. See also Touraine *mousseux* page 291.

Colour: Red, rosé and white.

Grape Varieties: (Red and rosé) Gamay, Cabernet Franc, Cabernet Sauvignon, Cot, Pinot Noir, Pinot Gris, Pineau d'Aunis, plus Groslot for rosé only; (white) Chenin Blanc.

Maximum Yield: 55 hl/ha.

Minimum Alcohol Level: (Red and rosé) 9°; (white) 9.5°.

Generic Touraine wine can be marvellous or dreary and can come from anywhere within the old province of Touraine, roughly bordered by Fontevraud and Blois to the east and west and Château-Renault and Loches to the north and south.

In such a large area, with so many different grapes and soils – though the clay-limestone mixture the French call *argillo-calcaire* predominates – it is difficult to generalise about Touraine's run-of-the-mill wines. From the top *négociants*, such as Plouzeau in Chinon, Pierre Chainier in Amboise, Paul Buisse in Montrichard, Bougrier (Caves de La Tourangelle) in Saint-Georges-sur-Cher and Monmousseau in Montrichard, come a range of wines, from Vin de Pays du Jardin de La France to varietal wines which are more than equal in quality and value-for-money to those of higher *appellations*. These firms often look after the vineyards and vinify and sell the wines of single growers whom they have under contract. Producers from outside the immediate area, such as Patrick de Ladoucette of Pouilly-sur-Loire and Moreau in Chablis, also make excellent Touraine wines.

Co-operatives, when they are good, can be very good. The Confrérie des Vignerons d'Oisly-et-Thesée produces a range of generic wines at different prices. Their top Sauvignon wines are not cheap, but they can be excellent, with a light, crisp, grassy flavour which is characteristic of this grape in the eastern end of Touraine. There are other reliable co-operatives at Civray and Francueil, near Bleré, at Onzain, at Limeray near Amboise, and at Saint-Georges and Saint-Romain on the Cher.

Other Producers of note

Domaine des Acacias/Charles Guerbois (Chémery), Domaine des Caillots/Dominique Girault (Noyers-sur-Cher), Domaine de La Charmoise/Henri Marionnet (Soings), Château de Chenonceau (Chenonceaux), Domaine des Corbillières/Maurice &

Dominique Barbou (Oisly), Domaine Daniel Delaunay (Pouillé), Domaine Pascal Gibault (Noyers-sur-Cher), Domaine de La Girardière/Patrick Léger (Saint-Aignan), Caves de La Grande Brosse/Mme Oudin (Chémery), Domaine Louet-Arcourt/Jean-Louis Arcourt (Monthou-sur-Bièvre), Domaine Jacky Marteau (Pouillé), Domaine du Petit Thouars (Saint-Germain-sur-Vienne), Domaine du Pré Baron/Guy Mardon (Oisly), Domaine de La Presle/Jean-Marie Penet (Oisly), Domaine Jacky Preys (Meusnes), Caves de La Ramée (Gérard Gabillet (Thésée), Clos Roche Blanche (Mareuil-sur-Cher), Domaine Alain & Philippe Sallé (Noyers-sur-Cher) and Domaine Sauvète (Monthou-sur-Cher).

NOBLE JOUÉ

Though not a separate *appellation*, this curiousity merits a separate mention. It is the story of the recreation of a rosé wine which had become extinct. Joué-Les-Tours is now a suburb of Tours itself and lies to the south, between the city and the Indre valley. The wine was well-known before the French Revolution, but the twin effects of phylloxera and urban development had led to its demise. In 1975, led by Michel Mousseau of the Clos de La Dorée near Esvres-sur-Indre, a group of growers decided to revive the wine, a *vin gris* blend of at least 50 per cent Gris Meunier (Champagne's Pinot Meunier), 30-40 per cent Pinot Gris (known locally as Malvoisie), and 10-20 per cent Pinot Noir.

In the best years – these Pinot grapes have to be fully ripe, and this requires a few more hours of sunshine than for Sauvignon Blanc – this is a dry, attractive, food-friendly wine and more than just a local curiosity.

COTEAUX DU LOIR AND JASNIÈRES

COTEAUX DU LOIR

Surface Area (1998): (Red and rosé) 38 ha; (white) 29 ha.
Production (1998): (Red and rosé) 1555 hl; (white) 1012 hl.
Colour: Red, rosé and white.
Grape Varieties: (Red and rosé) Cabernet Franc, Pineau d'Aunis, Cot, plus Grolleau for rosé only; (white) Chenin Blanc.
Maximum Yield: 55 hl/ha.
Minimum Alcohol Level: (Red and rosé) 9°; (white) 9.5°.

JASNIÈRES

Surface Area (1998): 50 ha.
Production (1998): 2096 hl.
Colour: White.
Grape Varieties: Chenin Blanc.
Maximum Yield: 52 hl/ha.
Minimum Alcohol Level: 10°.

North of the Loire between La Flèche and Vendôme lies the valley of a river confusingly called the Loir (or Le Loir as opposed to La Loire). This masculine tributary of a greater, feminine neighbour rises south of the city of Chartres and for much of its distance runs roughly parallel to the Loire before joining the river Sarthe north of Angers.

The Coteaux du Loir is a tiny *appellation* centred round the towns of Château-du-Loir and La Chartre about 40 kilometres north of Tours. Though the district covers twenty-two communes there are only some 50 hectares of vines. The soil contains a predominance of clay, while there is more flint in Jasnières. I find the wines unexciting. This region does not deserve to be AC.

Jasnières is a sub-region of the Coteaux du Loir and is a compact, more densely planted *appellation* covering just two communes, LHomme and Ruillé on the north bank of the river Loir, on limestone *tuffe* soil, rich in flint similar to that at Vouvray. The *appellation* covers white wines only.

On a few sites, well-exposed to the south, protected from the north winds and in the best vintages, the Chenin Blanc grape can ripen satisfactorily to produce a light, acidic wine, raspingly dry when young, but attaining a certain fatness and plumpness if allowed a few years' ageing in bottle. It is somewhat of an acquired taste, but one or two local growers do produce wine with at least some merit. This is really, though, at the northern limits of growing grapes in France, and there has to be a magnificent autumn before the wines produced are anything but over-tart and impossibly austere. In order to try and cover up their inherent lack of ripeness many are now being produced in a *sec-tendre* style, leaving behind some residual sugar.

Coteaux du Loir & Jasnières Producers of note
Domaine de Bellivière/Éric Nicolas (LHomme), Domaine Gaston Cartereau (LHomme), Domaine de La Charrière/Joël Gigou (La Chartre-sur-Le Loir), Domaine Jean-Jacques Maillet (Ruillé-sur-Loir) and Domaine Renard-Potaire/Nicolas Renard (Marçon).

Coteaux du Vendômois

Surface Area (1998): (Red and rosé) 120 ha; (white) 17 ha.
Production (1998): (Red and rosé) 7515 hl; (white) 1115 hl.
Colour: Red, rosé and white.
Grape Varieties: (Red and rosé) Pinot Noir, Cabernet Franc, Cabernet Sauvignon, plus Pinot d'Aunis and Gamay Noir à Jus Blanc for rosé only; (white) Chenin Blanc and Chardonnay.
Maximum Yield: (Red) 60 hl/ha; (rosé and white) 65 hl/ha.
Minimum Alcohol Level: (Red and rosé) 9°; (white) 9.5°.

The Coteaux du Vendomois (created VDQS in 1968) lies further upstream from Jasnières and the Coteaux du Loir, some 30 kilometres north-west of Blois. The vines are confined to sheltered slopes amid a sea of cereals, and few growers possess enough vines to enable them to survive independently of the local co-operative. The rosé – usually a blend of Pinot d'Aunis and Gamay – is the main wine. The quality of the wine is indifferent, no better than what one would expect from such a northerly winemaking region.

Cheverny and Cour-Cheverny

Cheverny

Surface Area (1998): (Red and rosé) 230 ha; (white) 172 ha.
Production (1998): (Red and rosé) 12,299 hl; (white) 9039 hl.
Colour: Red, rosé and white.
Grape Varieties: (Red and rosé) Gamay, Pinot Noir, Cabernet Franc, Cabernet Sauvignon (until 2000 only) and Cot plus Pineau d'Aunis and Pinot Gris for rosé; (white) Romorantin, Chenin Blanc, Menu Pineau (Arbois), Chardonnay and Sauvignon Blanc.
Maximum Yield: (Red and rosé) 55 hl/ha; (white) 60 hl/ha.
Minimum Alcohol Level: 9.5°.

Cour-Cheverny

Surface Area (1998): 43 ha.
Production (1998): 1982 hl.
Colour: White.
Grape Varieties: Romorantin.
Maximum Yield: 60 hl/ha.
Minimum Alcohol Level: 9.5°.

South of Blois and the former royal parks of Russy and Chambord lies the large area of Cheverny, covering twenty-three communes, and its smaller cousin, Cour-Cheverny, both created AC in 1993 and covering another eleven communes.

Most of the wines are more or less similar to the rest of the Touraine. The difference lies in the grape called the Romorantin. The town of Romorantin-Lanthenay lies not far away towards Vierzon but not within the *appellation*. I cannot say I am a fan. Romorantin produces a rather sour, white wine with a peculiar foxy taste, which is both green and acidic when young and tired and attenuated after a year or two more.

Cheverny and Cour-Cheverny Producers of note
Domaine de La Desoucherie/Christian Tessier

(Cour-Cheverny), Domaine de La Gaudronnière/
Christian Dorléans (Cellettes), Domaine des
Huards/Michel Gendrier (Cour-Cheverny) and
Domaine Le Petit Chambord/François Cazin
(Cheverny).

Valençay

Surface Area (1998): (Red and rosé) 98 ha; (white)
31 ha.
Production (1998): (Red and rosé) 5711 hl; (white)
2135 hl.
Colour: Red, rosé and white.
Grape Varieties: (Red and rosé) Cabernet
Sauvignon, Cabernet Franc, Cot, Gamay Noir à
Jus Blanc and Pinot d'Aunis; (white) Arbois

(Menu Pineau), Chenin Blanc, Sauvignon Blanc
and Chardonnay.
Maximum Yield: (Red and rosé) 45 hl/ha; (white)
50 hl/ha.
Minimum Alcohol Level: 9°.

Valençay (created VDQS in 1970) lies at the extreme
south-east of the Touraine, in the *département* of Indre,
south of the river Cher. It comprises 130 hectares of
vines spread over fourteen communes. The reds, mainly
from Gamay, are light and rustic, as are the whites,
though these come from a potentially interesting blend
of Sauvignon Blanc, Chardonnay, Chenin and Arbois.
Talleyrand, a noted gourmet, lived at the Château de
Valençay in the early nineteenth century. I doubt that
he thought much of the local wines either.

Sparkling Wines of the Loire

Both Touraine and the Anjou region produce
some excellent Champagne-method sparkling
wines. These can be sold either as Touraine or
Anjou *mousseux*, or, as is more usual, under more specific
district names such as Vouvray, Montlouis and Saumur.
There may be several *appellations* to cover sparkling wine
from the Loire but production methods, authorized
grape varieties and other details are similar, as is the end
result, so it seems logical to deal with these wines under
one heading, and at this point in the chapter, as we are
about to traverse the boundaries between the Touraine
and the Anjou.

Méthode champenoise, now rechristened *méthode traditionnelle* or Traditional method, describes the method used
to make sparkling wine in Champagne. It is defined as
the production of carbon dioxide (which vaporizes once
the cork and pressure within the bottle is released) by
means of inducing a second fermentation inside the bottle. Thereafter the wine never leaves this bottle until the
cork is drawn prior to drinking. This process is discussed
in greater detail on page 546.

The technique was brought from the Champagne
region to the Loire in Napoleonic times by a Belgian,

Jean Ackerman, who married a girl named Laurance
from Saumur. He produced his first sparkling wine in
Saumur in 1811. For thirty-seven years his was the only
local firm to make sparkling wine, and today Ackerman-Laurance, now largely owned by the Rémy family
of Rémy-Pannier, is still the largest sparkling wine firm
in the Loire, though now, naturally, there is considerable competition from other producers.

Originally, until the name of Champagne was protected early in the twentieth century in a series of
decrees, sparkling wine from the Loire was sold as
Champagne, with the Loire element played down to a
minimum. Among the Loire sparkling wines Saumur
has always been the dominant name.

What is curious, however, is that despite its increasing popularity, so little sparkling wine is sold compared
to Champagne. The whole of the Loire produces barely
one-tenth (25 million bottles) of that of Champagne.

Most of these sparkling wines are, of course, white,
and in Vouvray and Montlouis exclusively, and made
solely from the Chenin Blanc. Elsewhere black grapes
are permitted too, (usually to a maximum of 60 per cent
of the blend) and some *mousseux* rosé is produced as well

as a little red. Similarly, most Loire sparkling wines are made in the *brut* style, though in practice they are marginally sweeter than *brut* Champagnes.

SAUMUR D'ORIGINE

Surface Area (1998): 1133 ha.
Production (1998): (Red and rosé) 75,605 hl; (white) 3362 hl.
Colour: Red, rosé and white.
Grape Varieties: (Red and rosé) Cabernet Franc, Cot, Grolleau, Gamay Noir à Jus Blanc, Pineau d'Aunis and Pinot Noir; (white) all the above varieties except Gamay plus Chenin Blanc, Chardonnay and Sauvignon Blanc.
Maximum Yield: 60 hl/ha.
Minimum Alcoholic Level: 9.5°.

Sparkling Saumur – the name of the *appellation* was changed from Saumur Mousseux to Saumur d'Origine in 1975 – is perhaps the best-known French Champagne-method wine (outside Champagne itself). At present a dozen or so firms produce about eleven million bottles of Saumur d'Origine annually, a figure which has grown considerably since the Second World War. Some Champagne houses have had the foresight to diversify into sparkling Saumur – Taittinger own Bouvet-Ladubay (and Monmousseau who make other Loire sparkling wines in Montrichard) and Bollinger own Langlois-Château.

Most of the leading Saumur houses were founded in the second half of the nineteenth century – Bouvet-Ladubay in 1851, De Neuville in 1856, Veuve Amiot in 1882, Gratien & Meyer in 1884, and Langlois-Château in 1885. The exception is the Compagnie Française des Grands Vins who own the brand Cadre Noir. Together with Ackerman-Laurance, these six houses have formed the Comité du Vin de Saumur to maintain and promote the quality of sparkling Saumur. This association possesses a joint harvest reception centre on the outskirts of Saumur, for most of these producers prefer to buy grapes from the growers, not wine. Each house has its own extensive cellars, cut out of the limestone *tuffe* cliffs

on the left bank of the Loire, on either side of the town of Saumur. These cellars, often stretching back into the hillsides for several hundred metres, and comprising many kilometres of galleries, are great tourist attractions during the summer months. Gratien, Meyer even has an underground spring and can arrange banquets deep inside their caves.

Between them, these seven *grandes maisons* plus the co-operative at Saint-Cyr-en-Bourg produce practically all the sparkling Saumur. The wine will vary quite considerably in style depending on the balance of the grape varieties in the base wine. Most of the firms have a number of grades of quality, and as elsewhere you get what you pay for. At the lowest level the blend will normally be fairly four-square and uncomplicated, and ascending upwards in value as well as in finesse and delicacy of fruit until one reaches Crémant de Loire, the highest level. The top wines of Bouvet-Ladubay and Gratien & Meyer and the co-operative can be strongly recommended.

ANJOU MOUSSEUX

Surface Area (1998): 66 ha.
Production (1998): (Red and rosé) 3302 hl; (white) 151 hl.
Colour: Red, rosé and white.
Grape Varieties: (Red and rosé) Cabernet Franc, Cot, Gamay Noir à Jus Blanc, Grolleau, Pineau d'Aunis; (white) as above plus Chenin Blanc.
Maximum Yield: 65 hl/ha.
Minimum Alcohol Level: 9.5°.

The rules governing Anjou Mousseux are the same as those for Saumur. It is not a common *appellation*. Indeed the only ones I have come across are those made from base wine produced at the Union Agricole du Pays de Loire at Brissac by the Saint-Cyr-en-Bourg co-operative.

VOUVRAY MOUSSEUX AND MONTLOUIS MOUSSEUX

Surface Area (1998): (Vouvray Mousseux) 1124 ha; (Montlouis Mousseux) 155 ha.
Production (1998): (Vouvray Mousseux) 72,159 hl; (Montlouis Mousseux) 8609 hl.
Colour: White.
Grape Varieties: Chenin Blanc.
Maximum Yield: 65 hl/ha.
Minimum Alcohol Level: 9.5°.

Sparkling wine in Vouvray and Montlouis is a relatively recent development. According to Monsieur Cuvier, the retired director of the Cave Co-operative des Producteurs de Vins Fins at La Vallée Coquette, the idea was dreamed up by the Mayor of Vouvray, Monsieur Vavasseur, during the First World War, when there was a shortage of Champagne. Production has boomed since 1950, and now threatens to rival that of Saumur. Mousseux now makes up an important part of most Vouvray producers' portfolios.

One of the best sparkling Vouvrays comes from Château Montcontour, a handsome fifteenth-century château just outside the town on the road to Tours. Since being taken over by the Brédut family in 1989, the estate has expanded to some 140 hectares of vines, the largest holding in the Vouvray *appellation*. Their still wines, impeccably vinified by the most up-to-date methods, are also recommended.

Both the co-operatives, Château de Vandenuits and La Vallée Coquette, produce good examples of Vouvray Mousseux and also make the sparkling wines for several of the other local firms.

TOURAINE MOUSSEUX

Surface Area (1998): (White) 565 ha; (rosé) 68 ha.
Production (1998): (White) 32,740 hl; (rosé) 3829 hl.
Colour: Red, rosé and white.
Grape Varieties: (Red and rosé) Cabernet Franc, Cot, Grolleau, Gamay Noir à Jus Blanc, Pineau d'Aunis, Pinot Noir; (white) as above plus Chenin Blanc, Chardonnay and Sauvignon Blanc.
Maximum Yield: 65 hl/ha.
Minimum Alcohol Level: 9.5°.

The Touraine Mousseux *appellation* was created in 1974, and is now the third largest sparkling wine label in the Loire, after Saumur and Vouvray. The Brédut family own two important producers, Château Montcontour (see above) and J M Monmousseau at Montrichard on the Cher. Their best-known sparkling wine is the Brut de Mosny, a Blanc de Blancs.

CRÉMANT DE LOIRE

Surface Area (1998): 485 ha.
Production (1998): (Rosé) 61,035 hl; (white) 1702 hl.
Colour: Rosé and white.
Grape Varieties: Chenin Blanc, Cabernet Franc, Pineau d'Aunis, Pinot Noir, Chardonnay, Arbois and Grolleau (or Groslot).
Maximum Yield: 50 hl/ha.
Minimum Alcohol Level: 9.5°.

In 1975 a new and stricter *appellation* for a quality white sparkling wine was authorized, Crémant de Loire. The yield was restricted to 50 hectolitres per hectare, as against 60 hectolitres for Saumur Mousseux (as Saumur d'Origine was then called) and the weight of grapes required for 1 hectolitre of must was fixed at 150 kilograms as opposed to 130. A longer period of bottle-ageing was also required. Crémant has to remain on its lees before disgorging for a year while Saumur d'Origine needs only nine months.

The *appellation* excludes the inferior Cot grape and restricts the amount of Groslot to 30 per cent. The grapes can come from either Anjou or Touraine, though in practice Crémant seems to have become a sort of superior Saumur. As yet production is less than Saumur d'Origine but the improvement in quality, even over the best Saumurs and Vouvrays, is considerable. Ackerman-Laurance (Cuvée Privée and Cuvée Privilège), Bouvet-Ladubay and Gratien & Meyer all produce excellent examples.

Anjou and Saumur

The large province of Anjou lies between Touraine and the Pays Nantais or the Muscadet region, between Fontevraud Abbey in the east and the dungeon of Champtoceaux in the west, a distance of more than 100 kilometres. It includes the sweet wines of the Coteaux du Layon, the excellent dry whites of Savennières and the reds of Saumur-Champigny as well as a great deal of generic AC red, white and rosé wine of no great presumption, under the regional names of Anjou and Saumur.

The vineyards for the AC wines of Anjou occupy some 16,000 hectares. They lie almost entirely in the Maine-et-Loire *département* and produce some 900,000 hectolitres of wine a year. Forty-five per cent of this is rosé wine, with roughly 33 per cent red and 22 per cent white. This makes it the largest of the four main Loire regions, and even if most of this is fairly ordinary wine – or, at least, from a fairly basic *appellation* (Anjou) – there is much wine that is good, if not excellent, from an increasing number of enthusiastic, dedicated growers or from larger companies practising all the latest wine-making techniques.

Anjou is much like Touraine, a countryside of sleepy villages and old country mansions, gently undulating away from the wide, slowly meandering Loire. It is lush and fertile, gentle in its colours and with its climate. The soil is a heterogeneous mixture, generally more sandy than the Touraine to the east, less clayey than the Muscadet area to the west: a combination of shale, marl, sand, limestone and gravel. As well as vineyards there are fields of arable crops, cherry orchards and market gardens, and pasture for cattle. Here and there are greenhouses full of orchids and other exotic flowers, or quarries for the slate roofs of Angers and Saumur.

The capital of the province is Angers, a more elegant town than Tours. It possesses an impressive early medieval fortified castle, built under the direction of Saint Louis in the thirteenth century. The castle has seventeen squat round towers within whose wide battlements can be found a small vineyard.

Henry II of England was also Count of Anjou. His ascent to the throne of England in 1154 gave a great boost to the wines of the region, so much so that two centuries later a law was passed prohibiting the import into Anjou of wines from outside the region, in order to protect the local produce from adulteration with 'inferior' wines.

Some centuries later, while the French court was concentrating its attention on the Touraine and Orléans wines, and the English had diverted theirs to Bordeaux, the Angevins began to cultivate the Dutch. The Dutch traders, who would in the seventeenth century come in search of base wine for brandy as well as for table wine, could sail their shallow boats up to the Pont de Cé, just south of Angers, and the Low Countries became an influential export market. The Dutch traders would arrive as soon as the winter weather had improved, and swiftly depart with the pick of the new wine. This relationship was fostered by a strong Protestant presence in the area – Saumur is still one of France's most important Protestant centres – and it lasted, despite interruptions of war, until the French Revolution in 1789.

Traditionally, Anjou was a white wine region and for the most part this wine was sweet or semi-sweet. Red grapes for rosé, and, more recently, for red wine, is a twentieth-century innovation. It is only since the Second World War that the popularity of the soft, fruity, off-dry Anjou rosé has become so important. But if rosé is the first thing we associate with the Anjou, there is much else which is worth investigating.

Within the Anjou there are a number of viticulture sub-areas. Nearest to the Touraine is Saumur, producing not only generic and sparkling wine, but increasingly good Chinon and Bourgueil look-alikes under the Saumur-Champigny label.

Further west we come to Anjou proper, producing everything from simple table wines to good reds (Anjou-Villages) and excellent sweet wines (Coteaux du Layon, Bonnezeaux and Quarts de Chaume). Finally, north of the river Loire – the only important *vignoble* this side of the river except for Bourgueil and Saint-Nicolas-de-Bourgueil — is the dry white wine of Savennières. Throughout Anjou the white wines are produced almost exclusively from the Chenin Blanc, the best reds from Cabernet Franc and Cabernet Sauvignon.

SAUMUR APPELLATIONS

SAUMUR

Surface Area (1998): (Red and rosé) 870 ha; (white) 356 ha.

Production (1998): (Red and rosé) 55,452 hl; (white) 23,312 hl.

Colour: Red, rosé and white.

Grape Varieties: (Red and rosé) Cabernet Franc, Cabernet Sauvignon and Pineau d'Aunis; (white) Chenin Blanc (minimum 80 per cent), Sauvignon Blanc and Chardonnay.

Maximum Yield: (Red and rosé) 40 hl/ha; (white) 45 hl/ha.

Minimum Alcoholic Level: 10°.

COTEAUX DE SAUMUR

Surface Area (1998): 3 ha.

Production (1998): 138 hl.

Colour: White.

Grape Variety: Chenin Blanc.

Maximum Yield: 35 hl/ha.

Minimum Alcoholic Level: 11°.

CABERNET DE SAUMUR

Surface Area (1998): 95 ha.

Production (1998): 6294 hl.

Colour: Rosé.

Grape Varieties: Cabernet Franc and Cabernet Sauvignon.

Maximum Yield: 40 hl/ha.

Minimum Alcoholic Level: 10°.

Saumur, dominated by its castle, which is so magnificently illustrated in the prayer book, the Très Riches Heures, painted for Jean, Duc de Berry by Pol Limbourg and his brothers in 1416, is an attractive market town. It is host to the famous Cadre Noir Cavalry School, founded in 1814, now equally involved with modern tanks and mobile guns. The area is a centre for mushroom cultivation which is carried out in the multitude of caves dug out of cliffs on the left bank of the Loire. And the town is the home of all the important Saumur d'Origine producers.

Because of the importance of these sparkling wines (see page 289), Saumur is the largest centre of wine production in the Loire. About half of the grapes from the thirty-nine Saumur communes which run down from the river towards Montreuil-Bellay and beyond are used for *mousseux* and the remainder for still wine.

The regulations for Saumur are somewhat stricter than for generic Anjou. Unlike generic Anjou the Gamay is not authorized and neither are the Cot or Groslot/Grolleau. Saumur Blanc denotes a dry wine and Coteaux de Saumur a semi-sweet wine. Cabernet de Saumur is a superior rosé made, as you would expect from its name, solely from the two Cabernet varieties, Cabernet Sauvignon and Cabernet Franc.

Most of the local production of still wine is sold by the reliable Cave Coopérative des Vignerons de Saumur at Saint-Cyr-en-Bourg and much of the rest by the sparkling wine merchants themselves such as Bouvet-Ladubay and Gratien & Meyer, both of whom make attractive examples.

Saumur Producers of note

CLOS DE L'ABBAYE/JEAN-FRANÇOIS AUPY (LE PUY-DE-NOTRE-DAME), CHÂTEAU DE BEAUREGARD/PHILIPPE GOURDON (LE PUY-DE-NOTRE-DAME), CHÂTEAU DE BRÉZÉ (BRÉZÉ), CHÂTEAU DE MONTREUIL-BELLAY/BERNARD DE COLBERT (MONTREUIL-BELLAY), DOMAINE DE LA RENIÈRE/RENÉ-HUGUES GAY (LE PUY-DE-NOTRE-DAME) AND DOMAINE DU VIEUX-PRESSOIR/BRUNO ALBERT (VAUDELNAY).

SAUMUR-CHAMPIGNY

Surface Area (1998): 1375 ha.

Production (1998): 78,715 hl.

Colour: Red.

Grape Varieties: Cabernet Franc, Cabernet
Sauvignon and Pineau d'Aunis.
Maximum Yield: 40 hl/ha.
Minimum Alcohol Level: 10°.

Within the much larger general region of Saumur, in an
area roughly bounded by the forest of Fontevraud, the
Loire and river Thouet, lies Saumur-Champigny, the
best Anjou red wine. Here the soil is not the *tuffe* of
Bourgueil and Chinon but another much harder limestone, which is more heat retentive, and thus able to
produce riper grapes than the surrounding vineyards.
The name Champigny comes from *campus ignis*, the Latin
for 'field of fire', denoting a warm mesoclimate.

From the river Loire the land rises very steeply, giving
the appearance of a cliff in places, at the base of which
there are a number of troglodyte houses. The caves
behind are used for storing wine as well as cultivating
mushrooms. On the plateau above lie the vineyards, in
the ten communes of Champigny, Souzay, Dampierre-
sur-Loire, Varrains, Chacé, Saint-Cyr-en-Bourg,
Turquant, Parnay, Montsoreau and Saumur itself. There
is a large, up-to-date co-operative at Saint-Cyr-en-Bourg
which produces a significant proportion of the *appellation*
as well as generic Saumur, both still and sparkling.

The wine is quite different from Anjou-Villages as
well as from those of nearby Bourgueil and Chinon. It
is lighter and fresher than all three, very plummy in its
fruit but without either the tannic background of some
Anjou-Villages or the top Chinons' ability to age with
refinement. Yet it has an enormous fruity appeal and no
lack of elegance. The wine is at its best young, between
two and six years old.

Leading Saumur-Champigny Producers

DOMAINE DE BONNEVAUX

Commune: Varrains.
Owner: Camille Bourdoux.
Surface Area under Vine: 13 ha.
Wines: Saumur-Champigny and Crémant de
Loire.

Camille Bourdoux is a retired plumber. He makes at
least two different *cuvées* of Saumur-Champigny. What
I sampled were, I was assured, the 'old vines' *cuvées* but it
did not say so on the label. The wines were delicious:
round, balanced, complex, rich and stylish.

CHÂTEAU DES CHAINTRES

Commune: Dampierre-sur-Loire.
Owner: Baron Gaël de Tigny.
Surface Area under Vine: 17 ha.
Wines: Saumur-Champigny.

The château is one of the *appellation*'s finest buildings.
There is only one wine and it is tank-aged. I much
enjoyed the profound, classy 1997 and 1996, but I found
the 1995 rather bland and weedy, despite the success of
this vintage elsewhere.

★ DOMAINE FILLIATREAU

Commune: Chaintres.
Owner: Paul Filliatreau.
Surface Area under Vine: 50 ha.
Wines: Saumur-Champigny including Cuvée de
Printemps and Cuvée Vieilles Vignes, and Saumur
(red and white).

Paul Filliatreau is the *appellation*'s godfather. When I first
came into the wine trade in the 1960s and then started
buying wine in the 1970s Saumur reds were rustic and
rather unpleasant. It needed a very hot year like 1976
before they were even half decent. Then I visited Paul
Filliatreau and his attractive blonde Swedish wife, Lena
in Chaintres. Filliatreau was the pioneer of modern
Saumur-Champigny, bringing out all the fruit, not prolonging the maceration and eliminating the rustic
elements. Today his land includes Château Fouquet
which is in the Saumur *appellation* and which he bought
in 1987, replanting with Cabernet Franc in 1990. So far
the results are promising. There is a delicious Saumur-
Champigny Cuvée de Printemps and an old-vine wine
which is lovely and complex.

DOMAINE DES GALMOISE

Commune: Chacé.
Owner: Didier Pasquier.

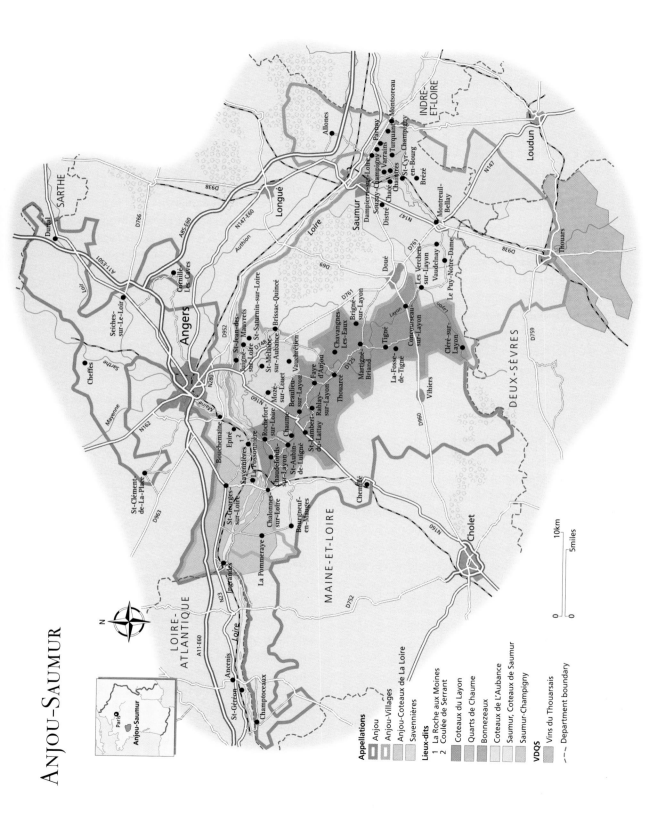

ANJOU-SAUMUR

Surface Area under Vine: 10 ha.

Wines: Saumur-Champigny including Secret du Caveau.

The youthful Didier Pasquier keeps his wine entirely in stainless steel, and bottles his better *cuvée*, Secret du Caveau after two years. The wines have depth and fruit.

★ CHÂTEAU DU HUREAU

Commune: Dampierre-sur-Loire.

Owner: Philippe Vatan.

Surface Area under Vine: 10 ha.

Wines: Saumur-Champigny including Cuvée des Fevettes and Cuvée Lisagathe, Saumur (white), Coteaux de Saumur and Saumur *mousseux*.

There have been Hureaus at this fine château for eight generations. The estate produces two of the best wines of the *appellation*. As well as the standard *cuvée*, a lush ripe wine for early drinking, there is the old-vine Cuvée des Fevettes which receives some barrique-ageing and Cuvée Lisagathe, from the best parcels of vines, which does not. The wines are almost entirely from Cabernet Franc and have plenty of definition and style.

DOMAINE DE NERLEUX

Commune: Saint-Cyr-en-Bourg.

Owner: Régis Neau.

Surface Area under Vine: 40 ha.

Wines: Saumur-Champigny including Clos Les Châtains.

Régis Neau's father, Robert helped found the local co-operative and ran it until his retirement in 1996 (his brother Marcel is now in charge). Régis Neau runs the family domaine and makes two *cuvées*. I find the better one, Clos des Châtains, from the older vines, proportionately much more interesting.

DOMAINE DES ROCHES NEUVES

Commune: Varrains.

Owner: Thierry Germain.

Surface Area under Vine: 8 ha.

Wines: Saumur-Champigny including Terres Chaudes and La Marginale, and Saumur (white).

Thierry Germain comes from Bordeaux and bought the domaine in 1991. The estate is entirely planted in Cabernet Franc. There are three *cuvées*: I like the basic one which is ripe and plump and the rich, ample and juicy Terres Chaudes, too. I have my reservations about La Marginale, which was very oaky under the previous owners and remains so today.

★★ CLOS ROUGEARD

Commune: Chacé.

Owner: Jean-Louis and Bernard Foucault.

Surface Area under Vine: 8 ha.

Wines: Saumur-Champigny, including Clos Rougeard, Les Poyeux and Le Bourg, and Coteaux de Saumur.

This is the leading estate in the *appellation* and one of the few to use new wood as well as achieving the correct balance of fruit and oak. The answer, of course, lies in low yields and hence properly concentrated wine. The vines are old, reproduced by massal selection. The wine is prouced in open wooden vats, using *pigeage* or treading down as in Burgundy and matured for up to two years. There is no filtration. There are three *cuvées*: Clos Rougeard (despite its name, not from a single vineyard), Les Poyeux and Le Bourg, both single-vineyard wines. Les Poyeux is aged in old wood and Le Bourg in new. These are very serious examples of Saumur-Champigny indeed and can keep for ten years.

★ DOMAINE SAINT-VINCENT

Commune: Dampierre-sur-Loire.

Owner: Patrick Vadé.

Surface Area under Vine: 10 ha.

Wines: Saumur-Champigny, including Les Trézéllières and Les Adrialys, and Saumur (white).

In the hands of the youthful Patrick Vadé this estate has risen in the last decade to be one of the *appellation*'s rising stars. Les Trézéllières forms 80 per cent of the total production and is a ripe, clean and beautifully balanced wine. The old-vine bottling, Les Adrialys, spends a few months partly in cask and is even better. Both are lush, elegant wines, without hard edges and just as all Saumur-Champigny should be.

CHÂTEAU DE TARGÉ
Commune: Parnay.
Owner: Édouard Pisani-Ferry.
Surface Area under Vine: 9 ha.
Wines: Saumur-Champigny.

Targé is a fine Renaissance château overlooking the Loire and has belonged to the Pisani-Ferry family since 1652. The wines are pleasant, medium-bodied and fruity. They are good but not in the top league.

DOMAINE DES VARINELLES
Commune: Varrains.
Owner: Claude and Laurent Daheuiller.
Surface Area under Vine: 30 ha.
Wines: Saumur-Champigny, including Cuvée Vieilles Vignes, and Crémant de Loire.

Daheuiller *père et fils* make their wine in a modern cellar complete with automatic plungers for the *pigeage*, a pneumatic press and thermo-regulated stainless steel vats. There are two *cuvées*, a basic Saumur-Champigny and a Vieilles Vignes and both are soft, rounded and stylish, the old-vine one with more definition, obviously. They are ready earlier than most Saumur-Champigny.

★ CHÂTEAU DE VILLENEUVE
Commune: Souzay-Champigny.
Owner: Jean-Pierre Chevallier.
Surface Area under Vine: 30 ha.
Wines: Saumur-Champigny, including Cuvée Vieilles Vignes and Le Grand Clos, and Saumur (white).

The château dates in part from the sixteenth century and stands alongside an eleventh-century belltower. Jean-Pierre Chevallier uses only Cabernet Franc for the Saumur-Champigny. There are three *cuvées*: the basic one is plump, rich and stylish and the Vieilles Vignes is aged partly in three-year-old wood. This is a gently cedary rather than oaky wine and is sophisticated without any hard edges. From a *lieu-dit* of old vines called Le Grand Clos comes an even more impressive wine, profound and classy, and matured in 500- and 300-litre barrels (40 per cent new each year). Even this wine is ready fairly early – the 1995 was delicious in 1998.

Other Producers of note
CAVE DES VIGNERONS DE SAUMUR (SAINT-CYR-EN BOURG), DOMAINE MICHEL AND JEAN-CLAUDE DUBOIS (SAINT-CYR-EN-BOURG), SCA FOURRIER & FILS/DOMAINE DES HAUTES VIGNES (DISTRÉ), GRATIEN & MEYER (SAUMUR), DOMAINE GILBERT LAVIGNE (VARRAINS), DOMAINE LANGLOIS-CHÂTEAU/RENÉ-NOËL LEGRAND (SAINT-HILAIRE-SAINT-FLORENT), DOMAINE DE LA PERRUCHE/ ALAIN ROUILLER (MONTSOREAU) AND DOMAINE SAINT-JEAN/JEAN-PIERRE ANGER (TURQUANT).

ANJOU APPELLATIONS

ANJOU
Surface Area (1998): 2828 ha.
Production (1998): (Red) 99,666 hl; (white) 58,234 hl.
Colour: Red and white.
Grape Varieties: (Red) Gamay Noir à Jus Blanc, Cabernet Sauvignon, Pineau d'Aunis and Cabernet Franc; (white) Chenin Blanc, Chardonnay and Sauvignon Blanc.
Maximum Yield: (Red) 40 hl/ha; (white) 45 hl/ha.
Minimum Alcohol Level: (Red) 10°; (white) 9.5°.

ANJOU-GAMAY
Surface Area (1998): 307 ha.
Production (1998): 16,784 hl.
Colours: Red and rosé.
Grape Variety: Gamay Noir à Jus Blanc.
Maximum Yield: 40 hl/ha.
Minimum Alcohol Level: 10°.

CABERNET D'ANJOU
Surface Area (1998): 2448 ha.
Production (1998): 142,568 hl.
Colour: Rosé (off-dry to sweet).
Grape Varieties: Cabernet Franc and Cabernet Sauvignon.
Maximum Yield: 40 hl/ha.
Minimum Alcohol Level: 10°.

ROSÉ D'ANJOU
Surface Area (1998): 2069 ha.

Production (1998): 129,511 hl.
Colour and Style: Rosé, off-dry to sweet.
Grape Varieties: Grolleau, Cabernet Franc,
Cabernet Sauvignon, Gamay Noir à Jus Blanc, Cot
and Pineau d'Aunis.
Maximum Yield: 50 hl/ha.
Minimum Alcohol Level: 10°.

ROSÉ DE LOIRE

Surface Area (1998): 821 ha.
Production (1998): 53,402 hl.
Colour and Style: Dry rosé.
Grape Varieties: Cabernet Franc, Cabernet
Sauvignon, Pinot Noir, Gamay Noir à Jus Blanc,
Grolleau and Pineau d'Aunis.
Maximum Yield: 50 hl/ha.
Minimum Alcohol Level: 9°.

Basic red, rosé and white wine form the base of the
Angevin wine pyramid. The vineyards lie almost
entirely south of the Loire from a line south of Chemillé
to the west towards Thouars and the Saumur boundary
on the east: some 195 communes, almost entirely in the
Maine-et-Loire *département*, but overlapping into the
Deux-Sèvres and the Vienne. Within this region lies
both Anjou-Villages, for superior reds, and the sweet
white wine regions of Coteaux de L'Aubance, Coteaux
du Layon, Bonnezeaux and Quarts de Chaume.

White Anjou is usually dry or *sec-tendre*. The reds are
passable at best. Unless the summer has been particularly warm it is best to seek out Anjou-Villages instead,
though some of the Gamay wines can be pleasant.

Anjou rosé, which can be *tendre* or even medium-
sweet, can be made from the same black grapes used for
the red wine, but normally comes from mainly Cot and
Groslot, particularly the latter. Gamay is also authorised. There is additionally a Rosé de Loire which can
come from either Anjou or Touraine. The *appellation* was
created in 1974 to meet the increasing demand for drier
wines. Rosé de Loire is bone-dry as opposed to Anjou
rosé which is off-dry, and must have a minimum of 30
per cent of Cabernet grapes in the blend. Cabernet
d'Anjou is another rosé and must be made exclusively

from the two Cabernet grapes. It cannot be bone dry
and must contain at least 10 grammes of residual sugar
per litre. Well-made, chilled Cabernet d'Anjou can be a
delicious, abundantly fruity wine, to be drunk in a
deckchair on a hot summer's day, or, alternatively, with
cold salmon at a smart picnic.

ANJOU-VILLAGES

Surface Area (1998): 180 ha; (Anjou-Villages-
Brissac) 98 ha.
Production (1998): 8741 hl; (Anjou-Villages-
Brissac) 4771 hl.
Colour: Red.
Grape Varieties: Cabernet Franc and Cabernet
Sauvignon.
Maximum Yield: 50 hl/ha.
Minimum Alcohol Level: 9.5°.

Red wine is new to Anjou. In the past such red grapes as
were grown were made into *rosé*. This market is now in
decline and since the 1980s growers have turned to red.
The Villages area occupies some fifty-six communes
including Savennières north of the Loire, the valleys of
the Layon and the Aubance and the area known as the
Coteaux de La Loire between Ingrandes and Chalonnes.
The two Cabernet varieties do particularly well here
where the soil is schistous. More Cabernet Sauvignon is
used for Anjou-Villages than in Saumur and this means
the wine is fuller, chunkier even, and needs a few years'
ageing. It is best at between three and six years old.

The producers of Brissac in the Aubance Valley,
where there is also an important co-operative, lobbied
successfully to get their village promoted to a sort of
super-Villages *appellation*: Anjou-Villages-Brissac which
was first used for the 1996 vintage.

Leading Anjou-Villages Producers

DOMAINE DE BABLUT

Commune: Brissac-Quincé.
Owner: Christophe Daviau.
Surface Area under Vine: 100 ha.

Wines: Anjou-Villages, including Château de Brissac, and Coteaux de L'Aubance.

The combined domaine of the Daviau family covers 100 hectares (this is large for the region). I remember buying old vintages of sweet *rosé* (1943, 1945 and 1947) from Christophe Daviau's parents in the 1970s. Now they produce a wine under the Château de Brissac label, from gravel soil, as well as those under the domaine name, from clay-limestone and schistous soil. The first has good blackberry fruit, and is elegant and of medium weight. The second is richer and more concentrated, with lots of depth. Both are very good, especially in 1996.

Domaine des Charbotières

Commune: Saint-Jean-des-Mauvrets.
Owner: Philippe Vintrou.
Surface Area under Vine: 10 ha.
Wines: Anjou-Villages including Les Richoux and Les Tuloires.

Philippe Vintrou, a biodynamist since 1993, is just beginning to use wood for ageing his wines. He produces two *cuvées*: Les Richoux is 100 per cent Cabernet Franc and Les Tuloires 100 per cent Cabernet Sauvignon. His 1996s are better than his 1995s and are indeed very stylish. Subsequent vintages have been just as good.

Domaine de L'Echalier

Commune: Rablay-sur-Layon.
Owners: L & F Lorent-Bureau.
Surface Area under Vine: 13 ha.
Wines: Anjou-Villages, Anjou and Coteaux du Layon.

This estate favours using a very large amount of Cabernet Sauvignon: 60 per cent for the basic Anjou red and 80 per cent for the Anjou-Villages. I find the wines good, but not stylish enough to be anything better than that. The Coteaux du Layon is good but not great.

Domaine Gaudard

Commune: Chaudefond-sur-Layon.
Owner: Pierre Aguilas.
Surface Area under Vine: 5 ha.
Wines: Anjou-Villages and Anjou.

Pierre Aguilas only makes red wine. His basic Anjou is quite good, but the Anjou-Villages, coming from a part of his domaine where the soil is limestone, is rather better, with a nice touch of oak.

Domaine de Haute Perche

Commune: Saint-Melaine-sur-Aubance.
Owner: Christian Papin.
Surface Area under Vine: 20 ha.
Wines: Anjou-Villages, Coteaux de L'Aubance and Anjou.

Christian Papin lives within the new Anjou-Villages-Brissac *appellation*. The soil here is a sort of clayey schist. These are round, rich wines with a good dollop of Cabernet Sauvignon in the blend. His basic Anjou red is a wine of lovely abundant fruit and no hard edges.

Domaine de Montgilet

Commune: Juigné-sur-Loire.
Owner: Victor Lebreton.
Surface Area under Vine: 8 ha.
Wines: Anjou-Villages, including Cuvée Barrique, Anjou and Coteaux de L'Aubance.

Victor Lebreton produces three red wines: basic Anjou, Anjou-Villages and Cuvée Barrique (both the latter can have as much as 50 per cent Cabernet Sauvignon in the blend). Vinification is in stainless steel vats, temperature-controlled at 30°. I liked all three 1997s – they struck me as very stylish, clean and clear-cut and the barriqued wine was not as woody as I feared. The 1996s were less interesting but other vintages rather better. These are wines that will last ten years or more.

Domaine Ogereau

Commune: Saint-Lambert-sur-Aubance.
Owner: Vincent Ogereau.
Surface Area under Vine: 20 ha.
Wines: Anjou-Villages and Coteaux du Layon.

Vincent Ogereau produces two Anjou-Villages: one 100 per cent Cabernet Franc, the other all Cabernet Sauvignon. I find them lush, ripe and smooth, almost too sweet but certainly very seductive. The Coteaux du Layon is also good.

CHÂTEAU PIERRE-BISE
CLOS DE COULAINE
Commune: Beaulieu-sur-Layon.
Owner: Claude Papin.
Surface Area under Vine: 35 ha.
Wines: Anjou, Anjou-Villages and Savennières.

Claude Papin is based in Beaulieu-sur-Layon but also owns the Clos de Coulaine in Savennières on the opposite side of the river Loire. Here he produces two red wines – one 100 per cent Cabernet Sauvignon, the other a blend of half Cabernet Sauvignon and half Franc, which I prefer, at least in the 1996 vintage. The Anjou-Villages Château Pierre-Bise wine, another 50:50 blend, is ripe and succulent. He also produces a splendid Anjou-Gamay from old vines and low yields. (See also pages 304 and 307.)

★ CHÂTEAU DE PUTILLE
Commune: La Pommeraye.
Owner: Pascal Delaunay.
Surface Area under Vine: 30 ha.
Wines: Anjou-Villages, Anjou Coteaux de La Loire and Anjou.

Pascal Delaunay's domaine is based in the Coteaux de la Loire *appellation* where there is volcanic rock as well as schist – a good environment. His vineyards contain a high percentage of Cabernet Sauvignon and the basic Anjou-Villages uses 50 per cent and the Cuvée Prestige 100 per cent. I like the wines here – they have plenty of character and the Prestige *cuvée* is very good indeed: full, generous and concentrated.

★ DOMAINE RICHOU
Commune: Mozé-sur-Louet.
Owner: Didier Richou.
Surface Area under Vine: 30 ha.
Wines: Anjou-Villages, including Vieilles Vignes, and Coteaux de L'Aubance.

Didier Richou produces one of the best Anjou-Villages. The Vieilles Vignes uses 20 per cent Cabernet Sauvignon and even in the abundant 1996 vintage the yield was under 40 hl/ha. These are wines with intensity, very pure classy fruit and lovely balance.

DOMAINE DES ROCHELLES
Commune: Saint-Jean-des-Mauvrets.
Owner: Jean-Yves Lebreton.
Surface Area under Vine: 35 ha.
Wines: Anjou-Villages including La Croix de Mission.

The star red wine in Jean-Yves Lebreton's portfolio is La Croix de Mission. Predominantly Cabernet Sauvignon (90 per cent in 1997), the wine is quite extracted, the product of the schistous soils around Brissac and needs five years' ageing in a good vintage. Is it a bit too big for its boots?

★ CHÂTEAU DE TIGNÉ
Commune: Tigné.
Owner: Gérard Depardieu.
Surface Area under Vine: 50 ha.
Wines: Anjou-Villages, including Mozart and Cyrano.

Château de Tigné, a splendid domaine in the southern Layon Valley, was acquired by the wine lover and actor Gérard Depardieu in 1989. The wine is made for him by Dominique Polleau, the mayor of Tigné. The vineyards are tended biologically, with low yields, green harvesting and very selective hand picking, and produce a range of excellent wines: the top *cuvées*, made from the oldest vines and only in the best years, are called Mozart (100 per cent Cabernet Franc) and Cyrano (a blend of Cabernet Sauvignon and Cabernet Franc). The latter is the sturdier of the two wines and is better in the warmer vintages. But does Mozart always have more finesse?

Other Producers of note
DOMAINE DES BEAUMARD (ROCHEFORT-SUR-LOIRE), LES CAVES DE LA LOIRE (BRISSAC), DOMAINE DES DEUX ARCS/MICHEL GAZEAU (MARTIGNÉ-BRIAND), DOMAINE DES EPINAUDIÈRES/ ROGER ET PAUL FARDEAU (SAINT-LAMBERT-DU-LATTAY), CHÂTEAU DE FESLES/VIGNOBLE GERMAIN (THOUARCÉ), DOMAINE DE GATINES/ MICHEL DESSÈVRE (TIGNÉ), DOMAINE DES HAUTES OUCHES/JOËL & JEAN-LOUIS LHUMEAU (BRIGNÉ-SUR-LAYON), DOMAINE LAFFOURCADE (ROCHEFORT-SUR-LOIRE), DOMAINE DES MAURIÈRES/FERNAND MORON (SAINT-LAMBERT-DU-

Lattay), Le Petit Clos/MM. Musset-Roullier (La Pommeraye) and Château La Varière/Jacques Beaujeau (Brissac).

Anjou Producers of note

Les Caves de La Loire (Brissac) and the reliable local merchants (such as Bouvet-Ladoubay and Gratien & Meyer) produce most of the generic anjou wines.

Individual growers Château du Beugnon/Jean-Marie Humeau (La Fosse-de-Tigné), Domaine des Bonnes Gagnes/Jean-Marc Héry (Saint-Saturnin-sur-Loire), Domaine Dittière/Joël & Bruno Dittière (Vauchrétien), Domaine des Epinaudières/Roger et Paul Fardeau (Saint-Lambert-du-Lattay), Château La Franchaie/Jean-Claude Chaillou (La Possonnière), Domaine du Fresche/Alain Boré (La Pommeraye), Château du Fresne/MM. Robin-Bretault (Faye-d'Anjou), Domaine des Hautes Ouches/Jean & Jean-Louis Lhumeau (Brigné-sur-Layon), Domaine Jolivet (Saint-Lambert-du-Lattay), Domaine Leduc-Frouin (Martigné-Briand), Le Clos de Motèles (Belleville-de-Sainte-Vierge), Clos du Moulin-Sainte-Cathérine/ Franck Perrault (Rochefort-sur-Loire), Domaine des Noëls/Jean-Michel Garnier (Faye-d'Anjou), Domaine du Sauveroy/Pascal Caillou (Saint-Lambert-du-Lattay) and Vignoble du Martinet/GAEC Bertrand (Beaulieu-sur-Layon).

ANJOU-COTEAUX DE LA LOIRE

Surface Area (1998): 40 ha.
Production (1998): 1064 hl.
Colour and Style: White, medium-sweet.
Grape Variety: Chenin Blanc.
Maximum Yield: 40 hl/ha.
Minimum Alcohol Level: 11°.

Similar medium-sweet wine to the Coteaux de L'Aubance comes under the label of Anjou-Coteaux de La Loire. This small *appellation* covers eleven communes

on mainly schistous soil, both north and south of the Loire from Savennières and Chalonnes-sur-Loire westwards to the Anjou/Muscadet border. One can't help feeling that these *appellations* are neither one thing nor another: too sweet for main dishes, too dry for puddings. Local producers can, of course, produce some of the other Anjou *appellations*, and some are now even making Sélection de Grains Nobles i.e. really luscious wines from grapes affected by noble rot.

Anjou-Coteaux de La Loire Producers of note

Domaine du Freshe/Alain Boré (La Pommeraye), Vignoble Musset-Roullier/Gilles Musset & Serge Roullier (La Pommeraye), Château de Putille/Pascal Delaunay (La Pommeraye), Domaine de Putille/Pierre Sécher (La Pommeraye) and Domaine Voisine-Harpin/Michel Voisine (Chalonnes-sur-Loire).

SAVENNIÈRES

Surface Area (1998): 130 ha.
Production (1998): 3878 hl.
Colour: White.
Grape Variety: Chenin Blanc.
Maximum Yield: 50 hl/ha.
Minimum Alcohol Level: 10°.

If most of the dry white wines of the Loire are wines made one year for drinking the next, one small area, at least, aspires to produce something a little more substantial, a little more serious: a white wine which, like those of Bordeaux or Burgundy, needs time to develop. This is Savennières.

Savennières lies on the north bank of the Loire, some 13 kilometres downstream from Angers. At this point the river is flowing roughly south-west, so the vineyards, in steep little side valleys whose streams debouch into the Loire itself, have an ideal exposure which is practically due south. The vines are protected from the wind and enjoy full sun from dawn to dusk.

The soil is volcanic in origin, and consists of a thin layer of loess, mixed with a peculiarly coloured, blue-violet schist, with veins of sandstone and granite. This sits on a more solid schistous base which, even in the hottest summers, retains enough humidity to succour the vines. The colour of the stones is, as far as I know, unique to Savennières: and certainly I have not met their like in any other vineyard area.

Savennières is a small *vignoble*, though it has tripled in size since 1980. The most important part of Savennières is the 17-hectare *lieu-dit* known as La Roche-aux-Moines. This site, as the name suggests, is a rocky promontory which dominates the Loire, roughly opposite where the Layon river enters it from the south near Rochefort. It is said to have been donated to the Abbey of Saint-Nicolas at Angers by one Buhard, a Breton squire in the service of Geoffrey Martell, Count of Anjou, in 1063. However, this legend has been disputed by modern historians who have shown that all the poor Buhard ever possessed in the way of land were two islands in the middle of the river, one of which still preserves his name, now corrupted into Béhuard.

At the beginning of the thirteenth century, during the wars between King John of England and King Philippe-Auguste of France, a fortress was built on the site, which successfully withstood several sieges by the hapless John. Both at La Roche-aux-Moines, and later at Bouvines, the English troops were defeated, as John fulfilled his destiny – to be known as Jean-Sans-Terre, or Lackland. At the end of the fourteenth century the land passed from a local *seigneur*, Guillaume de Craon, to Louis II, Duke of Anjou, and it was probably about this time that the site was first planted with vines on a large scale. A document from the mid-fifteenth century refers to the despair of local monks at the damage to the vineyard caused by a particularly bad storm. By this time the fortress and its dependencies had passed to Jean de Brie, Seigneur de Serrant, and it was one of his descendants, Pontus du Brie, who was authorized by Louis XI in 1481 to call the property La Roche du Serrant.

At the end of the sixteenth century, during the Wars of Religion between the Huguenots and the Catholics, the old fortress fell into disrepair and was largely dismantled. Only a few ruins remain to this day, notably a round tower which today stands guard over part of the vineyard known as the Clos du Château.

That the site was certainly a flourishing vineyard is shown by a story Hubrecht Duijker recounts in his admirable book on the *Loire, Champagne and Alsace*. Louis XIV is said to have proposed a journey to Savennières after having been much impressed by the quality of the wine when it had been presented to him at court. News of this project soon passed back to the region, and the local proprietors set about plans to receive the royal entourage. The owner of the Château de La Roche-aux-Moines actually went as far as building another storey on his mansion, and constructing new wings and towers to it. Unfortunately the king never arrived. His coach got stuck in the mud and frustrated and angry, the king was forced to turn back. Later still, at the time of the Revolution, the site was known as the Roche Vineuse. Once again, under Napoleon, the wine was enjoyed at court, for one of the Empress Josephine's ladies-in-waiting was the Comtesse de Serrant.

La Roche-aux-Moines still exists, as does the neighbouring 7-hectare vineyard of Coulée-de-Serrant, exclusively owned by the Joly family who are the current owners of the Château de La Roche-aux-Moines itself. They are both sub-*appellations* of Savennières itself and lie at the north-eastern end of the *appellation* between the villages of Savennières and Epiré. Epiré is next to the commune of Bouchemaine, nearest to Angers; further downstream is the commune of La Poissonière. Only the most favourable, protected sites within these three communes are suitable for the vine, and to all intents and purposes these are all in Savennières and Epiré.

When *appellation contrôlée* was bestowed on Savennières in 1952 the yield was fixed at 25 hectolitres per hectare, and a minimum alcohol level of 12.5°. This may seem parsimonious on the one hand, and presumptuous on the other. The explanation is that up until this time, most Savennières wines, like its neighbours in the Layon Valley, were sweet or semi-sweet, depending on the climate. It was not dry, though some, such as Coulée de Serrant, had been vinified dry for much longer. For most of the last thirty years most Savennières has been made as a dry wine, but more recently some producers have turned to making a wine which is off-dry or *tendre*, or even one which is sweeter still.

To produce a wine with a minimum alcoholic content of 12.5° in such a northerly region as the Loire Valley, at the very limits of successful grape-growing, is no easy thing. It means risking all to pick as late as possible, or, alternatively, ruining the balance and breed of the wine by excessive chaptalization. It is no wonder that making wine in Savennières is a precarious procedure. Indeed, the Joly family did not make any Coulée de Serrant in 1963, 1965 and 1972: the grapes were just not good enough. Frost also is a problem. Inevitably, in all but the luckiest years, some vineyards are damaged. Regrettably, more recently, the minimum alcohol level has been reduced to 10° as a result of local pressure. Surely 11.5° would have been a compromise?

Savennières is made exclusively from Chenin Blanc. When young the wine is very austere, bone dry, and the acidity is dominant. The 'old style' Savennières, as practised by Nicolas Joly at Château de La Roche-aux-Moines, is a wine which carries this austerity to an extreme. Because the wine is deliberately made as one to age, it is bottled with a high degree of sulphur and this combines with Chenin grape to produce a rather solid wine with a clumsy, wet-wool flavour – or so it seems for at least five years. Sometimes these ugly ducklings evolve into nothing better than ugly ducks: by the time the sulphur has disappeared, so also has the fruit. However, in the best years patience is eventually rewarded, and the wine opens out to show a firm, full, ripe, complex character with a flowery, greengage, aroma and with nuances of honey and lime trees.

Elsewhere in Savennières, the trend has been to produce something a little more supple. The results are more elegant. Most of the other producers are trying to bring the fruit to the fore, while still retaining the wine's ability to age. Some are now fermenting the wine in newish barrels. After a period when I felt the local growers were somewhat feeling their way, when the wine was neither a serious *vin de garde* nor a pleasant fruity wine for early drinking and when many wines seemed to be at their most elegant and enjoyable while still in cask, I now feel that the producers have got their collective act together. Savennières is not a cheap wine, and so it has a duty to be a fine one.

Leading Savennières Producers

★ DOMAINE DES BAUMARD
Commune: Rochefort-sur-Loire.
Owner: Florent Baumard.
Surface Area under Vine: 15 ha.
Wines: Savennières including Clos du Papillon and Clos de Saint-Yves. (See also Coteaux du Layon page 306.)

The Clos du Papillon is the third of Savennières' important *lieux-dits*, and is shared by the Baumards, the Domaine du Closel and Château de La Bizolière, now farmed by the Soulez family of Château de Chamboureau. There is a lot of quartz in the soil and perhaps as a consequence of this I find this a much more profound wine than the Clos de Saint-Yves. Baumard makes wines that are accessible young but they will keep in good vintages. Increasingly, the grapes are picked in successive visits to the vineyard and these *cuvées* are sometimes vinified and bottled separately.

★ CHÂTEAU DE CHAMBOUREAU
CHÂTEAU DE LA BIZOLIÈRE
Owner: Pierre Soulez.
Surface Area under Vine: 25 ha.
Wines: Savennières including Clos du Papillon *moelleux* and La Roche-aux-Moines.

Pierre Soulez offers three dry *cuvées*, Château de Chamboureau, Château de La Bizolière, which the family farms for Baron Brincard, and La Roche-aux-Moines. The holdings in the Clos du Papillon produce *moelleux* wines in the good years, *demi-sec* in the less good. These are very stylish wines. Fermented in wood, the Roche-aux-Moines is particularly good.

DOMAINE DU CLOSEL
Owner: Michèle de Jessey.
Surface Area under Vine: 16 ha.
Wines: Savennières including Les Coulées, Les Caillardières, Clos du Papillon and Cuvée Vieilles Vignes.

Quality is a bit uneven here, especially at the lower levels (Les Coulées), but it improves and becomes more reliable as you ascend the range. The Clos du Papillon can be very good indeed.

CLOS DE COULAINE
Owner: Claude Papin.
Surface Area under Vine: 4 ha (in Savennières).
Wines: Savennières. (See also Château de Pierre-Bise pages 300 and 307.)

Claude Papin, well-known for his Coteaux du Layon, rents these vines and harvests by successive sweeps through the vineyard. He produces a *demi-sec* wine under the Pierre de Coulaine label and aims to make a Sélection de Grains Nobles wine when the harvest permits.

★ CHATEAU D'EPIRÉ
Owner: Luc Bizard.
Surface Area under Vine: 8 ha.
Wines: Savennières including Cuvée Spéciale and Cuvée Armand Bizard (*moelleux*).

There have been Bizards here since before the French Revolution. The vines consist of three parcels: Le Parc, La Croix-Picot and Le Hu-Boyau, the latter lying above Coulée de Serrant. The wines are very clean and pure, with real style. They keep well too.

DOMAINE DES FORGES
Commune: Saint-Aubin-de-Luigné.
Owner: Stéphane Branchereau.
Surface Area under Vine: 1.5 ha (in Savennières).
Wines: Savennières including Clos des Mauriers, and Coteaux du Layon.

The Branchereau family set up here in 1994, planted a vineyard and produced their first wine the same year. I have tried all the vintages since. They are all good but different! As the vines mature and the winemaking settles down to a consistent style we can expect some good things here. The wines are fermented in (newish) wood.

DOMAINE AUX MOINES
Owner: Monique Laroche.
Surface Area under Vine: 7 ha.
Wines: Savennières including La Roche-aux-Moines.

Madame Laroche, once a pharmacist, has been here since 1981. Most of her land is in the Roche-aux-Moines *lieu-dit*, the better wine from there forming the superior of her two *cuvées*. The 1995 Roche-aux-Moines was good, but I have yet to be really enthused overall.

DOMAINE DE LA MONNAIE
Owner: Eric Morgat.
Surface Area under Vine: 2.5 ha.
Wines: Savennières.

Eric Morgat, whose parents own the Château du Breuil in the Coteaux du Layon, took over this small parcel of thirty-year-old vines in 1996. Watch this space.

★ CHÂTEAU DE LA ROCHE-AUX-MOINES
Owner: Nicolas Joly.
Surface Area under Vine: 13 ha.
Wines: Savennières including Coulée de Serrant *monopole*, Clos de La Bergerie and Becherelle.

Nicolas Joly, who took over responsibility here in 1976, is one of the pioneers of biodynamism, a viticultural approach which combines homeopathy with a planetary calendar, building on the more common biological techniques now employed by nearly all serious winemakers the world over. The property has been completely biodynamic since 1985. It also possesses a large slice of the Roche-aux-Moines (bottled as Clos de La Bergerie) and the exclusivity of the splendidly situated Coulée de Serrant vineyard.

So the domaine ought to produce three star wine. Er, no: good but not breathtaking. Too often I find the wines hard rather than rich and succulent, and with an excess of sulphur. They are uncompromisingly built to last. But neither the 1988, nor the 1989 nor the 1990, all very successful vintages, really struck me as brilliant when last sampled in the summer of 1999.

Other Producers of note
MOULIN DE CHAUVIGNÉ/SYLVIE TERMEAU (ROCHEFORT-SUR-LOIRE), CLOS DES PERRIÈRES/PIERRE-YVES TIJOK (LAYON), CLOS DES VARENNES/VIGNOBLES GERMAIN (THOUARCÉ) AND VIGNOBLES LAFFOURCADE (CHAVAGNES-LES-EAUX).

COTEAUX DU LAYON

Surface Area (1998): 1853 ha.
Production (1998): 52,772 hl.
Colour and Style: Sweet white.
Grape Variety: Chenin Blanc.
Maximum Yield: 30 hl/ha (25 hl/ha in Chaume).
Minimum Alcohol Level: Coteaux du Layon 11°;
Coteaux du Layon-Villages 12°.

If Savennières produces the best dry Loire white wine, so the Layon Valley provides the best sweet wines. In Vouvray the grapes which produce sweet wines are only very rarely, in exceptional years, attacked by *pourriture noble* but this noble rot arrives more frequently in the Layon Valley, as a result of its mesoclimate. Moreover, the Layon wines can only be sweet: for these growers there is not the alternative of making a dry or merely *tendre* wine in lesser years, though they are allowed to produce simple white Anjou.

The Layon is more of a stream than a river. It rises just over the border in the *département* of Deux-Sèvres, and flows north-west through some of the most beautiful Loire countryside for some 40 kilometres, as the crow flies, before reaching the Loire downstream of Rochefort. On the map this looks a relatively large area; much bigger than Chinon or even Saumur. Yet not all the area is suitable for sweet wine; in so northerly a region only the best-sited vineyards, conditioned by the mesoclimate of the valley itself and on precisely the correct soil, produce the correct combination of morning mists and hot, sunny afternoons late into October, which is necessary for noble rot to attack the grapes. Out of a total of some 3000 hectares of vines, only about half produce Coteaux du Layon or the superior communal *appellations* of Quarts de Chaume or Bonnezeaux. The rest produce *appellation contrôlée* Anjou.

As in Sauternes in the Bordeaux region, when noble rot attacks the grapes they shrivel up and then dry out, with both the sugar and acidity levels increasing and the action of the fungus imparts a particular spicy, luscious, honeyed, herbal flavour. The Layon wines never have the weight or richness of their Bordeaux rivals and are unsuitable accompaniments for any but the most delicate desserts. But, of course, they are marvellous as dessert wines on their own, and also as an aperitif.

In order to pick each bunch or part bunch of grapes at its peak of ripeness and noble rot, it is necessary to harvest through each row of vines several times – but in order to afford to do this, the growers need to be able to command a high enough price for their wine. Unfortunately the base price for a Layon wine is low. Usually there is only one picking, though this is made as late as possible. Only the top domaines can afford to make more than one passage through the vineyards. Happily a combination of good vintages and an increasing interest in Layon wines has encouraged more and more growers to take the measures necessary to produce wines at the top quality level.

The Layon vineyards stretch over twenty-seven communes between Les Verchers, south of Doué-La-Fontaine, and Chalonnes, on the Loire. The best are on the north side of the valley between Thouarcé and Rochefort on slopes which rise up to 100 metres above the river Layon. The soil consists of various clay-sand-limestone mixtures such as loess and marl over a subsoil of schist. In 1955, five years after Coteaux du Layon became a separate *appellation*, the INAO decreed that seven superior communes could be designated Coteaux du Layon-Villages. These communes are Rochefort-sur-Loire, Chaume, Saint-Aubin-de-Luigné, Saint-Lambert-du-Lattay, Beaulieu-sur-Layon, Rablay-sur Layon and Faye-d'Anjou. The wine from these communes must reach 12° of alcohol plus another one of unconverted sugar, as against 11° plus another one for straight Coteaux du Layon. Moreover, in Chaume itself the maximum yield was reduced to 25 hectolitres per hectare, the same as in Sauternes. Elsewhere the maximum is 30 hectolitres. Rather than sell their wine as Coteaux du Layon-Villages, it is more usual for the local growers to suffix the name of the commune; for example, Coteaux du Layon-Rablay, and so on.

The sweet Layon wines vary from communal Coteaux du Layon, as offered by one of the Loire *négociant*s or local co-operatives such as UAPL at Brissac, to the more substantial wines of the Coteaux du Layon-

Villages, Bonnezeaux or Quarts de Chaume, from a single domaine and a good vintage, made from grapes affected by noble rot. The lesser wines are made for early drinking: light, fruity and, one hopes, not overlaid with sulphur. The better wines are made to last, and in their youth, until the sulphur has been absorbed, may be ungainly. A venerable old bottle, a 1964, 1959, even a 1947 if you are really fortunate, is a great delight, with a soft, almost flowery fragrance, a high-toned, racy, delicate, peachy or greengagy fruit, and a pronounced freshness maintained by the wine's high acidity.

There are said to be pronounced — or at least discernible — nuances between the wines of the different communes in the Layon Valley. In my experience the styles vary as much from grower to grower as from village to village. Baumard's Quarts de Chaume, for instance, is quite a different wine, being less rich, more lemony, than that from Château de Bellerive.

Which is your yardstick? In general I must admit to finding Bonnezeaux more pedestrian — slightly earthier, less elegant — than Quarts de Chaume, and indeed than the best single-domaine Coteaux du Layon-Villages wines. This, however, may be my bad luck. Perhaps I have had the misfortune to meet too many pedestrian Bonnezeaux growers.

QUARTS DE CHAUME AND BONNEZEAUX

Surface Area (1998): (Quarts de Chaume) 40 ha; **(Bonnezeaux)** 99 ha.
Production (1998): (Quarts de Chaume) 693 hl; **(Bonnezeaux)** 2365 hl.
Colour and Style: Sweet white.
Grape Variety: Chenin Blanc.
Maximum Yield: 25 hl/ha.
Minimum Alcohol Level: 12°.

These are two *lieux-dits* lying within the Coteaux du Layon *appellation*. Quarts de Chaume is in the commune of Rochefort 5 kilometres inland from the river Loire. The name derives from the medieval practice of share-cropping. The local seigneurs were the Guerche family whose ruined castle can still be seen nearby. They demanded a quarter of the crop each year, exercising the right to choose the best grapes from their local tenants, the monks from the Abbaye du Ronceray.

Quarts de Chaume is a tiny *appellation*. The vineyards occupy land which contains more clay than the rest of the Layon Valley and are magnificently situated. The vines undulate gently down towards the river, away from the hamlet of Chaume, and face due south. On the other three sides the horseshoe-shaped hill of Chaume protects the vineyards from cold and wind. The maximum yield is the lowest prescribed for the entire Loire Valley. Understandably the yield is small, for here several passages through the vines are normal at harvest time, and only grapes affected by *pourriture noble* are used.

Bonnezeaux lies upstream from Quarts de Chaume in the commune of Thouarcé. The area is larger but the wines have less reputation: in the main less depth and concentration.

Leading Coteaux du Layon Producers

★ DOMAINE DES BAUMARD
Commune: Rochefort-sur-Loire.
Owner: Florent Baumard.
Surface Area under Vine: 44 ha.
Wines: Quarts de Chaume, Coteaux du Layon including Clos-Sainte-Cathérine, Savennières and Anjou-Villages. (See also page 303.)
The Baumard family are one of the biggest and one of the very best producers in this corner of the Loire Valley. Fanatical about preserving as much freshness as possible in their wines, they take great pains to preserve Chenin Blanc's primary spring blossom and Victoria plum aromas. The result is wines of impeccable purity, intensly flavoured but never hard. The sweet wine is delicious young but also keeps very well.

★ CHÂTEAU BELLERIVE
Commune: Rochefort-sur-Loire.
Owners: Serge & Michel Malinge.
Surface Area under Vine: 12 ha.

Wines: Quarts de Chaume including Clos de Chaume and Quintessence.

In May 1994 Jacques Lalanne sold his family property to resolve inheritance problems but he remains as wine-maker, with a completely free hand. Quality has not been compromised by the change of ownership and if anything the 1995 and 1996 wines are better than those of 1989 and 1990. The wines are fermented in old wooden barrels, Lalanne deliberately prolonging the vinification so that it takes three months or more. The result is splendid spicy-rich wines which take their time to come round, from what is reportedly the best corner of the Quarts de Chaume vineyard.

DOMAINE PHILIPPE DELESVAUX

Commune: Saint-Aubin-de-Luigné.
Owner: Philippe Delesvaux.
Surface Area under Vine: 14.5 ha.
Wines: Coteaux du Layon.

Philippe Delesvaux came to the Layon as a trainee and has been here ever since, setting up in 1983. He specialises in Sélection de Grains Nobles and the wines are very concentrated and fine, indeed.

★ CHÂTEAU DE FESLES

Commune: Thouarcé.
Owner: Bernard Germain.
Surface Area under Vine: 33 ha.
Wines: Bonnezeaux, Anjou-Villages, Anjou (white), Savennières (Clos de Varennes), and Coteaux du Layon-Chaume (Château de La Guimonière and Château de La Roulerie).

The legendary grower, Jean Boivin established the Coteaux du Layon as a quality sweet wine area. This tradition was ably continued by his son Jacques. Then in 1991 de Fesles was sold to Gaston Lenôtre, Parisien ex-pastry chef, as a result of inheritance problems. Lenôtre spent a fortune on Fesles and other properties, only to sell out a few years later to Bernard Germain and his associates. This second change of ownership in five years does not seem to have impaired quality, thankfully. The three sweet château wines are the best of a large range: the Bonnezeaux Château de Fesles is the best.

VIGNOBLES LAFFOURCADE

Commune: Chavagnes-Les-Eaux.
Owner: Pascal Laffourcade.
Surface Area under Vine: 34 ha.
Wines: Quarts de Chaume including Château L'Echardière, Anjou-Villages (Château Perray-Jouannet) and Savennières (Clos de La Royauté).

The Laffourcades are major producers in Anjou, but they used to be even more substantial, as they were once owners not only of Château L'Echardière, but of Le Suronde as well, which meant they owned half the Quarts de Chaume *appellation*. Anyway, the 1990s have seen a sea-change here and from light wines for early drinking we now have rich, positive wines that will keep well. The Laffourcades are now merchants in a small way as well.

DOMAINE DES PETITS-QUARTS-LADOUVE

Commune: Faye-d'Anjou.
Owner: Godineau Père & Fils.
Surface Area under Vine: 25 ha.
Wines: Bonnezeaux, including Melleresses and Malabé, Coteaux du Layon-Faye and Anjou (red).

Standards can be uneven here. I find a great difference in style as well as in lusciousness between the Coteaux du Layon and the Malabé, the richest of the Bonnezeaux *cuvées* (this can be brilliant, for instance in 1996).

★ CHÂTEAU PIERRE-BISE

Commune: Beaulieu-sur-Layon.
Owner: Claude Papin.
Surface Area under Vine: 35 ha.
Wines: Quarts de Chaume, Coteaux du Layon-Beaulieu, Coteaux du Layon-Chaume. (See also Château de Pierre-Bise and Clos de Coulaine pages 300 and 304.)

The name Pierre-Bise refers to a volcanic rock called *spilite*, one of the complex mix of rocks which underlies Claude Papin's vineyards. He makes a number of *cuvées* from Beaulieu (L'Anclaie and Les Soucheries) and Chaume (Les Tétuères and Les Rouannières), and sometimes in the best years a Sélection de Grains Nobles wine too. The man is a master.

CHÂTEAU DE PLAISANCE
Commune: Rochefort-sur-Loire.
Owner: Rochais family.
Surface Area under Vine: 28 ha.
Wines: Quarts de Chaume, Coteaux du Layon-Chaume including Les Zerzilles, Savennières, Clos des Mauriers, and Anjou-Villages.

Both the Quarts de Chaume and the Savennières are relatively new additions here, but I continue to think that the Zerzilles is the best wine here – and it is two-thirds of the price of the Quarts de Chaume.

DOMAINE DES SABLONNETTES
Commune: Rablay-sur-Layon.
Owner: Joël Ménard.
Surface Area under Vine: 13 ha.
Wines: Coteaux du Layon-Faye, including Quintessence and L'Aubépine, Coteaux du Layon-Rablay including Les Erables, Cabernet d'Anjou, Anjou-Villages and Anjou-Gamay.

A new star, the youthful, sympathetic Joël Ménard produces a range of excellent sweet wines from his holdings in Faye and Rablay. I find the wines clean, pure and beautifully poised.

DOMAINE DE LA SANSONNIÈRE
Commune: Thouarcé.
Owner: Marc Angeli.
Surface Area under Vine: 8 ha.
Wines: Bonnezeaux including Cuvée Mathilde, Coteaux du Layon, and Anjou (red and white).

Hailing from Provence, Marc Angeli was determined to produce sweet wine, and eventually settled in Thouarcé, producing his first wine in 1990. His vineyards are tended biodynamically. His top Bonnezeaux is Cuvée Mathilde, fermented in a mixture of new and newish barrels.

CHÂTEAU SOUCHERIE
Commune: Beaulieu-sur-Layon.
Owner: Pierre-Yves Tijou.
Surface Area under Vine: 33 ha.
Wines: Coteaux du Layon-Beaulieu, Coteaux du Layon-Chaume including Vieilles Vignes and Les Mouchis, Savennières, Anjou-Villages and Anjou (white).

In his fifties, Pierre-Yves Tijou is a member of the Coteaux du Layon aristocracy, being related to the Boivins, the Touchais and other leading winemaking families. His mansion is a fine *maison bourgeoise* commending a magnificent view of the Loire. Underneath, in a splendid cellar, the wines live up to their surroundings. The Chaume Vieilles Vignes (and they really are old: approaching their centenary) is especially lovely.

Other Producers of note
DOMAINE PIERRE AGUILAS (CHAUDEFONDS-SUR-LAYON), CHÂTEAU DU BREUIL/MARC MORGAT (BEAULIEU-SUR-LAYON), CHÂTEAU DE BROSSAY/RAYMOND & HUBERT DEFFOIS (CLÉRÉ-SUR-LAYON), DOMAINE PHILIPPE CADY (SAINT-AUBIN-DE-LUIGNÉ), DOMAINE DES CLOSSERONS/JEAN-CLAUDE LEBLANC & FILS (FAYE-D'ANJOU), DOMAINE COUSIN-LEDUC/OLIVIER COUSIN (MARTIGNÉ-BRIAND), DOMAINE DESMAZIÈRES/MARC GODEAU (BEAULIEU-SUR-LAYON), DOMAINE HERVÉ DULOQUET (LES VERCHERS-SUR-LAYON), DOMAINE DE L'ECHALIER/ISABELLE LORENT & FRANÇOIS BUREAU (RABLAY-SUR-LAYON), DOMAINE DES FORGES/CLAUDE BRANCHEREAU (SAINT-AUBIN-DE-LUIGNÉ), DOMAINE DES GAGNERIES/CHRISTIAN & ANNE ROUSSEAU (THOUARCÉ), CHÂTEAU DE LA GENAISERIE/YVES SOULEZ (SAINT-AUBIN-DE-LUIGNÉ), DOMAINE PIERRE JUTEAU (CHAUDEFONDS-SUR-LAYON), CHÂTEAU DES NOYERS/M CARLO (MARTIGNÉ-BRIAND), DOMAINE VINCENT OGEREAU (SAINT-LAMBERT-DU-LATTAY), DOMAINE DU PETIT VAL/VINCENT GOIZIL (CHAVAGNES-LES-EAUX), DOMAINE JO PITHON (SAINT-LAMBERT-DU-LATTAY), DOMAINE JOSEPH RENOU (SAINT-AUBIN-DE-LUIGNÉ), DOMAINE MICHEL ROBINEAU (SAINT-LAMBERT-DU-LATTAY) AND CHÂTEAU DES ROCHETTES/JEAN DOUET (CONCOURSON-SUR-LAYON).

COTEAUX DE L'AUBANCE

Surface Area (1998): 152 ha.
Production (1998): 4660 hl.
Colour and Style: Sweet white.
Grape Variety: Chenin Blanc.

Maximum Yield: 30 hl/ha.
Minimum Alcohol Level: 10.5°.

Parallel with the Layon, a few kilometres upstream, runs the Aubance river. The *appellation*, created in 1950, covers ten communes of schistous soil on the opposite bank of the Loire to Angers, and is for a medium-sweet wine from the Chenin Blanc grape. Though the area is of a reasonable size, many growers now concentrate on the production of the more popular red, rosé or dry white wines, selling them as Anjou or Anjou-Villages.

Leading Coteaux de L'Aubance Producers

★ DOMAINE DE BABLUT
Commune: Brissac-Quincé.
Owner: Christophe Daviau.
Surface Area under Vine: 100 ha.
Wines: Coteaux de L'Aubance, including Cuvée GN, Vin Noble, Anjou-Villages, Cabernet d'Anjou, Anjou (white) and Anjou-Gamay.

I bought old sweet rosés (1943, 1945 and 1947) from the Daviau family in the 1970s. The sweet whites today are even better. Partly fermented in new wood, they have a depth, a complexity, and indeed a lusciousness, which rival the best of those from the Layon.

DOMAINE DE MONTGILET
Commune: Juigné-sur-Loire.
Owners: Victor & Vincent Lebreton.
Surface Area under Vine: 35 ha.
Wines: Coteaux de L'Aubance, including Les Trois Schistes, Le Tertereaux and Le Clos des Huttières, Cabernet d'Anjou and Anjou (white).

These stylish Coteaux de L'Aubance wines are vinified in barrel (most of the lesser growers use stainless steel) and the wines have greater depth as a result. The Cabernet d'Anjou rosé is also good.

Other Producers of note
DOMAINE DE HAUTE-PERCHE/CHRISTIAN PAPIN (SAINT-MELAINE-SUR-AUBANCE), DOMAINE DIDIER & DAMIEN RICHOU (MOZÉ-SUR-LOUET), DOMAINE DES ROCHELLES/JEAN-YVES LEBRETON (SAINT-JEAN-DES-MAUVRETS) AND CHÂTEAU LA VARIÈRE/JACQUES BEAUJEAU (BRISSAC).

COTEAUX D'ANCENIS

Surface Area (1998): 257 ha.
Production (1998): (Red & rosé) 15,366 hl; (white) 226 hl.
Colour: Red, rosé and white.
Grape Varieties: (Red & rosé) Gamay Noir à Jus Blanc, Cabernet Franc and Cabernet Sauvignon; (white) Chenin Blanc and Pinot Gris (Malvoisie).
Maximum Yield: 40 hl/ha.
Minimum Alcohol Level: 9°.

Though officially the Coteaux d'Ancenis (VDQS 1954) is an Anjou wine, it would be more logical to consider it under the heading of Pays Nantais or Muscadet. Most of the land is also authorized for making Muscadet des Coteaux de la Loire, and much of it also for Gros Plant du Pays Nantais. Though half the area, that on the south bank of the Loire, lies in the *département* of Maine-et-Loire, the rest, on the north side, is in the Loire-Atlantique, which is definitely Muscadet country.

I have included it here with the other Anjou wines because it is mainly a red or rosé wine, which no Nantais wine can be (except for Fiefs Vendéens). The grapes authorized are typically Anjou – Gamay is the main red grape, but both Cabernets are also permitted. Chenin Blanc and the little known Malvoisie are the white wine grapes. The grape name must always follow the Coteaux d'Ancenis name on the label.

Malvoisie is the most interesting wine. The grape is said by the locals to be the same as the Malmsey grape of Madeira and other similar varieties grown round the Mediterranean (such as Italy's Malvasia). However, it has nothing to do with these varieties. It is, in fact, none other than the Pinot Gris. In Ancenis, and elsewhere in the Loire where I have occasionally seen it, it produces a wine of medium sweetness, soft, aromatic and slightly spicy; a curiosity well worth sampling. Frankly, the rest of the Ancenis wines are rather dull.

Coteaux d'Ancenis Producers of note

Domaine Pierre de La Grange/Pierre Luneau-Papin (Le Landreau) and Pierre Guindon (Saint-Géréon).

Vins du Haut-Poitou

Surface Area (1998): 443 ha.
Production (1998): (Red & rosé) 16,265 hl; (white) 17,081.
Colour: Red, rosé and white.
Grape Varieties: (Red and rosé) Gamay Noir à Jus Blanc, Pinot Noir, Cabernet Franc, Merlot, Cot and Grolleau; (white) Sauvignon Blanc , Chenin Blanc, Chardonnay and Pinot Blanc.
Maximum Yield: 50 hl/ha.
Minimum Alcohol Level: 9°.

There was a time when Poitou wines were rather a vogue in Britain. Ninety-five per cent of the production came from a very up-to-date co-operative, the Cave du Haut-Poitou, at Neuville, 16 kilometres north-west of Poitiers. The quality here was reliable, the wines clean and usually sold under their varietal label and everything seemed set fair for this VDQS – a recent creation in 1970. In 1988 the co-operative started producing single-vineyard wines (Château de Brizay, Le Logis, La Fuye) and other *têtes de cuvée* including cask-fermented Chardonnays. Then something began to go wrong. Rumours persisted that some members hadn't been paid for their harvest. In 1995 Georges Duboeuf of Beaujolais bought a 40 per cent share. The Cave du Haut-Poitou now operates as a merchant. The suppliers get paid and the wine, commercial as always, remains the same.

Vins du Thouarsais

Surface Area (1998): 24 ha.
Production (1998): (Red and rosé) 569 hl; (white) 435 hl.
Colour: Red, rosé and white.
Grape Varieties: (Red and rosé) Cabernet Franc, Cabernet Sauvignon and Gamay Noir à Jus Blanc; (white) Chenin Blanc and Chardonnay.
Maximum Yield: 50 hl/ha.
Minimum Alcohol Level: 9°.

South of Thouars, on either side of the river Thouet in the Deux-Sèvres *département*, fifteen communes can produce Vins du Thouarsais (promoted to VDQS 1966). In practice the locals prefer to grow cereals and other fruits, and production is tiny. Michel Gigon at Oiron is the only grower whose wines are seen outside the immediate neighbourhood.

Pays Nantais

More white wine is made in the Pays Nantais or Muscadet region than in Anjou and Touraine put together. The production of Muscadet wine is a quarter of the entire Loire harvest, including VDQS wines. Muscadet, then, is a prolific region; and the wine is one of the cheapest *appellations contrôlées* and one of the most popular wines, both in France and abroad.

The Muscadet area is the Pays Nantais, the last of the five main regions of the Loire. Here we are in the ancient Duchy of Brittany – the border was the old fortified town of Ancenis – long independent of the kings of France, and before them of the kings of England, to whom it was more closely allied. At Ancenis a treaty was finally agreed in 1468 between Duke François II of Brittany and King Louis XI of France, and the Bretons lost, if in legality only, their fierce independence. It is worth paying a nostalgic visit to the castle ruins.

Visually, the Pays Nantais is the least interesting part of the Loire Valley. The countryside has no forests and grand landscaped parks. There are few historic houses and monuments – though there is a charming cottage museum to Abelard and Heloise in Le Pallet, and the Château de Goulaine is worth a visit. In the main area,

PAYS NANTAIS

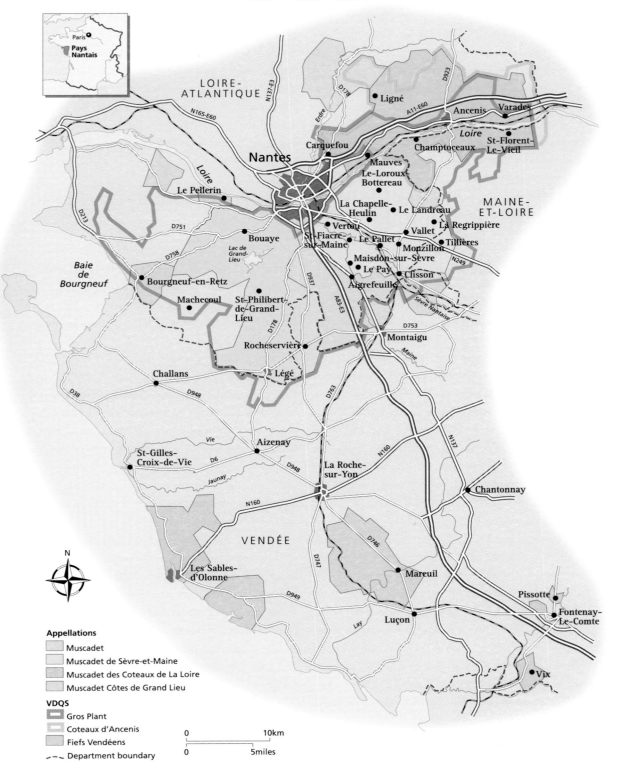

Paris
Pays
Nantais

LOIRE-
ATLANTIQUE

Ligné

Ancenis   Varades

Carquefou   Loire
Champtoceaux   St-Florent-
Le-Vieil

Nantes   Mauves
Le-Loroux-
Botterau

Le Pellerin   MAINE-
ET-LOIRE

La Chapelle-
Heulin   Le Landreau

Bouaye   Vertou   La Regrippière
St-Fiacre-   Vallet
sur-Maine   Le Pallet   Tillières
Lac de   Monzillon
Grand-   Maisdon-sur-Sèvre
Lieu   Le Pay
Bourgneuf-en-Retz   Clisson
Aigrefeuille

Baie
de
Bourgneuf   Machecoul   St-Philibert-
de-Grand-
Lieu

Rocheservière   Montaigu

Challans   Légé

Aizenay

St-Gilles-
Croix-de-Vie   La Roche-
sur-Yon

Chantonnay

VENDÉE

Les Sables-
d'Olonne   Mareuil

Pissotte
Fontenay-
Le-Comte

Luçon

Vix

N

Appellations

Muscadet

Muscadet de Sèvre-et-Maine

Muscadet des Coteaux de La Loire

Muscadet Côtes de Grand Lieu

VDQS

Gros Plant

Coteaux d'Ancenis

Fiefs Vendéens

– – – Department boundary

0   10km

0   5miles

the Sèvre-et-Maine, the villages are hemmed in by vines, with hardly a tree to break the landscape.

As elsewhere in the lower Atlantic end of the Loire Valley, the Dutch have had a strong influence. The vine was brought here by the Romans, but the original varieties produced only red wine grapes, which in the harsh local climate could not be said to have prospered, and whose produce gave rise to appropriately acidic comments in medieval texts. In the seventeenth century the Dutch, brandy drinkers, were forced to seek an alternative source of supply for their base wine, for the taxes in the Charente, now the home of Cognac, were becoming too prohibitive. The city of Nantes levied no duties on the export of wine, and the Dutch, already trading in the wines of the Anjou, persuaded the Nantais growers to switch to producing white wine.

Fortuitously a variety had recently arrived from Burgundy, where it was called the Melon. The story goes that following a catastrophic frost in the winter of 1709, which wiped out the unpopular red varieties, Louis XIV ordered that a new white grape should be planted instead. The Nantais christened it the Muscadet because it was said to have a musky flavour. It has no connection with any of the Muscat varieties nor with the Muscadelle of Bordeaux. Muscadet or the Melon de Bourgogne is actually a white cousin of the Gamay. The Muscadet grape prospered in the Pays Nantais. It suffered little from frost and ripened early, essential for successful cultivation in the Breton climate. It thrives on the predominantly clayey soil of the Pays Nantais and despite the region having the least summer sun of any wine area in France outside Champagne, it produces a wine which is by no means acid.

Until the early 1950s, Muscadet was a pleasant regional wine for drinking within the year and could only be found locally. It was seldom seen out of the region, even in other parts of France. Then came the boom. As a sort of white equivalent of Beaujolais, light, refreshing, uncomplicated and, above all, cheap, Muscadet has conquered the world. Muscadet, then, is not only the name of an area and a wine, but the name of the grape from which the wine comes. The grape is a fairly prolific variety and the maximum yield per

hectare for basic Muscadet wine is as high as 65 hectolitres. Only in Champagne and Alsace are there yields as high as this.

Mainly situated in the *département* of Loire-Atlantique, but also overlapping into the Maine-et-Loire and the Vendée, the entire area covers some 13,000 hectares and extends from the river Erdre in the north-east clockwise around the city of Nantes to Legé in the south and Machecoul in the west. Most of the vineyards and the best wines are found in the Sèvre-et-Maine district.

MUSCADET DE SÈVRE-ET-MAINE

Surface Area (1998): 10,544 ha.
Production (1998): 541,613 hl.
Colour: White.
Grape Variety: Muscadet (Melon de Bourgogne).
Maximum Yield: 55 hl/ha.
Minimum Alcohol Level: 9°.

Muscadet de Sèvre-et-Maine is named after the two small rivers, La Sèvre Nantaise and La Petite Maine, and consists of the four cantons of Clisson, Loreaux-Bottereau, Vallet and Vertou. The district is roughly bounded by the N137 road to Montaigu, the river Loire and the border of the Loire-Atlantique *département*. This is the source of some 75 per cent of all Muscadet wine and most of the best.

The Sèvre-et-Maine is a compact, undulating district, with a soil that is predominantly clay, particularly away from the Sèvre and Maine rivers, and mixed with sand and gravel. At its centre, at La Haie-Fouassière, it is worth climbing up the little hill of the Moulin du Breil. From its rocky summit, some 65 metres above sea level, there is an excellent panorama over the entire area.

Though seemingly 100 per cent cultivated, if not by the vine then with vegetables and fruit, there is still further potential for growth in this increasingly thriving part of the world, as every little patch of land, not only the south-facing slopes, comes to be planted, and as the inferior Gros Plant vine is replaced with Muscadet.

MUSCADET DES COTEAUX DE LA LOIRE

Surface Area (1998): 354 ha.
Production (1998): 17,144 hl.
Colour: White.
Grape Variety: Muscadet (Melon de Bourgogne).
Maximum Yield: 55 hl/ha.
Minimum Alcoho Level: 9°.

The Muscadet des Coteaux de la Loire occupies much the same region as that of the Coteaux d'Ancenis (see page 309). The vines lie on both banks of the Loire between Mauves in the west and Saint-Florent-Le-Vieil in the east, with Ancenis as its centre. The soil here contains less clay and more limestone and the wine is consequently lighter and more *primeur* in style than Muscadet de Sèvre-et-Maine.

MUSCADET CÔTES DE GRAND LIEU

Surface Area (1998): 334 ha.
Production (1998) 15,263 hl.
Colour: White.
Grape Variety: Muscadet (Melon de Bourgogne).
Maximum Yield: 55 hl/ha.
Minimum Alcohol Level: 9°.

This is a new *appellation*, created in 1994, and covers the region around Bouaye and extending south to Legé, south-west of Nantes. The Lac de Grand-Lieu, a large shallow lake and a nature reserve, is in the middle of the *appellation*. The soil contains less clay and more sand than in the Sèvre-et-Maine, and the wines are light and forward: no better than basic Muscadet.

MUSCADET

Surface Area (1998): 1689 ha.
Production (1998): 115,207 hl.
Colour: White.
Grape Variety: Muscadet (Melon de Bourgogne).
Maximum Yield: 65 hl/ha.
Minimum Alcohol Level: 9°.

The Muscadet vine is also found south and south-west of Nantes, in what is predominantly Gros Plant country. The wine labelled simply as Muscadet comes from these vineyards, and from one or two other isolated pockets. All four Muscadet *appellations* stipulate 12° as the maximum level of alcohol, as well as a minimum (9.5° for simple Muscadet, 10° for the other three wines). All Muscadet can be produced *sur lie*.

Muscadet *sur lie*

Sur lie means literally 'on the lees' and denotes a wine left on its lees throughout the winter before being bottled, usually early in the spring – by law this has to be done before 1 July. Normally a white wine must is left to settle before fermentation is allowed to commence (*débourbage*) and then, once completed, it is decanted off its lees – the sediment being predominantly dead yeast cells – into a new tank or vat. The malolactic fermentation then takes place, if the winemaker so wishes.

The rationale behind *sur lie* is two-fold. Muscadet is a fairly light, relatively anonymous wine. If this wine is allowed to feed on the dead yeast cells it will gain an extra element of richness and character. Also if the wine is left undisturbed in its original fermentation tank, some of the carbon dioxide released by both the original and by the malolactic fermentations will be retained within the wine in the form of carbonic acid. Thus the bottle will have a slight sparkle, and this will give an extra crispness and freshness to a wine which is sometimes slightly deficient in acidity. Genuine Muscadet *sur lie* cannot be fined, and in some cases is not filtered either. Muscadet *sur lie* requires modern fermenting and storage equipment, as well as a high standard of cleanliness in the winery. If the lees are not themselves 'clean', the wine will be ruined. Since the early 1980s most growers, particularly in the Sèvre-et-Maine, have changed to making their Muscadet *sur lie*. The result is a more interesting wine.

Muscadet wine at its best should be dry without being lean, should have a reasonable fullness without being fat or oily, and, if made *sur lie*, a suggestion of a yeasty richness. The character is neither herby nor fruity, and difficult to describe. Some suggest wild roses, others detect a hint of vanilla but I can find neither of these, though I do occasionally (but this is probably auto-suggestion) detect a faint crisp ozone whiff in some Muscadets. Above all the wine must be fresh – after as little as a year in bottle it begins to tire.

Muscadet is a large area of intensive production. Though there are a number of big *négociant* companies, the majority of the best wines are from single domaines, selling direct to the consumer in France or importer abroad. Among the many hundreds of worthy producers it is impossible to speak with personal authority about more than a few dozen, so the following list is not exhaustive.

Leading Muscadet Producers

★ DOMAINE CHÉREAU-CARRÉ
Commune: Saint-Fiacre-sur-Maine.
Owner: Bernard Chéreau.
Surface Area under Vine: 120 ha.
Wines: Muscadet de Sèvre-et-Maine including the Château de Loing (Cuvée de Saint-Hubert), Château de Chasseloir (Cuvée des Ceps Centenaires), Château de L'Oiselinière and others.

There is high class stuff here, but at a price, it has to be said. The Chéreaus, father and son both called Bernard, are merchants as well as considerable vineyard owners.

★ CHATEAU DU CLÉRAY
DOMAINE SAUVION ET FILS
Commune: Vallet.
Owners: Jean-Ernest & Yves Sauvion.
Surface Area under Vine: 30 ha.
Wines: Muscadet de Sèvre-et-Maine including Château du Cléray; plus merchant wines including the Découvertes and Allégorie ranges and Cardinal Richard.

Merchants as well as domaine owners, the Sauvion brothers believe in the variety of Muscadet. There are

wines for drinking young and ones for keeping: wine from last year and wines that are seven or eight years old. The latter I find tired and dull, but the young Château de Cléray Réserve and Cardinal Richard wines are fine.

★ DOMAINE DE L'ECU
Commune: Le Landreau.
Owner: Guy Bossard.
Surface Area under Vine: 20.5 ha.
Wines: Muscadet de Sèvre-et-Maine and Gros Plant.

Across the board from his simplest *primeur* wine upwards, Guy Bossard, one of the region's stars, produces stylish, fresh, profound wines. Atypically, they will keep for a few years.

CHÂTEAU DE LA GALISSONIÈRE
Commune: Le Pallet.
Owner: Pierre Lusseaud.
Surface Area under Vine: 30 ha.
Wines: Muscadet de Sèvre-et-Maine including Cuvée Prestige.

Pierre Lusseaud made fine Muscadet twenty years ago, when I used to buy wine from him. He continues to do so, and his prices are reasonable. The Cuvée Prestige is a special selection of the best old-vine *cuvées*.

DOMAINE DE L'HYVERNIÈRE
Commune: La Chapelle-Heulin.
Owner: Jean Beauquin.
Surface Area under Vine: 50 ha.
Wines: Muscadet de Sèvre et Maine including Clos des Orfeuilles and Château de L'Hyvernière, and Gros Plant.

Jean Beauquin produces very good wines – the Clos des Orfeuilles belongs to his wife, Marie-Madelaine – including one of the better Gros Plants in the region.

DOMAINE DE LA LOUVETRIE
Commune: La Haie-Fouassière.
Owner: Joseph Landon.
Surface Area under Vine: 24 ha.

Wines: Muscadet de Sèvre-et-Maine including Amphibolite, Hermine d'Or, Le Fief du Breuil and Cuvée Bois.

Domaine de La Louvetrie makes stylish, minerally wines, usually of high quality. The Cuvée Bois is too oaky for my taste. The *cuvées* relate as much to soil differences as to quality criteria: the Fief du Breuil, for instance, comes from vines planted on gneiss rock.

DOMAINE PIERRE LUNEAU-PAPIN
Commune: Le Landreau.
Owner: Pierre Luneau-Papin.
Surface Area under Vine: 30 ha.
Wines: Muscadet de Sèvre-et-Maine including Domaine Pierre de la Grange, Vieilles Vignes, Clos des Allées, Les Pierres Blanches, Le L d'Or and Manoir Pierre.

Pierre Luneau produces at least six different Muscadet de Sèvre-et-Maine *cuvées*. They are all stylish and often delicious. What is as important is that they are all consistently, subtly different. My vote goes to the Pierres Blanches. The L d'Or is also very good.

★ DOMAINE LOUIS METAIREAU
Commune: Maisdon-sur-Sèvre.
Owner: Louis Métaireau.
Surface Area under Vine: 29 ha.
Wines: Muscadet de Sèvre-et-Maine including Domaine du Grand Mouton Huissier, Cuvée L M and Cuvée No 1.

Louis Métaireau is a *négociant,* owning only 2 hectares of vines himself (the 27-hectare Domaine du Grand Mouton is jointly owned). His top merchant wine is called, appropriately, No 1. Cuvée L M is the cream of the rest. Grand Mouton is bottled by gravity, without filtering or fining, which is how all fine wine should be treated. These are splendid wines here and they keep too, in Muscadet terms.

DOMAINE DE LA QUILLA
Commune: La Haye-Fouassière.
Owners: Daniel & Gérard Vinet.
Surface Area under Vine: 12 ha.

Wines: Muscadet de Sèvre-et-Maine including Clos de la Houssaie and Le Muscadet.

The Domaine de la Quilla is the basic wine. Clos de La Houssaie, from a well-sited, single vineyard with gravelly soil, is rich but at the same time austere and minerally. Le Muscadet is a *tête de cuvée*, held back for a further year before release. I am not sure this is a good idea as few Muscadets benefit from age.

★ CHÂTEAU DE LA RAGOTIÈRE
Commune: La Regrippière.
Owners: Bernard, François & Michel Couillaud.
Surface Area under Vine: 61.5 ha.
Wines: Muscadet de Sèvre-et-Maine including Château de la Ragotière and Domaine de La Morinière, and Vin de Pays du Jardin de la France Chardonnay.

As well as some excellent Muscadets (the best of the Ragotière wines, called Premier Cru, comes in numbered bottles and has a black — as opposed to a white — label), the Couillaud brothers produce oaky Chardonnays. These are some of the more successful examples of Chardonnay in the region.

★ DOMAINE DE LA TOURMALINE
Commune: Saint-Fiacre-sur-Maine.
Owners: Michel & Christophe Gadais.
Surface Area under Vine: 32 ha.
Wines: Muscadet de Sèvre-et-Maine including Domaine de la Tourmaline, Grande Réserve and Vieilles Vignes, and Gros Plant.

Domaine de La Tourmaline makes three separate fine *cuvées* — the Vieilles Vignes is from hand-picked grapes (most Muscadet is picked by machine) and produced by *bâtonnage*. There is also a perfectly respectable Gros Plant.

Other Muscadet Producers of note
DOMAINE DE L'ABBAYE DE SAINTE-RADEGONDE/JEAN GUILBEAULT (LE LOROUX-BOTTEREAU), DOMAINE DE LA BRETTONNIÈRE/JOËL & BERTRAND CORMERAIS (MAISDON-SUR-SÈVRE), DOMAINE DE LA CHAPELLIÈRE (TILLIÈRES), DOMAINE CHINON (MOUZILLON), DOMAINE DES DONCES/FRANÇOIS & FRÉDÉRIC BOUILLAUT (VALLET),

DOMAINE DE LA FERTÉ/JÉRÔME ET RÉMY SÉCHER (VALLET), CHÂTEAU DU HALLAY AND DOMAINE DE LA COGNARDIÈRE/ DOMINIQUE & VINCENT RICHARD (LE PALLET), CHÂTEAU DE LA MERCREDIÈRE/FUTEUL FRÈRES (LE PALLET), DOMAINE DE LA RENOUÈRE/VINCENT VIAUD (LE LANDREAU) AND DOMAINE SAINT DONATIEN-BAHAUD (LA CHAPELLE-HEULIN).

GROS PLANT DU PAYS NANTAIS

Surface Area (1998): 2538 ha.
Production (1998): 156,758 hl.
Colour: White.
Grape Variety: Gros Plant.
Maximum Yield: 50 hl/ha.
Minimum Alcohol Level: 8.5°.

Until 1984 the Loire-Atlantique *département* had only one other *appellation* besides Muscadet, the Gros Plant du Pays Nantais VDQS. Gros Plant can come from throughout the Muscadet area, as well as from certain other ones to the south and west. It is normally an undistinguished wine with a pronounced, even savage acidity and a rather coarse flavour.

The Gros Plant vine was imported by the Dutch in the seventeenth century from the Charente region to the south, where it is known as the Folle Blanche (it is also the same variety as the Picpoul of southern France). The VDQS dates from 1954.

In the hands of some growers and *négociants*, Gros Plant in a good year such as 1998 or 1999 can be an agreeable wine. It is noticeably 'greener' than Muscadet, and this acidity can make a pleasant change, particularly if one is on holiday in the area. Gros Plant makes the perfect accompaniment for the local seafood. However, the difference in price between lesser Muscadet and Gros Plant is marginal, and I suspect the consumers would prefer the former.

Gros Plant du Pays Nantais Producers of note
See under Muscadet page 314.

FIEFS VENDÉENS

Surface Area (1998): 415 ha.
Production (1998): (Red and rosé) 17,692 hl; (white) 3096 hl.
Colour: Red, rosé and white.
Grape Varieties: (Red and rosé) Pinot Noir, Gamay Noir à Jus Blanc, Cabernet Franc, Cabernet Sauvignon and Grolleau Gris; (white) Chenin Blanc, Sauvignon Blanc, Chardonnay and Colombard.
Maximum Yield: 50 hl/ha.
Minimum Alcohol Level: 9°.

South of the Pays Nantais is the Vendée region. Les Fiefs Vendéens consist of four distinct vineyard areas based on clay, mixed with quartz boulders and schist. The area was elevated from Vin de Pays to VDQS in 1984. Most of the wine is red, *primeur* and Gamay-based. These are simple, somewhat rustic country wines for local drinking.

Fiefs Vendéens Producers of note
DOMAINE XAVIER COIRIER (PISSOTTE) AND LA FERME DES ARDILLERS/JEAN MOURAT & JEAN LARZELIER (MAREUIL-SUR-LAY).

VINS DE PAYS

Vin de Pays du Bourbonnais
This is a white wine from the Saint-Pourçain area of the Upper Loire in the Allier *département*. It is produced from the local grapes, Tressalier, Sauvignon Blanc, Chardonnay, Aligoté and Saint-Pierre-Doré .

Vin de Pays du Cher
This is a departmental *vin de pays* from the *département* of Cher around Bourges. Reds and rosés come from Gamay and whites from Sauvignon Blanc.

Vin de Pays des Coteaux Charitois
These are Sauvignon-based whites from Pouilly-sur-Loire in the Nièvre *département*.

Vin de Pays des Coteaux du Cher et de L'Arnon

This zonal *vin de pays* comes from the Reuilly-Quincy area in the Cher and Indre *départements*. Gamay is used for reds and rosés and Sauvignon Blanc for whites.

Vin de Pays des Deux-Sèvres

The Deux-Sèvres *département* lies south of Angers. These are mainly white wines, from Chenin Blanc, Muscadet, Gros Plant and Sauvignon Blanc.

Vin de Pays du Jardin de La France

This is the regional *vin de pays* of the Loire Valley and the most commonly seen Loire *vin de pays* outside France. The wines are mainly white and made from Chenin Blanc and/or Sauvignon Blanc. There are also some interesting Chardonnay-based wines.

Vin de Pays de L'Indre

A departmental wine from southern Touraine around Châteauroux. All three colours are made, mainly from Gamay, Sauvignon Blanc and Chenin Blanc.

Vin de Pays de L'Indre-et-Loire

A departmental wine from the heart of the Touraine. Red, rosé and white wines are made, mainly from Gamay, Sauvignon Blanc and Chenin Blanc.

Vin de Pays de La Loire-Atlantique

A departmental wine from the Muscadet region. Red and rosé wines are made from Gamay and Grolleau and whites from Muscadet and Folle Blanche (Gros Plant). There are some interesting Chardonnays.

Vin de Pays du Loir-et-Cher

A departmental wine from the eastern end of Touraine. All three colours of wine are made, mainly from Gamay, Sauvignon Blanc and Chenin Blanc.

Vin de Pays du Loiret

This departmental wine comes from the eastern end of the Loire basin, around the city of Orléans. Red and rosé wines come from Gamay and the whites from Sauvignon Blanc.

Vin de Pays de La Maine-et-Loire

A departmental *vin de pays* from the Anjou. Red and rosé wines come from Gamay, Grolleau and Cabernet Franc and the whites from Chenin Blanc, though Chardonnay is also found.

Vin de Pays des Marches de Bretagne

A zonal *vin de pays* from the Pays Nantais. These are mainly rather thin red and rosé wines from Gamay and Cabernet Franc.

Vin de Pays de La Nièvre

A departmental *vin de pays* from the Coteaux du Giennois/Pouilly-sur-Loire area. Red, rosé and white wines, mainly from Gamay and Sauvignon Blanc.

Vin de Pays du Puy-de-Dôme

The departmental *vin de pays* of the Auvergne. Mainly red and rosé wine, mainly from Gamay.

Vin de Pays de Retz

A zonal wine from the southern part of the Pays Nantais. The wines are mainly red and rosé from Grolleau and Cabernet Franc.

Vin de Pays de La Sarthe

A departmental wine from north of Anjou and Touraine. All three colours of wine are authorized, and a wide range of local varieties. I have never seen it.

Vin de Pays d'Urfé

A zonal *vin de pays* for the Forez/Roannaises area in the Upper Loire. Gamay is used for red and rosé wines.

Vin de Pays de La Vendée

A departmental *vin de pays* for reds and rosés from Gamay from south of the Muscadet area. I have not seen this wine since the Fiefs Vendéens VDQS was created in 1984.

Vin de Pays de La Vienne

A departmental *vin de pays* from the Haut-Poitou area. Mainly Gamay is used for the reds and rosés and Chenin Blanc and Sauvignon Blanc for the whites.

THE RHÔNE VALLEY

THE RIVER RHÔNE RISES IN THE VALAIS CANTON OF SWITZERLAND, enters France at Lake Geneva and travels at first in a generally south-westerly direction until it is joined by the river Saône at Lyon. Diverted by the Montagnes du Lyonnais it is then forced south, flowing initially through a narrow, steep-sided valley past the towns of Vienne, Tain, Tournon, Valence and Montélimar, while being joined by several major tributaries, among them the Isère and the Drôme. South of Montélimar the valley begins to widen out, particularly on the Alpine side, and the Rhône begins to slow and meander. At Avignon it is joined by the Durance, and we soon reach the wild, sandy flatlands of the Bouches-du-Rhône and the Parc Régional de la Camargue. At Arles the river splits into two; the smaller section, the Petit Rhône reaches the Mediterranean at the old gypsy rendez-vous of Sainte-Marie-de-La-Mer and the Grand Rhône at Port Saint-Louis, 800 kilometres from its source.

Viticulturally speaking, the Rhône Valley is that part between Lyon in the north and Avignon in the south, a distance as the crow flies of some 200 kilometres. The upper Rhône is dealt with under its more usual title of the Savoie (see page 558), the wines of the Rhône delta under Provence and Languedoc (see pages 382 and 406).

For most of its course – particularly between Lyon and Avignon – the immediate surroundings by the river are dull, unattractive, even despoiled. The Rhône is a major industrial and commercial artery. Large sections are canalised; hydro-electric dams, atomic centres, quarries, cement works, metallurgical industries and other factories pollute the river and send columns of smog into the atmosphere. It is noisy, dirty, arid and dusty – thoroughly unpeaceful, decidedly uncongenial.

Away from the river the picture is a total contrast. Even a five-minute drive away from the river up the winding roads into the hills above the northern Rhône Valley will bring one into an entirely different land. This is a countryside of meadows and pasture full of herds of cattle, walnut trees and orchards of peaches, apricots and cherries; of small hamlets apparently deserted except for the odd

tethered goat and free-range chicken; a pre-industrial countryside, a land of private smallholdings, tranquillity and agricultural plenty.

In the south the valley undulates its way between the Cévennes in the west and Mont Ventoux and the Dentelles de Montmirail in the east. Here the landscape is Provençal: the terrain of the olive and the cypress as well as the vine. The light is vivid and penetrating. The sky is more violet than blue. The smells are of lavender and wild thyme, rosemary and oregano. The well-irrigated fields on the flatter, more alluvial soils yield artichokes and melons, cucumbers, peppers and courgettes, asparagus, lettuce and tomatoes. The vines lie on the stonier, higher slopes, where the land has been prised away from its rightful owners, the heather, broom and scrub of the *garrigues*. Further inland and uphill, the countryside is spectacular, deserted and beautiful. Dense forests of pine, aspen and birch alternate with jagged outcrops of bare rock or the rounded bald expanse of ancient hills. This is France at its most dramatic, both savage and glorious.

HISTORY

The earliest historical roots in the Rhône Valley go back to the Ligurians, a savage, nomadic hunting people, originally from Asia, who arrived in the Rhône and Provence about 1600 BC. They were followed by the Celts, a more settled people who practised farming. The first cultivated vines together with the art of winemaking were probably introduced by Phocaean Greeks from the west coast of Asia Minor about 600 BC. Their chief trading post and settlement was Massilia (Marseilles) which can probably claim to be the oldest city in France. According to Herodotus, these Phocaeans were the first to undertake distant sea journeys, and introduced the vine to mainland Greece, Italy and the Dalmatian coast, as well as to northern Africa and Mediterranean Spain.

At this time the Lydian empire, which bordered on Phoenecaea, was a rich vine-growing country. After the defeat of the Lydian Croesus by Cyrus 1 of Persia in 546 BC, the Phocaeans came under Persian domination, and many of the itinerant traders settled permanently in southern France and began opening up trade routes to the north. Massalian coins from 500 to 450 BC have been found all the way up the Rhône Valley, and early Greek amphorae of the same period both in Marseilles and in Tain L'Hermitage.

The Phocaean colony prospered, but as time went on came under heavy pressure from the local inhabitants and sea pirates. About 150 BC the Massalians had to appeal to the Romans to come to their aid. Within a generation the latter had returned with an army to conquer the country for themselves. The Roman era lasted some six hundred years, and its legacy has been both striking and long lived. Many of the Roman ruins, at Vienne, Nimes, the Pont du Gard, Vaison-La-Romaine and Orange, are the most extensive outside Italy. Most of the important towns, roads, and, most importantly, the vineyards which exist today, were established in the Roman era.

By the early Christian era, Vienne was the capital of mid-Gaul, and its pitched wine, *vinum picatum*, was exported to Rome, where it became a fashionable drink of the time. The fall of Rome and the decline of civilisation in the fifth and sixth centuries AD was accompanied by a decline in winemaking and a reduction in communications and trade. France was colonised by the Germanic tribe, the Franks, and invaded from the south by Moors and Saracens, and even Vikings who sailed through the Straits of Gibraltar and are said to have reached almost as far north as the Hermitage vineyards.

Around the ninth century civilisation began to return with the Church emerging as the driving force behind the sophistication of agricultural techniques and the focus for stability and learning. In 1309 Bertrand the Goth, Archbishop of Bordeaux, was elected Pope Clément V. With relations badly strained between the king of France and the papacy in Rome, and Italy in a state of chaotic religious warfare, he elected to stay in France, and established his court at Avignon. His successor, John XXII, was able to improve the papal finances and set about enlarging the modest official residence in Avignon. He also built a summer palace nearby on the foundations of an old castle at Châteauneuf. This 'new château' was a huge construction and took fifteen years to build, and, of course, the surrounding vineyards went with the property.

The papal stay in Avignon lasted through seven popes until 1378, after which there were two anti-popes until the differences were healed with Rome in 1410, and during this time the city enjoyed an expanding and prosperous period. The Avignon area – together with a small parcel to the north around Valréas, which was purchased by the popes during their stay and remains, curiously, as part of the *département* of Vaucluse completely isolated from the rest – continued as part of the Papal states until 1791.

Rhône wines were exported to Italy in the sixteenth and seventeenth centuries, but exports to the north of France and England were virtually unknown until the opening of the Midi canal in 1681 gave access to the great sea route from Bordeaux (when the Bordelais chose to revive some of their ancient rights and reimpose quotas and duties on these 'up-country' wines). Later they used Rhône wine, particularly Hermitage, to add body and alcohol to their own wines.

Soon other trade routes opened. In 1710 work on the upper Loire made it navigable from Saint-Etienne, and canals provided a direct route to Paris; later came further canals and finally the railways. In the early eighteenth century the first Rhône names began to appear in England: Vin de Mure (a *négociant* in Tain), Vin de la Nerte, an estate in Châteauneuf-du-Pape, and Vin d'Avignon. In the 1730s the first grouping of villages under the generic name of Côtes du Rhône made its first appearance, and casks began to be marked 'CdR' with the vintage date.

The phylloxera bug first appeared in France in the *département* of Gard in 1863 and the Rhône vineyards were among the first to be devastated. One of the major research stations into combating the pest was at Montpellier, further down the Languedoc coast.

In 1923 the first quality controls, the origins of what were later to become the laws of *appellation contrôlée*, were self-imposed by the Châteauneuf *vignerons*, led by Baron le Roy of Château Fortia (who even had a statue erected to him during his lifetime). By 1936 the French had made the Châteauneuf quality controls broadly applicable to the whole country. Since the Second World War, and particularly since the early 1970s, modern viticultural and winemaking methods have arrived in the Rhône Valley and, as a result, there has been a well-deserved export success. Côtes du Rhône exports have climbed from under 100,000 hectolitres in 1964 to approaching 750,000 hectolitres today. The area has overtaken both Burgundy and Beaujolais in popularity in recent years and though it still exports less than Bordeaux, it is rapidly catching up. The main reason for this surge has been the remarkable value-for-money of Rhône wines compared with those of elsewhere. At all levels, whether at generic Côtes du Rhône (versus Bordeaux Rouge or Beaujolais) or at the summit of quality (a good grower's Hermitage or Côte-Rôtie versus a super-second red Bordeaux or *premier cru* Burgundy) Rhône wines are attractively priced, though regrettably less so today than a decade or two ago.

THE WINES

The Rhône Valley is largely a red wine region, and the reds befit their setting, being bold, solid and weighty, powerful and uncompromising. In the south, particularly at Tavel, a dry, masculine *rosé* is found; in the north there is a little white, some of which, that from Condrieu and Château Grillet, is among the most delicious of the entire country. But mainly the production is of red wine: from Châteauneuf-du-Pape, Gigondas, Vacqueyras, Lirac and the Côtes du Rhône-Villages in the south; from Hermitage, Côte-Rôtie, Cornas and Saint Joseph in the north. The northern Rhône grows one red grape variety, the Syrah (if we exclude some Gamay cultivated for *vins de pays*), and three white varieties: Roussanne and Marsanne – normally blended together – and Viognier (only in Côte-Rôtie, Condrieu and Château Grillet). In the southern sector the varieties used are many. There are no fewer than thirteen authorized for Châteauneuf-du-Pape. Chief of these are Grenache, Cinsault, Mourvèdre and again Syrah. There is also the Muscat, used to provide the *vin doux naturel* of Beaumes-de-Venise, and some minor white varieties for the small amounts of southern Rhône white wine. All these southern Rhône varieties are planted throughout the South of France.

For reasons of differences in climate and soil, grape variety and styles of wine, it is customary, indeed logical, to treat the Rhône Valley as two separate sections, divided by a vineless no-man's-land between Valence and Montélimar. The northern section, or Rhône *septentrional*, begins at Vienne and continues south for some 70 kilometres. It is a long, narrow region, the vines themselves clinging precariously to the steep sides of the valley itself. South of Donzère the southern section or Rhône *méridional* continues on to Avignon, a distance of

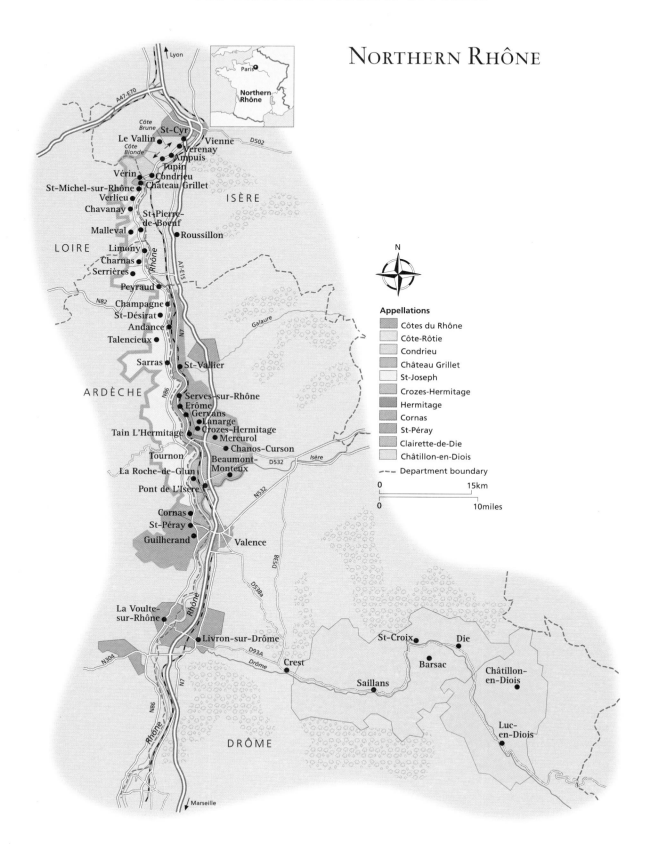

Northern Rhône

Paris

Northern Rhône

Lyon

A47-E70

Côte Brune

St-Cyr

Le Vallin · Vienne

Côte Blonde

Verenay

Ampuis

Tupin

Vérin · Condrieu

St-Michel-sur-Rhône · Château Grillet

Verlieu

Chavanay · St-Pierre-de-Bœuf

Malleval · Roussillon

Limony

Charnas

Serrières

Peyraud

Champagne

St-Désirat

Andance

Talencieux

Sarras · St-Vallier

Serves-sur-Rhône

Erôme

Gervans

Lanarge

Crozes-Hermitage

Tain L'Hermitage · Mercurol

Chanos-Curson

Tournon · Beaumont-Monteux

La Roche-de-Glun

Pont de L'Isère

Cornas

St-Péray

Guilherand · Valence

La Voulte-sur-Rhône

Livron-sur-Drôme

Crest

St-Croix · Die

Barsac

Châtillon-en-Diois

Saillans

Luc-en-Diois

ISÈRE

LOIRE

ARDÈCHE

DRÔME

Rhône

Galaure

Isère

Drôme

D502

D532

D538

D538a

D93A

N82

N7

N86

N304

N532

A7-E15

Appellations

Côtes du Rhône
Côte-Rôtie
Condrieu
Château Grillet
St-Joseph
Crozes-Hermitage
Hermitage
Cornas
St-Péray
Clairette-de-Die
Châtillon-en-Diois

- - - Department boundary

0   15km

0   10miles

Marseille

N

50 kilometres, and the vines lie on mounds and slopes upon the valley floor as well as its hillsides, a distance from east to west of 50 kilometres again.

The wines are now increasingly well made. A generation ago the cheaper Rhône reds were fiery, rustic and over alcoholic and the more expensive wines were very firm and dense – more often than not too solid for their own good. The rosés were hard and unstylish; the few whites heavy, oily and spirity.

Today the picture is different. The cheaper red wines are largely made using the carbonic maceration method and have fruit and colour without being too robust. The better wines are rich and elegant, without having lost their essential sturdiness; the rosés are supple and fruity and the whites crisp and aromatic.

The Rhône is a good hunting ground for the adventurous wine buyer looking for well-made, sensibly priced wines; the region has many dedicated, individual growers who have travelled and tasted widely and who understand that the public taste has changed and is more demanding, seeking wines of style rather than mere weight, and fruit rather than alcohol.

The wines of the Rhône Valley can be divided into the following groups. They are all *appellation contrôlée* unless indicated otherwise.

Northern Rhône

Right (west) bank Côte-Rôtie, Condrieu, Château Grillet, Saint-Joseph, Cornas and Saint-Péray.
Left (east) bank Hermitage and Crozes-Hermitage.
Valley of the river Drôme Clairette de Die, Châtillon-en-Diois, Coteaux de Die and Crémant de Die.

Southern Rhône

Right (west) bank Lirac, Tavel and Côtes du Rhône-Villages.
Left (east) bank Châteauneuf-du-Pape, Gigondas, Vacqueyras, Côtes du Rhône-Villages, Coteaux du Tricastin, Côtes du Ventoux, Rasteau (*vin doux naturel*) and Muscat de Beaumes-de-Venise (*vin doux naturel*).
Ardèche Valley Côtes du Vivarais.
Durance Valley Côtes du Lubéron and Coteaux de Pierrevert.

Côtes du Rhône This can come from both the northern and southern sections of the Rhône Valley. In practice it comes almost entirely from the South.

Surface Area and Production

Over 95 per cent of the Rhône Valley's vines are in the southern half of the region and over 95 per cent of the harvest comes from the south. Just over 5 per cent of the Rhône Valley harvest is white wine. Two-thirds of the entire harvest of the Rhône Valley is simple Côtes du Rhône red or rosé. In practice it is overwhelmingly red wine. Apart from simple 'Bordeaux' this is the most important single *appellation* in France, being larger than Champagne and more than three times as large as Beaujolais or Corbières. While French agricultural statistics do not separate red and rosé wine, it is estimated that 15 per cent of the grand total for red and rosé wine from the Rhône Valley is rosé.

In total, some 75,000 hectares are under vine, producing some 370,000 hectolitres of AC wine annually. Of this, only 2700 hectares lie in the northern section. The Rhône is dominated by its south. The whole of Hermitage produces no more wine than one of the largest Bordeaux estates. In terms of production, more wine is made in Châteauneuf-du-Pape alone than in all the northern section combined, and twenty times as much wine is declared as simple, generic Côtes du Rhône as is declared as Châteauneuf-du-Pape.

A comparison of today's figures with those of ten years ago show that while there has been very little change in the vineyards at Chateauneuf-du-Pape, Hermitage and basic Côtes du Rhône, the area under Côtes du Rhône-Villages has increased 50 per cent (despite the loss of Vacqueyras which is now an *appellation* in its own right), Crozes-Hermitage is up by 46 per cent, Cornas 50 per cent, Côte-Rôtie 43 per cent and Condrieu almost 500 per cent – up from 20 hectares to 98 hectares.

When to Drink the Wines

Rhône wines are not for the faint-hearted. They are full and assertive, rich and powerful, firm and muscular. In total contrast to Burgundy they are wines of heat and alcohol rather than fragrance and finesse. They show

SURFACE AREA AND PRODUCTION (1998 HARVEST)

APPELLATIONS	SURFACE AREA (HA)	PRODUCTION (HL)	
REGIONAL WINE		RED & ROSÉ	WHITE
CÔTES DU RHÔNE	41,606	2,210,820	44,942
NORTHERN RHÔNE			
CÔTE-RÔTIE	200	6929	–
CONDRIEU	98	–	2549
CHÂTEAU GRILLET	3	–	93
HERMITAGE	134	3853	976
CROZES-HERMITAGE	1225	52,503	4649
SAINT-JOSEPH	869	21,166	2412
CORNAS	91	6287	–
SAINT-PÉRAY	63	–	1501
TOTAL NORTHERN RHÔNE VALLEY	**2683**	**90,738**	**12,180**
		102,918	
DRÔME VALLEY			
CHÂTILLON-EN-DIOIS	1373	1918	1311
CLAIRETTE DE DIE	–	–	71,644
COTEAUX DE DIE	–	–	–
CRÉMANT DE DIE	–	–	4877
TOTAL DRÔME VALLEY	**1373**	**1918**	**77,832**
		79,750	
SOUTHERN RHÔNE			
CÔTES DU RHÔNE-VILLAGES	6917	268,153	5226
CHÂTEAUNEUF-DU-PAPE	3139	102,299	7847
GIGONDAS	1250	43,988	–
VACQUEYRAS	1159	39,453	337
LIRAC	546	22,895	1021
TAVEL	957	43,374	
COTEAUX DU TRICASTIN	2630	109,154	3066
CÔTES DU VENTOUX	7307	319,244	9781
CÔTES DU LUBÉRON	3756	150,686	30,251
COTEAUX DE PIERREVERT	315	12,853	1303
CÔTES DU VIVARAIS (VDQS)	663	19,859	1380
TOTAL SOUTHERN RHÔNE	**28,639**	**1,211,708**	**60,212**
		1,271,920	
VINS DOUX NATURELS			
MUSCAT DE BEAUMES-DE-VENISE	448	–	14,575
RASTEAU	102	3029	–
TOTAL VINS DOUX NATURELS	**550**	**17,604**	
		3,518,213	**209,741**
GRAND TOTAL	**74,851**	**3,727,954**	

their origins; whether from the baked granite cliffs of the north or the Mistral swept, boulder-strewn plateaux of the South.

The wines are almost entirely red. If from the north they are based almost exclusively on Syrah. If from Châteauneuf-du-Pape and its surrounding vineyards they are made from Grenache and other varieties. This produces two wines of quite distinctive styles. The Syrah makes a purple, tannic, austere wine: full-bodied and closed in its youth but with a good level of acidity. Young Syrah smells of blackcurrant leaves. As much as ten years or more is required before the leafy denseness — almost brutal at first — is replaced by warm fruit. And the wines will last for decades, as they mature taking up more and more of a complexity and character similar to that of a fine Bordeaux; though always a red Bordeaux with the voluptuousness of Château Mouton-Roth-schild or Cheval-Blanc rather than the restrained Cabernet Sauvignon of Château Latour.

The most precocious of the northern Rhône *appella-tions* is Crozes-Hermitage. A minor Crozes will be mature after four years. Saint-Josephs will begin to be ready a year or so after that and Côte-Rôties after six or seven years. The slowest-maturing wines are Cornas and Hermitage. These need a minimum of eight years' ageing. Grenache-based wines from the southern Rhône mature quicker and have an altogether different character. The wines are rich, warm, spicy, peppery and alcoholic, but the acidity level is lower and development is faster. Even today when the best wines have quite sig-nificant proportions of Syrah or the yet more brutally firm Mourvèdre blended in with Grenache and Cinsault a top Châteauneuf du-Pape will usually be mature after half a dozen years, while a minor Côtes du Rhône will be drinkable after a year. There is even some Côtes du Rhône Nouveau.

The majority of the white wines, like white wines everywhere, are for early drinking. This applies to most Condrieu, to white Crozes-Hermitage, to Saint-Péray and to all the white wines of the Rhône *méridional*, except one or two white Châteauneufs. It also applies to Tavel rosé. Only top, oak-aged, white Hermitage can last in bottle. I find these delicious when I taste them out of

cask, then ungainly for the first three or four years in bottle, and totally different — subtle, scented and aro-matic — after six or so years. They have an individual taste. It is almost a culture-shock, after Chardonnay!

Rhône Vintages

1998 Spring frost affected the vineyards in the north. The summer was then fine until the beginning of Sep-tember produced some much needed rain. The vin-tage took place in excellent conditions which lasted until the end of September, by which time the vast majority of the crop had been picked. A highly suc-cessful vintage at both ends of the valley — in Châteauneuf-du-Pape as well as in Hermitage as good as 1990. It will keep well.

1997 An early flowering but long and drawn out in inclement weather. This was followed by a generally hot, often too hot summer. After unsettled weather at the beginning of September the conditions during the vintage itself were favourable. Nevertheless, 1997 looks like being a year of only above-average quality, with ripe, healthy wine of medium body, without the dimension and concentration of a great vintage.

1996 The 1996 vintage was saved after a cold wet sum-mer by a sunny windy September. The result is wines, both red and white, with higher than normal acidity. The reds have good colour, but they lack richness and fat. They are better in the north than in the south, where they may come to resemble the lean but ulti-mately elegant and successful 1972s. The Châteauneufs are for the most part soft, ample and fruity; clean but for early drinking. The white Her-mitages and Crozes-Hermitages are fine, though.

1995 The best of the vintages since 1990. It was a small harvest as a result of poor weather during the flower-ing. But this inclement period was followed by fine weather right up until mid-September. From the north to the south of the Rhône Valley the reds are full, rich, concentrated and have the grip to last well. The whites are less exciting: indeed the 1996s are to be preferred. Drink the best of the whites from 1998 onwards.

1994 A larger, but less homogenous vintage than the 1995; but very good at its best. Rain interrupted the harvest. There is charm here, and a softness of fruit which is engaging. There are wines for the medium term, but they are nonetheless elegant, and they are well balanced. Drink soon.

1993 Good if not great in Côte-Rôtie and quite good in Châteauneuf-du-Pape, but more or less a disaster in Hermitage after a cool rainy summer and a vintage which was inundated by rain. A number of growers declassified their wine. Drink up.

1992 Another below average vintage. Drink up.

1991 This is a very good vintage, especially in Côte-Rôtie, where it is as good as 1990 in many cellars. The Châteauneufs, on the other hand, are unspectacular. Hermitage is also patchy, one leading grower not producing his *grande cuvée* this year. A vintage, therefore, to approach with caution. Now ready. It was a very good year for Condrieu but these are now old.

1990 A great Rhône vintage, and, as elsewhere in France both large and consistent as well. Properly substantial Rhône wines for ageing, with rich tannins, plenty of substance, good acidity and a nicely exotic cooked fruit. They should be in everyone's cellar. The best still need keeping.

1989 A fine vintage. The wines are less firm and long lasting than the 1990s and are more spicy and voluptuous. They lack a little acidity and therefore elegance. But they are rich and enjoyable nonetheless. The best are approaching maturity.

1988 A smaller crop, more reserved but more classic. The best wines, especially in the north, will repay further keeping. They are fullish, very well balanced and very elegant. It was a fine year for white wines, but only the top Hermitages will still be alive now.

GOOD, EARLIER VINTAGES

1985, 1983, 1982, 1981 (southern Rhône wines only), 1978, 1971, 1970, 1969, 1966, 1964, 1962 and 1961. Earlier than 1978 even the very top red Châteauneufs will now show age but the best wines of the North are still holding up well.

The Wine Regions
THE NORTHERN RHÔNE

CÔTE-RÔTIE

Surface Area (1998): 200 ha.
Production (1998): 6929 hl.
Colour: Red.
Grape Varieties: Syrah plus up to 20 per cent (usually 8 per cent or less, even none at all) Viognier.
Maximum Yield: 40 hl/ha.
Minimum Alcohol Level: 10°.

The most northerly vineyard in the Rhône Valley, up until recently one of its most neglected, is one of the most difficult to work. Yet it produces one of the finest wines not only of the Rhône but of the whole of France. Côte-Rôtie, or the 'Roasted Slope', is centred round and above the village of Ampuis on the west bank of the river a few kilometres south of Vienne, itself 25 kilometres south of Lyon. Côte-Rôtie produces a limited quantity of excellent, Syrah-based red wine, full-bodied but elegant; a wine which needs ageing in bottle. The vines occupy narrow terraces which have been hacked out of the wall of hillsides which rise abruptly up from the valley floor. These are the most precipitous vineyards in the Rhône Valley and probably the steepest in the whole of France. In places the incline is as much as 55 degrees. All the vineyards have to be maintained by hand, a costly process.

Nevertheless this is one of the oldest vineyards in the area. The city of Vienne was one of the first staging posts established by Phocaean traders based at Marseille in the south five centuries or so BC. Wine was originally brought to the upper Rhône from the Mediterranean vineyards. Later, certainly well before the Romans, the vine was cultivated in the Vienne region, and Vienne became the thriving capital of mid-Gaul and a place of great importance in the early days of the Roman Empire, its wine being exported back to the capital, laced with pitch to preserve it. The *vinum picatum* of Vienne is mentioned by Lucius Columella, Pliny and Martial in the first century AD. Vienne began to decline in eminence as Lyon rose to fame, and the wine, equally, sank into semi-obscurity, re-emerging as Côte-Rôtie in the writer Jullien's *Topographie de Tous Les Vignobles Connus* (1816) when he classified it among his *Deuxième Classe* along with the best of Châteauneuf-du-Pape, the Third Growths of Bordeaux and what today we would term the *premiers crus* of Burgundy. Only the best wines of Hermitage were deemed superior among local wines.

Phylloxera and the economic difficulties of the first half of the twentieth century hit Côte-Rôtie particularly hard. Rather than reconstitute the vineyard terraces with American rootstocks and wait five years for the first crop many local growers turned to fruit-growing. This trend was further accelerated, first by the ease of communication between Paris and the South, opening up the competition of the wines of the Midi, and then by the lack of labour after the First World War. The price of Côte-Rôtie sank to uneconomic levels and the terraces fell into disuse.

Since the 1950s, cautiously, slowly but surely, Côte-Rôtie has made a comeback. Production has increased from 1000 hectolitres in 1960 to over 7000 today and equally, the area under vine has been enlarged. At first this was on the ancient hillsides; terraces perhaps several hundred years old being cleared of bramble and scrub, the walls rebuilt and eventually the sites replanted. In the lasttwenty years, however, a disturbing new development has taken place: vines have been planted on the plateau above the slopes. Apparently the land, though unsuitable for quality wine, is, nevertheless, authorised for Côte-Rôtie, and, of course, it is easier to work. (The same problem has arisen further south in Saint-Joseph where, in addition, vines have been planted

in the more alluvial soil of the valley floor.) The wine resulting from these as yet immature plateau vineyards is thin, weedy, pale and attenuated. At the stage where top Côte-Rôtie can at last fetch prices which make production a profitable proposition, it would be tragic if the reputation of the wine were to suffer as a result of being debased with this inferior coinage. It is time the INAO exercised its authority.

Côte-Rôtie today comprises some 200 hectares in the communes of Ampuis, Saint Cyr-sur-Le-Rhône and Tupins-et-Semons, and has grown by 30 per cent in the last fifteen years. The best vineyards are those immediately above Ampuis itself. It has been customary to class these globally as either Côte Brune, the sector to the north, or as Côte Blonde, the sector to the south, leaving the vineyards further north still, above Verenay and even further to the south, above Tupin, as 'second division'. Many producers, notably Ets. E Guigal, the most powerful in the area, produce a Brune et Blonde *cuvée* as an intermediary between their generic Côte-Rôtie and their single-vineyard or super-*cuvées*. In fact both Côte Brune and Côte Blonde are distinct, if tiny *lieux-dits* in their own right. Currently the consumer does not know what he or she is getting. Here again the authorities should step in and tidy things up. As the name suggests, the soil in the Côte Blonde or southern section is lighter in colour. The bedrock of both is granite or gneiss, a hard metamorphic rock, but in the Côte Brune or northern section the soil is sand mixed with clay while in the Côte Blonde it is lighter and has more limestone and is usually planted with more Viognier.

The origins of these two names is Côte-Rôtie's best-loved legend. Many centuries ago the local *seigneur*, named Maugiron, had two daughters, as perfectly beautiful as they always are in fairytales. One was blond, vivacious and jolly, the other a brunette, quiet and reserved but passionate when aroused. Maugiron gave as a dowry his two best vineyards for his heiresses, and henceforth they were named after the daughters, particularly as the wines they produced were somewhat in character as well, that from the Côte Blonde being then and today, a more delicate, lighter wine which did not last as well as the fuller, more austere Côte Brune.

Côte-Rôtie is made principally from the Syrah grape, locally known as the Sérine, a name which would be unfamiliar even in nearby Hermitage. In Côte-Rôtie the Syrah can be blended with up to 20 per cent of the Viognier grape, a rare and wonderful white variety. In practice many growers have abandoned growing Viognier, for the yield is small and inconsistent, and it is now only found in isolated pockets, primarily on the Côte Blonde, and to the extent of perhaps a maximum of 8 per cent of the *appellation*.

The steep, small terraces of the Côte-Rôtie also make it impossible to train the Syrah in the usual way. Instead, the vines are trained up and around a framework of four poles tied together at the top, making a shape somewhat like that of a steep wigwam. Two or three vines may be trained up the same structure like runner bean plants, and there will be perhaps half a dozen such 'wigwams' per terrace.

Though leading growers such as Guigal and Rostaing do produce single-vineyard, separate Côte Blonde and Côte Brune wines, Côte-Rôtie today is normally a wine blended from the yields of several small parcels scattered over the *appellation*. The 200 hectares are divided between fifty or so families and holdings are small, barely economic for most, who need to supplement their activities as winemakers with other jobs such as growing fruit.

The wine is made by traditional methods, often being fermented with the stalks and macerated for two or even three weeks. Ageing can be in *barrique* or in *foudre* and for three or more years before bottling. In the *barrique* the wine has more contact with the air and it develops quicker. In the *foudre* which more often than not will be considerably encrusted with tartrate crystals, the wine ages more slowly; indeed, it can often remain dumb, drying out in fruit without softening in tannin and so deteriorate, if the winemaker is sloppy with his *élevage*. The last couple of decades, as elsewhere in France, have seen a decisive cleaning up of the winemaking process. The younger generation, who have all been to wine school, fully understand the importance of meticulous attention to detail during the maturation process, of keeping the barrels topped up, of temperature control, of the desirability of minimal handling at maturation. There are still some cellars where time seems to have stood still, but also an increasing number of highly commendable 'modern' wines combining the best of the old with the best of the new. There are some splendid wines coming from this *appellation* today.

Leading Côte-Rôtie Producers

★ DOMAINE GILLES BARGE

Commune: Ampuis.
Owner: Gilles Barge.
Surface Area under Vine: 6.75ha.
Wines: Côte-Rôtie including Côte Brune and Cuvée du Plessy, Saint-Joseph (red) Clos des Martinets, and Condrieu.

Up until 1994 some of the wines at this domaine were bottled under the name of Gilles' father, Pierre and some under his own name. They were two different wines. Pierre has since retired and the range has been rationalised, with one single superior *cuvée* from the *climat* of Côte Blonde as well as the basic Cuvée du Plessy. The Saint-Joseph, from a recently bought vineyard, is deliberately made to be drunk young. Yields have been reduced, the winemaking refined and there are now very good wines here.

DOMAINE PATRICK ET CHRISTOPHE BONNEFOND

Commune: Le Mornas.
Owner: Patrick & Christophe Bonnefond.
Surface Area under Vine: 7 ha.
Wines: Côte-Rôtie including Les Rochains, and Condrieu Côte Chatillon.

The brothers Bonnefond took over from their father in 1990 and have since increased production and started domaine-bottling. The grapes are entirely destemmed and the wine given fifteen to eighteen months in wood (all new for the Rochains *cuvée*). These are classy, modern Côte-Rôties. The Condrieu is also very good.

★ DOMAINE BERNARD BURGAUD

Commune: Le Champin, Ampuis.
Owner: Bernard Burgaud.

Surface Area under Vine: 4.20 ha.

Wines: Côte-Rôtie.

Bernard Burgaud's vines lie two-thirds on the hillside, one-third on the plateau, and he produces a single wine, mainly matured in small wood of which one-fifth is new. Yields are low. The wine is rich and concentrated and made to last. This is one of the best Côte-Rôties in the *appellation*.

★ DOMAINE JOËL CHAMPET

Commune: Ampuis.

Owner: Joël Champet.

Surface Area under Vine: 2.5 ha.

Wines: Côte-Rôtie La Viallière.

Joël Champet, son of Emile, now retired (you will see Emile's name on older bottles) lives halfway up one of the steepest vineyards in Europe, in the middle of his vines in the Viallière *climat*. There is one wine, aged in *demi-muids*. It is a substantial example, on the sturdy side.

★ DOMAINE CLUSEL-ROCH

Commune: Verenay.

Owner: Gilbert Clusel & Brigitte Clusel-Roch.

Surface Area under Vine: 3.75 ha – Côte-Rôtie including Les Grandes Places, and Condrieu.

Gilbert Clusel and Brigitte Roch are based in Verenay, north of Ampuis, and have vines in La Viallière and Champin, from which they produce their regular *cuvée*, and in Les Grandes Places where the average age is sixty-eight-years old. Maturation takes place in small wood, 25 to 50 per cent of which is new. The Condrieu is also matured in oak, but only three or four casks are made, from half a hectare of vines. These are serious wines which last well. Though the domaine is tiny, this is one of the best addresses in Côte-Rôtie.

★ DOMAINE ALBERT DERVIEUX-THAIZE

Commune: Verenay.

Owner: Dervieux-Rostaing family.

Dervieux' last vintage was 1989, but you may still find this one and older vintages, and they are well worth the search. He produced three Côte-Rôties: La Fongent, from the northern half of the *appellation*; La Garde, from the southern sector, and incorporating some Viognier; and, much the best but much the most brutal, La Viallière, from vines above his house. His vineyards are now exploited by his son-in-law, René Rostaing (see page 330).

★ DOMAINE MAURICE GENTAZ-DERVIEUX

Commune: Ampuis.

Owner: Gentaz-Rostaing family.

Maurice Gentaz is Albert Dervieux's brother (see above). He is also now retired and the vines are leased to René Rostaing (see page 330). Older vintages under the Gentaz label show old-fashioned, rustic Côte-Rôtie at its best: tiny harvests of very concentrated wine from venerable old vines, reared in old *demi-muids* and bottled by hand.

★ DOMAINE JEAN-MICHEL GERIN

Commune: Verenay.

Owner: Jean-Michel Gerin.

Surface Area under Vine: 9 ha.

Wines: Côte-Rôtie including Champin Junior, Champin Le Seigneur, La Landonne and Les Grandes Places, Condrieu and Côtes du Rhône.

Jean-Michel Gerin built up his domaine by a mixture of purchase, lease and inheritance and since 1990 has established himself as one of Côte-Rôtie's stars. The wines are matured in barrel (25 per cent new). The Condrieu is fermented and matured one-third in cask, two-thirds in barrel. These are very good 'modern' Côte-Rôties, especially the rich and concentrated Grandes Places.

★★★ ETS. E GUIGAL CHÂTEAU D'AMPUIS

Commune: Ampuis.

Owner: Guigal family.

Surface Area under Vine: 22 ha.

Wines: Côte-Rôtie including Brune et Blonde, La Landonne, La Turque, La Mouline and the Château d'Ampuis, Condrieu including La Doriane (from the *lieux-dits* of Châtillon and Colombier), Hermitage, Châteauneuf-du-Pape, Côtes du Rhône and other merchant wines from bought-in grapes, must and wine.

Marcel Guigal – perfectionistic, fanatical, pernickety – is the super-star of the *appellation* and probably sells more Côte-Rôtie under his own label than all the other growers combined. Despite this size, however, the quality is exemplary – as they should be at the prices he charges! He harvests late, insists on very low yields, and keeps the wines in a combination of barrel and small *foudres* and *demi-muids*, all newish wood, for up to three and a half years before bottling. There wines are so concentrated they can withstand this wait without drying out, and remain profound, rich and individual. La Landonne is the Brune, La Mouline the Blonde, La Turque a sort of hermaphroditic mixture. Usually my favourite is the Landonne. The Château d'Ampuis bottling combines elements of both the sectors of Côte-Rôtie, from vines in the *climats* of La Pommière, Le Pavillon, La Garde and Le Clos. The Condrieu La Doriane was first produced in 1994. It is an oaky example: one of the few Condrieux which keeps in bottle.

★ DOMAINE JEAN-PAUL & JEAN-LUC JAMET

Commune: Le Vallin.
Owner: Jean-Paul & Jean-Luc Jamet.
Surface Area under Vine: 6.5 ha.
Wines: Côte-Rôtie.

The winery of the brothers Jamet is located up on the plateau at the top of the slope, beyond that of Burgaud. They have vines all over the *appellation*, but produce one single wine, aged in a mixture of *demi-muids* and barrel. Things have been gently improving here since these Jamets took over responsibility from their father in the mid-1980s. The new, enlarged, temperature-controlled *cave*, completed in time for the 1996 vintage, has brought with it a rise in quality to star status.

DOMAINE ROBERT & PATRICK JASMIN

Commune: Ampuis.
Owner: Jasmin family.
Surface Area under Vine: 4 ha.
Wines: Côte-Rôtie.

Nothing seems to have changed here in 100 years. The old cellar contains mainly old *demi-muids* in which the rich, spicy but often rather rustic Jasmin wine, vinified with the stems, remains until ready for bottling. There are often several bottlings, drawn out over a year or more, of the same wine, and all will appear under the same label, though the bottlings will taste different. Robert Jasmin, father of Patrick, died in 1999.

★ DOMAINE MICHEL OGIER

Commune: Ampuis.
Owner: Michel Ogier.
Surface Area under Vine: 3.30 ha.
Wines: Côte-Rôtie including Côte Rosier, and Vin de Pays des Collines Rhodaniennes.

Michel Ogier produces a splendidly stylish 'modern' Côte-Rôtie: the fruit being destemmed and the wine aged in small oak casks. His wines have ripe tannins, splendid fruit and a velvety-smooth character. They come forward in the medium term, but last well. He also produces a pure Syrah *vin de pays* 'La Rosine', from a vineyard on the other side of the river, which I can enthusiastically recommend.

★★ DOMAINE RENÉ ROSTAING

Commune: Le Port, Ampuis.
Owner: René Rostaing.
Surface Area under Vine: 8 ha.
Wines: Côte-Rôtie including La Viallière, La Landonne and Côte Blonde, Condrieu and Vin de Pays des Collines Rhodaniennes.

Having taken over the land of Albert Dervieux and Maurice Gentaz (see page 329) on their retirement, René Rostaing now produces four different Côte-Rôtie wines, and these are made in a modern winery down by the river at Ampuis. Rostaing's wines – indeed his attitude towards their making – is a combination of the best of the old and the new. Old vines, low yields and a respect for nature on the one hand, stainless steel vats, a flexible attitude towards destemming and maturation in barrels, 30 per cent of which are new, on the other. Which is his best wine? For me the Côte Blonde, and I prefer the Landonne to the Viallière. Rostaing also produces a good Vin de Pays Syrah and red *vin de table* Les Lezardes.

Ets. J Vidal-Fleury

Commune: Ampuis.
Owner: Ets. E Guigal.
Surface Area under Vine: 10 ha.
Wines: Côte-Rôtie including Brune et Blonde and La Châtillonne, Condrieu, and other Rhône *appellations* from bought-in grapes, must and wine.

Marcel Guigal's father was the head *caviste* at Vidal-Fleury until he left to set up on his own (see Ets. E Guigal page 229). Some forty years later his son bought his father's ex-employer's domaine. Vidal-Fleury, in the capable hands of Jean-Pierre Rochias, is, however, both separate and independent. The Châtillonne, a Côte-Rôtie Blonde, is very good, but some of the merchant wines can be a bit dull.

Other Producers of note
Based within the appellation GAEC GUY BERNARD/GUY & FRÉDÉRIC BERNARD, DOMAINE DE BONSERINE, EDMOND DUCLAUX, HENRI GALLET, JEAN & CARMEN GARON, VINCENT GASSE AND DOMAINE LA ROUSSE (GEORGES DUBOEUF OWNS A SHARE).

Based outside Côte-Rôtie MAISON CHAPOUTIER (TAIN L'HERMITAGE), DOMAINE DE BOISSEYT/DIDIER CHOL (CHAVANAY), DOMAINE YVES CUILLERON (CHAVANAY), MAISON DELAS FRÈRES (SAINT JEAN-DE-MUZOLS), PIERRE GAILLARD (MALLEVAL), YVES GANGLOFF (CONDRIEU), PAUL JABOULET AÎNÉ – LES JUMELLES (TAIN L'HERMITAGE), DOMAINE DE MONTEILLET/ANTOINE ET STEPHAN MONTAZ (CHAVANAY), ROBERT NIERO (CONDRIEU), L DE VALLOUIT (SAINT-VALLIER), GEORGES VERNAY (CONDRIEU) AND FRANÇOIS VILLARD (CHAVANAY).

Condrieu

Surface Area (1998): 98 ha.
Production (1998): 2549 hl.
Colour: White.
Grape Variety: Viognier.
Maximum Yield: 37 hl/ha.
Minimum Alcohol Level: 11°.

Condrieu, home to one of the most rare and mysterious, intriguing, individual and delicious white wines of France, lies on the right or west bank of the Rhône adjacent to the vineyards of Côte-Rôtie, just where the river makes an S-bend after passing the town of Vienne. The name comes from *coin de ruisseau*, or corner of the stream – though one would be hard put, these days, to describe the wide, grey, muddy, polluted Rhône as a *ruisseau*.

As with many of the vineyards in this part of the Rhône, the precipitous hillsides topped with deciduous woods have had, until recently, a somewhat sorry, decayed aspect. A hundred years ago this was a flourishing vineyard. The difficulties of working the land and the lure of an easier 'nine-to-five' life in the factories and offices of Vienne and Lyon, together with the temptation today of high prices offered by real estate speculators intent on developing the land for holiday homes, have led to the abandonment of the slopes. Scrub and bramble cover the ancient terraces, the walls of which have crumbled away. Here and there the vines are planted but most is once again nature's domaine.

Until recently, then, Condrieu and its even smaller neighbour Château Grillet were names in books rather than wines we had actually tasted. Outside the local restaurants the wines were hardly obtainable. They were wines of myth and fable. Those who had enjoyed them – at the restaurant La Pyramide in Vienne and at the Beau Rivage in Condrieu itself – pronounced them fabulous. When I first began to encounter them, in the early 1960s, I could only agree.

The last twenty years have seen a renaissance in this part of the world. First it was the neighbouring Côte-Rôtie which was 'discovered'. Prices rose and rose again. Once more it became economical to plant vines on what are some of the steepest vineyard hills in Europe. A new generation of young, dedicated men and women could be seen gradually reconstructing the old terraces, increasing the land under vine cultivation.

Then it was the turn of Condrieu. The same thing happened. From a couple of dozen hectares under vine the *appellation* has increased by leaps and bounds, and is still expanding. Many growers combine wine production with that of soft fruit: apricots being a particular local success story. But at present the vast majority of the harvest comes from young vines.

Currently there are 98 hectares under vine within a delimited area of 200 hectares scattered over the communes of Vérin, Saint-Michel-sur-Rhône, Saint-Pierre-de-Boeuf and Chavanay in the *département* of Loire, Condrieu to the north in Rhône and Limony to the south in Ardèche. The southern two communes, Limony and Saint-Pierre, are also authorised for Saint-Joseph, and were added to the Condrieu *appellation* in 1953 in an effort to expand the production.

The Viognier is not an easy vine to grow, nor is it productive; and though it is authorized for cultivation in parts of the southern Rhône, and even in Provence and Languedoc, it is rarely found outside Condrieu and Château Grillet. According to local legend it is said to have been imported from Dalmatia in AD 281 at the behest of the Emperor Probus, perhaps as a compensation for the total destruction of the Condrieu vineyards by his predecessor the Emperor Vespasian. The Viognier is susceptible to both *coulure* (failure of the flower to set into fruit) and *millerandage* (shot berry); the latter more than the former for even after a successful flowering the grapes may remain shrivelled and undeveloped. It is, however, long-lived. Once established, the vine may last for fifty or even seventy years, and its best fruit will be provided between the ages of twenty-five and fifty. Yields are low, though. While the *appellation* laws permit a maximum yield of 30 hectolitres per hectare, the average yield over the last twenty years has been barely half that, and even in 1994, the most abundant year anybody can remember, Georges Vernay only produced 28 hectolitres per hectare, the most he has ever made in his long and celebrated career.

The vines are mainly planted in isolated pockets, facing south or south-east, and on slopes which run back perpendicularly from the river and so are protected from the wind. Viognier is trained along wires and pruned to a single cane with six buds (*guyot simple*). The soil is granite based, and carries a fine topsoil containing decomposed mica, known locally as *arzelle*. It is sandy-grey in appearance and washes away easily. John Livingstone-Learmonth (*The Wines of the Rhône*) quotes the

late André Dézormeaux, a grower who had 1¼ hectares in Saint-Michel. In 1972 he had to retrieve 100 cubic metres of soil from the bottom of his vineyard after the winter rains. 'I had to carry it all up on my back, and it makes me wonder what I did wrong to deserve such a penance,' he said ruefully.

CHÂTEAU GRILLET

Surface Area (1998): 3 ha.
Production (1998): 93 hl.
Owner: Canet family.
Colour: White.
Grape Variety: Viognier.
Maximum Yield: 37 hl/ha.
Minimum Alcohol Level: 11°.

Within the delimited area of Condrieu lies a single estate with its own *appellation contrôlée*. In this respect, so they claim, Château Grillet is unique in France, though as each of the *grands crus* of Burgundy has its own separate *appellation*, the Domaine de La Romanée-Conti could argue that they, too, have this exclusive right, and for two vineyards, La Romanée-Conti and La Tâche, while Mommessin can boast the same for the Clos de Tart. Château Grillet is often said to be the smallest *appellation* in France but this is not so. Fifteen years ago there were 1.75 hectares under vine at Château Grillet but since then the vineyard has been expanded to 3.08 hectares. Meanwhile La Romanée-Conti has remained at 1.6 hectares; and the adjacent La Romanée at 0.85 hectares. It is the latter which is the smallest *appellation* in France. Grillet has for long had a particular eminence, separate from the rest of Condrieu. The writer Jullien (1816) rates it a wine of his *première classe*. The wines can be made *liquoreux*, he says, but more often than not they are dry rather than sweet. Today, it is a dry wine, and seems to have been so since the early twentieth century.

Château Grillet's pre-eminence seems to have been consolidated by the arrival of the Neyret-Gachet family in 1820. Prior to this there are few records of the wine being held in any particular esteem though the estate and its wine must have been well established –

Livingstone-Learmonth (*op. cit.*) says that prior to 1820 it was always shipped in cask and adds that the château records date back to the time of Louis XIII (1610-1643) — nor, it seems, do we know who or what the original Grillet was. Perhaps like Côte-Rôtie ('roasted slope') the word Grillet is a corruption of *grillé* ('grilled'). Indeed it has often been mis-spelled as such. Yet by 1830 the wine was already being exported to Moscow and to the court of Saint James in London, an order of twelve dozen bottles being placed on behalf of King George IV. Ninety years later, with an arrogance only the French could adopt when talking about food and wine, the self-styled Prince of Gastronomes, Curnonsky, wrote that Château Grillet was 'quite simply the third (after Montrachet and Yquem) of the five best wines of France and *therefore of the world*' (my italics) — the other two being Coulée de Serrant and Château-Chalon.

The château of Grillet rests in the middle of its vineyard above the village of Saint-Michel-sur-Rhône. The soil, poorer than in Condrieu, is a decomposed, almost powdery granite rich in mica. The vineyard itself could not be more ideally situated. It is a natural amphitheatre, facing due south, steep, terraced, sheltered, a veritable sun-trap. With such a perfect setting, coveted jealously, so it is said, by the neighbouring Condrieu growers, it was natural that something out of the ordinary could be produced.

The building itself is a rather engaging architectural hotchpotch. Built on medieval foundations, the facade is Renaissance and, as Livingstone-Learmonth writes, 'subsequent owners built on as the fancy took them, their main criterion being size rather than charm'; and one might add, defence against local marauders, for the sides are heavily fortified. The Neyret-Gachet family is still the proud owner and the current incumbent, André Canet, who married Hélène Neyret-Gachet, is in his seventies. He has been gradually extending the area under vine by restoring ancient terraces on his domaine. From an average of 44 hectolitres per annum in the 1960s he can now make over 100 in a good year. In 1996, a prolific vintage, production was 124 hectolitres.

The grapes are collected in three days in late September (earlier than in Condrieu, so producing a wine with a higher acidity) by a team of some two dozen local harvesters who supplement the three full-time employees on the estate. The fruit is crushed in a modern pneumatic press and vinified in epoxy resin-lined steel vats, where the wine remains on its lees until the spring and when the malolatic fermentation has finished. It is then racked into small, old, oak barrels, and not bottled until after the second winter. Unlike Condrieu, Grillet uses a special 70cl brown, flute-shape bottle, not the formal *feuilles-mortes*, 75cl, Burgundy-shaped bottle.

It is this longer ageing which gives Grillet its distinctive character, different from Condrieu. The maturation in wood produces a darker colour and a richer and fuller flavour, at the expense, it could be argued, of the more racy and delicate fragrance of a Condrieu. Monsieur Canet would reply that at Château Grillet the bouquet and character becomes more aromatic and more complex, the wine has more weight and more depth, and it keeps better, though his own preference is to drink the wine young, generally before its fifth birthday, and never after eight years of age.

I have drunk some splendid Château Grillets: the 1969, the 1971 and the 1978, for example. Since then, I felt, and was it a coincidence that this coincided both with the expansion of the vineyard and an increase in yield per hectare, standards slipped somewhat. I think Monsieur Canet's policy of early harvesting is a mistake: the wines simply lacked substance; the grapes were not ripe enough. The 1985 was harvested later, however. The 1988 and 1989 were better than average, and the vintages of the 1990s I have seen so far — Monsieur Canet is reluctant to receive visitors and so my notes are mainly on wines in bottle — have been generally complimentary. But at twice the price of Condrieu? The answer is: not worth it.

At the outset, both Condrieu and Château Grillet are made in the same way. It is after the first fermentation that the processes diverge. First, most but not all, Condrieu wines undergo a malolactic fermentation (those that do not preserve a higher natural acidity, which may well be an advantage). Second, Condrieu is bottled earlier and most wines never see wood. As the growers will normally have sold their previous year's harvest, part of the crop will be bottled as soon as possible. These lighter wines are crisp and enticing in the spring and summer after the vintage, but will appear tired as little as a year after that. The rest of the wines will be bottled later in the summer and will last better, but even then are at their best almost as young as possible, though the locals would aver that the optimum is between two and four years old. Condrieu is both oak and tank-aged, and it is difficult to be hard and fast about which method is better. Vernay's young wines do not 'see oak' in the sense of being matured in small barrels. Other growers' wines are both fermented and stored in large wooden *foudres*, but these are normally so encrusted with tartrates that the influence of the oak is negligible. Some *négociants'* wines such as those of Guigal and Delas have a definite oaky taste and are all the better for it, but other wines, while oaky, lack style. Vernay's young Condrieu can be enticing but his special *cuvée*, the Coteau de Vernon, which is left for a year in cask, is one of the best Condrieux you can get.

I adore the wine. Young Condrieu is delicious. Difficult to describe but delicious nevertheless. The wine is paradoxical: quite high in alcohol, rather low in acidity; but instead of being heavy, as this might indicate, it is in fact rather delicate. Some talk about a combination of Vouvray and the Moselle with an added element of alpine flowers thrown in for good measure. Jonathan Livingston-Learmonth (*op. cit.*) says 'Young Condrieu gives the impression of slightly unripe pears or of eating the fruit near the pear skin'. When the wine is old, he adds, 'honey and apricots are sometimes mentioned by the growers.'

Personally, what characterises Condrieu for me is an aspect of candied peel, of citrus, even of marmalade. In my view it is best young. I don't think the wine ages well, though the oaky examples last longer than others. But a lot of this may well be a consequence of the young vines. When these come of age, and produce a more concentrated balanced wine, they may age better.

Condrieu and Château Grillet Vintages

Condrieu is a wine best drunk young. The oaky *cuvée* will last, but hardly more than three years after bottling. The non-oaked wines are best drunk as soon as they are released, or within the next twelve months.

1998 A reduced crop, as a result of spring frost, but good, rich, abundantly fruity wines, perhaps without quite the grip of 1997.

1997 A very good, even fine, vintage for Condrieu. The harvest season was fine, without interruption by rain. The wines are rich and round, fat and ample, but with good acidity.

1996 A very good vintage, especially for those with the courage to wait until their fruit was properly ripe, for together with maturity came a satisfactorily high acidity. Those who picked earlier made correspondingly thin and characterless wine which has evolved quickly. In general the wines are less concentrated than 1997: cooler in character.

1995 Very much a similar pattern to 1996, benefiting the later harvesters. Neither of these vintages was as good as 1994. Most wines are now becoming tired.

1994 A fine vintage, but except for superior oak-aged *cuvées*, now reaching its end.

1993 and 1992 Mediocre vintages: now passed their best.

1991 A fine vintage but now showing age. A few oaky *cuvées* may still be enjoyable.

1990 and earlier Too old.

Leading Condrieu & Château Grillet Producers

★ DOMAINE LOUIS CHÈZE

Commune: Limony.
Owner: Louis Chèze.
Surface Area under Vine: 20 ha.
Wines: Condrieu and Saint-Joseph (red and white) including the Cuvée Prestige de Caroline (Vieilles Vignes).

The sympathetic, energetic, forty-year-old Louis Chèze is based in Pangon, up in the hills behind Limony. Two hectares on the Coteau de Brèze are planted with Viognier. The vines are still young but the wine, vinified using 30 per cent new oak, is improving vintage by vintage. The Saint-Joseph white, made from 100 per cent Marsanne, is stylish. The basic Saint-Joseph red is soft and fruity, for reasonably early drinking. The Cuvée Caroline (named after his daughter) is rather more serious and is matured in oak.

★ DOMAINE YVES CUILLERON

Commune: Chavanay.
Owner: Yves Cuilleron.
Surface Area under Vine: 19.5 ha.
Wines: Condrieu including La Côte, Les Chaillets and Les Eguets (Vendange Tardive), Saint-Joseph (red and white) including Coteau Saint-Pierre, L'Amarybelle and Les Serines, and Côte-Rôtie, including La Viallière (Cuvée de Massron).

Yves Cuilleron took over his uncle's estate in 1986, and since then has established himself as one of the leading growers in the region. He is fortunate enough to have nearly 12 hectares in the Condrieu *appellation* (not all of this is yet planted) and therefore can produce three *cuvées*: La Côte (50 per cent wood, 50 per cent stainless steel), Les Chaillets (older vines, entirely fermented in oak, of which 30 per cent is new) and Les Eguets, which is collected at the end of October and is a *vin de garde*. This is gently sweet (more in the style of sweet Loire than Bordeaux) and will keep. The Saint-Josephs are good as well: Les Serines, from sixty-year-old vines, is particularly noteworthy.

★ DOMAINE PIERRE DUMAZET

Commune: Limony.
Owner: Pierre Dumazet.
Surface Area under Vine: 5 ha.
Wines: Condrieu including Clos La Myriade, Côte Fournet and Coteau Rouelle Midi, Côtes du Rhône, Vin de Pays Rhodanien Viognier, Côte-Rôtie and Cornas.

Pierre Dumazet, grey-haired, voluble and in his mid- to late-fifties, runs this domaine from a base in Limony, at the southern end of the *appellation*. He has now retired from his regular job in Lyon and can devote himself full time to his domaine. The Côte Fournet is Dumazet's best wine. This comes from sixty-five-year-old vines, and originating from granitic soil, not schist, has a power and a succulence lacking in many Condrieux.

★ DOMAINE PIERRE GAILLARD

Commune: Malleval.
Owner: Pierre Gaillard.
Surface Area under Vine: 13 ha.
Wines: Condrieu, Côte-Rôtie including Brune et Blonde and Rose Pourpre, Saint-Joseph (red and white) including Clos de Cuminaille, and Côtes du Rhône (white) from Viognier, Le Clos de Cuminaille.

The solid-looking, dark, intelligent Pierre Gaillard is based up in the hills near Malleval and is the owner of 2.5 hectares of Côte-Rôtie, much of it in La Viallière, and 1 hectare of Condrieu – this wine, though aged in oak, is not one of the greatest and the vines are still young. The star is awarded for the Saint-Joseph wines. The Rose Pourpre is lush and voluptuous: for the medium term.

DOMAINE JEAN-YVES MULTIER CHÂTEAU DE ROZAY

Commune: Condrieu.
Owners: Multier family.
Surface Area under Vine: 3.4 ha.
Wines: Condrieu and Côtes du Rhône.

Jean-Yves Multier produces two white *cuvées*: plain Condrieu and a wine bottled under the château name. These vines are situated on the Coteau de Chéry. Multier's father used to work with Georges Vernay (see page 336), until relations cooled in 1978. He then decided to go it alone. Quality is variable here, but the potential is fine.

★ DOMAINE ROBERT NIÉRO-PINCHON

Commune: Condrieu.
Owner: Robert Niéro.
Surface Area under Vine: 4.71 ha.
Wines: Condrieu including La Roncharde and Coteau de Chéry, Côte-Rôtie and Côtes du Rhône.

Handsome Robert Niéro, in his early forties, is one of the few growers who produces more Condrieu than red wine. In 1986, having worked as a banker, he took over the vines belonging to his father-in-law Jean Pinchon and has since enlarged the estate. His best Condrieu is the aromatic, quite powerful Coteau de Chéry.

★ DOMAINE ALAIN PARET
CHAIS SAINT-PIERRE

Commune: Malleval.

Owner: Alain Paret & Gérard Depardieu.

Surface Area under Vine: 36 ha.

Wines: Condrieu including Les Ceps du Nébardon and Les Lys de Volan, and Saint-Joseph (red and white) including Les Pieds Dendes, Les Larmes du Père and Domaine de La Couthiat.

Alain Paret, like Pierre Gaillard (see page 335), can be found in Malleval, up in the hills above Saint-Pierre-de-Boeuf. The super-star behind the domaine, however, is the actor Gérard Depardieu, a passionate wine lover. The two met in the 1970s, as supplier and client, and subsequently became partners. Of the 36 hectares Paret looks after 10 in Condrieu and the best wines are labelled Ceps du Nébardon and Lys de Volan, a real winner. The red Saint-Josephs, particularly the black cherry and raspberry, succulent Les Larmes du Père, are worth looking out for, too.

★★ DOMAINE ANDRÉ PERRET

Commune: Verlieu.

Owner: André Perret.

Surface Area under Vine: 10 ha.

Wines: Condrieu including Clos Chanson and Coteau de Chéry, and Saint-Joseph (red and white) including Les Grisières.

The genial, hospitable André Perret took over from his father in 1982. He lives in Verlieu, near Chavanay, and his domaine is equally divided between Condrieu and Saint-Joseph. Additionally, he is share-cropper for Robert Jurie de Camiers. Perret's wines are brilliant but unflamboyant and really subtle. Of the two Condrieux listed above I have a slight preference for the Coteau de Chéry. It is less expressive when young, but it has more depth.

★ DOMAINE CHRISTOPHE PICHON

Commune: Chavanay.

Owners: Pichon family.

Surface Area under Vine: 2 ha.

Wines: Condrieu and Saint-Joseph (red).

Christophe Pichon works alongside his father Philippe. Since 1996 there have been two separate *cuvées* of dry Condrieu. The family also like to produce a *moelleux* when weather conditions are suitable. This is one of the best examples of late-harvest Viognier available. The dry wine is made partly in wood, mainly in tank and is clean, stylish and harmonious.

★ DOMAINE PHILIPPE PICHON

Commune: Chavanay.

Owners: Pichon family.

Surface Area under Vine: 3 ha.

Wines: Condrieu and Saint-Joseph (red).

Philippe is the father of Christophe (see above). The wines also have much in common, being crisp and elegant, for drinking reasonably young. The Saint-Joseph is also commendable. As Christophe's parcel is so small, the grapes of both are vinified together, but the wine thereof is eventually bottled under two different labels.

★ DOMAINE GEORGES VERNAY

Commune: Condrieu.

Owners: Vernay family.

Surface Area under Vine: 14 ha.

Wines: Condrieu including Les Terrasses de L'Empire, Les Chaillées de L'Enfer and Coteau du Vernon, Côte-Rôtie including Les Maisons Rouges, Saint-Joseph (red) and Côtes du Rhône.

Now in his seventies, Georges Vernay is the guru of the *appellation*, and as little as twenty years ago just about its only producer. He has given enormous encouragement, lending equipment, not hesitating to offer advice, to the younger growers in the *appellation*, and as the one who kept the flame alive in the dark days, is naturally much revered. He is now being succeeded by his son Luc, daughter Christine and her husband, Paul Ansellem. Vernay's wines vary from light, unoaked *primeur cuvées* to the altogether more serious, oak-fermented (10 per cent new) Coteau du Vernon.

★ DOMAINE FRANÇOIS VILLARD

Commune: Monjoux.

Owners: Villard family.

Surface Area under Vine: 7 ha.

Wines: Condrieu including Coteau du Poncins, Les Terrasses du Palat, Le Grand Vallon and Quintessence, Saint-Joseph (red and white) including Reflet and Côtes de Mairlant, and Côte-Rôtie including La Brocade.

The youthful François Villard lives at Montjoux, near Saint-Michel-sur-Rhône, owns 3 hectares of Condrieu, and produces his oak-fermented, powerful Coteaux du Poncins from a site adjacent to Château Grillet. Les Terrasses du Palat is from the younger vines, Quintessence a sweet wine, produced occasionally. The reds are very good too. This is a splendid address.

Other Producers of note

Based within the appellation DOMAINE DU CHÊNE/MARC ROUVIÈRE (CHAVANAY), CHRISTIAN & MAURICETTE FACCHIN (VÉRIN), PHILIPPE FAURY (CHAVANAY), YVES GANGLOFF (CONDRIEU), DOMAINE DU MONTEILLET/ANTOINE MONTEZ (CHAVANAY), DIDIER MORION (CHAVANAY), HERVÉ RICHARD (VERLIEU) AND GÉRARD VILLANO (CONDRIEU).

Based in Côte-Rôtie PATRICK AND CHRISTOPHE BONNEFOND (LE MORNAS), DOMAINE CLUSEL-ROCH (VERENAY), DOMAINE JEAN-MICHEL GERIN (VERENAY), ETS. E GUIGAL, DOMAINE RENÉ ROSTAING (LE PORT, AMPUIS) AND J VIDAL-FLEURY (AMPUIS).

Based elsewhere MAISON CHAPOUTIER (TAIN L'HERMITAGE), MAISON DELAS FRÈRES (SAINT-JEAN-DE-MUZOLS) AND MAISON PAUL JABOULET AÎNÉ (TAIN L'HERMITAGE).

Many of the Condrieu-based growers noted above also produce Saint-Joseph (see page 345).

HERMITAGE

Surface Area (1998): 134 ha.
Production (1998): (Red) 3853 hl; (white) 976 hl.
Colour: Red and white.
Grape Varieties: (Red) Syrah, Roussanne and Marsanne; (white) Roussanne and Marsanne.
Maximum Yield: 40hl/ha.
Minimum Alcohol Level: (Red) 10.5°; (white) 11°.

The apogee of the Syrah grape is reached in Hermitage. Great Hermitage is truly great by any standards; in its own way as fine as a First Growth red Bordeaux, a top *grand cru* Burgundy and anything any other country or region might have to offer. According to Jonathan Livingstone-Learmonth (*op. cit.*) Tain L'Hermitage was already a thriving vineyard in Roman times, and the wine, then known as Tegna, is mentioned not only by Pliny, who wrote about agricultural matters in his *Natural History* in AD 77, but in Martial's *Epigrams*, which seem to indicate that it enjoyed more than a local fame. This is a part of France which is rich in Roman ruins. From Arles and Nîmes in the south to Vienne and even Lyon in the north, the Rhône Valley abounds in antiquities, and in Tain there is an ancient altar, known as the Taurobole, that was used for the sacrifice of bulls to the god Mithras. It may have been the Phocaeans who introduced the cultivated vine to southern France in the sixth century BC, but it was the arrival of the Romans which gave the impetus to organized viticulture.

Looming above the bustling town of Tain is the granite hill of Hermitage, rugged and bleak in winter. There are many legends accounting for the origin of its name. Without a scrap of evidence to support their claims, James Joyce and Maurice Healy, both Irish, each aver that the site was a resting place for Saint Patrick, on his way to convert the Irish to Christianity. Another story is of a Christian priest who, fleeing from the Romans, took refuge on the hill and was supplied with food by the wild animals around him. There was nothing to drink, however, and he was in danger of dying from thirst, when the good Lord intervened and sent down a band of angelic growers with vines which produced wine overnight. The best-known story is of the holy knight Gaspard de Stérimberg. Stérimberg was wounded in a crusade against the Albigensian heretics in 1224, and, disgusted with the follies of his fellow mortals, chose the hill of Hermitage as a place to build a small chapel of retreat, wherein he would pray for the souls of his fellow men. In due course he decided to plant vines on the surrounding steep slopes. The reputation of this wine soon spread, and the local peasants began to cultivate the remaining sections of the hill.

The modern era for the wines of Hermitage seems to date from 1642, when, a year before his death, Louis XIII stopped at Tain. As might be expected the local wine was offered as part of the royal refreshment. It was enthusiastically appreciated and orders were given for Hermitage to be included in the royal cellar. The reputation of the wine never looked back. Shipments were being exported as far as Russia only a couple of decades later and by the end of the seventeenth century it was established as one of the greatest red wines of France.

By the end of the eighteenth century Hermitage wine had found its way to Bordeaux. From 1780 until the time of phylloxera, it was used extensively to give a bit of muscle to the sometimes insipid Gironde wines. This blending was quite legal then – it was well before the introduction of the INAO laws. Even estate wines such as Château Lafite were offered either pure or *Hermitagé*.

The mid-nineteenth century saw a series of great vintages. Professor Saintsbury (*Notes on a Cellar Book*, 1920) described an 1846 (the year before he was born) as 'really a wonderful wine . . . the manliest wine I ever drank; and age (the bottle was forty years old) has softened and polished all that might have been rough in the manliness of its youth'. Red wines then were made bigger than they are today. The grapes were picked somewhat earlier, and so had a higher acidity; and the *cuvaison* was longer, so the wines were burlier and more tannic. Bottles of the best years, therefore, would last well into their third or even fourth decade. Hermitage, therefore, must have been one of the most indestructible of all wines. In 1981, at a pre-auction tasting which I presented in Chicago on behalf of Heublein Inc., an anonymous 1825 Hermitage was offered. The most badly ullaged bottle in the lot – a cache discovered in the back of a cellar near Lyon – was opened for tasting. Even that was still well-coloured, vigorous, recognizably Syrah, and still had fruit. And yet the wine was over 150 years old!

By a quirk of geography the hill of Hermitage is comprised of a granite base over which lies a thin layer of decomposed flint and chalk. Odd because the surrounding countryside is a mixture of limestone and clay. The explanation for this is that originally the river Rhône ran its course to the east of Hermitage. Geologically the hill is part of the right bank of the valley, and, indeed, shares the same soil structure as Saint-Joseph and Côte-Rôtie. At some stage, however, the river changed its direction, leaving Hermitage isolated on the left, eastern bank. The hill dominates a bend in the river. North of Tain, the river is flowing due south. Once past the town, it flows east for a kilometre or so before correcting itself. This leaves the prime vineyards of the granite hills of Hermitage with an exposure which is due south and bathed in sunlight from dawn to dusk.

The 130-odd hectares of vines are sub-divided into a number of *climats* or individual vineyards, and most of these are split between a number of owners. Each site produces wine which varies subtly from the others, and most growers and *négociants* make a wine which is a careful blend originating from a number of different plots. In *Topographie de Tous les Vignobles Connus* (1816), Jullien listed the three best *climats*: Les Bessards, at the western end of the hill, producing a full, sturdy wine; Le Méal, next door, with a deeper layer of flint and chalk, producing a wine of fine perfume; and Les Greffieux, below Le Méal, making generous, supple wine. The ideal is said to be a blend of these three.

Cultivation on the steep hill is a problem. While spraying these days is done by helicopter, the Jaboulets of Paul Jaboulet Aîné still reckon on one labourer per hectare on the hill rather than one per 10 hectares on the flatter Crozes vineyards. Though not as precipitous as Côte-Rôtie the terrain is steep and the fragile layer of topsoil has to be protected within terraces, or too much would be washed away every time there was a thunderstorm. The first machines which can work the soil efficiently are just beginning to be developed, and some of these have been invented by the Jaboulets themselves. But much of the ploughing is still done using horses and mules. Oxen were used as recently as a century ago.

The Syrah vine can be pruned by the *guyot* (cane) and *gobelet* (bush) methods and, on the steepest parts of Hermitage, trained up a single stake to help protect it

Hermitage and Crozes-Hermitage

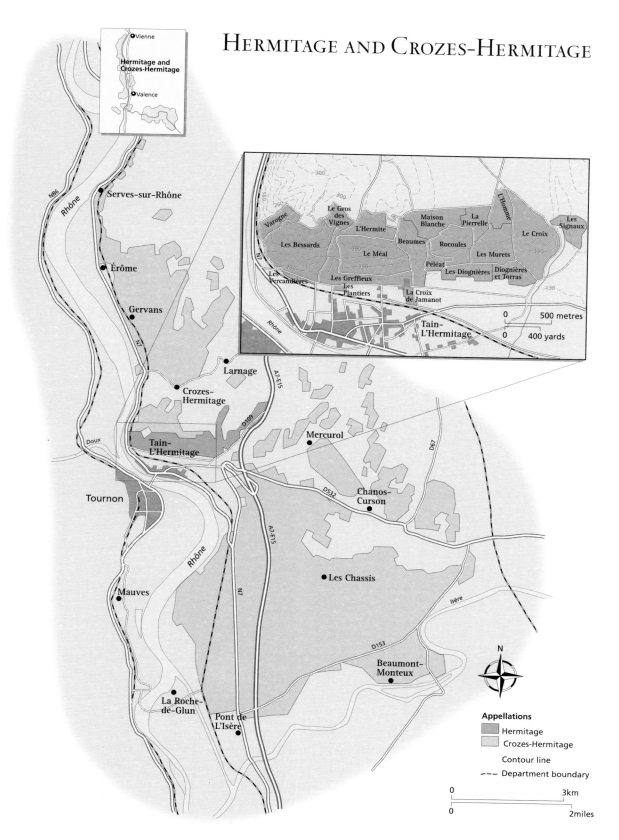

Vienne

Hermitage and Crozes-Hermitage

Valence

N86

Rhône

Serves-sur-Rhône

Érôme

Gervans

Larnage

Crozes-Hermitage

A7-E15

D109

Tain-L'Hermitage

Doux

Mercurol

Tournon

D532

Chanos-Curson

D67

Les Chassis

Mauves

A7-E15

Rhône

N7

Isère

La Roche-dé-Glun

Pont de L'Isère

D153

Beaumont-Monteux

N

Inset map

300

150

290

300

Varogne

Le Gros des Vignes

L'Hermite

Maison Blanche

La Pierrelle

L'Homme

Les Signaux

Les Bessards

Beaumes

Rocoules

Le Croix

200

Le Méal

Péléat

Les Murets

150

150

130

Diognières et Torras

Les Vercandières

Les Greffieux

Les Diognières

130

Les Plantiers

La Croix de Jamanot

Rhône

Tain-L'Hermitage

N7

0 500 metres
0 400 yards

Legend

Appellations

Hermitage

Crozes-Hermitage

Contour line

–‑‑ Department boundary

0   3km
0   2miles

339

against the strong Mistral winds. On the flatter land the vines can be trained along wires by the Cordon de Royat method to form the traditional hedge aspect somewhat similar to that in Bordeaux or Burgundy.

The hill of Hermitage makes both red and white wine. About 20 per cent of the total output is white, produced from a mixture of Roussanne and Marsanne grapes grown where the topsoil is rich in clay. The Marsanne is today the predominant variety. It produces a wine which is richer and has more structure if having less finesse than the delicate, alpine-flowery Roussanne and is less prone to disease. Traditionally, white Hermitage was a full-bodied wine, high in alcohol; a wine of muscle rather than finesse. Often it was aged too long before bottling and as a result was heavy and flat, with a rather oily aspect to add to the nutty, herby peach-kernel flavour. Maturation was in oak, but in large oak *foudres* rather than in new barrels.

Led by Paul Jaboulet Aîné, the leading *négociant*, production methods in the last twenty years have somewhat changed. Fermentation is now at a low temperature, storage is in a mixture of barrel, vat or tank, malolactic fermentation is discouraged and bottling is early. Moreover the wine is fermented in *barrique*.

A puzzling factor is the evolution of white Hermitage. When young the white wines can be delicious: crisp and fruity and youthful. After three years or so they seem to go through a prolonged awkward adolescence. White Hermitage becomes lumpy, hard, even resinny. Patience, however, provided the wine has been well made in the first place, will be rewarded. After four or five more years, i.e. after seven in bottle, the ugly duckling becomes a swan – once more clean and fruity, but now rich, mellow and profound. This curious process, which I put down to the side effects of an oxidation/reduction in bottle, does not often occur in Burgundy, though I have noticed it in some dry Bordeaux and in white Châteauneuf-du-Pape.

Theoretically, a maximum of 15 per cent of white grapes can be included in the vats for red Hermitage – a curious decree which does not pertain for any other red wine *appellation* except for Côte-Rôtie and Crozes in the northern Rhône. In practice few growers ever use more

than 5 per cent and I suspect that all the top wines such as Jaboulet's La Chapelle and those from Gérard Chave are made exclusively from Syrah.

Vinification methods for the red wines are still largely what might be termed 'old fashioned', with a long *cuvaison* in glass-lined concrete vats or large oak *foudres*, together with *pigeage* twice a day, the object being to produce a big, full-bodied, tannic wine – a wine of power and strength which will need a decade or more to mature. While today top growers such as Jaboulet and Chapoutier and (usually) Chave destalk entirely the result is nevertheless one of the fullest, densest and richest wines in the world. When young the colour is immense; a solid, viscous, almost black purple that continues to the very rim of the glass. The nose is leafy, with an undercurrent of unripe blackcurrants. The wine is full-bodied and very tannic, strong, powerful and alcoholic. The best examples are also oaky and despite their 'size' not the least fiery, robust or spicy. When mature, these retain their vastness of structure, but the flavour is now rich, ample, profound and aromatic with a depth of flavour and a concentration of character which has few rivals. The fruit is now a ripe and subtle combination of blackcurrants and blackberries with a hint of raspberry, all underpinned by a slightly baked smell, as if the wine could remember its origins as the sun slowly heated up the granite bed rock day after day as the grapes ripened.

What I find particularly memorable about top Hermitage of a good vintage is the way the wines manage to achieve an extraordinary retention of fresh, ripe fruit, even after fifteen or even twenty five years in bottle.

Until very recently Hermitage was a remarkably inexpensive wine. Despite the low production – 5000 hectolitres from 130 hectares – and despite the quality, it did not have the fame of top Bordeaux and Burgundy estates. The late 1980s and 1990s have seen prices climb somewhat, and the best older vintages reach premium prices on the rare occasions that they actually turn up at auction. Yet the wines are still marvellous value. All you need is a good cellar to store them in and the patience to wait the dozen years or more until they are fully mature.

CROZES-HERMITAGE

Surface Area (1998): 1225 ha.
Production (1998): (Red) 52,503 hl; (white) 4649 hl.
Colour: Red and white.
Grape Varieties: (Red) Syrah; (white) Roussanne and Marsanne.
Maximum Yield: 45 hl/ha.
Minimum Alcohol Level: 10°.

Surrounding the hill of Hermitage itself is the expanding *appellation* of Crozes – the largest one in the northern Rhône. The *appellation* covers eleven *communes* and takes its name from one of them, that nearest to the hill itself. To the north of Hermitage lies Crozes, Larnage, Gervans, Érôme and Serves-sur-Rhône; Mercurol and Chanos-Curson are to the east; Beaumont-Monteux, Pont de L'Isère and La Roche-de-Glun to the south. The vines occupy undulating gentle slopes situated on a mixture of soils, some of which, like that at Gervans, are of a similar granite to that of Hermitage itself, while in other parts – at Mercurol, for instance – sand can be found, making it a suitable commune for white wines. Elsewhere, in parts of Mercurol again, at Beaumont and at Les Chassis on the way to Pont de L'Isère, the soil contains a large amount of smooth pudding stones, these *galets* showing evidence of the Rhône's old route to the east of the Hermitage hill. Generally the soil is much less granitic than at Hermitage itself, and this, plus a less ideal exposure, helps explain the difference in the wines. The best reds are said to come from Gervans and Larnage, where the ground is heavier and contains more clay, while the best wine of the *appellation*, Jaboulet's Domaine de Thalabert, comes from their own domaine of the same name at Les Chassis. The same grapes are used as at Hermitage: Syrah (with 15 per cent white grapes allowed but rarely used) for the red wine and Marsanne and Roussanne (almost entirely the former) for the white. The *appellation* now produces about half of the total northern Rhône production.

Crozes-Hermitage, together with Saint-Joseph, is the lightest and the cheapest of the northern Rhône red wines. Prices compare to that of a lesser *cru* Beaujolais

and some of the wine, too, is made by carbonic maceration. In my view, however, this is a mistake as the Syrah grape does not take kindly to this vinification technique. It loses not only the character of its fruit but also any individuality deriving from the soil. The result is anaemic and anonymous wine, and, compared with some of the Syrah wines made in the South of France, very poor value for money.

The best wines are made by traditional methods, and along the lines of that of Hermitage, though Crozes, being less structured, needs to be bottled after a maximum of a year in cask, lest the fruit dries out. In good hands Crozes can be a very interesting wine, somehow less spicy and peppery, more refined than Saint-Joseph, and it is then excellent value. This sort of red is at its best after five or seven years. The best whites are those made by low-temperature fermentation, with no malolactic fermentation and with early bottling. These are similar in body, cost price and aspiration to a Mâcon Blanc-Villages. The difference lies in the grape varieties used, and in a soil which has less limestone and more sand. I find the flavour of white Crozes-Hermitage difficult to describe, particularly as one grower's wine may be quite different to that of his neighbour. At a stab, a mixture of hay and vegetables, plus a whiff of peaches and apricots, as well as their kernels. Jaboulet's Mule Blanche is an excellent example of white Crozes-Hermitage, and it is at its best within a couple of years after the vintage.

Leading Hermitage & Crozes-Hermitage Producers

★ DOMAINE ALBERT BELLE
Commune: Larnage.
Owner: Belle family.
Surface Area under Vine: 18 ha.
Wines: Hermitage (red and white) and Crozes-Hermitage (red and white) including Cuvée Louis Belle and Pierreles.

Albert Belle and his son Philippe work from a large, temperature-controlled, barn-like cellar at the top of a hill in Larnage. They also produce soft fruit. Their vineyards lie mainly in Crozes, but include 1.2 hectares of

Hermitage in the *lieux-dits* of Murets and Diognières. The wine business dates from 1990; prior to this they were members of the local co-operative. The red Hermitage is good and improving year by year. The white Hermitage is even better, one of the *appellation*'s stars, as is the Crozes Cuvée Louis Belle. These are modern, oaky wines.

★★ ETS. CHAPOUTIER

Commune: Tain.

Owner: Chapoutier family.

Surface Area under Vine: 80 ha.

Wines: Hermitage (red and white) including Le Pavillon, L'Ermite, Le Méal and La Sizeranne (all red) and Chante-Alouette and Cuvée de L'Orée (both white), Crozes-Hermitage (red and white) including Les Varonniers and Les Meysonnières, Côte-Rôtie including Modorée, Saint-Joseph including Les Granits and Deschants, Cornas, Châteauneuf-du-Pape, Barbe Rac, La Bernardine; plus other *appellations* from the southern Rhône and occasional Hermitage Vin de Paille.

This is an important domaine, but also a company which was in the doldrums until the diminutive, brash, dynamic Michel Chapoutier and his more sober brother Marc took over the family reins in 1989.

Since then the change has been dramatic – the wine-making process has been cleaned up, a number of super *cuvées* introduced and the vineyards are now farmed bio-dynamically. There are some brilliant wines at the top levels here. The Chapoutiers own some 30 hectares on the Hermitage hill, 60 per cent of which is planted with Syrah. The best vintages of the red wines produced under the new regime – Le Pavillon, L'Ermite and Modorée – are not yet fully mature, but the signs are that in character they fall between the lush, approachable, generously oaky style of Jaboulet's La Chapelle and the more austere, unflamboyant, only marginally woody personality of those of Gérard Chave. The range today is wide, consistent and competent. The Chapoutiers are now moving into Provence and Languedoc. In 1998 they took over Domaine Ferraton (see page 343). This is operated separately.

DOMAINE BERNARD CHAVE

Commune: Mercurol.

Owner: Bernard Chave.

Surface Area under Vine: 13 ha.

Wines: Hermitage and Crozes-Hermitage (red and white).

These Chaves (no relation to those below) live in Mercurol and are as much into soft fruit as into wine. Father Bernard concentrates on the latter, son Yann is responsible for the former. The family possesses 1.2 hectares on the Hermitage hill in the *lieux-dits* of Beaumes and Péléat. The red grapes are not de-stemmed (a mistake, in my view, unless the stems are fully ripe, which they are rarely) and the red wine reared in a mixture of *demi-muids* and small barrels. A good source but it could be better.

★★★ DOMAINE JEAN-LOUIS CHAVE

Commune: Mauves.

Owner: Chave family.

Surface Area under Vine: 15 ha.

Wines: Hermitage (red and white) including Cuvée Cathelin and Saint-Joseph; plus occasional Hermitage Vin de Paille .

There have been Chaves in the area since 1481, making this perhaps the oldest father-to-son wine domaine in France. It is also one of the greatest. There are few bottles quite as profound and as complex as a mature Chave Hermitage. Gérard Chave works with his son Jean-Louis. Their 10 hectares on the Hermitage slopes include vines in Rocoules, Beaume, L'Hermite, Péléat, Le Méal and Les Bessards, the best of which is sometimes isolated and bottled as Cuvée Cathelin. The wines are kept in a mixture of oak barrels (only new for some of the white wine) and *foudres* and handling is minimal. The white wine is elegant, flowery and gently oaky, the red Hermitage cool, slow to mature, long to show its richness and fruit, requires a minimum of ten years. The best vintages are even better after twenty years.

★ DOMAINE DU COLOMBIER

Commune: Mercurol.

Owner: Viale family.

Surface Area under Vine: 14 ha.

Wines: Hermitage (red) and Crozes-Hermitage (red and white) including Cuvée Gaby.

Florent and Gabriel Viale are relative newcomers, only having started to bottle seriously since the early 1990s. Their base is in Mercurol, and the estate includes 1.65 hectares of sixty-year-old vines from parcels in the *climats* of Diognières, Péléat and Beaume on the Hermitage hill. These are well-made wines, with nothing rustic about them. A domaine to watch.

DOMAINE COMBIER

Commune: Pont de L'Isère.
Owners: Combier family.
Surface Area under Vine: 13 ha.
Wines: Crozes-Hermitage (red and white) including Clos des Grives and Vieilles Vignes.

Maurice and Laurent Combier left the co-operative at Tain in 1990 and constructed a modern cellar behind the family house on the N7 road, which works as much as possible by gravity. The approach in the vineyard is fully *biologique*. These are well-made wines, especially for those who like plenty of new oak. There is 30 per cent for the basic blend and 100 per cent for the Cuvée des Grives and the old-vine *cuvée*.

DOMAINE DARD ET RIBO

Commune: Mercurol.
Owner: Jean-René Dard & François Ribo.
Surface Area under Vine: 5.35 ha.
Wines: Crozes-Hermitage (red and white), Saint-Joseph (red and white) and Hermitage.

Jean-René Dard and François Ribo joined forces in 1984 and work from a dilapidated cellar behind the Château Blanche-Laine, close to the *autoroute* at the foot of the Hermitage hill. From ¼ of a hectare of very old vines they produce a concentrated, intense Hermitage. The other wines are rustic but in the best sense: robust, muscular and no new wood.

★ ETS. DELAS FRÈRES

Commune: Saint-Jean-de-Muzols.
Owner: Champagne Deutz.
Surface Area under Vine: 22 ha.

Wines: Hermitage (red and white) including Marquise de la Tourette and Les Bessards, Côte-Rôtie including Cuvée Seigneur de Maugiron, Condrieu and Saint-Joseph (red and white).

Maison Delas possesses 10 hectares of Hermitage, chiefly in Les Bessards, and has a lease on 4 hectares in Condrieu and another 4 hectares in Côte-Rôtie from the Delas family. The range of northern Rhône wines includes a very good red Crozes-Hermitage, Cuvée Tour d'Albon, but the special bottlings are the stars of the range. I find the Hermitages (Les Bessardes is only produced in the best vintages) more interesting than the Côte-Rôtie, Cuvée Seigneur de Maugiron.

DOMAINE BERNARD FAURIE

Commune: Tournon.
Owner: Bernard Faurie.
Surface Area under Vine: 4.5 ha.
Wines: Hermitage (red and white) including Le Méal and Saint-Joseph (red and white) including Cuvée Vieilles Vignes.

Bernard Faurie, who operates out of a rather cramped cellar in Tournon, produces two *cuvées* of Hermitage, one from eighty-five-year old vines in Le Méal, the other from Les Greffieux, from where he also produces a couple of cases of white Hermitage each year. The winemaking here has been steadily improving during the 1990s.

DOMAINE FERRATON PÈRE ET FILS

Commune: Tain.
Owners: Ferraton family and Ets. Chapoutier.
Surface Area under Vine: 9.5 ha.
Wines: Crozes-Hermitage (red and white) including La Matinière, and Hermitage (red and white) including Les Miaux; plus occasional Hermitage Vin de Paille.

The Ferraton family own 4 hectares on the Hermitage hill, in Le Méal, Diognières and Beaume where they have planted Syrah, and in Diognières and Muret where they have Marsanne. These are individual wines, occasionally very good indeed. In 1998 Michel Ferraton retired, and the business was taken over by Chapoutier, though run independently by Michel's son Samuel. It now has a merchant's licence.

★ DOMAINE ALAIN GRAILLOT

Commune: Pont de L'Isère.
Owner: Alain Graillot.
Surface Area under Vine: 20 ha.
Wines: Crozes-Hermitage (red and white) including La Guiraude, Saint-Joseph and Hermitage.

Alain Graillot, brought up in Vienne, used to sell agricultural chemicals until he decided to become a winemaker in 1985. Since then he has become one of the stars of the northern Rhône. The exploitation is based on 18 hectares of Crozes-Hermitage, a domaine in Chassis which he used to rent but has since purchased. These wines, especially the special *cuvée* La Guiraude are among the best in the area. On the Hermitage hill he has a microscopic vineyard of old vines in Les Greffieux and a 1-hectare parcel of young vines nearby. As yet I prefer the better Crozes-Hermitage *cuvée*.

★★★ ETS. PAUL JABOULET AÎNÉ

Commune: La Roche-de-Glun.
Owner: Jaboulet family.
Surface Area under Vine: 91 ha.
Wines: Hermitage (red and white) including La Chapelle (red) and Le Chevalier de Stérimberg (white), Crozes-Hermitage (red and white) including Domaine de Thalabert, Domaine Roure and Mule Blanche (white), Saint-Joseph Le Grand Pompée (red and white), Cornas Domaine Saint-Pierre and Condrieu; plus, from bought-in grapes, must and wine, Côte-Rôtie Les Jumelles, Châteauneuf-du-Pape Les Cèdres (red and white), Côtes du Rhône Parallèle 45, Gigondas, Vacqueyras, Tavel and other wines.

One of the very finest domaine/merchants in the whole of France, Ets. Paul Jaboulet Aîné produce a complete range of Rhône wines, all of it at a very high level of quality indeed. The family owns 29 hectares on the Hermitage hill, making them the second largest proprietors after Chapoutier. The top wine from these holdings, mainly in Le Méal and Les Bessards, La Chapelle, is one of the best wines in the world. It is more oaky than that of Gérard Chave, easier to discern when young, but just as profound, just as glorious when mature (the 1978 took twenty years to come round). Both the single-domaine red Crozes-Hermitages are among the best of the *appellation*. The same can be said for the Cornas, where there is stiff competition today, and the whites are equally exciting. Jaboulet is thoroughly reliable and strongly recommended.

DOMAINE ETIENNE POCHON

Commune: Chanos-Curson.
Owner: Pochon family.
Surface Area under Vine: 15 ha.
Wines: Crozes-Hermitage (red and white) including Cuvée Château de Curson.

Two distinct styles of wine can be obtained from this tidy, modern cellar. That bottled as Domaine Pochon is for reasonably early drinking. Those under the Château de Curson label see more oak, have more body and depth and are meant to be kept a few years. These are well-made, stylish, clean wines.

DOMAINE DES REMIZIÈRES

Commune: Mercurol.
Owner: Desmeure family.
Surface Area under Vine: 20 ha.
Wines: Hermitage (red and white) and Crozes-Hermitage (red and white) including Cuvée Particulière.

Philippe Desmeure has been running this domaine since his father Alphonse retired in 1990. The family owns 3 hectares of vines in Hermitage, Syrah in the Rocoules and L'Hermite *climats* and Marsanne in Maison Blanche. This is one of those reliable estates that you wish would turn the corner and become really stunning.

★ DOMAINE MARC SORREL

Commune: Tain.
Owner: Marc Sorrel.
Surface Area under Vine: 4 ha.
Wines: Hermitage (red and white) including

Le Gréal (red) and Les Rocoules (white), and Crozes-Hermitage (red and white).

Marc Sorrel owns 2.5 hectares of land in Hermitage planted roughly 60:40 red and white. His top *cuvée*, Le Gréal (into which are blended some 7 to 8 per cent of white grapes), comes from Les Greffieux and Le Méal *climats*, whence its name. It can be one of the top wines of the vintage. The lesser wines are less good though.

Other Hermitage Producers of note

Domaine Fayolle (Gervans), Jean-Louis Grippat (Tournon), Ets. Guigal (Ampuis), Jean-Michel Sorrel (Tain), Ets. L de Vallouit (Saint-Vallier), Ets. J Vidal-Fleury (Ampuis) and Cave Coopérative des Vins Fins (Tain).

Other Crozes-Hermitage Producers of note

Domaine Jean-Michel Borja (Beaumont-Monteux), Cave des Clairmonts, Domaine Collonge (Mercurol), Domaine des Entrefaux/Tardy & Ange (Chanos-Curson), Domaine Fayolle (Gervans), Domaine du Pavillon/GAEC Cornu (Mercurol), Domaine Pradelle (Chanos-Curson) and Cave Coopérative des Vins Fins (Tain).

Saint-Joseph

Surface Area (1998): 869 ha.
Production (1998): (Red) 21,166 hl; (white) 2412 hl.
Colour: Red and white.
Grape Varieties: (Red) Syrah; (white) Marsanne and Roussanne.
Maximum Yield: 40 hl/ha.
Minimum Alcohol Level: 10°.

Saint-Joseph, an *appellation* created in 1956, lies on the west bank of the Rhône, centred around Tournon, but runs sporadically from south of Condrieu as far as Cornas, a distance of some 50 kilometres as the crow flies. In all there are twenty-three communes. This is the second largest *appellation* in the northern Rhône, after Crozes-Hermitage, and the grape varieties and regulations are the same.

Saint-Joseph, like Crozes, is an expanding *appellation*, the increase having been largely, and regrettably, in land not entirely suitable for fine wine, being predominantly on the flatter, more alluvial soils of the valley floor, rather than on the slopes themselves. As a result the wine of Saint-Joseph varies enormously, ranging from substantial wines for ageing from the steep slopes above Tournon itself, Mauves and Saint-Jean-de-Muzols, where the soil is essentially granite, to weaker wines made by carbonic maceration methods from the Cave Coopérative at Saint-Désirat-Champagne and others. There are those who think highly of the better wines from the Saint-Désirat co-operative (indeed, they are prolific gold medal winners at the annual Concours Agricole in Paris) but for me they lack the truly masculine character and depth of a northern Rhône wine.

At their best, however, after five years or so, Saint-Joseph can be very good, and, like Crozes, the wine is inexpensive. At the *négociant* level, prices are marginally more than for a simple Crozes but cheaper than a better Crozes, let alone Cornas.

In general, Saint-Joseph is a rugged wine, more open than Hermitage or Cornas, yet chewy and sometimes peppery. It lacks, for me, a certain finesse. Finesse may be a strange word to apply to the northern Rhône; yet the best wines of all the other *appellations*, underneath their sturdy character, seem to have it, and this is apparent when the wines are mature. Saint-Joseph has power without grace, size without, ultimately, class. There is a small amount of white Saint-Joseph, produced mainly from Marsanne. In character it is very similar to a white Crozes-Hermitage.

Leading Saint-Joseph Producers

Domaine Maurice Courbis et Fils GAEC Les Ravières

Commune: Châteaubourg.
Owner: Courbis family.
Surface Area under Vine: 22 ha.
Wines: Saint-Joseph (red and white) including Les Royes, and Cornas including Champelrose, Les Eygats and La Sabarotte.

This is an expanding and up-to-date domaine, producing wine in a modern warehouse in Châteaubourg, which is also used for storing the soft fruit produced by the family firm. One-third of the white is vinified in newish wood. The basic red is aged in a mixture of tank and barrel and Les Royes entirely in oak. Laurent and Dominique, Maurice's sons, also produce Cornas on the same site. The best *cuvée*, La Sabarotte, comes from fifty-year-old vines and is matured in 50 per cent new wood.

DOMAINE PIERRE COURSODON

Commune: Mauves.
Owner: Coursodon family.
Surface Area under Vine: 13 ha.
Wines: Saint-Joseph (red and white) including Paradis Saint-Pierre, L'Olivaie and La Sensonne.

This reliable domaine is located in Mauves' main square, right on the main road. The Paradis Saint-Pierre is a special *cuvée* from 1 hectare of vines planted on the granite hillsides behind the village. L'Olivaie, a red wine matured using about 15 per cent new or newish barrels, comes from the Olivet *climat* at Saint-Jean-de-Muzols, the other side of Tournon. La Sensonne, a special selection from these two *lieux-dits*, is matured in new oak.

★ DOMAINE JEAN-LOUIS GRIPPAT

Commune: Tournon.
Owner: Grippat family.
Surface Area under Vine: 6 ha.
Wines: Saint-Joseph (red and white) including Vignes des Hospices, and Hermitage (red and white).

Jean-Louis Grippat and his wife and their daughter, Sylvie (who is now in charge) make some of the best wines in the area, including the Vignes des Hospices from 100-year-old vines, and demonstrate the difference between Hermitage's class – they have 1.5 hectares in Les Murets *climat*, producing more white than red – and the rather more robust, less elegant wines of Saint-Joseph.

Other Producers of note
DOMAINE SYLVAIN BERNARD (SAINT-PÉRAY), DOMAINE FLORENTIN – CLOS DE L'ARBALESTRIER (MAUVES),

DOMAINE GONON (MAUVES), BERNARD GRIPA (MAUVES), PASCAL PERRIER (SARRAS), CAVE COOPÉRATIVE DE SAINT-DÉSIRAT (CASTILLON DU GARD) AND RAYMOND TROLLAT (SAINT-JEAN-DE-MUZOLS).

(See also Condrieu producers page 334 and Hermitage and Crozes-Hermitage producers page 341.)

CORNAS

Surface Area (1998): 91 ha.
Production (1998): 6287 hl.
Colour: Red.
Grape Variety: Syrah.
Maximum Yield: 40 hl/ha.
Minimum Alcohol Level: 10.5°.

The village and vineyards of Cornas are located between those of Saint-Péray and Saint-Joseph on the west bank of the Rhône, almost opposite Valence and 15 kilometres as the crow flies from the hill of Hermitage. Cornas is a red wine, and this being the northern Rhône, that means the Syrah grape. The wine is one of the fullest, sturdiest and most rewarding of the entire Rhône Valley: hard, tannic and unyielding when young, rich velvety with a heady scent of blackcurrant and raspberry, yet always sizeable and with a somewhat baked flavour, when mature. In good vintages the wines need ten years to reach optimum drinking.

One of the reasons for Cornas' bulk and concentration, and this baked flavour, is the mesoclimate. The steep slopes on which the vines lie are set well back away from the Rhône, facing due south and protected from the prevailing Mistral. It can be very dry here, and very hot too. The result is that the grapes at harvest time can be almost desiccated. The second factor is the soil: essentially granite debris over granite rock – gritty and friable, it is locally called *gore*. The rock absorbs the heat of the day only to release it at night, like a storage radiator. This serves well to ripen the grapes but it will also add to the baked, warm-brick character of the wine.

Cornas – the locals like to pretend that the wine was much appreciated by Emperor Charlemagne, and they may well be right, for it is mentioned in a document dated AD 885 – is an area of the small *vigneron*. Few growers have more than 5 hectares of vines and some of the best known, now the world over, only have a couple of hectares. This means that these are essentially one-man band operations, extra hands only being required at harvest time. Twenty per cent, representing 25 hectares, are members of the Tain co-operative. The village is dominated by its church and nothing much seems to have changed here for centuries. The cellars are small and cramped, earth-floored. Most wine is still matured in old wood, stored in large barrels called *demi-muids*. Much of the wine is still fermented with the stems on. It is only since the 1950s that the domaines have begun to bottle their own wine.

Today the vines are sprayed collectively by helicopter, which must take a great burden off the hands of the vineyard workers, but most of the rest of the operations can only be done by hand: the slopes are too steep for even the most hyper-modern tractors.

You can separate the vineyard area into four distinct parts, which, and logically, the locals call *quartiers*. Very often these place names, or *lieux-dits*, will be found on he labels of the superior *cuvées*. The southernmost is Les Reynards or Renards, the vines ascending to 300 metres, with the slope beginning at 125 metres or so. The granite here is topped in part with clay, with the odd patch of limestone, which helps to preserve some of the moisture in very dry years.

Next to Les Renards is the Coteau du Tezier, referred to by some simply as La Côte. Here the topsoil is almost entirely decomposed rock. North of the village is Les Mazards, again with some clay, and in patches sand, and above this is Les Chaillots, again with some limestone. Each of these produce a wine of slightly different character within the basic, sturdy, masculine Cornas spectrum. Most growers will offer a young-vine *cuvée* or one from the bottom of the slope (*pied de côte*) and one if not more from old vines and/or the name of the *quartier* itself on the hill.

While the Cornas *appellation* has grown in the last twenty years, it is a far cry from what it was a century ago and this is itself a long way short of the volumes produced in pre-phylloxera times. Back then, when labour was cheap and the attraction of a comfortable 'nine-to-five' job in nearby Valence rather less seductive, practically every nook and cranny on the hillside must have been planted with vines, for as late as the 1920 annual production was around 6000 hectolitres and vines were very much less prolific in those days. The 1970s yielded only a quarter of this figure. Since then the area under vine has increased from 50 to 90 hectares and with modern, disease-resistant clones production is back to the 6000-hectolitre mark. Yet a glance up at the hills behind the village will reveal a patchwork of vines, rock and scrub with more that belongs to nature than that cultivated by man.

Slowly but surely, as the decision to spray the hillsides collectively against crytogamic diseases such as mildew and oidium, and insect depradation, such as the grape-moth indicates, Cornas is modernising itself. But there is still a sharp contrast between the traditionalists and the modernisers. Jean Lionnat, one of the larger vineyard owners, vinifies in stainless steel. Most of the other growers ferment in closed concrete vats or old, open wooden containers. Lionnat also destems totally. Guy de Barjac destalks 80 to 100 per cent: what he leaves in is purely for its physical effect in aiding the fermentation process. Alain Voge destalks half or more of his crop. Marcel Juge, August Clape and René Balthazar, on the other hand, do not destem.

Lionnat and Jean-Luc Colombo believe in using new oak. There is a lot both in their cellars and in their wines, especially when you taste them young (Colombo even bottles his in a Bordeaux-shaped bottle rather than the traditional Burgundy shape). Alain Voge and Guy de Barjac, who is now retired, are less convinced but nevertheless use small barrels, with perhaps one new one in six and the rest newish. Noël Verset, Auguste Clape, Marcel Juge and René Balthazar, representing the traditionalists' approach, use old *demi-muids*, barrels about double the size of the usual Bordeaux *barrique* or Burgundian *pièce*, or small, fixed wooden *foudres* sized between 10 and 20 hectolitres. Others, such as Robert Michel, use barrels, but only old ones. These growers insist that the flavour of new oak has no place in the wine of Cornas.

A similar division can be discerned in other approaches to the winemaking and the resultant elevage or maturing before bottling. The old guard continues to prolong the maceration and will keep the wine eighteen months to two years before bottling. The modernisers have speeded things up. Today, they argue, the public should have access to a less robust Cornas. We need to keep the volume but clean the wine up so that the richness and concentration are not obliterated by coarseness and astringency. However, while some will fine gently with white of egg, few if any Cornas will have been filtered before bottling.

Cornas, then, has become a more civilised wine over the last twenty-five years or so. When I first started to explore the area and buy the wines in the early 1970s, they were brutal in their youth: almost black in colour, seriously tannic, very powerfully flavoured, occasionally too alcoholic for their own good. Today the wine is better mannered: still with the weight of Hermitage, a considerable step up in bulk from Saint-Joseph and Crozes-Hermitage but now revealing greater complexity and class. Compared with Hermitage and Côte-Rôtie it is competitively priced. For those with cellar space to store it for the obligatory eight to ten years the wine will give much pleasure. I would even call it a bargain. And the village contains a large number of good growers. Cornas has become a thriving *appellation*.

Back in 1763 the village priest, Monsieur Molin, recorded: 'The mountain of this village is almost entirely planted with vines which make a very good black wine. This wine is much sought after by the merchants and is very heady,' You could echo this today.

Leading Cornas Producers

★ DOMAINE THIERRY ALLEMAND
Owner: Thierry Allemand.
Surface Area under Vine: 3.9 ha.
Wines: Cornas including Le Reynard and Les Chaillots.
Thierry Allemand is one of the leading stars among the younger generation of Cornas growers. The wines are matured partly in cask and partly in stainless steel.

These are full, rich, tannic wines which need keeping. Of the two *cuvées*, Le Reynard is generally to be preferred. It is a brilliant site, and the vines are sixty-five to eighty-five years old.

★ DOMAINE RENÉ BALTHAZAR
Owner: Blathazar family.
Surface Area under Vine: 2 ha.
Wines: Cornas.
René Balthazar makes only one wine. From eighty-year-old vines and matured in *demi-muids*, it is a wine of succulent fruit, ample, balanced and fullish, and normally needs six or seven years to come round rather than the decade in some establishments.

★ DOMAINE GUY DE BARJAC
Owner: Guy de Barjac.
Surface Area under Vine: 1.5 ha.
Wines: Cornas.
Guy de Barjac produced his last vintage in 1991 and his vines are now exploited by Sylvain Bernard in Saint-Péray and Jean-Luc Colombo. The wines he used to make are very good – they have more finesse but often slightly lighter colour and density than many of the other wines of the village. This is to its advantage and old vines, low yields and minimal handling were the order of the day here.

★★ DOMAINE AUGUSTE ET PIERRE-MARIE CLAPE
Owner: Clape family.
Surface Area under Vine: 5.7 ha.
Wines: Cornas, Saint-Péray and Côtes du Rhône.
The seventy-year-old Auguste Clape is the doyen of Cornas. He has been bottling longer than most, is the name which put the *appellation* on the map and has been mayor of the village for longer than anyone can remember. Today it is his friendly, bearded son Pierre-Marie who makes the wine. As always there are four *cuvées*, from vines of different ages, which are eventually blended together after maturing for eighteen months in old barrels and *demi-muids*. In their attitude towards new wood (none) and destemming (only the young

vines) the Clapes are old-fashioned. But the wines are yardstick examples. They need a decade to come round.

★ DOMAINE JEAN-LUC COLOMBO

Owner: Jean-Luc Colombo.
Surface Area under Vine: 12 ha.
Wines: Cornas including Terres Brûlées, Les Ruchets and Cuvée Jean-Luc Colombo, Côtes du Rhône and merchant wines.

Very definitely Cornas with a modern touch here, even to the extent of a Bordeaux-shaped bottle rather than the usual Burgundian style. Twenty per cent new wood is used in the basic Terres Brûlées *cuvée*, 70 per cent in Les Ruchets, 100 per cent in the special *cuvée*, which some will argue is too much, for it hides the Cornas character. Nonetheless, these are very well-made, elegant wines. From a base in La Roche-de-Glun, Colombo runs a *négociant* business. The standard is good: the wines usually reasonably forward.

★ DOMAINE DUMIEN-SERRETTE

Owner: Serrette family.
Surface Area under Vine: 1.3 ha.
Wines: Cornas.

Gilbert Serrette used to sell to Jaboulet, but started bottling his own wines in 1993, having held back some of the 1990 (excellent) and 1991. I find the wines here poised, concentrated and elegant.

★ DOMAINE JACQUES LEMÉNICIER

Owner: Jacques Leménicier.
Surface Area under Vine: 3.05 ha.
Wines: Cornas and Saint-Péray.

Another member of the rising generation, the bearded Jacques Leménicier, who works with his wife Sylviane, destems entirely, but rears his wine in old wood and bottles it after a year to preserve the fruit. This is a very good Cornas, both full and rich, and stylish. It is ready after six or seven years rather than ten.

★ DOMAINE JEAN LIONNET

Owner: Jean Lionnet.
Surface Area under Vine: 14 ha.

Wines: Cornas including Domaine de Rochepertuis, Saint-Péray and Côtes du Rhône.

The tall, greying, handsome Jean Lionnet has one of the larger domaines in the *appellation*, owning 10 hectares in Cornas. In a modern cellar the grapes are destemmed, vinified in temperature-controlled, stainless steel vats, and matured using about 20 per cent new oak. The wines are looser-knit than some, which means that the oak is very obvious. They are lush and charming though, for drinking in the medium term.

★ DOMAINE ROBERT MICHEL

Owner: Michel family.
Surface Area under Vine: 7 ha.
Wines: Cornas including Cuvée des Coteaux and La Geynale, and Saint-Joseph.

After Clape, this is the senior domaine in Cornas because of the length of time it has been bottling seriously. Robert Michel, now approaching sixty, has been generous with his encouragement to the younger generation. Many of today's stars started as trainees here and still today borrow Michel's bottling-line and other machinery. Fifteen years ago this was an address for 'old-fashioned' Cornas, in the style of Clape: no destemming, long *cuvaison*, no new wood, brutal and tannic wines when young. Sometimes the wines could be too rustic and they were proportionately better in the really good vintages. Today most of the *demi-muids* are relatively new, destemming takes place more and more, and the wines are cleaner and purer.

★★ DOMAINE NOËL VERSET

Owner: Noël Verset.
Surface Area under Vine: 2 ha.
Wines: Cornas.

Now well into his eighties, and widowed, Noël Verset has rented off some of his vines – and sold some to Thierry Allemand (see page 348) – but he still continues to make some of the finest wines in the village. The bulk of his vineyard is between 85 and 100 years old. Yields obviously are tiny. The winemaking is 'old-fashioned' but the results are splendid, with an enormous intensity of fruit. The wines need at least ten years to mature.

★ Domaine Alain Voge

Owner: Alain Voge.
Surface Area under Vine: 13 ha.
Wines: Cornas including Vieilles Vignes and Vieille Fontaine, and Saint-Péray.

Although local, Alain Voge did not inherit any vineyards. Today in his late fifties, he has been bottling his own wine since he arrived in 1969. A lot of thought goes into his winemaking and flexibility is the key. The Vieille Fontaine is only made in exceptional vintages. These are rich, fat, concentrated wines, less brutal than some and easier to appreciate when they are young. They keep very well, however.

Other Producers of note

Sylvain Bernard (Saint-Péray), Ets. Chapoutier (Tain L'Hermitage), Laurent and Dominique Courbis (Châteaubourg), Ets. Delas Frères (Hermitage), Joël and Noël Durand (Châteaubourg), Paul Jaboulet Aîné – Domaine Saint-Pierre (Tain L'Hermitage) and Marcel Juge (Cornas).

Saint-Péray

Surface Area (1998): 63 ha.
Production (1998): 1501 hl.
Colour: White (still and sparkling).
Grape Varieties: Marsanne and Roussanne.
Maximum Yield: 45 hl/ha.
Minimum Alcohol Level: (Still wines) 10°; (sparkling wines) 9.5°.

Saint-Péray lies on the west bank of the Rhône opposite Valence. It is a small *appellation* and the wines are little seen outside the immediate area. Yet it was not always as obscure. There is a well-known story of Richard Wagner ordering 100 bottles to be sent to Bayreuth in 1877, where he was busy completing *Parsifal*. Napoleon was stationed as a cadet at Valence, and later spoke of Saint-Péray with affection as his first vinous discovery. Perhaps deliberately taking a contrary view, Wellington is said to have despised it. These references are to the Champagne-method sparkling wine, which makes up about

80 per cent of the wine. Some 200,000 bottles are made each year, always *brut*, and nearly always non-vintage.

Why is it that Saint-Péray, in a predominantly red wine area, is exclusively a white wine? One reason may be a change of soil. At Saint-Péray, whose vineyards also lie in the adjoining commune of Toulaud, the slope is more gentle than it is further north, and the soil less granitic. The *terroir* is made up from clay, sand, flint and stones, without any chalk or much limestone. This is similar to the sections in Hermitage and Crozes given over to white grapes. Another reason is the local competition. As a red wine, the quality could not compete with neighbouring Cornas. As a sparkling white, it has the field to itself. It has a round, herby, nutty flavour with a certain *goût de terroir* and a southern fullness.

Saint-Péray Producers of note

Jean-François Chaboud, Pierre Darona et Fils, Domaine de Fauterie/Sylvain Bernard, Jean-Marie Teysseire and Jean-Louis Thiers (all in Saint-Péray), Domaine Auguste et Pierre-Marie Clape, Jean Lionnet (both in Cornas) and Bernard Gripa (Mauves). (See also Cornas page 346.) There is also a local co-operative, but their wines have less distinction.

Clairette de Die and Châtillon-en-Diois

Clairette de Die

Production (1998): 71,644 hl.
Colour: White (sparkling).
Grape Varieties: Clairette and Muscat à Petits Grains.
Maximum Yield: 50 hl/ha.
Minimum Alcohol Level: 9°.

Coteaux de Die

Production (1998): Nil.
Colour: White.
Grape Variety: Clairette.
Maximum Yield: 50 hl/ha.
Minimum Alcohol Level: 10.5°.

CHÂTILLON-EN-DIOIS

Production (1998): (Red and rosé) 1918 hl; (white) 1311 hl.

Colour: Red, rosé and white.

Grape Varieties: (Red and rosé) Gamay (75 per cent of the blend) plus Syrah and Pinot Noir; (white) Aligoté and Chardonnay.

Maximum Yield: 50 hl/ha.

Minimum Alcohol Level: (Red and rosé) 10°; (white) 10.5°.

CRÉMANT DE DIE

Production (1998): 4877 hl.

Colour: White (sparkling).

Grape Variety: Clairette.

Maximum Yield: 50 hl/ha.

Minimum Alcohol Level: 9°.

Surface Area for all Diois appellations **combined (1998):** 1373 ha.

Halfway between Valence and Montélimar the river Drôme, flowing in from the Alps, reaches the Rhône near Livron. This marks the boundary between the northern and southern Rhône, and, if travelling south, is where the Midi effectively begins. Within the space of a few dozen kilometres the countryside changes completely. Walnut and cherry are exchanged for cypress and olive; the light becomes brighter and the sky bluer; the soil exudes heat and crickets begin incessantly to chirrup: we are in Provence. Before however we reach the southern Rhône we must make a little detour up into the Alps to survey the wines of Die.

The town of Die lies on the river Drôme some 50 kilometres up into the hills, just about at the point where deciduous forest – beech, birch, poplar and aspen – give way to larch and pine. Here the countryside is distinctly alpine, with chalets, meadows of lush grass, and jagged, snow-covered peaks in the distance.

Until the mid-1920s Clairette de Die was a still white wine, made, as the name suggests, from the Clairette grape, a variety more associated with southern France where it produces a soft, fruity wine which is rather deficient in acidity, and so for early drinking.

In 1926 the first sparkling wines were made, and from this date a second grape, the Muscat à Petits Grains, began increasingly to be used. A large and up-to-date co-operative was inaugurated in 1951, and this now produces three-quarters of the *appellation* which is now entirely sparkling wine. Two types of sparkling wine are made. The Brut, using at least 75 per cent Clairette, is made by the Champagne method and is a crisp, clean but rather neutral drink. The Tradition or Méthode Dioise Ancestrale is made using both Clairette and Muscat à Petits Grains, which can vary in proportions from three of Clairette to one of Muscat, to one of Clairette to three of Muscat. The Cave Coopérative de Die uses half and half. The difference between the two styles of Clairette de Die is quite marked, for even a wine with only a quarter of Muscat in the blend will have the very positive grapy character typical of Muscat, and the Tradition is always made *demi-sec*, or even sweeter. Those who prefer a mildly grapy wine should go for a blend with less Muscat. Those who really enjoy its pronounced flavour should seek a wine like that of Jean-Claude Vincent of Sainte-Croix which is made with 70 per cent Muscat and 30 per cent Clairette. Today, however, Tradition is less in favour, and the Brut, which started in 1960, now makes up 40 per cent of the total production of around six million bottles.

The Tradition method involves cooling the newly extracted must in isothermal vats at a temperature of minus 3°C for 48 hours, then centrifuging and lightly filtering to remove loose particles, and then allowing the wine to ferment very slowly. The wine is bottled in January before all the original sugar has been transformed into alcohol. During the nine months' bottle ageing the remaining sugar ferments and the malolactic fermentation occurs, thus producing carbon dioxide. Finally the deposits produced by this further fermentation are removed by filtration under pressure, before rebottling. There is only one fermentation.

The grapes themselves come from thirty-two communes stretching between Aouste, in the west near Crest, and Luc-en-Diois, south-east of Die along the Drôme Valley. The soil is predominantly limestone and clay on a hard rock base and becomes more meagre and the rock harder as the altitude increases. South and east of Die, around the town of Châtillon, alternative grapes for still wines have been planted. These wines, under the *appellation* of Châtillon-en-Diois, were promoted from VDQS status to full AC in 1974.

All this sounds rather promising, and some twenty years ago I made a special journey up the beautiful Drôme Valley to visit the Die co-operative, main producer, then and now, of Châtillon-en-Diois. They seemed rather surprised when I expressed interest in the still wines rather than the *mousseux*, and when I came to taste them I could see why. Not only were the wines weak, thin and unripe but they were also surprisingly rustic. The ripeness of the grapes, perhaps, was something over which the co-operative had little control. The cleanliness of the winemaking, or in this case the lack of it, was their responsibility. I regret to report that there has been little improvement. There is, however,

only a tiny amount produced and the vines are scattered among tiny artisanal parcels in eleven communes.

There are two further *appellations*, both dating from the mid-1990s. The first is Crémant de Die. This is supposed to replace the Clairette de Die Brut which is being phased out, but must henceforth come from 100 per cent Clairette grapes. From 1999, paradoxically, Clairette de Die will mean the Tradition i.e. with a fair amount of Muscat in the *encépagement*, while Crémant de Die will be the Clairette wine.

Coteaux de Die is the *appellation* for still wines from the Clairette grape. There is little of it, and what I have sampled I have found undistinguished.

Clairette-de-Die Producers of note
CAVE COOPÉRATIVE DE DIE (DIE), DOMAINE DE MAGORD/ JEAN-CLAUDE VINCENT (BARSAC) AND DOMAINE DE LA MURE/JEAN-CLAUDE RASPAIL (SAILLANS).

THE SOUTHERN RHÔNE

CHÂTEAUNEUF-DU-PAPE

Surface Area (1998): 3139 ha.
Production (1998): (Red) 102,299 hl; (white) 7847 hl.
Colour: Red and white.
Grape Varieties: (Red) Grenache Noir, Syrah, Mourvèdre, Cinsault, Counoise, Vaccarèse, Terret Noir, Muscardin, Clairette, Bourboulenc, Roussanne, Picpoul and Picardin; (white) Grenache Blanc, Terret Blanc, Bourboulenc, Clairette, Roussanne, Picpoul and Picardin.
Maximum Yield: 35 hl/ha.
Minimum Alcohol Level: 12.5°.

Châteauneuf-du-Pape, 20 kilometres north of Avignon, is both the geographical centre of the southern Rhône and its leading quality *appellation*. It is a large *vignoble*, its 3100 hectares producing over a million cases of wine a year. It is also, like Bordeaux, a region of large estates which are self-sufficient and individual in wine terms. The styles of the top Châteauneuf-du-Pape domaines contrast interestingly with one another, as do individ-

ual châteaux in Bordeaux, and for the same reason. Each reflects its own particular soil, mixture of grape varieties, mesoclimate, and, perhaps most important of all, differences in vinification techniques. Each, obviously, is a mirror of the personality and skill of the man who makes the wine.

While it was Bertrand de Goth, former Archbishop of Bordeaux – and owner of Château Pape-Clément in the Graves – who on taking up the papacy in 1309 decided to reside in Avignon rather than in Rome, it was his successor who built the summer palace and gave the impetus that went with papal patronage to the area. Pope John XXII first started to enlarge what was a relatively modest set of buildings in Avignon itself. The result, now being extensively renovated, is the magnificent papal palace we know today. With this complete, his thoughts turned to strengthening his defences in the surrounding countryside, and, *inter alia*, to building himself a residence wherein he could escape from the oppressive summer heat and stench of busy medieval Avignon and the duties of his office. A castle at

Châteauneuf already existed but was in ruins. Between 1318 and 1333 a 'new castle' was constructed. For a summer palace it was huge, but it also formed part of a defensive circle of fortifications surrounding Avignon.

Châteauneuf was already an important wine area. It has been estimated that 1000 hectares were under vine in the early part of the fourteenth century. The church, however, was the only important proprietor and most of the land was in tiny plots leased to the local peasants. There was a ready outlet for their wine, however, for the papal holdings, originally only 10 hectares, were totally insufficient for the papacy's needs.

The official papal stay at Avignon lasted until 1378, after which anti-popes resided until the schism was healed in 1410. Thereafter the area sank back into being a backwater and the wine into obscurity. The modern era for Châteauneuf-du-Pape begins in the eighteenth century with the rise of a number of individual estates. La Nerthe or La Neste was the first, and is said to have commenced 'château-bottling' in 1785. That Thomas Jefferson passed close by in May 1787, without stopping to taste the wines, would indicate that any reputation was but local. The writer Jullien in 1816 rated La Nerthe in the 'Comtat d'Avignon' as a *vin de deuxième classe* and names the *crus* of Saint-Patrice, Bocoup, Coteau Pierreux at Châteauneuf-du-Pape plus Coteau-Brûlé at Sorgues as wines of the third class. 'The wines of this area, coming from long-established local varieties and new ones from Spain, though warm are delicate, *fin* and show a pretty bouquet . . . the moment to drink them is when they are three or four years old and in their prime.' The recent Spanish arrival is obviously the Grenache or Garnacha, today the dominant grape of the entire Midi, as far as quality wines are concerned. The strange reference to Châteauneuf as being delicate would seem to indicate that this Grenache was not yet fully established as well as perhaps the absence of grapes which would give solidity such as Syrah or Mourvèdre (also a Spanish import).

At the time Jullien was writing there were some 2000 hectares of vineyards at Châteauneuf-du-Pape, a figure which was to remain constant until the onset of phylloxera, which struck the vineyards very soon after it was first noticed in the neighbouring *département* of Gard

in 1863. Pre-phylloxera levels of production were not attained once more until the 1950s, since when the area has reached almost saturation point.

Meanwhile, the local producers led by Baron Le Roy of Château Fortia imposed on themselves a system of voluntary *appellation contrôlée* in 1923, complete with the necessity for the wines to pass a tasting test (not a universal requirement elsewhere until recently). These were to become the basis of all French AC laws.

Châteauneuf-du-Pape can be made from a large number of different grape varieties. There are as many as thirteen authorized for the *appellation*, though several of these are now rarely encountered. Some of these are white varieties, added to the red wine to give it a bit of zip and freshness. The most important grape is the Grenache, widely grown throughout the South of France, in Provence as well as the Languedoc, and also in Spain. Next comes Syrah, the staple red wine grape of the northern Rhône, and then Mourvèdre and Cinsault. The other varieties are Counoise, Vaccarèse, Terret Noir and Muscardin (all red grapes) and Clairette, Bourboulenc, Roussanne, Picpoul and Picardin (all white). Grenache Blanc and Terret Blanc additionally are authorized for white Châteauneuf.

At the end of the nineteenth century a Commandant Duclos published a voluminous paper on the area, and recommended the following blend as likely to produce the optimum wine: 20 per cent Grenache and Cinsault, 'giving warmth, liqueur and mellowness'; 30 per cent Mourvèdre, Syrah, Muscardin and Vaccarèse, 'giving solidity, durability, colour and a pure refreshing flavour'; 40 per cent Cournoise and Picpoul, 'giving vinosity, charm, freshness and bouquet'; and 10 per cent Clairette and Bourboulenc, 'giving fire and brilliance'.

This was the 'ideal' *encépagement*. However, because much Châteauneuf was constantly shipped up to Burgundy (to be used as 'a bolster wine' and blended in with the wines of the area), the Grenache percentage was more habitually 80 per cent if not 90 per cent. The Grenache gives a wine of high alcohol and plenty of body, if low in acidity, ideal for making 'old-style' Burgundy – if you like that sort of thing. Nowadays, the normal blend is usually the following: 50 to 70 per cent

CHÂTEAUNEUF-DU-PAPE

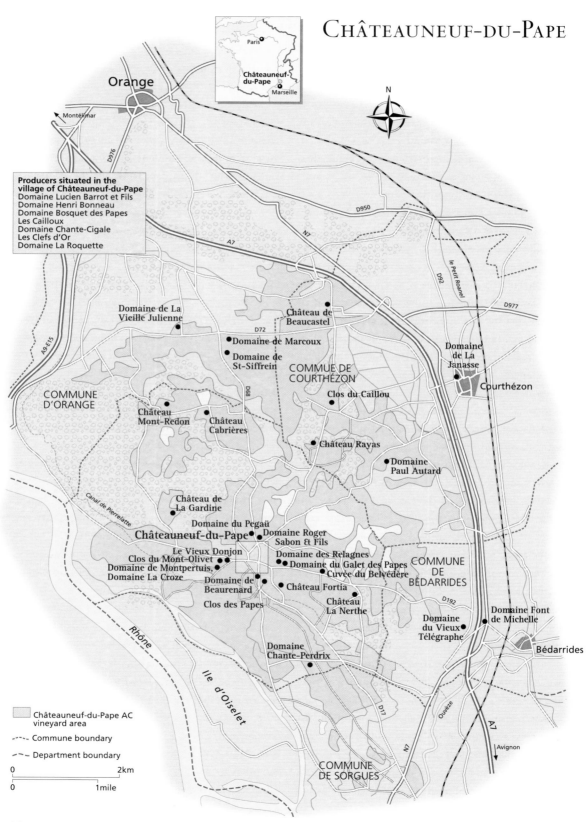

Paris

Châteauneuf-
du-Pape

Marseille

N

Orange

← Montélimar

D976

D950

N7

le Petit Roanel

D92

D977

A7

A9-E15

Canal de Pierrelatte

Producers situated in the village of Châteauneuf-du-Pape
Domaine Lucien Barrot et Fils
Domaine Henri Bonneau
Domaine Bosquet des Papes
Les Cailloux
Domaine Chante-Cigale
Les Clefs d'Or
Domaine La Roquette

Domaine de La
Vieille Julienne

Château de
Beaucastel

Domaine de Marcoux

Domaine de
St-Siffrein

COMMUE DE
COURTHÉZON

Domaine
de La
Janasse

Courthézon

D72

D68

Clos du Caillou

COMMUNE
D'ORANGE

Château
Mont-Redon

Château
Cabrières

Château Rayas

Domaine
Paul Autard

Château de
La Gardine

Domaine du Pegaü

Châteauneuf-du-Pape

Domaine Roger
Sabon & Fils

COMMUNE
DE
BÉDARRIDES

Le Vieux Donjon

Domaine des Relagnes

Clos du Mont-Olivet

Domaine du Galet des Papes

Domaine de Montpertuis,
Domaine La Croze

Cuvée du Belvédère

Domaine de
Beaurenard

Château Fortia

D192

Clos des Papes

Château
La Nerthe

Domaine Font
de Michelle

Domaine
du Vieux
Télégraphe

Bédarrides

Domaine
Chante-Perdrix

Rhône

Île d'Oiselet

D17

Ouvèze

A7

N7

↓ Avignon

COMMUNE
DE SORGUES

Châteauneuf-du-Pape AC
vineyard area

----- Commune boundary

--- Department boundary

0   2km

0   1mile

Grenache; 10 to 30 per cent Mourvèdre; up to 20 per cent Syrah, Cinsault, Cournoise and Vaccarèse (the latter two in very small proportions); and up to 10 per cent Clairette, Picpoul and Bourboulenc (all white grapes).

Led by the Perrins at Château Beaucastel, today's fashionable Châteauneuf grape is Mourvèdre. This means there are two factions in the *appellation*: those who insist on almost as much Grenache as possible, and those like the Perrins who are making their super-*cuvées* from 60 per cent or more Mourvèdre.

The soil in Châteauneuf is very varied. The Rhône Valley is some 50 kilometres wide at this point, and the vines are planted on undulating mounds rather than on the valley hillsides themselves. The Rhône river has changed its course many times over recent millennia, and the glaciers of succeeding ice ages have deposited stones over the alluvial debris left on the valley floor. Châteauneuf is a geological hotch-potch: there is gravel, clay, sand and limestone. South of the village in the direction of Avignon, gravel predominates; north, towards Orange, the soil is argillo-calcaire (clay and limestone); west of Châteauneuf is limestone and east is sand. Overall, especially to the north and north-east, the soil is covered by large quartzite boulders, the size of large baked potatoes, and beige or terracotta in colour. These stones or *galets* aid the maturity of the grapes, for they absorb the heat of the sun during the day and reflect it back onto the vines at night (like storage radiators). They also help to retain moisture in the soil, which would otherwise quickly evaporate in the heat of the day. On the other hand, these stones are an understandable hindrance in the mechanical working of the soil – the sharpened end of a plough-share hardly lasting 24 hours before being blunted to a stump during the weeding season.

The mesoclimate and hence the character of the wines also varies. It tends to be hotter and more arid on the eastern side and picking here commences a week earlier than around the town of Châteauneuf itself. As a generalisation, but remember that many estates have vineyard plots scattered all over the *appellation*, the wines from around Courthézon and Bédarrides are bigger and meatier than those from the western side.

One of the most original regulations of the *appellation contrôlée* code, self-imposed in Châteauneuf-du-Pape long before similar regulations elsewhere, was the stipulation of *triage*. A minimum of 5 per cent of the grapes, the least ripe and the rotten, must be discarded before fermentation, to ensure that the wine is made only of healthy, well ripened fruit. Châteauneuf is also distinguished by having the highest minimum alcoholic strength (12.5°) of all *appellation contrôlée* wines in France.

With such a choice of grapes, soils, and now, vinification methods – for there are some estates which seek to produce a more *primeur*, early drinking style of wine – it is not surprising that there is no such thing as a typical Châteauneuf-du-Pape. All wines, however, will be full in colour and full in body; somewhat fiery and peppery, robust with a warm rich southern flavour and a broad, spicy, slightly farmyardy aroma and character. Those estates with a high proportion of Grenache, and which keep the wine long in wood (large oak *foudres* rather than the *barriques* traditional in Bordeaux and Burgundy), make a wine with a pronounced, somewhat attenuated earthy character, full of guts but lacking in finesse, and not able to age gracefully. Others, adopting modern methods but not discarding the concept of Châteauneuf as it is known and appreciated, produce excellent wine, which, price for price, is undoubtedly one of the best value of the top reds in France.

There is, however, one problem, also found in the northern Rhône and elsewhere. Except for a few estates, the bottling of a particular vintage does not take place all at the same time. It may indeed be strung over several years. Many growers have neither the cellar space nor the funds to buy all the bottles, corks etc. in one go, nor the space to store all the bottled wine. While one can appreciate the problem, the result is not fair to the consumer, for the bottlings, ostensibly the same wine, will in fact differ. A wine bottled after eighteen months will be quite different from that bottled after thirty months. This is an issue which the local authorities and growers associations urgently need to assess. Meanwhile it is a point that the customer needs to keep in mind. If buying some more bottles of a Châteauneuf wine you have enjoyed, make sure you purchase the identical bottling. If this is no longer available, taste the wine before you buy.

There is, additionally, a very small amount of white wine. This can be made from a range of grape varieties and can, like the red, vary enormously in character. Only lately has it been anything other than heavy, hard and alcoholic. The best is now made by modern methods with an increasing amount of Roussanne, this variety often being fermented in barrel: the grapes are pressed immediately after picking, then fermented at 18°C for a month and the malolactic fermentation needs to be prevented, though it seldom seems to occur.

The result can be a decidedly fragrant wine, with a mountain herb flavour, a touch of spice and a crisp character reminiscent of peaches and nectarines, particularly when young. White Châteauneuf is, nevertheless, an assertive, full, uncompromising wine. It is also highly alcoholic. It is not the wine to drink as an aperitif in a deckchair on a warm summer's evening but rather as an accompaniment to *bouillabaisse*. I have to confess that it is not to my taste. Like white Hermitage it needs to be drunk either young, or, provided it is not solely a *primeur* wine, after seven years or so. Between three and seven years the white wines often do not show well, they seem very oily and resiny but this is a passing phase.

All estate-bottled Châteauneuf – that is wine from estates who bottle all the wine appearing under their labels – appears in a special Burgundy-shaped bottle with low, sloping shoulders and with the papal emblem (mitre and crossed keys) embossed on the shoulder.

Leading Châteauneuf-du-Pape Producers

Domaine Paul Autard

Commune: Courthézon.
Owners: Autard family.
Surface Area under Vine: 12 ha.
Wines: Châteauneuf-du-Pape (red and white) including Les Côtes Rondes, Cuvée Mireille and Cuvée Michèle.

Jean-Paul Autard, son of Paul, is now in charge. His headquarters are hidden in a little glen with cellars cut into the limestone rockface. There is a mixture of *foudres* and *barrique* in the cellar, some of the latter being new. He destems completely. The better *cuvées* are made with 40-50 per cent Syrah, 20-30 per cent Grenache, plus Mourvèdre and others. Improvements during the 1990s means that this is now classy winemaking.

★ Domaine Lucien Barrot et Fils

Owners: Barrot family.
Surface Area under Vine: 19 ha.
Wines: Châteauneuf-du-Pape (red).

Just one wine here, from a scattered domaine and from 80 per cent Grenache, 10 per cent Syrah and the remainder Cinsault and Mourvèdre. Today run by Régis Barrot, his sister and her husband, the wines are rich and substantial. Vinification takes place in a modern cellar in cement vats, retaining all the stems, and after that the wine is stored in 50-hectolitre wooden *foudres*. Be warned: not all the wine is bottled in one go.

★★★ Château de Beaucastel

Commune: Courthézon
Owners: Perrin family.
Surface Area under Vine: 80 ha.
Wines: Châteauneuf-du-Pape (red and white) including Hommage à Jacques Perrin (red) and Roussanne Vieilles Vignes (white); plus two Côtes du Rhônes, Cru du Coudoulet and Château du Grand-Prébois, and a range of merchant wines (La Vieille Ferme, Perrin Réserve and others).

The large, magnificent Beaucastel domaine, run by François Perrin and his older brother Jean-Pierre (Jean-Pierre concentrates on the merchant business), is found up in the north-east corner of the *appellation*. The soil here is rich in *galets* and suits the Perrin's fondness for the Mourvèdre grape. Unlike most Châteauneufs, which are based on Grenache, even if they may use a higher proportion of Syrah and/or Mourvèdre in their *de luxe cuvées*, Beaucastel is made from only 30 per cent Grenache, with 30 per cent Mourvèdre, 10 per cent Syrah, 10 per cent Counoise, 5 per cent Cinsault and the rest from the other permitted varieties. The percentages of Mourvèdre and Counoise are being increased in the vineyard. The Hommage à Jacques Perrin is made from 60 per cent Mourvèdre. The vineyard approach is biological and the winemaking meticulous: destemming for Mourvèdre and Syrah – these are the varieties whose stems are rarely properly ripe, small oak barrels for the Syrah but only the Syrah – it benefits from the extra oxidation, plus their own special system of flash-pasteurisation to kill off the oxidase enzymes in the wine. As important, the entire harvest is bottled at the same time, thus ensuring no bottle variation. The result is a wine which, while it has all the weight of traditional Châteauneuf-du-Pape, has as well the sophistication of fruit of a northern Rhône wine.

★ DOMAINE DE BEAURENARD

Owners: Coulon family.
Surface Area under Vine: 30 ha.
Wines: Châteauneuf-du-Pape (red and white) including Cuvée Boisrenard.

The Coulons are all very tall, welcoming and enthusiastic. Paul Coulon is now semi-retired and his son Daniel is in charge. The *encépagement* consists of 70 per cent Grenache, 10 per cent Syrah, 10 per cent Mourvèdre and the rest mainly Cinsault. The fruit is largely destemmed, fermented in stainless steel and matured in *foudres* and *barriques*, some of the latter, especially that housing the old-vine wine, Cuvée Boisrenard, being new. This is good modern Châteauneuf, plenty of size and depth, but not too weighty or rustic. Occasionally I find the Cuvée Boisrenard too oaky.

★★ DOMAINE HENRI BONNEAU

Owner: Henri Bonneau.
Surface Area under Vine: 6 ha.
Wines: Châteauneuf-du-Pape (red) including Réserve des Célestins and Cuvée Marie Beurrier.

The short, shrewd, bespectacled and self-opinionated Henri Bonneau is one of Châteauneuf's characters. Now in his seventies, he lurches (owing to an accident in the vineyard) from one small, scruffy cellar to another beneath his house in the village, pontificating about everything under the sun as he offers you samples of his wines. These are made from 80-90 per cent Grenache,

picked late, fermented traditionally and bottled later than most, after three years or more of ageing in a mixture of old small barrels, *demi-muids* and *foudres*. There is not much wine here, but it is very good indeed: old-fashioned winemaking at its very best. My own worry is that some vintages are bottled far too late.

★ DOMAINE BOSQUET DES PAPES

Owner: Maurice Boiron.
Surface Area under Vine: 25 ha.
Wines: Châteauneuf-du-Pape (red and white) including Cuvée Chantemerle.

This estate is spread out all over the *appellation*, and mostly leased. Maurice Boiron only owns some 8 hectares. The *encépagement* includes 80 per cent Grenache, 8 per cent Syrah and 7 per cent Mourvèdre. Vinification takes place with all the stems in cement vats and the wine is matured in a mixture of *foudres* and *demi-muids*. I am never struck by the white wine, but the reds can be good, especially the Cuvée Chantemerle, which is made from ninety-year-old Grenache, if on the rustic side. There are several bottlings of the same wine here.

CHÂTEAU CABRIÈRES

Owners: Arnaud family.
Surface Area under Vine: 65 ha.
Wines: Châteauneuf-du-Pape (red and white) including Cuvée Prestige.

Guy Arnaud and his sister Carole run this large estate in the north-west corner of the *appellation* from a custom-built cellar surround by a moonscape of *galets*. The grapes – 50 per cent Grenache, 12-15 per cent Syrah, 10 per cent Mourvèdre and 10 per cent Cinsault – are destemmed, the wine held in *foudres* and *barriques*, some new for the Cuvée Prestige, and bottled early. The wine is clean, medium-bodied but rather anonymous.

CLOS DU CAILLOU

Commune: Courthézon.
Owners: Pouizin family.
Surface Area under Vine: 7 ha.
Wines: Châteauneuf-du-Pape (red and white) and Côtes du Rhône.

Claude Pouzin is an engaging old boy whose 58-hectare domaine (mainly producing Côtes du Rhône red) has its headquarters inland from Courthézon, guarded, like the Roman Capitol, by a noisy herd of geese. The Châteauneuf is made from 70 per cent Grenache, 15 per cent Syrah, 5 per cent Mourvèdre, plus other varieties, and matured in cellars which stretch deep into the hillsides. These are neat, stylish wines, but not the greatest.

★★ LES CAILLOUX
Owner: André Brunel.
Surface Area under Vine: 21 ha.
Wines: Châteauneuf-du-Pape (red and white) including Cuvée Centenaire.
André Brunel is one of the *appellation*'s best and most thoughtful winemakers. He is planting more and more Mourvèdre whenever he can, but keeping the old Grenache. Following trials some years ago he persuaded himself that the stems did not contribute anything beneficial, so he now eliminates most, enabling him to extend the *cuvaison*. Once blended, the wine is kept in tank, under inert gas until bottled, so that separate bottlings differ as little as possible.

The *encépagement* is 65 per cent Grenache, 20 per cent Mourvèdre, 10 per cent Syrah and 5 per cent others. Some of the wine is aged in vat, some in oak, of which a proportion is new, especially for the exceptional Cuvée Centenaire, from vines planted in 1889. These are full wines with really very lovely, concentrated fruit.

DOMAINE CHANTE-CIGALE
Owners: Sabon-Favier family.
Surface Area under Vine: 40 ha.
Wines: Châteauneuf-du-Pape (red and white) including Cuvée Spéciale.
The Sabon-Favier family estate is planted with 80 per cent Grenache, 10 per cent Syrah, 5 per cent Mourvèdre and 5 per cent Cinsault. The grapes are not destemmed and the wine is matured in wooden *foudres*. Bottling takes place as and when the wine is required.

DOMAINE CHANTE-PERDRIX
Owners: Nicolet family.

Surface Area under Vine: 18 ha.
Wines: Châteauneuf-du-Pape (red and white).
Frédéric Nicolet is in charge here. The grape mix is 80 per cent Grenache, plus Syrah, Mourvèdre and Muscardin and the vines are situated in the south-west part of the *appellation* on lighter gravelly soil. This makes a medium-bodied, less sturdy Châteauneuf. The wine is very elegant, with particularly attractive fruit.

★ DOMAINE CHARVIN
Commune: Orange.
Owners: Charvin family.
Surface Area under Vine: 19.5 ha.
Wines: Châteauneuf-du-Pape and Côtes du Rhône (red).
Young Laurent Charvin is in charge, now that his father Gérard has retired. The Châteauneuf is from 80 per cent or more Grenache, the rest of the blend being Syrah, Mourvèdre and Vaccarèse. The wine is all bottled in one go and is rich and succulent. The red Côtes du Rhône is very good too.

★ LES CLEFS D'OR
Owners: Deydier family.
Surface Area under Vine: 25 ha.
Wines: Châteauneuf-du-Pape (red and white).
Pierre Deydier does not normally destem his grapes and vinifies them (80 per cent Grenache) in concrete. The wine is then stored in round 60-hectolitre *foudres* for eighteen months before bottling which continues over the following year or so. This is good, old-fashioned Châteauneuf. There is only one *cuvée*, the lesser wines being sold off in bulk.

CUVÉE DU BELVÉDÈRE
Owners: Girard family.
Surface Area under Vine: 4 ha.
Wines: Châteauneuf-du-Pape (red).
Robert Girard makes traditional Châteauneuf-du-Pape and only red. The vineyard is a single parcel called Le Boucou and is planted with 80 per cent Grenache, 15 per cent Counoise and 5 per cent Syrah. The wines are lush and spicy and are ready in the medium term.

★ DOMAINE FONT DE MICHELLE

Commune: Bédarrides.

Owners: Gonnet family.

Surface Area under Vine: 32.5 ha.

Wines: Châteauneuf-du-Pape (red and white) including Cuvée Etienne Gonnet.

The label says 'Les Fils d'Étienne Gonnet' and the *fils* are Jean and Michel, the latter, large, robust, bald and in his forties. The vineyard is planted with 65 per cent Grenache, 15 per cent Cinsault, 10 per cent Mourvèdre and 10 per cent Syrah. The large *cave* is temperature-controlled (so the whole vintage can be bottled in one go). The Cuvée Etienne Gonnet (no Cinsault here) is particularly rich and opulent. The Gonnets are cousins of their neighbours, the Bruniers of Domaine du Vieux-Télégraphe.

★ CHÂTEAU FORTIA

Owners: Bruno Le Roy and family.

Surface Area under Vine: 27 ha.

Wines: Châteauneuf-du-Pape (red and white).

Since Bruno Le Roy took over in 1994 there have been changes here, and one hopes for a return to the quality produced in the 1950s and 1960s (I cannot speak for earlier years). The grapes are now destemmed, and the proportion of Syrah in the vineyard increased. Now supervised by the oenologist Jean-Luc Colombo (see page 349), the wine has improved. Nevertheless, it is still held for over two years in a mixture of tanks and old oak casks and there is more than one bottling.

★ DOMAINE DU GALET DES PAPES

Owners: Mayard family.

Surface Area under Vine: 12 ha.

Wines: Châteauneuf-du-Pape (red and white) including Cuvée Vieilles Vignes.

Jean-Luc Mayard produces his wine in a modern cellar just outside the village of Châteauneuf-du-Pape. The basic *cuvée* comes from 80 per cent Grenache, 15 per cent Mourvèdre and 5 per cent Syrah, Vaccarèse and Cinsault. I like both the style and the atmosphere here and hope the Mayards soon get round to bottling their entire harvest in one go.

★ CHÂTEAU DE LA GARDINE

Owners: Brunel family.

Surface Area under Vine: 4 ha.

Wines: Châteauneuf-du-Pape (red and white) including Cuvée des Générations (red) and Cuvée Vieilles Vignes (white).

The Gardine estate, run by Patrick Brunel, lies in one parcel north-west of the village and is planted with 60 per cent Grenache, 15 per cent Syrah, 12 per cent Mourvèdre and 13 per cent 'other' varieties, the Mourvèdre, as elsewhere, being increased at the expense of the Grenache. This is modern winemaking: the fruit destemmed, the wine fermented in stainless steel with automatic *pigeurs* to tread down the cap into the wine and break it up, and maturation in oak barrels and *demi-muids*. The wine is bottled in a special irregular bottle. The wines are good, but sometimes I find the Cuvée des Générations too oaky. In 1998 Patrick and his brother, Maxime, bought the Château Saint-Roch estate in Lirac (see page 366).

★ DOMAINE DE LA JANASSE

Commune: Courthézon.

Owners: Sabon family.

Surface Area under Vine: 12 ha.

Wines: Châteauneuf-du-Pape (red and white) including Cuvée Vieilles Vignes and Cuvée Chaupin, and Côtes du Rhône-Villages.

Christophe Sabon, no immediate relation of the Sabons of Châteauneuf, also has a vineyard in the Côtes du Rhône *appellation* on the other side of the village. The Châteauneuf comes from 90 per cent Grenache, the fruit is not destalked and the wine matured in *foudre*, with a small percentage of new *barrique* for the Vieilles Vignes. From vines in Courthézon, now upgraded to Côtes du Rhône-Villages, he produces a stylish wine from one-third each Grenache, Syrah and Mourvèdre.

★★ DOMAINE DE MARCOUX

Owners: Armenier family.

Surface Area under Vine: 25 ha.

Wines: Châteauneuf-du-Pape (red and white) including Cuvée Vieilles Vignes.

Marcoux is run on biodynamic lines by two sisters, members of the Armenier family, who have been in the area for centuries. The *encépagement* is 75-80 per cent Grenache, with the balance in Cinsault, Syrah and an increasing amount of Mourvèdre. Yields are very low and the grapes are not destemmed. The winemaking, given that it must comply with the biodynamic calendar, is traditional. The red wines are splendidly intense and pure in fruit, full without being dense.

The whites are fine too. Recently there have been experiments with fermenting the Roussanne in cask. The results are very impressive.

★ Domaine de Montpertuis
Domaine La Croze
Owner: Paul Jeune.
Surface Area under Vine: 20 ha.
Wines: Châteauneuf-du-Pape (red and white) and Vin de Pays du Gard-Counoise.

Tall, bald and in his fifties, Paul Jeune produces an unusually large amount of white wine – it can be very good. There are two Châteauneufs: Montpertuis, which lies on the western side of the *appellation*, comes from 85-90 per cent Grenache and is more powerful than La Croze from the eastern side and from 70 per cent Grenache. Fermentation takes place with the stems in cement vats and the wine is then matured in cask. I like the style of wine here: masculine and tannic, but composed and elegant.

★ Clos du Mont-Olivet
Owners: Sabon family.
Surface Area under Vine: 25 ha.
Wines: Châteauneuf-du-Pape (red and white) including Cuvée du Papet.

Jean-Claude, Pierre and Bernard are the sons of Joseph Sabon, one of the grand old men of the *appellation*, and it is the first two who are now responsible for this domaine, Bernard producing apricots and asparagus from another family estate near Bollène to the north. The grape mix includes 90 per cent Grenache. This is traditional winemaking at its best, with no destemming and so on and the results, particularly the Cuvée du

Papet can be excellent. One reservation, however: the wine is bottled in several goes over a period of several years. *Caveat emptor*. The white wine is less exciting.

★ Château Mont-Redon
Owners: Abeille and Fabre families.
Surface Area under Vine: 130 ha.
Wines: Châteauneuf-du-Pape (red and white), Lirac (red and white) and Côtes du Rhône (red and white).

Mont-Redon, run by cousins Jean Abeille and Didier Fabre, is a large domaine. The grapes are completely destemmed; there is automatic *pigeage*; the wine is fermented in stainless steel; and matured in a mixture of vats and *barriques*, 25 per cent of the latter being new. This is round, mellow, generous medium-bodied wine: a civilised, elegant Châteauneuf, not great, but highly competent. It keeps well. In 1997 the cousins bought Château de Cantegril in Lirac. The wine from this estate is now sold under the Mont-Redon label.

Château La Nerthe
Owners: David et Foillard and associates.
Surface Area under Vine: 82 ha.
Wines: Châteauneuf-du-Pape (red and white) including Clos de Beauvenir (white) and Cuvée des Cadettes (red).

This is an estate whose wine has completely changed in style since it was taken over by a consortium including the Beaujolais shippers David et Foillard in 1985. The basic red wine is now matured entirely in barrel or tank, one-third of the wood being new. The Cuvée des Cadettes spends its *élevage* almost entirely in new wood. The results are good, but the wine tastes like a cross between a Châteauneuf and a super-Tuscan.

★★ Clos des Papes
Owners: Avril family.
Surface Area under Vine: 32 ha.
Wines: Châteauneuf-du-Pape (red and white).

Indisputably first division, the much morcellated Avril domaine is planted with 65 per cent Grenache, 20 per cent Mourvèdre, 9 per cent Syrah, Vaccarèse, Muscardin and Counoise. The cellar is *climatisé* and this is one of the few estates which always bottles the whole vintage in one go. The grapes are destemmed, the *foudres* are now renewed on a regular basis and there is a pneumatic press. This is confident, highly competent winemaking, producing wines of finesse which keep well, and the handsome Avrils, Paul and his son Paul-Vincent, are decidedly *sympas*. This is also a very good source for white Châteauneuf.

★ DOMAINE DU PEGAÜ

Owners: Féraud family.
Surface Area under Vine: 13.2 ha.
Wines: Châteauneuf-du-Pape (red and white) including Cuvée Laurence.

Paul Féraud and his daughter Laurence produce big, old-fashioned, rustic Châteauneufs from destemmed grapes, vinified in concrete vats and reared in *foudres*. The wines are full, firm and rich, quite alcoholic but lacking a little elegance. This style of Châteauneuf has many followers. I would be happier to recommend Pegaü more enthusiastically if I hadn't encountered too many different bottlings of the same wine, deteriorating the longer the wine was held in *foudre*. Cuvée Laurence is the same wine as the basic wine but bottled later.

★★ CHÂTEAU RAYAS

Owners: Reynaud family.
Surface Area under Vine: 11 ha.
Wines: Châteauneuf-du-Pape (red and white) including Château Pignan (red) and Côtes du Rhône Fonsalette (red and white).

The legend behind Château Rayas, Jacques Reynaud, died in 1997, and his nephew Emmanuel now runs this determinedly idiosyncratic estate. There are several very curious things about Rayas. First, the vineyard contains very few of the traditional Châteauneuf pudding stones or *galets* (legend has it that they were removed by Louis Reynaud, Jacques' father). Second, the wine is almost pure Grenache. Yet, such is the concentration, a result of low yields and old vines, that it does not lack acidity, nor indeed is it too alcoholic. Third, the cellar is in a state of disorder, the wine being kept in a mixture of very old

demi-muids and *foudres*. What you taste out of cask often does not inspire, being flat and oxidised, on occasion, just merely odd on others. Despite this, what you get in bottle is splendid. Château Pignan is, so to speak, the second wine, and can be excellent. Château Rayas is even better: essence of wine.

DOMAINE DES RELAGNES

Owners: Boiron family.
Surface Area under Vine: 13 ha.
Wines: Châteauneuf-du-Pape (red and white).

This is traditional Châteauneuf: no destemming, vinification and maturation in *foudres*, and bottling as and when necessary. If you capture a wine bottled when young you can find a good wine here. The proprietor is Henri Boiron, cousin of Maurice Boiron of Domaine Bosquet des Papes (see page 357).

★ DOMAINE LA ROQUETTE

Owners: Brunier family.
Surface Area under Vine: 30 ha.
Wines: Châteauneuf-du-Pape (red and white).

Roquette is based in the village of Châteauneuf-du-Pape and the vines lie nearby on quite different soils from those of the Brunier's other property in Béddarides, Domaine du Vieux Télégraphe. Harvesting starts a week later here. The young Bruniers have built a modern vinification cellar – first used for the 1998 vintage – and make ripe, stylish, harmonious, generous wine, though without the individuality of Vieux Télégraphe.

★ DOMAINE ROGER SABON & FILS

Owners: Sabon family.
Surface Area under Vine: 16.5 ha.
Wines: Châteauneuf-du-Pape (red and white) including, in ascending order, Cuvée Olivets, Cuvée Réserve and Cuvée Prestige.

Jean-Jacques Sabon has now succeeded his father at this commendable estate, working alongside his brothers Gilbert and Denis. The *encépagement* of the three *cuvées* varies slightly, diminishing in Grenache (80 to 60 per cent) and Cinsault, increasing in Syrah and Mourvèdre. All are matured partly in *foudres* and *barriques*, but not new

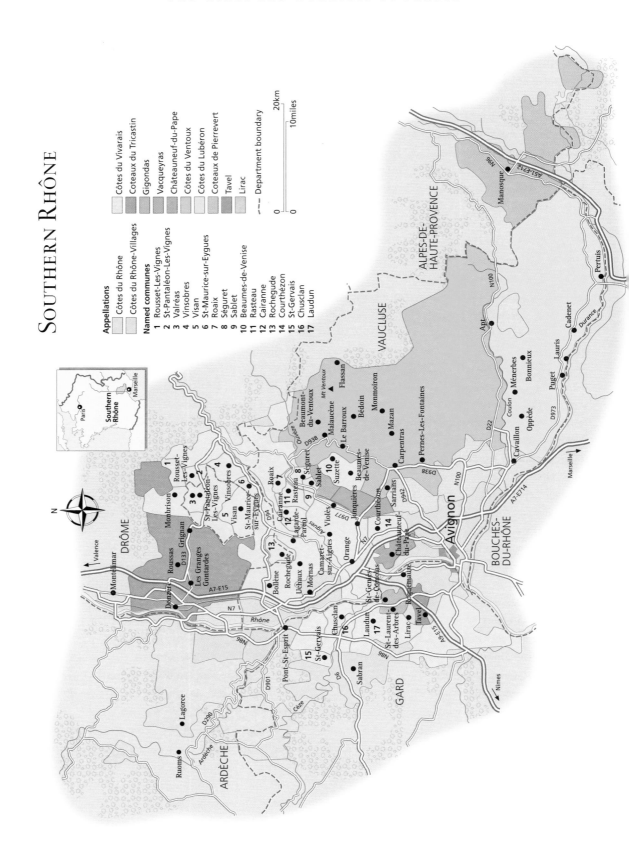

Southern Rhône

Appellations

| | Côtes du Rhône |
| | Côtes du Rhône-Villages |

Named communes
1 Rousset-Les-Vignes
2 St-Pantaléon-Les-Vignes
3 Valréas
4 Vinsobres
5 Visan
6 St-Maurice-sur-Eygues
7 Roaix
8 Séguret
9 Sablet
10 Beaumes-de-Venise
11 Rasteau
12 Cairanne
13 Rochegude
14 Courthézon
15 St-Gervais
16 Chusclan
17 Laudun

	Côtes du Vivarais
	Coteaux du Tricastin
	Gigondas
	Vacqueyras
	Châteauneuf-du-Pape
	Côtes du Ventoux
	Côtes du Lubéron
	Coteaux de Pierrevert
	Tavel
	Lirac
---	Department boundary

wood. The basic difference lies in the age and location of the vines. This is sensitive but traditional winemaking.

★ DOMAINE DE SAINT-SIFFREIN
Commune: Orange.
Owner: Claude Chastan.
Surface Area under Vine: 17 ha.
Wines: Châteauneuf-du-Pape (red and white) and Côtes du Rhône-Villages.

This is traditional Châteauneuf: no destemming and storage in a mixture of stainless steel, *foudres* and *barriques* (not new). The grape mix includes 60 per cent Grenache and 15 per cent each Syrah and Mourvèdre. The wines can be rich, profound and definitely praiseworthy. The Côtes du Rhône-Villages can also be recommended, but not, alas, the white Châteauneuf.

★ DOMAINE DE LA VIEILLE JULIENNE
Commune: Orange.
Owners: Daumen family.
Surface Area under Vine: 17 ha.
Wines: Châteauneuf-du-Pape (red and white) including Cuvée Réservée.

There have been improvements here since Jean-Paul Daumen took over from his father in 1990. The place has been tidied up, the grapes are destemmed, and, most important, the vintage is bottled in one go. The Cuvée Réservée is made from the 70- to 100-year-old vines and matured in new or newish oak. A property to watch.

★ LE VIEUX DONJON
Owners: Michel family.
Surface Area under Vine: 13.2 ha.
Wines: Châteauneuf-du-Pape (red and white).
I have long admired the quality of Lucien Michel's stylish, concentrated, splendidly fruity wines, as well as finding the man himself straightforward and sympathetic. The viticulture is organic, carefully preserving the high proportion of old vines. The *encépagement* is 80 per cent Grenache, 15 per cent Syrah and 5 per cent others, but the grapes are not destemmed. The wine is held in a mixture of tank and *foudre* until bottling two years later and keeps well.

★★ DOMAINE DU VIEUX TÉLÉGRAPHE
Commune: Bédarrides.
Owners: Brunier family.
Surface Area under Vine: 50 ha.
Wines: Châteauneuf-du-Pape (red and white).

The essential flavour of Châteauneuf, says Daniel Brunier, is of old-vine, non-destemmed Grenache. Here the other varieties, including the young Grenache vines, not the old, are destemmed. These *cuvées* are *pigées* (trodden down), the old Grenache is pumped over in what is still a very modern-looking winery, yet built in 1980. Maturation takes place in *foudres* and the entire vintage is bottled in one go. This is a first class property producing profound, long-lasting wines. On the eve of the 1998 harvest, the Bruniers, together with their American importer, Kermit Lynch, bought the Domaine de Paillères in Gigondas. The 1999 harvest is a distinct improvement on the beefy but unsophisticated 1998.

Other Producers of note
Within the *appellation* DOMAINE BOIS DE BOURSAN/JEAN-PAUL VERSINO, DOMAINE DE LA CHARBONNIÈRE, CUVÉE DE BOISDAUPHIN, CUVÉE DU VATICAN, DOMAINE DURIEU, CHÂTEAU DES FINES ROCHES, DOMAINE DE LA FONT DU LOUP, DOMAINE DU HAUT DES TERRES BLANCHES, DOMAINE COMTE DE LAUZE, CHÂTEAU MAUCOIL, DOMAINE DE NALYS, CLOS DE L'ORATOIRE DES PAPES, DOMAINE DU PÈRE CABOCHE, DOMAINE PONTIFICAL, DOMAINE SAINT-BENOÎT, CLOS SAINT-MICHEL, DOMAINE DE LA SOLITUDE, CHÂTEAU DE VAUDIEU, DOMAINE DU VIEUX LAZARET and DOMAINE DE VILLENEUVE.

Outside the *appellation* CHAPOUTIER – LE BARBE RAC AND LA BERNARDINE, PAUL JABOULET AÎNÉ – LES CÈDRES (BOTH TAIN L'HERMITAGE), DOMAINE DE LA MORDORÉE (TAVEL) AND TARDIEU-LAURENT (LAURIS).

TAVEL AND LIRAC

TAVEL
Surface Area (1998): 957 ha.
Production (1998): 43,374 hl.

Colour: Rosé.
Grape Varieties: Bourboulenc, Calitor, Carignan, Cinsault, Clairette, Grenache, Syrah, Mourvèdre and Picpoul.
Maximum Yield: 48 hl/ha.
Minimum Alcohol Level: 11°.

The second best known wine of the southern Rhône is Tavel, one of the few *appellations* in France for rosé wine alone. It lays claim to being the country's best and it is certainly the fullest and the firmest; the most 'masculine' perhaps.

Tavel lies south of Lirac on the western side of the Rhône in the *département* of Gard, some 15 kilometres north-west of Avignon. In contrast to the more market garden aspect of the countryside in the Vaucluse on the opposite side of the Rhône the appearance here is more similar to that of the Languedoc: arid, sparse, rocky *garrigues* within which parcels of land have been laboriously hacked out, flattened and planted with vines. Constant work is needed to prevent these plots from being reclaimed again by nature.

Tavel has been a well-known and prosperous vineyard area for many centuries, and considerable quantities of the wine were exported outside the immediate area to the Versailles court and beyond as early as the eighteenth century. After phylloxera the vineyards, as in so many other areas in France, largely fell into disuse and they declined from 750 hectares in the heyday of the nineteenth century to a mere 100 hectares in 1930. The formation of the local co-operative in 1937, which now makes 55 per cent of all Tavel, and the growth of the wine's popularity in the United States in the 1950s, encouraged the opening-up of new tracts of land in the hillsides, first north of the village on a well-exposed plateau known as the Vallongue and then to the south and west.

The soil is lighter than on the other side of the Rhône Valley. It consists predominantly of chalk, mixed with sand on the flatter land nearer to the village itself, clay north of the village and covered in parts with white, flat, crumbling stones. Grenache (maximum 60 per cent) and Cinsault (minimum 15 per cent) are the main-

stays of the recipe, though seven other varieties (Carignan to a maximum of 10 per cent, Syrah and Mourvèdre, the white Bourboulenc, Clairette and Picpoul, and the fast disappearing Calitor) are also permitted. The use of Syrah and Mourvèdre, authorized since 1969, is somewhat controversial. They certainly add colour and backbone to the wine, but is this not somewhat of a contradiction in terms, particularly as there has been a move away from the old-style, hard Tavel to a more supple, fruity, forward wine?

One of the myths that has done much disservice to Tavel is the notion that it is a wine to age. No rosé is, or should be, for keeping, certainly for more than two or three years after the vintage. The idea that Tavel is somehow better after five years in bottle is nonsense; the wine will have dried out, the fruit disappeared and all the fresh attraction gone. Equally a rosé, like a white wine, must be vinified at a cool temperature, aged in vat rather than oak *foudre*, and bottled early in order to retain the maximum amount of aromas and personality from the fruit. Many Tavel domaines produce Lirac, red and white, and vice versa. The Caveau Saint-Vincent in the centre of the village sells the wines of twenty-seven leading estates, plus those of the co-operative.

LIRAC
Surface Area (1998): 546 ha.
Production (1998): (Red and rosé) 22,895 hl; (white) 1021 hl.
Colour: Red, rosé and white.
Grape Varieties: (Red and rosé) Grenache, Mourvèdre, Syrah, Cinsault and Carignan; (white) Clairette, Grenache Blanc, Picpoul, Roussanne, Viognier and Bourboulenc.
Maximum Yield: 42 hl/ha.
Minimum Alcohol Level: (Red) 12°; (rosé and white) 11.5°.

Lirac, north of Tavel, covers four communes west of the Rhône and makes red, rosé and white wines. I suspect that some red wine is made on Tavel soil and bottled as Lirac and perhaps vice versa for rosé. Certainly many Tavel growers have land in Lirac and so offer a range of colours. The Lirac *appellation* extends over the communes of Lirac itself, Saint-Laurent-des-Arbres, Roquemaure and Saint-Geniès-de-Comolas, opposite Châteauneuf du-Pape, and is definitely an up-and-coming and expanding area. The main thrust behind this expansion has been the influx of ex-Algerian *pieds noirs* in the early 1960s after independence. Why there should be this enclave of North African expatriates here and not, say, in Vacqueyras or Gigondas, is curious, but perhaps the attraction of a ready-made if not widely known *appellation*, a dependable climate and a soil not dissimilar to what they had been used to, plus, above all, land that was cheap, proved irresistible.

Château de Clary at Lirac is said to have had the dubious honour of being the site in France where the phylloxera louse was first detected in 1863. The owner at the time was possessed of insatiable curiosity and planted all sorts of different varieties and species of vines, American as well as *vinifera*, thus letting the bug loose to devastate the non-resistant vines of France, and ultimately the whole of Europe.

The Lirac soil is similar to Tavel's but more sandy, and near the Rhône at Roquemaure, densely covered in the large pudding-stones or *galets* so familiar in Châteauneuf on the opposite bank. The *encépagement* is the usual southern Rhône mix of Grenache, chiefly, which with Cinsault, Mourvèdre and Syrah makes up the bulk of the blend, while white grapes such as Clairette, Bourboulenc and Picpoul add a little zip. The inferior Carignan is restricted to a maximum of 10 per cent.

John Livingstone-Learmonth in *The Wines of the Rhône* (*op. cit.*) describes Lirac wines as lighter-styled, softer and easier to drink than the wines on the opposite side of the valley from Cairanne or Vacqueyras. He puts this down to a large proportion of Cinsault vines dating from the expansion of the *vignoble* in the early 1960s in the blend. I cannot agree with this. In my experience Liracs are somehow more baked and have a more pronounced *goût de terroir* than the wines of Vacqueyras, and they can be harder too. I can see in Lirac similarities with the Costières de Nîmes, if at a superior level. Far from being easy to drink, I find Lirac a meaty and sturdy wine and it is more of an acquired taste.

French statistics do not differentiate between red and rosé wine so it is difficult to be exact about the breakdown in production between these two colours. One grower estimated the amount of Lirac rosé to be no more than 8 per cent, which is about the same as the amount of white wine produced. Both of these can be – should be – fresh and crisp and full of fruit: the rosé is similar to Tavel, the white is like a modern, *primeur*-style white Châteauneuf-du-Pape. Both are for drinking within a couple of years after bottling.

Leading Tavel and Lirac Producers

CHÂTEAU D'AQUÉRIA
Commune: Tavel.
Owners: Olivier family.
Surface Area under Vine: 65 ha.
Wines: Tavel and Lirac (red and white).
At this attractive château, between Tavel and Roquemaure, the Olivier family produce not only one of the most reliable Tavels but very good Lirac, the white distinguished by a good dollop of Roussanne in the blend.

CHÂTEAU BOUCARUT
Commune: Roquemaure.
Owner: Christophe Valat.
Surface Area under Vine: 30 ha.
Wines: Lirac (red, rosé and white) and Côtes du Rhône (Domaine Saint-Maurice).
Christophe Valat is one of the best of the new generation of Lirac producers. The full, rich and concentrated red wine, forming the bulk of the production, contains 30 per cent Syrah and is matured partly in oak casks, partly in stainless steel vats. It has plenty of personality.

DOMAINE DE LA FORCADIÈRE
Commune: Tavel.
Owner: Roger Maby.
Surface Area under Vine: 42 ha.
Wines: Tavel and Lirac (red and white) including Cuvée Prestige.
Roger Maby produces good, modern wines, the best Lirac reds from 50 per cent Mourvèdre, which he prefers

to Syrah. The white is made from equal amounts of Clairette, white Grenache and Picpoul plus a little Viognier. The Cuvée Prestige is aged using some new oak.

DOMAINE DE LA GENESTIÈRE

Commune: Tavel.
Owners: Garcin family.
Surface Area under Vine: 37 ha.
Wines: Tavel and Lirac (red and white).

A decade ago, in the time of Georges Bernard, this was one of the leading Tavel producers. Under the new ownership some of the flair has been lost. A good address nevertheless.

★ DOMAINE DE LA MORDORÉE

Commune: Tavel.
Owners: Delorme family.
Surface Area under Vine: 45 ha.
Wines: Tavel, Lirac (red and white) including Cuvée de la Reine des Bois, and Châteauneuf-du-Pape (red).

Christophe Delorme's Domaine de La Mordorée is the leading estate in Tavel, producing a delicious, juicy-fruity wine. The main vineyard, however, lies in Lirac. Here the basic red is a 50:50 Grenache-Syrah blend which is reared in a mixture of tank and old *barriques*. The special *cuvée* contains Mourvèdre in the blend and sees new oak. The white is good, as is the old-vine Châteauneuf.

CHÂTEAU SAINT-ROCH

Commune: Roquemaure.
Owners: Brunel family.
Surface Area under Vine: 40 ha.
Wines: Lirac (red, rosé and white), Châteauneuf-du-Pape and Côtes du Rhône.

Much has changed here since Patrick and Maxim Brunel of Chateauneuf's La Gardine bought this estate in 1998. The density of the vines has been increased and more Syrah, Roussanne and Viognier have been planted. There is a new press, a *table de trie* and temperature control of vinification and the cellars. Barrels have been introduced at the expense of *foudres*. There are now oaky *cuvées* for both red and white Lirac and all the grapes are now picked by hand. A comparison of the wines between the old and new regime shows a distinct increase in flavour.

CHÂTEAU DE SÉGRIÈS

Commune: Lirac.
Owner: Henri de Lanzac.
Surface Area under Vine: 19 ha.
Wines: Lirac (red, rosé and white).

This is one of Lirac's older domaines. The wine is made in a cramped cellar underneath the ruins of the old château and has been bottled on site since the 1950s. It spends all its time in vat (cement or enamelled steel) which I feel detracts from the possibilities for wines of individual character. But a good address nevertheless.

Other Producers of note

CHÂTEAU BOUCHASSY (ROQUEMAURE), DOMAINE DE CORNE-LOUP (TAVEL), DOMAINE DES GARRIGUES (ROQUEMAURE), PRIEURÉ DE MONTÉZARGUES (TAVEL), DOMAINE ROC-EPINE (TAVEL) AND CHÂTEAU DE TRINQUEVEDEL (TAVEL).

GIGONDAS

Surface Area (1998): 1250 ha.
Production (1998): 43,988 hl.
Colour: Red and rosé.
Grape Varieties: Grenache, Syrah and/or Mourvèdre , Cinsault and Carignan.
Maximum Yield: 35 hl/ha.
Minimum Alcohol Level: 12.5°.

After Châteauneuf-du-Pape, the most prestigious and the most expensive southern Rhône red wines come from Gigondas, a commune lying in the shadow of the jagged peaks of the Dentelles de Montmirail some 16 kilometres east of Orange. The vineyards lie beneath the village, on slopes which run down in a westerly direction towards the river Ouvèze, and border those of Vacqueyras and Sablet. The soil structure is varied, ranging from rich, yellowish clay in the highest vineyards, which can go up to 550 metres, to stony and sandy areas on the lower slopes and flatter ground.

Until 1971, Gigondas, like Sablet and other neighbouring hillside villages, was entitled to the Côtes du Rhône-Villages *appellation*, but then it was elevated to *appellation contrôlée* in its own right. Why this should have been so, and why, with the precedent set, it was not over the subsequent years joined by others – with the sole exception of Vacqueyras in 1990 – no-one seems to be able to explain. This singling out has certainly done the local growers good, for they obtain a substantially higher price for their wines over those enjoyed by their neighbours. Not all Gigondas is necessarily worth the extra money, and elsewhere in this part of the Rhône there are numerous fine domaines and dedicated proprietors making wine from the same mix of grapes. The intrepid wine lover can find Côtes du Rhône-Villages as equally good as Gigondas, and 30 per cent cheaper or so. The consumer, however, can rely on the fact that there are many good growers in Gigondas to choose from.

Most Gigondas is red, for the rosé is hardly a commercial proposition with a price which if based on the level of the red would greatly exceed that of Tavel. This red is well-coloured, similar to a lesser Châteauneuf, but without the intensity and structure of the best domaines. It is in general at its best between three and eight years old, though some individual vintages will keep for ten years or more. Like Châteauneuf, it often used to be kept two or more years – far too long – in wood. Today most growers bottle after a year and many are experimenting with *barrique*-ageing. Gigondas is a cheerfully prosperous and improving *appellation*.

Leading Gigondas Producers

DOMAINE LA BOUISSIÈRE
Owner: Faravel family.
Surface Area under Vine: 7.50 ha.
Wines: Gigondas including Le Font de Tonin.
Meaty but well-mannered wines with good black cherry fruit are made by Gilles and Thierry Faravel. The wines come largely from Grenache, plus Syrah and Mourvèdre. The Font de Tonin is made from fifty-year-old vines.

★ DOMAINE BRUSSET, LES HAUTS DE MONTMIRAIL
Commune: Cairanne.
Owners: Brusset family.
Surface Area under Vine: 79 ha.
Wines: Gigondas including Les Hauts de Montmirail, Côtes du Rhône-Cairanne and Côtes du Rhône.
The young Laurent Brusset is one of the southern Rhône's best winemakers, following in the footsteps of his father Daniel, who was one of the first in the region to use new oak for his top *cuvées*, including the Hauts de Montmirail. There are some splendid Cairanne wines here also, at two-thirds of the price of the Gigondas. There is also fine Côtes du Rhône Viognier.

★ DOMAINE DU CAYRON
Owner: Michel Faraud.
Surface Area under Vine: 15 ha.
Wines: Gigondas.
In several blind tastings laid on by local growers I have put this wine in first place. It is big and powerful, often almost at the limits of acceptable alcohol, with a rich, earthy *garrigues* flavour which immediately recalls its origins. There is a single *cuvée* made from 70 per cent Grenache and 15 per cent each Syrah and Mourvèdre, but it is bottled at several stages, as and when the wine is required.

★ DOMAINE DES ESPIERS
Commune: Vacqueyras.
Owner: Philippe Cartoux and family.
Surface Area under Vine: 9 ha.
Wines: Gigondas including Cuvée des Blaches, Côtes du Rhône-Sablet and Côtes du Rhône.
Philippe Cartoux started this estate in 1990 and began seriously domaine-bottling in 1994. The wine is made in his father-in-law's cellar at Domaine Montvac in Gigondas. These are good wines, especially the Sablet (60 per cent Grenache, 20 per cent Syrah, 15 per cent Mourvèdre and 5 per cent other grapes) and the barrel-aged Gigondas Cuvée des Blaches (65 per cent Grenache and 35 per cent Syrah).

★ DOMAINE DE FONT-SADE

Owners: Reysson and Cunty families.
Surface Area under Vine: 14 ha.
Wines: Gigondas including Cuvée Fûtée, and
Côtes du Ventoux.

Though the label still says G Reysson et Fille, Véronique Cunty (daughter of Gilbert) and her husband Bernard have run this estate for some years. The Ventoux is a serious example of this *appellation*. The Gigondas, roughly 65 per cent Grenache, 35 per cent Syrah, is a wine to keep. The old-vine, woody Cuvée Fûtée is a fine example.

★ DOMAINE LES GOUBERT

Owners: Cartier family.
Surface Area under Vine: 24 ha.
Wines: Gigondas including Cuvée Florence, Côtes du Rhône-Sablet, Côtes du Rhône-Beaumes-de-Venise and Côtes du Rhône (red and white).

The star here is not so much the basic Gigondas, which is perfectly acceptable, but the splendid Cuvée Florence. The vines here are said to be over 100 years old. The wine is a 80:20 Grenache/Syrah mixture, matured in oak, about half of which is new. Jean-Pierre Cartier also produces a white Côtes du Rhône from 100 per cent Viognier, which is well worth a try.

DOMAINE DU GRAPILLON D'OR

Owners: Chauvet family.
Surface Area under Vine: 15.5 ha.
Wines: Gigondas.

Bernard Chauvet was president of the growers' association on one of my visits in the mid-1990s, so it was gratifying to find out I had given his 1995 18 marks out of 20 when the bottles were uncovered. This is traditional winemaking: no destemming, but old vines and low yields, and the results are poised and classy.

DOMAINE DU PESQUIER

Owners: Boutière family.
Surface Area under Vine: 17 ha.
Wines: Gigondas.

Raymond Boutière's Gigondas, from 75 per cent Grenache and 20 per cent Syrah and reared in cement

vats and old oak casks, is one of the better of the more traditional Gigondas wines. There are two or three *cuvées* which may or may not be blended together before bottling. Perhaps son Guy, now that he has taken over, will regulate this. I would like to see one wine, all bottled at the same time, or specific *cuvées* under different names.

★ DOMAINE DE PIAUGIER

Commune: Sablet.
Owners: Autran family.
Surface Area under Vine: 25 ha.
Wines: Gigondas, Côtes du Rhône-Sablet and Côtes du Rhône.

Jean-Marc Autran's wine is kept entirely in cement vats and the grapes are not de-stemmed, which I regret, but it is made with a low *rendement* from forty-five- year-old vines, which I applaud. The result is a somewhat less rustic and burly version of Gigondas, nicely fresh. The Sablets, of which there are a number of different *cuvées,* are just a little cheaper and at least as good. The Ténébi *cuvée* is 95 per cent Counoise and is particularly splendid. An extension to the cellar, based in Sablet, has enabled him to mature the Syrah in barrel from the 1999 vintage.

DOMAINE RASPAIL-AY

Owners: Ay family.
Surface Area under Vine: 18 ha.
Wines: Gigondas.

Dominique Ay, one of the leading lights of the *appellation*, produces a Gigondas which comprises the best of the old and the new. There is no lack of weight but no lack of elegance or fruit either. The grapes (70 per cent Grenache, 15 per cent Syrah) is entirely destemmed. *Foudres* and old *demi-muids* are used for the *élevage*.

CHÂTEAU REDORTIER

Commune: Suzette.
Owners: de Menton family.
Surface Area under Vine: 35 ha.
Wines: Gigondas, Côtes du Rhône-Beaumes-de-Venise including Cuvée Prestige, Muscat de Beaumes-de-Venise, Côtes du Rhône and Côtes du Ventoux.

This is a puzzling estate in an enchanting valley the other side of the Dentelles de Montmirail, approached from Beaumes-de-Venise. The wine is made by an 'outsider', Etienne de Menthon. originally of Annecy in Savoie. The wine is made from destemmed grapes (60 per cent Grenache and 40 per cent Syrah). But it is then left for three years in cement vats. This is like strangling the wine at birth. Wine needs a gentle oxidation/reduction during its first eighteen months of life. The wines are very good yet I can't help feeling Château Redortier could be so much better.

CHÂTEAU DE SAINT-COSME
Owners: Barruol family.
Surface Area under Vine: 15.5 ha.
Wines: Gigondas including Cuvée Vabelle.
Louis Barruol's family have owned Saint-Cosme, which lies below the village guarding the little road up towards the Hôtel les Florets, since the fifteenth century. The chateau itself is built over Roman ruins. Cuvée Malbelle is aged half in new wood, half in one-year-old wood, which, for the 1998 in February 2000 seemed far too excessive. Monsieur Barruol acquired a merchant's licence in 1997.

★ DOMAINE SAINT-GAYAN
Owners: Meffre family.
Surface Area under Vine: 38 ha.
Wines: Gigondas including Cuvée Fontmarie, Côtes du Rhône-Rasteau, Côtes du Rhône and Châteauneuf-du-Pape (red).
Roger Meffre, the warm, hospitable, outgoing head of the family, comes from a long line. The family have been making wine at Saint-Gayan since 1400. His son Jean-Pierre is responsible for the winemaking. The vines (75 per cent Grenache) are old, the yields small and the wine aged in old oak barrels and *demi-muids*. It is a typical 'old-fashioned' Gigondas and a good one too — full, rich, fleshy and generous.

★ DOMAINE SANTA-DUC
Owners: Gras family.
Surface Area under Vine: 23 ha.

Wines: Gigondas including Prestige des Hautes Garrigues, Vacqueyras, Côtes du Rhône-Villages and Côtes du Rhône (red, rosé and white).
Yves Gras has brought this domaine to the fore since he took over from his father in 1985. His 1995 regular *cuvée* was the best wine of my vintage 1995 blind tasting. The wine is made from 70 per cent Grenache, 15 per cent Syrah and 15 per cent Mourvèdre (the top *cuvée* may have more Mourvèdre), aged in a rotation of cask, *foudre* and tank and has splendid fruit and intensity. The Prestige des Hautes Garrigues comes from a small parcel of fifty-year-old vines, cropped at half the usual yield.

DOMAINE DE LA TOURADE
Owners: Richard family.
Surface Area under Vine: 13 ha.
Wines: Gigondas including Font des Aïeux and Cuvée Morgan, and Vacqueyras.
André Richard's domaine is split between Gigondas and Vacqueyras. The recipe for the former is 65 per cent Grenache, 35 per cent Syrah and Mourvèdre and for Vacqueyras 80 per cent Grenache and 20 per cent Syrah and Mourvèdre. There are two prestige *cuvées*, Font des Aïeux, made from old vines on the slopes and Cuvée Morgan, aged in *barrique*. The premises, on the main road, are very well organised for selling to the passing tourist. The wines are good, but not special.

CHÂTEAU DU TRIGNON
Commune: Sablet.
Owners: Roux family.
Surface Area under Vine: 50 ha.
Wines: Gigondas, Côtes du Rhône-Rasteau, Côtes du Rhône-Sablet, Côtes du Rhône; plus 25ha at Châteauneuf-du-Pape, Domaine des Sénéchaux.
This branch of the Roux family (the Bruniers of Châteauneuf's Vieux Télégraphe have recently bought out the cousins at the Domaine Les Pallières) operates from a large modern winery in Sablet. Until 1994 most of the wine was made by the carbonic maceration method. Today 90 per cent is traditionally made. They disapprove of super-*cuvées* and there is one single wine in each *appellation*.

Other Producers of note

DOMAINE LA BASTIDE SAINT-VINCENT (VIOLÈS), DOMAINE DE LA GARRIGUE (VACQUEYRAS), CLOS DE JONCUAS (GIGONDAS), DOMAINE L'OUSTAU FAUQUET (VACQUEYRAS), DOMAINE LES PALLIÈRES (GIGONDAS), CHÂTEAU RASPAIL (GIGONDAS), DOMAINE DES TOURELLES (GIGONDAS), CAVE DES VIGNERONS DE GIGONDAS and CAVE DES VIGNERONS DE VACQUEYRAS.

(See also under Vacqueyras below.)

Outside the region CROS DE LA MÛRE (MONDRAGON), PAUL JABOULET AÎNÉ (TAIN L'HERMITAGE), DOMAINE PERRIN (JONQUIÈRES) AND TARDIEU-LAURENT (LAURIS).

VACQUEYRAS

Surface Area (1998): 1159 ha.

Production (1998): (Red and rosé) 39,453 hl; (white) 337 hl.

Grape Varieties: (Red and rosé) Grenache, Syrah and/or Mourvèdre, Cinsault and Carignan; (white) Grenache Blanc, Clairette, Bourboulenc, Marsanne, Roussanne and Viognier.

Maximum Yield: 35 hl/ha.

Minimum Alcohol Level: (Red) 12.5°; (rosé and white) 12°.

Vacqueyras, like its neighbour Gigondas, was promoted from Côtes du Rhône-Villages to a separate *appellation*, this time in 1990. For a long time it had been the leading contender, producing wine which is much like Gigondas, naturally, but a little less 'hot' and chunky, a little bit crisper and more elegant.

Leading Vacqueyras Producers

★ DOMAINE DES AMOURIERS

Owners: Heirs of Jocelyn Chudzikiewicz.

Surface Area under Vine: 22 ha.

Wines: Vacqueyras including Cuvée Signature, Cuvée Les Genestes, Cuvée Les Truffières and Cuvée Hautes Terraces.

Under the inspired leadership of the late Jocelyn Chudzikiewicz, Domaine des Amouriers quickly became established as one of the leaders in Vacqueyras with a series of super-*cuvées*, at very reasonable prices, one has to add, which became progressively more new oaky and Syrah dominated. Until 1995 everything was sold to the co-operative. I trust the new regime, under the *régisseur*, Patrick Gras, will continue the progress.

★ DOMAINE LE CLOS DES CAZAUX

Owners: Vache family.

Surface Area under Vine: 20 ha.

Wines: Vacqueyras including Cuvée St-Roch, Cuvée des Templiers, Cuvée Prestige and Cuvée Les Clefs d'Or (white), Gigondas including Cuvée de La Tour Sarrazine, and Côtes du Rhône Cuvée Mataro.

The Vache family make ample, fruity, modern-style Vacqueyras for the medium term. The Cuvée St-Roch contains 60 per cent Grenache, 35 per cent Syrah and 5 per cent other grapes, the Cuvée des Templiers is almost entirely Syrah and the Cuvée Prestige is the same but oak aged. The wines are matured for eighteen months in stainless steel. Since Jean-Michel Vache and his brother Frédéric have been in charge – almost a decade now – quality has been regularly at the top level.

DOMAINE DE LA CHARBONNIÈRE

Commune: Châteauneuf-du-Pape.

Owners: Maret family.

Surface Area under Vine: 12 ha.

Wines: Vacqueyras and Châteauneuf-du-Pape (red and white).

Michel Maret owns 4 hectares of Vacqueyras vines and makes the wine at his Châteauneuf-du-Pape winery. The wine comes from a 50:50 mixture of old-vine Grenache and Syrah and is ripe, balanced and succulent.

DOMAINE DE COUROULU

Owners: Richard family.

Surface Area under Vine: 19 ha.

Wines: Vacqueyras including Cuvée Vieilles Vignes, and Côtes du Rhône.

'Couroulu' is Provençal for curlew, of which there were many in the area before the locals shot and ate them.

Guy Richard started bottling his own wine as long ago as 1971, when he took over from his father. These are good, sturdy wines from roughly 70 per cent Grenache, 30 per cent Syrah plus a little Mourvèdre.

★ DOMAINE DE LA FOURMONE

Owners: Combe family.
Surface Area under Vine: 27 ha.
Wines: Vacqueyras including Trésor du Poète, Sélection Maître de Chais, Les Ceps d'Or and Cuvée Fleurantine (white), and Gigondas Domaine L'Oustau Fauquet.

Roger Combe, for long the doyen of the Vacqueyras *appellation*, has now retired and handed over to his daughter Marie-Thérèse. There are three red *cuvées*, of which the best is the Ceps d'Or: fifty-year-old vines, 100 per cent Grenache, eighteen months in vat followed by eighteen months in oak. This is a wine of splendid intensity, though I am normally wary of keeping anything three years before bottling. The Sélection Maître de Chai (70 per cent Grenache, 15 per cent each Syrah and Mourvèdre, one year in tank, one year in wood) is also very good. This is also one of the few producers I know who make a white Vacqueyras. It is a little four-square.

CHÂTEAU DE MONTMIRAIL

Owners: Archimbault family.
Surface Area under Vine: 45 ha.
Wines: Vacqueyras including Cuvée des Deux-Frères, Cuvée des Saints-Papes and Cuvée de L'Ermite, Gigondas including Cuvée des Beauchamp, and Côtes du Rhône.

Philippe Bouteille is in charge, alongside his mother at this well-established, if not quite first division, estate. The Deux-Frères *cuvée* does not see any wood. The Saints-Papes is essentially the same wine but matured in *foudres*. Cuvée L'Ermite (50 per cent each Grenache and Syrah) is the best wine.

DOMAINE DE MONTVAC

Owners: Dusserre family.
Surface Area under Vine: 24 ha.
Wines: Vacqueyras (red and white) including

Cuvée Vincila and occasionally Cuvée Grenache, Gigondas, and Côtes du Rhône (red, rosé and white).

Jean Dusserre, who runs this estate with his daughter Cécile, inherited the domaine from his father-in-law. Just before the Second World War, the Audiberts were one of the first in the area to start domaine-bottling. The basic Vacqueyras red (70 per cent Grenache, 25 per cent Syrah, 5 per cent Mourvèdre) does not see small wood. The white, which contains 40 per cent Roussanne, is vinified in oak, however. The Cuvée Vincila (a red from old Grenache and Syrah vines) is matured in oak. Both these are more than competent wines. Cécile is married to Philippe Cartoux of the Domaines des Espiers, whose wine is made in the same cellar (see page 367).

★ CHÂTEAU DES TOURS

Owner: Bernard Reynaud.
Surface Area under Vine: 40 ha.
Wines: Vacqueyras and Côtes du Rhône (red, rosé and white).

Emmanuel Reynaud, son of Bernard who is proprietor here, is also the nephew of the late Jacques Reynaud, of Châteauneuf's Château Rayas (see page 361). Today he is responsible for the winemaking at both establishments. Things are a little less haphazard-looking here in Vacqueyras, and the wine, made from low-yielding, 95 per cent Grenache, is sumptuous, concentrated and gamey. It lasts well.

DOMAINE DE VERQUIÈRE

Commune: Sarrians.
Owners: Chamfort family.
Surface Area under Vine: 30 ha.
Wines: Vacqueyras, Côtes du Rhône-Rasteau and Côtes du Rhône-Sablet.

Most of Bernard Chamfort's vines lie outside Vacqueyras and his winery is at Sarrians. I have been impressed by the neat style of these medium- to full-bodied, richly-fruity wines on several occasions. They are made from 75 per cent Grenache and bottled after almost a year in old barrels. The average age of the vines is young and the wines can only go on improving.

Other Vacqueyras Producers of note
Domaine La Bastide Saint-Vincent (Violès),
Domaine de La Garrigue (Vacqueyras), Domaine
La Monardière (Vacqueyras), Château des Roques
(Vacqueyras), Domaine Le Sang des Cailloux
(Sarrians), Domaine de La Tourade (Gigondas)
and Cave des Vignerons de Vacqueyras.
(See also under Gigondas page 366.)

Outside the region Paul Jaboulet Aîné (Tain
L'Hermitage), Domaine Perrin (Jonquières) and
Tardieu-Laurent (Lauris).

Côtes du Rhône-Villages

Surface Area (1998): 6917 ha.
Production (1998): (Red and rosé) 268,153 hl;
(white) 5226 hl.
Grape Varieties: (Red and rosé) Grenache, Syrah,
Cinsault, Mourvèdre and others; (white)
Clairette, Roussanne, Bourboulenc, Grenache
Blanc and others.
Maximum Yield: 42 hl/ha.
Minimum Alcohol Level: (Red) 12.5°; (rosé and
white) 12°.

The Côtes du Rhône-Villages *appellation* was first set up
in 1953 and comprised the wines of four communes:
Gigondas and its near neighbour, Cairanne, in the Vaucluse *département* and Chusclan and Laudun on the other
side of the Rhône Valley in the Gard. The *appellation*
applied at first, until 1984, to red and rosé wines only,
and its aim was to bridge the quality gap between
Châteauneuf-du-Pape and basic Côtes du Rhône. The
wines would need to reach 12.5° of alcohol rather than
11°, while the yield was restricted to 42 hectolitres per
hectare as opposed to 50 hectolitres for straight Côtes
du Rhône. The *encépagement* was made stricter than for
Côtes du Rhône. For simple Côtes du Rhône there are
fourteen recommended grape varieties plus a further
ten accessory varieties – some like Pinot Noir and

Gamay admittedly hardly ever used. A Villages wine
must be made with Grenache (maximum 65 per cent)
and Syrah, Mourvèdre and Cinsault (minimum 25 per
cent in total). The lesser varieties can only make up 10
per cent of the total. As far as the whites are concerned it
is interesting to note that a 100 per cent Viognier wine
cannot be Villages but mere Côtes du Rhône.

Gradually more communes were admitted to the
fold, while Gigondas was promoted to AC in its own
right in 1971 and Vacqueyras in 1990. There are now seventeen villages – part of Courthézon across the *autoroute*
from Châteauneuf-du-Pape has recently been added,
mostly on the higher slopes overlooking the valleys of
the rivers Ouvèze and Aigues (or Eygues), which run
down into the Rhône from the Alps. In *département* order
these are:

Drôme
Rochegude, Rousset Les-Vignes, Saint-Maurice-sur-
Eygues, Vinsobres and Saint-Pantaléon-Les-Vignes.

Vaucluse
Beaumes-de-Venise, Cairanne, Courthézon, Rasteau,
Roaix, Sablet, Séguret, Valréas and Visan.

Gard
Chusclan (including land in Orsan, Codolet, Bagnols-
sur-Cèze and Saint-Etienne-des-Sorts), Laudun
(including parts of Saint-Victor-Lacoste and Tresques)
and Saint-Gervais.

The wines can either be described as Côtes du Rhône-
Villages, indicating that the wine is a blend from any or
all of these villages, or as Côtes du Rhône- followed by
the name of a particular village. A Côtes du Rhône-
Villages is a much better wine than a simple Côtes du
Rhône. The soil is better, and better exposed, the wines
are in practice made almost entirely from 'noble' grapes,
often with a substantial proportion of Syrah, and the
result is something which is well coloured, well-structured, rich, ripe, warm, meaty and generous. While
most Côtes du Rhônes, certainly at the cheapest level,
are carbonic maceration blends, soft and fruity, and for

drinking young, a Villages wine is a wine to keep, if only for two or three years.

I have had many a happy time driving around in the rolling southern Rhône countryside visiting grower after grower in order to find good Villages wines. There are many, prices are very reasonable and the quality is very exciting. Many producers in the region will declare their best *cuvées* as Villages but produce a lighter wine for earlier drinking under the simple Côtes du Rhône *appellation*. Now that Vacqueyras has been a separate AC for a decade it is clear that the best remaining village is Cairanne. It is home to a number of top Villages domaines and also has an excellent co-operative.

Leading Côtes du Rhône-Villages Producers

★ DOMAINE DANIEL & DENIS ALARY
Commune: Cairanne.
Owners: Alarys family.
Surface Area under Vine: 25 ha.
Wines: Côtes du Rhône-Cairanne including La Réserve du Vigneron and Le Font d'Estévenas, and Côtes du Rhône Blanc de Blancs La Chèvre d'Or.
Cousins of the Alarys of L'Oratoire Saint-Martin (see below), Denis and Daniel are determined to make equally good wine. The wines are full-bodied, but not too sturdy and with lovely blackberry fruit.

DOMAINE DES BUISSERONS
Commune: Rasteau.
Owners: Bouquet family.
Surface Area under Vine: 15 ha.
Wines: Côtes du Rhône-Cairanne.
Pierre Bouquet lives in Rasteau but his vines are next door in Cairanne. The wine is full, firm, rich and powerful, from 65 per cent Grenache, 15 per cent each Syrah and Mourvèdre and 5 per cent Counoise.

DOMAINE DE CABASSE
Commune: Séguret
Owners: Haeni family.
Surface Area under Vine: 20 ha.

Wines: Côtes du Rhône-Séguret, including Les Anges, Cuvée Garnacha, Casa Bassa and Cuvée Bois, and Gigondas.
Alfred Haeni makes several wines – the Gigondas is nothing special but the pure Grenache is good and the Casa Bassa even better. These are abundantly fruity wines for drinking in the medium term.

DOMAINE DIDIER CHARAVIN
Commune: Rasteau.
Owner: Charavin family.
Surface Area under Vine: 50 ha.
Wines: Côtes du Rhône- Rasteau including Cuvée Prestige.
The vineyards are planted with 75 per cent Grenache and 25 per cent Syrah and produce refined wines with very good balance and most attractive fruit. These are ready in the medium term.

★ DOMAINE LES HAUTES CANCES
Commune: Cairanne.
Owners: Astart family.
Surface Area under Vine: 16 ha.
Wines: Côtes du Rhône-Cairanne including Cuvée Vieilles Vignes and Cuvée Col du Débat.
In the early 1990s Jean-Marie and Anne-Marie Astart stopped selling to the co-operative and set up on their own. These are civilised wines, with balance and richness and no lack of elegance.

★ DOMAINE DE L'ORATOIRE-SAINT-MARTIN
Commune: Cairanne.
Owners: Alary family.
Surface Area under Vine: 25 ha.
Wines: Côtes du Rhône-Cairanne including Cuvée Haut Coustias, Réserve des Seigneurs and Cuvée Prestige, and Côtes du Rhône (red, rosé and white).
This long established domaine is one of the best in the entire Villages area. The wines range from Côtes du Rhône to the Mourvèdre-Syrah Cuvée Haut Coustias, a splendid contrast to the Grenache-Mourvèdre Cuvée

Prestige, and are intense and concentrated, surprisingly sophisticated. At less than half the price of a top Châteauneuf this domaine offers splendid value.

Domaine Pélaquié

Commune: Laudun.
Owners: Pélaquié family.
Surface Area under Vine: 68 ha.
Wines: Côtes du Rhône-Laudun (red and white), Lirac and Tavel.

This is one of the few domaines with a good reputation for its white wine, made from Clairette and Viognier. The other wines are good but not compelling.

★ Domaine Rabasse-Charavin

Commune: Cairanne.
Owner: Corinne Couturier.
Surface Area under Vine: 68 ha.
Wines: Côtes du Rhône-Cairanne including Cuvée Laure-et-Olivier, Cuvée Les Amandiers-Cuvée pigée and Cuvée d'Estévenas, Côtes du Rhône-Rasteau, Côtes du Rhône-Villages (from Voilès) and Côtes du Rhône (red and white).

This is yet another Cairanne domaine with a fine reputation. The basic mix of grapes is 70 per cent Grenache and 10 per cent each Cinsault, Mourvèdre and Syrah, traditionally made, and stored in vat. The wines are full, rich, occasionally quite sturdy but with plenty of fruit.

Domaine Marcel Richaud

Commune: Cairanne.
Owners: Richaud family.
Surface Area under Vine: 41 ha.
Wines: Côtes du Rhône-Cairanne (red and white) including Cuvée L'Ebrescade and Cuvée Les Estrambords, and Côtes du Rhône (red and white).

The charming Marcel Richaud makes the usual range of wines but does it rather better than most, especially in white. The Estrambords was pure Grenache in 1996 but pure Mourvèdre in 1997. The Ebrescade is made from a plot of vines – one-third each Grenache, Syrah and Mourvèdre – planted in 1900. You can rely on these wines for their impressive, stylish fruit and consistency.

★ Domaine Sainte-Anne

Commune: Saint-Gervais.
Owners: Steinmaier family.
Surface Area under Vine: 33 ha.
Wines: Côtes du Rhône-Saint-Gervais including Cuvée Vieilles Vignes and Cuvée Syrah and Côtes du Rhône (red and white) including Viognier.

The Sainte-Anne domaine, now run by Jean Steinmaier, is famous for Viognier, one of the few examples of this increasingly modish grape which can stand up to a top Condrieu. The reds are also very good. The regular Villages wine is produced from 60 per cent Grenache, Syrah and a little Cinsault. There is more Syrah plus Mourvèdre in the Vieilles Vignes *cuvée*, and 60 per cent Mourvèdre in the excellent Saint-Gervais wine. The 100 per cent Syrah wine is even more sophisticated.

★ Domaine de La Soumade

Commune: Rasteau.
Owners: Andre Romero and family.
Surface Area under Vine: 30 ha.
Wines: Côtes du Rhône-Rasteau including Cuvée Prestige and Cuvée Confiance, Rasteau *vin doux naturel* (*doré* and red).

André Romero is now using more sophisticated techniques for his winemaking, destemming the grapes and vinifying at a slightly cooler temperature. The wines are made from 60 per cent Grenache, 20 per cent Syrah and 20 per cent other grapes and then matured for a year in (mainly old) oak casks. The top *cuvées* come from a selection of the best vats, usually from the oldest vines.

Domaine de Trapadis

Commune: Rasteau.
Owners: Durand family.
Surface Area under Vine: 18 ha.
Wines: Côtes du Rhône-Rasteau including Cuvée Les Adrats and Cuvée Confiance, Rasteau *vin doux naturel* (*doré* and red).

Helen Durand, a man despite his first name, runs this domaine increasingly on biodynamic lines. The vines are about thirty years old, the grapes are entirely destemmed and the wine reared in vat and bottled after eighteen months. The Cuvée Harys – look at the name in reverse – is entirely Syrah, a blend not officially allowed. I like the wines here but I can't help feeling that they would benefit from a six-month spell in oak.

Other Producers of note

Within the region DOMAINE D'AÉRIA (CAIRANNE), DOMAINE DE L'AMEILLAUD (CAIRANNE), DOMAINE BRESSY-MASSON (RASTEAU), DOMAINE BRUSSET (GIGONDAS), DOMAINE LAURENT BRUSSET (CAIRANNE), DOMAINE GOUR DE MAUTENS (RASTEAU), DOMAINE DE PIAUGIER (GIGONDAS), CHÂTEAU REDORTIER (GIGONDAS), DOMAINE SAINT-ESTÈVE (UCHAUX), DOMAINE SAINT-GAYAN (GIGONDAS), DOMAINE SANTA-DUC (GIGONDAS), CHÂTEAU DU TRIGNON (GIGONDAS) AND DOMAINE DE VERQUIÈRE (VACQUEYRAS); PLUS THE CAIRANNE AND BEAUMES-DE-VENISE CO-OPERATIVES.

From outside the region PAUL JABOULET AINÉ (TAIN L'HERMITAGE) AND TARDIEU-LAURENT (LAURIS).

CÔTES DU RHÔNE

Surface Area (1998): 41,606 ha.

Production (1998): (Red and rosé) 2,210,820 hl; (white) 44,922 hl.

Grape Varieties: (Red and rosé) Grenache Noir, Syrah, Mourvèdre plus Carignan, Cinsault, Counoise, Vaccarèse, Muscardin, Camarèse, Picpoul Noir, Terret Noir, Grenache Gris and Clairette Rosé; (white) Grenache Blanc, Clairette Blanc, Marsanne, Roussanne, Bourboulenc, Viognier, plus Ugni Blanc and Picpoul Blanc .

Maximum Yield: 52 hl/ha.

Minimum Alcohol Level: 11°.

Côtes du Rhône wine can come from anywhere in the Rhône Valley between Vienne and Avignon. In practice most comes from south of Bollène and Pont de L'Esprit, and from the flatter, less highly prized soils which lie between the Villages and the other more serious *appellations*. Côtes du Rhône is an enormous *appellation* – some 42,000 hectares are under vine, and some 2^1/$_2$ million

hectolitres of wine are produced each year. This represents about two-thirds of the entire Rhône Valley – even if one includes productive but peripheral areas such as the Ventoux and the Lubéron in the overall statistics.

The *appellation* covers red, rosé and white wine, though barely one per cent is white. The maximum yield per hectare and the register of authorized grape varieties, both 'recommended' and 'accessory', are generous. The maximum yield is 50 hectolitres per hectare (plus 20 per cent *plafond limite de classement*) and the list of varietals includes all the grapes listed above, provided Carignan is restricted to 30 per cent maximum and the 'recommended' varieties make up at least 70 per cent. In practice, Grenache, Carignan and Cinsault are the basic varieties used for Côtes du Rhône.

Not surprisingly in such a vast area, with almost every type and combination of soil, styles and aspirations, styles, qualities and prices can vary enormously. At the top level are wines which are as good as the best Gigondas, and will cost accordingly. Elsewhere, there are cheap generic wines, which can range in style from the traditional to those made by carbonic maceration and in character from the agreeable to the undrinkable.

For good basic wines, the co-operatives are the best source. There are some sixty-five in the Rhône Valley, the best of which, like that at Cairanne, produce a whole range of wines from *vin ordinaire* and *vin de pays* upwards. Almost every village has one. The Cellier des Dauphins in Tulette acts as a bottling and marketing centre for some ten of its co-operative neighbours.

More interesting, but more expensive, are wines from individual domaines. No-one can possibly know them all, but here is a selection of the best.

Leading Côtes du Rhône Producers

COUDOULET DE BEAUCASTEL
Commune: Courthézon.
Owners: Perrin family.
Surface Area under Vine: 35 ha.
Wines: Côtes du Rhône (red and white).
Only the *autoroute* separates the Coudoulet vineyard from that of Château de Beaucastel itself. The soils are very

similar, and the wine made by the Perrin brothers with the same amount of care. The red is produced from 30 per cent each Mourvèdre and Grenache and 20 per cent each Syrah and Cinsault. The white has improved considerably over the last decade as more and more Viognier and Marsanne has been included in the blend.

DOMAINE DE L'ESPIGOUETTE
Commune: Voilès.
Owner: Edmond Latour.
Surface Area under Vine: 21 ha.
Wine: Côtes du Rhône (red).
The hospitable Edmond Latour makes very good Côtes du Rhône from his domaine based on the flat plains at Plan de Dieu, below Gigondas. The basic blend is roughly 80 per cent Grenache, and it produces a warm fleshy wine which benefits from a year or two in bottle.

CHÂTEAU DE FONSALETTE
Commune: Lagarde-Paréol.
Owners: Reynaud family.
Surface Area under Vine: 11 ha.
Wines: Côtes du Rhône (red and white) including Cuvée Syrah.
This is the sister estate of Châteauneuf-du-Pape's Château Rayas. The basic red is made from 65 per cent Grenache and 35 per cent Cinsault. Both wines need several years' ageing before they are ready.

DOMAINE DE GRAMENON
Commune: Monbrizon-sur-Lez.
Owners: Philippe & Michelle Laurent.
Surface Area under Vine: 24 ha.
Wines: Côtes du Rhône (red and white) including Le Laurentides, Cuvée Sagasse, Cuvée Syrah and Ceps Centenaires.
Though they acquired the estate in 1978, Philippe and Michelle Laurent only started seriously estate-bottling their wines in 1990. Since then they have quickly achieved a high reputation for their splendidly intense, concentrated Grenache-based wines along with their hands-off attitude towards winemaking. One can only wonder that, if the Laurents can make wine so well at

Monbrizon off the beaten track up, why aren't they surrounded by a dozen other aspiring estates? The Viognier-based white wine is very good, too.

CHÂTEAU DU GRAND MOULAS
Commune: Mornas.
Owner: Marc & Yves Ryckwaert.
Surface Area under Vine: 30 ha.
Wines: Côtes du Rhône (red and white) including Cuvée Clos L'Ecu.
Marc and Yves Ryckwaert arrived at Mornas, north of Orange, from Algeria in 1958 and have created this estate from scratch, planting the red grapes in the ratio of 66 per cent Grenache and 33 per cent Syrah. They have since added Mourvèdre. Both the red and white wine (based on Roussanne and Marsanne) are vinified and aged in stainless steel. They are clean and abundantly fruity wines, not at all rustic.

DOMAINE LA RÉMÉJEANNE
Commune: Sabran.
Owners: Rémy and Ouahi Klein.
Surface Area under Vine: 30 ha.
Wines: Côtes du Rhône (red and white) including Les Chevrefeuilles, Les Arbousiers and Les Eglantiers.
Scattered over the hills south-west of Bagnols-sur-Cèze in the Gard, are the parcels which make up Domaine Réméjeanne. The reds are better than the whites, especially the superior *cuvées* such as Les Eglantiers (entirely Syrah). The wines are aged in a mixture of tank, *foudre* and smaller barrels.

CHÂTEAU SAINT-ESTÈVE D'UCHAUX
Commune: Uchaux.
Owners: Français family.
Surface Area under Vine: 60 ha.
Wines: Côtes du Rhône-Villages, Côtes du Rhône (red and white) including Cuvée Réserve, Cuvée Vieilles Vignes and Viognier.
A wide range of highly competent wines is produced by Marc Français at the family domaine north of Orange in a splendidly modern winery. The better *cuvées* are

made from roughly half Grenache and half Syrah and spend some of their life in oak. The lesser wines are matured in stainless steel. There is a very good, if expensive white from Viognier.

★ MAISON TARDIEU-LAURENT

Commune: Lauris.

Owners: Michel Tardieu & Dominique Laurent.

Michel Tardieu, the man on the spot, and Dominique Laurent of Nuits-Saint-Georges teamed up in 1993 with the aim of repeating Laurent's Burgundian *négociant* business in the Rhône Valley. Success has been swift. A full range of Rhône wines is offered and they are yardstick examples of their *appellations*. The wines are kept in the cellars of the château in nearby Lourmarin in the Lubéron.

DOMAINE DU VIEUX CHÊNE

Commune: Camaret-sur-Aigues.

Owners: Bouche family.

Surface Area under Vine: 30 ha.

Wines: Côtes du Rhône including Cuvée des Capucins and Cuvée Aux Haies des Grives, and Vin de Pays de Vaucluse.

The brothers Jean-Claude and Dominique Bouche took over from their father in 1978, when the domaine left the local co-operative and began to bottle its own wines. The Cuvée des Capucins is soft and juicy, made almost entirely from Grenache, while Aux Haies des Grives is a sturdier wine for keeping (60 per cent Grenache and 40 per cent Syrah).

Other Producers of note

MOST GIGONDAS, VACQUEYRAS AND CÔTES DU RHÔNE-VILLAGES PRODUCERS ALSO MAKE CÔTES DU RHÔNE, AS DO SOME CHÂTEAUNEUF-DU-PAPE ESTATES. LOCAL MERCHANTS WILL LIST ONE IF NOT SEVERAL CUVÉES – MAISON GUIGAL (AMPUIS) AND PAUL JABOULET AÎNÉ'S PARALLÈLE 45 (TAIN L'HERMITAGE) ARE WORTH TRYING. DOMAINE PERRIN AT JONQUIÈRES NEAR ORANGE PRODUCES SEVERAL VERY GOOD CÔTES DU RHÔNE WINES AS WELL AS CRU DU COUDOULET AND CHÂTEAU DU GRAND-PRÉBOIS (SEE PAGE 375).

MUSCAT DE BEAUMES-DE-VENISE

Surface Area (1998): 448 ha.

Production (1998): 14,575 hl.

Colour: White (*vin doux naturel*).

Grape Variety: Muscat à Petits Grains.

Maximum Yield: 30 hl/ha.

Minimum Alcohol Level: 15°.

Beaumes-de-Venise lies some 17 kilometres east of Orange at the southern end of the Dentelles de Montmirail, and produces what most people regard as the best French *vin doux naturels* or fortified sweet wine. As my translation shows, there is nothing 'natural' about a *vin doux naturel*; indeed, the wine is made on essentially the same lines as Port, the object being to retain the natural sugar of the ripe fruit by arresting the fermentation of the must with the addition of pure grape alcohol.

The Muscat grape is a relative newcomer to this area of the southern Rhône, dating from the early nineteenth century. The vineyards were then destroyed by phylloxera and despite the efforts of a few growers and the granting of the *appellation* in 1945, the situation was at almost rock bottom until 1956, when the Beaumes de Venise co-operative was founded. The Muscat variety used is the most elegant one, the Muscat à Petits Grains, of which there are two sub-varieties, the Grain Blanc and the Grain Noir. The difference in flavour between these two is slight. The Grain Noir produces more prolifically but by itself is considered to produce a wine of too pronounced a colour, so most growers prefer to have a combination of the two. These vines are planted in a variety of soils around the village, ranging from pure sand in the south, sand and stones in the east and heavy clay in the north. The Muscat is prone to disease, particularly odium and red spider. The skins are also fragile, rendering it susceptible to rot if it rains during picking.

The grapes are harvested late, not until mid-October, by which time the sugar is well concentrated, giving a potential natural alcohol level of 15°. The must is vinified slowly, being cooled if necessary, and then comes the *mutage*, or addition of 5 to 10 per cent neutral alcohol at a strength of about 96° volume. This will raise the potential alcohol level to 21.5° (the actual level is normally just over 15°) and must leave 125 grams of sugar per litre in the finished wine. Sometimes the *mutage* is done in one go, but some growers prefer to do it in stages, to avoid the spirit becoming too obtrusive. Thereafter the wine is racked as little as possible to avoid both the evaporation of alcohol and the dilution and coarsening of the Muscat flavour by oxidation. Some growers age their wines in vats – for the above reason wood is never used – for a year, others bottle after six or nine months.

Muscat de Beaumes-de-Venise was a mini-success story of the 1980s. In 1972 the co-operative shipped its first export order (twenty-five cases) to the wine merchant Robin Yapp in Britain. Today the co-operative exports by the pallet if not container load, and the wine is stocked by supermarkets the world over. The flavour of the Muscat grape is instantly recognizable, opulent and aromatic and it is the most 'grapy' of all grape varieties. A good *vin doux naturel* retains a fresh acidity, a ripe, welcoming fruit and is softly, generously sweet. It is delicious both as an aperitif and with desserts. Muscat de Beaumes-de-Venise is at its best while young and fresh, but once the bottle is open, the wine will keep for a fortnight, especially if stored in the refrigerator.

The co-operative now produces 90 per cent of all Muscat de Beaumes-de-Venise, which it sells in a rather unattractive screwtop bottle. The wine, however, is excellent, perhaps lighter and marginally less sweet than that of the leading growers, but fresh, balanced and full of fruit. And it is cheaper. The co-operative is also a good source of Côtes du Rhône, Côtes du Rhône-Villages and Côtes du Ventoux.

Leading Muscat de Beaumes-de-Venise Producers

DOMAINE DES BERNARDINS
Owner: Madame Renée Castaud.
Surface Area under Vine: 21.9 ha.
Wines: Muscat de Beaumes-de-Venise and Côtes du Rhône-Beaumes-de-Venise.

Madame Renée Castaud runs this small estate with a firm hand and makes a fatter, richer, more golden Muscat than most, a very *liquoreux* wine. Don't bother about the reds, which are severely rustic.

DOMAINE DE COYEUX
Owner: Yves Nativelle.
Surface Area under Vine: 70 ha.
Wines: Muscat de Beaumes-de-Venise, Gigondas and Côtes du Rhône-Beaumes-de-Venise.

Yves Nativelle produces a lighter, fragrant Muscat, more in the style of the co-operative's wine than that of Domaine des Bernardins or Domaine de Durban. It is fresh, balanced and *gouleyant*.

★ DOMAINE DE DURBAN
Owners: Leydier family.
Surface Area under Vine: 25 ha.
Wines: Muscat de Beaumes-de-Venise.

Bernard and Jean-Pierre Leydier produce what is generally regarded as the best Muscat de Beaumes-de-Venise. It is rich without being heavy, delightfully floral and perfumed without being thin. A yardstick example.

Other Producers of note
Growers DOMAINE DE BEAUMALRIC (BEAUMES-DE-VENISE), DOMAINE DE FENOUILLET (BEAUMES-DE-VENISE) AND CHÂTEAU SAINT-SAUVEUR (AUBIGNAN).
Merchants CHAPOUTIER (TAIN L'HERMITAGE), PAUL JABOULET AÎNÉ (TAIN L'HERMITAGE), VIDAL-FLEURY (AMPUIS) AND CAVE DES VIGNERONS DE BEAUMES-DE-VENISE.

RASTEAU

Surface Area (1998): 102 ha.
Production (1998): 3029 hl.
Colour: Tuilé (red) or Ambré (white).
Grape Varieties: Grenache Noir, Blanc and Gris, plus (to a maximum 10%) Syrah, Cinsault and Carignan .
Maximum Yield: 30 hl/ha.
Minimum Alcohol Level: 15°.

Rasteau, some 15 kilometres north of Beaumes-de-Venise is one of the seventeen villages in the Côtes du Rhône-Villages *appellation*, as is Beaumes-de-Venise. It too makes a *vin doux naturel*. The base for Rasteau is the Grenache grape (minimum 90 per cent) and the wine can be either *ambré* (white) or *tuilé* (red) like Rivesaltes and Banyuls. The *tuilé* is a little drier than the amber. The result is not nearly as appealing as Muscat de Beaumes-de-Venise, particularly when the wine is deliberately aged and oxidized so that it becomes *rancio*. The *vin doux naturel* makes up a very small proportion of Rasteau's production.

Producers of note
DOMAINE BRESSY-MASSON/THIERRY MASSON (RASTEAU).

COTEAUX DU TRICASTIN

Surface Area (1998): 2630 ha.
Production (1998): (Red and rosé) 109,154 hl; (white) 3066 hl.
Grape Varieties: (Red and rosé) Grenache Noir, Cinsault, Mourvèdre, Syrah, Picpoul Noir and Carignan, plus up to 20% white grapes; (white) Grenache Blanc, Clairette, Picpoul Blanc and Bourboulenc plus (to a maximum 30% combined) Ugni Blanc, Marsanne, Roussanne and Viognier.
Maximum Yield: 52 hl/ha.
Minimum Alcoholic Level: 11°.

Between Bollène and Montélimar lies a wine area entirely created since 1950. Tricastin takes its name from the Trois Châteaux of Saint-Paul. There had been vines here and further north near Donzère and Grignan in pre-phylloxera times but the vineyards declined, and when Côtes du Rhône was delimited in 1937, as there was nothing in the Tricastin area worth limiting, it was excluded. The *appellation* centres on the communes of Les Granges Gontardes and Roussas. In the early 1960s a number of families who left Algeria at independence decided to settle here. The soil is very similar to Châteauneuf-du-Pape's and in parts also completely covered in large pudding-stones or *galets*.

The usual Côtes du Rhône varieties were planted: Grenache, Cinsault, a little Mourvèdre and Carignan, plus a relatively high percentage of Syrah. Most Tricastin is made in the soft *vin de l'année* style, and is similar in style and price to Côtes du Ventoux or lesser Côtes du Rhône. Only the better wines, those with a large proportion of Syrah, are matured in wood and need more than a few months' ageing in bottle. There is a little rosé but Tricastin's reputation rests on its red wine.

Producers of note
CHÂTEAU DES ESTUBIERS (LES GRANGES-GONTARDES), DOMAINE DE GRANGENEUVE (ROUSSAS) AND DOMAINE DE LA TOUR D'ELYSSAS (LES GRANGES-GONTARDES).

CÔTES DU VENTOUX

Surface Area (1998): 7307 ha.
Production (1998): (Red and rosé) 319,244 hl; (white) 9781 hl.
Grape Varieties: (Red and rosé) Grenache Noir, Syrah, Cinsault, Mourvèdre and Carignan, plus Picpoul Noir, Counoise and white grapes; (white) Clairette, Bourboulenc and Grenache Blanc, plus Roussanne.
Maximum Yield: 50 hl/ha.
Minimum Alcohol Level: 11°.

The Côtes du Ventoux is a large area – three times the entire surface of the northern Rhône. It begins to the north-west of Mont Ventoux at Beaumont-du-Ventoux and Malaucène and continues south past Carpentras and Pernes-Les-Fontaines as far as Apt, covering some fifty-two communes. Most of the wine, however, comes from either the south side of Mont Ventoux itself, in a line between Beaumes-de-Venise and Flassan, or on the north side of the Plateau du Ventoux around Mormoiron. The lower land in the valley between is used for table grapes, grapes for *vin ordinaire* and fruit trees.

The vines are planted in soils which range between gravel, sand, clay, limestone and chalk. With a few exceptions Ventoux is an undemanding, easy-to-drink, light wine of *vin de l'année* style, a wine for which one can see little justification for the accolade of *appellation contrôlée* being granted as far back as 1974. The bulk of the production is in the hands of the local co-operatives.

Producers of note

DOMAINE DES ANGES (MORMOIRON), DOMAINE DE CHAMPAGA (LE BARROUX), DOMAINE DE LA FERME SAINT-PIERRE (FLASSAN), DOMAINE DE FONDRÈCHE (MAZAN), DOMAINE DE FONT-SANS (GIGONDAS), PAUL JABOULET AINÉ (TAIN L'HERMITAGE), DOMAINE PERRIN (JONQUIÈRES), DOMAINE PESQUIÉ (MORMOIRON) AND DOMAINE LE VAN (BÉDOUIN).

CÔTES DU LUBÉRON

Surface Area (1998): 3756 ha.
Production (1998): (Red and rosé) 150,686 hl; (white) 30,251 hl.
Grape Varieties: (Red and rosé) Grenache Noir and Syrah, plus 10% allowed of lesser varieties already planted; (white) Grenache Blanc, Bourboulenc, Ugni Blanc and Vermentino (Rolle), plus Marsanne and Roussanne.
Maximum Yield: 55 hl/ha.
Minimum Alcoholic Level: 11°.

The Montagne de Lubéron and the Durance Valley, on the northern slopes of which lie the vineyards, may be deemed Haute-Provence, and on the other side of the valley lies the Coteaux d'Aix-en-Provence *appellation*. The *département*, however, is Vaucluse, and the area covered by the Lubéron *appellation* shares the Vin de Pays de Vaucluse with Côtes du Ventoux. French government statistics list Côtes du Lubéron under the Rhône.

The *appellation* covers some thirty communes stretching east of Cavaillon on the north or right bank of the river Durance towards Manosque. Eighty-five per cent of the production is red or rosé, from broadly the same grape varieties and under the same other regulations as that of Ventoux or generic Côtes du Rhône.

While the red and rosé are very similar wines, if a little leaner and fresher, to those of the Ventoux, it is the whites that attract interest. According to the latest

INAO regulations these whites, as elsewhere in the southern Rhône, must come from Clairette and Bourboulenc, with Grenache Blanc, Pascal Blanc, Roussette and Ugni Blanc as tolerated 'accessory' varieties. In practice, more and more Chardonnay is being planted for *vins de pays*. It flourishes on the chalky, limestone hills of the upper Lubéron, particularly away from the more alluvial soils of the valley floor and on higher ground east of Cadenet where the temperature does not rise to quite such high levels during the summer. In recent years this area has seen much investment from outside. But as yet, most of the wine is made by the local co-operatives.

Producers of note

CHÂTEAU LA CANORGUE (BONNIEUX), DOMAINE DE LA CITADELLE/YVES ROUSSET-ROUARD (MÉNERBES), DOMAINE DE MAYOL/BERNARD VIGUIER (APT), DOMAINE DE LA ROYÈRE /ANNE HUGUES (OPPÈDE), CHÂTEAU DE TOURETTES/JEAN-MARIE GUFFENS (APT), CHÂTEAU VAL JOANIS/CHANCEL FAMILY (PERTUIS) AND CHÂTEAU LA VERRERIE/DESCOURS FAMILY (PUGET).

COTEAUX DE PIERREVERT

Surface Area (1998): 315 ha.
Production (1998): (Red and rosé) 12,853 hl; (white) 1303 hl.
Grape Varieties: (Red and rosé) Carignan, Cinsault, Grenache Noir, Mourvèdre, Oeillade, Petite Syrah and Terret Noir; (white) Clairette, Grenache Blanc, Marsanne, Picpoul, Ugni Blanc, Vermentino and Roussanne.
Maximum Yield: 50 hl/ha.
Minimum Alcoholic Level: 11°.

Further upstream from the Côtes du Lubéron, across the boundary into the *département* of Alpes de Haute-Provence, scattered over some forty-two communes round the city of Manosque, lies the Coteaux de Pierrevert, elevated from VDQS to full *appellation contrôlée* in 1997. Most of the wine is rosé, and this seems to be the most successful style.

So far I have found the wines dull at best, but some of the local growers are now planting Cabernet Sauvignon and Chardonnay to add to the indigenous Rhône varieties, so one hopes for more interesting wines in the future.

Producers of note

DOMAINE LA BLAQUE AND DOMAINE DE RÉGUSSE (BOTH PIERREVERT).

CÔTES DU VIVARAIS

Surface Area (1998): 663 ha.
Production (1998): (Red and rosé) 19,859 hl; (white) 1380 hl.
Grape Varieties: (Red and rosé) Grenache Noir, Syrah, Cinsault, Carignan (Grenache & Syrah 90% minimum combined; Grenache minimum 30%; Syrah min. 40%); (white) Clairette, Grenache Blanc and Marsanne (all 75% maximum).
Maximum Yield: 50 hl/ha.
Minimum Alcohol Level: 10.5°.

A drive up the Ardèche Valley from Pont Saint-Esprit is a breathtaking journey. The Gorges de l'Ardèche vie with the canyons of the Tarn as the deepest and most spectacular in France. Up beyond the famous Pont d'Arc, the countryside becomes less dramatic and the large fertile valleys, some 100 to 250 metres above sea level, form the wine land of the Ardèche.

Twelve communes in the *département* of the Ardèche and two more south of the river itself in the Gard are entitled to the *appellation*, planted with Rhône varieties such as Grenache, Cinsault and Carignan. This is good, holiday quaffing *vin de l'année* stuff, similar to that made in the Ventoux or the Lubéron. Frankly the Vin de Pays de L'Ardèche is just as good, and marginally cheaper.

Producers of note

DOMAINE DE BELVEZET/LÉON BRUNEL (SAINT-REMÈZE), DOMAINE CHRISTIAN GALLATY (LES GRANGES-GONTARDES), DOMAINE DE VIGIER/DUPRÉ & FILS (LAGORCE) AND LES VIGNERONS ARDÈCHOIS (RUOMS).

VINS DE PAYS

Vin de Pays des Alpes-de-Haute-Provence

This is a departmental *vin de pays* from the upper Durance near Manosque. The wines are mainly red, with some white and a little rosé – from Grenache, Cinsault, Carignan and Ugni Blanc, plus a number of other varieties.

Vin de Pays de L'Ardèche

A departmental *vin de pays* for mainly red wines from Gamay and southern French varieties. There have been interesting recent developments with both Chardonnay and Viognier.

Vin de Pays des Collines Rhodaniennes

This zonal *vin de pays* covers all the northern Rhône. The wines are mainly red from Gamay and Syrah. The small amount of white comes from Marsanne.

Vin de Pays du Comté de Grignan

This is a zonal *vin de pays* from the Tricastin area. The wines are mainly Grenache-based reds, with a little rosé and white from traditional southern French varieties.

Vin de Pays des Coteaux des Baronnies

This zonal *vin de pays* comes from the area around Nyons. The wines are mainly Grenache-based reds.

Vin de Pays de La Drôme

This departmental *vin de pays* covers the eastern side of the Rhône Valley between Tricastin and Valence. The wines are mainly Grenache-based reds.

Vin de Pays de La Principauté d'Orange

A zonal *vin de pays* covering two areas in the Vaucluse *département* formerly within the Papal states, including Châteauneuf-du-Pape. The wines are mainly Grenache-based reds.

Vin de Pays du Vaucluse

A departmental *vin de pays* covering the eastern part of the southern Rhône and the Côtes du Ventoux region. The wines are mainly Grenache-based reds.

PROVENCE & CORSICA

FROM A WINE POINT OF VIEW, Provence is that part of south-eastern France bounded on the east and west by Italy and the Rhône delta and on the north and south by the Alps and the Mediterranean. It includes the Riviera and the Côte d'Azur as well as Cézanne's Montagne-Sainte-Victoire near Aix-en-Provence. It is Marseille and Nice and Aix and Draguignan. It is Bandol and Cassis, the tiny *appellations* of Bellet and Palette and the large ones of Côtes de Provence and Coteaux d'Aix-en-Provence. Away from the bustling seaside resorts, this is a wild and rugged country-side; blazing hot in summer, bleak in winter; a land of olive groves and *garrigues* – a scrub land of bramble and broom, of stunted oaks and pine, of rocky outcrops with wild thyme, oregano and rosemary; at its prettiest in May and June when the land is still green and not yet parched, when flowers bloom and butterflies dally. It is a countryside of contrast. Here an ultra-modern development by Le Corbusier out of Clockwork Orange; a few miles away, a crumbling brigand castle, a beat-up Romanesque church or a secluded monastery.

Yet it is also a fertile country. Between the coast and the mountains, near where the *autoroute* thunders between Avignon and Marseille or Menton, the land is lush and the soil abundant. This is ideal country for the vine, the sort of land and climate the plant found in Kurdistan when it was first cultivated by Neolithic man. The vine can withstand the long periods of drought it often encounters in Provence. Its roots dig deep for the moisture needed to see it through the arid summers. The wines, like the climate, have tended to be larger than life – full and robust, fiery and alcoholic. Today, tamed by man and with modern viticultural and vinification methods, often with the use of *cépages améliorateurs* such as Cabernet Sauvignon to supplement the indigenous Grenache, Mourvèdre and other varieties, the standard is rising. Wines of elegance and depth are being made.

Bandol, Cassis, Palette and Bellet are quality *appellations*, confined to small areas, while the others are more general, regional ones. All produce predominantly red wine, a certain amount of rosé, especially

in Côtes de Provence, but little white. The one exception is Cassis, a curious *appellation* for the South of France in that its fame, and the bulk of its production, is its dry white.

When to Drink the Wines

Modern methods of vinification and *élevage* have largely tamed the undue robustness and fiery solidity of Provence wines. The wines are better balanced. They have a better acidity which preserves the freshness of the fruit. And this fruit is not submerged under the 'size' of the wine. This means both that the wines are ready for drinking earlier and that they will keep better. With such a variation in style across the region – from the lightish wines of some of the producers in Coteaux d'Aix, such as Château Fonscolombe, to the serious examples made at the top levels in Bandol – it is unwise to generalise. The rosés and the few whites should be consumed early. Many reds are equally delicious in the summer or the following winter, early after the vintage. The best reds, obviously, are made for keeping. In principle, unless the wine, like those in Bandol, is largely Mourvèdre-based or unless it is essentially a Syrah or Cabernet Sauvignon wine, I would drink them earlier rather than later, as soon as they have softened up, and this means at the age of five years or so for a good Côtes de Provence.

There are, of course, exceptions. Bandol wines can require a decade or more to soften up and here the particular vintage is more important. Fine vintages for Provençal red wines include 1998, 1997, 1995, 1993, 1990, 1989, 1988, 1985, 1982, 1978, 1975, 1971 and 1970.

SURFACE AREA AND PRODUCTION (1998 HARVEST)

APPELLATIONS	SURFACE AREA (HA)	PRODUCTION (HL)	
		RED & ROSÉ	WHITE
BANDOL	1500	45,303	2161
CASSIS	172	1685	4197
PALETTE	28	989	471
BELLET	32	810	414
CÔTES DE PROVENCE	19,000	840,264	30,324
COTEAUX D'AIX-EN-PROVENCE	3300	78,553	3530
COTEAUX VAROIS	1800	30,611	1013
LES BAUX-DE-PROVENCE	150	8648	–
TOTAL	25,982	1,006,863	42,110
		1,048,673	

THE WINE REGIONS

BANDOL

Surface Area (1998): 1500 ha.
Production (1998): (Red and rosé) 45,303 hl; (white) 2161 hl.
Colour: Red, rosé and white.
Grape Varieties: (Red) Mourvèdre, Grenache and Cinsault, plus Syrah, Carignan, Tibouren and Calitor; (rosé) Mourvèdre, Grenache and Cinsault plus Syrah and Carignan; (white) Bourboulenc, Clairette and Ugni Blanc plus Sauvignon Blanc.
Maximum Yield: 40 hl/ha.
Minimum Alcohol Level: 11°.

About two-thirds of the way between Marseille and Toulon, just across the boundary between the Bouches-du-Rhône and Var *départements*, lies the Mediterranean town of Bandol, both a holiday resort and fishing village. Like Bordeaux, Bandol has given its name to the wines which hitherto were despatched through its port, and these wines can justly lay claim to being not only the best of Provence but the most interesting of the whole of southern France. Based on the Mourvèdre grape, Bandol reds are full, rich, firm and long-lasting, and as such have more in common with the Syrah wines of the northern Rhône than the Grenache-based wines of Châteauneuf-du-Pape. That they are cheaper

is an added advantage. Strangely, however, the wines of Bandol have not yet received the recognition they deserve. In my view they are serious wines that age and I am sure that anyone who has experienced a ten-year-old Bandol wine will enthusiastically echo this view. The difficulty is trying to lay your hands on that wine!

I have had a particular fondness for the wines of Bandol for many years. In 1964 I spent a few days in Bandol after a holiday further up the coast *en route* towards Bordeaux, where I was to spend several months. I can't remember who I saw or what I tasted, as I didn't keep notes then in the methodical way I do today, but I still remember the flavour of one old wine a grower offered me. The aroma was a combination of a fine cigar and the cooked fruit of an old tawny port; the colour was more like hot chocolate sauce than wine; and the aftertaste was both ethereal – nuances wafted around the back of one's throat like a swirl of silk ribbon – and powerful, enveloping one in a warm cloud of alcohol.

The vine is generally considered to have been first cultivated in France around 600 BC when Phoenician traders established an outpost at Marseille, bringing with them the techniques of tending the vine and fermenting the juice to make wine. The Phoenicians were succeeded by the Greeks and then by the Romans. By this time Bandol had already been colonised, Julius

Caesar mentions Tauroentum, the Latin version of the Phoenician Taurois. This is present-day Bandol, and evidence of considerable activity in wine production is found in the quantity of amphorae brought up from the sea-bed and two dolia, stone fermenting-vats, dating from the Roman epoch, discovered in the hinterland. The French historian Abbé Magloire Giraud has suggested that the famous wine of Marseille, well-known throughout the empire, might have been at least in part the wine of Bandol.

In the aftermath of the collapse of the Gallo-Roman civilisation, the Mediterranean coast was prey to barbaric invasion, Saracen occupation and spasmodic, more entrepreneurial harassment from pirates. The inhabitants retreated into their hilltop towns so familiar throughout Provence – the one at Le Castellet is of Roman origin. Eventually life grew easier and under local war-lord or ecclesiastical settlement, peace, at least for most of the time, returned to the vineyards. Documents throughout the Middle Ages attest to commercial and proprietorial vinous transactions and reveal not only that what was produced enjoyed a high reputation, but that wine dominated the economy of the whole of this area.

Bandol always seems to have been a full and sturdy wine. The local *seigneur*, Monsieur de Boyer-Bandol, in a petition he addressed to the king at the beginning of the seventeenth century remarks that 'these wines keep well, and even improve during long journeys'. He adds that he 'exports them in large quantities to the French Antilles'. We do not know the success of Monsieur de Boyer-Bandol's petition but about a century and a half later there are accounts of Bandol being consumed at Versailles. Louis XV and the royal family, according to 'reliable sources', drank *only* (my italics) carefully prepared wine from the Rouve district (a *lieu-dit* in the commune of Le Beausset).

When a sycophantic courtier asked the king to what he owed his 'everlasting youth', the 'much-loved' monarch is supposed to have replied: 'Why, from Rouve wine. It gives me all the vital sap and wits I need.' According to contemporary documents the amount of Bandol consumed at Versailles continued to increase throughout Louis XV's reign. For a wine which not only would have had to have been shipped the long way round via the Straits of Gibraltar to northern ports such as Rouen or Le Havre, but also would have been facing forceful competition from Burgundy, the Loire and Champagne, this is no mean achievement.

Following the Napoleonic wars, an average of 1200 ships called at the port of Bandol each year, shipping 60,000 to 65,000 hectolitres of wine annually (this is half as much again as the current AC production). The casks were branded with the letter B which is still the symbol of Bandol wines.

The first serious reference to the wine appeared at the end of the eighteenth century. In a book entitled *The Geography of Provence, the County of Avignon, the Principality of Orange and the County of Nice*, written by a Monsieur Achard and published in 1787, we find: 'The soil of Bandol is very dry and stony. Its main product is first quality red wine, the most highly prized (in the area) . . .' Another writer of the time states: 'The climate of Bandol and its vicinity is particularly mild and sheltered; its limestone soil containing a high proportion of carbonate of lime. The intensity of sunshine on its slopes (which the immediate proximity of the sea protects from winter frosts), the salt and the iodine present in the air, all contribute to make the wines of this locality that famous product which the Provençal poets called 'bottled sunshine'. 'These wines have the consistency, bouquet and finesse appreciated by connoisseurs who look for true quality rather than the name on the label. They sum up quite simply the real virtues of the Provençal soil and its products: honesty, finesse and ardour.' You could echo this sentiment two centuries on today.

In 1816 the writer André Jullien placed the wines of Bandol among his *deuxième classe*: ' .... very deep colour, plenty of alcohol . . . full-flavoured, they keep well and acquire quality on ageing or being sent on a long sea-voyage'. Thereafter the wines seem to have gone into decline as far as the world at large was concerned. Oidium in the late 1860s followed by phylloxera in the early 1870s totally destroyed the Bandol vineyards and the area only recovered slowly in the difficult economic climate which followed. According to P Morton Shand in

PROVENCE

ALPES-
MARITIMES

Nice

St-Romain-
de-Bellet

Villars-sur-Var

VAR

VAUCLUSE

BOUCHES-
DU-RHÔNE

Marseille

Toulon

MEDITERRANEAN SEA

ILES D'HYÈRES

Ile de Porquerolles

Seillans

La Motte
Le Muy

Fréjus
St-Raphaël

Roquebrune-
sur-Argens

St-Tropez

La Faux
Gassin

Callas

Villecroze

Draguignan
Flayosc
Lorgues

Salernes

Cotignac

Châteauvert

Les-Arcs-
sur-Argens

Cabasse

Le Luc

Le Cannet-des-Maures

La Garde-
Freinet

Grimaud

Bormes-Les-
Mimosas

Le Lavandou

La Verrerie

La Londe-
des-Maures

Collobrières

Tavernes

Brignoles

Besse-
sur-Issole
Flassans

Pignans

La Roquebrussanne

Meounes-
Les-Montrieux

Solliès-Pont

La Crau

Hyères

Cuers

Esparron

Puyloubier

St-Maximin-
Ste-Baume

Nans-Les-Pins

Le Camp-
du-Castellet

Ste-Anne d'Evenos

Beausset

Ollioules

Rions
Vauvenargues

Jouques

Meyrargues

Aix-en-
Provence

Le Tholonet

Trets
St-Zacharie

Meyreuil

Allauch

La Cadière
d'Azur

Le Beausset
Ste-Anne du Castellet

Le Castellet

St-Cyr-
sur-Mer

Bandol

Le Puy-
Ste-Réparade

St-Cannat

Puyricard

Éguilles

Palette

Cassis

La Ciotat

Mazargues

Mallemont

Lambesc

La Fare-
les-Oliviers

Vitrolles

Rognac

Vernègues

Lançon

Istres

Etang
de
Berre

Martigues

Salon-
de-Provence

Eygalières

Mouriès

St-Rémy
Les Baux

Ste-Etienne-
du-Grès

Avignon

Arles

MARITIMES

Valence
Paris
Marseille
Provence

Appellations
- Côtes de Provence
- Les Baux-de-Provence
- Coteaux d'Aix-en-Provence
- Palette
- Coteaux Varois
- Cassis
- Bandol
- Bellet
- Department boundary

N

30km
20miles
0
0

A *Book of Wine* (1926), the most that could be said of Bandol (and a few other Provençal wines) was that they were 'the best of a bad lot'.

Nevertheless, a few pioneering spirits soldiered on, led by Monsieur Peyraud of Domaine Tempier and Monsieur Estienne of La Laidière. When the Comité National des Appellations d'Origine was set up in 1935, these Bandol growers were quick to respond. They established their own Syndicat de Producteurs des Vins d'Appellation d'Origine Contrôlée Bandol and between them set up laws which came into effect on 11 November 1941. With Cassis and the tiny vineyard areas of Palette and Bellet these were Provence's first AC wines.

The Bandol vineyards lie a few kilometres inland from the coast and run round in a sort of natural amphitheatre formed by a semi-circle of hills, the slopes of which overlook the motorway in the valley floor. Only these slopes are authorised for *appellation contrôlée* Bandol; the valley is merely *vin de pays*, and the 1500-odd hectares currently in production (getting on for double what it was twenty years ago) extend over eight communes. La Cadière d'Azur and Le Castellet are the principal centres; the communes of Bandol and Sanary and in part Le Beausset, Saint-Cyr-sur-Mer, Ollioules and Evenos are also authorised. Starting from the Golfe des Lecques in the west, rising to the Plateau du Camp and then curving towards Le Beausset, the boundary of the production area follows the N8, crosses the Gorges d'Ollioules and runs back to the sea along the river Reppe, ending to the east of Sanary.

Almost all this area consists of silico-calcareous soil, a complex mixture of flints, calcareous sandstone and sandy marl, lying on a harder rock of the same composition. The land is arid and well drained, and the vines, enclosed and protected by the hills behind them which rise up to a height of 400 metres, face towards the south and enjoy sunshine from morning to night. They receive more sunshine than any other locality on the French Riviera (3000 hours per annum). The views from some of the hilltop wineries or *bastides* (Provençal manor houses) are breathtaking. Red and rosé wines must be made from a minimum of 50 per cent Mourvèdre. In practice the percentage for the rosé is (unofficially of course) often less and that for the red is between 60 per cent and 70 per cent, in some cases 100 per cent. Even in the most prolific years Bandol's production rarely surpasses the maximum permitted yield of 40 hectolitres per hectare, plus *plafond limite de classement*.

When young red Bandol is well coloured, moderately high in alcohol and rather dense and unforthcoming. Frankly, it is rather aggressively solid, even a touch bitter, and seems to lack both richness and generosity. It must be kept for a minimum of eighteen months in wood before bottling. With time, in a successful vintage, it will mellow, acquire complexity, warmth, flesh and concentration. But it does need time. Mature Mourvèdre and therefore mature Bandol – a wine of ten-plus years of age – has a black fruit flavour: black cherries, blackberries and bilberries mixed with truffles, liquorice, cinnamon and a hint of peonies. Even when fully evolved and fully ripe there is an element of austerity though, a hint of masculinity. But so there is, in a different way, in a fine Pauillac.

Grenache and Cinsault are the other varieties for the red and rosé wines, the former adding a bit of warmth and alcohol in its robust and rather boorish way and the latter a touch of acidity and freshness. For the white wines Clairette, Bourboulenc and Ugni Blanc are the standard varieties and Sauvignon Blanc is also authorised. In practice it is the increasing use of Sauvignon which is helping to produce something less oily, heavy and 'southern' than the wines of yesteryear. Today Bandol produces about 45,000 hectolitres per annum of which perhaps 40 per cent is red and most of the rest rosé. The white wine production is about half that of nearby Cassis.

Fine Bandol vintages include 1998, 1997, 1995, 1993, 1990, 1989, 1988, 1985, 1982, 1978, 1975, 1971 and 1970.

Leading Bandol Producers

DOMAINE DE LA BASTIDE BLANCHE
Commune: Le Castellet.
Owner: Michel Bronzo.
Surface Area under Vine: 28 ha.
Wines: Bandol red, rosé and white.

In 1980 or so, looking for a Bandol to import on an exclusive basis, I selected Louis and Michel Bronzo's Sainte-Anne-de-Castellet domaine. Twenty years on, judging by comprehensive tastings made in 1997, I made a sensible choice. All their wines scored very well indeed.

The Bronzos arrived in 1970, reconstituted the vineyard, progressively planting more and more Mourvèdre (some red *cuvées* today contain 95 per cent) and installing a modern, temperature-controlled cellar. The vines are looked after biologically, with a particular attention to the *tri* at the time of the vintage. This is carried out three times: by the picker, by the person who fills the small plastic cases in which the grapes are transported to the winery, and on reception there on a *table de tri*.

One thing I remember from the early 1980s is that although there was then only one red wine, the *foudres* in the centre of the cellar always tasted better than those (exposed to the draught) at either end. Today there are three bottlings: the classic, a 'Longue Garde' and Cuvée Fontanieu, this latter usually being 95 per cent Mourvèdre. The top two *cuvées* are bottled unfiltered.

★ DOMAINES BUNAN, MOULIN DES COSTES, MAS DE LA ROUVIÈRE

Commune: La Cadière d'Azur.
Owners: Bunan family.
Surface Area under Vine: 77 ha.
Wines: Bandol red and Vin de Pays de Mont Caume-Cabernet Sauvignon.

The brothers Paul and Pierre Bunan left Algeria in 1961 and made their first vintage at the 25-hectare Moulin des Costes in 1966. Two years later they acquired the 29-hectare Mas de La Rouvière (the name Château La Rouvière is reserved for special *cuvées* in superior vintages) and they now also farm the Domaine de La Belouvre. The wines are kept separate – Moulin des Costes lies near La Cadière-d'Azur while Mas de La Rouvière is located on the other side of the valley and *autoroute* near Le Plan du Castellet – but vinification is centralised at the up-to-date, temperature-controlled Moulin des Costes.

Laurent Bunan, who lives with his wife in a modern mansion with a 360 degree view above the vineyards, has now joined his father Paul and is in charge of the winemaking.

This is a modern, go-ahead set up, consistently producing very good wines. The red Château La Rouvière, made entirely from fifty-year-old Mourvèdre vines adjoining the Peyraud's Tourtine vineyard (see Domaine Tempier page 389), is distinctly fine.

DOMAINE LAFRAN-VEYROLLES

Commune: La Cadière d'Azur.
Owner: Madame Claude Jouve-Férec.
Surface Area under Vine: 10 ha.
Wines: Bandol red, including Cuvée Classique and Cuvée Spéciale, rosé and white.

This is a domaine which can trace its history back to the seventeenth century, yet has only recently come to the forefront as a producer of good Bandol. The estate is the property of Mme Claude Jouve-Férec who makes the wine. Her husband looks after the vineyard. Like many neighbouring domaines all chemical products are banned. There are two red wine *cuvées*: the Cuvée Classique (from 80 per cent destemmed grapes) and the Cuvée Spéciale labelled Longue Garde (from 95 per cent Mourvèdre and non-destemmed).

★ CHÂTEAU DE PIBARNON

Commune: La Cadière d'Azur.
Owner: Comte Henri de Saint-Victor.
Surface Area under Vine: 45 ha.
Wines: Bandol red, rosé and white.

Comte Henri de Saint-Victor and his wife bought Pibarnon in 1977, restored both château and vineyard and now produce one of the very best red Bandols. The vines lie on some of the highest slopes of the *appellation*, at the end of a long sinuous road now also the approach to a large number of holiday houses. Curiously, here, as Comte Henri will enthusiastically explain to you, the bedrock has buckled, so that soil from secondary era, the Triassic, lies on top of that of the later tertiary era.

The château itself is a substantial Renaissance-style edifice, with thirteenth-century origins. Deep into the hills behind lie the cellars. There is only one *cuvée* of each wine, the red being 95 per cent Mourvèdre with 5 per cent Grenache. It is meaty, opulent and classy, and has consistently been among the top three red Bandols for the last twenty years.

CHÂTEAU PRADEAUX
Commune: Saint-Cyr-sur-Mer.
Owner: Comtesse de Portalis.
Surface Area under Vine: 18 ha.
Wines: Bandol red and rosé .

Château Pradeaux has belonged to the Portalis family since 1752. Today owned by the Comtesse Arlette and run by her nephew and adopted heir Cyril it remains – as it has done since I first encountered the wine in the 1970s – one of Bandol's enigmas.

The red is vinified almost entirely from Mourvèdre with some Grenache, without destemming in concrete vats in a very dirty cellar. At the outset the wine is dense, solid and seems stewed to death. Yet underneath there is undeniably good fruit. After ten years, provided the vintage has ripened the stems as well as the grapes, the ugly duckling then becomes a swan. It will then keep for another two decades.

★★ DOMAINE TEMPIER
Commune: Le Plan du Castellet.
Owners: Jean-Marie and François Peyraud.
Surface Area under Vine: 28.5 ha.
Wines: Bandol red, including Cuvée Spéciale, Migoua, Tourtine and Cabassaou, white and rosé.

The Peyraud family have been the driving force behind Bandol for so long that it is hard to imagine the area without them. Their domaine has the leading reputation and their wines command the highest prices. This attracts a little jealous commentary from some less fortunate neighbours but it seems to wash over the Peyrauds' heads and they are some of the most openly welcoming and charming people in the area.

Lucien Peyraud married Lucie (Lulu) Tempier in 1940, just before *appellation contrôlée* was bestowed on Bandol, and was largely instrumental in persuading the authorities to focus increasingly on Mourvèdre. He died in 1997 and has been succeeded by his sons Jean-Marie and François. The domaine, rich in old vines, produces

three special *cuvées*: Migoua, from a plot on top of the hill near the old church of Le Beausset, a wine of real elegance; Tourtine, a south-facing hillside site, with more Mourvèdre in the blend; and Cabassaou, 100 per cent Mourvèdre. The wines spend thirty months in *foudres* of various sizes before bottling, without fining or filtration. This is Bandol at its very best: rich, profound and very long-lasting.

DOMAINE DE LA VIVONNE
Commune: Le Castellet.
Owner: Walter Gilpin.
Surface Area under Vine: 25 ha.
Wines: Bandol red and white.

The Domaine de La Vivonne dates from 1956, when William Gilpin married Josette Lantéri, and acquired a neighbouring vineyard to add to that belonging to his father-in-law. It was not until 1979, however, that a cellar was constructed and the wine was vinified on the property. Today Walter Gilpin, son of the late William, is in charge and he produces a ripe, elegant, balanced, cedar-woody red Bandol, from 100 per cent Mourvèdre, which matures in the medium term. The basic wine, called Cuvée Spéciale, is also noteworthy and will last well. Finally, the Peyrauds produce one of the few rosés which is more profound than the average Côtes de Provence rosé. This will keep for two to three years.

Other Producers of note
DOMAINE BÉGUDE/VINCENT RACINE (LE CAMP-DU-CASTELLET), DOMAINE DU CAGUELOUP/PREBOST FAMILY (SAINT-CYR-SUR-MER), DOMAINE DE FRÉGATE/JEAN DE PISSY (SAINT-CYR-SUR-MER), CHÂTEAU DE LA NOBLESSE/ JEAN-PIERRE GAUSSEN (LA CADIÈRE-D'AZUR), DOMAINE DE L'OLIVETTE/DUMOUTIER FAMILY (SAINT-CYR-SUR-MER), DOMAINE RAY-JANE/RAYMOND CONSTANT (LE PLAN-DU-CASTELLET), LA ROQUE CO-OPERATIVE (THE BETTER CUVEES), CHÂTEAU SAINTE-ANNE/FRANÇOIS DUTHEIL DE LA ROCHÈRE (SAINTE-ANNE-D'EVENOS), DOMAINE DE TERREBRUNE/REYNOLD DELILLE (OLLIOULES), DOMAINE DE LA TOUR DE BON/MADAME HOCQUARD (LE BRÛLAT-DU-CASTELLET) AND CHÂTEAU VANNIÈRES/MME BOISSEAUX (LA CADIÈRE-D'AZUR).

CASSIS

Surface Area (1998): 172 ha.
Production (1998): (Red and rosé) 1685 hl; (white)
4197 hl.
Colour: Red, rosé and white.
Grape Varieties: (Red and rosé) Mourvèdre,
Grenache, Cinsault plus Carignan, Barbaroux,
Terret Noir; (white) Marsanne, Clairette, Ugni
Blanc, Sauvignon Blanc, Bourboulenc
(or Doucillon), Pascal Blanc, Terret Blanc.
Maximum Yield: 45 hl/ha.
Minimum Alcohol Level: 11°.

Elsewhere in this book (see page 440) I discuss Limoux, a Midi white wine region which is changing with the times to meet modern demands. In contrast the Cassis *appellation* is static and hidebound, the wine expensive and uninteresting. Some movement in the right direction can be discerned, but I fear that the changes are being made too slowly and too late.

Fifteen kilometres west of Bandol is the smaller and prettier fishing village of Cassis, pronounced without the final 's', to distinguish it from the blackcurrant liqueur. Cassis, like much of the Mediterranean coast, is in danger of losing its charm. A generation or two ago artists could afford to live and work there. Today it is a very self-conscious, mini-Saint-Tropez, full of expensive yachts with sugar daddies and their bimbos. East of Cassis overhangs the 360-metre Cap Canaille, the tallest cliff in France. Above and behind, up in the hills, precariously surviving in the midst of the continual expansion of holiday homes, a few brave souls continue to produce the wine of Cassis.

Vines are said to have been introduced to Cassis by a refugee Florentine family named Albrizzi in 1520, and from the start it seems to have been the white wine that caught on. This is doubly odd: it is hard to imagine that a Tuscan white grape (surely not the ubiquitous Trebbiano or Ugni Blanc) could have excited the Cassis farmers and their customers; and why a white wine? Ninety-nine per cent of the produce of the Midi is red or rosé. What isn't is usually a *vin doux naturel*. Perhaps, as

suggested by the American wine merchant Kermit Lynch, the wine was produced simply to provide a suitable accompaniment for the local fish soup, *bouillabaisse*.

Nevertheless it was the white wine which made Cassis famous. The wine writer, André Jullien (*Topographie de tous les Vignobles Connus*, 1816) is ignorant of any red wine. The Cassis whites, he states, are the best of the region and are three times as expensive as the local reds. He describes them as *liquoreux* i.e. sweet; while a contemporary document quoted by Philippe Muguier in *Vins de Provence* says, 'Les vins blancs de Cassis jouissent d'une certaine réputation; ils sont secs et très spiritueux.' – 'the white wines of Cassis enjoy a certain reputation; they are dry and very alcoholic'. Perhaps they were both right. The writer, M A Saurel, surveying the devastation at the height of the phylloxera epidemic sixty years later, writes of the highly regarded dry, white wine and the Muscat Noir, an amber-coloured sweet wine.

The best place to find Cassis, even today, is in the locality itself. Naturally it is the wine for the local *bouillabaisse* and *bourride*, as well as other seafood and shellfish dishes. Only recently has the wine begun to find its way outside the region as well as abroad.

The vineyards form an amphitheatre up and behind the village. The steeply sloping terraces are largely calcareous, consisting of various marls or limestone rock strewn with boulders. Up here there is a regular breeze which tempers the summer heat and drought, for this is one of the most arid parts of France, rain only falling in two brief periods, spring and late autumn. While the grape varieties are similar to Bandol, it is the white wine which holds sway, producing 65 per cent of the *appellation*. Clairette, giving freshness, and Marsanne, giving depth and class, are the favoured varietals, which together must make up 60 per cent of the white blend by 2005, of which 30 per cent must be Marsanne.

The reds and rosés of Cassis are almost indistinguishable from the lighter and lesser Bandols: very few show any real distinction. The white wine, however, is the flagship, and this is more serious, though not fermented and matured in oak, which is to its commercial disadvantage. The character is herbal and flowery, of medium weight, with reasonable freshness. Malolactic fermentation takes place after which it is held for six to nine months before bottling. The wines are intended for early consumption. Sadly I have to say that I find Cassis white wine expensive for what it is and essentially rather boring. It is the fault of the grape varieties used. The *appellation* should dispense altogether with neutral second division varieties such as the Ugni and perhaps insist on a more rapid transformation to a predominantly Marsanne-based *encépagement*.

Apart from the producers below there are only ten other members of the Syndicat des Vignerons de Cassis.

Leading Cassis Producers

DOMAINE DE LA FERME BLANCHE
Owner: François Paret.
Surface Area under Vine: 30 ha.
Wines: Cassis red, rosé and white including Blanc de Blancs and Cuvée Spéciale.

François Paret's family domaine is one of the few in Cassis to employ a trained oenologist, Philippe Garnier, and this must be a key to its success. As elsewhere in Cassis, 70 per cent of the wine is white, and there are two *cuvées* – the Blanc de Blancs (from 50 per cent each Clairette and Marsanne) has complex flowery fruit and a good nutty depth. The Cuvée Spéciale contains 70 per cent Marsanne and is even finer. Both are produced using a pneumatic press and matured in a temperature-controlled cellar.

CHATEAU DE FONTCREUSE
Owner: Jean-François Brando.
Surface Area under Vine: 19.5 ha.
Wines: Cassis rosé and white.

Jean-François Brando is the owner of one of the top Cassis domaines, lying on a north-facing slope – and so avoiding the full heat of the summer which is a good thing for white wine – on the road to La Ciotat. The wines are vinified, after *débourbage*, in stainless steel tanks thermo-regulated at 18°C. The rosés are bottled after six months, the whites after twelve. There is a soft, fruity-flowery character to the Fontcreuse white which shows the high proportion of Marsanne (up to 60 per cent).

CLOS SAINTE-MAGDELEINE
Owners: François & Georgina Sack-Zafiropulo.
Surface Area under Vine: 9 ha.
Wines: Cassis rosé and white.

Clos Sainte-Magdeleine has belonged to the Zafiropulo family since 1922 and is perhaps the best known of the Cassis estates. François Sack and his wife, Georgina Sack-Zafiropulo are the owners today. The extraordinary Art Deco-style château lies under the Cap Canaille, facing the bay of Cassis, with the vineyards on the slopes behind it. The white Clos Sainte-Magdeleine (one-third Marsanne, Clairette and Ugni Blanc) is firmer and fuller than most and lasts well.

PALETTE

Surface Area (1998): 28 ha.
Production (1998): (Red and rosé) 989 hl; (white) 471 hl.
Colour: Red, rosé and white.
Grape Varieties: (Red and rosé) Grenache, Mourvèdre and Cinsault, plus Castet, Manosquin, Syrah, Carignan, Muscat Noir and Cabernet Sauvignon; (white) Clairette, Bourboulenc, Ugni Blanc, Grenache Blanc and Muscat Blanc.
Maximum Yield: 40 hl/ha.
Minimum Alcohol Level: 11°.

Palette, situated on calcareous soil in Meyreuil, an eastern suburb of Aix-en-Provence, is an obscure *appellation*, the smallest in Provence. Its reputation, such as it is, is almost entirely based on one estate, Château Simone. Prior to 1987, the wine of the other main domaine, Château Crémade, was sold in bulk to a *négociant* in Rognes, and the end wine was innocuous but dull. A change of generation here has taken things in hand.

Moreover, a number of local small farmers have discovered that some of their land is entitled to the Palette *appellation*, and are starting to bottle their own wine separately for the first time instead of selling it off in bulk. Like many other southern French *appellations*, Grenache, Mourvèdre and Cinsault have to provide 80 per cent of the red blend and Clairette 80 per cent of the white.

Leading Palette Producer

Château Simone
Commune: Meyreuil.
Owner: René Rougier.
Surface Area under Vine: 16 ha.
Wines: Palette red, rosé and white.

Hard by the *autoroute* as it leaves Aix-en-Provence for Nice, located in a natural north-facing amphitheatre and worked biologically, lies Château Simone. René Rougier is the seventh generation of a family which has owned this estate, once a Carmelite monastery, since the early 1800s. The low-yielding vines are sixty years old on average and the vintage arrives late here, a fortnight after that of Bandol. After destemming, the red grapes are vinified together. The wine is then aged in a mixture of vats and casks for two years before bottling.

Even the white wine (from 90 per cent Clairette), which rarely undergoes malolactic fermentation, is aged for a year or more.

Approximately half of Château Simone's crop is red wine, 30 per cent rosé and 20 per cent white. The red varies: sometimes it can be soft, the tannins ripe but otherwise it can be tough. Given that it is quite expensive I would suggest it is only worth it in the best of vintages (1998, 1997, 1995, 1993, 1990, 1989, 1985, 1982 and 1978). Then we have a wine more akin to Châteauneuf-du-Pape than Bandol, but with a distinct acidity. In the lesser vintages the wine's fullness becomes unnecessary bulk. It is a bit hard. The rosé is unremarkable, a sort of dilute red. But the white can be interesting, intriguingly woody and maturing into something resembling a white Hermitage – despite the *encépagement*: not a bit 'southern' in style. All in all, though – as this is really the only serious wine estate of the *appellation*, and always has been – one wonders why the *appellation* authorities bothered in the first place.

Other Producer of note
Château Crémade/Christine Vidalin (Le Thonolet).

Bellet

Surface Area (1998): 32 ha.
Production (1998): (Red and rosé) 810 hl; (white) 414 hl.
Colour: Red, rosé and white.
Grape Varieties: (Red and rosé) Braquet, Folle Noire, Grenache and Cinsault; (white) Rolle and Chardonnay.
Maximum Yield: 40 hl/ha.
Minimum Alcohol Level: (Red and rosé) 10.5°; (white) 11°.

The Pays de Nice have been wrangled over for centuries, from the cousins Charles, one of Anjou, the other Prince of Naples in the fourteenth century, via Catherine Ségurant in the sixteenth century, a local peasant woman who mooned at Barbarossa (a Barbary pirate whose fleet captured Nice in 1543), to the counts of Savoy. Though briefly seized by the first Napoleon, it was not until the plebiscite of 1860 that Nice became permanently incorporated into France. And in 1947 the Tende region to the north was transferred from Italy allowing the French boundary to continue to its natural frontier, the centre of the ridge of the Mediterranean Alps.

As a consequence the wines of Bellet are a mixture: of French and Italian, similar in their own way to the wines of Corsica. For the red wine the base is the Braquet (*not* the same, as some would suggest, as the Brachetto of Piedmont). This is blended with the Folle Noire and the Grenache, with Cinsault being used for the rosé. The result is a wine on the one hand suggesting the southern Rhône – the soft raspberry peppery spice of the Grenache – and on the other the tar and roses of Piedmont.

The white wines are more interesting. Here we can have a wine of real seriousness, as well as one with the capability to last. The basic grape is the Rolle, otherwise known as the Vermentino. Until recently this was confined to Bellet and Corsica. Now it is found throughout the Midi from the Côtes de Provence to the Côtes du Roussillon, and its presence is one of the explanations behind the rise in interest of dry white Midi wines.

Together with up to 20 per cent Chardonnay – the law permits 40 per cent but if you were to use this much the wine would taste of pure Chardonnay – and a modicum of new oak, it makes an intriguingly new and satisfying blend, with a flavour of plums and quinces and a herbal suggestion of white Hermitage, while being underpinned by the oak and the nuttiness of the Chardonnay. The acidity level is nice and high (malolactic fermentation is usually discouraged). Like the wines of the Rhône it is delicious young and can be fine after a decade, but goes into an adolescent phase in the middle. It would be further improved if it was always fermented in oak, and if these casks were reasonably new: not the excessive oakiness of some Australian and Californian Chardonnays, nor that of *grand cru* Burgundy, but just a recognisable touch.

The vines of Bellet are neatly arranged with Cordon du Royat precision on the precipitous hillsides of one or two of a number of pre-Alp hills which point fingers out of the mountains down towards Nice. We are immediately to the east of the river Var. The soil is a grey silico-calcaire, a gritty mixture of mainly sand, together with limestone debris, into which are impacted pudding-stones as large as cricket balls.

The land is terraced, planted with a wild wheat variety of rough grass to avoid erosion, and jealously guarded against the ever-present pressure of being absorbed into yet another housing estate of holiday homes or obliterated under another *autoroute* to relieve the congested traffic along the coast.

Of perhaps 600 hectares of officially delimited land there are today a little over 30 hectares under vines, producing about 1200 hectolitres of wine, split roughly in thirds between the three colours.

Leading Bellet Producers

★ Château de Bellet
Commune: Saint-Roman-de-Bellet.
Owner: Ghislain de Charnacé.
Surface Area under Vine: 10 ha.
Wines: Bellet red, rosé and white including Baron G Cuvée.

The leading estate in the *appellation* was inherited by Ghislain de Charnacé's father Bernard, through his wife, descendants of the old Counts of Bellet. The red wine is made entirely from Braquet, produced by *sélection massalle* from the domaine's own vines. The grapes are destemmed, vinified in enamelled steel and stored in barrels of 450 litres (double the size of a Bordeaux hogshead), some of which are new. It is bottled after two years and in the best vintages such as 1990 and 1995 ready three or four years after that.

There are two white *cuvées*. The basic wine is made without any oak and sold in a clear Bordeaux bottle. The Baron G *cuvée*, only produced in the best vintages and from 100 per cent Rolle, is sold in a dumpy bottle. The wine spends a year in wood of which two-thirds are new. Both wines are good. The whole range is bottled with a minimum of sulphur and makes admirable food wines. Yet they also keep well. However, I would like to see Ghislain de Charnacé give all his whites the oak treatment.

Château de Crémat
Commune: Saint-Roman-de-Bellet.
Surface Area under Vine: 10 ha.
Wines: Bellet red, rosé and white.
At present a questionmark hangs over the future of the Château de Crémat, which, together with the Château de Bellet, used to be one of only two estates in the area. Now there are perhaps another half dozen smaller estates also making wine. Ex-proprietor Charles Bagnis, whose family had dealt with the wine when they were wholesalers, before acquiring the domaine in 1957, sold both Crémat and the merchant business in 1996 and at the time of writing, the estate is up for sale again.

In contrast to Château de Bellet, the red Château de Crémat in Bagnis's day was made from a blend of 60 per cent Folle Noire, 20 per cent Braquet and 20 per cent Grenache, while the rosé contained 60 per cent Braquet, 20 per cent Grenache and 20 per cent Cinsault. Moreover, while Château de Bellet red is bottled after two years, Château Crémat was kept in bulk as much as a further two years after that. Again, it is the white which is the most interesting, and this at Crémat used to always be a gently oaky wine. We shall wait and see what changes take place at the domaine in the future.

Other Producers of note

CLOS DOU BAILE/LUDOVIC CAMBILLO DOU BAÏLE, SCEA LES COTEAUX DE BELLET/HÉLÈNE CALVIERA, DOMAINE LA FOLOGAR/JEAN SPIZZO, CLOS SAINT-VINCENT/JOSEPH SERGI & ROLAND SICARDI AND DOMAINE DE LA SOURCE/JACQUES DALMASSO (ALL AT OR NEAR SAINT-ROMAN-DE-BELLET).

CÔTES DE PROVENCE

Surface Area (1998): 19,000 ha.
Production (1998): (Red and rosé) 840,264 hl; (white) 30,324 hl.
Colour: Red, rosé and white.
Grape Varieties: (Red and rosé) Grenache, Syrah, Cinsault, Mourvèdre, Tibouren, plus Cabernet Sauvignon and Carignan; (white) Rolle, Semillon, Ugni Blanc and Clairette.
Maximum Yield: 55 hl/ha.
Minimum Alcohol Level: 11°.

Threequarters of all Provençal wine – an average total of 100 million bottles a year – is bottled as *appellation contrôlée* Côtes de Provence. Of this 75 per cent is rosé, 20 per cent red and 5 per cent white. This is, therefore, not just the main generic *appellation* for the region, but probably (French statistics do not differentiate between red and rosé) the most important rosé *appellation* in the country.

Quite why Provence should have started to produce rosé in such volume – for it is a post-Second Word War phenomenon – while the Roussillon and the Languedoc did not, not only does no-one seem to know, no one seems to have addressed.

Nevertheless with modern methods of temperature control of the fermentation and a generally very dry and sunny climate producing ripe, healthy grapes, a delicious to look at, pale salmon pink, fruity, balanced, dry wine is produced and sold in the unmistakable 'Brigitte Bardot' curvaceous bottle which is almost entirely consumed on the spot by the locals and the hundreds of thousands of tourists who flock into the region every summer. Such Provence wine which is exported, and it is rather less than that of the Languedoc/Roussillon, is mainly red.

The Côtes de Provence area stretches from Aix-en-Provence and Marseilles in the west to Saint-Raphaël and Lake Saint-Cassien in the east, a distance of about 120 kilometres; but is interrupted by a gap containing the Coteaux Varois *appellation* in the middle, north and south of the *autoroute* between Saint-Maximin-La-Sainte-Baume and Brignoles. There are five district sub-regions, each with its own terroir and mesoclimate.

Côtes de Provence sub-regions

1. The area on the southern and eastern slopes of the Massif de Sainte-Victoire. The soil here is argillaceous sandstone on a limestone rock base.
2. Le Beausset basin, south of the Montagne de Sainte-Baume, between Cassis and Bandol. This is largely chalky-limestone.
3. The 'Vallée Intérieure'. This follows the *autoroute* that skirts the Maures mountains between Toulon and Le Muy: sandy clay and marl from the Palaeozoic era.
4. The coastal region from Toulon via the Saint-Tropez peninsular and along to Saint-Raphaël. These are ancient schistous and granitic soils.
5. The hills of the 'Haut Pays' north of the A8 *autoroute* between Brignoles and the Lac de Saint-Cassien. Here again the soil is calcareous on a limestone rock base.

In general the soils are stony and well-drained, poor in nitrogenous matter, and therefore suitable for cultivating the vine. The weather is also beneficial. This is a dry and warm part of France, with, on average, a mere 600mm of rain annually, falling mainly in the late autumn and in the spring, when it will encourage growth in the vine. The cold, dry Mistral is frequently present, especially in the western part of the region, and this evaporates moisture, helping the vine protect itself against disease.

As a consequence of this largely risk-free climate, a great many Provençal vineyards are now worked ecologically or biologically, without recourse to chemical fertilisers, insect sprays or herbicides. In contrast to the increasingly dead and polluted sea nearby, the land is healthy and full of micro-flora and micro-fauna.

Côtes de Provence red wines can be expensive – or seem so in comparison with those of the Languedoc and Roussillon – but they start out with a major advantage, the appearance of Cabernet Sauvignon in the recommended list of grape varieties. Cabernet Sauvignon, Syrah and Grenache, in various proportions and now with a modicum of new oak for the Réserve *cuvées* is the recipe for much Côtes de Provence. Mourvèdre is often used instead of Syrah in the hottest mesoclimates nearest to the coast where it can ripen properly. Provençal reds are harder to find outside the region than those of the Languedoc.

The rosés, produced by a *saignée* after 12 to 24 hours' maceration and with or without malolactic fermentation according to choice, can be very delicious, and they do travel, contrary to what exporters might think. But they are too expensive to compete with cheap blush and for some reason, while white and red present no problem, the consumer is loath to spend much money on a rosé wine.

The standard of the white wines has improved enormously since the arrival of modern winemaking methods. Today's whites are increasingly made from the two quality varieties: Sémillon and Rolle. Fifty-fifty blends, vinified in oak – and then often with the malolactic fermentation having taken place – or in tank regulated at 18°C, and the malolactic fermentation blocked (today the choice and the control rests with the winemaker) are the rule rather than the exception, and many are admirable. I find them of much greater interest than the whites of Cassis. It does however take a little extra dedication to produce fine white wine. In the Provençal sun the grapes race to maturity in September, and the window of perfect picking opportunity is in any case narrower for white grapes than red. What I drink on my annual summer holiday in the region is the rosé. They are not serious wines but are fun to drink.

Côtes de Provence Vintages
1997, 1995, 1993 (provided one picked early), 1990 (excellent), 1989, 1988, 1985, 1982 and 1978.

Leading Côtes de Provence Producers

CHÂTEAU BARBEIRANNE
Commune: Pignans.
Owner: François Sonniez.
Surface area under Vine: 29 ha.
Wines: Côtes de Provence red, including Cuvée Charlotte, rosé and white.

Lying on stony, clay-limestone soil in the Vallée Intérieure Château Barbeiranne produces a fullish, generous but slightly earthy basic red wine and a rather more superior one called Cuvée Charlotte. This is Cabernet Sauvignon- and Syrah-based and aged in small oak. There are Cuvées Spéciales also vinified and aged in wood for the other colours.

MAS DE CADENET
Commune: Trets.
Owner: Guy Négrel.
Surface area under Vine: 50 ha.
Wines: Côtes de Provence red including Cuvée Mas Negrel Prestige, and white.

Mas de Cadenet lies in Trets, south of the imposing Montagne-Sainte-Victoire. Guy Négrel makes two red wines; the basic one, simply called Mas de Cadenet, is clean and fruity and for early drinking. The Cuvée Mas Négrel Prestige is for laying down for as long as a decade – this wine is full but can sometimes be a little too heavily oaked.

★ DOMAINE DE LA COURTADE
Commune: Porquerolles.
Owners: Henri Vidal & Richard Auther.
Surface area under Vine: 33 ha.
Wines: Côtes de Provence red and white.

Henri Vidal's Domaine de La Courtade is located on the Ile de Porquerolles and is one of the star domaines of Provence. The red wine, made from 97 per cent Mourvèdre with a little Syrah, is full, profound and very classy, with a touch of Provençal herbs. The white wine, vinified in wood, comes from 100 per cent Rolle and is excellent too. Both wines will keep well – in the best years as long as ten years.

CHÂTEAU D'ESCLANS

Commune: La Motte.
Owners: Vin and Spirit AB (Rabiega Vin).
Surface area under Vine: 35 ha.
Wines: Côtes de Provence red including Carbase, Grebase and Mourbase, and white including Svala, and Vin de Pays d'Argens-Roussanne.

Lying outside La Motte in the Haut Pays on the road up to Callas and the Gorges du Verdun, and surrounded by other properties with Esclans in their name, this estate has belonged to the Swedish Rabiega Vin since 1995. Since 1996 it has produced three different prestige *cuvées*: Carbase (based on Carignan), Grebase (based on Grenache) and Mourbase (based on Mourvèdre); all from hand-picked old vines, low yields and aged in a mixture of French, Hungarian, Slovenian and even American oak casks, some new. Given that it is early days, and that the vineyard and cellars were in poor shape at the time of the purchase, all three wines are highly promising.

The white, Svala, from a mix of local varieties, is good, too, as is the Roussanne *vin de pays*.

DOMAINE GAVOTY

Commune: Cabasse.
Owners: Gavoty family.
Surface area under Vine: 50 ha.
Wines: Côtes de Provence red, including Grandes Orgues and Clarendon, and white.

Based at Cabasse near Le Luc in the Haut Pays this estate believes in releasing their wines only when ready for drinking, and in producing Prestige red wine *cuvées* only in the best vintages. Cuvée Clarendon is made from Syrah, Cabernet Sauvignon and Grenache, roughly in equal proportions. The Grandes Orgues is from 100 per cent Syrah. The new generation of the family, Pierre Gavoty and his sister Roselyne Gavoty-Bonnet, are making great strides here.

DOMAINE DES PLANES

Commune: Roquebrune-sur-Argens.
Owners: Christophe & Ilse Rieder.
Surface area under Vine: 35 ha.
Wines: Côtes de Provence red including Cuvée Reserve, rosé and white.

The Domaine des Planes lies between Roquebrune-sur-Argens and Saint Aygulf overlooking the bay of Fréjus. The best red wines are a pure Mourvèdre and a Cuvée Réserve which is from Mourvèdre and Cabernet Sauvignon, matured in new 50-hectolitre *tonneaux* for two years before bottling. The former has more austerity, as you might expect; the latter, in 1996, showed good, fresh, ripe spicy-mocha-caramel fruit.

★ DOMAINE RABIEGA

Commune: Flayosc.
Owners: Vin & Spirit AB.
Surface area under Vine: 10 ha.
Wines: Côtes de Provence red including Clos d' Ière No 1 and No 2, and white.

Domaine Rabiega lies at Flayosc near Draguignan, and was acquired by Vin & Spirit AB (the Swedish wine and spirits monopoly) in 1986 as a training and conference facility. Under winemaker Lars Torstenson it has established itself as one of the top domaines in the *appellation*.

This reputation is based on two wines: Clos d'Ière No 1, based on Syrah, and Clos d'Ière No 2, a wine made with Grenache and Carignan plus a little Cabernet Sauvignon. Both are aged in new or newish French, Slovenian, Hungarian or American oak. These are expensive wines, but worth it as they are cedary, ripe and full of finesse.

DOMAINE RICHEAUME

Commune: Puyloubier.
Owner: Henning Hoesch.
Surface area under Vine: 25 ha.
Wines: Côtes de Provence red, including Cuvée Columelle, rosé and white.

Henning Hoesch's beloved Château Richeaume lies directly under the grey limestone flank of the Montagne Sainte-Victoire east of Aix-en-Provence, and his Cuvée Columelle is one of the most consistent and stylish wines of the *appellation*. The fruit is cool and classy, the wine full, concentrated and gently oaky. It will need ten years to mature in the best vintages.

CHÂTEAU SAINTE-ROSELINE

Commune: Les Arcs-sur-Argens.
Owner: Bernard Teillaud.
Surface area under Vine: 40 ha.
Wines: Côtes de Provence red including Cru Classique and Cuvée Prieuré, rosé and white.

Since the tenth century Templars, Benedictines, Carthusians and other ecclesiastics succeeded each other in a long line and much remains of the old abbey, especially an exquisite cloister and some very impressive cellars. Proprietor Bernard Teillaud has been quietly and sensitively renovating the old and installing the new since he arrived in 1994. There is now a *chai à barriques* as well as the old *chai à foudres*, and an up-to-date *cuverie* of stainless steel vats.

All the wines are very good – the Cru Classé red (40 per cent Cabernet Sauvignon and 60 per cent Mourvèdre) is aged in *foudres* and has good structure, depth and length. This wine comes in the estate's own version of a Provençal bottle. The Cuvée Prieuré, from the same blend, spends twelve months in *barrique*.

Other Producers of note

DOMAINE DE LA BASTIDE NEUVE/HUGO WIESTNER (LE CANNET-DES-MAURES), DOMAINE LA BERNARDE/ GUY MEULNART (LE LUC), DOMAINE DES BERTRANDS/ PHILIPPE MAROTZKI (LE CANNET-DES-MAURES), DOMAINE DE CARPE DIEM/FRANCIS ADAM (COTIGNAC), COMMANDERIE DE PEYRASSOL/FRANÇOISE RIGORD (FLASSANS), CHÂTEAU FERRY-LACOMBE/F HOUDIN (TRETS), CHÂTEAU GRAND'BOISE /NICOLE GRUEY (TRETS), DOMAINE DU JAS D'ESCLANS/RENÉ & CHRISTIANE LORGUES-LAPOUGE (LA MOTTE), DOMAINE DE LA LAUZADE/ LOUIS ONZET (LE LUC), LES MAÎTRES VIGNERONS DE LA PRESQU'ILE DE SAINT-TROPEZ (GASSIN), CHÂTEAU MARAVENNE/JEAN-LOUIS GOURJON (LA LONDE-LES-MAURES), DOMAINE DE LA MAYONNETTE/H JULIAN & FILS (LA CRAU), CHÂTEAU MINUTY/ETIENNE MATTON (GASSIN), DOMAINE LA MOUTÈTE/GÉRARD DUFFORT (LE BEAUSSET), DOMAINE DE LA NAVARRE/PÈRE MICHEL DE LOUVENCOURT, DIRECTOR (LA CRAU), DOMAINE DE RIMAURESQ/MARC JACQUET (PIGNANS), DOMAINE SAINT-ANDRÉ DE FIGUIÈRE/ALAIN COMBARD (LA LONDE-LES-MAURES), CLOS SAINT-JOSEPH/ANTOINE AND CÉCILE SASSI (VILLARS-SUR-VAR), CHÂTEAU SAINTE-MARGUERITE/ JEAN-PIERRE FAYARD (LA LONDE-LES-MAURES), DOMAINE SORIN/LUC & SERGINE SORIN (SAINT-CYR-SUR-MER) AND LES VIGNERONS DE GRIMAUD.

COTEAUX VAROIS

Surface Area (1998): 1800 ha.
Production (1998): (Red and rosé) 30,611 hl; (white) 1013 hl (white).
Colour: Red, rosé and white.
Grape Varieties: (Red) Grenache, Syrah, Mourvèdre, Cabernet Sauvignon and Cinsault; (rosé) Grenache, Cinsault, Syrah, Cabernet Sauvignon; (white) Rolle, Ugni Blanc, Clairette and Sauvignon Blanc.
Maximum Yield: 55 hl/ha.
Minimum Alcohol Level: 11°.

The Coteaux Varois lies between the eastern and western halves of the Côtes de Provence *appellation*, an area spread over twenty-eight communes around Brignoles and Saint-Maximin-La-Sainte-Baume. It was originally intended to be part of the Côtes de Provence *appellation*, but the intransigence and independence of one Victorin Henri, mayor of Rougiers and president of the Fédération of Cave Coopératives of the Var resulted in this area being omitted because of the widespread plantation of non-noble varieties and even hybrids, which would have had to be grubbed up and replaced with better varieties.

The area languished as a mere *vin de pays* until 1984, but was elevated from VDQS to full *appellation contrôlée* in 1993. For the red wines Grenache, Syrah and Mourvèdre have to make a combined minimum of 80 per cent. Cabernet Sauvignon can be used up to 20 per cent of the blend. For the rosé Grenache and Cinsault have to make a combined minimum of 70 per cent, again with no more than 20 per cent of Cabernet Sauvignon in the blend. The white wines are less interesting.

This is the Var at its most attractive, undulating and forested, both deciduous and coniferous, and with a largely clay-limestone soil, with pockets of gravel and flint. The area extends between Tavernes in the north to Méounes-Les-Montreux in the south, with an additional pocket at Villecroze to the north-east.

Production continues to be dominated by the local co-operatives, who offer a range of different *cuvées*, but all of the fruity, supple, early-drinking style. During the 1990s a number of independent estates have been set up but few of these have much of a track record yet.

Leading Coteaux Varois Producers

★ DOMAINE DE TRIENNES
Commune: Nans-Les-Pins.
Owners: Michel Macaux, Jacques Seysses and Aubert de Villaine.
Surface Area under Vine: 43 ha.
Wines: Vin de Pays red, rosé and white.
The Domaine de Triennes lies south-west of Saint-Maximin in the heart of the Coteaux Varois *appellation*, but in order to have maximum flexibility with grape varieties its wines are produced as *vins de pays*. The property is co-owned by two Burgundian producers – Jacques Seysses of Domaine Dujac in Morey-Saint-Denis and Aubert de Villaine, co-owner of the Domaine de La Romanée-Conti in Vosne-Romanée, along with Michel Macaux, a Parisian businessman and wine lover.

Two varietal whites are produced, as well as a *vin gris* from Cinsault, and various reds: the Réserve is made with 65 per cent Cabernet Sauvignon and 35 per cent Syrah, the Aureliens from a 50:50 blend of these varieties; and there are varietal wines from Merlot, Syrah and Cabernet Sauvignon.

Domaine de Triennes was acquired in 1990 and things began to get serious in 1995. By 1997 when Rémi Laugier joined as manager and after seven years work by Christophe Morin, vineyard manager at Domaine Dujac and down here, quality really began to sing.

Other Producers of note
DOMAINE DU DEFFENDS/SUZEL DE LANVERSIN (SAINT-MAXIMIN), DOMAINE DU LOOU/DANIEL DI PLACIDO (LA ROQUEBRUSSANNE) AND CHÂTEAU ROUTAS/PHILIPPE BIELER (CHÂTEAUVERT).

COTEAUX D'AIX-EN-PROVENCE

Surface Area (1998): 3300 ha.
Production (1998): (Red and rosé) 78,553 hl; (white) 3530 hl.
Colour: Red, rosé and white.
Grape Varieties: (Red and rosé) Grenache, Cinsault, Counoise, Syrah, Mourvèdre, Carignan and Cabernet Sauvignon; (white) Ugni Blanc, Sauvignon, Sémillon, Clairette, Rolle, Grenache Blanc and Bourboulenc.
Maximum Yield: 60 hl/ha.
Minimum Alcohol Level: 11°.

Though dwarfed by Côtes de Provence the Coteaux d'Aix-en-Provence is comfortably the second largest vineyard area in Provence, occupying some 3300 hectares (almost twice that of the Coteaux Varois) and stretching from Esparron, north-east of Aix, to Eygalières north-west of Salon, and down to Martigues on the Mediterranean coast. The heart of the *appellation* lies between the Durance river and the A8 *autoroute* between Aix and Salon, directly opposite the Lubéron vineyards.

Away from the big cornurbations – though Aix-en-Provence has preserved much of its dignity and attraction – the countryside in this corner of Provence, especially near to the river Durance, has real charm. It is based on limestone, out-cropping at intervals, within which are a number of fertile valleys, secluded and peaceful. The vine does not dominate the landscape, the stony undulations covered in scrub and olive groves, being mixed with maize and sunflower fields and dotted with long half-cylinders of canvas sheltering the production of soft fruit and vegetables. Dry and sunny, theclimate is even more dominated by the Mistral than it is further east.

Coteaux d'Aix-en-Provence makes two styles of wine: first are those wines deliberately made for early drinking, which, however pleasant, cannot really be regarded as serious. Rosés and whites fall into this category as do some reds. Châteaux de Fonscolombe and du

Seuil make wines in this style, and there are many more less elegant examples from local merchants and co-operatives. (There are fifteen co-operatives who are responsible for 40 per cent of the 15 million bottles of Coteaux d'Aix produced every year.)

The second style is a wine for ageing and as serious as the best Côtes de Provence wines. Here Syrah is the important grape variety, with Cabernet Sauvignon planted to the official limit of 30 per cent or even more (the limitation dates from 1955). These wines are well worth seeking out and will keep for a decade.

Leading Coteaux-d'Aix-en-Provence Producers

COMMANDERIE DE LA BARGEMONE
Commune: Saint-Cannat.
Owner: Jean-Pierre Rozan.
Surface Area under Vine: 60 ha.
Wines: Coteaux d'Aix-en-Provence red and white.
The vineyard surrounding the thirteenth-century Templar fort alongside the N7 at Saint-Cannat has been created out of the *garrigue* since 1968 by Jean-Pierre Rozan. The vines are now mature and the wines are increasingly sophisticated. The red wine keeps for up to decade.

CHÂTEAU DE BEAUPRÉ
Commune: Saint-Cannat.
Owner: Baron Christian Double.
Surface Area under Vine: 36 ha.
Wines: Coteaux d'Aix-en-Provence red, including Cuvée Collection, and white.
Not far from the Commanderie de La Bargemone (see above) along the N7 road is Château de Beaupré which produces some of the top red wines of the *appellation*. The basic red is medium-bodied, fruity and agreeable. The Cuvée Collection (90 per cent Cabernet Sauvignon and 10 per cent Syrah) is rather more serious.

CHÂTEAU CALISSANNE
Commune: Lançon-de-Provence.
Owners: Groupe UAP & Groupe SHRM.

Surface Area under Vine: 100 ha.
Wines: Coteaux d'Aix-en-Provence red, rosé and white including Cuvee du Chateau, Cuve Prestige and Clos Victoire for all three colours.
This large estate, owned by an insurance group, lies between Lançon-de-Provence and the Etang de Berre. There are three *cuvées* each for red, rosé and white: Cuvée du Château is supple and juicy fruity for early drinking; Cuvée Prestige is rather more serious (the white includes some barrel-fermented Sauvignon Blanc and Sémillon; the rosé is mainly Syrah which has been saignéed; and the red is based on Cabernet Sauvignon); and the Clos Victoire, from the oldest vines (the red has 50 per cent each Cabernet Sauvignon and Syrah). This is an up-to-date establishment whose professional management is left to exercise its perfectionistic best.

CHÂTEAU REVELETTE
Commune: Jouques.
Owner: Peter Fischer.
Surface Area under Vine: 25 ha.
Wines: Coteaux d'Aix-en-Provence red, rosé and white, and Vin de Pays du Var.
Overlooking the river Durance in the north-east of the Coteaux d'Aix *appellation*, Château Revelette is the result of the dream of a German trained in California. In his early forties, Peter Fischer hails from Baden-Baden and he bought the domaine for hunting as much as for its vineyards in 1985. He has since added 10 hectares of vines (the Cabernet and Chardonnay) – and now produces a Grand Blanc (only *vin de pays* because of the Chardonnay) and a Grand Rouge, which is full and rich and a real keeper.

CHÂTEAU VIGNELAURE
Commune: Rians.
Owner: David O'Brien.
Surface Area under Vine: 64 ha.
Wines: Coteaux d'Aix-en-Provence red and rosé, and Vin de Pays des Coteaux du Verdon.
Poor old Château Vignelaure! This domaine has had so many ups and downs and so many changes of ownership! The estate was formed by Georges Brunet,

ex-Bordeaux's Château La Lagune, in 1964, planted entirely with Cabernet Sauvignon, and made splendid wines in the 1970s. In the 1980s the vineyard was enlarged from 28 hectares to 60, much of which had to be turned over to Syrah when Coteaux d'Aix was elevated to *appellation* status in 1985. Georges Brunet then sold to William Graulich, a businessman, and during his tenure standards declined. Another change of owner led to corners being cut: the domaine was no longer cultivated biologically and the time the wine spent in wood before bottling was reduced. Finally Hugh Ryman of Rystone, consultants since 1992, formed a consortium with David O'Brien to purchase the property. O'Brien bought out Rystone in 1998 and is now the sole owner.

After much investment, both in restoring the vineyard to its former glory, and in the introduction of small oak casks to replace the *foudres* in the cellar, there has recently been a return to Brunet standards and let us hope this potentially very fine estate can look forward to more settled times. As we can see from both the wines of Brunet's day and those made today the red Vignelaure is a serious *vin de garde*: at its best, in good vintages, after a decade of ageing.

Other Producers of note

CHÂTEAU BAS/GEORGES DE BLANQUET (VERNÈGUES), CHÂTEAU LA COSTE/PIERRE BORDONADO (LE PUY-SAINTE-RÉPARADE), CHÂTEAU DE LA CRÉMADE/MARQUIS LOUIS DE SAPORTA (LAMBESC), CHÂTEAU DE FONSCOLOMBE/MARQUIS LOUIS DE SAPORTA (LE PUY-SAINTE-RÉPARADE), CHÂTEAU DES GAVELLES/JAMES & BÉNÉDICTE DE ROANY (PUYRICARD), CHÂTEAU DE PONT-ROYAL/JACQUES-ALFRED JAUFFRET (MALLEMORT) AND CHÂTEAU DU SEUIL/PHILIPPE AND JONINE CARREAU-GASCHEREAU (PUYRICARD).

LES BAUX-DE-PROVENCE

Surface Area (1998): 150 ha.
Production (1998): 8648 hl.
Colour: Red and rosé.
Grapes Varieties: (Red and rosé) Grenache, Syrah, Cinsault, Mourvèdre, Counoise, Carignan and

Cabernet Sauvignon; (white) Rolle, Ugni Blanc, Sauvignon Blanc, Grenache Blanc and Clairette.
Maximum Yield: 50 hl/ha.
Minimum Alcohol Level: 11.5°.

Formerly part of the Coteaux d'Aix-en-Provence *appellation*, with the suffix Les Baux-de-Provence, the eight communes surrounding Les Alpilles in the Bouches-du-Rhône *département* gained independence in 1995, simplifying the name of the *appellation*. The regulations are much the same as for Coteaux d'Aix, though the maximum yield has been tightened up – Grenache, Syrah and Cinsault must provide a minimum of 60 per cent of the red blend. The restriction of a maximum of 30 per cent Cabernet Sauvignon has also barred the area's best known estate, Domaine de Trévallon, from labelling its wines as Les Baux de Provence.

As in Coteaux d'Aix, some of the thirteen domaines in Les Baux produce wines for early drinking and some wines for ageing. But none really excite me. Domaine Hauvette and the Cuvée Taven of the Domaine de Terres Blanches can be included in the latter category.

Leading Les Baux-de-Provence Producer

★★ DOMAINE DE TRÉVALLON

Commune: Sainte-Etienne-du-Grès.
Owner: Eloi Dürrbach.
Surface Area under Vine: 20 ha.
Wines: Vin de Pays du Bouches-du-Rhône red and white.

Domaine de Trévallon is one of the South of France's superstar estates, yet the wine is sold as mere *vin de pays* because the percentage of Cabernet Sauvignon in the red exceeds the official regulations. The blend for the red is 60 per cent Cabernet Sauvignon and 40 per cent Syrah, and there is no Grenache.

Eloi Dürrbach hails from Alsace, and originally trained as an architect in Paris. His parents had bought Domaine de Trévallon as a holiday home. In 1973 Dürrbach cleared some 3 hectares of scrub behind and above the garden, revealing a moonscape of broken limestone rock, and planted some vines. Over the years, and over a surface area of several square kilometres, the vineyard has been extended to 20 hectares in twenty different parcels, the most recent addition being 1 hectare of white wine varieties.

At first the wines were almost impossibly tough, yet showing an undeniable richness underneath. Over the years the tannins have been tamed and the wine has become more sophisticated, without losing its size or its firmness at the outset. Techniques include no destemming of the grapes and *pigeage* as well as *remontage*. The wine is then stored in *foudres* for eighteen months before bottling. The results are very fine.

Other Producers of note

DOMAINE HAUVETTE/DOMINIQUE HAUVETTE (SAINT-RÉMY-DE-PROVENCE), MAS DE LA DAME (LES BAUX-DE-PROVENCE), MAS DE GOURGONNIER (MOURIES), CHÂTEAU ROMANIN/C & J P PEYRAUD (SAINT-RÉMY-DE-PROVENCE), MAS SAINTE -BERTHE/MME DAVID (LES BAUX-DE-PROVENCE), DOMAINE DE TERRES BLANCHES/NOËL MICHELIN (SAINT-RÉMY-DE-PROVENCE).

CORSICA

As with so many wine regions the more beautiful the countryside, the more ordinary the wine. This holds as true in Corsica as it does on the mainland of France. Corsica is indeed an island of outstanding beauty. Stretching roughly 200 kilometres from north to south, and at its widest point almost 100 kilometres from east to west, Corsica is a mountainous land of wild and wooded beauty. Away from the holiday resorts along the coast – and there are still many secluded coves and beaches – the interior is lonely and spectacular. In parts it is rocky and arid, covered with a herby scrub known as *maquis*, like the *garrigues* of southern France; elsewhere densely forested as on the island of Madeira. It was probably the Phoenicians who first brought wine to Corsica, as they did to so much of the western Mediterranean. They named the island Korai, meaning 'covered in forests'. It became part of the expanding Genoese empire in 1347 and was to remain under Italian hegemony for four centuries. In 1768 the Genoese, having failed to subdue island unrest, sold Corsica to the French. Yet the island is still fiercely independent: neither Italian nor French; just Corsican.

The Italian influence persisted. It was not until well into the nineteenth century that Midi varieties, Grenache, Cinsault and Carignan, began to be planted alongside the Italian grape, Aleatico, which André Jullien described in the early nineteenth century as being from Florence, but today is only found further south in Puglia, and other Italian varieties. In Jullien's day some 13,500 hectares were under vine on the island, forming the backbone of its economy. Decimated by phylloxera some sixty years later prosperity suffered, and it was not until the arrival of hundreds of Algerian expatriates in 1960 that a revival began. These *pieds noirs* were only interested in making *vin ordinaire*, however, and it was not until the institution of *appellation contrôlée* in 1976 that the production of quality wine began to be encouraged.

Yet the amount of *appellation* wine is still tiny. There are now 2750 hectares of *appellation contrôlée* vineyards (up from 1600 hectares or so in 1988), producing some 125,000 hectolitres of wine. There is an equivalent amount of *vins de pays* and a similar quantity of *vin ordinaire*.

VIN DE CORSE

Surface Area (1998): (Red) 1019 ha; (rosé) 761 ha; (white) 297 ha.
Production (1998): (Red) 56,250 hl; (rosé) 32,520 hl; (white) 10,876.
Colour: Red, rosé and white.
Grape Varieties: (Red and rosé) Sciacarello, Niellucio, Grenache, Syrah, Cinsault, Carignan and Barbarossa; (white) Vermentino and Ugni Blanc.
Maximum Yield: 50 hl/ha.
Minimum Alcohol Level: 11.5°.

SURFACE AREA AND PRODUCTION (1998 HARVEST)

APPELLATIONS	SURFACE AREA (HA)			PRODUCTION (HL)		
	RED	ROSÉ	WHITE	RED	ROSÉ	WHITE
AJACCIO	128	53	24	3939	2095	864
PATRIMONIO	192	113	83	8258	5061	2958
VIN DE CORSE	1019	595	190	44,053	25,364	7054
TOTAL	1339	761	297	56,250	32,520	10,876
GRAND TOTAL	2397			99,646		
VINS DOUX NATURELS & MUSCAT DU CAP CORSE	-	-	84	-	-	2142

CORSICA

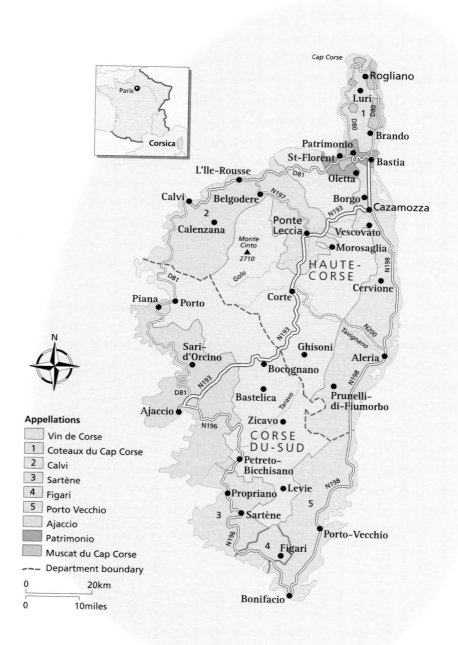

Cap Corse

Rogliano

Luri

1

D80

D80

Brando

Patrimonio

St-Florent • Bastia

L'Ile-Rousse

D81

Oletta

Calvi

Belgodere

N197

Borgo

N193

Cazamozza

2

Ponte Leccia

Vescovato

Calenzana

Morosaglia

Monte Cinto ▲ 2710

HAUTE-CORSE

N198

Golo

Cervione

Piana • Porto

Corte

D81

Sari-d'Orcino

Ghisoni

N193

Aleria

Tavignano

Bocognano

N200

D81

N193

Bastelica

Tavaro

Prunelli-di-Fiumorbo

N198

Ajaccio

N196

Zicavo

CORSE DU-SUD

Petreto-Bicchisano

Propriano • Levie

N198

3

Sartène

5

4

Figari

Porto-Vecchio

N196

Bonifacio

Paris • (inset map) **Corsica**

N

Appellations

- Vin de Corse
- 1 Coteaux du Cap Corse
- 2 Calvi
- 3 Sartène
- 4 Figari
- 5 Porto Vecchio
- Ajaccio
- Patrimonio
- Muscat du Cap Corse
- - - Department boundary

0   20km

0   10miles

403

AJACCIO

Surface Area (1998): (Red) 128 ha; (rosé) 53 ha; (white) 24 ha.
Production (1998): (Red) 3939 hl; (rosé) 2095 hl; (white) 864 hl.
Colour: Red, rosé and white.
Grape Varieties: (Red and rosé) Sciacarello, Nielluccio, Barbarossa, Vermentino, plus Grenache, Cinsault and Carignan; (white) Vermentino and Ugni Blanc.
Maximum Yield: 45 hl/ha.
Minimum Alcohol Level: (Red) 12°; (rosé and white) 11.5°.

PATRIMONIO

Surface Area (1998): (Red) 192 ha; (rosé) 113 ha; (white) 83 ha.
Production (1998): (Red) 8258 hl; (rosé) 5061 hl; (white) 2958 hl.
Colour: Red, rosé and white.
Grape Varieties: (Red and rosé) Niellucio, Grenache, Sciacarello and Vermentino; (white) Vermentino.
Maximum Yield: 50 hl/ha.
Minimum Alcohol Level: (Red) 12°; (rosé and white) 11.5°.

Vines are grown throughout the island on the lower, less mountainous slopes and coastal areas. There are two individual *appellations*, Ajaccio and Patrimonio, and five superior sub-areas of the generic Vin de Corse: Calvi, Coteaux du Cap Corse, Figari, Porto Vecchio and Sartène as well as Muscat du Cap Corse.

The grape varieties are a mixture of Italian and French ones – for red wines the Italian varieties are primarily Sciacarello and Niellucio. The former produces a wine which can be well-coloured, distinguished and fruity. Niellucio is said to be related to Tuscany's Sangiovese and produces quite alcoholic wines which lack colour and can lack guts. These, plus another Italian variety called Barbarossa, are blended with the French varieties, Grenache, Cinsault, Syrah and Carignan and the Italian white grape, Vermentino.

Authorities are divided as to whether the Vermentino – the Rolle of Provence – is the same as the Malvoisie or a distant cousin. Throughout the island it is the mainstay of the *appellation contrôlée* white wines, forming 75 per cent to 80 per cent of the blend, to which is added Ugni Blanc. The result is a full and sometimes rather deeply coloured wine with plenty of fruit, opulent but dry. Well vinified, and with enough Ugni to maintain the acidity, it can be pleasantly fragrant but often the result is coarse and blowsy.

Ajaccio, the region surrounding Corsica's capital of the same name on the west side of the island, produces medium-bodied red wines and a certain amount of rosé, predominantly from the Sciacarello grape. Patrimonio, west of Bastia on the north coast, on the other hand, concentrates on the Niellucio grape to make fuller, richer red wines, and some interesting rosés from clay and limestone soil. Further north, the schistous peninsula of Cap Corse is a source of the best white wine on the island, Clos Nicrosi. Here Jean-Noël Luigi makes a 100 per cent Vermentino wine. In the north-west, the gravelly soils near Calvi yield fruity, medium-bodied reds and one or two fresh, flowery (if occasionally somewhat neutral) whites. This is one of Corsica's largest winemaking areas. Sartène, Figari and Porto Vecchio are at the southern end of Corsica and produce more structured wines; at times somewhat rustic, with a strong smell of tobacco, almost as if someone had dunked their dog-end in the glass.

It is difficult to describe the general character of Corsican wine. The flavour is neither that of the South of France, nor that of any easily recognised area of Italy, and I can't say that I have ever been enthused enough by the value for money of a Corsican wine to buy any, either for myself or commercially. The most elegant red wines tend to be the most neutral: soft and fruity and more Italian than French, but without anything special or individual about them. For those on holiday on the island there are some perfectly drinkable rosés and white wines, but these are somewhat anonymous, if cleanly made.

Producers of note

Domaine d'Alzipratu (Calvi), Domaine Antoine Arena (Patrimonio), Clos Capitoro (Ajaccio), Domaine de Catarelli (Patrimonio), Clos Culombu (Calvi), Domaine Jean-Paul Gentile (Patrimonio), Domaine Yves Leccia (Patrimonio), Clos Nicrosi (Coteaux du Cap Corse), Domaine de Paviglia (Ajaccio), Domaine Comte Peraldi (Ajaccio), Clos Reginu (Calvi), Domaine Martin Santini (Ajaccio), Domaine de Tanella (Figari) and Domaine de Torraccia (Porto Vecchio).

VINS DE PAYS

DEPARTMENTAL VINS DE PAYS

Vin de Pays des Alpes-Maritimes

This is the *vin de pays* from around Nice. All three colours of wine are authorised. I have only seen it in red and rosé, made from the local Provençal varieties. This is a simple, slightly rustic brew and little is produced.

Vin de Pays des Alpes-de-Haute-Provence

Most of the wine comes from the east of the *département* in the Durance Valley. There are sturdy reds from Carignan and Grenache plus some rosé and very little white.

Vin de Pays des Bouches-du-Rhône

This *vin de pays* appears mainly as red, with a little rosé. The wines are made from the usual local varieties plus Cabernet Sauvignon. The Domaines Viticoles des Salins du Midi are the main producers. Domaine de Trévallon (see page 400) is the super-star.

Vin de Pays des Hautes-Alpes

Most of this *vin de pays* comes from the southern end of the *département* between Sisteron and Gap. There is not much wine made.

Vin de Pays de L'Ile de Beauté

This is an appropriate name for the Corsican *vin de pays*. It appears both as red and as rosé (there is also a little white

but I have never tried it) and it can be made from a large number of grape varieties. In my experience it is either rather light and neutral or fuller but somewhat rustic.

Vin de Pays du Var

This *vin de pays* is by far the largest – in terms of wine produced – of the Provençal *vins de pays*. The wines are mainly red, with some rosé, from Carignan, Cinsault and Grenache. There are some interesting wines made from 100 per cent Cabernet Sauvignon and Syrah.

ZONAL VINS DE PAYS

Vin de Pays d'Argens

This comes from the heart of the Var around the towns of Les Arcs and Vidauban in the Argens Valley. Mainly red and rosé wines are produced, from the usual local varieties. I have seen one or two interesting wines which have additionally incorporated Cabernet Sauvignon.

Vin de Pays des Maures

This comes from the eastern, coastal side of the Var. mainly from around Saint-Tropez. The wines are largely red, with some rosé, and from Carignan, Cinsault and Grenache. I have seen some good wines which have benefited from the addition of Cabernet Sauvignon.

Vin de Pays du Mont Caume

This is the zonal *vin de pays* of the Bandol area and the wines are similar in style to Vin de Pays des Maures. The Bunan family of Moulin des Costes produce an attractive pure Cabernet Sauvignon example.

Vin de Pays de La Petite Crau

This zonal *vin de pays* comes from the area around Les Baux. The wines are mainly red, with some rosé and some white, and made from the local varieties.

Vin de Pays des Coteaux du Verdon

This comes from an area in the northern Var between the Gorges du Verdon and the river Durance. I have only seen it as red and rosé wine and usually Carignan- and Grenache- based. The wines from Château Vignelaure wines are Cabernet Sauvignon-based.

LANGUEDOC

WHILE WHAT THE FRENCH CALL THE MIDI is what we roughly translate as the South of France, from a wine point of view the Midi is that part west of the Rhône and its delta, that half of the South which is not Provence or the Côte d'Azur. This is where the bulk of French *vin ordinaire* is produced but is also where an important wine revolution has been taking place over the last twenty years. In an arc bounded by the southern slopes of the Massif Central – the Cévennes and the Montagne Noire – by the Pyrenees and by the Rhône, the Mediterranean coast and the Spanish border, a total of 15 million hectolitres of non-*appellation contrôlée* wine is produced a year from the four *départements* of Gard, Hérault, Aude and Pyrénées-Orientales.

Vines here can produce yield way over the permitted maximum for the Pinot Noir in Gevrey-Chambertin or the Cabernet Sauvignon in Pauillac without raising a sweat. Prodigious quantities of wine are produced, much of it very ordinary indeed, and much of it ultimately destined for the EU Common Agricultural Policy's distilleries rather than even the most undiscriminating Frenchman's throat. Hitherto this liquid, weak, acidic and barely within the legal alcoholic limit of the word wine, was bolstered up with highly coloured, heavily alcoholic blends from Algeria and other sources in North Africa.

After Algerian independence in 1962 this trade was officially barred, and the new Muslim governments of these countries pursued a policy of neglect if not of destruction of their vineyards in favour of cereals and other crops. A large number of *pied-noir* growers, taking advantage of their French nationality while they still had time, upped sticks and moved to France. The *vin ordinaire* bottling factories of the Midi looked for an alternative source of blending wine within the EU and found it in the similarly rustic wines of southern Italy.

It soon became apparent, however, that as standards improved, this Italian wine was perfectly palatable in its own right – if one's standards were no higher than 11 or 12 degrees 'plonk' – and the Italian brews were substantially cheaper than the thin rubbish produced in the Languedoc. The result

eventually was that what looked like domestic *vin ordinaire* was made increasingly with almost entirely non-French wine, leaving the local brew and its producers quite superfluous. The consequence was confusion, occasionally erupting to riot as tankers of Italian wine en route from the ports of Sète and Marseille to nearby bottling factories were overturned by furious locals. The French government found themselves with a political hot potato.

Belatedly the French bureaucratic machine began to edge towards an answer to the problem. Encouragement was given to the local growers to plant better qualities of grapes and to reduce the size of their harvests. Loans at favourable rates were made available to facilitate the installation of modern equipment. The establishment of up-to-date co-operatives, viticultural and vinicultural research institutes and oenological departments in local universities was encouraged and a new and higher grading for *vin ordinaire*, the *vins de pays*, was introduced in 1973. This process has continued with the gradual but now accelerating elevation of local VDQS regions to full *appellation contrôlée*, and, one hopes, eventually to the situation where it will be truly economically viable for every local grower to go for quality rather than to continue to make enormous quantities of indifferent wine which nobody wants and for which he will have to be subsidized, only for it to be distilled into industrial alcohol or further swell the bulging storage vats of the European wine lake.

The result, as much I feel in spite of as because of the efforts of successive French governments, has been a positive, encouraging and frequently exhilarating improvement in the quality of Midi wines in the last generation. Perhaps the single most exciting thing that I have experienced in my wine trade career has been the enormous improvement in the standard of winemaking, *élevage* and bottling that has taken place in the South of France and elsewhere since the early 1970s. This means that the days are now firmly past when a venture off the beaten track was a gamble, when it was a risk to approve a wine on a mere cask sample and take the successful handling of the wine from then on for granted. There is now plenty of well-made wine of character in these lesser areas of France.

One of the positive hindrances to the improvement of quality has been the continued intransigence of the INAO. When the original laws were set up for *appellation contrôlée* in 1936 and for VDQS in 1949 the object primarily was to determine and codify existing practices, to limit growing areas to the soils and areas known to be the best, to establish a list of the proven suitable fine grape varieties, to legislate minimum levels of alcohol and maximum levels of production, and so on. By and large, for the mainstream quality wine regions of Bordeaux, Burgundy and elsewhere the laws are fine, though in my view they were slow to react to the consequence of the increases in quantity which could be obtained with better husbandry in the vineyard, more effective methods for controlling pests and diseases, and the development of more productive clones of vines. Where the AC and VDQS laws were too rigid was in their insistence that Midi wines should continue until time immemorial to be made with indigenous Midi grape varieties – Grenache, Carignan, Cinsault, Terret Noir and others for red and rosé wines, Clairette, Ugni Blanc, Picpoul, Maccabéo and others for whites. It was only belatedly recognised that the addition of non-local quality varieties (Cabernet Sauvignon, Merlot, Syrah and Mourvèdre for reds and Chardonnay, Chenin Blanc and Sauvignon Blanc for whites) could do much to raise standards. Even today, these improving varieties, called *cépages améliorateurs*, are not officially permitted or encouraged in certain *appellations*.

Yet it is by using these *cépages améliorateurs* that the more enterprising growers have started to produce the most interesting local wines. Often these are classified as *vin de pays* not *appellation contrôlée*, just as many of the 'new style' Italian wines are classified as *vini da tavola*. All the INAO seems to be able to do is to recommend the gradual decrease of rather boring grapes such as the Carignan and a corresponding increase in the use of Syrah and Mourvèdre which have always been allowed but only recently positively encouraged.

The result is currently a mess. More and more areas – starting with the Côtes du Roussillon and still continuing with the Côtes de Cabardès et de L'Orbiel in 1999 – have been elevated from VDQS to *appellation contrôlée* status. Yet the wines are no better, and no more expensive, than the best *vins de pays*.

The grower of *appellation* wine is often unduly restricted. Syrah is a high quality grape variety encouraged by the authorities. Yet in some *appellations* in the Languedoc or the Roussillon a wine made entirely from Syrah cannot qualify for the *appellation contrôlée* name. To do this it has to be blended with Grenache or another permitted variety. In addition there may be further regulations stipulating the time a wine must remain in cask or larger receptacle before bottling or release which the grower may find unnecessarily restrictive. Alien grapes such as Cabernet Sauvignon, though allowed in Provence, are banned from all Languedoc *appellations* (except those inland near Carcassonne). Cabernet Sauvignon grows well in the Aude and the Hérault but any wine made from it has to be labelled as *vin de pays*, as does white wine from the fashionable Viognier and ubiquitous Chardonnay.

So the result is a polarisation – *appellation contrôlée* wine from vineyards up in the hills following the official laws and regulations and *vins de pays* from vineyards down on the plain where almost anything goes, while the production of *vin ordinaire* is decreasing. There is not much difference in price between the best *vins de pays* and the best *appellation contrôlée* wines, which makes a nonsense of the concept of *appellation contrôlée*. Moreover, there is a bewildering array of these *vins de pays*: approximately sixty at the moment, mainly in the Hérault, plus the all-embracing regional Vin de Pays d'Oc. Do we really need this number?

Despite all this the Languedoc is now one of the most rewarding places to look for interesting, well-made new wines, and to encounter the independent spirits who make them. Every year I hear of another dozen or so new exciting domaines. It is hard to keep up! It is estimated that there are now over 1000 independent domaines in the region to add to the 190 co-operatives and dozens of local *négociants* and that one-third of the annual production (89 per cent red, 6.5 per cent rosé and 4.5 per cent white) is exported.

THE WINES

The wine region of the Languedoc spreads across three *départements*: part of the Gard and the whole of the Hérault and the Aude. In the Gard are the *appellations* of Costières de Nîmes and Clairette de Bellegarde. In the Hérault are the Coteaux du Languedoc and its *crus* — some of whose vineyards overlap into the Gard and the Aude — Clairette du Languedoc, Faugères and Saint-Chinian, Picpoul de Pinet and the sweet, coastal Muscat *vins doux naturels* of Lunel, Mireval and Frontignan. In the Aude are Corbières and Fitou, plus, further inland, Limoux and the newer *appellations* of Côtes de La Malepère and Côtes de Cabardès et de L'

Orbiel, the latter promoted from VDQS to full *appellation contrôlée* in 1999. The Muscat de Saint-Jean-de-Minervois *vin doux naturel* comes from the hills in the south-west Hérault, and the Minervois overlaps both the Hérault and the Aude.

Climate and Terroir

Most of the Languedoc enjoys a Mediterranean climate, mild in winter, hot in the summer — though not as warm or as sunny as in Provence — and generally dry, even arid in some quarters. But as you journey up into the mountains behind Montpellier and Béziers, or along

SURFACE AREA AND PRODUCTION (1998 HARVEST)

APPELLATIONS	SURFACE AREA (HA)	PRODUCTION (HL)	
		RED & ROSÉ	WHITE
COSTIÈRES DE NÎMES }	3270	214,817	10,818
CLAIRETTE DE BELLEGARDE }		–	2357
COTEAUX DU LANGUEDOC	8307	381,896	46,257
CLAIRETTE DU LANGUEDOC	90	–	3362
FAUGÈRES	1714	75,559	–
SAINT-CHINIAN	2714	130,123	–
MINERVOIS	4285	203,455	2827
CORBIÈRES	14,992	542,104	11,261
FITOU	2585	93,582	–
LIMOUX		–	1842
BLANQUETTE DE LIMOUX }	1429	–	37,407
BLANQUETTE MÉTHODE ANCESTRALE }		–	3213
CRÉMANT DE LIMOUX		–	19,525
TOTAL	39,386	1,641,536	137,869
		1,779,405	
CÔTES DE LA MALEPÈRE (VDQS)	515	41,062	–
CÔTES DE CABARDÈS & DE L'ORBIEL (VDQS)	302	19,038	–
TOTAL	817	60,100	
VINS DOUX NATURELS			
MUSCAT DE FRONTIGNAN	792	–	24,085
MUSCAT DE LUNEL	315	–	10,918
MUSCAT DE MIREVAL	266	–	7859
MUSCAT DE SAINT-JEAN-DE-MINERVOIS	165	–	5267
TOTAL	1538		48,129

the river Aude towards Carcassonne, the weather pattern changes. West of Carcassonne the influence of the Atlantic can be felt. It is cooler, especially at night, and as the autumn closes in at vintage time. As the river Aude bends and one ascends into the foothills of the Pyrenees around Limoux, and indeed in the Alaric part of the north-western part of Corbières around Lagrasse, there is a similar change in ambient temperature. The rainfall is also higher. Equally the difference in mesoclimate between the plain of Béziers and the *appellations* of Saint-Chinian and Faugères, or the temperatures and precipitation at Montpellier as opposed to the rocky hinterland of Pic-Saint-Loup and Montpeyroux is marked. Not all the Languedoc is as enervatingly hot as many of us may remember from our summer holidays on the beaches of Valras-Plage or the Cap d'Agde!

In a region as large as the Languedoc – and indeed as prolific in wine production terms – you would expect a wide variety of individual *terroirs*. The essential difference lies between the sandy, loamy, marly, alluvial soils of the plain around Béziers and the coastal areas, the centre for much of the cheaper *vins de pays*, and the mainly limestone-based rocky *garrigues* further inland.

In the Costières de Nîmes and further west along the coast near Montpellier the vineyards contain *galets* or pudding-stones, so familiar in nearby Châteauneuf-du-Pape. They can also be found at the Prieuré de Saint-Jean-de-Bébian near Pézenas. Between Béziers and the coast the soil contains volcanic admixtures, on which the vine thrives, while the Clape region between Narbonne and the sea is based on volcanic rock. Corbières is complex, combining shale and slate, schist, limestone rock and marl. Minervois, too, is large and has a varied soil. Saint-Chinian has *terroirs* of schist in the uplands and limestone-clay mixtures on the lower slopes, while Faugères is entirely schistous and the Cabrières, a Coteaux du Languedoc *cru* further east, is based on slate as well as schist.

Grape Varieties

Ninety-five per cent of the wines of the Languedoc is red or rosé and *appellation contrôlée* rules stipulate a base of three traditional varieties (Carignan, Grenache and Cinsault) along with the more recent introduction of Syrah and Mourvèdre as *cépages améliorateurs*. The Grenache gives the wine colour and alcohol, but low acidity; the Cinsault is light but aromatic, fruity and with good acidity while the Carignan gives body and weight, and is also well-coloured. The resulting blend, common across the whole of the South, up into the southern Rhône and across into Provence, is a wine which used to be fiery and harsh, often rustic, often attenuating quickly. But thanks to both better understanding of how these varieties perform and vinification techniques is today ripe and succulent, full and hearty, and often surprisingly sophisticated.

Carignan and Cinsault are today despised in some quarters, and there are moves to gradually reduce their influence in the blend. It is true that if vinified at 60 hectolitres per hectare, which is the permitted limit, including PLC, in most *appellations*, the results are dull. The Cinsault is a bit thin; the Carignan simply characterless. The *vin de pays* regulations allow much higher yields, up to 90 hl/ha, and the deleterious effect is even more pronounced.

Curtail the yield, use old vines and the improvement in quality is startling. Sylvain Fadat at Domaine d'Aupilhac in Montpeyroux (see page 418) makes a splendid Carignan from sixty-year-old vines which is reared entirely in tank. In 1991, his neighbour Olivier Jullien at Mas Jullien (see page 418) produced a 100 per cent, old-vine Cinsault. Traditionally made, both wines are original and delicious. In the Languedoc Carignan is often vinified by carbonic maceration methods. René Duchemin at Mas de Mortiès in the Pic-Saint-Loup area (see page 420) makes a 100 per cent Carignan from forty-year-old vines. Vinified by carbonic maceration and the wine is a revelation to those who consider Carignan a totally dispensable grape variety.

Much Cinsault is now used for rosé blends only, where its combination of lightness of touch, good acidity and high-toned fruit makes it a good base on which to graft other varietal flavours. But for those unconvinced by Cinsault as a red wine, I must mention Sylvain Fadat again. He doesn't often produce a pure Cinsault, but when he does it is worth trying.

Today, more and more Syrah and Mourvèdre, plus Cabernet Sauvignon and Merlot, are being used for *vin de pays*. There is also increasing use of small oak barrels. Growers edge warily around the corners of the regulations, some being quite open about the fact that they are being flouted. Others offer both both styles of wine — *tradition* (matured in bulk) and *réserve* (reared in barrel); and *vin de pays* wine alongside *appellation* wine. Many growers are now planting Syrah. Mourvèdre, however, will only ripen where the climate is very hot, as in Jonquières on one side of the Montpeyroux — for example, at Domaine Saint-Andrieu (see page 418) Charles Giner makes a splendid 70 per cent Mourvèdre wine called L'Yeuse Noire. Nearby, but up in the hills, at Yvan Poncé's Château La Sauvageonne (see page 422) growing Mourvèdre would be a disaster.

It is hard, even with modern methods, to produce interesting white wines within the *appellation contrôlée* laws. Most producers don't bother. Many *appellations* indeed — Faugères, Saint-Chinian and many of the Coteaux du Languedoc *crus* — are solely for red and rosé wine. Consider the ingredients for *appellation* whites: Bourboulenc, Clairette, Maccabéo, Ugni Blanc, Terret, Picpoul and Grenache Blanc. What an uninspiring collection! I would choose Viognier and Roussanne or Marsanne and Vermentino for a challenge; or, indeed, a Muscat à Petits Grains and made into a dry wine. Those who merely want to make money will plant Chardonnay. And all these wines will be labelled as *vins de pays*.

Some of these wines can be as boring as the mainly Clairette-based *appellation contrôlée* whites — some Chardonnays lack zip, grace and harmony and some are over-oaked; many Viogniers are thin and tasteless and Sauvignon Blanc doesn't seem to work in the Languedoc. I suspect it is too hot. But many white *vins de pays* are excellent and good partners to the large number of splendid *appellation* reds.

When to Drink the Wines

Most Languedoc wines, especially the whites and rosés, are made for drinking the moment they are put on the market, in the summer after the vintage for the whites and roses; six months later (i.e. twelve to fifteen months after the vintage) in the case of the reds. Only the top wines from the best domaines really benefit from any bottle-ageing. Even these wines are ready three years after the vintage and are old by seven or eight years. There are, of course, always the exceptions: these will come from blends dominated by Syrah and Mourvèdre, plus Cabernet Sauvignon in the case of *vin de pays*.

The best Muscat-based *vins doux naturels* should, like those of Muscat de Beaumes-de-Venise, also be drunk early in order to capture the freshness of this aromatic grape variety. And, once the bottle is broached, while it will keep for a few days in the refrigerator, it should nevertheless be finished up quickly.

Languedoc Vintages

The Languedoc is a huge region, and therefore it is dangerous to generalise about the wines, especially about those from further inland. Nevertheless the following is a useful guide.

1998 A small harvest in some areas as a result of poor spring weather. A fine vintage nevertheless.

1997 Good at best. Light, forward wines, but not without style.

1996 In some cases better than 1997; in others not as good. A satisfactory vintage. Drink soon.

1995 Very good indeed. Good ripe, rich reds which can still be kept for a year or two.

1994 Average to good. The tannins in the red wines are a bit unripe and astringent.

1993 Very good but sturdy reds.

1992 and 1991 Not good and the wines are now old.

1990 A fine vintage. Some red wines are still worth investigating.

The Wine Regions

Costières de Nîmes

Surface Area (1998): 3270 ha.
Production (1998): (Red and rosé) 214,817 hl;
(white) 10,818 hl.
Colour: Red, rosé and white.
Grape Varieties: (Red and rosé) Grenache Noir,
Syrah, Mourvèdre, Counoise , Terret Noir,
Carignan and Cinsault (the latter two maximum
50 per cent each); (white) Clairette, Grenache
Blanc, Ugni Blanc, Marsanne, Roussanne
(minimum 50 % of all five combined or separately),
Maccabéo and Rolle (maximum 50 % combined or
separately).
Maximum Yield: 60 hl/ha.
Minimum Alcohol Level: 11°.

The Costières de Nîmes (until 1989 called the Costières du Gard) lies in the Gard *département*. Some authorities, but not the INAO, regard it as part of the Rhône Valley but it fits logically into the Languedoc.

The area, roughly rectangular in shape, measuring 40 kilometres by 16, lies on a low ridge of hills south-east of Nîmes. The soils are complex: sand and chalk in the north-east, chalk and clay in the south-west, loess near Nîmes airport, but overall stony, the depth of stones determining the potential quality of the wine. Probably the best area in theory is that inland of the Vauvert-Saint-Gilles road, the N572, around Beauvoisin and Générac. Vines are planted on the more exposed and better-drained soils; on the richer, more alluvial land is a mixture of pasture, market gardening and orchards.

Most Costières de Nîmes wine is red – there is about as much rosé as there is white – and this can vary from a light, *primeur* style, probably made entirely by carbonic maceration, and at best pleasantly fruity, to wines based more on Syrah which you would be hard put to distinguish from a good Côtes du Rhône. Yet there is a certain baked hardness about the wine, not necessarily disagreeable, that I do not find elsewhere. Currently the *appellation* is good value, quality is improving and new young talent has arrived from outside the area.

Leading Costières de Nîmes Producers

Château de Belle-Coste
Commune: Caissargues.
Owner: Bertrand du Tremblay.
Surface Area under Vine: 60 ha.
Wines: Costières de Nîmes including Cuvée Saint-Marc.

There is something of an air of gentility fallen on hard times here, as you look round what is a fine *manoir provençal* in need of a little refurbishment. But the wines – the Tradition is sold without a vintage date, and intended for early drinking; the Cuvée Saint-Marc is rather more serious – are well-made and stylish. The white is gently oaky, largely from Roussanne, the rosé a *saignée* of Grenache and Syrah and the red from one-third each Grenache, Syrah and Mourvèdre. Honey, oil, *foie gras* and other delicacies are on sale as well as wine.

Mas des Bressades
Mas du Grand Pagnol
Commune: Manduel.
Owner: Cyril Marès.
Surface Area under Vine: 70 ha.
Wines: Costières de Nîmes including Cuvée Excellence, and Vin de Pays du Gard.

Cyril Marès's father, Roger, owns and runs Château Puy-Castéra in Bordeaux's Haut-Médoc. Having taken an oenology degree at Montpellier, Cyril decided to stay in the neighbourhood and is now married to Nathalie *née* Blanc of the Domaine du Mas Carlot (see page 413). Aged in wood, the Cuvées Excellence (90 per cent Roussanne for the white, 80 per cent Syrah for the red) are concentrated and stylish. Mas du Grand Pagnol is an alternative name for the same wines. Also on offer is a good *vin de pays* from two-thirds Cabernet Sauvignon and one-third Syrah.

CHÂTEAU DE CAMPUGET
CHÂTEAU DE L'AMARINE

Commune: Manduel.

Owner: Jean Dalle.

Surface Area under Vine: 150 ha.

Wines: Costières de Nîmes including Cuvée des Bernis (L'Amarine) and Cuvée Prestige (Campuget).

Campuget is a large, modern winery next to a château which is a mixture of the Renaissance and nineteenth-century Gothic. Jean Dalle bought Château de L'Amarine, whose vineyards lie nearer to Bellegarde, in 1996, the wines of both being vinified at Campuget.

Harvesting is by machine, the white wines being based on Grenache Blanc and the rosés on Grenache Noir. These are pleasant but not serious wines. The better red wine *cuvées*, from roughly equal proportions of Grenache and Syrah, are partly aged in *barrique*, some of which are new each year. These are soft and succulent, at their best three to five years after the vintage.

DOMAINE DU MAS CARLOT
CHÂTEAU PAUL BLANC

Commune: Manduel.

Owners: Paul Blanc and Nathalie Marès.

Surface Area under Vine: 72 ha.

Wines: Costières de Nîmes, red, rosé and white, and Clairette de Bellegarde.

Domaine du Mas Carlot, bought by Nathalie Marès' father in 1988, is next door to Mas des Bressades (see page 412). A full range of wines includes Château Paul Blanc, the superior, oaky red wine *cuvée*, first produced in 1996. The domaine also makes good Clairette de Bellegarde.

CHATEAU GRANDE CASSAGNE

Commune: La Grande Cassagne.

Owners: Laurent and Benoît Dardé.

Surface Area under Vine: 43 ha.

Wines: Costières de Nîmes including a pure Syrah cuvée.

West of Saint-Gilles, on the plateau south of the Nîmes-Arles *autoroute*, the land rises to expose a boulder-ridden plateau much like the one at Châteauneuf-du-Pape.

This is where the Dardé brothers installed themselves, their first vintage being 1993. Much progress has been made in a short time proving *inter alia* the wisdom of their choice of *terroir*. A domaine to watch.

CHÂTEAU MOURGUES DU GRÈS

Commune: Beaucaire.

Owner: François Collard.

Surface Area under Vine: 41 ha.

Wines: Costières de Nîmes including Terre d'Argence and Réserve du Château red, rosé and white.

On the lip of the Costières de Nîmes plateau, halfway between Bellegarde and Beaucaire, lies Mourgues du Grès, a seventeenth-century *mas* of substantial proportions and owned by the Collard family for nearly forty years. The Réserve du Château, largely from Syrah, can be recommended.

CHÂTEAU DE LA TUILERIE

Commune: Nîmes.

Owner: Chantal Comte.

Surface Area under Vine: 70 ha.

Wines: Costières de Nîmes including Cuvée Vieilles Vignes and Cuvée Eole, and Vin de Pays du Gard.

Château de La Tuilerie lies near Nîmes airport between orchards of kiwi fruit, apples, peaches and apricot. The vine feels only incidental. Adjoining the winery is an immense shop where you can buy a dinner service as well as the glasses to pour the wine into, and various home-made liqueurs and alcohols. In the good vintages Château de La Tuilerie produces very good wines, but it proportionately suffers in less good; the soil is a bit thin. Cuvée Eole, from 90 per cent Syrah and matured in *barrique*, is the wine to look out for.

Other Producers of note

DOMAINE DES AVEYLANS, DOMAINE DES CANTARELLES AND CHÂTEAU DES SOURCES (ALL HUBERT SENDRA AND HIS SON-IN-LAW JEAN-FRANÇOIS FAYEL AT BELLEGARDE), CHÂTEAU LAMARGUE/ANDERS BERGENGREN (SAINT-GILLES), CHÂTEAU DE NAGES/ROBERT GASSIER (CAISSARGUES),

Domaine Sainte-Colombe et Les Rameaux/Philippe Guillon (Saint-Gilles) and Château Saint-Cyrgues/Guy de Mercurio (Saint-Gilles).

Clairette de Bellegarde

Surface Area (1998): 40 ha.
Production (1998): 2357 hl.
Colour: White.
Grape Variety: Clairette.
Maximum Yield: 60 hl/ha.
Minimum Alcohol Level: 11°.

Bellegarde is a rather attractive town halfway between Nîmes and Arles on the Rhône-Sète canal. The *appellation* Clairette de Bellegarde lies within the Costières de Nîmes *appellation*, and is for white wines only, produced entirely from the Clairette grape. Compared with the Clairette du Languedoc white this is a lighter, more aromatic wine for even earlier drinking. Sadly production is in decline, most of it, and that no better than competent, being controlled by the local co-operative.

Leading Clairette de Bellegarde Producers

Château de L'Amarine/Jean Dalle (Manduel), Domaine du Mas Carlot/Paul Blanc (Manduel) and Domaine Saint-Louis-La-Perdrix/Philippe Larmour (Bellegarde).

Coteaux du Languedoc

Surface Area (1998): 8307 ha.
Production (1998): (Red and rosé) 381,896 hl; (white) 46,257 hl.
Colour: Red, rosé and white (the latter in certain communes only).
Grape Varieties: (Red and rosé) Carignan (maximum 50%), Syrah, Mourvèdre, Grenache, Lladoner Pebut, Cinsault (maximum 50%), Counoise and Terret Noir (both maximum 10%).
Grenache, Syrah and Mourvèdre must account for 50% of the blend; (rosé) same varieties as for red plus some white grapes allowed; (white) Bourboulenc, Clairette, Grenache Blanc, Ugni Blanc, Maccabéo, Picpoul, Roussanne, Marsanne, Terret Blanc, Rolle and Viognier.
Maximum Yield: 50 hl/ha.
Minimum Alcohol Level: 11°; 11.5° for the *crus*.

The Coteaux du Languedoc spreads patchily over a vast stretch of land mainly in the Hérault but overlapping at either end into the Aude and the Gard from south of Narbonne almost to the gates of Nîmes, a distance of some 125 kilometres as the crow flies. By no means all the land qualifies for *appellation contrôlée*. This is confined to the best areas, usually hilly, usually rock based, for the most part away from the alluvial plains of the coast. Moreover, many growers produce Coteaux du Languedoc from the indigenous grapes alongside *vins de pays* from Chardonnay and Cabernet Sauvignon.

Drive through the Hérault along the *autoroute* and all you notice, if you see anything growing at all, is a vast sea of undulating vines on rich alluvial soils which are mechanically harvested to produce prodigious quantities of indifferent *vin ordinaire*. Turn off the *autoroute* and wander inland into the hills where you will find a different world. The Languedoc landscape can be enchanting. It is the typical Midi mixture of rocky scrub (*garrigue*), limestone outcrops, sheltered valleys and farmsteads and sleepy towns. Vineyards share the hillsides with fields of sunflower, lavender or maize. Here the vines yield only a third of what they do on the plain, resulting in some interesting wines being made by a group of gifted and perfectionistic young winemakers.

Naturally, in such a vast region, there is a wide variety of soils and mesoclimates, and twelve sub-regions or *crus* can add their names to the basic *appellation*. Two stand out – Pic-Saint-Loup and Montpeyroux – and will probably become *appellations* in their own right one day, as happened to Faugères and Saint-Chinian. Another *cru*, Pinet is *appellation* only for its white wine, exclusively from the Picpoul variety. It would make sense for this *cru*, too, to have its own separate *appellation*.

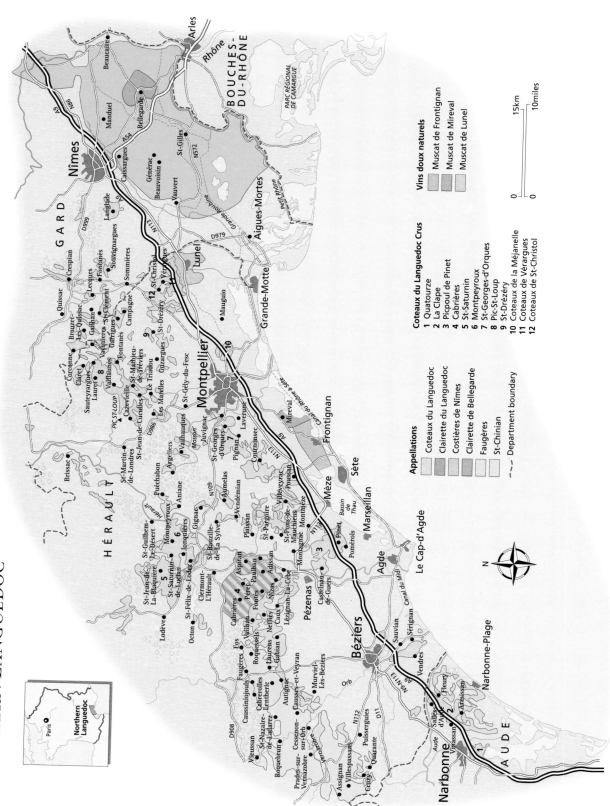

COTEAUX DU LANGUEDOC-CABRIÈRES

The *cru* of Cabrières lies north of Pézenas and is the continuation of the Faugères hills towards Clermont-L'Hérault. The Clairette de Languedoc *appellation* lies within it. In the upper slopes the soil consists of the same schist as in Faugères while elsewhere there is slate. Lower down as the land descends towards the river Hérault, the soil becomes more calcareous or siliceous clay-based, as in the Saint-Chinian *appellation*.

Leading Cabrières Producer

★★ PRIEURÉ DE SAINT-JEAN-DE-BÉBIAN
Commune: Pézenas.
Owners: Jean-Claude Le Brun and Chantal Lecouty.
Surface Area under Vine: 27 ha.
Wines: Coteaux du Languedoc-Cabrières and La Chapelle de Bébian.

This is one of the Languedoc's great estates and was bought in 1994 from the legendary and difficult Alain Roux, who had built it up with cuttings from other leading estates such as Château Rayas, Gérard Chave and Domaine Tempier. Techniques are now a little more sophisticated, there being a slight suggestion of new wood, and the beautiful tumble-down priory has been restored. The red wine, rich, full and long-lasting, contains roughly one-third each Grenache, Mourvèdre and Syrah plus a smidgen of all the other Châteauneuf varieties. Keep the best vintages for a decade.

Other Producers of note
LES VIGNERONS RÉUNIS CO-OPERATIVE — ESPECIALLY CUVÉE FULCRAND CABERNON (CABRIÈRES).

COTEAUX DU LANGUEDOC LA CLAPE

Between Narbonne and the sea lies an extinct volcano called La Clape. Here and on neighbouring limestone outcrops lies the *cru* of La Clape. Together with nearby Quartouze, this is the furthest south that the Coteaux du Languedoc stretches. We are in the Aude *département*, not the Hérault, and some of the land overlaps into what is officially the Corbières *appellation*. Evidence of this is the higher amount of Carignan planted here than further north in other *crus*. The reds can be a bit tough at first, requiring patience. The volcanic soil means that this is a better area than most for white wines.

Leading La Clape Producers

CHÂTEAU DE PECH-REDON
Commune: Narbonne.
Owners: Jean-Claude & Christophe Bousquet.
Surface Area under Vine: 42 ha.
Wines: Coteaux du Languedoc-La Clape including Cuvée Réserve, Cuvée Sélection and Cuvée 'Elevé en Fûts de Chêne', and Vin de Pays d'Oc.

Only a few kilometres from the beach on the one side, and from the noisy city of Narbonne on the other, but 150 or more metres higher up in the mountain of La Clape, lies the peaceful paradise of Château de Pech-Redon. I envy the Bousquets! They bought the estate in 1988 and make several interesting wines, including a good, crisp, unoaked Chardonnay. The Cuvée Sélection is 50 per cent each, old-vine Syrah and Grenache and needs time to soften. The oaky *cuvée* comes from 40 per cent each Syrah and Grenache and 20 per cent Carignan. Both wines are very good.

CHÂTEAU DE PECH-CÉLEYRAN
Commune: Salles-d'Aude.
Owner: Jacques de Saint-Exupéry.
Surface Area under Vine: 95 ha.
Wines: Coteaux du Languedoc-La Clape, and Vin de Pays d'Oc.

There are two Céleyran domaines next door to each other. They were once one estate which belonged to the Toulouse-Lautrec family. The domaine is large — over half the vines lie outside the Coteaux du Languedoc *appellation* and they are used to make a range of *vins de pays*:

Chardonnay, Viognier and *primeur* reds. The Coteaux du Languedoc red, from Syrah, Grenache, Carignan and Mourvèdre and not aged in oak, is medium-bodied, round, cool and stylish.

Other Producer of note

CHÂTEAU DE LA NEGLY/JEAN PAUX-ROSSET (FLEURY D'AUDE).

COTEAUX DU LANGUEDOC-MÉJANELLE

On the high ground east of Montpellier and north of its airport, in danger of being engulfed by the city's suburbs, lies the Méjanelle *cru*. The soil is a sort of sandy alluvion but rich in Châteauneuf-du-Pape-type boulders or *galets* and well-drained. Mainly red, these are good meaty wines.

Leading Méjanelle Producer

CHÂTEAU DE FLAUGERGUES

Commune: Montpellier.
Owner: Comte Henri de Colbert.
Surface Area under Vine: 30 ha.
Wines: Coteaux du Languedoc-Méjanelle including Cuvée Sélection, Cuvée Sommelière and Cuvée 'Elevé en Futs de Chêne'.

Henri de Colbert's family have owned the magnificent seventeenth-century Château de Flaugergues for 300 years. This is the best address in this sub-region. The vineyard is planted mainly with Syrah and Grenache with a little Mourvèdre and these varieties are used for the top *cuvées*. The basic wine, made mainly from Grenache, plus one-third Syrah, is called Cuvée Sélection and is dependable. The Cuvée Sommelière does not see small wood but is full, cool, rich and elegant. The woody Cuvée 'Elevé en Fûts de Chêne' (one-third new oak) is a little less sturdy, but balanced and stylish.

Other Producer of Note

CHÂTEAU LA CALAGE/PIERRE CLAVEL (SAINTE-AUNES).

COTEAUX DU LANGUEDOC-MONTPEYROUX

It is debatable whether Montpeyroux has been put on the map because of its special soil – it seems to be the same stony calcareous-marl, mixed in parts with gravel, *grès* and schist that you find elsewhere – or whether, as I suspect, it is the large number of very talented young growers in the area. What is more interesting is how fast this *cru* has progressed in a very short space of time. Even Sylvain Fadat of the Domaine d'Aupilhac (see page 418), did not really get going until 1989. Most of the other producers date their independence as individual domaine bottlers from more recently.

The *cru* lies due west of Montpellier, north of Clermont L'Hérault, above the river Hérault for the most part, and merges into another one, Saint-Saturnin, to the north-west. Montpeyroux produces firm, full, rich wines, which cry out for at least five years' ageing. I would argue that, along with Pic Saint-Loup, this sub-region deserves to be promoted to full individual *appellation* in its own right.

Leading Montpeyroux Producers

CHÂTEAU L'AIGUELIÈRE

Owners: Aimé Commeyras and associates.
Surface Area under Vine: 30 ha.
Wines: Coteaux du Languedoc-Montpeyroux including Cuvée Tradition – Elevé en Bois, Côte Dorée and Côte Rousse.

Aimé Commeyras was president of the local co-operative until he got fed up with their negative attitude towards excellence and struck out on his own in 1987. He vinifies his grapes parcel by parcel in a temperature-controlled modern cellar outside the village. The basic Montpeyroux is from 50 per cent Syrah, 40 per cent Grenache and 10 per cent Cabernet Sauvignon. The two Côte wines are from special vineyards, the Dorée being gravel and the Rousse clay-limestone and practically 100 per cent Syrah. They are full and virile, with succulent fruit and the flavour of eight months in new wood.

★ DOMAINE D'AUPILHAC

Owner: Sylvain Fadat.
Surface Area under Vine: 22 ha.
Wines: Coteaux du Languedoc-Montpeyroux,
and Vin de Pays du Mont Baudile.

Sylvain Fadat is a classic example of the new breed of Languedoc super-stars. His first vintage was in 1989 and he has quickly made a reputation for himself. His excellent Montpeyroux, from 28 per cent Mourvèdre, 28 per cent Syrah, 20 per cent Carignan and 14 per cent Grenache, is aged in a mixture of small *foudres* and *barriques* for seventeen months and is neither fined nor filtered. Even more interesting is his Vin de Pays du Mont Baudile from 100 per cent, very old Carignan, made in the traditional manner, with a long maceration and lots of *pigeage*. The yield is a very low 35-40 hl/ha, and the wine is a revelation to those who consider Carignan one of the bad boys of the vineyard scene.

MAS CAL DEMOURA

Commune: Jonquières.
Owner: Jean-Pierre Jullien.
Surface Area under Vine: 24 ha.
Wine: Coteaux du Languedoc-Montpeyroux.

Jean-Pierre Jullien was a member of the local co-operative until 1993 and he still has to give them 19 hectares' worth of grapes each year. With the remainder he makes one wine, so far, with only partially destemmed fruit. It comes from 22 per cent each Syrah, Grenache, Mourvèdre and Cinsault and 12 per cent Carignan. There is barrel-ageing for the Mourvèdre which now gives the wine a gently oaky touch.

DOMAINE FONT CAUDE

Owner: Alain Chabanon.
Surface Area under Vine: 22 ha.
Wines: Coteaux du Languedoc-Montpeyroux
including Font Caude Tradition, Esprit de Font
Caude and Les Boissières, and Vin de Pays d'Oc.

Alain Chabanon was the director of a co-operative in the Gard before setting up on his own here in 1992. For the time being two- thirds of his harvest goes to the local co-operative. He is cramped for space and looking for better sited vineyards. It is an open secret that in direct violation of the local wine laws his Font Caude Tradition and other wines contain Merlot as well as Syrah and Grenache. The Esprit de Font Caude *cuvée* contains 90 per cent Syrah and is aged in *barrique*. Les Boissières is 90 per cent Grenache from a very stony vineyard between Montpeyroux and Saint-Saturnin. These two need to be kept for at least five years before drinking.

★ MAS JULLIEN

Commune: Jonquières.
Owner: Olivier Jullien.
Surface Area under Vine: 15 ha.
Wines: Coteaux du Languedoc-Montpeyroux
including Les Cailloutis, Les Depierres and Les
Etats d'Ame, and Vin de Pays d'Oc.

Olivier Jullien, son of Jean-Pierre Jullien (see Mas Cal Demoura left), is another of the region's stars. The red wine *cuvées* are Les Cailloutis (one-quarter each Carignan, Grenache, Syrah and Mourvèdre); Les Depierres (schistous *terroir* for the 40 per cent Syrah and half of the 30 per cent Grenache; limestone and gravel soil for the rest of the Grenache and the remaining Cinsault and Carignan); and the very good Les Etats d'Ame (30 per cent old Carignan, 20 per cent Cinsault plus others and then matured in old *barriques* for six to ten months). In 1991 Olivier Jullien produced a revelatory 100 per cent old-vine Cinsault that lasted very well.

★ DOMAINE SAINT-ANDRIEU

Owner: Charles Giner.
Surface Area under Vine: 25 ha.
Wines: Coteaux du Languedoc-Montpeyroux
including Les Roches Blanches, Les Marnes Bleues
and L'Yeuse Noire.

Charles Giner was an engineer, taking over the estate on his father-in-law's death in 1982. At first he rented the vines out, then on retirement from his job took over personally in 1992, and from 1995, as he puts it himself, began to get it right. Vallougue is a *cuvée* for early drinking; Les Marnes Bleues comes from 80 per cent Mourvèdre; Les Roches Blanches from a more normal mixture, but neither wines use small wood, unlike the rather special L'Yeuse Noire, which comes from 70 per cent Mourvèdre. This will last at least for a decade.

DOMAINE LES THÉRONS
CHÂTEAU MANDAGOT
Owner: Jean-François Vallat.
Surface Area under Vine: 35 ha.
Wines: Coteaux du Languedoc-Montpeyroux, and Vin de Pays d'Oc.

The top wine here is Château Mandagot, from older vines (40 per cent each Syrah and Grenache and 20 per cent Mourvèdre) and made with a touch of *barrique-* ageing. This is a very good example of the sort of new wave Languedoc red: a wine that will improve in bottle and is meant for drinking after five years rather than two.

Other Producers of note
CHÂTEAU DE JONQUIÈRES/FRANÇOIS AND ISABELLE DE CABISSOLE (JONQUIÈRES) AND CAVE COOPÉRATIVE DE MONTPEYROUX – INCLUDING DOMAINE DE PÉROU, CHÂTEAU DE ROQUEFEUIL AND OTHERS (MONTPEYROUX).

COTEAUX DU LANGUEDOC-PICPOUL DE PINET

'*Son terroir, c'est la mer*' ('its *terroir* is the sea'), proclaims the brochure advertising the white Picpoul wines from six communes lying between Pézenas and the Bassin de Thau on the Mediterranean coast. Four co-operatives, at Castelnau de Guers, Pomérols, Montagnac and especially the Cave de L'Ormarine at Pinet itself, provide much of the annual 30,000 hectolitres. I have to say I find most of the wines rather undistinguished though the oak-aged Cuvée Hugues de Beauvignac from the Pomérols co-operative is well worth a try.

Producers of note
DOMAINE FÉLINES-JOURDAN/MARIE-HÉLÈNE JOURDAN (SAINT-GÉLY DU FESC), CLAUDE AND LUDOVIC GAUJAL – ESPECIALLY CUVÉE LUDOVIC GAUJAL (PINET), DOMAINE DE MONTREDON/BRUNO CENTIÉ (CASTELNAU DE GUERS), CHÂTEAU DE PINET/MADAME ARNAUD GAUJAL (PINET)

AND MAS SAINT-LAURENT/ROLAND AND NICOLE TARROUX (MONTMÈZE).

COTEAUX DU LANGUEDOC PIC-SAINT-LOUP

If Montpeyroux is worthy of being upgraded to *appellation contrôlée* in its own right, Pic-Saint-Loup can also surely justify promotion, both because of its superior *terroir* and a long and expanding list of good producers.

The Pic itself, a splendid piece of naked, jagged rock, lies equidistant between Saint-Martin-de-Londres and Valflaunès some 25 kilometres north of Montpellier, and the vineyard area lies south and east stretching between Saint-Gély-du-Fesc and Corconne, just over the *départmental* border into the Gard. This is a cooler area than most of the Languedoc, especially at night in the run-up to the vintage, and with a higher average annual rainfall as well. It is generally not hot enough for the Carignan here and, according to some locals, even in parts for the Mourvèdre. Ninety per cent of the red wine *encépagement* must come from Grenache, Syrah and Mourvèdre. The soil is based on clay and limestone, but there are different types: a deep band of reddish, very stony debris, lower down; porous, more rocky soil containing less clay, and greyer in colour further up the slope; and in parts a much cooler, less well-drained calcareous marl. This latter soil is a good environment for white grape varieties. The Pic-Saint-Loup *cru*, however, is for red and rosé only. White wines are labelled as straight Coteaux du Languedoc.

What I find distinctive about Pic-Saint-Loup wines is that they are substantial without being 'hot' or heavy. They are well-balanced and they can be surprisingly sophisticated. They will also last well.

Leading Pic Saint-Loup Producers

★ MAS BRUGUIÈRE
Owner: Guilhem Bruguière.
Commune: Valflaunès.
Surface Area under Vine: 10 ha.

Wines: Coteaux du Languedoc-Pic-Saint-Loup including Cuvée Vinum de Calcadis, Cuvée Classique and Cuvée 'Élevé en Fûts de Chêne'.

Next door to Hortus (see below) and in the hands of the Bruguière family since the Revolution, this vineyard is planted with Syrah, Grenache and Mourvèdre, plus Roussanne for the white wine. The Cuvée Vinum de Calcadis is for the young vines, and is partially vinified by carbonic maceration. The Cuvée Classique comes from 60 per cent Syrah and 40 per cent Grenache while the oaky blend contains less Grenache and 20 per cent Mourvèdre. This wine is intense, harmonious, profound and elegant and one of the Languedoc's best.

Château de Cazeneuve

Commune: Lauret.
Owner: André Leenhardt.
Surface Area under Vine: 35 ha.
Wines: Coteaux de Languedoc-Pic-Saint-Loup including Les Terres Rouges and La Grande Cuvée, and Coteaux du Languedoc white.

André Leenhardt acquired the Château de Cazeneuve in 1988 and has been making wine since 1992. In the meanwhile a major replanting programme has been underway, replacing the ignoble varieties with Syrah and Mourvèdre, plus Roussanne for the white wine.

There are two good *cuvées* of the white, one oaky and one with a faint suggestion of wood. These can only get better as the Roussanne vines become older. Les Terres Rouges is the label for the young vine red. The simple château label is used for non-oaked, 70 per cent Syrah wine. The Grande Cuvée comes from 90 per cent Syrah, aged in barrel, of which one-third is new each year. This is a rich, profound, poised and balanced wine. A domaine to watch.

★ Domaine de L'Hortus

Commune: Valflaunès.
Owner: Jean Orliac.
Surface Area under Vine: 32 ha.
Wines: Coteaux du Languedoc-Pic-Saint-Loup including La Grande Cuvée, and Vin de Pays du Val de Montferrand.

Towards the end of the 1970s Jean Orliac, a young agricultural engineer, discovered an abandoned valley hidden in the shadows of the Pic-Saint-Loup. He set about renovating the ancient vine terraces and had his architect sister construct an attractive wooden home there. He named his new domaine Hortus, after the Latin for 'garden', and a local place name. Until 1990 he sent his grapes to the local co-operative. Since then he has become one of the stars of the area. The Grande Cuvée Blanc (Vin de Pays du Val de Montferrand) is made from roughly equal amounts of Chardonnay and Viognier and vinified in barrel. It is one of the Midi's classiest white wines. Like the white, the Grande Cuvée is an exemplary wine. Made from almost equal parts of Syrah and Mourvèdre, plus 10 to 15 per cent Grenache, it is matured in oak (two-thirds new) for fifteen months.

★ Château de Lascaux

Commune: Vacquières
Owner: Jean-Benoît Cavalier.
Surface Area under Vine: 35 ha.
Wines: Coteaux du Languedoc-Pic-Saint-Loup including Les Nobles Pierres, and Coteaux du Languedoc (white) including Les Pierres d'Argent.

'Lascaux' means limestone rock, says Jean-Benoît Cavalier, who took over from his father in 1984 and extricated himself from the local co-operative some five years later. His vines lie north of the village (his cellar is near the church) on a series of very stony terraces rescued out of the *garrigues*. 'Finesse is everything', he says. The top white *cuvée* is made from Viognier, Marsanne, Rolle and Roussanne vinified in *barrique* and is delicious. The red equivalent contains 90 per cent Syrah and 10 per cent Grenache and is matured for twelve months in wood, 30 per cent of which is new. This is a wine of size with fine tannins and lots of finesse. It needs time to mature.

Mas de Mortiès

Commune: Saint-Jean-de-Cuculles.
Owners: Isabelle & Rémi Duchemin.
Surface Area under Vine: 26 ha.
Wines: Coteaux du Languedoc-Pic-Saint-Loup

including Cuvée Fût de Chêne, Coteaux du Languedoc and Vin de Pays d'Oc.

Mas de Mortiès lies on the southern side of the Pic Saint-Loup. The Duchemins, who work with a sister and brother-in-law, took over in 1993, since when there has been much replanting. The wine from the younger vines is sold as simple Coteaux du Languedoc, which leaves them with two *cuvées* sold as Pic-Saint-Loup. The basic one is ripe and succulent (from one-third each Syrah, Carignan and Grenache, the first two made by carbonic maceration) and the oaky *cuvée* contains a bit more Syrah, is riper and more chocolaty in flavour.

★ CHÂTEAU DE LA ROQUE

Commune: Fontanès.
Owner: Jack Boutin.
Surface Area under Vine: 42 ha.
Wines: Coteaux du Languedoc-Pic-Saint-Loup including Cupa Numismae and Cuvée des Vieilles Vignes, Mourvèdre, and Coteaux du Languedoc Clos des Bénédictins.

The Mas of La Roque has its origins in a Benedictine monastery founded in 1029. Today the château, up against the hillsides south of Fontanès, is painted with rather garish magenta shutters, with its cellar carved out of the rock underneath.

Jack Boutin bought the estate in 1983 and has replanted much of the vineyard with Mourvèdre, a variety in which he strongly believes. The white wines are from Marsanne, Rolle, a little Viognier and Grenache Blanc (none of the latter in the individual and delicious, gently oaky Clos des Bénédictins). The reds are from Syrah, Mourvèdre and Grenache (again none of the latter in the Cupa Numismae, named after a Gallo-Roman gold coin Jack Boutin found in the vineyard). This special *cuvée* is tannic, serious and impressive: needing five years' ageing. The old-vine Mourvèdre *cuvée*, a new introduction, is very good too and needs ageing too.

Other Producers of note

ERMITAGE DU PIC-SAINT-LOUP (CAZEVIEILLE), CHÂTEAU L'EUZIÈRE/MICHEL CAUSSE (FONTANÈS), DOMAINE DE LANCYRE/DURAND-VALENTIN (VALFLAUNÈS), CHÂTEAU DE LASCOURS/CLAUDE ARLÈS (SAUTEYRARGUES), MAS DE LAVABRE/OLIVIER BRIDET (CLARET) AND DOMAINE DES VIGNES HAUTES/SCA LA GRAVETTE (CORCONNE). ALSO JEAN-MARC BOILLOT OF POMMARD IN BURGUNDY BOUGHT LAND NEXT TO LA ROQUE IN 1998.

COTEAUX DU LANGUEDOC-QUARTOUZE

Quartouze is a small *cru* south of Narbonne. The soil is a stony quartz mixed with sandstone and the wine, big and burly, comes mainly from the Carignan grape. One of the few growers of note is Georges Ortola at Château Notre-Dame-du-Quartouze.

COTEAUX DU LANGUEDOC-SAINT-CHRISTOL, -SAINT-DRÉZÉRY AND -VÉRARGUES

North-east of Montpellier lie the adjacent *crus* of Vérargues, Saint-Christol and Saint-Drézéry, each based around a village of the same name. None is very large and even grouped together they do not equal the production of Pic-Saint-Loup, nor are they of great importance. The co-operatives are the main producers and most wines are light and made for early drinking.

Leading Saint-Drézéry Producer

CHÂTEAU PECH-HAUT

Commune: Saint-Drézéry.
Owner: Gérard Bru.
Surface Area under Vine: 50 ha.
Wines: Coteaux du Languedoc-Saint-Drézéry including Cuvée Tradition, Cuvée Prestige and Cuvée Succès.

This new domaine was established on very stony soil on a little hill in the mid-1980s by a Montpellier businessman, Gérard Bru, who suddenly got an itch for wine. He cleared the land, planted Syrah and Grenache and some Carignan for the reds and rosés, Viognier, Marsanne and Roussanne for the whites, and rebuilt stone by stone an attractive château in the eighteenth-century style. There is an impressive vinification cellar of stainless steel vats, a storage cellar of wooden *foudres*, and a barrel cellar too. All three reds spend a period in *barrique*. I like both the Prestige and the Succès, and am sure that the white wine will be fine when the vines age a bit. It just shows what you can do when there's a will — and there is a truffle forest nearby.

Other Producers of note

Domaine de La Devèze/Claudine Navarro (Vérargues) and Domaine Guinand/Domaine Salièga (Saint-Christol).

Coteaux du Languedoc-Saint-Georges-d'Orques

Five communes almost engulfed by the south-west suburbs of Montpellier are home to the *cru* of Saint-Georges-d'Orques, named after one of them. This is a small *appellation* (there are only seven private domaines and three co-operatives) for many of the original vineyards which enjoyed a good reputation 200 or more years ago have been absorbed by the expanding city. The soil consists of limestone, ridges rich in quartz pebbles, with gravel on the flatter land which gives the wine an attractive freshness.

Leading Saint-Georges d'Orques Producer

Domaine Henry
Commune: Saint-Georges-d'Orques.
Owner: François Henry.
Surface Area under Vine: 11 ha.
Wines: Coteaux du Languedoc-Saint-Georges-d'Orques including Cuvée Paradines and Cru Saint-Georges, and Vin de Pays d'Oc.
The Henry family, *vignerons* from father to son for more than ten generations, moved to Saint-Georges-d'Orques

in 1993, having read up on the ancient pre-phylloxera reputation of the wine. They had previously owned the Domaine Saint-Martin de La Garrigue at Montagnac. Cuvée Paradines, the name of a *lieu-dit*, is made from Grenache, Syrah and Cinsault plus a little Mourvèdre, and is ripe and sturdy. The Cru Saint-Georges is from older vines, and undergoes a *cuvaison* as long as a month, which is longer than most. This is also good: in the better vintages it is very good indeed.

Other Producers of note

Château de L'Engarran/Diane Losfelt (Lenserune) and Château de Forques/Lise Fons-Vincent (Juvignac).

Coteaux du Languedoc-Saint-Saturnin

West of Montpeyroux, round the town of Saint-Saturnin-de-Lucian, on good schistous and limestone debris soil, lies the *cru* of Saint-Saturnin. The area is dominated by two local co-operatives, at Saint-Félix-de-Lodez and at Saint-Saturnin, famous for its rather deep-coloured wine called Rosé d'Une Nuit. There are few individual growers. Château La Sauvageonne (below), although it lies firmly within the *appellation*, does not label its wine as Saint-Saturnin.

Château La Sauvageonne
Commune: Saint-Jean-de-La-Blaquière.
Owners: Gaëtan Poncé & Fils.
Surface Area under Vine: 35 ha.
Wines: Coteaux du Languedoc including Carte Noire and Cuvée Prestige, and Vin de Pays du Mont Baudile.
The hills around Saint-Jean-de-La-Blaquière are a marvellous russet-coloured schist and twenty-five years ago here at 350 metres above sea level, the Poncé family created a domaine from scratch. There is an interesting white *vin de pays*, made from Sauvignon Blanc with a dash of Muscat à Petits Grains. The Carte Noire comes from 50 per cent Syrah and a quarter each Grenache and

Cinsault. There is no wood used but the wine is ripe, ample and easy to enjoy. The Prestige red wine *cuvée* comes from 80 per cent Syrah and 20 per cent Grenache, and is ample and concentrated, even though no wood has been used.

Other Coteaux du Languedoc Producers

ABBAYE DE VALMAGNE
Commune: Mèze.
Owner: Philippe d'Allaines.
Surface Area under Vine: 70 ha.
Wines: Coteaux du Languedoc including Cuvée de Turenne, and Vin de Pays d'Oc.

Some 8 kilometres north-west of Mèze, which lies on the Bassin de Thau opposite Sète, is the Cistercian Abbaye de Valmagne, founded in 1138. The monks were the first to plant vines, and this tradition has been continued by Philippe d'Allaines, the present owner, whose family has owned it since 1838. The white Cuvée de Turenne, Roussanne vinified in *barrique*, is a good wine which will keep for a few years. Its red counterpart, half each Syrah and Mourvèdre, also oak-aged, is cool, classy and succulent. The Gothic church now houses the *foudres* wherein most of the wine is stored.

MAISON JEANJEAN
Commune: Saint-Félix-de-Lodez.
Owners: Bernard and Hugues Jeanjean.
Wines: Appellation Contrôlée and Vins de Pays from all over the Languedoc.

This is a large and long-established merchant which as well as providing literally millions of litre bottles of *vin ordinaire* and anonymous *vins de pays*, has the exclusivity for a number of good individual Languedoc domaines. These include Domaine Saint-Martin in Fitou, Domaine Adelaine in Corbières and Château Pierreru in Saint-Chinian. The standard of these wines is high.

CHÂTEAU DE MONTPEZAT
Commune: Pézenas.
Owner: Christophe Blanc.

Surface Area under Vine: 21 ha.
Wines: Coteaux du Languedoc and Vin de Pays d'Oc.

Christophe and Laurence Blanc took over the estate in 1988 and until then the wines had been sold off in bulk. The Coteaux du Languedoc comes from 100 per cent Mourvèdre and is a very good, classy example which can only improve as the vines mature. The *vins de pays* (Syrah/Grenache and Merlot/Cabernet) are good, too.

★★ DOMAINE PEYRE-ROSE
Commune: Saint-Pargoire.
Owner: Marlène Soria.
Surface Area under Vine: 24 ha.
Wines: Coteaux du Languedoc including Cuvée Les Cistes and Cuvée Clos Léone.

Peyre is a corruption of *pierre* (stone) and Rose is the name of Marlène Soria's mother. And *rose* (French for pink), and a garish one at that, is the colour of the paint on the storage tanks. Hacked out of uncompromising limestone *garrigue* in the late 1980s, the domaine is reached with difficulty at the end of a beaten track above the village of Saint-Pargoire. There is no temerpature control over the winemaking (they have to generate their own electricity), the yields rarely exceed 20 hl/ha and no oak is used. The wine, however, is exceptional. Les Cistes (85 per cent Syrah, 15 per cent Grenache) is usually fresher and more red fruity; the Cuvée Clos Léone (95 per cent Syrah, 5 per cent Mourvèdre) is more black fruity, more roasted and gamey. These are some of the greatest, and certainly some of the most original wines, to come out of the Languedoc.

LES VIGNERONS DE LA MÉDITERRANÉE, VAL D'ORBIEU
Commune: Narbonne.
Owners: Eric Brousse and Jean-Claude Guitard.
Surface Area under Vine: 4000 ha.
Wines: Appellation Contrôlée and Vins de Pays from all over the Languedoc.

Les Vignerons de la Méditerranée, which exports its wines under the name of Les Vignerons du Val d'Orbieu, is a grouping of some 190 domaines. There is a common warehousing and despatch depot on the outskirts of Narbonne, as well as facilities for winemaking and bottling. Standards are high. A number of leading estates belong, including Châteaux Les Oilleux-Romanis, Fontsainte and La Voulte-Gasparets, all in Corbières.

Other Coteaux du Languedoc Producers of note
DOMAINE DE BAUBIAC/SCEA PHILIP FRÈRES (BROUZET-LÈS-QUISSAC), DOMAINE BOIS D'ELEINS/SCA CRESPIAN (CRESPIAN), DOMAINE CELINGUET/PIERRE ROUQUETTE (ARGELLIERS), MAS DES CHIMÈRES/GUILHEM DARDÉ (OCTON), DOMAINE DURAND-CAMILLO/ARMAND DURAND (CAUX), CHÂTEAU GRÈS SAINT-PAUL/JEAN-PHILIPPE SERVIÈRE (LUNEL), DOMAINE DU PUJOL/KIM AND ROBERT CRIPPS (VAILHAUQUES), DOMAINE SAINT-MARTIN DE LA GARRIGUE/ UMBERTO AND GRÉGORY GUIDA (MONTAGNAC) AND DOMAINE DES TOURELLES/DIDIER CABANÈS (SAUVIAN).

CLAIRETTE DU LANGUEDOC

Surface Area (1998): 90 ha.
Production (1998): 3362 hl.
Colour: White.
Grape Variety: Clairette.
Maximum Yield: 50 hl/ha.
Minimum Alcohol Level: 12°.

On hillside slopes between Pézenas and Clermont L'Hérault, facing south-east towards the valley of the river Hérault, you will find the vineyards for Clairette du Languedoc, an *appellation* which is rarer today than it was in the 1940s and 1950s. The eleven communes can also produce red wine but this is sold as Coteaux du Languedoc. Clairette du Languedoc is usually dry, but can be medium-dry, sweet and even *rancio*, a maderised version. This is a more substantial wine than Clairette de Bellegarde produced on the coast at Bellegarde, but is still best drunk young as Clairette wines tend to age fast. Bernard Jany at Château La Condamine Bertrand at Lézignan-La-Cèbe is the best known producer. The co-operative at Adissan is another useful address.

FAUGÈRES

Surface Area (1998): 1714 ha.
Production (1998): 75,559 hl.
Colour: Red and rosé.
Grape Varieties: (Red and rosé) Carignan (maximum 40%), Syrah and Mourvèdre (minimum 20% combined), Grenache and Lladoner Pelut (minimum 20% combined) and Cinsault (maximum 60%).
Maximum Yield: 50 hl/ha.
Minimum Alcohol Level: 11.5°.

North of Saint-Chinian and higher in the foothills of the Cévennes, entirely on schistous soil, lies the *appellation* of Faugères. Like Saint-Chinian it was singled out from the Coteaux du Languedoc *appellation* and promoted to one in its own right in 1982.

The area is roughly the shape of a trapezium, confined by the communes of Fos, Laurens, Autignac and Cabrerolles. It is smaller than Saint-Chinian, not only in terms of its size and production, but even more so in the number of individual independent growers, but the standard of these producers, led by Domaine Alquier (see page 425), possibly the best producer of *appellation* wine in the whole of the Languedoc, is high. The name of Faugères, though, is not widely recognised on the export market. Perhaps this is to do with difficulties with the spelling and pronunciation of the name?

With a *terroir* and a mesoclimate much like the higher part of Saint-Chinian, and an equally desolate, rugged countryside, the wines have much in common. I find Faugères a little firmer and more structured, with a definite herbs-of-the-*garrigue* flavour: more original. Schist gives an elegant, mineral element to the tannins, while the wines produced from clay-limestone soils can be a bit tough and dense.

Modern winemaking and viticultural techniques have produced more sophisticated wines. Most of the fruit is now entirely destemmed and several leading producers also give their wines a period in *barrique*. But better techniques have not, thankfully, subdued the inner strength and individual personality of the wine. It keeps well.

Leading Faugères Producers

★★ DOMAINE JEAN-MICHEL ALQUIER
Owner: Jean-Michel Alquier.
Surface Area under Vine: 44 ha.
Wines: Faugères including Cuvée La Maison Jaune and Les Bastides, and Vin de Pays de L'Hérault.

Gilbert Alquier, father of Jean-Michel, is credited with being the driving force behind the creation of Faugères as a separate *appellation* in 1982. He had first planted Syrah in his vineyard as many as twenty years before with the intention of producing a wine from the Midi that could be as serious as a Côtes du Rhône, a novel idea at the time. This is one of the few cellars in the Languedoc which is entirely air-conditioned. Today his son Jean-Michel is in charge.

The oaky Maison Jaune *cuvée* is produced from 50 per cent Syrah, 30 per cent Grenache and 20 per cent Mourvèdre and the even better Les Bastides from 70 per cent Syrah and 15 per cent each of the other two varieties. This is expensive for a Faugères wine but well worth it. And the Alquiers are quite right: it does keep, and it has all the class and depth of a red Hermitage. There is, in addition, a good white *vin de pays*, from Roussanne and Marsanne with a dash of Viognier.

★ CHÂTEAU DES ESTANILLES
Commune: Lenthéric.
Owners: Monique and Michel Louison.
Surface Area under Vine: 22 ha.
Wines: Faugères including Cuvée Tradition, Cuvée Prestige, Cuvée Syrah and Cuvée Mourvèdre Rosé, and Coteaux du Languedoc (white).

Michel Louison was an electrician in the Touraine before setting up at the Château des Estanilles in 1978. This is a modern winery, with stainless steel vats and a *table de tri*, and the wines are cool, elegant and have plenty of fruit. The basic Cuvée Tradition is cool, fruity and elegant: not aged in wood. The oak-aged Cuvée Prestige is produced from 50 per cent Syrah and 25 per cent each Grenache and Mourvèdre. The pure Syrah wine spends thirteen months in *barrique* and is rich, succulent and individual.

CHÂTEAU GRÉZAN
Commune: Laurens.
Owners: Michel Lubac, Rémy Fardel and Jean-Louis Pujol.
Surface Area under Vine: 120 ha.
Wines: Faugères including Cuvée Arnaud Lubac, and Vin de Pays d'Oc.

This sizeable estate makes a big, meaty style of Faugères. The Cuvée Arnaud Lubac is aged in wood, one-third of which is new, and is rich, fat and concentrated. There are good *vins de pays* from Chardonnay, Merlot and Pinot Noir. The château itself dates from the twelfth century and there is a cafeteria-style restaurant in one of the outbuildings.

CHÂTEAU HAUT-FABRÈGUES
Commune: Cabrerolles.
Owners: André and Cédric Saur.
Surface Area under Vine: 66 ha.
Wines: Faugères including Sélection and Cuvée Prestige.

Haut-Fabrègues is a handsome early seventeenth-century château surrounded by its vines in the middle of nowhere. You taste in its splendid vaulted cellar. The basic *cuvée*, which contains some Cinsault, is agreeable: a lightish wine for early drinking. The Sélection, from older vines and the best sited parcels, is better still. But the oak-aged, half-Syrah half-Mourvèdre Cuvée Prestige is the wine that really excites me here. It has plenty of depth and potential for ageing.

CHÂTEAU DE LA LIQUIÈRE
Commune: Cabrerolles.
Owners: Bernard and Claude Vidal.
Surface Area under Vine: 60 ha.
Wines: Faugères including Cuvée des Amandiers, Cuvée Vieilles Vignes and Cuvée Cistus, and Coteaux du Languedoc (white) Cuvée Schistes, and rosé.

The Vidal family has been producing wine at La Liquière since the seventeenth century. The vineyard lies up in the hills at an altitude of 300 metres. The rich and intense Cuvée Vieilles Vignes is made from 40 per cent, seventy-year-old Carignan vines (produced by carbonic maceration), 40 per cent Grenache and 10 per cent each Syrah and Mourvèdre. The Cuvée Cistus is one of the best Faugères wines produced – it contains 60 per cent Syrah and is given fourteen months in *barrique*. The white Schistes, from 90 per cent Grenache Blanc, is lightly oaky and full of interest. The rosé is full and meaty: a good wine. A good address.

DOMAINE DU MÉTÉORE

Commune: Cabrerolles.
Owners: Ginette Coste and Geneviève Libès.
Surface Area under Vine: 19 ha.
Wines: Faugères including Cuvée Réserve and Cuvée Fûts de Chêne, and Coteaux du Languedoc (red).

Next to an impressive crater which is well worth a visit, the Mesdames Coste and Libès produce an excellent Mourvèdre-based Cuvée Réserve. This is a backward, concentrated, structured wine which in the best years needs seven or eight years to soften up.

DOMAINE OLLIER-TAILLEFER

Commune: Fos.
Owners: Alain and Luc Ollier.
Surface Area under Vine: 24 ha.
Wines: Faugères including Cuvée Grande Réserve and Cuvée Castel Fossibus.

Fos is in the extreme north-west of the *appellation* and this domaine seems to be the only private one in the commune. There are good wines here, especially Cuvée Castel Fossibus, which is velvety-rich, balanced and elegant. In a good vintage it needs five years.

DOMAINE RAYMOND ROQUE

Commune: Cabrerolles.
Owners: Raymond and Marc Roque.
Surface Area under Vine: 40 ha.
Wines: Faugères including Cuvée Marc François and Grande Réserve.

The Roques have two cellars, one at the top and one at the lower end of the village of Cabrerolles. The Grande Réserve *cuvée* has long enjoyed the reputation of being one of Faugères' top reds, and it is a stayer too. It comes from very old vines: 50 per cent Carignan and 25 per cent each Syrah and Grenache.

Other Producers of note

CHÂTEAU CHENAIE/ANDRÉ CHABBERT (CAUSSINIOJOULS), DOMAINE DE FENOUILLET/MAISON JEANJEAN (SAINT-FÉLIX-DE-LODEZ), DOMAINE DU FRAISSE/JACQUES PONS (AUTIGNAC), CHÂTEAU DES PEYREGRANDES/PIERRE BÉNÉZECH (ROQUESSELS) AND THE CO-OPERATIVE AT LAURENS.

SAINT-CHINIAN

Surface Area (1998): 2714 ha.
Production (1998): 130,123 hl.
Colour: Red and rosé.
Grape Varieties: Grenache, Lladoner Pelut, Syrah, Mourvèdre (to provide a combined total of not less than 60% of the blend, from 1998), Carignan (maximum 40%) and Cinsault (maximum 30%).
Maximum Yield: 50 hl/ha.
Minimum Alcohol Level: 11.5°.

Saint-Chinian lies up in the hills at the southern end of the *département* of Hérault, sandwiched between the Minervois and the Faugères. Like the latter, having been VDQS Coteaux du Languedoc, it was promoted to full *appellation contrôlée* in 1982. Named after the main town in the area which itself is named after an eighth-century Benedictine saint, Saint Benoît d'Aniane or Anhan. From twenty communes which stretch between Villespassans and Saint-Nazaire-de-Ladarez, and up to Vieussan in the hills, the wine has a long history as a wine in its own right.

The higher slopes, up to 250 metres high, are schist or *grès*, rocky and exposed to the south. The area is wild and depopulated, the vineyards having been planted on land rescued from the *garrigue*. Lower down limestone predominates, mixed with clay and bauxite and boulders brought down by the rivers Orb and Vernazobres. Sheltered from the north by the hills of the Caroux and L'Epinouse, this is an auspicious place to make wine.

There is an increasing number of good growers, and at least two excellent co-operatives.

With the growing concentration on *cépages améliorateurs* such as the Syrah – unlike neighbouring Faugères there is nothing in the Saint-Chinian legislation to stop growers making a pure Syrah wine – the improvement in the quality of the wine over the last fifteen years has been dramatic. In general, the wines are a little fuller than those of the Minervois, but not as firm – to the advantage of their finesse perhaps – as the average Faugères. The best are made by traditional methods (only the Carignan being vinified by carbonic maceration), but with full destemming and proper temperature control, and the top wines are barrique-aged in small wood. They keep well.

Leading Saint-Chinian Producers

CLOS BAGATELLE

Owners: Henry and Christine Simon.
Surface Area under Vine: 53 ha.
Wines: Saint-Chinian including La Gloire de Mon Père, and Muscat de Saint-Jean-de-Minervois.

The vineyard of Clos Bagatelle is almost equally divided between limestone and schistous soil and is planted with 35 per cent Carignan, 20 per cent Grenache, 20 per cent Syrah, 15 per cent Mourvèdre and 10 per cent Cinsault, the latter being used for the rosé wine. The top *cuvée*, La Gloire de Mon Père, is oak-aged and is full, rich and tannic, needing five years' ageing.

★ DOMAINE BORIE LA VITARÈLE

Commune: Saint-Nazaire-de-Ladarez.
Owners: Catherine Planes and Jean-François Izarn.
Surface Area under Vine: 12 ha.
Wines: Saint-Chinian, Coteaux du Languedoc and Vin de Pays d'Oc.

Domaine Borie La Vitarèle lies on the Faugères side of the *appellation* in a soil which is a mixture of limestone rich in fossils, white marl, and on the higher slopes Roquebrun schist. Cathy Planes and Jean-François Izarn arrived in 1990 and have quickly established their Saint-Chinian (usually 100 per cent pure Syrah) as one of the leading wines of the *appellation*. La Combe, a *vin de pay*, is made from 60 per cent Cabernet Sauvignon (still young vines) along with Syrah, Grenache and Merlot, and is very good too, as is the Coteaux du Languedoc, from 80 per cent Grenache and 20 per cent Syrah. The wines age well and need five years to mature in good vintages.

★ CHÂTEAU CAZAL-VIEL

Commune: Cessenon-sur-Orb.
Owners: Christine and Henri Miquel.
Surface Area under Vine: 90 ha.
Wines: Saint-Chinian including Cuvée Tradition, Cuvée Prestige Fût and Cuvée Georges Albert Aoust, and Vin de Pays d'Oc including Cuvée Finesse.

Laurent Miquel has now joined his parents at this family domaine – it has been in Miquel hands since 1797 – and is now responsible for the winemaking. The Saint-Chinians are made primarily from Syrah, with Grenache, Cinsault and Carignan making up the balance for the lesser *cuvées*, Mourvèdre in the Cuvée Georges Albert Aoust, and entirely Syrah for the Cuvée Prestige Fût. These are stylish wines, rich, oaky and concentrated. They keep well. The *vins de pays* include Sauvignon Blanc, Viognier, Syrah and Pinot Noir wines and the Cuvée Finesse is a Sauvignon and Muscat à Petits Grains blend. I prefer the Saint-Chinians.

MAS CHAMPART

Commune: Bramefan.
Owners: Isabelle and Mathieu Champart.
Surface Area under Vine: 16 ha.
Wines: Saint-Chinian, Coteaux du Languedoc and Vin de Pays d'Oc.

Isabelle and Mathieu Champart took over the family vineyards in 1976, ripped up the ignoble varieties and planted Mourvèdre and Syrah for the reds and more exotic strains such as Viognier and Marsanne for the whites. Some Cabernet Franc for *vin de pays* was planted in the late 1980s. The wines they produce themselves come from the better, schistous parcels, grapes from 7.5 hectares of their domaine being destined for the local co-operative. The Saint-Chinian comes from 70 per cent

Syrah and 30 per cent Grenache and is matured in a mixture of small wood and *demi-muids*. The wine is firm, somewhat old-fashioned, but not short of depth. The best vintages of the reds need five years' ageing before they are ready.

Domaine des Jougla
Commune: Prades-sur-Vernazobre.
Owner: Alain Jougla.
Surface Area under Vine: 40 ha.
Wines: Saint-Chinian including Cuvée Classique, Cuvée Tradition and Cuvée Signée, and Vin de Pays d'Oc.

The Jougla vineyards straddle the border between the Saint-Chinian's calcareous clayey, low-lying land and the schistous upper part. The basic *cuvée*, the Classique, contains 20 per cent Cinsault as well as Grenache, Carignan, Syrah and Mourvèdre, and is attractively fruity without being serious. The Tradition is better, from 35 per cent Grenache, 45 per cent Mourvèdre and 20 per cent Syrah, with the added bonus of a picture of Jougla himself on the label. Even better is the oaky Cuvée Signée from old vines (30 per cent Grenache, 55 per cent Syrah and 15 per cent Carignan) planted on schistous soil. What a difference this makes! Keep this wine for five years before drinking.

Château Maurel Fonsalade
Domaine de Fonsalade
Commune: Causses-et-Veyran.
Owners: Philippe and Thérèse Maurel.
Surface Area under Vine: 27 ha.
Wines: Saint-Chinian including Tradition, Fonsalade and Cuvée Frédéric, and Vin de Table (white).

Philippe Maurel is a wine merchant in Béziers. Château de Fonsalade has been in the hands of his family since the French Revolution. The vineyard, a heterogenous amalgam of clay with large stones, gravel, schist and clay, is planted mainly with Grenache and Syrah, these two comprising two-thirds of the total. The rest is Carignan and Cinsault for the red and rosé, Chardonnay, Chenin, Roussanne, Viognier and Muscat for the *vin de*

table. I prefer the Fonsalade to the Cuvée Frédéric. It is made with 70 per cent Syrah and is rich and subtle. Somehow, though, compared with the very best, the Fonsalade wine lacks a little grip.

Domaine G Moulinier
Owners: Joël & Guy Moulinier.
Surface Area under Vine: 21 ha.
Wines: Saint-Chinian including Cuvée des Sigillaires and Cuvée Les Terrasses Grillées.

Guy Moulinier has now taken over from his father, who created this domaine in the 1960s. He believes in training his vines a little bit higher than most, in order to maximise the size of the leaf canopy, the engine for the photosynthesis. The Sigillaires *cuvée* comes from 40 per cent Syrah and 30 per cent each Grenache and Mourvèdre. It is balanced and lively in its fruit. The Terrasses Grillées is a modern-style Saint-Chinian — fat, rich and ample with no hard edges — the *encépagement* is 85 per cent Syrah, 15 per cent Mourvèdre (100 per cent Syrah in 1995) and it undergoes malolactic fermentation while in *barrique* where it then stays for a year.

Les Coteaux du Rieu Berlou
Commune: Berlou.
Members: 80.
Surface Area under Vine: 600 ha.
Wines: Saint-Chinian including Schistell and Berloup Terroir, Vignes-Royales and Collection Rouge, Coteaux du Languedoc and Vin de Pays d'Oc.

This is one of the best and most up-to-date co-operatives, not just of the Saint-Chinian area but of the whole of France. Berloup (sic) Terroir comes entirely from old Carignan vines and is made by carbonic maceration and then matured in stainless steel. Vignes-Royales comes from old Carignan and Syrah, plus a little Grenache and again is aged in vat. The Collection *encépagement* is 55 per cent Syrah, 25 per cent Grenache and 20 per cent Mourvèdre and spends twelve months in *barrique*.

Cave Les Vins de Roquebrun
Commune: Roquebrun.

Members: 114.

Surface Area under Vine: 500 ha.

Wines: Saint-Chinian including Baron d'Aupenac, Château Roquebrun, Sir de Roc Brun, Domaine de La Serre, Cuvée Prestige, Cuvée Roches Noires and others, Coteaux du Languedoc and Vins de Pays.

Hidden away up in the hills where the river Orb is joined by one of its main tributaries, the Roquebrun area has entirely schistous soils: a promising environment for good wine. This energetic and modern co-operative offers a range of high-quality wines at reasonable prices. The top *cuvées* are aged in wood, the Prestige and the Sir du Roc Brun being based on Mourvèdre (60 per cent) while the Château Roquebrun and Baron d'Aupenac are based on Syrah.

Château Viranel

Commune: Cessenon-sur-Orb.

Owners: Danielle and Gérard Bergasse-Milhé.

Surface Area under Vine: 40 ha.

Wines: Saint-Chinian including Cuvée 'Élevé en Fûts de Chêne'.

The Viranel vineyard, above the river Orb, is a south-facing, clay-limestone terrace planted with Syrah and Grenache with some old Carignan vines (vinified by carbonic maceration) and a little Cinsault (which is used for the rosé). In good vintages such as 1995 Gérard Bergasse makes rich, concentrated, balanced and stylish red wines, both oaky and non-oaky.

Other Saint-Chinian Producers of Note

Château de Combebelle/Comte Cathare SA (Villespassans), Château Coujan/François Guy (Murviel-Lès-Béziers), Château Etienne La Dournie/ Annick & Henri Etienne (Saint-Chinian), Domaine du Landeyran/Patrice & Michel Soulier (Saint-Nazaire-de-Ladarez), Château Milhau-Lacugue/ Emilienne & Jean Lacugue (Puisserguier), Château Soulié des Joncs/ Rémy Soulié (Assignan) and the co-operatives at Cruzy, Les Vignerons du Pays Ensérune/Domaine de Fontcaude (Maraussan), Rieutort (Murviel-Lès-Béziers) and Quarante.

Minervois

Surface Area (1998): 4285 ha.

Production (1998): (Red and rosé) 203,455 hl; (white) 3287 hl.

Colour: Red, rosé and white.

Grape Varieties: (Red and rosé) Syrah, Mourvèdre, Lladoner Pelut, Grenache, Carignan, Cinsault, Picpoul Noir, Terret Noir, Aspiran Noir (the first four must provide a minimum of 60% of the blend, including a minimum of 10% Syrah and Mourvèdre and a maximum of 40% Carignan); (white) Bourboulenc, Maccabéo (minimum 50%), Marsanne, Picpoul, Clairette, Grenache Blanc, Terret Blanc, Listan Blanc, Muscat Blanc à Petits Grains and Muscat of Alexandria.

Maximum Yield: 50 hl/ha.

Minimum Alcohol Level: (Red and rosé) 11.5°; (white) 11°.

Lying mainly in the Aude *département* with some land in the Hérault, the Minervois is sandwiched between the Montagne Noire and the river Aude and the Canal du Midi. This is one of the oldest wine regions of France, the vine having been introduced in pre-Roman times by the Phocaeans, and the techniques of winemaking preserved and sophisticated by the Benedictines and others from the ninth century onwards. Promoted from VDQS to full *appellation contrôlée* in 1985, and with its central area recently promoted into a new superior Minervois La Livinière *appellation* (see page 430) this is now one of the most rewarding areas in the Midi for inexpensive but interesting wines.

The Minervois area comprises forty-five communes in the Aude and sixteen in the Hérault, and is roughly rectangular, beginning a couple of kilometres north-east of Carcassonne, and melding into Saint-Chinian almost due north of Narbonne, a distance of some 50 kilometres. The increasing influence of the 'Midi' as one moves towards the Mediterranean as well as the effect of altitude as one moves north into the foothills account for the difference in the character of the wines from one sector to another.

Minervois Sub-Areas

There are four, five or even six sub-areas of the Minervois according to which authority you consult. The central and best area became an *appellation* in its own right, Minervois La Livinière, in September 1998 and comprises the central communes of La Livinière, Cesseras, Siran, Félines, Azillanet and Azille. There are currently some 150 hectares of vines here, producing around 6000 hl of wine a year. Apart from a lower maximum *rendement* of 45 hl/ha, before PLC, regulations are the same as for Minervois itself.

Immediately west of La Livinière, continuing to Caunes and Laure, is another area, potentially almost as good; the climate is a little cooler, rainfall is a little higher, but there isn't much in it. Further west still, on the borders with the Cabardès *appellation*, the climate is certainly influenced by the Atlantic rather than the Mediterranean, and the wines are leaner.

On the east side of La Livinière, up in the hills above the D5 main road to Béziers and reaching up to Minerve – a splendidly picturesque small town perched on the top of cliffs overlooking two small canyons where the river Cesse is joined by one of its tributaries – and Saint-Jean-de-Minervois, a centre for *vins doux naturels* – is another of the sub-areas for quality wine. Here the heat of the Midi is tempered by the altitude, and though it tends to be both drier and hotter than at La Livinière, the rain, when it comes, pours down more violently. These wines are rich, full and robust but not clumsy.

Finally in the flatter lands along the Canal du Midi and the river Aude the climate is hot and dry. Like those in that part of the Corbières which lies directly opposite the wines can be somewhat baked. The wines resemble the countryside: they have less character than those from the hills.

Geologically the Minervois is largely limestone, very stony in parts. There is schist and white marble near Caunes, schist again in the extreme west at Salsigne, *grès* (a red-purple sandstone) in parts, and red clay limestone around Saint-Jean-de-Minervois.

I have long found the red wines of the Minervois more interesting, in general, than those of the Corbières. The whites are of lesser importance. They are cooler, less peppery, and also more flexible, less baked. Generalisations such as these are today becoming less important, as more and more classy domaines emerge, and the tendency to super-*cuvées* with ageing in new or newish oak threatens even more to hide differences in *terroir* behind modern techniques of winemaking. Yet in September 1998, when I followed several days of exploration in the Corbières with a similar trip into the Minervois the difference I had pinpointed when I first began to understand these wines still seemed to hold good. I found much to applaud.

Leading Minervois Producers

Abbaye de Tholomies
Commune: La Livinière.
Owners: Lucien and Micheline Rogé and Georges Forto.
Surface Area under Vine: 8 ha plus 30 ha in Minervois La Livinière.
Wines: Minervois La Livinière including Cuvée Mourvèdre, and Vin de Pays d'Oc.
The winemaking cellar has been converted out of the vaulted church of the old abbey, while next door a fine *salle de réception* has been created from what were once stables and dormitories. Georges Forto, brother of Madame Rogé, is now in charge, Lucien Rogé having retired. The wine is vinified in stainless steel and concrete vats, and subsequently matured in wood, in whole or in part. The quality is very high and there are splendid labels by the artist François Anton.

Domaine des Aires Hautes
Commune: Siran.
Owners: Gilles and Eric Chabert.
Surface Area under Vine: 25 ha.
Wines: Minervois La Livinière including Clos de L'Escandil, and Vin de Pays d'Oc.
This medium-sized estate in the heart of the region is well run by the Chaberts, father and son. I am more impressed by the Minervois wines than by the Sauvignon Blanc and Chardonnay *vins de pays*. The special *cuvée* the Clos de l'Escandil, can be a little over-oaky though.

★ CHÂTEAU COUPE ROSES

Commune: La Caunette.

Owners: Françoise Le Calvez and Pascal Frissant.

Surface Area under Vine: 32 ha.

Wines: Minervois including (red) Cuvées Bastide, Vignals and Prestige, rosé and white, and Vin de Pays.

This is one of the best domaines in the Minervois, run with quiet determination by Françoise Le Calvez and her partner who produce luscious wines. The vines, at 350 metres, with schist on the upper slopes, marl below, are low-yielding and, unusually for the Minervois region, the grapes are harvested by hand. The cellar works by gravity, stainless steel is used for fermentation and at the entrance are a few rows of barrels for the Syrah and the Grenache in the Prestige Cuvée. Both this wine and the Vignals are made from 50 per cent each Syrah and Grenache. The Bastide comes from 75 per cent Carignan and 25 per cent Cinsault.

★ CHÂTEAU FABAS

Commune: Laure-Minervois.

Owner: Roland Augustin.

Surface Area under Vine: 60 ha.

Wines: Minervois including (red) Cuvée Réserve and Cuvée Alexandre and (white) Cuvée Virginie, and Vin de Pays d'Oc.

Roland Augustin hails from Champagne and used to work on the marketing side for Moët et Chandon. He bought Château Fabas, which has the potential for another 30 hectares of vineyard, once he gets planting permission, early in 1996. The grapes are harvested by machine, destemmed and vinified traditionally before being aged in wood, a fair proportion of which is new or newish. Roland Augustin believes in high-training his vines so that the grapes can benefit from a larger leaf canopy. Among the reds, the Réserve is mainly Syrah and Grenache and spends six to seven months in barrel while the Alexandre is entirely Syrah and Mourvèdre and stays in wood for fourteen months. The white Virginie *cuvée* comes largely from the Vermentino grape and is aged in newish wood for eight to nine months, with the lees being stirred from time to time. The *vin de pays* is

pure Carignan. These are nicely cool, stylish, well-made wines, usually at their best four or five years after the vintage. They will then last for another five years or so.

★ CHÂTEAU DE GOURGAZAUD

Commune: La Livinière.

Owner: Roger Piquet.

Surface Area under Vines: 100 ha.

Wines: Minervois including Cuvée Réserve and Cuvée Mathilde, and Vin de Pays d'Oc.

Roger Piquet, erstwhile head of the wine merchants Chantovent, bought Château de Gourgazaud in 1973. He was the first in the area to plant Syrah and Viognier and has been one of the movers and shakers behind the new La Livinière *appellation*.

Harvesting is by machine, the grapes are destemmed, and the top *cuvées* matured entirely in barrique. Monsieur Piquet prefers a long vinification at low temperatures in order to obtain softer, more sophisticated tannins. Part of the wine is kept in a big underground cellar which also serves as a tasting room. This is a reliable source – all the reds are from 80 per cent Syrah and 20 per cent Mourvèdre and the Cuvée Réserve can be lovely. The *vin de pays* is from Viognier.

★ DOMAINE LACOMBE BLANCHE

Commune: La Livinière.

Owner: Guy Van-Lancker.

Surface Area under Vine: 10 ha.

Wines: Minervois including (red) La Chandelière, and Vin de Pays d'Oc including L'Enfer and Le Dessous de L'Enfer.

Guy Van-Lancker, from Charlerois in Belgium, arrived in the area in 1981 and at first sent his grapes to the co-operative. Little by little, from 1988 onwards, he kept back some to vinify and sell under his own label, and has been completely independent since 1995, when he also started to mature some of his wine in wood.

The winery is small and cramped within an old house in the centre of the village. There is a separate storage cellar, equally tight for space. The Minervois special *cuvée*, La Chandelière, comes from 60 per cent Syrah and also undergoes ageing in wood. This wine is not made every year. The white wine, from roughly Roussanne and Viognier, is vinified and matured in new wood, and new oak is used for L'Enfer, the *vin de pays* from Pinot Noir. The Dessous de L'Enfer comes from Tempranillo, the only French wine I have come across made from this Spanish grape. It is still early days here but Guy Van-Lancker has shown he can produce wines of quality. The Chandelière will keep for a decade.

★ Domaine Luc Lapeyre

Commune: Trausse-Minervois.
Owner: Luc Lapeyre.
Surface Area under Vine: 35 ha.
Wines: Minervois including (red) L'Amourier and (white) Nuit Blanche, and Vin de Pays.

Luc Lapeyre is a gentle, darkly-bearded giant. His vineyards, planted with 40 per cent Syrah, plus Grenache, Mourvèdre and Carignan, lie on a terrace of flint and *grès* (a red-purple sandstone) at an altitude of about 250 metres. In 1993 he extricated himself from the local co-operative, and stopped fining his wines after the 1996 vintage (he has never filtered them). The medium- to full-bodied wines spend a year in wood (newish rather than new) and they are of increasing interest and quality, with great style and very good fruit. They will keep for up to ten years. An address to watch.

Domaine Maris

Commune: La Livinière.
Owners: Comte Cathare SA and Robert Eden.
Surface Area under Vine: 60 ha.
Wines: Minervois including Carte Noire, Tradition and Prestige.

One of three domaines belonging to Comte Cathare (Colombelle in Saint-Chinian and Bégude in Limoux are the other two), Domaine Maris lies on clay-limestone soil at La Livinière. So far – but it is early days – the wines have been perfectly acceptable but not brilliant. The Carte Noire is made from 50 per cent Carignan, 20 per cent Syrah and 30 per cent Grenache; the Tradition has less Carignan in the blend and the Prestige comes from a blend of 80 per cent Syrah and 20 per cent Grenache.

★ Château d'Oupia

Commune: Oupia.
Owner: André Iché.
Surface Area under Vine: 60 ha .
Wines: Minervois including (red) Les Barons and Nobilis.

Château d'Oupia lies outside Olonzac, the vines planted nearby on a small hill. André Iché has planted Marsanne and Roussanne for his stylish white and Carignan, Syrah and Grenache for his red and rosé. There are more vines up in the hills at La Caunette which are used for the Barons *cuvée* (50 per cent Syrah, 35 per cent Carignan and 10 per cent Grenache – and matured in wood). Nobilis is a selection of the best *cuvées* of this wine, and aged entirely in wood, some of it new. Hats off to this. The other wines are good, too.

★ Domaine Piccinini

Commune: La Livinière.
Owners: Maurice and Jean-Christophe Piccinini.
Surface Area under Vine: 20 ha.
Wines: Minervois including (red) Clos d'Angély, Cuvée Line et Laëtitia, Vin de Pays d'Oc and Vin de Paille (Vendange Tardive).

Maurice Piccinini, president of the local co-operative for thirty years, went independent in 1991 and has now been succeeded by his son Jean-Christophe. The winery, opposite the garage in the middle of the village, is temperature-controlled (Jean-Christophe likes a slow fermentation), while there is a cramped storage cellar elsewhere. The grapes are harvested by hand, completely destemmed and then given a *cuvaison* of up to three weeks. The special *cuvées*, from 60 per cent Syrah, 20 per cent Grenache, 20 per cent old-vine Carignan and a dash of Mourvèdre, are matured in *barrique*. The basic difference between them is the age of the vines, the Line et Laëtitia being from older ones. There are some lovely wines here. This domaine is one of the *appellation*'s stars.

Domaine Sainte-Eulalie

Commune: La Livinière.
Owners: Isabelle and Laurent Coustal.
Surface Area under Vine: 34 ha.

Wines: Minervois including (red) Cuvée Tradition, Cuvée Prestige and Cuvée 'Elevé en Fûts de Chêne'.

Isabelle and Laurent Coustal, two young oenologists, bought the Sainte-Eulalie domaine in 1996. The vineyard, on a gentle, sheltered slope, faces due south and is planted with 36 per cent Carignan, 28 per cent Syrah, 28 per cent Grenache and 8 per cent Cinsault (the latter only used for the rosé). The basic red wine, Cuvée Tradition, is made from 40 per cent Carignan and 30 per cent each Syrah and Grenache. The better *cuvées* are mainly from Syrah. The first results since the takeover are encouraging. This is a property to watch.

CHATEAU VILLERAMBERT-JULIEN

Commune: Caunes-Minervois.
Owner: Michel Julien.
Surface Area under Vine: 75 ha.
Wines: Minervois (red and rosé).

The Juliens have been at the imposing, partly medieval Château Villerambert since 1852, and now share half of the chateau itself with some cousins, retaining two-thirds of the vineyard. Part of the land, to the west, is schistous; to the east there is clay and both are very good soils for Syrah. There is an additional vineyard at Trausse in a hotter mesoclimate which suits Mourvèdre.

Until 1994, the better *cuvée* was called Trianon. Now the Juliens have reverted to the Bordeaux tradition of a château wine, while the second wine is called L'Opéra du Château Villerambert. The *grand vin* is made from 60 per cent Syrah and 40 per cent Grenache and aged in wood. It is rich and meaty and needs time to mature. It will last a decade or more.

CHÂTEAU DE VIOLET

Commune: Peyriac-Minervois.
Owner: Emilie Faussié.
Surface Area under Vine: 40 ha.
Wines: Minervois including (red) Cuvée Clovis and Cuvée Vieilles Vignes.

Château de Violet is both a domaine and a hotel. Joseph, Emilie's husband, Joseph acquired the property in 1966, ripped out most of the ignoble varieties and planted Grenache and Syrah, plus Marsanne for the white wine. In 1991 Hélène Serrano arrived as winemaker, and in 1997 Jacques Bernard, Joseph and Emilie's son, took over responsibility for the vineyard from his father. The Cuvée Clovis is produced from 70 to 75 per cent Syrah, and not aged in wood, while the Vieilles Vignes contains a percentage of Mourvèdre and spends ten months in barrel. The Vieilles Vignes is not produced every year but when it is is rich and classy. There is more vintage variation here than at some estates, but in the successful years the results can be impressive.

Other Producers of note

FRANK BAZANETH (VILLENEUVE-DES-MINERVOIS), CHÂTEAU BELVIZE/JEAN-PAUL AMIEL (BIZE-MINERVOIS), DOMAINE BORIE DE MAUREL/MICHEL ESCANDE (FÉLINES), CHÂTEAU DE CESSERAS/JEAN-YVES & PIERRE-ANDRÉ OURNAC (CESSERAS), CELLIER DES COTEAUX DU HAUT-MINERVOIS co-operative (LA LIVINIÈRE), CLOS CENTEILLES/ PIERRE BOYER-DOMERGUE (SIRAN), DOMAINE PIERRE CROS (BADENS), CLOS D'ESPEROU/JEAN-LOUIS ALAUX (SALSIGNE), DOMAINE PAUL-LOUIS EUGÈNE (SIRAN), CHÂTEAU LAVILLE-BERTOU/NICOLE MARTIN (LA LIVINIÈRE), DOMAINE MURETTES/JEAN-LOUIS BELLIDO (LA LIVINIÈRE), DOMAINE SAINT-SERNIN/PHILIPPE SENNAT (TRAUSSE-MINERVOIS) AND DOMAINE LA TOUR BOISÉE/JEAN-LOUIS POUDOU (LAURE-MINERVOIS).

CORBIÈRES

Surface Area (1998): 14,992 ha.
Production (1998): (Red and rosé) 542,104 hl; (white) 11,261 hl.
Colour: Red, rosé and white.
Grape Varieties: (Red & rosé) Carignan, Grenache, Syrah, Mourvèdre, Cinsault, Terret Noir and Picpoul Noir; (white) Grenache Blanc, Malvoisié, Maccabéo, Muscat Blanc a Petits Grains, Muscat of Alexandria, Terret Blanc and Picpoul Blanc.
Maximum Yield: 50 hl/ha.
Minimum Alcohol Level: (Red and rosé) 11.5°; (white) 11°.

Corbières is by some way the largest *vignoble* in the Languedoc. It lies between the river Aude, where it marches with the Minervois, and the border between the Aude *département* and that of the Pyrénées-Orientales, a distance of almost 60 kilometres north to south; and some 70 kilometres from east to west, between the Mediterranean and Carcassonne.

Vines have been planted here since Phocean and Greek adventurers first established a trading post at Narbonne about 500 BC. Production reached a first heyday under the Romans, declined in the Dark Ages that followed, survived the Albigensian wars in the early thirteenth century, and then began to expand early in the eighteenth century. The opening of the Canal des Deux Mers in 1681, linking Bordeaux with the Mediterranean, had made communications easier. Bad vintages in the north of France and rising prosperity all over the country increased demand, and by the Revolution Corbières was one of the most important vineyard areas in France. The arrival of the railway in 1858 more than halved freight costs to the capital, while phylloxera dealt a fatal blow to those marginal vineyards in northern France which Corbières was quick to take advantage of. Appointed VDQS in 1951, promotion to *appellation contrôlée* occurred in 1985, along with many other areas of Languedoc. The *appellation* regulations of 1985 and amendments since then have encouraged the planting of noble grape varieties such as Syrah, Mourvèdre and Grenache at the expense of the indigenous Carignan.

Corbières Sub-Areas

There are a number of sub-areas within Corbières as a result of differences in *terroir* and mesoclimate. Furthest west, and influenced by the Atlantic, lie Les Corbières d'Alaric and Les Corbières du Val d'Orbieu. The soil here is limestone, and the red wines are aromatic and succulent, without the sometimes baked character of those from the rest of the region. As it is cooler here, this is a good area for whites and rosés too.

In the centre, roughly between Lagrasse and Montséret, the landscape is one of undulating foothills at first becoming flatter and drier as nearer the river Aude at Lézignan. This is one of the best areas and is home to many of the leading estates. The climate is dry and warm; the soil thin and stony. The wines are firm, rich and, where there is plenty of Syrah in the *encépagement*, capable of considerable improvement in bottle.

South of here, as one climbs up beyond Durban and Villeneuve towards Tuchan and Paziols, is the Hautes Corbières, and, at a higher altitude still, around Cucugnan, the Corbières Montagneuses. This is rivetingly lovely countryside, verdant even in October, the vine on the lower slopes giving way to limestone-based *garrigues* and rocky outcrops, overlooked by many an impressive ruined Cathar castle. The mesoclimate is drier and the wines full and sturdy. Again, with today's keen attention and imaginative winemaking, the wine can last well, as much as five to eight years. Much of the land around Villeneuve and Tuchan is schistous. It is also authorised for making Fitou.

Finally, separated from the west by a ridge of hills, is the Corbières Maritimes. This area lies between Narbonne and the border between the Aude and the Pyrénées-Orientales departments, and takes in the districts of Gruissan, Portel-des-Corbières and Roquefort-des-Corbières. South of La Palme lies the Maritimes half of the Fitou *appellation* where again the grower has a choice of *appellations*. Corbières and Fitou wines sell for roughly the same price. The climate here gives warm winters, dry, even arid summers, but tempered by the Mediterranean, cooler temperatures than further inland. The wines tend to be looser-knit and more forward than elsewhere in Corbières.

Overall the geology is diverse. Essentially limestone rock in the hills, stony and more alluvial in the Aude valley, it ranges from primary schist, to limestones and *grès* (a deep-coloured, hard sandstone rock) of the secondary era, plus marl of the tertiary and the post ice-age debris of the quarternary epochs. In general the best and most long-lasting wines come from the older soils.

Such is the complexity of soil and mesoclimate, not to mention the different aspirations of the individuals who tend the vines and run the wineries, it is difficult to generalise about the wines of Corbières today. Officially, though not always in practice, the red wine must be a blend of three varieties. It can range in style from a

Syrah-based *vin de garde* which would not be out of place alongside a good Côtes du Rhône-Villages capable of lasting for up to decade to a Carignan-based *vin de l'année* made by carbonic maceration and the standard wine made by the fifty or so Corbières co-operatives.

In general, however, the wines have a drier, more baked centre than those of the Minervois and they are less rich, concentrated and succulent than the best Côtes du Roussillon-Villages. Like all red wines of the Midi they can be dense, burly, clumsy, even rustic. But the progress during the 1990s or so has been considerable and this increase in quality is continuing. Like the rest of the Languedoc, Corbières is a happy hunting ground for value for money wines. In general, the whites and roses, nearly all made for drinking young, are less important than the reds.

Leading Corbières Producers

CHÂTEAU LA BASTIDE

Commune: Escales.
Owner: Guilhem Durand.
Surface Area under Vine: 70 ha.
Wines: Corbières (red) including Cuvée Durand.

Château La Bastide is a rather curious, partly ivy-covered building dating from 1830. It resembles a riding stables more than something medieval and fortified. The Durand family have owned the domaine since post-phylloxera times and make good rich, meaty red wines from a mixture of Grenache, Syrah and very old-vine Carignan, the last produced by carbonic maceration.

★ CHÂTEAU DE CARAGUILHES

Commune: Saint-Laurent-de-La-Cabrerisse.
Owners: Lionel and Galatée Faivre.
Surface Area under Vine: 125 ha.
Wines: Corbières including Cuvée Classique and Cuvée Prestige.

Caraguilhes is an imposing, if somewhat solid-looking, seventeenth-century château surrounded by 500 hectares of *garrigue* just where the land begins to rise up into the hills of central Corbières. The Faivres are firm ecologists, insisting on organic methods of farming, and

thereby reducing the crop to an average of 30 hl/ha. The Cuvée Classique contains 30 per cent each Grenache, Syrah and old-vine Carignan, plus 10 per cent Mourvèdre and is made without any wood. The Cuvée Prestige contains one-third each of the first three grapes and spends a year in oak barrels. These are only medium-bodied wines but certainly the Prestige has no lack of harmony and finesse.

★ CHÂTEAU CASCARDAIS

Commune: Saint-Laurent-de-La-Cabrerisse.
Owner: Philippe Courrian.
Surface Area under Vine: 22 ha.
Wines: Corbières (red).

Philippe Courrian, of Bordeaux's Château Tour-Haut-Caussan, bought Cascardais in 1992. One can well see why – it lies deep into a private valley, that of the river Nielle, of the most breathtaking beauty. There is just one wine, a red from old-vine Carignan, Grenache, Syrah, Mourvèdre and Cinsault and partly aged in oak barrels, some of which are new. It has a style and a freshness uncommon for Corbières.

CELLIER DU GRAND CORBIÈRES

Commune: Cucugnan.
Owners: Sichel family.
Surface Area under Vine: 18 ha.
Wines: Corbières including Domaine du Trillol and Réserve du Révérend.

High in the hills near the border with the Pyrénées-Orientales *département*, at altitudes of up to 450 metres, is the Domaine du Trillol, bought by the Sichels in 1991. The Sichels are part-owners of Château Palmer and sole owners of Château d'Angludet, both in Bordeaux's Médoc region. At first the wine was produced in association with the owner of the nearby Domaine du Révérend, but the liaison ceased in 1997. The Sichels still buy grapes from du Révérend to make the Réserve du Révérend *cuvée*. These are highly competent red wines, as one would expect from the Sichels, made from varying amounts of Syrah, Grenache and Carignan and produced in a custom-built, modern cellar. The white, from Roussanne, Marsanne and Maccabéo, is good, too.

CHÂTEAU COULON, CHÂTEAU DU LUC

Commune: Luc-sur-Orbieu.

Owner: Louis Fabre.

Surface Area under Vine: 110 ha.

Wines: Corbières including Château Fabre-Gasperets, Cuvée Irma Coulon and Cuvée Vieilles Vignes, and Vin de Pays d'Oc (Domaine des Rives).

Château Coulon and the associated Château du Luc are separately run by Louis Fabre along strictly ecological lines with no fungicides or chemical products. The soil consists of a thick bed of gravel, planted mainly with Carignan, plus some Syrah and Grenache, with Mourvèdre reserved for the Cuvée Irma Coulon. The standard wine is partly *barrique*-aged and the top *cuvées* entirely oak-aged. Sometimes the wines are a little too oaky, but the fruit underneath is cool, classy and succulent. Most of the *vin de pays* is Viognier and is worth noting, too.

CHÂTEAU ETANG DES COLOMBES
CHÂTEAU SAINT-JAMES

Commune: Cruscades.

Owners: Henri and Christophe Gualco.

Surface Area under Vine: 80 ha.

Wines: Corbières including Bois des Dames, Prieuré Saint-James and Cuvée Bicentenaire, and Vin de Pays.

The vineyards of Château Etang des Colombes lie on gently undulating, very stony, clay-limestone land west of Lézignan and are planted with Grenache, Syrah, Mourvèdre and Carignan for the red wines and Maccabéo, Bourboulenc, Grenache Blanc and Roussanne for the white wines, plus Viognier for *vin de pays*. Rare in the area, for the water table hereabouts is quite high, is a splendid, vaulted underground barrel cellar.

The Prieuré Saint-James *cuvée* (50 per cent Syrah) is given seven months in wood, the Bicentenaire which contains most of the Mourvèdre, ten months, and the Bois des Dames (from the oldest vines) fourteen months. All the reds are produced by carbonic maceration and are ripe, stylish and for the medium term. The Château Saint-James wines, such as the Prieuré Saint-James, are lighter and more elegant.

DOMAINE DE FONTSAINTE

Commune: Boutenac.

Owners: Yves and Bruno Laboucarié.

Surface Area under Vine: 41 ha.

Wines: Corbières including Réserve La Demoiselle and Rosé Gris de Gris.

Domaine de Fontsainte lies on an interesting soil, partly red sandstone, partly siliceous clay, partly limestone. The vineyard consists in the main of very old Carignan vines, some of them planted right at the beginning of the twentieth century. These venerable vines are the mainstay of the Réserve La Demoiselle wine. The basic *cuvée* comes from 70 per cent Carignan, 15 per cent Grenache, 10 per cent Cinsault and 5 per cent Mourvèdre and Syrah. The wines are rich and sturdy — old fashioned without being rustic.

★ DOMAINE DU GRAND CRÈS

Commune: Ferrals.

Owners: Pascaline and Hervé Leferrer.

Surface Area under Vine: 11.5 ha.

Wines: Corbières including (red) Cuvée Classique and Cuvée Majeure, and Vin de Pays d'Oc.

Hervé Leferrer was formerly the *régisseur* (bailiff) at the Domaine de La Romanée-Conti in Burgundy. In 1989 he bought 5 hectares of vines in the Corbières and has since planted another 6.5 hectares. The red wine is made from Syrah, Cinsault and Grenache and the white from Roussanne, Viognier and Muscat à Petits Grains. Barrel-ageing for between eight and thirteen months for the red wine follows, depending on the vintage, the variety and the *cuvée*. This is up-to-date, very clean winemaking and all the wines are exemplary.

CHÂTEAU GRAND-MOULIN

Commune: Luc-sur-Orbieu.

Owner: Jean-Noël Bousquet.

Surface Area under Vine: 57 ha.

Wines: Corbières including (red and white) Cuvée Vieilles Vignes Élevée en Fûts de Chêne and rosé.

Jean-Noël Bousquet's Château Grand-Moulin is a prolific winner of gold medals as well as showing consistently well whenever I have conducted a blind tasting. I find myself continually writing down the word 'juicy' when I sample his wines. The soil here is the usual undulating stony marl of the Lézignan area, and the white grape varieties (Grenache Blanc, Maccabéo and Vermentino) have been planted on the most pebbly parts. This white wine is produced by skin contact, *bâtonnage* and vinification in new wood: all new modern techniques, and is gradually becoming refined into something very praiseworthy. The reds, from Syrah, Grenache, Mourvèdre, and less Carignan than most, are stylish and attractive.

CHÂTEAU HAUT-GLÉON
Commune: Villesèque-Lès-Corbières.
Owner: Léon-Nicolas Duhamel.
Surface Area under Vine: 30 ha.
Wines: Corbières including Cuvée Spéciale, and Vin de Pays d'Oc.

Villesèque-Lès-Corbières is halfway up in the hills on the way to Durban, in country suitably endorsed by the name of the *vin de pays*: La Vallée du Paradis. Duhamel's vines lie amid 250 hectares of *garrigue*, wild thyme and rosemary and are planted not only with the usual Corbières grape varieties but also with Viognier, Chardonnay, Sauvignon, Merlot and even Pinot Noir for the *vin de pays* wines. The Corbières wines are good, particularly the firm, ample, oaky Cuvée Spéciale. Château Glenun and Domaine de La Passière are subsidiary labels for the same wine.

CHÂTEAU DE LASTOURS
Commune: Portel-des-Corbières.
Owner: Jean-Marie Lignère.
Surface Area under Vine: 104 ha.
Wines: Corbières including Chatellerie, Arnaud de Berre, Simone Descamps and Cuvée 'Elevé en Fûts de Chêne'.

This large estate, planted on stony, clay-limestone terraces protected from the wind, is a Centre d'Aide par le Travail, worked by some sixty handicapped people. There is a large number of *cuvées*, the actual Château label being the best (50 per cent each Grenache and Syrah) and from a special vineyard. This wine spends a

period in *barrique* and has a good, old-viney richness and intensity. The wines are held back before release until they are fully mature.

CHÂTEAU LES OLLIEUX
Commune: Montséret-Boutenac.
Owner: Mme Surbézy-Cartier.
Surface Area under Vine: 47 ha.
Wines: Corbières including Cuvée 'Elevé en Fûts de Chêne'.

Sheltered from the north by the hills of Roquestière, the marly soil of Château Les Ollieux, rich in *galets* of *grès rouge*, a hard sandstone, is planted with Cinsault, Grenache, Syrah and Carignan, the wine being made by carbonic maceration. The Cinsault is not used in the oak-aged *cuvée* which gives the wine a bit more definition, but even the basic Corbières is nicely cool, juicy and succulent.

CHÂTEAU LES OLLIEUX-ROMANIS
Commune: Montséret-Boutenac.
Owners: Jacqueline and François Bories.
Surface Area under Vine: 40 ha.
Wines: Corbières including Cuvée 'Elevé en Fûts de Chêne'.

Separated from Château Les Ollieux (see above) at the time of the French Revolution, this domaine has similar clay-limestone, gravelly soils facing south-east. There is a mini-railway in the vineyard which was built in 1896 to transport the grapes to the cellars. The cellars are impressive – 50 metres long and lined with huge oak *foudres*. The wines are made from Grenache, Mourvèdre, Syrah and Carignan, the latter vinified by carbonic maceration and the best *cuvées* given six months in *barrique*. These top wines are firm and rich, and last well.

★ CHÂTEAU LES PALAIS
Commune: Saint-Laurent-de-Cabrerisse.
Owners: Anne and Xavier de Volontat.
Surface Area under Vine: 130 ha.
Wines: Corbières including Cuvée Merville, Cuvée Bernard, Cuvée Tradition, Cuvée Randolin and Domaine Saint-Joseph.

On gently rolling country exposed to the south and south-east lies the small elegant Château Les Palais surrounded by its vineyards. The main grape variety is Carignan, which is then vinified by carbonic maceration. Xavier de Volontat produces splendidly poised, elegant wines, the Randolin *cuvée* being gently oaky, rich and profound. The Cuvée Merville and Domaine Saint-Joseph are made from the young vines.

★ Château Saint-Auriol

Commune: Lagrasse.
Owners: Jean-Paul Salvagnac and Claude Vialade.
Surface Area under Vine: 45 ha.
Wines: Corbières including Château Baronis, Domaine Montmija, Château Salvagnac and Château Saint-Auriol.

Château Saint-Auriol is a very up-to-date property in a particularly lovely, forgotten part of the Corbières. Claude Vialade and Jean-Paul Salvagnac gradually abandoned carbonic maceration in the mid-1990s and the wines are all the better for it. Château Saint-Auriol is now produced from half Syrah and half Grenache, plus a little Carignan, and ages for one year in *barrique*. Château Salvagnac comes from vines further east in the commune of Boutenac and from half Syrah and half Mourvèdre, matured in barrel and *demi-muids*. These are the two best wines. Château Baronis is pure Carignan. Claude's brother, Eric produces wine in the Limoux at Domaine des Terres-Blanches (see page 444).

★ Château La Voulte-Gasparets

Commune: Boutenac.
Owner: Patrick Reverdy.
Surface Area under Vine: 53 ha.
Wines: Corbières including Cuvée Romain Pauc and Cuvée Réserve.

Ten generations of Reverdys have run this domaine, one of the most reliable in the whole of Corbières. The basic *encépagement* is 60 per cent Carignan, 30 per cent Grenache and 10 per cent Syrah, all vinified by carbonic maceration. The Cuvée Réserve undergoes six months' oak-ageing; the Cuvée Romain Pauc, from older vines and from rather more stony soil, is matured in oak for a year. The wines are full and rich with plenty of character. They keep well.

Other Producers of note

Château La Baronne/Suzette Lignères (Fontcouverte), Château Gléon-Montanié/ Jean-Pierre & Philippe Montanié (Villesèque), Domaine du Grand Arc /Bruno Schenck (Cucugnan), Château Hélène/ Marie-Hélène Gau (Barbaira), Caves Rochère – especially Terra Vinea (Portel-Les-Corbières), Domaine Rouire-Segur/ Geneviève Bourdel (Lagrasse), Celliers Saint-Martin – especially Tresmoulins (Roquefort-des-Corbières), Celliers des Demoiselles – especially Blanc de Blancs (Saint-Laurent-de-La-Cabrerisse) and Cave Pilote de Villeneuve – especially Marquis de Villecor and Haute Expression (Villeneuve-Les-Corbières).

Fitou

Surface Area (1998): 2585 ha.
Production (1998): 93,582 hl.
Colour: Red.
Grape Varieties: Carignan, Grenache (a combined minimum of 90%, with a maximum for Carignan of 75%), Cinsault, Mourvèdre and Syrah (all maximum 10%).
Maximum Yield: 45 hl/ha.
Minimum Alcohol Level: 12°.

Fitou is a curious *appellation*. It is split into two distinct halves: a coastal area, known as Fitou Maritime, covering five communes, including Fitou itself; and an inland area, Fitou Montagneux, sandwiched into the Corbières *appellation*, which stretches from Cascastel and Villeneuve to Tuchan and Paziols. The soil is essentially limestone, though there is schist in the Fitou Montagneux at Tuchan, and there can be gravel and sandstone, quartz and gypsum in parts. But it is the mesoclimate, rather than the soil, which varies greatly between the two areas. The coastal area is bare of trees, very arid and can be quite hot, though the influence of the Mediterranean tempers the extremes. Fifteen kilometres inland, directly across the mountains, the countryside is quite different, altogether more attractive. It is cooler, lusher and the rainfall is higher. Here, curiously, much of the land is authorised for both Corbières and Fitou. This is an anomalous situation, especially as the basic regulations for the wines are similar. Most growers offer both wines. One wonders how often it is just the same wine!

The name Fitou comes from the Latin word *fita* meaning the 'limit' i.e. the former frontier between France and Spain. The area has been *appellation contrôlée* since 1948, far longer than any other *vignoble* in Languedoc-Roussillon, and at the beginning of the twenty-first century, one wonders why it should have been so signalled out. The wine was based almost exclusively on Carignan, though it had to be oak-aged for nine months, and, even more than any other *appellation* in the region, production was centred on the local co-operative movement. Even today, 90 per cent of Fitou comes from seven co-operatives, and one, Les Producteurs du Mont Tauch, is directly responsible for over 45 per cent of the entire sales, as well as probably supplying many of the local *négociants* with their Fitou wine. There are now some twenty-two individual domaines.

Today Carignan is being gradually replaced by more noble varieties: Syrah in the Fitou Montagneux and both Mourvèdre and Syrah in the Fitou Maritime. By 2007 there must be a minimum of 10 per cent (and a maximum of 30 per cent) Syrah in the blend. Meanwhile, the percentage of Carignan is being reduced from a maximum of 75 per cent to a minimum of 40 per cent.

The style of Fitou varies considerably. The basic co-operative *cuvées* start off almost as cheap as you can get and are not surprisingly light and anonymous at best. At the other end of the scale Fitou can be full-bodied, undergoing successful *barrique*-ageing (though, strangely, the locals seem more reluctant than most to age in small oak, generally preferring the *foudre*) and is rich and luscious. These *cuvées*, obviously, will cost four or five times more than basic Fitou, but are still no more more expensive than a top Côtes du Roussillon-Villages or Corbières. I find the wines from Fitou Maritime somewhat dull, lacking character and definition. Inland, however, there are some lovely wines.

Leading Fitou Producers

★ DOMAINE BERTRAND BERGÉ
Commune: Paziols.
Owner: Jérôme Bertrand.
Surface Area under Vine: 30 ha.
Wines: Fitou, Corbières, Vin de Pays d'Oc and Muscat de Rivesaltes.

Half of Jérôme Bertrand's vineyards are licenced for the production of Fitou, made from 60 per cent Carignan and 40 per cent Grenache and by traditional methods. There is no *barrique*-ageing. Yet despite this the wines, rich, ample and succulent, have a mellowness which almost suggest the presence of the *barrique*.

DOMAINE LERYS
Commune: Villeneuve-Lès-Corbières.
Owners: Magny and Alain Izard.
Surface Area under Vine: 50 ha.
Wines: Fitou including Cuvée Tradition and Château Lerys, Corbières and Muscat de Rivesaltes.

As well as wine, the Izards offer *chambres d'hôtes* (bed and breakfast). The basic Tradition *cuvée* comes from 60 per cent Carignan (vinified by carbonic maceration) and 40 per cent Grenache, the Château wine from 60 per cent Syrah and 40 per cent old-vine Carignan. There is no *barrique*-ageing but the wines are structured and ripe with very good fruit.

LES PRODUCTEURS DU MONT TAUCH
Commune: Tuchan.
Members: 300.
Surface Area under Vine: 2000 ha.
Wines: Fitou including Château de Ségure, Corbières, Rivesaltes, Muscat de Rivesaltes and Vin de Pays d'Oc.

This organisation, founded in 1913, combines the products of the four co-operatives at Tuchan, Paziols, Villeneuve-Lès-Corbières and Durban who are between them responsible for 45 per cent of wine produced in the Fitou *appellation*. A large number of individual domaine names and other brands are on offer, culminating in the

Prestige de Paziols. In all 72,000 hl of wine are produced a year. The general standard is good.

★ Château de Nouvelles

Commune: Tuchan.
Owner: Robert Daurat-Fort.
Surface Area under Vine: 75 ha.
Wines: Fitou, Corbières, Rivesaltes and Muscat de Rivesaltes.

This is the senior estate in the Fitou *appellation*, and lies up in its own special valley in magnificent countryside off the D611 road between Durban and Tuchan.

The rich, fat and concentrated Fitou is produced from 50 per cent Carignan, 35 per cent Grenache and 15 per cent Syrah and Mourvèdre and aged in wooden *foudres*. It is not released until fully mature. It is a Midi wine in the best senses of the world and lasts well. The Rivesaltes is traditionally made and aged to the point where a touch of oxidation is apparent. The Muscat, though, is properly fresh.

Domaine de Rolland

Commune: Tuchan.
Owner: Louis Colomer.
Surface Area under Vine: 25 ha.
Wines: Fitou including Cuvée Spéciale.

Louis Colomer produces good, hearty, concentrated and individual wines. The basic Fitou wine is made from a blend of 50 per cent Carignan, 30 per cent Syrah and 20 per cent Grenache. The Cuvée Spéciale comes from 60 per cent Syrah and 40 per cent Carignan (from very old vines). Yields are low, and the wines are all the better as a result.

Cave Pilote de Villeneuve

Commune: Villeneuve-Lès-Corbières.
Members: 100.
Surface Area under Vine: 460 ha.
Wines: Fitou including Domaine des Trois Filles and Château Montmal, and Corbières including Marquis de Villecor.

The top wines from this co-operative are labelled Haute Expression and are worth seeking out, especially the Château Montmal and the Corbières wines (70 per cent Grenache and 30 per cent Syrah which is *barrique*-aged).

Other Producers of note

Co-operatives at Fitou, Lecaute and La Palme, Domaine de Gauthier (Treilles), Marie-Antoinette Maynadier (Port-La-Nouvelle) and Cellier de Roudène/Jean-Pierre & Bernadette Faixo (Paziols).

Limoux

Blanquette Méthode Ancestrale

Production (1998): 3213 hl.
Colour and Style: Dry white, gently effervescent.
Grape Variety: Mauzac.
Maximum Yield: 50 hl/ha.
Minimum Alcohol Level: 10°.

Blanquette de Limoux

Production (1998): 37,407 hl.
Colour and Style: Dry to medium-dry white, sparkling.
Grape Varieties: Mauzac (minimum 70%), Chardonnay and Chenin Blanc (maximum 20% each).
Maximum Yield: 50 hl/ha.
Minimum Alcohol Level: 10°.

Crémant de Limoux

Production (1998): 19,525 hl.
Colour and Style: Dry white, sparkling.
Grape Varieties: Mauzac, Chardonnay and Chenin.
Maximum Yield: 50 hl/ha.
Minimum Alcohol Level: 10°.

Limoux

Surface Area (1998): 1429 ha (all the Limoux ACs).
Production (1998): 1842 hl.
Colour: White.
Grape Varieties: Chardonnay, Chenin and Mauzac (minimum 15%).
Maximum Yield: 50 hl/ha.
Minimum Alcohol Level: 10°.

There are few white wine-only *appellations* in the South of France. Eliminate the *vins doux naturels* and you are left with Limoux, Cassis, Picpoul de Pinet and a couple of Clairettes. Limoux is the most interesting, if perhaps the least known. Yet we have all probably drunk the wine, if unwittingly, hidden behind the label of a Vin de Pays d'Oc Chardonnay. Today there is lots of Chardannay planted in the Limoux. The cool limestone slopes of the Limoux region have proved to be a natural environment for this ever so popular varietal.

Twenty-five kilometres south of Carcassonne, in the Haute Vallée of the river Aude, lies the town of Limoux. This has been a centre for sparkling wine for some 250 years. The reputation for this, attested by the contemporary historian Froissart in 1388, dates back to the Middle Ages, long before, so the locals will be quick to point out, anyone had heard of Champagne. The altitude here is high, the climate a cross between that of the Atlantic and the Mediterranean, and so this is the one area in the Languedoc where the grapes can achieve a high-enough acidity necessary for sparkling wine.

Originally Limoux was just a wine that had been bottled early, finishing its first fermentation in bottle and the carbon dioxide generated only escaping in the form of effervescence once the cork had been released. This style is known as Blanquette Méthode Ancestrale and is still produced today. The word 'Blanquette' refers to the indigenous Mauzac grape, and to the white downing underside of its leaf.

As sparkling winemaking evolved in the Limoux region Blanquette de Limoux was increasingly produced by the Champagne method, now called Traditional method or *méthode traditionnelle*, when yeast and sugar is added to a finished wine, thus inducing a second fermentation in the bottle. *Appellation contrôlée* for this wine was bestowed in 1938, the first one in the Languedoc-Roussillon area. Originally the wines had to be made almost entirely from Mauzac, with Clairette as a subsidiary variety.

Local growers, however, began to lobby for the introduction of Chardonnay, which had proved itself highly successful as a (still) *vin de pays*, and also for Chenin Blanc. The law was then changed in 1975 to allow up to 20 per cent of each variety or 30 per cent combined and the use of Clairette was dropped.

This amendment was not enough for the Chardonnay lovers and in 1989, a separate sparkling *appellation*, Crémant de Limoux, was created. This allowed for an unlimited percentage of Chardonnay, though it was felt that a certain amount of Mauzac should be left to ensure a certain special typicity. The idea was that Mauzac-dominated blends would be called Blanquette de Limoux, while those made with mainly with Chardonnay would be labelled Crémant. Whatever the laws intended, however, Crémant de Limoux has failed to catch on, as the figures show, two-thirds of the sparkling wine is still declared as Blanquette. As this in practice can contain any proportion of the grape varieties listed the current position is an absurd muddle and needs sorting out.

Most Blanquette and all Crémant are dry wines, in my experience. Most, also, is sold as non-vintage.

Meanwhile, lobbying was also taking place on the still wine front. A small amount of still Blanquette de Limoux, made from the Mauzac grape, had always been produced. There was little demand and growers increasingly and with great success turned to Chardonnay, which was sold as *vin de pays*. In 1993 a new *appellation*, called simply Limoux, was created to apply to the still wines of the Blanquette production area. Moreover, for the first time in any *appellation* decree barrel fermentation and *élevage* in these barrels until 1 May of the subsequent year was prescribed.

Unlike Crémant, this was an *appellation* which became an instant success. Chenin Blanc has been forgotten and in many cases the Mauzac provision is being quietly set aside as well. And there are still some splendid Chardonnays sold as *vin de pays*.

The Limoux area is confined on the west by the hills of the Chalabrais, to the east by those of Lecamp and to the south by the foothills of the Pyrenees. It begins at Rouffiac to the north, extends into the mountains beyond Espéraza and up into various valleys on both sides. Down on the main road, the D118, the views are unprepossessing, and the town of Limoux is no beauty. But away from the hurly-burly lies a different world:

where the vine shares the countryside with maize and sunflowers or merely pasture. It is rural and peaceful: *La France profonde*.

Research promoted by the major producer in the area, the excellent Caves du Sieur d'Arques, has differentiated seven different mesoclimates in the region: two Mediterranean-influenced areas on the eastern side, an Atlantic-influenced area on the western side, the essential Limouxin (note the 'x', to differentiate it with Limouzin) in the middle, around the Aude Valley; behind the Haute Vallée to the south-east and the Pyrenean hills to the south-west. As a result Les Caves du Sieur d'Arques now make four separate Chardonnays to illustrate the differences. The Haute Vallée is the best area as it has the coolest climate.

The soil varies too. Essentially it is alternatively marl, limestone or *grès*, with clay in some areas, and in parts very stony, with the sort of *galets* (pudding-stones) found in Châteauneuf-du-Pape. Altitude also plays its part and affects the end result. The vines can be found at up to 450 metres, which is high, the wines getting progressively more steely the higher the altitude of the vines and therefore the cooler the mesoclimate. Limoux is an area still feeling its way but shows great potential.

The Mauzac produces a light, crisp, appley but somewhat anonymous wine. I find the Mauzac-dominated Blanquette rather dull and the more Chardonnay in the blend the better. Currently I have some reservations about the still wines. Despite the altitude some of the Chardonnays can be almost as tropical fruit in style as those from the Languedoc plain between Narbonne and Montpellier. Without careful vinification they can be rather heavy. Quite often I find myself preferring the *vin de pays* Chardonnay which are lighter but cooler and more stylish. On the whole, all Limoux wines, whether still or sparkling, should be drunk within a year of the time of bottling.

Vintages in Limoux are not necessarily the same as those in the rest of the Languedoc: 1989 was very good, 1992 and 1993 not good, the rest at least good. Contrary to the rest of the Languedoc, 1997 was picked without a day of rain, and is a very successful vintage. 1998 promises well too.

Leading Limoux Producers

DOMAINE DE L'AIGLE
Commune: Roquetaillade.
Owner: Jean-Louis Denois.
Surface Area under Vine: 20 ha.
Wines: Crémant de Limoux including Tradition, Limoux including Cuvée Classique and Les Aigles, and Vin de Pays d'Oc Terres Rouges.

Jean-Louis Denois established his vineyard, up in the hills in the Haute Vallée in 1989. Some of the vines are planted at up to 450 metres above sea level. His Limoux wines are entirely from Chardonnay and aim to achieve the fruit of the New World along with the acidity of Chablis. The soil is very clayey, with only some 20 per cent of limestone, and so it is very cold and very heavy. As a result he has planted some Pinot Noir vines, of which I noted in 1998 'These are the closest to Burgundy in style I have even seen outside that area, despite the vines being young.' The Pinot Noir is used for the Terres Rouges *cuvée* and also blended with Chardonnay for the sparkling Tradition wine.

He has also planted Riesling, Gewurztraminer and Pinot Gris, only to find himself in hot water with the authorities. For some reason, while it has always been assumed – by the logical outsiders anyway – that you could plant anything you liked in the Midi for *vin de pays*, these Alsace varieties are not permitted. French bureaucracy can be most absurd at times! Surely the proof should be the quality of the wines.

DOMAINE COLLIN
Commune: Tourreilles.
Owner: Philippe Collin.
Surface Area under Vine: 20 ha.
Wines: Blanquette de Limoux including Cuvée Prestige and Cuvée de Réserve, Limoux and Vin de Pays d'Oc.

Philippe Collin is a Champenois and his wife Marie-Hélène is from Perpignan. They set up here in 1980 and built a splendid new winery on a little bluff outside Tourreilles in 1992. The soil is marl, and we are on the cusp between the Haute Vallée, the Atlantic and the

SOUTHERN LANGUEDOC

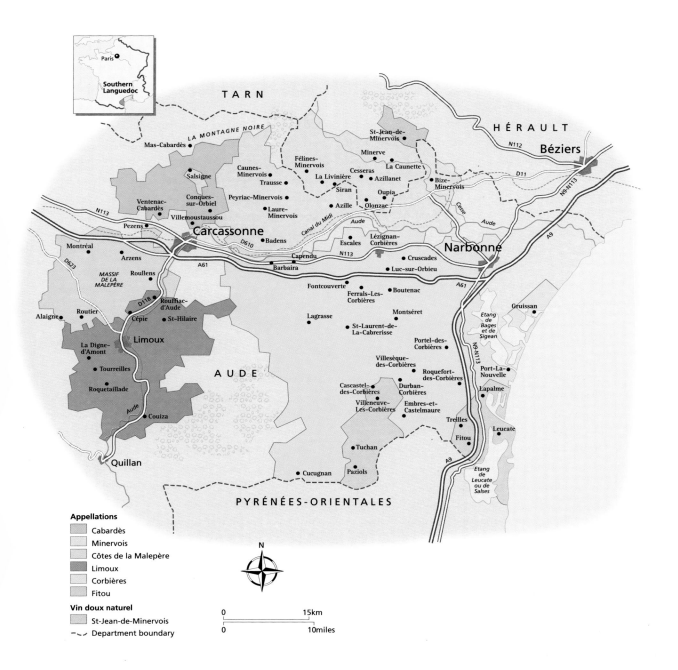

Paris

Southern
Languedoc

TARN

LA MONTAGNE NOIRE

HÉRAULT

St-Jean-de-
Minervois

N112

Béziers

Mas-Cabardès

Minerve

Félines-
Minervois

La Caunette

Caunes-
Minervois

Cesseras

D11

Salsigne

La Livinière

Azillanet

Bize-
Minervois

N9-N113

Trausse

Siran

Oupia

Conques-
sur-Orbiel

Peyriac-Minervois

Azille

Olonzac

Ventenac-
Cabardès

N113

Laure-
Minervois

Canal du Midi

Aude

A9

Aude

Villemoustaussou

Pezens

Carcassonne

D610

Badens

Lézignan-
Corbières

Narbonne

Montréal

Escales

Cruscades

D623

Arzens

Capendu

N113

Luc-sur-Orbieu

MASSIF
DE LA
MALEPÈRE

Roullens

Barbaira

A61

Roullens

D118

Rouffiac-
d'Aude

Fontcouverte

Boutenac

A61

Etang
de
Bages
et de
Sigean

Gruissan

Routier

Cépie

St-Hilaire

Ferrals-Les-
Corbières

Alaigne

Lagrasse

Montséret

N9-N113

Limoux

St-Laurent-de-
La-Cabrerisse

Portel-des-
Corbières

Port-La-
Nouvelle

La Digne-
d'Amont

Villesèque-
des-Corbières

Tourreilles

AUDE

Roquefort-
des-Corbières

Lapalme

Roquetaillade

Cascastel-
des-Corbières

Durban-
Corbières

Aude

Villeneuve-
Les-Corbières

Embres-et-
Castelmaure

Couiza

Treilles

Leucate

Fitou

Quillan

Tuchan

Fitou

A9

Cucugnan

Paziols

Etang
de
Leucate
ou de
Salses

PYRÉNÉES-ORIENTALES

Appellations

- Cabardès
- Minervois
- Côtes de la Malepère
- Limoux
- Corbières
- Fitou

Vin doux naturel

- St-Jean-de-Minervois
- Department boundary

N

0   15km

0   10miles

Limouxin mesoclimates. I find his Limoux excellent, as is the Cuvée Prestige, from 75 per cent Chardonnay and 25 per cent Pinot Noir (unofficially, of course).

DOMAINE DE LA NOUREILLE
Commune: Tourreilles.
Owner: Reynold Jumelle.
Surface area under Vine: 8 ha.
Wines: Limoux and Vin de Pays d'Oc.
Reynold Jumelle's vineyards, planted entirely with Chardonnay, lie higher up the hill on the other side of the village from Domaine Collin. He started in 1986 and still hasn't got round to building his own winery. When I visited in 1998 he was having his wine made for him by Hugh Ryman and his team at La Cave du Casse at Ville-longue d'Aude. His Chardonnay is very stylish.

★ LES CAVES DU SIEUR D'ARQUES
Members: 460.
Surface Area under Vine: 3200 ha.
Wines: Blanquette de Limoux including Renaissance, Crémant de Limoux, Blanquette Méthode Ancestrale, Limoux and Vin de Pays d'Oc.
Responsible for 70 per cent of the total Limoux production, this is a powerful and ambitious co-operative, selling to the public under the Aimery label and to hotels and restaurants under the Sieur d'Arques and Sieur de Limoux labels.

On offer is a wide variety of wines at different price levels from the prestige Cuvée Grande Renaissance, a non-vintage blend of 60 per cent Mauzac, 20 per cent Chardonnay and 20 per cent Chenin and aged for at least eight years before release. Leading the still wines are four Limoux wines under the Toques et Clochers label, representing four of the local mesoclimates. The *vins de pays* are sold as a range of seven wines, covering different varietals, called Les Sept Soeurs, with attractive labels based on paintings by Renoir.

DOMAINE DES TERRES BLANCHES
Commune: Cépie.
Owner: Eric and Claude Vialade.
Surface Area under Vine: 20 ha.

Wines: Blanquette de Limoux, Limoux, and Vin de Pays d'Oc.
Owned by Eric Vialade and his sister Claude (of Corbières' Château Saint-Auriol see page 438), Domaine des Terres Blanches lies south of Limoux high up in the hills at 375 metres above sea level in the area influenced by the Atlantic climate. The soil consists of clay-sandstone containing plenty of *galets* (or pudding-stones) as at Châteauneuf-du-Pape. The Blanquette comes from 90 per cent Mauzac, 10 per cent Chardonnay; the Limoux from 85 per cent Chardonnay, 15 per cent Mauzac. The wines are clean, fresh and stylish.

Other Producers of note
GÉRARD AVERSENG (LA DIGNE D'AMONT), DOMAINE BEGUDE/COMTE CATHARE SA (CÉPIE), SA BROUETTE PETIT FILS/MAISON JEAN BABOU (LIMOUX), DOMAINE DE MARTINOLLES/VERGNES FAMILY (SAINT-HILAIRE) AND GFA ROBERT (PIEUSSE).

CÔTES DE LA MALEPÈRE

Surface Area (1998): 515 ha.
Production (1998): 41,062 hl.
Colour: Red and rosé.
Grape Varieties: Cot, Cinsault, Merlot (minimum 60% combined), and Cabernet Sauvignon, Cabernet Blanc, Grenache and Syrah (maximum 30% combined).
Maximum Yield: 50 hl/ha.
Minimum Alcohol Level: 11°.

South-east of Carcassonne, and directly north of the Atlantic-influenced sections of the Limoux vineyard lies an isolated wooded hill, 442 metres high. This is the Massif de La Malepère. There are vineyards on all sides, on gravelly and clay-limestone soil and these are divided into four sub-areas according to their aspect. The north-east area is the Terroir de Carcassonne; the south-east La Belle Aude; the south-west the Terroir de Razès and the north-west the Terroir Dominican. These are the most westerly vineyards in the Languedoc and the Atlantic influence, especially on that side of the

Malepère hill, is very marked. So this is the meeting place of the Midi and the South-West, not just in climate but also in terms of the choice of grape varieties.

Most of the growers in the thirty-one communes which comprise the *appellation* send their wine to two co-operatives, the Cave de La Malepère at Arzens and the Cave du Razès at Routier, and the top *cuvées* of these establishments (Domaines du Foucauld and de Montlaur for the former; Domaine de Fournery and Château de Montclar at the latter) are among the best in the *appellation*. There are not many individual properties. Château de Cointes/Anne Gorostis at Roullens and Château de Routier/Michèle Lezerat at Routier are worth noting. The Domaine Virginie in Béziers offer the wine from the Domaine des Bruyère.

The Côtes de La Malepère is in the process of being upgraded to full *appellation contrôlée* from VDQS. Ninety per cent of the production is red wine. I find them light and somewhat lacking definition. The rosé is even less inspiring. Both styles should be consumed early.

CÔTES DU CABARDÈS ET DE L'ORBIEL

Surface Area (1998): 302 ha.
Production (1998): 19,038 hl.
Colour: Red and rosé.
Grape Varieties: (Red and rosé) Merlot, Cabernet Sauvignon and Cabernet Franc (combined 40% minimum), Grenache and Syrah (combined 40% minimum), Malbec (Cot), Cinsault and Fer Servadou.
Maximum Yield: 50 hl/ha.
Minimum Alcohol Level: 11°.

West of the Minervois and north of Carcassonne, as the land begins to climb up towards the Montagne Noire, lies the Côtes du Cabardès et de L'Orbiel, usually shortened to Cabardès. Like Côtes de La Malepère the area is in the process of being upgraded to full *appellation contrôlée* status. This is also a meeting-place of the Midi and the South-West, in respect of climate and grape varieties.

The *appellation* is spread over fourteen communes on soils which are calcareous and marly lower down and granitic, schistous or gneiss further up in the hills. The climate is benign and sunny, but the heat of the Languedoc is tempered by the influence of the Atlantic, and the wines are a similar mixture of the styles of both regions.

The wines, almost entirely red, are on the light side, and neither one thing nor another: neither proper Midi – in the sense of a good Minervois or Saint-Chinian – nor anything else. The blend of Bordeaux and Languedoc varieties does not seem to produce anything with any real character or individuality. The terrain, particularly up in the hills, is geologically promising, however. Perhaps it is only a question of time. However, they are already better than the wines of the Malepère.

Cabardès Producers of note

CHÂTEAU DE PENNAUTIER/LORGERIL FAMILY (PENNAUTIER) IS THE MAIN PRODUCER. CHÂTEAU LA BASTIDE IS OWNED BY THE SAME FAMILY. ALSO WORTH NOTING ARE CHÂTEAU JOUCLARY/ROBERT GIANESINI (CONQUES-SUR-ORBIEL), CHÂTEAU RIVALS/CHARLOTTE TRONCIN (VILLEMOUSTAUSSOU) AND CHÂTEAU VENTENAC/ALAIN MAUREL (VENTENAC); PLUS GOOD CO-OPERATIVES AT PEZENS AND CONQUES.

VINS DOUX NATURELS

MUSCAT DE FRONTIGNAN
Location: On the coast just north-east of Sète.
Surface Area (1998): 729 ha.
Production (1998): 24,085 hl.

MUSCAT DE LUNEL
Location: On alluvial land between Montpellier and Nîmes.
Surface Area (1998): 315 ha.
Production (1998): 10,936 hl.

MUSCAT DE MIREVAL
Location: Between Frontignan and Montpellier.
Surface Area (1998): 266 ha.
Production (1998): 7859 hl.

MUSCAT DE SAINT-JEAN-DE-MINERVOIS

**Location: Up in the hills close to the border
between Minervois and Saint-Chinian.
Surface Area (1998): 165 ha.
Production (1998): 5267 hl.**

As elsewhere in the South of France, the Languedoc
makes its fair share of *vins doux naturels* or VDNs. There are
four in the Languedoc, all based on the Muscat Blanc à
Petits Grains. They are not made in such a large quantity as Muscat de Rivesaltes in Roussillon or with such
elegance as that from Beaumes-de-Venise in the southern Rhône. But nevertheless they are worth seeking
out. Most of the wines are made by the local co-operatives and most are inexpensive.

Production details vary, but essentially the principle
behind the winemaking is the same. The must, which
needs to have a minimum alcoholic potential of at least
14°, is partly fermented. At approximately 5 per cent of
volume of alcohol the fermentation is stopped by the
addition of between 5 and 10 per cent neutral grape alcohol of a minimum strength of 96 per cent. This process is
called *mutage*. It produces wine with an alcoholic
strength of about 15° and sufficient residual sugar to a
potential of 21.5°. The resulting wine is rich, sweet, aromatic and very fruity, but it retains the natural grape
acidity, so, like good sweet wines anywhere, it is not
cloying. These Muscat wines are best drunk as young as
possible as freshness is the essence of their delicacy.

There is as much difference between the wines of one
producer and the next as there is in principle between
the Muscats of Frontignan, Lunel and Mireval, Frontignan producing more than twice as much as the other
two. In general I find them a little sweeter and more
raisinny than Muscat de Beaumes-de-Venise, but then
they are less expensive.

Saint-Jean-de-Minervois, a very pretty village up in
the hills and in equally impressive countryside, produces
a lighter style of wine, but with a lovely floral bouquet. I
prefer it to the other Languedoc *vins doux*. The wine from
the 16.2 hectare domaine of Marie-Thérèse Miquel de
Barroubio has long been the finest producer of fortified
Muscat in the whole of the Languedoc, if not France.

Vin doux naturel Producers of note
Frontignan CHÂTEAU DE LA PEYRADE/YVES PASTOUREL
& FILS, CHÂTEAU DE STONY/NODET FRÈRES AND CAVE
COOPÉRATIVE DE FRONTIGNAN — ESPECIALLY CHÂTEAU DE
MEREVILLE.
Lunel CLOS BELLEVUE AND DOMAINE LACOSTE/FRANCIS
LACOSTE, CHÂTEAU GRÈS SAINT-PAUL/JEAN-PHILIPPE
SERVIÈRE AND CAVE COOPÉRATIVE DE LUNEL — ESPECIALLY
CHÂTEAU TOUR DE FARGES.
Mireval DOMAINE DU MAS NEUF/HUGUES & BERNARD
JEANJEAN AND DOMAINE DU MOULINAS/LES FRÈRES AYMES.
Saint-Jean-de-Minervois DOMAINE DE BARROUBIO/
MARIE-THÉRÈSE MIQUEL AND CAVE COOPÉRATIVE LE
MUSCAT.

VINS DE PAYS

The Languedoc region comprises the departments of
Aude, Hérault and part of the Gard and covers more
than fifty different *vins de pays*. Some of those in the Gard
more properly belong to the chapter on the Rhône Valley. Moreover there is, in addition, the important
regional *vin de pays*, Vin de Pays d'Oc.

I consider this far too many. The Corbières, to take
an example, is a known and defined *appellation*. Is there
really a need for 14 separate *vins de pays* within its confines? Are they really that different? Commercially, too,
I can't help feeling that this plethora of names is
counter-productive. A single domaine may rejoice in
the idea of being able to produce Vin de Pays des Hauts
de Badens. But most of the rest of us have no idea where
the Badens Heights are; nor do we care. Any company
seeking to create a brand suitable for selling to supermarkets worldwide will be forced to source from several
areas and therefore sell under all-embracing Vin de Pays
d'Oc label.

There is now an increasing dichotomy in the presentation and pricing of *vins de pays*. On the one hand there
are wines tailormade to fit a flavour and price-point:
whites from the ubiquitous Chardonnay or, increasingly, Viognier; reds from a mixture of local grapes and
cépages améliorateurs such as Cabernet Sauvignon and
Syrah. This is the mass production end of the market.

The Chardonnays can indeed by very good, though it pays to buy up to one of the better houses such as Fortant de France or the domaines of Jacques and François Lurton. It is now estimated that there are 4000 hectares of Chardonnay planted in the Languedoc. This is more than the surface area of Saint-Chinian (approximately 2900 hectares) and getting on for that of the Minervois (approximately 5200 hectares). Most *vins de pays*, however, and by a long way, is red wine.

On the other hand are the wines from perfectionist domaine owners such as Laurent Vaillé of the Domaine de La Grange des Pères at Aniane, north of Montpellier. These growers find they cannot make their best wine within the local *appellation* rules – they may want to blend Cabernet Sauvignon with their Syrah, they may want to make a wine from just Syrah or just Mourvèdre wine whereas the *appellation contrôlée* rules require the use of three varieties.

Led by Aimé Guibert at Mas de Daumas Gassac (see right) – and by Eloi Dürrbach at the Domaine de Trévallon in the Bouches-du-Rhône (see page 400) – these growers have followed their Italian counterparts and as well as super-Tuscan wines (that is wines of high quality and price but sold under a simple *vin de pays appellation*), we now have super-Midi wines.

Most of the Languedoc domaines noted elsewhere in this chapter produce *vins de pays* as well as their *appellation contrôlée* wines. Here is a selection of those producers who concentrate on making *vins de pays*.

Leading Vins de Pays producers in the Languedoc

DOMAINE DE L'ARJOLLE

Commune: Poulolles.
Owner: Louis-Marie Teisserenc.
Surface Area under Vine: 45 ha.
Wines: Vin de Pays des Côtes de Thongue.
Louis-Marie Teisserenc and his partners set up in 1974 and now operate a sizeable domaine halfway between Béziers and Faugères. There is a wide range of different varieties planted, including, so they claim, the only French plot of Zinfandel, a variety more normally

associated with California. The star wines include the Muscat à Petits Grains, Chardonnay Delphine de Margon and Cabernet Cuvée de L'Arjolle, an oaky blend of 80 per cent Cabernet Sauvignon and 20 per cent Cabernet Franc.

★ DOMAINE DE BARUEL

Commune: Tornac.
Owner: Rainer Pfeffercorn.
Surface Area under Vine: 10 ha.
Wines: Vin de Pays des Cévennes.
Rainer Pfeffercorn established his domaine on schistous marl west of Uzès in 1990 and is in the process of selling it as the book goes to press. The vines, Cabernet Sauvignon and Merlot, are much older though, and with yields pruned to the bone, provide a wine somewhat similar to Domaine de Trévallon (see page 400) in intensity but with less brutal tannins. Ageing is in *foudres*, not *barriques*, as at Domaine de Trévallon.

DOMAINE DE CLOVALLON

Commune: Bédarieux.
Owner: Catherine Roque.
Surface Area under Vine: 12 ha.
Wines: Vin de Pays d'Oc.
Catherine Roque started up in the late 1980s, buying out her brother-in-law from land inherited by her husband's family. She then proceeded to plant Chardonnay, Viognier, Syrah and in particular, Pinot Noir; the latter on *grès rouge*, the Syrah on schist and the Chardonnay on dolmitic limestone. The vineyard lies at an altitude between 250 and 450 metres, north of the Faugères *appellation*. The results are promising.

★ MAS DE DAUMAS GASSAC

Commune: Aniane.
Owner: Aimé Guibert.
Surface Area under Vine: 27 ha.
Wines: Vin de Pays de L'Hérault.
Mas de Daumas Gassac is the super-star of the super-Midi estates. Planted as long ago now as 1971, and yielding its first vintage in 1978, this Cabernet Sauvignon-based wine became an instant success when first

released in 1981. The soil is a curious glacial deposit, a very porous reddish-pink powder, free of stones and other admixtures, and the wine is a mongrel but nevertheless noble mixture of Bordeaux and the Languedoc, yet with only a *soupçon* of a southern French grape, and Syrah at that, in the *encépagement*. I have sampled the full series of Mas de Daumas Gassac vintages on a number of occasions. The wines have become softer as the vines have aged and the tannis are consequently less tough. Curiously while they were very Bordeaux-like at first (and usually from 90 per cent Cabernet Sauvignon) they are less so now.

There is also a good Chardonnay/Viognier white and in recent years a wide range of other wines sourced, *inter alia*, from the nearby co-operative of Villeveyrac.

★ FORTANT DE FRANCE
Commune: Sète.
Owner: Robert Skalli.
Suppliers: 140.
Average annual Production: 670,000 hl.
Wines: Vin de Pays d'Oc.

Robert Skalli established his business in Sète in the mid-1970s, and in 1988 set up Fortant de France, dealing exclusively in Vin de Pays d'Oc wines from some 140 suppliers in the region and from a wide range of grape varieties, including Chardonnay and Viognier for the whites (and Sauvignon Blanc but I consider this to be less successful) and Cabernet Sauvignon and Merlot for the reds. This is a very modern establishment, with all the control one would wish, and quality is high. The wines are balanced, discreet, intensely flavoured and not a bit too oaky.

★★ DOMAINE LA GRANGE DES PÈRES
Commune: Aniane.
Owner: Laurent Vaillé.
Surface Area under Vine: 10 ha.
Wines: Vin de Pays de L'Hérault.

Laurent Vaillé's family vineyard, abandoned at the time of phylloxera, and not resurrected until 1989, lies near to Mas de Daumas Gassac (see page 447) and would be entitled to the Coteaux du Languedoc *appellation*.

Laurent has planted Cabernet Sauvignon, however, alongside his Mourvèdre and Syrah (the blend is 20:40:40), reduces his yield to the minimum, keeps his wine 26 months in wood, and neither fines nor filters. The results are spectacular: rich, concentrated, fresh and very classy. There is also a very impressive Roussanne-based white wine.

DOMAINE LA GRANGE DE QUATRE SOUS
Commune: Assignan.
Owners: Hildegard Horat and Ernst Wirz.
Surface Area under Vine: 8 ha.
Wines: Vin de Pays d'Oc.

The first vines were planted in 1983. Two whites are offered: Chardonnay and Le Jeu du Mail (60 per cent Viognier, 25 per cent Marsanne, 15 per cent Roussanne) aged in newish *demi-muids* of 500-litre capacity. Les Serrottes is made from 70 per cent Syrah and 30 per cent Malbec, and Lo Molin from half each Cabernet Sauvignon and Cabernet Franc, again aged in oak. This is intelligent winemaking and good wines all the way down the range.

DOMAINE DE LIMBARDIE
DOMAINE DE GRANGENEUVE
Commune: Cessenon-sur-Orb.
Owner: Henri Boukandoura.
Surface Area under Vine: 20 ha.
Wines: Vin de Pays des Coteaux de Murviel.

Henri Boukandoura started out at Murviel, closer to Béziers, and produced his first vintage in 1987. He moved to Grangeneuve, up on a hill outside Cessenon, in 1993, and has since bought land in the neighbourhood. Only reds and rosés are produced. The Merlot-Cabernet blend is good; the pure Merlot, Cuvée Tradition, aged in *barrique*, is even better.

★ MAISON JACQUES & FRANÇOIS LURTON
DOMAINE DE POUMEYRADE
Commune: Vayres (Bordeaux).
Owners: Jacques & François Lurton.

Jacques and François Lurton, sons of André Lurton of Châteaux Bonnet, La Louvière, Couhins and others in

Bordeaux, produce, as well as a range of other wines from elsewhere in France, Argentina, Australia, Rueda in Spain and even in Uruguay, some of the best *vins de pays* from the Midi. These are available in a wide range of exclusive own labels and domaine titles. *Inter alia* there is a delightful Chardonnay wine called Domaine d'Horte-Neuve. This company proves that not all the flying-winemaker geniuses are Australian!

DOMAINE DE RAVANÈS

Commune: Thézan-Lès-Béziers.
Owner: Guy Benin.
Surface Area under Vine: 54 ha.
Wines: Vin de Pays des Coteaux de Murviel.

The Benins came from Algeria in 1955 and established themselves in an imposing mansion north of Béziers, specialising in the Bordeaux varietals. There is a pure Merlot, a pure Cabernet Sauvignon and even a pure Petit Verdot (an experimental parcel planted in 1982). There is also a late-harvest white produced from fifty-year-old Ugni Blanc vines.

DOMAINES VITICOLES DES SALINS DU MIDI

Commune: Listel, Sète and Aigues-Mortes.
Surface Area under Vine: 1700 ha.
Wines: Vin de Pays des Sables du Golfe du Lion.

If anything proves that with attention to controlled vinification and the selection of the better grape varieties one can make good wine almost anywhere in the world it is the Domaines Viticoles des Salins du Midi. As the name suggests, the main business of the parent company, the Compagnie des Salins du Midi, is the manufacture of salt, which is produced literally on the edge of the land in the extensive sand-flats of the Camargue, by making very shallow reservoirs of sea water which then evaporate, leaving behind salt.

Under the direction of one of the most engaging wine geniuses I have ever met, the now-retired Pierre Jullien, Domaines Viticoles des Salins du Midi decided after the Second World War to turn its attention to making quality rather than quantity. The company had moved into wine production at the time of the phylloxera epidemic, when the remainder of France's vineyards were under threat, as it was found that vines planted in sand were immune from the devastation of the phylloxera louse. But with the re-establishment of the usual Midi vineyards, now under grafted vines, they found they could not compete at the basic level.

The operation is vast. The vineyards total more than 1700 hectares and it is the largest wine estate in France. There are two enormous vinification, storage and bottling factories, one at Aigues-Mortes and the other at Sète, and almost exclusive production of the Vin de Pays des Sables du Golfe du Lion. Particular attention has been given to *cépages améliorateurs*: Cabernet Sauvignon, Sauvignon Blanc, Chardonnay, and even Riesling. The wines are inexpensive and impeccably made and are sold under the name of Listel, with the best boasting a domaine or château name such as Jarras or Villeroy.

Other Producers of note:

DOMAINE DE BACHELLERY/BERNARD JULLIEN (BÉZIERS), DOMAINE DE LA BAUME (SERVIAN), DOMAINE DE LA BAUMIÈRE (BÉZIERS), DOMAINE DE CAPION/PHILIPPE SALASC (ANIANE), CHANTE CIGALE/DOMAINE DU BOSC/PIERRE BEZINET (VIAS), DOMAINE CHARTREUSE DE MOUGÈRES/SARAH BONNE TERRE (CAUX), DOMAINE LA CHEVALIÈRE (BÉZIERS), DOMAINE DE LA CONDAMINE L'EVÊQUE/GUY & MARIE-CLAUDE BASCOU (NÉZIGNAN-L'EVÊQUE), DOMAINE L'ENCLOS D'ORMESSON/JÉRÔME D'ORMESSON (LÉZIGNAN-LA-CÈBE), DOMAINE DE L'ENGARRAN (LAVERUNE), DOMAINE DES FONTAINES/BERNARD MONTARIOL (LIEURAN-LÈS-BÉZIERS), DOMAINE DE MOULINES/SAUMADE (MUDAISON), DOMAINE DU MOULIN DE PERIÉS/JEAN-JACQUES & MICHELINE ORTIZ-BERNABÉ (NISSAN-LÈS-ENSÉRUNE), DOMAINE LA PROVENQUIÈRE/BRIGITTE & CLAUDE ROBERT — PARTICULARLY FOR WHITE WINES (CAPESTANG), DOMAINE SAINT-JEAN DE CONQUES/F R BOUSSAGOL (QUARANTE), DOMAINE DE SAINT-LOUIS/PIERRE CAPTIER (LOUPIAN), DOMAINE SAINT-MARTIN DE LA GARRIGUE/JEAN-CLAUDE ZABAGLIA (MONTAGNAC), DOMAINE SIMONET/CHRISTOPHE BARBIER (LES CABANES DE FLEURY) AND DOMAINE VIRGINIE (BÉZIERS).

VINS DE PAYS

REGIONAL
Vin de Pays d'Oc.

DEPARTMENTAL VINS DE PAYS
Vin de Pays du Gard.
Vin de Pays de L'Hérault.
Vin de Pays de L'Aude.

ZONAL VINS DE PAYS
Gard
Vin de Pays des Cévennes: Around Alès up in the foothills of the Cévennes.

Vin de Pays des Coteaux de Cèze: Right bank of the Rhône between Bagnols-sur-Cèze and Roquemaure.

Vin de Pays des Coteaux Flaviens: Covers much of the Costières de Nîmes *appellation*.

Vin de Pays des Coteaux du Pont du Gard: Around Remoulins.

Vin de Pays des Côtes du Vidourle: Around Sommières.

Vin de Pays Duché d'Uzès: Between the Cévennes and the town of Uzès.

Vin de Pays des Sables du Golfe du Lion: The Camargue region.

Vin de Pays de La Vaunage: East of Nîmes.

Vin de Pays de La Vistrenque: From Nîmes to Aigues-Mortes.

Hérault
Vin de Pays de L'Ardailhou: Between Béziers and the coast.

Vin de Pays de La Bénovie: Above Lunel on the Gard border.

Vin de Pays du Bérange: Around Castries.

Vin de Pays de Bessan: Inland from Agde.

Vin de Pays de Cassan: In the hills behind Pézenas.

Vin de Pays de Caux: Also in the hills behind Pézenas.

Vin de Pays de Cessenon: The central part of the Saint-Chinian *appellation*.

Vin de Pays des Collines de La Moure: South-west of Montpellier as far as the Etang de Thau.

Vin de Pays des Coteaux de Bessilles: Around Montagnac.

Vin de Pays des Coteaux d'Enserune: West and south-west of Béziers.

Vin de Pays des Coteaux de Fontcaude: Southern part of the Saint-Chinian *appellation*.

Vin de Pays des Coteaux de Laurens: The Faugères *appellation*.

Vin de Pays des Coteaux du Libron: Around the town of Béziers.

Vin de Pays des Coteaux de Murviel: The eastern part of the Saint-Chinian *appellation*.

Vin de Pays des Coteaux de Peyriac: Western part of the Minervois *appellation*.

Vin de Pays des Coteaux du Salagou: Around Lodève.

Vin de Pays des Côtes du Brian: Eastern part of the Minervois *appellation*.

Vin de Pays des Côtes du Ceressou: Around Clermont L'Hérault.

Vin de Pays des Côtes de Thau: North of Agde.

Vin de Pays des Côtes de Thongue: Béziers and Pézenas.

Vin de Pays des Gorges de L'Hérault: Around the town of Aniane.

Vin de Pays de La Haute Vallée de L'Orb: Around Bédarieux.

Vin de Pays du Mont Baudile: North of Clermont L'Hérault.

Vin de Pays des Monts de La Grage: Western part of the Saint-Chinian *appellation*.

Vin de Pays de Pézenas: Around Pézenas.

Vin de Pays des Sables du Golfe du Lion: Coastal area between Agde and Gard border.

Vin de Pays du Val de Montferrand: North of Montpellier, around the Pic Saint-Loup.

Vin de Pays du Vicomté d'Aumelas: East of the Hérault river and Clermont L'Hérault.

Aude

Vin de Pays de La Cité de Carcassonne: Around Carcassonne.

Vin de Pays des Coteaux de La Cabrerisse: Around Saint-Laurent-de-La-Cabrerisse in the Corbières *appellation*.

Vin de Pays des Coteaux du Littoral Audois: Coastal area between Grussan and Leucate.

Vin de Pays des Coteaux de Miramont: Around Capendu in the Corbières *appellation*.

Vin de Pays des Coteaux de Narbonne: Around Narbonne.

Vin de Pays des Coteaux de Peyriac: Western part of the Minervois *appellation*.

Vin de Pays des Côtes de Pérignan: South-western Corbières.

Vin de Pays des Côtes de Lastours: Cabardès and extreme eastern Minervois.

Vin de Pays des Côtes de Prouille: East of Carcassonne around Fanjeaux.

Vin de Pays de Cucugnan: Deepest Corbières hills.

Vin de Pays d'Hauterive: West of Narbonne as far as the Massif des Corbières.

Vin de Pays de La Haute Vallée de L'Aude: The Limoux *appellation*.

Vin de Pays des Hauts de Badens: North of Capendu.

Vin de Pays du Torgan: Around Tuchan in the high Corbières.

Vin de Pays du Val de Cesse: North-east of Narbonne around Ginestas.

Vin de Pays du Val de Dagne: Eastern end of the Corbières.

Vin de Pays de La Vallée du Paradis: Around the commune of Durban in the south-east of the department.

THE ROUSSILLON

THE DEPARTMENTAL BOUNDARY between the Aude and the Pyrénées-Orientales – roughly a straight east-west line that bisects the Etang de Leucate – marks the end of the *appellations* of Corbières and Fitou and the start of the Côtes du Roussillon. It also marks the border between the French Midi and one which is much more definitely Catalan. The Roussillon was part of the kingdom of Majorca until 1642. Catalan is still spoken, as it is across the border in Spain, and the local cuisine, rich in garlic, tomatoes and red peppers, is as much Spanish as French.

The capital of the region is Perpignan, the sunniest city in France, around which is a large fertile plain, largely given over to market gardens and orchards. Across this terrain a number of rivers flow out of the Pyrenees into the Mediterranean: the Agly, the Têt and the Tech, and it is largely in the hinterland, the uplands beyond the plain, that the best wines are found, particularly in the upper part of the region, the valley of the Agly and the northern part of the valley of the Têt. This is the area of the Côtes du Roussillon-Villages, and, in the upper Agly, the *vin doux naturel appellation* of Maury. South-east, as the Pyrenees mountains fall into the sea, close to the Spanish border, are the *appellations* of Banyuls – another *vin doux naturel* – and Collioure.

In between, throughout the rest of the Pyrénées-Orientales, other *vins doux naturels* are produced, reds from Grenache, whites from Muscat: Rivesaltes and Muscat de Rivesaltes, respectively. More popular domestically than on the export market, many of these *vins doux naturels*, especially Rivesaltes itself, are in decline. But, as if to compensate, the standard of the red table wines is rising, with an encouraging amount of new vibrant domaines emerging every year to sell their own wine in bottle. In addition there are now a number of interesting white wines under the Côtes du Roussillon label, and, as elsewhere in the Midi, an increasing interest in single-varietal *vins de pays* made from non-indigenous quality grapes. As in the Languedoc, the flatter lands closer to the Mediterranean tend to be cultivated today with a view to producing *vins de pays* wines. The AC wines are from vines on the hills behind.

Nevertheless, this continues to be a wine area dominated by the co-operatives. It is estimated that 70 per cent of the Roussillon harvest is controlled by co-operatives. Many of these are very good. Few, however, demonstrate the *esprit de corps*, either at director or at member level, of the top individual estates.

The soil structure in Roussillon is complex, as are the mesoclimates. Away from the plain, which can be bakingly dry and boiling hot in the summer, the uplands can be refreshingly cool, and the average rainfall is significantly higher. The Tramontane, the dry wind from the hills, is neither as fierce or as frequent as the Mistral, and can play its part in concentrating the fruit. The Marinara, the wind from the sea, can refresh the summer heat.

Down in the plain are alluvial soils, clay and *limons* (clay-sandstone mixtures), sand and gravel and larger *galets* or pudding-stones as found at Châteauneuf-du-Pape. Inland the hills are mainly limestone rock or light-coloured schist, though granite and *grès* is to be found. There is marl and in the Agly Valley black schistous debris. The four superior sub-areas of the Côtes du Roussillon Villages each have their own different soils – Caramany has gneiss, Latour de France is black schist, Lesquerde has granite and Tautavel, which extends up to Vingrau, is limestone rock and clay-limestone (*argilo-calcaire*).

It is in the uplands, on the rock and its deposits, that the best red wines are found, superior to the rest of the Midi. While it is hot during the day, it is not baking hot; and the nights are cool, allowing the vine to relax. This prolongs the gestation of the vine, preserving the acidity and resulting in something of greater complexity. Roussillon reds are full-bodied but lush, rich and balanced, lacking the hot peppery character of much of the Languedoc. The tannins are more sophisticated, and they age better. And they are not necessarily any more expensive.

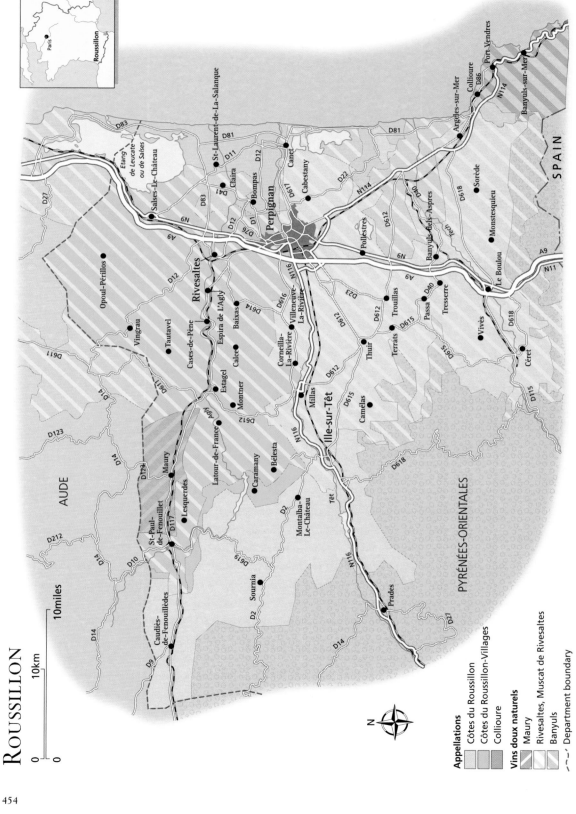

ROUSSILLON

Paris

Roussillon

AUDE

PYRÉNÉES-ORIENTALES

SPAIN

Étang
de Leucate
ou de Salses

Salses-Le-Château

St-Laurent-de-La-Salanque

St-Paul-de-Fenouillet

Caudiès-de-Fenouillèdes

Lesquerdes

Maury

Latour-de-France

Caramany

Bélesta

Montalba-
Le-Château

Sournia

Prades

Estagel

Montner

Calce

Baixas

Espira de L'Agly

Cases-de-Pène

Rivesaltes

Vingrau

Tautavel

Opoul-Périllos

Cornailla-
La-Rivière

Villeneuve-
La-Rivière

Millas

Ille-sur-Têt

Camélas

Thuir

Terrats

Troullias

Passa

Tresserre

Vivès

Céret

Le Boulou

Monstesquieu

Sorède

Banyuls-dels-Aspres

Pollestres

Perpignan

Canet

Cabestany

Bompas

Claira

St-Laurent-de-La-Salanque

Argelès-sur-Mer

Collioure

Port Vendres

Banyuls-sur-Mer

Têt

Tech

10km

10miles

N

Appellations

Côtes du Roussillon

Côtes du Roussillon-Villages

Collioure

Vins doux naturels

Maury

Rivesaltes, Muscat de Rivesaltes

Banyuls

Department boundary

SURFACE AREA AND PRODUCTION (1998 HARVEST)

APPELLATIONS	SURFACE AREA (HA)	PRODUCTION (HL)	
		RED & ROSÉ	WHITE
COLLIOURE	325	11,925	–
CÔTES DU ROUSSILLON	4309	183,385	10,830
CÔTES DU ROUSSILLON-VILLAGES	2071	89,891	–
TOTAL	**6705**	**285,201**	**10,830**
		296,031	
VINS DOUX NATURELS			
BANYULS & BANYULS GRANDS CRUS	1346	24,043	–
MAURY	1715	48,086	–
MUSCAT DE RIVESALTES	4854	–	144,744
RIVESALTES	9951	–	163,760
GRAND ROUSSILLON		2779	–
TOTAL	**17,866**	**74,908**	**308,504**
		383,412	
GRAND TOTAL	**24,571**	**679,443**	

Surface Area and Production

Despite the high potential of Roussillon red wines, the *vins doux naturels* form the majority of the region's production. Over the last ten years there has been a serious decline in the demand for Rivesaltes, yet the *vins doux naturels* from Muscat, like others elsewhere, have increased in popularity. Production of table wines, except in recently discovered Collioure, has remained static in *appellation contrôlée* terms. What the figures do not show is a substantial increase in the demand for Catalan *vins de pays*.

When to Drink the Wines

Drink the whites and rosés early, during the calendar year after the vintage. They are not made for keeping. Most of the reds are also for drinking in the relatively short term, between two and five years after the vintage. The very best Roussillon-Villages reds will keep for as long as eight years.

Muscat de Rivesaltes, like all Muscat wines, should be drunk young. The older Banyuls and Maurys, once bottled, will not normally improve any further but can be kept for a couple of years. Once you have broached a bottle of *vin doux naturel*, finish it within the week.

Roussillon Vintages

1998 As elsewhere in the Midi the harvest was on the small size but of good concentrated quality. The wines will keep well.

1997 A wet September, threatening both mildew and rot effectively diluted the crop in all but Collioure and Banyuls. The vintage is good here; but somewhat lightweight elsewhere. The Muscat grape was particularly badly hit.

1996 Good but not remarkable.

1995 Bigger, sturdier wines, though sometimes with rather clumsy tannins.

1994 A cooler year. Paradoxically a combination of more elegant wines but with a less ripe tannic structure than either 1995 or 1993.

1993 Big sturdy wines, as in 1995.

1992 A light year. Many wines now past their prime.

The Wine Regions

CÔTES DU ROUSSILLON

**Surface Area (1998): 125 communes covering
4309 ha.**
**Production (1998): (Red and rosé) 183,385 hl;
(white) 10,830 hl.**
Colour: Red, rosé and white.
**Grape Varieties: (Red and rosé) Carignan,
Grenache Noir, Lladoner Pelut, Cinsault, Syrah
and Mourvèdre; (white) Maccabéo, Malvoisie du
Roussillon (Tourbat), Grenache Blanc,
Roussanne, Marsanne and Rolle (Vermentino).**
Maximum Yield: 50 hl/ha.
**Minimum Alcohol Level: (Red and rosé) 11.5°;
(white) 10.5°.**

Essentially there are two types of red Côtes du Roussillon: a lighter wine produced by carbonic maceration
which is plump and freshly fruity, without a tannic
structure, and which is drinkable after six months in
bottle; and a wine produced by traditional methods,
sometimes aged in small wood, a percentage of which
can of course be new, and which needs ageing for a minimum of a year or two after bottling. This will have not
only more tannin but a greater dimension, the fruit
flavours being more of cooked plums.

Many growers vinify their Carignan grapes by the
first method, their other varietals by the second, later
blending the two. An increasing number produce three
blends: a carbonic maceration wine, a 'traditional' wine,
and a traditional wine matured in new and newish
wood – this last wine destined for ageing in bottle.

South of the river Têt, which flows through Perpignan, the wines tend to be lighter, looser knit and less
interesting. Most of the best Côtes du Roussillon comes
from the Roussillon-Villages area to the north.

Three varieties must be used for the red, including at
least 20 per cent Syrah or Mourvèdre – the former is
generally preferred as being better adapted to the climate and soils of the region than the later-ripening
Mourvèdre – and a maximum of 60 per cent Carignan.

Up to 10 per cent white Maccabéo (or Macabeu, as it is
pronounced and spelt locally) can be incorporated but
today most locals make their reds from only red grapes.

Most Côtes du Roussillon rosé is produced by *saignée*
(bleeding) methods rather than by a short maceration
with the skins, and is best drunk in the summer after
the vintage, when its qualities of lightness, freshness and
fruitiness are pronounced. By and large it is more reliable than the local *appellation contrôleé* whites, though
these have much improved in the last decade.

Roussanne and Rolle (Vermentino), the latter the
most aromatic of the local varieties, plus Macabeu to
give the necessary acidity, are the grapes which make
the most interesting whites. Most of these wines are
vinified in tank and bottled early to be drunk quickly. A
few pioneering estates, such as Sarda-Malet (see page
462) are experimenting with using new and newish oak.
The last four grapes in the list for white Roussillon cannot make up more than 50 per cent of the *encépagement*.

Many of the best dry Roussillon whites, such as the
delicious, gently oaky Grenache/Roussanne blend Les
Magdaléniens from Alain Razungles of the Domaine des
Chênes in Vingrau (see page 459), are classified as *vin de
pays*, which allows a freer use of grape varieties – as well
as Muscat, Chardonnay and Viognier are increasingly
popular. There is even Sauvignon Blanc, which in my
view, is a mistake as the climate in the Roussillon is too
warm. It is necessary to pick the Chardonnay at 12-12.5°
in order to obtain a wine with sufficient acidity. If the
harvest takes place much later, the sugar content of the
grapes would produce a much more alcoholic wine,
which would also have a heavy, oily character. At the
same time the acidity level would have decreased to a
point where it would be necessary to acidify the wine: a
process frowned upon as the results are rarely elegant.

Fine dry Muscat is difficult to produce in the Roussillon. The window of opportunity for harvesting when
all the elements of flavour, acidity and finesse are available in balance is very short. Nor do these elements
always arrive at optimum at the same time.

CÔTES DU ROUSSILLON-VILLAGES

Surface Area (1998): 32 communes in the northern part of the region covering 2071 ha.
Production (1998): 89,891 hl.
Colour: Red.
Grape Varieties: Carignan, Grenache Noir, Lladoner Pelut, Cinsault, Syrah and Mourvèdre; plus up to 10% white Maccabéo if desired.
Maximum Yield: 45 hl/ha.
Minimum Alcohol Level: 12°.

The *appellation* of Côtes du Roussillon-Villages applies to the red wines only of the northern, more mountainous section of the Pyrénées-Orientales *département*. The same grape requirements apply as for red Côtes du Roussillon. Three varieties must be used, including at least 20 per cent Syrah or Mourvèdre – the former is generally preferred as being better adapted to the climate and soils of the region than the later-ripening Mourvèdre – and a maximum of 60 per cent Carignan. Up to 10 per cent white Maccabéo (or Macabeu, as it is pronounced and spelt locally) can be incorporated.

A lower yield than for Côtes du Roussillon is stipulated, but not, strangely, a higher proportion of *cépages améliorateurs* (Syrah and Grenache) and a correspondingly lower amount of Carignan. One of the explanations may well be that old-vine Carignan, cropped low, can indeed produce very good wine, a real surprise to those who have never encountered it and who only heard this variety slagged off as the bad boy of the Midi.

At its best – as seen in the wines of Domaine Gauby in Calce and the superior *cuvées* of estates such as Força-Réal, Mas Crémat, Domaine Cazes, the Domaine des Chênes and the Château de Caladroy (see pages 458-461) – Roussillon-Villages deserves its greater reputation and higher price. The co-operative wines are less expensive but there is little difference between a Roussillon-Villages and a Côtes du Roussillon except a bit more weight and a bit more new oak.

The *appellation* has four superior sub-areas – Caramany, Latour de France, Lasquerde and Tautavel. Each

has its own particular soil. Each in principle is slightly different but these differences tend to be obscured by the fact that most of the wines are made by co-operatives. They are competent but do not show meticulous *terroir*-expressive winemaking.

RIVESALTES

Surface Area (1998): Throughout the entire Roussillon region (an area of 9951 ha) with the exception of Banyuls and Collioure.
Production (1998): 163,760 hl.
Colour: Red, white, ambré and tuilé.
Grape Varieties: Grenache Noir, Grenache Gris, Grenache Blanc, Muscat à Petits Grains, Muscat of Alexandria, Maccabéo, Tourbat, plus a combined maximum of 10% Carignan, Cinsault and Syrah.
Maximum Yield: 30 hl/ha.
Minimum Alcohol Level: 15°.

Rivesaltes is the generic *appellation* for the Roussillon *vins doux naturels* which are not delimited geographically (Banyuls, Maury) or varietally (Muscat de Rivesaltes) and production amounts to half of all France's *vins doux naturels*. The wine can be red or white, *ambré* or *tuilé* (amber or tawny), 'vintage' or aged in cask, fresh or *rancio* (slightly oxidised), and on the dry side – intended as an aperitif – or properly sweet. You will also find it with a vintage and without. Red Rivesaltes is made in the same way as Maury (see page 463), the white that of Muscat de Rivesaltes (see 458).

Styles vary. There are 'vintage' wines such as those of Domaine Gauby (see page 460), not a bit too sweet; indeed, more like a liquid but alcoholic red fruit jelly. There are youthful, clean Rivesaltes Blancs, such as the Roc du Gouverneur of Les Vignerons du Rivesaltais (see page 463). And there are older, richly mature wines which have a touch of fine *oloroso* sherry coupled with an orangepeel nuance (from the Muscat grape). Joseph Puig of Domaine Père Puig in Claira (see page 462) gives his Grenache Noir nine months of maceration with the skins and harvests at 9 hl/ha. The wines are marvellously subtle and individual.

Most of the larger companies produce a wide range of Rivesaltes, from the cheap and cheerful to the old and profound. Les Vignerons du Rivesaltais, under the inspired leadership of Fernand Baixas, is responsible for about 60 per cent of the Rivesaltes production. Personally I prefer my Rivesaltes not oxidised and *rancio* is a taste I have no wish to acquire.

Muscat de Rivesaltes

Surface Area (1998): Throughout the Pyrénées-Orientales wine area, covering 4854 ha.
Production (1998): 144,744 hl.
Grape Varieties: Muscat of Alexandria and Muscat à Petits Grains.
Maximum Yield: 30 hl/ha.
Minimum Alcohol Level: 15°.

While sweet *vin doux naturel* Muscat wines are now increasingly popular the variety is difficult to grow. It suffers from excessive heat, necessitating a *gobelet* pruning with plenty of leaves to prevent the grapes from getting scorched. These leaves, however, tend to retain humidity round the bunch, rendering it susceptible to mildew. Moreover the thin skins can easily lead to rot, if, as in 1997, the run-up to the vintage is very wet.

Two sub-varieties are grown in Roussillon, Muscat of Alexandria and the Blanc à Petits Grains. The former withstands drought stress better, developing later than Petits Grains. Both are best planted on cold clayey soils such as around Salses, near the Etang de Leucate, or around Bompas, north-east of Perpignan.

The wine is made by *mutage*, decanting the juice off into a vat containing sufficient grape alcohol to ensure a finished alcoholic degree of 15°, the unfermented sugar leaving the final wine sweet. In order for the wine not to be too heavy, the acidity level must be high enough to balance the sugar. Cold fermentation is used in order to retain finesse, perfume, and delicacy.

There has been much progress in the quality of the Languedoc-Roussillon Muscats, of which Rivesaltes is far and away the most important one, in recent years. But I still consider that the Beaumes-de-Venise version

(from the southern Rhône and made entirely from the superior Petits Grains variety) has the edge. Beaumes-de-Venise is, of course, made exclusively from the Petits Grains sub-variety of Muscat, grown here in Roussillon, *inter alia*, by Raymond Laporte at Château Roussillon, producer of one of the best Muscat de Rivesaltes (see page 461). Many other estates, as at Domaine Cazes Frères (see page 459), who make perhaps the most delicious dry Muscat, prefer the Alexandria variety for the table wine. Perhaps the solution is to plant both, but to use the latter for the dry wine and the Petits Grains for the *vin doux naturel*.

Grand Roussillon

Surface Area (1998): Throughout the Roussillon, Banyuls area. The official figures do not disclose the size of the appellation, including it within that of Rivesaltes.
Production (1998): 2779 hl.
Colour: As for Rivesaltes.
Grape Varieties: As for Rivesaltes.
Maximum Yield: 30 hl/ha.
Minimum Alcohol Level: 15°.

Grand Roussillon is a rare *appellation*. It can come in various colours, fresh or *rancio*, as with Rivesaltes, to which, to all extents and purposes, it is undistinguishable. Most local producers prefer to use the Rivesaltes name.

Leading Roussillon Producers

Château de Caladroy
Commune: Bélesta.
Owners: Olivier Arnold and Mathilde Moulle.
Surface Area under Vine: 120 ha.
Wines: Côtes du Roussillon (red and white), Côtes du Roussillon-Villages, Rivesaltes and Muscat de Rivesaltes.
Built in the twelfth century to defend the then border between France and the county of Barcelona, the Château de Caladroy dominates a hill at 360 metres above sea level, with a commanding view over the plain

towards Perpignan and to the south. This is a proper castle – a *château fort* in French – with high, sheer walls and an impressive tower on the north-west side.

Winemaking at a serious level is a recent development and improving – barrel-ageing was only introduced in 1998 and much of the vineyard is recently planted. The vines are located on arid limestone and schistous slopes, at an altitude of 250 metres where it is difficult to produce yields over 25-30 hl/ha. So there is potential here.

DOMAINE LA CASENOVE
Commune: Trouillas.
Owner: Etienne Montes.
Surface Area under Vine: 50 ha.
Wines: Côtes du Roussillon including (red) Cuvée Jaubert and white, and Vin de Pays Catalan.
Adjacent to the *autoroute* south of Perpignan the Casenove estate occupies undulating land which consists mainly of clay sand and gravel surrounding rather a fine château, parts of which date back to the sixteenth century. It has belonged to the Montes family for many generations.

I find the red wines better than the whites and the *vins de pays*. The whites are fermented and aged partly in small oak, partly in tank; the reds being matured likewise. The top red wine is Cuvée Commandant Jaubert, named after Etienne's grandfather: this is a burly wine with the *tabac* flavour reminiscent of the smoking room of a gentlemen's club.

★ DOMAINE CAZES FRÈRES
Commune: Rivesaltes.
Owners: André and Bernard Cazes.
Surface Area under Vine: 150 ha.
Wines: Côtes du Roussillon (red, white and rosé), Côtes du Roussillon-Villages, Rivesaltes, Muscat de Rivesaltes and Vin de Pays des Côtes Catalanes (Chardonnay, Muscat Sec and red wines).
André and Bernard Cazes are based in a little back street in Rivesaltes and produce a full range of the local wines, almost all of it to a very high standard. The Muscat Sec is one of the best of its kind, as is the gently woody,

Vermentino-based white Côtes du Roussillon. The *vins de pays* include Le Canon du Maréchal, a clever blend of Cabernet Sauvignon, Merlot, Syrah and Grenache, plus an oaky Cabernet Sauvignon and Merlot Le Crédo. The Côtes du Roussillon-Villages come as both oaked and non-oaked and are clean and full of character.

There are some delicious *vins doux naturels* too, particularly the Rivesaltes Cuvée Aimé Cazes 1975, a wine without a hint of age when last sampled. I felt it would last a further thirty years.

★ DOMAINE DES CHÊNES
Commune: Vingrau.
Owner: Razungles et Fils.
Surface Area under Vine: 30 ha.
Wines: Côtes du Roussillon-Villages, Rivesaltes, Muscat de Rivesaltes and Vin de Pays des Vals d'Agly.
The village of Vingrau lies on the edge of a gentle amphitheatre of vines sheltered by limestone hills, a part of the northern Roussillon of truly outstanding beauty. The Razungles domaine is the leading name in the area, and can be singled out for two delicious whites, Les Sorbiers, from 50 per cent each Grenache Blanc and Macabéo, vinified in *cuve* but given four months in wood, and Les Magdaléniens, 50 per cent each Grenache Blanc and Roussanne, vinified in wood and kept on its fine lees until bottling.

There are two Roussillon-Villages *cuvées*: Les Grand-Mères, containing 60 per cent old-vine, *macération carbonique* Carignan, a wine for early drinking, and Les Alzines (meaning 'green oak' in Catalan), made from 30 per cent each Carignan, Grenache and Syrah, plus 10 per cent Mourvèdre. This wine needs keeping for three or four years. Both wines are very good, as are the Rivesaltes Tuilé and the Muscat de Rivesaltes.

DOMAINE DU MAS CRÉMAT
Commune: Espira de L'Agly.
Owners: Jean-Marc Jeannin-Mongeard.
Surface Area under Vine: 37 ha.
Wines: Côtes du Roussillon (red), Muscat de Rivesaltes and Vin de Pays des Côtes Catalanes.

Jean-Marc Jeannin and his wife (daughter of Jean Mongeard-Mugneret, a grower in the village of Vosne-Romanée in the Côte de Nuits) bought Mas Crémat in 1990 and are slowly converting the black schistous *vignoble* to table wine and tastefully restoring the old *mas* or farmhouse.

I have admired much of what has been achieved here. There is a fine and concentrated, gently oaky, pure Grenache Blanc as well as a dry Muscat (both *vins de pays*), and their intention, subject to permission from the authorities, is to produce two top red-wine *cuvées*, one from the black schist (called Cuvée Terres Noires) and one from the limestone soils (Cuvée Terres Blanches). According to Jean-Marc, the former gives finer tannins. The current top red *cuvée* is made from 40 per cent Syrah, 40 per cent Grenache and 20 per cent Mourvèdre.

GAEC DES FLO
DOMAINE FERRER-RIBIÈRE
Commune: Terrats.
Owners: Denis Ferrer and Bruno Ribière.
Surface Area under Vine: 30 ha – Côtes du Roussillon (red and white) including Cuvée Jacques V and Cuvée Caroline, Muscat de Rivesaltes and Vin de Pays Catalan.
Situated on the slopes of the hills that lie beneath Mont Canigou, and formed by two *vignerons* who decided to work together, the Domaine Ferrer-Ribière grows Syrah, Mourvèdre, Grenache and Carignan. The Côtes du Roussillon Cuvée Jacques V, round and voluptuous, is made for drinking three to six years after the vintage. The Cuvée Caroline has no Carignan, and is more serious, firmer and classier. The Muscat de Rivesaltes is elegant. They are all well-made.

DOMAINE FONTANEL
Commune: Tautavel.
Owners: Pierre and Marie-France Fontaneil.
Surface Area under Vine: 35 ha – Côtes du Roussillon-Villages, Rivesaltes, Muscat de Rivesaltes and Vin de Pays des Côtes Catalanes.
Up in the hills, the Fontanel estate produces good wines including a lightly oaked pure Grenache Blanc from

sixty-five-year-old vines and a Côtes du Roussillon-Villages-Tautavel from 60 per cent Syrah, 20 per cent Grenache and 20 per cent Carignan. There is one-fifth new wood, and fining and filtration are not used unless clearly necessary.

★ DOMAINE FORÇA RÉAL
Commune: Millas.
Owners: Jean-Paul Henriquès.
Surface Area under Vine: 38 ha – Côtes du Roussillon (red, white and rosé), Côtes du Roussillon-Villages, Rivesaltes and Muscat de Rivesaltes.
Jean-Paul Henriquès, now working with his son Cyril, has a dual role as a *négociant* as well as a grower. He bought Força Réal in 1989, when the vineyards consisted of only 10 hectares of Muscat vines, and in these early days, before he built his own winery in 1992, the wine was made by a neighbour.

Today's Força Réal, magnificently perched on a schistous hill surrounded by vines, olive groves and scrub overlooking the Têt Valley, is still a bit of a building site. Four table wines are produced as well as the *vins doux naturels*: Mas de La Garrigue is a 'traditional' Côtes du Roussillon-Villages made from 50 per cent Grenache, 20 per cent Carignan, Syrah and Mourvèdre, without any wood; the Domaine Força Réal is a well-structured Syrah and Mourvèdre-based wine; Les Hauts de Força Réal is an oak-aged wine from 80 per cent Syrah. Both the latter two wines keep well. The white tropical-flavoured Les Hauts is made from 80 per cent Malvoisie and the vines are still relatively young.

★ DOMAINE GARDIÉS
Commune: Vingrau.
Owner: Jean Gardiés.
Surface Area under Vine: 45 ha.
Wines: Côtes du Roussillon-Villages and Muscat de Rivesaltes.
Jean Gardiés, who set up in 1990, and started bottling in 1993, has vines in two distinct soils, the marl and limestone of Vingrau (AC Côtes du Roussillon-Villages-Tautavel), and black schist in land near Espira d'Agly.

Les Millères (50 per cent Syrah and 25 per cent each Mourvèdre and Grenache) comes from the latter. It is matured in tank but is nevertheless a wine of real depth and style: one that will keep. The *encépagement* in the Tautavel is the same, but the wine has a longer maceration and is reared in wood, one-third of which is new. This is even more impressive. Cuvée J G is produced from 60 per cent Syrah and is even better. This is a star.

★★ DOMAINE GAUBY

Commune: Calce.
Owners: Gérard and Ghislaine Gauby.
Surface Area under Vine: 45 ha.
Wines: Côtes du Roussillon, Côtes du Roussillon Villages, Rivesaltes and Vin de Pays Catalan.

I came across the charming Gaubys and their excellent wines almost by chance. I had written to the local syndicat, asking them to set up a blind tasting of Roussillon-Villages wines, and, by chance or by design, the Gauby domaine, in the hills above Baixas, was chosen as the venue. Lo and behold the Gauby wines got my best marks and we hit it off from the first moment. Five years on in late1998 their wines were better than ever.

There are various whites, including a Muscat Sec and Coume Gineste (meaning 'the valley of the broom'), a high class, pure Grenache Blanc, which will keep well. The reds include a classy Vieilles Vignes, only lightly oaky, and the more woody, 95 per cent Syrah called Muntada. Their Syrah vines are young – the first vintage was 1995 – but this is a splendid, ripe, cool, sophisticated example. It just shows how good the wines can be from the limestone, schistous granitic *garrigues* of the Roussillon-Villages area.

In addition there is the Rivesaltes. This is produced in the early-bottled version the locals call 'vintage'. It is not a bit too sweet: like a red-fruit jelly with a touch of dark chocolate. It needs drinking within three years. Domaine Gauby is one of the region's superstars.

DOMAINE DE JAU

Commune: Cases-de-Pène.
Owners: Dauré family.
Surface Area under Vine: 134 ha.

Wines: Côtes du Roussillon, Côtes du Roussillon-Villages, Muscat de Rivesaltes (Château de Jau), Collioure, Banyuls (Les Clos des Paulilles), Rivesaltes (Mas Christine) and Vin de Pays.

This is a newish domaine set up by the Dauré family, Bernard, Sabine and daughter Estelle who have expanded from the Agly Valley into Banyuls and its surroundings. The Roussillon vineyard is still young, however, and at first the Daurés were content to sell the wine without the Villages designation.

The style throughout the range can be described as commercial. The basic Jau red blend is 40 per cent Syrah, 30 per cent Mourvèdre, 20 per cent Grenache and 10 per cent Carignan, but the wine is of medium body only and develops quickly. The Collioure comes from 90 per cent Mourvèdre but is of similar weight. The Banyuls wines are made in the oxidised style. The range as a whole is competent but far from exciting.

DOMAINE LAPORTE

Commune: Château Roussillon.
Owner: Raymond Laporte.
Surface Area under Vine: 41 ha.
Wines: Côtes du Roussillon, Rivesaltes, Muscat de Rivesaltes and Vin de Pays Catalan.

On gently undulating essentially alluvial clay and sandy soil mixed with *galets*, between Perpignan and the sea, the Domaine Laporte is an exemplary modern set up. There *terroir* doesn't exist, says Raymond Laporte. But with controlled vinification techniques he makes, *inter alia*, a very fine Muscat Sec, from pure Muscat of Alexandria, a balanced, opulent Côtes du Roussillon, a finely-balanced Muscat de Rivesaltes and a Rivesaltes Ambré Vieux, fermented and matured in wood and very intense and vigorous.

DOMAINE PIQUEMAL

Commune: Espira de L'Agly.
Owners: Franck and Pierre Piquemal.
Surface Area under Vine: 52 ha.
Wines: Côtes du Roussillon (red), Côtes du Roussillon-Villages, Rivesaltes, Muscat de Rivesaltes and Vin de Pays des Côtes Catalanes.

You will find the Piquemal brothers and their neat, modern set-up in a cul-de-sac in the back streets of Espira de L'Agly where the schistous *garrigues* of the Roussillon-Villages begin to merge into the flatter lands of the plain. The wines are good here, but not inspired. The Cuvée 'Élevé en Fût de Chêne' is in principle from the same wine as the non-oaky bottling.

There are some very good *vins doux naturels* though. The Muscat de Rivesaltes Coup de Foudre, aged in newish wood for two years, has a vanillary richness which echoes Sauternes.

DOMAINE PÈRE PUIG
Commune: Claira.
Owner: José Puig.
Surface Area under Vine: 52 ha.
Wines: Côtes du Roussillon, Rivesaltes and Vin de Pays des Côtes Catalanes.

José Puig produces a modern range of mainly *vins de pays* from the alluvial soils of the plain north-east of Perpignan. The whites include a Viognier which is rather more flavoursome and profound than most and the interestingly complex Cuvée Marie-Laure, from Malvoisie, Chardonnay and very old Grenache Blanc. There are Merlot and Cabernet for the reds while the Côtes du Roussillon, Cuvée Sainte Anne has 80 per cent Syrah. Skin contact, *bâtonnage*, keeping the wine on its lees, early bottling and a sensible use of new wood are the order of the day here: fresh, competent, carefully-made wines.

CLOS SAINT-GEORGES
Commune: Trouillas.
Owners: Dominique and Claude Ortal.
Surface Area under Vine: 57 ha.
Wines: Côtes du Roussillon (red, white and rosé) and Vin de Pays d'Oc.

The soil structure here consists of very large stones (*galets*) on a clay-siliceous bed, and it reminds the Ortals of Châteauneuf-du-Pape, where they used to work, though they were not vineyard proprietors at the time. While the *vin de pays* Cuvée Eva, from Cabernet Sauvignon, is matured in small wood, the Côtes du Roussillon is not. It is produced from 70 per cent Grenache and 30 per cent Syrah and is not sold until well-matured. Similar examples from other sources tend to be coarse and rustic, but the Ortals' 1989, in 1998, was fresh, cedary and well-balanced.

DOMAINE SALVAT-TAÏCHAC
Commune: Villeneuve La Rivière.
Owner: Jean-Philippe Salvat.
Surface Area under Vine: 70 ha.
Wines: Côtes du Roussillon, Rivesaltes, Muscat de Rivesaltes and Vin de Pays des Pyrénées-Orientales.

Jean-Philippe Salvat's domaine is split between land at Villeneuve, overlooking the river Têt, inland from Perpignan, and vineyards at Saint-Paul de Tenouillet in the upper Agly Valley. Here you will find some cleanly-made, competent reds and whites for early drinking; a good Côtes du Roussillon red matured using 25 per cent new wood (Syrah 45 per cent, Grenache 35 per cent, Mourvèdre 20 per cent) and some neat *vins doux naturels*. The Muscat de Rivesaltes can be particularly recommended.

DOMAINE SARDA-MALET
MAS SAINT-MICHEL
Commune: Perpignan.
Owner: Suzy Malet.
Surface Area under Vine: 38 ha.
Wines: Côtes du Roussillon and Rivesaltes.

Just south of Perpignan, on the right bank of the river Têt the clay-calcareous and clay-siliceous soils of Domaine Sarda-Malet produce surprisingly good red and white Roussillon wines. Terroir Mailloles, the *tête de cuvée*, is only produced in the best vintages. The white is made from a mixture of Maccabéo, Malvoisie, Roussanne, Marsanne and Viognier vinified in wood. The red is 50:50 Syrah and Mourvèdre with a token amount of Grenache to satisfy the *appellation* regulations. A curiosity is L'Abandon, a late-harvest Malvoisie picked by *tris*.

LES VIGNERONS CATALANS
Commune: Perpignan.
Members: 2000.

Surface Area under Vine: 10,600 ha.

Wines: A wide range of branded and single-domaine wines covering all the *appellations* in the region.

Les Vignerons Catalans was set up in the early 1960s as an association of wine producers. It claims to have 'invented' carbonic maceration in 1964. The firm deals with a large number of individual domaines and local co-operatives and the general standard is competent, if rarely of the top-most quality. The wines are made for consumption in the short to medium term. Among the individual domaines marketed by Les Vignerons Catalans I would single out Château Cap de Fouste, Château de Blanes and Château de Castelnou.

LES VIGNERONS DU RIVESALTAIS

Commune: Rivesaltes.

Members: 800.

Surface Area under Vine: 3500 ha.

Wines: Côtes du Roussillon, Côtes du Roussillon-Villages, Rivesaltes, Muscat de Rivesaltes and Vins de Pays des Côtes Catalanes.

Though responsible for 60 per cent of the production of Rivesaltes and the Côtes du Roussillon *appellations*, and covering 75 per cent of the local AC surface area, this is a quality establishment, the better *cuvées* being bottled under the Arnaud de Villeneuve name. The reds are made for the short to medium term, but there are some fine old Rivesaltes. The 20-year-old Hors d'Age, from one-third each Grenache Noir, Grenache Blanc and Muscat, is particularly noteworthy.

Other Producers of note

BERNARD VAQUIER (TRESSERRE), DOMAINE DE ROMBEAU/PIERRE HENRI DE LA FABRÈQUE (RIVESALTES) AND CHÂTEAU DU CANTERAINE/MAURICE COMTÉ – SPECIALISTS IN OLD VINTAGES (TROUILLAS); PLUS VARIOUS CO-OPERATIVES, NOTABLY LESQUERDE (ESPECIALLY CUVÉE GEORGES POUS), LATOUR DE FRANCE (WHICH HAS A CONTRACT WITH LANGUEDOC NÉGOCIANT JEAN-JEAN), ESPIRA D'AGLY (LES CHAIS SAINTE-ESTELLE), CALCE, LES VIGNERONS DE BAIXAS, LES VIGNERONS DE PEZILLA AND LES VIGNERONS DE CORNEILLA-LA-RIVIÈRE.

MAURY

Surface Area (1998): 1715 ha.

Production (1998): 48,066 hl.

Colour: Tuilé.

Grape Varieties: Grenache Noir, Carignan, Macabeu plus other local grapes.

Maximum Yield: 30 hl/ha.

Minimum Alcohol Level: 15°.

Beyond Estagel as you journey into the hills, the Agly Valley, between the last limestone of the Corbières and the first schistous slopes of the Pyrenees, becomes both lusher and wider. It is cooler here. One can feel the influence of the Atlantic as well as the Mediterranean. The valley floor is black schist and marl debris and this is the base for one of France's last undiscovered delights, a red *vin doux naturel*.

Sweet red wine, until one thinks of Port, sounds like an oxymoron, disgusting to boot. Maury, with its silky-smooth rich flavours of black cherries, mocha and chocolate – usually a little oxidised, and deliberately so – is a delight. This is one of the rare wines which can accompany chocolate desserts. It keeps well too, for up to thirty years or more depending on the *cuvée*. Once bottled and put on the market, however, like tawny Port, the shelf-life is relatively short: not more than eighteen months. Once opened, drink the wine within the week.

The blend for the wine must include at least 75 per cent of Grenache Noir but in practice most wines are made from 90 to 100 per cent. The grapes are picked at a minimum of 14.5° alcohol. Five to ten per cent of grape alcohol is added to the fermenting must.

This allows the winemaker to prolong the maceration for up to thirty days, extracting colour, tannin and aroma by continuing to *piger* (plunge down the pulp into the wine) and pump over. The resulting alcohol is about 16.5°. The wine is then left in concrete vats for the rest of the winter.

The next stage of the process is to bottle the 'vintage' *cuvée*. This is a fresh, raspberry-flavoured wine, a little rough and ready perhaps, for drinking cool and young.

At some establishments, notably Domaine Mas Amiel (see below), as in Banyuls, part of the crop is decanted into large glass *bonbonnes* (demijohns) which are left out in the hot sun all summer to oxidise. The colour falls out (the deposit is left in the *bonbonne* in order to give extra colour to next year's crop) and the wine is then usually blended back with wine which has spent its life in *foudres* (large casks). It can otherwise be bottled separately as Maury Rancio. Most Maury is aged in bulk. Some is aged in small new or newish wood.

With the exception of the 'vintage', most Maury spends its adolescence and maturity in vat and is sold under such names as Réserve or Cuvée Spéciale, with a bottling date but not a vintage date, vintages being blended together to create a continuity of character and flavour. Like old tawny Port, the wines become more refined and more rarified as they age. Old Maury can be quite delicious. It exhibits superior tannins to the wines of Banyuls and often has a deeper colour. The base wine itself, coming from where it does, is more classy. The local co-operative, Les Vignerons de Maury, dominates production.

Leading Maury Producers

★ DOMAINE MAS AMIEL
Owner: Vignerons de Val d'Orbieu and associates.
Surface Area under Vine: 155 ha.
Wines: Maury and Vin de Pays des Pyrénées-Orientales.

After many years of being up for sale, Mas Amiel was finally sold by Charles Dupuy in 2000 to a consortium which includes the giant Vignerons de Val d'Orbieu based in Narbonne. This is the best place to sample all the possible variations of Maury on the market. A very high standard it is too. As well as Vintage, the styles include the 6-year-old Réserve, the 10-year-old Cuvée Spéciale and the 15-year-old Hors d'Age. I much admire the cool, black cherry and black chocolate style of Mas Amiel's Maury. The base wine is very sophisticated.

DOMAINE MAURYDORÉ
Owner: Madame Paule de Volontat.

Surface Area under Vine: 25 ha.
Wines: Maury.

Madame Paule de Volontat, a vigorous old lady of great charm and generosity, inherited this estate through her paternal grandparents. Her main sales are of vintage Maury, and, at a price, she can still offer vintages back to 1925. The oldest I have sampled is the 1939, and it was very lovely: mellow, sweet and fragrant, without a trace of undue spirit.

Other Producers of note
DOMAINE DE LA PLEÏADE/JACQUES DELCOUR AND THE LOCAL CO-OPERATIVE, LES VIGNERONS DE MAURY.

BANYULS AND BANYULS GRAND CRU

Surface Area (1998): 1346 ha.
Production (1998): 24,043 hl, of which about one-tenth is Banyuls Grand Cru.
Colour: Red or white.
Grape Varieties: Grenache Noir, Grenache Blanc, Grenache Gris, Maccabéo, Tourbat, Muscat of Alexandria and Muscat Blanc à Petits Grains, plus Carignan, Syrah and Cinsault.
Maximum Yield: 30 hl/ha.
Minimum Alcohol Level: 15°.

These arid, schistous hills – the end of the Pyrenees mountains as they fall into the Mediterranean sea – are home to two *appellations*: Banyuls and Collioure. Production of the latter is increasing at the expense of the former, but nevertheless Banyuls is one of France's great red *vins doux naturels*, with more depth, concentration and interest than most Rivesaltes and a warmer, richer, more cooked character than Maury.

Grenache Noir must make up 50 per cent of the blend and 75 per cent for Banyuls Grand Cru. A wide range of styles is made: Banyuls can be red or white, turning tawny or amber as it ages, fairly dry or quite sweet, can be deliberately oxidised (*rancio*) or fresh and sold with a vintage date or not. A Banyuls Grand Cru must be aged in wood for at least thirty months. There are no limits on how long the other Banyuls wines may be kept. As in Maury and Rivesaltes a relatively recent departure is to offer a young, early-bottled vintage version. The Coume of Jean-Michel Parcé's Domaine du Mas Blanc (see right) is a good example.

I find these early bottled styles do not age well. For an old Banyuls one should seek a version matured in *foudre*. Those of the other branch of the Parcé family, Domaine de La Rectorie (see page 466), the Coopérative L'Etoile (see page 466), who offer a total of eleven different Banyuls, and the Vin de Méditation of the Domaine La Tour Vieille (see page 466), are recommended examples. The great vintages of Banyuls include 1997, 1995, 1993, 1991, 1988, 1986 and 1982.

COLLIOURE

Surface Area (1998): As Banyuls, covering 325 ha.
Production (1998): 11,925 hl.
Colour: Red and rosé.
Grape Varieties: (Red) Grenache Noir, Syrah and Mourvèdre, plus Carignan Noir, Cinsault and Syrah; (rosé) the same varieties as for red plus Grenache Gris.
Maximum Yield: 40 hl/ha.
Minimum Alcohol Level: (Red) 12°; (rosé) 11.5°.

Just north of the border with Spain, Collioure is named after the pretty old fishing village and artists' colony on the Côte Vermeille, guarded by Vauban castles. It was once one of the most obscure of all France's *appellations*, but is today thriving and expanding. The terraces *en friche*, left untended since phylloxera, have been cleaned and replanted, and many Banyuls producers have switched from making *vins doux naturels* to table wine, to their commercial advantage.

While there is a little rosé, most Collioure is red wine, and this varies from light, early-drinking blends with soft tannins which are produced in tank, to more serious examples matured in wood, some of which can be aged in new *barriques*. Grenache Noir, Syrah and Mourvèdre must make up 60 per cent of the blend.

The wine has its own distinctive personality, fullish, sturdy and spicy, with those with a high Mourvèdre percentage in the *encépagement*, such as the Domaine du Mas Blanc's splendid Clos du Moulin (see below), providing an interesting contrast with a top Bandol. This Parcé (Jean-Michel) is perhaps the best source, with three distinct high quality Collioure wines. The cousins at the Domaine de La Rectorie (see page 466), and Christine Campadieu and Vincent Cantié at the Domaine La Tour Vieille (see page 466), can also be recommended.

Leading Collioure and Banyuls Producers

★ DOMAINE DU MAS BLANC
Commune: Banyuls.
Owner: Jean-Michel Parcé.
Surface Area under Vine: 8 ha.
Wines: Collioure and Banyuls.

The late Dr André Parcé was the driving force behind the Banyuls and Collioure *appellations* for more than a generation. The domaine is now run by his son, Jean-Michel who is in his forties, and who had already been in charge of winemaking for several years before his father's death in 1998.

There are three *cuvées* of Collioure: my favourite, Cosprons Levants (from 60 per cent Syrah, 30 per cent Mourvèdre and 10 per cent Counoise), Clos du Moulin (from 80 per cent Syrah and 20 per cent Counoise from vines planted on sand and gravel debris over schist, a rather special combination) and Les Junquets (from 90 per cent Syrah and 5 per cent each Marsanne and Roussanne, from vines planted on schistous soil with veins of clay at Collioure's higher altitudes). The grapes are picked at a low yield of 30 hl/ha and the wines aged in one-year-old barrels from Château Belair in Bordeaux's Saint-Emilion. All these are proper *vins de garde*.

Parcé's Banyuls include La Coume, an early-bottled version, the slightly oxidised Mise Tardive, the sumptuous Vieilles Vignes, Cuvée de Saint-Martin (the aroma of the 1981 is like walking into an orangery) and the old *oloroso*, toffee-flavoured Hors d'Age Vieilli en Solera. Prices are high, but worth it.

Cave Co-Opérative L'Etoile

Commune: Banyuls.
Members: 130.
Surface Area under Vine: 152 ha.
Wines: Collioure, Banyuls and Vin de Pays.

The Etoile co-operative, with Marcel Centène in charge, concentrates on making Banyuls, of which they offer eleven different versions. Even their better Collioure 'Vieilli en Montagne' is unexceptional.

The Banyuls are another matter. This is a prime source. My favourites are the Cuvée 75ème Anniversaire, the Grande Réserve, 1982 and the Select Vieux, 1979. It is the Macaré Tuilé, currently the 1988, just a touch *rancio*, which wins all the prizes. Part of the production is aged in large glass *bonbonnes* laid out on terraces exposed to the hot sun.

Domaines et Châteaux du Roussillon, Cellier des Templiers, Groupement Interproducteurs Collioure et Banyuls

Commune: Banyuls.
Members: 900.
Surface Area under Vine: 2400 ha.
Wines: Collioure and Banyuls.

The names above represent different faces of the same organisation, an association of properties which claims to represent two-thirds of Banyuls production and 80 per cent of that of Collioure.

Domaine de Baillauny (a blend of 75 per cent Grenache and 25 per cent Mourvèdre) and Castell des Hospices (from Grenache and Carignan) are two of the *cuvées* produced. Cuvées Régis Boucabeille, Christian Reynal and Castell des Hospices are names for the Banyuls. I have yet to see anything which really excites me from this source.

★ Domaine de La Rectorie

Commune: Banyuls.
Owner: Parcé Frères
Surface Area under Vine: 26 ha.
Wines: Collioure, Banyuls and Vin de Pays de La Côte Vermeille.

In his late forties, Marc Parcé boasts a splendid moustache and sports a *béret* set with angular flair. He and his brother Thierry, cousins of the Parcés at Domaine du Mas Blanc, set up on their own in 1984, the land being inherited from their grandparents who had been tied in to the local co-operative until 1976.

Originally the domaine produced only Banyuls, made almost entirely from Grenache. They favour their Banyuls fresher, not oxidised, and make two good *cuvées*: Parcé Frères and Léon Parcé, bottled six months and twelve months after the vintage respectively.

Today two-thirds of their production is table wine. There is a white *vin de pays* 'L'Argille' produced from Grenache Gris, partly fermented in wood, and a stylish example. Three different *cuvées* of Collioure cover the range from Col de Bast, a wine for early drinking, from 30-40 per cent Carignan through Le Seris, to the fine, oaky La Coume Pascole which is made using 30-40 per cent Syrah.

★ Domaine La Tour Vieille

Commune: Collioure.
Owners: Vincent Cantié and Christine Campadieu.
Surface Area under Vine: 12 ha.
Wines: Collioure, Banyuls and Vin de Pays de La Côte Vermeille.

Domaine La Tour Vieille is one of the best sources for Collioure. Its *têtes de cuvée* Puig Orio (from a blend of 65 per cent Grenache and 35 per cent Syrah) and Puig Ambeille (from Grenache, Mourvèdre and Carignan) — Puig, pronounced 'push', meaning 'hill' in Catalan — having plenty of backbone, depth and class. The Banyuls Cuvée Francis Contié contains wine which has spent a year in large glass *bonbonnes* and is naturally slightly oxidised, but a very good example of this style. The Banyuls Vin de Méditation, a wine which has spent forty years in barrel, is is rare, intense, individual and simply delicious.

Other Producers of note

Domaine Piétri-Géraud (Collioure), Domaine de Traginer/Jean-François Deu (Collioure) and Vial Magnères (Banyuls).

VINS DE PAYS

REGIONAL VIN DE PAYS
Vin de Pays d'Oc.

DEPARTMENTAL VIN DE PAYS
Vin de Pays des Pyrénées-Orientales.

ZONAL VINS DE PAYS
Vin de Pays Catalan
This is the centre and southern part of the department.

Vin de Pays de La Côte Vermeille
This covers the Collioure and Banyuls *appellations* in the far south of the department.

Vin de Pays des Coteaux de Fenouillèdes
The hills of the north-west of the department.

Vin de Pays des Côtes Catalanes
The northern part of the department, roughly the eastern sector of the Côtes du Roussillon-Villages area.

Vin de Pays des Vals d'Agly
The western sector of the Côtes du Roussillon-Villages area, between the two zonal *vins de pays* above.

The South-West

THE SOUTH-WEST WINE REGIONS OF FRANCE can be defined as everything south of Cognac and the Massif Central, with the exception of Bordeaux itself, and west of an imaginary watershed somewhere between Toulouse and Carcassonne where the climatic influence becomes Atlantic rather than Mediterranean.

As in the South of France there has been a revolution in quality in the last couple of decades. Old vineyard areas such as Cahors, which following phylloxera, the slump and the 1956 frost had almost entirely died out, are now vigorous and expanding. New ones such as Irouléguy and Marcillac, whose wines hitherto were more read about in books than available in the shops, have found an enthusiastic market. Others such as Jurançon and Madiran have found a new modern identity. And throughout the region a new generation of scientifically trained, perfectionist winemakers is working wonders. South-west wines are still not very widely seen in the world's wine lists. Twenty-five years ago one could have said that this neglect was no more than what the wines deserved. Today it is a different story.

The wines of the South-West can be divided into three regions. First is the Far South-West, beginning on the Spanish border at Irouléguy, and moving northwards through Jurançon and Madiran to the edge of the Landes on the one side and the Armagnac country on the other. Red wines here come chiefly from the Tannat grape; whites from the Gros and Petit Manseng and the more rustic Petit Courbu and Arrufiac. Next comes the region of the Bordeaux Satellites: Bergerac, Monbazillac, Duras, the Marmandais and Buzet. The grape varieties here are Bordelais; so too, largely, are the wines. They are at their most interesting when the wines are not precisely 'lesser Bordeaux' in character, as in the sweet wines of Monbazillac and Saussignac, the dry white wines of the better Bergerac producers and Côtes du Marmandais. Third is the Haut Pays region covering Cahors, Fronton, Gaillac and other wines. The wines here are quite distinct from the other two areas, as they are from each other. Fronton is the home of the Négrette grape. In Cahors the Malbec or Cot, known here as the Auxerrois, comes into

its own. Gaillac, a wine region as yet without a definite identity, grows a number of varieties, red and white, Midi and Atlantic, and the growers are free to blend them as they wish.

The South-West is the most varied wine region in France, and caters for all tastes. Few of the wines are expensive and most are no more expensive than a Mâcon Blanc-Villages or a *cru* Beaujolais. And quality has increased by leaps and bounds in the past twenty years. There are three compelling reasons why the South-West deserves further interest. Moreover, the countryside is beautiful, the weather normally benign and the local food hearty and – if not entirely healthy, for this is the land of goose fat, *foie gras*, cassoulet, garlic and truffles – certainly delicious.

APPELLATIONS OF THE SOUTH-WEST

THE FAR SOUTH-WEST	THE BORDEAUX SATELLITES	THE HAUT PAYS
IROULÉGUY	BERGERAC, CÔTES DE BERGERAC	CÔTES DU FRONTONNAIS
BÉARN AND BÉARN-BELLOCQ	AND MONBAZILLAC	LAVILLEDIEU (VDQS)
JURANÇON	SAUSSIGNAC	CAHORS
MADIRAN AND PACHERENC DU	PÉCHARMANT	COTEAUX DE QUERCY (VDQS)
VIC-BILH	ROSETTE	GAILLAC
TURSAN (VDQS)	MONTRAVEL, HAUT-MONTRAVEL	MARCILLAC
CÔTES DE SAINT-MONT	AND CÔTES DE MONTRAVEL	ENTRAYGUES ET LE FEL
	CÔTES DE DURAS	(VDQS)
	CÔTES DU MARMANDAIS	ESTAING (VDQS)
	BUZET	CÔTES DE MILLAU (VDQS)
	CÔTES DU BRULHOIS (VDQS)	

SURFACE AREA AND PRODUCTION (1998 HARVEST)

APPELLATIONS	SURFACE AREA (HA)	PRODUCTION (HL)	
		RED & ROSÉ	WHITE
THE FAR SOUTH-WEST			
IROULÉGUY	200	6143	624
JURANÇON	800	–	41,712
BÉARN	202	5112	199
BÉARN-BELLOCQ	–	2451	179
MADIRAN	1512	69,888	–
PACHERENC DE VIC-BILH } (INCLUDED ABOVE – APPROX. 200)		–	10,021
TURSAN (VDQS)	240	11,024	2385
CÔTES DE SAINT-MONT (VDQS)	824	44,768	8284
THE BORDEAUX SATELLITES			
BERGERAC	7506	335,828	103,341
CÔTES DE BERGERAC (RED)	367	23,637	–
CÔTES DE BERGERAC (MOELLEUX)	1741	–	81,284
MONBAZILLAC	1769	–	43,830
SAUSSIGNAC	62	–	1518
PÉCHARMANT	391	17,247	–
ROSETTE	18	–	523
MONTRAVEL	360	–	17,121
HAUT-MONTRAVEL	60	–	3523
CÔTES DE MONTRAVEL	54	–	1091
CÔTES DE DURAS	1585	66,748	50,729
CÔTES DE MARMANDAIS	1398	85,994	3819
BUZET	1836	111,797	4861
CÔTES DU BRULHOIS (VDQS)	211	10,825	–
THE HAUT PAYS			
CÔTES DU FRONTONNAIS	2054	116,661	–
VIN DE LAVILLEDIEU (VDQS)	170	2278	–
CAHORS	4236	248,336	–
GAILLAC	2260	118,207	45,131
MARCILLAC	140	5224	–
VIN D'ENTRAYGUES ET DU FEL (VDQS)	20	648	336
VIN D'ESTAING (VDQS)	15	470	57
CÔTES DE MILLAU (VDQS)	30	1489	89
TOTAL APPELLATION CONTRÔLÉE	28,551	1,225,819	399,485
TOTAL VDQS	1510	71,502	11,151
GRAND TOTAL	39,961	1,297,321	410,636
		1,707,957	

THE FAR SOUTH-WEST

IROULÉGUY

Surface Area (1998): 200 ha.

Production (1998): (Red and rosé) 6143 hl; (white) 624 hl.

Colours: Red, rosé and white.

Grape Varieties: (Red and rosé) Tannat, Cabernet Franc and Cabernet Sauvignon; (white) Gros Manseng, Petit Courbu and Petit Manseng.

Maximum Yield: (Red and rosé) 50 hl/ha; (white) 55 hl/ha.

Minimum Alcohol Level: (Red) 10°; (white and rosé) 10.5°.

I first visited Irouléguy in 1982. At the time the co-operative was the only source of wine, and this wine was cheap, attenuated and rustic. I was not encouraged to revisit. I then heard that Ets. Brana, a local *négociant* and distiller, was taking an interest in the *appellation*. The local two-star restaurant in Saint-Jean-Pied-de-Port announced in successive Michelin guides that it featured Irouléguy wines. Something was astir.

Irouléguy is a staging post below an important – *the* most important perhaps – pass in the Pyrenees. This was the route the pilgrims, each with their identifying scallop shell, climbed through the mountains on their way to Santiago de Compostella. A few miles away, across the border, is the impressive abbey of Roncevaux. On the French side, on protected south-facing slopes over four communes between Saint-Jean-Pied-de-Port and Saint-Etienne-de-Baïgorry, lie the vines of Irouléguy. Most of them lie in the commune of Ispoure.

As you approach Irouléguy, either from Bayonne on the coast, or from the direction of Bellocq, due north, the countryside becomes more and more attractive. All the road signs are in Basque as well as French. The mountainslopes are quite steep and there are few vines. The landscape is mostly pastureland – particularly for sheep (the local cheeses are delicious) – and the houses, white with tiles, beams and doors picked out in a blood-rich terracotta, give the impression of Swiss chalets.

The soil is a clay-schist mix, very stony and rich in iron. It is also well-drained, which is handy, as precipitation is high. One of the *vignerons'* problems is to keep the growth of weeds, herbs and grass at bay. The vines are trained high, to avoid the risk of frost, and the rows are widely spaced, to reduce contamination of the fruit by cryptogamic diseases.

Irouléguy can be dry white or rosé. In fact it is almost entirely red, based on the Tannat, with Cabernet Franc and/or Cabernet Sauvignon as the subsidiary grape variety. The top *cuvées* are often pure Tannat. As well as the co-operative, which produces a number of *tête de cuvée* domaine wines (Domaine Mignaberry is the best), there are some half a dozen independent growers.

Leading Irouléguy Producers

DOMAINE ARRETXEA
Owners: Thérèse & Michel Riouspeyrous.

Surface Area under Vine: 6 ha.

Wines: Irouléguy including (red) Cuvée Haitza.

The domaine is run on biodynamic lines in its white wine vineyards (85 per cent Gros Manseng, 10 per cent Petit Courbu and 5 per cent Petit Manseng), but simply *biologique* (with no chemical fertilisers) in red. It makes its own compost, and the vines are ploughed rather than herbicides being employed. The basic red (50 per cent Tannat) is plump and fruity, with no hard edges. The oak-aged Cuvée Haitza (meaning 'oak' in Basque) is 80 per cent Tannat and an impressive Irouléguy.

DOMAINE BRANA
Commune: Ispoure.

Owners: Jean & Martine Brana.

Surface Area under Vine: 40 ha.

Wines: Irouléguy including the Harri Gorri range and the superior Domaine range.

The Branas have been wine merchants since the 1980s, and distillers since 1974. In 1985 Jean and Martine Brana, brother and sister, started planting a vineyard on a very steep slope facing south over Saint-Jean-Pied-de-Port and looking towards Spain. The soil, based on *grès*, a purple-coloured sandstone, contains little clay and is very acid and very porous. The vineyard is worked biologically. Jean Brana takes a different view about *encépagement* from his peers, preferring more Cabernet Franc, which he avers was planted here before the Tannat. This results in supple, easy-to-drink wines. They are well-made but lack the personality of the Tannat-based examples you can find elsewhere. There is a good, clean, non-oaky white made from Gros Manseng and Petit Courbu.

DOMAINE ETXEGARAYA
Commune: Saint-Etienne-de-Baïgorry.
Owners: Marianne & Joseph Hillau.
Surface Area under Vine: 7 ha.
Wines: Irouléguy including (red) Cuvée Lehengoa.

The Hillaus used to send their grapes to the co-operative, but went independent in 1984. Their estate, hidden up against the side of the hills in a little corner of paradise, well off the road between Irouléguy and Saint-Etienne-de-Baïgorry, contains some 100-year-old vines. The soil is *grès* rather than limestone, so only red grape varieties are planted. The Hillaus do not use wood, even for the superior *cuvée* Lahengoa (which means 'yester year' in Basque) but their wines are rich, fat and succulent. In the best years give them five years' ageing.

DOMAINE ILARRIA
Owner: Peio Espil.
Surface Area under Vine: 8 ha.
Wines: Irouléguy including (red) Cuvée Bixintxo.

Peio Espil was the first member of the co-operative to go independent in 1982, and is the senior local grower. The vineyards are planted to 70 per cent Tannat, which makes for a good, juicy rosé and a nicely round, standard red, which has four or five months' barrel-ageing. The Cuvée Bixintxo ('x' being pronounced 'ch' in Basque, and the word being equivalent to Vincent, patron saint of the village) is from 100 per cent Tannat, aged for fourteen to sixteen months in *barrique*. This is currently Irouléguy's best wine.

Other Producers of note
DOMAINE ABOTIA/JEAN-CLAUDE ERRECART (ISPOURE) AND LES MAÎTRES VIGNERONS D'IROULÉGUY/DU PAYS BASQUE (SAINT-ETIENNE-DE-BAÏGORRY).

BÉARN AND BÉARN-BELLOCQ

Surface Area (1998): 202 ha.
Production (1998): (Red and rosé) 563 hl; (white) 378 hl.
Colour: Red, rosé and white.
Grape Varieties: (Red and rosé) Tannat, Cabernet Franc, Cabernet Sauvignon and Pinenc (Fer Servadou); (white) Gros Manseng, Petit Manseng, Rousselet de Béarn and Raffiat de Moncade (Arrufiac).
Maximum Yield: 50 hl/ha.
Minimum Alcohol Level: 10.5°.

In theory the wines of Béarn can come from any one of seventy-four communes in the Pyrénées-Atlantiques *département*, six in the Hautes-Pyrénées and three in the Gers. This includes such red wine as is produced in the Jurançon area, and a little white from the Madiran which is not declared as Pacherenc du Vic-Bilh. In practice most wine comes from south of the delimited Madiran *vignoble* in a swathe which stretches west to Orthez and Salies-de-Béarn. Bellocq and its co-operative which produces most of the *appellation*'s wines are located near Salies-de-Béarn, guarded by a ruined castle which was once the home of Jeanne d'Albret, mother of Henri IV of France.

All but a token quantity of Béarn is red or rosé, the latter having been very fashionable in the *bistros* of Paris in the late 1940s, while Madiran and Jurançon were little known. Even the red is a light *vin de l'année*, quaffable at best but not really serious. The parallel would be a young vine or minor Madiran. Nearly all Béarn is made by co-operatives, mainly the one at Bellocq, and also others such as that at Crouseilles in the Madiran *appellation*, and its counterpart at Gan in the Jurançon. A few local growers in both Madiran and Jurancon, such as Richard Ziemek-Chigé at the Cru Lamouroux in the Jurançon, produce Béarn. Béarn-Bellocq is a sub-area from vineyards around the town of the same name. I find little difference between the wines of both areas.

Leading Béarn Producers

DOMAINE GUILHÉMAS
DOMAINE LAPEYRE

Commune: Salies-de-Béarn.
Owner: Pascal Lapeyre.
Surface Area under Vine: 11 ha.
Wines: Béarn (red, rosé and white).

This is one of the very few independent producers of Béarn, and the only one not producing Jurançon or Madiran as well. There are two ranges of wines, the Lapeyre red and rosé containing more Tannat than the Guilhemas. The whites are from Gros Manseng and Rousselet de Béarn: 80:20 for the Guilhémas *cuvée*, the proportions reversed for the Lapeyre white.

JURANÇON

Surface Area (1998): 800 ha.
Production (1998): 41,712 hl.
Colour: White.
Grape Varieties: Gros Manseng and Petit Manseng.
Maximum Yield: (*moelleux*) 40 hl/ha;
(*sec*) 60 hl/ha.
Minimum Alcohol Level: (*moelleux*) 12°;
(*sec*) 11°.

Pau, capital of Béarn and the birthplace of Henri IV of France, lies in the *département* of Pyrénées-Atlantiques. It was to the ancient château, once a proper *donjon* or fortified castle but extensively reconstructed both in the Renaissance and again by Louis-Philippe and Louis Napoleon in the nineteenth century, that Jeanne d' Albret, wife of Antoine de Bourbon and daughter of Marguerite d'Angoulême, retired to have her important child. On 13 December 1553, after nineteen days of travelling in a carriage from the battlefields of Picardy to Pau in the foothills of the Pyrenees, she was safely delivered of the future king, whose lips, as was the custom, were duly rubbed with garlic and moistened with the local wine. Grandfather d'Albret then held up the child before the waiting crowds and cried: '*Voici le lion enfanté par la brebis de Navarre*' (Here is the lion which has been borne by the ewe of Navarre)'. This was in response to the crowd's insolent reaction on the birth of Jeanne: 'A miracle, a cow [the heraldic motif of the Béarn] has given birth to a ewe!' Thirty-six years later Henry proclaimed himself King of France and Navarre. Henri remained in Béarn throughout his childhood and retained fond memories of his *jeunesse paysanne* all his life.

From the Boulevard des Pyrénées in Pau you can enjoy one of the most impressive views in the whole of France. Looking south, the land falls steeply away into a gulley through which flows the Gave de Pau. Beyond, across the river, is the town of Jurançon itself, a suburb of Pau. Behind this is a gently rolling landscape, at first sight rather too densely wooded for an important vineyard area. In the distance, encased in sunlight if you are lucky, are the mountains: the Pic du Midi d'Osseau in the middle is the most spectacular but the panorama stretches from the Pic de Bigorre to the left to the Pic d'Anie on the right. These are the real Pyrenees (the Pic du Midi d'Osseau is almost 3000 metres high, and snow-capped even in the height of summer).

The vines on the Jurançon hills are planted at a mere 300 or 400 metres high, about the same altitude as the Hautes-Côtes vineyards in Burgundy, and yet these are truly mountain wines. The proximity of the Pyrenees produces frosts in the spring and a first half of the year which is wetter than most of the South-West. Happily the autumn is mild and dry, influenced both by the Atlantic and warm winds which float across the mountains from the plains of Spain.

The vineyard area extends over twenty-eight communes south and west of Pau between two rivers, the Gave de Pau and Gave d'Oloron. This is a lush country-side of mountain foothills, hidden valleys and swiftly running streams, with the vineyards facing the mountains, to the south and south-east, on slopes which run from north to south.

The Jurançon vineyards have doubled in area in the last fifteen years, and yet this is not by any means a monocultural wine region. On the flat lands the fields are largely given over to maize or pasture, though there are other crops such as apples, peaches and sweet chestnuts. In Béarnais style the farmhouses and ancillary buildings are often built in the form of a hollow square.

This is a large area, some 20 kilometres long on all sides, and the geology is varied. Essentially there is marl or loam, mixed together with glacial debris, gravel and large pudding stones or *galets* similar to those found at Châteauneuf-du-Pape. Areas which are too calcareous can be a problem: the vine takes longer to reach maturity here and can be susceptible to the disease chlorose. In general, there are two main areas of production: around Monein to the west and around Chapelle de Rousse on the eastern side. One of the best estates, however, Clos Guirouilh, lies 8 kilometres south of Lasseube, right at the edge of the Jurançon area. In general the soils around Monein are less acid than elsewhere.

Despite what the occasional palm tree might suggest, the Jurançon hills are prone to spring frosts, and the vines are trained high as a result so that the buds and consequently the grapes are about $1^1/_2$ metres off the ground. The ancient metal stakes with their macabre cross pieces – in winter the vineyards seemed to echo the military graveyards of the Somme – have been replaced by ones of acacia wood and the vines are trained along wires running between them.

Jurançon is produced from the Gros Manseng and Petit Manseng, with the addition of a little Petit Courbu. The Gros Manseng, as its name suggests, produces a larger berry and the wine from it matures more quickly. The Petit Manseng fruit is more widely spread on the cane, and is less productive, but the alcohol level of the wine (and therefore the amount of potential sugar) is higher. Both varieties have thick skins. In principle, therefore, dry Jurançon is made mainly with Gros Manseng, the Petit Manseng being reserved for the sweeter wine.

Until recently, Jurançon was exclusively a sweet wine. This sweetness came not from noble rot, but simply from a process called *passerillage*: the autumns are normally warm and dry here and the grapes are left to dry out gradually on the vine. The thick skins help prevent the grapes from rotting and also enable the fruit to withstand any rain. As this drying process happens, the acidity level remains constant. And the result is a wine which can range from quite sweet to seriously *liquoreux*, fuller than a sweet Loire wine, but nevertheless Loire-ish in style rather than resembling a Sauternes. The wines that have no oak-ageing or where the oak is just a light touch, are fresh and flowery, with the fruit suggesting fruit salad, or plain peaches and apricots, sometimes with a hint of crab apple or quince. The richer and more luscious the wine, the more the new oak and the more the wine resembles a Cérons or Sainte-Croix-du-Mont from Bordeaux, yet it always has a more zippy acidity and higher-toned flowery fruit. They are at their best at five to ten years old.

Following the twin vicissitudes of first phylloxera and then the economic depression, the fashion for Jurançon declined, demand evaporated, and the vineyard area contracted. When the co-operative at Gan was founded in 1950, the local growers were advised to produce dry wine as well as sweet. At first it was rather hard and neutral but in the last couple of decades, as pioneers like Henri Ramonteu at the Domaine Cauhapé (see page 476) have shown, dry white Jurançon can be a delicious, clean, crisp, individual wine for drinking young. His is still the best example, as are his sweet wines. But there is now plenty of competition.

Sweet Jurançon Vintages

1998 This is a very good year, though with reduced quantity.

1997 The wines are a little lighter than 1998 or 1996, with a slight lack of zip.

1996 This is a very good year and the wines are classy.

1995 A very hot year and the wines are rich and concentrated but lacking a little acidity.

Earlier vintages of note

1994 was a good but not spectacular vintage, but better than 1993, which itself is much better than the rain-affected, dilute results from 1992 and 1991. 1990, 1989 and 1988 were fine vintages.

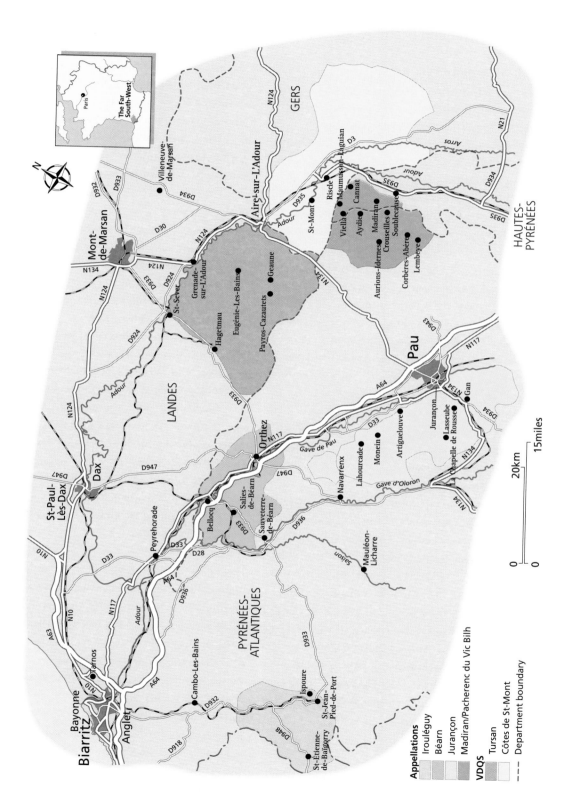

THE FAR SOUTH-WEST

The Far South-West

Paris

GERS

Aire-sur-L'Adour

Villeneuve-de-Marsan

D932
D933
D934

Mont-de-Marsan

D30
D924
D933
D124

N134

N124

D924

St-Sever

Grenade-sur-L'Adour

Engénie-Les-Bains

Hagetmau

Geaune

Payros-Cazautets

N124

N134

Adour

D935

D935

St-Mont

Riscle

Maumusson-Laguian

Cannat

Viella

Aydie

Madiran

Crouseilles

Soublecause

Aurions-Idernes

Corbères-Abères

Lembeye

HAUTES-PYRÉNÉES

N21

Arros

D934

D935

D943

Pau

N117

N134

Gan

D934

D33

Jurançon

Artiguelouve

Monein

Lasseube

La Chapelle de Rousse

N134

Lahourcade

Navarrenx

Gave de Pau

Gave d'Oloron

Orthez

N117

D947

LANDES

Dax

St-Paul-Lès-Dax

N124

Adour

D947

Salies-de-Béarn

Bellocq

Sauveterre-de-Béarn

D933

D936

Saison

Mauléon-Licharre

Peyrehorade

D33
D28
D936
A64

PYRÉNÉES-ATLANTIQUES

D933

Cambo-Les-Bains

D932

Ispoure

St-Jean-Pied-de-Port

D48

St-Étienne-de-Baïgorry

D918

Biarritz

Bayonne

Anglet

Tarnos

N10

A63

N117

N10

A64

Adour

15miles

20km

0

0

Appellations

Irouléguy

Béarn

Jurançon

Madiran/Pacherenc du Vic Bilh

VDQS

Tursan

Côtes de St-Mont

Department boundary

Leading Jurançon Producers

★ DOMAINE BELLEGARDE

Commune: Monein.
Owner: Pascal Labasse.
Surface Area under Vine: 18 ha.
Wines: Jurançon including (dry) Cuvée Tradition and Cuvée Bois and (*moelleux*) Cuvée Thibault and Sélection DB.

Domaine Bellegarde was acquired by the Labasse family in 1926. It was originally polycultural, with only a couple of hectares of vines, and the wine was made by the local co-operative. In 1986 Pascal Labasse set up on his own, constructed a new cellar, and set about acquiring more land. The bias in the vineyard is towards Petit Manseng, and in the cellar towards *moelleux* wines. The wines here are stylish and the dry Cuvée Bois (70 per cent Gros Manseng, 30 per cent Petit Manseng) is one of the *appellation*'s best examples: nice and lean – like all the wines of this domaine – and not too oaky, and with the capacity to develop.

DOMAINE BRU-BACHÉ

Commune: Monein.
Owner: Claude Loustalot.
Surface Area under Vine: 7 ha.
Wines: Jurançon including Cuvée Casterrasses, Cuvée La Quintessence and Cuvée L'Eminence.

This estate was created above Monein on the northern side by Georges Bru-Baché in the 1960s. Estate-bottling started in 1973, followed a decade later by barrel fermentation. In 1994 Monsieur Bru-Baché retired, handing over the reins to a distant cousin, Claude Loustalot. The steep, schistous vineyard contains a large proportion of Petit Manseng and production is concentrated on the sweeter wines, which I find more successful than the dry ones. The Cuvée L'Eminence, made from Petit Manseng grapes picked in December, is very sweet and luscious.

DOMAINE CASTÉRA

Commune: Monein.
Owner: Christian Lihour.
Surface Area under Vine: 9.5 ha.
Wines: Jurançon including Cuvée Privilège.

The Castéra domaine is south-east of Monein surrounded by fields of maize and pasture. The splendid slate-roofed Béarnais *manoir* encloses a courtyard, the wall reinforced with the pudding-stones dug out of the surrounding soil. Christian Lihour's winemaking philosophy is to preserve the fruit, and so he dislikes the use of new wood. This gives his sweet wines a fresh, slightly herbal character, without the vanilla under-pinning you find elsewhere. The dry wines are very dry: to the point of real austerity. But they keep well.

★★ DOMAINE CAUHAPÉ

Commune: Monein.
Owner: Henri Ramonteu.
Surface Area under Vine: 32 ha.
Wines: Jurançon including (dry) Chant des Vignes, Sève d'Automne and Noblesse du Temps and (*moelleux*) Ballet d'Octobre, Symphonie de Novembre, Noblesse du Temps and Quintessence.

Domaine Cauhapé is the leading Jurançon estate, and one of the largest, with vineyards in several locations. Henri Ramonteu's parents bought the estate in 1957, when it was polycultural and with only some 4 hectares of vines, mainly hybrids. Henri took over in 1981, and has since revolutionised both Cauhapé and Jurançon as a whole, introducing techniques such as skin contact, temperature-controlled fermentation, clean handling of the wine during its *élevage* and the use of new oak. That dry Jurançon is increasingly popular throughout the world is largely as a result of his wine and his genius for promotion. He is also largely responsible for the cleanliness and style of today's sweet Jurançon wines.

Chant des Vignes, from 100 per cent Gros Manseng and no oak, is a very stylish basic wine. Sève d'Automne is also solely from Gros Manseng but with about 70 per cent of the grapes being barrel-fermented. Cuvée Noblesse, entirely from Petit Manseng, is 100 per cent barrel-fermented and has a dry, Sauternes-type nose and richness. It needs time to age. The four sweet wines are the result of successive visits to the vineyard and increasingly sweet and concentrated.

DOMAINE DU CINQUAU

Commune: Artiguelouve.

Owner: Pierre Saubot.

Surface Area under Vine: 8 ha.

Wines: Jurançon including both dry, *moelleux* and Cuvée 'Elevé en Fûts de Chêne'.

Pierre Saubot lives in Paris, leaving his family domaine in the hands of his *régisseur*, Alain Baute. There are good oaky *cuvées* in both dry and sweet styles, the latter entirely from Petit Manseng. My only reservation is with the basic dry wine, made from 70 per cent Gros Manseng and 30 per cent Petit Courbu. The Courbu, I fear, is a mistake and it adds a rather coarse, tropical aspect. Otherwise, a good address.

★ CLOS GUIROUILH

Commune: Lasseube.

Owner: Jean Guirouilh.

Surface Area under Vine: 7 ha.

Wines: Jurançon including Cuvée Réserve and Vendange Tardive, and Béarn (red and rosé).

One of Jurançon's best and most interesting estates lies up in the hills in spectacular countryside south of Lasseube at the southern end of the *appellation*. The Guirouilh family have been here for over four centuries, and until recently the main crops were apples and peaches along with rearing cattle. Vines are now the sole source of income.

There is one dry Jurançon wine: unoaked, it is a full, rich example, with plenty of depth and less *primeur* than Domaine Cauhapé's dry wine. The sweet wines, from both Gros and Petit Manseng, spend as much as eighteen months in newish wood. Both the sweet and dry wines keep well. In the best vintages the Réserve/Vendange Tardive (the latter designation only permitted since 1995, and tightly controlled) is like biting into a fresh honeycomb. Jean Guirouilh also makes a little Béarn red and rosé, from half Tannat, half Cabernet Franc, both rarities now in the area.

CHÂTEAU JOLYS

Commune: Gan.

Owner: Pierre-Yves Latrille.

Surface Area under Vine: 36 ha.

Wines: Jurançon including Cuvée Jean and Vendange Tardive.

In his seventies, Pierre-Yves Latrille is the grand old man of Jurançon, and almost a caricature of the charming, elderly French gentleman, with a continual twinkle in his eye. With its elegant château the domaine is perched on the spine of a north-south ridge above Gan and like its owner is the doyen of Jurançon.

Soon after Monsieur Latrille bought it in 1959, he replanted the derelict vineyards. At first the wine was made by a neighbouring merchant, Louis Menjucq, and sold as an exclusivity but in 1982 Latrille constructed some cellars and started to make the wine himself. All the usual techniques such as sorting the grapes after picking and *macération pelliculaire* or skin contact have been carried out here for ages. Unusually for Jurançon the wine undergoes malolactic fermentation as Latrille regards the wines as too acid and malic without it. He doesn't like to de-acidify (i.e. add tartaric 'artificial' acid to the must) and he finds the fruit rounder and softer as a result. The wines are good – the Vendange Tardive is really quite sweet and concentrated – but they lack the flair of the best.

CRU LAMOUROUX

Commune: La Chapelle-de-Rousse.

Owner: Richard Ziemek-Chigé.

Surface Area under Vine: 6 ha.

Wines: Jurançon including Cuvée Amélie-Jean, and Béarn (red and rosé).

Cru Lamouroux was founded in 1895 by the great-grandfather of Mme Ziemek (*née* Chigé) and lies at the end of a little drive, on the flank of a south-west-facing hill, overlooking its vines. Her husband arrived at the estate in the mid-1970s and then took over the domaine five years later. Sweet wines are the main business here and they are mainly sold to private customers in France. Ziemek dislikes the vanilla flavour of new wood and thinks it has nothing to do with the flavours from the grapes. Curiously, I preferred the 1995 *moelleux* to the richer, purer Petit Manseng, Cuvée Amélie-Jean from the same vintage.

★ CLOS LAPEYRE

Commune: La Chapelle-de-Rousse.
Owner: Jean-Bernard Larrieu.
Surface Area under Vine: 12 ha.
Wines: Jurançon including Cuvée Sélection,
Cuvée Vitatge Vielh and Cuvée Vendange Tardive.

With the decline of interest in Jurançon during the economic depression of the inter-war years, the Larrieu family decided to entrust the winemaking and distribution to the local co-operative and to concentrate on growing strawberries instead. The domaine began winemaking again when Jean-Bernard Larrieu took over in 1985. The basic dry wine is admirable. The Vitatge Vielh is an oaky dry wine from very old Gros Manseng, rich and capable of ageing in bottle. There are two *moelleux* wines, a semi-sweet, aperitif-style example and the ultra-rich Vendange Tardive. A fine address.

★ DOMAINE NIGRI

Commune: Monein.
Owner: Jean-Louis Lacoste.
Surface Area under Vine: 10 ha.
Wines: Jurançon including Cuvée Réserve (both dry and *doux*).

The Lacoste family have been at Nigri, south of Monein, just off the main road, the D9, for four generations. Jean-Louis, a qualified oenologist, took over running the domaine in 1994. Unlike most domaines in the area, there is a small amount of the early-ripening Camaralet and Lauzet, subsidiary Jurançon varieties, in the vineyard, 'to soften the rigidity of the Gros Manseng in the dry wine', though the Courbu has been dispensed with. These are stylish, supple, relatively early-maturing wines. A good source.

CLOS UROULAT

Commune: Monein.
Owner: Charles Hours.
Surface Area under Vine: 7 ha.
Wines: Jurançon including (dry) Cuvée Marie and (sweet) Clos Uroulat.

Charles Hours is a tall, stocky, welcoming man in his fifties. There is no nonsense about him or his wines.

There is one dry wine called Cuvée Marie, and one of sweet, Clos Uroulat (meaning 'chestnut tree' in Béarnais). Both wines are vinified in wood and bottled after twelve months. Charles Hours likes to produce wines with good acidity and enough volume to accompany food. If he dispensed with the 10 per cent of Courbu the wines would be even better. At present I find the *moelleux* better than the dry wine.

Other Producers of Note

DOMAINE BORDENAVE AND CLOS BAYARD/GISÈLE BORDENAVE-MONTESQUIOU (MONEIN), DOMAINE CAPDEVILLE/CASIMIR CAPDEVILLE (MONEIN), DOMAINE LARREDYA/JEAN-MARC GRUSSAUTE (LA CHAPELLE-DE-ROUSSE) AND CLOS DE LA VIERGE/ANNE-MARIE BARRÈRE (LAHOURCADE).

MADIRAN

Surface Area (1998): 1512 ha (including Pacherenc du Vic-Bilh see page 480).
Production (1998): 69,885 hl.
Colour: Red.
Grape Varieties: Tannat, Cabernet Franc (Bouchy), Cabernet Sauvignon and Fer Servadou (Pinenc).
Maximum Yield: 55 hl/ha.
Minimum Alcohol Level: 11°.

North of Pau and Tarbes, near the junction of four *départements* (Landes, Gers, Pyrénées-Atlantiques and Hautes-Pyrénées) is Madiran, the best Béarnais red wine *appellation*. Like Cahors but unlike Fronton and Gaillac, this is a wine for ageing.

The river Adour and its tributaries flow through the *appellation*, dividing this green and unspoilt region into numerous gentle valleys. Mixed woodland alternates with pasture, cornfields and vineyards. Ancient homesteads, small Romanesque churches and the occasional fortified manor house decorate the landscape and show evidence of an unhurried, self-sufficient way of life which seems barely to have changed for centuries.

The name Madiran is derived from the Latin *mariae donarium* meaning the 'gift of the mayor'. Vines have been grown here since Gallo-Roman times. There is evidence of commercial winemaking in the eleventh century and when a Benedictine abbey was established in the town in 1030 the Tannat grape makes its first recorded appearance. The author Hubrecht Duijker suggests that this might have been transported from a brother establishment at Burgundy. Others say it came from Bordeaux where it was still certainly cultivated as recently as the nineteenth century.

Communications were good and the reputation of the wine was propagated by pilgrims who encountered it on their journey through the South-West to Santiago de Compostella. The wine could be taken overland to the river Garonne for shipment down to Bordeaux as one of the many Haut Pays wines, which were often used to bolster up the lighter wines of the Gironde, or sent directly down the river Adour to Bayonne. It was exported to the Low Countries and Germany, particularly to Hamburg and Bremen, to Britain and even as far afield as Finland and Russia as early as the sixteenth century. In 1816 the writer Jullien (*Topographie de Tous les Vignobles Connus*) judged Madiran the most important of the Béarnais wines. According to him they were rich in colour, *âpre et pâteux* (tart and inky) but would keep for eight or ten years in cask or bottle and eventually soften, comparing to advantage with wines which enjoyed a higher reputation. Often they were softened up by blending in a little white wine. They were much in demand in Bayonne to give colour and body to some of the weaker wines of the South-West.

Despite the creation of a Syndicat de Défense of the wine in 1906 and, indeed, the award of *appellation contrôlée* in 1948, phylloxera and its aftermath almost wiped out the vineyards of Madiran. The first half of the twentieth century was a depressing time. The Tannat grape, in particular, was on the point of extinction. By 1953 the vineyard area was down to 6 hectares. Only in the last thirty years have horticulturalists mastered the technique of reproducing the Tannat on a commercial scale in the greenhouse.

For many years the co-operative at Crouseilles was the sole source of the wine, and even when I first started visiting the area in 1974 or 1975, there were few private estates apart from the Laplace family at Château d'Aydie. As in Cahors and elsewhere in the South-West, there has been a resurgence of the *appellation* since 1970. By then there were 100 hectares under vine, a decade later the figure was 700 and today more than 1500. There are now many individual domaines bottling and selling there own wine, though few are on a really large scale.

This part of South-West France enjoys a mild winter and a long, dry summer, though it suffers from a wet spring. The valleys are prone to frost so are left as grazing for cattle or planted with wheat and maize. Most of the vineyards are on the slopes which are limestone of various types, mixed with clay and sand, very stony in parts. Thirty-seven communes, forming the shape of a rough shield beginning just below Saint-Mont and Riscle and extending southwards to Lembeys, are entitled to produce Madiran.

Madiran is not a monocultural region. As at Jurançon the hills run north to south, with streams draining the lower land between them. The vines are planted largely on the eastern-facing slopes, and on the higher land at that. Maize is much more widely planted. Moreover it is to the north of the village of Madiran itself, at Aydie, Viella and especially Maumusson that the best domaines congregate, at somewhere between 150 and 300 metres above sea level. Here, on the edges of the Gers *département*, the climate is the driest, the sunniest and the warmest. As in the Jurançon, spring frosts can be a problem, and so the vines are trained high, along wires, the fruit bunches being a metre or so above the ground for the Tannat (*demi-hautain*), higher still for some reason for the white wine varieties.

The chief and, until recently, dominant grape variety is the Tannat, the classic red wine variety of the extreme South-West. Tannat on its own produces a very full, solid, astringent wine. Today, the *appellation* laws decree a maximum of 60 per cent in the blend and a minimum of 40 per cent. This, however, is in the vineyard. Some growers, particularly those who use a lot of new wood, make superior blends with quite a bit more Tannat in the *encépagement*. The Cuvée Vieilles Vignes of Château Bouscassé, contains 100 per cent Tannat, for example. Traditionally the other grape used has been

Cabernet Franc, known locally as the Bouchy. This softens the burly Tannat and adds to the wine's bouquet. Recently, more and more Cabernet Sauvignon has been planted. Until 1975, Madiran had to spend eighteen months in wood or vat before bottling, but this has since been reduced to one year. Growers now have the freedom to make the wines as they choose.

Two vinification improvements have made today's Madiran much more sophisticated, without undermining its essential character. The first is *microbillage*, a process whereby oxygen is gently released through the wine by a device in the middle of the vat. The second is *délestage*, a process of pumping over whereby the entire vat-load of liquid is emptied and returned rather than the wine being merely extracted from underneath and sprinkled over the top in small doses. The principle underlying both techniques is that Tannat is a variety which requires rather more oxygen than most during vinification in order to avoid it making too dense and inky a wine. Coupled with this, of course, has been a general increase in the amount of new oak used.

Today, while firm and masculine, full and sturdy, Madiran is solid without being robust. The elements of denseness and bitterness are still there in the young wine – a cross between Saint-Estèphe and Châteauneuf-du-Pape in flavour – but the wines are richer and more concentrated, the fruit classier and more positive. A good Madiran still needs a decade to mature but will now produce an unexpectedly fine bottle.

PACHERENC DU VIC-BILH

Surface Area (1998): approximately 200 ha (included with Madiran see page 478).
Production (1998): 10,021 hl.
Colour: White.
Grape Varieties: Petit Manseng, Gros Manseng, Petit Courbu, Arrufiac and Sauvignon Blanc.
Maximum Yield: 40 hl/ha.
Minimum Alcohol Level: 12°.

Pacherenc du Vic-Bilh is the white wine of the Madiran region, and is enjoying a renaissance, production

having increased tenfold in the last twenty years. We don't know precisely where the *Vic* or *canton* (a canton is a group of communes or parishes in France) was, for it has disappeared, though it covered what is now the Madiran area. *Bilh* means 'old' in the local dialect. Today the name is used for the white wine, and though hitherto only dry, it is now increasingly seen as a sweet wine.

Traditionally the wine was the product of the Arrufiac grape variety. Sadly this produces a very rustic wine, as does the Petit Courbu. As far as I am concerned, and a number of locals not only agree with me but have uprooted the variety entirely, despite the so-called tradition, the less Arrufiac the better. On the other hand, we don't want a sort of second division Jurançon, which is what happens if the wine is made solely from the Manseng varieties. But I have to admit that these make the wines my palate likes the best.

Most growers, as in both Jurançon and Vouvray, produce several styles of wine ranging from dry to *doux* (the latter to differentiate them from sweet Jurançon which is called *moelleux*) by picking at intervals from late in September onwards. The Arrufiac, Petit Courbu and Sauvignon Blanc, which only a few growers have planted, go into the dry wines, along with some Gros Manseng. The Petit Manseng is used for the sweeter wine.

I love Madiran, a wine I consider one of today's real red wine bargains, and I am a great fan of well-made Jurançons, especially the drier versions which make excellent aperitifs. But I find Pacherenc difficult to come to terms with. Happily for the locals, I am not the only potential customer.

Leading Madiran and Pacherenc du Vic-Bilh Producers

★★ CHÂTEAU D'AYDIE
DOMAINE FRÉDÉRIC LAPLACE
Commune: Aydie.
Owners: Jean-Luc, François, Bernard and Marie Laplace.
Surface Area under Vine: 45 ha.
Wines: Madiran and Pacherenc including Cuvée Frédéric Laplace.

The Laplace family has been farming in the region since at least 1759, the date of construction of the present château, and it is still a working farm, as well as a winery. In 1961 Frédéric Laplace was one of the first growers to set up independently of the local co-operative and to start selling his own wine in bottle. Even two decades later his son Pierre still seemed to be the only grower who appreciated the potential quality of the *appellation*.

Today the grandchildren are in charge: Jean-Luc of the wine, François of the administration. The dry *cuvée* Frédéric Laplace Pacherenc comes from 40 per cent Gros Manseng, 25 per cent each Arrufiac and Petit Courbu and 10 per cent Petit Manseng fermented and matured for six to eight months in wood, after skin contact. It has good depth and style and will keep. The Château d'Aydie, one of the best Madiran wines, is now made almost entirely from Tannat and bottled after two years of oak-ageing. It needs a good five years in bottle.

The second wine, called Ode d'Aydie, is available as both red or white. Fleury-Laplace is the name for a parallel range of merchant wines, from bought-in grapes.

★★ CHÂTEAU BARREJAT

Commune: Maumusson.
Owner: Denis Capmartin.
Surface Area under Vine: 17 ha.
Wines: Madiran including Cuvée des Vieux Ceps, and Pacherenc.

Everything has changed at this long-standing domaine since the arrival of Denis Capmartin (brother of Guy, see right) in 1992, including ageing the wine in oak. More recently, the techniques of *délestage* and micro-oxygenation have been introduced.

The basic Madiran wine (60 per cent Tannat, 40 per cent Cabernet Franc and Cabernet Sauvignon) comes in a tank version (Cuvée Tradition) and an oak version, called Sélection. The malolactic fermentation of the Cuvée des Vieux Ceps, from 80 per cent Tannat, takes place in barrel, 50 per cent of which are new. The sweet Pacherenc is entirely from Petit Manseng and the dry from almost 100 per cent Gros Manseng. I find all the wines here wholly admirable: one of the *appellation*'s super-stars.

★ DOMAINE BERTHOUMIEU

Commune: Viella.
Owner: Didier Barré.
Surface Area under Vine: 25 ha.
Wines: Madiran including Cuvée Charles de Batz, and Pacherenc including Symphonie d'Automne.
The youngish, voluble Didier Barré is the sixth generation at Berthoumieu, the name of his great grandmother, and is one of the region's better *vignerons*.

The fine Madiran Cuvée Tradition is the basic wine: made from 60 per cent Tannat, 35 per cent Cabernet Sauvignon and Cabernet Franc and 5 per cent Fer Servadou, the grapes are macerated for three to four weeks and then kept half in tank, half in *barrique*. Named after a real-life d'Artagnan musketeer, the Charles de Batz wine is made from forty- to eighty-year-old Tannat vines and matured in barrel, 60 per cent of which are new. Didier Barré believes that fermentation must be at high temperatures otherwise too much astringency and bitterness is extracted. The Tannat also needs plenty of oxygen so he racks the wine eight or nine times in the first year (four would be common in Bordeaux). It is a splendid wine.

The dry Pacherenc is a little neutral, but cleaner and less funky than most. The sweet wine, the Symphonie d'Automne from 70 per cent Petit Manseng and 30 per cent Petit Courbu is also noteworthy.

★ DOMAINE CAPMARTIN

Commune: Maumusson.
Owner: Guy Capmartin.
Surface Area under Vine: 7 ha.
Wines: Madiran including Vieilles Vignes and Cuvée du Couvent, and Pacherenc including Cuvée du Couvent.
Guy Capmartin is the older brother of Denis at Château Barréjat and set up on his own beside an old convent in 1987. His Madiran contains less Tannat than those of most of the neighbouring domaines: only 40 per cent in the basic *cuvée*, rising to 70 per cent in the Cuvée du Couvent. This gives the wines less strength, but allows all the lush fruit to show itself relatively early. These are seductive wines.

★★ DOMAINE LA CHAPELLE LENCLOS DOMAINE MAURÉOU

Commune: Maumusson-Laguian.
Owner: Patrick Ducournau.
Surface Area under Vine: 18 ha.
Wines: Madiran and Pacherenc.

'The magician of Madiran' is how the *Revue du Vin de France* (France's leading wine magazine) describes Patrick Ducournau. In 1986 he took over the domaine his father had bought and replanted the vineyards in 1968. He was concerned about the frequent rackings necessary to aerate the Tannat, which he felt would never allow the lees to settle properly and so developed, together with the Laplaces of Château d'Aydie, the techniques of *microbillage* or micro-oxygenation now widespread not only here but in Cahors and even in Bordeaux.

Domaine Mauréou is the name of a lesser wine from very chalky, badly-drained soil. The grapes producing Chapelle Lenclos (almost 100 per cent Tannat) comes from better land. I have watched Ducournau's wines become more sophisticated during the 1990s and today they are highly commendable. This is one of the leading domaines of the area.

DOMAINE DU CRAMPILH

Commune: Aurions-Idernes.
Owner: Alain Oulié.
Surface Area under Vine: 28 ha.
Wines: Madiran including Cuvée Vieilles Vignes and Cuvée Baron, and Pacherenc.

Domaine du Crampilh lies to the south of the *appellation*, an island of vines amid a sea of maize. Lucien Oulié left the co-operative in 1970, becoming one of the first growers in the region to convert to estate-bottling. His son Alain took over in 1989 and is now assisted by his son Bruno, his daughter-in-law Marie-Claude and other members of the family. The basic and the old-vine *cuvée* contain 40 and 55-60 per cent Tannat respectively while the Cuvée Baron has as much as 90 per cent, plus 40 per cent new wood. The Ouliés use the technique of micro-oxygenation for their Madiran wines. I find the wines good, but they lack the sparkle of the best, and a bit of real concentration.

DOMAINE DE GRABIEOU

Commune: Maumusson-Laguian.
Owners: René & Frédéric Dessans.
Surface Area under Vine: 16 ha.
Wines: Madiran including Cuvée Prestige, and Pacherenc.

During the 1960s René Dessans completely replanted the vineyards and then in 1970 started estate-bottling his wines. The style of the wines is old-fashioned – there is no wood, no *microbillage* and the wine is bottled only when it is two years' old or more. The Prestige *cuvée* comes from 100 per cent Tannat. The wines have won their fair share of medals but I find they lack a bit of succulence – they could have more sex appeal.

★ DOMAINE LABRANCHE-LAFFONT

Commune: Maumusson.
Owner: Christine Dupuy.
Surface Area under Vine: 11.5 ha.
Wines: Madiran including Cuvée Tradition and Cuvée Vieilles Vignes.

You might assume a feminine touch to the wines here, *oenologue*-trained Christine Dupuy having taken over from her mother in 1992, but you would be mistaken. The Cuvée Tradition comes from 60 per cent Tannat, and, despite being aged in tank, is rich, ripe and elegant. The Vieilles Vignes is made from 80 per cent Tannat and matured for a year in barrel (one-third new). One of the best Madirans, it is profound and full-bodied, splendidly sophisticated. The key is the use of techniques such as *délestage* and micro-oxygenation.

CHÂTEAU LAFFITTE-TESTON

Commune: Maumusson.
Owner: Jean-Marc Laffitte.
Surface Area under Vine: 40 ha.
Wines: Madiran including Tradition, Vieilles Vignes and Cuvée Joris Laffitte, Pacherenc including Ericka, Béarn (rosé) and Vin de Pays des Côtes de Gascogne.

Jean-Marc Laffitte, a big, burly, ex-rugby player in his late forties, inherited 9 hectares of vineyard in 1983, and has much enlarged his *vignoble* since then, necessitating the construction of a large underground cellar, over which is a folly of a château and a splendid reception room overlooking the vines. His wines mature early, lacking the depth and concentration of some of his neighbours'. The Vieilles Vignes is pure Tannat.

★★★ CHÂTEAU MONTUS
CHÂTEAU BOUSCASSÉ
DOMAINE MEINJARRE
Commune: Maumusson.
Owner: Alain Brumont.
Surface Area under Vine: 160 ha.
Wines: Madiran including Vieilles Vignes (Bouscassé) and Cuvée Prestige (Montus), Pacherenc and Vin de Pays des Côtes de Gascogne.

Others were there before him, but it was Alain Brumont who put Madiran on the wine map. He left the family domaine at Bouscassé in 1980, dissatisfied by his father's lack of any ambition for quality, and set up on his own. In a mere twenty years, Brumont has succeeded by a combination of breathtaking chutzpah and brilliant winemaking in creating the largest fine wine domaine in the South-West and establishing without a doubt that Tannat is a first division quality grape variety.

The basic Bouscassé (70 per cent Tannat) and Montus (75 per cent) are matured in 50 per cent new wood, and are very fine. The better *cuvées*, both 100 per cent Tannat and aged in new wood, are brilliant. The dry Pacherencs come from 100 per cent Petit Courbu, and are not to my taste. Alain Brumont has pioneered Pacherenc *moelleux* and these are more interesting.

CHÂTEAU PEYROS
Commune: Corbère-Abères.
Owner: Denis de Robillard.
Surface Area under Vine: 25 ha.
Wines: Madiran including Le Couvent.

Northwest of Lambaye, this is the most southerly of the important Madiran domaines. The domaine is based at a well-preserved priory near the remains of an old castle and is a large polycultural enterprise. Maize and cattle-rearing are as, or more important than, the vine. The basic Madiran contains only 40 per cent Tannat and is

tank-aged. The superior Cuvée Le Couvent, from 100 per cent Tannat, is aged in wood, 25 per cent of which is new. This wine needs time before it is ready. It can be very good.

DOMAINE PICHARD
Commune: Soublecause.
Owners: René & Bernard Tachouères.
Surface Area under Vine: 12.5 ha.
Wines: Madiran including Château Vigneau Pichard, and Pacherenc.

René Tachouères' uncle, Monsieur Vigneau, was perhaps the first grower in the region in modern times to practise estate-bottling. From the beginning of the 1960s he followed a policy of holding back a proportion of most vintages in order to offer wines ready for drinking, which his nephew and grand-nephew still continue. The vineyard, south of the village of Madiran, is on a relatively steep slope for the *appellation*, facing south-west, and produces rich but spicy wines, a shade on the dense side, but they keep well.

★ DOMAINE SERGENT
Commune: Maumusson.
Owner: Gilbert Dousseau.
Surface Area under Vine: 14 ha.
Wines: Madiran, including Cuvée Vieilles Vignes Elévé en Fûts de Chêne, Pacherenc and Béarn (rosé).

Gilbert Dousseau has been estate-bottling his wines since 1975, and is now assisted by his daughter Corinne, who trained at Rutherglen in Australia and Marlborough in New Zealand after taking her oenology degree. Modern techniques such as *délestage* and micro-oxygenation are used and the wines are both cool and elegant, while still fat and concentrated. The Pacherencs, solely from Petit Manseng and Gros Manseng and vinified in wood, are stylish, too.

Other Producers of note
DOMAINE DAMIENS/ANDRÉ BEHEITY (AYDIE), CHÂTEAU DE DIUSSE (AYDIE), DOMAINE DE FITÈRE/ROGER CASTETS (CANNET), DOMAINE LAOUGUÉ/PIERRE DABADIE (VIELLA),

CHÂTEAU DE PERRON/RICHARD CROUZET (MADIRAN) AND DOMAINE TAILLEURGUET/FRANÇOIS BOUBY (MAUMUSSON); PLUS THE PRODUCTEURS PLAIMONT CO-OPERATIVE (SAINT-MONT) AND THE CAVE DE CROUSEILLES (CROUSEILLES).

TURSAN

Surface Area (1998): 240 ha.
Production (1998): (Red and rosé) 11,024 hl; (white) 2385 hl.
Colours: Red, rosé and white.
Grape Varieties: (Red and rosé) Tannat, Cabernet Sauvignon and Cabernet Franc; (white) Barroque, Sauvignon Blanc, Gros Manseng, Petit Manseng and Sémillon.
Maximum Yield: 50 hl/ha.
Minimum Alcohol Level: (Red and rosé) 10.5°; (white) 11°.

The Tursan region, rich and polycultural, and only recently of any serious note from a wine point of view, lies west of Aire-sur-L'Adour in the Landes *département* and became VDQS in 1958. The reds are similar to the lighter, more *primeur* styles of Madiran. The Barroque grape, which you rarely see elsewhere, can produce rather heavy wine unless vinified with care, and, for my palate, a little of this white wine goes a long way.

Leading Tursan Producers

CHÂTEAU DE BACHEN
Commune: Aire-sur-L'Adour.
Owner: Michel Guérard.
Surface Area under Vine: 20 ha.
Wines: Tursan (white) including Baron de Bachen, and Vin de Pays des Coteaux de L'Adour (rosé).
Michel Guérard of the famous restaurant at Eugénie-les-Bains lives 5 kilometres away at Bachen in a carefully restored manor house whose origins go back to the thirteenth century. Here he has planted a vineyard. At first the wine was made by the Plaimont co-operative, but Michel Guérard now has his own winery and wine-

maker, the young Véronique Vialard. The vines are young, having been planted between 1984 and 1986 (white varieties only at first which are now being T-grafted to produce a 50:50, red-white equilibrium). At present, all the wines are white, except for a *vin de pays* rosé. The Baron de Bachen is the superior oak-fermented *cuvée* and has a certain style.

Other Producers of note
DOMAINE DE PERCHADE-POURROUCHET/ALAIN DULUCQ (PAYROS-CAZAUTETS) IS THE ONLY OTHER INDEPENDENT ESTATE; PLUS LES VIGNERONS DE TURSAN CO-OPERATIVE (GEAUNE).

CÔTES DE SAINT-MONT

Surface Area (1998): 824 ha.
Production (1998): (Red and rosé) 44,768 hl; (white) 8284 hl.
Colour: Red, rosé and white.
Grape Varieties: (Red and rosé) Cabernet Sauvignon, Cabernet Franc, Tannat and Fer Servadou; (white) Petit Courbu, Petit Manseng, Gros Manseng and Arrufiac.
Maximum Yield: 60 hl/ha.
Minimum Alcohol Level: 10°.

North of Madiran, on either side of the river Adour in the extreme south-west corner of the Gers *département*, is the Côtes de Saint-Mont region, a VDQS since 1981. The soil here is more alluvial than in Madiran, with a mixture of marl and gravel. This soil, combined with the wine spending a shorter period in vat, produces a lighter wine than Madiran, but similar in flavour. The whites are similar but more anonymous than those of Pacherenc de Vic-Bilh.

Côtes de Saint-Mont producers of note
THE PLAIMONT PRODUCTEURS CO-OPERATIVE (SAINT-MONT) – THIS UP-TO-DATE ESTABLISHMENT OFFERS A FULL RANGE OF WELL-MADE WINES FROM VINS DE PAYS TO MADIRAN AND PACHERENC, INCLUDING SEVERAL SINGLE-ESTATE LABELS.

VINS DE PAYS

Vin de Pays du Comté Tolosan

This is the regional *vin de pays*. It covers all the South-West as far inland as Millau apart from the Landes *département*. As a result it varies greatly depending on the grape varieties used and the wine can be red, rosé or white.

Vin de Pays des Landes, Vin de Pays des Terroirs Landais

The zonal Vin de Pays des Terroirs Landais, made up of four areas in the south of the Landes, the largest being Les Coteaux de Chalosse east of Dax, is rather more important than the departmental Vin de Pays des Landes. Reds and rosés come from Cabernet Sauvignon, Cabernet Franc and Tannat; the whites from Ugni Blanc, Colombard, Gros Manseng and Barroque. The local co-operative at Mugron, Les Vignerons des Coteaux de Chalosse, is the main source.

Vin de Pays des Pyrénées-Atlantiques, Vin de Pays du Gers, Vin de Pays des Côtes de Gascogne

The first of these covers the Irouléguy, Jurançon and Béarn regions, producing lighter, more anonymous versions of the local *appellation* wines.

The Gers and Côtes de Gascogne wines come from the Armagnac brandy country. Most are from Ugni Blanc and Colombard, which produces a refreshing, fairly acidic white for drinking within the year. These are deservedly some of the most popular French country whites. The co-operative at Riscle, allied to the Plaimont Producteurs at Saint-Mont and Domaines Grassa (see below) are the main sources.

Vin de Pays de Bigorre

This zonal *vin de pays* comes from the other side of the river Adour from Madiran between Tarbes and Riscle. The reds come from both Cabernet Sauvignon and Franc and Tannat, the whites from Colombard, Gros Manseng, Listan, Ugni Blanc, Sauvignon Blanc, Sémillon and Muscadelle. The Plaimont Producteurs and Les Vignerons de Tursan at Geaune are the main producers.

Leading Vin de Pays Producer

DOMAINES GRASSA
Commune: Eauze.
Owner: Pierre Grassa and family.
Surface Area under Vine: 350 ha.
Wines: Vin de Pays des Côtes de Gascogne, including Château de Tariquet, Domaine de Rieux, Domaine de Planterieu and La Jalousie.

Pierre Grassa helped put the Côtes de Gascogne on the wine map. From a mere 5 hectares in the 1950s Grassa has built up a formidable empire based on the original Château de Tariquet. The wine is white, made from Ugni Blanc and Colombard, and is refreshingly crisp, fruity and *primeur*. Its success has led to other *vins de pays*: Sauvignon Blanc, a Chardonnay-Sauvignon Blanc blend, barrel-fermented Chardonnay, Cuvée Bois from Gros Manseng, Colombard and other grapes, and a 100 per cent Gros Manseng.

THE BORDEAUX SATELLITES

BERGERAC REGION

BERGERAC
Surface Area (1998): (Red and rosé) 5670 ha; (white) 1836 ha.
Production (1998): (Red and rosé) 335,828 hl; (white) 103,341 hl.
Colours: Red, rosé and white.
Grape Varieties: (Red and rosé) Cabernet Sauvignon, Cabernet Franc, Merlot and Malbec; (white) Sauvignon Blanc, Sémillon, Muscadelle, Chenin Blanc and Ugni Blanc.
Maximum Yield: (Red and rosé) 55 hl/ha; (white) 60 hl/ha.
Minimum Alcohol Level: 10°.

CÔTES DE BERGERAC

Surface Area (1998): (Red and rosé) 367 ha;
(white) 1741 ha.
Production (1998): (Red and rosé) 23,637 hl;
(white) 81,284 hl.
Colours: Red, rosé and white.
Grape Varieties: (Red and rosé) Cabernet
Sauvignon, Cabernet Franc, Merlot and Malbec;
(white *moelleux*) Sauvignon Blanc, Sémillon and
Muscadelle.
Maximum Yield: 50 hl/ha.
Minimum Alcohol Level: 11°.

East of Bordeaux, across the departmental border from the Gironde into the Dordogne, lies Bergerac, the most prolific wine region in the South-West, apart from Bordeaux itself, as well as producing wines the closest in character to Bordeaux. This is the southern and western part of the ancient province of Périgord, a land that becomes progressively more unspoiled and more dramatic as one journeys upstream towards the Massif Central. It is a country rich in prehistory – the world-famous Lascaux caves with their wall-paintings near Montignac (you can only visit a replica now), and those at Les Eyzies de Tayac (with its celebrated restaurant Centenaire), lie upstream from the town of Bergerac in a land of impressive beauty.

This is one of the most hospitable parts of France and despite its popularity not too crowded with tourists even in the height of summer. The locals know how to eat well. There are *cèpes* and truffles, walnuts, plums and home-made cheeses, river trout, goose and duck, the fish steamed *au bleu,* the fowl often served as a *confit,* not forgetting *foie gras.* Along the winding, wooded valley of the river Dordogne and its tributaries lies many a feudal stronghold – old walled villages perched on a rock, or a *château fort,* splendid in its isolation.

Elsewhere, there are medieval ruins, grand Renaissance palaces which rival those of the Loire, and solitary peaceful hamlets a century away from the bustling civilisation of the cities of Bordeaux or Toulouse. West of the confluence of the rivers Vézère and the Dordogne, beyond the impressive meander of the Cingle de

Trémolat, the hills subside into an undulating countryside of orchards, wheat and maize fields and vineyards. Here, the land is less wooded, the views are more wide-ranging, the atmosphere is bucolic rather than raptorial. Dordogne, the prehistoric and picturesque, has given way to Bergerac the *vignoble.*

Bergerac, like Cahors and other wines of the Aquitaine hinterland, was part of the Haut Pays. In medieval times, there was much rivalry between Bergerac and Bordeaux. Sometimes there was a great need for the Bergerac wines to beef up the rather lighter wines of the Gironde. At other times, as a protectionist measure, the Bordelais imposed taxes on the border between French and English territory and these taxes continued even after the English left in the 1450s.

The only port out of which the wines could be shipped was Bordeaux whose merchants jealously guarded their privileges, imposing all sorts of restrictions on the unfortunate producers. The Dordogne wines, for instance, were prohibited from being sent down river until after Christmas, long after the annual fleet, carrying the Gironde harvest, had departed for the northern markets. Taxation was by the hogshead rather than volume, and it was decreed that the Haut Pays container should be smaller than that used in Bordeaux. Despite all this, wine was still a profitable commodity and business flourished. The area under vine in the sixteenth century and even later in the nineteenth century was vastly more extensive than it is today and the chief markets – the British disdaining anything other than 'quality wines' – were Holland, Scandinavia, Hamburg and the Baltic Ports.

The Bergerac wine area lies mainly south of the river Dordogne and extends from Lalinde, 20-odd kilometres east of the town itself, to Sainte-Foy, 24 kilometres to the west. Beyond Sainte-Foy, as far as Castillon, the right bank of the river is within the Dordogne *département,* so the wine is *appellation contrôlée* Bergerac, or one of the various Montravels; the left bank of the river is within the Gironde, so qualifies for the Bordeaux *appellation.*

The basic regional *appellation* is Bergerac, covering red wine and also, in practice, dry white. Just about all the growers in Monbazillac and Saussignac, smaller,

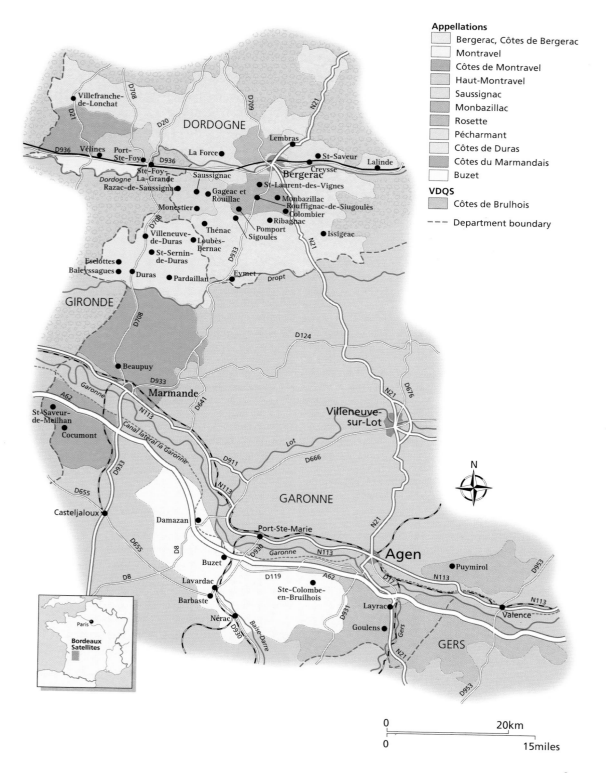

THE BORDEAUX SATELLITES

Appellations

Bergerac, Côtes de Bergerac
Montravel
Côtes de Montravel
Haut-Montravel
Saussignac
Monbazillac
Rosette
Pécharmant
Côtes de Duras
Côtes du Marmandais
Buzet

VDQS

Côtes de Brulhois

--- Department boundary

Villefranche-de-Lonchat

DORDOGNE

D708

D709

N21

D20

D21

Vélines

D936

Port-Ste-Foy

La Force

Lembras

St-Saveur

Lalinde

Creysse

Ste-Foy-La-Grande

Dordogne

Saussignac

Bergerac

Razac-de-Saussignac

St-Laurent-des-Vignes

Gageac et Rouillac

Monbazillac

Rouffignac-de-Siugoulès

Monestier

Colombier

Ribagnac

Thénac

Pomport

Villeneuve-de-Duras

Loubès-Bernac

Sigoulès

Issigeac

St-Sernin-de-Duras

N21

Esclottes

Baleyssagues

Duras

Pardaillan

Eymet

Drop

D933

D708

GIRONDE

D708

D124

Beaupuy

D933

Garonne

Marmande

D641

A62

N113

St-Saveur-de-Meilhan

Villeneuve-sur-Lot

N21

D676

Canal latéral à la Garonne

Cocumont

Lot

D933

D911

D666

N113

GARONNE

D655

Casteljaloux

D655

Damazan

Port-Ste-Marie

Agen

D8

D930

Garonne

N113

Puymirol

D953

Buzet

N21

D17

N113

Lavardac

D119

A62

Barbaste

Ste-Colombe-en-Bruilhois

Layrac

Baïse-Darre

Nérac

D930

D931

Valence

N113

Goulens

Gers

GERS

N21

D953

N

Paris

Bordeaux Satellites

0   20km
0   15miles

superior *appellations* for sweet white wine, produce Bergerac or Côtes de Bergerac as well and these wines are the mainstay of their production. Côtes de Bergerac red, and Côtes de Bergerac white, in practice a medium-sweet white wine, are superior *appellations* to basic Bergerac, requiring a higher minimum alcohol. The parallel is Bordeaux and Bordeaux Supérieur.

I note most of the best domaines under these smaller, more select *appellations*. Below are the best domaines which concentrate almost exclusively on dry white wines, as opposed to sweet, as well as red.

Leading Bergerac and Côtes de Bergerac Producers

★ CHÂTEAU DE LA COLLINE
Commune: Thénac.
Owner: Charles Martin.
Surface Area under Vine: 17 ha.
Wines: Bergerac (dry white), Bergerac (red) including Carmine, Côtes de Bergerac (*moelleux*) Confit de La Colline.

Charles Martin used to work for Nick Ryman at Château La Jaubertie (see below). In 1994 he bought the appropriately named Château de La Colline – it is the highest vineyard in the Aquitaine at 183 metres above sea level. He has built up the domaine gradually since then, and now also makes the wine for the nearby Château La Tour Monastier, and at the Domaine des Anges in the Côtes du Ventoux.

The rich and stylish Carmine red is from 95 per cent Merlot; the oak-fermented dry white (80 per cent Sémillon, 14 per cent Sauvignon and 6 per cent Muscadelle) is admirable, and the luscious Confit de La Colline, from botrytis-affected Sémillon from eighty-year-old vines, is quite delicious.

CHÂTEAU LA JAUBERTIE
Commune: Colombier.
Owners: Hugh Ryman and family and associates.
Surface Area under Vine: 50 ha.
Wines: Bergerac (red) and (dry white) including Cuvée Mirabelle, and occasional Monbazillac.

This domaine was sold in early 2000. It belonged formerly to Nick Ryman and then to Rystone, a firm jointly owned by Ryman's winemaker son Hugh and Esmé Johnstone, owner of Bordeaux's Château des Sours. The difficulties surrounding Château La Jaubertie in recent years are nothing short of tragic. The property was acquired by Nick Ryman in 1973, and he soon established it as one of the leading sources of dry, modern-style white wine in the area. Indeed, it is no exaggeration to say that it was Jaubertie that put Bergerac on the commercial map in the 1970s. Subsequently Nick fell out with his son but then eventually sold the property to Rystone. It now belongs to a consortium headed by Hugh and his father-in-law. The future is uncertain, but in good hands there is no reason to suppose that Château La Jaubertie will not continue to provide some of Bergerac's best wines.

CHÂTEAU DE PANISSEAU
Commune: Thénac.
Owners: Groupe Suez.
Surface Area under Vine: 70 ha.
Wines: Bergerac (red, rosé and dry white) and Côtes de Bergerac (*moelleux*).

The Bercher family had been making and exporting Bergerac longer than most until they sold out to the Groupe Suez company in 1990. The large estate – double the area under vine – surrounds a thirteenth-century castle which has been lovingly restored. The new owners have entrusted the management to Sylvie and Frédéric Labat who now run the domaine with considerable autonomy. The vineyard has been enlarged, a new *chai à barriques* constructed and a wood-aged white and red added to the range. I find the dry whites more interesting than the reds, but not up with the very best in the area.

★ CHÂTEAU TOUR DES GENDRES
Commune: Ribagnac.
Owner: Luc de Conti.
Surface Area under Vine: 45 ha.
Wines: Bergerac (white) including Cuvée Moulin des Dames and Cuvée Anthologia, and Côtes de

Bergerac (red) including Cuvée Moulin des Dames and Cuvée La Gloire de Mon Père.

Château Tour des Gendres was acquired by the de Conti family, more or less derelict, in 1981. The vineyard has since been enlarged by Luc de Conti and by trial and error he has discovered that sweet wines do not work here. He also has a strong preference for Sémillon rather than Sauvignon Blanc and for Cabernet rather than Merlot. The vineyard is biologically cultivated – the one producing Anthologia, a 100 per cent Sauvignon Blanc wine with the grapes individually picked at 10 hl/ha, is biodynamic – and the wines are produced on their lees with no sulphur. The red wines are made by *pigeage* and micro-oxygenation, with the malolactic fermentation taking place in oak, and the barrels are never racked. All in all this is a domaine of great originality and splendid wines across the board.

Other Producers of note

CHÂTEAU LA RAYRE/JEAN REVOL (COLOMBIER).
See also Monbazillac below and Saussignac page 492.

MONBAZILLAC

Surface Area (1998): 1769 ha.
Production (1998): 43,830 hl.
Colour and style: Sweet white.
Grape Varieties : Sémillon, Sauvignon Blanc and Muscadelle.
Maximum Yield: 40 hl/ha.
Minimum Alcohol Level: 12.5°.

To the south of the town of Bergerac, across the river Dordogne, lies the now thriving area of Monbazillac. The name is a corruption of the Gascon name 'Mont Bazailhac' which is said to mean 'mountain of fire' or 'mountain of gold'.

This is an ancient vineyard area, renowned for centuries and the wines were exported. Two pilgrims from the area, at an audience with the Pope in the sixteenth century, found he was already acquainted with the wine and Talleyrand is said to have served it as a 'wine of peace' at the Congress of Vienna in 1814. At this time,

according to André Jullien (*op. cit*, 1816), it was already better than a mere sweet white wine, for Jullien describes the grapes being left on the vine until they turned brown and the fruit was almost rotten. He also mentions that during the harvest each section of the vineyard was picked over a number of times, just as happens today in Sauternes and Barsac.

Despite its reputation, which some have dubbed the poor man's Sauternes, quality and demand declined abruptly after the phylloxera epidemic and the First World War, and by the 1960s production was a mere echo of its heyday. The establishment of the Cave Coopérative de Monbazillac in 1940 and perhaps, more important, its amalgamation with a number of other local establishments under the umbrella of Unidor (Union des Coopératives Vinicoles de La Dordogne) in 1965 did much to promote Monbazillac's revival.

To its great credit, the co-operative followed a policy of quality, not only keeping separate the grapes from the Château de Monbazillac, a splendid sixteenth-century building which now houses a restaurant and a museum, but also from a number of other domaines which it sells under single-estate names. This did much to revive interest in Monbazillac and encourage other growers in the area to resurrect the concept of sweet wines.

Twenty years ago Monbazillac was a sweet wine, often quite alarmingly deep golden in colour, even when young, with a flavour of barley sugar. It lacked not only the balance and elegance of Sauternes, but its richness. Nor was there much evidence of new oak. All this was put down not only to a lack of money but also to an over-preponderance of the Muscadelle grape, viewed by the Sauternais as 'common'. Monbazillac continues to be made with much higher proportions of Muscadelle than Sauternes. Now that the growers have been able to clean up their winemaking we can hail the Muscadelle as making a quality contribution rather than ruining the *cuvée*. It prevents the wine from being heavy and gives it its characteristic *fondant* and coffee flavour. The poor man's Sauternes no longer exists!

The *appellation* covers some 1750 hectares in the communes of Rouffignac-de-Sigoulès, Colombier, Pomport and Saint-Laurent-des-Vignes, as well as Monbazillac itself, the best vines lying on north-facing slopes as the *plateau* descends towards the Dordogne. It is here that the morning mist, so necessary for the formation of noble rot, is the most prevalent in the early mornings of autumn. Monbazillac, in its less oaky versions, is delicious young. The more serious examples will keep for ten years or more. In poor vintages the wines are vinified dry and sold as Bergerac *blanc sec*.

Leading Monbazillac Producers

★ Château Belingard

Commune: Pomport.
Owner: Comte Laurent de Bosredon.
Surface Area under Vine: 90 ha.
Wines: Bergerac (dry white) including Cuvée Blanche de Bosredon, Bergerac (rosé), Côtes de Bergerac (red) including Cuvée Blanche de Bosredon and Cuvée Prestige, and Monbazillac including Cuvée Blanche de Bosredon.

The name 'Belingard' means 'Garden of the Gods' in the ancient Celt language. Druids worshipped on the rocks nearby a thousand years later and subsequently the Benedictines built a monastery on the site. This is one of the oldest vineyards in the area, and one of the finest, Laurent de Bosredon incorporating the best modern techniques as well as the best traditional ones. 'Having spent most of the 1970s reducing the number of vines per hectare, I am now increasing the density,' he told me. The best *cuvées* are hand-harvested and fermented and/or matured in barrel. The Cuvée Prestige has 100 per cent new wood. The fine Monbazillacs come from 90 per cent Sémillon with 10 per cent Muscadelle.

Château La Borderie

Owner: Armand Vidal.
Surface Area under Vine: 70 ha.
Wines: Bergerac (dry white), Côtes de Bergerac (red), and Monbazillac including Cuvée 'Elevé en Fût de Chêne'.

There have been family disagreements recently and Dominique Vidal, who used to make the wine here, has now exiled himself to nearby Château Fonmourgues (see below), leaving his father Armand at La Borderie, and the family's other property Château Treuil Le Nailhac. Armand Vidal is getting on a bit now and there is a certain temporary hiatus, while the grandchildren grow up. More wine is being sold *en vrac* than hitherto to the local merchants. Most of the remaining wine is kept in *foudres*. The wines are good but not great.

Château Le Fagé

Commune: Pomport.
Owner: François Gérardin.
Surface Area under Vine: 40 ha.
Wines: Bergerac (dry white), Côtes de Bergerac (red) and Monbazillac including Grande Réserve.

Château Le Fagé lies on the top of the slope, with a splendid view northwards, while the *cave* is halfway down. It has belonged to the same family for two centuries and has been run by François Gérardin since 1983. There are two dry whites, neither woody (a deliberate choice): one pure Sémillon, the other pure Sauvignon Blanc. He has only just begun to use wood for his red wine, which is made from 65 per cent Merlot, plus both Cabernets and Malbec. There are two sweet wines, the superior Grande Réserve being full with a tendency to be a little four-square, after twenty-six months in cask.

★ Château Fonmourgues

Owner: Dominique Vidal.
Surface Area under Vine: 19 ha.
Wines: Bergerac (dry white), Côtes de Bergerac (red) and Monbazillac.

Dominique Vidal used to be responsible for Château La Borderie (see left), but after a quarrel with his father set up on his own in 1994. The red wines are quite marked by oak but I like the Monbazillac which is intense, luscious and balanced.

Clos Fontindoule

Owner: Gilles Cros.
Surface Area under Vine: 17 ha.
Wines: Monbazillac.

A visit here is a journey into the past. The eightysomething Gilles Cros and his wife live in an old farmhouse at the bottom of a little gulley. The set-up is artisanal in the extreme and ultra-traditionalist, the wine being held in bulk in stainless steel or polystyrene vats for three years and then in old *demi-muids* for another two at least, bottling taking place when stock is required. Early in 1999 Gilles Cros could still offer you a 1990 wine out of barrel. Despite this the wines are unexpectedly good!

★ DOMAINE GRANDE-MAISON

Owner: Thierry Després.

Surface Area under Vine: 20 ha.

Wines: Bergerac (dry white) including Cuvée Sophie, and Monbazillac including Cuvée des Anges.

Thierry Després arrived at Domaine Grande-Maison, a thirteenth-century building, in 1990, and since then has more or less replanted the vineyard from scratch. The mesoclimate produces a very precocious harvest here: ten days in advance of the Saint-Emilion area of Bordeaux, twenty in advance of his neighbours.

His vinification methods are individual, too: a super-extraction of the must, produced by almost freezing the grapes, then half cask fermented, the rest in tank, with micro-oxygenation, followed by seven months on the lees, with *bâtonnage*. The result is a wine which will keep. The dry Bergerac is fat but bone-dry, with hints of a dry Sauternes. There are usually three *cuvées* of Monbazillac, corresponding to different *tris*. The wines are splendidly concentrated, very clean and pure. Thierry Després is a fanatic, as well as an individualist, but he makes very good wines.

DOMAINE DU GRAND-MARSALET

Commune: Saint-Laurent-des-Vignes.

Owner: Jean-Pierre Nadal-Ode.

Surface Area under Vine: 100 ha.

Wines: Bergerac (dry white), Bergerac (red) including Cuvée Prestige Élevée en Fûts de Chêne, and Monbazillac including Château Bel Air, Cuvée Exception and Cuvée Prestige Élevée en Fûts de Chêne.

There have been recent changes for the better here, including modernising the *chais* and introducing temperature control and more new oak. These improvements have been reflected in the standard of the wines but as yet they are competent rather than fine.

DOMAINE DU HAUT-MONTLONG

Commune: Pomport.

Owner: Alain and Josy Sergenton.

Surface Area under Vine: 36 ha.

Wines: Bergerac (dry white), Bergerac (red) including Cuvée Laurence and Cuvée 'Elevé en Fûts de Chêne', Côtes de Bergerac (*moelleux*), and Monbazillac including Cuvée Audrey and Cuvée 'Elevé en Fûts de Chêne'.

This is a friendly set-up, daughters and their husbands working alongside Alain Sergenton and his wife. Quality has been steadily improving over the years, especially since the arrival of a pneumatic press. On the white side they concentrate on the sweet wines, the woody Monbazillac being from eighty-year-old vines: wood is not yet used for the dry white. The red oaky *cuvée* is from the same original blend as the unoaked Cuvée Laurence.

CHÂTEAU POULVÈRE

Owners: Borderie family.

Surface Area under Vine: 86 ha.

Wines: Bergerac (red, rosé and dry white), Côtes de Bergerac (*moelleux*), Monbazillac including Cuvée Tradition and Pécharmant (under the label Domaine Les Grangettes).

Jean Borderie retired in 1994 and the family domaines, which include Châteaux de Haute-Brie and du Caillou and Domaine Les Barses, as well as Domaine Les Grangettes (6 hectares in Pécharmant) are now run by his four children. Most of the Monbazillac and Bergerac is now sold under the Château Poulvère label. The better sweet wine *cuvée*, Cuvée Tradition, is very good. I would like to see the Grangettes (from one-quarter each Merlot, both Cabernets and Malbec) matured in wood, too. Currently it lacks a bit of sophistication.

CHÂTEAU THEULET

Owners: Serge and Pierre Alard.

Surface Area under Vine: 34 ha.

Wines: Bergerac (dry white) including Cuvée Prestige, Côtes de Bergerac (red) including Cuvée Prestige, Monbazillac including Cuvée Prestige.

Château Theulet has been in the hands of the Alard family since 1848. The vineyard was almost entirely reconstructed after the disastrous frost of 1956. Serge is more or less retired, and Pierre has just been joined by the seventh generation, his oenologist son Antoine.

This is an up-to-date establishment, with a pneumatic press and full thermo-regulation of the fermentation. The dry whites are made using modern techniques such as skin contact and lees-stirring; the sweet from 75 per cent Sémillon and 25 per cent Muscadelle. The red wine is aged in wood following micro-oxygenation in tank. There are good wines across the board here, sweet and dry, as well as two associated domaines, Rauly-Marsalat and Haut-Rauly.

★ Château Tirecul-La-Gravière

Owners: Claudine & Bruno Bilancini.
Surface Area under Vine: 9 ha.
Wines: Monbazillac including Cuvée Madame.

Here is a property which has exploded into the public eye, the wines – only in 50cl bottles – now selling for impressively high prices thanks to an enthusiastic reception from the wine critics. Bruno Bilancini studied in Bordeaux but never trained in a sweet wine château. He took over the vineyard in 1992 and then bought it in 1997. The Monbazillac is made from at least 50 per cent Muscadelle, most of it very old vines, and then matured in 30-40 per cent new wood for two years. In very good years part of the crop, but sometimes only three or four barrels, will be given 100 per cent new wood and labelled Cuvée Madame. The wine is quite different from a Sauternes: rich, high-toned and with a toffee flavour.

Cave Coopérative de Monbazillac

Members: 100.
Surface Area under Vine: 800 ha.
Wines: The full range of Bergerac wines including the single estates of Châteaux Haut-Marsalet, Monbazillac, Monrepos, La Sabatière, Septy and Le Tournon.

The Monbazillac co-operative, located on the main road south of Bergerac, the N21, is responsible for 30 per cent of the Monbazillac *appellation*, including the 22-hectare Château de Monbazillac itself. The overall quality of the wines is high and the Château de Monbazillac wine would clearly merit a star. Seventy per cent of the production is sweet wine.

Other Producers of note

Domaine de L'Ancienne Cure/Christian Roche (Colombier), Château Bellevue/Gérard Lajonie (Monbazillac), Château La Brie/Lycée Viticole, (Monbazillac), Château Haut-Bernasse/ Jacques Blais (Monbazillac), Château Le Mayne/Jean-Pierre Martrenchard (Sigoulès), Domaine de Pécoula/René Labaye (Pomport) and Château Vari/Vignobles Jestin (Monbazillac).

SAUSSIGNAC

Surface Area (1998): 62 ha.
Production (1998): 1518 hl.
Colour and Style: White *liquoreux* and *moelleux*.
Grape Varieties: Sémillon, Sauvignon Blanc and Muscadelle.
Maximum Yield: 50 hl/ha.
Minimum Alcohol Level: 11.5°.

Between Monbazillac and the boundary with the Gironde *département* (and the Entre-Deux-Mers wine region) lies the Saussignac *appellation*, covering the communes of Saussignac, Razac-de-Saussignac, Gageac, Monestier and Rouillac. It covers approximately the same surface area as Monbazillac but production is much, much lower, many growers simply ignoring the possibility of sweet wines, or sticking with the Côtes de Bergerac *moelleux* label rather than the as-yet-little-known Saussignac, an *appellation* dating from 1982. Pierre-Jean Sadoux at the long-established and sizeable Château Court-de-Mûts has been one of the pioneers of the new *appellation*, and he has now been joined by one or two enterprising outsiders. Saussignac is not quite so luscious as Monbazillac but it can have a better acidity.

Often it exhibits a most enticing quince-apple flavour. A parallel is perhaps the difference between Barsac and Sauternes. Saussignac can either be *moelleux* (medium-sweet) or *liquoreux* (very sweet, from botrytis-affected grapes). The wine can be lovely drunk quite soon after bottling but it will also keep for a decade.

Leading Saussignac Producers

DOMAINE DU CANTONNET
Commune: Razac-de-Saussignac.
Owner: Jean-Paul Rigal.
Surface Area under Vine: 16 ha.
Wines: Bergerac (dry white) including Tête de Cuvée Sauvignon, Côtes de Bergerac (red), and Saussignac including Cuvée Prestige.

Jean-Paul Rigal makes a very good dry Sauvignon-based Bergerac, one of the best in the area, from his modern premises outside Razac, but his Saussignac Cuvée Prestige is even better: splendidly floral and perfumed, very clean and elegant.

CHÂTEAU COURT-DE-MÛTS
Commune: Razac-de-Saussignac.
Owner: Pierre-Jean Sadoux.
Surface Area under Vine: 68 ha.
Wines: Bergerac (dry white) including Cuvée 'Elevé en Fûts de Chêne', Côtes de Bergerac (red) and Saussignac.

Court-de-Mûts is an old estate, but it was somewhat run-down when Pierre-Jean Sadoux's father bought it on his return from Algeria in 1960. Pierre-Jean, a trained oenologist, started estate-bottling when he took over in 1972. I find the wines good but not brilliant. There can be a somewhat heavy hand with the sulphur in the sweet wines. Châteaux Bramefont and Petite-Borie are affiliated estates, also in Saussignac.

★ CHÂTEAU LES MIAUDOUX
Owner: Gérard Cuisset.
Surface Area under Vine: 18 ha.
Wines: Bergerac (dry white), Côtes de Bergerac (red) and Saussignac.

Gérard Cuisset made a wonderful Saussignac in 1990 from fully botrytised grapes and has been determined to repeat the exercise ever since, even in uneconomic vintages such as 1992. Happily for him recent years have been very good for sweet wine in Saussignac. He also makes a very good dry white Bergerac.

★ DOMAINE DE RICHARD
Commune: Monestier.
Owner: Richard Doughty.
Surface Area under Vine: 17.5 ha.
Wines: Bergerac (dry white), Côtes de Bergerac (red), and Saussignac including Cuvée Harmonie and Cuvée Coup de Coeur.

Richard Doughty was an oil geologist before he decided to switch careers. He studied at the oenological school at Château La Tour-Blanche in Sauternes before buying land in Monestier in 1988. He produces an excellent woody, dry Bergerac from 95 per cent Sémillon, a good barrel-aged red and some very delicious Saussignac. The domaine is entirely organic.

★ CLOS D'YVIGNE
Commune: Gageac et Rouillac.
Owner: Patricia Atkinson.
Surface Area under Vine: 21 ha.
Wines: Bergerac (dry white), Côtes de Bergerac (red), and Saussignac.

James and Patricia Atkinson's first vintage was 1990, when they only possessed 5 hectares of vines. Patricia now runs Clos d'Yvigne on her own and has recently quadrupled its size. Both the dry whites – one oaky, one not – are very stylish. The reds, mainly Merlot, are fruity and succulent and the Saussignac balanced and luscious. A fine address.

PÉCHARMANT

Surface Area (1998): 391 ha.
Production (1998): 17,247 hl.
Colour: Red.
Grape Varieties: Cabernet Sauvignon, Cabernet Franc, Malbec and Merlot.

Maximum Yield: 45 hl/ha.
Minimum Alcohol Level: 11°.

Clinging to the suburbs north and north-east of the town of Bergerac lies the *appellation* of Pécharmant: the Pech, or hill, being 300 metres above sea level. It covers the communes of Lembras, Creysse, Saint-Saveur and Bergerac itself. The soil is a sandy gravel, rich in iron, lying on a clay base. The wines can be quite sturdy, if at the expense of finesse, but with this goes a good acidity. This means that they can age well, up to a decade in the best vintages.

Leading Pécharmant Producers

Château de Tiregand
Commune: Creysse.
Owner: Xavier de Saint-Exupéry.
Surface Area under Vine: 31 ha.
Wines: Pécharmant including Clos de la Montalbanie.
Almost entirely replanted after the 1956 frosts, and now run on biological lines, Château de Tiregand is the senior property in the *appellation* as well as one of the largest. Clos de La Montalbanie is the young-vine *cuvée*. The top wine, sold under the château name, comes from 50 per cent Merlot and 25 per cent each of the two Cabernets, and is matured in oak, one-sixth of which is new.

Domaine du Haut-Pécharmant
Commune: Bergerac.
Owner: Michel Roches.
Surface Area under Vine: 45 ha.
Wines: Pécharmant including Cuvée Prestige and Cuvée Vieux Roches.
Only the Prestige *cuvée* is matured in wood here, making the basic wine, which has 10 per cent Malbec, somewhat dense and four-square. It is kept for three years before being bottled. The wines last well, however, and do eventually come round. Clos Peyrelevade and Château Haut-Citar are affiliated properties, also in Pécharmant.

Rosette

Surface Area (1998): 18 ha.
Production (1998): 523 hl.
Colour and style: White *moelleux*.
Grape Varieties: Sémillon, Muscadelle and Sauvignon Blanc.
Maximum Yield: 40 hl/ha.
Minimum Alcohol Level: 12°.

To clear up any confusion at the outset, Rosette is not a rosé wine. The *appellation* covers the same land as Pécharmant north and north-east of the town of Bergerac, on either side of the N21 to Périgueux, but very little wine is made nowadays. Like most Saussignac until recent times and most Coteaux du Layon Rosette is not usually made from nobly rotten fruit and so is *moelleux* rather than *liquoreux*. This means, unfortunately, that unless you can be persuaded to drink it as an aperitif, Rosette is neither a wine for food nor a dessert or *digestif* wine. This, plus Bergerac's burgeoning suburbs, which like in Pécharmant are threatening to take over the vineyards helps to explain the *appellation*'s moribund position today.

Montravel

Montravel
Surface Area (1998): 360 ha.
Production (1998): 17,121 hl.
Colour and Style: Dry white.
Grape Varieties: Sémillon, Sauvignon Blanc and Muscadelle.
Maximum Yield: 50 hl/ha.
Minimum Alcohol Level: 10°.

Côtes de Montravel
Surface Area (1998): 54 ha.
Production (1998): 1091 hl.
Colour and Style: White, *demi-sec* to *moelleux*.
Grape Varieties: Sémillon, Sauvignon Blanc and Muscadelle.
Maximum Yield: 50 hl/ha.
Minimum Alcohol Level: 12°.

HAUT-MONTRAVEL

Surface Area (1998): 60 ha.

Production (1998): 3523 hl.

Colour and Style: White *liquoroux*.

Grape Varieties: Sémillon, Sauvignon Blanc and Muscadelle.

Maximum Yield: 50 hl/ha.

Minimum Alcohol Level: 12°.

North of Sainte-Foy and continuing westwards to the departmental boundary are the Montravel *appellations* (the 't' is not sounded, as in Montrose and Montrachet). Montravel itself comes from the flatter, more alluvial land between the river Dordogne and the main road to Bordeaux, the D936. Côtes de Montravel lies on the slopes north of this road nearer to Sainte-Foy and Haut-Montravel is on even higher ground and further to the west. The terrain here is marly. It is an attractive part of the world with mixed farming. I have always found it somewhat curious why there should be this abrupt change from red to white at the departmental border of the Gironde and the Dordogne, particularly when there are few if any producers in Montravel who can compete with their peers in dry or sweet white in the Monbazillac-Saussignac area.

Montravel Producers of note

CHÂTEAU PUY-SERVAIN/DANIEL HECQUET — GOOD SWEET WINES (PONCHAPT).

CÔTES DE DURAS

Surface Area (1998): 1585 ha.

Production (1998): (Red and rosé) 66,748 hl; (white) 50,729 hl.

Colour: Red, rosé and white.

Grape Varieties: (Red) Cabernet Sauvignon, Cabernet Franc, Malbec and Merlot; (white) Sauvignon Blanc, Sémillon and Muscadelle.

Maximum Yield: (Red and rosé) 55 hl/ha; (dry white) 60 hl/ha; (sweet white) 50 hl/ha.

Minimum Alcohol Level: (Red) 10°; (white and rosé) 10.5°.

The Duras *appellation* lies east of the Entre-Deux-Mers region, south of Sainte-Foy. It is a secluded, peaceful land of gentle hills and mixed farming which only failed to be part of the Bordeaux region as a result of being placed in the *département* of Lot-et-Garonne rather than in the Gironde when the departmental boundaries were drawn up after the Revolution. As far as reputation and the export market are concerned, this is largely dry white wine country, the local varieties, mainly Sauvignon Blanc with some Sémillon and the odd row of Muscadelle, being at home in the essentially limestone soil. Yet, as across the border in the Entre-Deux-Mers, there is an increasing concentration on red wine. The proportions used to be 70:30, white and red respectively in the 1960s but today they are half and half. Growers will point out to you that there are 10 per cent more hours of sunshine than in Bordeaux. Despite this, I find the end results in both colours a bit lean.

Though there are a number of good individual domaines the reputation of Duras rests mainly on the wine produced by the local co-operatives. There are two rival establishments, the Cave at Landerrouat and the Cave Berticot at Duras itself. The latter is certainly a quality-conscious concern, having been a pioneer of modern methods in the *appellation* and the driving force behind the trend towards crisp, fragrant, dry wine produced mainly from Sauvignon Blanc.

The area has been *appellation contrôlée* since as early as 1937, yet is still looking for an identity other than as a cheaper alternative to Bordeaux. Bergerac has managed this, so why not Duras?

Leading Côtes de Duras Producers

DOMAINE AMBLARD

Commune: Saint-Sernin-de-Duras.

Owner: Guy Pauvert.

Surface Area under Vine: 75 ha.

Wines: Côtes de Duras.

Guy Pauvert is gradually handing over responsibility to his son, Fabrice as he heads towards retirement. In the 1960s Amblard was a 15-hectare, polycultural domaine. Today the Pauverts own 52 hectares of vines and lease another 23. As yet no oak is used, and there is one single cuvée of each style which includes a sweet wine and a sparkling wine. A new vinification cellar was built for the 1999 vintage and Fabrice has more ambitious plans. Currently the wines are no more than competent.

CAVE BERTICOT
Commune: Duras.
Members: 130.
Surface Area under Vine: 1000 ha.
Wines: Côtes de Duras including Duc de Berticot, and single-estate Bergerac (Château La Dime and Château Beauchamp).

Drive through Duras, on the way to Sainte-Foy, past the splendid moated, Renaissance-fronted palace of the local dukes and you will soon come to the *cave*. There are some good dry Sauvignon Blancs (Cuvée Première and Cuvée Vieilles Vignes), a delicious but not serious Merlot made by carbonic maceration and the oaky Duc de Berticot red from 70 per cent Cabernet Sauvignon and 30 per cent Merlot.

DOMAINE DE DURAND
Commune: Saint-Jean-de-Duras.
Owner: Michel Fonvielhe.
Surface Area under Vine: 10 ha.
Wines: Côtes de Duras including (red) Cuvée Élevée en Fûts de Chêne, (dry white) Muscadelle, (*moelleux*) and (*liquoreux*) La Dame Saint-Jean.

In the 1970s Michel Fonvielhe's father was one of the first in the *appellation* to start estate-bottling his own wines. Since then the family has built a modern *chais*-cum-shop on the main road, the D708, to attract passing tourists. Michel Fonvielhe's other passion is ballooning – and this he also offers to passers-by. The domaine is farmed biologically. The wines are competent but not great.

DOMAINE DU GRAND-MAYNE
Commune: Villeneuve-de-Duras.
Owner: Andrew Gordon (for Wineshare Ltd)
Surface Area under Vine: 33.5 ha.
Wines: Côtes de Duras, including oaked *cuvées* of Sauvignon and red wine.

Andrew Gordon, a British wine merchant, fulfilled a lifetime's ambition when he acquired the near derelict domaine in 1985. The vineyard has been entirely replanted and then enlarged in 1993. The bulk of the wine goes to Mr Gordon's investors, under the Wineshare agreement. They are good but not brilliant.

CHATEAU LA GRAVE-BÉCHADE
Commune: Baleyssagues.
Owner: Daniel Amar.
Surface Area under Vine: 64 ha.
Wines: Côtes de Duras including (red) Les Hauts, Les Compagnons and Cuvée Abdon Béchade.

Daniel Amar's father, Abdon Béchade, arrived at Château La Grave-Béchade in 1962, on his return from north Africa. At first both white and red wine were made but the Sauvignon Blanc vines are being ripped up and replaced with Cabernet Sauvignon and Merlot. Henceforth the domaine will produce only red wine, which in the case of the top *cuvées* is gently oaky.

★ DOMAINE DE LAULAN
Commune: Duras.
Owner: Gilbert Geoffroy.
Surface Area under Vine: 30 ha.
Wines: Côtes de Duras, including Cuvée Emile Chariot and Cuvée Duc de Laulan.

This is the best address in the neighbourhood, the reason being the insatiable curiosity and determined perfectionism of the jolly, hospitable, bearded Gilbert Geoffroy. Geoffroy arrived in 1974 from the Auxerrois in Burgundy to resurrect a derelict domaine. He has been using newish oak since 1988, experimenting with different sources and toasts, and has tried, but rejected, using the technique of skin contact. He has now invested in a pneumatic press and will try the technique again. The white wines are entirely from Sauvignon Blanc and are excellent, both oaked and non-oaked. I am yet to be convinced about the reds.

CHATEAU LA MOULIÈRE
Commune: Duras.
Owner: Patrick & Francis Blancheton.

Surface Area under Vine: 26 ha.

Wines: Côtes de Duras including _moelleux_.

This is one of the few estates in the area to have a sizeable proportion of Sémillon and Muscadelle as well as Sauvignon Blanc which gives Château La Moulière a wider palette of flavours to play with. In suitable vintages a sweet wine is produced. The dry white and the reds are good, too.

DOMAINE DU VIEUX BOURG

Commune: Pardaillan.

Owner: Bernard Bireaud.

Surface Area under Vine: 30 ha.

Wines: Côtes de Duras (colours) including Cuvée Sainte-Anne and Cuvée Vendange Tardive.

Bernard Bireaud's father bought this domaine in 1952, but there have been Bireauds in the area for seven generations. No oak is used (so far) and the wines are fresh, stylish and fruity. The Bireauds are justifiably proud of their Vendange Tardive wine.

Other Producers of Note

CHÂTEAU BELLEVUE-HAUT-ROC/BRUNO ROSETTO (ESCLOTTES), CHÂTEAU LAFON/PASCAL GITTON (LOUBÈS-BERNAC) AND DOMAINE DES SAVIGNATTES/MAURICE DREUX (ESCLOTTES).

CÔTES DU MARMANDAIS

Surface Area (1998): 1398 ha.

Production (1998): (Red and rosé) 85,994 hl; (white) 3819 hl.

Colour: Red, rosé and white.

Grape Varieties: (Red) Cabernet Sauvignon, Cabernet Franc, Merlot, Malbec, Abouriou, Fer Servadou and Syrah; (white) Sauvignon Blanc, Sémillon and Muscadelle.

Maximum Yield: (Red and rosé) 56 hl/ha; (white) 66 hl/ha.

Minimum Alcohol Level: 10°.

Between Duras and Buzet, marching with the Entre-Deux-Mers but at the eastern limit of the Lot-et-Garonne _département_, lies the _appellation_ of Côtes du Marmandais. Like the Côtes de Duras, this is another area excluded from the Bordeaux region merely by the whim of a Parisian bureaucrat in 1790. In 1990 it was promoted from VDQS to full _appellation contrôlée_.

The _appellation_ straddles both banks of the Garonne and takes its name from Marmande, a busy market town. In the gently rolling countryside, the vine has to share the predominantly marly, gravelly soil with a number of other fruits, and though the delimited area looks large on the map and covers some twenty-seven communes, there are only about 1400 hectares under vine. The grape varieties are chiefly the Bordeaux ones, though interlopers such as Abouriou, Fer Servadou, Gamay and even Syrah are allowed in small amounts. Production is almost exclusively in the hands of two co-operatives. The one at Cocumont on the left bank, where the soil contains more gravel on a sandstone base, enjoys a higher reputation than the one at Beaupuy.

The wines, especially the reds, have more personality than those of the Duras and are quite different from those of Buzet: in part this is because most of the wine is red, but also the gravel in the soil on the south (left) bank of the Garonne is finer than further north. It may also be the judicious use of non-Bordelais grape varieties.

Leading Côtes du Marmandais Producers

CHÂTEAU DE BEAULIEU

Commune: Saint-Saveur-de-Meilhan.

Owners: Robert & Agnès Schulte.

Surface Area under Vine: 28 ha.

Wines: Côtes du Marmandais including Cuvée L'Oratoire.

The Schultes arrived here in 1991, and, with a certain amount of difficulty, extracted themselves from the local co-operative. Their red wines have the great benefit of _not_ being Bordeaux look-alikes. Both _cuvées_ are matured in _barrique_. The classy Cuvée L'Oratoire contains a little less Malbec and a little more Cabernet Franc than the standard wine, the grapes are picked by hand and the wine is matured in new oak.

Cave de Cocumont

Commune: Cocumont.
Members: 150.
Surface Area under Vine: 1100 ha (plus 100 ha of appellation contrôlée Bordeaux).
Wines: Côtes du Marmandais including Beroy and Château Sarrazière.

The Cave de Cocumont is an up-to-date establishment situated on the left bank of the Garonne river, the local terrain being red *graves* mixed with clay, well-drained and with a good sunny aspect. The white wines are produced almost entirely from Sauvignon. Ninety-five per cent of the production, however, is red. The Beroy *cuvée* (from 75 per cent Cabernet Sauvignon) is matured in wood (40 per cent new) and is very good. The Château Sarrazière is also mainly Cabernet Sauvignon and is up to the standard of a good *cru bourgeois* Médoc. The first vintage of this wine was 1995.

Buzet

Surface Area (1998): 1836 ha.
Production (1998): (Red and rosé) 111,297 hl; (white) 4861 hl.
Colour: Red, rosé and white.
Grape Varieties: (Red) Cabernet Sauvignon, Cabernet Franc and Merlot; (white) Sauvignon Blanc, Sémillon and Muscadelle.
Maximum Yield: 55 hl/ha.
Minimum Alcohol Level: (Red and rosé) 10°; (white) 9.5°.

Midway between Agen and Casteljaloux a small tributary approaches the Garonne from the woodlands of the Gers and reaches the river near the town of Buzet. The thriving Buzet *appellation* covers some twenty-seven communes here on the south or left bank of the Garonne. In general the vines are confined to well-exposed sites in the gentle valleys that ripple away from the Garonne but the amount of land under vine is increasing. The soil is varied: gravel, clay and limestone mixed with alluvial soil and stony in parts, becoming more sandy to the west where the vineyard area meets the eastern edges of the Landes forest. It is marly to the south where it overlaps into Armagnac country.

Like Duras, the wines of Buzet suffered from being located outside the Gironde *département*. As Haut Pays wines they had to pay a forfeit to be sent down the river or were even excluded from the Bordeaux wine trade altogether. Unlike Duras this is an area of almost exclusively red wines. *Appellation contrôlée* was awarded in 1973.

Leading Buzet Producers

Les Vignerons de Buzet

Commune: Damazan.
Members: 257.
Surface Area under Vine: 1600 ha .
Wines: Côtes de Buzet including Château de Gueyze, Château La Padère, Marquis du Grez and and Grande Réserve.

Buzet is dominated by its co-operative which is responsible for over 95 per cent of the wine produced in the *appellation*. It was set up in 1955, two years after Buzet was promoted to VDQS and from the start adopted a policy of quality, using the best modern methods, including oak-ageing for the top wines and a severe selection for the *appellation* wine.

Château Sauvagnères

Commune: Sainte-Colombe-en-Bruilhois.
Owners: Bernard & Jacques Thérasse.
Surface Area under Vine: 20 ha.
Wines: Côtes de Buzet.

The rather dilapidated warehouse wherein the wines of Château Sauvagnères are made and matured can be found only with some difficulty. The set-up is rather haphazard, without it seems much interest in barrel-ageing (I counted a grand total of sixteen) or in the very highest quality. The wines are almost entirely red and from 40 per cent Merlot, and 30 per cent each Cabernet Sauvignon and Franc. But I am sure they could make good wine here. The location seems promising.

Other Producers of note
Château du Frandat/Patrice Sterlin (Nérac).

CÔTES DU BRULHOIS

Surface Area (1998): 211 ha.
Production (1998): 10,825 hl.
Colours: Red and rosé.
Grape Varieties: Cabernet Sauvignon, Cabernet Franc, Merlot, Malbec, Tannat and Fer Servadou.
Maximum Yield: 50 hl/ha.
Minimum Alcohol Level: 10°.

Côtes de Brulhois is a relatively recent VDQS, having been elevated from *vin de pays* in 1984. The area adjoins Buzet, and continues south of the Garonne, past Agen, as far as the departmental boundary between Lot-et-Garonne and Tarn-et-Garonne. Production is mainly in the hands of the Goulens-en-Bruilhois co-operative a few kilometres south of Agen in the valley of the Gers. Agen is a centre for plums — and indeed for peaches and table grapes — rather than for wine.

The wines are somewhat unstylish reds or rosés and made from the three Bordeaux varieties plus Fer Servadou, Malbec and Tannat.

VINS DE PAYS

Vin de Pays de La Dordogne
This is the departmental *vin de pays* for the Bergerac region. The wines are mainly dry white, from Sémillon, Sauvignon Blanc, Muscadelle and Ugni Blanc; the reds come from the Bordeaux *encépagement* of Cabernet Franc, Cabernet Sauvignon and Merlot.

Vin de Pays des Landes du Lot-et-Garonne
This *vin de pays* covers the Lot-et-Garonne *département* and the *appellations* of Côtes de Duras and Côtes du Marmandais. The wines are mainly red, from Cabernet Franc, Cabernet Sauvignon, Merlot, Abouriou and Fer Servadou; the whites come from Sémillon, Sauvignon Blanc, Colombard, Gros Manseng and Ugni Blanc.

Vin de Pays de L'Agenais
This zonal *vin de pays* is found at the western end of the Lot-et-Garonne *département*, around the town of Agen. The wines are mainly red, from the same grape varieties as above.

THE HAUT PAYS

CAHORS

Surface Area (1998): 4236 ha.
Production (1998): 248,336 hl.
Colour: Red.
Grape Varieties: Malbec (Auxerrois or Cot) minimum 70%, Merlot, Tannat (both maximum 20%) and Folle Noire (Jurançon Rouge or Dame Noire) maximum 10%.
Maximum Yield: 50 hl/ha.
Minimum Alcohol Level: 10.5°.

A number of the Garonne's tributaries flow due westwards out of the Massif Central. After the river Dordogne the two most important are the Tarn, with its own main tributary the Aveyron, and the Lot. The Lot has its source near the town of Mende in the *département* of Lozère, not far from that of the river Allier, a major tributary of the Loire. It flows through spectacularly wild, empty and beautiful country before reaching the old fortified town of Cahors, capital of the *département* which takes its name from the river. Cahors, in the old French region of Quercy — named after *quercus*, the Latin word for 'oak' — is the Lot's major wine region whose red wine lays claim to be the best and most interesting of all those made in the South-West.

The Cahors *appellation* comprises 4000 hectares in forty-five communes in the cantons of Cahors itself, Catus, Lalbenque, Luzech, Montcuq, and Puy-L'Evêque- and is equidistant (200 kilometres), as the crow flies, from the Atlantic Ocean, the Pyrenees and the Mediterranean. The vineyards are mainly west of Cahors itself, spread on both banks of the weaving, meandering river for about 50 kilometres, the western boundary being near Fumel where the Lot meets the Lot-et-Garonne.

The Cahors climate, though governed by the Atlantic Ocean, and in many respects similar to that of Bordeaux, nevertheless differs in some important respects. Chiefly, and crucial to the quality of the wine, is the incidence of warm, dry wind from the south-east during September and October. While no hotter than Bordeaux – on average Cahors is marginally cooler throughout the year, probably because of the higher altitude – September and October are considerably drier, not only by comparison with Bordeaux but also with Montpellier in the Languedoc. The prevailing westerly rain-bearing clouds appear to pass to the north of the region and the annual rainfall in Aurillac, Brive or Figeac can be as much as three times the 500 or 600 mm of Puy L'Evêque, further south in the middle of the Cahors region. Frost is always a threat, though the region is protected for most of the year from the cold winds issuing from the Massif Central and the river itself often swathes the valley in an insulating blanket of fog.

Just as the more exposed *causse* or limestone plateau is more susceptible to frost than the valley, so it is to hail. Hail appears to be more frequent in the south-east corner of Cahors and steps are in hand for united action by means of helicopters, despatched to seed hail-bearing clouds before they devastate the vineyards.

The Lot has carved a narrow, steep-sided, fertile valley into the dusty, more arid, limestone bedrock of the Quercy region, and the vineyards lie both on the flatter, more alluvial soil of the serpentine valley floor and on the hillsides and plateaux overlooking the river. The soil structure is complex; gravel and quartz mixed with sand and limestone in the valley, limestone debris on the hillsides, and Kimmeridgian soil comprised of limestone rubble, clay and marl on the plateau. Nowhere is the top soil more than a few metres deep at most. Everywhere the base is limestone rock. Parts of the valley are too alluvial for the cultivation of quality wine and have never been included in the *appellation*. The local Comité Interprofessionel, now that the Cahors *vignoble* has been re-established, wants more vineyards in the richer soil of the valley to be declassified.

Historically Cahors has been an important vineyard area for a long time. Indeed, it was flourishing in Gallo-Roman times, even before Bordeaux became established as a major wine region and the wines of the Haut Pays were shipped through the port of Bordeaux. The region was producing the equivalent of 1.4 million hectolitres in the Middle Ages, and in 1816, according to the author André Jullien, there were more vineyards in the Lot (40,000 hectares) than in the Pyrénées-Orientales, the Aude or the Bouches-du-Rhône. This was the era of the fabled 'black wine' of Cahors. It was made by concentrating part of the must and lightly fortifying it with grape spirit. It was able to last for up to thirty years in wood, or fifty in bottle. It was a wine for blending to bolster up the thinner wines of Bordeaux.

From the phylloxera epidemic onwards, however, Cahors went into decline. 'Direct producers' (hybrids between *Vitis Vinifera* and a phylloxera-resistant species of vine) replaced the noble vines, and the area under plantation disappeared almost completely. What could have been the final straw was the terrible February frost of 1956 and in 1958 the whole of Cahors produced barely 650 hogsheads of wine (less than 200,000 bottles).

The renaissance of the Cahors vineyard since then has been impressive. The area under vine has risen from 200 hectares in 1960 to over 4000 today and is currently increasing by an average of 150 hectares per annum. Production now comfortably tops 200,000 hectolitres – a pittance perhaps compared with the Middle Ages but we are talking now about *appellation contrôlée* wine, analysed, blind-tasted and approved by the local office of the INAO. Currently the region produces 4 per cent of France's total of *appellation contrôlée* wine.

The resurgence of Cahors has been two-edged. On the one hand there were the co-operatives, on the other the indomitable spirit of the late Jean Jouffreau at the Clos de Gamot (see page 504), one of the few growers who had soldiered on through the depression. Jouffreau was a traditionalist and a perfectionist. Clos de Gamot had been in his family since 1610; and when he saw the area beginning to revive he set out to encourage other growers to remain independent of the co-operatives and to aspire to the quality end of the market.

The Côtes d'Olt co-operative ('Olt' is an old form of 'Lot') at Parnac was established in 1947. Approximately half the region's 600 or so growers are members of the co-operative. It has a research station and experimental vineyards, and has been in the forefront of developing disease-resistant and more prolific strains of the vine by clonal selection, establishing the most suitable root-stocks for each variety and soil type, and introducing and promoting *cépages améliorateurs* such as Merlot and Tannat to complement the *appellation*'s indigenous quality variety, Auxerrois.

As the vineyards have expanded, so has the quality of the wine improved and the aspirations of those who make it. Cahors was one of the original VDQS *appellations* created in 1949, and was then elevated to *appellation contrôlée* in 1971.

The principal grape in Cahors is known locally in the Quercy as Auxerrois. This is the Cot of the Loire Valley and the same as the Gironde's Malbec, Pressac or 'Cahors'. Why it should be called Auxerrois here – for as far as I can find out it has no connection with Auxerre near Chablis – history and legend do not relate, though legend has it that it is derived or even directly descended from the Latin vine Aminée from which was made the famous Falernian wines of the ancients. Auxerrois forms a loose cluster of sizeable berries, is prone to downy mildew and rot – and particularly *coulure* – and produces a satisfactory quantity of sturdy, well-coloured, quite tannic wine. Auxerrois must make up 70 per cent of the Cahors blend. It is planted particularly on the slopes where *coulure* is less prevalent as the humidity is lower, and where there is less danger, as the soil is more meagre, of too vigorous a yield.

The secondary varieties stipulated in the original *appellation contrôlée* legislation included a number which have since been banned: Valdiguié or Gros Auxerrois, Abouriou or Gamay du Rhône, Syrah and Négrette (the Côtes du Frontonnais grape). Since 1979 only three subsidiary varieties have been permitted: Jurançon, Merlot and Tannat. Jurançon Rouge (also known as the Folle Noire, and here in the Quercy as the Dame Noire) is a variety which has nothing to do with the wine called Jurançon, which is white and made from Gros and Petit Manseng. Jurançon Rouge forms a tight cluster, and for this reason, and because of its thin skin, it tends to rot in

wet and humid weather, so it is little grown on the valley floor. It is better on the stony slopes away from the river. It produces well and regularly but the wine is light and forward and tends to attenuate rapidly. Acreage is decreasing and is estimated today to be less than 5 per cent of the *appellation*.

Merlot is a relative newcomer to Cahors. As in Bordeaux the wine it produces is rich and alcoholic, soft and aromatic in character and matures quickly, though by no means as fast as the Dame Noire. It is planted on the richer soils. The third subsidiary variety is Tannat, the main grape of Madiran and other red wines of the Béarn and Pays Basque. Though, from the ampelographical point of view, a distant cousin of Auxerrois, Tannat has a more compact bunch and the wine it produces is less alcoholic than that from Auxerrois and Merlot. The wine is tough, tannic and astringent and when young gives the Cahors blend muscle and stuffing, and, because of its good but not high level of acidity, longevity. Tannat ripens last of all, often not entirely successfully.

All these vines are trained and pruned to the *taille* Guyot, both single and double, though here and there in the vineyards some *gobelet* (bush-shaped) old vines can be seen. There is increasing use of machine-harvesting (in some vineyards 4 hectares a day can be covered) which means the vines must be planted further apart and trained higher off the ground. First of all, the vines are pruned to eight or ten buds per cane, i.e. up to a maximum of twenty per vine, but this number, particularly rigorously in the best properties, is pruned back once the danger of frost has passed.

Cahors no longer produces the fabled black wine of yesteryear (must concentration is now forbidden) and is sometimes – from a valley vineyard and at the basic level of the *appellation* – rather on the weak side. This is a result of the extensive vineyard enlargement since the early 1960s – much originally in the valley rather than on the hillsides. Moreover, a lot of the generic Cahors of the 1970s – and still today – was never matured in wood so lacked density and staying power. In good years such as 1982, 1990 and 1995 the wine was acceptable, but in other years when there was not enough sunshine during the late summer, or rain during the vintage, such as 1992 and 1993, it was thin and insipid. It did the reputation of the *appellation* an injustice.

Better, indeed a totally different animal, is the sort of Cahors obtainable as a *négociant*'s 'Réserve' wine, one that has been matured using new oak, provided it is not kept in wood excessively long. Traditionally Cahors was aged in large wooden *foudres* or vats and, somewhat in the Italian or Spanish manner, was left there until mature. A few growers still use this method, believing that more Bordeaux methods using new *barriques* are foreign to the true character of Cahors and that keeping a wine in wood does not necessarily dry it out or lose all its fruit. Today, inevitably, the trend has changed towards barrel-ageing and to bottling before the wines are ready, though growers are still shy of using too much new wood. Most of the best properties use a combination of *barrique* and *foudre*, secondhand casks from Bordeaux being preferred to new wood.

The best Cahors are the single-vineyard or domaine wines, often from long-established estates, and from vines planted on the hillsides or the *causse*, though the wines from the *causse* tend to lose in style what they gain in robustness. These wines give one an idea of the 'manly' wines produced in pre-phylloxera times.

Just because Auxerrois is one of the grape varieties used in the lesser, eastern regions of Bordeaux does not mean to say that there is any resemblance with the loose-knit wines of the Saint-Emilion satellites. Cahors is, or should be, a solid wine: and a Cahors from the *causse* is as solid by comparison with a wine from the valley.

A solid Cahors wine is strong, baked, full-bodied, rich and sturdy, yet not without warmth and even elegance if allowed to mature and to round off the muscle and density of the wine in its youth. It lasts well, often being not at its best before seven or ten years, and will keep another decade thereafter. This is the sort of Cahors which is worth pursuing and cellaring.

Leading Cahors Producers

CLOS CARREYRÈS
Commune: Vire-sur-Lot.
Owner: M. and Mme Edmond Hartmann.

Surface Area under Vine: 8 ha.
Wines: Cahors.

This is a small estate (until recently with only 5 hectares) run by Monsieur and Madame Edmond Hartmann and their son-in-law, Thierry Dulac. Their Cahors is made from 90 per cent Auxerrois and 10 per cent Tannat and it needs time to mature. The 1995 is very good indeed. Merlot is used in lesser *cuvées*.

★ CHÂTEAU DU CÈDRE
Commune: Vire-sur-Lot.
Owners: Pascal and Jean-Marc Verhaeghe.
Surface Area under Vine: 25 ha.
Wines: Cahors including Cuvée Le Prestige and Cuvée Le Cèdre.

Much has happened for the better at this leading domaine since the Verhaeghe brothers took over from their parents in 1987. Yields have been significantly reduced. Though the grapes are still partly mechanically harvested, they are sorted on arrival in the winery, *pigeage* and *microbillage* have been introduced, and the malolactic fermentation takes place in wood (one-third of which is new) for the Prestige *cuvée* (90 per cent Auxerrois and 10 per cent Tannat). In 1996 the Verhaeghes introduced Le Cèdre, a 100 per cent Auxerrois wine from very old vines and made with 100 per cent new wood. It is an impressive wine.

CHÂTEAU DE CHAMBERT
Commune: Floressas.
Owner: Joël Delgoulet.
Surface Area under Vine: 60 ha.
Wines: Cahors.

This is a large estate, worked biologically, up in the hills south of Puy-L'Evêque. Marc Delgoulet has retired and his son Joël, assisted by oenologist Vincent Neuville, is now in charge. For reasons of limited storage, the domaine has traditionally bottled its wines later than most (bottles take up more space than wine stored in bulk), but a new cellar was constructed in 1999. I hope this will help give the wine a bit more personality, something it presently lacks. Les Hauts de Chambert and La Tour Chambert are second wines. The *négociants* Menjucq, who are shareholders, distribute the wine.

THE HAUT PAYS

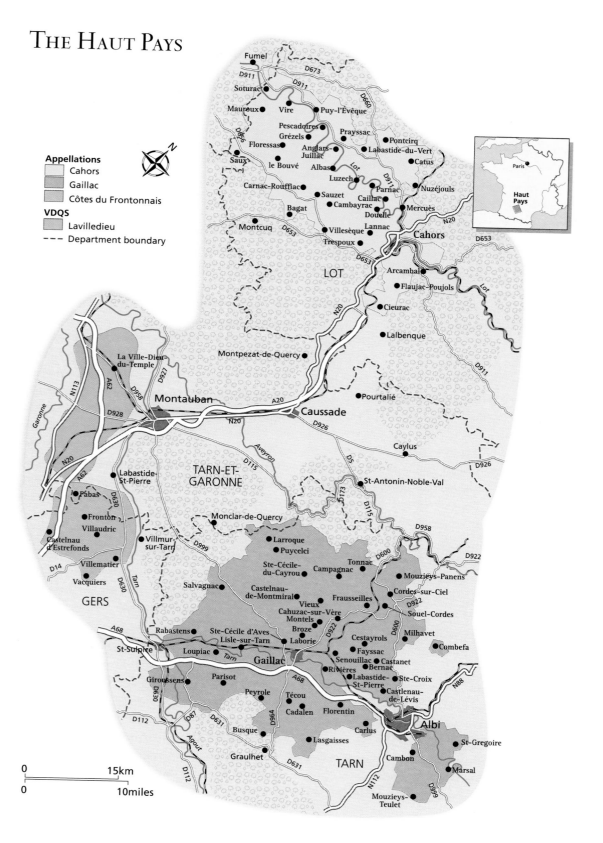

Appellations
- Cahors
- Gaillac
- Côtes du Frontonnais

VDQS
- Lavilledieu
- - - - Department boundary

Fumel

Soturac

Mauroux   Vire   Puy-l'Évêque

Pescadoires   Prayssac
Grézels
Floressas   Anglars-   Pontcirq
Juillac   Labastide-du-Vert
Saux   le Bouvé   Catus
Albas   Luzech
Carnac-Rouffiac   Parnac   Nuzéjouls
Sauzet   Caillac
Bagat   Cambayrac   Mercuès
Douelle
Montcuq   Villesèque   Lannac
Trespoux   Cahors

LOT

Arcambal
Flaujac-Poujols

Cieurac

Lalbenque

La Ville-Dieu-
du-Temple   Montpezat-de-Quercy

Montauban   Pourtalié

Caussade

**TARN-ET-
GARONNE**   Caylus

Labastide-   St-Antonin-Noble-Val
St-Pierre
Pàbas
Fronton   Monclar-de-Quercy
Villaudric
Castelnau   Villmur-   Larroque
d'Estrefonds   sur-Tarn   Puycelci
Villematier   Ste-Cécile-   Tonnac   Mouzieys-Panens
du-Cayrou   Campagnac
Vacquiers   Salvagnac   Cordes-sur-Ciel
Castelnau-   Frausseilles   Souel-Cordes
GERS   de-Montmiral
Vieux   Milhavet
Cahuzac-sur-Vère
Montels   Combefa
Rabastens   Ste-Cécile d'Aves   Broze
Lisle-sur-Tarn   Laborie   Cestayrols
St-Sulpice   Loupiac   Fayssac
Giroussens   Parisot   **Gaillac**   Senouillac   Castanet
Rivières   Bernac
Peyrole   Labastide-   Ste-Croix
Técou   St-Pierre
Cadalen   Florentin   Castelnau-
de-Lévis
Busque   Carlus   **Albi**
Lasgaisses   St-Gregoire
Graulhet   Cambon
Marsal
TARN
Mouzieys-
Teulet

Paris

Haut
Pays

0 ____ 15km

0 ____ 10miles

LES COTES D'OLT

Commune: Parnac.
Members: 300.
Surface Area under Vine: 1100 ha.
Wines: Cahors including Comte André de Monpezat, Impérial, Château Les Bouysses and Château Beauvillain-Monpezat.

The co-operative Les Côtes d'Olt was founded in 1947. It represents some 60 per cent of the local growers and produces about one-third of *appellation contrôlée* Cahors. Much of this, inevitably, is fairly standard stuff, but there are a number of commendable superior *cuvées*: Comte André de Monpezat, Impérial (100 per cent Auxerrois and aged in new barrels for twelve months), Château Les Bouysses and Château Beauvillain-Monpezat. My vote goes to the Bouysses.

★ CLOS LA COUTALE

Commune: Vire-sur-Lot.
Owners: Jean Valmy and Philippe Bernède.
Surface Area under Vine: 54 ha.
Wines: Cahors.

Clos La Coutale has been a leading Cahors estate for a long time, the Aymard family (from whom the Bernèdes are directly descended) winning a prize for their wine in 1895. The vineyard surrounds the winery, the soils being limestone scree at the upper levels, gravel lower down, and the grapes are mechanically harvested, which is rare among the very top estates here. Fermentation takes place in temperature-controlled, stainless steel vats, after which the wine is matured for a year in cask, 20 per cent of which is new. These are elegant, succulent wines, and yet nicely substantial. They keep well.

CHÂTEAU EUGÉNIE

Commune: Albas.
Owners: Jean and Claude Couture.
Surface Area under Vine: 30 ha.
Wines: Cahors including Cuvée des Tsars.

The Couture brothers produce rich, meaty wines from their domaine whose vineyards lie one-third each in the valley, on the gravel terraces above and on the *causses*. The vines are planted in the ration of 80 per cent Auxerrois, 14 per cent Merlot and 6 per cent Tannat. The wines are bottled after twelve to eighteen months in barrel. The elegant Cuvée des Tsars, commemorating sales to the Russian court from a vineyard now owned by the Coutures, comes from twenty-five-year-old vines on the *terrasses*. Domaine Boissor, next door, is a centre for the handicapped and co-owned by the Coutures.

★ CLOS DE GAMOT
CHÂTEAU DU CAYROU

Commune: Prayssac.
Owner: Yves Hermann.
Surface Area under Vine: 10 ha (Clos de Gamot) and 30 ha (Château du Cayrou).
Wines: Cahors including Cuvée des Centenaires (Clos de Gamot).

Clos de Gamot and its late owner Jean Jouffreau, who died in 1997, have a special place in the history of Cahors. Despite the slump and neglect, Jouffreau carried on, convinced that Cahors had a place in the world market. In the early 1970s he offered some old Cahors wines for sale at Christies, not just to raise capital to purchase Château du Cayrou, but also to generate publicity for Cahors. Clos de Gamou is pure Auxerrois and in good years there is a special *cuvée* from 100-year-old vines. Château du Cayrou was planted in 1971 on more gravelly soil (73 per cent Cot, 20 per cent Merlot, 7 per cent Tannat). Harvesting of both vineyards is by hand, the maceration long and there is no *barrique*-ageing, fining or filtration. These are old-fashioned wines that need time. They can be mightily impressive and last for up to twenty years in the best vintages.

CHÂTEAU DE GAUDOU

Commune: Vire-sur-Lot.
Owner: René Durou.
Surface Area under Vine: 30 ha.
Wines: Cahors including Tradition, Cuvée Prestige and Cuvée Renaissance.

There are three wines, full, generous but sometimes a little four-square, from respectively 80 per cent, 85 per cent and 100 per cent Auxerrois and an increasing amount of new wood. The château is most attractive.

CHÂTEAU GAUTOUL

Commune: Puy-L'Evêque.

Owner: Eric Swenden.

Surface Area under Vine: 30 ha.

Wines: Cahors including Le Chatenet.

The celebrated chef, Alain Senderens, used to be the proprietor here. He sold to a Belgian named Swenden in 1998 but continues as a consultant. The wine is made from 85 per cent Auxerrois, 10 per cent Merlot and 5 per cent Tannat. This is a modern set-up, currently being re-organised. The 1995 Château Gautoul is very good indeed. Le Chatenet is a *tête de cuvée* released later and for laying down for seven to eight years.

CHÂTEAU LES IFS

Commune: Pescadoires.

Owners: EARL de La Laurière, Buri & Fils.

Surface Area under Vine: 10 ha.

Wines: Cahors including Cuvée Prestige.

Resurrected by Jean-Paul Buri, who died in 1996, and still with fairly young vines (80 per cent Auxerrois, 20 per cent Merlot) this domaine can produce very good ample, stylish wine. The fermentation is thermo-regulated and there is automatic *pigeage*. Worth watching.

★ CHÂTEAU DE LAGREZETTE

Commune: Caillac.

Owners: Alain-Dominique Perrin.

Surface Area under Vine: 65 ha.

Wines: Cahors including Cuvée Dame Honneur.

Lagrezette is an impressive, restored, medieval château lying up in a little valley north of the river Lot. This is the source of one of the best Cahors. Nearby, built into the side of a slope underneath part of the vineyard, is an impressive, three-storey underground cellar, working by gravity. Michel Rolland, the wine guru from Pomerol, is a consultant.

Harvesting for the *grand vin*, the Dame d'Honneur and superior *cuvées* (the second wine is called Chevalier Lagrezette) is by hand. There is a *table de tri* for sorting the grapes, controlled fermentation at 30°C, and one-third new wood for all but the second wines. These are nicely substantial, but nevertheless sophisticated wines.

★ CHATEAU LAMARTINE

Commune: Soturac.

Owner: Alain Gayraud.

Surface Area under Vine: 30 ha.

Wines: Cahors including Cuvée Particulaire and Cuvée Expression.

This is a leading Cahors estate as well as being one of the oldest. Alain Gayraud's grandfather was instrumental in getting Cahors established as a VDQS in 1949 and he was estate-bottling his wines even then. At the western end of Cahors, the domaine enjoys a warmer climate than most and harvests ten to fifteen days in advance of estates, say, at Parnac. The top *cuvées* use both micro-oxygenation and *délestage*, as well as plenty of new oak to bring out all the fruit. I find the results excellent.

DOMAINE DU PEYRIÉ

Commune: Soturac.

Owners: Christian and Pascal Gilis.

Surface Area under Vine: 16 ha.

Wines: Cahors.

The bearded Christian Gilis and his brother Pascal produce their Cahors from 90 per cent Auxerrois, 7 per cent Tannat and 3 per cent Merlot. The wine is vinified and matured in concrete vats. These are good, fullish, round and ample wines.

★ DOMAINE PINERAIE

Commune: Puy-L'Evêque.

Owner: Jean-Louis Burc.

Surface Area under Vine: 37 ha.

Wines: Cahors including Château Pineraie and L'Authentique.

The blend for the château wine is 85 per cent Auxerrois, 15 per cent Merlot; for the Authentique *cuvée* 95:5 per cent and from older vines. The wines are matured in oak, 30 per cent of which is new for the Authentique. These are wines with most impressive, elegant fruit; rich and substantial without being too sturdy. A fine source.

CLOS RESSÉGUIER

Commune: Sauzet.

Owner: Jean-Claude Rességuier.

Surface Area under Vine: 13.5 ha.
Wines: Cahors including Cuvée Vieillie en Fûts de Chêne.

Sauzet lies up on the plateau, and in total contrast to the predominantly limestone soils here, the Clos is a rich, deep, clayey hollow, planted with 75 per cent Auxerrois, 20 per cent Merlot and 5 per cent Tannat. The Rességuiers have farmed this parcel for over four generations. These are good wines, the oaky *cuvée* having the same origin as the basic wine. In 1998, after trials in 1997, *délestage* was used for the first time on all the wines.

CHÂTEAU LES RIGALETS
Commune: Prayssac.
Owners: André and Jean-Luc Bouloumié.
Surface Area under Vine: 25 ha.
Wines: Cahors including Cuvée Prestige and Cuvée Quintessence.

Situated next to the Clos de Gamot on the Prayssac peninsular, Château Les Rigalets is planted 80 per cent Auxerrois, 15 per cent Merlot and 5 per cent Tannat. The Prestige and Quintessence *cuvées* come from better sited parcels and older vines, and are oak-aged (100 per cent new wood for the Quintessence). There are progressive bottlings of the basic and Prestige *cuvées*, as and when sales necessitate. I would rather they bottled the entire crop in one go.

★ DOMAINE DES SAVARINES
Commune: Trespoux.
Owners: Danielle Biesbrouck-Borde.
Surface Area under Vine: 4 ha.
Wines: Cahors.

Up on the plateau in a wild and forgotten part of Cahors, Domaine des Savarines is hard to find. The vines are farmed biodynamically. There is newish rather than new wood here, and the wines, from 70 per cent Auxerrois and 30 per cent Merlot, are lovingly hand crafted and very delicious. They need time to mature.

★ CLOS TRIGUEDINA
Commune: Puy-L'Evêque.
Owner: Jean-Luc Baldès.

Surface Area under Vine: 60 ha.
Wines: Cahors including Cuvée Prince Probus.

There have been seven generations at this splendid estate since Etienne Baldès first planted vines in the area in 1830. Jean Baldès, father of Jean-Luc, created the first prestige Cahors *cuvée*, Prince Probus, in 1976, and doubled the size of the estate. This wine comes from 100 per cent Auxerrois, old vines and new oak, and is still one of Cahors' finest examples. Clos Triguedina (75 per cent Auxerrois, 20 per cent Merlot, 5 per cent Tannat) reared in a mixture of *foudres* and barrels is full, rich and satisfying, too. Domaine Labrande is the second label for the younger vines.

GEORGES VIGOUROUX
CHÂTEAU DE MERCUES
CHÂTEAU DE HAUTE-SERRE
Commune: Cahors.
Owners: Georges and Bertrand-Gabriel Vigouroux.
Surface Area under Vine: 106 ha (Château de Mercues 40 ha; Château Haute-Serre 66 ha).
Wines: Cahors including Château de Mercues, Château de Haute-Serre and others.

The Vigouroux family have been in the wine business since 1861, but Georges Vigouroux has transformed it into a large organisation.

In 1971 he planted Château de Haute-Serre, derelict since phylloxera. The acquisition of Château de Mercues followed in 1983 and since then a joint venture has been established with the Monpezat family (Château Leret-Monpezat) and an agreement with HRH Prince Henrik of Denmark to sell the latter's Château de Caix.

More recently the Vigouroux family have leased Château Pech de Jammet and set up a large wine shop called L'Atruim on the outskirts of Cahors, which sells wines from throughout the South-West, including Bertrand-Gabriel Vigouroux's Buzet estate, Château Tournelles. The wines, however, lack soul and are no more then competent.

Other Producers of note
CHÂTEAU LA CAMINADE/RESSES & FILS (PARNAC), DOMAINE GÉRARD DECAS (LANNAC), CHÂTEAU DIDIER-PARNAC/

RIGAL & FILS (PARNAC), CHÂTEAU LATUC/COLIN AND
PENNY DUNS (LABORIE) AND DOMAINE DE PAILLAS/SCEA
DE ROBERT (FLORESSAS).

COTEAUX DE QUERCY

Colour: Red and rosé.
Grape Varieties: (Red and rosé) Auxerrois,
Tannat, Cabernet Sauvignon, Cabernet Franc,
Merlot, Jurançon Rouge and Gamay.
Maximum Yield: 50 hl/ha.
Minimum Alcohol Level: 11°.

This area lies between the Aveyron and the Lot south of
Cahors and includes the Cahors *appellation*. In 1999 it was
promoted from *vin de pays* to VDQS. The wines are almost
entirely red, and from the usual Cahors grape varieties
plus a few others. The co-operatives at La Ville Dieu and
Montpezat are important sources, as is the *négociant*
Georges Vigouroux on the outskirts of Cahors. I have
yet to sample it.

CÔTES DU FRONTONNAIS

Surface Area (1998): 2054 ha.
Production (1998): 116,661 hl.
Colour: Red and rosé.
Grape Varieties: Négrette, plus (between 30 and
50%) Cabernet Franc, Cabernet Sauvignon
(maximum 20% together or combined), Syrah,
Gamay and Tannat.
Maximum Yield: 50 hl/ha.
Minimum Alcohol Level: 10.5°.

Halfway between Montauban and Toulouse, on a predominantly gravel plateau between the rivers Tarn and
Garonne, is the up-and-coming Côtes du Frontonnais
appellation which was created out of two local VDQS *appellations* in 1975. The *appellation* covers the wines of both the
Fronton and neighbouring Villaudric areas and the label
will denote one or the other in a suffix. The fourteen
Fronton communes lie to the north and west of the six
in Villaudric.

The combined area contains two distinct soil types.
First, there is weathered sand and clay, very pebbly, a
rather nondescript grey in character. Second, a dirty
pinkish, crumbly stone, rich in iron and quartz. There
are some particularly good gravels near to the *autoroute*,
west of the town of Fronton. On the other side, nearer
to the Tarn, the soil is heavier, marginally less well-
drained. At Villaudric the soil is particularly poor and
very stony, the size of these boulders being akin to those
at Châteauneuf-du-Pape.

There was a time when the towns of Fronton and Villaudric were deadly enemies. During the Wars of
Religion in the sixteenth century Fronton was
destroyed, though Villaudric spared. During the siege
of Montauban, Louis XIII had his headquarters in one,
and his minister Richelieu in the other and they used to
send each other complimentary hogsheads of wine.
With the expansion of Toulouse in the nineteenth century the wines of neighbouring Fronton enjoyed a
boom, and after the restrictions imposed by the Bordelais on Haut Pays wines were lifted, they began to be
exported abroad. The arrival of phylloxera, though,
dealt a deadly blow. The traditional local grape, the
Négrette, took badly to its grafted rootstocks, and the
region went into decline. Revival began after the Second
World War. A Fronton co-operative was started up in
1947, followed by one at Villaudric two years later – this
has since been shut down and its activities transferred to
the one at Fronton. It is really only since the arrival of
appellation contrôlée that anyone outside the region has
begun to take notice of these wines.

Fronton is based on the Négrette grape, a variety little seen elsewhere. Négrette gives a wine which is
abundant in aroma but meagre in tannin and low in
acidity. Despite the legislation there are some red Fron-
tons (and more rosés) which are 100 per cent Négrette. It
produces a delicious *primeur*-style wine with a mouthfeel
a little like Beaujolais. Correctly vinified, the wine is an
abundantly fruity, supple, aromatic wine without a
great deal of tannin. It is bottled early and is intended for
drinking cool within eighteen months of bottling. Fronton does not age gracefully – there are other wines for
this purpose.

Leading Côtes du Frontonnais Producers

★ Château Bellevue-La-Forêt

Commune: Fronton.

Owner: Patrick Germain.

Surface Area under Vine: 112 ha.

Wines: Fronton (red and rosé) including Ce Vin, Cuvée d'Or, La Sélection and Prestige.

Bellevue-La-Forêt lies on a splendid gravel mound over-looking the *autoroute*, and has been one of the *appellation*'s leading domaines since being bought by Patrick Germain in 1974. It claims to be the largest estate in one block (*d'un seul tenant*) in the South-West. The lesser wines (Ce Vin is 100 per cent Négrette) do not use any wood. La Sélection (30 per cent Négrette, 10 per cent Syrah, 20 per cent Cabernet Franc and 40 per cent Cabernet Sauvignon) has six months' barrel-ageing. Prestige (10 per cent Négrette, 15 per cent Syrah, 25 per cent Cabernet Franc and 50 per cent Cabernet Sauvignon) spends one year in wood. This particular wine can be kept. A fine range and the basic château *cuvée* (50 per cent Négrette) is exemplary.

★ Château Baudare

Commune: Labastide-Saint-Pierre.

Owner: Claude Vigouroux.

Surface Area under Vine: 35 ha.

Wines: Fronton including Cuvée Tradition, Cuvée Aristide and Cuvée Prestige Élevée en Fûts de Chêne, and Vin de Pays du Comté Tolosan.

The young Claude Vigouroux produces very good wines. His office is in his house, a simple bungalow surrounded by vines. The cellar is in the nearby village of Campsas. The Tradition and the Cuvée Aristide wines both contain 50 per cent Négrette, 30 per cent Cabernet Sauvignon and 20 per cent Cabernet Franc: the difference being older vines and a light oak-ageing for the Aristide. The Cuvée Prestige, from 50 per cent Négrette, 40 per cent Cabernet Sauvignon and 10 per cent Tannat, spends fourteen months in new wood and is not bottled until three years old. The *vins de pays*, reds, whites and a rosé, are good too.

Château Cahuzac

Commune: Fabas.

Owner: Claude Ferran.

Surface Area under Vine: 57 ha.

Wines: Fronton including Cuvée Tradition, Cuvée Authentique and Fleuron de Guillaume.

Ten generations of Ferrans have succeeded each other as *vignerons* here. The vines were first planted in 1766. The Ferrans started domaine-bottling in 1978. The Fleuron de Guillaume is matured in new wood for six months. This is an up-to-date set up producing good wines.

Domaine de Callory

Commune: Labastide-Saint-Pierre.

Owner: Guy Pérez.

Surface Area under Vine: 27 ha.

Wines: Fronton and Vin de Pays du Comté Tolosan.

Georges Pérez, who runs de Callory today, inherited the property from his wife's family. It was her father who first started domaine-bottling in the 1970s. The basic *cuvée* is the non-vintage called Saveurs. The domaine wine is made from 40 per cent Négrette, 30 per cent Cabernet Sauvignon and 30 per cent Syrah, matured, as yet, in bulk. This is a good wine which lasts well.

Chateau La Colombière

Commune: Villaudric.

Owner: Baron François de Driesen.

Surface Area under Vine: 25 ha.

Wines: Fronton including Réserve du Baron and Cuvée Baron de D.

Baron de Driesen bought Château La Colombière in 1984 and is one of the few growers in the *appellation* who ferments both his Négrette and his Gamay by carbonic maceration. This produces wines for early drinking. Even the old-vine Baron de D is fully ready after a year.

Château Ferran
Château Montauriol

Commune: Fronton.

Owner: Nicolas Gélis.

Surface Area under Vine: 35 ha (Château Montauriol); 25 ha (Château Ferran).

Wines: Fronton including Mons Aureolos (Château Montauriol).

Having bought and rescued the derelict Château Ferran in 1994, Nicolas Gélis acquired Montauriol (potentially rather larger than a mere 35 hectares of vines) at Villematier in 1998. There is currently one red wine *cuvée* of Ferran, which is unoaked. The two Montauriols have more structure than the Ferran. The Mons Aureolos spends a year in wood and is rich and profound.

Château Joliet

Commune: Fronton.
Owner: François Daubert.
Surface Area under Vine: 19 ha.
Wines: Fronton including Cuvée Négrette and Cuvée Élevée en Fûts de Chêne, Vin de Pays du Comté Tolosan, Dernière Cueillette de Mauzac.

Hitherto suspicious of maturing Négrette in wood François Daubert produced his first oaky *cuvée* in 1997 and very good it is. The late-harvest, sweet Mauzac, Dernière Cueillette is also oak-aged. A good domaine.

Château Plaisance

Commune: Vacquiers.
Owner: Marc Pénévayre.
Surface Area under Vine: 20 ha.
Wines: Fronton including Cuvée Thibaut.

Like most Frontonnais growers, Marc Pénévayre picks his grapes by machine, but unlike some, he does not destem them. The result is a fairly sturdy wine. The oaky Cuvée Thibaut is named after Marc's young son.

★ Château Le Roc

Commune: Fronton.
Owner: Frédéric Ribes.
Surface Area under Vine: 18 ha.
Wines: Fronton including Cuvée Réservée and Cuvée Don Quichotte.

Frédéric's father and uncle slowly removed themselves from the co-operative, and from 1988 the domaine has been completely independent. It is now one of Fronton's best. The Cuvée Réservée comes from specially selected parcels of vines (50 per cent Négrette, 25 per cent each

Syrah and Cabernet Sauvignon), spends a year in oak, and has excellent depth and dimension. Don Quichotte was first made in 1999, from 50 per cent each Négrette and Syrah, and using *pigeage*. Both wines last very well.

Other Producers of Note

Domaine Caze/M. Rougevin-Baville (Villaudric), Château Flotis/Küntz family (Castelnau d' Estrefonds), Château La Palme/Martine Ethuin (Villemur-sur-Tarn), Château Peyreaux/Vovette Linant de Bellefonds (Villematier); plus the co-operative at Fronton offers some single-estate wines.

Lavilledieu

Surface Area (1998): 170 ha.
Production (1998): 2278 hl.
Colour: Red and rosé.
Grape Varieties: Négrette, Gamay, Syrah, Cabernet Franc and Tannat.
Maximum Yield: 45 hl/ha.
Minimum Alcohol Level: 10.5°.

North-east of Fronton on the other side of the Toulouse-Montauban *autoroute*, the A20, is an obscure VDQS which seems to have but one source of supply: the local co-operative. The *appellation* is Lavilledieu (one word), covering thirteen communes surrounding the town of La Ville Dieu (three words) du Temple. VDQS was conferred in 1947 and the Cave Co-operative opened in 1949. Its basic Lavilledieu wine is made from 10 per cent Négrette, 25 per cent each of Gamay, Syrah and Cabernet Franc, plus 15 per cent of Tannat, and comes both in an unoaked version and an oaked one (Cuvée des Capitouls). The co-operative also produces *vins de pays*. Across the board standards could be better.

Gaillac

Surface Area (1998): 2260 ha.
Production (1998): (Red and rosé) 118,207 hl;
(white) 45,131 hl.
Colour: Red, rosé and white.

Grape Varieties: (Red) Duras, Fer Servadou
(Braucol), Gamay, Syrah (these four must provide
60% of the total, but after 2000 the 60% must come
from the first three), Cabernet Sauvignon,
Cabernet Franc and Merlot; (white) Mauzac,
Len de L'El, Muscadelle, Sémillon, L'Ondenc
and Sauvignon Blanc.
Maximum Yield: (Red and rosé) 55 hl/ha; (white
and sparkling) 60 hl/ha; (sweeter whites) 45 hl/ha;
Gaillac Premières Côtes: 45 hl/ha.
Minimum Alcohol Level: (Red and rosé): 10.5°;
(white and sparkling) 10°; (sweeter whites) 11°;
Gaillac Premières Côtes: 11°.

Until the phylloxera epidemic at the end of the nineteenth century Gaillac was one of the largest vineyard
areas in France. It is also one of the oldest. From the
Roman settlements on the coast near Narbonne, only
some 120 kilometres away, the vine made its way up the
Aude Valley and across the mountains to the Tarn, finding rich agricultural land near the ancient city of Albi.

Geographically, despite the proximity to the
Mediterranean, this is the extreme south-east of the
Aquitaine basin. The land is protected from the north,
east and south by the *causses* and the Montagne Noire,
but open to the west, in the direction of the flow of the
river, and the climate is more Atlantic than Mediterranean. As in Cahors winters and springs can be cool
and wet, with an ever-present danger of frost. Come the
summer one can sense the nearby presence of the Midi.
It is hot and dry, and autumns are long and sweet.

The rose-brick city of Albi is one of France's loveliest
and the western gateway to the spectacular Gorges du
Tarn. By the time the river Tarn has reached Albi, it
flows through an undulating landscape of cereals, fruit
and vegetables. Other crops such as saffron, anise, mad-
der and hemp are also cultivated as well as the vine.

In 1852 the Gaillac region produced 12,500 hectolitres
of white wine and no less than 4.48 million hectolitres
of red. There must have been 150,000 hectares under
vine at the very least. Today the AC production can
reach 150,000 hectolitres in a good year (of which 60 per
cent approximately is red), denoting a surface area of

2200 hectares, though there is additional land given over
to a very acceptable Vin de Pays des Côtes du Tarn,
which produces approximately 125,000 hectolitres of
wine. The vineyards extend over seventy-eight communes west of Albi, an area which reaches as far north as
Cordes and downstream to beyond Rabastens.

Gaillac comes in a mixture of styles and colours and
from a wide palette of grape varieties. The red wines are
based on Duras and Braucol (the local name for Fer Servadou), plus Syrah. These produce wines of body and
substance, if on the rustic side. Gamay, Merlot and the
two Cabernets are subsidiary varieties. The whites are
from Mauzac (the Blanquette of Limoux), the quaintly
named Len de L'El (Langue d'Oc for 'out of sight'), Muscadelle, Sauvignon Blanc, Sémillon and L'Ondenc.

Gaillac reds cover both *primeur*-style wines, largely
based on Gamay and made by carbonic maceration, and
sturdier ones. The Duras grape produces a wine with
medium colour and body, which is soft yet quite alcoholic, with pleasing, aromatic fruit. The Braucol has
better acidity, more body and tannin but can be a bit
herbaceous at the start, even hard and rustic. When
properly ripe and well-vinified there is a good, quite
blackcurranty fruit. There is no concensus on the correct blend of Duras and Braucol or the desired amount
of Cabernet or Syrah in quality red Gaillac for ageing.

The whites also range in style, this time from fairly
dry to *moelleux* (Gaillac Premières Côtes is a superior version) and can be still, *perlé* (gently sparkling) or fully
sparkling. These sparkling versions are produced either
by the Traditional method or by the *méthode gaillacoise*, a
more artisanal technique – the wine is bottled when it
has only partially finished its first fermentation, without the addition of extra sugar. This results in a
semi-sweet wine. There are today an increasing number
of *doux* if not *liquoreux* wines, though some, like that of
Domaine de Gineste (see right) are *vins de table*.

Most popular on the export market is the gently *pétillant* dry white *perlé*, of which one is most likely to see the
examples of the co-operatives at Labastide-de-Levis or
Rabastens. Based on the Mauzac grape, and bottled early
before all the malolactic fermentation is complete, or
with the addition of a jet of carbon dioxide, this is a

somewhat anonymous but clean, slightly herbal wine without excessive acidity. Drink within the year.

Gaillac Premières Côtes

Eleven communes in the heart of Gaillac can call their wines Premières Côtes, and are subject to stricter rules on yield and minimum alcohol level. In practice you rarely see the words 'Premières Côtes' on any label. The communes are: Bernac, Broze, Cahuzac-sur-Vère, Castanet, Castayrols, Fayssac, Gaillac, Labastide-de-Levis, Lisle-sur-Tarn, Montels and Senouinac.

Leading Gaillac Producers

DOMAINE DE BALAGÈS
Commune: Lagrave.
Owner: Claude Candia.
Surface Area under Vine: 14 ha.
Wines: Gaillac (red) including Cuvée Rêveline.
Domaine de Balagès is situated on the left bank of the river Tarn, and, as the name of the village suggests, profits from a splendid gravel *croupe*. It was bought by Claude Candia's father on his return from Algeria in 1963.

Only red wines are produced, and the only ones to be matured in cask are the very concentrated years of Cuvée Rêveline – for example, 1995 and 1998. This is Syrah, Braucol and Cabernet Sauvignon country and there are no Duras vines. The wines are well-balanced, and nicely stylish.

DOMAINE ALAIN GAYREL-PHILIPPE
Commune: Gaillac.
Owner: Alain Gayrel-Philippe.
Surface Area under Vine: 60 ha.
Wines: Gaillac.
Alain Gayrel-Philippe is a merchant who has his cellar on the site of a now defunct co-operative. He owns two domaines, Les Meritz and Vigné-Laurac, but is more interested in showing you his generic Gaillac wines: red wine from 30 per cent each Braucol and Merlot and 20 per cent each Syrah and Duras. No oak is used in the winemaking and these are competent rather than brilliant wines.

DOMAINE DE GINESTE
Commune: Técou.
Owner: Vincent Laillier and Dominique Bellevret.
Surface Area under Vine: 23 ha.
Wines: Gaillac including (white) Cuvée Pourpre and Cuvée Fût, and La Coulée d'Or (*vin de table*).
Vincent Laillier and his wife Dominique Bellevret hail from the Jura and came to Gaillac in 1991. Técou is on the left bank of the Tarn, and its gravel soils suit red wines more than white. There are good reds, based on the Braucol rather than the Duras, and also a rich sweet wine from Mauzac (called La Coulée d'Or) and a Chardonnay, both *vins de table*.

★ DOMAINE DE LABARTHE
Commune: Castanet.
Owner: Jean Albert & Fils.
Surface Area under Vine: 42 ha.
Wines: Gaillac including L'Héritage, Cuvée Guillaume and Les Grains d'Or.
Jean-Paul Albert is in charge at this domaine which can trace its history back 750 years. The white Héritage is made from 100 per cent Sauvignon, the Guillaume from 100 per cent Braucol, with twelve months' barrel-ageing, one-quarter of which is new. Les Grains d'Or is a sweet wine from 100 per cent Mauzac and given a year in barrel. These are lovely clean wines across the range.

DOMAINE DE LONG-PECH
Commune: Lisle-sur-Tarn.
Owner: Christian Bastide.
Surface Area under Vine: 14 ha.
Wines: Gaillac including (white) Cuvée C. Bastide and (red) Cuvée Jean-Gabriel, and Vin de Pays des Côtes du Tarn.
The Bastide family have been making wine at the Domaine de Long-Pech since 1810. The Cuvée C. Bastide is 100 per cent Sémillon, and is available in an oaked version. The Cuvée Jean-Gabriel, from 50 per cent Braucol, 30 per cent Merlot and 20 per cent Cabernet Sauvignon, is similarly oak-aged. This is good. The dry Gaillacs do not convince me. There is a Gaillac Doux, largely from Mauzac, and a Chardonnay *vin de pays*.

CHÂTEAU DE MAYRAGUES

Commune: Castelnau-de-Montmiral.
Owner: Alan and Laurence Geddes.
Surface Area under Vine: 15 ha.
Wines: Gaillac including Clos de Mages.

Alan and his wife Laurence, after more than two decades globetrotting in the petroleum industry, bought the medieval castle of Mayragues in 1980. The superior Clos de Mages white is a pure Mauzac, vinified in barrel, and is one of the best whites in the region. Its red equivalent comes from half each Braucol and Cabernet Sauvignon, while the basic red is made from 45 per cent Duras and 55 per cent Syrah. Both reds are matured in cask. These two are good, as is the Gaillac Doux, from Len de L'El.

★ CHÂTEAU MONTELS

Commune: Souel-Cordes.
Owner: Bruno Montels.
Surface Area under Vine: 22 ha.
Wines: Gaillac including Cuvée Prestige.

There have been Montels here for ten generations, according to young Bruno Montels, in charge of the winemaking. Len de L'El is the basis for the ordinary *cuvée*; the Prestige (usually 60 per cent Sauvignon Blanc and 40 per cent Len de L'El) is fermented in older wood. The basic red *cuvée* is from 10 per cent Syrah, 30 per cent each Braucol, Cabernet Sauvignon and Merlot, the Prestige from half each Braucol and Cabernet Sauvignon, matured for a year in *demi-muids*. Good wines here.

DOMAINE DU MOULIN

Commune: Gaillac.
Owner: Jean-Paul Hirissou.
Surface Area under Vine: 35 ha.
Wines: Gaillac (red, dry and sweet white).

Jean-Paul Hirissou's new winery, tourist-tasting centre and *cave* lies north of Gaillac, on a hill commanding a splendid view along the Tarn Valley. Like many of his neighbours he confines his Duras and Syrah grapes to the basic red *cuvée*, the oaky one being made from half each Braucol and Merlot. The Gaillac *doux* comes from Muscadelle, the dry white from Sauvignon Blanc. These are good 'modern' wines for the medium term.

MAS PIGNOU

Commune: Gaillac.
Owners: Jacques and Bernard Auque.
Surface Area under Vine: 35 ha.
Wines: Gaillac including Cuvée Mélanie (red and white).

Jacques Auque and his son Bernard are at least the fifth and sixth generation of growers at Mas Pignou. The superior *cuvées* are named after a great-grandmother. The white comes from 50 per cent each Len de L'El and Sauvignon Blanc; the red from about 50 per cent Braucol plus Duras, both Cabernets and Merlot. These are fairly sophisticated wines but for the medium term.

CAVE DE RABASTENS

Commune: Rabastens.
Members: 950.
Surface Area under Vine: 1290 ha.
Wines: Gaillac including Baron de Lyssat and Marquis d'Oriac (red and white).

The impressively up-to-date co-operative, founded in 1923, is now by far the largest wine establishment in the area, controlling 50 per cent of the *appellation*. The best wines are the Baron de Lyssat and Marquis d'Oriac ranges plus various single estates vinified separately: Château de Bra, Château La Peyre, Domaine de Cassagnols and Château d'Escabès. Not all the wines are *barrique*-aged. Standards are competent.

DOMAINE DE RAMAYE

Commune: Sainte-Cécile-d'Aves.
Owner: Michel Issaly.
Surface Area under Vine: 5.20 ha.
Wines: Gaillac including La Quintessence, and Vin de table.

This is an old-established family who have been based in the area since 1847. Today the domaine concentrates on sweet wines, one 100 per cent Mauzac and the other from L'En de L'El. Some of these wines are matured in acacia barrels (rare today). Vin d'Oubli is a wine from Mauzac kept in nine-year-old barrels, without topping up, like a *vin jaune*, but more oxidised, the Mauzac being rather prone to oxidation.

DOMAINE DES TERRISSES

Wines: Gaillac.
Owner: Alain Cazottes.
Surface Area under Vine: 40 ha.
Wines: Gaillac including Cuvée Saint-Laurent.

Alain Cazottes has recently doubled his vineyard from 28 to 40 hectares. The white Saint-Laurent is made from 60 per cent Len de L'El, 40 per cent Sauvignon Blanc, with *macération pelliculaire* and *bâtonnage* when the wine is still young. The basic red comes from 60 per cent Duras, 30 per cent Braucol and 10 per cent Syrah, while the Cuvée Saint-Laurent is from 80 per cent Braucol and 20 per cent Syrah and is matured in one-third new oak. This is a good source.

★ DOMAINE DES TRÈS CANTONS

Commune: Cahuzac-sur-Vère.
Owner: Robert Plageoles.
Surface Area under Vine: 20 ha.
Wines: Gaillac including Le Vin d'Antan and Le Vin de Voile.

Robert Plageoles is an energetic man in his early sixties with curly white hair. The wine is made in concrete vats and stored in *demi-muids* of 600 litres capacity. Increasingly bottled as Les Vins de Robert Plageoles his production is mainly white wine, often sweet, sometimes *vin jaune* in character, such as his Le Vin de Voile. They are very stylish indeed.

Other Producers of note

DOMAINE DE CAUSSE MARINE/PATRICE LESCARRET (VIEUX), DOMAINE D'ESCAUSSES/DENIS BALARAN (SAINTE-CROIX), CHÂTEAU LES MERITZ/PHILIPPE GAYREL (CAHUZAC-SUR-VÈRE), CAVE DE TÉCOU (GAILLAC) AND CHÂTEAU VIGNE-LOURAC/ALAIN GAYREL (CAHUZAC-SUR-VÈRE).

MARCILLAC

Surface Area (1998): 140 ha.
Production (1998): 5224 hl.
Colour: Red and rosé.
Grape varieties: Fer Servadou (Mansoi) and Braucol plus 10% maximum each Cabernet Franc,

Cabernet Sauvignon and Merlot.
Maximum Yield: 50 hl/ha.
Minimum Alcohol Level: 10°.

Three of the most isolated and obscure French country wines are found north of Rodez, capital of the *département* of Aveyron. Further north still lies the Auvergne, but there are no vines until Clermont-Ferrand and the upper reaches of the river Loire and its tributaries. Gaillac and Cahors are equally far away to the south and west. Why has winemaking persisted here? Why should Marcillac have been promoted from VDQS to *appellation contrôlée* in 1990? This is wild and rugged countryside and is not promising terrain for the vine.

Nevertheless north-west of Rodez, in a valley sheltered from the wind from the north, there are slopes where the vine can thrive. In pre-phylloxera times it did so very successfully, there being a ready market in Rodez. This continued even after the arrival of the pest, for a new market for the local wines was found among the miners at Decazeville but when the mine closed in 1962 the bottom fell out of the Marcillac market.

To encourage the few growers who remained VDQS status was awarded in 1968, three years after a co-operative was set up. Hybrids and lesser vines were slowly but surely weeded out, with the result that the vineyards are today almost entirely planted in Mansoi, the local name for Fer Servadou. Since *appellation contrôlée* was awarded in 1990, the area under vine has grown. But it is still a shadow of what it was a century or more ago.

The vines are planted on the slopes, in a soil which comprises the hard red sandstone called *grès* (from which most of the houses are built), limestone rock and compacted clay at about 450 metres above sea level. Here the Mansoi produces a surprisingly sophisticated wine, full and fruity, but supple at the end.

Leading Marcillac Producers

CAVE DES VIGNERONS DU VALLON

Commune: Valady.
Members: 35 to 40.
Surface Area under Vine: 110 ha.

Wines: Madiran including Domaine de Ladrecht and Cuvée 'Elevé en Fûts de Chêne'.

André Metge, enthusiastic and *sympa*, has been in charge here since the co-operative's inception in 1965. The lesser *cuvées* are made without any oak. This is reserved for selected *cuvées* from the better sited as well as older vines.

DOMAINE DU CROS

Commune: Goutrens.
Owner: Philippe Teulier.
Surface Area under Vine: 21 ha.
Wines: Marcillac including Cuvée Spéciale and Lo Sang del Païs.

Philippe Teulier has built up this domaine from 1 to 21 hectares since he took over in 1982. The basic *cuvée* Lo Sang del Païs is stored in stainless steel and the Cuvée Spéciale in *foudres* for ten months. The wines are rich, meaty and concentrated.

DOMAINE LE VIEUX ROCHE

Commune: Bruéjols.
Owner: Jean-Luc Matha.
Surface Area under Vine: 14 ha.
Wines: Marcillac including Cuvée Spéciale.

Jean-Luc Matha started making wine in 1975, and claims to have been the first to produce 'modern' Marcillac, using vinification without the stems and at a controlled temperature. His Cuvée Spéciale – from old vines, low yields and matured in *foudre* – is very good indeed.

Other Producers of note

CLAUDINE COSTES (COMBRET) AND JEAN-MARC REVEL (MERNAC).

ENTRAYGUES ET LE FEL

Surface Area (1998): 20 ha.
Production (1998): (Red and rosé) 648 hl; (white) 336 hl.
Colour: Red, rosé and white.
Grape Varieties: (Red and rosé) Cabernet Sauvignon, Cabernet Franc, Gamay, Négrette and Fer Servadou; (white) Chenin Blanc.

Maximum Yield: 45 hl/ha.
Minimum Alcohol Level: 9°.

Entraygues lies 45 kilometres due north of Rodez – it is a breathtakingly beautiful drive – at the point where the river Lot is joined by the Truyère. A few kilometres downstream, up on the *causses*, is the hamlet of Le Fel. Wine has been made here for 1000 years but production today is tiny. A few brave souls struggle on, including François Avallon and Jean-Marc Viguier. On sampling the wines you wonder why they bother.

ESTAING

Surface Area (1998): 15 ha.
Production (1998): (Red and rosé) 470 hl; (white) 57 hl.
Colour: Red, rosé and white.
Grape Varieties: (Red) Cabernet Sauvignon, Cabernet Franc, Gamay, Fer Servadou and Pinot d'Estaing; (white) Chenin Blanc and Mauzac.
Maximum Yield: 45 hl/ha.
Minimum Alcohol Level: 9°.

Further upstream from Entraygues, the other side of the Gorges du Lot, lies Estaing. It is an attractive town, but this is an even smaller vineyard area. The soil is schistous. Most of the wine is made by Le Caveau du Viala, managed by Pierre Rieu.

CÔTES DE MILLAU

Surface Area (1998): 30 ha.
Production (1998): (Red and rosé) 1489 hl; (white) 89 hl.
Colour: Red, rosé and white.
Grape Varieties: (Red and rosé) Gamay, Syrah (30% minimum of each), Cabernet Sauvignon (maximum 20 per cent) and Fer Servadou; (white) Chenin Blanc and Mauzac.
Maximum Yield: 60 hl/ha.
Minimum Alcohol Level: (Red and rosé) 11°; (white) 10.5°.

Côtes de Millau was promoted from *vin de pays* to VDQS in 1994. The vines lie in and above the valley of the Tarn on either side of the town of Millau, and are mountain, cold-climate wines. The co-operative at Aguessac, just north of Millau, the Cave des Vignerons des Gorges du Tarn, is the major source. This is an up-to-date establishment, eager to put the *appellation* on the map.

VINS DE PAYS
DEPARTMENTAL VINS DE PAYS
Vins de Pays du Gers, du Tarn-et-Garonne, du Lot, de L'Aveyron, de La Haute-Garonne
These are the local departmental *vins de pays* for the Haut Pays. Most of the wine is red, from whichever varieties are grown in the local *appellations*. The few that I have encountered are light and uninspiring.

ZONAL VINS DE PAYS
Vin de Pays des Côtes du Condomois, Vin de Pays des Côtes de Montestruc
These *vins de pays* come from the countryside around the towns of Condom and Montestruc in Armagnac country. I have never come across them.

Vin de Pays de Saint-Sardos
Saint-Sardos is a small village on the south bank of the river Garonne between Montauban and Auch. Production centres round the co-operative. The red wines (from Syrah, Tannat, Cabernet Franc, Gamay and Arbourieu) are the most interesting. Application has been lodged for promotion to VDQS.

Vin de Pays des Coteaux et Terrasses de Montauban
The area covers Fronton and Lavilledieu and extends north to the river Aveyron. The chief producer is the co-operative at La Ville Dieu. The wines are mainly red and rosé from Cabernet Franc, Merlot, Gamay, Tannat, Syrah and Jurançon Rouge.

Vin de Pays de Thézac-Perricard
This *vin de pays* lies west of Cahors in the Lot-et-Garonne.

Production is in the hands of a local group called Les Vignerons de Thézac-Perricard. The wine, in fact, is made at the co-operative at Toulens, south of Agen, and is similar to a lightweight Cahors.

Vin de Pays des Coteaux de Glanes
The village of Glanes, and its co-operative Les Vignerons du Haut-Quercy, are north-west of Cahors in the Lot. This is the sole source of this soft red wine, from a blend of Gamay, Merlot and Ségalin (a cross between Jurançon and Portugais Bleu).

Vin de Pays de Corrèze
This *vin de pays* comes from Branceilles, hilly truffle country between Brive and the Dordogne Valley. A small co-operative movement produces a *primeur*, fruity red wine, based on Merlot, called Mille et Une Pierres.

Vin de Pays des Côtes du Tarn
This covers the Gaillac area. The local co-operatives such as Labastide-de-Lévis, Cunac and Técou are the chief sources. I find the dry whites, from local varieties such as Mauzac and Len de L'El, better than the reds, if a bit neutral. The reds can come from the two Cabernets, Merlot, Duras, Fer Servadou, Gamay and Portugais Bleu.

Leading Vin de Pays Producer

DOMAINE DE RIBONNET
Commune: Beaumont-sur-Lèze.
Owner: Christian Gerber.
Surface Area under Vine: 40 ha.
Wines: Vin de Pays du Comté Tolosan and Vin de Pays de La Haute-Garonne.
South of Toulouse, this domaine has just about every quality grape variety imaginable in its vineyards, even Riesling, Gewürztraminer, Pinot Gris and Sylvaner which have been outlawed in the Limoux. There are interesting wines from these grapes (called Les Epicuriens), as well as from Chardonnay, Pinot Noir, Cabernet Sauvignon, Merlot and Syrah. Cuvée Cabirol is made from the last three varieties plus Tannat and Cot and needs time to mature.

ALSACE

A
LSACE IS ONE OF THE LOVELIEST PARTS OF FRANCE. Its plains are covered in orchards of walnut, cherry and plum, its lower hillsides with vines and the higher slopes with pine and beech, larch and ash, spruce, maple and fir. In the uplands of the Vosges, the mountains which protect Alsace from the west, there are deep, lonely lakes beside alpine meadows, bestrewn in the spring with flowers, on which graze the cattle which give the milk for Munster cheese, one of the most powerful as well as the most delicious in France. Sheltered by the Vosges, the Alsace region enjoys an exceptional climate. This gives the countryside a feeling of richness and plenty, an abundance which extends to the people, who are generous and welcoming.

The foothills and side valleys are dotted with attractive villages, some in a mixture of architectural styles, others almost pure Renaissance with gables, half-timbered houses and cobbled courtyards, as at Riquewihr. Throughout, Alsace is festooned with flowers, from window boxes, hanging baskets, on balconies and in parks, squares and gardens.

Alsace has been fought over for centuries. The Vosges and the Rhine form natural boundaries, and it is the Vosges rather than the Rhine which is the natural barrier between the French language, culture and cuisine and that of Germany. Be that as it may, the region is loyally French, despite remaining staunchly independent, and the wine, like the local cooking – and this is one of the great gastronomic centres of the world – is a subtle combination of German ingredients and French flair. It is this flair, with noble grape varieties such as Riesling, Pinot Gris and Gewurztraminer, which makes Alsace one of Europe's finest wine regions.

You can divide Alsace, longitudinally, into three parts. The plain is that of the Rhine Valley, together with its tributaries, chief of which is the river Ill. This is fertile land, but unsuitable for the vine. The Vosges, whose summits mark the frontier with neighbouring Lorraine, are gently rounded, well weathered and much eroded. They rise to not much more than 1000 metres, and stretch from the Saar border

to the Belfort gap. Between this chain of low mountains and the plain, at altitudes of between 200 and 400 metres, are the vineyards lying on south-eastern-facing slopes, in a continuous line some 100 kilometres long by 3 or 4 kilometres wide. The vineyards begin at Thann, west of Mulhouse, and run north for some 100 kilometres to Nordheim, west of Strasbourg, with a further isolated pocket in the extreme north near Wissembourg on the German border. Most of the vineyards (8500 hectares), and the southern and better section, lies in the *département* of Haut-Rhin. North of Sélestat lies the Bas-Rhin with 5500 hectares. Here there is less protection from the Vosges and so the climate is marginally less warm and less dry, and a lower proportion of the best varieties such as Riesling and Gewurztraminer are planted. The heart of the Alsace vineyards lies just either side of Colmar, in the geographical centre of the region. The villages of Ribeauvillé, Hunawihr, Riquewihr, Kaysersberg, Ammerschwihr, Turckheim, Wintzenheim and Eguisheim follow each other along the wine route and produce many of the finest wines in Alsace.

Alsace, although one of France's smaller provinces, is a major wine region. Now divided into the *départements* of Haut-Rhin and Bas-Rhin, the region occupies 14,390 hectares of vines, yielding on average of well over a million hectolitres of wine per annum. This is 5 per cent of the total AC production of France (around a quarter of the total white wine figure). The wines are almost entirely *appellation contrôlée* whites and dry, fruity and aromatic; they are all bottled in the region itself, and they are largely named after the grapes from which they are made. There is one basic *appellation*, that of AC Alsace itself, though better wines are deemed Alsace *grand cru*, a new *appellation* introduced in 1981. Alsace, like Burgundy and Champagne, is a region where the producer's name on the bottle is all important. The producer decides where the wine is to come from and how the blend is to be made up, and all the consumer has to do once having chosen a grape variety, is choose a category of quality, from basic to Réserve Exceptionnelle.

History

The history of Alsace is violent and bloody, and in parts tragic. The wine it has produced has suffered along with its people, who have been forced to change nationality almost as often as another frontier people, the Poles, and have consequently frequently had to adjust their winemaking to the decrees of foreign oppressors. The first mention of a form of the name Alsace occurs in the time of the Frankish and Merovingian kings when it was termed Alesia. This is thought either to derive from Alisa, or from a combination of 'Ill' from the river, and Sass, old German for 'resident'. In medieval times the wine was known in England and the Low Countries as Aussey.

Clovis, having defeated the Alamans near Wissembourg in AD 496, established Alsace for the Franks at the same time as Christianity was beginning to become a force in the area. The next few centuries, particularly after his successor Charlemagne became Holy Roman Emperor in 800, saw the establishment of numerous monasteries and other religious institutions, all of which required the produce of the grape both for religious use and for the diet of the clergy and their guests – for the many abbeys were the chief hostelries for travellers – as well as for wine's use in medicine.

In 843, the Treaty of Verdun divided the empire of Charlemagne, and Alsace was ceded to Louis the German 'in order that he might have wine in his new kingdom', and for the next seven hundred years was nominally under Teutonic rule, though in practice local dukes and other feudal lords held the sway. Both bishops and nobles owned land and encouraged the cultivation of the vine. Export markets developed, for the wine could be shipped via the Rhine as far as England and Denmark, perhaps even into the Baltic. By 1400 according to the historian Monsignor Médard Barth, there were 430 communes producing wine in the Alsace region. At this time the wines of Mainz and Worms were of little importance and probably most of what was 'Rhenish' came from Alsace. It was a prosperous time, and not only the clergy and the nobility, but the merchants and smallholders were also able to benefit. But it was not to last.

First there were invasions by bands of marauding Armagnacs, then there were a series of natural disasters, a great freeze followed by a terrible flooding when the thaw came in 1480, a six-month-long frost in 1487/1488 and a peasants' revolt in 1525, when 20,000 were killed. Finally the local nobility grew too greedy. Customs duties were raised and raised again – at one period between Strasbourg and Cologne there were sixty-two points along the route when dues had to be paid. Then Strasbourg decreed that all Alsace wine had to pass through its gates, in order to collect a levy, and in addition decided that a proportion of each shipment had to be sold to the inhabitants at a knock-down price. Alsace had killed the golden goose, and north Germany began to develop its own vineyards.

Worse was to follow. Alsace was one of the battlefields of the Thirty Years War (1618-1648), devastated, pillaged, looted and burned. The vineyard owners deserted the countryside for the safety of the towns, production fell to negligible totals and the misery was increased by outbreaks of plague.

Peace was restored by the Treaty of Westphalia, and Alsace passed into the French kingdom. There was a concerted move to encourage people, especially Catholics, to settle in the area – for the population had declined to barely a quarter of a million – and this seems to have been successful, settlers arriving from Austria, Lorraine and particularly from Switzerland, which as the northern market had evaporated was to become an important export target. On a visit to Alsace, Louis XIV was to exclaim: 'Ah, l'Alsace . . . quel beau jardin', echoing Montaigne, who in 1584 had noted: 'the beautiful and extensive plain, bordered on the left by slopes covered in vines'.

It was about this time that a number of well-known, present-day wine firms first set up in business (Trimbach in 1626, Hugel in 1639, Dopff around the turn of the century) and specific grape varieties begin to be first mentioned. Riesling had been recorded in 1477, Muscat in 1523, Traminer in the seventeenth century and Tokay about 1750. In 1766 a decree defined the viticultural area of Alsace, discouraged the planting of inferior, high-yielding varieties and promoted vineyard expansion on the slopes. The area under vines began to expand, and this expansion accelerated after the French Revolution, when the property of the nobility and the church was sequestered and sold off, and when the trade associations and guilds were abolished, leaving 'each person to carry on such business or pursue such profession, art or craft as he thinks fit'. Unfortunately a by-product of the fragmentation of these large domaines and the introduction of the Code Napoléon, regulating that an equal share of an estate must pass to all heirs on the death of the owner, was a division and sub-division of the Alsace vineyard into ever-smaller and inefficient units, a problem which persists today.

In 1870, as a result of the Franco-Prussian war, Alsace was annexed by Germany. This was a sad time for the province. The Germans imposed their language, their restrictions and their culture in a particularly harsh and unpleasant manner. One in every eight inhabitants fled the country. For the vine-grower the situation was even worse. Though most of the expansion during the previous half-century had been on the plain, and with inferior grapes, there had at least been some move towards the planting of noble varieties. This was discouraged. And then, to exacerbate the situation further, came phylloxera. In the 'Land of Unshed Tears', as an American put it, the *vignoble* declined to 18,700 hectares by 1900 (there had been 65,000 hectares in 1870), and what it produced, for the most part, was fairly ordinary wine, largely from Burger (Ebling), with some Chasselas and Sylvaner.

After the First World War Alsace returned to France, and the growers found themselves in a difficult position. Under German rule they had been the dominant wine-producing area, providing 40 per cent of the total crop of what was then Germany. Now they were once again part of the most prolific quality wine-producing country in the world, and had to compete on an equal basis with the cheap wines of the Midi and French North Africa – and with wines which were unknown, as well as very different from those from the rest of France.

In 1925 the decision was taken to go for quality rather than quantity, with the encouragement of the Station de Recherches Oenologiques and the Institut Vinicole de Colmar. The growers' association opted to concentrate on planting noble grape varieties and condemned the planting of hybrids. The vineyard area continued to fall, but the standard of the wine considerably improved.

The regime imposed by the Nazi occupation forces in the Second World War was harsher still than it had been during the 1870-1918 period. Everything French, even the language, was prohibited. The Alsatian dialect, incomprehensible to an outsider, was banned and young men were sent to serve on the Russian front, where many perished and others ended up in labour camps. In the last winter of the war, as the Germans retreated across the Rhine, many villages, including Ammerschwihr, Bennwihr, Sigolsheim and Mittelwihr, were almost totally destroyed, as was much of Colmar. When the allied troops arrived in Strasbourg they were reminded by a poster put up by the Mayor, 'Soldiers, do not forget you are in a French town, though you may hear a German language'.

Since 1945 the policy of quality has been continued. Regulations were drawn up in that year prohibiting the Burger (Ebling) – a large number of prolific German varieties had already been banned in 1932 – and draft proposals on the definition and delimitation of the area, rules and regulations for the planting of the vine and the making of the wine, were established. This was eventually codified into the INAO statutes, and Alsace became *appellation contrôlée* in 1962, the last of the great French vineyard areas to be so covered.

In 1972 the decision was taken to make bottling of Alsace wines in the region mandatory – in order to keep control of the entire process in local hands. This was an unusual and imaginative step, and still unique except for Champagne and the Bordeaux 1855 classed growths which must be château-bottled. More recently certain sites have been designated *grand cru* and the necessary criteria for the usage of the words Vendange Tardive and Sélection de Grains Nobles have been established.

The Wine Region

Aglance at a map of Alsace will show that the Rhine basin is confined on the west by the Vosges and on east by the hills of the Black Forest. Both these ridges are comprised of either granite or *grès rouge*, a very compact red sandstone, much used in the local buildings. In the Tertiary period about 60 million years ago, as the Alps were suddenly forced above the surrounding waters, the Black Forest and Vosges chains rose as well, but leaving a fault between them. This remained flooded, and was later further eroded and deposited as glaciers came and went.

The result of these geological movements is a soil structure which is varied and complex. Somewhere in Alsace is almost every type of soil composition: clay and limestone, sand and gravel, chalk, marl and loess. There is granite at Turckheim and Wintzenheim, adjoining soil which is largely limestone; at Riquewihr there is more limestone as well as marly clay-limestone mixtures; there are zones of loess, a greyish yellow loam at Guebwiller and to the north of Molsheim; more limestone, rich in fossils, at Eguisheim and Barr; and *grès rouge* as well as schistous soil can be found in the region of Andlau. A commune can have several types of soil, making the choice of variety and rootstock complicated, but this gives the local growers the chance of having a wide range of grapes to play with. Each variety is suited to a particular soil and site: Gewurztraminer to the richer, more alluvial clayey soil nearer to the valley floor, the Riesling to the chalk and limestone of the upper slopes, the Sylvaner to a heavy loam, and so on. The soil determines the grape variety, as well as the yield, quality and style of the wine produced.

What this means is that the character and flavour of an Alsace wine will vary considerably as one journeys through the region; for example, a Gewurztraminer from Ribeauvillé or Riquewihr, regardless of producer, will be markedly less perfumed – what the French call *pommadé* – than one from land to the south. As there are a number of different styles, particularly for this grape, and some may be more to your taste than others, it makes sense to have an idea of where one's source lies along the wine route from Thann, west of Mulhouse, northwards to Nordheim, west of Strasbourg. Most of the *négociants* buy in grapes, must or wine, from within a small area, and, for obvious reasons, individual growers and co-operatives are even more restricted.

The Alsace climate is largely determined by the protection given by the Vosges from the prevailing westerly winds. Alsace enjoys a propitious climate, and a weather pattern which is far drier and sunnier than other regions of France on the same latitude. After Perpignan in the Roussillon, Colmar is the driest city in France. Precipitation measures 500mm per annum in Alsace while it is 2000mm on the western side of the Vosges.

Though Alsace is on the same latitude as Paris – and is the northernmost vineyard region in France after Champagne – the climate is continental, with long, hard winters, warm, sunny summers and often exceptionally fine autumns. While the mean average temperature in Colmar is not exceptionally warm at 10.8°C – the same as Dijon's but a whole degree Celsius less than Angers – it is the weather between April and October which is crucial to the production of quality wine, and particularly the weather after the grapes have changed colour at the beginning of September. Here Alsace is favoured, with on average fifty more days of sunshine during the entire summer season than in the Rheingau, and better ripening conditions than Dijon, the Loire and even Hermitage in the Rhône.

Frost, hail and poor weather during the flowering can be more of a problem. Though a really hard winter's frost is rare, and has occurred only three times since 1918 to the extent of damaging the vines, spring frost can be a hazard. By planting the vines on the slopes above the valley the danger is reduced, and as an added precaution the vines are trained high, one to two metres above the ground. Many of the Alsace grape varieties, particularly the Muscat, are extremely susceptible to both *coulure*, failure of the flowers to set into fruit, and *millerandage*, failure of the fruit to develop, and this problem is made worse if the weather is wet and humid during the flowering season in June. Hail is unpredictable and can cause one vineyard to be completely devastated, while leaving a neighbour's untouched. In Alsace there are two means of insurance against this: first, most growers have plots of vineyards in several areas, so they are unlikely to experience a total destruction of their crop. Second, some combine forces with neighbours to hire small aeroplanes to seed the hail-bearing clouds.

In Alsace the grape variety is of even more crucial importance than in the rest of France. In Bordeaux and Burgundy the variety is taken for granted, the site is all important, and the wine is sold under a vineyard or château name. In Alsace the wines are sold under the names of the grapes from which they are made, together with some indication of a level of quality such as *grand cru*, Réserve, and so on. The site is of less interest.

There are either eight grape names or eleven varieties, depending on how you look at it, for *appellation contrôlée* Alsace wine. The eight are Gewurztraminer, Riesling, Pinot Gris, Muscat, Pinot Blanc, Sylvaner, Chasselas and Pinot Noir. Tokay d'Alsace is made from Pinot Gris and Muscat can be made from either Muscat Ottonel or Muscat d'Alsace à Petits Grains, or from both. Chasselas comes from either the white or rosé version, while Pinot Blanc can come from Pinot Noir vinified as a white wine, or from Pinot Auxerrois or even from Pinot Gris, as well as from Pinot Blanc itself.

SURFACE AREA AND PRODUCTION (1998 HARVEST)

APPELLATIONS	SURFACE AREA (HA)	PRODUCTION (HL)	
		RED & ROSÉ	WHITE
ALSACE	11,705	89,238	953,128
ALSACE GRAND CRU	750	–	44,445
CRÉMANT D'ALSACE	1940	15,633	154,206
CÔTES DE TOUL (VDQS)	97	4686	722
VIN DE LA MOSELLE (VDQS)	21	431	1169
TOTAL	14,513	109,988	1,153,670
		1,263,658	

BY GRAPE VARIETY	1969		1998	
	(HA)	(%)	(HA)	(%)
MIXED CULTIVATION (MAINLY CHASSELAS)	755	8.0	259	1.8
CHASSELAS	1001	10.6	144	1.0
SYLVANER	2577	27.3	2044	14.2
PINOT BLANC	1039	11.0	3037	21.1
RIESLING	1199	12.7	3354	23.3
PINOT GRIS	387	4.1	1440	10.0
MUSCAT	340	3.6	331	2.3
GEWURZTRAMINER	1945	20.6	2534	17.6
PINOT NOIR	198	2.1	1252	8.7
TOTAL	9441	100	14,395	100

NORTHERN ALSACE

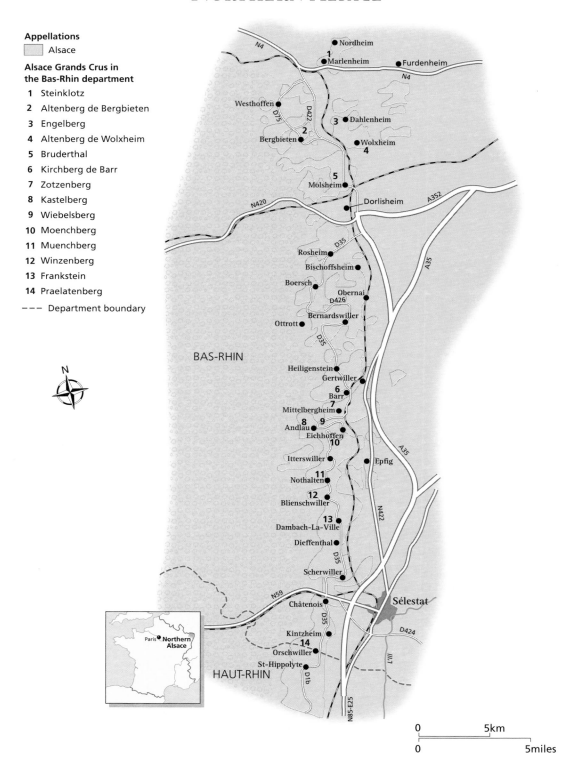

Appellations

Alsace

Alsace Grands Crus in the Bas-Rhin department

1 Steinklotz
2 Altenberg de Bergbieten
3 Engelberg
4 Altenberg de Wolxheim
5 Bruderthal
6 Kirchberg de Barr
7 Zotzenberg
8 Kastelberg
9 Wiebelsberg
10 Moenchberg
11 Muenchberg
12 Winzenberg
13 Frankstein
14 Praelatenberg

--- Department boundary

N4
Nordheim
1
Marlenheim
Furdenheim
N4
Westhoffen
D75
D422
3 Dahlenheim
2
Bergbieten
Wolxheim
4
5
Molsheim
Dorlisheim
A352
N420
D35
Rosheim
Bischoffsheim
Boersch
Obernai
D426
Bernardswiller
Ottrott
D35
BAS-RHIN
Heiligenstein
Gertwiller
6
Barr
7
Mittelbergheim
8 9
Andlau
Eichhoffen
10
Itterswiller
Epfig
A35
11
Nothalten
12
Blienschwiller
13
Dambach-La-Ville
Dieffenthal
D35
Scherwiller
N422
N59
Châtenois
Sélestat
D35
Kintzheim
D424
14
Orschwiller
III.1
St-Hippolyte
D1b
HAUT-RHIN
N85-E25

Paris Northern Alsace

0   5km

0   5miles

THE WINES

ALSACE AC

Surface Area (1998): 11,705 ha.

Production (1998): (Red and rosé) 89,238 hl; (white) 953,128 hl.

Grape Varieties: (Red) Pinot Noir; (white) Riesling, Gewurztraminer, Pinot Gris (Tokay d'Alsace), Muscat, Pinot Blanc, Sylvaner and Chasselas.

Maximum Yield: 100 hl/ha.

Minimum Alcohol Level: 8.5°.

The Alsace *vignoble* has grown by over 35 per cent in the last thirty years, and the proportions of the lesser, 'ignoble' varieties such as Sylvaner and Chasselas have diminished considerably, being replaced with Pinot Blanc and Riesling and, more recently, Pinot Noir. It is estimated that 80 per cent of the total production is from unblended varieties. If not, the term Edelzwicker can be used or the varietal left off the label altogether.

When the *appellation contrôlée* decrees became law in 1962, they established a single *appellation* for the whole of Alsace – Alsace, or Vin d'Alsace. The maximum yield is fixed at 100 hectolitres per hectare, regardless of grape variety, but, unlike anywhere else in France, this can be averaged out over the total holding of any one grower, whatever the grape variety; for example, if his Riesling vineyard only produces 50 hectolitres per hectare, theoretically, another of Gewurztraminer can legally yield 150 hectolitres per hectare. If the grape variety name is stated on the label, then the wine has to consist of 100 per cent of that variety, and if a vintage year is stated, then the wine must come solely from that vintage.

ALSACE GRANDS CRUS

Surface Area (1998): 750 ha.

Production (1998): 44,445 hl.

Grape Varieties: (White only) Riesling, Gewurztraminer, Pinot Gris (Tokay d'Alsace) and Muscat.

Maximum Yield: 70 hl/ha.

Minimum Alcohol Level: 10° for Riesling and Muscat. 12° for Gewurztraminer and Pinot Gris.

A decree of 1982, which, like the 1962 *appellation* regulations, largely followed the original order drawn up in 1945, set out the definition of *grand cru*. To be called *grand cru* a wine had to attain a minimum natural strength of 10 degrees for Riesling and Muscat, and 12° for other varieties, but can only be made from Pinot Gris, Muscat, Gewurztraminer, Riesling and Pinot Noir. The maximum yield was reduced to 70 hectolitres per hectare.

In 1975 the first moves were made towards redefining *grand cru* and restricting it to the produce of certain specific well-favoured sites. A list of some ninety-four vineyards thought suitable for classification was drawn up, and the new proposals were originally intended to come into force from the 1978 vintage. As a result of considerable opposition, largely from the merchants who would be then deprived of the opportunity of making their own, large-scale, *grand cru* blends, this initiative floundered somewhat. A decree of 1983 defined twenty-five *lieux-dits*. This was expanded by a further twenty-five in November 1985.

Vendange Tardive and Sélection de Grains Nobles

The culmination of long years of lobbying by a number of producers, pioneered by the late Jean Hugel, resulted in a framework which became law in 1984, defining the necessary criteria for the production of Vendange Tardive or late-harvested Alsace wines and Sélection de Grains Nobles (from individually selected, nobly rotted grapes). These can only be produced from Gewurztraminer, Pinot Gris, Riesling and Muscat.

In the case of the first two, the grape juice must achieve a ripeness equivalent to 14.3° of potential alcohol in order to be labelled Vendange Tardive, and 16.4° for Grains Nobles. For Riesling and Muscat the levels are 12.9° and 15.1°.

THE ALSACE GRANDS CRUS

LISTED GEOGRAPHICALLY FROM NORTH TO SOUTH

NAME	VILLAGE	SIZE	SOIL
STEINKLOTZ	MARLENHEIM	24 HA	STONY LIMESTONE
ENGELBERG	DAHLENHEIM	11 HA	STONY MARLY LIMESTONE
ALTENBERG DE BERGBIETEN	BERGBIETEN	29 HA	GYSUM RICH MARLY CLAY
ALTENBERG DE WOLXHEIM	WOLXHEIM	28 HA	STONY CALCAREOUS MARL
BRUDERTHAL	MOSHEIM	19 HA	STONY CALCAREOUS MARL OVER LIMESTONE
KIRCHBERG DE BARR	BARR	40 HA	CALCAREOUS MARL OVER LIMESTONE ROCK
ZOTZENBERG	MITTELBERGHEIM	34 HA	LIMESTONE AND MARL
KASTELBERG	ANDLAU	6 HA	STONY SILICEOUS SOIL OVER SLATY SCHIST
WIEBELSBERG	ANDLAU	2 HA	SILICEOUS TOP SOIL, MARLY QUARTZ OVER SANDSTONE
MOENCHBERG	ANDLAU/EICHHOFFEN	12 HA	LIMEY SILTY CLAY OVER GRANITE
MUENCHBERG	NOTHALTEN	18 HA	OLD WEATHERED SOIL INCLUDING TUFA RICH IN VOLCANIC DEBRIS
WINZENBERG	BLIENSCHWILLER	5 HA	GRANITIC AND MICACEOUS SOIL AND GRANITE
FRANKSTEIN	DAMBACH-LA-VILLE	53 HA	MICA-GRANITE
PRAELATENBERG	ORSCHWILLER/KINTZHEIM	12 HA	STONY SILICEOUS SOIL WITH GRAVEL
GLOECKELBERG	RODERN/ST-HIPPOLYTE	23 HA	SAND, CLAY AND SCHIST OVER GRANITE ROCK
ALTENBERG DE BERGHEIM	BERGHEIM	35 HA	CALCAREOUS MARL OVER LIMESTONE ROCK
KANZLERBERG	BERGHEIM	3 HA	GYPSUM AND MARL OVER LIMESTONE
GEISBERG	RIBEAUVILLÉ	9 HA	STONY CLAY OVER GYPSUM-RICH MARLY SANDSTONE
KIRCHBERG DE RIBEAUVILLÉ	RIBEAUVILLÉ	11 HA	STONY CLAY OVER MARL AND SANDSTONE LAYERED WITH GYPSUM
OSTERBERG	RIBEAUVILLÉ	24 HA	STONY CLAY OVER CALCAREOUS MARL
ROSACKER	HUNAWIHR	26 HA	STONY CALCAREOUS MARL OVER LIMESTONE
FROEHN	ZELLENBERG	13 HA	CLAYEY AND SCHISTOUS MARL
SCHOENENBOURG	RIQUEWIHR	40 HA	STONY, SILICEOUS SOIL OVER MARL, LIMESTONE AND SANDSTONE
SPOREN	RIQUEWIHR	22 HA	DECALCIFIED MARLY CLAY
SONNENGLANZ	BEBLENHEIM	33 HA	HEAVY MARL OVER LIMESTONE
MANDELBERG	MITTELWIHR	12 HA	CALCAREOUS MARL OVER LIMESTONE
MARCKRAIN	BENNWIHR	45 HA	CALCAREOUS MARL OVER MARLY LIMESTONE
MAMBOURG	SIGOLSHEIM	65 HA	PEBBLY MARL OVER LIMESTONE AND MARL

NAME	VILLAGE	SIZE	SOIL
FURSTENTUM	KLENTZHEIM/SIGOLSHEIM	27 HA	PEBBLY MARL OVER LIMESTONE AND MARLY SANDSTONE
SCHLOSSBERG	KAYSERSBERG/KLENTZHEIM	80 HA	CLAYEY SAND OVER GRANITE BEDROCK
WINECK-SCHLOSSBERG	KATZENTHAL	24 HA	GRANITE AND MICACEOUS SOIL OVER GRANITE
SOMMERBERG	NIEDERMORSCHWIHR/ KATZENTHAL	28 HA	GRANITE SAND OVER GRANITE AND MICA
FLORIMONT	INGERSHEIM	15 HA	STONY CALCAREOUS MARL OVER LIMESTONE ROCK
BRAND	TURCKHEIM	60 HA	MICA OVER GRANITE; GRANITIC SAND OVER LIMESTONE AND MARL TO THE EAST
HENGST	WINTZENHEIM	76 HA	PEBBLES OVER CALCAREOUS MARL
STEINGRUBLER	WETTOLSHEIM	19 HA	STONY CALCAREOUS MARL OVER LIMESTONE
EICHBERG	EGUISHEIM	58 HA	PEBBLY SCREA OVER CALCAREOUS MARL
PFERSIGBERG	EGUISHEIM	56 HA	CALCAREOUS MARL OVER RENDZINA AND LIMESTONE
HATSCHBOURG	HATTSTATT/ VOEGTLINSHOFFEN	47 HA	GRAVELLY LOESS OVER CALCAREOUS MARL
GOLDERT	GUEBERSCHWIHR	45 HA	CALCAREOUS–CLAY OR SANDSTONE OVER LIMESTONE
STEINERT	PFAFFENHEIM	38 HA	SAND AND STONES OVER LIMESTONE
VORBOURG	ROUFFACH/WESTHALTEN	72 HA	CALCAREOUS MARL OVER SANDSTONE AND LIMESTONE
ZINNKOEPFLÉ	SOULTZMATT/WESTHALTEN	62 HA	SANDY AND CALCAREOUS CLAY OVER SANDSTONE AND LIMESTONE
PFINGSTBERG	ORSCHWIHR	28 HA	CALCAREOUS AND MICACEOUS SANDSTONE OR CLAYEY SANDSTONE
SPIEGEL	BERGHOLTZ/GUEBWILLER	18 HA	SANDY CLAY OVER SANDSTONE AND MARL
KESSLER	GUEBWILLER	29 HA	RED SANDY CLAY OVER SANDSTONE AND LIMESTONE ROCK
KITTERLÉ	GUEBWILLER	26 HA	SAND OVER QUARTZ, RICH SANDSTONE, SCHISTOUS VOLCANIC ELEMENTS TO THE WEST
SAERING	GUEBWILLER	27 HA	STONY SANDSTONE OVER CALCAREOUS MARL
OLLWILLER	WUENHEIM	36 HA	RED SANDY CLAY OVER MARL AND SAND
RANGEN	THANN	19 HA	ESSENTIALLY VOLCANIC WITH SOME SAND
TOTAL, in theory if not currently declared in practice		**1614 HA**	

These are the top Alsace wines, the very epitome of excellence. Vendange Tardive wines will occur in most good years, and are roughly the equivalent of German Auslese wines, though the requirements are for much riper grapes, and as Alsace wines are fermented out as dry as the yeasts will go, the wines will be rich rather than sweet. Sélection de Grains Nobles, made from botrytized grapes, will only occur in exceptional years such as 1976, 1983, 1989. 1994 and 1995. The wines are sweet, and with the power and intensity of character more like Sauternes than German Beerenauslese.

Réserve, Cuvée Spéciale and others

Most producers, whether merchants or co-operatives, make a wide range of wines of different qualities from many, if not all, of the Alsace grape varieties. Designations such as Réserve or Cuvée 'this and that' are used to differentiate between the qualities, but they have no legal definition.

Edelzwicker

Edelzwicker is an Alsace wine made from a blend of the better grape varieties, most commonly from Pinot Blanc and Sylvaner but perhaps also from the lesser *cuvées* (such as young vines) of the nobler grapes such as Riesling and Pinot Gris. It is often sold under a brand name such as Hugel's Flambeau d'Alsace or Beyer's Spéciale Fruits de Mer.

Klevner de Heiligenstein

In and around Heiligenstein in the Bas-Rhin some 13 hectares are planted with the Savignin Rosé, a variety related to the Gewurztraminer and used further south in the Jura to make Vin Jaune. In Heiligenstein the wine is dry, white and fairly spicy, though without any great definition or distinction. The firm of Charles Wantz in Barr is the only source of Klevner I know.

CRÉMANT D'ALSACE

Surface Area (1998): 1940 ha.
Production (1998): (Red and rosé) 15,633 hl;
(white) 154,206.

Grape Varieties: (Rosé) Pinot Noir; (white) Pinot Blanc, Riesling, Pinot Noir, Pinot Gris.
Maximum Yield: 100 hl/ha.
Minimum Alcohol Level: 8°.

The pioneer of Alsace sparkling wines was Julien Dopff of Dopff au Moulin. He was a lifelong friend of the Heidsieck family of Reims and, having seen the Champagne method demonstrated at the Paris Exhibition in 1900, started to make his own sparkling wines in Alsace. The wine has had its own AC since 1976, since when production has expanded enormously. In 1983 sales topped 5 million bottles for the first time, a fivefold increase since 1977. Today the figure is approaching 18 million bottles.

Crémant d'Alsace is a Champagne- or Traditional-method wine that is fully sparkling, that is the pressure would be in the region of five to six atmospheres. It is normally made largely if not exclusively from Pinot Blanc and this base wine must conform to the standards required by a still Alsace wine. Other permitted varieties are Riesling, Pinot Gris and Pinot Noir, and Pinot Noir exclusively for the rosé version. I find it one of the best of the French Traditional-method sparkling wines.

When to Drink the Wines

For most Alsace wines the variation in style and quality from one vintage to the next is negligible. As with inexpensive white wine produced elsewhere – in Muscadet, Bergerac or the Mâconnais – modern techniques of vinification and early bottling ensure crisp, fruity Edelzwickers and basic qualities of Pinot Blanc, Sylvaner and Riesling year in, year out and these are produced for drinking within a couple of years. Gewurztraminer, though, does need a good *fin de saison* to fully ripen, otherwise it will be somewhat hard and lacking charm. Few vintages in Alsace, luckily, are really disastrous.

Alsace Vintages

The following notes apply to the better grades of wine, labelled Réserve, Vendange Tardive and so on. These can be kept – and indeed should be – to mature in bottle.
1998 After a successful flowering and a fine summer, hopes were high, only to be dashed by changeable

weather during the harvest. The grapes remained healthy, however, and quality is certainly good especially in Riesling (though less so in Pinot Gris). A good sized crop; 10 per cent above average.

1997 The third in a succession of very fine vintages and the best of the trio for Gewurztraminer. A hot and sunny August was followed by almost perfect conditions in September and October. The grapes were exceptionally ripe, producing high alcohol degrees and plenty of wines at Vendange Tardive level. The wines are lush and fat but with acidities on the low side. An average-sized crop. The best will still keep well, however.

1996 A relatively cool but very sunny and very dry September and October produced wines with both a high degree of ripeness and a notable acidity level. No botrytis but very elegant, healthy wines which will keep exceptionally well. Superb Rieslings and fine Pinots Gris. The Gewurztraminers are less exciting. An average-sized crop.

1995 At the time the best vintage since 1990. A hot August was followed by a humid September but a fine, sunny October. Best in Riesling and Pinot Gris, and for Vendange Tardive and Sélection de Grains Nobles. These wines have depth and concentration and will last well. Less good for Gewurztraminer. An average crop.

1994 After a year with less sun and more rain than usual Alsace enjoyed its usual dry autumn. The fruit was clean but nevertheless not really very concentrated. Most of the wines lack real depth. Good but not great, in short; but best of all in Gewurztraminer and Pinot Gris. Here some fine Sélection de Grains Noble have been produced. The rest though need drinking soon.

1993 Another year of quality which can be summed up as a good average. Better than 1991 and 1992 and fairly uniform across the varietals. Drink them now.

1992 Rain at the beginning of September and at the end of October plus a large harvest produced a vintage of only quite good quality. The wines lack depth and concentration. The Rieslings and Pinot Gris are clean and elegant. The Gewurztraminers are rather one-dimensional. Drink up.

1991 Another medium to good vintage, but not, as elsewhere in France, a short one. Better Gewurztraminers than in 1992, but the other varietals are rather thin and lean. They are now showing age.

1990 A truly great vintage, and one which still has plenty of life to it. A splendid summer was followed by a near perfect autumn. It was also – in Alsatian terms – a small crop: 15 per cent less than in 1989. There was much less botrytis than in the previous year, but better acidities, a firmer structure, and great depth and finesse. The best wines still need keeping.

1989 A large harvest, and a very successful one, on a par with 1988 and 1983, and like them the wines will keep well. The vintage is at its most successful in Riesling. Large quantities of Vendange Tardive and Sélection de Grains Nobles have been produced.

1988 A large harvest which could have been of very fine quality had it not been for heavy rain just before the start of the harvest. This had the effect of diluting the quality the acidity and the concentration – and increasing the quantity. Nevertheless, thereafter the weather improved and some very good late-harvest wines have been made. Not an outstanding vintage but better than 1987 and with more depth than 1986.

1987 After a variable summer the harvest was quite large and of above average quality. The wines were balanced, if not of exceptional depth, but are now too old.

1986 As in 1987 the climate was variable, though there was less rain. It was a large harvest. As a result some wines were a little dilute. Fine weather later in the season produced some very good late-harvest wines, especially the Rieslings. Now getting old.

1985 The greatest vintages of the 1980s are 1989, 1985 and 1983. Fine dry late summer weather extended late until the autumn, and together with a smaller than average harvest this produced some splendid wines, full, rich and concentrated, with higher alcohol levels than usual, but with superb balancing acidity. Though there was a large quantity of late-harvest wines there were fewer Sélection de Grains Nobles. The Rieslings, in particular, are excellent. The wines will still keep well.

1984 The one disappointing vintage of the 1980s. Uneven flowering followed by a lack of sun produced wines with a high acidity and a lack of ripeness which aged fast. Now too old.

1983 An excellent vintage. A hot dry summer produced big, spicy, concentrated wines with good balancing acidity. They are full, fat and rich, the Gewurztraminers and Tokays being particularly successful, while there are fine Rieslings. A large quantity of both Vendange Tardive and Sélection de Grains Nobles. All will still keep well.

GOOD, EARLIER VINTAGES

The best years are 1981, 1979, 1976 (superb), 1975, 1971 (excellent) and 1967.

The Wine Trade

Like most of France, the dissolution of the large ecclesiastical and lay estates after the Revolution and the effects of the Code Napoléon have led to a region of smallholdings. Since 1969 concerted efforts have been made to reduce the number of tiny plots by encouraging amalgamation, and at the same time the vineyard area has expanded. In 1969 12,000 growers shared 9500 hectares of vineyards, producing 700,000 hectolitres. In 1998 8000 growers shared 14,350 hectares of vineyards and production now averages a million hectolitres. Yet, still today 65 per cent of growers have less than 1 hectare of vines each, and only a few hundred own more than 5 hectares. Few proprietors, therefore, can make a living solely out of wine. Most work their vineyards as a weekend 'hobby'. Some 1870 growers sell their own wine (about 30 per cent of the total production, though 80 per cent of this growers' total is accounted for by only 175 proprietors). The *négociants* buy both wine and grapes and sell 40 per cent of the harvest, leaving 30 per cent to the co-operatives, who have some 2500 members.

The co-operative movement started at the beginning of the twentieth century, during the period of German occupation, but has really only come to the fore since the Second World War. The first two co-operatives were in Eguisheim and Dambach-La-Ville, and originally they were merely central, collective storage units for the surplus production over and above what the *négociants* were immediately prepared to buy. After 1945 growers of Bennwihr and Sigolsheim, two villages devastated in the last six months of the war, grouped together to create a couple of vinification units, primarily with the aim of selling in bulk to their traditional customers, the merchants. Faced with a reluctance on the part of the latter, they began to bottle and sell the wines themselves. There are now seventeen in the Alsace region, and many of these have justifiably high reputations – especially Eguisheim, Beblenheim, Pfaffenheim, Westhalten and Bennwihr. Recently, two *négociants*, Kuehn of Ammerschwihr (by the Ingersheim co-operative) and Heim of Westhalten, have been absorbed by their local co-operatives. Additionally there is the Union Vinicole Divinal at Obernai, a union of seven other co-operatives from the Alsace region. Of these the best are Pfaffenheim and Turckheim.

Leading Alsace Producers

DOMAINE LUCIEN ALBRECHT
Commune: Orschwihr.
Owners: Albrecht family.
Surface Area under Vine: 26 ha including Grand Cru Pfingstberg.
Most of Jean Albrecht's wines are sold to private clients in France. I rate this estate good in Riesling and fine in Pinot Gris/Tokay. The Pfingstberg soil, Albrecht points out, is *grès*, a red sandstone rock. This produces a wine with plenty of fat but, austere at first, it needs time to develop. The top wines include Tokay, Clos Renaissance and Gewurztraminer Cuvée Martine Albrecht.

MAISON JEAN BECKER
Commune: Zellenberg.
Owners: Becker family.
Surface Area under Vine: 16 ha including Grands Crus Froehn, Schoenenbourg and Sonnenglanz.
Zellenberg, near Riquewihr, is surrounded by the Froehn *grand cru*, whose soil is predominantly clay-limestone. The Becker domaine is largely situated here and on the more clayer Schoenbourg *grand cru*. The Beckers also buy in grapes. A subsidiary label is Gaston Beck. A very good source.

DOMAINE LÉON BEYER
Commune: Eguisheim.

Owners: Beyer family.

Surface Area under Vine: 20 ha including Grands Crus Eichberg and Pfergsiberg.

Marc Beyer is passionate about the importance of vinifying most Alsace wines dry and not neglecting the wine and food compatibility. I find some of the lesser *cuvées* somewhat one-dimensional and the Gewurztraminer *pommadé*. The Réserve and Vendange Tardive are proportionately better. This is one of Alsace's most important *négociants*, selling some 800,000 bottles a year.

★ DOMAINE PAUL BLANCK

Commune: Kientzheim.

Owners: Blanck family.

Surface Area under Vine: 31 ha including Grands Crus Schlossberg, Furstentum and Mamburg.

Since the outgoing Philippe Blanck (in the vineyard) and his more reserved cousin Frédéric (who is responsible for the wines) took over from their parents in the early 1990s yields have been reduced and the winemaking cleaned up. The result is greater finesse and greater definition. This once humdrum property has now become one of Alsace's stars. The pick of the bunch are the minerally Schlossberg and Furstentum Rieslings; but in fact the whole range is now exemplary.

DOMAINE BOTT-GEYL

Commune: Beblenheim.

Owners: Bott-Geyl family.

Surface Area under Vine: 12.8 ha including Grands Crus Sonnenglanz, Mandelberg, Schoenenbourg and Furstentum.

Jean-Christophe Bott makes rich, full, powerful wines from Pinot Gris and Gewurztraminer in the heavy soils of the Sonnenglanz, sometimes a little over-sweet for my taste, but they are made for keeping and they do last. The Rieslings from the Mandelberg are good, too.

★ DOMAINE ALBERT BOXLER

Commune: Niedermorschwihr.

Owners: Boxler family.

Surface Area under Vine: 9.5 ha including Grands Crus Sommerberg and Brand.

Nestling in a valley up in the hills, surrounded by steep granitic slopes clinging with vines, lies the headquarters of the Boxler domaine. Jean-Marc Boxler admits Niedermorschwihr is not a suitable terrain for Gewurztraminer and he would rather forgo it entirely, but his customers insist on it. Instead, the domaine concentrates on marvellously steely, austere Rieslings, the purest expression of this varietal and the local soils. These wines are hard to beat. One of the very best domaines in the region.

DOMAINE ERNEST BURN

Commune: Gueberschwihr.

Owners: Burn family.

Surface Area under Vine: 9 ha including Grand Cru Goldert.

The Burn domaine includes 6 hectares of *grand cru* Goldert, within which is the Clos Saint-Imer, a monopoly. This is a gem of a piece of land, south-east-facing terraces with well-drained, stony calcareous soil. The best wine from here is the Cuvée La Chapelle. The Burn style is for big wines, bottled later than most, but certainly rich. I find their Pinot Gris and Gewurztraminers better suited to this approach than their Rieslings.

★ DOMAINE MARCEL DEISS

Commune: Bergheim.

Owners: Deiss family.

Surface Area under Vine: 20 ha including Grands Crus Schoenenbourg and Altenberg de Bergheim.

The charming but decidedly eccentric Jean-Michel Deiss is one of the most perfectionistic growers in Alsace. He is now cultivating more and more by biodynamic methods and also returning to complantation, mixing different varieties in one plot and vinifying them together – 'to increase the complexity'.

If you crop as low as 40 hl/ha (as he does), you will get a potential alcohol level of 18° and there will be a corresponding level of sugar in the wine. You therefore need to let the wines age, which his do splendidly, so that this sweetness becomes less apparent. The Rieslings are perhaps the best wines. But this is a fine domaine. The wines can be difficult to sample when young.

SOUTHERN ALSACE

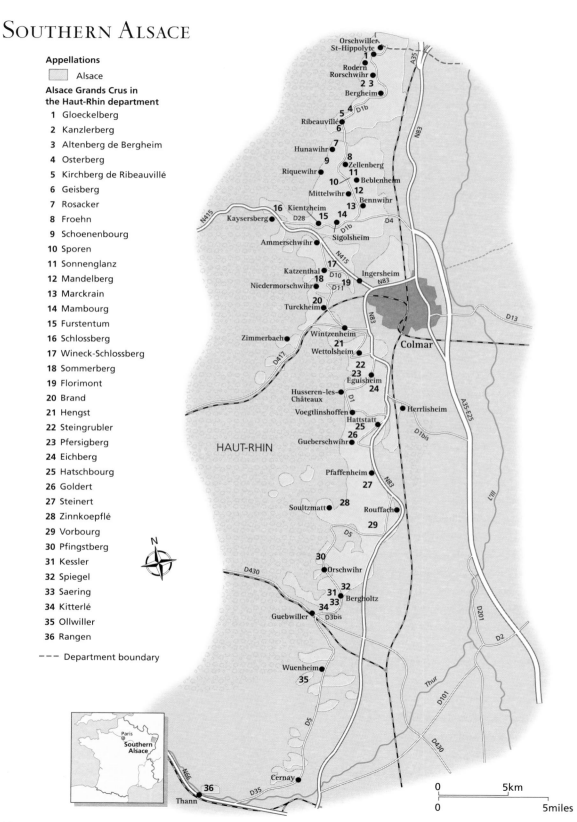

Appellations

Alsace

**Alsace Grands Crus in
the Haut-Rhin department**

 1 Gloeckelberg
 2 Kanzlerberg
 3 Altenberg de Bergheim
 4 Osterberg
 5 Kirchberg de Ribeauvillé
 6 Geisberg
 7 Rosacker
 8 Froehn
 9 Schoenenbourg
10 Sporen
11 Sonnenglanz
12 Mandelberg
13 Marckrain
14 Mambourg
15 Furstentum
16 Schlossberg
17 Wineck-Schlossberg
18 Sommerberg
19 Florimont
20 Brand
21 Hengst
22 Steingrubler
23 Pfersigberg
24 Eichberg
25 Hatschbourg
26 Goldert
27 Steinert
28 Zinnkoepflé
29 Vorbourg
30 Pfingstberg
31 Kessler
32 Spiegel
33 Saering
34 Kitterlé
35 Ollwiller
36 Rangen

– – – Department boundary

DOMAINE JEAN-PIERRE DIRLER

Commune: Bergholtz.

Owners: Dirler family.

Surface Area under Vine: 7.4 ha including Grands Crus Spiegel, Kessler and Saering.

Bergholtz lies just north of Guebwiller at the southern end of the Alsace vineyard, and Dirler's *grands crus* lie on the weathered sandstone *grès* of the Guebwiller hills. The Saering Riesling is floral, the Kessler minerally and the Spiegel concentrated and classy. There are good Gewurztraminers too.

MAISON DOPFF AU MOULIN

Commune: Riquewihr.

Owners: Dopff family.

Surface Area under Vine: 74 ha including Grands Crus Sporen, Schoenenbourg and Brand.

Dopff au Moulin virtually invented Crémant d'Alsace, and are still the brand leaders. For a long time the table wines were four-square and fruitless, but in the last few years they have improved. Choose the top ones such as the Rieslings and Gewurztraminers from the Brand and Schoenenbourg *grands crus*. The turnover is some 3 million bottles, making them one of Alsace's largest.

DOMAINE ANDRÉ & RÉMY GRESSER

Commune: Andlau.

Owners: Gresser family.

Surface Area under Vine: 10 ha including Grands Crus Kastelberg, Wiebelsberg and Moenchberg.

'We try to respect the soil and the *cépage*', say the Gressers 'and to produce wines for drinking with food'. Andlau is Riesling territory, and the Gressers excel in making thes wines. They are both ample and racy, and keep well.

DOMAINE MATERNE HAEGELIN & SES FILLES

Commune: Orschwihr.

Owners: Materne Haegelin family.

Surface Area under Vine: 15 ha including Grand Cru Pfingstberg.

I was first led to this estate by a Pinot Auxerrois I much enjoyed in a restaurant in London. The domaine is run by the charming Régine Garnier-Haegelin and her brothers-in-law. A superior bottling is called Cuvée Eliane, while the Lippelsberg is a Riesling from a special sector of the Pfingstberg.

★ MAISON HUGEL & FILS

Commune: Riquewihr.

Owners: Hugel family.

Surface Area under Vine: 25 ha including Grands Crus Sporen and Schoenenbourg.

Hugel, which celebrated its 350th anniversary in 1989, is one of the most important (one million bottles a year) as well as one of the oldest Alsace merchants. A new generation, Etienne and his brother Marc, took over at about that time and are now firmly in charge. The style remains constant: soft, aromatic, sometimes a little bland at the lower levels. I like my Alsace to have a bit of bite! They prefer to label their wines according to their own hierarchy: Tradition, Jubilée and so on. It is when one gets to the Vendange Tardive and Sélection de Grains Nobles, which to a very large extent the Hugels pioneered, that the wines begin to really excite.

MAISON JOSMEYER

Commune: Wintzenheim.

Owners: Meyer family.

Surface Area under Vine: 32 ha including Grands Crus Hengst and Brand.

Jean Meyer – it was his grandfather who was Joseph, contracted to Jos – persists in planting non-noble varieties such as Chasselas and Pinot Auxerrois in his *grands crus*, and designating them by the letter H for Hengst, for instance. These are very good wines. Among the noble varieties I like his Rieslings, always nice and steely, the best. The firm sells around 350,000 bottles annually.

★★ DOMAINE ANDRÉ KIENTZLER

Commune: Ribeauvillé.

Owners: Kientzler family.

Surface Area under Vine: 10 ha including Grands Crus Geisberg, Kirchberg and Osterberg.

Beautifully pure, understated, persistent wines right across the range of grape varieties can be found here.

André Kientzler is an intelligent, meticulous wine-maker, and the results, from his Swiss chalet-type premises in the middle of the vineyards under the Osterberg, are long-lived wines of great elegance. One of Alsace's super-star domaines.

★ DOMAINE MARC KREYDENWEISS

Commune: Andlau.

Owners: Kreydenweiss family.

Surface Area under Vine: 11 ha including Grands Crus Wiebelsberg, Moenchberg and Kastelberg.

Marc Kreydenweiss' grandfather was one of the pioneers of domaine-bottling in Alsace. Now run on biodynamic lines, this estate produces clear-cut, austere wines which keep well from the *grès* of Wiebelsberg, the more exposed *grès* and glacial deposits in the Moenchberg and the slate and schistous (rare in Alsace) soils of Kastelberg. The Rieslings are particularly fine. There is also that rarity: Klevener, a variety of Pinot Auxerrois; and the Val d'Eléon, a blend of 70 per cent Riesling and 30 per cent Pinot Gris.

★ MAISON KUENTZ-BAS

Commune: Husseren-Les-Châteaux.

Owners: Bas and Weber families.

Surface Area under Vine: 12 ha including Grands Crus Eichberg and Pfersigberg.

Christian Bas runs the commercial side of this company and his cousin Jacques Weber makes the wine. They buy in grapes to triple the quantity from their own vineyards and have a turnover of some 350,000 bottles. This is one of the very best *négociant* houses, producing ample, full, long-lived wines right across the range. The Vendange Tardive wines are bottled as Cuvée Jérémy and the Sélection de Grains Nobles blends as Cuvée Caroline.

DOMAINE SEPPI LANDMANN

Commune: Soulzmatt.

Owners: Seppi Landmann and family.

Surface Area under Vine: 8.5 ha including Grand Cru Zinnkoepfle.

Not only is this one of the best addresses for Sylvaner in Alsace but it is also a source for some splendidly rich,

flowery, almost scented Zinnkoepfle Gewurztraminers. Seppi Landmann is a 'character', and not surprisingly his wines have plenty of personality in them, too.

MAISON GUSTAVE LORENTZ

Commune: Bergheim.

Owners: Lorentz family.

Surface Area under Vine: 30 ha including Grands Crus Altenberg and Kanzlerberg.

Gustave Lorentz sell around 2 million bottles a year, making them one of the largest firms in Alsace, and the quality, especially in Gewurztraminer and the Altenberg Rieslings, is better than merely good. As well as their own considerable domaine, the firm buys in grapes or must from about fifty growers in the immediate region.

DOMAINE ALBERT MANN

Commune: Wettolsheim.

Owners: Barthelme family.

Surface Area under Vine: 19 ha including Grands Crus Schlossberg, Furstentum, Hengst and Steingrubler.

Jacky Barthelme and his brother Maurice are in charge here. Progress has continued throughout the 1990s and there are now a number of finely fruity and definitive wines made here. The Vendange Tardive wines are steely and ripe: not a bit too sweet.

DOMAINE MEYER-FONNÉ

Commune: Katzenthal.

Owners: Meyer family.

Surface Area under Vine: 9 ha including Grand Cru Schlossberg.

Félix Meyer trained at Zind-Humbrecht and elsewhere and since he has been in charge here the wine has taken on more quality and definition. Good wines across the board include the Schlossberg Rieslings.

DOMAINE MITTNACH KLACK

Commune: Riquewihr.

Owners: Mittnach family.

Surface Area under Vine: 10 ha including Grands Crus Rosacker, Sporen and Schoenenbourg.

Jean and Annie Mittnach run their estate from a modern house outside the cobbled antiquity of Riquewihr. They make fine, pure, austere wines which keep well. A good if little-known address.

MAISON RENÉ MURÉ
CLOS SAINT-LANDELIN

Commune: Rouffach.

Owners: Muré family.

Surface Area under Vine: 21 ha including Grand Cru Clos Saint-Landelin, part of Vorbourg.

The top wines come from their own domaine, a clay-limestone slope above the winery. I regularly see good notes on these wines elsewhere but every time I call I am disappointed as I find the wines lack grace.

★ DOMAINE ANDRÉ OSTERTAG

Commune: Epfig.

Owners: Ostertag family.

Surface Area under Vine: 10 ha including Grand Cru Muenchberg.

Ostertag belongs to the new generation of innovators. His search follows two paths: the effect of vinifying Pinot Blanc and Pinot Noir in barrel, and the continuing refinement necessary to express the *terroir* of his *vins de garde*. I was dubious about the wood when I first began to visit him regularly in the mid-1980s but now he seems to have got the technique right. And the *vins de terroir*, especially from the *grès* and volcanic soils of the *grand cru* Muenchberg, kept long on their lees, with regular *bâtonnage*, can now be very fine. The Pinots Gris and the Rieslings are better than the Gewurztraminers (Epfig is not Gewurztraminer land). And there is a lovely Vieilles Vignes Sylvaner. The lesser *cuvées*, for drinking young, are termed *vins du fruit*; the Vendanges Tardives and Sélections de Grains Nobles are called *vins du temps*.

DOMAINE ROLLY-GASSMANN

Commune: Rorschwihr.

Owners: Rolly-Gassmann family.

Surface Area under Vine: 19 ha.

This estate is the combination of the inheritances of Marie-Thérèse Rolly and Louis Gassmann. The wines sell well in Britain and the USA but they have never struck me as anything better than round and ripe and pleasant, with quite a bit of residual sugar, even at the lower levels.

DOMAINE MARTIN SCHAETZEL

Commune: Ammerschwihr.

Owner: Jean Schaetzel.

Surface Area under Vine: 6 ha including Grand Cru Kaefferkopf.

Jean Schaetzel is professor of oenology at the wine school in Rouffach. The domaine makes two *cuvées* of Riesling from the nearby Kaefferkopf: one from vines planted on marl, the other from the more usual granite. Cuvée Isabelle, Cuvée Catherine and Cuvée Nicolas indicate special bottlings. These are good wines here.

DOMAINE ANDRÉ SCHERER

Commune: Husseren-Les-Châteaux.

Owners: Scherer family.

Surface Area under Vine: 8 ha including Grands Crus Eichberg and Pfersigberg.

Christophe Scherer is in charge here, the family buying in wine to raise what they have to sell to the equivalent of 25 hectares, i.e. the equivalent of 200,000 bottles. Both Pinot Auxerrois and Pinot Gris are vinified in *barrique*, but so far they are not as sophisticated as those of, for instance, Ostertag (see left). Time will tell, no doubt. The Rieslings, traditionally made, are good.

DOMAINE SCHLUMBERGER

Commune: Guebwiller.

Owners: Schlumberger family.

Surface Area under Vine: 140 ha including Grands Crus Kessler, Kitterlé and Saering.

There cannot be many domaines in France with over 100 hectares of prime vineyard land. Schlumberger claim to be the largest estate on a slope. They are located in the extreme south of the region and make a speciality of late-harvested Gewurztraminers, labelled Cuvées Christine (Vendange Tardive) and Anne (Sélection de Grains Nobles). These can be fine but I find the lesser wines lack real refinement.

★ DOMAINE SCHOFFIT

Commune: Colmar.

Owners: Schoffit family.

Surface Area under Vine: 15 ha including Grand Cru Clos Saint-Théobald (Rangen de Thann).

Robert Schoffit produces the world's greatest Chasselas. This may not be of earth-shattering importance, but he also makes some splendidly serious wines from the volcanic Clos Saint-Théobald *grand cru* on the steep slopes of the Rangen de Thann.

DOMAINE GÉRARD SCHUELLER & FILS

Commune: Husseren-Les-Châteaux.

Owners: Schueller family.

Surface Area under Vine: 7 ha including Grands Crus Eichberg and Pfersigberg.

Gérard Schueller (beware of homonyms: there are other Schuellers in the village) eschews the use of chemical sprays, herbicides and fertilisers in order to be mean with the harvest and to persuade the vines to develop their own complex root-system, and to build up their own personal resistance to diseases. Good definitive wines across the range here.

DOMAINE SICK-DREYER

Commune: Ammerschwihr.

Owners: Dreyer family.

Surface Area under Vine: 13 ha including Grands Crus Kaefferkopf and Mambourg.

Pierre Dreyer took over from his late uncle Joseph Sick in 1989. Cuvée Joseph Dreyer indicates a special bottling. At the top levels the wines have no shortage of depth but the cheaper *cuvées* can be a little bland.

DOMAINE JEAN SIPP

Commune: Ribeauvillé.

Owners: Sipp family.

Surface Area under Vine: 22 ha including Grand Cru Kirchberg.

Not to be confused with Maison Louis Sipp, also in Ribeauvillé, Jean Sipp makes understated, stylish wines. The Rieslings from Kirchberg are minerally and classic. The Tokay from Trottsacker (not a *grand cru*) is also good.

★ DOMAINE BRUNO SORG

Commune: Eguisheim.

Owner: Sorg family.

Surface Area under Vine: 10 ha including Grands Crus Eichberg, Pfersigberg and Florimont.

This man is a rising star. He excels in many quarters, not least with that elusive variety, the Muscat which is one of the very best in the region. There are fine Rieslings from the Pfersigberg and Gewurztraminers from the Eichberg too.

★★★ MAISON F E TRIMBACH

Commune: Ribeauvillé.

Owners: Trimbach family.

Surface Area under Vine: 27 ha including Grands Crus Geisberg, Osterberg and Rosacker (Clos Sainte-Hune).

For most of my professional life I bought most of my Alsace wines from Trimbach. Trimbach is, along with Comtes Lafon in Burgundy, albeit in different ways, at the summit of dry white winemaking. The Clos Sainte-Hune is simply the world's top dry Riesling. From father to son since 1626, and now with Pierre at the helm in the cellar and his brother Jean as the 'public face', this firm has no ambition to be the biggest in Alsace: merely the best. They usually vinify their wines bone dry and disdain the idea of labelling their wines as *grand cru*, having already established brands such as Riesling Frédéric-Emile and Gewurztraminer Cuvée des Seigneurs de Ribeaupierre. Even the basic Pinot Blanc is one of the best aperitif wines on the market.

★★ DOMAINE WEINBACH
CLOS DES CAPUCINS

Commune: Kaysersberg.

Owners: Madame Colette Faller and family.

Surface Area under Vine: 24 ha including Grands Crus Schlossberg and Furstentum.

Madame Colette Faller and her two daughters make a formidable team, youngest daughter Laurence now being in charge in the cellar. There are a number of different names (such as Théo and Sainte Cathérine) and an even greater number of different *cuvées*, all variations on the theme of the *grand cru* Schlossberg and the surrounding terrain. The wines are sparkling and pure, dry but splendidly fruity, and of great class.

★★ DOMAINE ZIND-HUMBRECHT

Commune: Turckheim.

Owners: Zind-Humbrecht family.

Surface Area under Vine: 30 ha including Grands Crus Rangen, Goldert, Brand and Hengst.

In 1959 Léonard Humbrecht married Geneviève Zind, thus creating one of the greatest domaines in Alsace, now run by their son Olivier. The family is dedicated to low yields (average 30 hl/ha), specifically to allow the *terroir* to express itself, and to allow the wine to ferment out naturally. And the wines keep remarkably well.

In no other cellar in Alsace can you learn as much about how *terroir* affects taste and character. Their Rieslings, for example, offer the granite of Brand, the volcanic schist of the Clos Saint-Urbain in the Rangen, the muschelkalk of the Clos Winsbuhl above Hunawihr (not yet a *grand cru*), the marl of the Clos Hauserer, close to the Hengst (not a *grand cru* either), the different limestones of the Hengst and the Goldert, the gravel of the Herrenweg in Turckheim and the flatter land in Wintzenheim. None are alike, and if you sample the range at a basic level and then try the wines blind, in a different order at a better level, you can recognise the *terroir* signature: a fascinating lesson.

Other Producers of Note

ADAM (AMMERSCHWIHR), DOPFF ET IRION (RIQUEWIHR), CHARLES KOEHLY (RODERN), DOMAINE DU MANOIR/ MARINA & TOM THOMANN (INGERSHEIM), PREISS-ZIMMER (RIQUEWIHR), RIEFLÉ (PFAFFENHEIM), CHARLES SCHLERET (TURCKHEIM), LOUIS SIPP (RIBEAUVILLÉ) AND WILLM (BARR).

VIN DE LA MOSELLE

Surface Area (1998): 21 ha.

Production (1998): (Red and rosé) 431 hl; (white) 1169 hl.

Grape Varieties: (Red and rosé) Gamay, Pinot Meunier, Pinot Noir and Pinot Gris; (white)

Auxerrois, Gewurztraminer, Muller-Thurgau, Pinot Blanc and Pinot Gris.

Maximum Yield: 60 hl/ha.

Minimum Alcohol Level: 8.5°.

The VDQS wines of the French Moselle, covering three small areas near Sierck, Metz and Vic-sur-Seille in the *département* of Moselle, are a brief echo of those of neighbouring Luxembourg. The wines are of little consequence and with great difficulty, I managed to track down some on a recent visit but was not impressed.

CÔTES DE TOUL

Surface Area (1998): 97 ha.

Production (1998): (Red and rosé) 686 hl; (white) 722 hl.

Grape Varieties: (Red) Pinot Meunier and Pinot Noir; (rosé) Gamay, Pinot Meunier, Pinot Noir and white grapes; (white) Aligoté, Aubin and Auxerrois.

Maximum Yield: 60 hl/ha.

Minimum Alcohol Level: 8.5°.

The Côtes de Toul VDQS, from nine communes near the town of Toul, between Bar-Le-Duc and Nancy in the *département* of Meuse, is as obscure as Vin de La Moselle. Once upon a time these Lorraine wines were of some importance, and they certainly can boast a long history. The Vin Gris is an agreeable, light, fruity, Gamay-flavoured wine.

VINS DE PAYS

Vin de Pays de La Meuse

This obscure departmental *vin de pays* hails from the valley of the river Meuse west of Metz and Nancy. The varieties used are the same as for Côtes de Toul.

Vin de Pays du Bas-Rhin, Vin de Pays du Haut-Rhin

These two departmental *vins de pays* are obscure, with an estimated annual production of 50 hectolitres each.

CHAMPAGNE

THERE IS SOMETHING SPECIAL ABOUT CHAMPAGNE, and this something – which is unique to Champagne, not just to sparkling wines in general – has, I suspect, always been there, ever since Champagne as we know it today first began to be produced in the later half of the seventeenth century. Champagne is the celebration wine. It launches ships; it commemorates anniversaries; it toasts weddings. As Talleyrand, foreign minister of France in 1814, said, it is a civilising wine; an elevating wine, as Jorrocks neatly put it ('champagne certainly gives one very gentlemanly ideas'). It can even change principles: 'I'm only a beer teetotaller, not a Champagne teetotaller' (Candida). And it can lead to flights of fancy which no other wine can match. John Arlott in his book on Krug quotes a schoolgirl's first experience of Champagne: 'It's like icicles of rainbow in my mouth.' What a marvellous expression! I wish I'd thought of it!

Above all, Champagne is a joyful and luxurious wine – and by that I do not mean one has to live in the lap of luxury to be able to afford it. It is not pricey; indeed it is much less expensive by comparison with other top wines than it was ten or twenty years ago. By luxurious I mean that it induces a feeling of luxury, of well-being and gracious living, in the same way as dressing-up for dinner does. André Simon, Champagne promoter and connoisseur par excellence, coined the phrase 'The Art of Good Living'. No wine is more an example and a celebration of this art than Champagne.

Champagne is both a province and a wine. La Champagne is the region; le champagne is what is produced. The reason for the change of gender is that le champagne is really short for *le vin de la Champagne*. The name is derived from the Latin *campania*, meaning plain, and the region is one of the historic provinces of France, bounded by Belgium and Luxembourg on the north, Lorraine on the east, Burgundy to the south and Picardy and the Ile de France to the west. At the Revolution France was divided into *départements* – the province of Champagne was split between the *départements* of Ardennes, Marne, Aube, Haute-Marne and parts of Aisne. *La Champagne viticole* is almost entirely centred on the Marne with

about 75 per cent of the potential total vineyard of 30,700 hectares. The Aube has 17 per cent and the rest are scattered between the Aisne, Seine-et-Marne and Haute-Marne.

Theoretically, the total production of Champagne could reach 400 million bottles a year (see page 546). In practice, in a region at the extreme northern limits of grape-ripening, frost and other weather hazards bite into the potential crop. Harvests in recent years have been as low as 152 million bottles (1985), and even in super-abundant vintages such as 1982 and 1983, only the equivalent of some 300 million bottles were produced. The annual average for the five years 1993 to 1997 was 258 million bottles, and that is before allowing for the inevitable loss and evaporation between harvest and bottling. Meanwhile consumption climbed from 237 to 270 million bottles between 1988 and 1997. So supply is hardly keeping pace with demand. Another short crop will be a disaster.

This is perhaps the place to highlight the other important sparkling wines found in France. The Loire Valley (sparkling Vouvray, Saumur and others) is a major source. Crémant de Bourgogne comes closest in character to Champagne (the same grape varieties are used). Those of Alsace and Limoux can be delicious. Those from Die, a valley halfway down the Rhône Valley are less so. Champagne, though, considerably outsells the combined total of all these wines.

Nearly all France's *appellation contrôlée* sparkling wines are made by the Champagne method (though one is no longer allowed to use the phrase *méthode champenoise* or a translation thereof — other regions now have to use the term *méthode traditionnelle* or Traditional method). Lesser wines are made by the *cuve close* or Charmat method, the second fermentation taking place in bulk, in tank rather than in bottle, prior to filtration and bottling under pressure.

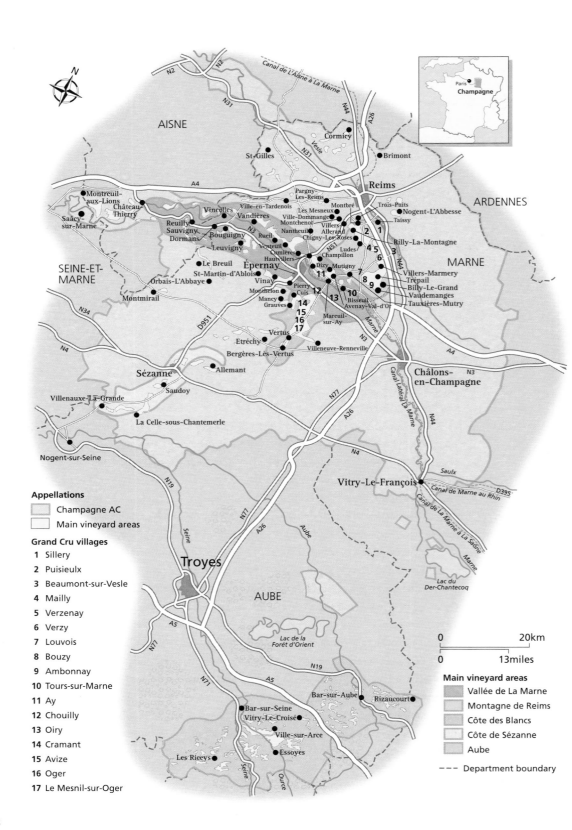

N

Canal de L'Aisne à La Marne

AISNE

ARDENNES

Cormicy

St-Gilles

Brimont

Reims

Montreuil-
aux-Lions

Château-
Thierry

Saâcy-
sur-Marne

Vincolles

Vandières

Pargny-
Les-Reims

Montbré

Trois-Puits

Ville-en-Tardenois

Les Mesneux

Nogent-L'Abbesse

Ville-Dommange

Taissy

Reuilly
Sauvigny
Dormans

Bouguigny

Rueil

Nantheuil

Montchenot

Villers
Allerand

Chigny-Les-Roses

2

1

Rilly-La-Montagne

MARNE

Leuvigny

Venteuil

Cumières

Ludes
Champillon

4 5

3

Le Breuil

Hautvillers

Dizy

Mutigny

6

SEINE-ET-
MARNE

St-Martin-d'Ablois

Epernay

11

7

Villers-Marmery

Orbais-L'Abbaye

Vinay

Pierry

8 9

Trépail

Montmirail

Montbelon

Cuis

12

10

Billy-Le-Grand

Mancy

13

Bisseuil

Vaudemanges

Grauves

14

Avenay-Val-d'Or

Tauxières-Mutry

15

Mareuil-
sur-Ay

16

17

Vertus

Etréchy

Villeneuve-Renneville

Bergères-Lès-Vertus

Châlons-
en-Champagne

Sézanne

Allemant

Villenauxe-La-Grande

Saudoy

La Celle-sous-Chantemerle

Nogent-sur-Seine

Vitry-Le-François

Canal de Marne au Rhin

Saulx

Troyes

AUBE

Lac du
Der-Chantecoq

Lac de la
Forêt d'Orient

Bar-sur-Aube

Rizaucourt

Bar-sur-Seine

Vitry-Le-Croisé

Ville-sur-Arce

Les Riceys

Essoyes

Appellations

Champagne AC

Main vineyard areas

Grand Cru villages

1 Sillery
2 Puisieulx
3 Beaumont-sur-Vesle
4 Mailly
5 Verzenay
6 Verzy
7 Louvois
8 Bouzy
9 Ambonnay
10 Tours-sur-Marne
11 Ay
12 Chouilly
13 Oiry
14 Cramant
15 Avize
16 Oger
17 Le Mesnil-sur-Oger

0   20km
0   13miles

Main vineyard areas

Vallée de La Marne
Montagne de Reims
Côte des Blancs
Côte de Sézanne
Aube

– – – Department boundary

HISTORY

While it is possible that the odd vine-cutting might have found its way up the Rhône, through Burgundy and into Champagne in pre-Roman times, it is highly unlikely that there was any large-scale vine cultivation before AD 50, and in a new vineyard, with forests to be cleared and the correct match of variety and site to be established, initial progress must have been slow, exacerbated by the edict of Emperor Domitian in AD 92 that all colonial vines must be uprooted. Appropriately this law was rescinded by a gardener's son, the Emperor Probus, in AD 202. In Reims, in celebration, a temple to Bacchus was erected, and on one of the columns of the Porte Mars, constructed about the same time but now destroyed, there is known to have been a vineyard scene. The years following were the first heyday of the *Champenois*. The wine, then red, but light and fruity, was exported to Rome where no doubt it was appreciated as a contrast to the heavy, alcoholic Italian brews, which were often spiced with resin and herbs, or laced with sea water.

Already, however, even in Probus' time, Champagne, so vulnerable to attack from the east, was subject to raids from Alamans and Franks. One wonders if the search for wine – for it was originally forbidden to sell wine to the barbarians – was a spur to these incursions. At first these invasions were easily repelled, but as the Roman Empire decayed, communications evaporated and requests for help and reinforcements became increasingly ignored, so the pressure, the numbers and the frequency of this aggression mounted. Reims was burnt to the ground in AD 355 and sacked again in 406. The European tribes had already made some permanent settlements throughout Gaul and Iberia. It was a further series of waves of invaders from Asia forcing the first barbarian settlements westwards which was to become the real threat to the Roman Empire, and it was in the Champagne district that a decisive battle was fought between Attila and his Asiatic Huns and the Gallo-Romans and their European barbarian allies, commanded by the Roman general Aetius. This battle

– with perhaps as many as a million men in the field, and it is estimated that 200,000 never left it alive – was of a size and savagery probably unparalleled before, and not equalled thereafter until the senseless brutality of the First World War was fought on the same soil.

Though Attila was defeated, the tide had irretrievably turned for the Romans. In the ensuing interregnum Clovis, king of the Franks, emerged as the master of northern Gaul. His conversion to Christianity by Saint-Rémi, Bishop of Reims, in AD 496 – his baptism is said to have taken place roughly where the cathedral now stands – was as important and far-reaching as that of Constantine a century and a half earlier. It ensured for the Champagne country a continuing prosperity, for Reims the prestige of being the spiritual centre of France, and for the French vineyards as a whole the continuity of the Church, for it was through the monastic orders that the techniques of viticulture and winemaking were preserved, refined and transferred through the succeeding generations. The barbarian domination was not then in the end as hostile or unpropitious to viticulture as is generally supposed. With the monastic movement gaining force throughout the seventh century, Champagne became a centre of new orders, and hardly had the first stone of a new monastery been laid than the monks would snap up the best land for their vines. Had it not been for them the story would have been entirely different.

In the middle of the ninth century, on the death of Charlemagne, the Frankish Empire was divided. Champagne was ruled by local counts, and because of its geographical position was gradually sucked into the kingdom of France. In 1285 Jeanne, heiress of Champagne and Navarre, married Philip the Fair, heir to the French throne, and the absorption was complete.

Dom Pérignon, of course, did not 'invent' Champagne. What he possessed, however, was an undoubted genius for knowing where the vine would flourish best, which soils would produce the best vines, the vinification, handling and maturation of wine, and, above all, for the blending of different wines to make up a whole which was infinitely more than the sum of its constituent parts. Pierre Pérignon was born, it is thought, in the late autumn of 1638, into a family of lawyers and local government officers. He entered the Saint-Vannes monastery at Verdun at the age of nineteen and some ten years later was appointed to the post of cellar-master at the Abbey of Hautvillers, near Epernay, where he remained until his death in 1715. The position of cellar-master was second only in importance to that of the abbot himself. Pérignon was responsible not only for the vineyards and the wine, but for all procurement – food, clothing and implements – for maintenance of the abbey and even for the abbey finances. He must have been highly regarded to have been given that position at the young age of thirty or so.

Under Dom Pérignon's aegis the wines of the Hautvillers Abbey soon became the most sought-after in the area, fetching prices up to four times that of its neighbours. Until his arrival the local wine, though made from red grapes, was not exactly red in colour. It must have been a sort of rosé, for only in exceptional years would the fruit have been ripe enough, the skins pigmented enough, to give the resulting must a really ruby colour. What Pérignon developed was, first, the technique of making white wine from red grapes; second, that of mixing young wines from different provenances and even ages to make a quality blend; and, third, the importance of maturing this wine so that instead of a harsh, rough, youthful brew, one would get a mellow, richly flavoured, mature wine. He was helped in his experiments by three factors: the considerable stock at his disposal, for the abbey's own holdings were sizeable, and this would be increased by the donations of wine they received in tithes; that in 1673 a very large underground cellar, called the Biscomettes *cellier*, was constructed beneath the abbey in the chalk subsoil; and because, early in his life, Dom Pérignon gradually went blind. He was obviously blessed with an exceedingly fine palate and, as can happen, this sense developed unusual powers to compensate for the other loss.

Additionally, the period of office of Dom Pérignon coincided with two important new developments.

There was the arrival of a new technique of glass-blowing developed in England, which resulted for the first time not only in a container which can be properly called a bottle, as we know it today – rather than a carafe or decanter – but one of a thickness and strength much tougher and more consistent than hitherto. And then there was the cork, a stopper certainly known to the Romans, but out of fashion and memory since the Dark Ages. Corks once again began to be used at the same time. The stage was set for the initiation of the wine we call Champagne; for the bottling of a carefully vinified and blended wine – a white wine from black grapes – which would at first be bottled before the first fermentation had entirely been completed, easy enough in Champagne's cold climate where the initial chemical reaction and certainly the malolactic fermentation would be temporarily halted by the winter snows, and then, increasingly be bottled with a little extra yeast and sugar, so that the amount of carbonic acid created would produce the fizz we expect today.

Whether Dom Pérignon actually was the first to bottle effervescent wine we do not know. We can certainly credit him with the turning of Champagne's greatest weakness, the insipidity of its wine – and whose popularity would come under increasing threat as communications developed and the wines of Burgundy and further south could easily reach Paris – into its greatest strength. The success of Champagne was not exactly instant, but once the sober regime of the elderly Louis XIV and his purse-lipped mistress, Madame de Maintenon, had given place to the debauched Regency of Louis d'Orléans, Champagne rapidly became the beverage of fashion. The ladies, in particular, liked the wine. It made them drunk without bringing too much of a flush to their cheeks. Champagne, said Madame de Pompadour, is the only wine that leaves a woman beautiful after drinking it. Once Voltaire had given the wine a splendid notice after visiting Epernay in 1737, and the Champenois had geared themselves up to meeting the demand from all corners of France, the prosperity of the wine was well and truly established.

The eighteenth and nineteenth centuries – for the Revolution and its consequences hardly affected the market for the wine – saw the consolidation of this early fame, the establishment of most of the firms we know today and the creation of an export market. Ruinart was founded in 1729, Moët in 1743 and the origins of Roederer and Lanson (the latter originally Delamotte Père et Fils) date from the 1760s; while Taittinger stems from Forest, Fourneaux et Cie which began as Jacques Fourneaux in 1734, and Philippe Clicquot, a banker and textile merchant, started a Champagne business in 1772. The original Heidsieck concern was founded in 1785, while Bollinger, Mumm, Krug and others followed in the early decades of the nineteenth century.

The early shippers were gentlemen (and ladies) of great personality, initiative and drive. They thought nothing of travelling enormous distances by stagecoach (in those days it would take three days to reach Orléans from Reims, and a fortnight to make the trip to Vienna) and journeyed to Russia, the United States and, later, to South America to promote their wares, always with great panache and extravagance. Bohne, the traveller for the widow Clicquot, went to Moscow to impress the Tsar and pick up his business only months after the retreat of Napoleon. Charles-Henri Heidsieck also cultivated the Russian market, on a white horse. Later the shippers of Moët & Chandon sent a trainload of the house brand to the survivors of the San Francisco earthquake in 1906. By this time no soirée, party or night-club extravaganza was complete without fizz, as the Victorians called it, bubbly as it was christened by the Edwardians, or champers as the gay young things of the 1920s named the wine. George Leybourne, as Champagne Charlie, sang the praises of Moët (or indeed any other marque you cared to name, for a shilling). A rival, the Great Vance, extolled Clicquot, and Edward VII was followed on shooting parties by the 'boy' with a basket of bottles.

Meanwhile in Champagne itself, there was unrest. Champagne was Big Business, and big business meant big profits. Yet the growers, then, as now, mainly small peasant landowners, with holdings of barely a hectare each on average, were being paid derisory amounts for their grapes. Not only this, but as demand continued to grow, as well as the area under vine expanding, some unscrupulous firms began to bring in wine from outside the Champagne area and incorporate it into *cuvées* destined to be made into Champagne. Unrest turned to fury, and fury to riot. Despite the creation, with the blessing of the honest Champagne houses, of a Syndicat Général des Vignerons, and government legislation – the first attempts at a definition of a delineated Champagne area – in 1908 and 1911, the tocsin began to beat. A fearful night of arson and looting took place in Ay, though the house of Bollinger (as they had been fair) was spared. Suddenly the normally temperate *vigneron* had become anarchist. The threat of continuing insurrection was swiftly dealt with. Accounts differ as to how many troops were drafted in (20,000 to 40,000), but the Champagne district became an armed camp. Additionally, further legislation, more satisfactory to the Marne growers, was proposed.

Enough has already been written about the First World War. I merely need to remind the reader that the Battle of the Marne, the first decisive event in the war, took place in the middle of the Champagne vineyards, with the grapes already having turned colour and almost ready to be picked. For the next three years the front line ran along the Reims to Châlons road, around Reims and along the Aisne-Marne canal. By the end of the war half the houses in the city were in ruins and it is a wonder that the cathedral, started in 1211 and finally completed in the fifteenth century, managed to survive.

The 1930s saw Prohibition in the United States and the slump on the one hand, but the establishment of the rules and regulations of *appellation contrôlée* on the other. It also saw the start of attempts to prohibit the use of the word 'Champagne', even with a qualifying prefix, by wines from outside the district. This culminated in the celebrated Spanish Champagne Case in London in 1958, which the Champenois originally lost, but then won two years later on appeal.

In 1941, in the dark days of the Second World War, a new organisation, the Comité Interprofessionnel du Vin de Champagne (CIVC), was established. The responsibilities of this body include organising and controlling both the production and the sales of Champagne 'with the constant aim of ensuring that honest and traditional practices are adhered to and quality is maintained', organising and disciplining the relations between grower and shipper, taking action in years of plenty or meagre yield to stabilise prices, and deciding the price to be paid to the growers each year for their grapes. The Council of the CIVC consists of five representatives from each side, from the vineyard owners on the one hand and the Champagne producers on the other. Since the Second World War production has increased sixfold, and so have sales. Exports have increased even more, though while in 1900 they represented two-thirds of total sales, now they make up only 40 per cent.

Meanwhile, some of the well-known Champagne houses, the Grandes Marques, have lost the family character they had possessed since their inauguration. There have been amalgamations and takeovers, mergers and public flotations. The giant Moët Hennessey group owns Mercier and Ruinart, as well as Christian Dior, and is itself associated with the Louis Vuitton group which owns Veuve Clicquot (LVMH is the name of the overall group). Seagrams, the North American spirit conglomerate, owned until recently Mumm and Perrier-Jouët. Rémy Martin have a controlling interest in Krug and in 1985 bought Charles Heidsieck; Taittinger owns Irroy just as Lanson owns Masse and Roederer Deutz; Laurent-Perrier owns shares in Castellane. Six firms are quoted on the Paris *bourse* (stock exchange) and a number of Champagne houses have interests in the Loire Valley and further afield, in California's Napa Valley, for example. The changes have become necessary as a result of the considerable sums of money involved. Most firms have a stock-holding of some three or four times their annual sales. Money is required for investment in increasingly sophisticated plant and machinery and for the ever more ruthless and expensive costs of maintaining and improving the brand image. Champagne is not a wine which can be successfully made, if quality is to be the keynote, on an artisanal scale.

THE CHAMPAGNE DISTRICTS

The three most important districts within the Champagne area are the Montagne de Reims, the Vallée de La Marne and the Côte des Blancs. The Montagne de Reims begins at Montchenot, south of Reims on the Epernay road, and runs clockwise round the side of the Montagne itself until Bouzy and Ambonnay. Here it meets the Vallée de La Marne district, which runs west along the banks of the Marne and the Marne-Rhine Canal towards Dormans. South and east of Epernay a range of hills runs south perpendicular to the river valley. The vineyards on these south-eastern-facing slopes make up the Côtes de Blancs. There are several smaller areas. South-west of Reims around the village of Ville-Dommange is the Petite Montagne; south-west of Epernay are the Cubry and Grauves valleys. Beyond Dormans lie the Aisne vineyards and to the south, around Sézanne, is the Côte de Sézanne. Finally, some 100 kilometres to the south, halfway to Dijon, is the district of the Aube around the two Bar townships: Bar-sur-Aube and Bar-sur-Seine.

The Montagne de Reims

The mountain of Reims is a hill some 20 kilometres wide from east to west and 10 kilometres long from north to south. Though it is a flat plateau on its thickly wooded top where there is a wild boar sanctuary, the sides of the Montagne rise steeply away from the surrounding countryside, from the valleys of the river Vesle on the north and Marne on the south. Near Verzy, on the eastern side, the forest is very curious. Strange, stunted, withered parasol beeches of considerable age, known as the Faux de Verzy, are to be found. A viral infection has produced this deformed growth, and I originally assumed the word *faux* (French for 'false') was a statement of description. I now find (from Patrick Forbes' excellent book *Champagne, The Wine, The Land and The People*, 1967) that the word is the plural of the old French for beech, *fay*. On the western side of Verzenay stands a disused windmill, now owned by Heidsieck Monopole & Co. This is an excellent place to stop and regard the vineyards, which stretch before and to the side in an unbroken succession. In the distance, through the smoke of Reims, one can see the cathedral.

The vines begin hard by the Epernay to Reims road, in the village of Montchenot, and continue through Villers-Allerand, Rilly, Chigny-Les-Roses, Ludes, Mailly, Verzenay, Verzy, Villers-Marmery, Trépail, Louvois, Tauxières, Bouzy and Ambonnay; lower down lie Sillery, Puisieulx and Beaumont-sur-Vesle. At first, unusually for a French wine area, the aspect is to the north, then to the east – only from Trépail onwards is it properly to the south. The Montagne de Reims is a region of mainly black grapes – Pinot Noir and Pinot Meunier. Indeed, Bouzy produces the best-known Coteaux Champenois or still red wine. The Champagnes from here are powerful, rich and full of depth.

CHAMPAGNE DISTRICTS
SURFACE AREA IN HECTARES (1998 HARVEST)

MONTAGNE DE REIMS	4047
VALLÉE DE LA MARNE (RIVE GAUCHE)	2138
VALLÉE DE LA MARNE (RIVE DROITE)	2870
CÔTE DES BLANCS	3162
PETITE MONTAGNE	2751
RÉGION D'EPERNAY	1233
RÉGION DE CONGY	1007
AISNE VINEYARDS	2851
CÔTE DE SÉZANNE	1367
AUBE VINEYARDS	6717
ISOLATED VINEYARDS	2980
TOTAL	31,220

(These are the figures for vineyards in production.)

SURFACE AREA (HA) BY DÉPARTEMENT (1998 HARVEST)

DÉPARTEMENT	SURFACE AREA (HA)
MARNE	22,442
AUBE	5877
AISNE	2030
HAUTE-MARNE	21
SEINE-ET-MARNE	20
TOTAL	30,370

(These are the figures accompanying the declaration of appellation contrôlée wine.)

The Vallée de La Marne

Beyond Bouzy and Ambonnay, whose vineyards already have a southerly as opposed to easterly aspect, the Vallée de La Marne begins. This stretches between Tours and Dormans, a distance of some 35 kilometres. The Vallée de La Marne district can be divided into two sections. The more easterly, and better section, known as the Vins de La Rivière, lasts until Cumières. From Damery westwards, the soil and aspect is poorer. Vineyards continue on both sides of the river bank until Dormans, where they become the Aisne département, and stretch intermittently onwards for nearly another 25 kilometres, past Château-Thierry until Nanteuil which lies just within the border of the Seine-et-Marne département. Here we are only 50-odd kilometres, as the crow flies, from Notre Dame in Paris.

The important Vallée de La Marne communes are Tours-sur-Marne, Bisseuil, Avenay, Mareuil-sur-Ay, Ay, Mutigny, Dizy, Champillon, Hautvillers and Cumières. Like the Montagne de Reims this is a black grape district. Though the resulting white wine is less powerfully bodied than that from the Montagne de Reims, it is nevertheless full, and is finely perfumed and of fine, elegant character.

The Côte des Blancs

As the name suggests, the Côte des Blancs is the white grape district. While there are some Chardonnay vineyards among the Pinot ones of the Montagne de Reims and the Marne Valley, in the Côte des Blancs you will hardly find a single red grape. The vines cling to the eastern side of a hill approximately 20 kilometres long and form a strip no more than a couple of kilometres wide, not unlike the Côte d'Or in shape. The main villages, running north to south, are Chouilly, Cramant, Avize, Oger, Le Mesnil-sur-Oger and Vertus.

Soil and Climate

What distinguishes the Champagne area from the surrounding countryside, and what gives its wines their special character, is the nature of the soil, the subsoil, and its climate. Much of northern France – and indeed southern England – has a chalky or limestone soil dating from the Upper Cretaceous era, roughly 65 million years ago. It is also fairly flat. At the end of the Tertiary period (30 million years ago) earthquakes of considerable violence struck at the eastern side of the Paris basin, forcing the land to buckle and rise up above the surrounding countryside. This chain of hills, the Falaises de Champagne, consists of a particular type of chalk, Belimnita Quadrata, not found in the outlying areas. The Montagne de Reims, the Côte des Blancs and the other Champagne hills are also the only important hills between Normandy and the Vosges. The tops of these hills are thickly wooded which helps protect the vines on the slopes below.

The chalk subsoil, rich in minerals and trace elements, is covered by a very thin layer of surface soil, nowhere more than a metre thick and in places hardly 15 centimetres. This often washes away in the heavy winter rains and laboriously has to be replaced. The soil varies marginally between the three main regions described above. In the Côte des Blancs there is clay, in the Marne Valley sand and on the Montagne de Reims cendres noires, a sort of impure lignite. These nuances, as well as the dissimilarities in mesoclimate, help explain the differences between the wines.

Chalk is a soil which is excellent for a vine-growing area, particularly one at the northern limits of successful cultivation. It drains well, yet does not dry out; it is loose and friable, enabling the vines' roots to penetrate deep; and it is heat-retentive, radiating the heat of the day back on to the vines in the cool of the night.

The climate in Champagne is what you would expect in an area only a few degrees south of the 50 degrees latitude line generally agreed as the northern limit for successful vine cultivation. It is wet, it is cold and grey for much of the year, and it is prone to frost. Yet the mean average temperature on the vineyard slopes is a good half a degree Centigrade above the minimum required for the cultivation of the vine, and the vines are for the most part sheltered from the prevailing westerly winds. Rain, however, is a problem, as is late spring frost. It rains for 160 days a year on average, with July being the wettest month of all. This makes hail an additional hazard, and renders spraying of the vines against mildew

and other diseases a constant necessity. Frost damage is something the Champenois, like their colleagues in Chablis, just have to accept. Hardly a year goes by without some devastation just as the buds are beginning to shoot in the spring (it is less of a problem while the vine is dormant).

Grape Varieties

The three grape varieties of Champagne are the black Pinot Noir and Pinot Meunier and the white Chardonnay. Overall, the black varieties predominate, with about 75 per cent of the vineyard region, the Pinot Noir found particularly in the Montagne de Reims and the Aube and the Pinot Meunier in the Vallée de La Marne. The Chardonnay is king in the more clayey soil of the Côte des Blancs. It is the Pinot Noir which gives backbone, richness of flavour, depth of character, finesse and the ability to age for a decade or more, as anyone who has tasted a really good Blanc de Noirs will know.

The advantage of the Pinot Meunier is that it will grow on land which the more fussy Pinot Noir would disdain. It is hardy and it buds late – an advantage in such a northerly climate. The wine from it is very scented but has less breed, and it ages more rapidly than the Pinot Noir. Nevertheless, some Champagne houses, Krug and Deutz, for instance, would not be without it. It is the most widely planted variety, accounting for 44 per cent of Champagne's surface area (Pinot Noir covers 30 per cent and Chardonnay 26 per cent).

The Chardonnay buds earlier than the other two, making it the most susceptible to frost, but takes longest of all to complete its cycle from shoot to ripeness, hence its higher acidity, which is so necessary for quality sparkling wine. Normally the harvest on the Côte des Blancs does not take place until a week after the Montagne de Reims. Chardonnay produces wine of less alcohol but great delicacy, finesse and freshness. Champagne made solely from the Chardonnay, called Blanc de Blancs, is noted for its light, almost ethereal, filigree character, and a subtle, unmuscular complexity of fruit. Most Blancs de Blancs, though there are exceptions such as Taittinger's Comtes de Champagne, do not last as long as Chardonnay/Pinot blends.

Champagne Growers

Champagne is a region of the small husbandman. There are some 19,000 growers in an area of 30,700 hectares, an average of 1.6 hectares each. Take away the roughly 3700 hectares, one-eighth of the area, which are owned by the Champagne houses themselves, and the average holding falls even more. Most growers can only work part-time in their vineyards, and have jobs in Reims, Epernay or Châlons during the day. Few, obviously, can be self-sufficient in wine terms, and though an increasing number now sell their own Champagne, one suspects that the majority of these may be own-label wines but produced in a local co-operative. Tom Stevenson, in his monumental *World Encyclopedia of Champagne and Sparkling Wine* (1998) puts the number of independent growers selling their own individual wine at 2124.

Of the 261 or so Champagne firms, some sixty have vineyard holdings, and these are concentrated more in the best areas. In the Montagne de Reims and Côte des Blancs, for instance, these firms own one-fifth of the *vignoble* as against one-eighth over the whole region. The size of their holdings, naturally, is very much larger. The Champagne houses who have extensive land of their own, will, of course, assure you of the wisdom and good fortune of this fact. They are able to control the entire process from start to finish. They are less reliant on the vagaries of the open market and the increasing competition for the best grapes of the best growers. Those who have no vineyards will be equally adamant that theirs is the best policy: total flexibility to purchase only the best and in whatever quantities they wish depending on the quality of the vintage and the state of the market.

Most of the large Champagne houses do have vineyard holdings. The amount of grapes these provide, relative to production, can be as much as 80 per cent in the case of Louis Roederer and 70 per cent in the case of Bollinger, though the figure is usually far less. Some (Alfred Gratien, Charles Heidsieck and Piper Heidsieck, for instance) possess no vineyards at all. I don't think the presence or lack of a large in-house landholding has any bearing on the quality of the label.

The Champagne houses own 12 per cent of the land but are responsible for 71 per cent of all sales. On the export market, however, the shippers are supreme, accounting for 88 per cent of the total, only the co-operative at Mailly on the Montagne de Reims being any rival, in the sense that it sells under its own name rather than supplying Buyer's Own Brand Champagne (B.O.B.).

Classifications

The communes in the Champagne area were first classified in 1911, originally into Hors Classe (today *Grand Cru*), Première Catégorie (or *Premier Cru*) and Deuxième Catégorie (or *Deuxième Cru*). Later this was refined into percentages, with the Hors Classe communes being given a 100 per cent rating, the *premiers crus* between 90 and 99 per cent, and so on. It is on this basis that the *négociant* and grower agree a price for the grapes which are produced. Each year just before the vintage commences, the CIVC fixes a price for a kilo of grapes from a 100 per cent *cru* – in 1999 it was 25.50FF – taking into account the current world and Champagne's economic and stock position, and the potential size and quality of the harvest. The price of grapes in the rest of the area follows according to the rating of each vineyard.

There are seventeen *grands crus* or 100 per cent communes: Avize, Cramant, Chouilly, Oiry, Oger and Le Mesnil-sur-Oger (white grapes only) in the Côte des Blancs, Ay and Tours-sur-Marne (black grapes only) in the Vallée de La Marne, and Ambonnay, Beaumont-sur-Vesle, Bouzy, Louvois, Mailly, Sillery, Puisieulx, Verzy and Verzenay on the Montagne de Reims. Those with 95 per cent and above include Vertus (white grapes only) in the Côte des Blancs, Grauves and Cuis (white only) in the Cubry/Grauves valleys, Mareuil-sur-Ay and Dizy in the Vallée de La Marne, and Tauxières, Trépail and Villers-Marmery on the Montagne de Reims.

Personally I feel this classification is too simplistic. It would be like decreeing that all Vosne-Romanée in Burgundy is 100 per cent while Nuits-Saint-Georges, adjacent, only merited 95 per cent. This is, of course, ridiculous. Parts of Ambonnay, Avize and Ay, to take the first three villages alphabetically, are of course capable of making first class wine but not every site in these villages. It is time the Champagne authorities moved to a stricter assessment of every vineyard.

CHAMPAGNE PRODUCTION

CHAMPAGNE

Surface Area (1998): 30,370 ha.

Production (1998): 332 million bottles (2,515,151 hl).

Colour: White and rosé.

Grape Varieties: Pinot Noir, Pinot Meunier and Chardonnay.

Maximum Yield: 13,000 kg/ha (86.66hl/ha).

Minimum Alcohol Level: 11° after second fermentation.

Surface Area and Production

The Champagne area and its production has expanded over the last twenty years or so. There is perhaps a theoretical maximum of some 35,000 hectares of suitable land. While this would give 400 million bottles of wine per annum in theory – or even more in a really abundant vintage – what, given the vagaries of the Champagne climate, would be the average? 350 million? And how much of this increase would be of acceptable quality? Demand is continuing to grow. It was probably (official figures were not out as we go to press) 300 million bottles in 1999, pre-millennium. Sadly, on past

CHAMPAGNE PRODUCTION

YEAR	SURFACE AREA (HA)	PRODUCTION (MILLION BOTTLES)
1998	30,370	332
1997		229
1996		270
1995	30,709	286
1994		244
1993		257
1992		288
1991		278
1990	27,542	288
1989		275
1988		224
1986	25,250	259
1985	26,398	152
1983		302
1982		295

experience, the Champenois will have to take steps to reduce demand and that means by raising prices. My suggestion is to try other increasingly well made Champagne- or Traditional-method wines from elsewhere in France or from other parts of the world.

How Champagne Is Made

The key to making Champagne, indeed any non-artificially carbonated sparkling wine, is the induction of a second sugar-alcohol fermentation, producing carbon dioxide, and the retention of this carbon dioxide within the wine, in the form of carbonic acid, until the cork of the bottle is released. Once that pressure is off, the carbonic acid can revert back to water and carbon dioxide and the carbon dioxide escapes in the form of tiny bubbles which well up mainly from the bottom of the glass. This is the fizz. There are 250 million bubbles (says Tom Stevenson, *op. cit.*) in an average bottle of Champagne.

What is special about the Champagne method is that the second fermentation takes place in a bottle and that the wine remains in the same receptacle from the moment the bottling takes place until the moment of consumption. The problem, and one of the causes of the expense of such a wine, multiplied in the case of Champagne by the high price of the base fruit, is that this second fermentation produces a sediment which has to be eliminated without losing the carbon dioxide.

Champagne is first made like any other white wine, the difference again between most other sparkling white wines – whether made by the Champagne method or not – being that the main ingredient is usually black grapes, not white. Most varieties of grapes, however, all that are white and most that are black, whatever the colour of their skins, have white juice. The pigmentation causing the red colour in red wines comes from these skins, and so the first task is to ensure a quick and uncomplicated pressing to extract juice without allowing the skins to colour the must.

The traditional Champagne press consists of a round or square base, loose planks which can be inserted on their sides to enclose the platform, and a vertical screw press which descends to press the grapes. Nowadays these presses are being replaced by horizontal machines. The regulations stipulate that 4000 kilograms of grapes are required in order to produce 2950 litres of must. The first pressing yields 2050 litres of the best quality and is termed the *cuvée*. The second pressing will give a further 500 litres and is called the *taille*. The rest is the *deuxième taille*. The best Champagnes are made from just the *cuvée*.

The next step, after the must, or grape juice, has been allowed to settle so that some of the gross lees can be racked off, is the fermentation. This takes place in concrete or stainless-steel tanks at 15°C to 20°C and usually with the aid of special yeasts – of the main houses only Krug and Alfred Gratien, to my knowledge, still vinify their entire harvest in oak – and is followed, if the winemakers desire, by a malolactic fermentation. So far, apart from the separation of the pressings, the process has been similar to white winemaking all over the world. But now comes the first important divergence, the *assemblage* or blending.

Nowhere is the winemaker's expertise more of an art than in the blending of Champagne. Champagne is an area of three grape varieties, many different subtle variations of soil and mesoclimates. Most houses will have contracts with growers from all over the region, as well as grapes from their own vineyards. Their aim, with this variety of base ingredients, and despite the difference in the weather pattern from year to year, is to produce a standard, consistent and quality blend which typifies the style and personality of their house; and they have to do this with young wine, harsh, raw, acid and unpalatable. It is a skill unparalleled in modern winemaking.

Once the blend has been prepared – in the case of non-vintage wine this will almost certainly require the use of older reserves of wine especially kept back for the purpose – the wine is bottled, and at the same time a carefully calculated amount of *liqueur de tirage*, sugar and yeast dissolved in wine, is added. This will produce the second fermentation, and because of the build-up of pressure of carbon dioxide, the by-product, the bottle will need to be tougher than usual, and the closure firmly attached. Most closures these days are a sort of crown cork but in the past, only today for some de luxe *cuvées*, a cork, secured by a metal clip (*agrafe*) was used. The bottles are then binned away, the second fermentation takes place and the wines are allowed to mature, feeding on the lees or sediment of dead yeast cells left over after this fermentation process.

Next comes the elimination of the sediment. It has first to be collected into a compact little cup, on the underside of the closure, and then removed without allowing the gas to escape. In order to shake down the sediment, an operation known as *remuage*, the bottles are put into *pupitres*. These consist of two rectangular planks of wood a little smaller than a door, fastened together at the long ends, and stood upright in an A-shape, into which have been cut a number of angled holes. The bottles are inserted into the holes, which are wide enough to trap them by the neck, and at first lie horizontally. The task of the *remueur* is to give each bottle a series of turns, shakes and tilts so that over a period of two or three months the bottles are lifted from horizontal to vertical, neck downwards, and the sediment shaken down so that it rests on the underside of the closure.

By passing the bottles, still upside down, through a freezing solution, the *dégorgement*, or removal, of the original closure and sediment can be simply accomplished as the bottom inch or so of the wine, including the sediment, forms a little block of icy slush. The bottles are then topped up, normally with a little sugar solution (the *liqueur d'expédition* or *dosage*), corked and then given a rest for several months before labelling and shipping.

This is the process in a nutshell, and, as can be seen, it takes time, it requires space for the hundreds of *pupitres* – and it is expensive. An experienced *remueur* is said to be able to handle 30,000 bottles a day, but in terms of the millions of bottles exported each year this is negligible, particularly if the *remuage* process is to last for the full three months. Today, *remuage* is speeded up, in many houses, to five or six weeks, or is being done mechanically. Mechanical systems, using gyropalettes, are increasingly widely used, and consist of hexagonal metal bins, holding 500-odd bottles, which rotate and oscillate mechanically every few hours, day in and day out, and reduce the process of shaking down the sediment to a week. Another technique, still experimental, is to introduce the yeast for the second fermentation encapsulated in a small ball. The membrane of these balls or *billes* allows the yeasts to do their work in the wine without allowing the deposit to escape, and it is hoped that this will make the work of *remuage* easier still.

The penultimate process before the final resting and labelling is the introduction of the *liqueur d'expédition*. This will determine how sweet the Champagne is to be. Champagne, even though it undergoes two fermentations, is a fully fermented wine, so it will be bone dry. As a wine from such a northern area it would also normally be unduly austere. A little sweetening will round the wine off and accentuate the fruit.

Most Champagne has a pressure of between five and six atmospheres. Until 1992 the term Crémant in Champagne used to refer to a wine with a little less pressure, four to five atmospheres, but now the term can only be used by other French wine regions (for instance, Alsace, Die, Bourgogne, Loire and Limoux) for their Champagne-method sparkling wines bottled at full pressure at five to six atmospheres .

CHAMPAGNE STYLES

Champagne can vary widely in style. Not only will there be differences according to the quality – vintage, non-vintage or de luxe – but also according to the grapes used. Moreover Champagne changes character as it ages. Additionally each house has its own particular style, and just as the discerning eye can differentiate between Monet and Renoir, so can (though I must personally confess with rather more difficulty) the discerning palate distinguish between, say, Bollinger and Pol Roger, and identify Krug without seeing the label.

Which style and which vintages you prefer are as much a question of personal taste as inherent quality. In the profiles of the leading producers (see page 551) I attempt to give an indication of the house style as well as denoting which are my particular favourites. In fact my taste for Champagne is extremely catholic. It is the supreme wine to drink alone or in company, at any time of the day or night, with or without food.

Pink Champagne

There is an increasing vogue for both Champagne rosé and Champagne produced exclusively from white grapes, Blanc de Blancs. The rosé is produced by mixing a little red wine with the white before bottling (Champagne is the only French wine where this is allowed), although it can be produced by making a rosé in the usual manner and then applying the Champagne method to that. In my view, though this is not stipulated in the legislation, it should also be produced entirely from the Pinot Noir grape, and those which are do stand out as more elegant and interesting examples. For some reason which I do not fully understand, rosé Champagne is more expensive than the normal wine. It can be both vintage and non-vintage. Recommended wines: Billecart-Salmon, Lanson, Perrier-Jouët, Pol Roger, Pommery's Cuvée Louise Pommery, Roederer, Taittinger's Comtes de Champagne and Veuve Clicquot.

Blanc de Blancs

Blanc de Blancs, made exclusively from the Chardonnay grape, is, or should be, lighter and slimmer than ordinary Champagne, delicate as well as elegant. There are some delicious Blancs de Blancs which fully justify the extra price, for if they come from the Côte des Blancs exclusively they are bound to be expensive. Other examples, though, seem rather thin and pale in character when drunk alongside a good non-Blanc de Blancs wine. It can be both vintage and non-vintage. Recommended wines: Billecart-Salmon, Krug's Clos de Mesnil, Mumm's Mumm de Cramant, Bruno Paillard, Pol Roger, Salon and Taittinger's Comtes de Champagne.

Blanc de Noirs

Blanc de Noirs, literally 'white of blacks', is a Champagne made entirely from either or both Pinot Noir and Pinot Meunier. There are very few of these wines. Bollinger produces a delicious but very, very expensive wine from a small plot of *vieilles vignes françaises* (ungrafted vines). The colour is golden, rather than straw-yellow and the wine is full-bodied, intensely flavoured, and very rich but not sweet: certainly a Champagne for food rather than for drinking as an aperitif.

Non-Vintage

Champagne can be sold with or without a vintage date, though if it is to have a vintage date 100 per cent of the blend needs to come from that vintage. If non-vintage, it cannot be put on the market until twelve months after 1 January following the harvest. If vintage, the stipulation is a minimum of three years. All Champagne houses produce a range of Champagnes from a basic non-vintage wine upwards. The non-vintage wine is the mass-produced brand, and therefore in this sense the flagship wine of the house. Non-vintage Champagne probably makes up 85 per cent or more of the market.

Vintage

Vintage Champagne, like vintage Port, is something special. It is, or should be, only declared in exceptional years, say, three or four times a decade, and it should be a wine of high quality, left to mature until it is round, complex, richly textured and full-flavoured. It should not be drunk as an aperitif, before the taste buds are ready to appreciate it, but with food or perhaps after a splendid meal when it can receive the full attention it deserves. Top vintage Champagnes need ten years to mature. The best include Bollinger, Alfred Gratien, Pol Roger, Roederer and Veuve Clicquot.

De Luxe

The same ageing period applies to the increasing number of prestige brands or de luxe wines. Led by Dom Pérignon, Moët & Chandon's de luxe brand, created as long ago as 1935, nearly all houses now produce a superior vintage, often in a fancy bottle, usually with a fancy name. All are expensive, some are delicious. Krug vintage, because of its price, must be considered a de luxe brand. My other favourites include Bollinger RD, Moët & Chandon Dom Pérignon, Laurent-Perrier Cuvée Grande Siècle, Pol Roger Sir Winston Churchill, Pomméry Cuvée Louise, Taittinger Comtes de Champagne and Veuve Clicquot La Grande Dame. In my view, sadly, rather too many, and that applies also to ordinary vintage Champagne, are put on the market too young. All vintage and de luxe Champagnes should have at least five years on their lees and further age thereafter.

Reading the Label

Small initials preceding a code number on the label indicate what sort of producer has made the wine.

NM Négociant-Manipulant A producer who buys in grapes and makes his own Champagne.

RM Récoltant-Manipulant A producer who makes Champagne from his own vineyards.

CM Coopérative-Manipulant The producer is a co-operative.

SR Société de Récoltants A partnership (often members of the same family) sharing premises and producing wine jointly.

ND Négociant-Distributeur The company is selling wine it did not make itself.

MA Marque d'Acheteur The wine is sold under the house or brand name of the purchaser such as a restaurant, wine merchant or supermarket. This applies also to Buyer's Own Brand (B.O.B.) Champagne.

LARGER BOTTLE SIZES FOR CHAMPAGNE

MAGNUM	2 BOTTLES
JEROBOAM	4 BOTTLES
REHOBOAM	6 BOTTLES
METHUSELAH	8 BOTTLES
SALMANAZAR	12 BOTTLES
BALTHAZAR	16 BOTTLES
NEBUCHADNEZZAR	20 BOTTLES

A Jeroboam of Champagne is a different size from a Jeroboam in Bordeaux, which used to be six bottles (4.5 litres) until 1989 but is now $6\,^2/_3$ bottles (5 litres).

CHAMPAGNE SWEETNESS

	RESIDUAL SUGAR G/L
EXTRA BRUT (NOT DOSED)	0–6
(also called Brut Intégral, Brut Nature, Brut Non-Dosé and others)	
BRUT (DRY)	3–15
EXTRA SEC (OFF-DRY TO MEDIUM DRY)	12–20
SEC (MEDIUM-DRY)	7–35
DEMI-SEC (QUITE SWEET)	35–50
DOUX (RICH AND SWEET)	50-PLUS

Nearly all Champagne is produced as Brut or Extra Sec. Only a little sweeter Champagne is produced, to accompany dessert courses.

Coteaux Champenois

Surface Area (1998): Not quoted separately.
Production (1998): (Red, rosé and white) 721 hl.
Colour: Red, rosé and white.
Grape Varieties: (Red and rosé) Pinot Noir and
Pinot Meunier; (white) Chardonnay.
Maximum Yield: 13,000 kg/ha (86.66 hl/ha).
Minimum Alcohol Level: 10°.

To some extent, Coteaux Champenois may be deemed the surplus wine from the Champagne area, for in order to keep supply and demand for the sparkling wine in equilibrium, the CIVC decides annually how many kilograms of grapes per hectare may be made into Champagne. The rest is used for still wine or Coteaux Champenois. Production, therefore, varies widely from one vintage to another. Sometimes it can be several thousand hectolitres. Sometimes hardly anything at all.

A generation ago the wine had a certain notoriety. At that time most Coteaux Champenois was white, produced as a generic wine by the Champagne houses themselves, Laurent Perrier and Moët & Chandon (under the Saran label) being the best known. Today most is red, and more is made by individual growers. Some of these can be recommended, particularly the Bouzy from Georges Vesselle, the local mayor. There are also one or two rosés. The white does not stand up to comparison with white Burgundy. It seems austere, as well as a little thin. Sadly it is also considerably more expensive.

Rosé des Riceys

Surface Area (1998): Not quoted separately.
Production (1998): 471 hl.
Colour: Rosé.
Grape Variety: Pinot Noir.
Maximum Yield: 13,000 kg/ha (86.66 hl/ha).
Minimum Alcohol Level: 10°.

Rosé des Riceys is a separate *appellation* for still wine, centred on the village of Riceys in the Aube *département*. I find it undistinguished.

When to Drink Champagne

Though it is said that fifteen years is the maximum life span for Champagne, I have found that to be unduly pessimistic. I have had Champagnes of almost 100 years old (admittedly only in the region itself) which have shown no sign of decay or lack of *mousse*, and I have had many wonderful Champagnes with twenty years or more bottle age. Old Champagne is delicious, and a year or two's landed age given to a raw non-vintage Champagne can work wonders.

Champagne Vintages

1998 Champagne escaped the frost and hail which had reduced the crop in Chablis and further south. After a good August but a rainy September there was a record crop. Quality, reflecting this volume, is merely fair.

1997 A small harvest. After a poor summer fine September weather produced wines high in both alcohol and acidity. Very good quality at best: but variable.

1996 A good-sized harvest. Excellent weather during the run up to the vintage produced very healthy ripe fruit. Never before have there been musts with such high sugar readings and such high acidities. Fine quality. Almost certainly to be declared as vintage.

1995 A large harvest. After a shaky start – frost in April and again in May – the flowering was successful and the summer warm and dry. After a rainy start to September the harvesting weather was benign. Very good quality. Probably to be declared as a vintage.

1994 A small harvest. The summer was largely fine, but the weather deteriorated in September and then improved at the end of the picking period. Nevertheless rot was widespread and a severe sorting out of the fruit was vital. Average quality only.

1993 An average harvest. The summer was uneven, odium and mildew prevalent, and heavy rain set in just as the harvest was about to commence, causing widespread rot, and lowering the acidity of the wines. Not great, but a stop-gap vintage for some houses.

1992 A large harvest. An early harvest after a generous good summer was a little interrupted by rain but nevertheless produced a satisfactory if not outstanding crop, best in the Chardonnays of the Côte de Blancs.

Declared by some houses as vintage.

1991 A large harvest, despite frost in late April. After a good summer the harvest, which began late, was spoilt by rain. Quality is only fair.

1990 A large harvest. After a poor spring, including frost in early April, the summer weather was excellent. The harvest was early, the fruit ripe, the level of potential alcohol high, as were the acidities. A splendid vintage of very high quality: firm, beautifully balanced, elegant wines which will keep for a long time.

EARLIER VINTAGES OF NOTE

1989, 1988, 1986, 1985, 1983, 1982, 1979, 1976, 1975, 1973, 1971, 1970, 1969, 1966 and 1964.

LEADING CHAMPAGNE HOUSES

★ BILLECART-SALMON
Commune: Mareuil-sur-Ay.
Owners: Billecart family.
Annual Sales: 720,000 bottles.
Vineyard Ownership: 10 ha.

Billecart-Salmon is a small, family-owned house the quality of whose wines has made enormous strides in the last twenty years. There have been Billecarts in the area since the sixteenth century but the Champagne firm dates from 1818 and a joint venture between Nicolas-François Billecart and his brother-in-law Louis Salmon. With a large proportion of Chardonnay in the blends, the range is noted for its purity of flavour and very good acidity. These are wines which are both delicate and intense. The de luxe wines are the Cuvée N.F. (Nicolas-François) and the Elizabeth Salmon Rosé.

★★ BOLLINGER
Commune: Ay-Champagne.
Owners: Bollinger family.
Annual Sales: 1.2 million bottles.
Vineyard Ownership: 142 ha.

The original Bollinger, Joseph (later changed to Jacques when he took French nationality), was a young German who was engaged by Admiral Count Athanase de Villemont to supplement the family fortunes by making wine on his estates. In 1829 Jacques Bollinger set up in business on his own, and later married the Admiral's daughter. One of Champagne's best-loved characters was Lily Bollinger, the wife of Jacques' grandson who ran Bollinger from the death of her husband in 1941 until her own death at the age of seventy-eight in 1977.

Bollinger's own vineyards have an average quality rating of 97 per cent, and produce two-thirds of their own requirements. They include two small plots of ungrafted Pinot Noir, the vines being reproduced by layering, or *provinage*. This produces the Vieilles Vignes Françaises, a Champagne of great breed and immense depth of character. Bollinger's vintage Champagne is called Grande Année, a reference to the fact that vintage Champagne is, or should be, only declared in the finest years. Bollinger R.D. is one of my all-time favourite Champagnes – the initials stand for *récemment dégorgé* (recently disgorged) and indicate a wine which has been kept longer than normal – up to as much as ten years – between bottling and disgorging. All this time it has been feeding off the lees, and the result is a wine of great complexity, concentration and richness. Bollinger were the first to publicise the idea and have in fact registered the words R.D. as a trademark. The R. D. is a personal favourite of mine. It was first launched in 1962 with the 1953 vintage. Année Rare is a wine kept even longer on its lees. Bollinger do not use the second and third pressings, even in their non-vintage Spéciale Cuvée; 80 per cent of their production is vinified in wood, and the firm has a stockholding equivalent to five years' sales. A subsidiary company is the sparkling Loire firm of Langlois-Château.

Bollinger is one of the great Champagne houses, producing firm, full, meaty wines which last well. Even the Spéciale Cuvée needs keeping, and it has occasionally been put onto the market a little early. The Vintage and de luxe wines are truly classic, especially in masculine vintages such as 1990, 1982, 1975 and 1970.

★ ALFRED GRATIEN

Commune: Epernay.
Owners: Seydoux family.
Annual Sales: 150,000 bottles.

Alfred Gratien is by no means a large Champagne house but it is one of the very best and one of my favourites. Winemaking is traditional: vinification is in oak; *remuage* and disgorgement are by hand; and the Champagne is not put on the market until fully mature, the Vintage not until almost ten years after the vintage, which virtually allows them (if they were permitted so to do) to call every vintage bottle R.D.! The composition of the vintage wine varies with every year. Gratien was founded in 1864 and is a subsidiary of Gratien & Meyer of Saumur. The Gratien style is for rich, full, firm wines, always fully mature.

HEIDSIECK & CO. MONOPOLE

Commune: Reims.
Owner: Paul-François Vranken.
Annual Sales: 1.2 million bottles.
Vineyard Ownership: 110 ha.

CHARLES HEIDSIECK

Commune: Epernay
Owner: LVMH.
Annual Sales: 2 million bottles.

PIPER-HEIDSIECK

Commune: Reims.
Owner: LVMH.
Annual Sales: 5 million bottles.

Florens-Ludwig Heidsieck, a German wool merchant, set up Heidsieck and Company in the years just before the French Revolution, and the firm passed to three nephews in the 1830s, each of whom went their separate ways. Piper is now the largest of the three. Its de luxe wine is called Florens-Louis. Heidsieck and Co. Monopole was taken over by Mumm in 1972 and now belongs to Paul-François Vranken. The prestige marque is called Diamant Bleu and the top wine Champagne Charlie.

Charles Heidsieck is my favourite of the three – though none would be in my superstar league – and the wines are fresh, generous, fruity and medium-bodied. Heidsieck and Co. Monopole makes standard, dependable wines. I find the wines of Piper-Heidsieck a bit green and find that they age less gracefully than the others.

★★★ KRUG

Commune: Reims.
Owners: LVMH.
Annual Sales: 500,000 bottles.
Vineyard Ownership: 15.5 ha.

Quality is the keynote in this small but prestigious house. Fermentation is in oak, no malolactic fermentation is allowed to occur, and no wines are put on the market until they have had considerable bottle age. Only vintage and de luxe Champagnes are produced. The de luxe marque, which used to be called Private Cuvée but was redesigned and relaunched as Grande Cuvée in the late 1990s, is an elegant, refined, complex wine which makes an excellent aperitif. I prefer the more masculine, fuller and firmer richness and depth of the vintage wine, always held back six to eight years before being sold. Recent additions to the range are a rosé and an elegant, harmonious single-vineyard Blanc de Blancs, Clos du Mesnil. Krug is not a cheap Champagne – which is why I refer to their non-vintage as a de luxe marque. Personally, good as it is, I can think of a number of vintage Champagnes I would rather spend my money on. The vintage wine, despite its even higher price, is worth it, and it lasts and lasts.

LANSON

Commune: Reims.
Owner: Marne-et-Champagne.
Annual Sales: 6 million bottles.

The house of Lanson was originally that of François Delamotte, founded in 1760. One of their employees, Jean-Baptiste Lanson, took over on the death of the last of the Delamottes, and began trading under his own name in 1838. Originally almost the entire production went to England but under the chairmanship of Victor Lanson – reputed to have drunk over 70,000 bottles of Champagne during his lifetime – sales expanded worldwide. After his death in 1970 the Lanson ownership changed regularly. The house finally emerged, without its 210 hectares of vineyards, in the hands of Marne et Champagne in 1991. At Lanson, as at Piper-Heidsieck and Krug, the base wine does not undergo a malolactic fermentation. The firm was one of the last to produce a de luxe marque, Noble Cuvée being launched in 1982.

The Lanson style is for light, flowery, quite forward wines – feminine, if you wish. The non-vintage Black Label is standard, but not one I would number in my first division.

LAURENT-PERRIER
Commune: Tours-sur-Marne.
Owners: de Nonancourt family.
Annual Sales: 6 million bottles.
Vineyard Ownership: 80 ha.

Laurent-Perrier is one of Champagne's recent successes. The house, family-owned though founded in 1812, was small, and business was moribund when Bertrand de Nononcourt took over in 1939. Even in 1959 annual production was only 400,000 bottles. Since then the growth has been spectacular yet without losing the family atmosphere of the business or the personality of the wines. Laurent-Perrier's rosé is one of the few to be made from an original genuine still rosé. Their prestige cuvée, Grand Siècle, also unusually, is a blend of several vintages, though it sells under a vintage label in the USA.

The non-vintage is a good dependable wine, marginally sweeter than some. It is soft and fresh, medium-bodied and fruity, without perhaps the depth and *élan* of the very best. I love the Cuvée Grand Siècle, however. This is an excellent, multifaceted wine, rich and profound. Laurent-Perrier owns the Champagne firms of de Castellane, Delamotte and Salon.

MARNE & CHAMPAGNE
Commune: Epernay.
Owner: Marne et Champagne S A.
Annual Sales: 12 million bottles.

This house sells its wines, not as Marne et Champagne, but under over 100 different labels or as Buyer's Own Brands (B.O.B.) Champagnes. Names include Alfred Rothschild, Pol Albert, Eugène Clicquot, Denis Père et Fils, Gauthier, Pol Gessner, Giesler and Giesmann. Qualities and styles vary, as you might expect. The buyer can dictate what he requires and prices are keen. Marne et Champagne additionally owns Lanson (see page 552) and Besserat-de-Bellefon.

★ MOËT & CHANDON
Commune: Epernay.
Owner: LVMH.
Annual Sales: 24 million bottles.
Vineyard Ownership: 291 ha.

Moët, even without its subsidiary companies Mercier and Ruinart – not to mention its association with the Louis Vuitton group which owns Veuve Clicquot and others – is by far the largest Champagne house. Moët's vineyards produce about 20 per cent of its needs. Pierre-Gabriel Chandon, son-in-law of Jean-Rémy Moët, himself the grandson of the founder of the firm, bought the Abbey of Hautvillers in 1823 – the monks had previously supplied his father-in-law with wine. Jean-Rémy was a personal friend of Napoleon who decorated him with the Légion d'Honneur. At the suggestion of Lawrence Fenn, an English journalist, the firm launched Dom Pérignon in 1935 to celebrate the centenary of its agency in Britain. This wine, from a blend of roughly half Pinot Noir and half Chardonnay and only from their own 100 per cent rated vineyards, is one of the best, as well as the best known, of the de luxe brands. It was also the first.

Despite the quantity produced, the standard and consistency of the non-vintage Moët is high: a medium-bodied, fruity wine, not absolutely bone dry, which I would put at the top of my second division. It is estimated that the quantity of Dom Pérignon sold equals more than the combined total of all the other de luxe brands put together. Despite this it really is a top-notch wine, worth every penny of its sadly inflated price.

MUMM
Commune: Reims
Owner: Hicks, Muse, Tate and First group.
Annual Sales: 7.5 million bottles.
Vineyard Ownership: 219 ha.

Mumm was founded in 1827 by Herr P A Mumm, a German from the Rheingau. After the launch of Cordon Rouge in 1873 the firm prospered only to find itself confiscated as enemy property in the First World War as none of the Mumm family had taken up French citizenship. The new director, René Lalou, after whom the firm's prestige brand is named, gradually acquired a majority holding but sold this in 1973 to the Canadian distillers Seagram who also own Perrier-Jouët (Seagram have recently sold both these to Hicks, Muse, Tate & First group). Mumm also produce a Crémant de Cramant (now relaunched as Mumm de Cramant), an excellent Blanc de Blancs.

The style of Mumm's Champagne is for something mild and soft, fruity and on the sweeter side, as far as their non-vintage Cordon Rouge Brut is concerned. I do not find it very stylish. Nor have I ever been particularly struck by the Vintage, though the René Lalou is better. This makes the finesse of the Mumm de Cramant all that more surprising.

★ PERRIER-JOUËT

Commune: Epernay.
Owner: Hicks, Muse, Tate and First group.
Annual Sales: 3 million bottles.
Vineyard Ownership: 108 ha.

Founded in 1811, Perrier-Jouët, like Mumm, now belongs to the Hicks, Muse, Tate and First group. The house has two de luxe brands: the Belle Epoque, also produced in rosé, sold in a delightful bottle with an embossed Art Nouveau flower motif; and the Blason de France. The house style is for elegant, fragrant wines on the delicate side. Fine quality throughout the range.

★★★ POL ROGER

Commune: Epernay.
Owners: Pol Roger family.
Annual Sales: 1.3 million bottles.
Vineyard Ownership: 85 ha.

Pol (another spelling for Paul) Roger founded this company in 1849 at the age of nineteen. Pol Roger's most famous customer was Sir Winston Churchill, and on his death a permanent black band was added to the label of their non-vintage White Foil, when shipped to England. Churchill did much to promote the brand, even naming one of his race horses Pol Roger. Not unnaturally one of the house's prestige *cuvées* is named after him. The other, rarely seen for obvious reasons in Britain, is PR.

All the Pol Roger wines have great finesse, a beautiful mousse and a fine depth. Their non-vintage is excellent, the vintage Blanc de Blancs called Chardonnay one of the very best examples, the 'ordinary' vintage superb, and the Cuvée Sir Winston Churchill truly excellent.

★ POMMERY & GRENO

Commune: Reims.
Owner: LVMH.
Annual Sales: 6 million bottles.
Vineyard Ownership: 307 ha.

Pommery & Greno, like Veuve Clicquot, is another firm whose fortunes were in the hands of a young widow in its early years, and it was one of the first to sell a really dry wine, its 1874 Nature, destined for the English market. The headquarters in Reims, built in 1878, is a gigantic folly largely based on two Scottish castles, Inverary and Mellerstain. André Simon was the Pommery agent in Great Britain between 1902 and 1932.

Now part of LVMH, Pommery is another first-division house. The wines are dry and austere, though not as firm and masculine as, say, Bollinger. The non-vintage is full and rich and the prestige wine, Cuvée Louise Pommery, which also comes in a delicious rosé, is ample, elegant and with real depth and complexity.

★★★ LOUIS ROEDERER

Commune: Reims.
Owners: Roederer family.
Annual Sales: 2.6 million bottles.
Vineyard Ownership: 185 ha.

Roederer's history goes back to 1765 when a Champagne firm called Dubois et Fils was founded. In 1827 Louis Roederer joined his uncle in the business and from then on it prospered greatly. It is now in the fortunate position of being able to produce 80 per cent of its requirements from its own vineyards, which have an average quality rating of 98 per cent. Louis Roederer's most famous wine is its excellent Cristal, a de luxe Champagne sold in a clear bottle.

Roederer is indisputably one of the great Champagne houses, and its non-vintage Brut Premier together with Pol Roger is, in my view, currently the best of the major non-vintage wines on the market. This is a firm wine of depth and maturity. Cristal, a lighter wine, is produced in almost every vintage, a practice of which I disapprove, as it seems to make a nonsense of the idea of 'vintage' or 'de luxe' being only the most successful years. Curiously, the lesser vintages have produced excellent Cristal, while in vintages when it can be compared with others it scores well but fails to number in the top two or three. I prefer the 'ordinary' vintage: always one of the best. Roederer also owns Deutz Champagne, Ramos-Pinto in Portugal and Château de Pez in Saint-Estèphe.

Ruinart

Commune: Reims.
Owner: LVMH.
Annual Sales: 2 million bottles.
Vineyard Ownership: 15 ha.

Founded in 1729, Ruinart is the oldest Champagne firm of the leading houses. In 1963 Moët & Chandon bought 80 per cent of the equity and took over completely ten years later so it is now in the hands of LMVH. The prestige brand is Dom Ruinart, a Blanc de Blancs. Like Taittinger, Ruinart wines are Chardonnay-based, light, fruity and elegant.

★ Salon

Commune: Le Mesnil-sur-Oger.
Owner: Laurent-Perrier.
Annual Sales: 120,000 bottles.
Vineyard Ownership: 1 ha.

Salon is in many ways unique: it produces a single wine, a Blanc de Blancs, sourced solely from the village of Le Mesnil-sur-Oger, and a vintage. But it does not produce wine every year. The house was established in 1921 by Louis-Aimé Salon but originally only as a hobby. When Salon is not declared the wine goes to the neighbouring house of Delamotte, also owned by Laurent-Perrier.

Salon is an austere wine so it is no surprise to hear there is no malolactic fermentation. It simply cries out for fifteen years' ageing and then it can be magnificent.

★ Taittinger

Commune: Reims.
Owners: Taittinger family.
Annual Sales: 4.2 million bottles.
Vineyard Ownership: 250 ha.

Pierre Taittinger took over the business of Fourneaux Forest in 1932 and the group, now run by his son Claude, has since bought the Champagne house of Irroy and the Loire businesses of Monmousseau and Bouvet-Ladubay. Taittinger is one of the houses which is better known for its prestige wine – in this case, the excellent Blanc de Blancs, Comtes de Champagne – than for its non-vintage. Brut Absolu is a wine with a nil dosage.

All Taittinger wines, like those of Ruinart, contain a large proportion of Chardonnay in the blend. I find the non-vintage elegant, fruity and reliable. The Comtes de Champagne is very full and rich, not obviously a Blanc de Blancs: a very fine example which lasts well.

★★ Veuve Clicquot-Ponsardin

Commune: Reims.
Owner: LVMH.
Annual Sales: 1 million bottles.
Vineyard Ownership: 280 ha.

The famous widow Clicquot was left on her own with a young daughter in 1805 at the age of twenty-seven. Thanks to the ingenuity of her salesman, Monsieur Bohne, 20,000 bottles reached Saint-Petersburg during the autumn of 1814 (having set off in defiance of a Russian embargo on French imports), where they sold for 12 roubles a piece, and Clicquot soon dominated the Russian market, though at the time it hardly sold at all within France. Madame Clicquot is also credited with the development of *pupitres* in order to facilitate *remuage*. All the Champagnes are impeccably made, from the non-vintage to the prestige label, La Grande Dame. The house style is for full, rich and firm wines but not as austere as, say, Bollinger. The non-vintage is consistent and one of the very best. A subsidiary is Canard-Duchêne.

Other Champagne Houses of note

Ayala, Henri Blin (the co-operative at Vincelles in the Marne Valley), Boizel, Château de Boursault, Cathier – especially the single-vineyard Clos du Moulin, Charles de Cazenove, Veuve A Devaux – the marque of twelve co-operatives in the Aube, Drappier – particularly the Grande Cendrée, Duval-Leroy, Gosset, Georges Goulet, Henriot, Jacquart/ Coopérative Régionale des Vins de Champagne, Jacquesson – the marque of the co-operative at Avize, Leclerc-Briant – especially the single-vineyard range Les Authentiques, Mailly co-operative (Mailly), Bruno Paillard, Palmer/co-operative of Avize, Pannier, Philipponnat – especially the single-vineyard Clos des Goisses, and de Venoge.

Individual Growers' Champagnes

Every street in the Champagne villages seems covered in signs advertising individual growers' Champagnes. Many of these, however, are members of the local co-operatives, who have taken some of the general wine for putting up under their own label. Many of the others – perfectly genuine individual wines – are not very good, for Champagne is difficult to produce at a high quality on a small scale unless you are blessed with a splendidly sited vineyard. But there are good *récoltants-manipulants*, and their wines can compete with all but the very finest of the merchants' de luxe brands. Under a strange quirk of the law an individual Champagne grower can purchase up to 5 per cent of his production from elsewhere without having to become a *négociant*: so a grower in a predominantly red grape village has a chance to buy in some Chardonnay to add to his blend.

Michel Arnould

Commune: Verzenay.
Owner: Patrick Arnould.
Surface area under Vine: 12 ha.
Champagne: Brut Réserve, Grand Cru; Brut Rosé, Grand Cru; Grande Cuvée, Grand Cru; and Carte d'Or Millésimé, Grand Cru.

The Arnould family have produced own-label Champagne since 1928. All the vineyards are in Verzenay (*grand*

cru) and a little wine is bought in from Cramant in the Côte de Blancs, also a *grand cru*. Only the *cuvée* or first pressing is used: the remainder sold under a *sous-marque*. Most of the wines are Blancs (or Rosés) de noirs. Fermentation is in stainless steel tanks with no malolactic. Fine quality: long, positive, elegant and fragrant wines.

★ Champagne et Villages

Commune: Epernay.
Owner: Paul & Françoise Couvreur.

This is an enterprising and high-class establishment, founded in 1988. Having worked for twenty-five years in the business, Patrick Couvreur set up on his own and has struck a deal to market the wines of local growers. This is a prime source for wines of *terroir* and diversity.

The growers represented include

Breteau-Huat – 100% Pinot Meunier from the Marne Valley (Leuvigny), José Dhondt – 100% Chardonnay from the Côte des Blancs (Oger), Bernard Girardin – mainly Chardonnay from the Marne Valley (Mancy), Jean Hanotin – largely Pinot from the Montagne de Reims (Verzy), Lecomte Père & Fils – from the Marne Valley (Vinay), Xavier Lecomte – 90% Pinot Meunier from the Marne Valley (Bouguigny), Thierry Massin – 100% Pinot Noir from the Aube (Ville-sur-Arce), Camille Savès – 90% Pinot Noir from the Montagne de Reims (Bouzy) and Vazat-Coquart – 100% Chardonnay (Chouilly).

Pierre Gimmonnet & Fils

Commune: Cuis.
Owners: Michel, Didier & Olivier Gimmonet.
Surface Area under Vine: 26 ha.
Champagne: Brut, Cuis, Premier Cru, Non Vintage; Brut Gastronome Millésimé; Brut Fleuron Millésimé and Champagne Maxi-Brut Oenophile Non Vintage.

The Gimmonets are cousins of the Larmandiers in Vertus (see page 557) and sell some of their wine as Larmandier Père & Fils. The vines lie in Cuis, a *premier cru*, and Cramant and Chouilly (both *grands crus*): entirely Chardonnay. These are good wines – the Oenophile is non-chaptalised, non-dosed and held back before drinking. Currently this is based on the 1990 vintage: powerful, rich, aromatic and very impressive.

HENRI GOUTORBE
Commune: Ay.
Owner: Henri René Goutorbe.
Surface Area under Vine: 20 ha.
Champagne: Cuvée Traditionnelle non-vintage; Cuvée Prestige non-vintage; Rosé; Blanc de Blancs non-vintage; Millésime Rare; Club Millésimé; and Coteaux Champenois, Ay Rouge.

Emile Goutorbe, vineyard manager for Perrier-Jouet after the First World War, embarked on a sideline as a vine-stock nurseryman (*pépiniériste*). As this prospered he gave up his job with Perrier-Jouet, and with the profits invested in vines. These lie mainly in Ay, but extend as far as the Côte de Sézanne. Today his son and grandson are in charge, together with their wives.

The wines are vinified and matured in tank, malolactic fermentation is encouraged and *remuage* is by gyropalettes. The basic blend is roughly two-thirds Pinot Noir, one-third Chardonnay, with a little Pinot Meunier. There are good wines, especially the older Non-Vintage, the Cuvée Prestige and the Club Millésimé made exclusively from Ay fruit, but I regret their habit of making some vintage wine every year.

LARMANDIER-BERNIER
Commune: Vertus.
Owner: Pierre Larmandier.
Surface Area under Vine: 11 ha.
Champagne: Brut Tradition non vintage; Brut Blanc de Blancs, Premier Cru; Terre de Vertus, Non-Dosé, Premier Cru, non vintage; Grand Cru Cramant Millésimé, Extra Brut, Vieilles Vignes; Brut Spécial Club Millésimé and Coteaux Champenois, Vertus Rouge.

The Larmandier family have been growing grapes and making wine since the eighteenth century. Their vines are situated in Vertus, a *premier cru* and Cramant, Chouilly, Oger and Avize, all *grands crus*. Their average age is thirty-one years: 85 per cent Chardonnay, 15 per cent

Pinot Noir. The wine is made and matured in tank, with malolactic fermentation taking place. These are carefully made wines, stylish and fruity. The Vintage *cuvées* are especially lovely.

★ JACQUES SELOSSE
Commune: Avize.
Owners: Corinne & Anselme Selosse.
Surface Area under Vine: 6.30 ha.
Champagne: Extra Brut, Blanc de Blancs non vintage; Tradition non vintage; Millésimé and 'Origine'.

Anselme Selosse and his sister Corinne have been in charge at this domaine since the death of their father Jacques, and have continued his very personal biological approach to winemaking. The vineyard is a patchwork of holdings in Cramant, Avize, Oger, Ay and further south at Saudoy in the Côte de Sézanne.

Vinification takes place in barrel, using natural yeasts, with no malolactic fermentation, and dosages are kept to a minimum. The wines both fine and splendidly original. The Origine is a *cuvée* produced by the solera method, 22 per cent of the blend being extracted for bottling every year (and replaced with younger wine).

VILMART ET CIE.
Commune: Rilly-La-Montagne.
Owner: Laurent Champs.
Surface Area under Vine: 11 ha.
Champagne: Grande Réserve non vintage; Cuvée Grand Cellier non vintage; Coeur de Cuvée Millésimé and Cuvée Grand Cellier d'Or Millésimé.

Five generations of Vilmarts have made wine at Rilly since 1890, the youthful Laurent Champs being a great great-grandson of the original founder. All the vines lie in Rilly, a *premier cru*, planted 60 per cent Chardonnay and 40 Pinot Noir, the vineyard being worked by biological methods. Fermentation takes place in large and small wood, with the malolactic fermentation blocked. All the wines spend at least ten months in barrel. The Grande Réserve contains 70 per cent Pinot Noir, the Cuvée Grand Cellier 70 per cent Chardonnay. The Vintage wines are also mainly Chardonnay.

THE JURA AND SAVOIE

E AST OF BURGUNDY, 50 KILOMETRES ACROSS A FLAT, GRASSY PLAIN through which flows the Saône and its tributary, the Doubs, the land begins to rise again. On these slopes, facing south-west, lie the vineyards of the Jura, a region of impressive beauty, horseshoe-shaped cliffs and other mysterious rock formations. This is one of the forgotten corners of France, seldom exported. Mention Jura and most wine lovers will think of Henri Maire, the largest producer of Jura wine, or alternatively of *vin jaune*; geologists will be reminded of a particular epoch when dinosaurs roamed the earth, the Jurassic; chemists will recall Pasteur, he who penetrated the complexities behind the fermentation of beer, provided the explanation of why milk turned sour, and, incidentally, discovered the antidote to rabies. The traveller will remember one of the most dramatically beautiful and private corners of France, a land of gentle alpine uplands, sudden limestone cliffs descending hundreds of feet into the valleys below; a lush region of pasture, vineyards and rushing rivers lying between the flat plains and sleepy lakes and lagoons of the Plaine de Bresse and the mountains which form the barrier between France and north-west Switzerland.

Historically and geographically the Jura was part of the Middle Kingdom: France to the west, Germany to the east and a line which ran from the Low Countries, through Alsace, to Switzerland and the Savoy in the middle. When Charlemagne's empire was divided among his children in AD 843 this Middle Kingdom was born and the seeds were sown for a millennium of strife between east and west. The Jura became part of Burgundy, itself soon to be divided between the Duchy – Burgundy proper - and the Comté, the 'Franche-Montagnes', fiercely independent of its liberty, be it from the suzerainty of the Holy Roman Emperor or of the French king. It was not until the Peace of Nijmegen in 1678 that Louis XIV's dominance over the Jura was finally assured.

Until the arrival of phylloxera in the late nineteenth century this was an important vineyard area. In 1836 the Jura possessed over 18,000 hectares under vine. In 1998 the figure had declined to just over 1600

hectares. Phylloxera, followed by the increasing availability of more inexpensive wines owing to the railway and other means of cheap transport between the Midi and the north of France including the capital, dealt an almost mortal blow. As the vineyards of northern Burgundy between Dijon and Chablis declined to a few straggly rows of vines used for *vin ordinaire* for local consumption, so the vineyards of the Jura declined. Today, chiefly at the hands of Henri Maire, there has been a renaissance, but the wines of the Jura are still little exported, and rarely seen on wine lists and restaurants outside the region.

According to official figures there are some thousand growers in the Jura of whom a quarter are members of one of the five main co-operatives at Arbois, Pupillin, Voiteur, Poligny and L'Etoile. Most of the rest, one imagines, are contracted to Henri Maire. Only about a dozen growers have more than a dozen hectares under vine.

Very much the biggest producer of Jura wines (and of other non-*appellation*, branded wines such as the sparkling Vin Fou) is Henri Maire at Château-Monfort at Arbois. The Henri Maire enterprise can be measured in millions rather than thousands of bottles, and the bulk of this is sold by mail order direct to private customers in France. Production is based on Maire's own domaines which cover some 300 hectares of vineyards. These names are now used as brands for the top *cuvées*: Domaine de Grange Grillard for white wine, Croix d'Argis, Domaine de Sorbief for a red made from a blend of Poulsard and Trousseau and Monfort for Pinot Noir.

I find Henri Maire's wines, frankly, dull; and frequently rather tired as well. They are pasteurised and therefore do not keep well in bottle. The reds are suspiciously sweet. Their success demonstrates not so much a public awakening of the excellence of Jura wines, than the efficacy of aggressive marketing. Paradoxically, in the long term, the presence of Henri Maire may be counter-productive to the growth of a quality Jura wine business.

THE WINES

The Jura vineyards extend in a thin line from north of Salins-Les-Bains to south of Saint-Amour (no relation to the Beaujolais *cru* of this name), a distance of 80 kilometres. The most important section lies in the north between Arbois and Lons-Le-Saunier, a town which lies halfway between Beaune and Geneva. As you approach from the west and cross into the Jura *département*, the countryside changes, the land begins to rise. In the distance are the Jura mountains. These are precursors of the Alps, a ridge of hills – few rise above 1000 metres – which runs from the valley of the upper Rhône east of Lyon to Basle in roughly a north-easterly direction. The Jura vineyards are on the western slopes of these hills.

The basic *appellation* is Côtes du Jura, the wines of which can be red, rosé or dry white as well as sparkling, *vin jaune* and *vin de paille*. In the north of the region lies the Arbois *appellation*, while in the middle, just north of Lons-Le-Saunier, is the tiny white wine *appellation* of L'Etoile. Nearby is Château-Chalon, for *vins jaunes* only.

The soil in the lowlands is almost pure clay. As the altitude increases it becomes progressively more calcareous, on a bedrock of oolitic limestone. This marl is mixed with sand and clay to the north, gravel and other pebbles in the south of the area. The vineyards face the setting sun at an altitude of 300 to 450 metres, not in a continuous line, as in Burgundy, but much interrupted by sudden valleys, above which a limestone cliff might rise a hundred metres into the sky, or by isolated village enclaves, woodland copses and tumbling streams issuing from underground springs deep in the hills.

Grape Varieties

Jura's grape varieties are the same as those commonly found in Burgundy: Chardonnay and Pinot Noir, plus several indigenous and, dare I say it, for the red wines at least, inferior varieties. As well as Pinot Noir, locally known as Gros Noiren, there are Trousseau and Poulsard for the red wines. The Trousseau, which is mainly found on gravelly soils around Arbois would not inspire any newly married man with great delight. It makes a lumpy, well-coloured, tannic wine, full-bodied perhaps, but without the quality to age gracefully. It oxidises fast and loses its colour quickly; the fruit, always rustic in character, soon dries out. While the autumn is generally sunny in the Jura, the region otherwise suffers an abundance of rain, particularly compared with Alsace which though further north is sheltered from the west by the Vosges mountains. Trousseau wines, like those reds from the central Loire Valley, are frequently stringy in their tannins and have an absence of fat. Poulsard makes a lighter wine with higher acidity. Never highly coloured, even in the best years, it resembles rosé rather than red, and is often labelled as such. When fresh it can have merit but with age it makes a dispiriting bottle. Both the red and rosé are often kept far too long in wood.

The whites are much more interesting. Now largely from Chardonnay (locally called the Melon d'Arbois) with the possibility of some Savagnin added at the time of the *écoulage* (descent from the fermentation vat into barrel or tank) or by means of *ouillage* or topping-up, they are rather like a full and spicy Mâcon – the more Savagnin, the more individual, the less quasi-Burgundian. Pinot Blanc is also used. Jura whites are either 100 per cent Chardonnay or a blend. If the first, they should be bottled early in the spring after the vintage and consumed within a year or two. If the latter, they will take age both in barrel and in bottle, and can mature to something with real character and merit. Sadly not all the Chardonnay or Chardonnay-Savagnin wines are bottled as early as they should be. Many are aged for two or even three years before bottling, even bottled in stages when sales demand. Only a few wines can stand this abuse.

The Savagnin grape, however, is the Jura's own special variety. Savagnin Blanc is said by ampelographical experts to be the Traminer of Alsace – the Savagnin rosé makes a particular, rather uncommon wine in Alsace (see Klevner de Heiligenstein, page 526), but is said not to be a true relation. It is sometimes known locally as Naturé. Legend has it that it was brought from Hungary to France by Benedictine monks in the tenth century. It is a late developer and a poor cropper but produces a wine powerful in both alcohol and flavour. I find it has little in common with the Traminer, but that is not to say that it does not have either quality or individuality. You will rarely see it on its own as a table wine. As the 'onlie begetter' of *vin jaune*, however, it is incomparable.

Vin Jaune

Vin jaune is peculiar to the Jura and, in its own way, great. The wine is made exclusively from Savagnin and the grapes are picked late, though without *pourriture noble*. The wine is then vinified slowly after which it is racked off into old oak barrels which are sealed up and left in a cool cellar for a minimum of six years. A film of yeasts – a flor similar to that in *fino* sherry – forms on the top of the wine. This imparts a particular flavour of oxidation to the wine but otherwise protects it from turning into vinegar. The result is something which is dry but fat and rich in extract, with a green walnut flavour akin to a dry sherry, though the wine is not fortified; nor does a *vin jaune* have sherry's pronounced acidity.

The cellar should be dry. If it is humid a sort of osmosis will take place, causing the alcohol level to dilute. Not all the casks attract flor, however, as in Jerez. Those which do not are pulled out and the wine blended with Chardonnay or sold as a pure Savagnin table wine.

I find *vin jaune* simply delicious. The wine is a deep yellow in colour; it is mellow but pungent in flavour, powerful, subtle and complex. They are delicious when young – recently bottled at the age of six years, that is – with a ripe, alpine-flower fragrance and a certain racy crispness. As the wine ages it becomes rounder and softer, the nutty elements are joined by flavours of crab-apple, camomile and elderflower and it becomes more and more multi-dimensional. I have had wonderfully complex twenty-year-old examples. They even last, for a week or two at least, after the bottle has been opened. *Vins jaunes* are bottled in a special dumpy 62-cl bottle known as a *clavelin*. The wines are expensive and hard to find, but they are worth the effort.

Vin de Paille

Vin de paille is another Jura speciality as well as being uncommon elsewhere. A little is made in the northern Rhône more as a curiosity than as a commercial proposition. After harvesting ripe but not botrytized grapes the bunches are left to dry out before pressing, for a minimum of two months. This was originally on straw mats – hence the name *vin de paille* (straw) – but as often now they are dried hanging from the rafters or alternatively in shallow trays in a well-ventilated room. This drying has the effect of concentrating the sugars and other elements in the grapes. Pressing and fermentation then takes place; because of the concentration of sugar the latter often taking months if not years.

The resulting wine has a deep gold or even amber colour and is full and rich; not just very sweet but with a nutty, raisiny quality with good balancing acidity. While it doesn't have the complexity of Sauternes, it certainly in its own way has merit as well as character. Naturally, it is expensive and production, sadly, is in decline.

SURFACE AREA AND PRODUCTION (1998 HARVEST)

APPELLATIONS	SURFACE AREA (HA)	PRODUCTION (HL)	
		RED & ROSÉ	WHITE
CÔTES DU JURA	710	7105	26,262
CRÉMANT DU JURA	152	1012	14,067
ARBOIS	826	24,140	24,647
L'ETOILE	78		4583
CHÂTEAU-CHALON	42		1803
TOTAL	1808	32,257	71,362
		103,619	

The Wine Regions

COTES DU JURA AND CRÉMANT DU JURA

CÔTES DU JURA

Surface Area (1998): 710 ha.
Production (1998): (Red and rosé) 7105 hl; (white) 26,262 hl.
Colour: Red, rosé and white.
Grape Varieties: (Red and rosé) Pinot Noir, Trousseau and Poulsard; (white) Chardonnay, Savagnin and Pinot Blanc.
Maximum Yield: (Red and rosé) 55 hl/ha; (white) 60 hl/ha; (vin de paille) 20 hl/ha.
Minimum Alcohol Level: (Red, rosé and white) 10°; (vin jaune) 11°; (vin de paille) 14.5°.

CRÉMANT DU JURA

Surface Area (1998): 152 ha.
Production (1998): (Rosé) 1012 hl; (white) 14,067 hl.
Colour: White and rosé.
Grape Varieties: (Rosé) Pinot Noir, Trousseau and Poulsard; (white) Chardonnay and Savagnin.
Maximum Yield: 65 hl/ha.
Minimum Alcohol Level: 10°.

The generic *appellation* of the Jura is the Côtes du Jura, a delimited area of twelve cantons, from Villers-Farlay and Salins in the north-east to Saint-Julien and Saint-Amour in the south-west by way of Arbois and Lons-Le-Saunier. Most of the wine is white, based almost exclusively on Chardonnay. Where growers do not make a 100 per cent Chardonnay wine, the Savagnin wine, pressed and vinifed separately, is blended in later, when the wines are racked.

While much of the wine is fairly mundane, if not downright artisanal, there are nuggets to be unearthed. Two of Jura's most respected quality growers, Jean Bourdy and the Comte de Laguiche, are based at Arlay which lies outside the more specific *appellations* of Arbois, L'Etoile and Château-Chalon listed below.

Leading Côtes du Jura Producers

★ CHÂTEAU D'ARLAY

Commune: Arlay.
Owners: Comte Renaud and Alain de Laguiche.
Surface Area under Vine: 5 ha.
Wines: Côtes du Jura (red, rosé and white), Vin Jaune and Vin de Paille.

Directly west of Château-Chalon an almost conical hill rises a few hundred metres above the local countryside. Once there was a magnificent castle on top, but this was destroyed in the time of Louis XI. The present château lies at the base of the northern, wooded side of the hill, while vines occupy the south-facing slopes. Comte Renaud de Laguiche (a cousin of the Laguiches in Montrachet in Burgundy and also related to the Moëts and Chandons of Champagne) acquired the estate in 1960. The table wines are clean and fruity, the red, called Corail, coming from 100 per cent Pinot Noir. But the *vin jaune* is the most interesting wine and a fine example, equal of the best Château-Chalons. It keeps very well.

★ DOMAINE JEAN BOURDY

Commune: Arlay.
Owners: Jean-François and Jean-Philippe Bourdy.
Surface Area under Vine: 10 ha.
Wines: Côtes du Jura (red and white), Arbois (rosé), Vin Jaune and Château-Chalon.

There have been Bourdys in Arlay for more than five hundred years. Today the estate is managed by Jean-François, who looks after the commercial side, and his brother Jean-Philippe, responsible for vines and wine. The Bourdys also have a merchants' licence: hence the Arbois and the Château-Chalon.

The table wines spend three years in *foudre* before bottling, but this does not seem to harm them. They are good wines to accompany food. The *vins jaunes* are fine, and it is interesting to compare their own wine with their Château-Chalon made from bought-in grapes. The latter has more vigour, depth and complexity.

THE JURA

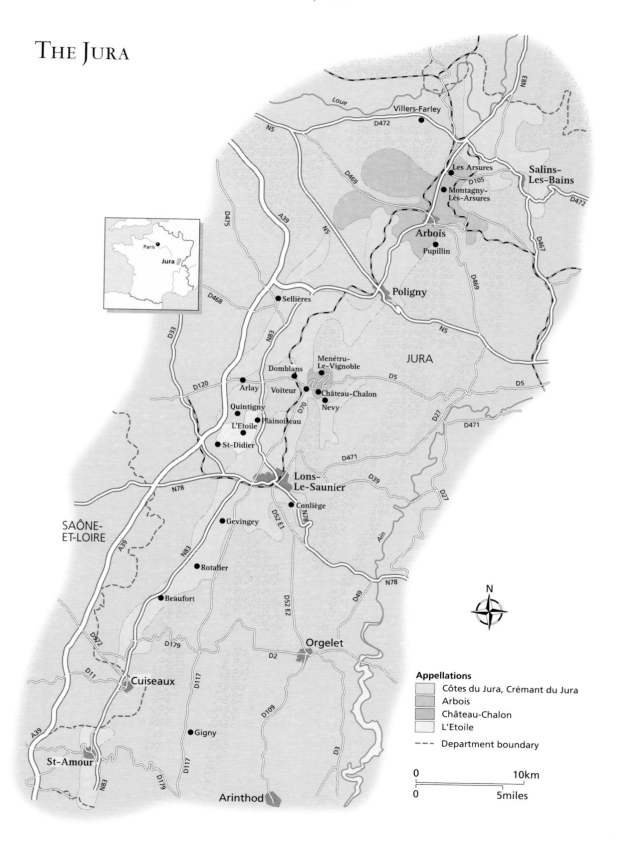

Villers-Farley

Salins-Les-Bains

Les Arsures

Montagny-Lès-Arsures

Arbois

Pupillin

Poligny

JURA

Sellières

Menétru-Le-Vignoble

Domblans

Voiteur

Château-Chalon

Arlay

Nevy

Quintigny

Plainoiseau

L'Etoile

St-Didier

Lons-Le-Saunier

Conliège

Gevingey

SAÔNE-ET-LOIRE

Rotalier

Beaufort

Orgelet

Cuiseaux

Gigny

St-Amour

Arinthod

Paris

Jura

Appellations

Côtes du Jura, Crémant du Jura

Arbois

Château-Chalon

L'Etoile

– – – Department boundary

0   10km

0   5miles

Domaine Xavier Reverchon

Commune: Poligny.
Owner: Xavier Reverchon.
Surface Area under Vine: 6 ha.
Wines: Côtes du Jura (red and white), Arbois (red), Vin Jaune and Vin de Paille.
Xavier Reverchon's grandfather founded the domaine about a century ago. There is a little Arbois, but the majority of the vines, biologically tended, are for Côtes du Jura. There are reds from both Poulsard and Pinot Noir (Les Trouillots and Les Freins) and a clean, vigorous Chardonnay. The *vin jaune* is very good indeed.

Other Côtes du Jura Producers of note

Domaine Richard Delay (Gevingey) and Domaine Voorhuis-Henquet (Conliège).

Crémant du Jura Producers of note

Château de L'Etoile (L'Etoile), Domaine Rolet Père & Fils (Montigny-Lès-Arsures) and Domaine André & Mireille Tissot (Montigny-Lès-Arsures).

Arbois

Surface Area (1998): 826 ha.
Production (1998): (Red and rosé) 24,140 hl; (white) 24,647 hl.
Colour: Red, rosé and white.
Grape Varieties: (Red and rosé) Pinot Noir, Trousseau and Poulsard; (white) Chardonnay and Savagnin.
Maximum Yield: (Red and rosé) 55 hl/ha; (white) 60 hl/ha; (vin de paille) 25 hl/ha.
Minimum Alcohol Level: (Red and rosé) 10°; (white) 10.5°; (vin jaune) 11.5°; (vin de paille) 14.5°.

The canton of Arbois is entitled to its own *appellation* and is the nucleus of the Jura winemaking area. Arbois itself is a bustling, picturesque town with plenty of medieval features and lies near the foot of one of the most spectacular of Jura's many *cirques*, the curious horseshoe-shaped cliffs which jut out of the countryside. Louis Pasteur is the local hero. He was born at Dole but brought

to Arbois at the age of five in 1827. His statue in the centre of Arbois is worth a nostalgic visit. His research provided the basis for the understanding of wine and was the start of making wine by modern methods. Arbois-Pupillin is a sub-*appellation* for wines made from grapes harvested in the commune of Pupillin.

The *appellation* covers thirteen communes in the northern part of the Jura. As with Côtes du Jura (though generally with a marginally more strict degree of ripeness of the fruit) the *appellation* covers red, rosé, white, sparkling (called Arbois Mousseux), *vin jaune* and *vin de paille*. Unlike the generic *appellation*, about half the wine produced is red or rosé. The white, though, is the most interesting wine.

Leading Arbois Producers

Domaine Lucien Aviet
Cave de Bacchus

Commune: Montigny-Lès-Arsures.
Owner: Vincent Aviet.
Surface Area under Vine: 6 ha.
Wines: Arbois (red and white) and Vin Jaune.
Five hundred years ago the Aviets were farmers for the local monks, says Vincent Aviet, presiding over his large *cave*, which was once a granary. This estate was one of the first in the area to bottle its own wine. The red wines, Poulsard and Trousseau kept separately, are bottled after eighteen months, as is the Chardonnay; the Savagnin, which I prefer, is bottled later. All the wine is aged in large wood.

Domaine Foret

Commune: Arbois.
Owner: Frédéric Foret.
Surface Area under Vine: 13 ha.
Wines: Arbois (red, rosé and blanc) and Vin Jaune.
The Foret domaine was created by Frédéric's father, now retired, and is based in the centre of Arbois. There are rosés from both Poulsard and Trousseau (the latter the more interesting), a blended red called Rubis, Trousseau and Pinot Noir on their own and whites from Chardonnay, Savagnin and a blend of the two. The results are

mixed, mainly because the wines are held too long before bottling. But there are very good *vins jaunes*.

DOMAINE DE LA PINTE
Commune: Arbois.
Owners: The Roger Martin family.
Surface Area under Vine: 30 ha.
Wines: Arbois (red, rosé and white), Vin Jaune and Vin de Paille.

Domaine de La Pinte lies on a hill south of Arbois, commanding splendid views to the west. Created in 1953 by Roger Martin to produce *vin jaune*, the domaine now grows other varieties as well as Savagnin and is managed by the magnificently moustached Philippe Chatillon. Underneath the offices, reception rooms and *cuvier* is a series of vaulted cellars. This is a modern set-up, using barrels, some new, for the table wines. The reds and the Chardonnays are bottled after one and a half to two years, the Savagnin, which I like, after two and a half years.

DOMAINE JACQUES PUFFENEY
Commune: Montigny-Lès-Arsures.
Owner: Jacques Puffeney.
Surface Area under Vine: 7.5 ha.
Wines: Arbois red including Assemblage Vieilles Vignes and white, and Vin Jaune.

The curly-bearded Jacques Puffeney has built up his domaine since he inherited from his father in 1962. The Chardonnay is bottled from eighteen months onwards, the reds from two years. All the wine except the Savagnin is stored in old, round *foudres*. The Vieilles Vignes red *cuvée* is noteworthy, and the best whites hold up well. The *vins jaunes* are delicate but splendidly balanced.

★ DOMAINE ROLET PÈRE & FILS
Commune: Montigny-Les-Arsures.
Owners: Rolet family.
Surface Area under Vine: 62 ha.
Wines: Arbois and Côtes du Jura (red, rosé and white), Crémant du Jura, L'Etoile, Vin Jaune and Vin de Paille.

Founded in 1945 by Désiré Rolet, and now managed by his children, the Rolet domaine possesses 36 hectares in Arbois, 21 in the Côtes du Jura, and now 5 hectares in L'Etoile, which makes them the second largest domaine in the Jura area. Barrels are used, though not new ones, for the Chardonnay and Pinot Noir, as well as, of course, for the *vin jaune*. This is an up-to-date, efficient set-up making good wines across the board, including very good *vins jaunes* and *vins de paille*.

DOMAINE ANDRÉ & MIREILLE TISSOT
Commune: Montigny-Lès-Arsures.
Owners: André and Mireille Tissot.
Surface Area under Vine: 28 ha.
Wines: Arbois (red and white), Côtes du Jura Pinot Noir, Crémant du Jura, Vin Jaune and Vin de Paille.

There are many Tissots in the Arbois area, a grandfather Tissot having four children, from whence have come four individual domaines. André Tissot and his wife set up independently and started winemaking in 1962. Their son Stéphane is now in charge. This is a modern winery, with Burgundian *pièces* (some new) in the cellar and a biological approach in the vineyard, making a range of good wines. Look out for *cuvée* Lea, half Chardonnay, half Savagnin. La Cave de la Reine Jeanne is a merchants' business, with a splendid vaulted cellar in Arbois.

Other Producers of note
DOMAINE DANIEL DUGOIS (LES ARSURES), FRUITIÈRE VINICOLE D'ARBOIS (THE LOCAL CO-OPERATIVE), DOMAINE PIERRE OVERNOY (PUPILLIN), DOMAINE DÉSIRÉ PETIT & FILS/JEAN-MICHEL PETIT (PUPILLIN), DOMAINE JACQUES & PHILIPPE TISSOT (ARBOIS) AND DOMAINE DE LA TOURNELLE/PASCAL CLAIRET (ARBOIS).

L'ETOILE

Surface Area (1998): 78 ha.
Production (1998): 4583 hl.
Colour: White.
Grape Varieties: Chardonnay, Savagnin and Poulsard.
Maximum Yield: (White and vin jaune) 60 hl/ha; (vin de paille) 20 hl/ha.

Minimum Alcohol Level: (White) 10.5°; (vin jaune) 11.5°; (vin de paille) 14.5° .

Just north-west of Lons-Le-Saunier, surrounding the hill of Mont Musard, are the communes of L'Etoile, Plainoiseau and Saint-Didier. Based largely on limestone soil they form the white wine-only *appellation* of L'Etoile. The area is rich in fossils, including one long shell in the form of a five-pointed star. It is from this that the *appellation* is named. The wines are very similar to Côtes du Jura whites, though there seems to be more of a tendency not to top up the Chardonnay barrels, a procedure I regard as suspect as it leads to premature oxidation and ageing of the wine. They are also, in my view, often bottled too late and therefore lack freshness.

Leading L'Etoile Producers

Château de L'Etoile
Owners: Georges and Bernard Vandelle.
Surface Area under Vine: 26 ha.
Wines: L'Etoile, Côtes du Jura (red and rosé), Vin Jaune, Vin de Paille and Crémant du Jura.
You drive up to the top of Mont Musard expecting to find something imposing. Perhaps there was once. What greets you is a collection of buildings vaguely resembling a Victorian vicarage, much extended. Here live, work and play the Vandelle family, whose ancestors bought the estate in 1832. The Chardonnay casks are not topped up. I prefer the Réserve de Mont Musard, a Chardonnay/Savagnin blend, and the *vins jaunes*.

Domaine Michel Geneletti & Fils
Owners: Michel and David Geneletti.
Surface Area under Vine: 12 ha.
Wines: L'Etoile, Côtes du Jura (red) and Vin Jaune.
David Geneletti is the third generation of an Italian family to run this domaine, his grandfather having married a local *mademoiselle* Duffort shortly after World War Two. The Chardonnay barrels are not topped up and are quite delicate wines, which makes you wish they had been bottled earlier. There are good *vins jaunes*.

Other Producers of note
Domaine Claude Joly (Rotalier) and Château de Quintigny/Cartaux-Bougaud family (Quintigny).

Château-Chalon
Surface Area (1998): 42 ha.
Production (1998): 1803 hl.
Grape Variety: Savagnin.
Maximum Yield: 30 hl/ha.
Minimum Alcohol Level: 12°.

Some 15 kilometres north-west of Lons-Le-Saunier lies Château-Chalon, an *appellation* rather than a single property, producing *vin jaune* only and, unlike other *vins jaunes*, from the Savagnin grape only. The area covers the communes of Menétru, Domblans, Voiteur and Nevy as well as that of Château-Chalon itself, a village on top of a hill once surmounted by a splendid castle built to protect a Benedictine abbey to which the local nobles would send their children to be educated.

The slopes below the abbey consist of *marnes bleus*, a marl with a light blue-green colour, and the vines thereon are splendidly sited. This *appellation* is *vin jaune* at its best – more intense, finer in flavour and with a greater capacity to age than elsewhere. A Château-Chalon wine should have a nose which suggests *fino* sherry and also green walnuts, a palate which hints at *morilles* (morels) and a length and complexity which is both round and vigorous, with no more oxidation than you would expect in a fresh *fino*.

Château-Chalon, which like other *vins jaunes*, is bottled in a special dumpy *clavelin* bottle containing 62cl (as opposed to the normal 35cl), is an expensive and rare wine. But it is quite delicious. The so-called Prince of Gastronomes, Curnonsky, decreed it along with Château d'Yquem, Coulée de Serrant (in Savennières), Le Montrachet and Château Grillet as the five best wines in France *and therefore* (my italics) of the whole world. Perhaps the man was unaware that Château-Chalon was an *appellation*, and not a single estate!

The wine, left in sealed casks under the famous *vin jaune* flor for a minimum of six and a half years before bottling, will last for ages. The best recent vintages are 1990, 1989, 1983, 1982, 1979, 1973, 1969, 1967 and 1964. The wines from the vintages of 1974, 1980 and 1984 were declassified to Côtes du Jura.

Leading Château-Chalon Producers

DOMAINE BAUD PÈRE & FILS
Commune: Le Vernois.
Owners: Alain and Jean-Michel Baud.
Surface Area under Vine: 16 ha.
Wines: Côtes du Jura (red and white), Vin Jaune, and Château-Chalon.

There have been eight generations of the Baud family at Le Vernois, dating back to before the French Revolution. The brothers currently in charge of the domaine produce good table wines – the Chardonnays are matured partly in barrel, partly in *foudre*, and there are also very good *vins jaunes*. Here you can taste a Château-Chalon alongside a Côtes du Jura *vin jaune*. Perhaps you will agree with me that the Château-Chalon is worth the 20 per cent extra cost.

★★ DOMAINE BERTHET-BONDET
Owner: Jean Berthet-Bondet.
Surface Area under Vine: 9 ha.
Wines: Côtes du Jura (red and white), Château-Chalon and Vin de Paille.

Now in his forties, blond, bespectacled Jean Berthet set up on his own and produced his first vintage in 1985. In my view he is the super-star of the *appellation*. As well as splendidly intense *vins jaunes* he produces fine Chardonnay, matured in cask, an even better blend of Chardonnay and Savagnin and also a pure Savagnin. His *vin de paille* is equally excellent.

DOMAINE DANIEL & PASCAL CHALANDARD GAEC DU VIEUX PRESSOIR
Commune: Le Vernois.
Owners: Daniel and Pascal Chalandard.
Surface Area under Vine: 7.5 ha.
Wines: Côtes du Jura (red and white), L'Etoile and Château-Chalon.

The father and son Chalandard team work their vineyards by *lutte raisonnée*, a biological approach to viticulture. They believe that pure Chardonnay wines have no place in the white wines of the Jura and use interesting labels on their bottles based on old monastic engravings. There is a worthy Pinot Noir, a good Chardonnay-Savagnin mix, and some fine, if not the very best, Château-Chalons.

★ DOMAINE JEAN MACLE
Owners: Jean and Laurent Macle.
Surface Area under Vine: 14 ha.
Wines: Côtes du Jura (white) and Château-Chalon.

In his sixties, the greying Jean Macle resembles an old-fashioned American priest, with a beard largely under his chin rather than on his cheeks and upper lip. His son Laurent, about to take over the domaine, will be the seventh generation of a family which arrived in the area through marrying into the locality, and were originally barrel-makers. The white wine is a blend of 85 per cent Chardonnay and 15 per cent Savagnin and it is complex, balanced and succulent. If only all the other Jura whites were this good! The Château-Chalons are excellent.

Other Producers of note
DOMAINE VICTOR CREDOZ (MENÉTRU-LE-VIGNOBLE) AND DOMAINE DURAND-PERRON/JACQUES DURAND (VOITEUR).

SAVOIE AND BUGEY

The wines of the French Alps and their foothills, of the upper Rhône and the river Ain, of Chambéry and Aix-Les-Bains, and of the shores of Lake Geneva (or Lac Léman) are little seen outside their region of production, the *départements* of Savoie and Haute-Savoie, Isère and Ain.

The *vignoble* is small and fragmented and the sub-*appellations* unnecessarily complicated. There are a number of different grape varieties and an even larger number of local grape names. Yet for all its obscurity and eccentricity of nomenclature this is an area well worth pursuing. There are signs recently that the outside world is beginning to take the area seriously and local producers are becoming less insular in their attitude to the idea of selling their wines elsewhere.

The wines of all these separate *appellations* are largely white and have a certain similarity despite being made with a number of different grape varieties. They are mountain wines: light, floral, evanescent, often better out of cask than in the bottle, frequently with a slight *pétillance*. Their essence is their youthful fragrance and the summer after the vintage is the optimum moment to drink them as they will not keep.

VIN DE SAVOIE

Surface Area (1998): 1725 ha.

Production (1998): (Red and rosé) 37,681 hl; (white) 85,553 hl.

Colour: Red, rosé and white.

Grape Varieties: (Red and rosé) Gamay Noir à Jus Blanc, Mondeuse, Pinot Noir, Persan, Cabernet Franc and Cabernet Sauvignon. Additionally, for the *département* of Isère: (Red) Etraire de la Dui, Syrah (Servarin or Serène) and Joubertin; (white) Roussette (or Altesse), Jacquère (or Cugnette or Abymes), Chardonnay, Aligoté, Molette, Roussanne (or Bergeron), Malvoisie (or Veltliner rosé), Mondeuse Blanche, Chasselas (or Fendant), Grignet (or Savagnin), Marsanne and Verdresse.

Maximum Yield: (Red and rosé) 60 hl/ha; (Vin de Savoie Cru) 55 hl/ha; (white) 65 hl/ha; (Vin de Savoie Cru) 60 hl/ha.

Minimum Alcohol Level: 9°; (Vin de Savoie Cru) 9.5°.

There are fifteen *cru* villages which can add their name to the Vin de Savoie *appellation*. The regulations are the

PRODUCTION AND SURFACE AREA (1998 HARVEST)

APPELLATIONS	SURFACE AREA (HA)	PRODUCTION (HL)	
		RED & ROSÉ	WHITE
VIN DE SAVOIE	1725	37,681	85,553
ROUSSETTE DE SAVOIE	145	–	1881
CRÉPY	72	–	2203
SEYSSEL	68	–	260
SEYSSEL MOUSSEUX	14	–	575
TOTAL	2024	37,681	92,814
		130,495	
BUGEY			
VIN DE BUGEY (VDQS)	445	13,093	15,517
GRAND TOTAL	4277	83,031	179,693
		262,724	

same except for a reduced yield of 55/60 hl/ha and an increased alcohol level of 9.5°. The *crus* are as follows: Abymes, Apremont, Arbin, Ayze, Charpignat, Chautagne, Chignin, Chignin-Bergeron (Roussanne only), Cruet, Marignan, Montmélian (Chasselas only), Ripaille (Chasselas only), Saint-Jean-de-La-Porte, Saint-Jeoire-Prieuré and Saint-Marie-d'Alloix.

The red Savoie wines, like those of the Jura, are in my view spoiled by a reliance on Gamay or Mondeuse. Both varieties will reduce the finesse of Pinot Noir which on its own could produce a delicious quasi-rosé. Equally the Cabernets have no quality place here. It is best to stick to the white wines.

ROUSSETTE DE SAVOIE

Surface Area (1998): 145 ha.
Production (1998): 1881 hl.
Colour: White.
Grape Varieties: Roussette (or Altesse), Chardonnay and Mondeuse Blanche.
Maximum Yield: 50 hl/ha; Roussette de Savoie Cru 45 hl/ha.
Minimum Alcohol Level: 10°; Roussette de Savoie Cru 10.5°.

It seems very odd that a wine calling itself Roussette should come from Mondeuse Blanche and Chardonnay as well as the Roussette, but such is the idiocy of some obscure corners of the French *appellation contrôlée* system. Roussette and Chardonnay individually can only make up 50 per cent of the blend.

There are four Roussette *crus* (Frangy, Marestel or Marestel-Altesse, Monterminod and Monthoux) which can add their name to the *appellation*. These wines must be made exclusively from the Roussette grape from a maximum yield of 45 hl/ha and have a natural alcohol level of 10.5°.

These are the two general *appellations* covering the entire Savoie region. The main centres for wine production are as follows:

South of Chambéry and along banks of the river Isère

Here you will find the villages of Apremont, Abymes, Saint-Jeoire-Prieuré, Chignin, Montmélian, Arbin, Cruet and Saint-Jean-de-La-Porte. I find this the most satisfying part of the Savoie. There are good whites, largely from Jacquère, Roussette, or Roussanne grapes (Chignin-Bergeron) and some quite respectable reds from the Mondeuse (more successful than the Pinot Noir here and more interesting than the Gamay). Sometimes the better Mondeuse *cuvées* are oak-aged.

On either side of the Lac du Bourget

The villages of Marestel (a *cru* for Roussette de Savoie) and Chautagne (a red wine centre) are in this section.

In the Haute-Savoie south and south-west of Bellegarde

Here lies the *cru* of Frangy and the separate *appellation* of Seyssel. The wines made here are mainly white and almost entirely from the Roussette grape.

Above Bonneville between Geneva and Chamonix

This isolated vineyard area includes the *cru* of Ayse. Again these are mainly white wines and largely from the Roussette grape.

The Lake Geneva vineyards

These vineyards lie on gentle slopes on the south bank of the lake near Thonon. Ripaille is a Vin de Savoie *cru* and Crépy is an *appellation* in its own right. Here Chasselas is the main grape variety.

Leading Savoie Producers

MAISON JEAN PERRIER & FILS
Commune: Abymes (Les Marches).
Owner: Gilbert Perrier.
Surface Area under Vine: 21 ha.
Wines: Abymes, Apremont, Arbin from their own vineyards, plus a complete range of Savoie (not Haute-Savoie) wines.

Gilbert Perrier's firm has been at Les Marches on the Savoie-Isère border south of Chamonix since 1853. This is an exemplary, modern set-up: not so large that the enthusiasm and dedication of the proprietor is dissipated. A good source of Savoie wines.

DOMAINE LOUIS MAGNIN
Commune: Arbin.
Owner: Louis Magnin.
Surface Area under Vine: 6 ha.
Wines: Montmélian (Jacquère), Roussette de Savoie, Chignin-Bergeron (Roussanne) and Arbin (Mondeuse) including Vieilles Vignes.

The friendly, able Louis Magnin took over the family domaine in the early 1990s and then started estate-bottling his wines. There are plenty of old vines here, and on steep slopes which can only be worked by hand. The 1997 Roussette weighed in at a natural 13.5°. The Vieilles Vignes Mondeuse is good, and would be even better if aged in wood.

★ DOMAINE ANDRÉ & MICHEL QUÉNARD
Commune: Torméry-Chignin.
Owner: Michel Quénard.
Surface Area under Vine: 20 ha.
Wines: Chignin (Jacquère, Gamay, Pinot Noir and Mondeuse) and Chignin-Bergeron (Roussanne).

Torméry is a hamlet just south of Chignin on the south-west facing slopes of the Massif de Bauges and is the heart of the Chignin-Bergeron *cru*. The soil is very stony – a scree of limestone debris. The view south over the valley of the river Isère is spectacular. In his forties, Michel Quénard picks his Roussanne in stages, when each bunch is at its optimum, and matures his wines in temperature-controlled cellars hacked out of the mountainside. The wines include delicious Chignin-Bergeron, produced by suppressing the malolactic fermentation and capable of taking bottle age, and good reds, especially those from the Mondeuse grape.

DOMAINE RAYMOND & PASCAL QUÉNARD
Commune: Chignin.
Owners: Raymond and Pascal Quénard.

Surface Area under Vine: 10 ha.
Wines: Chignin (Jacquère, Gamay and Mondeuse) and Chignin-Bergeron (Roussanne).

The Quénards are an extensive family. Father and son Raymond and Pascal work in tandem, but bottle their wines separately. Both the Chignin-Bergeron wines undergo malolactic fermentation. There are good wines here, and the oak-aged Vieilles Vignes Mondeuse can be very good.

Other Producers of note
DOMAINE BLARD & FILS (LES MARCHES), DOMAINE PIERRE BONIFACE (LES MARCHES), LA CAVE DU PRIEURÉ/RAYMOND BARLET & FILS (JONGIEUX), DOMAINE NOËL DUPASQUIER (JONGIEUX), DOMAINE CHARLES GONNET (CHIGNIN), DOMAINE CHARLES TROSSET (ARBIN), DOMAINE JEAN & ERIC VALLIER (BONNEVILLE), DOMAINE PHILIPPE VALLIET (APREMONT) and CHÂTEAU DE LA VIOLETTE/DANIEL FUSTINONI (LES MARCHES).

CRÉPY

Surface Area (1998): 72 ha.
Production (1998): 2203 hl.
Colour: White.
Grape Variety: Chasselas.
Maximum Yield: 55 hl/ha.
Minimum Alcohol Level: 9°.

Chasselas is not a very interesting grape variety, being dry and neutral, and it is hard to justify a separate *appellation d'origine contrôlée* being bestowed on Crépy, a district of three communes (Ballaison, Douvaine and Loisin) on the southern shores of Lake Geneva in the Haute-Savoie. The Vin de Savoie *cru* of Ripaille lies close by between Thonon and Evian. I find the wines very dull.

SEYSSEL
SEYSSEL MOUSSEUX

Surface Area (1998): (Seyssel) 68 ha; (Seyssel Mousseux) 14 ha.

SAVOIE AND BUGEY

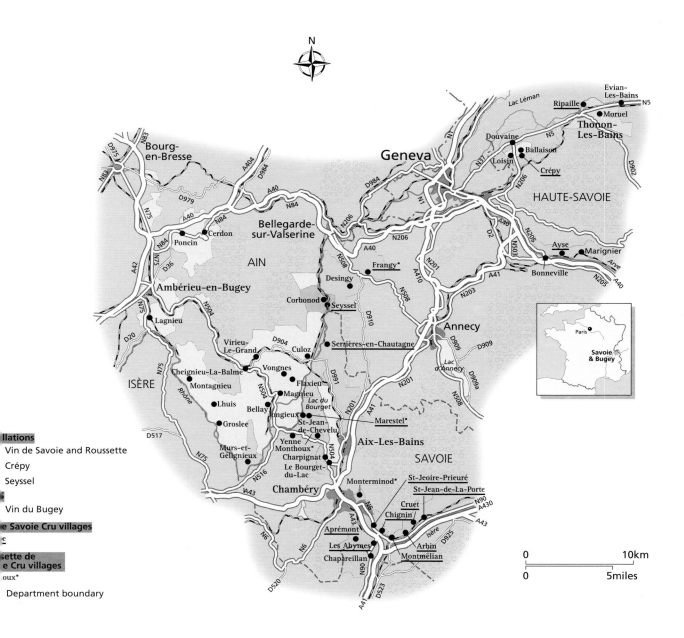

N

Evian-
Les-Bains
N5
Lac Léman
Ripaille
Moruel
Thonon-
Les-Bains
Douvaine
Ballaison
N5
Loisin
Crépy
D902
HAUTE-SAVOIE
Bourg-
en-Bresse
Geneva
Cerdon
Poncin
Bellegarde-
sur-Valserine
Ayse
Marignier
Bonneville
N205
Arve
A40
AIN
Frangy*
Ambérieu-en-Bugey
Desingy
Corbonod
Seyssel
Annecy
Lagnieu
Serrières-en-Chautagne
Virieu-
Le-Grand
Culoz
Lac
d'Annecy
Cheignieu-La-Balme
Vongnes
Flaxieu
ISÈRE
Montagnieu
Magnieu
Lhuis
Bellay
Longieux
Lac du
Bourget
Marestel*
Groslee
St-Jean-
de-Chevelu
Murs-et-
Gélignieux
Yenne
Monthoux*
Aix-Les-Bains
Charpignat
SAVOIE
Le Bourget-
du-Lac
Monterminod*
St-Jeoire-Prieuré
Chambéry
St-Jean-de-La-Porte
Cruet
Chignin
Aprémont
Arbin
Les Abymes
Montmélian
Chapareillan

Savoie
& Bugey
Paris

0   10km
0   5miles

Production (1998): (Seyssel) 2602 hl; (Seyssel Mousseux) 575 hl.
Colour: White.
Grape Varieties: (Seyssel) Roussette; (Seyssel Mousseux) Roussette, Chasselas and Molette.
Maximum Yield: (Seyssel) 45 hl/ha; (Seyssel Mousseux) 65 hl/ha.
Minimum Alcohol Level: (Seyssel) 10°; (Seyssel Mousseux) 8.5°.

Divided by the river Rhône, the Seyssel *appellation* covers the two communes of Seyssel and the parish of Corbonod on the steep slopes of the upper Rhône Valley. The soil is silico-calcareous and clay-siliceous, and from here the wines, both still and sparkling – the latter the most interesting – can be fresh and elegant but they are ephemeral and best almost as soon as they are in bottle. Most are consumed locally.

Seyssel Producers of note
MAISON MOLLEX (CORBONOD).

BUGEY

Surface Area (1998): 445 ha.
Production (1998): (Red and rosé) 13,093 hl; (white) 15,517 hl.
Colour: Red, rosé and white.
Grape Varieties: (Red and rosé) Pinot Noir and Gamay; (white) Roussette (or Altesse), Roussanne, Chardonnay, Jacquère and Molette.
Maximum Yield: (Red) 45 hl/ha ; (Vin de Bugey followed by name of a *cru*) 40 hl/ha; Roussette de Bugey followed by a name of a *cru*) 32 hl/ha.
Minimum Alcohol Level: (Red, rosé and white) 9°; (Vin de Bugey followed by the name of a *cru*) 9.5°; (Roussette) 10°; (Roussette followed by the name of a *cru*) 10.5°.

The VDQS of Bugey extends in the form of a U, along the banks of the Ain and Rhône rivers, from Cerdon, south-east of Bourg-en-Bresse, to Genissat, north of Seysses and well north of the Lac du Bourget. All this

lies within the borders of the *département* of Ain, if nicely on these borders. The main centres of activity are:
The commune of Vongnes, Flaxieu and Marignieu
Mid-way between Belley and Culoz and stretching up to Vineu-Le-Grand.
The south-west-facing slopes around Groslée and Lhuis.
Above the river Rhône as it flows north-west.
Montagnieu
A little further downstream from the above.
Cerdon
On the left bank of the river Ain.

There are several sub-*appellations* – Montagnieu makes a sparkling wine from the Roussette grape; and Cerdon a sparkling rosé. The Roussette de Bugey and the sub-*appellation* of Manicle at Cheignieu-La-Balme, north of Belley cover wines exclusively from this grape.

I find there is little difference in style or in quality between the Bugey wines and the non-Chasselas wines of the Savoie. The most interesting wines are the whites from Roussette and Roussanne, which can be admirable if fresh and youthful. The Chardonnays do not impress me as they seem ephemeral and age quickly, nor do the reds or rosés.

Leading Bugey Producer

DOMAINE DE MANICLE
Commune: Cheignieu-La-Balme.
Owners: Christian and Christine Beaulieu.
Surface Area under Vine: 10 ha.
Wines: Vin de Bugey, Cru de Manicle, (white) Roussette and Chardonnay, (red) Pinot Noir and Mondeuse, and Mondeuse rosé, Cuvée Caroline.
The Beaulieus live in a charming castle at Mers, on the southern tip of the Bugey slopes, but their vineyard, largely replanted since they took over in 1989, lies north of Belley. The land once belonged to the renowned nineteenth-century philosopher and gourmet Brillat-Savarin, and before that to the Carmelite monks.

Manicle is one of the Vin de Bugey sub-*appellations*, and most of the wine comes from this domaine (there is one other, the old boy who sold most of his vineyard to the Beaulieus). Christian Beaulieu is trying to produce a *vin de garde* with his Burgundian grapes but the 1996s were already a little tired three years later.

Other Bugey Producers of note

DOMAINE MAXIME ANGELOT (MARIGNIEU), LE CAVEAU BUGISTE (VONGNES) AND DOMAINE HUBERT & PHILIPPE MONIN (VONGNES).

VINS DE PAYS

Vin de Pays d'Ain

This is the departmental *vin de pays* of the Bugey area. A small amount of light white wine is made from the local grape varieties.

Vin de Pays d'Allobrogie

This zonal *vin de pays* is the main one of the Savoie region and is divided between the *départements* of Ain, Savoie and Haute-Savoie. The wine can come in all three colours — the reds and rosés from Gamay, Mondeuse and the other Savoie grapes; and the white, which makes up 95 per cent of the wines produced, comes mainly from the Jacquère grape.

I have had some well-made whites, even if they were rather ephemeral and acidic. The reds and rosés are weak, thin and rustic.

Vin de Pays des Balmes Dauphinoises

This is a zonal *vin de pays* from the Isère *département* south-east of Lyon. I have seen — and rejected — some thin, Gamay-based reds and rosés, but enjoyed crisp, dry, flowery whites made from Jacquère, Chardonnay and other varieties.

Vin de Pays des Coteaux du Grésivaudan

This zonal *vin de pays* comes from the Isère and Savoie *départements* around Grenoble. The reds and rosés, usually from Gamay, are thin and the whites are Jacquère-based. I have not sampled many wines.

Vin de Pays de Franche-Comté

Franche-Comté, comprising the *départements* of Jura and Haute-Saône, is one of France's most obscure regions, a no-man's land north of the Jura proper, equidistant between Dijon and Mulhouse.

Yet there are vines, if you look hard, as there are in almost every part of France, and this zonal *vin de pays* has at least one reputable grower, Pierre-Marie Guillaume at Charcenne on the marly slopes of the Coteaux de Gy. Monsieur Guillaume possesses 12 scattered hectares in what was formerly part of the estate and summer palace of the Archbishops of Besançon. I have enjoyed recent vintages of the Chardonnay and Pinot Noir. The former can fairly be compared with a lightweight Mâcon; the latter is more in the style of a red wine from Alsace than a Burgundy. There is also a Gamay and a sparkling wine.

Appendix One
The Starred Domaines

Three Stars ★★★

Bordeaux
Château Cheval-Blanc, Saint-Emilion
Château Haut-Brion, Pessac-Léognan
Château Lafite-Rothschild, Pauillac
Château Latour, Pauillac
Château Léoville-Las-Cases, Saint-Julien
Château Margaux, Margaux
Château Petrus, Pomerol
Château d'Yquem, Sauternes

Burgundy
Domaine d'Auvenay/Maison Leroy, Auxey-
  Duresses
Domaine des Comtes Lafon, Meursault
Domaine Leroy, Vosne-Romanée
Domaine de La Romanée-Conti, Vosne-Romanée
Domaine Armand Rousseau, Gevrey-Chambertin
Domaine Comte Georges de Vogüé, Chambolle-
  Musigny

The Loire Valley
Domaine Didier Dagueneau, Saint-Andelain
  (Pouilly-Fumé)

The Rhône Valley
Château de Beaucastel, Châteauneuf-du-Pape
Domaine Jean-Louis Chave, Mauves (Hermitage)
Ets. E Guigal, Ampuis (Côte-Rôtie)
Ets. Paul Jaboulet Aîné, La Roche-de-Glun

The South-West
Château Montus/Château Bouscassé,
  Maumusson (Madiran)

Alsace
Maison F E Trimbach, Ribeauvillé

Champagne
Krug, Reims
Pol Roger, Epernay
Louis Roederer, Reims

Two Stars ★★

Bordeaux
Château Canon, Saint-Emilion
Château Certan-de-May, Pomerol
Domaine de Chevalier, Pessac-Léognan
Château Climens, Sauternes
Château Cos d'Estournel, Saint-Estèphe
Château Ducru-Beaucaillou, Saint-Julien
Château L'Eglise-Clinet, Pomerol
Château L'Evangile, Pomerol
Château La Fleur-Petrus, Pomerol
Château Grand-Puy-Lacoste, Pauillac
Château Lafaurie-Peyraguey, Sauternes
Château Lafleur, Pomerol
Château Latour-à-Pomerol, Pomerol
Château Laville-Haut-Brion, Pessac-Léognan
Château Léoville-Barton, Saint-Julien
Château Léoville-Poyferré, Saint-Julien
Château Magdelaine, Saint-Emilion
Château La Mission-Haut-Brion, Pessac-Léognan

CHÂTEAU MOUTON-ROTHSCHILD, Pauillac
CHÂTEAU PALMER, Margaux
CHÂTEAU PICHON-LONGUEVILLE, COMTESSE DE
  LALANDE, Pauillac
CHÂTEAU RAUZAN-SÉGLA, Margaux
CHÂTEAU RIEUSSEC, Sauternes
CHÂTEAU TROTANOY, Pomerol
VIEUX-CHÂTEAU-CERTAN, Pomerol

BURGUNDY

DOMAINE DU MARQUIS D'ANGERVILLE, Volnay
DOMAINE DU COMTE ARMAND, Pommard
DOMAINE BONNEAU DU MARTRAY, Pernand-
  Vergelesses
DOMAINE JEAN-FRANÇOIS COCHE-DURY, Meursault
DOMAINE JEAN-JACQUES CONFURON, Nuits-Saint-
  Georges, Prémeaux
DOMAINE RENÉ & VINCENT DAUVISSAT, Chablis
MAISON JOSEPH DROUHIN, Beaune
ETS. GEORGES DUBOEUF, Romanèche-Thorins
  (Beaujolais)
DOMAINE DUJAC, Morey-Saint-Denis
DOMAINE RENÉ ENGEL, Vosne-Romanée
DOMAINE JOSEPH FAIVELEY, Nuits-Saint-Georges
DOMAINE HENRI GOUGES, Nuits-Saint-Georges
DOMAINE JEAN GRIVOT, Vosne-Romanée
DOMAINE ANNE GROS, Vosne-Romanée
MAISON LOUIS JADOT, Beaune
DOMAINE EMMANUEL ROUGET, Flagey-Echezeaux
DOMAINE MICHEL LAFARGE, Volnay
DOMAINE MÉO-CAMUZET, Vosne-Romanée
DOMAINE LOUIS MICHEL & FILS, Chablis
DOMAINE HUBERT DE MONTILLE, Volnay
DOMAINE DENIS MORTET, Gevrey-Chambertin
DOMAINE DR GEORGES MUGNERET/MUGNERET-
  GIBOURG, Vosne-Romanée
DOMAINE JACQUES-FRÉDÉRIC MUGNIER, Chambolle-
  Musigny
DOMAINE RAMONET, Chassagne-Montrachet
DOMAINE FRANÇOIS RAVENEAU, Chablis
DOMAINE GEORGES ROUMIER ET FILS, Chambolle-
  Musigny

THE LOIRE VALLEY

DOMAINE/MAISON COULY-DUTHEIL, Chinon
DOMAINE HUET, Vouvray
DOMAINE CHARLES JOGUET, Sazilly (Chinon)
CLOS NAUDIN, Vouvray
CLOS ROUGEARD, Chacé (Saumur-Champigny)

THE RHÔNE VALLEY

DOMAINE HENRI BONNEAU, Châteauneuf-du-Pape
ETS. CHAPOUTIER, Tain L'Hermitage
DOMAINE AUGUSTE ET PIERRE-MARIE CLAPE, Cornas
DOMAINE LES CAILLOUX, Châteauneuf-du-Pape
DOMAINE DE MARCOUX, Châteauneuf-du-Pape
CLOS DES PAPES, Châteauneuf-du-Pape
DOMAINE ANDRÉ PERRET, Verlieu (Condrieu)
CHÂTEAU RAYAS, Châteauneuf-du-Pape
DOMAINE RENÉ ROSTAING, Ampuis (Côte-Rôtie)
DOMAINE NOËL VERSET, Cornas
DOMAINE DU VIEUX TÉLÉGRAPHE, Bédarrides
  (Châteauneuf-du-Pape)

PROVENCE

DOMAINE TEMPIER, Le Plan du Castellet (Bandol)
DOMAINE DE TRÉVALLON, Saint-Etienne-du-Grès (Vin
  de Pays)

LANGUEDOC

DOMAINE JEAN-MICHEL ALQUIER, Faugères
DOMAINE LA GRANGE DES PÈRES, Aniane (Vin de Pays)
DOMAINE PEYRE-ROSE, Saint-Pargoire (Coteaux du
  Languedoc)
PRIEURÉ DE SAINT-JEAN-DE-BÉBIAN, Pézenas (Coteaux
  du Languedoc)

ROUSSILLON

DOMAINE GAUBY, Calce (Côtes du Roussillon-Villages)

THE SOUTH-WEST

CHÂTEAU D'AYDIE, Aydie (Madiran)
CHÂTEAU BARREJAT, Maumusson (Madiran)
DOMAINE CAUHAPÉ, Monein (Jurançon)
DOMAINE LA CHAPELLE LENCLOS, Maumusson-
  Laguian (Madiran)

ALSACE
DOMAINE ANDRÉ KIENTZLER, Ribeauvillé
DOMAINE WEINBACH, Kaysersberg
DOMAINE ZIND-HUMBRECHT, Turckheim

CHAMPAGNE
BOLLINGER, Ay-Champagne
VEUVE CLICQUOT-PONSARDIN, Reims

THE JURA
DOMAINE BERTHET-BONDET, Château-Chalon

ONE STAR ★

BORDEAUX — MÉDOC
CHÂTEAU D'ANGLUDET, Margaux
CHÂTEAU BRANE-CANTENAC, Margaux
CHÂTEAU CHASSE-SPLEEN, Moulis
CHÂTEAU CLERC-MILON, Pauillac
CHÂTEAU DAUZAC, Margaux
CHÂTEAU DURFORT-VIVENS, Margaux
CHÂTEAU DUHART-MILON, Pauillac
CHÂTEAU FERRIÈRE, Margaux
CHÂTEAU GRUAUD-LAROSE, Saint-Julien
CHÂTEAU HAUT-BATAILLEY, Pauillac
CHÂTEAU HAUT-MARBUZET, Saint-Estèphe
CHÂTEAU LABÉGORCE-ZÉDÉ, Margaux
CHÂTEAU LA LAGUNE, Haut-Médoc
CHÂTEAU LAGRANGE, Saint-Julien
CHÂTEAU LANGOA-BARTON, Saint-Julien
CHÂTEAU LYNCH-BAGES, Pauillac
CHÂTEAU MALESCOT-SAINT-EXUPÉRY, Margaux
CHÂTEAU MONBRISON, Margaux
CHÂTEAU MONTROSE, Saint-Estèphe
CHÂTEAU PICHON-LONGUEVILLE (BARON), Pauillac
CHÂTEAU PONTET-CANET, Pauillac
CHÂTEAU POUJEAUX, Moulis
CHÂTEAU SOCIANDO-MALLET, Haut-Médoc
CHÂTEAU TALBOT, Saint-Julien

BORDEAUX — GRAVES
CHÂTEAU COUHINS-LURTON, Pessac-Léognan

CHÂTEAU DE FIEUZAL, Pessac-Léognan
CHÂTEAU HAUT-BAILLY, Pessac-Léognan
CHÂTEAU PAPE-CLÉMENT, Pessac-Léognan
CHÂTEAU LA TOUR-HAUT-BRION, Pessac-Léognan

BORDEAUX — SAUTERNES
CHÂTEAU COUTET
CHÂTEAU DOISY-DAËNE
CHÂTEAU DOISY-DUBROCA
CHÂTEAU DOISY-VÉDRINES
CHÂTEAU DE FARGUES
CHÂTEAU LAMOTHE-GUIGNARD
CHÂTEAU DE MALLE
CHÂTEAU NAIRAC
CHÂTEAU RABAUD-PROMIS
CHÂTEAU RAYNE-VIGNEAU
CHÂTEAU SIGALAS-RABAUD
CHÂTEAU SUDUIRAUT
CHÂTEAU LA TOUR-BLANCHE

BORDEAUX — SAINT-EMILION
CHÂTEAU ANGÉLUS
CHÂTEAU L'ARROSÉE
CHÂTEAU AUSONE
CHÂTEAU BEAU-SÉJOUR-BÉCOT/LA GOMERIE
CHÂTEAU BEAUSÉJOUR-DUFFAU-LAGARROSSE
CHÂTEAU BERLIQUET
CHÂTEAU CANON
CHÂTEAU FIGEAC
LA MONDOTTE
CLOS DE L'ORATOIRE
CHÂTEAU PAVIE
CHÂTEAU PAVIE-MACQUIN
CHÂTEAU LE TERTRE-ROTEBOEUF
CHÂTEAU TROPLONG-MONDOT
CHÂTEAU DE VALANDRAUD

BORDEAUX — POMEROL
CHÂTEAU CERTAN-DE-MAY
CHÂTEAU CLINET
CHÂTEAU LA CONSEILLANTE
CLOS L'EGLISE
CHÂTEAU LA FLEUR-DE-GAY

CHÂTEAU GAZIN
CHÂTEAU LA GRAVE-À-POMEROL
CHÂTEAU NENIN
CHÂTEAU LE PIN

BURGUNDY — CHABLIS

DOMAINE J BILLAUD-SIMON, Chablis
LA CHABLISIENNE, Chablis
DOMAINE DANIEL-ETIENNE DEFAIX, Milly
DOMAINE/MAISON DROUHIN, Beaune
DOMAINE GÉRARD DUPLESSIS, Chablis
DOMAINE WILLIAM FÈVRE, Chablis
DOMAINE JEAN-PIERRE GROSSOT, Fleys
DOMAINE DES MALANDES, Chablis
DOMAINE DES MARRONNIERS, Préhy
DOMAINE LOUIS MOREAU, Beines
DOMAINE PINSON, Chablis
DOMAINE SERVIN, Chablis

BURGUNDY — CÔTE DE NUITS

DOMAINE DE L'ARLOT, Nuits-Saint-Georges, Prémeaux
DOMAINE ROBERT ARNOUX, Vosne-Romanée
DOMAINE DENIS BACHELET, Gevrey-Chambertin
DOMAINE GHISLAINE BARTHOD, Chambolle-Musigny
DOMAINE ALAIN BURGUET, Gevrey-Chambertin
DOMAINE SYLVAIN CATHIARD, Vosne-Romanée
DOMAINE JEAN CHAUVENET, Nuits-Saint-Georges
DOMAINE ROBERT CHEVILLON, Nuits-Saint-Georges
DOMAINE BRUNO CLAIR, Marsannay
DOMAINE BRUNO CLAVELIER, Vosne-Romanée
DOMAINE JACKY CONFURON-COTÉTIDOT, Vosne-
   Romanée
DOMAINE BERNARD DUGAT-PY, Gevrey-Chambertin
DOMAINE CLAUDE DUGAT, Gevrey-Chambertin
DOMAINE DES ESTOURNELLES/FRÉDÉRIC ESMONIN,
   Gevrey-Chambertin
DOMAINE RÉGIS FOREY PÈRE ET FILS, Vosne-Romanée
DOMAINE JEAN-CLAUDE FOURRIER, Gevrey-
   Chambertin
DOMAINE VINCENT GÉANTET-PANSIOT, Gevrey-
   Chambertin
DOMAINE ROBERT GROFFIER PÈRE ET FILS, Morey-
   Saint-Denis

DOMAINE MICHEL GROS, Vosne-Romanée
DOMAINE ALAIN HUDELOT-NOËLLAT, Vougeot
MAISON DOMINIQUE LAURENT, Nuits-Saint-Georges
DOMAINE HUBERT LIGNIER, Morey-Saint-Denis
DOMAINE GÉRARD MUGNERET, Vosne-Romanée
DOMAINE PHILIPPE NADDEF, Couchey
DOMAINE HENRI PERROT-MINOT, Morey-Saint-Denis
DOMAINE PONSOT, Morey-Saint-Denis
DOMAINE DANIEL RION ET FILS, Nuits-Saint-Georges,
   Prémeaux
DOMAINE JOSEPH ROTY, Gevrey-Chambertin
DOMAINE CHRISTIAN SÉRAFIN, Gevrey-Chambertin
DOMAINE THOMAS-MOILLARD, Nuits-Saint-Georges
DOMAINE JEAN & JEAN-LOUIS TRAPET, Gevrey-
   Chambertin

BURGUNDY — CÔTE DE BEAUNE

DOMAINE ROBERT AMPEAU ET FILS, Meursault
DOMAINE SIMON BIZE, Savigny-Lès-Beaune
DOMAINE JEAN-MARC BOILLOT, Pommard
MAISON BOUCHARD PÈRE ET FILS, Beaune
DOMAINE MICHEL BOUZEREAU ET FILS, Meursault
DOMAINE YVES BOYER-MARTENOT, Meursault
DOMAINE LOUIS CARILLON ET FILS, Puligny-
   Montrachet
DOMAINE CHANDON DE BRIAILLES, Savigny-Lès-
   Beaune
CHÂTEAU DE CHOREY-LÈS-BEAUNE/DOMAINE JACQUES
   GERMAIN, Chorey-Lès-Beaune
DOMAINE MARC COLIN, Saint-Aubin
DOMAINE MICHEL COLIN-DELÉGER, Chassagne-
   Montrachet
DOMAINE DE COURCEL, Pommard
DOMAINE DIDIER DARVIOT-PERRIN, Monthelie
DOMAINE MAURICE ECARD, Savigny-Lès-Beaune
DOMAINE JEAN-NOËL GAGNARD, Chassagne-
   Montrachet
DOMAINE JACQUES GAGNARD-DELAGRANGE,
   Chassagne-Montrachet
DOMAINE VINCENT GIRARDIN, Santenay
DOMAINE PATRICK JAVILLIER, Meursault
DOMAINE CHARLES ET RÉMI JOBARD, Meursault
DOMAINE FRANÇOIS JOBARD, Meursault

Domaine Hubert Lamy-Monnot, Saint-Aubin

Domaine Leflaive, Puligny-Montrachet

Domaine Michel Niellon, Chassagne-Montrachet

Domaine Thierry Matrot, Meursault

Domaine Pierre Morey, Meursault

Domaine Albert Morot, Beaune

Domaine Jean-Marc Pavelot, Savigny-Lès-Beaune

Domaine Paul Pernot et Fils, Puligny-Montrachet

Domaine Jean and Jean-Marc Pillot, Chassagne-Montrachet

Domaine Rapet Père et Fils, Pernand-Vergelesses

Maison Remoissenet Père et Fils, Beaune

Domaine Guy Roulot, Meursault

Domaine Etienne Sauzet, Puligny-Montrachet

Burgundy — Côte Chalonnaise

Domaine Jean-Claude Brelière, Rully

Domaine de la Croix Jacquelet, Mercurey

Domaine de la Folie, Rully

Domaine du Gardin, Givry

Domaine Henri & Paul Jacquesson, Rully

Domaine Jean-Marc & Vincent Joblot, Givry

Domaine Emile Juillot, Mercurey

Domaine Michel Juillot, Mercurey

Domaine François Lumpp, Givry

Domaine Jean & François Raquillet, Mercurey

Maison Antonin Rodet, Mercurey

Cave des Vignerons de Buxy, Buxy

Domaine A & P de Villaine, Bouzeron

Burgundy — Mâconnais

Domaine de la Bon Gran, Quintaine

Domaine André Bonhomme, Viré

Domaine Roger Cordier, Fuissé

Domaine Corsin, Davayé

Domaine J A Ferret, Fuissé

Château de Fuissé, Fuissé

Domaine Jean-Marie Guffens-Heynen, Vergisson

Domaine Pascal Renaud, Pouilly

Domaine Thibert Père & Fils, Fuissé

Domaine Valette, Chaintré

Maison Verget, Sologny

Beaujolais

Un Eventail de Vignerons Producteurs, Corcelles

Château des Jacques, Moulin-à-Vent

The Loire Valley — Central Vineyards

Domaine/Maison Henri Bourgeois, Chavignol (Sancerre)

Domaine Alain Cailbourdin, Maltaverne (Pouilly-Fumé)

Domaine Cotat Frères, Chavignol (Sancerre)

Domaine/Maison Lucien Crochet, Bué (Sancerre)

Domaine/Maison Alphonse Mellot, Sancerre

Domaine Vincent Pinard, Bué (Sancerre)

Domaine Vacheron, Sancerre

The Loire Valley — Touraine

Domaine Yannick Amirault, Bourgueil

Domaine des Aubuisières, Vouvray

Domaine Baudry & Fils, Cravant-Les-Coteaux (Chinon)

Domaine du Bourg, Saint-Nicolas-de-Bourgueil

Domaine Cathérine et Pierre Breton, Restigné (Bourgueil)

Domaine Didier Champalou, Vouvray

Domaine Delétang, Saint-Martin-Le-Beau (Montlouis)

Domaine Pierre-Jacques Druet, Benais (Bourgueil)

Vignoble de la Jarnoterie, Saint-Nicolas-de-Bourgueil

Clos Habert, Montlouis-sur-Loire (Montlouis)

Domaine de la Lande, Bourgueil

Domaine Moyer, Montlouis-sur-Loire (Montlouis)

Domaine Joël Taluau, Saint-Nicolas-de-Bourgueil

The Loire Valley — Anjou-Saumur

Domaine de Bablut, Brissac-Quincé (Coteaux de L'Aubance)

Domaine des Baumard, Rochefort-sur-Loire (Coteaux du Layon)

Château Bellerive, Rochefort-sur-Loire (Quarts de Chaume)

Château de Chamboureau, Savennières

Château d'Epiré, Savennières

CHÂTEAU DE FESLES, Thouarcé (Coteaux du Layon)

DOMAINE FILLIATREAU, Chaintres (Saumur-Champigny)

CHÂTEAU DU HUREAU, Dampierre-sur-Loire (Saumur-Champigny)

CHÂTEAU PIERRE-BISE, Beaulieu-sur-Layon (Coteaux du Layon)

CHÂTEAU DE PUTILLE, La Pommeraye (Anjou-Villages)

CHÂTEAU DE LA ROCHE-AUX-MOINES, Savennières

DOMAINE RICHOU, Mozé-sur-Louet (Anjou-Villages)

DOMAINE SAINT-VINCENT, Dampierre-sur-Loire (Saumur-Champigny)

CHATEAU DE TIGNÉ, Tigné (Anjou-Villages)

CHÂTEAU DE VILLENEUVE, Souzay-Champigny (Saumur-Champigny)

THE LOIRE VALLEY — PAYS NANTAIS

DOMAINES CHÉREAU-CARRÉ, Saint-Fiacre-sur-Maine (Muscadet de Sèvre-et-Maine)

CHÂTEAU DU CLÉRAY/DOMAINE SAUVION ET FILS, Vallet (Muscadet de Sèvre-et-Maine)

DOMAINE DE L'ECU, Le Landreau (Muscadet de Sèvre-et-Maine)

MAISON LOUIS MÉTAIREAU, Maisdon-sur-Sèvre (Muscadet de Sèvre-et-Maine)

CHÂTEAU DE LA RAGOTIÈRE, La Regrippière (Muscadet de Sèvre-et-Maine)

DOMAINE DE LA TOURMALINE, Saint-Fiacre-sur-Maine (Muscadet de Sèvre-et-Maine)

NORTHERN RHÔNE VALLEY

DOMAINE THIERRY ALLEMAND, Cornas

DOMAINE RENÉ BALTHAZAR, Cornas

DOMAINE GILLES BARGE, Ampuis (Côte-Rôtie)

DOMAINE GUY DE BARJAC, Cornas

DOMAINE ALBERT BELLE, Larnage (Crozes-Hermitage)

DOMAINE BERNARD BURGAUD, Ampuis (Côte-Rôtie)

DOMAINE JOËL CHAMPET, Ampuis

DOMAINE LOUIS CHÈZE, Limony (Condrieu)

DOMAINE DU COLOMBIER, Mercurol (Crozes-Hermitage)

DOMAINE JEAN-LUC COLOMBO, Cornas

DOMAINE YVES CUILLERON, Chavanay (Condrieu)

DOMAINE CLUSEL-ROCH, Verenay (Côte-Rôtie)

ETS. DELAS FRÈRES, Saint-Jean-de-Muzols

DOMAINE ALBERT DERVIEUX-THAISE, Verenay (Côte-Rôtie)

DOMAINE PIERRE DUMAZET, Limony (Condrieu)

DOMAINE DUMIEN-SERRETTE, Cornas

DOMAINE PIERRE GAILLARD, Malleval (Condrieu)

DOMAINE MAURICE GENTAZ-DERVIEUX, Ampuis (Côte-Rôtie)

DOMAINE JEAN-MICHEL GERIN, Verenay (Côte-Rôtie)

DOMAINE ALAIN GRAILLOT, Pont de L'Isère (Crozes-Hermitage)

DOMAINE JEAN-LOUIS GRIPPAT, Tournon

DOMAINE JEAN-PAUL ET JEAN-LUC JAMET, Le Vallin (Côte-Rôtie)

DOMAINE JACQUES LEMÉNICIER, Cornas

DOMAINE JEAN LIONNET, Cornas

DOMAINE ROBERT MICHEL, Cornas

DOMAINE ROBERT NIÉRO-PINCHON, Condrieu

DOMAINE MICHEL OGIER, Ampuis (Côte-Rôtie)

DOMAINE ALAIN PARET, Malleval (Condrieu)

DOMAINE CHRISTOPHE PICHON, Chavanay (Condrieu)

DOMAINE PHILIPPE PICHON, Chavanay (Condrieu)

DOMAINE MARC SORREL, Tain L'Hermitage

DOMAINE GEORGES VERNAY, Condrieu

DOMAINE FRANÇOIS VILLARD, Monjoux (Condrieu)

DOMAINE ALAIN VOGE, Cornas

SOUTHERN RHÔNE VALLEY

DOMAINE DANIEL & DENIS ALARY, Cairanne (Côtes du Rhône)

DOMAINE DES AMOURIERS, Vacqueyras

DOMAINE LUCIEN BARROT ET FILS, Châteauneuf-du-Pape

DOMAINE DE BEAURENARD, Châteauneuf-du-Pape

DOMAINE BOSQUET DES PAPES, Châteauneuf-du-Pape

DOMAINE BRUSSET, Cairanne (Côtes du Rhône)

DOMAINE DU CAYRON, Gigondas

DOMAINE LE CLOS DES CAZAUX, Vacqueyras

DOMAINE CHARVIN, Orange (Châteauneuf-du-Pape)

LES CLEFS D'OR, Châteauneuf-du-Pape

DOMAINE DE DURBAN, Beaumes-de-Venise (Muscat de Beaumes-de-Venise)

Domaine des Espiers, Vacqueyras

Domaine Font de Michelle, Châteauneuf-du-Pape

Château Fortia, Châteauneuf-du-Pape

Domaine de La Fourmone, Vacqueyras

Domaine du Galet des Papes, Châteauneuf-du-Pape

Domaine de La Gardine, Châteauneuf-du-Pape

Domaine Les Goubert, Gigondas

Domaine Les Hautes Cances, Cairanne (Côtes du Rhône)

Domaine de La Janasse, Châteauneuf-du-Pape

Clos du Mont-Olivet, Châteauneuf-du-Pape

Château Mont-Redon, Châteauneuf-du-Pape

Domaine de Montpertuis/Domaine La Croze Châteauneuf-du-Pape

Domaine de La Mordorée, Tavel

Domaine de L'Oratoire-Saint-Martin, Cairanne (Côtes du Rhône)

Domaine du Pegaü, Châteauneuf-du-Pape

Domaine de Piaugier, Gigondas

Domaine Rabasse-Charavin, Cairanne (Côtes du Rhône)

Domaine La Roquette, Châteauneuf-du-Pape

Domaine Roger Sabon & Fils, Châteauneuf-du-Pape

Domaine Sainte-Anne, Saint-Gervais (Côtes du Rhône)

Domaine Saint-Gayan, Gigondas

Domaine Santa-Duc, Gigondas

Domaine de La Soumade, Rasteau (Côtes du Rhône)

Maison Tardieu-Laurent, Lauris

Château des Tours, Vacqueyras

Domaine de La Vieille Julienne, Orange (Châteauneuf-du-Pape)

Le Vieux Donjon, Châteauneuf-du-Pape

Provence

Château de Bellet, Saint-Roman-de-Bellet (Bellet)

Domaines Bunan, La Cadière d'Azur (Bandol)

Domaine de La Courtade, Porquerolles (Côtes de Provence)

Château de Pibarnon, La Cadière d'Azur (Bandol)

Domaine Rabiega, Flayosc (Côtes de Provence)

Domaine de Triennes, Nans-Les-Pins (Coteaux Varois)

Languedoc

Domaine d'Aupilhac, Montpeyroux (Coteaux du Languedoc)

Domaine de Baruel, Tornac (Vin de Pays)

Domaine Bertrand Bergé, Paziols (Fitou)

Domaine Borie La Vitarèle, Saint-Nazaire-de-Ladarez (Saint-Chinian)

Mas Bruguière, Valflaunès (Coteaux du Languedoc)

Château de Caraguilhes, Saint-Laurent-de-La-Cabrerisse (Corbières)

Château Cascardais, Saint-Laurent-de-La-Cabrerisse (Corbières)

Domaine Cazal-Vieil, Cessenon-sur-Orb (Minervois)

Château Coupe Roses, La Caunette (Minervois)

Mas de Daumas Gassac, Aniane (Vin de Pays)

Château des Estanilles, Lenthéric (Faugères)

Château Fabas, Laure-Minervois (Minervois)

Fortant de France, Sète (Vin de Pays)

Château de Gourgazaud, La Livinière (Minervois)

Domaine du Grand Crès, Ferrals (Corbières)

Domaine L'Hortus, Valflaunès (Coteaux du Languedoc)

Domaine Lacombe Blanche, La Livinière (Minervois)

Mas Jullien, Jonquières (Coteaux du Languedoc)

Domaine Luc Lapeyre, Trausse-Minervois (Minervois)

Château de Lascaux, Vacquières (Coteaux du Languedoc)

Maison Jacques et François Lurton/Domaine de Poumeyrade, Vayres, Bordeaux (Vin de Pays)

Château de Nouvelles, Tuchan (Fitou)

Château d'Oupia, Oupia (Minervois)

Château Les Palais, Saint-Laurent-de-La-Cabrerisse (Corbières)

Domaine Piccinini, La Livinière (Minervois)

Château de La Roque, Fontanès (Coteaux du Languedoc)

Domaine Saint-Andrieu, Montpeyroux (Coteaux du Languedoc)

Château Saint-Auriol, Lagrasse (Corbières)

Les Caves du Sieur d'Arques, Limoux

Château La Voulte-Gasparets, Boutenac (Corbières)

ROUSSILLON

DOMAINE MAS AMIEL, Maury

DOMAINE DU MAS BLANC, Banyuls

DOMAINE CAZES FRÈRES, Rivesaltes

DOMAINE DES CHÊNES, Vingrau (Côtes du Roussillon-Villages)

DOMAINE FORÇA RÉAL, Millas (Côtes du Roussillon-Villages)

DOMAINE GARDIÉS, Vingrau (Côtes du Roussillon-Villages)

DOMAINE DE LA RECTORIE, Banyuls

DOMAINE LA TOUR VIEILLE, Collioure

THE SOUTH-WEST

CHÂTEAU BAUDARE, Labastide-Saint-Pierre (Côtes du Frontonnais)

CHÂTEAU BELINGARD, Pomport (Monbazillac)

DOMAINE BELLEGARDE, Monein (Jurançon)

CHÂTEAU BELLEVUE-LA-FORÊT, Fronton (Côtes du Frontonnais)

DOMAINE BERTHOUMIEU, Viella (Madiran)

DOMAINE CAPMARTIN, Maumusson (Madiran)

CHÂTEAU DU CÈDRE, Vire-sur-Lot (Cahors)

CHÂTEAU DE LA COLLINE, Thénac (Bergerac)

CLOS LA COUTALE, Vire-Sur-Lot (Cahors)

CHÂTEAU FONTMOURGUES, Monbazillac

CLOS DE GAMOT, Prayssac (Cahors)

DOMAINE GRANDE-MAISON, Monbazillac

CLOS GUIROUILH, Lasseube (Jurançon)

DOMAINE DE LABARTHE, Castanet (Gaillac)

DOMAINE LABRANCHE-LAFFONT, Maumusson (Madiran)

CHÂTEAU DE LAGREZETTE, Caillac (Cahors)

CHÂTEAU LAMARTINE, Soturac (Cahors)

CLOS LAPEYRE, La Chapelle-de-Rousse (Jurançon)

DOMAINE DE LAULAN, Duras (Côtes de Duras)

CHÂTEAU LES MIAUDOUX, Saussignac

CHATEAU MONTELS, Souel-Cordes (Gaillac)

DOMAINE NIGRI, Monein (Jurançon)

DOMAINE PINERAIE, Puy-L'Evêque (Cahors)

DOMAINE DE RICHARD, Monestier (Saussignac)

CHÂTEAU LE ROC, Fronton (Côtes du Frontonnais)

DOMAINE DES SAVARINES, Trespoux (Cahors)

DOMAINE SERGENT, Maumusson (Madiran)

CHÂTEAU TIRECUL-LA-GRAVIÈRE, Monbazillac

CHÂTEAU TOUR DES GENDRES, Ribagnac (Bergerac)

DOMAINE DES TRES CANTONS, Cahuzac-sur-Vère (Gaillac)

CLOS TRIGUEDINA, Puy-L'Evêque (Cahors)

CLOS D'YVIGNE, Gageac et Rouillac (Saussignac)

ALSACE

DOMAINE PAUL BLANCK, Kientzheim

DOMAINE ALBERT BOXLER, Niedermorschwihr

DOMAINE MARCEL DEISS, Bergheim

MAISON HUGEL ET FILS, Riquewihr

DOMAINE MARC KREYDENWEISS, Andlau

MAISON KUENTZ-BAS, Husseren-Les-Châteaux

DOMAINE ANDRÉ OSTERTAG, Epfig

DOMAINE SCHOFFIT, Colmar

DOMAINE BRUNO SORG, Eguisheim

CHAMPAGNE

BOLLINGER, Mareuil-sur-Ay

CHAMPAGNE ET VILLAGES, Epernay

ALFRED GRATIEN, Epernay

MOËT & CHANDON, Epernay

PERRIER-JOUËT, Epernay

POMMERY & GRENO, Reims

SALON, Le Mesnil-sur-Oger

JACQUES SELOSSE, Avize

TAITTINGER, Reims

THE JURA

CHÂTEAU D'ARLAY, Arlay

DOMAINE JEAN BOURDY, Arlay

DOMAINE ROLET PÈRE & FILS, Montigny-Lès-Arsures

DOMAINE JEAN MACLE, Château-Chalon

SAVOIE

DOMAINE ANDRÉ & MICHEL QUÉNARD, Torméry-Chignin

APPENDIX TWO

FRENCH WINE STATISTICS

These are the official INAO statistics.

That they do not correspond exactly to the figures summarised in each chapter is explained by the vineyards listed under 'extra', which I have included in their appropriate place.

REGION	SURFACE AREA BY REGION (1998) SURFACE AREA (HA)				
	AC	VDQS & ARMAGNAC	WINES FOR COGNAC WINES	OTHER	TOTAL
ALSACE	14,505	27		286	14,818
BEAUJOLAIS	21,713	–		241	21,954
BURGUNDY	27,006	97		601	27,704
BORDEAUX	113,775	–		1841	115,616
CHAMPAGNE	30,231	–		153	30,384
CORSICA	2474	–		3940	6414
THE JURA	1831	–		266	2097
SAVOIE	2034	448		1807	4289
LANGUEDOC-ROUSSILLON	6552	1123		162,342	229,017
PROVENCE	26,975	–		17,428	44,403
THE SOUTH-WEST	29,818	1418		31,071	623,07
LOIRE VALLEY	47,168	4922		19,221	71,311
RHÔNE VALLEY	78,222	630		71,529	150,381
TOTAL REGIONS ABOVE	461,304	8665	83862	310,726	864,557
EXTRA	1658	195		6383	8216
TOTAL FRANCE	462,962	8860	83,862	317,089	872,773

PRODUCTION BY REGION (1998)

PRODUCTION (HL)

REGION	AC		VDQS		WINES FOR COGNAC & ARMAGNAC	VIN DE PAYS		OTHER WINES		TOTAL		OVERALL TOTAL
	RED/ROSÉ	WHITE	RED/ROSÉ	WHITE		RED/ROSÉ	WHITE	RED/ROSÉ	WHITE	RED/ROSÉ	WHITE	
ALSACE	109,557	1,152,501	431	1169		–	–	5195	64,480	115,183	1,218,150	1,333,333
BEAUJOLAIS	1,324,298	15,396	–	–		384	55	61,824	1678	1,386,506	17,129	1,403,635
BURGUNDY	659,153	856,109	–	6876		744	1267	26,539	56,230	686,436	920,482	1,606,918
BORDEAUX	5,741,128	911,922	–	–		505	–	260,580	65,563	6,002,213	977,485	6,979,698
CHAMPAGNE	471	2,443,732	–	–		–	–	4950	242,234	5421	2,685,966	2,691,387
CORSICA	87,365	12,936	–	–		160,985	47,064	71,033	4888	319,383	64,888	384,271
THE JURA	32,333	72,825	–	–		100	270	5853	5103	38,286	78,198	116,484
SAVOIE	37,716	92,949	13,093	15,517		4673	11,448	62,503	26,680	117,985	146,594	264,579
LANGUEDOC-ROUSSILLON	1,800,593	420,006	60,100	–		6,531,529	837,654	1,492,813	75,514	9,885,035	1,333,174	11,218,209
PROVENCE	1,165,664	49,100	–	–		684,990	47,666	208,990	17,789	2,059,644	114,555	2,174,199
SOUTH-WEST	1,223,329	407,661	71,490	11,145		362,632	931,003	522,265	188,364	2,179,716	1,538,173	3,717,889
LOIRE VALLEY	1,110,192	1,488,067	108,260	189,241		321,385	278,202	370,956	73,593	1,910,793	2,029,103	3,939,896
RHÔNE VALLEY	3,619,363	216,470	27,651	1380		3,125,713	313,406	1,302,930	66,079	8,075,657	597,335	8,672,992
TOTAL REGIONS	16,911,162	8,139,674	281,025	225,328	9,354,249	11,193,640	2,468,035	4,396,431	888,195	32,782,258	21,075,481	53,857,739
EXTRA	49,211	42,811	8189	5		34,535	99,219	167,746	11,549	259,681	153,584	413,265
TOTAL FRANCE	16,960,373	8,182,485	289,214	225,333	9,354,249	11,228,175	2,567,254	4,564,177	899,744	33,041,939	21,229,065	54,271,004

Glossary

Words in SMALL CAPITALS have their own entries elsewhere in the glossary. The winemaking process is explained in further detail between pages 19 and 27.

Acid, Acidity Essential constituent of a wine (though not in excess!). Gives zip and freshness and contributes to the balance and length on the palate.

Alcoholic strength Alcohol content of a wine, usually expressed in degrees or as a percentage.

Appellation d'Origine Contrôlée Often abbreviated to AOC or AC. French legislative term referring to the top category of quality wines and the controls surrounding their production. *Appellations* are based on geographical areas.

Argile French for 'clay'.

Aroma The smell or 'nose' of a wine.

Aromatic Flavours/constituents of smell; more than just the grape variety.

Assemblage French for 'blend'.

Astringent Dry taste and finish of a wine which has lost some of its fruit.

Auto-pigeante Mechanical form of treading down and breaking up the CAP of grape-skins, pips etc. during fermentation.

Backbone Structure of a wine, implying body and grip.

Balance The harmony of a wine; its balance between body, fruit, alcohol and ACIDITY.

Barrique Wooden barrel, usually of about 225 litres (49.5 Imperial gallons) in capacity. Especially associated with Bordeaux. See also HOGSHEAD.

Bâtonnage The periodic stirring-up of the fine LEES of a very young wine in barrel. Applied to white wines more than red.

Bien national Term given to the estates sequestered and then sold by the state at the time of the French Revolution.

Biodynamism A philosophical approach to viticulture, derived from the theories of Rudolf Steiner, involving homeopathy and the movements of the moon and the planets.

Bitter Self-explanatory, but if not in excess, not necessarily a bad thing in an immature red Bordeaux wine.

Blackcurrants These are said to be the characteristic fruit taste of Cabernet Sauvignon.

Blanc de Blancs White wine made from white grapes only. Term especially associated with Champagne-method wines.

Blanc de Noirs White wine made from black grapes only. Term especially associated with Champagne-method wines.

Body The 'stuffing' or weight of a wine.

Botrytis cinerea A fungus which attacks grapes and which can cause 'noble rot' in certain climatic conditions. Noble rot is responsible for the luscious sweet wines of Sauternes and elsewhere.

Bouquet The smell or 'nose' of a wine. Also a French term used for mature wine.

Bouqueté French for 'aromatic'.

Brut French term for very dry, especially associated with Champagne-method wine.

Calcaire French for 'limestone'. Associated particularly with the soils of Champagne.

Canton A French administrative district within a DEPARTMENT.

Cap The accumulation of grape skins and other debris etc. which tends to rise to the top of the MUST during the fermentation process.

Carbonic maceration/*macération carbonique* A particular fermentation process that takes place without the presence of air. The fruit is uncrushed and the fermentation begins inside the berry, resulting in wines with colour but without a lot of TANNIN, as in Beaujolais.

Cave French for 'cellar', whether below or above ground.

Cépage French for 'vine variety'.

Cépage améliorateur A quality or 'noble' grape variety.

Chai French for 'cellar' or above ground winemaking and barrel and bottle storage facilities.

Chapeau French for CAP. .

Chaptalisation Addition of sugar to the must. with a view to increasing the eventual alcoholic content of a wine.

Character The depth or complexity of a wine.

Château French for 'castle' but also means a wine estate, including its outbuildings and vineyards, no matter how big or small. Mostly associated with Bordeaux.

Climat French for 'vineyard site', particularly used in Burgundy.

Clone In a wine context a specially reared and refined version of the grape variety.

Clos French for 'enclosed'; in wine denotes a vineyard enclosed within a wall. Most common in the Côte d'Or, as in Clos de Vougeot.

Coarse A wine lacking finesse and possibly not very well made.

Code Napoléon French law of succession abolishing primogeniture.

Cold maceration/Cold soaking/ *macération à froid* A process whereby the skins, pulp and juice macerate together before the fermentation gets under way.

Comité Interprofessionnel Professional body or organisation, representing wine growers or promoting the wines of a region.

Commune French for 'parish'.

Cordon du Royat A system of vine-training whereby a branch of old wood is arranged horizontally, the fruit coming from a series of spurs at intervals along this branch.

Côte or coteau French for 'slope' or 'plateau'.

Coulure Failure of a vine's flowers to set into grapes, following poor, humid weather during the flowering period.

Courtier French for 'broker'.

Creamy A richness and concentration in a wine's character and flavour as a result of old vines.

Croupe French for 'mound' or 'ridge', often of gravel.

Cru French for 'growth', or vineyard or the vines thereof.

Cru Classé A 'growth' that has been classified. Often further qualified, as in *premier* and *deuxième cru* in Bordeaux.

Cuvaison The length of time a red wine macerates with the skins.

Cuve French for 'wine vat'.

Cuve close/**Charmat method** A way of producing sparkling wines in bulk.

Cuvée The contents of a wine vat; used to denote a blend or particular parcel of wine.

Débourbage A process whereby the LEES are allowed to settle, after which the clear juice is racked off into another vat, or into cask.

Délestage The evacuation of juice from the vat, allowing the cap to fall and break up, after which the juice is returned to the vat.

Demi-muid Large barrel, double or more the size of a BARRIQUE.

Demi-sec French for 'medium-dry'.

Department/département French administrative area, equivalent to an English county.

Deuxième cru Second 'growth' in a classification.

Deuxième cuvée/**second wine** The produce of less mature vines or less good vines.

Domaine French for 'wine property' or 'estate'.

Douceâtre French for 'soft and sweetish'.

Doux French for 'sweet'.

Dry Opposite of sweet. Sometimes, when used of wine, indicates a lack of fruit.

Dumb Used for an immature wine which has character but which is still undeveloped.

Earthy A character of wine, not always pejorative, deriving from the nature of the soil.

Ecoulage The running off of the free-run juice after fermentation, leaving the skins, pips etc. behind.

Egalisage French for 'equalising'; i.e. mixing all the elements together to ensure a standard blend.

Elevage French for 'rearing'; in wine used to denote the length of time and processes undergone between vinification and bottling.

En fermage Leasing arrangement for a vineyard.

En métayage Share-cropping for a vineyard. See also MÉTAYAGE.

En primeur Sale of the young wine within the first few months of the harvest.

Encépagement French term for the proportion of different grape varieties planted on an estate or used in a blend.

Fat Full in the sense of high in glycerine, ripeness and extract.

Fermage A leaseholding arrangement.

Finish The 'conclusion' of the taste of a wine on the palate.

First growth or *premier cru* In Bordeaux the top wines in a classification. In Burgundy it refers to

Extra Dry and Brut are drier styles of Champagne.

Sec-tendre French for 'off-dry, soft and fruity'. Many Chenin Blanc wines from the Loire Valley are made in this style.

Sélection de Grains Nobles/SGN Wine made from nobly rotten fruit, especially in Alsace.

Sélection massalle Selection of new vine plants from a variety of existing stock.

Silex Flint.

Skin contact/macération pelliculaire A method whereby the fruit rests after picking for a period of hours to allow the juice to come into contact with the skins, thus augmenting the final flavour.

Sommelier French for 'wine waiter'.

Sous-bois French for 'undergrowth'; a tasting term implying a damp vegetative smell associated with many older red Burgundies and Rhône wines.

Soutirage French for 'racking'.

Stalky A 'green', rather raw, possibly stewed flavour particularly noticeable in young wine. Can result from over-long maceration with the stalks.

Sulphur, sulphites Sulphur is both an anti-oxidant and protects against bacterial contamination.

Sur lie See LEES CONTACT.

Sur-maturité French for 'overripe'.

Table de tri Conveyor belt on which the grapes are laid out so that TRIAGE can take place.

Taille French for 'pressing'. In Champagne, in fact, it is the second pressing after the CUVÉE or first pressing. Also means pruning.

Tannin An essential constituent of young red wine. An ACID deriving from the skins of the grape which leaves an astringent, chewy taste in the mouth. Adds to the weight of the wine. Broken down and mellowed by ageing.

Tartaric acid Natural ACID in grapes and the base by which the acidity is measured.

Tendre French for 'soft', usually used in the context of a wine which is a little weak in ACIDITY and will mature early.

Tête de cuvée Literally French for 'the juice of the first pressing', and therefore the best, and used as such in Champagne. Elsewhere it indicates the grower's best wine.

Tonneau A larger wooden barrel or vat which can be used for both vinification and storage. Also the measure of production of a Bordeaux wine estate.

Tri/Triage The process of eliminating the bruised, unripe and rotten from the healthy fruit.

Ullage The gap of air between the cork and the wine in a bottle. 'On ullage' means the wine left in a partially consumed bottle.

Velouté French for 'velvety'.

Vendange French for 'harvest'.

Vendange tardive French for 'late harvest'. Most common in Alsace.

Vendange verte French for 'green harvest'; also the knocking-out of excess fruit just before the VÉRAISON at the end of July.

Véraison The process whereby the grape changes colour from green to black, or from green to green-gold, usually in August.

Verjus Second generation of fruit, left unpicked, because it is unripe, at the time of the harvest.

Vignoble Vineyard area.

Vin de l'année The wine of the previous year's vintage.

Vin de garde A wine made for keeping, which is capable of improving in bottle.

Vin de goutte The non-press wine. See ÉCOULAGE and VIN DE PRESSE.

Vin de pays French country wine. A superior VIN DE TABLE.

Vin de presse Press wine.

Vin de table Table wine. The lowest category of French wine.

Vin Délimité de Qualité Supérieure / VDQS The second category of quality wine after *appellation contrôlée*.

Vin doux naturel A wine that has been sweetened but not by any natural process. The wine is, in fact, fortified.

Vin ordinaire The basic wine, produced without any APPELLATION.

Viniculture Everything to do with the production of wine.

Vinification The process of wine-making.

Vinifié/Elevé en fûts de chêne Wine vinified and/or matured in oak barrels.

Vintage The year of the harvest.

Viticulture Everything to do with the growing of vines.

Measurements

Surface Area

1 hectare (ha) = 100 ares (a) = 10000 sq metres = 2.471 acres.

One *ouvrée* corresponds to the amount of land one worker can cultivate by hand in one day. It measures 4.285 ares.

One *journal* (plural *journeaux*) is the equivalent of the area one worker can cultivate per day with the help of a horse and plough. A *journal* equals 8 *ouvrées*. There are 2.92 *journeaux* per hectare

Capacity

1 hectolitre (hl) = 100 litres = 22 gallons = 133.3 bottles = 11.1 cases.

1 cask (called a *barrique* or hogshead in Bordeaux, a *pièce* elsewhere in France) is normally approximately 225 litres (it varies from region to region) which will give 300 bottles or 25 cases. A *feuillette* is a half-size cask; a *quarteau* a quarter-size cask. A *queue* is two *pièces*, a *tonneau* four.

Yield

In general one vine will yield one bottle of wine. In most years 300 kg of grapes will yield one cask (225 litres) of wine. Sometimes the grapes contain less juice, in which case 12 or 13 containers (360-390 kg) are required.

Bibliography

This is not a list of all the books I have consulted, but a note of useful additions to the library which are at least reasonably up to date.

Bordeaux

Grands Vins, The Finest Châteaux of Bordeaux and Their Wines, Clive Coates MW, Weidenfeld & Nicolson (UK); University of California Press (USA), 1995.
Bordeaux and Its Wines (English translation of the 15th French Edition), Editions Féret (Bordeaux); John Wiley and Sons (USA), 1998.
Bordeaux, David Peppercorn MW, Second Edition, Faber and Faber (London and Boston), 1991, (new edition 2000).
The Wines of Bordeaux, Edmund Penning-Rowsell, 6th Edition, Penguin, 1989.
Bordeaux, A Comprehensive Guide, Robert M. Parker Jr., 3rd Edition, Simon and Schuster (USA); Dorking Kindersley (UK), 1998.
The Bordeaux Atlas and Encyclopaedia of Châteaux, Hubrecht Duijker and Michael Broadbent MW, Ebury Press (UK) 1997.
Sauternes, Stephen Brook, Faber and Faber (London and Boston), 1995.

Burgundy

Côte d'Or, A Celebration of the Great Wines of Burgundy, Clive Coates MW, Weidenfeld & Nicolson (UK); University of California Press (USA), 1997.
Burgundy, Anthony Hanson MW, Second Edition, Faber and Faber (London and Boston), 1995.
The Great Domaines of Burgundy, Dr Remington Norman MW, Second Edition, Kylie Cathie, 1996.

Rhône

The Wines of The Rhône Valley, Robert M. Parker Jr., Second Edition, Simon and Schuster (USA); Dorling Kindersley (UK), 1997.
The Wines of The Rhône, John Livingstone-Learmonth, 3rd Edition, Faber and Faber (London and Boston), 1992 (new edition 2000).
Rhône Renaissance, Dr Remington Norman MW, Mitchell Beazley (UK), 1995.

Loire

A Wine and Food Guide to the Loire, Jacqueline Friedrich, Henny Holt (USA); Mitchell Beazley (UK), 1996.

Alsace

The Wines of Alsace, Tom Stevenson, Faber and Faber (London and Boston), 1993.

Champagne

Christie's World Encyclopaedia of Champagne and Sparkling Wine, Tom Stevenson, Absolute Press (UK), 1998.

The Rest of France

Wines of South-West France, Paul Strang, Kylie Cathie (UK), 1994.
The Wines of Languedoc-Roussillon, Liz Berry MW, Ebury Press (UK), 1992.
French Country Wines, Rosemary George MW, Faber and Faber (London and Boston), 1990. **Wines of the South of France** (also Faber) published late 2000.
L'Atlas des Terroirs du Languedoc, APE Editions (Montpellier), 1997.
Le Vin de Cahors, José Baudel, Les Editions de La Bouriane, Gourdon, 1995.

General

The World Atlas of Wine, Hugh Johnson, 4th Edition, Mitchell Beazley (UK), 1994.
Terroir, The Role of Geology, Climate and Culture in the Making of French Wines, James E. Wilson, University of California Press (USA), Mitchell Beazley (UK), 1998.
The Oxford Companion to Wine, Second Edition, Ed. Jancis Robinson MW, Oxford University Press, 1999.

INDEX

Page references in **bold** indicate main entry, those in *italic* entry in a table. The words Château, Domaine, Cave, Vignerons, Clos and Mas have been inverted in the index and the item entered under the next word of the heading other than prepositions etc.